Warfare by Other Means

Warfare by Other Means

South Africa in the 1980s and 1990s

Peter Stiff

GALAGO

Books by Peter Stiff

Fact
Tommy Goes Home
Selous Scouts: Top Secret War
See You In November
Taming the Landmine
Nine Days of War
The Silent War
Cry Zimbabwe
Warfare by Other Means

Fiction
The Rain Goddess
The Road to Armageddon

ISBN 1 919854 01 0

First published by Galago December 2001

Galago books are published by Galago Publishing (1999) (Pty) Ltd
P O Box 404, Alberton, 1450, RSA

The Galago logo is a registered trademark

Type transferred electronically from Galago computer setting by CTP Pre-Press Cape Town

Colour and black and white photographs reproduced by Full Colour Graphics,19 St John Rd, Houghton Estate, Johannesburg

Printed and bound by CTP Book Printers (Pty) Ltd, Caxton Street, Parow, Cape

Electronic DDC20: 355.496

Book and dust cover design: Francis Stiff and Madelain Davies
Maps: Madelain Davies
Cover photography: Justyn Davies
Model: Mike J'Arlet Joy

For Francis, my wife
the special and beautiful lady I love . . .
A vital part of my books and all of my life

Whom God would destroy, He first sends mad

James Duport
(1606 – 1679)

Picture Credits

The following are credited for the use of photographs and illustrations: Associated Press, Dave Anderson (Andy), Kobus Bodenstein, Justyn Davies, Attie Dippenaar, Peter Dixon, Paul Dubois, Dries Kriel, Mossie Mostert, *Paratus* magazine, the former SADF Directorate of Public Relations, *Rapport* newspaper by the kind permission of its editor, Tim du Plessis, the South African Police, Peter Stiff and the Peter Stiff collection. The copyright holders of a few photographs are not acknowledged, although the publishers have made every effort to establish authorship which has been lost in the mists of time or blown away by the winds of war. However, the publishers will gladly amend or add credits in subsequent editions and make the necessary arrangements with those photographers who were not known at the time of going to print, or who had not been traced.

Acknowledgments

The following in alphabetical order and by no means in order of importance or in rank, are thanked by the author:

Ace investigative journalist, Geoff Allan, who generously made his own research documents on *Operation Katzen* available to the author; Brigadier Johan Beyers (retired), formerly Director of the SADF's Public Relations Department who facilitated the author's research in Namibia in 1989; ex-Detective Inspector John Birch, BSAP/SB; Colonel (later Brigadier) Dr Wouter Basson, who explained the unique medical equipment developed for Special Forces by 7-Medical Battalion; Colonel (later Brigadier-General) Andre Bestbier, who explained the early days of the Republic of Zimbabwe from a South African military point of view; Colonel Jan Breytenbach (retired), a legendary soldier and a good friend and the author of four books who gave the author numerous interviews over the years and frankly explained information unavailable from other sources.

Major Brian (*nom de guerre*), who was the first to introduce the author to the workings of *Project Barnacle*; Joseph Chiole, who clarified the relationship between the *Afrikaner Volksfront* and the SADF in April 1994; Colonel Eugene de Kock, who with the author as he did with the Truth and Reconciliation Commission, revealed much that would otherwise have remained lost in the dustbin of South African history and Colonel Lourens du Plessis, a fountain of knowledge regarding the SADF's 'dirty tricks' in the Eastern Cape in the 1980s.

Major-General (later Lieutenant-General) Daan Hamman, who spoke frankly about the SADF's involvement in 'Mad Mike' Hoare's coup attempt in the Seychelles; Major-General Bantu Holomisa, who provided a wealth of documentation on the Eastern Cape in the 1980s (called the 'Major-General Bantu Holomisa papers' in the bibliography); Colonel Gerrie Hugo, who provided a treasure of documentation on Military Intelligence operations in the Eastern Cape (called the 'Colonel Gerrie Hugo papers' in the bibliography); Johnny (*nom de guerre*), a brave man indeed whom I spoke to when times were different and who I have been unable to trace for permission to use his name; Dries Kriel, who spoke frankly about his AWB sabotage operations and allowed the author unlimited access to his unpublished manuscript, *Diary of a White Terrorist*, Mossie Mostert, another who spoke frankly about his AWB connections; friend and ace journalist, De Wet Potgieter, who traced documents that the author was unable to get from other sources and Colonel Jerry Puren, who discussed various aspects of the Seychelles coup attempt.

Colonel Bert Sachse, a good friend who willing supplied information, James Selfe, for permission to quote his material; Mike Tippett, who explained the circumstances surrounding the death of his brother Dave; Colonel Piet Uys, another who went into the *Afrikaner Volksfront*'s relationship with the SADF in early 1994; Colonel Sybie van der Spuy who spoke about 2-Recce's involvement in the Seychelles coup attempt; General Constand Viljoen, who explained with considerable frankness the Afrikaner right-wing's military planning before the April 1994 election; Anton van Zyl who detailed the frailties of the AWB's military planning in April 1994 and Colonel Craig Williamson, who revealed his involvement in the Seychelles and told why the South African authorities wanted no more mercenary interference there after Colonel Hoare's failure.

There were literally dozens of others interviewed by the author. Intelligence and Special Forces operators lead secretive lives — some lead double lives. Some came to see the author voluntarily and others he sought out. Most find it difficult to break a lifetime culture of secrecy — even though most, 'on the face of it', are no longer involved. It is for such reasons that their names do not appear, but this in no way diminishes that which in many instances have been invaluable, often unique, contributions.

Contents

Colour and black and white pictures

In-text maps, illustrations, cartoons and diagrams

Foreword

Warfare by Other Means is not an apologia — it is a history, much of it oral and straight from the mouths of those involved. This wide-ranging and explosive book is Peter Stiff at his best. It tells you everything you did not know about the last years of South Africa's total onslaught apartheid era. It deals with a swathe of assassinations — the ruthless killings of friends and foes alike — and of destruction and mayhem committed both at home and abroad. How anthrax letters were mailed to enemies of the State.

It tells how it joined the disastrous attempt by Colonel Mike Hoare's mercenaries to overthrow the René regime in the Seychelles because it was 'an anti-communist coup going begging' and how 'it was a shame to waste it'. How it secretly paid ransom to secure the release of captured mercenaries under sentences of death. How it foiled future coup attempts because, to the envy of the CIA and MI6 and the chagrin of the Soviets, it had amazingly managed to take over and run the Seychelles intelligence services through an SADF front company, Longreach.

It expands on the SADF's co-operation with and the roles of surrogate forces like Inkatha in KwaZulu-Natal, the *Witdoekies* in the Cape Flats, the *Ama-Afrika* in the Eastern Cape, the *Iliso Lomzi* in Transkei, the African Democratic Movement in Ciskei and many more in combatting the 'total onslaught'.

It shows the passing parade of the National Party government's allies in the 'independent' homeland states and the money it shovelled in to support them. There were corrupt rulers like President Kaiser Matanzima and Prime Minister George Matanzima in Transkei and President Lennox Sebe in Ciskei. It explains how they milked their territories (and the South African taxpayer) for their personal benefits. It tells how they were deposed in military coups by General Bantu Holomisa and Brigadier Oupa Gqozo. It also explains, how having failed to turn Transkei into a bastion against the ANC, the SADF turned to Ciskei and introduced a Military Intelligence front company there that effectively controlled the government.

Stiff writes about a great variety of Military Intelligence front organisations. How 'Veterans for Victory' was formed to infiltrate and 'destroy' the End Conscription Campaign. How right-wing churches were cultivated and covertly funded whenever it suited the SADF's purpose. He explains how the CCB was uncovered by the media only after it began to explore the drive-by shootings of Dr David Webster in South Africa and Advocate Anton Lubowski in Namibia.

Finally, revealed for the first time, are the murderous subversive activities of a diversity of right-wing organisations. There was Eugene Terre'Blanche's AWB and General Constand Viljoen's *Afrikaner Volksfront*, both of which came close to toppling South Africa into Civil War before the first democratic election in April 1994.

There is much, much, more in its 600 pages.

It is essential reading for all South Africans.

1

Operation Anvil
Seychelles
An anti-communist coup going begging
1977-1981

The Seychelles archipelago of 92 islands is scattered north to south in the blue waters of the Indian Ocean 1 800km east of Mombasa, Kenya. Some 1 200km separates the most northern from the southernmost island. The capital city of Victoria is on Mahé, the largest island, which is 35km long by 12km wide.

The population of 65 000 is principally Creole, but most business and political interests were and largely still are in the hands of the traditional ruling class known collectively as *les grands blancs*, although after more than 100 years of carefree miscegenated living, few remain truly *blanc*. Languages spoken are French, English and Creole. After being part of the British Empire for 165 years, the Seychelles Islands were granted self government in 1971. Independence followed on 28 June 1976.

There were two political parties contesting the country's first general election — James Mancham's Seychelles Democratic Party and the socialistic Seychelles People's United Party led by Albert France René. Both leaders came from the white grandee group.

It could hardly be classed as a bitterly fought campaign, but rather a relaxed one conducted in a manner that suited the gentle people of the islands. The results were inconclusive so the contending parties, on the British Government's suggestion, agreed to form a coalition government. James Mancham became the first president and Albert René his prime minister.

The amicable establishment of this first administration did not signal a lack of political differences between the two leaders. Mancham was for the continuance of friendly cultural and commercial ties with Great Britain and France, while René wanted to sever such links and swing towards the Marxist/Leninist/African socialist policies of President Nyerere of Tanzania.

Both agreed, however, that the government's priority was to contend with the massive economic problems that had accrued to the minuscule state with the arrival of independence. This was because no economy worth speaking of had existed in the colonial days and the islands and islanders had subsisted primarily on handouts by London.

President Mancham believed the answer lay in developing the tourist industry, which despite the paradise-like conditions prevailing in the islands, had not been seriously tackled in the past. It is easy to blame the former colonisers, but until the late 1960s the vast majority of people travelling abroad, whether for business or pleasure, went by ship. For reasons of economics the ships, excepting the occasional cruise liner, plied the most economic routes — which rarely included backwaters like the Seychelles.

The only ships calling at Mahé were the British India Steamship Line's *Kampala* and *Karanje*, which serviced the mail contract and docked at Mahé on alternate months. The arrival of wide-bodied jetliners revolutionised the tourist industry worldwide. The process was assisted locally by the British building the Pointe Larue International Airport on Mahé in 1972. President Mancham saw the moment and grasped the opportunities presented by such aircraft. He became the father of the rapidly mushrooming tourist industry.

But Mancham had his weaknesses, mostly relating to a playboy lifestyle. At the independence ball he promised his guests that his official residence would be 'the swinging-est State House in the whole world'. He cultivated rich Arabs as friends, people like international arms dealer Adnan Khashoggi. In a whim of largesse he sold islands to relatives of the Shah of Iran. After divorcing his English wife he turned to Hollywood starlets, international models, air hostesses and even a lady called Fiona Richmond, 'Britain's nudest dancer'.[1]

In early 1977 the island paradise was uncharacteristically disturbed by several bomb outrages in Victoria. No arrests were made but it was believed that René adherents, still agitating vigorously for a policy of African socialism, were responsible.

In May 1977 President Mancham was told that the sound of rifle fire had been heard emanating from a small island adjacent to Mahé. This was certainly unusual. There was no game on the islands so there were no hunters. There was no rifle range either and no defence force because the state had no enemies. In addition, the private ownership of firearms was forbidden. So Mancham, a charming and handsome man with a penchant for vacillation, dismissed the report as false or of no significance. He continued his preparations to attend the Commonwealth Prime Ministers' Conference in London in early June.

It was a bad mistake.

On 5 June 1977, when by Marcham's own account he was in a Savoy Hotel bed with a 'tousled blond', some 20 heavily armed Tanzanian soldiers smuggled secretly into the islands by Albert René mounted a *coup d'éta*t They achieved complete surprise; the mostly unarmed police force presented no opposition worth speaking of. All key installations in Victoria, including the radio station and police headquarters, fell to the rebels within four hours. The cost was one dead and one wounded on either side.

James Mancham's 11-month term of office as president was rudely terminated by *force majeure* and Albert René assumed office in his stead. Mancham's cabinet ministers were rounded up and arbitrarily deported, their land and property was confiscated by the state. In their place René appointed a cabinet of Marxist and Soviet sympathisers.

Commissioner of Police, Patrick Somerville, and four other British police officers were also arrested and bundled off to Britain with Chief Justice Aidan O'Brien Quinn, who was tactless enough to describe the new leaders as 'people with long criminal records'.[2]

To their collective sorrow various Arab personages and the Shah's relatives had their recently acquired islands of paradise expropriated without compensation.

To allay Western fears that he might transform the Seychelles into a communist state, which would have slammed shut the lids of the British and French aid chests and bruised his financial fingers, René announced that his government was adopting an internal policy of what he euphemistically called 'Indian Ocean and African Socialism'. He announced a foreign policy of strict neutrality and non alignment. The Seychelles would stand in the middle between the great superpowers. But these were only words couched to camouflage his true intentions.

Youths were despatched to Algeria and the Soviet Union for military training and children in their early teens were sent to Cuba for communist indoctrination. A general curfew was proclaimed and political opponents of the new regime 'disappeared' in mysterious circumstances. The main independent weekly, *Weekend Life*, was banned and its editor, Bernard Verlaque, detained.

The Catholic Church accused René of trying to eradicate the Christian faith among the people of Seychelles, most of whom were Catholics.

The Soviet embassy in Victoria was permitted an inflated staff, most of them KGB technical personnel monitoring the movement of US warships in the Persian Gulf and Indian Ocean. President René made official visits to the Soviet Union, Algeria, Libya and Cuba, throwing in his lot with the Warsaw Pact. He approved the Soviet invasion of Afghanistan, applauded Libyan aggression in Chad and praised the oppressive communist regime in Cambodia.

Without the approval of the electorate, nationalisation followed and the government took control of everything important in the tiny economy — shipping, lighterage, transport enterprises, taxis, fishing and agriculture. Cooperatives were established and the selling of one's own produce became a crime. A 200 nautical mile exclusive fishing zone around the islands was planned, but this was abandoned when the tuna market collapsed. This signalled the end of the new state-owned fishing industry.

Elections were promised, but instead a one-party state was declared.

The radical changes dramatically affected tourism. The 12 000 monthly visitors of Mancham's days were slashed by half when René arbitrarily cancelled South African Airways' landing rights. Tourists from elsewhere also stayed away, undoubtedly because of the state's new slant towards Marxism. Soon they were getting less than 4 000 visitors a month.

Libya and Algeria provided loans to boost the economy. The bulk of the state's financial support still came from Britain and France which continued their aid despite René's virulent anti-Western stance at the UN. Another major source of revenue was the rent paid by the US Government for NASA's tracking station at Mahé.

Enter 'Mad Mike' Hoare

Colonel 'Mad Mike' Hoare, then living at Hilton near Pietermaritzburg in Natal and practising as a chartered accountant, was approached by former Seychelles cabinet minister, Gonzangue D'Offay, and asked his opinion on the feasibility of a counter-coup to restore the Mancham presidency. D'Offay suggested the unoriginal idea of flying in a force of mercenaries in a C-130 à la the Israeli raid on Entebbe — a film of which was still the talk of the time. Mike Hoare dismissed this as impractical. He told D'Offay politely that while a counter-coup was a possibility it required three ingredients — a good plan, men of political integrity with the courage to back it and plenty of money — perhaps as much as US$5 million.

D'Offay, who was flying to London later that week, said he would talk it over with James Mancham. On his return he reported that the ex-president had shown no enthusiasm at all for a coup attempt.

The 'London Group of Exiles' came into the picture as an alternative to Mancham. They asked if Colonel Hoare would, as a first step, conduct a feasibility study and provide a plan supported by a detailed budget. While they could not reward him for such preliminary work, they were willing to pay expenses.

He failed to date this but mentioned that 'almost 15 months' had passed since the 5 June 1977 coup, which put it around August/ September 1978. In direct contradiction, however, a letter dated 12 May 1978 handed in at the hijack trial, which according to D'Offay, Hoare had written to him, said:

> Dear Gonzangue,
> I am enclosing Plan No. 2 which I would like you to consider. It seems a very workable plan to me . . .
> I would like you to know that I have excellent connections in Rhodesia with the top people and a close connection with the man who owns and runs a small airline . . .
> Please tender my sincere respects to the president and let him know my services are entirely at his disposition . . .
> M
>
> P S. Beware of a man named Banks in Britain. He is very dangerous and bad news in our line of country.[3]

He also mentioned that he had 'some pull with BOSS'— the South African Bureau of State Security.

So by May 1978 Colonel Hoare had been far more active than he has ever admitted, having already formulated two plans to cause René's downfall. The small airline owner was obviously Jack Malloch, a buccaneering pilot who played a big part in busting sanctions against Rhodesia after UDI in 1965. Hoare's mention of Banks shows he was both wary and aware of the possibilities of competition in the mercenary arena.

He called on Jerry Puren who had a motor business in Durban and asked him to accompany him on a reconnaissance of Mahé. Colonel Puren, a veteran of the South African and Royal Air Forces during World War II, had taken up arms in the service of Moise Tshombe and the breakaway Congolese province of Katanga in 1961, eventually becoming Tshombe's principal adviser. For seven years Puren was involved as a mercenary commander in the Congo (later Zaïre, now the Democratic Republic of Congo) in ground, air and advisory roles for Tshombe, Mobutu and vicariously for the CIA.

According to Puren Mike Hoare said: 'The conspirators wanted a feasibility plan drawn up and were prepared to pay hard cash for it. After that there was the possibility of actually taking part in the coup.' [4] Colonel Hoare was reticent about naming the backers but said the key one was in London.[5]

Puren had remained an *éminence grise* in the mercenary world by choice. This allowed him to travel freely without raising inquiring eyebrows. Mike Hoare on the other hand had always adopted a high profile — which made disguise essential. He grew a beard and altered the name in his passport to Michael Thomas Bernard Boarel — by amending an H to a B and adding L to the end of his surname.[6]

They flew British Airways to Mahé on 24 September 1978, sitting apart for security reasons, and, joining up only after they had left the terminal building on completion of immigration formalities.

They booked into the Reef Hotel and hired a Mini Moke. Ostensibly they were tourists, but if seriously challenged about their extensive wanderings, they intended saying they were businessmen sizing up the tourist market. Mike Hoare concentrated on getting an overview of the military situation, while Puren, because his cover was deeper, began a series of meetings with local dissidents to gauge support.

Through an intermediary, Madame Marie Ange, Puren contacted the Chief Immigration Officer, Gerard Hoarau, a former priest. He gladly passed on intelligence regarding troop strengths and dispositions, insisting the islands were 'ripe for revolt'.[7] He was also certain that elements within the police would actively help the plotters. [8] He next looked up Frank Puren — a distant relative and a prominent Mahé businessman. Appointed managing director of the Victoria Bus Company after nationalisation, he was sacked when it failed to make a profit. He was still, nevertheless, a foundation member of Albert René's Seychelles People's United Party, so he had political clout. Hoare hints that Frank was brought into the plot. Jerry Puren, however, maybe for reasons of family loyalty, insisted it was no more than a social visit to renew blood ties.

Also on the scene was Colonel Bob Noddyn — a Belgian mercenary associate dating back to the Congo days. He commanded and trained an élite praetorian guard for Albert René, so he was the last man they wanted to see. His use lay in his owing Jerry Puren a favour for saving his life in the Congo. Noddyn was also an old comrade of Colonel Bob Denard from 6-Commando days. Puren thought Denard untrustworthy, because he had abandoned his comrades to their fate when they were surrounded by Mobutu's forces at Bukavu in 1967. Commercially speaking, of course, he was also potential competition.

They criss-crossed Mahé in the Mini Moke, checking out army bases and the military camp in Liberation Road where 50 Tanzanian instructors were staying. Later they gave the Seychelles People's Defence Force HQ, the police headquarters, the radio station and other key installations the once-over. Two 20mm anti-aircraft heavy machine guns were emplaced at the military barracks overlooking the eastern end of Pointe Larue Airport. They explored approaches, worked out fields of fire and noted possible base-plate positions for mortars.

The Seychelles People's Liberation Army was not impressive. It had an establishment of ten officers and 190 other ranks, many of whom were former convicts. The majority were illiterate. Turnout was generally poor and discipline lax. Morale was said to be high, but loyalty to the president suspect — a contradictory titbit that smacked of wishful thinking on Gerard Hoarau's part. Their principal weapon was the AK47 with which they were largely unpractised because of the absence of a rifle range. The force possessed no mortars or other support weapons.

There was also the People's Militia with an estimated strength of 400, mostly young boys aged between ten and 15. They were issued with 1914 pattern bolt action Mausers. Their job was to patrol secluded beaches at night and look for intruders.[9]

On their return to South Africa, Jerry Puren compiled a relief map of Mahé, plotting in all military dispositions and features of interest, while Mike Hoare concentrated on the main report.[10] Hoare gave no credit to Puren in his book and said that he himself had formulated a plan for execution within the next six to nine months. The cost would be US$5 million.

Broadly speaking, this plan entailed the recruiting of 200 mercenaries in Europe and the USA for a six-month contract. Hoare regarded recruitment in South Africa as politically unwise. He intended to base his group in a 'friendly Arab country in the Persian Gulf', where a training camp in a remote coastal area had been provided. They would be trained in complete secrecy over a period of four months in the intricacies of mounting an amphibious assault. He intended to acquire a fleet of six fishing trawlers, one with a helipad and a helicopter. Zodiac inflatables would be used for the beach landings.[11]

Jerry Puren, contrarily, said they developed a five-phase plan which bears little resemblance to Hoare's model. It was based on the assumption that Hoarau's contention — that elements of the police would throw their weight behind them and that the civilian population would rise in support of a coup — was correct.

Phase One called for the infiltration of an advance party of about 15 men into Mahé. They would secure safe houses. In the following days weapons would be landed secretly from yachts and cached strategically around the island.

Phase Two required the same advance party, on receipt of a code word, to recover the cached weapons. They would drive to the airport and seize the control tower, then guide in an aircraft carrying the main force of mercenaries. It would have taken off from somewhere nearby, probably Kenya or the Comores.

Phase Three would commence with the arrival of the main force. After the issue of weapons they would be sent to knock out the heavy weapons dominating the airfield and the Tanzanian Army base.

Phase Four involved mercenary elements racing into Victoria, seizing key installations and capturing the President, his advisors and senior police officers loyal to the regime.

Phase Five covered a 'spontaneous' civilian uprising that would mop up any remaining points of resistance.

The cost was estimated at US$3 million. The manpower complement would be 120 men. Puren's role would be to lead the advance guard.[12]

The two plans had little in common, but Puren's one is remarkably similar to the one Hoare would submit to the SADF at a later date.

Hoare's plan was ambitious. An 'amphibious assault', the inclusion of a helicopter — presumably a gunship — and four months' training hardly implies a covert landing. It seems more like a forced landing bulldozed through to completion against opposition, should it become necessary. The operation appears risky to the point of foolhardiness. It seems probable that this was merely an opening gambit to maximise the finances — a negotiating ploy which, when the money was to hand, would have seen to the plan being watered down to a more economic level with a consequent enhancement of personal profit.

One can assume that both schemes plotted an escape by sea if things went wrong, but neither specified it.

Colonel Hoare sent his plan to London for approval. Meanwhile, he flew to America to help promote *The Wild Geese*, a film on mercenary soldiering for which he acted as an adviser. While he was in America, Eddie Camille, formerly of the Seychelles Foreign Office in London, phoned and requested he come to London and see the ex-President.

Hoare was kept hanging around London for 11 days, after which James Mancham again changed his mind about a coup attempt and decided there was no longer any point in meeting him. Hoare nevertheless had several meetings with Eddie Camille who had been nominated by the London Group of Exiles to coordinate efforts to bring about the René regime's downfall. Mancham's jaundiced viewpoint did nothing to dampen their enthusiasm. Hoare advised Camille to enlist the help of a big power, perhaps the USA or South Africa, although aid from the latter would bring them disfavour at the OAU.

But why would America be interested?

There was an ongoing race between the Soviets and the United States for strategic influence in the Indian Ocean. Great Britain and France had formerly ruled the waves of the Indian Ocean unchallenged for more than a century. But in the 1960s the Royal Navy had withdrawn its ships for reasons of waning British influence and financial stringency.

The United States stepped forward to fill the vacuum. An ideal naval base in the region would have been Simon's Town in the Cape with all its highly sophisticated facilities, but the apartheid policies of the South African Government put paid to that. In 1965 Great Britain offered to lease them Aldabra Island for development as a naval base, but withdrew the offer after pressure from conservationists. They had not realised it was the unique habitat of the giant turtle. The island of Diego Garcia in the Chagos Archipelago, some 2 000km due east of the Seychelles, was offered in its stead.

The Americans developed a base on Diego Garcia large enough to accommodate a Rapid Deployment Force consisting of their Indian Ocean fleet of 29 warships, including two aircraft carriers, and its Marine Amphibian Brigade. Kenya also granted them port facilities at Mombasa and Somalia did the same at Berbera on the Red Sea.

But the Soviets were not idle either. In the wake of decolonisation, they achieved substantial influence in states within the general region, such as Tanzania, Zambia, Mozambique, Angola, South Yemen and Madagascar. They obtained the use of naval facilities once belonging to Britain's Royal Navy in several 'non aligned' countries. They constructed a submarine base at Dahlak on the Red Sea and built a military base on Socotra Island off the Horn of Africa. Farther south they established themselves at the former Portuguese Naval Base of Nacala in Mozambique and at Diego Suarez in northern Madagascar.

Soviet influence in the Seychelles had shown a marked increase since Albert René's rise to power. This was evidenced by their expanded diplomatic mission and work under the supervision of Soviet and Cuban construction engineers that had commenced on a large military and air force base on Coetivy Island — assumed to be their answer to Diego Garcia.

It was not surprising that the Americans were displeased.

On his return to South Africa, Colonel Hoare tried to raise American money, unsuccessfully lobbying a series of CIA officers stationed at the US Embassy in Pretoria. Robin Moore, author of the best-selling books, *The French Connection* and *The Green Berets*, wrote and said he was standing as a US senator. Colonel Hoare asked for his support, requesting he use his influence in certain unspecified Arab states.[13]

In the first half of 1979 there were the beginnings of an underground movement in Mahé. Whether this gained spontaneous momentum because of Albert René's repressive regime, or whether it was orchestrated from outside, is open to speculation. Broadsheets denigrating René and his administration appeared on Victoria's streets. They accused him of rigging the elections which had recently returned him to office by an overwhelming majority, embezzling state funds and so on.

The French Government, undoubtedly in an act of one-upmanship directed at the

British, answered a René appeal and donated a 500-ton armed fisheries protection vessel, the *Topaz*. It came complete with 12 French officers who together with 19 locally recruited personnel made up its crew. Its role was to patrol the approaches of Victoria Harbour and restrict yachts to daytime sailing to prevent coup attempts. The immediate effect was a further drop in tourism.

In early April 1979 Eddie Camille asked Hoare to approach the South African government and ask for their support in mounting a coup. Hoare wrote to the Director General of the National Intelligence Service, Alec van Wyk, and made arrangements to see him on 17 May 1979.

Hoare laid out the exiles' case and asked what the government's attitude would be towards a coup. If they viewed it favourably, would they consider helping the plotters financially with US$3 million?

For South Africa it would mean a sympathetic voice at the OAU, the resumption of SAA's interrupted landing rights, special trade links and a share in the development of the oil field off Platte Island. It would also give it a firm base from which to destabilise Tanzania, the main host country of the ANC.[14]

Van Wyk examined the documentation, including a listing of the shadow cabinet, but excluding James Mancham who was still suffering from a severe attack of indoubtitis. There were other items, like the subversive leaflets and broadsheets circulating around Victoria. He said the matter would be presented to the cabinet and the State Security Council for discussion and consideration.

Ten days later Hoare got his answer. It was negative.[15]

President René took everyone by surprise by declaring martial law in November 1979. He contended that a plot ‘sponsored from abroad with the cooperation of mercenaries standing ready in Durban' had been foiled. Over 80 Seychellois were detained, including Gerard Hoarau.

The 12 French sailors crewing *Topaz* were numbered amongst those arrested on suspicion of involvement in the alleged coup attempt. Two months later they were deported after allegedly confessing their involvement in preparations for the coup attempt. They repudiated their ‘confessions’ on their return to France.[16]

The news shocked Jerry Puren, but Mike Hoare assured him it did not spell the end of their plans. René, he said, had got the wrong end of the stick.[17]

Colonel Hoare believed that financial aid for a coup bid was not forthcoming principally because the various factions opposing René lacked cohesion. The only person of stature capable of establishing that cohesion was James Mancham . . . and he was not interested.

Consequently, it came as a pleasant surprise when at the end of January 1980 Eddie Camille reported that Mancham had again reconsidered his position. He was now committed to re-assuming the presidency, although he had no desire to retain it for long. He would re-establish himself, hand over to a carefully groomed understudy and retire to Britain. Before committing himself irrevocably, however, he required an assurance that he would have the support of at least one big power.

So Eddie Camille asked Hoare to make another approach to the South Africans. Hoare reiterated that they would be better off speaking to the Americans. Camille, however, insisted he approach Pretoria.

Hoare had a friendly relationship with Martin Donaldson, a Yugoslavian-born National Intelligence Service officer based in Durban whose real name was Martin Dolinchek. He variously used other *noms de guerre* like Malcolm Donaldson, Eddie Smith, Martin van Rensburg, Martin van der Merwe and Frans Zajc.[18] Dolinchek said they first met in 1974 when Colonel Hoare was attempting to put together an International Brigade to fight in Rhodesia. BOSS chief, General Hendrik van der Bergh, despatched him to warn Hoare to keep his nose out of Rhodesian affairs.[19]

Colonel Hoare asked him to arrange a meeting with his Durban chief. A few weeks later Dolinchek reported to him that his chief thought he would probably find it more fruitful to speak to the SADF instead. Arrangements were made for him to see a Brigadier Daan Hamman in Pretoria.

A man in civilian clothes met him when he arrived at Pretoria station. He did not introduce himself and Hoare gained the impression he was a sergeant clerk in the brigadier's office. They spoke briefly and inconclusively in the railway station cafeteria and parted company. Hoare had said nothing, believing his interviewer was too lowly in rank to make decisions. So nothing was achieved.

Frustrated by the lack of progress, on 11 March Hoare flew to London to see James Mancham, who confirmed his eagerness to regain the presidency. Mancham agreed that the venture depended entirely on money. He suggested approaching his old friend Adnan Khashoggi, the billionaire arms dealer, when he next visited America. He felt sure that US$5 million would mean little to a man of his financial standing. Besides, René had expropriated Khashoggi's Seychelles property without compensation and to add insult to injury, declared him *persona non grata* — so he had an old score to settle.

In June Eddie Camille phoned and said they were out of luck. Khashoggi was going through a messy divorce and right at that moment was short of a spare US$5 million. To complicate things even further, the vacillating Mancham had changed his mind yet again. He no longer wished to face the perils inherent in taking up his old office again.

Robert Frichot, Mancham's former Attorney General, then living in Australia, took over as coup organiser. Camille remained as the coordinator in London.[20]

Hoare quietly dropped Jerry Puren from the team in about April or May 1980. He said it was on orders from London because Puren had been 'alarmingly indiscreet' at an old soldiers club.

Puren, on the other hand, who was as yet unaware that his services were no longer required, said he had, with Hoare's concurrence, made discreet enquiries about the recruitment of personnel. He had approached some white policemen who frequented the bar at the Assegai MOTH Shell Hole on the Bluff in Durban. Six volunteered but, unbeknown to Jerry, they checked with their station commander to see if there would be any official objections. His view was that, provided they did it in their own time, it would be okay. Not surprisingly, word soon got around in security circles, which caused Dolinchek to warn Hoare of what he regarded as a security breach.[21]

Puren said he had introduced his potential recruits to Gerard Hoarau, but he must have been mistaken because Hoarau was under detention in the Seychelles until September 1980. It was more likely D'Offay.

Robert Frichot asked Hoare to attend the independence celebrations in Mahé on 5 June 1980. He decided to travel alone and at his own expense to assess the army's recently acquired Soviet weaponry that would be on show for the first time.

The independence day parade proved useful. The Seychelles People's Liberation Army displayed six smartly turned out platoons, wearing camouflage uniforms and Soviet-pattern steel helmets. They were armed with well-used AK47s and had three RPG-7 rocket launchers per platoon.

Three Soviet BTR-40 armoured cars, armed with 14,5mm and 7,62mm machine guns, but without radio communications, were on parade. He spotted another nine parked in the barracks. Also there were six multiple-barrelled anti-aircraft guns — probably 14,5mm ZPU-4s, six 50 calibre machine guns towed by Land-Rovers and six new 75mm recoilless rifles mounted on Mini-Mokes. No grenades, light machine guns, pistols, mortars or grenade launchers were in evidence. The 200 or so People's Militia with their old and outdated weapons were little more than a rabble.

He conducted another detailed reconnaissance, updating intelligence gained during the first one. On his return he prepared a military appreciation and sent it to Eddie Camille. If local assistance was available, and given the element of surprise, a bloodless coup would probably be possible.

With this report to hand Frichot flew from Australia to England and Germany in July to negotiate with unnamed financiers. He phoned Colonel Hoare from Germany and asked that he revise his budget, saying he would find it easier to get US$3 than US$5 million. Hoare produced a reduced budget, but pointed out that the risk factor increased proportionally as the budget decreased.

Frichot achieved partial success. His German contact promised him money, but not as much as US$3 million — and it was conditional on the plotters gaining Kenya's political backing. For its part, Kenya was expected to promptly recognise the new government and fly in armed troops and police to support it.

In November after they had been detained without trial for 240 days, President René released 20 political prisoners and summarily deported them. Amongst their number was a vengeful Gerard Hoarau who settled in Durban and Bernard Verlaque who took up a strategically useful appointment with the Reuters news agency in Nairobi.[22]

Notable successes were achieved in Kenya during the month of November, undoubtedly as a direct result of Verlaque's groundwork. A delegation headed by Robert Frichot and including Hoarau, Verlaque and David Joubert — a former Minister of Tourism and Aviation in the Mancham administration — met people whom Hoare described as 'certain Kenyan government officials'.[23]

The leader of the Kenyan delegation was probably the colourful government minister, Charles Njonjo, a dandy rarely seen without the affectation of a red carnation in his buttonhole. Kenya's elite, half affectionately and half sarcastically, called him 'Sir Charles' because he modelled himself on their former British colonialists. His political clout, nevertheless, was considerable, probably exceeding that of Vice President Mwai Kibaki. It was also pertinent that Njonjo was a friend of James Mancham.[24] Kenya's Police Commissioner, Ben Gethi, also attended the meeting.[25]

Frichot said the outcome was 'highly satisfactory'. They had gained all the necessary backing, plus certain other unspecified concessions. [26] Politically the plan called for the restoration of the presidency to Mancham with Hoarau becoming vice president and Frichot prime minister.[27]

Colonel Hoare's mercenaries 'would act rapidly and decisively and then withdraw'. Kenya would place troops and police on standby to fly in, take over from Colonel Hoare and 'restore order'.[28]

Hoarau flew to London to see Mancham. He confidently expected to persuade him to change his mind about reclaiming the presidency. The friendly relationship enjoyed by Njonjo and Mancham must have been a key factor in the Nairobi discussions, so Frichot's delegation probably failed to mention Mancham's lack of enthusiasm.[29]

Frichot's German backers were satisfied with the Kenya discussions, but demanded the budget be trimmed to US$2 million. Hoare reluctantly complied, but viewed the cuts with misgivings.[30]

Although Jerry Puren had been dropped from the plot, the Durban exiles — principally Gerard Hoarau, his brother Owen and D'Offay — at times dropped in at his garage for a chat. Puren said they often discussed using other mercenary leaders, not having finally signed off on Mike Hoare. One name that came up was George Schroeder, then a successful businessman in Cape Town, who had succeeded Peters as the commander of 5-Commando in Congo days.

Tullio Moneta, an Italian born in Yugoslavia, had served with Hoare in V Commando and had maintained regular contact.

William Dunlop-Paul, a karate 3rd Dan and the owner of several health studios, was also friendly with Tullio. He was a Citizen Force corporal attached to South Africa's 2-Reconnaissance Commando in a support capacity. He had tried selection but had failed.

Moneta, Dunlop-Paul and Kurt Priefert, another former mercenary serving in 2-Recce, visited Schroeder in Cape Town. Schroeder said he was planning to overthrow President René but was very vague about his plans, which somehow involved the United States' Indian Ocean base of Diego Garcia. Schroeder offered each of them a down payment of R20 000 with another R20 000 to come on completion of the mission. Nothing was finalised but arrangements were made to meet again later.[31]

Tullio Moneta, unaware that Mike Hoare was hatching his own plans for a coup, phoned him and mentioned briefly what had occurred in Cape Town.[32] Hoare, who did not explain Tullio's own role, was furious when he heard of the involvement of 'Mr X' — Schroeder in his book. He immediately phoned London and told Eddie Camille he considered Schroeder's involvement to be 'a grave security risk which could prove fatal to the operation'. He suspended his involvement pending an assurance that Camille was not negotiating with Schroeder. The assurance was not readily forthcoming.

In February 1981 Hoare heard on the grapevine that Robert Frichot was paying a secret visit to South Africa to conduct negotiations with Schroeder. Schroeder introduced Frichot to Brigadier Daan Hamman of the SADF. He heard, too, that the SADF had paid for David Joubert to fly from London to Cape Town to take part in these discussions.[33]

Brigadier Hamman made no mention of Schroeder to the author, but he did say that Hoare had not been his preferred choice of commander for the operation. The man he wanted, presumably because of his close association with the SADF over the Comores takeover, was Colonel Bob Denard. In fact, he said, he did everything possible to swing the coup attempt over to Denard. He failed because of Mike Hoare's deep involvement with the plotters and their trust of him. There is no suggestion that he had negotiated directly with the exiles.[34]

Moneta, Dunlop-Paul and Priefert met Schroeder for a second time at the Rand International Hotel, Johannesburg. Tullio again reported to Mike Hoare, saying that Schroeder was evasive and he had learned little about his plans.[35]

Annoyed over being double crossed, Hoare sent his resignation to Eddie Camille. The plotters, however, hastily reassured him that their negotiations with Schroeder were of no consequence. Neither had they breached security — which seems highly unlikely in the circumstances.[36]

It seems probable that Hoare's threat to withdraw happened at a crucial time. Perhaps Brigadier Hamman had tried to off-load the services of Bob Denard on the plotters, causing them to back off in alarm. Perhaps, too, the exiles became concerned that if they continued their double dealing, they might end up militarily leaderless. Despite this, according to Hoare, Hoarau continued secret negotiations with Schroeder, before finally dropping him in mid 1981.[37]

Anthony Mockler said that Charles Njonjo had paid a secret visit to South Africa.[38] He said it was 'almost certain' he came to have discussions with the plotters in Durban, but this seems unlikely because Njonjo was a powerful and important man. If he had wanted to see them, he would have told them to fly to Nairobi, which would have been less politically perilous than his flying to South Africa. On the other hand, this would have been more feasible if he had gone there to conduct high level discussions with the South African government about coordinating their respective actions for the coup attempt.

Robert Frichot's German backers lost interest during the course of 1981, so the situation returned to square one. In June 1981 he told Hoare that US$200 000 would become available in August. It had apparently been pledged by a secret backer in South Africa. Hoare insisted Frichot reveal the identity of the financier. Frichot reluctantly told him it was the National Intelligence Service.[39] It was not much money to mount a mercenary operation with, but it was better than nothing.

In July or August 1981 Hoare met Tullio Moneta, whom he had earmarked as his deputy commander, at the Balalaika Hotel, Sandton. Hoare revealed his plans saying he was in touch with various leaders of the Seychelles Resistance Movement in different parts of the world. Tullio had visited the island and knew many of the personalities involved. He was keen to take part if the coup had the backing of the South African government.

Hoare confirmed that this was the case, adding that a US Congressman, a neighbour of US Secretary of State, General Alexander Haig, had also lent his tacit support to the operation. He envisaged a 130-strong mercenary group, of which 20 or 30 would comprise an advance party. Moneta expressed disquiet, believing that an attempt to raise such a large force would most likely leak to the press.[40]

Could the right type of men, trained and willing to take part in a coup attempt, be found at short notice? More importantly, would they agree to payment afterwards instead of in advance? Tullio had doubts that this would be acceptable to more than 30 or 40 of the men he had in mind.

Assuming that the necessary willing volunteers could be found, Hoare made plans for a cut-price coup costing US$300 000. He forwarded the proposal to Eddie Camille in London. He suggested that all expenses except for wages be met from the capital sum. 90% of the wages would be paid into Swiss bank accounts 14 days after the coup. The remaining 10% would be retained and paid after 60 days, providing the men had remained discreet. Per man this would amount to US$1 000 on engagement, US$9 000 on the successful completion of the contract and a final US$1 000 after 60 days.[41]

The 'spontaneous' uprising of several hundred members of the resistance was envisaged once the coup was under way.

A meeting of exiles chaired by Gerard Hoarau was convened in Durban and Hoare's proposals were discussed. They decided that paying the mercenaries after successful conclusion of the coup would not pose a problem. They would raise government loans, or make personal appeals to certain wealthy citizens who would feel an obligation to comply.

Both Gerard Hoarau and Colonel Hoare believed it vital that James Mancham, as the only unifying figure, be part of the coup. Hoarau flew to London to try to persuade him. Mancham changed his mind yet again, agreeing to take office with Hoarau as his vice-president. After six months, Hoarau would take over as president, allowing James Mancham to retire to England. Frichot, who pledged his loyal support to Mancham, would become ambassador to Australia.

Mike Hoare and Tullio Moneta flew to Mahé for a final reconnaissance on 10 September 1981. Hoare said they would meet there with an officer of the Zimbabwe Air Force who would assist with the planning. This officer knew the island well, because he often fished there. The officer turned out to be a former commander of the Rhodesian SAS and later a top CIO operative, Major Dudley Coventry, then in command of Zimbabwe's 1-Parachute Battalion.[42]

They met the local head of resistance in Mahé who assured them support would be forthcoming when the time came.

Two basic problems remained. The first was the means by which they would get arms to the island. The second was how to get the mercenaries there. The first problem was solved after they spoke to a member of the resistance. He imported bulk goods from South Africa and his merchandise was rarely checked because of a chummy relationship he shared with the local customs chief. He handed Hoare a supply of blank pro-forma invoices.

Hoare said he decided to restrict armaments to 100 automatic rifles with 90 rounds of ammunition per weapon. Foolishly, he decided to dispense with grenades and support weapons like RPG-7 rocket launchers and 60mm mortars. He believed that if the rifles and ammunition were packed and spread unobtrusively throughout a number of crates. They would likely escape detection. In Mahé they would be cached in a safe house.

The mercenaries would enter the country unarmed and[43] in small groups over a period of several days and disperse to a variety of hotels to avoid attention. Later they would hire Mini-Mokes — ideal for transporting two or three armed men around — and conduct final studies of their particular targets.

Tullio Moneta confirmed by reconnaissance that President René was guarded by a 30-strong élite unit. Their quarters above State House were protected by a high security fence with a mounted spotlight. There were some anti-aircraft gun positions and a few tanks. Fifty troops were based at the Tanzanian Army barracks. Montena looked at the Cable and Wireless station. He obtained a plan of State House and various other useful documents, presumably through his contacts in the resistance. He estimated the staff at the Soviet Embassy at 105.

More pertinent to his mercenary calling, he was promised favours by members of the resistance which would handsomely supplement the fees being paid to him by Colonel Hoare. This included a shareholding in a local hotel and the promise of facilities to open a business for the export of granite.[44]

Mike Hoare, after spending three days on Mahé, flew on to Harare. Moneta remained to complete the reconnaissance. It is unknown if Hoare was accompanied by Dudley Coventry.

In Harare Hoare saw Jack Malloch of Air Trans Africa and asked him to provide an aircraft to fly in the new government-in-waiting from Nairobi on D-day. He also enquired where arms could be acquired. Colonel Hoare said Malloch suggested Libreville instead of Nairobi. This seems unlikely for several reasons — despite Gabon being the main base for Affretair, Air Trans Africa's trading name in that country.

Firstly, there was a need to position the post-coup administration in Mahé without delay. A flight from Libreville, on Africa's west coast, added 4 800km — plus the extra flying time — to a 1 800km flight from Kenya. Secondly, Kenya was backing the coup and flying in troops afterwards, so why bother with Gabon?

Hoare said he came to terms with Malloch, but was reticent about what they were. Intriguingly, he mentioned a second trip to Zimbabwe a few weeks later (probably late September or early October 1981) to talk 'arms and aircraft' with Malloch, but he did not expand on its purpose.[45] One thing appears certain, though. He did not need another arms supplier because the SADF was involved by then.

There were two possible scenarios. The first was to arrange for Jack Malloch to fly the armed mercenaries directly into Mahé's Pointe Larue Airport, copying Denard's unsuccessful assault on Cotonou, Benin, on 5 January 1977.[46] The second was to have him circling overhead when the coup was launched so he could evacuate them if things went wrong. Mike Hoare had certainly kept Malloch in mind throughout his years of plotting and planning, as was witnessed by his 1978 letter to Gonzanque D'Offay. Three unnamed mercenaries, part of Hoare's old Congo clique and apparently the only ones he kept in the know, confirmed Malloch's involvement to the South African *Sunday Times*.

'He was heavily involved in the plot', one said, 'but pulled out mysteriously about a week to ten days before the operation was to be launched, causing a delay in our plans. I never really found out his reasons. Although the op seemed risky he was not really taking much of a chance as he would have landed straight after a coup and there would have been no record of his ever having been there. After it was over, he would have carried on his business in Zimbabwe as usual and no one would have been any the wiser.'

'Our plan was to have the plane overhead within half an hour', another said, 'because we wanted to be out of there as quickly as possible. I knew Captain Malloch from Rhodesia and there is no way he pulled out because he got cold feet.'

It was also suggested Malloch would have flown the mercenaries to Kenya where they would have been paid off after the coup had been successfully concluded.[47]

It remains an open question whether the original plan called for two aircraft. One would be piloted by Jack Malloch to fly in the main force and be available afterwards as an escape contingency if things went wrong. The other would wait at Nairobi to bring in the post-coup administration. It seems likely this was the case.

Hoare said his arrangement with Malloch to fly in the new administration fell through because the Zimbabwe Government nationalised Air Trans Africa and its associate companies a few weeks after their discussions.[48] The Zimbabwe Government obviously believed the substantial investments made in the company via the Central Intelligence Organisation during the Bush War years justified the move.

Anyway, it is doubtful whether a wild card like Jack Malloch — who took exuberant delight in using his own restored Spitfire to beat up the first Soviet aircraft to land after independence as it taxied in at Salisbury Airport — would have been popular with the new regime. He died tragically in an air crash involving the same Spitfire in 1982.

A first consignment of arms, a small truckload originating from a Rhodesian source introduced by Jack Malloch, arrived at Hoare's Hilton home during September 1981. It is believed an ex-Rhodesian stole a large quantity of ex-communist arms from Security Force stocks in Rhodesia. In the confusion of independence, he smuggled them from the country and warehoused them in the garage of his new Swaziland home. He had been keeping them, waiting for the right customer to come along.[49]

Colonel Hoare said he was forced to liquidate his personal share portfolio, raising US$14 000, to finance necessary expenditure because the National Intelligence Service money had not appeared.[50] The 'necessary expenditure' was not specified, but it is assumed it was to pay for the arms consignment.

Hoare ordered Moneta to begin discreetly recruiting key personnel in the Transvaal and the latter discussed his requirements with William Dunlop-Paul. Dunlop-Paul suggested they use the Citizen Force operators of 2-Recce and he put Tullio in contact with Sergeant Brian Walls — a Johannesburg jeweller in civilian life. He suggested they use the experienced and tough former Recce, Major Willy Ward, as a senior leader. He was then the commander of the SADF's Citizen Force 3-Parachute Battalion.

Willy Ward, Brian Walls, William Dunlop-Paul, Kurt Priefert and Pieter Doorewaard — a staff sergeant with 2-Recce — attended a meeting arranged by Moneta at Kyalami Ranch near Johannesburg. Hoare expanded on his plan and detailed his requirements. Willy Ward would lead one group and Tullio Moneta the other. Pay would be R40 000 each, with sub-leaders like Doorewaard getting R20 000.

Everyone was enthusiastic. It is believed Willy Ward offered to raise as many as 70 Recce operators for the operation should they be needed.[51] But according to Moneta, he along with Priefert, Dunlop-Paul and Doorewaard took the lead in recruiting the Recces.[52]

Willy Ward insisted, however, that the operation be approved by the SADF before he would take part.[53] Hoare assured him the approval existed, which — initially at least — satisfied him. He later asked to speak to Gerard Hoarau and the other local exiles to satisfy himself that the operation was justified. This was arranged. National Party parliamentary candidate Norman Reeves accompanied him during these discussions. Moneta regarded this as a serious breach of security, but Hoare was unconcerned.[54]

Hoare then commenced a low key recruiting campaign in Natal. He mentioned the possibility of an 'operation' to Peter Duffy, a freelance photographer and former officer with 5-Commando. 'How long and how much?' Duffy asked. In the end he declined. He was settled in civilian life and deeply involved in his own work.

Next was Barney Carey, another ex-Congo hand, who promptly volunteered. According to him many ex-Rhodesian soldiers, mostly battle hardened ex-SAS and ex-6-Reconnaissance Commando operators, used the Riviera Hotel in Durban as a watering hole. Hoare asked him to discreetly enquire about their availability. He reported back that most were unemployed and experiencing lean times. The manpower available from this source was probably four or five times greater than their needs.

Barney Carey, Ken Dalgliesh and Mike Webb eventually conducted most of the recruiting in Natal.[55] Because of budgetary considerations and for reasons of security, no one was engaged until the last moment.

Having some weapons to hand, Mike Hoare next formed an import/export company, through which he would export merchandise to his Mahé contact. He estimated he needed 50 to 60 packing cases in which to conceal the weapons and ammunition. Having ordered sufficient trade goods, he engaged a discreet carpenter to make the crates.

When the crates were ready and the merchandise was to hand, he packed some according to the bills of lading, but concealed the arms and ammunition amongst the goods.

A second and final consignment of weapons was due from his Rhodesian source, but the shippers said the packing cases had to be delivered to their Durban warehouse by Saturday 10 October 1981. If they arrived late, the consignment would miss the *SS Range* because it was due to sail five days after that. The consignment would arrive in Victoria about the end of October, which was right for the proposed *coup* dates. The second consignment of arms, unfortunately, would not be in time for the *SS Range*'s departure deadline.

Gerard Hoarau, who had developed a close liaison with the National Intelligence Service, flew to Pretoria at Hoare's request. He asked them for another 75 automatic rifles, either AK47s or FNs, with 100 rounds of ammunition for each.[56]

The NIS arranged a top level conference at the Elangeni Hotel, Durban, on 19 September under the chairmanship of their Mr Rothman. Hoare's requirements were discussed and his indent scrutinised by someone of a higher rank or status who remained incognito in an adjoining room. Whoever he was, he approved it.

After that it went to the State Security Council for approval. This body was due to meet in Cape Town on Tuesday 22nd and an answer was expected by the following day.

On the 23rd, JY 'Jimmy' Claasens, number two NIS, phoned Hoare and asked him to fly to Pretoria for a meeting. 'The Cabinet has given it the okay and the Prime Minister [P W Botha] is right behind it', Claasens told him over lunch. Asked if he meant 'in principle', Claasens replied: 'No, no, no! Not only in principle. He is right behind the whole project. All the way.' Hoare would get everything he had asked for, probably at no charge. Hoare said in his book that this occurred at a Pretoria roadhouse, which contradicted his court evidence when he said it was at the Burgers Park Hotel.[57]

Late that afternoon there was an unexpected change of plans. The Prime Minister, to Claasens' disappointment, had ordered the NIS to hand over the project to the SADF.

The next morning Claasens took Hoare to Zanza Building, Proes Street, where he introduced him to Brigadier Daan Hamman and the 'sergeant' he had last seen at Pretoria railway station. He turned out to be Brigadier Martin Knoetze.

Claasens explained the State Security Council's decision and passed on the Prime Minister's orders. The SADF was to make arms, ammunition and equipment available to Colonel Hoare. Brigadier Knoetze baulked, demanding a written instruction from the Prime Minister's office. Hoare was asked to wait in an outer office while the order was clarified. When it had been confirmed, Hoare rejoined them and Claasens left.[58]

Brigadier Daan Hamman asked Hoare to outline his needs. Hoare requested hand-held radios, weapons, ammunition and thunder flashes. He needed them by 7 October to give him time to pack and deliver them to the shipping agents by 10 October.

The brigadiers recommended the use of communist weapons because their origins were virtually impossible to trace.[59] Hoare agreed, saying he preferred AK47s with folding butts. He asked for four magazines per weapon, which posed no problem. The AKs, ammunition and radios would be drawn from stock captured in Angola, but they could not help with thunder flashes.

They met the next day for further discussions. Hoare went through his plan in greater detail, but avoided specifics of his intentions on D-day as he felt it was none of their business.

He wanted a remote camp where the recruits could be taken for training and rehearsals. That would also put them beyond reach of the press. He had in mind a private game ranch belonging to a friend in Naboomspruit in northern Transvaal. Brigadier Knoetze, however, offered him the better alternative of an SADF training camp in north-western Transvaal.

Hoare testified later that he had planned to recruit about 73 South African soldiers 'because their motivation would have been right'. The brigadiers, however, restricted him to recruiting a maximum of 12 to 15 South Africans, preferably with foreign passports. 'It was a question of keeping South African involvement to a minimum'.[60] In his book, though, he said he told the brigadiers his plan involved 100 men with a small reserve. He made no mention of the recruitment of South African soldiers.[61]

That evening the brigadiers brought a senior officer to his hotel to meet him and have a few drinks. The officer was the SADF's Military Intelligence chief, General Pieter van der Westhuizen. No business was discussed.[62]

There was much media speculation later about why the South African government agreed to help with the *coup*. Why would they interfere in a place like the Seychelles? Many reasons were advanced.

There was the advantage of overthrowing a Marxist government in the region, in keeping with the declared principle of 'total onslaught'; the restoration of SAA's landing rights; the potential of Mahé as a staging post for imports and exports if more stringent UN sanctions were imposed against South Africa; its use as a listening post for monitoring the Soviet fleet; the value of a friend at the OAU; its worth as a base from which to destabilise ANC-supporting Tanzania; and so on.

The truth was less complicated from the SADF's viewpoint.

The toppling of the René regime was not a priority and it did not even appear on the list, although Seychelles had been mentioned occasionally. The first time it came under serious consideration was when Mike Hoare appeared with his proposals. The short view was that the René administration was Marxist, so an overthrow would accrue some advantages to South Africa even if they were only minor. While South Africa would certainly not go out of its way to mount a coup by itself, somebody else had come forward to do it for them. It was a cut price deal, virtually for the cost of the arms, which would be captured stuff anyway.

It was an anti-communist coup going begging . . . it seemed a shame to waste it. So they did not![63]

The phone rang at Colonel Hoare's home at 07:00 on 6 October 1981. The caller warned him to stand by for 'a delivery' within the hour. He sent his servants away and an hour later a civilian type five ton truck entered his drive and drove onto the front lawn, rutting it deeply. The driver, who introduced himself as Sergeant- Major van der Merwe, and a co-driver had driven overnight from Pretoria. Both were dressed in civvies.

With Hoare's assistance they began to unload their cargo into the wine cellar.[64] It comprised 60 folding butt AK47s of Romanian origin, 15 Hungarian AMD 7,62 X 39mm rifles, five RPG-7 rocket launchers, 60 AK47 cleaning kits, 240 AK47 magazines, 60 AK47 slings, 23 800 rounds of AK ammunition, 20 hand grenades, 102 rockets for the RPG-7s and 15 two-way radios with batteries and plugs.

Much later Tullio Moneta noticed that ten AK47s were stamped with the mark of the Palestine Liberation Organisation (PLO). Three were marked 'MCL'.[65] This raises the possibility that the SADF had obtained some stock from the Israelis.

To Hoare's astonishment, considering the covert nature of the operation, Sergeant Major van der Merwe asked him to sign an issue voucher that fully detailed the consignment as a receipt. The Sergeant-Major, being a true bureaucrat, handed him a copy for his retention.[66]

Hoare commented that he got 'far in excess' of what he had asked for and estimated the value of the weapons at R1 million.This was a puzzling statement. Gerard Hoarau, at Hoare's suggestion, had asked for 75 rifles. He got them together with cleaning kits and rifle slings, 100 rounds of ammunition per weapon and 15 two-way radios. Hoare added the extra requirement of four magazines per weapon, presumably the standard 30 round variety. This meant he had increased his basic operational needs to 120 rounds per weapon, as carrying empty magazines would have been pointless. This brought his basic ammunition requirement, as far as the SADF supplied weapons were concerned, to 9 000 rounds.

But what about ammunition for the weapons bought from the ex-Rhodesian? These arms must have included at least 25 AK47s, because his plan involved 100 mercenaries. This would have raised the operational requirement by 3 000 rounds to at least 12 000.

The SADF expected the mercenaries would be taken to a camp in north-western Transvaal after recruitment, so a training allowance of 11 800 rounds of ammunition — a mere 118 rounds per man, to turn a group of strangers into a homogeneous fighting unit — seems mean rather than excessive.

Sergeant-Major van der Merwe had been ordered by Brigadier Hamman to return with a detailed copy of Hoare's operational plan, so while Mrs Hoare busied herself cooking them breakfast, the Colonel drew one up.

It was virtually identical to the one he had already discussed with Brigadier Hamman. The weapons would be shipped to the Seychelles by the *SS Range* and hidden in safe houses. The mercenaries would follow in small groups posing as tourists. For the first time, though, Hoare introduced two contingency plans in case the first fell through. This raised more questions than answers.

The first involved 'the purchase of an ocean-going yacht into whose false bilges the arms and ammunition would be stowed'. One is left wondering why, when he was poised to consign arms via the *SS Range*, he suddenly raised the possibility of this falling through? If he really intended to ship the weapons, why did he omit RPG-7 rocket launchers, rockets and grenades from the packing cases? [67] Surely the inclusion of such items would have posed no difficulties. That he did not, indicates that he probably never really intended shipping weapons on the *SS Range*.

While an ocean-going yacht would have provided a means of escape for some, although certainly not all the mercenaries, where was the money to buy it? The budget was already stretched.

His second contingency plan involved getting the arms and the men to the island simultaneously, but he provided no details of this.[68] The late introduction of this contingency suggests he had already decided that the men and the weapons would enter Mahé simultaneously. It was certainly risky, but it was also the cheapest way and the one which would leave Hoare with the greatest profit after the operation.

If the *SS Range* option had fallen through, it would have been due only to increased customs or military activity — if word of the impending coup had leaked to the authorities. And if that had happened, a new yacht in the area would also have attracted the unwelcome attention of the authorities. Such a scenario would have also substantially increased the risk of smuggling in weapons with personal baggage.

Mad Mike Hoare was a mercenary and in business for the money, whatever else he might have suggested to the contrary. With the National Intelligence Service holding the purse strings so tightly, there was not much cash left in it for him so he was obviously skimping on budgets.

It was essential that all weapons, particularly these secondhand captured weapons, were checked and tested. A discreetly remote rifle range was needed. This posed a major problem considering the large quantity of arms involved, but Martin Dolinchek solved it by arranging for the disused La Mercy Airport north of Durban to be used. Hoare, along with his sons Bruce, Chris and Simon, Bob Sims — his brother-in-law and a former jockey — and Martin Dolinchek, range-tested them there.[69]

Martin Dolinchek, Hoare said, offered his services as a security man and volunteered to report secretly on the mercenaries' behaviour once on the island. Hoare said he found the suggestion distasteful and refused. Dolinchek persisted, saying he would take leave from 5 November to 17 December and go in his private capacity.

At his Seychelles trial Dolinchek testified that he told his friends he was going elephant hunting in Botswana's Tuli Block. He said his superiors were not aware of his plans and they would not have approved his going.[70]

In the end Colonel Hoare, despite his distaste, took him on and paid him US$1 000 advance like the rest. Dolinchek possessed a forged passport in the name of Anton Lubick.[71] Hoare said he was unable to properly use him in a mercenary capacity because he was a 'fumbling amateur' and not a highly trained soldier. This does not ring true. He was a serving a member of the National Intelligence Service and an ex-member of the SAP, so he must have been a practised professional — certainly more so than most of the boys of the old Congo brigade. When one examines his actions after the coup bid, however, it is easy to understand why Hoare (and the NIS for that matter) played down his expertise.

Hoare said it was the intention of the NIS to have Dolinchek and three 'special experts' break into the Soviet embassy in Victoria. It was there, the NIS believed, that the Soviets coordinated their plans for subverting Africa, which explained the inflated diplomatic staff. Dolinchek had even persuaded Peter Duffy to come along as one of the 'experts'. His task was to photograph secret documents, which as a professional photographer he was well able to do.

Peter Duffy was less illuminating and only said that Dolinchek had contacted him. He said he was feeling ill from blood poisoning, to which Dolinchek retorted he should get better because he had a 'specific task' in mind for him. He told him to get his passport in order, obtain an international driving licence and get his yellow fever injections up to date.[72] Whether he was to be paid by the NIS or by Hoare is open to speculation. It seems improbable that Hoare would have made payments to men who were primarily engaged on NIS business from his niggardly US$300 000. It is more likely that the NIS picked up the tab for all four, including Dolinchek.

Hoare said he forbade breaking into the embassy because of the dangers of treading on the toes of the Soviet Union and dismissed Dolinchek variously as an 'anti-communist fanatic' . . . 'a little unbalanced' . . . 'a nut.'

Yet despite this 'specific task' having fallen away, Duffy and Dolinchek were still on track to go. So were the other 'special experts', 'Blue' Kelly, an Australian and Jan Sydow, a Swede. Both, it was suggested, were full time National Intelligence Service operators brought in by Dolinchek.[73] It is open to conjecture what Dolinchek's plans really were, but they might not have been as harebrained as suggested by Hoare.

Breaking into the Soviet embassy might indeed have been a mission impossible, but this was probably a red herring. Targeting a particular KGB officer's house and rifling his safe or filing cabinet would have been a far more useful exercise. Perhaps their task was to check records in the Seychelles Foreign Ministry, the papers of the Foreign Minister and perhaps in the office of the President himself. It would have been an ideal opportunity to check Communist Bloc connections and gather intelligence relating to the OAU's efforts to bring about South Africa's downfall. They would have had a free hand and plenty of time to do the job during the lull after the mercenaries took control and before the incoming administration assumed office.

Dolinchek obviously had an open brief, which is underlined by Colonel Hoare saying he had 'no official role to play in the operation'. He would be there merely as an observer. But why did he need an observer?

Who was he observing for?

Why recruit him at all?

To add to the confusion, Martin Dolinchek testified while on trial for his life in the Seychelles that he had agreed to be 'Colonel Hoare's driver, intelligence officer and bodyguard'.[74] Earlier, however, he had told the UN commission of enquiry investigating the coup, probably more truthfully, that he had been there on 'official business', not as a mercenary.[75]

Significantly, neither Peter Duffy nor 'Blue' Kelly appeared to have set roles to play in the coup. Both were seemingly loosely available. Jan Sydow was attached to Hoare's staff, but no one knew why. Perhaps he was a NIS liaison officer.[76]

Patrick Henrick, who disliked Blue Kelly from previous dealings he had had with him, specifically asked why he was involved. Hoare answered that 'security' had placed him there.[77]

Kelly when asked in court if he belonged to the National Intelligence Service, replied: 'I have nothing to say'. Later he changed his mind and said he had not gone to Seychelles on the instructions of the 'Security Branch'. He said nothing about the NIS.[78]

Once involved, though, Kelly did some recruiting of his own and was the first to broach the question of a 'job' to Rich Stannard, ex-Rhodesian SAS and 6-Recce operative.[79]

Another indication that Martin Dolinchek had a special role, was that Colonel Hoare did not even introduce him to Moneta, his second in command. Despite this, posing as 'Anton from New York', he made a frequent nuisance of himself by phoning Moneta to obtain the names of Recce recruits for security clearance purposes. Tullio indignantly queried his authority, but it is significant that Hoare confirmed it by telling him 'he was a member of security'.[80]

According to Hoare, Brigadier Daan Hamman phoned on Thursday 8 October 1981 with 'highly reliable information' that the Mahé importer had come under suspicion from the Seychelles' authorities. He advised Hoare to abandon any ideas of smuggling weapons in through him.

Hoare said he complied reluctantly, but only after getting an identical tipoff from an unidentified foreign diplomat in Pretoria. In his book, he was reticent about the diplomat's identity, but at his trial he testified that he maintained close contacts with a CIA agent in Pretoria. He said: 'I submitted reports to him and kept him fully posted on developments in the same way as I did with BOSS [National Intelligence Service].'[81]

There is only Hoare's word that he actually received such warnings. Daan Hamman has said not a word and neither has the CIA. Anyway, whatever the case, he abandoned his first plan and switched to the alternate one.

The next day Brigadier Knoetze withdrew his offer to provide a military training camp. Someone had changed his mind. Hoare, in his book, complained that this destroyed all chances of getting to know his men before the operation. He stressed the importance of leaders getting to know their men and vice versa.[82] Curiously enough, he said nothing about the vital necessity of men training and rehearsing together before an operation — particularly mercenaries who had drifted in from the street and hardly knew each other. It was even more curious that he did not try to revert to his original intention of using his friend's Naboomspruit game farm as a training area.

So the training he had at first deemed so essential was whittled down from the initial four months in the Persian Gulf to no training whatsoever.

He decided to use Bob Sims to test a plan he had been 'considering for some time'. This meant stripping down an AK47 and packing it at the base of a holdall in a block of polystyrene a few centimetres thick, the folding butt model fitting perfectly in such a bag. He professed not to have restricted himself to considering the AK47 only, but said he also examined the Heckler and Koch HK54, the Schmeiser MP40 and the Israeli Uzi.[83] His decision to use the AK, he said, 'turned largely on the availability of ammunition', because captured ammunition would fit that and not the other weapons.[84]

This appears strange because since September, when he had received the AK47s from Jack Malloch's ex-Rhodesian contact and more later from the SADF together with 23 800 rounds of 7,62-mm short ammunition, he had been irrevocably committed to the AK. In fact, unless lavish sums of extra money had suddenly become available, switching to another weapon type was impossible. His experiments with packing weapons into bags confirms that his idea of flying in fully armed men was a plan of long standing.

On Saturday 31 October Hoare put his method to the test in a full-dress rehearsal. Robert Sims with his girlfriend Susan Ingles, alias Sims, and Barney Carey flew into Mahé posing as holiday-makers. Each had a doctored holdall with an AK47, two magazines and an additional 120 rounds of ammunition concealed in the base. They were waved through customs without being subjected to a baggage check.[85]

The Sims pair had rented a small villa called Fairview at La Misère, a village on the island's central high ground close to NASA's satellite tracking station. Colin Whiting, an associate of Gerard Hoarau, had arranged the lease. It belonged to the Savvys who lived next door. They would later recall that they scarcely saw the Sims during their visit.[86]

They hid two smuggled AKs, the magazines and the ammunition in a cellar beneath the house. Susan Ingles called at the Standard Bank, Victoria, where she opened two bank accounts in her name and paid US$10 000 into each. The money had been telexed to her by the Swiss Banking Corporation, Geneva, on the behalf of their client, M Thomas Hoare.[87] It was to cover the expenses of the advance guard as they drifted into the island. Their task would be to conduct final reconnaissances and take photographs of targets, strategic points and so on. Barney Carey stayed a week, putting up at the Reef Hotel south of the airport, before he flew back to Durban.

The next to arrive was Martin Dolinchek, who travelled as Anton Lubick. He also posed as a tourist and was booked on a fortnight's package tour with Budget Tours. For the first week he was booked in at the Reef Hotel, for the second, at the Beauvallon Bay Hotel on the far side of the island. His task, he said later, was to 'evaluate the political, social economic and military situation for Mike Hoare'.

And probably to follow the National Intelligence Service's agenda!

He said later that Hoare tricked him into taking a holdall with a concealed AK47, by handing it to him just before he boarded, when it was too late to back out. Hoare denied this, but as he later pulled the same trick on everyone else, he probably did.

Dolinchek recklessly decided to declare cigarettes and liquor he had bought duty free in South Africa and made for the Red channel at Mahé Airport. Not accepting his declaration at face value, the customs officer decided to search his baggage for a spear gun which is a prohibited import to the islands. Luckily for Dolinchek he found nothing.

Robert Sims and Susan Ingles met him outside the airport and provided money for car hire and personal expenses. They relieved him of his weapon and concealed it at their safe house along with the rest.[88]

By Hoare's account, the NIS, working through Gerard Hoarau, came up with the solution to how the main force should be infiltrated. This was three weeks before the operation, around the first week of November. They would introduce the weapons to the island by means he, Hoarau, had been 'considering for some time'. Enlarging on this, he said the mercenaries would pose as members of a mens' club called The Chauvinist Pigs. They would wear ties with a distinctive club motif. The NIS undertook to arrange their manufacture.

The NIS would organise a bus, using a travel agent who had worked for them in the past, and ease the party's movement through the border post into Swaziland. They would depart for Mahé from Moreru Airport, Manzini, in an F-29 passenger aircraft chartered from the Royal Swazi National Airways. It could only carry 50 passengers, which would reduce the force to less than 60, including the advance party. Each would carry one of the special holdalls with a concealed AK47.

Hoare professed a dislike for the suggested name of the club and opted instead for Ye Ancient Order of Froth Blowers as an alternative. The Froth Blowers was an organisation of beer drinkers that was formed to raise money for children's charities in England between the two world wars.

It would be a Johannesburg drinking and rugby club, with particular emphasis on the former. Their cover story would be that they chartered an aircraft each year and went on boozy holidays to different destinations, distributing toys to local orphanages. Hoare nominated Peter Duffy, a man renowned for his wit and bonhomie, as 'tour' leader. To enhance their cover sterling silver lapel badges and suitcase stickers illustrated with a foaming beer tankard and the letters AOFB were prepared.[89]

Whether or not the NIS came up with the AOFB ties is unknown. The ties and lapel badges would have proved of little use anyway, because photographs of the mercenaries disembarking at the Pointe Larue International Airport — when their cover was most needed — show them in shirt sleeves, which was hardly a suitable attire for blazered club men.

Mike Hoare prepared the special luggage in his home workshop and bought a large quantity of lightweight toys to pack in them to divert attention from the concealed weapons.[90]

It was about this time that Brigadier Daan Hamman sent for Colonel Jan Breytenbach, then commanding 44-Parachute Brigade. He instructed him to visit Hoare at Hilton and undertake a proper appreciation of his plans. Brigadier Hamman had developed some worrying doubts over Colonel Hoare.

Hoare went over his plans with Breytenbach. He said the weapons and ammunition were already on the island and the men would fly there in the guise of tourists.

Breytenbach asked about the lack of a 'back door' in the plan. If things went wrong, how would they get out?

Hoare said his back door was President Daniel Arap Moi, because Kenya was flying in troops immediately afterwards.

How could he rely on this? The Kenyans might change their minds and not even go, particularly if things turned sour. What had been done about the group's training? What about rehearsals? How could weapons be zeroed if they had been shipped already?

Hoare dismissed the queries with a non committal shrug and stressed that it was a simple in and out operation. He was only using experienced soldiers, so he regarded training and rehearsals as unimportant. The weapons had been checked on the range so he did not regard zeroing as essential.

If flying in the weapons concealed in items of luggage with the mercenaries was a NIS suggestion, why did Hoare not advise Colonel Breytenbach or Brigadier Hamman, of that. Why did he say the weapons had already been shipped?

Undoubtedly, intense rivalry existed between Military Intelligence and the National Intelligence Service, but it seems unlikely the latter would have co-assisted Hoare to such a great extent without providing details to the former — particularly as they had already handed the operation over to the SADF on the Prime Minister's orders.

It also seems remarkably coincidental that Hoare had already conducted a dummy run with 'special luggage' using Sims and Carey before the NIS had allegedly made their suggestion.

Jan Breytenbach reported back to Brigadier Hamman, suggesting that he should 'laugh it off'.

Hamman took his advice and immediately demanded that Hoare return all the SADF's arms and equipment. Hoare replied that it was too late for that as everything was already on the water — he presumably meant the *SS Range*. He said that stuff he had not used, like the RPG-7s, surplus ammunition etc. was still at his house and they were welcome to collect it. They apparently did, but whether this was before or after the operation is unknown.

What was particularly significant, was that by Robert Sims's account, Hoare had removed 80 AK47s from his house and cached them at the Sims home in Hillcrest, Durban.[91] Hoare made no mention of this in his book.

This raises two interesting questions. Did Hamman really tell Hoare the Mahé importer had come under suspicion by the authorities? Or was this a ploy by Hoare to explain why he adopted the foolhardy method of trying to smuggle the guns through customs?

Jan Breytenbach discovered that Major Willy Ward, one of his battalion commanders, had been recruited for the operation. Ward firmly believed the operation had been given the official nod, particularly as the Chief of Staff Intelligence had provided the weapons. Jan told him to pull out, whether that approval existed or not, because there was no contingency escape plan if things the operation turned sour.[92] Major Ward contacted Hoare immediately and asked for details of his contingency plans. When pressed he admitted that none existed. Ward promptly withdrew from the operation.

About this time, according to Hoare, he had another meeting with Brigadier Hamman who again asked him to restrict the number of South African nationals taking part to a maximum of 15. If this caused problems, the Brigadier said, he would provide R30 000 to recruit more mercenaries in Europe. Hoare said he rejected the offer because it had come too late. This suggests he did not enlighten the brigadier on how many South Africans he had recruited.

Daan Hamman told the author, however, that SADF aid was conditional on Colonel Hoare recruiting no South Africans whatsoever. The question of recruiting serving members of the SADF, which he considered was preposterous, was not even mentioned.[93]

Like the cuckolded partner in a marriage when everyone insists 'he/she must have known', maybe Brigadier Hamman really did not know. Maybe people were hesitant to speak out about the almost open recruiting being conducted within the ranks of the SADF.

Perhaps they reasoned that if it was a Military Intelligence 'secret', it would be wise to pretend ignorance!

The proposed coup itself was certainly not much of a secret. The late Eschel Rhoodie, Secretary for Information, said he heard about it from Japanese businessmen in London long before it occurred. It triggered him into writing to General Geldenhuys on New Berners Hotel stationery 'warning him that if the coup was going to take place, the repercussions would irritate and antagonise the Reagan administration and the Thatcher government.' [94]

By mid-November recruiting for the operation was almost complete. The applicants were all personally interviewed by Hoare before final acceptance. The eventual number comprised 13 operators including two doctors from 2-Reconnaissance Commando, six operators or former operators from 1-Reconnaissance Commando, seven former operators from the disbanded 6-Recce — mostly ex-Rhodesian SAS — two ex-members of the British South Africa Police (Rhodesia) three ex-Selous Scouts, also from Rhodesia, three former members of the Rhodesian Light Infantry, two former Rhodesian Air Force pilots, seven ex-Congo mercenaries and a variety of others. Sven Forsell, a film producer-director without military experience, was permitted to go along unarmed for the ride to get the feel of mercenary operations.[95] Making up the final number was Martin Dolinchek and his three NIS agents. With Colonel Hoare and the Sims, there were 57 in all — 56 men and one woman.

The 2-Reconnaissance Commando operators were: 2/Lieutenant J L P 'Vic' de Beer, Staff Sergeant Pieter Doorewaard, Staff Sergeant Alan Mann, Sergeant Alex Deacon, Sergeant (Dr) Steyn de Wet, Sergeant (Dr) Chris de Jager, Corporal Johan Fritz, Corporal Keith Macleod, Corporal Des Walker, Lance-Corporal Bernard de Vos, Lance-Corporal Kurt G H Priefert, Lance-Corporal Patrick G B Henrick and Lance-Corporal William Dunlop-Paul.

The members and ex-members of 1-Reconnaissance Commando were Jochemus Dekker (a reserve officer), Christo Hillebrand (a former operator), Louis Boucher (a reservist who later rejoined), Kevin Beck (a reserve officer), Fred L Gouws and Dr Theo van Huyssteen.

The ex-members of 6-Reconnaissance Commando were Richard Stannard, Don Kenny, Nick Wilson, Barry Gribbin, Jacobus du Toit, Charlie Dukes and Roger England.

By Mockler's account, there were several last minute hitches in Kenya. The two turboprop aircraft originally scheduled for the operation (clearly Jack Malloch's) had been stood down and a Kenyan of note had withdrawn his support. The problems, he said, were resolved by Njonjo paying a visit to South Africa. Maybe also by Hoare visiting Nairobi, where he was said to have stayed at the Hotel Fransea in Moktar Daddah Street.

Hoare, however, contended he had no idea who in Kenya was helping with the coup bid and denies he went there. He confirmed, though, that Gerard Hoarau arrived in Nairobi a few days before the coup and arranged for the mustering of James Mancham's administration. He also got clearance from Nairobi's air traffic control for their aircraft to take off for Mahé at short notice.[96]

Under the new arrangement that came about after the nationalisation of Jack Malloch's Air Trans Africa by the Zimbabwe Government, a Beechcraft Super King 200, callsign Caroline Alpha, was leased from Captain Peter Lucas of Sunbird Charters. It would stand by at Nairobi until the code word for success, *Cloudburst*, was transmitted from Mahé. This would be acknowledged by the code words *Fairy Belle*, when they would take off for the Seychelles.

Hoare said the pilot was an old friend of Peter Duffy, but he did not identify him. He described him as 'not only highly experienced but also courageous and thoroughly reliable and, I may say, a legend in his own lifetime as an aviator of outstanding ability'. His fee was US$ 40 000.[97]

On 18 November 1981 Colonel Hoare presided over a meeting of the Durban group at the Riviera Hotel. Tullio Moneta presided over another for the Johannesburg group at his house. They explained the general terms and conditions of the contract and outlined the current political situation in the Seychelles. They told the men that Kenya was backing the coup and that it would fly in troops afterwards.

Many of the recruits demanded confirmation that the operation had been approved by the South African authorities. They were assured that Colonel Hoare had been working on his plans for three years with the support of the National Intelligence Service, the cooperation of Military Intelligence and with the backing of Prime Minister P W Botha and his cabinet. For obvious reasons they could not openly lend official support to a covert operation. Hoare said that if anyone doubted that the backing existed, they could check it out with any contacts they might have in high places. This, of course, was virtually impossible.[98]

Some, particularly the ex-Rhodesians who had already lost their homeland in a particularly vicious war, went to great lengths to confirm it. They were uncomfortably aware that if they got involved in anything illegal, they could be deported from South Africa and end up stateless. Most, however, being experienced Special Force soldiers and used to the tenets of covert warfare, did not expect evidence of South African involvement to be made freely available.

Barry Gribbin, a US citizen who had seen service in the Rhodesian SAS and 6-Reconnaissance Commando, was typical of most. When asked in court later — in the cool, clear light of day as it were — why he had accepted such skimpy information, he said reasonably: 'Last year troops from this country (they were from 6-Reconnaissance Commando — see Chapter 19 The Silent War, by Peter Stiff for the full story) drove into Maputo and killed 11 people. Was that legal? I don't know if it or the coup attempt was legal.' [99]

No one dropped out after those initial meetings.

They were warned to attend final briefings in Durban and Johannesburg on 23 November and advised they would be flying to the Seychelles on Wednesday 25 November.[100] Weapons, they were told, had already been smuggled into Mahé.

Colonel Hoare planned to commit a six-man advance party. They would operate in three teams of two and conduct final reconnaissances of the various targets. Later, when the main force arrived, they would join the groups responsible for the targets.

The first team comprised Ken Dalgliesh, manager of the Riviera Hotel and formerly of the BSA Police Special Branch and Aubrey Brooks, formerly a Selous Scout and later a Grey Scout in Rhodesia. He was a master controller in broadcasting, having learned his skills working for the Rhodesian Broadcasting Corporation. It was an essential skill for use after the coup succeeded. The second team was Charlie Dukes and Roger England, both ex-Rhodesian SAS and 6-Recce. The final duo was Barney Carey and Des Botes, an ex-member of the British South Africa Police.[101]

At the briefing of the advance party Hoare revealed his bombshell that their weapons would be accompanying them through customs on to the island. Des Botes protested, pointing out that there was a danger of detection at Louis Botha (Durban International) Airport, Jan Smuts (Johannesburg International) Airport and Mahé Airport.

Colonel Hoare reassured him, saying that provided the baggage intended for the hold was not found overweight at the check-in, it was put straight onto the conveyor belt and moved directly to the hold without examination. Only hand luggage was subject to X-ray. He told them that Barney Carey had already done the trip once without detection, so there was no need to worry. In the unlikely event of a weapon being detected, the person concerned should stay calm and he (Hoare) would soon have someone on the spot to sort things out.[102]

On 21 November Dalgliesh, Brooks, Carey and Botes, sitting apart on the same aircraft, flew to Mahé. The next day Dukes and England arrived there via the island of Réunion. They passed through customs carrying their holdalls without incident.

Some 2-Recce operators experienced difficulties in getting time off from their employment because they could not produce official call-up papers. Lieutenant Vic de

Beer, a member of the unit's support staff, took it on himself to overcome the problem. He approached the unit's only full time employee, Mrs Koen — reputed to be a meticulous worker — and demanded 18 or 19 blank forms of the standard DD 308 call-up papers.

Mrs Koen demurred, querying his request.

'It is no concern of yours . . . it's secret . . . you have no need to know . . . just give them to me.'

She handed them over, but noted the time and date in her diary.

The unit's OC, Commandant Sybie van der Spuy, was in America on arms procurement business for the Recces at the time.

Lieutenant De Beer provided call-up papers to anyone who experienced difficulties with his employer, including some men from other units. He stamped them with the unit's official date stamp and forged the signature of Major Bitten, the responsible officer.[103]

Mike Hoare personally conducted the final briefings for both the Durban and Johannesburg groups, the latter on 23 November 1981. He told them about their cover as the Froth Blowers and explained that they would be taking toys with them for orphans and underprivileged children. To enhance their respectability, because they were such a large group, arrangements had been made with the Seychelles Ministry of Tourism for the Minister of Tourism himself to hold a reception in their honour after their arrival.[104]

They were booked to stay at the Reef Hotel for a fortnight-long prepaid package tour. Hoare would stay at Auberge, a remote inn near the Sims' villa at La Misère. They would soak up the sun for a few days as tourists, then at midday on D-day — he did not specify the date — the operation would be launched. It would be during the heat of the day when it was anticipated that most enemy soldiers would be off guard and probably dozing.

Martin Dolinchek revealed later that Friday 27 November 1981 had been the planned D-day. Hoare imparted the sobering titbit that a battle fleet of Soviet warships was cruising in the area of the islands, but he did not believe it posed a threat to the operation's success.[105]

He explained his plan using papier maché models of the island.

Group One under Barney Carey's command was responsible for seizing the radio station at Unionvale, a few kilometres north of Victoria. Resistance from the 16-strong garrison guarding it was expected to be minimal.

Once in their control, Aubrey Brooks would broadcast a recorded message that announced the oppressive René regime had been overthrown by a popular uprising of the people. This would be followed by a recording of James Mancham proclaiming his return to the island and an appeal for calm. In traditional coup style, martial music would be played. Tapes chosen by Hoare himself, included *The World of Military Bands*, with marches by the massed bands of the Brigade of Guards, the bands of the Parachute Regiment and the Royal Marines.[106]

Group Two was 20 strong and commanded by Mike Webb, a former officer in the 15/19 The Kings Royal Hussars and a commando commander in the Rhodesian Light Infantry. Richard Stannard was his number two.

Group Two was broken down into three subgroups. The first, 12 strong, was commanded by Peter Hean, also an ex-RLI officer. He was tasked to neutralise the Seychellois Army barracks and secure and hold the airport perimeter.

The next subgroup, two former Rhodesian Air Force officers, Vernon Prinsloo and Charles Goatley, were tasked to take over the airport control tower. They would control air traffic and allow only authorised aircraft to land.

The final subgroup, a stick of six men under Simon Willar, formerly an officer in the Selous Scouts, would attack the two houses occupied by the Tanzanian contingent near the Pointe Larue camp. No particular problems were expected to arise provided they achieved and maintained the element of surprise.

Group Three, commanded by Tullio Moneta, was responsible for targets in Victoria. These included the army barracks, army headquarters, police headquarters, the presidential palace (if President René was not abroad as expected) and the parliamentary complex. The entire cabinet was expected to be there in session at 'H' hour.

Photographs and posters showing Albert René and his six cabinet ministers were displayed for identification purposes. Ogilvy Berlouis, the Minister of Youth and Defence, and James Michel, the Minister of Education and Information and Army Chief of Staff, were regarded as the most dangerous. The task of neutralising them was given to Pieter Doorewaard and his 2-Recce operators. Hoare ordered that the ministers should be taken prisoner and shot only if their resistance made it unavoidable.[107]

Hoare explained that the Seychellois were gentle people. A bloodless coup was the first prize, but this would occur only if strict security was maintained and they acted with the greatest speed and surprise.

Mike Hoare's HQ group comprised himself, Don Kenny for close protection, Jan Sydow for undisclosed reasons and Sven Forsell, who would act as administration officer and later as liaison officer to the incoming Mancham administration after the coup had been successfully completed. They would establish themselves in the Cable and Wireless offices from where they would control all external telephone and telex calls.[108]

Simon Willar asked: 'Is there a way out?'

Hoare told him that the aircraft flying in the new government 'would provide the means of escape if that was found necessary on D-day'. He added that if things went seriously wrong after touchdown, the advance party would be capable of causing a diversion. He made no attempt to explain how he would manage to cram nearly 60 mercenaries, plus James Mancham's administration, into a Beechcraft Super King 200.

Training and detailed rehearsals for an operation are essential, but none were conducted for *Operation Anvil*. It is imperative, too, that soldiers, no matter how experienced, have recently practised handling the weapons they are likely to use during an operation. It is probable that the serving Recce operators, who would have been training continually, fell into this category. The rest, even though they might have been away from weapons for just a few months, needed the chance to brush away the cobwebs.

Colonel Hoare produced an AK47 and passed it around to ensure that everyone knew how to strip and assemble it. He said: 'I timed a few of them and found they could assemble it in 20 seconds flat.'

Kevin Beck, a former 1-Recce officer, contradicted this. He said that he had taken the AK47 away from Hoare to demonstrate it, because 'some of the chaps present did not know how to handle it'. Nevertheless, despite his greater and more recent experience, Beck distinguished himself by fracturing his thumb during the demonstration. Beck was unimpressed with the soldierly qualities of the majority of them, describing them as 'a lot of old men'. With two in their 60s, one in his 50s, at least eight in their 40s and a dozen or so in their 30s, he was not far wrong.[109]

The worst fighting material — although many had probably been fine soldiers in their day — were the boys of the old 5-Commando brigade, including Mike Hoare himself. Few had seen a shot fired in anger since their glorious advance on Stanleyville in the Congo 20 years before. It is a sad but inevitable fact of military life that yesterday's heroes are not always the best material for fighting today's battles.

The rest, although fewer critical fingers can be pointed at their experience, varied in degrees of military rustiness. The ex-Rhodesians, depending on whether they became civilians on Robert Mugabe's sudden rise to power or continued their military service with 6-Recce or another SADF unit, were anything from a few months to two years distanced from military service.

Undoubtedly, everyone needed re-training and rehearsals.

The mercenaries were ordered to assemble at Jan Smuts (Johannesburg International) Airport at 14:00 on 24 November.

Colonel Jerry Puren did not attend the final briefing, having only been offered a part to play on 20 November. This was contrary to the advice of Dolinchek who had warned Hoare before he flew out that he should not 'take an old crazy like that!' Puren said he was allocated the task of taking and securing the control tower at Mahé Airport. Afterwards he would liaise with Bob Noddyn and Frank Puren to 'keep them out of circulation'. He was also tasked to be Peter Duffy's assistant master of ceremonies for the Froth Blowers.

Hoare contrarily maintained that Jerry Puren did not have a fighting role. His only task was to collect the debt of honour owed to him by Colonel Bob Noddyn, for saving his life all those Congolese years ago, by keeping him away from where the action was. This was something that Puren saw no difficulty in doing.

Hoare's version seems the most likely, because Puren's tasks at 'H' hour, as laid out by him, presented radically opposing priorities. They would have been impossible to attend to simultaneously. By his own account, he was also unarmed.

Hoare briefed Jerry Puren separately at his Hilton home, telling him that about 50 men would fly in with them and that a large advance party was already on the island. With the assistance of the local resistance movement they could count on having between 100 and 150 men. Puren was offered US$15 000 for his part, US$1 000 paid in advance and the balance when the job had been successfully completed.[110]

Froth Blowers blow the froth

On Wednesday 24 November 1981 the mercenaries rendezvoused at Jan Smuts (Johannesburg International) Airport. They numbered 47 in all and were dressed casually in shorts, open necked shirts, running shoes and sandals. By Jerry Puren's approving assessment they were a 'tough and competent looking bunch', but he knew none of them personally. Peter Duffy nominated Puren to call the roll and tick their names off on a roster as they boarded a chartered bus.

Their first scheduled destination was Ermelo in the Eastern Transvaal, but the mercenaries demanded a refreshment stop at a bottle store in the small town of Ogies where they took aboard a generous supply of beer. Puren, who from experience gained over many years in the military, believed that serious soldiering and serious drinking did not go well together. He glanced inquiringly at Peter Duffy.

Peter shrugged.

Other than nominating Tullio Moneta as his number two, Colonel Hoare had done nothing whatsoever to institute a command structure for his merry (and rapidly getting merrier) band of men, so nothing was said or done to bring the party to order.

Duffy and Puren, as master and assistant master of ceremonies, did not have the authority and neither did Mike Webb or any of the other officers. Their command authority apparently only kicked in once the coup attempt got going.

Only Moneta could have acted with the authority of his absent leader, but there is nothing to suggest he did. The real blame, however, lay with Hoare. Having created a flexible command structure, he should have been present when they mustered at the airport. He should either have assumed direct command, or nominated officers who could command in his absence if he was unable to accompany them on the first leg.

Mercenary units are never composed of angelic choir boys, but of tough and hard drinking military men — something Colonel Hoare should have known better than most. It seems incredible he did not take advance precautions to curb excessive drinking. Mercenaries might be notoriously difficult to discipline, but they were still in it for the money, so a threat to kick them off the bus would have quickly brought them into line.

On arrival at Ermelo's Holiday Inn, as Jerry Puren so aptly put it, the 'task force launched their first assault — against the ladies bar'.

Hoare arrived much later at around 17:00, driving a hired VW Combi. It was loaded with 50 holdalls plastered with AOFB labels. Snugly concealed in polystyrene beds in the bases were AK47s camouflaged by layers of toys. He carried 15 two-way radio sets loose. In the event of a customs query they had labels showing they were for delivery to a yacht due to dock in the Victoria Yacht Basin.

An emergency loomed as Hoare walked into the foyer.

Peter Duffy reported that a drunken mercenary had laid out a man after an argument over a woman in the bar. To make matters worse the injured party, a man of substance in the Ermelo community, was angrily demanding that the management call the police so he could lay charges. That could result in the operation being aborted.

Hoare got the smooth-talking Duffy to offer the aggrieved party R500 for 'medical expenses'. Peter explained apologetically that as a charity organisation, the AOFB could not afford to be involved in a scandal. Fortunately, the man decided to take the money.[111]

It was an unauspicious start.

The advance party was also not imbued with the principles of temperance. As Martin Dolinchek noted in his diary, the men were continually drunk and were more interested in women than in reconnaissance. Robert Sims, he said, was habitually in a drunken stupor. Barney Carey, irritated by Dolinchek's criticisms of his drinking habits, told him to butt out or he would take him out later in the crossfire. On the other hand, according to Colonel Hoare, the other members of the advance party had complained of excessive drinking by Dolinchek himself.

Peter Duffy, as head of the Froth Blowers, conducted a pre-dinner talk in a private conference room at the Holiday Inn. He belatedly cautioned the men about heavy drinking and apparently brought them under control. It was remarkable that Hoare had nothing to say about what was obviously a serious potential for disaster.

Duffy warned the men to be ready for a 04:30 start.

Jerry Puren said Mike Hoare showed a marked lack of security consciousness. He took a call in his room from Gerard Hoarau, who presumably phoned from Nairobi. Hoare updated him on the open line with the latest details and assured him that everything was going according to plan. Hoarau, for his part, assured him that everything was all right at his end. They were all in Nairobi and waiting for Hoare to make his move. All this took place on a public telephone system when it was common knowledge that the South African intelligence services taped all incoming and outgoing calls from states in black-ruled Africa. Also, it must be said, most black-ruled African countries taped all calls emanating from South Africa.

Hoare ordered an O group for his 'officers' in Jerry Puren's room at 24:00. It commenced with a bombshell. Producing an AOFB holdall he demonstrated how the weapons and magazines were concealed in the polystyrene bases. Each man would take a bag through customs at Mahé. The weapons were not, as he had said earlier, already on the island.

'No customs man is going to rumble that', he said. He told them that anyone who did not like it could withdraw from the operation. No one liked it, but no one pulled out.[112]

The men were awakened in the early hours of Wednesday 25 November. Just before they moved out to head for Swaziland it was the turn of the rankers to be told the news of the change of plans and issued with their loaded holdalls. Their feelings ranged from glum acceptance, to every extreme of unhappiness.[113] Sergeant (Dr) Chris de Jager of 2-Recce was the most dissatisfied — he opted to withdraw and go home. Hoare later dismissed him as a 'a rather scruffy individual' who had been 'evasive with his answers' on recruitment, insinuating he was glad to be rid of him. He blackened his character further by suggesting he had been spying to curry favour with the government or the NIS. This was completely baseless.

What Hoare conveniently overlooked was that a contract, even a mercenary one, is a two-way agreement. He had broken the covenant by lying about the weapons already being on the island. This introduced a new and potentially dangerous factor for intelligent consideration. The changed circumstances demanded a reassessment, the need to sum up the risks anew and make a fresh judgement. This was precisely the route taken by Chris de Jager. Unlike the rest who reluctantly swam on with the tide, he more sensibly concluded that the additional dangers posed by the 'change of plan', took the risks to an unacceptable level. This, as time and events would show, proved a more intelligent judgement than that of Mike Hoare.

An interesting but unanswered question is how Hoare intended to arm the resistance. He mentioned that a revolt in support of the mercenaries was expected. But what sort of support would that have amounted to if they were unarmed? Surely he had not intended to rely solely on the uncertainty of captured weapons? This poses the question of whether he really was expecting any help from the resistance. If he was, surely it would have been the prime task of the advance party to rally them. More to the point, did an effective resistance organisation with a fighting potential actually exist?

The mercenary busload passed through the Oshoek border post into Swaziland later in the morning and eventually arrived at Matsapa Airport. Awaiting them on the apron in front of the arrival hall was a Royal Swazi National Airways 60-seater F-28 Fokker Friendship. It was an aeroplane close to the heart of that fledgling airline. It was their flagship — the largest aircraft in the fleet.

The Froth Blowers and five other luckless passengers boarded without incident and took their seats. For a few tense moments it seemed that their bags were about to be scrutinised by metal detectors before being loaded into the hold, but this turned out to be a false alarm. Shortly afterwards they were airborne.

They had scarcely cleared Swaziland's mountains when the mercenaries again turned to the solace of booze. Hoare still made no effort to intervene. At the least, one would have expected him to make a contingency plan to switch his reservation from the remote Auberge Inn to the Reef Hotel so he would be available to curb indiscipline among his fellow adventurers, should the need arise.

They landed and refuelled in the Comores, where another passenger boarded.[114]

2

Operation Anvil
Seychelles Coup Attempt
The Execution
25 November 1981

The Fokker Friendship touched down at Pointe Larue International Airport at 16:00 on Wednesday 25 November 1981.

The mercenaries disembarked and led by Colonel Mad Mike Hoare they began dawdling slowly through the green 'nothing to declare' route. Customs officers cursorily examined a few bags, but on seeing the toys and on hearing they were for orphans and underprivileged children, they casually waved them through.

Hoare passed through the glass doors of the entrance and made his way out into the bright sunlight of the parking area. The advance party was waiting with several vehicles, with weapons smuggled in on the dry runs snugly concealed in the boots. Barney Carey approached as if greeting an old friend. The rest — Martin Dolinchek, Bob Sims, Aubrey Brooks, Ken Dalgliesh, Charlie Dukes and Roger England — only nodded furtively.

According to Martin Dolinchek, he spoke briefly to Hoare who told him he planned to bring the operation forward by one day to Thursday 25 November, because the mercenaries were such a boozy mob. Hoare said nothing about this in his book.

Des Botes said he took Hoare's luggage and loaded it in his hired vehicle. Three tour buses were waiting in front of the terminal building and as the mercenaries filtered out they put their luggage on the roof rack and took their seats.

According to customs officer Vincent Pillay, everyone except Kevin Beck — the last member of the party — passed through the Green route. Beck, Pillay said, went through the Red route and asked if he should declare scuba diving equipment. Peter Hean and Sven Forsell, on the other hand, said they were immediately behind Beck and he went via the Green route. Beck also said he went through the Green route, so maybe Pillay was mistaken.

Hoare, however, said the customs had picked on Beck because the passenger in front of him in the queue who had boarded in the Comores had tried to smuggle in fruit — a prohibited import in the Seychelles.[1]

Neither Beck, Hean nor Forsell mentioned this.

Whatever the case, it is clear that when Beck broke his thumb earlier he should have taken it as an ill omen and ducked out of the operation.

Whatever the case Vincent Pillay opened Beck's bag which contained his passport and toiletries. Then he turned his attention to the Froth Blower holdall.

Peter Duffy, sensing trouble was looming, tried to divert Pillay's attention to himself. He opened his own bag, pulled out toys and waved them around, cheerfully explained to anyone willing to listen how much those poor little orphans would appreciate them.

Vincent Pillay, suddenly assuming the character of nemesis, ignored him and continued his search. He poked a finger deep into the bag and raked it around the bottom, hooking out a piece of polystyrene.

'What's this?' he asked.

'It's to protect my bottles when I go diving on the island', Kevin replied innocently.

Pillay dipped his hand in again and broke off a larger segment of polystyrene, which now revealed a glimpse of gunmetal with an unmistakable profile.

'And what is this?' he asked severely.

'I don't know. I have never seen it before', Beck replied truthfully.

Pillay spoke rapidly in Creole to a female security officer, asking her to alert the airport security chief, Sergeant Kerchan Esparon, and tell him to stop the buses parked outside from leaving.

Kevin Beck accompanied him without protest to an office. Pillay handed him over to Sergeant Esparon and the woman officer and returned to his post. It appears that Esparon had gone straight to the office, without going out to the buses.

Rooting around in the holdall, Esparon wriggled the AK47 from its snug polystyrene nest, then yanked it into the open.

'What is this? What is this?

'I really don't know', Beck replied.

'So what do you intend doing with it?' the sergeant asked.

Things were clearly getting out of hand for Beck.

'I really don't know . . . but there are 44 others outside!'

Sergeant Esparon obviously was not paying attention, because he began to compare Beck's AK with his own issue weapon on the office desk.[2]

Somebody ran to the front and began bawling that everyone should return inside for further checks. Not everyone, including Mike Hoare, heard.

Jerry Puren reacted with alacrity.

'Get out the toys! Get out the toys! Get down, boys, the game's up!' he began to shout.

'For God's sake, colonel, stop him! Stop him! He's gone mad', someone said to Hoare.

Colonel Hoare rushed to the bus, suddenly realising the situation had gone seriously wrong. Some of the men were already on top of the buses throwing holdalls down to the rest. Most calmly sought out their own numbered holdalls and dug out the AKs. For a moment there was a lull, as men knelt and assembled their weapons, then clipped on loaded magazines.

Patrick Henrick struggled with his because the mechanism was faulty or damaged — which says little for the tests conducted before the operation.

There was the crash of a single shot. It was an AD (accidental discharge), or as the British Army nowadays more accurately calls it, a ND (negligent discharge), fired by an ex-member of 6-Recce.

It shattered the plate glass door of the terminal building and hit Johan Fritz of 2-Recce who dropped to the ground. The round had penetrated his chest and heart, causing massive damage to the aorta. He was mortally wounded. Poor Johan had paid the ultimate penalty for his commander's failure to take the elementary precaution of retraining his men before the operation.

There was a kaleidoscope of happenings, some occurring simultaneously or within a few minutes of each other.

Sergeant Esparon, apparently in reaction to the commotion, rushed from his office with Beck's AK47 in his hands, leaving Beck alone with the woman officer. There was a second shot and Sergeant Esparon spun around clutching a bloody wound in his shoulder.

Patrick Henrick jettisoned his faulty weapon and dashed into the terminal brandishing a knife. He found the grievously wounded Johan Fritz who was bleeding profusely. They were close friends, buddies, who had been on many operations together. He tried without success to staunch the blood flow. Steyn de Wet, a Recce doctor, took over but he could do nothing and Johan died within minutes.

Patrick Henrick took Johan's AK47 and assembled it. His friend no longer needed it.

Kevin Beck, meanwhile, nodded politely at the AK on the office desk.

'How about supplying me with the weapon? I need it.'

'We only keep one . . . but it is not loaded', the woman security officer said almost apologetically.[3]

He ducked from the office and ran outside where he grabbed an AK from an unclaimed holdall.

When the shooting started, Bob Sims got back in his car and drove for his safe house in the hills. With Susan Ingles's help, he concealed all the cached weapons in a nearby cave.

Martin Dolinchek also drove off for healthier climes.

Colonel Hoare told Des Botes to take a car, not his own, drive out on the Victoria Road and abandon it as a temporary roadblock. Botes complied but on returning, he discovered that his own vehicle — in which he had left his AK47 and Hoare's baggage — was missing.

There is considerable confusion about what followed — some of it created, perhaps, by the smoke of battle but also because the way events unfolded suggest that few of the mercenaries had been fully briefed regarding targets or their significance.

Mike Hoare himself conceded that he had made no proper contingency plan in the event of detection at the airport. He professed to having a vague plan which he said he had imparted only to Tullio Moneta, perhaps because of its complexity. If someone was caught 'we would have one or two of our larger types handy to seize that man. This would have worked very well barring the accident.' He offered no suggestion on how the other 'smaller types' would have disposed of the other 60 civilians and airport staff.[4]

During his reconnaissance with Jerry Puren. Hoare had noted that the soldiers of the Seychelles People's Liberation Army were based at barracks overlooking the 'eastern' end of the airport. Their 50 Tanzanian instructors were quartered in a private house (or two) between the airport and the barracks.

Hoare said he had no option but to immediately launch the coup bid. His priority objectives were the capture of 'the barracks' and the airport. Afterwards he would rally the resistance movement and advance on Victoria.

He despatched four of the advance party — Aubrey Brooks, Roger England, Ken Dalgliesh and Charlie Dukes — in a vehicle to seize the 'Tanzanian Army base' to the 'south' of the airport. Someone suggested they were sent to 'block the entrance gates' and another that they were to prevent troops leaving the base. No one appeared to know who was in command.[5]

Hoare says nothing in his book about sending this party to the barracks, but there seems little doubt that he did. They probably used Des Botes' vehicle, which would explain how it came to be missing. In retrospect it is impossible to say if the target was the Tanzanian instructors' quarters or the main SPLA base, but most likely it was the latter.

The plan, if it can be called that, apparently depended entirely on the element of surprise. It is speculated that they intended roaring up to the guardroom in the grand old Congo style, then after blocking the gates with the vehicle and using it as cover from which to shoot, they would spring out and order the sentries to surrender. If they followed the style of the disorganised, poorly led, badly trained and mutinous *Armée Nationale Congolaise* or the Simba Rebels of the old Congo days, they would probably have done just that.

If the opposition failed to cooperate, they would mow them down and roar through the barracks with guns blazing, herding before them all those who had thrown down their arms and surrendered.

'We drove up to the entrance to the camp. I think there were two or three men standing there', Roger England said. 'We got out of the car and told them to stand still. A man behind a wall let rip and wounded two of us. We took cover but five minutes later we came under fire from a Russian 12,7mm heavy machine gun.'

Events at the airport had evidently alerted the garrison and as it turned out the sentries had more iron in their souls than was expected.

Aubrey Brooks took shrapnel in his thigh and Charlie Dukes suffered a painful but less debilitating gunshot wound in his upper arm.

The mercenaries withdrew to a clump of big trees and rocks and returned fire. The enemy within, unlike the mercenaries, had no ammunition limitations. It was not long before Ken Dalgliesh, for one, found his magazines were empty.

Aubrey's wound was serious, but he could still hobble, so after it was dressed he decided to make his own way back to the airport. Despite a brave effort, the shock and loss of blood proved too much for him and he blacked out and collapsed several times. Eventually he found a cave, crawled into it and spent the night there.

'Gee, Colonel', said Charlie Dukes, giving his version of the action later to Hoare, 'it was just like the movies. We went in four abreast, all guns blazing, and beat up the guardroom. But a burst of fire from nowhere hit us on one side and we could not get enough support to go in again.'

Meanwhile, Mike Webb, who according to the original plan was responsible for neutralising the Tanzanians, apparently ordered Rich Stannard to take three or four men in a Mini-Moke to attack 'the barracks to the south of the airport' where they were quartered'. He did not tell Hoare what he was doing.[6]

It is also possible Rich used Des Botes' vehicle.

Hoare, virtually simultaneously, decided to rake up a larger 14-strong group. Sven Forsell said they attacked the 'island's garrison'. Steve Biddlecombe called it 'the Seychelles barracks'. Nick Wilson, a trainee pilot with the Zimbabwe Air Force, described it as 'the barracks'. Louis Boucher said it was 'the barracks' to the south of the airport.

Everyone said that Colonel Hoare took command, but in his book he spoke vaguely of the 'officer who was to command the group' without naming him. The force got into tour buses and set off, overtaking and picking up Richard Stannard and his team en route.[7]

To add to the confusion, Hoare said that shortly afterwards he decided to follow and went in a vehicle driven by Barney Carey. By his own account, he made no attempt to leave comprehensive orders for those remaining at the airport. He gave a few seemingly incidental orders while preparing to go with Carey. Andrew Standish White, he said, 'intercepted me on the way to the car' and received approval for his suggestion to mount a roadblock on the Victoria Road. Vernon Prinsloo asked if he should follow the original plan and take over the control tower. Hoare told him to take three men and do it.

Tullio Moneta also 'stopped me just before we pushed off' and asked for orders. He was told to place the terminal in a state of all round defence and put barrels on the runway to prevent aircraft from landing. Moneta contradicted this and said he took five men and went south intending to attack the barracks from the beach. It is unclear if he did this on his own initiative or on the orders of Colonel Hoare.[8] Whatever the case, the runway was not obstructed with barrels, either then or later.

Hoare 'raced off' towards the barracks with Barney Carey, noting that only 14 minutes had elapsed since Johan Fritz was shot. 'A few bursts of fire passed harmlessly over the top' as they passed the house used by the Tanzanians. This suggests that vital target had been left alone by the mercenaries. It also showed the opposition were alert and the element of surprise had been lost. Hoare did not explain why the Tanzanian house had lost its status as a priority target.[9]

It seems the mercenaries in the tour buses en route to the 'barracks' were fortunate indeed that they did not come under heavy RPG-7 and machine gun fire when they passed the Tanzanian quarters.

Hoare said Carey stopped their vehicle 50m from the barracks gate and they took cover in a palm grove. The main assault group, meanwhile, was mounting an attack on the barracks from one flank. He said they had already attacked the main gate but had been beaten back, suffering two wounded.

60mm mortar fire followed, but the bombs were not primed so they failed to explode. Then, by Hoare's account, an ex-Soviet BRDM armoured personnel carrier nudged its way from within the barracks and took up a position between the gates.

They had no anti-tank weapons, so Hoare decided he had no alternative but to withdraw to the airport, place it in 'a strong state of defence' and mount another attack 'at first light using maximum strength'. No one else mentioned mortar fire or the BRDM.

Richard Stannard only said they fanned out in a line in an attempt to neutralise the barracks, but abandoned the attack 'because the light was bad' and 'the group did not have radios'.

Ken Dalgliesh said they decided against attacking the barracks in a flanking movement. It was dark and 'the risk of shooting each other was too great'.

Sven Forsell, whose baptism of fire it was, merely dismissed the mission as 'unsuccessful'. It seems reasonable to suppose that if he had found himself staring down the hostile gun barrel of a monstrous Soviet armoured vehicle, he would have thought it worthy of a mention.

Tullio Moneta withdrew his beach assault force to the airport after hearing from an unspecified source that the main assault had been successful. When he got back, though, he discovered it had failed.[10]

Jerry Puren placed the blame for the failure squarely with Mike Hoare. He believed that by conducting the attack piecemeal, it resulted in the enemy being fully alert when the backup force arrived, making a fierce firefight inevitable. To compound this tactical error, he used men 'who had not handled rifles for months — in some cases years', instead of committing his 23 highly trained Recces — tough experienced soldiers who could have handled the job in minutes.[11]

Meanwhile, Vernon Prinsloo, Charles Goatley and probably Simon Willar made their way to the control tower. The door was locked, so they forced an entrance and found three terrified female air traffic controllers hiding under a table.

Vernon reassured them, saying everything would be okay.

'You are all right, but what about the Tanzanians? They are all armed with hand-grenades and rocket launchers', Margaret, the senior controller, retorted.

She told them the Air India Boeing 707 flight from Harare to Bombay was due to land at Mahé Airport later that evening.

Shortly after that, a light aircraft piloted by the Seychelles Director of Aviation, Maurice Loustau-Lalanne, landed and he and his passengers alighted. They watched with concern as two customs officers suddenly ran across the runway and jumped the fence. In addition firemen were dashing around helter-skelter on the apron.

Suddenly there were shots.

Loustau-Lalanne reboarded the aircraft, radioed the control tower and asked what was going on. An unfamiliar male voice ordered them to report to the control tower. When they got there they were confronted by armed men, who escorted them to the main terminal building. Loustau-Lalanne was later allowed to return to the control tower to take over from the female traffic control officers, who he said, were in a serious state of shock.[12]

Jerry Puren searched for Hoare after he had left for the barracks, but no one knew where he was. More importantly, no one was in charge. Mercenaries were firing haphazardly, civilian lives were being endangered and even more important, precious ammunition was being wasted. Puren took command.

In contradiction to Hoare, Puren said it was he who detailed a section to establish a roadblock on the Victoria Road and secure the perimeter. But whoever ordered it, the roadblock commander was Andrew Standish White. They stopped several cars and captured some AKs and an unspecified quantity of ammunition.

Puren ordered William Dunlop-Paul, whom Hoare had nominated as his sergeant major, to take men and seize the control tower. Despite holding that rank as a mercenary, Dunlop-Paul was actually a support soldier and not a warrior, which makes it unlikely that trained Recce operatives would have accepted him as their commander. This probably explains why Patrick Henrick, a senior operative, took command of the group.

The door of the control tower was locked so they shot out the windows and burst in to find Vernon Prinsloo, Charles Goatley and three distraught ladies already there.

Jerry Puren, concerned for the safety of the civilians and airport employees, many of whom were sobbing and terrified, ordered them to be assembled in an inner room for safety. He apologised, promising they would be safe. Much was said later about the taking of hostages, but Puren said this was not so. He was only concerned for their safety.[13]

Puren then checked the terminal building, switching off lights to diminish its target profile. He bumped into Peter Duffy. They held a hurried 'O' group and decided to issue radios to the control tower and the roadblock parties.

By the time Colonel Hoare and the others returned from the abortive attack on the barracks, it was dark. He reprimanded Puren for ordering the men to collect their bags and their weapons from the buses. He insisted it was unnecessary, but Puren convinced him otherwise.

Hoare established his HQ in a small room off the main reception hall. Peter Hean said Hoare mentioned that the attack on the barracks had failed, so they would have to launch another at first light.[14]

Puren became concerned when the control tower picked up alerts being broadcast to military units around the island. From experience he knew that if they delayed their next move for too long, the authorities would consolidate their forces and mount a major attack. The situation was precarious because they lacked anti-tank weapons. To make matters worse AK ammunition was running dangerously low.

'What now?' he asked Hoare.

According to Puren, Hoare panicked. The unexpected had unsettled him. He had no fall-back plan and was experiencing difficulty in handling the complex problems being thrust at him for decisions.

He was carrying a 'hit list' of 100 to 150 names and tapes from James Mancham (it turned out afterwards to be Hoarau) for broadcast once the radio station was captured. Puren suggested he destroy the list and hide the tapes until he could be certain they would not be needed.

Puren repeated his question. What were they going to do?

'I'll wait for tomorrow', Colonel Hoare replied.

'You can't wait', Puren told him. 'If you wait, you are lost. There is plenty of transport available to get the men into town, buses, cars, everything. The whole island is in confusion and they don't know our strength. If we can move quickly we can still pull it off.'

'I will go to town tomorrow', Colonel Hoare said. 'I will first regroup.'

'You've already regrouped!' Puren snapped.

He suggested they have another go at the Tanzanians at the Pointe Larue Base, but Hoare refused, saying it would be too bloody.

'Well, what then?' Puren demanded.

Hoare said an Air India Boeing was due in later. He did not say so outright, but the insinuation was they would fly out on that.

Puren did not fancy this, believing it would put civilian lives at risk, but they had to do something if Hoare was calling off the coup.

'What about trying for a deal with the Seychelles Government?'

Hoare, he said, agreed it should be given a try.

On Puren's orders external telephone communications had already been cut to prevent civilians from passing information to the authorities. The nearest functioning phone was at a garage across the road from the airport. The owner was a Seychellois, Manuel Laluette, who had been unwillingly roped in while the mercenaries were establishing their perimeter.

Hoare and Puren, accompanied by Laluette and 'Mercenary Steyn' — probably Steyn de Wet — went to the service station. Puren got through to the Reef Hotel and asked for the pilot of their Air Swazi Fokker Friendship. He explained they were mercenaries and were there to overthrow the government. The airport had been secured and they wanted to speak to the government. Could he arrange it?

It was understandable that the pilot did not exactly jump at the chance of involvement, but he was persuaded to try. Fifteen minutes later he phoned back. No one wanted to talk.

Puren, ever the optimist, changed tack and asked if he would consider returning to the airport and flying them out in his Fokker. This suggestion made the pilot almost hysterical, so Puren put the phone down.

Hoare ordered Puren, 'Mercenary Steyn' and Manuel Laluette to remain by the telephone in case anything happened. Meanwhile, he would return to the terminal to update himself and return later. It was what Puren called 'the beginning of the big wait'.[15]

Hoare's version, written *after* the publication of Puren's book, is diametrically opposed. He contended that Puren and two other unnamed mercenaries (he makes no mention of Laluette) were defending the service station as part of the perimeter. He went there to pull them back to the main body, but found Puren trying to get through on the phone to their Air Swazi pilot.

He said that as Puren's role was a non combative one, he was not really a group member, so he gave him permission to melt away into the bush if he wanted to. He could get his cousin Frank to hide him 'until the confusion died down'. Puren, however, refused to walk away from a fight.

Hoare said he explained that he was expecting to capture the barracks at dawn and subdue the remaining opposition by midday. He said he left Puren with an order to report to the terminal with his men when he had finished phoning the pilot. It is a matter for conjecture why he would have suggested to Puren that he exchange the obvious safety of the group for the hazards of the bush when he was confident of capturing the island in less than 24 hours. Hoare made no mention in his book of a potential deal with the Seychelles government.

The two mercenaries, Hoare said, returned to the airport a little later and reported that Puren had 'vanished'.

We will pick up Puren's version of the story presently.

There was a report that infantry had debussed from a truck — some say three trucks — far down the runway. Soon 20 to 30 soldiers, presumably Tanzanians, were seen advancing towards the airport buildings in extended line formation.

Patrick Henrick, Christo Hillebrand, Alex Deacon and others took up positions in the thick undergrowth fringing the runway. When the soldiers drew near, they challenged them, intending to take them prisoner. But the soldiers opened fire. The mercenaries returned fire and the soldiers fled, some throwing away their AK47s to gain greater speed and mobility. One truck was abandoned, apparently inadvertently, in a blocking position on the runway.[16]

Barney Carey explained to Ken Dalgliesh and Des Botes that Colonel Hoare's holdall had unwittingly been left in a car abandoned earlier — probably the one Des Botes had loaded Hoare's luggage into before Johan Fritz was shot. It is presumed this conversation was motivated by Hoare, but he did not mention it in his book.

The holdall contained several sensitive documents, including Hoare's forged 'Boarel' passport, an international health certificate and, most important of all, evidence of the coup's Kenya connection. Also included were details of the callsign of the Beechcraft Super King standing by at Nairobi as well as matters like the code word *Cloudburst* and the acknowledging *Fairy Belle*.[17] Someone had to go and get the documents.

Ken Dalgliesh thought it too dangerous and said so.

Barney Carey suggested that he and Des Botes go unarmed, which prompted a heated discussion. Carey said that if they carried weapons they might end up being shot on sight. Botes eventually decided, with reluctance, to go alone. He was older than the rest so it was more likely he would get away with a cover story. He handed over his AK47 for safekeeping and left. He soon found movement outside the immediate area of the airport which made it hazardous to continue, so he returned to the safety of the group. To his chagrin, he discovered that his AK47 had disappeared. So for the second time that day he was left unarmed.

Ken Dalgliesh thought of a simpler solution. He put together a largish sum of money, handed it to a local youth he had befriended in the bar and asked the lad to go and get the holdall. The youngster eagerly consented and took the money, but he never returned.[18]

There were bursts of incoming 14,5mm fire from the Pointe Larue barracks. The gunners were targeting the control tower. There were a few hits and some penetrated the brickwork, going through from one side to the other. Fortunately, they had difficulty with elevation, so those in the tower were unharmed. It was enough to give them a major fright, though, and Vernon Prinsloo, Charles Goatley and the ladies hurriedly evacuated. Maurice Loustau-Lalanne, however, was too petrified to move. He crawled under a desk and pulled a dustbin over his head for protection.[19]

Let us now return to Jerry Puren. After he had been at the service station with Manuel Laluette and Steyn de Wet for an hour his companions began to get impatient. Jerry Puren said there was a bizarre interlude when a young man emerged from the darkness and handed him an AK47. He explained he was not really a mercenary, having only joined them at the airport, and he thought the time had come to leave. Puren solemnly thanked him for his help and he faded into the darkness.[20]

A half hour later he heard someone faintly calling his name from the terminal and he decided to return with his two companions. They halted when they heard the noise of powerful engines and an armoured car emerged from the darkness.

They were not the first to see it.

Two BTR-40 armoured cars had prowled up the runway towards the terminal building, moving in protective tandem. The leading car, after drawing no fire from the defenders, paused briefly by the control tower, then detoured around the terminal building and stopped on the forecourt. The second car remained on the runway, its crew ignoring the dictates of mutual protection demanded in armoured warfare. It opened fire with its 12,7mm heavy machine gun and its shells pounded the airport building.

Patrick Henrick, in cover by the runway, decided to neutralise it, but before he could make a move it reversed wildly, then turned about and withdrew. The lead armoured car, its commander clearly not appreciating that his number two had retreated, paused at the front of the terminal which was shrouded in darkness, then moved to the front parking area. The defenders speculated that the crew was looking for targets by the minimal glimmer of their headlights.

Only five metres away, Colonel Hoare and 15 mercenaries crouched low in cover, helpless in the face of the heavy armaments. If the BTR crew saw them and opened fire they would be dead ducks. But fortunately for them, it suddenly reversed from the parking area, turned about and headed up the main road towards Victoria, halting by the mercenaries' roadblock. It opened fire and blazed away at the roadblock, then swung its gun and targeted the airport building.

Patrick Henrick and Tullio Moneta, meanwhile, collected empty bottles from the bar and passed them to some others who were making Molotov cocktails. They syphoned fuel from parked cars, filled the bottles and inserted rag wicks.

The BTR began to reverse towards the terminal building, but its rear wheels left the tar and bogged down in the mud. Instead of using his gears to rock the car out, the driver panicked and revved continuously, the wheels gouging ever deeper into the mud. For the moment it was helpless.

Mercenaries gave covering fire while Peter Rohwein, carrying great handfuls of mud, ran forward and jumped aboard the back of the car. Safe from its guns, he smeared mud on the visors, effectively blinding the crew. Others shot out its tyres to stop it moving.

Hoare ordered Moneta to hammer on the sides and yell out in French for the crew to surrender, telling them they would come to no harm. When this drew no response, he used a Seychellois at the terminal to repeat the message in Creole. This did not work either. Instead they opened fire blindly, bullets hammering everywhere.

Paddy Henrick and Tullio Moneta lobbed Molotov cocktails at the car, which burst brightly into flame as the bottles shattered. The crew, however, remained obstinately battened down. Henrick or Rohwein clambered back aboard, poured petrol around the groove of the cupola and struck a match. It flared up, as no doubt, did the petrol that had leaked into the interior. This was obviously a good hint to the crew that a fiery death had become a positive option. The lid slammed wildly open.

According to Hoare the commander, a young Seychellois officer named Antel, popped up in the turret and opened fire, shooting blindly at all and sundry. The mercenaries, he said, returned fire and killed him. Jerry Puren, on the other hand, said the evidence suggested he had been executed.

Meanwhile, Puren and his two companions moved to the rear of the service station and huddled around a small pond in an attempt to get out of the line of fire. In the heat of the engagement, Steyn de Wet opted to take his chances and make his way back to the terminal. First he went in the direction of Victoria, then doubled back and eventually got back to the main body of mercenaries.

Puren and Manuel Laluette decided to put distance between themselves and the mainstream of battle, particularly when 75mm recoilless rifle shells fired from the barracks began exploding in their general area. It became apparent they were cut off from the others. Because of the blackness of the night, Puren was unable to see where he was going and he slipped down a ravine, badly injuring his knee. Telling Laluette to continue on his own, which he reluctantly did, Puren crawled slowly and agonizingly until he found cover.[21]

Colonel Hoare, after the surrender of the armoured car crew, interrogated the prisoners. He explained they had come to the island to reinstate James Mancham as President.

The prisoners said the barracks were held by 60 Tanzanians. The Seychellois had run away. This clearly did not include them all, because the armoured car crews, of whom one was the barracks commander, were Seychellois.

Hoare explained that they were facing 300 mercenaries and 300 members of the resistance. If the garrison failed to surrender, they would be attacked in the morning. He then released them.

Whether the Tanzanian and Seychellois joint high command spent much time pondering on this gem of intelligence when they heard about it from the freed prisoners is a moot point. They might have spent more time wondering how 300 mercenaries had managed to cram themselves into a single Fokker F-28!

Tullio Moneta and some others tried to get the BTR-40 serviceable again so they could benefit from its firepower, but its electrical wiring had been fire damaged. Its 14,5mm gun could only be used for single shots. To make matters worse, its tyres had been shredded by bullets, so it could not be driven. Having no other alternative, they pushed it to the front of the terminal and positioned it tactically.

When the situation calmed, Vernon Prinsloo and Charles Goatley returned to the control tower. Maurice Loustau-Lalanne was still there, but he was in deep shock, having lived through what was virtually a mini-war.[23]

The irritated radio operator on Air India flight AI 224 from Harare to Bombay, was trying to raise Mahé.

Goatley called him up and he was sternly rebuked.

He had been calling for 20 minutes. Where had they been?

Maurice Loustau-Lalanne had ignored the calls.

He asked for clearance for the aircraft to land.

'Wait one', Goatley said.

He sent a runner to Colonel Hoare because their walkie-talkie communications were subject to chronic interference. What should he do? Should he give the aircraft permission to land?

Hoare, by his account, sent Alan Mann back with a strongly negative verbal message. The aircraft must not be allowed to land under any circumstances. He repeated his order three times to ensure there was no confusion. Whilst the enemy soldiers remained ensconced in their barracks and dominated the southern end of the runway with their guns, any landing attempt would be suicidal. The enemy would reasonably believe that the incoming aircraft was bringing in mercenary reinforcements.

They would shoot it out of the sky.

And what about the abandoned truck that blocked the runway only 600m from the barracks? Hoare also professed to have military reasons. Men would fight to the last if they had no alternative. The aircraft would offer an avenue of escape that would shatter morale. Besides, he did not believe the situation was truly serious. The Seychellois and Tanzanians were hardly first-rate opposition. When daylight came he was confident his forces would be able to sort them out.[24]

Having given the order, he said he attempted to phone his contacts in the resistance. Where were they? Why had they not turned out? Not a single rebel had appeared to support the mercenaries. No one answered when telephoned.

He said he was reluctant to write them off as non-existent, but maybe he should have checked this possibility earlier. But even if they had arrived, they would have been unarmed.

Alan Mann, according to Hoare, returned to the control tower. Against orders, he told Prinsloo and Goatley to allow the incoming flight to land.

Prinsloo received a confirmatory command on his walkie-talkie at 22:00.

'Bring that plane in', it said.

He believed it was Colonel Hoare, but in reality it was Mike Webb.

Mike Webb and Rich Stannard were on perimeter guard on the apron. They had heard about the incoming flight but when they detected the distant murmur of aircraft noises, both experienced second thought worries. Maybe it was flying in Tanzanian reinforcements.[25]

Neither Vernon Prinsloo nor Charles Goatley had ever brought a big jet in to land, so they asked Maurice Loustau-Lalanne for the airport's landing instructions. But they gave this up as hopeless when they realised his shocked state.

Loustau-Lalanne, however, said he pleaded with them to divert the aircraft and refuse it permission to come in, even as it was already preparing to land.

Okay, they said, if he would not assist, it could land by itself. Goatley took control. Loustau-Lalanne, feeling 'under threat', provided the correct information and this was relayed to the aircraft. He switched on the runway, approach and taxi lights.

Meanwhile, Alan Mann, Kurt Priefert and another man sprinted down the runway to the abandoned truck. They could not start it because they lacked ignition keys, so they pushed it clear. (Citizen 29/6/82)

Meanwhile, Charles Goatley talked the aircraft down as best he could.

Captain Saxena, the Boeing's captain, said he was cleared to land three times.

Concerned there might be other obstructions on the runway, Loustau-Lalanne asked Goatley to instruct the pilot to land 'deep', which he did. Goatley, however, said he did it because he was afraid the aircraft might be fired on from the barracks.

Just before touchdown, a red flare — a standard warning that it was dangerous to land — was fired from the barracks. It was followed by a few short bursts of anti-aircraft fire. Then, according to Simon Willar, they fired first at the airliner's tail, and then at its substantial belly.[26]

Despite this, Captain Saxena did not abort his landing. In any case, the presence of an unfamiliar air traffic controller who lacked the basic knowledge of landing procedures must have brought home to him that all was not well on the ground.

On short haul flights, international air traffic regulations demand that aircraft have sufficient fuel aboard to return to their point of departure. It appears the Air India jet did not. This might have been because of the high price of fuel in Harare, but whatever the reason it appears Captain Saxena had no option but to touch down.

Complying with the control tower's instructions to land deep, the captain committed to his approach. In the final stage when it was too late to abort, he suddenly saw the truck on the runway. 'Jumping' it was impossible. If he had tried to pull up, momentum would have crashed the wing into it. This would almost have certainly caused fire to break out, probably resulting in fatal consequences for the passengers and crew.

Fortunately, the wing only clipped the truck. Saxena angrily asked the tower why they had given him clearance to land when the runway was blocked.

Goatley ignored the question and merely responded that the passengers would not be allowed to disembark.

After the Boeing had taxied to a halt, a 75mm recoilless rifle opened fire on the airport, apparently targeting the jet.

Peter Duffy reported the landing to Colonel Hoare at his command post. Hoare was upset and insisted the aircraft should not have been allowed to land. (Star 18/5/82) He instructed Duffy to see the captain and personally tell him that the passengers would not be allowed to disembark. His aircraft would be refuelled and he would have to fly out again immediately.[27]

Peter Duffy, Mike Webb, Stephen Biddlecombe, William Dunlop-Paul and Richard Stannard went out to the apron. They manhandled a wheeled stairway to the cockpit hatch and Duffy, Webb and Biddlecombe went aboard.

The captain and co-pilot introduced themselves as Captains Saxena and Misra.

Duffy did not return the compliment, telling them only that they had landed in the middle of a revolution. He gave no details of the attempted coup, nor did he enlighten them regarding the origins of the mercenary force.

Peter Duffy and Biddlecombe walked through to the first class section, reassuring the passengers and telling them they had no reason to panic. Yes, they had landed at a 'rough time', but they would only be on the ground for a few minutes while the aircraft was being refuelled.[28]

The pilots left the Boeing with the mercenaries.

'Welcome to the Seychelles', Rich Stannard said to Captain Saxena, cheerfully slapping him on the back as he came down the stairway.

Duffy cast an eye at the incoming 75mm recoilless fire and suggested they switch off all the aircraft's lights, otherwise there was a good chance the plane would be hit. Sven Forsell, on the other hand, said Captain Saxena ordered the lights turned off to conserve power.

A passenger, Arthur Reid, said the gunfire and explosions were intermittent and occurred at 15 to 20 minute intervals. Kevin Beck, who was manning a solitary OP on high ground above the airport, said a few shells landed near the airport, but most were dumped in the sea.

Duffy and Dunlop-Paul escorted Captains Saxena and Misra to Hoare's command post.

'Those Tanzanian bastards are firing at us', Hoare said introducing himself as 'Tom'.[29]

The pilots expressed concern about the safety of their passengers. Colonel Hoare said he shared their concerns but attempted to allay their fears. He explained that there was no danger and no one would come to any harm, provided they cooperated and obeyed instructions.

Hoare described their relationship as cordial. He said he asked Captain Saxena if he would leave if permission was forthcoming from Victoria for him to take off. The captain readily agreed, but stressed there was a need to refuel. It would also be necessary to inspect the damaged wing to see if the aircraft was still airworthy.

Ken Dalgliesh, Nick Wilson, Des Botes, Peter Duffy, Patrick Eurelle and some others assisted with the refuelling under Captain Misra's supervision. Dalgliesh declined the request of an airport official that he sign for the fuel. Someone else could pay! A tractor towed the aircraft to an area out of sight of the barracks where it would be safer.

Hoare required a go-between to negotiate with the authorities, so he sent for Maurice Loustau-Lalanne who agreed to assist. He spent the next two hours on the phone trying to track down someone in authority.

Suddenly the gunners found their range — which gave the exotic fish swimming around the coral reefs a respite. A 75mm shell burst on the runway 300m from the jetliner; a second fell closer still and a third rattled the windows of the command post, prompting the occupants to throw themselves to the floor.

Tullio Moneta ran in and gave a sitrep (situation report). He said there was no doubt that if the aircraft suffered a direct hit, most of the passengers would end up burning to death.

'I know, Tullio', Hoare replied, according to his book. 'And if that happens, there won't be a place in the whole wide world you and I will be able to hide after that. They will say we did it — deliberately!'[30]

Despite this, he made no effort to order an evacuation of passengers — surely the obvious course of action. He merely left them aboard in their seats to face the hazards of the shelling.

Maurice Loustau-Lalanne handed the telephone to Hoare. He had got Ogilvy Berlouis, the Minister of Youth and Defence, on the line. Hoare introduced himself as 'Tom' and asked for an immediate cease-fire so the Boeing could take off.

The Minister refused point-blank. His soldiers, he said, were actually aiming for the aircraft and as far as he was concerned, both the aircraft and passengers were illegitimate and expendable. He accused Colonel Hoare of holding them as hostages.

The shelling became progressively more accurate. It was suddenly supplemented by mortar fire. Steyn de Wet, taking bearings on the gun flashes and noting the flight time of the shells, reckoned the 75mm recoilless was sited somewhere near the President's house at San Souci. Hoare asked Loustau-Lalanne to try to get President René himself on the line and he succeeded a few minutes later.

Hoare asked the president 'in the name of humanity' to order a cease-fire. He reassured him that neither the Boeing nor its passengers were associated with the mercenaries.

Albert René, discussing the situation as if were hypothetical, told Hoare that he and his mercenaries had been grossly misled . . .

Hoare cut him short, saying they were on the brink of a catastrophe. If the aircraft was hit it would not only shock the world, but would also ruin the fledgling tourist industry of the Seychelles.

Captain Saxena whispered that he should tell the President that a VIP, Mrs Shamuyarira, the wife of Zimbabwe's Minister of Tourism, was one of the passengers. Hoare passed it on.

Albert René told him to phone back in half an hour.

The shelling and mortaring continued unabated.

Hoare, inexplicably, still made no attempt to evacuate the passengers. There is no doubt the situation was serious. Nor is there any question of his exaggerating the risks faced by the passengers. William Dunlop-Paul, for one, emphatically confirmed this in evidence later, saying that if Colonel Hoare had failed to arrange a cease-fire, the jet would have been destroyed and its passengers killed.

The shelling abruptly ceased ten minutes later.

Hoare phoned Albert René and thanked him.

The President responded by saying that he still had not decided whether to allow the aircraft to take off or not.

Hoare said he was annoyed. His efforts to save the aircraft had been time consuming. He had directed his energies in an unprofitable direction when he should have been planning for a dawn attack on the barracks.[31]

If he was seriously considering an assault on the barracks, it seems strange he made no attempt to delegate the preliminary planning and preparation to a subordinate while he was otherwise engaged. If he really intended staying on the island, his only possible defence was to attack.

The President demanded that Captain Saxena be put on the phone so he could speak to him. He questioned him thoroughly to confirm that 'Tom' was telling the truth. He only gave permission for the aircraft to leave once he was completely satisfied.

Hoare said in evidence he also negotiated telephonically with the island's chief of police, James Pillay, but he made no mention of this in his book.[32]

Captains Saxena and Misra inspected the aircraft and satisfied themselves that it was still airworthy, despite its damaged wing. Saxena refused to take off, however, until he had personally inspected the runway to check that it was now clear. He asked President René for permission to conduct the inspection and requested he give orders that no one fire on them. The President assured him he could conduct the inspection in safety.

A vehicle was found and the pilots drove it slowly, headlights ablaze, from one end of the runway to the other. They discovered five vehicles obstructing it and a sixth abandoned on the far side of the strip. Alec Mann had not noticed these earlier because of the pitch darkness.[33] It was miraculous that Captain Saxena had landed the aircraft without it resulting in a major disaster. A party of mercenaries got to work and cleared the runway of obstructions.

The President phoned back. Permission to take off was subject to Hoare giving his word of honour that none of the mercenaries would leave on the aircraft.

Hoare agreed, asking on his part for an assurance they would not fire on the aircraft during the take off. President René agreed.

Sven Forsell, Don Kenny and Jan Sydow congratulated the pilots on their bravery when they returned from the runway inspection. It had been a lonely and risky task and it was a miracle that neither had been shot dead by the trigger-happy soldiery.

'Can you take us out? Have you enough room on the aircraft?' Sven Forsell asked.

Captain Saxena replied that he only had 65 passengers, so many seats were free.'It's no problem to take you out — if you can get us out of here.' He could fly them to anywhere within a radius of about 1 000km.

Forsell said later that Saxena only had two options. He could either 'team up with us or the other side. It was better to join us, rather than those trying to kill you . . . without us he would be facing certain death. With us he stood a chance.'[34]

Tullio Moneta, Hoare said, relayed the offer to him. He said that if he opted to stay and fight, Peter Duffy, Kurt Priefert, him and 'quite a few others' would remain behind. The rest, he said, were wavering. They thought it best to get out while the going was good.

Moneta, on the other hand, said the first he knew about it was when he overheard a pilot saying to Hoare: 'You have saved us, now we will get you out.' Colonel Hoare, he said, asked him to canvas the men for their opinions. Should they accept Captain Saxena's offer and abandon the coup attempt or what?

Most wanted to get out while they still could. They had lost the element of surprise, failed to turn the captured armoured car to their own use and were short of ammunition. It was a game of soldiers that had gone on long enough.

Some, however, including Pieter Doorewaard and Nick Wilson, were willing to stay and give the coup a chance. They did not believe the situation was desperate.[35]

Hoare discussed possible destinations with Saxena. The captain suggested Bombay, but Hoare rejected that without hesitation because he knew the Indian Government would return them to Mahé on the next flight — probably in irons.

James Mancham and Eddie Camille had both spoken of the Sultan of Oman as a friend and a sympathiser, someone who would bail them out if problems arose. This thought was scotched by a mercenary personally familiar with Oman. He said the British ran the place and they, like the Indians, would pack them aboard a RAF Hercules and return them to Mahé within hours.

Someone else suggested the Comoros, controlled by French mercenary Bob Denard. While this would have been ideal, it was vetoed by Captain Saxena because the runway was too short to take a Boeing 707.

Then there was Mauritius, but it was likely its communist administration would also have been rudely unsympathetic. No one suggested Kenya, which seems surprising. This was probably fortunate for the mercenaries, because their failure would have made them an embarrassment. They might even have found themselves being handed back to President

René as a peace offering — a gesture of Kenyan innocence designed to repair their tainted political relationship. The consensus was for Durban.

Captain Saxena, Hoare said, agreed to fly them to Durban although some confusion remains about this. He later said Saxena first set course for Jan Smuts (Johannesburg International) Airport, but while in flight discovered it was closed in by mist. He suggested Bloemfontein as an alternative, but switched to Durban when he found out the flying time was less.

Hoare said he opted to remain behind with a few men to rally the resistance. He believed he had no option, having given Albert René his word that he would phone him while the aircraft was taking off to confirm that at least he had remained behind. He told Tullio Moneta that he had friends on the island with whom he could seek shelter and who would ultimately aid his escape.

At his trial he was more frank and contended that he had aborted the coup because of the loss of the element of surprise. He also put forward a 'humanitarian' reason, suggesting that if he had carried out his plan in broad daylight it would have resulted in too much bloodshed. While confident he could overrun the opposition, he had estimated his own anticipated casualty rate at an unacceptable 20%. After consultations with his senior captains, he ordered that everybody had to leave on the Air India Boeing.

The prosecution, on the other hand, suggested his main reason for leaving was to save his own skin and those of his men — not for high-minded humanitarian reasons. Hoare conceded this was a possible explanation.[36]

Hoare testified that Captain Saxena suggested he make his phone call, then climb aboard at the last minute by means of a rope ladder he would leave dangling from the door, but he declined. He said he ordered his men to destroy their weapons and not take them aboard the aircraft. All secret codes and other papers were also to be destroyed, he said. It appears to have slipped his mind that the codes were still in a car abandoned earlier somewhere outside the barracks.

By Colonel Hoare's account the mercenaries began to bend their AK barrels, remove firing pins and throw breech blocks into the bush. In truth few did, because Mike Webb immediately questioned the order with Tullio Moneta.

What if the aircraft was shot at?

What if it failed to get off the ground because of the wing damage? This would leave them disarmed, stranded and helpless at the end of the runway. They would like be sitting ducks just waiting for the enemy to come and pluck them.

Moneta countermanded the order, but did not tell Colonel Hoare.

Peter Duffy and Barry Gribbin cleared it with Captain Saxena. It was vital they take their weapons aboard in case takeoff was aborted.

'Okay', Saxena agreed, 'but no explosives.'

In the event, 38 of the 43 mercenaries who boarded were armed. Some carried their weapons loaded and with actions cocked. Between them they had a total of 2 435 rounds of ammunition.[37] None of the mercenaries, few of whom were party to the discussions between Hoare and Saxena anyway, regarded it as a hijacking. The majority — their trial judge accepted at least 34 — regarded it as a deal struck between Colonel Hoare and Captain Saxena. Others believed it was a contingency escape plan arranged in advance by the South African government. An honest minority — like Stephen Biddlecombe — did not give a damn either way. They went aboard because the last thing they wanted was to be left behind on Mahé.

Vic de Beer asked for permission to take the body of Johan Fritz aboard.

Captain Saxena consented but stipulated it should be stowed in the hold to avoid upsetting passengers. Patrick Henrick wrapped the body in canvas before it was taken aboard. The mercenaries boarded in pitch darkness.[38]

While the aircraft was being readied for takeoff, Tullio Moneta and Kurt Priefert stayed with Hoare while he made his promised call to President René. After replacing the receiver they insisted that Hoare board with them.

Hoare adamantly maintained that the Boeing was their only means of escape. He ignored the very real danger of all the passengers and crew being killed if it was shot down during takeoff. He made no mention of the Air Swazi F-28 nor that the pilot had already refused to fly them out. Nevertheless, they could have used that to get out, because there were several pilots amongst the mercenaries. If they had flown to the Comoros in the F-28, Bob Denard would certainly have looked after them.[39]

There remains a lingering probability, particularly as he refused permission for the passengers to disembark during the shelling, that Hoare was effectively using them as hostages and banking on the likelihood that President René would not want to see them harmed. That, of course, would not have applied to the F-28. With a load of mercenaries aboard he would not have hesitated for a moment to order his gunners to destroy it.

Barney Carey volunteered to stay behind, believing he had an obligation to look for Aubrey Brooks who was wounded and had been missing since the first contact.[40]

Hoare said he believed the Boeing was easy meat for an RPG-7 gunner during takeoff and preferred to take his chances on the island. No one would know he had taken part in the attempted coup, so he planned to get back to his hotel and resume his 'holiday'. Needless to say, he did not.

Roger England was another who made a last minute decision to stay. He also intended using the remaining hours of darkness to get clear of the airport and be back into his hotel bed before daylight.

Hoare instructed Charles Goatley to act as liaison officer with the crew to ensure they stayed on course for Durban. In fact, he stayed in the cockpit for most of the flight. The crew said he monitored their radio transmissions, but he denied it.[41]

As the aircraft screamed down the runway for takeoff, many of the mercenaries stamped their feet in a rugged staccato, following the ritualistic parody of paratroopers edging towards the door for a jump.

'One, two . . . one, two, three . . . one, two . . . one, two, three', they chanted.

There was a rousing cheer as they became airborne. It was just after 02:30. There was much congratulatory back-slapping and hand-shaking.

A parachute flare went up from the barracks during takeoff and red curls of tracer fire reached up abortively towards the aircraft. Firing ceased when they reached an altitude of 1 600m and the aircraft cleared the airport. Arthur Reid, a passenger, said the pilot performed an astonishingly steep takeoff.[42]

Louis Boucher, who had brought a bottle of whisky in his bag, ritualistically polished it off with the help of a fellow Recce the moment they were airborne.

3

Operation Anvil
Seychelles Coup Attempt
Unhappy landings In Durban

It was only after takeoff that Colonel Hoare discovered that Tullio Moneta had countermanded his order about taking weapons aboard. So he arranged with Captain Saxena for the weapons to be collected, stacked behind the front cockpit and covered with a blanket. Live rounds were later found in the chambers of 12 weapons. Three primed Chinese stick grenades were also discovered in the stack, despite the captain forbidding explosives.

Sven Forsell walked around conversing with the passengers and apologising for the inconvenience suffered. He said they were all 'calm and collected'.

Hoare sat in his seat, lonely and deep in thought with tears in his eyes — presumably over the failure of his mission.

Peter Duffy asked Captain Saxena to radio Louis Botha (Durban International) Airport and ask for 'a particular security officer' to meet them when they landed. This was so the failed coup attempt could be explained in confidence and to let him know that the South African government knew about it.[1]

The only information available at Louis Botha (Durban International) Airport, was a terse notification by Jan Smuts (Johannesburg International) that an Air India flight had diverted to Durban with mechanical problems. Suspected hijackers were aboard.

Durban was closed for the night, but a 'stage B full emergency procedure' was set in motion. Emergency crews, ambulances, fire engines and the Police Task Force were called out. Before the landing Phase 3 — full emergency procedures — were implemented. Emergency vehicles including an ambulance lined the runway.

The Air India flight touched down at Durban just after 05:00. In compliance with a suggestion by Peter Duffy, Captain Saxena taxied to the Amamzimtoti side of the runway.

Hoare, according to Ken Dalgliesh, was 'exhausted . . . he looked a broken man'.

A fire tender appeared and halted in front of the aircraft to prevent it from taking off again. The fire chief later ordered its removal to avoid his crews being exposed to unnecessary dangers. Fifteen minutes later stairs were brought to the aircraft and Dalgliesh and Duffy left the aircraft. They were met by Colonel Mouton of the Railway Police (then responsible for airports) and Hilton Hardy, the airport's Chief Security Officer.

They explained in confidence to Colonel Mouton the South African government's involvement in the coup bid and said 13 or 14 Recces were involved. They requested an aircraft so they could 'fly anywhere' to prevent the passengers and crew becoming aware of South African involvement.

Time ticked slowly by. The scrambled telephone lines between Durban and Pretoria burned red hot as a top-level damage control exercise ground slowly into gear.

Blue Kelly left the aircraft to phone National Intelligence Service headquarters in Pretoria, but returned shortly afterwards without news.

The passengers and crew were allowed to disembark three to four hours after the landing and were bussed to the terminal building. The mercenaries, however, remained aboard.[2] At 10:00, almost five hours after the 707 landed, a SAAF C-130 touched down and a 50-strong detachment of Task Force policemen deplaned and deployed tactically around the Boeing. It was obviously an exercise done for show. The707 was towed to a hanger where the mercenaries disembarked. They insisted on keeping Johan Fritz's body with them.

Colonel Olckers, commander of 1-Reconnaissance Commando, addressed them privately, telling them they were to be flown to Pretoria.[3]

Brigadier J S Visser, the SAP Divisional Commander for Port Natal, recorded their names and particulars, then formally arrested them for hijacking. They were escorted aboard a SAAF C-130 Hercules and flown to Waterkloof Air Base, Pretoria. From there they were taken to Sonderwater Prison and held incommunicado under South Africa's draconian security laws.

At the request of General Zietsman, the CID chief, they all made statements explaining what had happened — apparently without being cautioned. The statements, nevertheless, were later produced in evidence.

After six days in detention, General Zietsman unconditionally released all but five of them. Peter Hean said the general advised those freed to keep a low profile and promised that the police would not reveal their identities to the press. They did not, but the authorities in the Seychelles did so instead.[4]

The unfortunate five who remained in custody — Mike Hoare, Tullio Moneta, Peter Duffy, Ken Dalgliesh and Charles Goatley — were to be arraigned on charges of 'manstealing' (kidnapping). A magistrate remanded them for a month. Bail of R10 000 was granted to Colonel Hoare and R5 000 for each of the others.[5]

The government did everything to play down the episode. Minister of Law and Order, Louis le Grange, announced that only the leaders would be charged. The rest had been freed, he explained facetiously 'because the police could not find they had contravened any laws. They only shot out some windows and ran around in the bush. You tell me what laws they broke in South Africa?' he asked.

Someone soon obliged.

On 5 January 1982, without prior warning, the Security Police rounded up all the freed mercenaries in a series of predawn swoops.

The manstealing charges were hurriedly withdrawn against the five and the whole lot were remanded on bail on four charges under the Civil Aviation Act. The charges alleged they had seized or exercised control of an aircraft at Mahé, interfered with the crew in the performance of their duties, performed acts jeopardising the safety of Mahé Airport, the aircraft or persons or property in it, jeopardised the safety of the aircraft or persons or property in it and were in unlawful possession of harmful articles (weapons), etc., at Durban airport. Each offence carried a maximum penalty of 30 years' imprisonment. The time for facetiousness was over.

Pretoria's volte-face had resulted from intense international pressures it had not anticipated. South Africa was a signatory to the international convention on hijacking and had no option but to take action. If she had refused or failed to fulfill her obligations, moves would have been set in motion immediately to sever her precious international air links.[6]

The trial, until that time, was reputed to be the longest and most expensive in South African legal history. It opened before Mr Justice James and two assessors in Pietermaritzburg on 10 March 1982.

The State based its case on the furtherance of a common purpose — that the accused had unlawfully diverted the Air India Boeing from its flight to Bombay to escape liability for the coup attempt. No doors were opened for passenger disembarkation at Mahé, so it was the State's contention that the aircraft had been in continuous flight from Harare to Mahé to Durban.

The defence asked for particulars of other people or organisations involved in the attempted coup or alleged hijacking, or to name them and explain their role, but the prosecution ignored the request.

After the trial had commenced, the Attorney General of Natal announced that Theo van Huyssteen and Steyn de Wet, the only two medical doctors involved, would become State witnesses. In the event they were not called to give evidence. It was obviously a ploy by the government to get at least a couple of the mercenaries off the hook.[7]

Voluminous evidence was introduced during the trial. Had the South African Government and the SADF been in the dock along with the mercenaries facing charges of complicity in the coup attempt, the evidence would have proved them guilty beyond all reasonable doubt. The charges, however, concerned only the actual hijacking and there was no evidence that the government and the SADF had complicity in that.

Judge James pointed out to the accused that most of the evidence before him, related to occurrences in South Africa before they had flown to the Seychelles. 'The charges only relate to the circumstances of how you left Mahé, not how you got there. The question of what happened before is only peripheral to this case.'

He found it difficult to believe that Captain Saxena had departed from his flight schedule, effectively cheating his company of the considerable costs involved, without his being under duress.[8]

The Indian government refused to allow Captain Saxena and his crew to attend court in South Africa, so their evidence was taken on commission in the Seychelles.

Many telling points were conceded by the beleaguered mercenaries during the marathon trial. Perhaps the most incriminating was Mike Hoare's admission that from the time they boarded the aircraft at Mahé, Captain Saxena and his crew were under his command. Another was Mike Webb's concession agreement that the mercenaries were in total control of Mahé airport and that the Boeing would have been unable to refuel or take off without their assistance.[9]

The Minister of Defence, General Magnus Malan, intervened and banned the cross-examination of 23 serving or ex-Recce operators on military operations they had been involved in before Seychelles.[10]

The trial ground on for months and defence costs mounted, beggaring Colonel Hoare and most of his men. He said that he spent R60 000 defending himself and 32 of his men. Legal aid was refused by the State, so when their personal financial resources were exhausted, most reverted to conducting their own defences. Significantly, 2-Recce personnel were separately defended from the outset with monies paid from secret SADF funds.[11]

The judge finally handed down his judgement on 27 July 1982, finding that the Air India Boeing had indeed been hijacked. Mike Webb and Vernon Prinsloo were instrumental in getting the aircraft to land. Peter Duffy had boarded the aircraft bearing arms, ordered the passengers to remain seated pending a decision by the mercenaries and in concert with others exercised general control over the aircraft.

Captain Saxena had acted under duress and it was not an act of benevolence when he agreed to fly the mercenaries to Durban. Moneta and Webb had countermanded Hoare's order that weapons should not be taken aboard, so most of the mercenaries were armed after takeoff. If this had resulted in a firefight, it would have seriously jeopardised the safety of the aircraft and its occupants. After boarding Hoare had ordered Charles Goatley to remain in the cockpit in a monitoring capacity to ensure the crew flew it to Durban. Even after it landed at Durban the aircraft remained under mercenary control.

The judge dismissed government involvement in the coup attempt saying: 'Most of Colonel Hoare's evidence regarding the knowledge or involvement in his plans by various governments, government departments and individuals is unsupported and the court has little or no belief in any unsupported statements made by him. Even on [Colonel Hoare's] own story he heard indirectly through Dolinchek that the government had refused to be involved in the affair many months before it took place.

'It is clear that Colonel Hoare does not claim to have had any direct contact with Mr P W Botha and the cabinet and any allegation that he has made about their involvement is purely hearsay.'[12]

Nevertheless the judge found it 'impossible to escape the conclusion that the delivery of the AK47s and other equipment to Colonel Hoare's house at Hilton on 6 October 1981 followed upon his contacts' with Brigadiers Hamman and Knoetze. Despite this he accepted that the brigadiers had neither been aware of Colonel Hoare's plans, nor had they actively assisted with them. He also attached little importance to the receipted SADF issue voucher, which clearly went far beyond being just a hint of official support for the operation.[13]

While these factors would not have influenced the subsequent convictions, they were surely mitigating factors as far as sentencing was concerned, particularly as the judge found the hijacking was unplanned and opportunistic.

Charlie Dukes, who could only have been a hijacker by association because he was *hors de combat* from wounds at the time, was found not guilty and discharged. The rest were convicted under the Civil Aviation Act, 1972.

More than a few people in government heaved sighs of relief that it was over. Sentences were passed on 28 July 1982.

Colonel Mike Hoare was sentenced to ten years' imprisonment on one count and five years on each of two other counts, the sentences to run concurrently.

Tullio Moneta, Peter Duffy and Pieter Doorewaard each drew five years, Ken Dalgliesh and Charles Goatley got 30 months each and Vernon Prinsloo 12 months.

The other 34 were given six months with another 54 months conditionally suspended for five years.[14]

On a scale of one to ten the feelings of the press regarding Mike Hoare's downfall were mixed, ranging from *The Star*'s contemptuous headline 'The last whimper of a fading hero', to the *Daily Dispatch*'s kinder 'Mike Hoare: Sad end to a heroic saga'.[15]

We must now return to the night of 25-26 November 1981. Jerry Puren was lying wounded in his hide, listening to the sounds of jet engines. He searched the night sky and saw the rapidly receding port lights of a large aircraft. He guessed it was the Air India Boeing, which had probably assessed the situation on the ground and decided to divert to somewhere less dangerous. From his position he could not see the airport and it did not occur to him that it had landed and taken off again.

Shortly afterwards a ferocious firefight erupted near the barracks. Puren assumed it was the mercenaries staging their second attack, but in reality it was jumpy Seychellois and Tanzanian patrols shooting at each other and scoring own goals.

Two hours later there was complete silence over by the airport, which led him to conclude that the remaining mercenaries had been captured.[16]

At the time, Robert Sims and Susan Ingles lay sleepless in bed, listening to the radio and wondering apprehensively what had happened.[17]

Aubrey Brooks was still in the cave, badly wounded.

Barney Carey and Roger England did what they could to find Aubrey Brooks, but there were too many troops around. Carey tried to make his way back to his hotel, but gave up because of the patrols and hid in the bush for the night.

Roger England thought of a route to safety. He plunged into the sea and swam parallel to the beach until he arrived at the hotel. He walked in just after dawn, pretending he had just come from an early morning dip, and went to bed.[18]

Martin Dolinchek stayed in his hotel room, playing the innocent visitor.

When daylight came Jerry Puren was surprised to discover that his hide was quite close to the bullet-pocked terminal building. There was a hive of activity below him and troop carriers and armoured cars were tactically deployed on the approach road.

He assumed that the attack on the barracks had failed and decided to surrender, knowing he stood little chance of survival out there on his own with a badly injured knee. He stood up and shouted to soldiers that he wanted to surrender, but needed help.

A Jeep commanded by an officer drove up and stopped below him.

'We don't give a damn about capturing you . . . we just want to kill you!' he bawled.

Jerry ducked into cover as fire commenced, but fragments of shrapnel wounded his wrist and surgically punctured a balloon of fluid in his damaged knee, immediately relieving the pressure. He applied wound dressings and waited patiently for what he knew would be the end. Eventually, when no one came, he cautiously raised his head and looked down. The troops were forming up to advance on the terminal. From his grandstand position he watched the armoured cars advance and shell the building, while the troops laid down a blanket of covering fire with their lighter weapons.

The Royal Swazi National Airways F-28 Fokker Friendship shuddered as shells shattered its tail. It would still be at Mahé four months later, disabled and unable to fly, while the Swaziland government tried to negotiate the return of the pride of their fleet.[19]

In half an hour the unrequited battle was over. The wrecked terminal had suffered R1,4 million worth of damages, according to a claim later put in to the UN by the Seychelles government. They claimed another R16 million for losses in tourism revenue.[20]

Unknown to Jerry Puren, both Barney Carey and Aubrey Brooks were also spectators to this one-sided battle.

Roger England was lying innocently in his hotel bed. He had two days of freedom before the police took him in for questioning. Not believing his story, they beat him up savagely.

Barney Carey was arrested the next day after walking into an ambush. His captors worked him over, fracturing all his ribs and beating his face into a bloody pulp.

Aubrey Brooks, wounded and delirious, spent a night and a day in his cave, before surrendering to a local. He was escorted under armed guard to a hospital, but his wounds did not save him from a merciless beating.[21]

Barney Carey and Aubrey Brooks were placed in solitary confinement, occasionally being taken out and threatened with execution. On occasions they were spirited away by Tanzanian troops for sessions of vicious assaults.

Robert Sims and Susan Ingles were next on the list. Hoare telephoned his wife at the first opportunity. She phoned her brother, Bob Sims, updated him and told him to get rid of all arms and evidence in their safe house.

Neither Sims nor Ingles handled the situation intelligently. Either they felt their existing hiding places were good enough, or they were too frightened to look for others in broad daylight. Hoare believed it was because Sims was a firearms fanatic who could not bring himself to 'destroy all those lovely weapons'. He also said he 'hung on too long' thinking that as no one knew him he would be left alone.

The police came the next morning. They admitted their involvement, but no evidence of this was found at the house. The investigation was sloppy in the extreme, but the beating meted out to Sims was of sterner stuff. No one touched Susan Ingles. Superintendent Jean Larue returned with Sims three days later after he had broken down under interrogation. This time he conducted a more thorough search of the house and found an envelope. It was addressed in Dolincheck's hand to Susan Ingles and contained a note dated 15 November 1981 and addressed P O Box 514, Westville, which read: 'As mentioned on the telephone this morning, John and I would be grateful if you would meet our friend Anton Lubick on arrival on the BA [British Airways] flight today. I am sure you will remember him from our last party.' It asked her to pay Lubick 1 000 rupees and hire him a car for the duration of his stay.

The superintendent also found a nominal roll of the mercenaries and, probably on indications by Robert Sims, four AK47s in a cave.[22] Their amateurishness, as Jerry Puren put it, was responsible for the authorities landing their biggest fish, Martin Dolinchek of South Africa's National Intelligence Service.

The only one still free was Colonel Jerry Puren, a sexagenarian, who refused to give up. He remained on the run for 17 days, hiding and sleeping in the bush, dodging enemy foot patrols and evading tracker dogs. By the end he was starving and almost dying of thirst, having been forced to sustain himself on wild fruit and berries. He could take no more, so he surrendered to a civilian, ending a remarkable saga of endurance and survival for anyone, let alone a man over 60.

Colonel Hoare suggested in his book that Puren had probably sought and found shelter, either with his cousin Frank or his old friend Colonel Bob Noddyn, and that he had not existed alone in the bush for all that time. If this was true their hospitality must have been truly stingy, because Puren's ordeal had melted some seven kilograms from his already spare frame.[23]

Martin Dolinchek avoided beatings after capture, probably because he eagerly told them everything they wanted to know, including that he was a senior NIS officer on official business. He confirmed this at a news conference shortly afterwards, saying he had come to the Seychelles on a reconnaissance to assess the chances of mercenaries toppling the government.

The National Intelligence Service's first reaction was to concede he was a senior agent, but said he had been dismissed from the service before the raid. This was soon proved a lie, when it was revealed his wife was still drawing his salary cheques.[24]

The Seychelles authorities later claimed that two senior NIS officers, identified as Gerhardus H Rothman and Evert Johannes de Wet, had slipped into Mahé during February 1982 as tourists.

Significantly, it was Gerhardus Rothman who had chaired the 19 September 1981 conference at the Elangeni Hotel, Durban, when it was recommended that the State Security Council provide Colonel Hoare with arms. If that fell within his area of responsibility, it follows he was also involved in the provision of the R300 000 to bankroll the coup. Their brief, so the story went, was to liaise with the resistance and others to discover how much Dolinchek had said about South African involvement in the Seychelles and assess the damage to their intelligence network. They were also required to find out if belated legal assistance to Dolinchek would recover the situation. Or maybe to see whether he could be disposed of?

They contacted a major in the Seychelles People's Liberation Army and tried to get the results of Dolinchek's interrogations both by the army and the police. The major suggested he advise Dolinchek that they were on the island, but they begged him not to.

Contradicting this, one newspaper suggested that the NIS officers were wangled into the prison for a brief interview with Dolinchek on the pretext that they were his legal advisers.[25] They spent a week on the island before returning to South Africa.

Although perhaps a resistance sympathiser, it seems probable that the major's loyalties were in a state of flux after the failure of the coup. So for safety's sake, he played off one side against the other. While he reported them, it seems he left it until the last possible moment, waiting until they were airborne. This explains how, in press parlance, they got out 'only hours ahead of the local police', because, significantly, there was only one flight per week out of the island . . . and they were on it.

It seems surprising that the NIS was prepared to risk the capture — and all it would have entailed — of an officer as high up the ladder as Gerhardus Rothman. It might indicate that Martin Dolinchek's role in the Seychelles was pivotal and not as scatter-brained as the South African government's damage control exercise implied.

This was largely confirmed by a report in the *Pretoria News*. It said that a source high in the intelligence community had claimed that Jimmy Claasens, Deputy Director-General NIS, was aware Dolinchek was going on the Seychelles mission. It is interesting that a newspaperman's notes regarding this were seized on the orders of the NIS chief.[26]

In June 1982, only two months later, the media discovered that Jimmy Claasens was no longer at his desk at the NIS. The switchboard operator said he had taken early retirement for 'health reasons'. This was later confirmed by a NIS spokesman. There had been no advance notification of his going — the normal practice when a senior officer reaches the end of a distinguished career. A spokesman blandly insisted his retirement had nothing to do with the Seychelles.[27]

When interrogators told him of the visit, Dolincheck was frightened the National Intelligence Service planned to eliminate him and he agreed to make a statement. In it he described the two officers as 'yes men'.

Soon afterwards, perhaps to make it known there was a possible threat to his life without publicising the visit by the senior intelligence officers, Dolinchek was allowed to speak to the press. He said someone had phoned from South Africa and warned that Dr Niel Barnard, the new NIS chief, had ordered that he be dealt with 'severely', for revealing secrets under interrogation. He said he feared not only for his own life, but for the lives of his wife and children in South Africa.[28]

He also came up with two major position statements. Firstly, he retracted much of what he had said about official South African involvement. Secondly, he offered to become a state witness at the trial of his fellow mercenaries. This, he said, was conditional on political asylum and Seychelles' citizenship being granted for both himself and his wife, so he would not have to return to South Africa.

This offer seems to have been considered and rejected, without the authorities admitting it had been made. Dolinchek and the Seychelles Attorney General both later denied that any offers had been made.[29]

There could have been a simpler explanation for the visit by the two NIS officers. They were probably there with the full knowledge of President René to conclude a ransom deal for the mercenaries — which was finalised later — meaning that everything else was disinformation.

It is of interest to note that Colonel Hoare wrote in his book that Brigadier Hamman had told him during February 1982 that 'high level negotiations were going on behind the scenes with regard to their [the imprisoned mercenaries'] release, negotiations which involved a very large sum of money'.[30] More of this later.

The mercenaries who had not left the islands first appeared in court on 5 January 1982 for formal remand. In early February they were notified they would be facing charges of treason, for which they could face the death penalty on conviction.

Their defence counsel, his fees paid from monies raised by Mike Hoare, argued against these charges. He submitted that it was impossible for a non-citizen, someone who held no allegiance to the state, to be found guilty of treason. The Chief Justice of the Seychelles, Judge Earl Seaton, disagreed, ruling that even visitors could be charged, creating what amounted to new common law. Counsel's next tactic was to submit it would be impossible to find an impartial jury in the islands. He drew attention to a news report which said that 10 000 people at a Mahé public meeting the day before had bayed for the mercenaries' blood. The island's adult population was only 20 000, so this was a substantial percentage of them.[31]

The Judge rejected that argument as well.

Martin Dolinchek stood aloof, having opted to defend himself.

Eventually the time came for the accused to plead. The press speculated that a deal had been worked out. If Brooks, Carey, England and Puren pleaded guilty, Susan Ingles and Robert Sims would be freed. A noble gesture indeed, but it was not so.

On 20 June 1982 Aubrey Brooks, Barney Carey, Roger England and Jerry Puren pleaded guilty to treason — Brooks and Carey for being part of the attack on the barracks and England and Puren for being involved in the assault on the airport. They were all found guilty according to their pleas.

Robert Sims pleaded not guilty to treason, but guilty to an alternative charge of smuggling arms of war into the country. The judge found him guilty on the alternative charge.

Martin Dolinchek pleaded guilty, but the judge rejected his plea after he made a statement amounting to a denial, so a plea of not guilty was entered.

Charges against Susan Ingles were withdrawn and she was deported to South Africa. The Attorney General said the case had been withdrawn on President René's instructions. He refused to give reasons without presidential permission, which was not forthcoming.[32]

Sentencing of all accused was postponed until the completion of Martin Dolinchek's trial.

Dolinchek's defence was that he had neither been involved in the planning, nor in any of the attacks. He presented a particularly unedifying spectacle, attacking Colonel Hoare for double-crossing him and the National Intelligence Service for failing to provide money for his defence. He obligingly implicated Kenya in the plot, condemned the evils of apartheid — despite having worked for years in its security system — and said the coup attempt was shameful — despite his having been an eager participant. On 5 July 1982 he was acquitted of treason, but convicted of aiding and abetting in the levying of war.

The prisoners were brought together for sentencing.

First Aubrey Brooks, then Roger England, then Jerry Puren and finally Barney Carey were sentenced to death. Martin Dolinchek was given 20 years and Robert Sims drew a ten-year term.

Counsel for the prisoners awarded the death sentence, gave notice of an appeal against sentence. On 27 July 1982 the death row prisoners were escorted to Government House for a secret meeting with President René. He said their appeals were causing his government embarrassment and promised that if they withdrew them, they would be free and home by September 1982. He gave them a week to consider it. They all accepted his word and signed letters withdrawing their appeals.

René had good reason for his largesse. In April 1982 he had appealed to President P W Botha on humanitarian grounds not to execute three MK guerrilla — Ncinibithi Lubisi, Petrus Mashigo and Naphtali Manana — all under sentence of death for attacking Soekmekaar Police Station in January 1980. President Botha's response was uncharacteristically mild. Political observers regarded this as the first step in State-to-State manoeuvres designed to save the lives of the captured mercenaries. President Botha commuted the death sentences to life imprisonment in June 1982, before sentences were passed on the mercenaries in the Seychelles.[33]

There was a hiccup when an army revolt against the Seychelles government failed in August 1982. For political reasons September became too soon for René to pardon and release the mercenaries. It was finally done only in July 1983, when the last six of Mike Hoare's raiders filed aboard a scheduled flight to Johannesburg.

The truth behind Albert René's benevolence remained undisclosed for nine years until July 1992, when he revealed that South Africa had indeed paid a ransom — US$3 million for the reprieve, release and safe return of the mercenaries. On 14 October 1997 in testimony to the Truth and Reconciliation Commission ex-Foreign Minister Pik Botha confirmed that 'between US$3 million and US$6 million' was paid to the Seychelles for their release. 'My recollection', he said, 'is that the National Intelligence Service and/or Defence Force were involved.'[34]

On the other hand, former Director-General National Intelligence Service, Dr Niel Barnard, professed in testimony to the TRC that neither he nor the NIS had any prior knowledge of the coup attempt. He said that during a routine visit to the Service's Durban office he had been asked to meet Colonel Mike Hoare, who told him of plans for a coup and asked for NIS help. Barnard said he refused. He also said Dolinchek's involvement had been unauthorised.

On his return to Pretoria, Barnard went to see Premier P W Botha with a senior colleague, told him what they knew and said there was a possibility of military involvement. 'He told me he would discuss this on a political level with his colleagues, because this could have negative results for South Africa. That was the last I heard about the Seychelles incident.'[35]

Whether true or false, and the author is inclined to the latter, Niel Barnard turned out to be not been much of a spy chief either way.

In South Africa those mercenaries sentenced to six months imprisonment were committed to Diepkloof Prison outside Soweto. With one-third remission for 'good behaviour', they only served four months.

The commander of 2-Recce, Commandant Sybie van der Spuy, rallied around his imprisoned men. He knew their wives and children by their Christian names, he had attended family christenings and been a welcome visitor in their homes. He thought of them as family. They were comrades-in-arms, volunteer civilian soldiers and warriors. They had been through much together.

There were unit whip-rounds to pay mortgage instalments on houses, to stop insurance policies from lapsing and for other financial help. A friend of the unit put one operator on his payroll the day he entered Diepkloof, to ensure he had a salary while serving sentence. It was not solely 2-Recce personnel who needed help — there were 1-Recce men and ex-Recces as well. Many people in the greater SADF contributed to the kitty. The Welfare Department of the SADF also helped out.

All this, unfortunately, as Sybie van der Spuy put it, 'stank of involvement, of the guilty conscience'. His conscience, unlike some others around, was clear. The Seychelles had not been his party. He was merely an officer who believed his first duty lay with the welfare of his men, and unlike many others more senior than him, practised his beliefs.[36]

Even with the benefit of the proverbial 20/20 vision available in hindsight, it is still difficult to say whether the SADF secretly lent official financial assistance to the men in their times of trouble. In fact many office-bound bureaucrats went out of their way to show their disapproval of the coup attempt and make things difficult for those involved. In one jarring note, a staff officer (and by inference the SADF chief himself), sanctimoniously ignored the SADF's involvement in the coup and gleefully discovered somewhere in the small print that winners of the *Honoris Crux* sentenced to terms of imprisonment could have their awards cancelled. This was solemnly done for the first time in UDF/SADF history in the case of a former officer of 6-Recce who had done his duty and fought bravely for South Africa. That he was an English-speaking ex-Rhodesian and not an Afrikaans speaking South African appeared to ease the process for some.

Yet on completion of their sentences, those who wished to, were allowed to continue their service with 2-Recce. The Permanent Force men who felt the same way rejoined 1-Recce.[37]

Former mercenary Charles Goatley, when serving as a helicopter pilot in the SAAF with the rank of captain, was awarded a well deserved Air Force Cross for saving lives at sea during the sinking of the cruise ship *MTS Oceanos* off the Transkei coast in 1991.[38]

These men serving longer sentences were released progressively. Those with five-year sentences went home after 22 months. Finally only Colonel Mike Hoare remained behind bars. His release came with a presidential amnesty in May 1985, after he had done just short of three years.[39]

At the end of it all the last word on *Operation Anvil* should go to Don Kenny, an old soldier. When testifying in his own defence during his trial for hijacking, he said he had made it clear he had not wanted to be part of a 'Mickey Mouse' mission.

The judge asked politely if he meant a badly planned one.

'Yes', Kenny replied, 'an operation that contained Mickey Mouse, Donald Duck, cowboys and Indians and Goofy.'[40]

4

Operation Anvil
Seychelles Coup Attempt
After the coup was over

In February 1983 the Leader of the Opposition PFP (Progressive Federal Party) in South Africa, Dr Frederick van Zyl Slabbert, put the government under extreme pressure during a five-day, parliamentary no confidence debate. He introduced a motion that the Seychelles coup attempt illustrated the government's incompetence.

'Here', he said, 'we have a coup planned at the level of brigadier in the SADF and where top people in the National Intelligence Service were aware of it. If Brigadiers Hamman and Knoetze and Warrant Officer van der Merwe acted in a manner prejudicial to the security of the State, the Minister of Defence must accept responsibility. The same argument applies in respect of senior officers of the National Intelligence Service.

'If, as has been averred, neither the cabinet nor the State Security Council were aware of the move, notwithstanding the prior knowledge of the SADF and National Intelligence Service — and notwithstanding easily obtained police evidence of a pending coup — then this points either to a distortion of the facts or to unbelievable incompetency and inefficiency on the part of the SADF, National Intelligence Service and even the State Security Council.'

Dr Slabbert posed various questions to the Prime Minister:

1. Was Martin Dolinchek in the employ of the National Intelligence Service when the raid took place?
2. If not why did his wife continue to receive his salary cheques?
3. Why did Mr Rothman and Mr de Wet of National Intelligence Service reportedly travel to the Seychelles to try to 'silence' him?
4. Why did the police seize newspapermen's notes on Dolinchek at the behest of the chief of the National Intelligence Service?
5. Did Dolinchek write a report on Colonel Hoare's plan and submit it to the National Intelligence Service and the SADF?
6. If so, to whom were these reports submitted?
7. Did the reports get submitted to the State Security Council?
8. Why was the information not acted upon?
9. Did Major George Schroeder tell the 'authorities' of the raid plans?
10. If so, who did he tell and why was the information not acted upon?
11. What was the involvement of Brigadier Hamman, Brigadier Knoetze and Warrant Officer van der Merwe?
12. In what section of the SADF are these officers employed?
13. How was it possible for Colonel Hoare to draw weapons of this nature [AK47s etc.] from an SADF store without authorisation?
14. If there was authorisation, is it possible for any member of the public to draw AK47s from SADF stores?
15. If the weapons were delivered to Colonel Hoare fraudulently and/or in contravention of SADF and Treasury regulations, what disciplinary steps have been taken against SADF personnel responsible for such fraud and/or contraventions?
16. What was the involvement of Mr Alex van Wyk and Mr Claasens in the coup bid?

17 In what capacities were these officers employed in the National Intelligence Service?
18 Did either Mr van Wyk or Mr Claasens report the planned coup to the State Security Council or to the cabinet?
19 If so what action did the State Security Council take?

Prime Minister Botha studiously avoided answering any of the questions, but instead rambled on long and inconclusively, quoting lengthy passages from the trial judgement of the mercenaries, the UN commission of enquiry and the report of the International Civil Aviation Organisation. All this, he contended, was proof that the government was not involved.

Departmental investigations, he said, had confirmed that no state funds had been used and action had been taken to prevent future undesirable contacts with such undertakings. 'I do not deem it to be in the public interest to make known steps taken against the officials involved and the rectifications which were carried out, because they affect delicate sections of our security service.' He repeated an old promise that his government would introduce legislation to prohibit members of the SADF from becoming mercenaries and ended by saying it was 'not in the interests of the Republic to discuss the matter any further'.

Dr Ferdi Hartzenberg, a Conservative Party front bencher and a former Minister of Education and Training in P W Botha's cabinet at the time of the coup attempt, had told the press on 4 May 1982 that the cabinet had not discussed the proposed coup at any meeting attended by him. He suggested it might have been discussed by groups or committees of which he was not a member (presumably he was referring to the State Security Council).[1]

He suggested that although the 'cabinet' might have no knowledge, this did not preclude individual ministers from knowing. Ferdi Hartzenberg looked directly at General Malan across the floor of the House and asked if he had known.

The general replied firmly in the negative.

Dr Hartzenberg turned to Prime Minister P W Botha.

'Did you have any prior knowledge, arising from your being the political head of the National Intelligence Service, which has been implicated through Dolinchek?'

P W Botha sat dumbly without answering. Eschel Rhoodie, quoting an eye witness, said he 'sat white faced, his hands trembling'.[2] Another report described him as stony-faced. *Hansard* recorded unemotionally that he refused to reply.

Perhaps he was thinking of the man he succeeded, John Vorster, and how his life and reputation came tumbling down after lying to parliament over the Information Scandal.

'I receive no reply from the Prime Minister', Dr Hartzenberg hunted on ferret-like, refusing to let go.

'He does not wish to reply?

'He does not wish to say yes or no?'

Dr Hartzenberg questioned him interrogatively: 'The Prime Minister says the cabinet did not know, but will not say whether *he* knew. The only conclusion I can draw from that is that he did know.'

The Prime Minister remained grimly silent, allowing Dr Hartzenberg to speak without interjection or challenge. Nine months earlier P W Botha had evaded vigorous questioning by the opposition PFP, when they demanded a Parliamentary Select Committee investigate alleged government authorisation of SADF and intelligence involvement in the coup attempt. He avoided their demands then by saying the matter was *sub judice*, adding: 'You are lending your ears to petty gossip stories.'[3]

This time he made no mention of 'petty gossip'.

CP Defence Spokesman Koos van der Merwe called the Prime Minister's assurances unconvincing. The Supreme Court had found that certain members of the SADF had helped the mercenaries, yet the Prime Minister had chosen to overlook it. It was 'astounding and inexplicable' that the Parliamentary Select Committee investigating the matter had found that no responsible official had approved the abortive coup — yet court evidence showed two brigadiers were involved. Even more astonishing, he said, both were still serving in the SADF. One had recently been awarded the Southern Cross Medal for outstanding service. The committee's finding that no state funds were used 'must be seriously doubted'.

Another crucial question, he said, was whether General Malan had prior knowledge, because the indications were he 'was aware, or reasonably aware' of it. He called on him to resign.

Dr Slabbert said the Prime Minister's responses in reply to the no-confidence debate had been 'hopelessly inadequate'. He revealed to the House that he had turned down an offer, made to him as Leader of the Opposition, to be privy to confidential information.

'We have to clear our [South Africa's] name in public. We have to clear our name in Parliament. We have to demonstrate quite clearly that we were not involved', Dr Slabbert said.

The PFP's and CP's demand for a probe was ignored by the government, so Dr Slabbert decided to force the Prime Minister to answer all the questions he had refused to answer during the no confidence debate and announced he would devote his whole allocation for the next three parliamentary question periods to the coup attempt.

He tabled the following questions:

- Was Dolinchek employed by the National Intelligence Service at the time of the attempted coup or prior to it?
- Did Dolinchek submit a report to the National Intelligence Service before the coup attempt?
- Was any action taken as a result?
- Would the Prime Minister furnish names?

On 9 February 1983, Prime Minister Botha made a statement saying that:

- Dolincheck was employed by the National Intelligence Service at the time of the Seychelles'coup.
- He was involved in the collection of intelligence.
- He was answerable to the National Intelligence Service regional representative in Durban.
- He was employed before the Seychelles coup and left the employ of the National Intelligence Service on 31 July 1982 . . . six months afterwards.
- He was dismissed on grounds of misconduct in contravention of section 9 of Act 104 of 1978 . . . apparently for being absent without leave.
- He submitted a report to the National Intelligence Service regarding the planned coup on 21 July 1978, via the regional representative in Durban to the National Intelligence Service head office in Pretoria.
- The report revealed a representative of the deposed Seychelles president, James Mancham, said that he and his council were planning a *coup d' état* in the Seychelles.
- On 24 July 1978 the former head of National Intelligence Service had issued instructions that the service should not be involved. They monitored the situation until it was confirmed all planning had ended.

P W Botha refused to confirm or deny the report had been submitted to the State Security Council or the involvement of certain individuals, whom he declined to name, in the coup attempt. He was not prepared to discuss anything on the State Security Council's agenda, nor mention the names of anyone in the National Intelligence Service. He said it would endanger their lives and impede their work.

In answer to other questions by Dr Slabbert, he said National Intelligence Service employees taking leave were obliged to supply a contact address. Dolinchek had not and the National Intelligence Service had no idea where he was. He denied the National Intelligence Service knew he had a passport in the name of Anton Lubick.

Regarding the activities of National Intelligence Service officers Rothman and Van Wyk, he refused to say if 'certain individuals' had visited the Seychelles in early 1982, give their names or state the purpose of their visit.

He also refused to say if Colonel Hoare or anyone else had approached any National

Intelligence Service employee regarding his coup plans, who that employee was and what action Mr Botha had taken.

Defence Minister Magnus Malan said that while the officer who authorised the delivery of SADF weapons to Colonel Hoare had the necessary authority, he had made an 'error of judgement'. He confirmed departmental steps had been taken, but said he did not believe it fair to name the officer and subject him to more embarrassment.

If he was referring to Brigadier Daan Hamman, which he obviously was, the departmental steps meant great big ones, like promotion to the rank of major-general and the award of the Southern Cross Medal for outstanding service as already mentioned by Koos van der Merwe, MP.

General Malan said a junior Citizen Force officer (Lieutenant Vic de Beer) who had issued unauthorised call-up papers had resigned. What he did not say was that the SADF had been anxious that Lieutenant de Beer, an obvious scapegoat for much of the flak taken over the Seychelles' affair, be charged with the theft of the leave forms. This was despite their value being a fraction of a cent. The matter was referred to the Attorney General for instructions and the SADF was sanctimoniously enraged when he ordered the case withdrawn on the principle *de minimus non curat lex* — the law should not concern itself with trifles.[4]

During 1983 Philip Myburgh asked Defence Minister General Magnus Malan if any of the Seychelles accused were still in the employ of the SADF. Malan replied in the affirmative, but refused to disclose their names.

Mr Myburgh said he was astounded because the men had been 'disloyal to the country and had seriously embarrassed' it internationally.[5]

Assassination of Gerard Hoarau: 1985

Gerard Hoarau would not live to fulfill his ambition of becoming President of the Seychelles. He survived an assassination bid in Cannes, France, but in 1985 he died violently when he was gunned down while walking in a quiet London street.[6]

Hello, Ian Douglas Withers alias John Douglas

MI-5, in the guise of the Anti-Terrorist Branch of Scotland Yard, raided Christopher Robin Investigations, the London office of Ian Douglas Withers alias John Douglas. MI-5's interest in Withers related to his having once been President René's National Security Adviser. His career had been chequered and his curriculum vitae, if written honestly, would have recorded numerous convictions for bugging telephones in cities as far afield as Hong Kong and London.

It was said, too, he had worked for other masters, including General Hendrik van den Bergh's BOSS (Bureau for State Security), for whom he admitted devising a system of 'pre-employment screening' of members of Britain's Anti-Apartheid Movement.

MI-5 arrested Wither's unfortunate 17-year-old receptionist, the only one remaining at his London office, and detained her in their detention centre (the Paddington Green Police station cells) for interrogation. Later, three men describing themselves as security consultants who admitted they had been hired by Withers — Bill Underwood, Dave Coughlan and Dave Richards — were jailed for bugging Hoarau's home before his assassination. They all claimed they had acted with the approval of the 'Foreign Office', which is probably the story Withers told them.

Withers shut down his Dublin-based operation in a hurry and retired to Mahé, where he opened the *La Perle Noire* restaurant. He also obtained the agency for Taylor's US ice-cream machines. He resumed his old business of 'security consultancy', regularly jetting to Tanzania, India, Sri Lanka, Panama and elsewhere — but not to London.

There seems little doubt that Withers was working for the South African National Intelligence Service, probably resulting from a secret deal worked out between President

René and Gerhardus Rothman and Evert de Wet, when ransoms for the captured mercenaries were apparently discussed.

Withers' prospects of long-term employment with the Seychelles government were clouded by the National Intelligence Service and Military Intelligence being in direct competition.[7]

Enter Colonel Garth Barrett

Certainly powerful forces in the National Intelligence Service and the SAP had been working hand in hand to ensure that another Military Intelligence-sponsored coup failed. Colonel Garth Barrett had retained his links with the SADF's Chief of Staff Intelligence (CSI), through the Rev Ndabaningi Sithole's dissident forces who partnered RENAMO and mounted pin prick attacks against Zimbabwe in the north-east. When his plans for another SADF sponsored coup attempt against the Seychelles were nearing fruition he was arrested on the orders of Minister of Police Louis Le Grange. He was kept in detention for a few days, but by the time he was released the National Intelligence Service had ensured the prospects for another coup had been well and truly blown.[8]

Enter Craig Williamson and Longreach

Major Craig Williamson, head of the G1 Branch of the Security Police, concerned with foreign intelligence operations, resigned his police commission on 31 December 1985. The following day he joined the Military Intelligence's DCC — Department of Covert Collection with the rank of commandant (lieutenant-colonel). He was later promoted to full colonel. He was put in charge of AL (*Ander Lande* — other lands, which meant the whole world except for Zimbabwe, Zambia and Angola).

Longreach, a company registered in Great Britain, was established with Williamson as chairman. Behind the scenes, though, he was the prime mover for the DCC. The managing director and front man was an Englishman, Michael Irwin. A former officer with the Royal Marine Commandos and a veteran of the Falklands War, he had impeccable references. At one time he had played for the same polo team as Prince Charles. Irwin later claimed he had moved on from Longreach when 'unsavoury people' appeared on the scene. He claimed he had no idea it was a South African Military Intelligence front.[9] An office was established in a very upmarket glass building at 31 Princess of Wales Terrace, Parktown, Johannesburg, opposite the Sunnyside Park Hotel.

Once established Williamson began to recruit operators and sources from scratch. He quietly took the odd source from the police, but he could not steal too many because it would have been undiplomatic. Nor could he take over and continue the good intelligence operations he had developed while with the Security Police. There was nothing, however, to stop him from mirroring them for the DCC. In many ways the mirrored operations were more effective. In the SAP he had been up against dinosaur structures in the senior ranks, elderly Afrikaans-speaking officers who had little idea of the modern concepts of intelligence. They regarded him with hostility and suspicion. It was bad enough having young officers who had matriculated, but having an *Engelsman* (Englishman) with a university degree put him beyond the pale! The job was clearer in the military and he was left to get on with it. As his team developed, Longreach rapidly spread its intelligence tentacles into Europe, the USA and many African countries.

In Uganda Longreach recruited former Ugandan army officers and set up shop for them near the ANC's Solomon Mahlangu School in Tanzania. They gathered intelligence from ANC students 'for corporate clients considering investment in the region'. Longreach used Ghanaians and Malawians to recruit spies in London and Britons to recruit agents in African territories where the ANC was active.

Introducing Giovanni Mario Ricci

On what the notorious CCB (Civil Corporation Bureau) would later call the 'Blue Plan' side of his business life, Craig Williamson, with the office of deputy chairman, looked after the South African interests of the giant GMR, an international commodities, financial and property group, owned by its chairman, Giovanni Mario Ricci, a controversial Italian billionaire. They were good friends.

Ricci, when a young man, had been convicted of offences relating to bankruptcy and the possession of forged currency notes in Italy and Switzerland. He came to prominence during dramatic civil court proceedings in London when he was alleged to have acted against Seychelles dissidents on behalf of his close friend, President Albert René. But Ricci was not a man to fool around with. At least two major newspapers who inferred that he had serious criminal connections discovered this when he sued them for defamation and won substantial damages when they failed to produce evidence of any wrongdoing.

After moving to South Africa in 1986, Ricci embarked on a multi-million rand spending spree, reputedly buying a private game farm near Potgietersrus in the northern Transvaal and luxury mansions in Bryanston and Midrand, both in the Johannesburg area.

Craig Williamson arranged Ricci's application for a South African permanent residence permit which made no mention of his previous convictions. It was granted in January 1987. Williamson said he did not know about these and had checked his record with Interpol 'before I agreed to be employed by him or to give him a character reference'. Ricci's criminal record, Williamson contended, had been routinely expunged in both Italy and Switzerland because of the long time-lapse which led to his 'technical error'. Ricci's residence permit was not withdrawn. The convictions were old and he was a man of influence. Military Intelligence undoubtedly threw their considerable weight behind his application because of his value to DCC, but it must also have been of assistance that President P W Botha counted Ricci as a close friend.[10]

Longreach (Pty) Ltd and GMR were formally associated and the former acted as security consultants for the latter. Both companies used the same post office box at Bryanston post office in Sandton, north of Johannesburg.[11]

Ricci had a genuine interest in protecting the Seychelles, which he had fallen in love with on his first visit. To him it was heaven on earth . . . but it was run like hell!

He made it his personal mission to do something about it, heavily investing there to boost its economy, starting a highly successful tea industry and doing much to boost tourism. To this end he published an expensive coffee table book in full colour and titled *Seychelles Images*. He dedicated it: 'To the Seychelles Islands the ultimate paradise with love. Meeting you, I fell in love with you. Getting to know you I found eternal peace.' Many thousands were printed at his personal expense and given away free to promote the islands.

Craig Williamson (on South Africa's behalf) takes over Seychelles' Intelligence

Mario Ricci's friendship with President René was Williamson's entree to the Syechelles. The Seychelles was a member of South Africa's main enemy, the OAU — Organisation for African Unity — and was regarded by the West as a Soviet client. The whole Indian Ocean region, including India and Madagascar, was inclining towards the Soviets at the time.

Understandably, René was paranoid about prospects of a *coup d'etat*, having seen too many attempts since taking office. Following the Mike Hoare debacle, tourist revenue — the country's main source of income — had dropped by 60%.

Ricci strongly recommended Williamson and his associates to René. He knew they were South Africans, but not that their company was a South African Military Intelligence front, although he might have suspected it. Nevertheless, they were obviously well connected in Pretoria, which on its own was an important reason to employ them. Williamson emphasised that they were professionals. If the Seychellois were paying them, they would be on the side of the Seychelles. If the South Africans, the British, the Americans, the Soviets or anyone else started planning a coup they would find out and tell him. They would also add professionalism to the job of training his own people.

Ricci's recommendation ensured that Williamson swung a deal with Albert René for Longreach to handle all security matters and intelligence for the island group. The price negotiated was US$40 000 to 50 000 a month. In real international terms it was peanuts, but it was all that the Seychelles could afford. Anyway, although President René might not have known it, Longreach would gladly have done the job for nothing!

Williamson's amazing coup put South Africa in an unbelievably strong position when dealing with the CIA, MI-6 and other Western intelligence agencies. It is a contradiction in terms, but there are few secrets in the intelligence business, and it was not long before other intelligence agencies put two plus two together and came up with the right answer.[12] Ant White, a former captain in Rhodesia's Selous Scouts, became Longreach's director of operations for the Seychelles. Although not holding the office *per se*, he also became the Seychelles' *de facto* Director-General, Intelligence.

Military Intelligence's Longreach did a good job for the Seychelles, effectively displacing its rivals, the National Intelligence Service and Ian Withers. With Williamson in Ricci's shadow the NIS stood no chance. Despite this, René allowed Withers to remain in the Seychelles, looking after his business interests and no doubt continuing to feed the odd intelligence titbit back to René. He was undoubtedly also tasked by the NIS to keep on eye on Williamson, whom those in office were — and probably still are — convinced was working for British Intelligence.

In 1991 the US pressured President René into democratising the Seychelles and allowing opposition groups — including James Mancham — to return from overseas exile. This prompted Withers to make a swift return to the Emerald Isle, probably in case a democratic free and fair election returned Mancham to power. If this had occurred, Mancham might well have dusted off the disused extradition treaty the Seychelles had with Great Britain in terms of the Fugitive Offenders Act, 1897, and shipped Withers back to Britain for MI-5's attention.[13] With the opposition back in the islands, it was also possible someone might start looking around for an opportunity to avenge Hoarau's death — by assassinating him! Besides, the NIS funds that had been sustaining him began drying up after the bans on the ANC and other black nationalist organisations were lifted in 1990. So, even though the palms might still have been waving over the Seychelles' balmy beaches, the palmy days were over. In the event Withers need not have worried about Albert René being shunted from office, because he remains President at the time of writing.

Longreach brought out big league security consultants to assist the Seychelles. Amongst them was an eminent retired British major-general and the influential Evelyn le Chene, who with her husband had served with Britain's Special Operations Executive (SOE), during World War II. She was politically highly influential and moved in the same circles as Margaret Thatcher.

No Longreach operators were ever based in the Seychelles, but the organisation maintained an office there. There was, however, a continual movement of operators both in and out, advising on training, guiding their intelligence people, providing intelligence and so on. For South Africa, of course, it was two-way traffic.

Longreach remained in operation until the Goldstone Commission triggered its shutdown in the early 1990s.[14]

This signalled the end of South Africa's Seychelles connection.

5

Total Onslaught — Total Response National Security Management System

There was nothing new in a 'total strategy' or a 'total response' towards a 'total onslaught'. Winston Churchill did it when Great Britain faced Nazi Germany's total onslaught in World War II. He harnessed every physically able-bodied Briton, male or female, young or old, to the war effort. While those who were able served in the armed forces or the merchant navy, 80% per cent of the civilians remaining, both men and women, served in the Home Guard, as fire watchers in the Air Raid Police (ARP), with the National Fire Service, with the rescue services or as auxiliary nurses — ready for the nightly air raids of Hitler's *blitzkrieg*. Often such duties were performed after long shifts at munitions factories or in other reserved occupations. Paradoxically, in London, Liverpool, Southampton and many other areas joining the armed forces often became a respite from danger.

The Truman Doctrine was adopted by the USA after World War II to stave off a Soviet-orchestrated Armageddon. The feeling of the time was aptly summed up by American Soviet expert George F Kennan who described the Soviets as fanatical, neurotic and determined that the 'internal harmony of our society be disrupted, our traditional way of life be destroyed, the international authority of our state be broken'.[1]

The doctrine demanded a (total) global commitment on America's part. Under-Secretary of State Dean Acheson explained: 'Like apples in a barrel infected by one rotten one, the corruption of Greece would infect Iran and all to the east. It would also carry the infection to Africa through Asia Minor and Egypt to Europe.' To combat this pernicious threat a strategy of 'containment' was adopted. It was designed to stop the Soviets expanding into every possible nook and cranny by the 'adroit and vigilant application of counter-force at a series of constantly shifting geographic and political points'.[2] In short, every time a Marxist-inspired insurgency reared its head anywhere in the world, it was treated with maximum force. It was a bit like the old game of under-the-blanket, except that when an interesting shape appeared, you did not just feel it, you whacked it as hard as you could and without warning.

The 'Eisenhower Doctrine' followed but it was virtually the same as its predecessors. 'Behind everything', Eisenhower wrote, 'was our deep-seated conviction that the communists were principally responsible for the trouble.'

Even President Kennedy, who hardly entered the White House as a Cold War warrior, said after the Bay of Pigs: 'It is clearer than ever that we face a relentless struggle in every corner of the globe that goes far beyond the clash of armies or even nuclear armaments. The armies are there, and in large numbers. The nuclear armaments are there. But they serve primarily as a shield behind which subversion, infiltration and a host of other tactics steadily advance, picking off vulnerable areas one by one in situations which do not permit our own armed intervention. Power is the hallmark of this offensive, power and discipline and deceit.' [3]

This belief in the necessity of responding whenever communist involvement was real or suspected took the UN to Korea, led to the Anglo-French landings at Suez in 1956, triggered the landing of 14 300 US Marines in the Lebanon in July 1958, and sparked numerous brush fire confrontations elsewhere in the world.[4] It also led America into the bloody morass of Vietnam.

Unfortunately for South Africa, when its communist threat began to escalate in the 1970s, the West began to wrongly perceive that its own threat from communism was on the wane.

In an astonishing act of weakness, comparable to Chamberlain's grasping at straws to attain 'peace in our time' at Munich in 1938, the USA and 33 European states signed the 'Final Act' with the Soviet Union at Helsinki in 1975. This ominous-sounding item of international law put the rubber stamp of legality and respectability on the Soviet Union's unlawful occupation and rape of central and eastern Europe in the 1940s. Effectively, they had won the first stage of the Cold War, which left them poised to move on to Stage 2.[5] Southern Africa — as history now proves although many deny it — was the next stepping stone on their road to communist world domination.

South Africa, along with many other third world countries, faced a real threat from communist expansionism. The situation was exacerbated because all African nationalist movements were allied to or supported by the Soviet Bloc or Red China. The editorials of *Pravda* and *Izvestia* had made the Kremlin's intentions clear. They intended to destroy the apartheid regime in South Africa and SWA/Namibia and replace it with Communist People's Republics under the control of the ANC/SACP and SWAPO. They had achieved this in Angola, Mozambique and elsewhere, so why not in South Africa and Namibia?

The man responsible for forging Soviet policy in Africa was Vassili Solodovnikov, a KGB officer senior enough to don the mantle of any government department convenient to the task in hand. For years the UN headquarters in New York, where he promoted the causes of African nationalist liberation movements, was his front line.

He next moved to Lusaka as the Soviet Ambassador to Zambia, where he orchestrated Soviet logistical support and training for the liberation movements based there, principally ZAPU, SWAPO, ANC and FRELIMO.

Solodovnikov, in an interview with David Bryce Jones, maintained that the Soviet Union's sponsorship of liberation movements and terrorism gave them an edge. The underlying interest was not material but ideological. 'We were sure', he said, 'we were weakening the rich West whose economies were based on colonialism and cheap natural resources. The costs to us were less than might be thought. It was not big money. The military equipment was not first class, and many people in those countries have now received their education in our institutions.'

The Cold War, he said correctly, was fought by Africans, Arabs, Afghans, Vietnamese and Cambodians. They were the victims. To the West, however, what happened in remote areas of jungle or bush was of far less significance to them than the continuation of the atomically armed stalemate in Europe.[6] In the end the unrestrained effects of the Final Act on the Soviet Union contributed more to the misery and degradation of Angola, Mozambique and other southern African countries than anything else.

The South African government, because it was being targeted, knew only too well that its estrangement from its traditional Western allies, by reason of its apartheid policies, had increased the threat tenfold. Despite this it was not prepared to bend and do anything about it.

Many white South African liberals who abhorred apartheid and communism in equal measure — and there were many in that category — believed the National Party government had painted the country into a corner that left them with few choices. Theirs was the paradox of longing for democratisation while the spectre of communism hung over the sub-continent like the sword of Damocles.

During his prolonged term as Minister of Defence before becoming Prime Minister, P W Botha developed a close relationship with the military. In the process he became the mentor of General Magnus Malan. Malan, in his younger days, had unusually been posted for a spell with the US Army's command and had undergone a staff training course at Fort

Leavenworth, Kansas. In 1962/63 he was attached to an armoured division in Colorado in and later to French forces in Algeria. Malan had long preached a doctrine, based on ideas picked up abroad and from the works of authors like Beaufre and Kitson, that South Africa was facing the threat of a 'Total Onslaught' from the Soviet Bloc and to a lesser extent from Red China. The idealism of Beaufre was soon eclipsed in SADF circles by the work of a US Army officer, John J McCuen, *The Art of Counter-Revolutionary War*, that preached counter-terrorism and the elimination of revolutionaries.

General Malan and many of his officers were convinced that the Soviets were riding on the twin backs of black nationalism and decolonisation as it spread inexorably southwards towards South Africa itself. By infecting the neighbouring black states with Marxism they hoped to attain dominance over South Africa and achieve their ultimate goals of controlling the subcontinent's strategic minerals and the Cape sea route.

To combat this threat, they argued, the South African response had to be a total strategy that would meet the threat in not only the military sphere, but in the political, economic and psychological arenas as well. They believed, in effect, that South Africa was at war with the Soviet Union. They were facing multi-dimensional attacks on the diplomatic front (increasing isolation and moves to get South Africa out of SWA/Namibia), the economic front (sanctions and boycotts), the propaganda front (the Anti-Apartheid Movement, and later the End Conscription Campaign, etc.) and the war front (low intensity war and military support of surrogates like MK, SWAPO, Angola, Mozambique etc.).[7]

James Selfe succinctly summed up this viewpoint as follows:

- The NATO and Warsaw Pact Blocs were effectively at war, but neither could attack the other by conventional means because of nuclear deterrence.
- Each competed with the other for regional political advantage, with the object of securing diplomatic advantage and of denying the other access to strategic resources.
- Because direct military aggression might provoke counter-action, both powers, engaged in indirect warfare.
- This involved using diplomatic, political, economic and propaganda levers to disadvantage the other.
- To promote deniability, many of these activities were conducted via surrogates, which were given extensive diplomatic and military support with which to wage guerrilla campaigns.

South Africa fitted into this pattern as follows:

- South Africa was an aggressively anti-communist state (even if this distinction did not automatically qualify it for membership of the West).
- The country was richly endowed with strategic minerals and was located midway along the oil route to the West.
- As such, South Africa was a target of Soviet expansionism via indirect warfare.
- South Africa was, as a result, facing a multi-dimensional attack from the Soviet Bloc on the diplomatic (increasing isolation), economic (sanctions and boycotts), and propaganda (the anti-apartheid campaign) fronts. In addition, Soviet support from the ANC's military wing (MK) ensured a campaign of low intensity warfare against South Africa.
- Since the Soviet Union was a totalitarian state, it could control and direct all the resources of the State to achieve its objectives in South Africa.
- South Africa was therefore facing a total onslaught from the Soviet Union, in which the ANC was the surrogate agent of its campaign of indirect warfare.

This had three important implications that would shape South African state policy, state institutions and State action in subsequent years.

Firstly, South Africa's military and, increasingly, its political leadership came to regard the country 'as being at war with the Soviet Union' and by implication with the ANC. Already a banned organisation, it became cast 'as the enemy, against whom maximum force could be legitimately employed in accordance with the conventions of war'.

Secondly, in the same way as the Soviets were able to 'deny that the activities of its surrogates were attributable to its main if concealed objective, so too, the State began to set up institutions which were likewise wholly deniable'.

Thirdly, the 'military and political decision-makers increasingly regarded themselves as under siege, and a garrison-state mentality took hold. This in turn affected budget priorities and led to the adaptation of state structures. Because the Soviet Union was engaged in a total onslaught' against South Africa, 'the South African state's response needed to be equally comprehensive, coordinated and total'.[8]

They viewed the threat to South Africa in the same way as Truman, Eisenhower and Kennedy had looked at the communist threat to the continued existence of the free world. The difference was that the South Africans were not concerned with the world, only with their own small sphere of influence in the sub-continent.

P W Botha and General Malan had tried to sell their brand of 'Total Strategy' to Premier Vorster, but without success. Either he did not understand or he was uninterested.

The all-powerful State Security system

P W Botha, in contrast to Vorster whose style was personalised, secretive and often haphazard, was a team and systems man. So after taking office as premier in 1978, Botha immediately plunged into a reorganisation to establish systems and enhance the decision making process by broadening input.

One of his first tasks was to establish an 'Office of the Prime Minister'. It was provided with a director-general and staff and given a role in the policy making process — something that had not existed in the homespun organisations of previous prime ministers.

To provide support and continuity for the cabinet, which had been lacking, he created a long overdue cabinet secretariat to bring order out of chaos and established five permanent cabinet committees. This consolidation replaced the haphazard arrangements of his predecessor who while in office had appointed 20 committees on an *ad hoc* basis, then ignored their existence and opinions. The new cabinet committees were the State Security Council, Social Affairs, Internal Affairs, Economic Affairs and Finance. He later amalgamated the latter two, which left four in all.

Under Vorster it was the duty of the committees to recommend action to the prime minister, but in 1979 Botha invested them with their own extensive executive powers.[9] In general they consisted of ministers and heads of departments. Each had its own interdepartmental working group made up of departmental heads and specialists coopted to assist with investigations or surveys demanded by the cabinet committees on an as-required basis.

The committees were linked laterally to planning branches in the Office of the Prime Minister. The State Security Council was linked with the Security Planning Branch, the Economic Affairs Committee with the Economic Planning Branch, the Social Affairs Committee with the Social Planning Branch and the Internal Affairs Committee with the Constitutional Planning Branch. Consequently the Office of the Prime Minister became a powerful focus of government decision making.

The purpose of the new system, according to a directive quoted by Brian Pottinger, was: 'that every member of the cabinet must know the extent of the policy and programme decisions over which he has co-responsibility, irrespective of whether it is in his specific field of authority or that of a colleague and . . . that every minister must have the opportunity to take part in the decision making process and to make his contribution'.[10]

The State Security Council (SSC), which became the senior and most important cabinet committee, was not new. It was originally established by Vorster in 1972 in terms of the Security Intelligence and State Security Council Act, but it had met infrequently. It was, nevertheless, the only cabinet committee established by statute and the only one chaired by the Prime Minister. Its responsibilities in those earlier days were confined to a narrow field of security matters. Under the new arrangement it was mandated to advise government on policy and strategy relating to the 'security of the Republic' in 15 fields ranging through military, economic, educational, social and so on.[11]

Besides the Prime Minister (later the President) its permanent membership consisted of the Ministers of Defence, Law and Order, Foreign Affairs, Justice, Finance, the senior cabinet minister if not already included, the Directors-General of Foreign Affairs, Justice and the Office of the Prime Minister, the Chief of the SADF, the service chiefs, the Director Military Intelligence, the Commissioner of Police and the Director-General of the National Intelligence Service.[12]

In addition, Premier Botha coopted the Ministers of Finance, Constitutional Development and Planning, and Cooperation and Development.[13] Other cabinet ministers and departmental heads, when matters relevant to their portfolios were on the agenda, might attend its twice-monthly sessions, but they would be there strictly by invitation of the Prime Minister only.The SSC had four branches with responsibility respectively for strategy, national intelligence interpretation and strategic communications and administration. In 1985 its permanent secretariat comprised 87 officials.[14]

During a no-confidence debate in Parliament in January 1984, the PFP leader and leader of the opposition, Dr Frederik van Zyl Slabbert, claimed the cabinet and Parliament was being bypassed and primacy given to the secretariat of the State Security Council. He alleged that 70% of the SSC's membership was drawn from the military, 20% from the NIS and 10% from the Department of Foreign Affairs. He accused the SSC of involving itself in a far broader range of matters than just security, including controversial proposals to transfer portions of South Africa to another state. He was referring to the proposed transfer of KaNgwane and Ingwavuma to Swaziland in 1984.[15] This astonishing move was intended as a *quid pro quo* for Swaziland's conclusion of a non-aggression pact with South Africa, signed in February 1982 but not made public until March 1984. This incorporation would have given the inland state a corridor to the sea.[16] Howls of outrage from the South Africans whom the State Security Council had been arbitrarily intending to turn into Swazis, and their supporters, effectively killed the idea.

In reply, Prime Minister Botha denied the military was paramount in the SSC and said its secretariat's composition was 56% from the National Intelligence Service, 16% from the Defence Force, 11% from Foreign Affairs, 11% from the Security Police, 5% from the Railway Police and 1% from the Prison Service.

He said the SSC's prime purpose was to enable government institutions to consult with each other. The SSC submitted its recommendations to the cabinet which acted on them.[17] What he avoided saying was that it had become his practise to convey SSC decisions *orally* to his cabinet, rarely if ever showing them the Council minutes. It became his prerogative to decide how much he would divulge, to whom he would divulge it and whether he would tell anyone outside the closed ranks of the SSC anything at all.

The SSC's bimonthly meetings occurred whether Parliament was sitting or not and whether cabinet meetings were scheduled or not. Decisions did not require ratification by the full cabinet, so most cabinet ministers only learned of them historically. And although they were deviously approved by the State President, all-important decisions were made in practice by an elitist handful of senior cabinet ministers and grey eminences from the military, security and foreign affairs. These men wielded enormous power. In theory, if a cabinet minister expressed serious reservations, the State President could, at his discretion, reconvene the SSC for the matter to be reconsidered. But it was a brave minister who queried a decision of *Die Groot Krokedil*'s — P W Botha's — State Security Council. That type of courage was sparse in the upper echelons of the governing Party.[18]

This explains, perhaps, why in later years ministers doggedly declined to accept ministerial responsibility for irregularities and illegalities occurring within their departments — to the puzzlement of the uninitiated. It becomes clearer when one realises that, in many cases, responsibility actually rested with P W Botha and the State Security Council and not with the so-called responsible minister. It says little, of course, for the integrity of such ministers that they meekly allowed themselves to be sidelined and by doing so, subjected

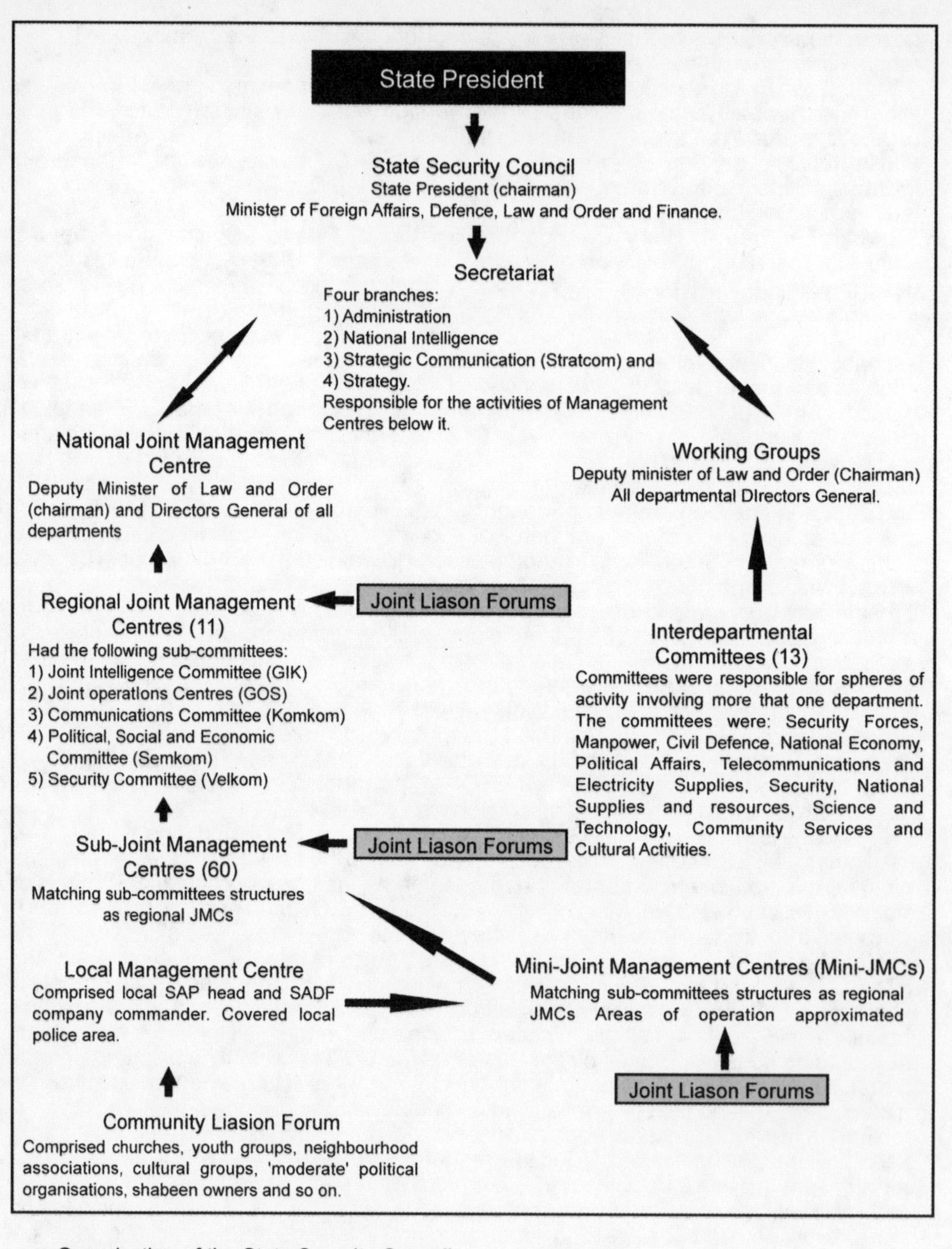
State President
State Security Council
State President (chairman)
Minister of Foreign Affairs, Defence, Law and Order and Finance.
Secretariat
Four branches:
1) Administration
2) National Intelligence
3) Strategic Communication (Stratcom) and
4) Strategy.
Responsible for the activities of Management Centres below it.
National Joint Management Centre
Deputy Minister of Law and Order (chairman) and Directors General of all departments
Working Groups
Deputy minister of Law and Order (Chairman)
All departmental Directors General.
Regional Joint Management Centres (11)
Had the following sub-committees:
1) Joint Intelligence Committee (GIK)
2) Joint operations Centres (GOS)
3) Communications Committee (Komkom)
4) Political, Social and Economic Committee (Semkom)
5) Security Committee (Velkom)
Joint Liason Forums
Interdepartmental Committees (13)
Committees were responsible for spheres of activity involving more that one department. The committees were: Security Forces, Manpower, Civil Defence, National Economy, Political Affairs, Telecommunications and Electricity Supplies, Security, National Supplies and resources, Science and Technology, Community Services and Cultural Activities.
Sub-Joint Management Centres (60)
Matching sub-committees structures as regional JMCs
Joint Liason Forums
Local Management Centre
Comprised local SAP head and SADF company commander. Covered local police area.
Mini-Joint Management Centres (Mini-JMCs)
Matching sub-committees structures as regional JMCs Areas of operation approximated
Joint Liason Forums
Community Liasion Forum
Comprised churches, youth groups, neighbourhood associations, cultural groups, 'moderate' political organisations, shabeen owners and so on.

Organisation of the State Security Council.

South Africa to a creeping totalitarianism.

Chillingly, it might also explain why so-called 'mad dogs' in the Security Forces — who would be revealed in the declining days of National Party rule, usually by the press, as having committed serious criminal offences — were often prosecuted only with extreme reluctance after routine cover-ups and the maximum dragging of heels. When and if they were brought to court, they would be defended on a no expenses spared basis by the State Attorney or by counsel briefed by him. Sometimes, too, when the situation looked bleak for an accused, the authorities hurriedly shipped him out of the country, thereby blatantly defeating the ends of justice.

One wonders how often it occurred to those officially approving such things that their actions rendered them punishable as accessories before and after the fact to the crimes committed.

A senior SADF officer headed the SSC's secretariat. In 1985 it was General A J van Deventer and when he retired in June of that year he was replaced by Lieutenant General Pieter W van der Westhuizen. This appointment was highly significant, because Van der Westhuizen was moved from the key post of Chief of Staff Intelligence to take over the secretariat. In November 1987, the incumbent was Major-General Charles Lloyd.[19]

It was the head of the secretariat's responsibility to sift through the various items submitted by departmental heads and decide what should be placed on the agenda for discussion by full sittings of the State Security Council.

From an early stage the SADF's general staff — not the National Intelligence Service — were responsible for preparing the biweekly 'national threat assessment' — called the 'gloom sheet' by the irreverent — and recommending what actions should be taken. While this was scrutinised by an inter-departmental working group before being laid before the SSC, it still gave the SADF planners the opportunity to emphasise aspects of particular interest to them. It also gave them the advantage of having the first crack at recommending solutions and actions.[20]

The secretariat operationalised decisions of the SSC with the assistance of the relevant interdepartmental committee or committees whose job it was to translate them into coherent directives to the government department or departments concerned.

Joint Management Centres were originally established in the 1970s to monitor the black schools' uprising, but they fell into disuse after that. 1984 marked their reappearance and the establishment of the National Security Management System (NSMS). This was on a much grander scale and it was designed to allow the SSC's tentacles to reach down to grass roots so it could effectively deal with the escalating unrest in South Africa's black townships.

General Magnus Malan, the Minister of Defence, in reply to a question in the Parliament on 11 March 1986, said the State Security Council had established 12 main Joint Management Centres (JMCs), chaired by senior SADF or SAP officers, in Bloemfontein, Cape Town, Durban, Johannesburg, Kimberley, Nelspruit, Oudtshoorn, Pietersburg, Port Elizabeth, Potchefstroom, Pretoria and Walvis Bay. Their boundaries in ten out of 12 of the JMCs coincided with SADF areas of command in South Africa including Walvis Bay. Additional JMCs concerned external areas like Namibia and other unspecified African countries.The JMCs and their substructures were composed of the military, the police and all government departments. They elected their own chairmen and vice chairmen. In 1987 11 of the 12 JMC chairmen were serving SADF brigadiers.[21] They reported to General Pieter van der Westhuizen at the State Security Council.

General Malan told *The Star* in an interview that 60 sub-JMCs and 354 mini-JMCs had been set up in the smaller towns and cities. He said their purpose was to 'coordinate joint government action at regional level'. He added that they possessed no executive powers and 'execution of government action still occurs at the level of responsible government institutions'. They had no authority to enforce decisions.

At a press interview with Magnus Malan and Pieter van der Westhuizen, it emerged that the JMC network acted as the government's early warning system for internal threats to state security and as a 'highly mobile mechanism to defuse revolutionary unrest'. The JMCs, they said, were a decentralisation of the SSC at regional and local level with the function of coordinating the implementation and management of security at those levels.

Malan said that no secret funds were used and nothing was hidden from Parliament or the general public.[22] Directives were passed down the line from the SSC's secretariat, through the NSM System to the JMCs, sub-JMCs, and mini-JMCs (later Joint Coordination Centre (JCC)) in the relevant area.

The JMCs, sub-JMCs and mini-JMCs each comprised five main components: Executive Committee, Security Committee (GIK-COM), Joint Intelligence Committee, Communication Committee (COMCOM) and Constitutional, Economic and Social Committee (CESCOM)

They were the eyes and ears of the State Security Council, the grass roots early warning system of issues with potential security implications. It might be a military matter, a police matter, a social issue, a political issue, of economic importance or anything else. It could be something apparently minor, like the need of a water tap in a squatter settlement, or something more important like an upsurge of UDF activity in a black urban township.

Recommendations emanating from the JMCs would be channelled through to the SSC and down to the relevant interdepartmental committee where they would be given immediate attention.

Combined Management Boards (CMB) were also set up to coordinate security management with the four independent homelands. They were established in the SADF's Far Northern Command to cover Venda, North-Western Command for Bophuthatswana, and Eastern Province Command for Transkei and Ciskei. Their main task was the coordination of training and the development of the homeland defence forces.[23]

In reality on the ground everything was not so ideal. Colonel Lourens du Plessis who for several years acted as secretary to the JMC in Port Elizabeth told the author: 'We were all-powerful, I am telling you.' Speaking of *Operation Katzen* (see Chapter 10) he said: 'Even with myself as a staff officer, people were currying for favours because the system worked that way. You could drop them at any time if they didn't hurry and execute when decisions were made. It was all manipulation. They [everyone involved] just had to do it and they were scared all the time that they would get into trouble. The system lent itself to that. The military were in charge everywhere from command level down to the smallest town. [At] each JMC or mini-JMC or area command — whatever they were called — there would be a Commando member or some other military guy in charge as chairman.They had police members there, but they were marginalised. They did not have the capabilities. They were not properly trained in comparison to the Defence Force members who were all staff qualified. That sort of thing. They did not stand a chance.'[24]

In an interview with *The Weekly Mail*, State Security Council secretary, Lieutenant-General Pieter van der Westhuizen, explained the philosophy of the National Security Management System. South Africa, he said, was confronted by a threat from four fronts. Her enemies had adopted a coordinated strategy to attack the country's constitutional, economic, social and security power bases. The government was convinced, he continued, that such a threat could be met and turned back only by applying the identical strategies in the same fields.[25]

Deputy Minister of Defence, Adriaan Vlok, said in April 1986 that 13 interdepartmental committees had been established to assist the secretariat on matters relating to manpower, the security forces, civil defence, transport, security, national supplies and resources, government funding, national economy, telecommunications and electrical power supply, science and technology, community services, culture and political affairs.

The new constitution, for the first time, had introduced non-whites into the cabinet, but in reality it gave ministers of colour no political clout. To ensure power remained safely in white hands, P W Botha, by now the executive State President, used the SSC as a cabal — an inner cabinet and sinister hidden hand — which made all the important decisions, particularly those affecting national security and foreign policy.

The SSC was also back-handedly given the ultimate in State authority — the authority to make war. It was able within its terms of reference, to approve or deny SADF requests to launch major cross-border military offensives. Significantly, in December 1985 it was the SSC, not the State President or cabinet, which formally warned neighbouring states that they would pay a 'heavy price' if their support of the ANC continued.[26]

In February 1988 it was the SSC which ordered the banning of the UDF. Immediately afterwards, British Ambassador Robin Renwick spoke to a group of National Party MPs on the steps of Parliament. None of them had been informed, let alone consulted.[27]

It was sinister that the enhanced power of the State Security Council remained a State secret and that President Botha never took the South African electorate into his confidence and explained why he had diminished the power of the Parliament they had elected to office.

Mrs Helen Suzman, of the opposition PFP, described the National Security Management System as a 'sinister and disturbing . . . development', which had created a 'creeping [military] *coup d'état* by consent'.[28]

President Botha, perhaps, should have remembered, when he enhanced the power of his SSC technocrats and securocrats, what he had once said about BOSS chief General Hendrik van den Bergh during the Vorster era: 'Who the hell elected him? How many votes did he get in the last election?'[29]

The most significant result of the NSMS' creation was the marked increase in power, in particular for the SADF, but also for the SAP and the NIS. Expenditure mushroomed and the Defence Vote was regularly overspent. Astronomical sums were utilised for upgrading equipment, improving personnel levels, providing funds for secret projects and so on.

The 1983/84 budget of R3 092 million rose by more than a billion to R4 274 million in the 1985/86 estimates. This was only the tip of the financial iceberg, however. Much of the cost of military operations as well as the maintenance of the SWA Territorial Force and the police counter-insurgency unit, Koevoet — although administered by Pretoria — was met by the SWA/Namibian administration from huge subsidies paid by the South African government.[30]

The SWA Territorial Force was no minor military muscle. Its strength of 22 000 men was recruited from all racial groups. It comprised a logistics brigade (including an engineer and a signals battalion), a motorised infantry brigade (three battalions of motorised infantry and a battalion with armoured cars), a mixed Citizen Force and regular parachute battalion, six light infantry battalions, a specialist unit, a Recce battalion, artillery support units and 26 area counter-insurgency units.[31]

Inevitably much of the money poured into the SADF went down the drain. In February 1984 the Auditor General, A P Ellis, criticised SADF spending during the 1982/83 financial year, stressing 'unauthorised, fruitless and irregular expenditure, thefts, unreliable stocktaking and weak internal control. He said he was unable to audit the Special Defence Account which funded secret projects. It was overdrawn by R150,5 million.

Initially, the State Security Council concerned itself with matters external to South Africa — approving Recce raids into adjacent territories against ANC and SWAPO targets etc. In the wake of South Africa's Angolan intervention, South Africa's 1977 Defence White Paper identified the need 'to maintain a solid military balance relative to neighbouring states and other states in southern Africa'.

It recommended 'economic action . . . action in relation to transport services, distribution and telecommunications' to promote 'political and economic collaboration among the states of southern Africa'. Formalised as CONSAS — Constellation of Southern African States, it was envisaged that it would consist of South Africa, the homeland states, Rhodesia, SWA/Namibia, Botswana, Lesotho and Swaziland — the three members of the customs union — Malawi and hopefully Zaire (now the Democratic Republic of Congo) and Zambia.

Its economic objectives were expected to lead to a southern African common market, in particular, to an enlarged market for South African manufactured goods. A defence pact was envisaged, with all member states signing a non aggression treaty with South Africa. They would be expected to recognise apartheid, extend recognition to the 'independent' homeland states and to internal settlements in SWA/Namibia and Zimbabwe-Rhodesia.[32]

Unfortunately for South Africa there was no mad rush to join CONSAS and hopes for it were fatally dashed when Robert Mugabe assumed power in Zimbabwe in 1980. This led to the founding in April 1980 of the rival SADCC — Southern African Development Coordination Conference (SADCC), later SADC, which the six 'Frontline' States — Angola, Botswana, Mozambique, Tanzania, Zambia and Zimbabwe — together with Malawi, Lesotho and Swaziland, joined. Instead of forming a common front with South Africa as envisaged by CONSAS, the goal of its member states became to 'liberate our economies' from dependence on South Africa, 'overcome the imposed economic fragmentation' brought about by colonialism and 'coordinate our efforts towards regional and national economic development'. 'Economic liberation', it was stressed, was as vital as political freedom.

They were to work towards reducing trade with South Africa and their dependence on South Africa's ports, roads and transport services. Their first priority was the rehabilitation and upgrading of ports, roads and rail routes that already existed in Mozambique, Tanzania and Angola.[33]

This was easier said than done. UNITA was astride Angola's Benguela Railway and RENAMO — the rebel opposition group in Mozambique — with South African assistance, would see to it that Zimbabwe's rail links from Mutare to Beira and from Rutenga to Maputo would either operate at only a fraction of their capacity or would be closed altogether. Joshua Nkomo's ZIPRA (Zimbabwe People's Revolutionary Army) in Zimbabwe (supported and armed by South Africa's Military Intelligence — *See Cry Zimbabwe: Independence — Twenty Years On* by Peter Stiff for the full story) would play a role in sabotaging the rail route to Maputo, between Rutenga and Sengo within Zimbabwe. The line running south from Rutenga to South Africa which carried South African exports, was treated as sacrosanct.

South Africa's plan was to sabotage the SADC's initiatives, forcing hostile black-ruled states in the region to remain economically reliant on South Africa's road and rail transport and on its port infrastructure.

Through the NSMS, the SSC put more emphasis on internal matters when violence inspired by the UDF (United Democratic Front) erupted in the townships in 1984. It involved both the velvet glove and the iron fist.

The velvet glove involved the anticipation and identification of potential points of unrest before they mushroomed into major issues. The JMC's task was to identify and neutralise activists in the townships and win the hearts and minds of the black populace. In areas like Alexandra (Johannesburg), New Brighton (Port Elizabeth), Mamelodi (Pretoria) and Bontheuwel (Western Cape) JMCs triggered the expenditure of vast sums of money which was used to establish sporting facilities, cultural facilities and churches and to finance political bodies willing to propagate government policies.[34]

In the financial year 1987/88 the government spent R3,2 billion in areas earmarked by JMCs as needing special attention. A staggering R16 billion was allocated to the Department of Constitutional Development and Planning for upgrading 200 townships.

Speaking during a House of Assembly debate in March 1986, Defence Minister Malan said the purpose of the military's presence in the townships, was to prevent the intimidation and manipulation by radicals of the 'vast uninvolved masses of the townships'. They were there to create confidence amongst the masses and to build up goodwill by being friendly and helpful. He claimed that the radical SACP/ANC/UDF alliance was seeking 'to separate auxiliary and protection services from the population' and gain the 'sole right to threaten, to intimidate, to terrorise and to manipulate people in black areas'.[35]

The National Party government regarded itself as comparable to any Western democratic administration, but over the years it had drifted far from that. Through legislation and regulations it had allowed the Security Police to become a law unto themselves. They had facilities for collecting information that would have been the envy of most intelligence services outside the Soviet Bloc. Files on tens of thousands of activists — or perceived activists — were kept up to date on a daily basis both in its Pretoria HQ and at 110 branches round the country. Millions of rands were budgeted to sweeten a widespread network of sources who continually fed their intelligence machine with information.

With *carte blanche* authority, Security Police tapped phones through the offices of the SAP's Technical Services, opened mail and clamped a control verging on totalitarianism over the population, both black and white — without most of the latter even realising it.

In a truly Orwellian move, Military Intelligence's DCC even financed the establishment of the best press clippings library in the land at the University of the Orange Free State. All they asked in return was the supply of regular reports on what subjects authors and journalists using the facilities were currently researching.

They interrogated and turned captured ANC and PAC guerrillas to the South African cause, to become what they called 'Askaris'. It was not much of a choice for captured guerrillas, because if they rejected the turncoat option, they were arraigned before the Supreme (now High) Court on terrorism charges. If convicted they were invariably sentenced to death. Many who refused to cooperate were shot out of hand.

The Askaris were based at the Security Branch's counter-insurgency unit, Section C10, at Vlakplaas, where they were deployed to fight a no-holds-barred war against the ANC, PAC and surrogates of these organisations. This would ultimately lead to its last commander, Colonel Eugene de Kock — appointed to its command in July 1985 — being convicted of 89 charges including murder, conspiracy to commit murder, fraud, gun running, sabotage, intimidation. He was sentenced to two life sentences plus 212 years' imprisonment. The TRC (Truth and Reconciliation Commission) granted amnesties to him for all his convictions, barring one for murder. Despite his conviction, there is no doubt whatsoever that he had been acting on the unlawful orders of higher authority. Unlike the trials of the major Nazi war criminals after World War II where the Allies started with Hitler's top command structures and worked down, in South Africa they started at the bottom structures and never worked up. The top people, political and military, got clean away with it.

At Security Branch HQ in Pretoria's Compol (Commissioner of Police) building, the heads of regional desks and other heads of departments met daily to discuss the countrywide security situation, the events and happenings of the past 24 hours and to plan strategy and tactics to counteract the 'total onslaught'. It was the ultimate Security Police planning committee — on the top floor and thus the closest to heaven. This prompted a wag to dub it *Sanhedrin* after the supreme council and highest court of justice in ancient Jerusalem. It was a nickname that stuck.

In 1985 or 1986 the top secret Coordinating Intelligence Committee (CIC) of the State Security Council under the chairmanship of the Director National Intelligence Service, Dr Niel Barnard, was established. Its purpose, according to Barnard, was to coordinate the gathering of intelligence by the police, the military and presumably the NIS.

Below it and still the responsibility of Dr Barnard, was a top secret subcommittee known as TREWITS, an acronym for the Afrikaans *Teen-Rewolusionêre Inligtings Teiken Sentrum* — Counter-revolutionary Intelligence Target Centre, formed to evaluate intelligence reports and provide target intelligence for the Security Forces. It was commanded by a senior police officer with representatives from Military Intelligence, National Intelligence and Special Forces. Its first commander was Major-General Jac Buchner, a highly experienced police officer.

At first it concentrated on targets within neighbouring countries, but as the security situation within South Africa deteriorated and showed signs of fulfilling the ANC's ambition of a 'People's War' developing, ANC and UDF activists operating internally were also identified and noted on 'priority lists' for targeting. External target intelligence was referred to Special Forces, while internal target intelligence went to the relevant Security Police regional headquarters.

Monthly meetings were held within the various Security Branch regions to update priority lists. If it was found a target was about to move from Botswana to Angola for instance, his name would be moved down on the list because of difficulties in reaching him.

Dr Niel Barnard, however, in evidence to the TRC denied TREWITS had been involved in the murder of activists. 'TREWITS was established to coordinate security intelligence and to establish an information data base. I am not going to say the information collected by TREWITS led to the death of people. I could not ask the line function departments what they did with the information.'

It is significant, though, that officers involved in operations emanating from TREWITS directly contradicted him. Major Henri van der Westhuizen, the former secretary of TREWITS is of particular significance, because he applied to the TRC for amnesty for the murder of activists identified for elimination by that body.[36] It would be incredible that the major applied for amnesty merely to embarrass his former chief!

The TRC also questioned Dr Barnard about a top-secret State Security Council document titled 'Draft counter-revolutionary strategy', which said activists in the townships should be 'neutralised' through *Operation Vasvat*. It suggested they could be clandestinely made the target of vigilantes from organisations like Inkatha. Barnard, as with the rest of his colleagues in similar circumstances, insisted that in the context, 'neutralise' meant to 'take away their ability to strengthen the revolutionary climate'.[37]

The foot soldiers accepted without question that the State Security Council's apparently well ordered and regulated command and control system in relation to internal operations was lawful in terms of the laws of South Africa. They had been told, and they believed, that murdering by numbers equalled command and control. It had to be because their leaders said so. By the time they realised they had been grossly misled and that many of their actions were, in fact, unlawful, they had already been abandoned to their fate by their erstwhile political masters and by most, although not all, of the Security Forces' commanders.

The Afrikaner understood regulation and control. He had been disciplined from childhood not to answer back, to obey his father, his teacher, his church and anyone else in authority. He did not question authority, nor did he rock the boat, and he believed implicitly in his leaders. He was also steadfast in the belief that he was engaged in a just fight for the survival of South Africa. It was *ons land* — our land, the promised land the Voortrekkers had fought for and won with God's help.

The authorisation for Security Forces operations commenced with discussions at the State Security Council's top level, then filtered down through the various committees to TREWITS, went from there to Sanhedrin, and finally to the regions and to the foot soldiers who did the dirty work in the field.

Orders from the SSC and its subordinate bodies to assassinate activists were invariably similar, always verbal and euphemistic instead of crude and blunt. It would be suggested that the target be 'eliminated', 'taken out' or 'neutralised'. Those responsible should 'make a plan' or 'shorten the list'.

Former senior police and military intelligence officer, Colonel Craig Williamson, described the language of instructions used in counter-insurgency operations as deliberately 'all encompassing'. He believed the P W Botha administration had sought to keep itself at arms length from covert operations, so it could deny knowledge or responsibility. 'The operational procedures were designed by people who knew the law, in order to circumvent proof of legal responsibility for the deed by the upper echelon.

'With the benefit of hindsight, it appears that the upper echelons, especially the politicians, were so keen to be at "legal arms length" from covert action that they abdicated their responsibility to exercise close operational supervision of such actions and so lost significant operational control.'

He was not wrong.

Many pertinent records of the State Security Council were destroyed or went missing, but others survived. A report back on the national state of emergency dated 8 September 1986 was one that did. The first heading was: 'List of politically sensitive people'. The minutes noted that the list 'had to be shortened' and that methods other than detention should be considered. Future President F W de Klerk was at this meeting. One wonders what they had in mind as a means to 'shorten the list' other than murder.

When asked by the TRC whether lists of 'politically sensitive people' were ever drawn up, De Klerk replied 'not to my knowledge'.[37]

Foreign Minister Pik Botha, a permanent member of the State Security Council of long standing, insisted during testimony to the TRC that 'too much power has been attributed to the State Security Council. SSC decisions were useless, of no validity, until the cabinet (approved) them'. He denied the National Party cabinet had approved the killing of specific politicians, but said that none could claim they never suspected the police of engaging in irregular activities. 'The question is', he said, 'whether we should have done more to ensure it did not happen.' He was another who engaged in an exercise in semantics, maintaining that where 'eliminate' or 'neutralise' was used in connection with a hot pursuit or a cross-border raid, it would have meant the killing of guerrillas. When used in respect of actions within the country they could 'indeed, mean detention without trial.'[38]

Former Law and Order Minister of the day, Adriaan Vlok, was yet another who described it as a 'misunderstanding', for which he apologised to the TRC. The 'misunderstanding' caused the Security Police to eliminate anti-apartheid suspects believing they had been ordered to do so by the government. 'I myself never knew anything about those crimes that came to light. I would never have tolerated them and would have acted against them.' He averred that when using the words 'eliminate' and 'neutralise' it was never the SSC's intention that it should be taken to mean that activists should be murdered. He maintained that police commissioners serving under him, namely Generals Coetzee and Van der Merwe, had never mentioned that policemen had been engaged in unlawful actions against activists.

Vlok's credibility level was never high, particularly considering his amnesty application for the Khotso House bombing where the part he played was criminal and where he found the testimony of witnesses impossible to deny.[39] (Khotso House in Johannesburg is the headquarters of the South African Council of Churches which was bitterly opposed to the National Party government).

Roelf Meyer, deputy to Adriaan Vlok from 1986 to 1988 and who was responsible for the National Security Management System, was more frank. He admitted that fear had dictated the government's response to the liberation struggle, resulting in a no-holds-barred 'dirty war' with no questions asked. He conceded that political leaders should take 'political responsibility' for some atrocities committed by the Security Forces, and that everyone in government should share the blame for contributing to the climate in which such atrocities were committed. He denied there had been an organised attempt by the government to identify specific targets for destruction.[40]

Leon Wessels, who became Deputy Minister of Law and Order after Roelf Meyer in 1988, contradicted his former chief, Adriaan Vlok, by saying: 'The relationship between the Security Forces and National Party politicians in general was not an open transparent one and therefore we did not manage the Security Forces/Intelligence services properly.' He refused to condemn soldiers and policemen who had committed violent, unlawful acts. 'I cannot disown them because we were on the same side and fought for the same cause, namely law and order as we saw it, and also to ensure that this country would not be made ungovernable.'

Regarding illegal actions by the Security Forces, Wessels said: 'I do not believe the political defence of "I did not know" is available to me because in many respects I believe I did not want to know. In my own way I had my suspicions of things that had caused discomfort in official circles, but because I did not have the facts to substantiate my suspicions, or lacked the courage to shout from the rooftops, I have to confess that I only whispered in the corridors.'[41]

Colonel Eugene de Kock confirmed this to some extent by suggesting that sections within the Security Forces establishment wielded more power than the politicians during the apartheid years. They even launched operations without political approval when they believed it was in the national interest. Law and Order ministers Louis le Grange and his successor Adriaan Vlok were frequently only told about operations after they had been completed. The Security Police chiefs were concerned they might inform Parliament and stop the operation. 'The commissioner, the head of the Security Police, the operation commander and the men in the team doing the operation were the only ones who knew. Military Intelligence and the Security Police were the untouchables', Eugene de Kock said. 'They were the mightiest groups in the country and even dictated policy to the cabinet. 'We protected the constitution by unconstitutional means.' [42]

It was significant that the responsible ministers and commanders never relieved any one of their commands, nor recommended that criminal action be taken against them. As Leon Wessels so correctly said, they did not want to know.

General Johan van der Merwe, Police Commissioner and a member of the State Security Council from 1991 until its dissolution before the 1994 elections, agreed in his testimony that the words 'eliminate' and 'neutralise' had been used in SSC policy documents. He described them as an 'unfortunate choice of words' and blandly maintained he had always taken them to mean 'arrest and detain'. 'However', he conceded, 'police on the ground . . . in a life and death struggle, could have seen it [the word 'eliminate'] as an order to kill. If you tell a soldier "eliminate your enemy", depending on the circumstances, he would take that to mean kill.' He admitted ordering the bombing of Khotso House, but said this was done on the direct orders of President P W Botha, relayed to him by Law and Order Minister Vlok.[43]

President P W Botha was also implicated by Colonel Eugene de Kock in the bombing of COSATU (Congress of SA Trade Unions) House in Johannesburg. His instructions, he said, had come from his immediate superior who said the President had ordered it.[44]

General van der Merwe's predecessor, General Johan Coetzee, turned to two Afrikaans dictionaries to seek salvation and also suggested that 'eliminate' meant no more than to remove. 'The word *per se*', he said, 'does not mean when used in connection with a person that person should be assassinated. But I agree it could have been misconstrued.' He added: 'I have never given any illegal instruction or unlawful instruction to kill a person.'

Two of the commissioners' former subordinates, Brigadiers Alfred Oosthuizen and Willem Schoon, forthrightly disagreed. They said bluntly that the terms 'eliminate' and 'take out' were not open to misinterpretation — they were commonplace euphemisms for killing.[45] Anyone who has served in the armed forces anywhere in the English-speaking world, be it South Africa, Rhodesia, Great Britain, America, Australia or anywhere else, would agree.

Colonel Jack Cronje, one-time Security Police chief in Northern Transvaal, a former C-10 commander and a 'foot soldier', said activists identified for elimination within South Africa were those involved in very serious actions. Killing them was the only way they could be effectively removed from society. 'To prosecute a person through the normal court structure was too much trouble and sometimes totally impossible . . . it was necessary to act outside the confines of the legal system. The object was to protect the State and the National Party, so the State would not be overthrown by the liberation movements.

'If they were not eliminated, they would not be permanently neutralised by security legislation, detention and the normal legal system', Colonel Cronje testified: 'The legal system was not equipped to deal with these situations and to counter the soldiers of the ANC, SACP and PAC.

'The government's approach was [that] there was a total onslaught and we were involved in a war', Colonel Cronje continued. 'During this period the country was infiltrated by activists who tried to make the country ungovernable. Their actions had to be countered by the SAP. They were forced to act in a way that was not in line with normal conduct in times of peace.

'Underlings were told to take whatever steps were necessary to deal with the situation . . . the orders were couched in general terms and meant that permission did not have to be sought for a specific operation . . . authority was delegated down the line and officers were increasingly confronted with general orders in terms of which they could act within broader parameters than would have been the case under normal circumstances.'

Colonel Cronje testified that reports on a unit's activities were sent on a daily basis to Security Branch HQ. 'Every incident of the previous day was mentioned in the report. If an activist was killed or his house burnt, that information would have been passed to head office and discussed by Sanhedrin.' Sanhedrin routed the reports to the State Security Council where they were included in the biweekly 'national threat assessment'. The files were destroyed on the orders of Security Branch head office in 1994, before the ANC government took power.[46]

The Security Branch and Military Intelligence's intentions were often frustrated by representatives of other government departments squabbling amongst themselves for the right to lead or influence activities within the Joint Management system, both at State Security Council and local levels.

The SADF's strategy during the apartheid years was described in a submission to the TRC, made on its behalf by the SANDF. It said:

> 'The RSA government made it clear that the RSA was not pursuing a policy of aggression against any state or group of states, or contemplating any territorial expansion, but that the RSA would defend its people against any threat. In this regard the Security Forces should have the means to preserve the highest democratic body, i.e. Parliament and afford it an opportunity to bring about changes to the RSA's political dispensation in an evolutionary way, so as to meet the constitutional and cultural needs of its people. The SADF was pre-eminently a peacekeeping task force, but owing to the perceived threat and the increasing instability in southern Africa, the SADF's strategy was directed at ensuring the safety of the people of the RSA by taking offensive pro-active steps.'

It went on to provide the following information:

SADF's three spheres of influence

SADF strategy, in terms of the SANDF's submission to the TRC, identified three spheres in which it might be required to act.

The first, its 'area of responsibility' — defined as South African territory including Prince Edward and Marion islands, the National States (the homelands that were not 'independent' e.g. Kwa Zulu), the TBVC states (Transkei, Bophuthatswana, Venda, Ciskei) and adjacent maritime areas and air space. In such areas the SADF was required to:

- Conduct conventional military operations
- Conduct counter-insurgency operations
- Conduct intelligence operations
- Conduct strategic communication operations and
- Support the SAP in maintaining law and order.

The second, its 'area of influence' — defined as Botswana, Lesotho, Swaziland, Angola, Zambia, Zimbabwe, Mozambique, Malawi and the adjacent maritime area. The SADF was required to be in a position to conduct:

- Restricted conventional operations in support of counter-insurgency operations
- Special and retaliation operations
- Conventional preemptive operations
- Full-scale conventional operations, if necessary and
- Strategic communication (STRATCOM) operations.

The third, its 'area of interest' — defined as Zaïre (now Democratic Republic of Congo), Rwanda, Burundi, Tanzania, Gabon, Congo (Brazzaville), Uganda, Kenya, the Comores,

Mauritius and adjacent maritime areas. Here, the SADF was to conduct intelligence and, if necessary:

- Exercise special and retaliatory operations
- Exercise air and maritime reconnaissance
- Deploy ground forces (restricted) and render air and maritime support to friendly governments.

Namibia was regarded as part of the South African State and thus within its area of responsibility. Consequently, Namibia's involvement in Angola fell within the SADF's 'sphere of influence'.

External operations

Authority for the conduct of operations within South Africa's 'area of influence' was contained in a directive approved by the State Security Council in 1979. Its initial purpose was to cover operations in southern Angola but it was later amended to encompass other countries. The authority of the Chief of the SADF was limited to immediate 'hot pursuit' operations. The approval of the Minister of Defence was required for reconnaissance operations into those countries within the 'area of influence'. The planning for all other military operations required the approval of the chairman of the State Security Council (the President), in consultation with those of its members he decided to involve.

Planning

A key strategic document was the 'Forecast of Operations', approved by the Chief of the SADF in 1980 and updated annually. It laid out the objectives and tasks set out in 'National Strategy and the Strategy for Southern Africa'. It served as the planning point of departure for force design and development of the operational planning of the SADF and defined the operational responsibilities of the arms of the service.

In 1980 more specific strategies and guidelines on the basis of national directives were introduced to replace the 'Forecast of Operations'. They were still based on total strategies and were prepared by the Chief of the SADF's planning staff for his approval. They were distributed as Military Strategic Documents (MSDs). Each arm of the service was responsible for its own strategic planning and implementation, in accordance with its role and functions, after approval by the Chief SADF.

SADF strategy was based on the Defence Act, 1957, and strategic guidelines issued by the State Security Council. It clearly said that 'no component of the SADF strategy existed independently from the national strategy or any other guidelines or commands of the State'.

The elements of the SADF's strategy were drawn from the National Strategy and the Strategy for Southern Africa. If the SADF identified a need for additions, it could make representations to the Working Group (WG) of the SSC or to the Council itself through its representative on the Interdepartmental Committees (IDCs). Alternatively, the Chief of the SADF could take the matter up directly with the secretary of the SSC who was, in any case, a senior SADF officer.

This meant that the SSC determined SADF policy and not the cabinet or Parliament. The government's guideline to the SADF was that the country's national security interests should be furthered through a pro-active posture. The strategy emphasised that the promotion, development and maintenance of South Africa's security interests should be achieved through military action, primarily outside the country's borders.

Authorisation for security actions

A policy directive approved by the Prime Minister in December 1969, and as amended from time to time, laid down the division of responsibility between the SADF and SAP for the conduct of internal operations. Within South Africa's borders the SAP had the primary responsibility for urban operations. The SADF was responsible for rural operations and border protection.

Regionally, responsibility and authority for the conduct of military operations were delegated to regional commanders in specific command directives and guidelines that accorded with approved defence policy, strategy, and directives.

Interdepartmental coordination

This was affected at regional and local levels through the National Security Management System. The JMCs were responsible for ensuring stability and security in their areas and for normalising local situations. Authority and accountability were based on the line functions of the departments represented.

State of Emergency

In terms of a State of Emergency declared in 36 magisterial districts in July 1985 members of the Security Forces were given enhanced powers. The *Government Gazette* confirmed members of the SADF, when being used in a police function, would have the same powers as policemen. State President Botha, in his announcement, said it was the duty of the State to ensure the re-establishment of normal community life. The unrest situation would be normalised to ensure there was a climate for continued dialogue.[47]

6

Section of Pseudo Operations to D40 D40 to Project Barnacle 1979-1986

Establishment of Project Barnacle: April 1979

Major Neil, commander of the Selous Scouts' recce troop, resigned from the Rhodesian Army in 1978. After a short spell with the Special Branch of the British South Africa Police he moved to South Africa and joined 1-Reconnaissance Regiment at the Durban Bluff as a group commander.

In April 1979 the Commanding General Special Forces, Major-General Fritz Loots, called him to Pretoria. They went together to see the Minister of Defence, General Magnus Malan, who told him he had a plan in mind to form a new covert organisation as an adjunct to Special Forces. It would be used to put into practice lessons learned regarding clandestine operations in Rhodesia. In particular the Minister wanted to establish a long-range deep-penetration reconnaissance capability, something the Selous Scouts had successfully achieved. Major Neil, of course, had commanded this group and many of its successes could be attributed to him. His most renowned operator, Captain Chris Schulenburg, who had won Rhodesia's equivalent of Great Britain's Victoria Cross — the Grand Cross of Valour — for bravery, had often operated some 500km behind enemy lines for several weeks at a time without the benefit of logistical support or contact with his own forces.

The organisation's task would be to identify guerrilla infiltration routes, pin-point and infiltrate training camps and direct air strikes on them.

So Major Neil became the unit's first director. It was cumbersomely labelled the Section of Pseudo Operations. This was changed to D40. Then, after a random selection from a list of registered code words, it became *Project Barnacle*. Its initial objectives became the collection of intelligence and long-range reconnaissance, but other objectives were soon added. In the coming years there would be few operations undertaken by Special Forces in which operators from *Project Barnacle* did not pay a vital role — particularly in the collection of intelligence.

The need-to-know principle was so strictly enforced within *Project Barnacle* that if someone at EMLC (a division of Special Forces) had been tasked to make some special equipment, he would have no idea who would use it or when and where it would be used. Conversely, the operator concerned would never get to know who had made the equipment.

Neil was soon joined by another officer, Johan Möller, but he left after a few months.

General Magnus Malan gave his personal authorisation for the purchase of Renosterspruit Farm, Broederstroom, south of Hartbeespoort Dam and north of Johannesburg, as a base from which D40 would operate. There were two houses already on the property, but facilities were expanded with the construction of mechanical workshops, detention cells, an operations room, a radio room, a specially constructed armoury, administrative offices and other infrastructure. Security was paramount and a wall four metres high by half a metre thick was built around the complex. It was patrolled by guard dogs. A considerable amount was spent on improvements.

Johan Theron, a totally ruthless officer who ran the security and counter-intelligence section of Special Forces, worked closely with *Project Barnacle*. He was appointed as the project officer for the construction of the Renosterspruit base. This was a natural progression as he was also the project officer for Speskop, the Special Forces HQ that was in the process of construction just outside Pretoria. Special Forces took it over and moved in during early 1980. According to Theron, Speskop had to house 'many disciplines', including a workshop for the Special Forces' technical company, Electronic Magnetic Logistical Component Technical Consultants and Manufacturers (Pty) Ltd (EMLC). EMLC made or procured the equipment and gadgets akin to those supplied or procured by 'Q' in the James Bond movies. EMLC was run by Commandant Sybie van der Spuy.

Major Neil, on instructions, set up a front company as a cover for *Project Barnacle*'s operations. The initial cover was an estate agency called NKJM Estates. This was clearly inappropriate, not only because of the high walls and attacker dogs protecting the 'agency', but also because nobody there had the slightest inkling of what the property business was about. It then became, for a short while and only slightly more appropriately, NKTF Security Consultants. The cover story was that the black operators were security guards and the white operators were training staff and suchlike.

The arrangement did not work. Paperwork was not one of Neil's strong points, scanty records were kept and it was not long before the administration degenerated into shambles. Major-General Loots appointed Colonel Raubenheimer as NKTF's chief executive officer to bring order out of chaos and handle administrative and financial matters. This left Major Neil free to concentrate on his operational responsibilities.

NKTF Security soon became President Security Consultants (Pty) Ltd with a head office in Verwoerdburg (now Centurion), near Pretoria. Like his operational colleagues Colonel Raubenheimer worked in civvies. He employed his brother and a few secretaries. President Security Consultants was funded entirely by the SADF. There were a few other covert organisations, smaller than *Project Barnacle*, that fell under the Special Forces umbrella and Raubenheimer and his staff also looked after their administrative functions.

Neil embarked on a recruiting drive. His intention was to recruit ex-Rhodesian and South African operators who were either no longer capable of hard operating, or who no longer wished to, but who possessed a wealth of experience in the intelligence fields. With the rapidly changing political situation in Rhodesia, it was expected that many experienced Rhodesian operators would be seeking new homes in South Africa.

Trevor Floyd, the Regimental Sergeant Major of 1-Recce and a founder member of the SADF's Special Forces, was operational in the SWA/Namibia-Angolan border area when he was summoned to attend an urgent meeting with General Loots at the Ondangwa Air Base. *Project Barnacle*'s concept was explained to him and he was told it was intended the organisation would undertake operations that were even more clandestine than those he had already taken part in while serving as a Recce. He was invited to join Major Neil as the unit's third member. Initially, he was offered a three-month trial period, as acceptance of the posting meant a major adjustment for himself and his family. It required a move from Durban to Pretoria. More importantly it would be necessary for him to move from the military environment to a civilian one. He would no longer wear uniform, nor live on a military base and he would have to cut his ties with the military. There would be no further socialising in military messes and things like that. He would have to turn his back on old friends. His wife and children would have to accept that he would be away on long missions, perhaps for months at a time.

Floyd accepted the three-month trial period and decided to stay on. For the first six months he lived in his own caravan on Renosterspruit Farm. In January 1980 his family moved from Durban into a house in Centurion that was bought with *Project Barnacle* funds. Mrs Floyd had objected to the family living in a non-military house at full rental instead of the subsidised one she had been used to. The house was bought to accommodate her wishes and Floyd paid a nominal military rental for it.

The need for *Project Barnacle* to have its own light aircraft was identified by Major Neil. He explained to General Loots that it would not always be possible to get agents in and out of Zimbabwe by road. There was also a need to move quickly. *Project Barnacle*'s recruitment drive was in full swing and having their own aircraft would obviate the need to use commercial or military aircraft. It would also be useful for inserting or picking up agents across borders without having to involve air force helicopters. Major Neil, the holder of a private pilot's licence, located a six-seater Piper Seneca that was for sale at the right price. It would have been nice, he said, to have had a King Air, but 'that kind of expenditure could not be justified'. It was bought with *Project Barnacle* funds and housed in a hangar at Lanseria Airport.

Johan Theron had joined the SADF in 1962 and served as an infantry instructor until 1969 when he was recruited into the counter-intelligence section of Military Intelligence by General Loots, the Director of Intelligence at the time. Theron qualified as a private pilot in 1972 and passed selection for Special Forces in 1978. He spent the next ten years of his service there. He was appointed as the Special Forces' security officer and his office at Speskop was next to that of General Loots. By his own job description, his primary task was to deal with security risks in the ranks of the SADF. He was also involved in 'ultra sensitive' operations and 'many' eliminations of SWAPO prisoners of war and own force members (ex-Zimbabweans, ex-Moçambicans and ex-Angolans) as well as some members of *Project Barnacle*. He was involved in *Operation Savannah* — South Africa's intervention in Angola — and the smuggling of weapons in Zimbabwe as well as to South Africa after the imposition of the UN arms embargo. He also had the joint responsibility of being *Project Barnacle*'s security officer.

Project Barnacle: eliminations

Operations were initially restricted to deep penetration reconnaissance. In time, the identification and elimination of external targets were added to *Project Barnacle*'s tasks. Major Neil refused to have anything to do with internal assassinations. 'I'm a soldier, not a policeman', he said.

On 12 December 1980 a directive signed 'Serfontein' repeated the nature of *Project Barnacle*'s work, but wrapped its objectives in rhetoric with phrases like: 'The RSA is in a state of war . . . World opinion notwithstanding . . . Certain tasks must be carried out in such a manner that they cannot be traced back to the SADF or compromise the government . . .' It mentioned eliminations, ambushes, intelligence gathering, combat intelligence and, significantly, 'conducting/carrying out chemical operations'. (*Die voer van chemiese operasies*).

On 9 January 1981 Major-General Fritz Loots issued a 'Top Secret' directive formalising *Project Barnacle*'s operational tasks as follows:

A **Purpose**: To manage extremely sensitive operations.

B **Functions**:

(i) Eliminations.

(ii) Ambuscades against individuals of strategic importance.

(iii) 'Operativeness' as instructed in super sensitive operations.

(iv) Gathering of combat information regarding the abovementioned operations.

(v) Gathering of information as assigned in cases where other sources could not be utilised.

(vi) The conducting of certain special security tasks, such as observation of sources/agents and the performance of certain special tasks, such as observation of 'at random' security, experiments as instructed for Special Forces.

This was followed by a further classified directive on 18 February 1981 which specifically spelt out the elimination of identified enemies of the State. It again mentioned 'super sensitive' covert operations. Soon after, the organisation also became responsible for the elimination of any members of 'own forces' who had become a threat to clandestine operations. It was specifically stated in directives that the director of *Project Barnacle* was not authorised to make decisions regarding the elimination of targets. That lay solely within the province of the Commanding General Special Forces.

Major Neil said that although elimination was never questioned by operators, it did lead some to ask if 'they [the senior officers] were mad?'[1]

Special Forces' Medical Unit, 7-Medical Battalion and Project Coast

When constructing facilities at Speskop provision was made to house five laboratories concerned with the medical aspects of Special Forces and the embryo chemical and biological warfare (CBW) programme, *Project Coast*. Dr Wouter Basson, the commander of the Special Forces' medical unit, was placed in charge of all this. During the construction of Speskop General Loots instructed Johan Theron to liaise with Basson regarding the acquisition of laboratory equipment. They worked well together, became good friends and visited each other's homes.

The medical unit became 7-Medical Battalion in 1985 and the facilities connected to *Project Coast* moved out of Speskop at about the same time. In brief, *Project Coast* came about in the late 1970s when the SADF received indications that its troops were facing a threat of possible chemical attacks from Cuban, Soviet and Soviet Bloc supported forces in Angola. The SADF possessed no defences against such attacks and the Defence Command Council appointed Dr Basson to investigate what was needed to provide counter-measures.

After travelling extensively aboard and visiting all the major powers, Basson submitted a proposal to the Minister of Defence who approved the establishment of *Project Coast*. Its purpose was to provide South Africa with a comprehensive defence capability, making provision for all aspects of chemical and biological warfare.

Everything would be conducted clandestinely through front companies, which would allow scientists free access to the international scientific community and draw top scientists into the projects. But remuneration offered by the military would never have been enough.

Basson's investigation had revealed three types of chemical weapons: lethal, incapacitants and irritants like teargas. The major powers had moved away from lethal weapons in favour of incapacitants, particularly those capable of being used in the dual role of disabling troops and controlling rioters.

Initial approval was given for the establishment of two front companies that would be untraceable to the SADF. The first, Delta G Scientific, was established for offensive chemical research in the area of chemical agents, toxins and biological organisms. The second, Roodeplaat Research Laboratories (RRL), was to research all aspects of defensive biological programmes. Infladel, a new front company, and companies that succeeded it, became the information and technology arm of *Project Coast* and the conduit through which secret funds were channelled into it by the SADF. Both programmes continued to run from the laboratories at Speskop until the mid-1980s when they moved to their own premises elsewhere. RRL's facilities cost some R7 million to build, covered some 10 000 square metres and were in use from the beginning of 1986. The first sophisticated synthesis projects were launched in mid-1984 from a rudimentary but well-equipped temporary laboratory in part of the original Roodeplaat farmhouse.

Dr Andre Immelman, a professor in veterinary pharmacology and toxicology at Pretoria University, joined Intralab, which became RRL, as one of four inaugural directors in 1984 because it offered him the opportunity to become involved in full-time research. He knew from the outset that it was a SADF front. He wanted to establish an anthrax research laboratory but had lacked the funding, so involvement with RRL offered a perfect opportunity. For RRL it also offered an ideal smokescreen to obscure whatever else might be going on. Other covers included 'soft' projects like the discovery of various vaccines and formulas which, because RRL did not possess the necessary large-scale facilities to produce them commercially, were sold off to pharmaceutical manufacturing companies.

The other three inaugural directors were Dr Daan Goosen, formerly a lecturer at Pretoria University's veterinary faculty and a director of the HA Grové Animal Research Centre attached to the then H F Verwoerd Hospital, Pretoria, Dr Schalk van Rensburg a veterinary surgeon and formerly a toxicologist with the Medical Research Council; and David Spamer, once secretary of Pretoria University's Medical faculty. Daan Goosen was appointed managing director. He lasted only until early 1986 when he was replaced by Dr Wynand Swanepoel. Goosen was moved to Roodeplaat Breeding Enterprises (RBE) because of a suspicion he had taken kickbacks from the civil engineers who constructed RDL. At RBE he engaged in breeding guard dogs and focussed on a programme designed to save the chimpanzee from extinction. In 1988, though, he was asked to return to RRL to sort out problems in the animal research centre. This lasted until February 1989 when he was asked or told by Surgeon-General Niel Knobel to quit *Project Coast* because of a 'serious security breach'. Goosen believes this arose from an ongoing dispute he had with Wynand Swanepoel over the latter's sloppy approach to internationally prescribed standards of good laboratory practice.

Nevertheless, from the outset RRL conformed to international scientific standards and every possible safety measure governing work with dangerous chemicals was introduced. The 'Com Lab' was planned by Immelman to work on noxious substances like Sarin, Tabun and VX. The laboratory was visible through a large plate glass window from an adjoining room where scientists would don protective suits with independent air supplies before entering. A qualified nursing sister was on duty watching for mishaps and a medical doctor was always on call whenever the laboratory was in use. Access was restricted and there were only two keys, one kept by Dr Immelman and the other by Dr Staan Wandrag.

Dr Wouter Basson was the SADF contact man who supplied research guidelines to the facility. Basson normally liaised through Dr Immelman during his frequent visits but later, at Immelman's suggestion, he began to liaise directly with the various heads of departments. Basson was more than just a contact man, however, for he was the only one in contact with the research scientists. Only he identified priorities and supplied guidelines for research, supplied budgets and the equipment and chemicals required. It was within his authority to identify suppliers worldwide and negotiate with them for whatever he wanted. Most of these activities involved sanctions-busting or purchasing on the black market. He was the oracle and was relied on entirely as to whether prices were fair and whether black market buys were necessary. He was also the only person who knew whether the purchases had actually been made.

From March 1981 to December 1987, Basson fell under the operational command of the Commanding General Special Forces. So he could also be tasked to supply the operational requirements in respect of *Project Coast* to the Chief of the SADF, the Chief of Staff Intelligence, the Commissioner of Police, the Security Police Chief and the National Intelligence Service.

In the mid-1980s Basson instructed Immelman not only to look for defences against chemical weapons of mass destruction, but also to seek defences against bio-weapons that might be used against VIPs like top-ranking military officers and cabinet ministers. He claimed that there had already been such attacks so he would identify the type of research that should be conducted. He invited Immelman to identify substances for research. They looked at products that were easily available and could likely be used against VIPs.

The evaluation of the suitability of substances for covert use was ambiguous, for the differences between offensive and defensive bio-weapons were blurred.

Dr Mike Odendaal became the fifth director of RRL. He had worked for three years at the Onderstepoort Veterinary Institute and another three at the H A Grove Research Centre in Pretoria. He came to know DrWouter Basson while he was at the latter facility. He was head-hunted by Dr Daan Goosen in January 1983 to become the head of RRL's immunology/microbiology research. He was aware it was a SADF front company. He commenced with a staff of eight in the biological department. By 1993, when he resigned, the staff had risen to 15.

Odendaal saw his task as developing a defensive capability in the biological field by identifying bio-agents that could be used against the South African Security Forces and neutralising their dangers. Literature on biological warfare is scarce, so from the outset he focussed on collecting cultures. He cultured and freeze-dried a wide variety of samples of bio-agents. His laboratory was especially equipped to allow for work with pathogens at a PL3 safety level. The approach in CBW programmes was to concentrate on micro-organisms and viruses. No viruses were developed at RRL.

At first, defensive aspects assumed prime importance, but gradually the emphasis shifted towards the offensive use of biological agents. Lacking clear guidelines from management, scientists working for Odendaal generally went their own way and worked on projects of their own choice. For Odendaal this was cattle vaccine.

Odendaal was not convinced the dangers posed by biological agents were as grave as is generally thought. Virtually all known bacteria respond to treatment. Their effectiveness is generally limited because the amount ingested is usually too small to be lethal. An exception was a catastrophic accident at Russia's Sverdlosk CBW plant where anthrax spores escaped into the nearby town. Hundreds of people died after inhaling them.

Anthrax is the most effective of the pathogens that attack the lungs. In the initial stages, Odendaal's research on anthrax was done in cooperation with the Kruger National Park where it is endemic. The results were openly published. He was, at the time, considered to be the authority on anthrax in South Africa. There was another expert in Namibia, but the acknowledged world expert was a Briton. At one stage he came to South Africa to consult with Odendaal. He had 46 different anthrax cultures and was seeking an oral vaccine. RRL had the same agenda, but when the quest proved unsuccessful, the search was abandoned. So much for its defensive programme.

Odendaal's team of scientists worked on the A and B types of clostridium botulinum which affects humans and the C and D types which affect animals. Botulinum, by Odendaal's account, is one of the most toxic substances on earth. Only six molecules are required to incapacitate and kill someone. Its toxicity was tested with various liquids. The results were good when it was added to water, milk, beer and wine, but unsatisfactory with alcohol of greater purity like whisky or gin, because of visible flocculent.

Dr van Rensburg was Odendaal's immediate superior, but Dr Immelman passed instructions he received from the SADF via Dr Wouter Basson directly to him. Immelman controlled all 'H' or hard projects and orders for them were always passed on verbally and never reduced to writing. In general, Immelman never confided in him the purposes of specific pathogens he required. Once, though, he asked for salmonella and said it was for adding to the sugar at an ANC meeting. Odendaal believed the meeting was in Soweto. Immelman told him later the stuff had worked well and all the delegates had fallen ill.

Cigarette filters, one or two per packet, were contaminated with anthrax spores. After being resealed to conceal signs of tampering, they were infiltrated into ANC bases in Zambia and Angola. Odendaal also supplied Immelman with soft-centred chocolates injected with anthrax or botulinum, orange juice contaminated with vibrio cholera, orange juice with aldicarb, orange juice contaminated with a brucella bacillus and letters containing anthrax spores.

Odendaal was frustrated because Immelman failed to provide him with a clear plan for hard projects. He estimated they took up no more than five percent of his time. He had the best equipment money could buy and some of South Africa's best scientific brains, but all they wanted, said Odendaal, was 'toxins in little bottles'. RRL, he said, had the potential of becoming one of the best research facilities in the world, but its biological warfare programme was nothing to be proud of. Insufficient was produced to sustain either a defensive or an offensive programme. The small quantities involved would only have been enough for a minor campaign of bio-terrorism. As Odendaal said: 'No great skills are required to manufacture anthrax spores and botulinum.'

Projects related to the identification of toxins, establishing how they worked, whether they could be traced through forensic examination, their stability when added to food and drink, and methods suitable for their application — orally, by inhalation or sub-cutaneously by intramuscular or intravenous introduction. In 1985 there were ten projects including research into the toxicity of paraoxon in baboons and ionophore antibiotics. It had been shown that an overdose of the latter attacked the heart muscles of ruminants and when used in an experiment on a horse, the animal almost died of heart failure. Tests were conducted on baboons. When ionophore antibiotics were mixed with alcohol and administered intravenously, the baboons died within six hours. The substance was undetectable by post mortem examination.

The 40 projects in 1986 included paraoxon synthesis, data bases for organophosphates and psycho-tropic substances, and evaluation of the anti-fertility potential of various substances — some suggested the aim was to find an ethnically selective vaccine that only worked on pigmented people. There was, at the time, much talk about a population explosion amongst the black population and it was felt that an ethnically sensitive vaccine could be politically useful. There was also an investigation into the toxicity of Brodifacum, normally used for rodent control. It has anti-coagulant properties and when ingested orally causes internal and external haemorrhaging from all the membranes, nose, eyes, mouth, genitals and anus. The reaction would not be immediate, however, and it could take up to 14 days to appear.

Synthesis of paraoxon was an ongoing project and plentiful supplies were always available. Paratheon, an organophosphate commonly used as an agricultural insecticide, only becomes toxic when metabolised in the body to form a paraoxon. RRP synthesised paraoxon as an active ingredient because it was reasonably easy to make, required a fatal dose of only one milligram per kilogram of body weight, was quickly absorbed and if detected on post mortem could always be attributed to paratheon.

Research into paratheon also offered an ideal cover for the establishment of the laboratory for research on Sarin, Tabun and VX, since the same stringent standards applied as when working on the nerve gasses. RRL achieved a world breakthrough by finding a new way of treating organophosphate poisoning through hydrolysis.

Paraoxon was experimentally added to lip balm, shampoo, roll-on deodorant and clothing. Research was also conducted into doctoring tobacco and alcohol with it. Experiments were carried out into lacing beer and whisky with thallium or colonicine. It was used in the treatment of gout but the slightest overdose leads to kidney failure. Orange juice was laced with aldicarb. Paraquat, an agricultural chemical, was another tried in whisky — fibrosis of the lungs and kidney failure resulted from ingestion. Other toxins like Dixogin and Cantharadine (Spanish Fly) were subjected to experimentation and delivered to agents for deployment. A vial of freeze-dried HIV-infected blood was provided by Dr Wouter Basson. It was stored but never used.

Dr Goosen said that as scientists, he and his colleagues agreed very early on and very clearly that they had no wish to be told anything about target details. When asked to supply a substance, all they needed or wanted to know were the circumstances under which it would be administered, as this could influence the dosage required. The advantage of this decision was that the scientists remained uncompromised. The disadvantage was that they never had precise data to work with, such as the weight of the target and the climate in which the substance was to be used.

Goosen said he discussed this arm's length method of operating with both the Surgeon-General and Basson and they all agreed that the need-to-know principle should be strictly applied. Despite this, the RRL directors were still worried about the selection of targets (as they might well have been) and Goosen sought reassurances from Basson that the targets were legitimate, in terms of the prevailing political climate, and that they would be selected with utmost responsibility. Nevertheless, during informal discussions, ANC leaders and known communists were mentioned as possible targets, but never by name. There was some general talk among the scientists about the difficulties of getting Joe Slovo (head of the MK, the ANC's military wing, who was operating from Mozambique) — and what could be used if the assassin only had a minute to use a substance. There was mention of a possibility that Nelson Mandela might somehow get cancer before his release from prison. If he did, he would no longer pose a problem. Although this was passed off as idle talk, Dr Schalk van Rensburg was instructed by Wynand Swanepoel to research carcinogens with a view to inducing cancer in possible targets. Van Rensburg said that he played along, but knew from the outset, because of his many years of work with animals in this area, that it was impossible to use carcinogens in this way.

Extensive experiments were conducted in the field of peptide synthesis, where methods of broadcasting mood and emotion altering drugs could be devised. Research in this field under *Project Baxil* was believed to be far more advanced than in America or elsewhere. Such substances are regarded as the holy grail of warfare. Taken to their ultimate, they held the possibility that, in time of civil disturbances rioters could be drugged into docile obedience — to say nothing of whole armies in the event of war. To advance research the police, through General Lothar Neethling of the police forensic science laboratory, supplied the project with confiscated drugs like cannabis (up to nine tons), Mandrax (methaqualone — up to 500 000 tablets), Ecstasy (an amphetamine) and cocaine. Delta G Scientific possessed the capacity for the large-scale production of incapacitates, but only two, methaqualone in 1986/87 and Ecstasy in 1992, were manufactured in greater than laboratory quantities.

Recommendations about the type of incapacitates to be produced for *Project Coast* were made by members of the Technical Work Group, the final decisions by the CMC. According to Basson, Ecstasy causes a sense of euphoria, while Mandrax dulls all emotions and might even induce sleep. Benzodiazepines cause altered perception, hallucinations and emotional mood swings. Cocaine has the same effect as Ecstasy but is more intense. Basson claimed that experiments where cocaine was mixed with BZ lowered aggression levels. A rioting mob, once it was exposed to Ecstasy, would lose the desire to throw stones.

Dr Basson, according to Dr Immelman, had access to all pathogens and toxins produced by RRL. Immelman had personally delivered several to him. Nothing left RRL without Basson's approval.

In the mid 1980s Immelman began to question the legitimacy of RRL's work and voiced his doubts to Basson. He assured Immelman that all projects had the approval of the State Security Council, which he accepted — despite having no idea what the SSC was. Basson also reminded him that an arms dealer could hardly be held liable for the irresponsible use of weapons by someone else.

On one occasion Dr van Rensburg heard Basson and Swanepoel deriding the calibre of Special Forces' recruits, complaining that they were 'not what they used to be'. Some had apparently refused to obey orders to poison people and were showing resistance to covert operations, 'protesting that it's murder'. Basson and Swanepoel agreed that it was not murder, but war.

Arising from a fear of compromising the project's security, no member of the SADF's Coordinating Management Committee (CMC) who were responsible for *Project Coast*, ever inspected or even visited front companies to verify that equipment Basson said he had bought even existed. Such supervision was delegated to the secretary of the CMC, who was none other than Basson himself. Once a year the CMC reported the progress of *Project Coast* to Minister of Defence Magnus Malan. Basson in his capacity as secretary kept the minutes of its meetings and as the only member in direct contact with the front companies, the CMC (and thus the minister) was totally reliant on him regarding information on operations, financial transactions, purchases, progress and so on. The multi zillions of rands lavishly spent was foolishly taken as evidence in itself that progress was being made.

Confusion became greater and more widespread as the number of front companies proliferated to more than 70, some registered in South Africa and others in the United Kingdom, the United States, Belgium, Ireland, Switzerland, Luxembourg and the Cayman Islands. Shares in most of them were assigned to nominees, but in some of them Basson held 100% of the equity. This left a confusing pattern of ownership and virtually impossible tracks along which to trace the course of investments. Yet, ironically, the confusion naïvely pleased the SADF because the more total the confusion became, the less likely it would be that the companies could be traced back to the SADF. Many of the 'experts' drawn in for the project were recently qualified doctors who had performed their national service with 7-Medical Battalion and the preceding medical unit. They were effectively Basson's men. Many became very wealthy top executives with the front companies, particularly after they were privatised in the early 1990s. (The buyout was aided by an SADF loan of R12 million.) One of those fortunate executives was ex-Special Forces doctor, Philip Mijburgh, Defence Minister Magnus Malan's nephew. Mijburgh was appointed managing director of Delta G Scientific in 1985.

Eventually, the whole unsteady edifice of what had once been *Project Coast* came under intense scrutiny both before and after the 1994 elections. This resulted in the laying of criminal charges and what became the longest and most expensive criminal trial in South African history with Dr Wouter Basson facing multiple criminal charges, including dealing in Mandrax allegedly obtained from *Project Coast* sources. The trial started in 1999 and was still ongoing at the time of publication of this book.

Is it coincidental that in recent years Mandrax abuse in South Africa has become endemic?

When RRL was shut down in late 1992, all toxins and pathogens were destroyed in the furnace. The SADF opted to capture all data relating to its projects in-house. Immelman bought two blue steel trunks, fitted them with heavy padlocks and packed them with the project files. They were removed from RRL by Wouter Basson and Philip Mijburgh. Investigators found them in the garage at Basson's home. Of the 203 project files found, 177 related to chemical and biological weapons and only 26 could be linked to 'soft' or cover projects that could be classified as commercial. According to Dr Daan Goosen who was called in by the investigators to examine the contents, it proved beyond doubt that *Project Coast* was about the development of weapons. It also proved that in the 1980s South Africa was a world leader in some aspects of biological research.[2]

The full story of *Project Coast* falls outside the scope of this book.

7-Medical Battalion's achievements

While much of the activities and advances relating to *Project Coast* became infamous, there were other developments in the advancement of medical science by the medical unit and 7-Medical Battalion which South Africans can be proud.

Because of the deep penetrations into enemy territory carried out by the Recces and the consequent distances from medical care and lack of casevac (casualty evacuation) facilities, doctors undergoing national service were encouraged to apply for the Recces and many passed selection. Where possible, such doctors formed part of long-range penetration teams to give them the benefit of 'built-in' medical care. There were few, if any, other Special Force units in the world involved in operations, more than 1 000km from their home borders. If they occasionally were, like US Special Forces during *Desert Storm* and in Somalia, lavish air support was invariably available.

In Special Forces, it became the philosophy for medical men to form part of the operational decision making team. While the provision of medical teams was 7-Medical Battalion's primary mission, this eventually developed into what became an all-encompassing support system for Special Forces.

Prior to this, negative aspects had been numerous. The worst was the almost complete absence of medical and human sciences support, which was only provided on an ad hoc basis. Missions were planned in the classical military manner and shortly before deployment, somebody would say as an afterthought: `Oh, where's the medical back-up?' On the few occasions when doctors had been committed to Recce operations before this, the operators had come to regard them as nuisances and security risks. They were of little practical use either when accompanying teams, because they lacked the fighting abilities of Special Forces. While they were keen and tried hard, when things happened to them en route they invariably ended up as passengers because of their lack of training.

An initial problem faced by Special Forces, apart from the lack of medical personnel, was the absence of medical equipment adapted for their special needs. Opening a patient's chest in 1-Military Hospital, Pretoria, where there was a minimal danger of damage to the chest or to the equipment, posed far less of a challenge than conducting the same procedure in the field. In the bush there were no sterile facilities either.

A Recce operator/doctor had to master the art of practising medicine under extreme conditions. He would be positioned by means that no ordinary doctor could pretend to enjoy perhaps by walking 300km, or by parachute drop. Once deployed he would have to work with relatively few instruments under very unfavourable conditions and with no short-term access to sophisticated facilities or specialist support. Operators, too, tend to get upset with doctors using lights at night, seemingly insensitive to the fact that light is essential for even the simplest of medical procedures.

This necessity for improvisation in the field, instead of relying on casualty evacuation, arose from the clandestine nature of Special Forces' operations. A word monitored on the radio by the enemy at the wrong time, or an aircraft detected while flying in or out, could blow an important operation.

Resuscitation and surgical equipment are heavy, bulky and manufactured from metal. The average surgical kit used in hospitals weighs in excess of 22kg, which makes it far from portable for a doctor deployed in the field. There was a need to develop lightweight or sometimes miniaturised equipment from various alloys, which was an expensive exercise.

Certain surgical instruments which are especially bulky and heavy, like the retractors used to open the abdomen to enable a surgeon to work deep down, were adapted. The outcome was a special purpose deep manual retractor suited for use in both the abdomen and the chest. Special anti-shock trousers made of lightweight durable materials were another development; so was a lightweight air-droppable operating table and special stretchers for casualty evacuation.

Lighting for surgery purposes remained a problem. Ear, nose and throat specialists use a small lamp that concentrates light, but it was not suitable for use in major surgery. Then progress was made through joint development work with the Department of Mines and a really potent light suitable for field use was the result.

Certain anti-bacterial agents were developed, as were a number of rapid diagnostic techniques used to test for various poisons in the field. This arose from *Project Coast* research.

Anaesthetic techniques involving the use of light intravenous anaesthetics, frowned on in hospitals, were also adopted for field use, the operator/doctors being trained to anticipate and handle any complications that might arise. The most radical procedure was a move away from the classical morphine type pain killers to local blocks. With morphine patients often become confused and noisy. They also have to be carried.

Local blocks produce no such side effects. A man might have his forearm blown off, but by infiltrating the correct nerves in his shoulder with a drip — a little like going to a dentist — he would remain wide awake and aware of what was going on while experiencing no pain whatsoever. For psychological reasons wounds were strapped up to prevent the casualty from seeing their fullest and often ghastly extent. The casualty would retain the use of his non-injured limbs, but more important for Special Forces' operations, he would still be capable of trudging out of a dangerous area for pick-up — as long as he still had two legs!

A local block is a technique used, although not extensively, in highly sophisticated hospitals, but it has scarcely been utilised in military medicine. This meant the operator/doctor had to be fully trained in the technique to ensure he knew precisely what he was doing and did not end up doing more harm than good. One operator casualty who was put under local block while deep inside Angola, remained on his feet and walked for 12 hours until a casevac could be organised.

The advantages of medical doctors accompanying Recce teams on deep penetrations were manifold. Operational medics are trained to render primary aid and arrange evacuation. But they have insufficient training to make sophisticated assessments. Their job is to pass the patient back to surgical teams.

So the difference between an operationally trained doctor and an ops medic is the operational advice they can give. On an overnight raid it makes little difference because they will return in 24 hours anyway, but on a prolonged deployment the differences can be considerable. A doctor is trained to evaluate. He might say a patient will be all right for 24 hours, enabling an operation to continue. On the other hand he might conclude that a patient will die if not evacuated, but assess an 80% probability of that happening anyway. The next move would then be a decision by the ops commander.

The presence of a doctor in adverse conditions, where it would not normally be practical, considerably enhances medical support.

75% of doctors undergoing Special Forces' selection passed. It is true that they underwent more preparation than usual, about six months in all, because their services were too valuable to lose. Coming after six or seven years in university, a fairly sedentary period because of studying demands, they required an enhanced programme to get them up to physical scratch. Nevertheless, doctors are usually healthy, sporty types, well balanced physically, emotionally and intellectually.[3]

Recruits from Rhodesia

Brian, a Detective Inspector in the Special Branch of the British South Africa Police, Rhodesia, like many of his contemporaries in the run-up period to the 1980 British supervised election, had not believed for a moment that Robert Mugabe's Marxist ZANU-PF would win the political battle and become the first government of the new Zimbabwe.

Besides, he had been led to believe there were contingency plans to keep Mugabe out. The assembly points where the guerrillas had been gathered under British supervision were being monitored on an ongoing basis and if things went wrong they would be attacked and the enemy forces wiped out while they were concentrated.

Stationed in Bulawayo, Brian ran a Special Branch pseudo team of regular detectives, both black and white, as well as captured guerrillas who had been turned to the Rhodesian cause. These were the 'turned' or 'tame terrs' of Security Forces' parlance. Their task, to infiltrate guerrilla groups and bring about their downfall, was the same as that of the Selous Scouts, except that they concentrated on external threats while the Scouts operated internally. Sometimes, however, they worked jointly.

Brian's group and similar groups in Matabeleland operated mainly against ZIPRA, which drew its fighters from that tribal region. ZIPRA mounted its infiltrations into Rhodesia from

Zambia and Botswana, so the groups concentrated on those countries, pin-pointing their camps and infiltration routes. The ANC also came in for attention because they were ZIPRA's comrades-in-arms. There were similar Special Branch pseudo groups in Mashonaland and Manicaland who concentrated on ZANLA, which was Mashona tribally based, and they operated cross-border into Mozambique.

The election results put Brian and his colleagues into a state of shock. Suddenly the enemy was within the gates. His officer commanding did not improve his state of mind when he returned from a Salisbury trip, announced he had met the prime minister designate, and said what a nice chap he was. Not long before, Brian had brought in the bodies of three of his operators killed in action and he was not yet ready to be so forgiving to his erstwhile enemy. The unexpected change of heart by his commander proved the last straw. He went straight to his typewriter and banged out a terse letter of resignation. Similar things happened elsewhere in the country.

Brian's mind turned to a certain SADF liaison officer based in Bulawayo during the late 1970s, who had surreptitiously approached him with a job offer. The SADF had wanted him to accept a commission in Special Forces. He had rebuffed the offer angrily, never suspecting for a moment the time would come when Rhodesia would collapse. He told the liaison officer tersely that if he tried that trick again he would report him to the proper authorities and have him booted out of the country.

He searched his desk, found the relevant details scribbled in his personal phone book and dialled a Pretoria number.

'Yes, the offer is still open.'

Major Neil was visiting Rhodesia on a recruiting drive at the time and he arranged for several former Selous Scouts and Special Branch detectives to be flown to Pretoria for interview by General Fritz Loots. The general had done his homework and was well informed. He knew Brian had been running a pseudo team and that he had operated extensively against the ANC in Botswana and Zambia.

Would he be interested in joining Special Forces?

The general told him he was interested in recruiting a team of professional clandestine operators from the Rhodesian Security Forces. There was no question of them having to go through the training rigmarole, neither would they have to wear uniforms and put up with army bull. It was too early to detail exactly how things would work. Nor had he figured out how he would keep the unit clandestine once its members became members of the Permanent Force. Would it be feasible, he asked, for Brian to persuade his old team to come to South Africa with him?

Brian was reasonably certain that at least some of his regular black detectives would be interested. They were unified in their unhappiness with the changes taking place in Rhodesia. The country was being stood on its head. But how many would actually come was another story. The long term loyalties of the turned guerrillas were less easy to predict. Maybe they would, maybe they would not. He would only be able to tell after speaking to them.

He returned to Bulawayo to serve out his notice and spoke to some of his black and white operators. Ideally, most of the white operators preferred to remain in Zimbabwe — whether they were in the police, the army or just farmers. They would work for the new unit covertly, providing intelligence and so on.

The undertaking given by General Loots and repeated later by General Liebenberg was that if anything went wrong and they lost anything or everything they would be fully compensated and so would any family members who might become inadvertently involved. In effect, even though they remained in place in Zimbabwe, they would be Special Forces operators. If they had to leave the country they would be given Permanent Force appointments.

They were paid what was virtually an honorarium of about R600 per year, but most of those recruited were more interested in bringing Mugabe down than in the cash. The money, paid in rands in South Africa, was nevertheless useful for holidays and so on, considering that in Zimbabwe a family's holiday allowance of foreign currency was restricted to about Z$300. Besides, they were still drawing normal salaries in Zimbabwe. In later years the South African government reneged on those unwritten promises and many operators who were due compensation came short.

The majority of Brian's black operators — both detectives and turned guerrillas — agreed to leave, although some changed their minds later. Most of the black policemen were married, while the ex-guerrillas were single. The transportation of wives and families to South Africa was arranged.

While Brian was engaged with his team, setting up cells, recruiting and so on, several other Special Branch officers were serving out their notices and doing the same elsewhere in the country. Still being in place in the force while finishing their time placed them in ideal positions to complete their work.

When they finally came down south with their teams, complete intelligence set-ups would remain in place not only in Zimbabwe but also in Botswana, Zambia and Mozambique. Brian joined the organisation in July 1980. His counterparts like Pete, Winston and others had done much work in Mashonaland and Mozambique, while Johnny and others had worked in Matabeleland, Botswana and Zambia.

The agents-in-waiting in Matabeleland spent their notices fruitfully. In those days of sudden political transition, orders came from high authority to destroy classified files, but instead copies and often the originals were trucked down to South Africa. They had duplicate keys cut of every cell block of every police station and prison in the province. They also obtained, on the off chance they might prove useful later, duplicate ignition keys of every CID and Special Branch vehicle in Bulawayo.

They obtained detailed plans, often architects' drawings, of every police station, army base, railway bridge, road bridge, railway line and so on. For bridges they even obtained the strengths and thicknesses of struts etc., in case they might one day have to return and blow them up. Frustratingly, when Brian later needed this material for operational purposes, he discovered it had been packed away somewhere for safekeeping and the South Africans responsible could not remember where they had put it.

With the influx of ex-Rhodesian servicemen into South Africa, plans within *Project Barnacle* changed. The idea was to form all the men recruited from Rhodesian Intelligence into one unit to work with and provide operational intelligence for 3 and 6-Reconnaissance Commandos — the former Selous Scouts and the Rhodesian SAS (Special Air Service). The idea was for the Rhodesians to work on their own, without South African involvement.

This idea soon fell through, however, and the intelligence officers not involved in *Project Barnacle* were absorbed by the Chief of Staff Intelligence (CSI). This created a rift and some jealousies between those former Special Branch officers doing their own thing with the Rhodesians of *Project Barnacle* and those absorbed by the greater SADF. The *Project Barnacle* posts were considered plumb jobs.

The organisation devolved into three wings. In the operational wing Brian, with the rank of major, was in charge of urban operations in Zimbabwe, Botswana and Zambia. Other officers commanded rural operations in the various areas. Major Pete handled operational intelligence.

The intelligence wing, commanded by Major Winston, had a staff consisting of Dan, Butch, Dave, Johnny, Phil, Mike and others. They gathered intelligence from their own and other sources and were also fed information by the operational wing. In turn they passed operational intelligence coming to hand to Major Pete.

Finally, there was the long range reconnaissance wing, which operated only in Angola. Initially only two ex-Rhodesians, Tim and Chris, were involved, but they were later joined by Lieutenant Andre Diedricks of the Recces. Former Selous Scout, Major Boet Swart, became the commander of this wing.

The regular detectives, both blacks and whites, began drifting in to Renosterspruit in June and July 1980, after their periods of notice in Zimbabwe had expired. In all, 40 members of Brian's team filtered down during the next 12 months. In the end, the former regular policemen comprised the minority, the majority being ex-guerrillas from both ZIPRA and ZANLA. Operators from many other teams also arrived at the farm.

In early 1981 the authorities decided to centralise the housing of the single black operators on the farm. Until then their accommodation had been costing the SADF a small fortune. They had been staying in hotels in Hillbrow, while the whites had been dispersed to houses in the Fourways area and elsewhere. Until then only a few of the senior operators like Neil, Brian, Pete and a couple of others were at Renosterspruit. Houses for married black operators were found in various black townships.

Nothing had been resolved as to the operators' conditions of employment. They had not been attested into the SADF and were taken on the books of Armscor as 'procurement officers', although they procured nothing but intelligence. They belonged to Armscor's medical aid scheme and their salary cheques were drawn on Armscor's bank account. Despite this, Armscor never saw them in the flesh and none of them ever saw Armscor.

Many operators, Brian in particular, often travelled to Zimbabwe conducting reconnaissances, gathering intelligence and photographing targets. Brian alone was handling between 50 and 100 operators, mostly in Zimbabwe but a few in Zambia and Botswana.

The visiting operators were welcomed-back into the old police and army circles they had always mixed in, which was not surprising because many had become paid sources. Nevertheless, such mixing posed certain dangers and Brian and the rest soon became concerned about their covers.

Armscor also become nervous. It was an organisation whose representatives frequently travelled secretly around Africa, setting up arms deals and so on. The last thing they needed was an employee being caught as a spy. This led to their Armscor covers being dropped and their being signed on as members of the SADF's Permanent Force.

While it suited the ex-Rhodesians to retain only tenuous links with the SADF and not have the obligation of attending courses at the Military Academy or wherever, what they had not realised was that they were being disadvantaged by a lack of advancement. They were getting far less pay and promotion than those pursuing a less hazardous way of life in safer branches of the service. In the Permanent Force, some officers were attaining their majorities or becoming commandants shortly after their mid-20s, but there were no rapid promotions in *Project Barnacle*.

None of them knew either that although they had signed on as Permanent Force soldiers, unlike their brothers-in-arms in the Recce commandos, the SADF had no intention whatsoever of acknowledging them if things went wrong. They were Rhodesians — surrogates forces — and even more disadvantageous, not members of the Afrikaner *volk*.

Brian's personnel records, which he examined quite by chance many years later, identified him correctly in only one respect — his name. All other particulars were manifestly wrong. In reality he was a 35-year-old married man with three children, holding the rank of acting major, but his records showed him as a 22-year-old captain, single and without children.

The inferences that can be drawn regarding the likely action of the South African authorities if he had been unfortunate enough to be captured are obvious. They would have denied all knowledge of him, insisting that the man of that name and number was a much younger man, and washed their hands of him. This is traditional, perhaps, for the spy, but they were neither told this nor rewarded appropriately.

During the post-election period in early 1980 while Lord Soames governed Zimbabwe before handing over to Premier Robert Mugabe and the new Zimbabwe National Army was being phased in, Major Neil, Trevor Floyd and Johan Theron spent much of their time taking convoys of heavy trucks to Zimbabwe, collecting equipment, particularly special equipment, and taking it to Renosterspruit for storage. Much of it comprised weapons captured by the Selous Scouts and Rhodesian SAS and there was some special equipment too. The Rhodesian Army assisted the movements by utilising low loaders to move much of the stuff themselves.

It seemed to some that the new ZANU-PF government knew about the South African movements, even to the extent of help having been provided by the Commonwealth Monitoring Force. But it was so involved in taking over the reins of power that it turned a blind eye to such things — and so did the British. Much equipment was flown out from the Fylde Air Base by SAAF C-130 and C-160 transports.

Some 800 brand-new MAGs (general purpose machine guns), most still in packing grease, lay in military stores around Zimbabwe-Rhodesia. This was more than the total in service with the SADF, so it was understandable that they were anxious to get them back. It was the same situation with Eland armoured cars, mounted with powerful 90-mm guns, which had been given to the Rhodesian Army on permanent loan. The SADF had no wish to leave their own sophisticated weaponry with an army which in the fullness of time might well become their military opponents.

A senior Rhodesian general officer arranging the removals got cold feet and withdrew his offer to help. He had time to serve before qualifying for a pension and had no wish to prejudice himself. He apologised for letting the South Africans down, but shrugged and said that times had changed. Many guerrilla commanders from ZANLA and ZIPRA had been promoted to the ranks of colonel, brigadier and general officer. Many of the white officers remaining were obsequiously trying to get in their good books and preserve their positions. Looking after number one became an obsession. The telling of tales about one's white brother officers became sickeningly widespread.

So to the chagrin of the South Africans, the MAGs and Elands remained where they were.

The SADF's liaison officer in Salisbury, Commandant André Bestbier, became aware of deep resentment on the part of many senior Rhodesian officers because so many others were leaving to join the SADF and because South Africa was recovering its equipment. They accused South Africa of disloyalty . . . of taking away their teeth . . . of stabbing the Rhodesian whites in the back. Most confidently predicted that their futures were secure. But they were wrong, for the new regime ruthlessly axed all but a handful of them within the next two years.[4]

On the other hand, it was clear that resentment remained in the SADF over the loss of its armoured cars to a country which might, one day, turn against South Africa.

After independence there was a large-scale movement of equipment from *Project Barnacle* back to Zimbabwe. D-40 merely turned it around and sent it back. It was not just weapons — there were powerful SSB radio sets, Zimbabwean police and army uniforms and other kit, explosives and so on. It was sent to different teams who cached it at various places in the country.

Some intelligence found its way to *Project Barnacle* from the Chief of Staff Intelligence, but the operatives often found it suspect, even unreliable. Majors Brian and Pete had both enjoyed excellent relationships and close liaison with the Security Police during their Rhodesian Special Branch days and many lasting friendships had developed.

The SADF did not like that at all. There was a general antipathy, verging on hatred, of the police as a service. The SADF's general staff had forbidden liaisons with them, except at the highest command levels. Even at that high level, though, the army barely tolerated the police and vice versa. Each service continually battled the other, jostling for political advantage and position.

If results were required, the simple solution, they decided, was to ignore orders which, in their option, verged on stupidity. So if intelligence was required on the ANC in Lesotho *Project Barnacle* consulted the Security Police in Ladybrand, Port Elizabeth or Bloemfontein. If Swaziland was the target they went to Pretoria, Ermelo and Nelspruit. If their eyes were on Botswana and Zambia they relied on Potchefstroom and Zeerust. For Zimbabwe they relied on their relationships with Messina and Pietersburg.

Naturally, it became a two-way street, and they fed military information back to the

Security Police. They made a particular point of concealing their sources of information at post-operational debriefs. In military circles they soon earned themselves the reputation of being particularly clever fellows.

Operational authority

Unlike the Rhodesian situation, virtually no operational freedom was granted to Special Forces. Even a general's authority was often insufficient. In Brian's time, except for *Operation Gericke*, which was authorised by Major-General Loots alone, not a single operation involving *Project Barnacle* went ahead without the personal authority of the Prime Minister, later the State President, P W Botha. Brian was often flown to Cape Town in the presidential jet to brief P W Botha on pending operations before approval was granted. Brian found this presidential involvement irksome, even inexplicable at times.

When times changed, it was also denied.

Operation Dual: The killing machine

During the 1970s South African Special Forces adopted the Rhodesian Selous Scouts' concept of infiltrating pseudo SWAPO gangs into suspect areas of SWA/Namibia and southern Angola in an attempt to root out the enemy. (For full details of *modus operandi* see *Selous Scouts: Top Secret War*, Lt Col Ron Reid Daly as told to Peter Stiff)

Most operations were conducted from Fort Rev, 5-Recce's forward operational base on the periphery of the Ondangwa Air Base in Owamboland. It was a 'Top Secret' operation, probably the most closely guarded secret of the border war, and few people in the ranks of the SADF knew anything about pseudo operations. On capture SWAPO prisoners were blindfolded and transferred as quickly as possible to 5-Recce custody at Fort Rev They were detained in an attached detention barracks with interrogation rooms.

Prisoners were sorted out. Those considered suitable were offered an alternative to the stern penalties they would face if they were put on trial in the criminal courts for terrorism offences. The alternative was to come over to the government side and fight against their former comrades. Most elected to do so. These men were immediately deployed with a pseudo gang, comprising 5-Recce soldiers and turned guerrillas kitted out with SWAPO uniforms and weapons. Their job was to track down their former comrades who had been fortunate enough to evade capture. It was always ensured that those just turned had an active part in any killing that took place, so that for them there could be no turning back.

Part of Johan Theron's job was his involvement with Special Forces' counter-intelligence at Fort Rev The question of the Recces using pseudo operations had to be kept secret from SWAPO 'at all costs'. If they tumbled to what was going on, it would not only have put the lives of the operators at risk, but would also have jeopardised the lives of the local population. This created a problem. When SWAPO guerrillas refused to be turned, or ones that had been turned became untrustworthy with the risk of them re-turning, it was impossible to feed them back into the SWA/Namibian prison system. If that had been done, word of 5-Recce's *modus operandi* would soon have spread like wildfire back to SWAPO in Angola.

Theron suggested to General Loots, after long deliberations, that 'redundant' SWAPO members should be disposed of 'without trace'. He suggested that the bodies be got rid of by dumping them in the sea. He had researched the matter carefully. He had visited naval headquarters at Silvermine in the Cape to obtain accurate information about tidal drifts. This was used to calculate the chances of a 'package' (weighing as much as an average man) being washed up on the shore after it was dumped in the ocean. The final formula required an aircraft to fly some 100 nautical miles out to sea before throwing a body out.

The idea was for a prisoner to be sedated for the flight and killed with a lethal injection shortly before being dumped. The use of firearms was out of the question. Invariably other people would be around and discharging one posed a danger not only to them but to the aircraft itself. In the unlikely event that a body was found knife and bullet wounds might prove difficult to explain. There was also the question of the mess made by blood.

Project Barnacle already had its own Piper Seneca, so to check on the practicality of furthering his ideas, Theron contacted the aircraft's manufacturers to investigate the possible dangers of flying the Seneca without the rear door in place. He explained that it was intended to use the aircraft for sky diving purposes. The manufacturers assured him that flying without the door would not pose any particular problems.

General Loots approved the idea and the scheme became *Operation Dual*.

Major Neil was briefed by General Loots after the discussions. He was told he should recce the situation, piloting the aircraft with Theron as co-pilot, to see if the idea was feasible. It was suggested they find a suitable landing ground on the long, remote and deserted beaches of SWA/Namibia's Skeleton Coast . They should land, remove the rear door, take off and head out to sea and dump the 'package', returning to recover and refit the door and head for home. The bodies were always referred to as 'packages that needed to be put into the system'. Certain 'key members' of the police counter-insurgency unit, Koevoet, and 5-Recce were briefed on the plan.

The first mission came unexpectedly via a radio call from the South African Police after the completion of their opening recce. They had already identified several suitable landing sites along the Skeleton Coast. They landed at Otjivelo, took over two 'packages' in body bags, flew out to sea for 100 nautical miles as planned and routinely dumped them from an altitude of about 4 000m.

At first orders to dump bodies were passed to Major Neil personally by General Loots. Once the system was in place, however, Johan Theron would tell him when a trip was needed. Neil never knew nor enquired about the identity of the victims. He described the dumping of bodies at sea as 'just doing a job'.

The next operation occurred in August 1980 and concerned a SWAPO detainee. Theron obtained a tranquilliser dart of the type used on wild animals from his contact, Jan Coetzee at EMLC. Coetzee assured him that the dosage in the dart would easily kill a man. Neil never enquired nor was told what prisoners were being injected with.

With Major Neil at the controls, they landed in the Etosha Game reserve and picked up a SWAPO prisoner from a SAP captain and a lieutenant. Theron had a hypodermic syringe with a red plunger and when they were airborne, he stuck it into the man's backside as Coetzee had instructed. It had absolutely no effect and the prisoner put up a mighty struggle as Theron tried desperately to subdue him.

'Just don't shoot him!' an alarmed Neil was shouting from the front.

Theron first tried to throttle the prisoner with his bare hands. When this did not work, he curled a strong plastic cable tie, normally used to bind a victim's hands, around the man's neck. He used pliers to tighten and exert maximum pressure on it, but the man would not die. It took about 15 minutes before he stopped kicking, threshing about and wetting himself. Eventually Theron was unable to detect a pulse. The remainder of the flight to the Skeleton Coast landing ground was uneventful. When they landed to strip the body before dumping it, the tie was so deeply embedded in the victim's neck that Theron experienced considerable difficulty in removing it.

Theron was a trained paratrooper and he was aware that an object plummeting from the sky could be seen from a considerable distance out on the open sea. So when they reached the planned drop area, Theron asked Neil to fly in a wide circle to ensure no ships were in the vicinity before he pushed the body through the door. They watched until it disappeared beneath the waves.

'Where are you getting this stuff?' an annoyed Neil asked Theron afterwards.

Theron promised to 'speak to Dr [Wouter] Basson about using something better' in future.

This incident was followed by the collection from Etosha of another six 'packages' delivered by Koevoet. Theron physically strangled to death all six with plastic restraints while they were still on the truck that had brought them. It took three flights to dispose of the bodies, two at a time. Neil's log book indicates he was not the pilot on that occasion.

Neil knew Wouter Basson as the Special Forces' medical officer. Some weeks later while on a visit to Speskop, he happened to bump into Basson in a corridor. Still feeling annoyed because the incident had posed a real danger to the aircraft, he told him: 'Make sure the stuff that's being used works next time. We can't afford problems when we are in the air.'

Basson promised he would 'take care of it'.

Theron reported to General Loots that the mid-air struggle could have jeopardised the whole operation. If the aircraft had crashed, it would have exposed everything. He also said that strangling the prisoners had 'totally traumatised' him. It was 'not the way I wanted to fight my enemy'. It was necessary to find a more humane way of eliminating prisoners.

Loots summoned Dr Basson into his office and they spoke alone. After this Theron was called in. Basson said he would give him Scoline and Tubarine in future. These were Schedule 7 (dangerous) drugs. Both were used during open heart surgery to collapse the lungs, but were lethal in an overdose. They could only be obtained via a doctor's prescription, in this instance through Dr Basson. Basson told him to use two ampules of each per victim, both to be injected intravenously. From then on Theron got regular supplies of ampules together with syringes from Basson. If Basson was not available Theron collected them, on Basson's instructions, variously from Doctors Kobus Bothma, Wynand Swanepoel or Wouter 'Buks' Lombard. The latter left Special Forces in 1980 and moved to the Department of Health. Theron kept a supply of the ampules in his strongroom and used them as required.

The drill was refined so that the victim was sedated before being loaded aboard the aircraft. When it landed on the Skeleton Coast, the door would be removed and hidden in the sand. The victim would be stripped of clothing and reloaded in the plane either before or after another — this time fatal — injection. After dumping the body at sea they would return to the beach, recover and refit the door, splash aviation fuel on the victim's clothing and burn it.

Theron had received rudimentary training as a paramedic in Special Forces, but the injections frequently posed problems. Many of the victims delivered to him were suffering from severe shock, which made it almost impossible to find a vein. For this reason he once had to inject the drugs directly into the victim's heart. Dr Basson, he said, had shown him how to do it and how to find the aorta in case of such a contingency arising.

Eventually, almost all the 'packages' delivered to Theron were sedated. This could be attributed to a supply of a strong sleeping draught that Theron called M3, which he alleged had been delivered to him by Dr Basson. Basson warned him, on one of the many occasions he allegedly supplied the tablets, that an overdose could prove fatal. This, of course, was strictly academic considering the circumstances!

At the trial of Dr Wouter Basson , an employee of EMLC, identified only as 'Mr Q' (after his James Bond counterpart), told how he had been called to Dr Phillip Mijburgh's office and asked to drill a tiny hole in a can of 'Game' — a non-aerated enery drink. He said he wanted the job done on the spot and not in the workshop. Mr Q obliged and drilled a tiny hole in the seam. He watched while Mijburgh injected a substance through the hole. He soldered it shut so professionally that it was all but impossible to find — even when one knew it was there. Mr Q said he did it on 'two or three occasions'. According to Theron, Basson had told him that 'Game' mixed well with sedatives. Cans of beer were also doctored. After seeing how it was done, it appears that Dr James Davies took over and used a dental drill on cans and bottles. Working as a team, Dr Immelman injected them with toxins — Paraoxon, anthrax, Brodifacum or other stuff — and Davies would soldier them shut.

There was an occasion, though, according to Trevor Floyd, when he and Major Neil had to kill three victims with hammers because the latter had forgotten the sedatives.

With the use of Scoline and Tubarine operations went more smoothly and victims died more humanely. The situation of people struggling for their lives soon became a thing of the past.

In November 1980 Neil told Floyd a security problem had developed with a Zimbabwean *Barnacle* operator who was suspected of preparing to expose the unit's activities in Zimbabwe. He had already committed a serious breach of security by making numerous calls to Zimbabwe on *Project Barnacle*'s phones. There was an unacceptable risk that he might reveal the identities of their agents in Zimbabwe.

On 13 November, Neil took off for SWA/Namibia from Lanseria Airport in the Piper Seneca with Floyd and the suspected traitor aboard. During the flight the suspect complained of a headache and Neil gave him a white tablet. They landed at an unnamed SWA/Namibian airfield where Theron and 5-Recce's intelligence officer, Dave Drew, awaited them with two prisoners in a panel van.

The two joined the *Barnacle* operator at the aircraft and Theron fatally injected all three. It is assumed the bodies were dumped in the Atlantic Ocean.

Neil said that he only picked up victims in South Africa once. That was at Lanseria Airport on 25 July 1981. He insisted in advance that the passengers be sedated and not dead. He had no wish to have to explain the presence of dead bodies in the event of an emergency landing. The four victims were brought to Lanseria by Theron. Floyd helped Neil prepare the aircraft by removing two of the passenger seats to make space. They flew to Windhoek and refuelled. From there they went to an abandoned airstrip near the deserted mining settlement of Toscanini. Theron injected the victims, stripped them naked, bundled them back in the aircraft and dumped them at sea. On their return they burnt the clothing with aviation fuel.

In July 1981 Floyd was ordered to rendezvous with Sergeant-Major Chris Pretorius, the head of 5-Recce's detention centre, at a spot on the Great North Road near Warmbaths. He was to take over some prisoners. Once they were in his custody he was to hand them cans of Game laced with sedatives. Floyd was puzzled at the choice because it was an energy drink used almost exclusively by sportsmen. Neil explained that 'Basson recommends it' because it disguised the taste of the sedatives.

On the night of 28 July Floyd met Pretorius as arranged and transferred three SWAPO prisoners to his Land-Rover. Theron said they included *Barnacle* operators 'who had to be moved into the system'. Floyd gave each a can of Game for refreshment. They drank the contents and soon fell asleep.

Floyd drove straight to the hangar at Lanseria Airport where the Piper Seneca was housed. Major Neil and Theron arrived shortly afterwards, followed by the latter's second in command, Eric Kennelly. Theron said one of the 'packages' was already dead. Kennely saw only two black men dressed in SADF browns seated on the floor of the hangar. Theron told the prisoners they were going for a trip in the aircraft. Turbulence was expected so he was giving them a sedative. Kennelly watched as Theron injected them intravenously and they both 'keeled over' almost immediately. Floyd thought they had been injected with long-lasting sedatives. The men were loaded into the aircraft. Floyd did not go on the flight.

Before take-off Theron gave Kennelly the syringe, needles and one or two empty ampules and told him to destroy them. He drove to Speskop and in a far corner of its spacious grounds he crushed them into the ground with the heel of his shoe. He had previously noticed similar ampules in Theron's walk-in safe.

Just prior to this incident, Theron had told him that a top secret project existed. It was designed to eliminate certain people with chemical substances and was called *Project Dual.* The files relating to it never left his office and were always kept in his personal strongroom. This was unlike other Special Forces files which, by order, had to be returned to Speskop's registry nightly. Kennelly believes Theron introduced him to *Project Dual*, and had him attend at Lanseria Airport as insurance in case he was transferred. Kennelly would than haven been enabled to take over the project. He was not, however, involved in any similar operations again.

Neil landed along the Skeleton Coast. Theron injected the victims with Scoline and Tuberine and stripped them naked. They were flown out to sea and dumped. Theron remembered the trip vividly because one of the still living victims had developed 'terrible bad breath' as a reaction to the initial sedatives.

Neil piloted the Seneca for Theron on what he said were seven or eight victim disposal trips before he resigned from *Project Barnacle*.

The Speskop HQ included a large furnace designed for the destruction of documents. One day, Theron alleged, Dr Basson told him he had a body to dispose of. They waited until the evening when all the staff had left. Basson arrived in an ambulance from which he and Theron removed the naked body of a black man that was already in *rigor mortis*. They had something of a struggle to get the body into the furnace but eventually succeeded. It took about 30 minutes for the body to cremate. They scraped together any remaining bone fragments and burned them again. When everything had been reduced to ashes, these were scraped up and put in a container.

Before leaving they went to the Special Forces pub and joined some of their colleagues who were having after- work drinks.

'What have you been up to — burning a body that you are so red in the face?' a colleague joked.

Theron muttered something about them destroying chemicals.

Theron scattered the ashes through his car window as he drove home.

Commandant Matie van der Linde was transferred to Special Forces at Speskop as Senior Staff Officer (Air Operations) on 12 January 1981. He had joined the SAAF in 1961 and had served with distinction. He had held the posts of Commanding Officer of 41 and 17 Squadrons and the Flying School at Dunottar. His principle task at Speskop was to liaise with the SAAF in arranging air transport/support for Special Forces' operations. Through his duties he soon became aware of the existence of *Project Barnacle* and that it was involved in covert operations. He met Major Neil who mentioned the Piper Seneca in a hangar at Lanseria Airport. Being a pilot, it was natural that Van der Linde displayed a professional interest in aircraft.

He had nothing to do with *Project Barnacle* operations *per se* until Major-General Loots called him in one day and asked if he was qualified to fly the Piper Seneca. He replied in the affirmative and was ordered to accompany Neil as co-pilot on an operational flight. Neil was not rated for night flying.

After Neil's resignation from *Project Barnacle* in August 1982, Major-General Kat Liebenberg, the new GOC Special Forces, called him in and told him there were 'certain tasks' that the Special Forces security officer, Johan Theron, had to do from time to time. In future, Van der Linde would pilot the Piper Seneca for him on such operations. With Neil's resignation *Project Barnacle* was without a pilot. It appears that this led to the Piper Seneca becoming a general Special Forces aircraft, despite it remaining on *Barnacle*'s inventory.

On his first mission, Theron told Van der Linde they were flying to Otjivello to pick up bodies. They would fly out over the South Atlantic and dump them. Theron explained to him on this and subsequent occasions that they were 'enemies of the State' who could not be processed normally through the system. Neither then nor later did Van der Linde enquire about the identities of victims, nor was he told. He made a fine point of never looking at faces.

Van der Linde said he was a 'professional soldier' and could not refuse the order.

He was hazy about the number of death flights he played a part in, but suggested it might have been as many as ten. With the exception of one instance he never even examined the 'cargo'. He professed to have no idea how many bodies were loaded. 'My job', he said, 'was to fly the plane.' On most occasions the bodies were dumped in the Atlantic Ocean, but on two occasions it was in the Indian Ocean.

In May 1982 Van der Linde flew Theron, Dr Basson and Trevor Floyd to Windhoek in the Seneca. From there Van der Linde flew on to Otjivello with Floyd. Theron said that he and Basson continued by car to Fort Rev at Ondangwa. The trip was undertaken so that Basson could monitor Theron's methods and assess how well he was handling his job from a psychological viewpoint. Four SWAPO detainees were used as guinea pigs.

The night before the four were due to receive lethal injections, they were taken to an interrogation room that could be observed through a two-way mirror. Theron watched through it while Basson gave them sedative tablets. When Basson left the room, the prisoners hid the tablets in the legs of their chairs. Basson returned, retrieved the tablets and watched until they swallowed them.

The next day, when it was time to administer the fatal injections, Basson demonstrated the correct procedures to Theron by administering the Scoline and Tubarine himself. Theron observed laconically that 'they were dead afterwards'.

His observations of these four unfortunates led Dr Basson to realise that while Scoline and Tubarine were effective, when given in the overdoses necessary to cause death, they inflicted great pain on the victims. It prompted him to recommend that in future Theron should first anaesthetise his victims with an injection of Ketelaar. It seems strange that despite being an acknowledged medical expert, Dr Basson took so long to discover that the people he was helping to put to death were actually suffering pain!

The bodies were routinely disposed of at sea.

On their return to Pretoria Theron said that he and Basson reported the results of their trip to Major-General Kat Liebenberg.

At his trial Dr Basson denied involvement or that he had even gone to Fort Rev

Rita Engelbrecht was employed by Military Intelligence in a civilian capacity. Theron told her at one stage that she should not believe that death came quickly when you murdered someone. He told her that his work included flying out to sea and dumping the bodies of terrorists into the ocean. He also said he was extremely good at injecting terrorists as Dr Wouter Basson had told him how to do it.

Danie Phaal had joined the SADF in 1977, straight from school. He qualified as an instructor before joining the Special Air Task Force commanded by Major-General Tienie Groenewald. His work with this unit involved air reconnaissance of external airfields and aircraft crash sites. He also underwent advanced training as a medic, learning how to suture and insert intravenous drips. He passed courses in the use of explosives and bush survival. In 1980 he passed a test to determine if he was capable of 'eliminating enemies of the State' and was trained in the use of silenced weapons. At the end of 1980 when the Special Air Task Force was disbanded, he joined Special Forces. He was highly recommended by Major-General Groenewald and gladly accepted by Major-General Loots to undergo selection. He passed and was also parachute trained.

In 1982 he joined Special Forces counter-intelligence where Theron was his commanding officer. Officers in the section at various times he remembers were a Colonel du Toit, Eric Kennelly, André 'Pine' Pienaar, a General Engelbrecht and May van Vuuren. Tasks included training, counter-intelligence, the issue of false identity documents to operators for use on covert missions, the supply of vehicles that could not be traced back to the SADF and electronic and photographic surveillance. He also investigated members of the SADF who had 'loose lips' or who were considered a threat to clandestine operations.

At Speskop he became aware of *Project Barnacle* through 'gradual exposure'. He noticed its operators wore civilian clothes and did not work at Speskop. At some stage he saw various restraints and balaclavas in the walk-in strongroom in Theron's office and learned they were used by *Barnacle*. He noticed blood on a pair of handcuffs in the vault. He also became involved in supplying the unit with special equipment, false identity documents, non traceable vehicles and restraints. Phaal became involved in the para training of *Barnacle* operators. Through such activities he got to know Major Neil as well as Trevor Floyd and several black operators. Floyd was also involved in such training.

He also conducted a parachuting course at Speskop for doctors in 7-Medical Battalion, including Dr Wouter Basson himself and Doctors van Aartweg, Blunden and Philip Mijburgh. He gave Basson an abbreviated one-on-one Special Forces training course at Fort Doppies in the Caprivi. He developed a good working relationship with Basson and they socialised once or twice.

In due course Theron made Phaal aware that *Project Barnacle* was involved in eliminations and that it was 'a very sensitive matter'.

During February 1983 information was received that Christopher, a Zimbabwean operator who was about to go to Zimbabwe on leave, was planning to desert. He also intended to blow the whistle to the CIO on details of *Project Barnacle*'s covert operations in Zimbabwe. It was decided he had to be eliminated as the risks posed by him were too great.

Theron ordered Danie Phaal to rendezvous with Trevor Floyd late on the afternoon of 14 February. It was Phaal's first operation as a fully fledged *Barnacle* operator. Floyd, driving a converted ambulance, had Christopher with him when they met. He was dressed in civilian clothes and was carrying a suitcase. The pretext for the meeting was that as he and Phaal were driving to Messina to conduct an operation, they would be able to give Christopher a lift to the border.

It would turn out to be not much of a St Valentine's Day for him.

Once out on the Great North Road, Floyd offered Phaal and Christopher cans of beer. Phaal knew they had been doctored so he declined. Christopher, however, accepted one and was soon asleep. Some time later Floyd became concerned that Christopher might wake up before they reached Zeerust and he pulled the vehicle off the road and stopped. Phaal injected Christopher intravenously with Ketelaar given to him by Basson. The idea was to keep him sedated until they rendezvoused with others at first light on 15 February at the Zeerust Airfield. Somewhere along the way, though, he stopped breathing.

Theron had warned Phaal that this might happen. He said that if it did, he should fold the body into a foetal position before *rigor mortis* set in to make it easier to handle. This was particularly true as far as Christopher was concerned because he was a very tall man. Phaal did as he had been instructed and strapped him in that position. But by the time they arrived at the airfield Phaal was tense and nervous. He said he did 'just about anything I could' to take his mind off events. This situation was particularly upsetting for him because he had put Christopher through his parachuting course and had become quite friendly with him. He recalled eating grapes that his wife had packed for him in a Tupperware container, despite feeling utterly nauseous.

While waiting for the aircraft to arrive, Sergeant-Major Chris Pretorius, who was in charge of 5-Recce's detention barracks, arrived in a van with three heavily sedated prisoners. Shortly after first light the Seneca, piloted by Van der Linde, arrived with Theron as the co-pilot. Phaal assisted Theron by injecting the three prisoners from Phalaborwa in the neck and heart, then stripped and loaded them into the aircraft. This was the only occasion on which Van der Linde left the cockpit to check that the 'cargo' was properly hidden under a tarpaulin. He knew that while en route to the Skeleton Coast he would have to land at Eros Airport in Windhoek to refuel. He was concerned that someone there might spot the bodies.

After the Piper's take-off at Zeerust, Floyd and Phaal drove back to Pretoria, stopping for breakfast in Rustenburg. They burnt Christopher's clothes and his suitcase at a municipal dump north of Pretoria.

Van der Linde routinely touched down at Eros. After refuelling he took off and flew west, crossed the coast and headed out to sea. To his and Theron's dismay, a fleet of Soviet fishing trawlers was sighted in the normal dumping area. This necessitated him turning and flying along the coast almost as far south as Swakopmund before it was deemed safe enough to toss the bodies out.

In July 1982 the Mozambique news agency claimed that Lieutenant Adriano Bonaventura Bomba, who had defected to South Africa in 1981 bringing a MiG 17 jet fighter with him, was the head of RENAMO, the Mozambique liberation organisation. It went on to say that Bomba was using South Africa as a base from which to launch attacks on Mozambique.[5] There is no doubt that the SADF capitalised on Bomba's defection, but the truth was there was a lot of in-fighting amongst RENAMO people in South Africa who were vying for positions. In April 1984 this culminated in RENAMO's secretary-general, Orlando Cristina, being gunned down at its base at Montana Farm outside Pretoria.[6] The farm belonged to the SADF. There had been a major gun battle there between factions vying for supremacy. Doctors from 1-Military Hospital were sent out to treat the wounded. Order was reimposed.

Theron knew the police had arrested the Cristina assassins and that one had ended up in the intensive care unit of 1-Military Hospital. When he recovered, Dr Basson went with Theron and a national serviceman, Paul Heyns, to fetch him from hospital. The prisoner was handcuffed to Heyns and the four drove in Theron's car to the Zwartkop Air Force Base where a light SAAF aircraft awaited them on the runway.

Theron was told they were going to Bloemfontein. The prisoner was handcuffed to a seat. During the flight the prisoner became extremely aggressive and fought hard to free himself. Basson told Theron his condition resulted from an overdose during a chemical interrogation in which he and Doctors Kobus Bothma and Philip Mijburgh had played a part. Theron had a special interest in interrogation techniques because of what Special Forces' operators might have to face if captured. He asked Basson how much could be obtained from a prisoner with the help of chemical substances. Basson said that with his method 'everybody talks', but specialised medical skills were required.

Commandant Jan Anton Nieuwoudt of the Military Intelligence's DCC was involved in the investigation. He was based at Fontana Farm outside Pretoria which was close to Montana. Basson visited him there on a couple of occasions. At one stage of the probe, there were fears of an outside infiltration by RENAMO forces and an infantry platoon was assigned to Nieuwoudt to prevent this. He deployed them in ambush for a week, but no one came.

After Bomba's arrest, his station wagon was left at the farm. Some time later a member of the Chief of Staff Intelligence's Directorate of Special Tasks came and removed the vehicle. It clearly did not suit the SADF for someone from that faction, probably Bomba himself, to take over as RENAMO's secretary-general. In the event, a man more to their liking, Evo Fernandes, took over the job.[7]

Adriano Bomba and his colleagues were never seen alive again. On the completion of the investigation, the alleged assassins were subjected to a mock court martial in the SWA/Namibian operational area, found guilty and summarily executed.

In December 1984, Dr Kobus Bothma took three drugged unidentified victims who 'had been put into the system' from Pretoria by minivan to the Dukuduku Military Base in northern Natal. Theron travelled there in a separate vehicle. During the drive one of the sedated victims partially recovered consciousness and made a half-hearted attempt to attack Bothma, despite being completely incoherent and disorientated.

He and Theron had a good laugh about it later.

They used a section of the base that Theron declared as 'off limits' to members of the Zulu Battalion housed in the camp. Their purpose was to experiment with two different chemical substances in ointment form which they thought might be useful in eliminating victims. If the guinea pigs died in the process, it was of no great moment as their bodies could be disposed of in the usual manner. The ointments, together with doses of Scoline and Tubarine, had been brought by Bothma.

They spent the day smearing the ointment at set intervals on the bodies and between the legs of the victims. They wore rubber gloves as a precautionary measure, but despite this they got some ointment on their own skins but suffered no ill effects. Nor did the guinea pigs, who had been far more liberally contaminated than they.

It was the day of the Tricameral Referendum and during the course of the day Theron and Bothma managed to slip away from their work to vote at the Mtubatuba town hall.

In the evening the prisoners were chained to trees, apparently with leg irons and handcuffs. Theron claims they were given food, clothing and blankets but this seems unlikely. In the circumstances it seems more likely that they were once again heavily sedated and left alone. The callous behaviour of Bothma and Theron, after a hard day's furthering the cause of science, hardly indicates they would have allowed the welfare of their prisoners to disturb their own evening meals, maybe a few cold beers and a good night's sleep.

They returned to the prisoners the next morning to finish them off, no doubt after hot coffee and a hearty breakfast. They were academically surprised to find that one of the prisoners had spent the entire night trying to free himself. In desperation he had almost succeeded in sawing through the tree with his chains.

Theron and Bothma, indifferent to their prisoners' fate, took turns injecting them with fatal doses of Ketelaar, Scoline and Tubarine. Meanwhile, Matie van der Linde had arrived from Pretoria with the Seneca and the bodies were loaded aboard. Van der Linde flew out to sea and the bodies were dumped off St Lucia.

On an operation some time between '1983 and 1986', Theron ordered Phaal to be at Pretoria's Waterkloof Air Base early one morning. He was told that he would be met by 'someone' who would hand him a substance. It was something they wanted to test. He was to fly with this substance to Ondangwa in SWA/Namibia where the victim would be identified to him. The 'someone' who met him turned out to Dr Wouter Basson himself, who was attired in civvies. Basson handed him a small bottle about the size of an eyedrop dispenser. He was told to mix the substance with orange juice and induce the victim to drink it. He was to wait at Ondangwa until the victim showed signs of illness, then take him over and return with him by the first available flight to Pretoria where he would be admitted to 1-Military Hospital.

Phaal presented himself at the detention centre at Fort Rev and introduced himself as a doctor. An intelligence officer who was expecting him, took him to see a SWAPO soldier in the cells. The man appeared to be in good health. After conversing with him for a while, he offered him an orange juice laced with the substance from Basson. The prisoner drank it gratefully.

The next morning an alarmed intelligence officer summoned Phaal to the detention centre and told him the prisoner was ill. When he entered the cell, he saw he was in bad shape. There was blood on his calves, in the toilet bowl and on the floor. It was apparent he had suffered an extensive loss of blood. Phaal arranged for him to be flown by the first available transport aircraft to the major military base at Grootfontein. From there he accompanied him when he was casevaced to Pretoria. During the flight he injected him with a substance a doctor at Ondangwa had given him. An ambulance awaited his arrival at Waterkloof Air Base and the crew took over the patient. Phaal did not know any of them. Some time later Basson told Phaal that the prisoner had died.

During 1985 plans were made to eliminate Peter Kalangula, a SWAPO-sympathising local administration official in SWA/Namibia. Trevor Floyd was briefed by Major-General Kat Liebenberg in person. He furnished details of Kalangula's car and where it was parked during office hours. His house presented a difficulty because it was guarded around the clock. What would he need to assassinate the man, General Liebenberg asked.

Floyd asked if there was a toxin available which if smeared on the car's door handle and touched could prove fatal.

General Liebenberg said he would ask Basson.

Dr Daan Goosen was party to discussions at Roodeplaat Research Laboratories with Doctors Basson and Immelman regarding something to smear on car door handles. The substance chosen was drawn from the range of organophosphates, because prior research had shown it was easily absorbable through the skin. An ointment was needed as a carrier, so dimethyl sulphate oxide (DMSO) was selected because its absorbing properties were akin to the toxin.

One Sunday afternoon Floyd took his wife with him to visit Basson at a townhouse in what he recalled was the Sunnyside suburb of Pretoria. A woman employed as a secretary at Speskop was there with him. Mrs Floyd chatted to her while Floyd and Basson discussed business.

Basson gave him a small plastic pill box of dark brown ointment, a pair of white surgical gloves and a pair of black gloves. He told him how the ointment should be applied to a doorhandle and warned him it was essential he wear both pairs of gloves as a precautionary measure. He provided him with an antidote for immediate use in case of accidental contamination, but warned that in that event, he should also seek immediate medical attention as the stuff was potent. He promised it would start to work virtually immediately after contact was made with the skin.

Floyd flew to Tsumeb, picked up a car and drove to Ondangwa. He found the parking lot and after locating Kalangula's car outside the administration offices, he pulled in next to it. Unfortunately, a security guard was vigilantly patrolling the lot which made it difficult for him to get out and apply the ointment. It was an open area and his tampering would have been observed. Another problem was that Ondangwa, being a main SAAF as well as a Recce base, had numerous SADF personnel stationed there who would recognise him. He waited for as long as he dared, then abandoned the plan and drove back to Tsumeb. He telephoned General Liebenberg to report his failure and was told to abort the mission.[8]

Major Brian knew of another occasion when such ointment was utilised. He had seen a *Project Barnacle* eliminator, Sergeant Rocky van Blerk, in possession of a small plastic bottle similar to those used for ladies' face creams. It contained a clear jelly-like substance intended for application to front door or car door handles. Van Blerk also possessed a small syringe in a packet which was an antidote, he told Major Brian.

In November 1985 Major-General Joep Joubert took over from General Kat Liebenberg as the Commanding General Special Forces.

Project Barnacle 1982

Project Barnacle operators were stretched thin on the ground. This was not surprising because they were responsible for areas as widely spread as Lesotho, Swaziland, Mozambique, Botswana, Zambia and Zimbabwe.

Trained intelligence and reconnaissance operators were at a premium. The majority of *Barnacle's* people were fighters from the Rhodesian Security Forces, from ZANLA or from ZIPRA, who were untrained in intelligence work. Despite this they had no option but to utilise as best as they could those who showed promise.

They would have dearly liked to recruit trained operatives from the ex-Rhodesian community — policemen with intelligence experience and former Selous Scouts — people of their own kind. But this was forbidden, despite the rapid escalation of their success rate. It is fair to say that their contribution to the SADF's intelligence coffers was almost inestimable.

Their comrades-in-arms in the ranks of the Recces soon recognised their worth, both operationally and in the intelligence field, and it was not long before they were given the nickname of the 'Super Recces'. High praise indeed from such seasoned fighters, but militarily, it was justified.

On 31 July 1981 they assassinated Joe Gqabi, the ANC's chief representative in Harare, in an operation carried out against an ANC facility in Mabelreign, Harare.[9]

On the night of 16-17 August 1981 there was a huge explosion at Inkomo Barracks. The barracks, the former home base of the Selous Scouts, had been used as the main national armoury for the countless tons of military equipment, weapons and ammunition handed in by both guerrilla armies after ZANU-PF's win in the 1980 elections. It had been moved there from dozens of assembly points around the country. In addition, ZANLA's Mozambique armouries from the war days had been emptied and the contents brought there by the trainload for storage. The air force also kept a stock of 455kg and 900kg bombs there. It had all been stored in underground bunkers. Its value in total was estimated at Z$36 million.

The police arrested the culprit, Captain Patrick Gericke. He was an officer with the Zimbabwe Engineers, but he was also a covert member of South Africa's Special Forces. In a daring rescue *Barnacle* operators kidnapped the police officer investigating the case, forced him to release Gericke from the police cells and then flew them all, including the policeman and his family, to South Africa.[10]

In May 1982 *Barnacle* operators mounted an impeccably planned raid on the Air Force of Zimbabwe's base at Thornhill, Gweru, and all but destroyed its strike jet capability.[11] (The full story of these operations can be found in *Cry Zimbabwe: Independence Twenty Years On* by Peter Stiff)

By the end of 1982 the then new Commanding General Special Forces, Major-General Kat Liebenberg, addressed the staff shortages by concentrating on the introduction of South Africans into the system as understudies. Areas were split up. The urban scene remained under Brian, but sub-commanders were introduced to handle different countries. Mozambique had an officer, Botswana another, Lesotho someone else and so on.

The South Africanisation of the organisation proceeded without subtlety. The commander, Major Neil, was a senior officer with hardened experience in covert warfare, but he neither trusted nor got on with Major-General Liebenberg. He also made it plain that he opposed Lieberberg's plan to turn *Project Barnacle* into a unit conducting operations within South Africa.

Major Charl Naudé was drafted in from the Recces as Neil's second-in-command. Shortly afterwards, to Neil's chagrin, Charl was promoted to commandant, suddenly reversing their positions. Not surprisingly, Neil resigned his commission in August 1982 and *Project Barnacle* lost its founding commander.

His parting message was: 'If anyone ever wants to talk to me about [returning to] *Barnacle*, they had better come with a wheelbarrow full of gold.'

He put his military career behind him and became a successful businessman.[12]

Operations: Mozambique/Swaziland: late 1980s

Johnny, a former detective inspector with the Special Branch of the British South Africa Police of Rhodesia and a South African by birth, commenced duties with *Project Barnacle*'s intelligence wing and was later given a false identity and infiltrated into the ANC to work in Mozambique and Swaziland. He pointed out that although agents such as the SAP's Colonel Craig Williamson had infiltrated the ANC and did an excellent job working with their intellectuals in Geneva, the dangers there bore little comparison to being side by side with MK in black states like Mozambique, Tanzania and Zambia. In that situation, law meant nothing and a single mistake meant your untimely death.

Craig Williamson, however, was once responsible for saving his life. The SAP's Vlakplaas commander, Captain Dirk Coetzee and his turned MK guerrillas — 'Askaris' — were heavily committed to anti-ANC operations in Swaziland. Askaris at the border post spent their time behind one-way glass seeking out ANC sympathisers. While Johnny was living in an ANC safe house in Swaziland he passed through the border from South Africa and was indicated as a dangerous MK cadre by an Askari who had worked with him in Mozambique. He was targeted for assassination by the Security Police's C1 unit based at Vlakplaas.

Fortunately, Craig Williamson was liaising with the military at about this time and it was mentioned by someone that they had an agent engaged in intelligence work staying in the safe house in question. Williamson told the police and there was all hell to pay between the Security Police and the SADF. The police regarded Swaziland as their turf because of their excellent relationship with the Swaziland Police; they were upset that the army was operating there without their knowledge.

Johnny heard later that the police squad tasked to kill him were actually standing by at the border awaiting the word to go when they were told to stand down. Staying at the same house was Damian de Lange, an important MK cadre whose activities were until then unknown to the South African authorities. It was Johnny who fingered him to *Project Barnacle* who passed the information on to the Security Police.

Johnny moved in and out of Mozambique regularly, using the cover of being involved in an 'import and export' business. He was trusted and mixed with dignitaries in high places, both in the ANC and with the Mozambican authorities. On several occasions he was even entertained in the house of Graça, the widow of Samora Machel who later married Nelson Mandela.

On one unfortunate day Johnny was in a flat with FRELIMO military people he was collaborating with and a top ANC cadre who was their contact man. There was an unexpected knock on the door and soldiers with rifles and fixed bayonets barged in. A man tried to escape prompting the soldiers to open fire at random, but fortunately hitting no one.

A four and a half month spell of imprisonment in a Mozambique hell-hole followed. Johnny's main problem was the ANC contact man who had been in the flat, because they had no cover story of sufficient persuasion to explain his presence. In prison Johnny was isolated from the main body of prisoners and was guarded day and night by intelligence officers, who interrogated him constantly. He experienced a very rough time, but had little to say about the methods used in their attempts to break him, except that they were the 'usual' ones.

There were other South African whites in the prison with him, including a member of the notorious Stander gang of bank robbers. Some, including one who had only been caught in possession of a hunting rifle, had been there for seven years. Some of the others were South African intelligence officers, but not agents from *Project Barnacle*.

Being an experienced intelligence officer himself, it took Johnny little time to piece together what the opposition knew and what they did not know and he rigidly maintained his cover story. He also got word to his ANC colleague in detention with him, telling him he had not broken and urging him to also stick to their joint cover story. If either broke, they would both be doomed. Johnny was only too well aware that prisoners of FRELIMO's military wing were automatically assumed to be spies unless the contrary was proved and they were liable to be hauled before a firing squad without notice.

He listed his Maputo contacts for his interrogators and they were all approached and questioned about him. Fortunately they insisted he was one of the 'good guys'. The ANC even interfered in an attempt to broker their man's release, but FRELIMO would have none of it.

They interrogated Johnny continually for months. What concerned him most was that he was not being detained in the prison proper, which meant they could kill him without anyone being aware that he had ever been there. One morning he solved this problem by indulging in a sudden outburst of shouting and swearing at his interrogators. This, as expected, prompted them to transfer him to the prison punishment block for a spell of solitary confinement. Solitary or not, he soon found opportunities, by whispers and the surreptitious passing of notes, to make his identify known to other prisoners. Prisoners of FRELIMO, because of their odious conditions of confinement, were all brothers under the skin. One of them managed to pass word of his predicament to his family in South Africa, and through them to *Project Barnacle*.

There was no outburst of media publicity, but the South African government put immediate pressure on Mozambique for imprisoning an 'innocent' South African citizen. Much of the pressure arose from agreements contained in the Nkomati Accord.

While he was in the punishment block the Red Cross demanded entrance to the prison to establish the condition of prisoners there. FRELIMO were unable to refuse because of recent negotiations they had been conducting with the Red Cross. They steered them clear of the punishment block, but Johnny managed to toss a note out through the bars of his cell window which a Red Cross official picked up and read. He immediately demanded the right to inspect the punishment block, but the jailers refused saying it only contained newly arrested prisoners who had not even been processed. Days later FRELIMO was pressured into agreeing and the Red Cross did the inspection. But by then the detainees had been moved out for the duration of the inspection and the place had been cleaned up.

Then suddenly, after four and a half months in detention, warders broke the news to Johnny and another prisoner that they would soon be seeing their families again. They were being put on an aircraft and flown to South Africa. But the news did not delight Johnny because he knew there were no scheduled flights of any description that day, either in or out of Maputo.

Both prisoners were driven to the airport under armed guard. Johnny asked and was permitted to go to the toilet. Certain they were about to be shot, he decided to climb through the window and make a run for it. Once inside, though, he changed his mind because he did not want to desert his companion. So he left the toilet and returned to the guards, ready to take his chances. To his astonishment and relief, however, they were handed over to some South African officials of the Foreign Affairs Department and flown by chartered aircraft to South Africa.

Despite his narrow escape from death, it was Johnny's last operation. Shortly afterwards, in keeping with unofficial *Project Barnacle* policy, his services with the organisation were terminated. The SADF knew from experience how easy it had been to 'turn' captured MK and SWAPO cadres, so they harboured real fears that the enemy might successfully do the same with their own captured operators. Consequently former prisoners, as a matter of routine, were no longer trusted.[13]

Anti-ANC operation goes wrong: Zambia: January 1986

In late 1978 Sergeant Isaiah Moyo, a South African-born operator with 5-Recce, was moved to an undercover position to conduct external intelligence work. The TRC said he was a former member of the Rhodesian African Rifles, but this was untrue.[14] A black operator was more effective than a white one in black states like Zimbabwe and Botswana because it was easier for him to blend with the locals. He was moved to *Project Barnacle* shortly after its establishment.

After training as a driver, he was placed with a long distance road haulage company, Southern Enterprises, Alberton, on 10 January 1979. This was part of the process to building up his intelligence cover, civilianising him and teaching him the ropes. Sometimes the proprietors of such haulage companies were aware of the identities of their drivers, at other times not. Later, the SADF formed its own transport companies as cover for intelligence operations beyond South Africa's borders. In 1979, however, they were still feeling their way. Rhodesian Intelligence had found such driver-agents invaluable during the years of the Bush War. Not only were they well positioned to seek intelligence, but their vehicles were available for smuggling weapons, explosives and so on in cleverly concealed compartments, into the countries they visited.[15]

Moyo's job involved driving to countries as far afield as Botswana, Swaziland, Malawi, Zaïre and Zambia, where he built up sources and established new contacts. Zambia, where the ANC was headquartered, was an especially important area.

Moyo mixed well and made friends easily. Through contacts with the ANC, established by himself or passed on to him by South African Intelligence, he provided his handler with a steady stream of intelligence.

On 15 January 1986, using the genuine cover that he was on leave for three months, he went to Zambia on an intelligence gathering operation. He was provided with ample funds that he had every reason to possess. As a driver he was well paid and received leave pay, generous trip bonuses and 'nights out' payments.

Driving a Datsun 1400 pick-up registered in Botswana, Moyo drove into Lusaka on 17 January. He booked into the Masiya Motel in the Lilanda Compound to the west of the city. He was given room 13, a number that would certainly be unlucky for him. The motel offered several advantages. Firstly, it was cheap, with tariffs ranging from 13 to 25 Zambian Kwacha per night. Secondly, and more relevant to the collection of intelligence, it was owned by Mrs Betty Kaunda, the President's wife, and was used as a watering hole by ANC exiles. Many active members of MK living under the auspices of the United Nations High Commissioner for Refugees, attended regularly.

Being South African and a voice from home, he soon developed friendships and contacts. He had plenty of money so he could afford to be generous when it came to rounds of drinks. The exiles possessed little or nothing, so he passed on well received gifts of clothing and money.

It seems likely that as well as making friends, some of whom he managed to recruit as South African agents — a ticklish and dangerous task when alone and beyond assistance in a hostile foreign country like Zambia — Moyo also aroused suspicions. Undoubtedly, the longer he stayed the greater were the chances of him being unmasked as a spy. His persistent questioning of exiles was undoubtedly reported to the authorities, who probably placed him under surveillance.

Whatever the case, he planned to drive back to South Africa via Botswana, on Monday 31 March. He intended making an early start, leaving the motel at 04:30. His departure was no secret and he spent a lot of time saying cheerful goodbyes to his friends in the bar on the Sunday evening. At 23:30, just after he had retired for the night, his room was cordoned by a 30-strong task force of heavily armed policemen from the secret C5 Group. Soldiers burst in and arrested Moyo without a warrant on 'government orders' as an 'espionage suspect'. They confiscated his belongings including clothing, blankets, a radio and R4 000 in cash and travellers cheques. At the police station they shared out his cash and belongings while he looked on. When he protested, saying they were treating him as if he were dead, they assured him he soon would be.

In April 1986, a month after Moyo's arrest, *Project Barnacle* became the CCB.

Moyo was detained variously at the Kamwala Remand Prison, the Lilayi Police Training Centre, C-5s 'anti-robbery' centre and the Mukobeko Maximum Security Prison. They did everything they could to break him — to get him to confess he was a South African spy. He was assaulted continually, hung upside down with his head in a bucket of water, beaten with rubber hoses, had his private parts tied with cord and subjected to a tug o' war, branded with hot irons and had his toe and finger nails ripped out with pliers.

At the Lilayi Police Training Centre, when all other methods failed, they called in police recruit squads to work him over with their boots. Resulting from this he began vomiting blood and was taken to a hospital. One wonders if such officially authorised torture was regarded as standard training by the Zambian Police.

During his travails he witnessed other prisoners under interrogation being subjected to far worse horrors, like being forced to eat their own noses, ears and private parts. Many died at the hands of their interrogators. What undoubtedly saved his life was being gazetted as a 'State President's Prisoner'. This made him a political pawn and too valuable to murder.

On 7 August 1987 he appeared in the High Court on a charge of espionage relating to allegations that he had spied on the ANC — a particularly questionable charge considering the ANC did not even possess the status of a government-in-exile in Zambia. The 'confessions' Moyo had made 'freely and voluntarily' to his interrogators were rejected after he showed the court branding-iron marks on his body and displayed his lack of toe and finger nails.

Despite this, after a trial where uncorroborated hearsay evidence was admitted throughout the proceedings, he was found guilty as charged on 28 March 1988. The learned judge sentenced him to 75 years in prison. The even more learned judges of appeal reduced this to a mere 50-year term. This was despite the maximum sentence for espionage under Zambian law being 25 years. So much for legal learnedness!

Amnesty International espoused his cause as did the Rev Peter Hammond of Frontline Fellowship, Cape Town, who met him in prison when he was himself detained for conducting 'subversive' Christian missionary activities.

The SADF, at first, did what they could behind the scenes, but a senior officer told the author that during the late 1980s their efforts dropped to virtually zero, only to be occasionally revived by the agitation of his former comrades in 5-Recce. Perhaps it was because when he was arrested he belonged to *Project Barnacle*, so the CCB did not consider him one of their own.

After 5-Recce's commander, Colonel Corrie Meerholz, died in questionable circumstances on 21 November 1989, Colonel Bert Sachse again took over the regiment as commanding officer. Sergeant Moyo's wife had been given employment with the unit at Phalaborwa after his capture. She asked Sachse if he could do anything about getting him released. He looked into the matter and discovered that Moyo, no doubt because he was black and not white, was a forgotten prisoner. The SADF was doing virtually nothing.

Sachse spoke to the Red Cross, the Department of Foreign Affairs and generally made a nuisance of himself, demanding that they engineer Moyo's release.

In 1990, following Nelson Mandela's release from prison in South Africa, all South African political prisoners, except for Isaiah Moyo, were released from Zambian prisons. But 5-Recce's agitation finally paid off when he was finally given a presidential pardon on 7 April 1991. He was released and deported to South Africa. He credited his survival to his unquestioning Christian faith.[16]

On his return to 5-Recce, because he had not seen his wife for more thanfive years, the two of them were booked into a small hotel in Pretoria for a few days with the minimum of publicity; then they went off together with their children to Durban for a well-deserved holiday. Afterwards Moyo was put through the standard 'head-shrinking' process with army psychologists, before resuming duty with the regiment as a uniformed sergeant.

Eventually he received back pay for his five years in prison, but a sour note crept in when the Staff Officer Finance SADF refused to authorise payment to him of operational allowances for the time he spent in prison. It had been standard practice in such cases, because although the man had been imprisoned, he had clearly been operational. An even sourer noter intruded when Moyo examined his pay slip and was concerned to discover that all expenses relating to his Durban holiday had also been deducted. Despite representations by Colonel Sachse, the deductions remained.

So much for a grateful SADF. It must be said that white Afrikaans-speaking prisoners on their return from captivity were certainly not treated in the same scurrilous manner.[17]

Zambian Reconnaissance: 1986

During early 1986 Brian and a colleague conducted a reconnaissance in Zambia. Their task was to seek out ANC targets, noting and photographing them. They posed as visiting South African businessmen intent on expanding business with Zambia.

In Zambia, police and army roadblocks were commonplace and negotiating a passage through them was routine. One merely presented identification and produced the other necessary papers and one was waved through. Unfortunately, at one roadblock, an over-zealous, young and distinctly anti-white Zambian policeman arrested them on suspicion of being spies without any grounds whatsoever.

Six weeks of beatings and torture involving the 'water treatment' and electrodes being attached to various parts of their bodies followed. They were crammed with as many as 80 other prisoners into cells designed to hold a fraction of that number. Invariably one or two corpses were removed from the cells each morning. Eventually, after Brian's wife in South Africa got word of his predicament, she sent 20 000 Kwachas from her own resources to a Zambian lawyer to get them out. They were released after being in custody for six weeks.

Special Forces never refunded the 20 000 Kwachas to Brian. This and other factors decided him to resign from *Project Barnacle*. He handed over to his number two, Alan.

Brian advised his sources on leaving that he was out of the picture. Having been through the particularly bad personal experience in Zambia, he advised them to follow his example and 'duck out' too as he did not believe the South Africans would look after them if things went wrong. However, most decided to continue.[18] Some would live to regret it.

7

Absolute Power/Absolute Corruption
Transkei and Ciskei
1970s and 1980s

Quest for apartheid's Utopia

Many inexplicable things have occurred in South Africa, but perhaps the strangest was when in the quest for apartheid's Utopia, John Vorster's National Party administration declared Transkei a state independent of South Africa. On 26 October 1976 at the stroke of a pen — despite a storm of protests nationally and internationally, some three million native South Africans of Transkei origin — were transformed overnight into foreigners in the land of their birth.

It turned the territory into a dumping ground for workless black 'foreigners' unwanted in greater South Africa. Both the Transkei and South African governments insisted that the popular support by Transkeians for the independence move was overwhelming. But this was based on political interest and the flimsiest of foundations.

Chief Kaiser Matanzima had been South Africa's protégé, their man in Umtata for many years. In 1956 he was officially reprimanded for posing as the Chief of the Emigrant Thembus, but within two years Pretoria confirmed him in that appointment over the head of his paramount chief. He was closely related to the ANC leader, Nelson Mandela, and the land that had spawned them both had been the cradle of the ANC and the PAC.[1]

In pursuance of the National Party government's policy of supporting tribal institutions and the hereditary tribal élite — which was a means of offsetting the influence and popularist support for the ANC and PAC — in 1955 it ensured that Transkei's Bunga was packed with chiefs and headmen. When considering a self-governing constitution for the territory, they recommended that a future parliament should comprise 64 chiefs and only 45 elected members. In the first election in 1963, Matanzima's Transkei National Independence Party (TNIP) was brought to power, with himself as Chief Minister, by the support of 42 chiefs and only 12 elected members. Understandably satisfied with the way things had worked out, Matanzima entrenched the system.

That he would gain the support of the majority of chiefs against opponents with more democratic processes in mind was inevitable. Their futures depended on him. The Transkei, more so than in many other African states, had perpetuated the traditionalist aspects of African productive practices, as well as the organisational linchpin of such practices, viz the chieftainship principle. So the political leadership in the Transkei was vitally dependent upon the support of this traditional leadership category and from the point of view of its own political survival, the TNIP would, to put it bluntly, be committing political suicide were it to fly in the face of traditionalism and all that it entails.

Chiefs were effectively protected against boisterous criticism at election meetings by the provisions of the notorious Proclamation R400 which provided that any person 'who makes a verbal or written statement, or does any act which is intended or which is likely to have the effect of subverting or interfering with the authority of the State . . . or any chief or headman, is guilty of an offence.' This proclamation also laid down that official permits had to be obtained for all meetings at which ten or more 'natives' were present. Needless to say, the opposition Democratic Party (DP) experienced great difficulty in obtaining such permits.[2]

A major issue in Transkei was the question of illiterate voters, where according to Benbo, a South African government research body, there was an illiteracy rate of 56,1% in 1970.[3] Elsewhere in Africa, to ensure voting secrecy and as an alternative to using names, easily recognisable symbols representing particular political parties or candidates — elephants, cockerels and so on — were and are printed on ballot papers. In the interests of secrecy the voter marks 'X' against his chosen symbol, folds his vote and drops it into the box.

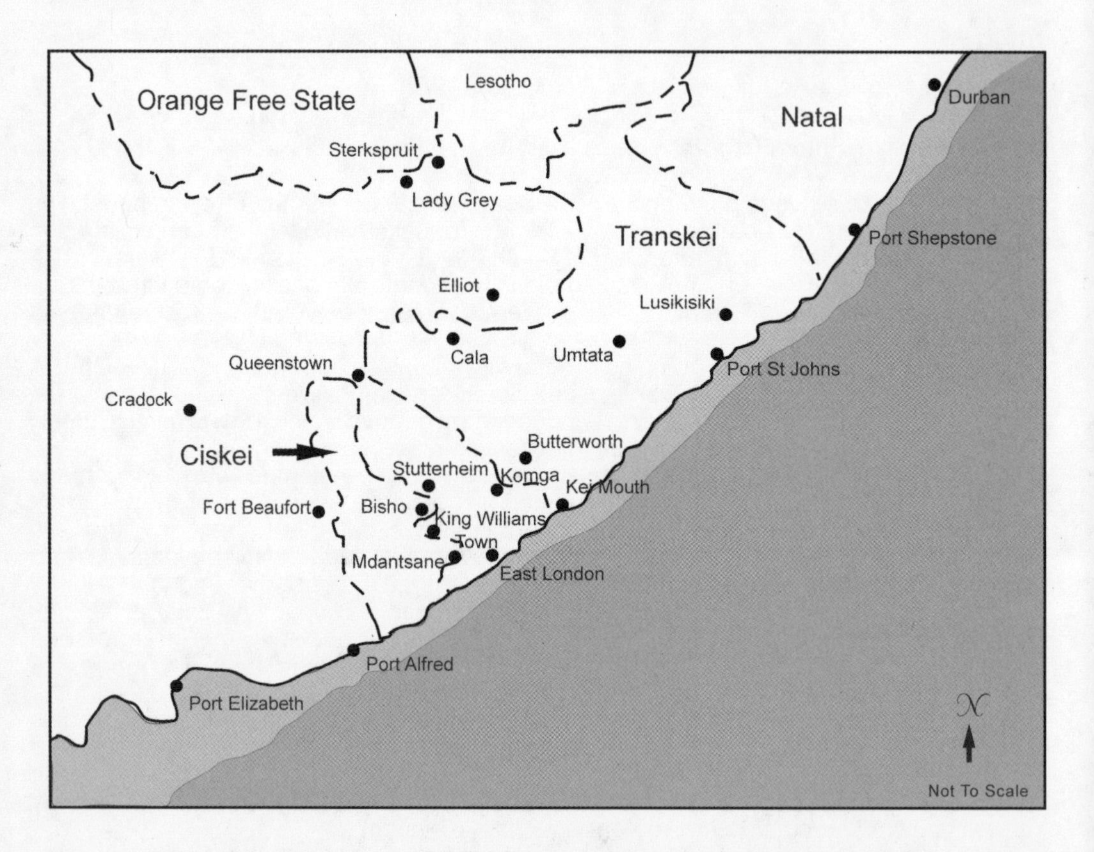

Map of the Eastern Cape showing the former Republics of Transkei and Ciskei.

This idea was rejected in Transkei in favour of the candidates' names being read to the voter by an election official in the presence of two witnesses. The voter notified his choice, the official completed the ballot paper on the voter's behalf and the witnesses confirmed the correctness of the vote. For more than half the electorate this clever system dispensed with the conceit of polling booths, secret ballots and other election frippery.[4]

The election officials were either headmen or Transkei civil servants, many of whom held office at the behest of the ruling TNIP. In the case of headmen, the peasant voters relied on them exclusively for their land, tribal largesse and miserable subsistence existence. So at polling stations where an election official had a known party loyalty, when the ballot boxes were opened and the votes counted, it was no surprise to anyone that his party sometimes achieved a 100% vote.[5]

While the 1976 elections were not in themselves rigged in favour of Matanzima's TNIP, the electoral system most certainly was. The Legislative Assembly by then was composed of 75 chiefs, elected by an electoral college of Transkei's traditional leaders, and 75 popularly elected members.[6]

There was also the regime's reckless use of the Emergency Regulations. Shortly before the 1976 election, Chief Minister Matanzima issued a stern warning in the Legislative Assembly that those opposed to his policies should use constitutional means to express themselves. Immediately afterwards the police launched a three-day round up of members of the opposition Democratic Party. Thrown into the cells were the DP's only two members of the Legislative Assembly and four other candidates besides. This prevented all six from being nominated for the election and scared off most of the other DP candidates. Three others who managed to register were also immediately arrested and detained. It was a miracle, and a disappointment to Matanzima, that the DP got even one seat.[7] But with the election attracting a mere 43,4% poll, the TNIP could hardly boast of a landslide victory.

Matanzima, nevertheless, welcomed the results as an 'unqualified victory for independence'. To ensure it remained unqualified, he side-stepped a referendum, putting the question instead to meetings of tribal bodies, public bodies, urban boards, the civil service association — some 229 bodies in all. All meetings were publicly held under the frightening umbrella of pro-Matanzima chiefs, all armed with draconian powers which they were only too willing to use against dissidents.

The published results surpassed belief, with 148 of the bodies polled failing to raise a single dissenting voice against the independence issue. Of the 60 urban boards scattered around the country, 53 registered unanimously affirmative verdicts.[8]

On the eve of independence, students at Jongilizwe College in Umtata held a debate on the issue. The vice-head prefect was remembered by his fellows as being vehemently opposed to it. He was the son of Chief Bazindlovu Holomisa of the Amagebe clan, a young man named Bantubonke, but more usually called Bantu.[9]

Paramount Chief Botha Sigcau became Transkei's first president and Chief Kaiser Matanzima its first prime minister.

The popularity of South Africa's independence grant was best illuminated by the 30 000 people of the Herschel district who fled to the remote Thornhill area of the Ciskei rather than live in Matanzima's independent wonderland of Transkei.[10]

Independence brought the benefit — if it can be called that — of the pomp and ceremony of a South African ambassador to the state capital of Umtata. As an equal of his brother diplomats in Washington, London and Paris, the ambassador affected a tailcoat with a broad green sash and a Paul Kruger-type high hat for ceremonial occasions — prompting the South African drag artiste and political satirist, Peter Dirk Uys, to appoint himself as ambassador to the imaginary homeland state of Bapeticosweti.

It also brought Matanzima the windfall of a R2 million palace, built at the South African taxpayer's expense, which with great pomp and ceremony was handed over by Foreign Minister Pik Botha. It had been designed as a prestigious status symbol that was said to be 'the best of its kind in the whole of southern Africa'. It was, perhaps, a little too prestigious for an area described as one of the poorest in the world.[11] It would be pertinent to ask who got the construction contract and how it was awarded. The building of luxury palaces for homeland leaders was par for the independence course. This applied equally to the construction of 'Independence Stadiums', a horrendously expensive essential, that no self-respecting homeland leader could function without — particularly as it was financed by the South African taxpayer. Even KwaZulu got an Independence Stadium, even though it resisted moves to push it into 'independence'. Those behind the construction company's bit obviously could not wait.

Many of Transkei's newly promoted black bureaucrats, barely tutored in the administrative rules of running things, set out to emulate the systems of their predecessors. At the new border post on the Kei River Bridge they introduced

'Arrival/Departure' forms identical to those used at ports of entry by the South African Immigration Department. The South African versions were passed to BOSS — Bureau of State Security — who used them as a tool to keep track of 'undesirables' — whatever that term meant at the time. The Transkei versions, which were badly photocopied from the South African example, had a less sinister destination as the author learned to his relief in 1977 after completing a form preparatory to crossing the Kei River Bridge to enter the territory.

'What happens to those things?' he asked.

The uniformed policeman, doubling as an immigration official, obligingly flung open the door of a huge cupboard. It was jammed-packed from top to bottom with dusty and yellowing bundles of the same forms.

'We put them in the cupboard', he volunteered obligingly.

Matanzima consolidated his position and silenced his opponents by rubber-stamping legislation through Parliament. The most important items were the Republic of Transkei Constitution Act that banned any meaningful discussion about the president and the Public Security Act that made it treasonable to advocate the reunification of Transkei with South Africa. Except for this, the act was a rework of South African security legislation. He embarked on a tyrannical campaign of preventative detentions, prosecutions and persecutions. Those convicted were stripped of official, tribal or other offices held — even though, usually, their only crime lay in suggesting that Matanzima was an ass. This high minded policy of dispensing with tainted administrators, however, had not prejudiced his brother George's appointments first as the minister of justice and later as prime minister. Big brother conveniently overlooked his having been ignominiously struck off the roll of attorneys in the Eastern Cape in 1963 for the peccadillo of fraudulently misappropriating trust funds.[12]

Another effective tool was the banishment of opponents to remote areas of the Transkei where they were out of the way and could not create further problems for the regime. Those remote areas became Transkei's Siberia. As Colonel Ngceba, the Transkei's Commissioner of Police, so chillingly said in 1979: 'The government has the right to banish anybody.'[13]

Economically the territory was a disaster. In 1976 its per capita domestic product was a mere R70 per annum and its per capita income was little better at R175 per annum. It was overpopulated, had a minimum of industry and its top soil was fast eroding into the sea from over grazing. Its main source of revenue was derived from the remitted salaries of Transkeians working in South Africa. Its second-best revenue source was dagga (marijuana) which even grows wild there. The true value of this crop is difficult to assess, because it is illegal in all aspects — growing, possession, dealing and smoking — but in 1981 it was estimated at between R6 and R12 million rand per annum.

Transkei's politicians, many of whom made fortunes from the drug, tended to close their eyes to the trade. In 1979 Colonel Funani of the Transkei Police remarked that there was even an informal auction market for it in the Libode area where dealers bid against each other to get the best. This illustrates the depth of the problem.[14]

In 1976 South Africa paid the Transkei subsidies to the tune of R135 million to keep it afloat. By the financial year 1980/81 this had risen to R231 million and the subsidies continued to rise by leaps and bounds every year. Transkei's economy was inextricably bound up with South Africa's. It was not separate and never could be.

Waste, nepotism and corruption became the hallmarks of Transkei. President Kaiser Matanzima, Prime Minister George Matanzima and other leaders made personal fortunes for themselves while, as Paramount Chief Sabata Dalindyebo accurately and publicly put it: 'Everyone else was living on shit'.

For that gem of *crimen majestatis* he was convicted of acts 'calculated to violate the dignity or injure the reputation of the President of Transkei' and deposed from office as paramount chief. Poor Chief Sabata eventually died in exile in Zambia.[15]

In 1979 Kaiser Matanzima proclaimed himself president, then in an exercise of grand nepotism, he appointed his younger brother George as prime minister. Kaiser retained executive powers, though, and cabinet meetings were normally held in his office.

Their late father, Chief Mhlolo Mvuzo Matanzima Mtirara, was another man with an eye for the main chance. He named his eldest son, who was born in 1915, after Kaiser Wilhelm when he believed Germany would win in World War I. He named his younger son, born in 1918, after King George V, when he saw that Great Britain was coming out the winner.

Not only were the Matanzimas paid large state incomes, plus tribal incomes and given luxurious mansions at the expense of the long-suffering South African taxpayer. They also acquired a string of private farms, substantial interests in a hotel chain, and dug their thieving fingers deep into the pies of untold other business enterprises. When the *Sunday Times* lifted the lid on some of this, it prompted President Kaiser Matanzima to ask plaintively: 'What is wrong with ministers of state taking shares in public and private companies?'

In 1987, after their removal from office, a judicial commission of enquiry identified a total loss to the country since 1976 of R45 million as a result of 'legally doubtful' directives from the Matanzimas. For example, the commission cited numerous directives, many only verbal, ordering the sale of properties bought by the South African government for disposal through the Transkei Development Corporation. On average they were sold at 10% of their market value, many to companies in which the Matanzimas held majority interests. The Transkei Breweries, with an established value of R7 million, was bargain-basemented at a mere R700 000. There were kickbacks or *lobola* (bride price), as it was euphemistically called in Transkei government circles. For the exclusive gambling rights to the Wild Coast Sun and its assignee, which ultimately became the Sun International subsidiary Transun, Kaiser demanded a R2 million kickback from the multi-millionaire entrepreneur Sol Kerzner for himself and his cronies.[16]

On 20 February 1986 Kaiser Matanzima resigned his presidency to resume his paramount chieftaincy of Western Thembuland. Paramount Chief Tutor Ndamase was elected to take his place. Despite this Kaiser retained his seat in the national assembly and remained the power behind the throne of Prime Minister George.[17]

Ciskei joins the homelands club

Since the earliest days of white rule, Transkei and Ciskei had been administered separately. Deep-seated hostilities, differences and blood feuds going back nearly 200 years were said to exist between the two Xhosa factions. Whatever the truth of that the reality in the late 1970s was that Transkei's leaders favoured the idea of all Xhosa-speaking people being unified in a single homeland, while Ciskei's leaders favoured it becoming a separate state. In opting for independent homeland status, the leaders of both territories adopted identical positions. While they were in favour of ending white domination in South Africa as a whole, it would take many years to achieve. In the meantime, opting for homeland independence was an interim stage by which blacks could achieve partial self rule without having to wait until white power was toppled.

In 1978 Chief Minister Lennox Sebe, leader of the Ciskei National Independence Party (CNIP) and Pretoria's favoured leader, appointed a commission of enquiry under the chairmanship of Professor G Quail, to enquire into the feasibility of Ciskeian independence.[18] It presented its report on 11 February 1980, but its findings for an independent Ciskei were discouraging. Infant mortality was high, more than 30% of infants were suffering from malnutrition, health services were inadequate, there was a serious housing shortage, there was-overcrowding due to a shortage of land, farm land was over-grazed and over-cultivated and the per capita output was worth no more than R40 per annum. 25% of the population were unemployed.

The commission was critical of the proposed citizenship agreement with South Africa that would come into force on independence, calling it 'denationalisation on ethnic lines'. A survey by the commission to test Ciskei public opinion found the overwhelming majority were opposed to independence. 90% favoured universal adult suffrage in a unitary political system (within South Africa). 70% opted for a federal structure as the next best alternative. Dealing with the question of one ethnic grouping dominating others, 60% insisted that Africans, whatever their tribal roots, were one people.

The commissioners ruled out independence unless the majority of Ciskeians, including those living outside the territory, voted affirmatively in a 'carefully supervised referendum', satisfactory citizenship arrangements were negotiated with South Africa, Ciskei was enlarged, the rights of Ciskeians to work in South Africa were retained and South Africa agreed to provide equitable financial support.

In an appendix, commissioner Professor Robert Rotberg lashed out at the use by Lennox Sebe's administration of preventative detention and banishments of the political opposition. He said the 'human rights of Ciskei' had been violated and 'breaches of accepted forms of democratic behaviour' were commonplace. Sebe said he viewed Rotberg's recommendations with contempt and had thrown them in his wastepaper basket.[19]

Sebe ignored the negative implications of the Quail Report and said that if South Africa accepted Ciskei's land claims, he would order an independence referendum. He said he would oppose independence if it meant surrendering South African citizenship and insisted on Ciskei's continued membership of the rand monetary area.

He repeated this on 30 September 1980 after meeting Dr Piet Koornhof, South Africa's Minister of Cooperation and Development. While not agreeing to all land incorporations demanded, Koornhof said R80 million would be used to buy another 100 000ha of land for the territory. Berlin, East London, King William's Town, Mdantsane, Zwelitsha and Ciskei would be promoted as a common economic development area for everyone within the region.[20]

A referendum was held on 4 December 1980. There were 503 000 registered voters, of whom 295 891 voted in favour of independence and 1 642 against. The percentage poll was 59,5%. Lennox Sebe's veiled threat to imprison those voting against independence played no small part in the result. The inexperienced opposition boycotted the poll instead of urging its supporters to vote 'no'.

In September 1980, after another meeting with Koornhof, Sebe announced a package deal. Ciskeians would retain dual nationality, the territory would include the land between the Stormberg and the Indian Ocean and all land between the Great Kei and the Great Fish Rivers. This included the so-called 'white corridor' of towns and farms running between Ciskei and Transkei.[21]

Before independence, this package deal, as Minister of Agriculture Rev Wilson Xaba would say, was 'stripped naked' by Koornhof and his team of experienced negotiators. Ciskeians lost their South African nationality and King William's Town and the white corridor between Transkei and Ciskei remained outside Ciskei.

Transkei's Prime Minister George Matinzima warned Sebe that the 'march of time would catch up on him'. He described the independence moves as the culmination of a systematic defiance of the natural leaders of Ciskei, who were scared of [Sebe's] wrath'.[22]

The Transkei made two thinly disguised bids through the Supreme (now High) Court to frustrate Ciskei's pending independence. The first related to boundary changes. In the second the court was asked to rule that independence was unlawful because it divided the Xhosa nation in breach of the Promotion of Black Self-Government Act, 1959. The court ruled that independence was a unilateral action by the South African government and neither Ciskeian citizens nor the Ciskeian government had any choice.[24]

Ciskei became 'independent' in December 1981. The only heads of state at the independence celebrations were South Africa's State President, Marais Viljoen, and

President Mphephu of Venda. The Transkei government declined an invitation to attend as the Matanzima brothers refused to sit down with Sebe.[25]

President Lennox Sebe announced the formation of the Central Ciskei Intelligence Service (CCIS) shortly afterwards. It would be in place of South Africa's Bureau for State Security (BOSS).[26]

President Kaiser had announced in October 1981 that he would be stepping down as president of Transkei in 1982, but shortly before Ciskei's 'independence', he changed his mind and said he would be staying on. Whether the Ciskei situation had anything to do with it is a moot point.

In terms of Ciskei's new constitution, the national assembly, like Transkei's, was loaded with traditional leaders to keep the African nationalists out. It consisted of 22 elected members, 33 nominated chiefs, a paramount chief and five members nominated by the president. Lennox Sebe was unanimously elected executive president. He appointed Rev Wilson Xaba vice-president.[27] In 1983 Sebe was elected life president by the National Assembly.

Two other 'independent' homeland states were created in the same era, Bophuthatswana and Venda. The four together, Transkei, Bophuthatswana, Venda and Ciskei, were called the 'TBVC' states. The driving idea behind the creation of homelands was to divide and rule the black population. Ostensibly, though, it was to allow the different 'tribal nations' to rule themselves. Some homelands, like KwaNdebele, KwaKwa and KwaZulu were granted self-governing status, but they did not become 'independent' like the TBVC states. The government had long wanted the Zulus to become independent, but led by the opposition of Chief Minister, Dr Gatsha (Mangosuthu) Buthelezi, this had long been resisted. Tribal areas, by their nature, are spread throughout South Africa in penny packets, some bits of the same ethnicity being hundreds of kilometres apart. Encompassing them into single ethnic homelands resulted in most being geographically fragmented.

It naturally followed, in all fairness, that if the black tribes had their own homelands, then it would be right and just for the white Afrikaner *volk* to also have theirs. And this would comprise the rest of non-tribal South Africa including all the major cities and ports, the best farmlands, most of the gold and other mines and the engines of industrial production. Places like Port Elizabeth, East London and the Border region in general were initially included, but that was envisaged as only a short term measure. These parts of the Eastern Cape were regarded as 1820 Settler country and the National Party government since its takeover in 1948 had deliberately marginalised the area as a means of weakening the 'English liberal vote'. As far as they were concerned, it could eventually be swallowed up by the homelands, or as they preferred to call them, the national states.

SADF establishes the Transkei Defence Force

Prior to independence the Transkei Defence Force (TDF), was established and trained by South Africa. A non aggression pact between the two countries followed, perhaps as a precautionary move to ensure that Transkei's 254 soldiers did not take it into their heads to launch a preemptive strike against South Africa!

With a defence budget of R1 342 000 in 1977, Kaiser Matanzima, wearing his cap as Minister of Defence, outlined plans for creating a Civil Defence division. In 1978, armed with an almost tripled defence budget of R3 651 000, he introduced moves to more than double the TDF's size to an establishment of 720 officers and men — the size of an enlarged infantry battalion. Plans were also made to create a second battalion.

From the outset Matanzima introduced a policy of commissioning chiefs' sons as officers in the TDF to gain and retain the support of chiefs.[28]

In 1979 preparations began to establish military bases in each of the Transkei's nine regions. In 1980 a form of national service was introduced. It was, George Matanzima the new Defence Minister, announced, to fight 'the terrorist onslaught' and Marxism which was the cause of 'disaster, destruction of innocent lives, robbery, banditry, orphans, widows and above all, chaos'. National service should be regarded as a 'fulfilment of a national obligation by Transkeian patriots'.[29]

There seems little doubt that the marked increases had been prompted by South Africa's desire for the Transkei to play its part in South Africa's 'total strategy' for dealing with the 'total onslaught'. There was, however, a particular need for the TDF to establish effective patrols along its vulnerable border with Lesotho, which MK had already been using as an infiltration route into South Africa.[30] In fact, if MK had gained free access by default of the TDF, there was a distinct danger they would have set up rear bases in some of the remoter areas of the Transkei.

The roles of the TDF fell conveniently within the parameters of South Africa's total strategy policy and were outlined in 1976 by the TDF's first chief, Brigadier Phil Pretorius, who had been seconded to take command by the SADF. He saw it as having a wider role than just defence, providing essential services like medical attention and supplies to rural communities and assisting where needed. The TDF would maintain roads, repair bridges and maintain farming equipment. 'Defence', he said, 'is not only with weapons, but through the hearts of the people'. This coincided exactly with the way the SADF felt about such matters.

The TDF's other role, of more direct concern to the Matanzimas, was its political one of keeping them in power no matter who opposed them, whether it was the ANC or an internal opposition party. But strengthening the army increased the possibility of a military coup.There was a reminder of this in January 1980 when three soldiers were arrested for distributing anonymous pamphlets calling for the military overthrow of the government.

Prime Minister Kaiser Matanzima broke off diplomatic relations with South Africa in 1978 after a refusal to hand land in Griqualand East over to Transkei. He also had expectations of attaining international recognition at the time and wrongly believed that would help to facilitate it. He followed this by cancelling the non aggression pact. He barred South African military aircraft from Transkei's airspace and its ships from its territorial waters. He also terminated an agreement by which the SADF trained the TDF.

The SADF withdrew Brigadier Pretorius. Brigadier Rodney Keswa, former chief of Transkei's Prison Service, assumed command of the TDF. Trained by the SADF as an understudy to succeed Brigadier Pretorius, he was untainted by allegations of corruption and inefficiency. He was also highly thought of in SADF and South African political circles and regarded, in the long term, as a possible successor to Kaiser Matanzima.

In March 1980 the non-aggression pact between Transkei and South Africa was reinstated. The Prime Minister and Minister of Defence, George Matanzima, said his ministry was studying a ten-year development plan for the TDF which would include the establishment of schools for infantry, signals, military engineers and armour.

Brigadier Keswa had began making military contacts all over the world. He travelled frequently to various countries for discussions on military matters and to arrange training courses. Major Bantu Holomisa, as he was then, frequently accompanied him on such missions and also travelled to foreign places alone as did other officers.

General Holomisa now believes this drew the attention of the SADF's Military Intelligence to Keswa, which began to harbour suspicions that he was an ANC sympathiser.[31]

Enter Abe Isaac Kaye and his pals

Doing good business with Transkei was Johannesburg tycoon, Abe Isaac Kivelowitz Kaye. Kaye's sprawling Greatermans Stores chain had a branch in every major South African town. His business empire's second leg was the pharmaceutical giant, Alumina.

Like the sharp businessman he was, Kaye saw numerous opportunities for turning a profit from the increasingly complex political situation. He had formed an association with

Gideon Henry 'John' Erasmus, an ex-Regimental Sergeant Major and heavyweight boxing champion of the Rhodesian Light Infantry. Commissioned at the tail end of his service, Erasmus moved to the Rhodesian Prime Minister's office after retirement and was posted to Johannesburg to assist RISCO (Rhodesian Iron and Steel Corporation), with its sanction-strapped exports.

Isaac Kaye twice financially supported National Party candidates in attempts to unseat Bryanston's PFP MP Horace van Rensburg. One of the unsuccessful hopefuls was John Erasmus.

By February 1980 Erasmus and SAP pensioner, General Johannes Frederick Kleinhans, were involved in Double S (Pty) Ltd, which specialised in security consultancy. The company had evolved from a wholly owned Greatermans subsidiary company originally formed as Hilson and Taylor in 1927. It had undergone various name changes and periods of dormancy before Erasmus and Kleinhans entered the scene. Isaac Kaye, as the major shareholder of Double S, made space for them in Greatermans' offices in Conlyn House, 156 President Street, Johannesburg. The name Double S (Pty) Ltd was changed to one with a better ring, Security Specialists International (Pty) Ltd.

Meanwhile, Lieutenant-Colonel Ronald Francis Reid Daly, the former commander of the Selous Scouts, had resigned from the Rhodesian Army in November 1979 and launched actions for civil damages against the Prime Minister and Minister of Defence, Bishop Abel Muzorewa; the army commander, Lieutenant-General John Hickman; and six other senior officers. This had arisen because Military Intelligence suspected the Selous Scouts 'were gun running, ivory poaching or even worse'. They bugged his telephone but Reid Daly found out.[32]

His subsequent direct action at an officers' cocktail party involving General Hickman, led to his court-martial. Ken Flower, Director of the Central Intelligence Organisation, suggested he had 'berated Hickman, with other officers present.' [33] More colourful media reports suggested the two had squared up 'medal to medal'.[34] Reid Daly put it that he had 'addressed those' present causing a 'wave of shock and consternation to my brother officers'.[35]

In June 1979 the court-martial found Reid Daly guilty and sentenced him to a reprimand. While this might appear a mere rap over the knuckles to the uninitiated, for a senior officer it is sufficient to spell an ignominious end to a career.

General Hickman, Ken Flower maintained, 'was not responsible for the [unconstitutional] bugging, yet General Walls, who was responsible for the Scouts and the Military Intelligence activities in question, let his brother officer [Hickman] take the rap to the extent that he was dismissed [from the service] on irrelevant evidence shortly afterwards.'[36]

Reid Daly's application to sue was refused by Mr Justice Waddington, who noted that he had not denied the ivory and weapons allegations in papers before the court. He appealed against this and was granted leave to sue, but by then 'I was forced by the circumstances of no longer being resident in the country of my birth, into dropping the matter'.[37]

Rhodesia's collapse led him to a job in Johannesburg with Security Scouts (Pty) Ltd, owned by ex-Selous Scout captain, Ant White. In April 1980 while addressing students at the Rand Afrikaans University, Reid Daly tactlessly referred to Premier Robert Mugabe and his former guerrillas as 'smelly gooks'. This prompted a *Sunday Times* editorial to thunder: 'No more gook talk here, Reid Daly'. The adverse publicity led to his resignation from Ant White's company. He never learned his lesson and as late as 1999 he was still persisting with the use of the racially offensive term 'gook' in public utterances.[38]

In June 1980 MK launched their spectacularly successful sabotage attack against Sasol. This won Security Specialists International (Pty) Ltd a contract to improve the security of the Sasol II installations at Secunda. A military notable was needed to front the operation and Reid Daly was available. Fortunately Reid Daly and Erasmus were old buddies, having served together as corporals in the Rhodesian Army.

Reid Daly joined the company as a director/security consultant. Erasmus and Kleinhans each had four shares, Reid Daly five and Veritas of Cape Town, wholly owned by Isaac Kaye, a generous15.

Reid Daly recruited several notable ex-Selous Scouts who both impressed and scared Sasol executives by crawling in and out of key areas of the complex, with blackened faces, at will and without detection. Obviously much was needed to improve security.

Meanwhile, a major contract to train the Transkei Defence Force began to simmer early in 1981. It appears the Matanzima brothers had begun to suspect their TDF commander, Brigadier Rodney Keswa, and other senior officers were not only playing free with army funds, but were also involved with the ANC. This view was undoubtedly encouraged by the SADF's Military Intelligence.

According to a 'Top Secret' document submitted to the TRC by Major-General Griebenauw of the Eastern Cape Security Police, Reid Daly had provided him with a summary of events which said that 'while in Secunda he was contacted by the Attorney-General of Transkei who introduced him to K D Matanzima. He wanted to know without a question of a doubt that it had the approval of the RSA. When returning to the RSA he discussed this incident with Brigadier [Daan] Hamman [Military Intelligence]. Brigadier Hamman promises to discuss this incident with his superiors. A few days later he was invited by Brigadier Hamman for lunch in Pretoria with Admiral du Plessis (Military Intelligence), Brigadier Francois Steenkamp (Security Police) and Brigadier Daan Hamman. After discussions with several Transkei cabinet ministers a contract was signed and his team took up service in the Transkei. He said a tight bond was built between the Transkei Defence Force and the SA Defence Force'.

The author understands it was not quite so open and shut as that.

Isaac Kaye certainly played a role in the introduction of Security Specialists International to the Matanzima brothers. With his silken tongue it must have been simple for him to boost the company's expertise in the military and intelligence fields, particularly considering that the almost legendary 'tough as teak' ex-commander of the Selous Scouts was on the board.

Major-General Holomisa says that an important role player was an ex-Rhodesian, Transkei's Government Attorney, Mr G Ford — who apparently had the ear of the Mantanzimas — and made suggestions regarding Reid Daly's suitability. He also suggested that Ford wrote the first draft of the contract between Transkei and Security Specialists Transkei (Pty) Ltd.[39]

According to the TDF pay records for 'white advisers', two experienced Selous Scout operators, ex-Sergeants Peter McNielage and Andy Balaam, began work in Transkei on 1 March 1981 — two months before the rest went there. It is reasonable to assume their job was to launch an undercover operation to check on Brigadier Keswa and his brother officers. They were probably acting as handlers for sources the Matanzimas already had in the ranks of the TDF.

It seems a reasonable assumption that offers to send a team to retrain the TDF, sort out a praetorian guard for the Matanzimas and establish a Special Forces unit for Transkei under the direct supervision of Reid Daly were attractive propositions. Reid Daly confirmed this during the Minutes of Evidence of the Transkei's Public Accounts Committee on 3 May 1983 saying: '. . . I figure very prominently in the contract. It was my presence that was the main object of the contract'.

That matters in the Transkei were coming to a head was confirmed to the author during March, April and May 1981 when he was writing the book *Selous Scouts: Top Secret War* in association with Ron Reid Daly. Reid Daly, Erasmus and former Selous Scout captain Chris Gough — later a non shareholding director with Security Specialist International — were on tenterhooks. They spoke often, although guardedly, about mysterious ongoing and highly profitable developments in Transkei.

In anticipation, John Erasmus prepared paperwork for the formation of a company by the name of Security Services Transkei (Pty) Ltd with himself as the sole director. The main business of the new company was described on the application form as 'security service consultants' and its proposed main object was 'to operate as consultants and advisers in setting up security services and the training of security personnel and to engage in all aspects of the provision of security services'. Johannes Kleinhans joined Erasmus as a director on 1 July 1982.[40]

It cannot be denied that SADF approval was essential for the type of contract that Security Services Transkei was seeking. It is doubtful, though, that this occurred to anybody in the place. Transkei was an 'independent republic' and the Matanzimas made up their own minds. Nevertheless, it would have been easy for Military Intelligence's Comops to have put an adverse spin on the security outfit. That would have ensured that it would not have been touched even with the proverbial barge pole.

Brigadier Alex Potgieter, SADF Eastern Cape Commander interviewed Reid Daly and gave his approval and so did Colonel Lourens du Plessis.[41] Brigadier Daan Hamman certainly had something to do with giving final Military Intelligence approval for Reid Daly to become engaged in Transkei, because he said so during a visit to the author's home.

Interestingly enough, as an aside and long before the name *Operation Katzen* entered the public domain, when the author asked him, the by then General Hamman professed to know absolutely nothing about a plot to murder President Lennox Sebe! [42]

The situation seemed to have taken longer to come to the boil than expected and it was only in late May 1981 that Brigadier Keswa and two of his senior colonels were arrested. Keswa described his cell after the first bitterly cold night in detention: 'When dawn eventually broke, I had the first opportunity of looking around my cell. What I saw still haunts me to this day. The wall on the one side of my cell was smeared with faeces. The spot where the night soil bucket stood was a pool of urine . . . The blankets were old, threadbare, smelly, dusty, coarse with tell-tale signs of perverse sexual acts. I tried walking towards the door, but I staggered about sick to the bottom of my gut . . . I remembered stories about tactics of killing someone without laying a finger on them'.[43]

The first anyone in the TDF knew about the arrest was when shortly after it occurred they were paraded for an inspection by Prime Minister George Matanzima. Major Holomisa was the then second in command of Transkei's 1-Battalion. Accompanying the Prime Minister was Lieutenant-Colonel Ron Reid Daly. Prime Minister George introduced him as a major-general and as the new commander of the TDF. Reid Daly told the author contemporaneously that this rank had been decided on a 'select-a-rank' to enable him to deal with senior SADF officers on an equal footing.

Prime Minister George addressed the parade. He told the troops that Brigadier Keswa and the colonels had been arrested. The arrests had obviously been synchronised with Reid Daly's arrival to allow for continuity of command to prevent trouble from brewing. The Prime Minister explained that Keswa and the colonels had been plotting against the State and so on. They would be charged and severely punished.

Major Holomisa and his brother officers were thrown into a state of shock by the unexpected happenings. They felt certain Brigadier Keswa was no traitor, but were so bewildered by the rapid turn of events that few questions were asked. Holomisa remains convinced that the SADF's Military Intelligence played a key role in Keswa's overthrow.

The next day Holomisa was told to report to Captain Lavisa of the Security Police in Umtata. Captain Lavisa and another officer questioned him about trips that he and Brigadier Keswa had made abroad. What was the purpose of the trips? What was done? Whom did you deal with? Where did you go?

'Many countries', Holomisa told him. 'So what's the problem?'

'We have arrested Brigadier Keswa and the others.'

'Yes, but why was he arrested? The officers want to know and so do the troops.'

Holomisa cooperated and began to tell them everything they wanted to know. Almost as soon as he started talking, both officers abruptly got up and walked out of the office. About half an hour later he saw them leaving a Colonel Pulati's office. Holomisa went through and asked the colonel what had happened to Captain Lavisa. Lavisa reappeared.

'Look', Holomisa told him, 'this is not fair. You said I should be here at 08:30 and I was here. Then you left the office. What is going on?'

'We were told by Colonel Mtirara [the most senior black army officer left in the TDF after the arrests] to take statements from you', Captain Lavisa said.

'If you want one', Holomisa retorted, 'you can come and get it at the base. I'm leaving.'

'But Colonel Mtirara said we must take a statement from you', Lavisa said.

'So since when have the police been controlled by the army? Why must Mtirara send you to take a statement from me? Why can't he call me? I am not going to stay here because I am sick and tired of these tricks. I think it must be true what the people are saying — that you are [George] Matanzima's dogs.If you want a statement you can come and take it at the base'.

He saluted the colonel and left.

Captain Lavisa came to the base and took the statement. He returned with it after it had been typed and asked Holomisa to sign it. On reading it he discovered that all sorts of things had been added in that he had not said — untruths that incriminated Brigadier Keswa and the two colonels.

'Captain', he said, 'if you still want to be in your police force you should rather do things professionally. I am your senior in rank. I did not say this. I did not say that. Why have you changed it? I do not lie. If I knew anything more, I would have told you'.

General Holomisa heard several years later that his negative attitude towards the Security Police resulted in urgent discussions between them and Major-General Ron Reid Daly. The question was: with Brigadier Keswa and his colonels out of the way, who else will give us trouble? Had Major Holomisa plotted with the rest? It was apparently touch and go at one stage as to whether he would be detained or not.[44]

In July 1981 Brigadier Keswa and his colleagues were charged jointly with conspiring to defraud Transkei of R3 139 590. The court released them on bail but they were immediately re-detained under security legislation. They were refused access to attorneys, even after they came up for third remands in September 1981.[45]

On 3 May 1983 Reid Daly spoke guardedly to the Transkei's Public Accounts Committee about the Security Services Transkei's contract: 'I spoke to the Prime Minister before coming to this session and told him I would have to answer questions. He asked me to pass on to you, Mr Chairman, a copy of a letter which will explain the background to this. That, sir, is the background to this contract . . . '

'So that was the background before the contract was concluded?' the chairman asked.

'Sir', said Reid Daly, 'this covers in essence what happened'. The contract had not been finalised when 'we had the unfortunate episode where the commander of the Transkei Defence Force was detained'.

Beyond this little was revealed and the public was left to assume that the 'disgraced' and disgraceful Brigadier Keswa had finally got his just deserts for criminal activities. The truth was somewhat different. The brigadier was innocent. The charges against him had been rigged.

In the Minutes of Evidence of the Transkei Public Accounts Committee on 23 January 1985, under paragraph 25 (3) — 'Fruitless Expenditure — R67 334,60', General Reid Daly, in his capacity as the TDF's accounting officer, was asked the somewhat embarrassing question: 'General, could you please furnish full particulars indicating why the former commander of the TDF continues to draw salary without his services being utilised? Why after a period of more than three years has it not been possible to bring his suspension to an end?'

General Reid Daly said he had mentioned it to Prime Minister George Matanzima in 1983, who said he would 'resolve the issue at Presidential level'. At the Prime Minister's request, Reid Daly sent him a report in September 1983, which he copied to President Kaiser. After this was 'lost' by the President's secretary, a copy was submitted. 'In view of the delicacy of the issue and the high-level attention it is receiving, it is considered that any further action on my part would have been inappropriate'. He did not explain why it was 'delicate', but one can suppose that when an innocent man has been railroaded and imprisoned it would fall into that category.

Ten months later on 11 July 1984, after an audit query, Reid Daly wrote to the Auditor General 'putting to him the position in which we found ourselves regarding this matter, as well as the action taken by the department'.

The 'delicate situation' was finally resolved in 1985, apparently more by the persistence of the Public Accounts Committee than by the accounting officer of the TDF, General Reid Daly. In paragraph 14 (4) — 'Fruitless Expenditure' of the Minutes of Evidence of the Transkei Public Accounts Committee for 1985 Reid Daly reported: 'Mr Chairman, as a result of the work of this committee I am pleased to report that the former commander has returned to duty and is mustered as the Deputy Director of Civil Defence, which is a section within the Defence Force'.

This after a suspension on full pay for nearly four years!

Brigadier Rodney Keswa had clearly been subjected to a gross injustice. Disregarding the allegations of massive frauds, if there had been the slightest taint of association with the ANC, he would not have been reinstated and appointed to a key post in the Civil Defence Directorate. Reid Daly, in view of the TDF's counter-insurgency role, would not have been pleased about it either.

All this leaves a host of open questions regarding the competency of those who gathered the information that put Keswa behind bars in the first place. For Transkei, which paid him his full salary for the three and a half years when he was under suspension, his detention might well have been a fruitless operation. For Security Services Transkei (Pty) Ltd, to borrow some Rhodesian Army slang, it was certainly no 'lemon'.

It brought them a golden contract on 10 June 1981 between the Government of the Republic of Transkei — represented by Prime Minister George in his capacity as Minister of Defence — and Security Services Transkei (Pty) Ltd, a wholly owned subsidiary of Security Specialists International (Pty) Ltd, represented by Gideon Henry 'John' Erasmus.

Transkei's Auditor General, Mr J Maqubela, cited the Keswa case when explaining to Parliament in 1985 that 'indifference' on the part of accounting officers was one of the main failings in the problematic financial administration of Transkei.[46]

Certainly no one involved with Security Services Transkei had reason to complain about the contract. There were later protestations that it was not a mercenary contract, that neither Reid Daly nor his men were mercenaries, but this was a question of semantics.[47] Its preamble certainly made it sound like a mercenary contract. It allowed that the company had access to men with 'experience, skills and motivations of seasoned veterans in the matters of security and related activities', which Transkei wished to employ for the purpose of 'restructuring, training and deploying the armed forces of the Republic of Transkei'. The main business and objectives of Security Services Transkei (Pty) Ltd are also significant.

The contract was deemed to have commenced on 1 March 1981, the date Peter McNielage and Andy Balaam started work there. It was for an initial period of six years, subject to automatic renewal after the first three, unless either party objected. The company's duties and responsibilities fell into two parts, which the contract confusingly called phases.

The first phase was for the establishment of the praetorian guard, to provide security for the Matanzima brothers and a select few, or as the contract phrased it, 'certain persons nominated by the government'. The company would also 'select and specially train personnel drawn from the army and police force of Transkei' for that purpose. Initially, at least, the specially trained personnel would fall under the command of the company until the 'restructured defence force' assumed responsibility and reabsorbed them.

The second part allowed for the 'specific object of establishing and thereafter maintaining at a high operational level the land and sea defence forces of Transkei, with particular reference to a special counter-insurgency unit'. The mind boggles at what the 'sea defence force' was.

The contract allowed for Colonel Reid Daly, at the pleasure of commander-in-chief President Kaiser Matanzima, to be appointed as general officer commanding and given a virtual free hand.

The Rhodesian Light Infantry's former Regimental Sergeant Major, 'John' Erasmus, achieved remarkably accelerated promotion to Chief Liaison Officer with the rank of Brigadier. Brigadier Erasmus' duties, whether part time or full, were conveniently left to the discretion of General Reid Daly.

Although Erasmus drew no salary in terms of the contract, it was an appointment which allowed him to continue living in Johannesburg and deal with the day-to-day running of their parent company, Security Specialists International (Pty) Ltd. It was not entirely a sinecure, though, because he was designated to act as the secretary/convenor of Transkei's Defence Council, established in terms of the contract. The Council comprised President Kaiser Matanzima as Commander-in-Chief, Major-General Reid Daly as GOC the TDF, George Matanzima as Prime Minister and Minister of Defence, Major-General Martin Ngceba the Commissioner of Police and the Senior Government Legal Officer. On the Defence Council's order of seniority, Reid Daly's name was listed below the president, but above the Prime Minister.

The contract allowed for the government to appoint a representative to the board of Security Services Transkei (Pty) Ltd at the salary of not less than R100 per month. The Transkei government allowed this generous offer to slip through its fingers.

Reid Daly, in collaboration with the President, became responsible for appointing officers to the TDF. The President designated their ranks. Reid Daly had the overall say in the appointment of NCOs.

The company was contracted to supply non-Transkeian officers and NCOs to the TDF. They were drawn from Security Services Transkei's 'personnel pool' to which they would be returned after 'serving their purpose in Transkei' if needed elsewhere. Reid Daly's salary at the commencement of the contract in 1981 was R3 000 per month, which rose to R6 217 by April 1986. By then lieutenant-colonels in Transkei were drawing R3 940 per month, majors R3 453 and the lowest paid sergeant-majors, R2 183 per month.[48] They had the perks of free accommodation and free medical care. Travelling expenses, household removals and bonuses or gratuities for good service were subject to the approval of the Defence Council. They were handsome salaries indeed for the time. After resignation they could be considered for a land grant with freehold title in Transkei.

Clause 19, the most generous of all clauses, said: 'The remuneration payable to the company and the salaries or wages payable to non-Transkeian personnel *attested* into the armed forces in terms hereof shall be free of company, personal or income tax in any form'. This clause was subsequently amended by an addendum so that salaries for advisers and administrative fees for the company would be regarded as net after tax deductions — making them not liable for *further* taxation.

By March 1987 the monthly salary bill submitted by Security Services Transkei to the government for between 25 to 30 personnel supplied to the TDF was R101 684 per month — R1 220 208 per annum — only R121 792 less than Transkei's entire Defence Vote for the year after it became independent.

Attestation involved taking the prescribed oath of allegiance to Transkei, after which a soldier became subject to the disciplinary code. There is some doubt that any of Security Services Transkei's employees, including Reid Daly, actually attested and signed the oath of allegiance. After they were ignominiously bundled out of Transkei, Major-General Bantu Holomisa ordered an investigation, but no record of any attestations could be found. Neither Reid Daly nor his former employees have produced anything to contradict this. In May 1988 *Scope* magazine asked ex-Brigadier Erasmus in writing if he had been properly attested. He declined to answer.

One wonders if Major-General Reid Daly really did attest and fulfil all the contractual conditions pertaining to his appointment as a general officer. Whatever the case, he promptly reverted to using his old Rhodesian Army courtesy title of 'lieutenant-colonel' after his untimely exit from Transkei.

The issue of attestation could be crucial. If the advisers were not attested, the question of clause 19's validity is purely academic as it applied only to 'attested' personnel. So if they were not attested there can be no argument that they still owe a lot of tax to South Africa.

The maximum number of white ex-Rhodesian advisers the company posted to Transkei for duty with the TDF at any one time, it has been said, was 42. Mostly it averaged between 25 and 30 men. Some were former Selous Scouts, but others were ex-SAS and ex-Rhodesian Light Infantry.

Chris Gough was made responsible for administering the Sasol II security contract. There was no question of the Sasol II contract being 'broken' as a result of Reid Daly's move to Transkei as he suggested to the Public Accounts Committee. Everything just carried on as normal under Chris Gough.[49]

Reid Daly coyly suggested to the Public Accounts Committee that he had been reluctant to move to Transkei, only going after President Matanzima had personally intervened. This was far from the truth. He had anticipated going, he wanted to go and he had high-tailed it there with alacrity.

For the provision of services to Transkei, in addition to salaries, the government agreed to pay the company an administration fee subject to an escalation clause. The fee commenced at R8 000 per month for the first phase and R20 000 per month for the second. In time it rose to R46 948 per month.

To ensure Transkei honoured payments when they became due, a Defence Fund was established at a mutually agreed bank, into which it was agreed that not only the full amount due to Security Services Transkei (Pty) Ltd for the forthcoming year would be paid, but the entire Defence Vote as well. This was credited to the account immediately after the national assembly approved the Defence Vote. The TDF/Company Liaison Officer, Brigadier Erasmus, was made first signatory to the account. The second was a choice between 'one or more persons appointed or approved by the government'.

As an additional assurance for Security Services Transkei (Pty) Ltd, and of course, for Isaac Kaye, the government agreed to furnish them with a guarantee by a mutually agreed financial institution 'in a form approved by Security Services Transkei' as security for the following year's remuneration.

There was a cancellation clause, subject to arbitration, which allowed for termination if the company failed 'in its prime function of restructuring, training and maintaining at high operational level the armed forces of Transkei or being guilty of conduct prejudicial to the safety and security of Transkei'.[50]

The highly experienced investigative journalist, Geoff Allen, in a two-part serialisation in *Scope* magazine in May and June 1988 entitled: *The Rotten, Rotten Transkei* and *The Transkei-Ciskei "Invasion" Fiasco*, aptly dubbed Reid Daly and his colleagues of Security Services (Transkei) (Pty) Ltd as the 'Greatermans Grenadiers'. In truly incisive articles he blew the whistle on the corruption and mismanagement of the so-called 'independent Republic of Transkei' [51] Reid Daly threatened to sue and to Geoff Allen's fury, *Scope*'s proprietors decided it was more expedient to settle rather than fight and they paid Reid Daly R15 000 to drop the case. As a matter of journalistic ethics they should have stared him out.

Perhaps not surprisingly considering the times, no other publications took up the story. What undoubtedly had something to do with it was an unwritten and chummy 'don't rock the boat' arrangement between editors, through their SADF-approved military correspondents. They had been advised that an unofficial 'D' notice had been placed on stories relating to 'conflict between Transkei and Ciskei' for reasons of national security. This should have effectively killed the story in any publication. *Scope*, however, was regarded as a 'girlie' magazine, not a publication that engaged in serious investigative journalism, so it had not even occurred to Military Intelligence to put the kibosh in there.

President Kaiser delayed the official announcement that he had appointed white military advisers until August 1982, when he told the national assembly that a number of 'military experts' had been secured. Their task was to restructure and train the TDF and to neutralise internal unrest or external aggression. This had been necessitated, he said, because southern Africa's changing political climate had exerted increased pressure on Transkei.[52] It had been an open secret known widely for a long time.

Two years later a storm broke over the contract when the Commissioner of Inland Revenue, Transkei, issued the company with tax assessments for the years 1982 and 1983. The company claimed that both they and their employees were exempt.

No one but Security Services (Transkei) (Pty) Ltd, however, had a copy of the contract. This was revealed by the Minutes of Evidence of Transkei's Public Accounts committee of 3 May 1983 when General Reid Daly was summoned before it.

The chairman asked: 'General, it is observed in the report that Transkei government entered into an agreement with a firm of Security Services under some contract involving payments . . . which according to the report were unauthorised since the contract had no Treasury approval:

(a) Was it not your responsibility as accounting officer to see that before the contract was implemented Treasury authority was obtained?
(b) What delayed your reply to the Auditor General's inquiry on such an important issue with financial implications of the nature now revealed in the report?'

Reid Daly conveniently overlooked his close business and old mate corporal-in-arms relationship with John Erasmus and professed ignorance of events surrounding the signing of the contract. He explained that 'the Prime Minister [George Matanzima], for reasons of his own, gave instructions that this matter [the contract] was only to be dealt with at the highest levels. A copy of the contract was handed to the Secretary for Finance with instructions that all queries on this would be dealt with at this level'. Reid Daly implied it was far too secret to give to the Public Accounts Committee. He conceded that Auditor General Mr Maqubele had accused him of being obstructionist in the past, but he denied this.

Mr Maqubela refused to accept the answer and bluntly insisted that in terms of the Exchequer and Audit Act he had the right to see the contract. Where was the act of Parliament that said it was secret? he asked.

In the face of such determination, Reid Daly crumbled and agreed that 'there was nothing secret about it. It is just a straightforward contract'.

The chairman irritably ordered him to produce it.

Dealing with his responsibilities as the TDF's accounting officer, Reid Daly said: 'I know . . . the accounting officer is responsible for contracts but here is another situation that is beyond my control, and . . . I was placed in a very invidious position'.

There was much wrangling and seeking of legal opinions. Transkei's Commissioner of Inland Revenue's view was that the contract had not been ratified by the Cabinet or the National Assembly nor was it approved by the Treasury. President Kaiser and Prime Minister George had viewed an amendment to the contract differently. It was signed and approved by George without witnesses in April 1984, but endorsed by Kaiser on 10 April 1984: 'I do not agree to this amendment'.

Mysteriously, Cabinet Resolution 4/6/84 dated 11 April 1984 was passed without any legal authority to regularise the matter. This must have been realised at some stage, because no copy was sent to Treasury!

The Receiver of Revenue, Pretoria, opined that the Transkei government had 'no power to exonerate Security Services (Transkei) nor its employees from the payment of income tax leviable upon taxable income derived from sources within Transkei'.

Floundering for a solution, some suggested the company should be paid additional monies to cover their tax commitments. Others, however, rightly insisted they had no lawful authority to pay the company or its employees extra money. Why should they anyway? Besides, if they did, that would attract additional taxation.

The government, as the taxing body, was not entitled to waive taxation in respect of remuneration. To give them that right the National Assembly would have to pass special legislation. There was no way around it, no matter what had or had not been signed by whoever. Security Services (Transkei) (Pty) Ltd itself and its mercenary advisers were obliged to pay their taxes. Despite this, not a penny was paid.[53]

Ultimately, after Security Services Transkei (Pty) Ltd and its advisers were summarily ejected from Transkei in April 1987, the new administration under General Bantu Holomisa ordered the collection of all taxes due. To affect this, the Commissioner for Inland Revenue requested the Transkei's Department of Foreign Affairs to request South Africa's assistance. In their Note 800 of 2 August 1988 they formally asked the South African Department of Foreign Affairs to approach 'the relevant authorities' to recover from Security Services Transkei (Pty) Ltd the sum of R4 755 312 in taxes due.[54]

The South African government, despite its own Receiver of Revenue agreeing with Transkei and confirming that the tax was due — as with many other dirty dealings that occurred in the apartheid era — never responded. The reasons for this become apparent later in this chapter. Nevertheless, the taxes remain collectable and any offences arising from their non-payment can be prosecuted. The offences only become proscribed after 20 years from their dates of commission.

In December 1981, after concluding the TDF deal, Isaac Kaye also sealed what the press called the 'deal of the year'. He sold Greatermans Stores to Kirsh Industries through the Volkskas Merchant Bank for R25 million. Natie Kirsh intended merging it with his Checkers chain of supermarkets. The sale was concluded through Griffon, a Kaye holding company, to which all Veritas shares (the majority shareholder in Security Services Transkei) had been ceded.

1982 would not be such an exhilarating year for Kaye, as matters from the past began crowding in on his present and intruding on his likely future. April 1982 signalled the re-entry of Volkskas Merchant Bank into his life. They were called in by Kirsh to re-examine the books of Greatermans Stores. Their audit confirmed that the last half-yearly trading figures had been grotesquely distorted, considerably enhancing the company's value. Kirsh promptly renegotiated the price, dropping it by a hefty R10 million to R15 million.

The auditors then discovered that R26,9 million had been milked from shareholders' accounts over a period of nine months. A secret inquiry in terms of the Companies Act was set up to investigate what had happened. The Commercial Branch of the South African Police was called in to investigate fraud charges.

Checkers Stores also issued a summons to recover R2 million from Isaac Kaye and others. It was claimed this represented fraudulent loans advanced to themselves while 'recklessly' conducting a subsidiary company, Rehabilitation Equipment, which manufactured wheelchairs.

Kaye tried in vain to cancel the deal and buy back Greatermans.

Another knock came when a judicial commission of enquiry was appointed to enquire into bribes and kickbacks paid to provincial authorities and private doctors by Alumina, his pharmaceutical giant. According to undisputed testimony at the commission, he had established a plant to manufacture X-ray film at Rustenburg on the border of the independent homeland state of Bophuthatswana. With the onset of UN trade sanctions, government had adopted a policy of giving import protection to industries producing strategic materials. In addition, by reason of its location, his business became eligible for tax concessions applicable to border industries. Yet it was impossible for Kaye's factory to produce film, because he lacked the prohibitively expensive plant required to manufacture it. To overcome this, he arranged for the Reef-based US multi-national, 3-M, to import huge bulk rolls of the film which he cut, packaged and sold as a South African product.

When a business colleague nervously mentioned that they lacked the capability to manufacture film, Kaye replied: 'Yes, but they'll never know that in Pretoria!'

Of course, he was right.

Kaye left the country in mid 1982, apparently for London. He vowed he would return and testify at the Alumina enquiry to clear his name, but needless to say, he never did. He had resigned most of his directorships, but there is nothing to indicate he had resigned from another of his companies called Veritas or that it had ceased operations. No company returns have been submitted since 1982.

Veritas and another company called ABC Securities (Pty) Ltd, which was not even incorporated until five months after the negotiations began — both fronted by Kaye's close associate, John Erasmus — were utilised in a failed attempt to take over the security division of the Transkei Development Corporation in 1986. It would have been another golden contract. The scheme envisaged by Erasmus was that the Transkei's TDC would finance the takeover in its entirety, spend R1 million to build accommodation for ABC's security guards and pay a hefty monthly fee for its services.

As General Holomisa later put it: 'We would supply everything, pay for everything and they would repay us at some later date!' [55]

The SAP's Commercial Branch allegedly laboured for five years to unravel Kaye's complex financial empire, but to this day no charges have been laid and no attempt has been made to issue a warrant of arrest as a preliminary to extraditing him from Great Britain. It is clear he knew too much about too many sensitive things. The old apartheid regime preferred him out of the way in the obscurity of England, instead of in the dock where he might easily spill the beans over whatever and drag everyone else down with him. Yet, if the authorities still have a mind to do it, and he has a case to answer, he can still be extradited and prosecuted for fraud.

The TDF's Special Forces unit, established in terms of the contract, was to be based at Port St Johns. There was no military infrastructure there and until it was built, houses in the area were utilised for offices and quarters.[56]

Those entering the unit were put through the same selection process as had been developed by the Selous Scouts of Rhodesia.

Why a Special Forces unit was required for a homeland state like Transkei boggles the mind. It was no doubt envisaged that it would have a pseudo guerrilla role and be used against the MK and APLA in the same way as the Selous Scouts had operated against ZANLA and ZIPRA during the Rhodesian War. It seems, too, that men of the Lesotho Liberation Army (LLA), were trained, based there and operationally stiffened by TDF Special Forces' personnel.

By late 1982 Bantu Holomisa had been moved from Transkei's 1-Battalion and placed in charge of training and operations. In 1978 he had attended a two-month combat commanders' course at the Rhodesian Army's School of Infantry in Gwelo (Gweru) during Brigadier Keswa's days as commander. At the school he was introduced to what was called the 'Anti-Rhodesian Indoctrination Document'. This involved identification of the enemy, what organisations were involved, what they stood for, the personalities, what they looked like and so on.

At an officers' conference General Reid Daly announced that he was introducing a similar system in the TDF. In this case the plainly identified enemy was the ANC and its related organisations. Pictures and posters and other stuff relating to them would be placed in barracks, administration offices and similar places. This was obviously the SADF's idea.

Bantu Holomisa, the only black officer there who knew anything about such things, stood up and objected.

'If we listen to Chief George, the Prime Minister, he attacks apartheid every day. He attacks apartheid continually', he told Reid Daly. 'You say we must introduce the anti-revolutionary forces' doctrine within our army, but don't you think this is a contradiction?

If you want to do this, write a memorandum to the Prime Minister and ask for his permission so that we are in the clear'.

Holomisa discussed the question with the black officers afterwards and explained what it was all about. He suggested they individually lobby Prime Minister George and other cabinet ministers to get the idea quashed.

This is precisely what happened. Chief George disapproved of the idea because of the exploitation of blacks under apartheid. He believed the conflict was between white South Africans and black revolutionary forces. It was not Transkei's battle. Transkei was an independent state and the TDF had not been established to fight South Africa's wars.[57] In fact, while a unit from the Ciskei Defence Force was posted for a tour of duty on the Namibian/Angolan border, none from the Transkei ever served there.

Operation Latsa: formation of Lesotho Liberation Army: 1979

May 1979 marked the appearance of the Lesotho Liberation Army (LLA), which Ntsu Mokhehle claimed through the South African press was the military wing of the Basotho Congress Party (BCP). Its aim, he said, was to topple Chief Leabua Jonathan's administration. Its first targets were Maseru's central post office, two electricity pylons and the headquarters of the electricity corporation, followed by bomb attacks on some bridges, telephone poles and power lines in the north. Before this, the BCP's supposed 'military wing' had comprised a riffraff of militant supporters who, with knobkerries, sticks and antique firearms, had invariably been worsted by the disciplined Police Mobile Unit. The BCP's resurgence heralded a switch to sophisticated rockets, automatic weapons, mortars, explosives and men well trained in their use.

Significantly, its activities abruptly ceased after a meeting between Chief Jonathan and Prime Minister P W Botha on the Peka Bridge crossing the Caledon River in August 1980. This signalled a brief improvement in relations between the two countries.[58]

There was a sudden resumption of LLA activity in August and September 1981, when a bomb was planted at the US Cultural Centre and another in the West German Ambassador's car. A brazen mortar attack on a PMU unit near Maseru was mounted in October 1981.

On 19 August 1981 Lesotho's Foreign Minister, Mooki Molapo, met South Africa's Foreign Minister, Pik Botha. According to Molapo, Botha produced photographs of an LLA training camp in QwaQwa — a South African black homeland — and said 'there would be no LLA if you removed all [ANC] refugees from Lesotho. If you want us to do something about the LLA camps, you must do something about the ANC'.[59] If true, this was the first and only time that South Africa admitted that the LLA was operating from its soil.

Mooki Molapo insisted that Lesotho would continue granting asylum to South African refugees, provided they did not use the country as a springboard for attacks against their home states. He admitted, after a subsequent investigation, that he had found certain ANC members had violated their asylum conditions by printing a leaflet calling on black South African workers to take part in a work stay away. Following this, the Lesotho government charged South Africa through the UN with arming and training the LLA.

In a letter to the UN Secretary General, Foreign Minister Pik Botha pointed out that Chief Jonathan had suspended Lesotho's constitution after his defeat in the first and only election since independence. 'The smouldering opposition which has persisted since then has recently grown in intensity and become more sophisticated and better organised'. He suggested the Lesotho government 'should look closer to home' for those responsible.[60]

But the truth was that South Africa had formed, trained, armed and deployed the Lesotho Liberation Army in cooperation with BCP leader Ntsu Mokhehle. It was placed under the wing of the Special Tasks Division of the Chief of Staff Intelligence, SADF. The responsible officer in 1981 was formerly a senior officer with Rhodesia's Special Branch of the British South Africa Police and the Central Intelligence Organisation — Colonel Ricky May.

Some training was undertaken at the Security Police base at Dithotaheng in QwaQwa and at a camp on Ferndale Farm near Bergville, Natal.

Major-General Reid Daly was asked to visit Military Intelligence in Pretoria where he had routine discussions on Transkei matters with a General van der Westhuizen and a Brigadier Roux. Afterwards he was taken to another office where he met Colonel May, whom he had known from the Rhodesian War days.

The situation relating to the Lesotho Liberation Army was explained to Reid Daly. He was asked whether it would be possible to arrange for the LLA to have rear-bases in Transkei. On his return to Umtata, he discussed the question with President Kaiser and Prime Minister George. They gave permission for him to go ahead. According to Reid Daly, 'bases were erected and training and operations started under the joint command of Reid Daly and Ricky May.[61]

Whether a separate base was established for the LLA is not known for sure, but it is likely they were based, trained and operated from Transkei's Special Forces Base at Port St Johns, or somewhere attached to it. Officers of Security Services Transkei who were involved in at least some of their deployments on Transkei's border with Lesotho were Captains Bob Mackenzie and Peter Cole, both ex-Rhodesian SAS and ex-6-Recce.

Although limited in scope, the exercise was apparently expensive, although it might have been that the private company controlling Reid Daly and his men made expensive demands. It is significant that in the 1982/83 financial year, not only did South Africa allocate the Transkei R50 million — R1 million for the Transkei Defence Force — through the Economic Co-Operation Loan Fund, but it also provided an additional R30 million in direct aid to 'strengthen' the TDF.[62]

MK was incapable of launching guerrilla attacks against South Africa when they were rear-based in Tanzania and Zambia. They could only commence attacks after they were granted such facilities in Mozambique, Botswana, Zimbabwe and Lesotho. All of these countries consistently denied they had allowed MK bases on their territory, but whatever it was they granted them, it served the purpose.

No one suggested the LLA was operating from 'liberated areas' in Lesotho, because that was obviously untrue. The country is landlocked and bounded on three sides by South Africa (which includes a boundary with the former Qwa Qwa Homeland) and on the remaining side by the Transkei. So common sense indicates the attacks could only have been launched from South Africa, Qwa Qwa or the Transkei.

This was confirmed by a survey of *The Star*'s Africa News Service. The Johannesburg newspaper found that, of the 19 LLA attacks during 1981, all but two had occurred within four kilometres of the South African border. A few involved mortar bombardments from South African territory and others took place only a few metres within Lesotho. The remainder occurred within easy escaping distance of the border.[63]

South African support for the LLA was not always plain sailing and in many instances, the left hand had no idea whatsoever what the right was doing.

In November 1981 LLA cadre Seisa Seisa and others bombed a bus stop in Lesotho. Afterwards they fled to Clarens in the Free State to avoid arrest. Ironically, they were arrested there by the SAP, taken to Bloemfontein and tortured by the Security Police because it was suspected they belonged to MK. Despite discovering that their leader, Ntsu Mokhehle, was working with the SADF, they decided to strike a separate deal with Chief Leabua Jonathan to swop the LLA cadres for Chris Hani, a senior communist and MK agitator. Jonathan refused, so the Security Police switched to 'Plan B' — they equipped Seisa Seisa and his comrades with a limpet mine and returned them to Lesotho to continue their work.[64]

In 1981 Hani was promoted to the Politburo of the South African Communist Party (SACP), a move that recognised the sterling work he had done for the Party and the ANC in Lesotho.[65]

During 1982 LLA attacks against Lesotho became bolder. In May they assassinated J K Rampeta, Lesotho's Minister of Works and two aides. In July they attacked Chief Jonathan's country home. Chief Jonathan announced he was taking steps to tighten security to counter the 'foreign-backed' campaign of abduction and assassination.

The war of words between Lesotho and South Africa continued unabated, with the former repeatedly charging South Africa with complicity in LLA attacks. Chief Jonathan described the attack on his country home as 'an act of aggression by South Africa against Lesotho'. He also charged that Mr Rampeta's assassin, who had been killed in Lesotho, had oscillated between Soweto and Qwa Qwa from where he had organised hit and run raids.[66]

In 1982 Chris Hani was appointed Political Commissar and Deputy Commander of the MK. In May he was transferred to Maputo to work with Joe Slovo, MK's Chief of Staff.[67] A potted biography, for which he probably supplied or checked much of the information, would later say that while in Lesotho he 'created a network of couriers' and arranged for 'cadres entering South Africa' to be 'assisted by guides'.[68] Zola Nqini, a former Robben Island prisoner, took over as the ANC's chief representative in Lesotho.[69]

Major-General Reid Daly said that after approximately nine months of supporting the LLA, Prime Minister George summoned him and ordered him to stop operations as the Lesotho government had become aware of Transkei's involvement. George told him he had been visited by Lesotho's Foreign Minister who asked him to 'reduce' Transkei's support of the LLA. In return Lesotho would try to assist to get Transkei's 'independence' recognised by the Organisation of African Unity.

Reid Daly said he advised Military Intelligence accordingly.[70]

Major-General Holomisa, however, told the author that LLA personnel were staying at the Special Forces base at Port St Johns for a long time after that.

Rumblings in Ciskei

In June 1981 Ciskei Chief Minister Lennox Sebe announced that a group from the Ciskei Central Intelligence Service (CCIS), was being trained in 'underground operations'. He warned that 'top figures' in Ciskei government were on a 'hit list'. It was assumed that if such a hit list existed, it was an MK or APLA one. Subsequent events indicate it was probably of Transkei origin.

Lennox Sebe, as Commander-in-Chief, had placed Ciskei's combined forces, the CCIS, the Ciskei Police force, the Special Airborne Group and the Ciskei Traffic Division directly under his command. Later, he appointed his half brother, Charles Sebe, Director-General of State Security, promoted him from brigadier to major-general and placed him in charge of the combined forces.[71]

Relations between Ciskei and Transkei deteriorated. In May 1982 students at the University of Fort Hare stoned President Sebe's motorcade at a graduation ceremony. Police opened fire, wounding two and arrested 1 500. Transkei's Prime Minister George Matanzima challenged Ciskei's jurisdiction over the university, saying it belonged to the Xhosa nation as a whole. He described events as 'a brutal display of power'.[72]

Lennox Sebe answered that the Butterworth area was a 'haven for terrorists' and threatened to launch his forces across the Transkei and Lesotho borders to sort them out. Transkei described this as an extreme case of aggression.[73]

Ciskei, following Transkei's example, began recruiting whites from the ex-Rhodesian community. In this way they acquired ex-Selous Scout, Major Dennis Croucamp, who was tasked to form, train and command a new Special Forces anti-terrorism squad, *Ikrele Le Sizwe*. Besides its anti-terrorist duties, it would conduct clandestine missions and provide bodyguards for Ciskei's cabinet ministers.[74] Dennis Croucamp and his former boss, Ron Reid Daly, were not on the best of terms, which was a decided advantage for the major's new employers.

President Lennox Sebe began to develop ties with Israel, which he played down as unofficial. In July 1983 he cut short a visit to Israel and rushed home, after hearing news of an armed attack against Foreign Minister B N Pityi's home.

He accused his half brother, General Charles Sebe, of plotting his overthrow. The attack against Pityi, he said, had been planned within Charles Sebe's Ciskei Central Intelligence Service (CCIS). It was said that enmity between Charles and the President had arisen after a fist fight between the President's son Lolo and Charles' son Khambashe. Lolo was beaten so badly that medical treatment was called for.[75] The President also denounced Vice President Rev Wilson Xaba for his involvement.

Disbanding the CCIS, he nullified the sweeping security and military powers of Charles Sebe granted in terms of the National Security Act. Brigadier Harvey Tamsanqa, the CCIS' deputy chief, and three of his aides were arrested and detained along with the Defence Force Chief.

As an interim measure General Charles Sebe was appointed head of the newly formed Ciskei National Intelligence Service (CNIS), which replaced the CCIS. It had an intelligence gathering function, but no powers of arrest.

On 19 July 1983 both Charles Sebe and his senior adviser, Major-General Taileffer Minnaar, a white South African, were arrested. Vice-President Xaba was despatched on 'sick leave' and his son, Lieutenant Mbulelo Xaba, joined the rest of the mob in prison.

Major-General Minnaar had experienced a meteoric rise in rank. He had started as a second-lieutenant in South Africa's Parachute Battalion. Charles Sebe had taken a liking to him and offered him the rank of lieutenant-colonel in Ciskei. His rapid promotion did not impress everyone and he complained to General Charles Sebe that Commandant Lourens du Plessis of Eastern Cape Command, was not giving him the respect he merited. This resulted in a written request to Brigadier Alex Potgieter asking him to please ensure that his officers treat Lieutenant-Colonel Minnaar with respect.

But he was heading for a fall.

In a second hasty reorganisation, the Defence Force, the Special Forces, the Air Wing and the CNIS were placed under the control of Justice Minister, David Takane.

The SAP's Security Branch Chief, Major-General F Steenkamp, confirmed that his men were 'advising and assisting' in Ciskei. The SAP's Commissioner, General Johan Coetzee, and General Steenkamp met President Lennox Sebe, his Cabinet and Ciskeian police officers on 21 July 1983. Details of the meeting were not disclosed.[76]

In 1984 Foreign Minister Pik Botha 'deeply offended' Lennox Sebe by telling Israel that South Africa did not consider itself responsible for Ciskei's foreign debts. This followed a proposal by Lennox Sebe to spend R25 million on the construction of an international airport at Bisho. Ciskei was a recipient of Pretoria's financial aid, so South Africa had a duty to demand they applied sound procedures and policies.

Lennox Sebe retaliated by claiming that Pik Botha and Generals Coetzee and Steenkamp had twice visited Bisho to appeal for leniency for Charles Sebe, suggesting his case be dealt with by way of a judicial enquiry, instead of by a trial in open court. Lennox Sebe said Botha had insulted him by playing the matter down as a family affair. He had been left with the distinct impression that 'Charles Sebe was working for South Africa'.

Pik Botha retorted that he had become concerned about the escalating unrest in Ciskei after President Sebe had sought his advice. He agreed he had favoured Charles Sebe being treated with leniency, but suggested the 'Ciskei government should ask itself whether the image that it is creating for Ciskei is an image that does justice to the people of Ciskei'.

President Sebe denied there was an unrest problem and he brushed Botha's statement aside 'with the contempt it deserved'.[77]

Further investigations resulted in the arrest of Lieutenant Colin Sebe — General Charles Sebe's son — and two other members of the president's family for the attack on Foreign

Minister Pityi's home. An application to Ciskei's Supreme Court for the release of Charles Sebe and seven other detainees was refused.

A doctor certified that Major-General Taileffer Minnaar was displaying suicidal tendencies, so he was transferred to the security ward of Weskoppies Mental Hospital, Pretoria, on 17 August 1983. The general was not as mad as he looked, however, and his wife immediately lodged a writ of *habeas corpus* with the Pretoria Supreme Court. The judge ordered his release from custody.

The SAP immediately rearrested him for extradition to Ciskei to face nine charges under the Explosives and the Arms and Ammunition Acts. In terms of the protocol between South Africa and Ciskei, extradition could be refused in political cases. At the enquiry General Minnaar denied knowledge of a plot to assassinate Lennox Sebe. Yes, he had stored arms at his house and office, but this was because other facilities were inadequate.

Despite opposition by the South African government he was released on R10 000 bail. The case dragged on until February 1984 when the court threw out the extradition application, finding that Minnaar had been keeping the arms lawfully in the course of his duties as a security adviser. He also held licences for most of the firearms.[78]

In July 1983 Vice President Wilson Xaba was accused of misappropriating funds from the ruling Ciskei National Independence Party (CNIP). He was expelled from the party and sacked as Vice President in March 1984. Six months later he fled to Transkei and asked for political asylum. He said he had been harassed by the police to the extent that he was in fear for his life.[79]

On 31 August 1983, the Minister of Transport and national organiser of the CNIP, Lennox Sebe's half brother, Namba Sebe, was arrested. In December of that year he was remanded on charges of corruption, theft and fraud and granted R10 000 bail, conditional on his not leaving Ciskei. He was rearrested on 17 January 1984 and his bail declared forfeit after he travelled to his farm using a route outside Ciskei. Some five months later he was again released on R10 000 bail, but this time he also fled to Transkei and asked for political asylum.[80]

On 4 October 1983 the 17 year old son of Namba Sebe was arrested and remanded on charges of corruption, theft and fraud. In December Major Ntobelo Mlotana of the disbanded Ciskei Central Intelligence Service, Lieutenant Mbulelo Xaba and Corporal Khambashe Sebe, Charles Sebe's son — both members of the Special Forces unit, *Ikrele Le Sizwe* — were remanded on charges under Ciskei's National Security Act. They appeared in Ciskei's Supreme Court in February 1984, together with Toni and Koli Sebe, on charges relating to the armed attack on the house of Foreign Minister Pityi the previous 14 July. Mbulelo Xaba was acquitted. The rest were sentenced to terms of imprisonment ranging from ten to 26 years. On appeal, Khambashe Sebe's sentence was reduced to 15 years.[81]

Charles Sebe appeared in court for remand in January 1984, the first time since his detention. The following month Lennox Sebe ordered that both he and Brigadier Harvey Tamsanqa be reduced to the ranks and dismissed the service retrospective to the dates of their arrest. Tamsanqa was released shortly afterwards.

Charles Sebe's trial in the Supreme Court began on 1 May 1984. Penniless, he appealed to Amnesty International for legal assistance, but they declined as it was against their policy to provide legal aid. They said substantial allegations of torturing detainees had been made against him and his security command. Nevertheless, despite his dubious background they still regarded him as a political prisoner who merited a prompt and fair trial.

On 15 June he was found guilty of intending to endanger the authority of the state, by inciting police and army officers to release his deputy, Harvey Tamsanqa, by force from the Mdantsane police cells. He was sentenced to 12 years' imprisonment. However, he was acquitted on the main charge of attempting to overthrow the state. Leave to appeal was refused. It is ironic that at the end of it all, ex-Brigadier Tamsanqa was the only one of those arrested who remained a free man.

In January 1985 the commander of the Ciskei Defence Force on secondment from the SADF, Brigadier A Nel, and two of his officers, Colonel P Hall and Captain S R Barnhard, were suspended because Ciskei was no longer satisfied with their services. This arose from a commission of enquiry appointed to investigate the deaths in December 1984 of two Ciskei soldiers. It uncovered 'gross irregularities' and insufficient control at the Sandile and Mapaso bases. In a tit for tat move South Africa withdrew all 44 seconded SADF personnel. They accused Ciskei of violating principles of international law and understandings reached between them. President Sebe replied that the withdrawal had caused a serious disruption of the service.

Relations with Transkei, Lennox Sebe commented, would only improve when they stopped giving sanctuary to Wilson Xaba and Namba Sebe. Neither, he said, could be described as political refugees.[82]

In March 1985 Chief Lent Maqoma was arrested and detained for three days. He, too, fled the country and was granted political asylum by Transkei.[83]

On 5 December 1985 the *Eastern Province Herald* reported that Ciskei's cabinet had split into two factions after a bitter power struggle. One was led by Chief D M Jongilanga and the other by Ray Mali, chairman of the ruling CNIP. The cabinet and the executive of the CNIP met in joint session on 6 December, expressed full support for Lennox Sebe's administration and condemned the 'despicable smear campaign' by the *Eastern Province Herald*. Ray Mali and Chief Jongilanga insisted there was no dissent within the party, nor was there a power struggle.

Three days later, however, Ray Mali was arrested, but the CNIP's party caucus insisted it had nothing to do with a power struggle. He was charged with the theft of R300 000 and fraud involving R255 000 of government monies. He was suspended as a cabinet minister.[84]

Other senior Ciskei government officials and notables were not immune from arrest at Lennox Sebe's whim and found themselves detained for varying periods. They included, W M Zantsi, the secretary-general of the ruling Ciskei National Independence Party (CNIP); E S Ntlabati, the Director-General of Education who was released a month later and demoted but not charged; LM Fani, the traditional councillor of Chief Lent Maqoma; S Lucas and K Myoyo, respectively the Director-General and Deputy Director-General of Finance; L F Siyo, a former cabinet minister and president of the Mdantsane Chamber of Commerce; L M Yako, the deputy chief whip in the national assembly; Professor C H J Lalendle, rector of the Lennox Sebe Training College; Miss N Goya, the new MP for Zwelitsha who was released and sworn in as an MP a few days later; and H M Mdleleni, the Director-General of Health.[85]

In 1984 President Kaiser Matanzima suffered a slight at the hands of President Lennox Sebe. He had intended going to Ciskei to attend a funeral, but Sebe had refused to allow him to enter the country. In a fit of temper Matanzima ordered Major-General Reid Daly to muster 200 armed troops on his farm. When Reid Daly asked why, he was told they were to attack Ciskei.

Reid Daly has said he threatened to resign, so President Kaiser cancelled the invasion.

In December 1984, after Security Services Transkei's contract had run for almost four of its six years, it was announced that Reid Daly was handing over command of the TDF to Colonel Zondwa Mtirara, Kaiser's nephew. He was promoted from colonel to major-general overnight. Although not written into the contract, it was tacitly understood that the company would train the TDF through its advisers until it could produce its own black commanders. After this Reid Daly and his men would remain in an advisory capacity.[86] Major-General Holomisa told the author, however, that one of the main reasons behind the change was because the advisers had displayed an abysmal lack of knowledge and appreciation of local African customs.

Meanwhile, Major-General Taileffer Minnaar was still thirsting for revenge against Lennox Sebe over his sacking and detention in 1983. In January 1985, only a month after the change of command, he went to see the Matanzimas and offered to overthrow Lennox

Sebe. He would do it for a fee of R1 000 000, paid in advance, plus a contract allowing him to take over the training of the TDF from Security Services Transkei (Pty) Ltd, should they refuse to assist with the overthrow plan.

He was promised a cheque for R1 000 000 and the contract. President Kaiser was obviously still smarting over the slight he had suffered at Lennox Sene's refusal to allow him to attend a funeral in Ciskei.

The first Reid Daly knew about it was when he was called to the office of Colonel Ngceba, the Director-General of Transkei's Intelligence Services. He showed him a cheque for R1 000 000 that he was making out to T Minnaar and the contract. He asked for Reid Daly's advice and requested he tell the South African government what was going on.

Understandably shocked that his own contract might be in jeopardy, Reid Daly advised him to make a deliberate mistake on the cheque to ensure the bank declined to cash it. He reported the incident to the South African Ambassador in Umtata. A week later Colonel Ngceba showed him a returned cheque for R700 000 made out to the same person, that had already been cashed.

Needless to say, no coup was mounted and Minnaar faded from the scene.[87]

8

SADF
Internal Surrogates/Proxy Forces
A Culture of Impunity
1983-1986

The Witdoekies at Crossroads

The shanty towns of tin, wood and plastic sheeting that sprang up in the sand dunes near D F Malan (Cape Town International) airport were symptomatic of the times. Black 'foreign' work-seekers had long been 'illegally' flooding into the Cape Peninsula from the depressed areas of the Transkei and Ciskei. By 1983 an estimated 76 000 illegals were within the city's environs. This influx was virtually impossible to control because agreements with the Ciskei and Transkei allowed their 'citizens' to pay 14-day visits to the Cape Peninsula.[1] The mechanics of checking by the authorities were all but impossible. There were no immigration posts impeding free movement, so not surprisingly anyone questioned had 'just arrived' on a 14-day visit.

5 882 black families were on the official waiting list for houses, but an unofficial estimate suggested 19 000 families were in need of homes. If every black person had been tyre-levered into the official housing stock available, each house would have had to accommodate 146 people. Inevitably squatter camps mushroomed around Cape Town to cater for the accommodation of both legals and illegals.[2]

The government evinced a complete lack of sympathy or understanding about the problem. Dr George de V Morrison, the Deputy Minister of Cooperation and Development, announced in September 1983 that the government had no intention of making the squatter encampments at Crossroads a permanent township. He called it 'a symbol of provocation and of blackmail of the government'. In pursuit of government policy, officials of his department demolished 6 448 structures during 1983 and another 8 597 in the first six months of 1984. Many squatters were arrested and charged.[3]

Widespread opposition to a proposal to move squatters from Crossroads to a new township at Khayelitsha developed. In December 1982, Johnson Ngxobongwana, leader of the Crossroads Executive Committee and the unofficial mayor of Crossroads , said that if the government wanted to move them they should 'bring the army and shoot us'. The UDF soon became a natural home for Ngxobongwana after it was formed in 1983, particularly as he was already working with those of its affiliates and various Western Cape youth groups who had been allied to him in his opposition to removals from Crossroads.[4]

Fighting broke out between the supporters of Oliver Memani's residents' association and the Crossroads Executive Committee of Johnson Ngxobongwana in December 1983. In June 1984 more than 12 000 Crossroads residents signed a UDF-sponsored declaration saying that they refused to move to Khayelitsha.[5]

Harassment of squatters continued, shacks were destroyed and fines levied, but the problem did not go away. Criticising the government's policy, opposition MP Helen Suzman fittingly described it as 'a crude and useless way to tackle what was obviously a housing crisis'.[6]

In February 1985 there was a major outbreak of violence there with serious street clashes occurring between thousands of residents and the police. The clashes had been triggered by rumours that a convoy of vehicles was on its way to move residents to Khayelitsha. When the trouble petered out after three days of rioting, 18 civilians were dead and another 250 had been injured by police action. Six policemen were injured and 28 police vehicles damaged.

Young UDF radicals virtually took over control of Crossroads. It became a no-go area for the Security Forces and at night well-armed pro-UDF comrades openly patrolled the streets.

The dominance of this youthful element, however, was not to the taste of everyone in Crossroads, including many former UDF and ANC-sympathising supporters and particularly amongst the older people. A clique calling themselves the Comrades organised street committees and quickly gained a terrifying reputation for brutality and fanaticism. In enforcing a boycott of white-owned businesses, they systematically stopped and forced homecoming residents of the squatter camp to open their shopping bags. In many documented instances, the youthful Comrades set about elderly shoppers and forced them to eat the cooking oil and soap powder they had purchased in defiance of the boycott.[7]

Johnson Ngxobongwana, for one, resented his loss of control. Suddenly too, according to a senior police officer, the authorities came to realise that things had gone too far.

The Comrades and the UDF were on the verge of declaring Crossroads a liberated area. It was known that the UDF had smuggled in many firearms already. The police had been fired on and it was concluded that savage fighting and unacceptably heavy Security Force casualties would inevitably result from any attempt to regain control.

Someone advanced an alternative.

Johnson Ngxobongwana's rabble were the underdogs in what had happened so far. Now if the Security Forces lent them covert support and treated them as a surrogate organisation, the government's agenda could be followed but the blame for any violent consequences would rest with Ngxobongwana's gang. It was inevitable he would agree to the offer because it was the only way he could regain control of his rapidly sliding position of influence. He would also be amply rewarded and financed with money channelled through his Crossroads Executive Committee.

It was accepted that with the adoption of such a plan, the launching of civil actions by aggrieved parties against the police would be inevitable. The author was told in confidence by a senior police officer who was in a position to know, that 'high authority' had agreed to set aside R7 million to deal with such cases. If settlements (without any admission of responsibility) were possible, this would be the preferred route. On the other hand if claimants opted to fight it out in court, they would be rigorously opposed and the case stretched out until the media and the general public lost interest. Then the police would make substantial offers of settlement that would be difficult to refuse.[8]

December 1985 heralded the first clashes between the radicalised Comrades and the 'Fathers', a newly formed vigilante group. Members of the Fathers, it was said, had got tired of being pushed around by their children. In truth neither group was identifiable by age — there were substantial constituencies of young and old in both. It should surprise no one that the genesis of the Fathers was Johnson Ngxobongwana's Crossroads Executive Committee.[9]

At first some headmen, unwilling to accept Ngxobongwana's authority, aligned themselves with the Comrades. But most of them turned to the Fathers once the radical nature of the Comrades became apparent.

On 30 December 1985, sparked by the Christmas Eve killing of a community councillor called Siqaza, the Fathers instructed women to remain in their houses and ordered their menfolk to join patrols to hunt down the Comrades. They rampaged through the camp, indiscriminately assaulting anyone assumed to be a Comrade. A Crossroads resident, a

Mrs Benge, alleged that the police refused to intervene to assist the beleaguered Comrades.

On New Year's Eve the Comrades retaliated and attacked a group of 300 Fathers. A hand grenade blast injured five of them. Violence escalated, but the police sat it out on the periphery, displaying a 'let 'em get on with it' attitude.

On 18 May 1986, the Fathers launched a violent campaign against the Comrades, other supporters of the UDF and Crossroads residents who opposed Ngxobongwana's leadership. Soon a state of open warfare existed at Crossroads and at KTC, Nyanga Bush, Portland Cement and Nyanga Extension squatter camps.

Eye witnesses spoke of the Fathers burning down shacks with the help of the Security Forces. While the Fathers rampaged through the squatter townships, at least five Casspirs and two Buffels stood by in support. Police denied the report. By the end of the day, 14 were dead and 20 000 people had been made homeless.

In a sudden change of nomenclature, the Fathers became the *Witdoekies*, recognisable by white cloth bands around their heads. This was to ensure that they were easily identifiable as 'allies' by Security Forces personnel operating in the area. The conflict continued unabated for a week.

On 21 May the Western Province Joint Management Committee sent a secret signal to the State Security Council Secretariat confirming that the Witdoekies had succeeded in driving the Comrades from Crossroads, leaving 600 homeless in the process. It continued: 'Fathers are well disposed towards the Security Forces and they are not a security risk as they want law and order. Fathers cannot be openly supported due to the hostility of the leftist press.' [10]

On 25 May the Supreme Court in Cape Town issued a temporary interdict preventing the Witdoekies and soldiers from attacking people or property in the KTC squatter camp.

On 27 May 1986 the opposition PFP (Progressive Federal Party) and other bodies, called on the government to declare Crossroads and adjacent squatter camps disaster areas. They also demanded a commission of inquiry into the fighting, repeating widespread accusations that the police had been assisting the Witdoekies.

Not all policemen were aligned with or involved in unlawful activities. Leonard Knipe, commanding a special police unit investigating murders and other violence in Guguletu Township, raided a shack in Crossroads which comprised 'cells and a courtroom and was obviously used as a "people's court"[Kangaroo court]'. He seized court books, canes, tyres (for 'necklacing') and suchlike as exhibits. Investigations revealed that Johnson Ngxobongwana was in charge of the court so he arrested him, finding him in possession of a military-issue pistol. He reported this to the divisional CID chief, Brigadier Ronnie van der Westhuizen who received the news with enthusiasm. Knipe opposed bail, but later, on the instructions of a clearly agitated Brigadier van der Westhuizen he was instructed to ensure Ngxobongwana was immediately released on bail. Van der Westhuizen said the order had originated from either President P W Botha or Law and Order Minister Louis le Grange. Bail of R50 was granted. Knipe later discovered the police docket had been destroyed.[11]

The PFP spokesman on African Affairs in the Western Cape, Ken Andrew, labelled the Crossroads problems as '1986-style forced removal', with the Witdoekies doing the 'dirty work . . . taking the place of the government's front end loaders of the past'.

The Minister of Constitutional Development and Planning, Chris Heunis, condemned accusations that government institutions had played a role in the Crossroads violence. He said there was no need to declare Crossroads, or parts of it, a disaster area because facilities for those left destitute were available at Khayelitsha 20km from Cape Town. He said the government's offer was being portrayed as a 'forced removal' but it was no such thing. Negotiations with the private sector to upgrade Crossroads were advanced, but decreasing the population density in the first phase of the upgrading was necessary.[12]

On 29 May a body of 39 clerics and church workers issued a statement claiming the Security Forces were supporting the Witdoekies — they had not been dispersed or tear-gassed by the Security Forces, who had allowed them to set up roadblocks and stood by while they committed atrocities.

Another outbreak of violence occurred on 9 June when a pitched battle was fought between a swarm of 2 000 Witdoekies supported by white men wearing civilian clothes and armed with rifles, and 8 000 Comrades. At least five people died in the day's fighting.

The secretary of the Western Cape Joint Management Committee, Commandant R P du Plessis, sent a signal classified 'top secret' to the State Security Council on the same day advising that they were arranging a victory feast for the Witdoekies. 'The cost has not been finalised but it is estimated at about R3 000. It will be appreciated if the necessary funds could possibly be made available for this. Finality will, however, not be reached until 11 June 1986 when we will be in contact with you again.'[13]

On 10 June a freelance ex-Rhodesian news cameraman was attacked by the Witdoekies at the KTC squatter camp sustaining injuries from which he subsequently died. The following day the Witdoekies launched a major assault against the KTC camp. They destroyed 75% of the shacks and left in their wake 20 dead and some 30 000 homeless. Shortly afterwards Bishop Desmond Tutu brokered a cease-fire between the warring factions.

During the savage internecine fighting during May and June 1986, more than 60 people were killed, thousands of shacks were destroyed and at least 70 000 people were left homeless.[14]

Affidavits filed in the Cape Town Supreme Court in October 1986 claimed that members of the SAP and the SADF had actively assisted the *Witdoekies* in their attacks on residents' homes, or had stood by and declined to intervene. They alleged that refugee squatters attempting to erect new shelters were hounded from relief centres by police and the Witdoekies. According to Josette Cole of the Surplus People's Project, squatters who attempted to rebuild their shacks at Brown's Farm, several kilometres from the site of their previous homes, had them broken down by officials of the Cape Divisional Council. The officials threatened that they would be attacked by the Witdoekies if they failed to move to Khayelitsha. According to Cole, the violence achieved what the State had been unable to do for the best part of a decade — which was the removal of the 'three most coherent and consistently resistant squatter communities in the Crossroads complex'.[15]

In March 1989 attorneys acting for former residents of the KTC squatter camp against Minister of Law and Order, Adriaan Vlok, subpoenaed a SADF commander to testify and produce all Joint Management Committee documents that referred to events occurring near the KTC and Crossroads squatter camps during June 1986. Deputy Minister of Law and Order, Roelf Meyer, responded by issuing a certificate in terms of the Internal Security Act 1982 that blocked access to such documents in the interests of State security.[16] If the hands of the State Security Council and the Joint Management Committee concerned had been clean, a blocking action would have been unnecessary.

Finally, in March 1990, a settlement totalling R2 million was announced. In terms of it, the former residents of KTC and the police agreed to the case being stopped 'in the public interest'. Instead of incurring further costs, which had already risen to R2,5 million, the government offered to establish a fund to provide assistance for community development programmes for the communities of KTC, Nyanga Bush Camp, Nyanga Extension Camp and Portland Cement Camp. It also offered *ex-gratia* compensation to residents who had suffered loss as a result of damage or loss of property during the events occurring between 17-21 May 1986 and 9-11 June 1986.

As a *quid pro quo* the squatters withdrew their action and their allegations against the police. Each party agreed to pay its own costs.[17]

The action had been regarded as a test case because of 3 000 outstanding claims totalling R5 million by KTC residents. Because of the terms of the settlement, such residents had no option but to accept such ex-gratia payments as they were offered. Clearly few had enough money to tackle the government themselves.

While not exactly an admission of guilt, it seems unlikely that the police — despite having access to unlimited public funds — would have entered into such a settlement out of the goodness of their hearts. If they had not been guilty of criminal conduct, why settle at all?

The police, it seems, had stayed well within the R7 million budget allotted to them by 'high authority'. One is left to ponder who this 'high authority' was. Whoever it was, Minister Vlok must have known about it. Yet, when testifying to the Truth Commission in October 1997, he said: 'I at no time had any evidence of any support by the police for the Witdoekies'.[18]

Project Henry: Black Crisis Centre/AZANYU/Ama-Afrika: Eastern Cape

The Azanian People's Organisation (AZAPO), which owed its origins and its creed of Black Consciousness to the late Steve Biko, was easy meat for *agents provocateurs* of the Security Police.

There were fundamental differences between the UDF/ANC/SACP alliance and AZAPO. The former professed adherence to the non-racial Freedom Charter which called for the land to be shared by all who lived on it, while the latter had the radical objective of repossessing all land from whites for the benefit of the black indigenous people.

AZAPO's policy, at times denied, was that the whites were irrelevant. It advanced this view to a stage where, in 1984, it expressed criticism of the liberal Progressive Federal Party for defying the provisions of the Prohibition of Political Interference Act 1968 by opening its membership to all racial groups.

During 1984 dissension between the UDF and its allies and AZAPO surfaced publicly. In June 1984 the ANC announced plans to protest after it learned that AZAPO's Natal vice president, Imraam Moosa, had been allowed to address a UN conference on action against apartheid. In September 1984 AZAPO criticised the UDF affiliated Mandela Committee for calling for a work stay away without consulting all sectors of the community. It did the same, together with 15 other Black Consciousness organisations, at a meeting in Soweto in November 1984. This epitomised its attitude towards the countrywide UDF inspired eruptions of township violence against government authority. It professed to support the action in principle but in almost every aspect was critical of the UDF's methods.[19]

In Port Elizabeth the Security Police took advantage of this by distributing bogus pamphlets in the name of AZAPO alleging that the UDF was being 'manipulated by liberals'.[20]

The SAP formed an unlikely alliance with the Rev Ebenezer Muzondile Maqina's Black Crisis Centre, an affiliate of AZAPO. With the help of SAP supplied finance and weapons, it soon came to control some of the most radically inclined black areas of Port Elizabeth.

When it became apparent to the ANC that Maqina's movement had gained the upper hand over its UDF rivals in this constantly swaying battle for supremacy in the townships, it appealed to *Umkhonto we Sizwe* (MK) for help in fighting Maqina's gangs.

Chris Hani was in favour, believing that Maqina, by fighting the ANC aligned comrades, was fighting the government's fight. This was opposed by both Joe Slovo and Joe Modise, top MK lieutenants. The question was passed to the ANC's Political Military Council (PMC) where it was decided 'the powerless should not be encouraged to fight the powerless'.[21]

Divisions between AZAPO and the UDF were first publicly exposed in January 1985 when US Senator Edward Kennedy was visiting South Africa. While the UDF hosted him at various centres, AZAPO staged protests condemning his visit. A meeting hosted by Bishop Desmond Tutu in Soweto was called off because of disruptions.

Violence between UDF and AZAPO erupted in April 1985 when the UDF refused to allow AZAPO to take part in the funerals of victims of police shootings in Langa and Uitenhage.[22]

Shortly afterwards Mono Badela, a former journalist and a UDF supporter, was abducted by AZAPO and taken to the Rev Maqina's house. After interrogating him, Maqina ordered his followers to 'necklace' him. (Necklacing was the charming practice of putting a tyre around the victim's neck, filling it with petrol and lighting it.) They put him in a van and drove away, but fortunately for Badela, not all his captors agreed and after an argument they let him go.[23]

During May 1985 UDF supporters attacked 19 AZAPO members in the Eastern Cape, killing four, and put the homes of 33 AZAPO supporters to the torch.[24]

On 7 June 1985 a meeting to discuss the conflict between the UDF and AZAPO was held at the SADF's Eastern Cape command. It was chaired by Brigadier Joffel van der Westhuizen. In the minutes it stated: 'Informers report that about 200 women were at Rev Ebenezer Maqina's and that he said the conflict between AZAPO and UDF will continue until the heads of five UDF activists have rolled.' He named the five as Eastern Cape UDF president Edgar Ngoyi, his deputy Henry Fazzie, Mono Badela (a UDF supporter and secretary of a non racial rugby club), Africa Maqolo of the Port Elizabeth Black Civic Organisation and Mkuseli Jack — president of the Port Elizabeth Youth Congress.[25] It seems Maqina remained determined to get Badela who had earlier only escaped necklacing by the skin of his teeth.

In January 1986 AZAPO and the UDF found common ground and reached a peace agreement, enabling them to present a common front against the government. This, needless to say, suited neither the Security Police nor Rev Maqina and his 'Africanist Group' who in February 1986 splintered his recently formed Azanian National Youth Unity (AZANYU), away from AZAPO. Some said he was expelled.

Rev Maqina explained the break by saying AZAPO had 'betrayed the Africanist position by pleading for a non-racial solution to South Africa's problems. They might just as well join the UDF now'. So AZAPO also became the enemy and the ruthless conflict was extended to them. In February 1986 at least eight people died.[26]

AZANYU first came to public prominence in December 1985 when some of its members were killed in clashes with UDF supporters in Paarl in the south-west Cape. The UDF claimed that AZANYU was receiving support from the police in Paarl, a claim AZANYU strenuously denied. A lower key mention of the organisation had been made in March 1985 when the Ciskei arrested and detained some of its officials for two weeks.[27]

Eventually, it was said, an MK cell in Port Elizabeth, acting without the authority of the ANC's PMC, attacked Rev Maqina and his AZANYU and for while drove them from the Port Elizabeth townships.

Soon Rev Maqina expanded into Uitenhage near Port Elizabeth where he took over the coordination of another Security Police surrogate, the Ama-Africa vigilante group. Needless to say, like AZANYU, it violently opposed the UDF and its allies.[28]

For 18 months Uitenhage's black township, Kwanobuhle, had been a scene of seemingly never ending UDF inspired civil unrest. It was marked by vicious bouts of political murders, general lawlessness, necklacings and the destruction of property.

In 1985 Kelman Befile owned shops in the old shack area of Langa. They were burned down together with his father's house after it was alleged he had 'colluded with the police against the people of Langa' to avoid criminal charges. Following this, he moved to Tent Town, a new section of Kwanobuhle, where he once more set up business. Again his shop was burned down.

The embittered Befile and his friends became the core of Ama-Afrika and were involved in a number of skirmishes with groups of comrades.

On Wednesday 31 December 1986, a group of comrades wearing identifying red T-shirts stopped Befile's car, burnt it out and abducted the driver, his brother Kid. Later in the day Kid was located in the custody of Comrades and released. Whether this was by police or Ama-Afrika vigilantes is unknown, but after his release the police and Ama-Afrika were certainly working together. The vigilantes beat up the Comrades responsible while the police looked on. Afterwards the police arrested some of the Comrades.

Between 03:00 and 05:00 on Sunday 4 January 1987, groups of Ama-Afrika vigilantes armed with guns, some wearing masks, and operating from 9 Sogcwayi Street and 5 Solilo Street, knocked on the doors of all residents of Khayelitsha and Tent Town and ordered them to march on Kwanobuhle. They were told to 'go and clean out old Kwanobuhle'. They had nothing to fear because the police would accompany them. Their job would be to 'challenge the youth' who stopped buses and organised boycotts, and the like.

No one was given the option of not going. It was straightforward intimidation — the general practice of both the UDF and its affiliates and its opponents. Two people, Tiban Johnson and Samuel Mpushe, were typical of those present. They were told: 'If you don't go, we will come back for you.' The threat was unmistakable.

Before setting off, the crowd was addressed at Kelman Befile's house by Mandla Nkonki who said 'we know who we want' (at Kwanobuhle). Variously estimated at between 1 000 and 5 000 people, they were told to arm themselves with sticks and follow their Ama-Afrika leaders, Luyunda Mgobo and Mandla Nkonki. Men coming off night shift and others on their way to church were forced to join the marchers.

They entered Old Kwanobuhle at about 07:00, headed for the Angola section and then spread out into other areas. Ama-Afrika used a commandeered taxi and a van from which to control the crowd and liaise with members of the SAP and the local Municipal Police who followed the marchers. They were using 'Hippo 88' (probably an army Buffel) and two 'mellow yellow' personnel carriers (probably police Casspirs).

One of the marchers, Makaya Sam, said the police 'were almost everywhere — not dispersing [the] crowd, just monitoring the situation. They would take particulars where property was destroyed. The police felt it was in the interests of stopping the consumer and school boycotts and the mindless violence they couldn't stop.'

The Ama-Afrika leaders led or personally supervised attacks. UDF supporters were 'beaten and hacked' and handed over to the SAP as prisoners. It was said that four were killed which prompted the march leaders to caution the crowd that 'the SAP didn't want you to burn or kill people'.

At times a police helicopter circled protectively overhead.

Finally at about 13:00 the crowd was addressed by their Ama-Afrika leaders in a Khayelitsha street and told there would be no more consumer or school boycotts.

The relatives of two of the fatal casualties, John Maya (14), and Siphiwo Loom (20), told human rights workers that by Friday 9 January — five days after the events — the police had not interviewed anyone in connection with the deaths. It is unlikely they ever did.

The phone of Rev A F Diko, the Methodist minister at Kwanobuhle, was probably being monitored by the Security Police. On the 5 January 1987 he phoned Rory Riordan, the director of the Human Rights Trust, Port Elizabeth, and arranged to meet him that afternoon in Uitenhage to discuss the happenings.

Fifteen minutes before the appointed time he was arrested by Security Police Colonel Strydom and two others and questioned about the pending meeting and asked his view on the events of the day before. Strydom said the police had no desire to get involved 'in friction between two groups of black persons' and warned Rev Diko that he would find himself in trouble if he spoke to the press about the happenings. Following this, Ama-Afrika supporters accosted him at his home and accused him of being an informer. They threatened to run him out of Uitenhage if they found out he had been harbouring UDF members.

Many believed that despite the resultant deaths and injuries, the community as a whole approved the outcome. The Comrades had gotten out of hand. Now 'people can go to town and shop, trucks and buses will enter the township, kids will return to school.'[29]

The actions of the SAP and their surrogates, however, did not result in the peace they had hoped for, but in the escalation of violence. Kwanobuhle was plunged into a protracted period of Ama-Afrika inspired violence, with assaults and murders becoming commonplace. Despite this, the SAP made no attempt to prosecute those responsible.[30]

Colonel Lourens du Plessis, then running Comops (Communication Operations) in the SADF's Eastern Cape Command, Port Elizabeth, said Rev Maqina eventually became an embarrassment to the Security Police. They asked Colonel du Plessis to take over from the SAP's Major Herman du Plessis as Maqina's handler, but he refused. Nevertheless, after this, finance for Rev Maqina's group was channelled through the Military Intelligence's Eastern Cape front company, Eduguide CC, Port Elizabeth, under the code name *Project Henry*. Maqina, Colonel du Plessis said, was eventually dropped altogether by the SADF after he refused to submit balance sheets and provide reconciliations of monies given to him.[31]

1987 was the high point of Ama-Afrika inspired violence and groups monitoring its activities collected many affidavits. In September 1987, for example, three members of the UDF-aligned Uitenhage Women's Congress were abducted by 15 armed vigilantes and taken to Ama-Afrika's HQ where, after repeated assaults with blunt and sharp instruments, they were 'beaten to a pulp'.[32]

On one occasion the Department of Health made funds available, presumably on the recommendation of the Eastern Province Joint Management Committee, for the purchase of food parcels to be distributed in the townships by the Rev Maqina.[33]

In October 1987 a former member of Ama-Afrika told journalists he had been forced to join a group in an attack on Tyoksville, a Uitenhage shanty town. The result was five UDF supporters dead and at least one other seriously injured.

'The municipal police did nothing while we were looking for comrades', he said. 'They just milled around while we continued with our raid.'

In November 1987 there were reports that the Rev Maqina was chairing a sub-committee of Port Elizabeth's Join Management Committee.[34]

Peace of a kind was eventually restored in the townships and squatter camps around Port Elizabeth and Uitenhage by ANC activist and local community leader, Raymond Mhlaba, who brokered a peace agreement between the Comrades and Ama-Afrika after his release from detention in 1990.

For a brief time Rev Maqina dropped from sight, but he reappeared in 1991/92 and opened offices for his Peace Foundation for Youth in North End, Port Elizabeth. This organisation was probably funded by various state departments.[35]

In March 1994 the Rev Maqina, by then a National Party supporter, questioned an ANC candidate during a pre-election discussion programme screened on SATV's Newsline. The uproar from the predominantly black audience at his appearance was such that he had to ask the chairman for protection.

Maqina had travelled a long and winding road from the black exclusiveness of AZAPO to take his stand in the ranks of the Afrikaner dominated National Party.

9

Operation Marion
Security Forces' support for Inkatha
1985-1988

Pretoria created the self governing homeland of KwaZulu on 31 March 1972 and formed an Executive Council headed by Chief Gatsha (Mangosuthu) Buthelezi. Unlike his counterparts in other homelands, Buthelezi refused to countenance full independence for what he aptly called a 'polka dot' state — a territory consisting of 44 isolated land pockets around the Tugela River. The resurrection of the Zulu state (about 10% of Shaka's old empire of the 1820s) was symbolised by the erection of a legislative assembly building at Ulundi. Buthelezi's rejection of full independence was a slap in the face for Pretoria, whose international credibility and internal policies were inextricably bound up with the creation of Bantustans for the black 'nations' of South Africa.[1]

Buthelezi, a chief in his own right and a grandson of Dinuzulu — Cetshwayo's unrecognised heir — had been a protégé of Nobel Prize winner Chief Albert Luthuli[2] and a member of the ANC's Youth League. In the 1960s when the voice of the ANC was silenced by the imprisonment or exile of its leaders, Buthelezi emerged as apartheid's most vocal black critic. Despite this he remained a Zulu first and an African nationalist second.[3] While genuinely attempting to widen his appeal to other tribal factions, his constituency remained predominantly Zulu. His appeal came from reminding them of their inherited discipline, their history, their traditions and above all their glorious warrior past.

He did not share the ANC's viewpoint that the powerful apartheid regime could be broken by military means. It was too powerful for that. He thought the only way forward was to exert pressure against the country's economy and for the African people to passively increase their resistance against the system itself. His views were not appreciated by the authorities who withdrew his passport from 1966 to 1971. In 1973 he called for the release of Nelson Mandela and other black leaders from Robben Island and for the granting of immunity to Oliver Tambo, president of the ANC, to enable him to return from exile.

President Kenneth Kaunda of Zambia told Buthelezi that he lacked a constituency. In March 1975 this prompted him to revive *Inkatha ka Zulu* — a short-lived Zulu cultural society formed in 1924 as *Inkatha ya KwaZulu* — this time called a 'cultural liberation' movement. The name was derived from *Inkatha yezwe* — the sacred grass coil symbolising Zulu unity, passed down from Shaka's time and unwittingly burnt by the British Army as they advanced on Ulundi in July 1879.[4]

Shortly afterwards the name was amended to *Inkatha ye Nkululeko ye Sizwe* — a subtle change of meaning from 'Ring of the Zulus' to 'Ring of the Nation'. In English it became the Inkatha Freedom Party (IFP). Buthelezi was summoned to Pretoria by Law and Order Minister, Jimmy Kruger, who warned him to confine its membership to Zulus.[5]

Refusing to be cowed, Inkatha adopted the black, green and gold colours of the ANC. It based its constitution on the ANC's Freedom Charter. Its aim was to foster 'the spirit of unity amongst the people of KwaZulu throughout southern Africa, and between them and all their African brothers'. It would 'cooperate with any movement or organisation for the improvement of the conditions of the people . . . and for the eradication of all forms of colonialism, neo-colonialism, racialism, imperialism, discrimination and to strive for the attainment of African unity'. Buthelezi told the press: 'Inkatha plainly declares itself to be an instrument of liberation. The business of black liberation is our business.'

Virtually all of Natal's old ANC establishment — from Selby Msimang, a founding father of 1913, to former Robben Islanders and men disillusioned about the ANC's communist links — flocked to Inkatha's standard.

Buthelezi's political moves were endorsed by Mandela in prison and byTambo in exile. He was received with enthusiasm everywhere. The high watermark of his popularity was in early 1976 when he was given a tumultuous reception after delivering an outspoken oration to an audience packed into Soweto's Jabulani Stadium.

Then came the Soweto Uprising of June 1976.The violent actions of youths protesting the compulsory use of Afrikaans as the learning medium in black schools, shoved elders like Buthelezi into the political back seat. The opening violence, which could not be long sustained against the well armed and organised Security Forces, was soon replaced by youth inspired strikes, work stay aways and boycotts. Such action, enforced by violence and intimidation was aimed at disrupting the white economy, drawing international attention to South Africa and ultimately bringing down the apartheid regime.

Militant youth intimidated Zulu hostel dwellers into a work stay-away in September 1976. But when calls came for a second stoppage in October, the Zulus refused. They could not afford the loss of wages. The youthful militants attacked them on their way home. The Zulus of Mzimhlophe hostel launched counter-attacks. Several youths were killed. Significantly the police stood aside and let the Zulus get on with it.

Buthelezi flew to Johannesburg to mediate an uneasy peace, but he was a Zulu and his impartiality was suspect.[6]

In 1977 Pretoria extended greater powers of self government to KwaZulu and Buthelezi as chief minister headed a cabinet responsible for its own police force, the civil service, finance, justice, education, the interior, public works and health. Buthelezi still resisted full independence, but having his own police force was the close to having his own army.[7]

In 1979 Buthelezi and an Inkatha delegation went to London to meet Oliver Tambo and other ANC leaders. They each had something to offer. The ANC regarded Buthelezi as a potential ally, while Buthelezi needed ANC recognition to counter allegations that he was a stooge of the apartheid government.

For their part the ANC explained that *Umkhonto we Sizwe* (MK) guerrillas were infiltrating South Africa from Mozambique, but when they asked if KwaZulu could be used for the same purpose, or at least as a safe haven, Buthelezi refused.

For his part, Buthelezi asked the ANC to publicly acknowledge Inkatha as a 'vital force in the struggle', cooperate on shared intelligence and warn new militant groups like AZAPO that it was not in the black interest to attack Inkatha. He explained his opposition to the armed struggle and his belief in passive resistance as espoused by Albert Luthuli. This meant he could never allow KwaZulu to host MK guerrillas. There was an unspoken arrogance on the part of Inkatha's leaders. Its paid up membership, estimated at a quarter of a million, was the largest of any party in South African history. This inclined Buthelezi and his delegation towards the belief that Inkatha was at the least equal with the ANC, but more likely its superior.

The ANC agreed to mull over the points made by Inkatha and reply later. On returning to South Africa, Buthelezi declared publicly that the problems between the ANC and Inkatha had been resolved. This was, however, a serious case of over-optimism, because his going public had seriously irritated the ANC. They never replied to Inkatha and in July 1980 Oliver Tambo announced from Zambia that Buthelezi had 'emerged on the side of the enemy against the people'.[8]

Dr Frank Mdlalose, Inkatha's national chairman, later said after the failure of the conference, that KwaZulu and Inkatha were targeted for destabilisation by the ANC. 'The differing strategies to overcome apartheid proved irreconcilable at that conference . . .

Inkatha was singled out as an enemy because it refused to crook its knee to the ANC, or accept its strategy of armed struggle and the destruction of the South African economy.'[9]

In Natal, as elsewhere in South Africa, the 1980s were marked by large-scale movements of blacks from the rural to the urban areas. They brought with them blood feuds and faction fights that until then had mostly been restricted to the country districts.

Broadly speaking, Buthelezi was handicapped by the burden of two agendas. On the one hand, as Chief Minister he was Pretoria's agent and had a statutory responsibility — to say nothing of a moral responsibility to its people — to see that KwaZulu was well governed and that its structures were not targeted by insurrectionists. On the other hand if he had allowed Inkatha to be the 'liberation' movement he so often suggested it was, he would have had to give cognisance, even active assistance, to 'progressive groupings', reject narrow Zulu nationalism and help make the apartheid state — including KwaZulu — ungovernable. With his 90% tribal constituency, this was impossible.

Inkatha's balancing act ended abruptly in April 1980 when pupils in KwaMashu joined a nationwide school boycott. Buthelezi (whose cabinet was responsible for education) rejected it. He claimed it was being orchestrated by outside agitators and demanded that the pupils return to their studies. When they refused, an Inkatha impi armed with assegais, shields, knobkerries and axes moved into KwaMashu and sjamboked the striking pupils back to their desks.

In another incident, Buthelezi, who was also Chancellor of the University of Zululand, was scheduled to speak on campus. The students demonstrated against his impending visit. In the early morning of 29 October 1983 an Inkatha impi appeared and hacked and stabbed its way through a hostel, killing five students and wounding many others.[10]

With the rise of the UDF/COSATU (Congress South African Trade Unions) alliance Chief Buthelezi and Inkatha found their dominance in the politics of Natal and KwaZulu seriously challenged. This was particularly so in the townships, informal settlements and sprawling squatter camps around Durban and Pietermaritzburg. There was an informal declaration of war when the UDF announced it would work with any black political organisation except Inkatha.

What was going through Chief Buthelezi's mind at the time can be assessed by a speech he made to the KwaZulu Legislative Assembly in May 1984. He said: 'We must prepare ourselves to hit back with devastating force at those who destroy our property and kill us. It will be a sad day when a brother has to defend himself against his brother. This is what we will be forced to do if this kind of incident escalates. If and when we have a fully operational paramilitary wing in our police force, we will not be a soft option for any Tom, Dick or Harry who wants to attack us.'[11]

On 1 August 1985 prominent UDF activist and human rights lawyer, Victoria Mxenge, was assassinated outside her Umlazi home by operators of the Security Police's C1 unit. The Azanian Student's Organisation (AZASO) and the Congress of South African Students (COSAS) called for a seven day school stay-away as a period of mourning commencing on 5 August. Mobs of school children swollen by unemployed youths marched the streets of KwaMashu, Umlazi, Clermont, Lamontville and other KwaZulu 'polka dots' around Durban. Government structures were targeted, cars were stoned and Indian stores looted. The police battled to contain the extensive rioting and struggled to disperse the crowds. In Umlazi, Wellington Sabelo, a KwaZulu MP, brought an impi of Inkatha supporters to assist.

On Wednesday 7 August a heavily armed 300 strong Inkatha impi attacked mourners at the memorial service for Victoria Mxenge, killing 17 and wounding many others.

The rioting continued all day Thursday. By evening councillors and traders had begun to mobilise Inkatha supporters. By Friday Inkatha was in control of Ntuzuma. In KwaMashu 1 000 spearmen routed the rioters and began house to house searches for loot. At Inanda, meanwhile, the police managed to persuade a mob ransacking the Gandhi Phoenix Settlement to disperse. As they started to filter away, an Inkatha impi from Lindelani appeared and attempted to turn their withdrawal into a rout. The heavily armed Inanda crowd, however, fought back and inflicted savage casualties on the impi. Smarting from their defeat, they returned at 02:00 to mount a surprise attack. But they were expected and once again the community repulsed them, killing 12. By the time calm returned 67 had been killed, 1 000 were seriously injured and 180 businesses had been destroyed. Damage was estimated at more than R25 million.[12]

After August 1985 the populace of Natal and KwaZulu's township and informal settlement areas would be polarised into two hostile camps — Inkatha and the UDF/COSATU alliance. That a person might be apolitical — that his sympathies might not lie with either grouping, was irrelevant.

Tribal problems followed. For many years there had been a gradual migration of Pondos from the Transkei into Natal and KwaZulu. Most had settled in the Malakazi, Umbogintwini No. 5, and Umbumbulu squatter settlements and worked or sought work in the Durban or greater Durban area. Some had bought land and many were loyal members of Inkatha, but in those troubled times political loyalties no longer mattered. They were not Zulus and the Transkei was regarded as an ANC/UDF stronghold, so it was not difficult for Inkatha to regard the Pondos as enemies.

Trouble started after a Pondo man molested a Zulu woman in Malakazi in November 1985. A Zulu stabbed the molester and this sparked widespread fighting between the two factions. The Pondos fled Malakazi and sought refuge in Umbogintwini Number 5. A Zulu attack on the camp was routed and the Zulus left behind seven dead. On Christmas Day 1985 there was a bloody full-scale battle involving 5 000 Pondos and Zulus in Umbogintwini Number 5, which left 60 dead.

In January 1986 Pondos attacked Zulus on an Umbumbulu-bound train. A Zulu impi drove Pondos from Msahweni and looted and burnt their shacks. On 22 January a Pondo was burned alive by Zulus at the Isipingo railway station. In response 500 Pondos attacked KwaMakutha, but were repulsed. Pondo women fearing attack, fired their shacks and fled into the bush. The fire raced through the settlement and about 10 000 shacks were destroyed. 42 people died in the holocaust and 40 000 were left homeless. Peace was only restored after representatives from the Transkei and KwaZulu met for peace talks and there was a massive influx of police into the Natal Midlands.[13]

Buthelezi was a worried man as civil strife began to escalate out of control. Top security branch policeman, Brigadier Jac Buchner, was appointed head of the KwaZulu Police Security Branch by Pretoria. Later, as a major-general, he became the KwaZulu Commissioner of Police until his retirement.[14]

Although Inkatha allegedly had a quarter of a million paid up members, it had a relatively small constituency compared to the six million Zulus in the province. Its real power lay in KwaZulu's bureaucracy. Chief Minister Buthelezi and everyone in the KwaZulu Legislative Assembly were Inkatha members. The chiefs, the headmen and civil servants and KwaZulu policemen were only appointed if they belonged to Inkatha, thus giving the party total control over access to land, employment and trading opportunities. This approach was allied completely with the separate development policies of the National Party government — which were rooted in the policy that blacks should live in and be ruled by their own traditional leaders within their tribal homelands.

Clearly, with such backing there was no room in KwaZulu's bureaucracy for people tainted either by association or membership of the UDF/COSATU alliance. Such people were the enemy, the ANC. Association or membership of the opposition was assumed if they did not hold Inkatha cards.

To increase its constituency, Inkatha latterly aimed at incorporating the remaining black areas still falling within Natal's jurisdiction. The most important, probably, was the Edendale Valley west of Pietermaritzberg. It was no easy target for the tribally inclined Inkatha, because of Edendale's detribalised *kholwa* or Christian tradition that had existed for more than 100 years. The 100-strong Edendale contingent, which fought with the British Army against Cetshwayo in the war of 1879, were the only troops, black or white, who retired as a compact fighting force from the disastrous field of Isandhlwana.[15] So few, if any, Edendale folk had any wish to become retribalised in the new Zululand.

In the Edendale valley, Vulindlela and other areas of KwaZulu and Natal, an unofficial bloody war for political supremacy was waged in which at least 14 000 people died. At first it was fought between the warlords and vigilantes of Inkatha and the comrades of the UDF/COSATU Alliance. Later, though, it evolved into a fight between Inkatha supporters and ANC supporters. Both organisations denied lending support to the combatants.

There were no saints in this conflict and helpless civilians, women and children, were frequently targeted by both factions. At the start, the weaponry on both sides was crude. It ranged from shotguns and home-made pistols down to assegais, axes, pangas, iron bars, knives and stones. In later years Natal and KwaZulu became awash with modern firearms. AK47s could be bought for R5 000 and R1s for between R1 800 and R2 000. The price of a R4 was between R1 400 and R1 500. Rounds of ammunition went for between four and five rand a round.[16]

The Director of Military Intelligence, General Tienie Groenewald, saw Buthelezi at Ulundi on 25 November 1985 at the latter's request. Groenewald told him and the acting KwaZulu Police Commissioner, General Sipho Mathe, that MK was training specialist units in Mozambique to assassinate him (Buthelezi), KwaZulu cabinet ministers, their deputies, various government officials and other VIPs. They also planned to destroy KwaZulu government buildings. If true this was an extraordinary volte-face for the ANC, who until then had believed that killing Buthelezi would make him a martyr. Chief Buthelezi confirmed that he had received information to this effect.[17]

Deputy President Thabo Mbeki denied to the TRC in September 1996 that the ANC had ever considered such plans. He contended the story was a plot by senior military officers of the former regime to get Buthelezi on side. Chief Buthelezi refuted this. The Rev Londa Shembe, leader of one of the largest independent churches in South Africa, had maintained covert links with the ANC and MK. Shembe had heard that the ANC had assigned Terence Tyrone, an MK operative, to assassinate him. Shembe's family rejected the claim. He was, they said, totally loyal to the ANC and he would not have betrayed their plans. Chief Buthelezi, however, produced a warning letter from the Rev Shembe and a file of secret intelligence reports confirming the assassination plot.

Chief Buthelezi asked the SADF to provide him with close protection as he did not trust his existing SAP-trained bodyguards. On a broader plain, he required an intelligence service, a defence force and his own State Security Council for KwaZulu with which to facilitate and coordinate counter-insurgency actions. In addition he asked that a battalion of Zulu troops be based at Jozini.[18]

Groenewald briefed the Chief of Staff Intelligence, Vice-Admiral Dries Putter, on his discussions with the Chief Minister. He recommended the SADF meet Buthelezi's needs by secretly training a defensive unit of between 50 and 100 men and an offensive unit of ten to 20 men. In turn Vice-Admiral Putter spoke to SADF chief, General Jannie Geldenhuys, on 27 November and suggested that either he or Defence Minister Magnus Malan seek an urgent meeting with Chief Buthelezi to capitalise on the new spirit of goodwill and cooperation he was displaying.

The next day an extraordinary meeting of the SSC was convened at Tuynhuys, Cape Town, and Chief Buthelezi's requirements were discussed. The council mandated Defence Minister Malan, Constitutional Development and Planning Minister Chris Heunis and Law and Order Minister Louis le Grange to help Buthelezi create a security force for KwaZulu. A special interdepartmental committee was appointed to implement decisions. In turn this committee set up a sub-committee to investigate Buthelezi's special needs, including a paramilitary unit and the power to issue firearms licences.

General Malan described the negotiations as 'highly sensitive' and a 'huge political risk', because although Buthelezi was a target of the ANC he was also publicly opposed to the

resident René of the Seychelles examines a bloodstained shirt of the Ancient Order of the Froth Blowers following ol Mike Hoare's failed coup attempt.

Colonel Craig Williamson found a better way to control the Seychelles – he made a successful bid for their Intelligence service through a Military Intelligence front company.

President P W Botha arrives by SAAF Puma for a *Bosberaad* at Alldays, Northern Transvaal, in the mid 1980s.

Finding he was down to his last packet of sliced biltong President Botha sets out to shoot a buck or fifty.

Later, dining on venison with Law and Order Minister Adriaan Vlok.

remain incognito the
esident and his ministers
sguised themselves as
nerican tourists with David
vingstone-type pith
lmets. Pith helmets (l to r)
reign Minister Pik Botha,
esident P W Botha,
efence Minister Magnus
alan and Minister of Co-
peration and Development
et Koornhoff.

Minister Piet Koornhoff (centre) explains some of the niceties surrounding the 'independence' of the Republic of Ciskei.

oreign Minister Pik Botha
vearing Lincoln green) in a
ensive mood.

Above – General Jannie Geldenhuys (SADF Chief) (left) and Lt Gen Dewan Prem Chand of India (UNTAG Force Commander) discuss military arrangements in Windhoek during April 1989

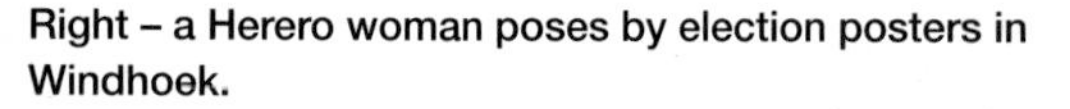

Right – a Herero woman poses by election posters in Windhoek.

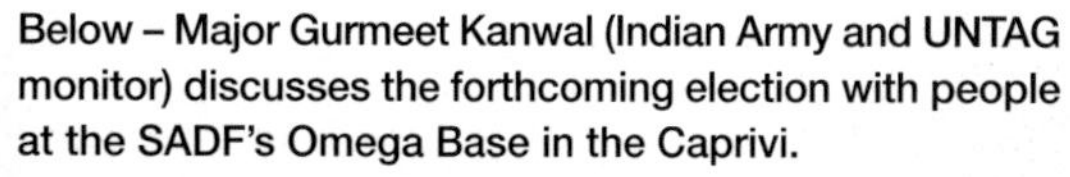

Below – Major Gurmeet Kanwal (Indian Army and UNTAG monitor) discusses the forthcoming election with people at the SADF's Omega Base in the Caprivi.

Top right – Bastion Building in Windhoek. Nerve centre for the SADF's Comops' (Communications Operations) plans to swing the election in the DTA's (Democratic Turnhalle Alliance) favour.

Top left – UNTAG monitors the voting to ensure it is free and fair.

Centre – DTA celebrates in advance of the results.

Below – DTA's hopes lie in the dust as its 9 000 votes in Owamboland are swamped by SWAPO's 196 169.

The End Conscription Campaign was constantly monitored by Military Intelligence through Veterans for Victory. People w stopped at its stands were photographed and their car registration numbers noted. This picture, one of thousands taken, shot with a telephoto lens.

Veterans for Victory were responsible for this Johannesburg bus. The PFP (Progressive Federal Party) complained and the artwork was removed within 24 hours.

Left – Rob Brown, Veteran's for Victory organiser, took parties of right-wing Americans to visit Jonas Savimbi at his Jamba HQ in southern Angola. Seen here with his UNITA bodyguard.

Below – after the signing of the Protocol of Brazzaville relative to Namibian independence on 22 December 1999, Rob Brown was instructed to orchestrate a visit there by the right-wing missionary group, Frontline Fellowship. It was expected they would give a positive spin to the forthcoming political campaign. It did not work out that way. Rev Peter Hammond far right and Colonel Jan Breytenbach far left.

KWELA
BUTCHERY

GROCERIES
LET US SHARE
Coca-Cola

ft page – the UDF's orchestrated
mpaign of civil disobedience and
lence in the 1980s turned many black
vnships into no-go areas for the
curity Forces. The police even provided
ned guards for firefighters.

o – some security policemen were
sponsible for horrific excesses when
hting to regain control of the security
uation. This often occurred on the
ders of higher police and political
thority, but was latterly denied. Facing
music at the TRC amnesty hearings
Steve Biko (l to r) Capt Daniel Siebert,
Col Gideon Nieuwoudt and Col Harold
yman. Those standing are bodyguards.

ght – KwaZulu's Chief Minister, Dr
tsha (Mangosuthu) Buthelezi. His
atha Freedom Party and the ANC/UDF
ance fought a bitter undeclared war
oughout the late 1980s and early 1990s.

Prime Minister John Vorster welcomes Presid
Kaiser Matanzima as a member of the Homela
Club. Then he only took Vorster's hand, but la
he took an arm and a leg.

Prime Minister George Matanzima of Transkei. He took the other arm and a leg. His training, having been struck off the roll of attorneys for serious frauds, was excellent.

Foreign Minister Pi
Botha charms
President Lennox S
and Mrs Sebe of th
Republic of Ciskei
an official function.
Shortly afterwards
State Security Cour
of which Botha wa
permanent membe
approved a plan to
murder him.

Gen Joffel van der Westhuizen. His *Operation Katzen* (named after General Liebenberg and himself) was designed to
rcibly incorporate Transkei, Ciskei and the 'white corridor' between into a single state. It also involved murder.
oove right – Vice Admiral Dries Putter, Chief of Staff Intelligence, strongly reprimanded Brigadier Johan Deyzel for reporting
at someone was planning to murder President Lennox Sebe.
elow – Gen Kat Liebenburg, the other half of *Operation Katzen*. He was tried and acquitted of the KwaMakutha massacre
ong with other notables. Seen here with a bodyguard.

Left – Gen Bantu Holomisa took over the Transkei in a bloodless coup. He kicked out military adviser Major-General Reid Daly and his men for their involvement in *Operation Katzen*.

Left below – Brig Oupa Gqozo took over Ciskei in a bloodless coup.

Above – Brig Johan Deyzel blew the whistle on the *Operation Katzen* plan to murder President Lennox Sebe.

Left – General Charles Sebe was lured into Ciskei and murdered by Br Gqozo and Military Intelligence. 'He was poison . . . we blew him!'

Left – Colonel Joe Verster, managing director of the CCB and below – Maj Gen Eddie Webb, Chairman of the CCB. Only they can say if every operation was approved by the chairman. Unfortunately, each contradicts the other.

Top left – Ferdi Barnard clearly a CCB member althoug it has been denied. He was convicted of the murder of David Webster. Not a man to tangle with.

Above – Calla Botha (left) with his attorney. Ferdi sai Botha drove the car when he shot David Webster.

Left – Staal Burger (standing), Regional Manager for the CCB's Region 6. Seen here with his predecessor at the elité Brixton Murder and Robbery Squad, Krappies Engelbrecht. Engelbrecht and Lt Gen Witkop Badenhorst 'investigated' the CCB on behalf of the Chief of the SADF.

ove – CCB victim Dr David Webster, gunned down in
hannesburg.

Above – CCB victim Advocate Anton Lubowski, gunned down in Windhoek.

ight – UN Special Representative in Nambia, Martti Ahtisaari,
as nearly a CCB victim. Plans were in hand to firebomb
s car.

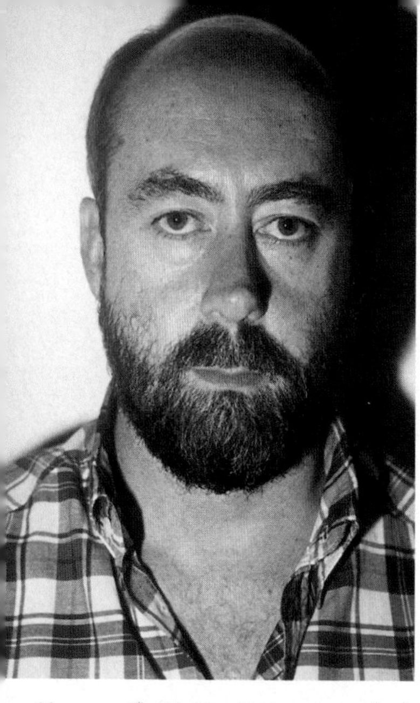

Above – Dr Wouter Basson supplied chemical and biological agents to *Project Barnacle* and the CCB.

Above right – CCB agent Leslie Lesia, arrested in Zimbabwe with his especially modified car.

Above – the burnt-out car of highly decorated war hero, Colonel Co[r]
Meerholz. Only his Rolex watch survived the blazing inferno.

Left – the late Colonel Corrie Meerholz (when still a major) with his R
watch. Was he murdered by his former CCB colleagues?

apartheid government. This meant he could have changed his political mind at any time, come to a deal and formed an alliance with the ANC virtually overnight. This would have placed any such force at the ANC's disposal. It also would have meant that the government would indirectly be supporting the 'revolutionary onslaught' against itself.[19]

The sub-committee assembled in Ulundi in early January 1986 and issued a report listing Buthelezi's needs that should be met. They included the paramilitary unit and the blanket authority to issue firearms' licences. The sub-committee believed it vital to create the impression that KwaZulu was assuming its new powers and functions legally.

The recommendations were accepted by the special interdepartmental committee, but said that Ministers Heunis and Malan should personally discuss the question of the proposed paramilitary unit with Chief Buthelezi. This suggestion was given the green light by the SSC who wanted the ministers to evaluate the chief minister's requirements and aims in respect of the paramilitary unit.

General Groenewald was instructed to clear the ground. In a preliminary meeting Chief Buthelezi requested a 'contra-mobilisation capability' and an intelligence capability. The offensive capability was required to prevent the UDF disrupting Inkatha meetings, destroying property and terrorising, attacking or murdering Inkatha members. It was agreed the Chief Minister would select 200 candidates for special training.

General Groenewald reported back to General Malan who demanded more details about the proposed paramilitary unit and how it would be financed, stipulating that he 'must be able to sell the proposals to Mr Heunis'. The SADF set up a special task group under army chief General Kat Liebenberg to provide the information required.

The 'top secret' Liebenberg Report, which was handed to SADF Chief General Jannie Geldenhuys, said the unit was required to 'neutralise' the UDF. It would have the capacity to mobilise people of 'Zulu culture' and would include about 30 men to operate covertly against the UDF. They would form the basis for a future KwaZulu defence force. The SADF would benefit because it would make it more effective against the UDF. If successful, it would pave the way for similar projects in other 'national states'.

The report stipulated that the Department of Constitutional Development and Planning would be responsible for the overall coordination of the project. It was important to create the impression that the unit had originated in KwaZulu and that it could not be traced back to the SADF or the South African government. The objective was to have a small unit of well trained troops that could act offensively against the ANC, the UDF and their allies. A cover organisation responsible for the paramilitary training would be established.

A R3,5 million opening budget was allocated to neutralise the UDF in Natal. The report also proposed that the black 121-Battalion based at Lenasia should become the core of a future Defence Force for KwaZulu. In future only proven Inkatha loyalists should be recruited into its ranks.[20]

General Malan prepared a summary of the report for Minister Heunis, but left out references to the paramilitary unit. He explained to Heunis that 'this' information was not included as it was 'of a departmental nature and due to [its] sensitivity'. This indicated that Heunis knew the details, but they were too sensitive to be circulated in writing outside the ranks of the SADF. After discussions between Vice-Admiral Putter and Chief Buthelezi the plan, by then code named *Operation Marion*, was accepted. From the South African point of view the objective was to make Inkatha self sufficient and to de-link its military capacity from the South African government.[21]

Chief Buthelezi's personal assistant since 1976 and later Inkatha's Deputy Secretary General, Zakhele 'MZ' Khumalo, was appointed as Inkatha's liaison officer for the operation. He had learnt his trade under Eschel Rhoodie in the Information Department. MZ Khumalo helped to recruit and screen 206 young men deemed 'loyal to the KwaZulu government'. Daluxolo Luthuli was appointed their political commissar, but overall they remained under the control of MZ Khumalo. At first, MZ Khumalo maintained that he had no idea the SADF would be involved in training them. The impression he was given was that a Mr Swart of Swart Security would employ instructors to train the recruits in Caprivi.

This was confirmed by Captain Opperman, a former Recce intelligence officer, who was appointed second in command of *Operation Marion* for the training phase, but he made no mention of Mr Swart. Whatever the case, Opperman was certain MZ Khumalo had finally concluded that the operation was an SADF one — despite the initial cover story. He said that as a 'political man' put in charge of troops — some highly trained in offensive warfare — Khumalo had been 'caught between the devil and the deep blue sea'.[22]

The recruits were briefed that they would be undergoing a tough training course. If they passed successfully it would qualify them as members of the KwaZulu Police. Khumalo later stringently denied that it was intended to train the group for 'hit squad attacks'. He insisted their main purpose was to win hearts and minds.[23]

On 16 April 1986 the contingent was moved to D F Malan Airport (Durban International) in closed troop carriers. They were backed up to waiting SAAF C-130 transports.Hidden from the view of even the casual onlooker, the recruits filed aboard.

They had no idea where they were going, although a rumour that they were en route to Israel was encouraged. After several hours flying time the aircraft landed in darkness at the Immelmann airstrip near the Recce's Fort Doppies base in Caprivi. A flare path of torches marked the airstrip for their arrival, but these were extinguished as soon as the aircraft landed. They disembarked and were shepherded into waiting trucks by drivers in nondescript camouflage uniforms.

An hour later they arrived at Hippo Base on an island in the Kwando River. It was part of the San Michelle guerrilla training school commanded by Colonel Jan Breytenbach. The trainees had no idea where they were and no one enlightened them. Guerrillas from other organisations, UNITA in particular, were also undergoing training elsewhere in the extensive base area. They never came into contact with them or even learned they were there.

After spending a night in the open, they offloaded tents from the trucks and set up a camp. The course fell under former Recce and RENAMO specialist, Major Jake Jacobs. The officer responsible to the Chief of Staff Intelligence (CSI) for *Operation Marion* was General Neels van Tonder, assisted by Colonel Cor van Niekerk. The latter was CSI's Director of Special tasks, a specialist in guerrilla surrogate organisations who had taken over RENAMO from the Rhodesians in 1980. The instructors used code names and wore the same nondescript uniforms as the drivers who had collected them.

Captain J P Opperman and Sergeant Cloete joined the programme midway through the training. Opperman was briefed in Pretoria before flying out and was told the trainees would be used as 'force which we would use to [counter] the onslaught against our country'. He travelled to Hippo Base where he was met by Major Jacobs and the 'project manager' Colonel Hennie Blaauw.

First, everyone underwent a period of basic military training. This in all likelihood included infantry training and elements of guerrilla warfare. After all, San Michelle's *raison d'être* was to train guerrillas. Later the 206 men were divided into four groups that specialised respectively in offensive, defensive, contra-mobilisation and VIP protection.

The 30-strong Offensive Group was given advanced training in urban and guerrilla warfare. This included house clearing, training in the use of G3 and AK47 rifles, hand-grenades, the use of explosives and landmines. While under training they were told to behave as if they were shooting a 'Hani' or a 'Tambo'.[24]

The Defensive Group was trained in the covert collection of intelligence, the analysis of target information, the use of codes, cover stories and the development of dossiers on people targeted for elimination.[25]

The 120 strong Contra-Mobilisation Group was trained to promote Inkatha amongst the people for and on behalf of the Military Intelligence front company, Adult Education Specialists. Their activities had little to do with education, but much to do with propaganda.

As far as possible the training of the different groups was kept separate and the recruits were told not to discuss its nature with the members of other groups. Two recruits were injured during the training and were moved to a security ward at 2-Military Hospital, Cape Town. Security wards were used for the treatments of wounded from organisations like UNITA, RENAMO and so on.[26]

Their salaries of R300 per month were paid by MZ Khumalo. He claimed the money came from Mr Swart of Swart Security. A contract for the training was, in fact, signed between the KwaZulu government and Swart Security — a Military Intelligence front company, but the contract disappeared — probably into the shredder. R300 000 a month was allocated to the programme by CSI who channelled the money from Military Intelligence through Armscor. From there it was paid into various Inkatha accounts. A variety of accounts were used to give the impression that the monies had been contributed by Inkatha branches around the country. Khumalo visited the trainees in the Caprivi three times. He also attended their passing out parade.[27]

They were returned to KwaZulu after seven months' training. According to trainee Bhekisisa Alex Khumalo, Chief Buthelezi personally welcomed them back. 'When he [Buthelezi] arrived we were introduced to him. He then shook our hands and thanked us for having returned [from the Caprivi]. He then showed us a beast that he was going to slaughter on our behalf'.[28]

Members of the Offensive and Contra-mobilisation groups, who were first drafted as special constables, went on another six-week training course in Cape Town. They posed as school leavers 'to enable Inkatha to identify its targets'.

Shortly afterwards Colonels Cor van Niekerk and John More visited Chief Buthelezi and presented him with the gift of a bullet-proof vest. The Chief expressed his gratitude to them for training the 206 men, which he regarded as a boost to his safety.[29]

President F W de Klerk and Foreign Minister Pik Botha were both at a 1986 meeting of the State Security Council where *Operation Marion* was discussed.[30]

In 1996 General Magnus Malan and 19 others were charged in the Supreme Court for the murder of 13 people killed in what became known as the KwaMakutha massacre of 1987. Chief Buthelezi called the use of his name in court documents the 'biggest poppycock I have ever heard of'. He affirmed he had possessed information that people were 'actually plotting my murder and wanted to kill my cabinet colleagues'.

He had already declined offers of 'independence' for KwaZulu so 'I did not have my own army' and 'only had a small police force. When the violence started in 1985 I had a duty not only to see to my own protection but the protection of other people . . . so we selected the 200 young people for training. Where they were trained and how they were trained — I was not involved in that.

'Now if some of the people decided then to break the law and do what they did, then that is a matter for them, because that's a matter of law, which needs to be resolved in court. To try to drag in my name merely because I did that . . . there was nothing sinister about that. I have a very clear conscience about it. I was threatened, people were dying and they were asking what we were doing about that. With only a small police force, the acting commissioner at that time decided we should approach the military.'

In direct contradiction 'a highly placed Inkatha source' told *The Weekly Mail* in 1991 that when they returned from the Caprivi, the trainees were told their task was 'to kill Inkatha opposition, to propagate its policies and to recruit and mobilise for it. Some were also trained as aides'.[31]

MZ Khumalo travelled to Cape Town and met a staff officer of General Malan and other unidentified officers. He requested SADF assistance in the establishment of a permanent base for the new force. The officers were worried that the meeting had even taken place. An SADF report classified 'top secret' explained: 'Mr Khumalo was under the impression that military intelligence personnel could help him at a departmental level to acquire land for a base camp. It has since been explained to him that these actions will immediately link the army to the land. He must carry out the acquisition through KwaZulu channels.' This confirms the 'Mr Swart' deception did not last for long.[32]

Having nowhere to house them, MZ Khumalo allegedly told the men to return to their homes and reintegrate into their communities until they were needed.General van Tonder said they were not deployed immediately after their training. No formal structures, as envisaged by the SSC when it approved *Operation Marion* in 1986, had been established by the KwaZulu government for them. Such structures included a joint intelligence network and a joint security management system.[33]

This did not preclude Captain Opperman and Sergeant Cloete from the continuation of training for the new force. This would have been impossible if they had been dispersed to their homes. This was confirmed in a report in *The Weekly Mail* in 1991 which said the trainees were moved to a secret base on Etshanini Farm at Mkuze. Funds of between R200 000 and R300 000 were provided by Guy Boardman's Creed Consultants to refurbish the base. Creed, another Military Intelligence front, bought vehicles for the base and 'donated' others to MZ Khumalo. Six were bought for the unit's use. They were all registered in the name of MZ Khumalo of Etshanini Farm, Mkuze. Most equipment provided had SADF markings. The existence of the secret base was confirmed by Captain Opperman, but he did not name it or say where it was.[34]

Military Intelligence supplied toy laser guns for training purposes, as well as binoculars, waterproof torches, searchlights, clothing and Military Intelligence identity documents known as 'James Bond' cards. They identified the holders as members of MI and requested they be assisted in their official duties. The cards guaranteed the holders unquestioned access to military buildings. Another issue was an identity card showing they were employees of Omega, a non existent security company. This was a cover to explain periods of absence and the source of their salaries to their families.[35] The unit's clandestine nature demanded that its members always wore civilian clothes, kept their hair long and did not adhere to established military procedures.

Captain Opperman said he had lunched with *Operation Marion*'s chief military intelligence officer, Colonel Hennie Blaauw, and a wealthy German businessman sympathetic to the Inkatha cause in October 1986. The German agreed to supply, and was said to have supplied, highly sophisticated radio equipment for bodyguards, bullet proof vests and other equipment worth millions of rands.[36] That the donor was really a benevolent German businessman is unlikely. In 1996 Colonel John More, the senior staff officer for *Operation Marion*, testified that the minutes of a meeting indicating he had told Chief Buthelezi that funds from a foreign donor had been deposited in an account for the operation were untrue. The money had actually originated from the 'Scraper Fund' — used for classified Military Intelligence operations.[37]

Captain Opperman and Sergeant Cloete were ordered to spend the first month after the return from Caprivi familiarising themselves with Durban and its environs. They were to pose as tourists and get to know the areas in which they were going to operate.

Defence Minister Malan testified that in late 1986 Chief Buthelezi had thanked the South African government, through him, for having adopted *Operation Marion* and training paramilitary soldiers for him, thereby demonstrating the SADF's support for Inkatha.

The thought that the SADF's involvement in *Operation Marion* could be unlawful occurred to Major-General Tienie Groenewald who suggested in a paper that the paramilitary actions envisaged might be unconstitutional, and that members of the SADF might expose themselves to criminal prosecution by their involvement.[38]

After the trainees returned from the Caprivi, apparently towards the end of 1986, Captain Opperman testified that MZ Khumalo approached him and said that 'they [the Inkatha recruits] wanted to strike back . . . they were trained and sitting idle'.[39] He allegedly approached Colonel John More and asked permission to launch an operation. Colonel More, he alleged, gave permission for planning to commence on operations targeting 'persons whose death would have a positive impact on the Inkatha Freedom Party'.[40] Colonel More later denied all knowledge of this.

Captain Opperman described the operation as probably the most sensitive plan ever approved by the former government and its military, especially at a time when the SADF was reducing support for foreign resistance movements. 'All hell would have broken loose if anything had leaked from the KwaMakutha massacre and was traced back to the military . . . It would have been terrible.'[41]

Captain Opperman then instructed the group's political commissar, Daluxolo Luthuli, to select four targets 'whose death would have a positive impact on Inkatha'. Four members of the defensive group were nominated to compile target dossiers. After all the target dossiers had been submitted, Captain Opperman asked Military Intelligence and the Security Police to check and ensure that none of the proposed targets were informers. He could not remember the names of two of the targets, but one was Billy Nair (later an ANC MP), then a member of the UDF's national executive and on the run from the police. He had once served a 20-year sentence on Robben Island. 'It was obvious', Captain Opperman said, 'that Billy Nair was conscious that he was either under surveillance or there was a threat against him, because he readily changed vehicles.' Such vigilance saved his life.[42]

Bhekisisa Alex Khumalo reconnoitred the house of UDF activist Victor Ntuli who lived in KwaMakutha. The dossier on Ntuli, allegedly a UDF paymaster for operations against Inkatha and a trained MK operator,[43] was the next most comprehensive. So he was also chosen as a target. The dossier failed to mention that the target house belonged to Rev Willie Ntuli. Victor was only a lodger.

Captain Opperman testified that Colonel More gave him the final go-ahead in Pretoria. More, he said, arranged for the issue of AK47s and ammunition from Ferntree — a secret military base close to the Drakensberg Mountains — by a Colonel Gerrit Griesel. Griesel agreed he had made the issue but, presumably on a need-to-know basis, had not been told the stuff was required for a hit-squad attack. Opperman said it was planned to take the weapons to Pretoria for destruction in a furnace at Iscor (the state-owned Iron and Steel Corporation) after the operation. In court Colonel More described Captain Opperman's allegations as 'laughable and absurd'. If he had wanted rifles he would have got them from Steyn's Park armoury in Pretoria. It had a holding of 'tens of thousands' of rifles.[44]

Captain Opperman said he liaised with MZ Khumalo on several occasions during the planning stages when they discussed the attack.[45]

With Sergeant Cloete and MZ Khumalo, Opperman rendezvoused with the 12-man hit squad in a dry river bed near Ulundi on 20 January 1987. Political commissar, Daluxolo Luthuli, and the guide Bhekisisa Alex Khumalo, were there. They issued weapons and taped torches to the barrels so the target could be illuminated. Opperman and Cloete briefed them on how to conduct the attack.[46] The layout of Ntuli's house was drawn in the sand. Final rehearsals were conducted and the squad members were allowed time to practise and test weapons.

Sergeant Cloete had conducted the preliminary training. He said Captain Opperman had ordered him to train a squad to penetrate the home of Victor Ntuli. They were to 'kill all the occupants of the house', including the women and children. He said that 'under the circumstances it seemed to be a legal order', particularly as Opperman told him the attack had been authorised by Pretoria. In answer to a question he said: 'Yes, I thought he [Opperman] was mad.' He described the order as the most outrageous he had ever received.[47]

A white Combi was used for the operation. Specially prepared posters advertising a disco were pasted to its sides and number plates stolen by Captain Opperman earlier were attached. A member of the group, Peter Msane, was handed a chit on which was written 'Chapter 1 verse 1'. He was ordered to leave it behind after the attack. The wording is an indication that it was the group's first operation.

Afterwards, Captain Opperman and Sergeant Cloete went to the Malibu Hotel where they met Major Louis Botha, the Security Police's liaison officer for *Operation Marion*. His task, Opperman testified, was to divert normal police patrols and to 'sweep' the scene for incriminating evidence before the police got there. Captain Botha later denied knowing anything about it or about *Operation Marion*.[48]

Victor Ntuli had been in hiding for a month and was away. His brother, Rev Willie Ntuli, however, was at home. A lot of women and children were staying the night because of a late night prayer meeting.

Anna Khumalo was asleep when she was awakened by a bang on the door and a fusillade of shots. She quickly grabbed her toddler and tried to get out of the house, but so many people were asleep on the floor that she could not get past them. So she ducked into a wardrobe, her baby in her arms, and cowered down. She heard a frightening crescendo of gunfire and screams.

Meanwhile, Bhekisisa Alex Khumalo, the guide, waited in the Combi while the ten-man offensive team smashed its way inside and sprayed shots at the unfortunates there.[49]

Neighbours alerted by the shooting came out, but they were driven back into the safety of their homes by the gunfire. Thembinkosi Mkhize, an Inkatha member, saw a minibus arrive at the Ntuli house at about 02:00. 'Three or four men got out. When I saw they were armed with firearms I hid under the bed. I was afraid.' He did not leave his house again until the police arrived.[50]

Silence eventually returned, but Anna Khumalo was petrified and she remained with her baby in the doubtful safety of the wardrobe. Several hours later she plucked up enough courage to leave it and was confronted by a charnel house of 12 bodies, including five children under the age of ten.

Rev Willie Ntuli and his three children aged six, 16, and 19 were amongst the dead. His wife, Ethel Ntuli survived as did her one-year-old granddaughter, Nomvula. They were saved because a body fell and covered them. A church elder, Ernest Thusini, his wife Faith and their children Nomfundo (10), Phumzile (8), Vukile (7), twins Mbuso and Nombuso (6) and Sanele (4) were asleep when the room was sprayed with bullets. Ernest, Faith and Nombuso survived. Nomfundo became the 13th fatal casualty when she was declared brain dead after more than a week on a life support machine. Ten-year-old Ernest Ntuzhini, whose four siblings were less fortunate, also escaped with his life after hiding in a wardrobe.

Ironically, although he survived that attack, Victor Ntuli was shot dead at a political rally in 1990. No one has been arrested for his murder.

Captain Opperman said Major Botha diverted police patrols away from the scene. If he did, he was highly successful because Major Allan Alford of the Amanzimtoti murder and robbery unit only got there five hours after the shooting. This was despite Amanzimtoti Police Station being only a ten-minute drive away. Major Alford described the carnage of bodies scattered around bedrooms. A child, her stomach ripped open by a bullet, lay among them. Only a sudden movement as she briefly opened her eyes alerted him to the realisation that she was still alive.

It was not like a normal investigation, Major Alford recalled. Senior officers arriving at the scene behaved in a 'confused' manner and could not make up their minds as to who should take charge of the investigation. 'It was disgusting, the way the scene was handled, for the offence we were dealing with.' He agreed that he might have been partly responsible for the chaotic situation because he had failed to secure the crime scene before 30 to 50 other policemen arrived. 150 AK47 cartridge cases were found at the scene.[51]

At a much later stage, after the bodies and exhibits had been removed, Captain Sipho Mbele was detailed to take over the docket. It surprised him that the Security Police had not taken it over as the discovery of AK47 cartridge cases was a sure sign the case was politically motivated and involved 'ANC terrorists'. In his experience the Security Police had always handled such cases. The Security Police, however, advanced the improbable theory that it was just a 'plain murder' case. They suggested the person responsible was Victor Ntuli, because his father, one of the victims, had expelled him from the house.[52]

This theory became even more improbable when it was discovered that Ntuli's father was not even amongst the victims.

A week later, despite facing obvious obstacles, the tenacious Captain Sipho Mbele arrested Ephraim Buthelezi for possession of an unlicensed firearm and as a suspect in the murders. He was a cousin of Chief Gatsha Buthelezi and his praise singer. Oddly enough on the night of the massacre it was alleged that the KwaZulu Police were guarding his house, which was only a 100m from the Ntuli home.[53]

The next day Captain Mbele's commander, Captain Phillip Oosthuizen, called him into his office at the Amanzimtoti police station. Ephraim Buthelezi and an unnamed senior Inkatha legislator were there. 'The station commander was in a very bad mood and wanted to know why I [had] arrested Buthelezi. He told me Buthelezi was a very important person and he ordered me to take him to court immediately to have the case withdrawn.'

Captain Mbele's investigations were further handicapped when the Security Police arrested two policemen assisting him in the investigation under the Emergency Regulations. The arrests were for no apparent reason.[54]

Political commissar Daluxolo Luthuli said some of those who had planned the massacre had lived with Ephraim Buthelezi before the attack. He also said that Ephraim had assisted in identifying opponents of Inkatha in KwaMakutha.[55]

Captain Opperman said the hit squad rendezvoused after the massacre with himself and Sergeant Cloete under a freeway bridge. They reported that everything had gone well, except that Msane had forgotten to leave the 'Chapter 1 verse 1' chit at the scene. They cleaned the Combi of disco posters and removed the stolen registration plates. They drove to Umhlanga Rocks where they burnt the posters and disposed of the number plates. Their next stop was MZ Khumalo's shop at Ulundi. There was no formal debrief, only informal discussions. It was revealed that Victor Ntuli had escaped death, but women and children had been killed. MZ Khumalo asked Captain Opperman to give him money to buy a goat. He would arrange for it to be ceremonially slaughtered as a gesture of mourning over the deaths of the women and children.[56]

'I was horrified', Captain Opperman said. 'If we knew, if intelligence had shown there were women and children in the place, the operation would never have taken place.' Despite this, he said, 'the operation was successful, but the wrong people were killed . . . all that went wrong is that they shot women and children and missed the target. I was 100 per cent satisfied with the operation, except for the women and children shot'. His superiors were happy with the operation's execution because it was carried out without a risk of those behind the killings being exposed.[57]

Captain Opperman and Sergeant Cloete withdrew the squad's weapons, packed them in a steel trunk and at a rendezvous behind the old Durban Prison, handed it to the Natal Command's Senior Military Intelligence chief, Colonel Jacobus Victor. Opperman later went with Commandant Jan van der Merwe to Natal Command. He collected the trunk and loaded it in the boot of his car. With Van der Merwe following, they drove to a lonely stretch of road between Durban and Ulundi where the trunk was transferred to Van der Merwe's car. It was his job to convey the trunk to Pretoria for the weapons to be smelted in an Iscor furnace. Van der Merwe denied he had done such a thing. Colonel Victor agreed he had accepted the trunk from Opperman, but said he had no idea what the contents were.[58]

Captain Opperman said General Neels van Tonder, the Director of Intelligence Operations, congratulated him on the success of the operational planning and for the security aspects, but 'not for the people killed'. General van Tonder later denied that he had authorised the KwaMakutha attack or that he had congratulated Opperman. Colonel Cor van Niekerk also denied authorising the attack.[59]

Billy Nair, himself a target considered for assassination, suggested there were probably wider reasons for the massacre. The killings almost derailed a landmark meeting for exploratory talks between exiled ANC president, Dr Oliver Tambo, and US Secretary of State, George Schultz. The South Africans insisted the killings were (ANC) 'terrorist related' and 'the Americans were very keen to find out the facts'. The UDF called an urgent press conference. It was addressed by the intended victim, Victor Ntuli, who had lost his family so cruelly. What he said convinced the Americans that the ANC was not involved. The Schultz/Tambo meeting took place as scheduled.[60]

Captain Opperman alleged that on General Magnus Malan's instructions, Colonel Cor van Niekerk ordered an end to all offensive operations relating to *Operation Marion* after the KwaMakutha attack.[61]

Opperman had given MZ Khumalo ammunition on at least five occasions. In 1987 he gave him more than a 1 000 AK rounds, 250 rounds of 9mm ammunition and several hand grenades.[62]

Bhekisisa Alex Khumalo claimed in evidence that some time after the KwaMakutha attack, he had moved to Johannesburg and worked as a bodyguard for Themba Khoza, a senior Inkatha official. He had also dealt in home-made firearms and distributed ammunition to Inkatha-controlled hostels. While there he had shared a flat with Peter Msane, who had also taken part in the KwaMakutha massacre.[63]

During a meeting in January 1988, Chief Buthelezi allegedly asked the Chief of Staff Intelligence, Vice-Admiral Putter, for the training of more members of Inkatha, so as to swing the ongoing conflict against the UDF in the black townships in Inkatha's favour. In March 1988 General Malan said he believed Inkatha was not doing enough about the situation in Natal and suggested they should 'climb in'.[64]

MZ Khumalo testified that although in charge of the Caprivi trainees, he had found them difficult to control. This prompted Chief Buthelezi to set up a meeting between Khumalo and General Malan in August 1988. During the five-minute meeting Khumalo outlined problems with the 'restless' trainees. 'We had heard that they were getting involved in the fighting that was going on in their [home] areas. Some would just disappear for weeks.' Most only returned to Ulundi to collect their salaries at the end of each month.[65] He also complained that the SADF was not committed to *Operation Marion*. This resulted in an officer being posted to Natal Command to take control of the Caprivi trainees. They were rounded up and sent to a camp. Intermittent training, including by the SAP, continued until most of them were integrated into the KwaZulu Police in 1989. Despite this, the SADF continued to finance *Operation Marion* until at least 1991, perhaps longer. What appears to have happened, although there is no firm evidence, was that from 1988 control of the trainees, and probably others that followed, was progressively passed from the SADF to the SAP.

MZ Khumalo denied the trainees had ever been involved in hit squad activity. Their sole purpose, he said, was to protect dignitaries and the buildings of the KwaZulu government. 'We had received reports that the UDF would attack KwaZulu installations.'[66]

He omitted to mention that the unit's 'demobilisation' only took place after 'security problems' threatened to compromise the whole *Operation Marion* exercise. This followed the arrest of trainees, including political commissar Daluxolo Luthuli, for crimes committed during the course of offensive actions.

Captain Opperman testified that '[Major] Louis Botha told me [Daluxolo] Luthuli had been arrested and was telling everyone' in the cells who cared to listen about *Operation Marion*.[67] 'They tried to convince us Luthuli was going to blow *Operation Marion* wide open', he said. 'The security threat to the country would have been immense. General Buchner [the KwaZulu Police Commissioner] suggested we kill Luthuli. If it should have come out, the Defence Force would have taken a helluva knock, the National Party would have taken a helluva knock and Inkatha would have gone down the drain.'

Both he and Major Botha were in favour of the idea, Opperman said.[68] 'We [Military Intelligence] told Botha we would not carry it out without a specific written order from the police.' The embryo plan, Captain Opperman testified, was finally sunk after a meeting with MZ Khumalo. 'Khumalo was shocked and was definitely not keen for such a thing [the murder] to take place.'

A signal dated 31 August 1988 from the office of the Minister of Defence, General Malan, to the Chief of the SADF, General Jannie Geldenhuys said there was a need to 'temporarily remove' a member of the *Marion* group. Senior military officers and the Commissioner of Police, General Johan van der Merwe and his Deputy, General Basie Smit met to make arrangements. It is significant that the military and the police at the highest level were willing to meet and conspire to subvert the course of justice.[69]

Daluxolo Luthuli was eventually spirited away from police custody and taken to a farm. He was 'kept busy with TV, video and a lot of magazines' while plans for *Operation Marion* continued. After *Operation Marion* had petered out he was frequently seen paying visits to an ANC office.

'In 1994 the newspapers were full of hit squad developments. Luthuli was going to talk', Captain Opperman said. He asked the military if they were prepared to safeguard his position. They refused to give him such a reassurance, so he resigned and voluntarily handed himself over to the police task unit investigating murder squads in KwaZulu Natal. He agreed to turn state witness and for a long time lived under a witness protection programme in Denmark.[70] The existence of a right-wing plot to assassinate him was confirmed.

A 'Top Secret' memorandum presented verbally to General Malan by Vice-Admiral Putter in October 1988, warned that although cut-off points were being built in to protect those involved 'this does not eliminate the possibility that the Chief of Staff Intelligence [Putter himself] and officers involved by virtue of their planned responsibility in *Operation Marion* may be charged with a capital crime'. The handwriting of SADF Chief General Jannie Geldenhuys also appears on the document, referring to an informal meeting with General Malan when they discussed its contents.[71]

In a 'Top Secret' letter to General Malan from General Geldenhuys in March 1990, Geldenhuys said: 'As you know, the present State President [F W de Klerk] has been briefed on two occasions about a broad spectrum of sensitive projects and reacted as follows: "Approval in principle has been given for the running of Stratcom projects . . . the Defence Force must continue with the operations".'

Fort-five 'approved' projects were listed in an annexure. *Operation Marion* was number 41. It noted that R6,5 million had either been spent or was due to be spent during the period 1987-1991. Its stated aim was: 'to put Inkatha in a position to neutralise the onslaught against it from *Umkhonto we Sizwe*.' The remaining 44 projects were deleted from the annexure before its production in court. The expenditure was approved by Generals Malan, Geldenhuys and Minister of Finance Barend du Plessis, who signed it.[72]

On 2 May 1990 Colonel Mike van den Berg, a staff officer, compiled a memo summarising a visit to Ulundi by the Chief of Staff Intelligence, Vice-Admiral Dries Putter, on 31 October 1989. It said: 'The Chief Minister [of KwaZulu, Gatsha Buthelezi] was worried because he was losing the armed struggle and intimated that "offensive" steps were still a requirement; meaning the use of "hit squads".' He recorded that MZ Khumalo purportedly said: 'At the minimum, cells were required that could take out undesirable members . . .' There was no explanation for the six month delay in compiling the memorandum.[73]

On 5 November 1995, more than ten years afterwards, 20 people appeared in the Supreme Court, Durban, for remand on charges relating to the KwaMakutha massacre.

Accused 1 Major Louis Botha, formerly head of the Security Police in Durban and liaison officer for *Operation Marion*.
Accused 2 Brigadier John Reeves More, formerly a colonel in the Chief of Staff Intelligence's Directorate of Special Tasks.
Accused 3 Zakhele 'MZ' Khumalo, former personal assistant to Chief Buthelezi who was in charge of the Caprivi trainees.
Accused 4 Peter Msane, Caprivi graduate and alleged hit squad member.
Accused 5 Celukwanda Ndhlovu, Caprivi graduate and alleged hit squad member.

Accused 6 Martin Thulani Khanyile, Caprivi graduate and alleged hit squad member.
Accused 7 Prince Phezukwendoda Mkhize, Caprivi graduate and alleged hit squad member.
Accused 8 General Magnus Malan, former Minister of Defence.
Accused 9 General Kat Liebenberg, former Chief of the Army.
Accused 10 General Jannie Geldenhuys, former Chief of the SADF.
Accused 11 General Tienie Groenewald, former Director of Military Intelligence.
Accused 12 General Neels van Tonder, former Director of Intelligence Operations.
Accused 13 Vice Admiral Dries Putter, former Chief of Staff Intelligence.
Accused 14 Brigadier Cor van Niekerk, as a colonel former Director of Special Tasks - Unit 2 - in the office of the Chief of Staff Intelligence.
Accused 15 Colonel Johannes Victor, former senior Military Intelligence Chief of Natal Command.
Accused 16 Colonel Jake Jacobs, the chief instructor of the Caprivi trainees when a major.
Accused 17 Colonel Jan van der Merwe, a Military Intelligence operative as a commandant.
Accused 18 Colonel Dan Griesel, former commander of the secret Ferntree military base.
Accused 19 Hloni Andreas Mbuyazi, Caprivi graduate and alleged hit squad member.
Accused 20 Alex Vulindiela Biyela, Caprivi graduate and alleged hit squad member.

On 11 March 1996 the accused were called on individually to plead to the charges — the attempted murder of Victor Ntuli, alternatively conspiracy to commit murder, 13 counts of murder including those of six children under ten years and the attempted murder of four survivors. There were also supplementary charges of conspiracy that occurred between December 1985 and June 1989 when *Operation Marion* began to wind down.

The accused entered pleas of 'not guilty' to all charges and the alternatives.[74]

It appears the SADF documents relating to *Operation Marion* had been shredded, because the investigation task unit probing the murders failed to locate the files when they searched Military Intelligence's HQ in Pretoria during June 1995.

Colonel Cor van Niekerk, to protect himself, had taken the precaution of secretly removing a selection of *Operation Marion* documents from there in 1992. Most were important documents that had been signed by notables like General Magnus Malan, General Jannie Geldenhuys, Vice-Admiral Dries Putter and other senior officers in the military hierarchy. None of them referred to the massacre at KwaMakutha. He had concealed them in a fake circuit box in his Pretoria home when allegations began to surface in the press about links between *Operation Marion* and resistance movements in southern Africa. There was talk of murder squads and a 'third force'.

Without prompting, Van Niekerk handed the documents over to the investigation task unit saying: 'I kept them in case I needed them one day.' The colonel obviously knew enough of the character and culture of his senior military colleagues, to say nothing of his political superiors, to realise they were more likely to feed him to the sharks than toss him a lifebelt if he needed assistance.[75]

The defence claimed that the military assistance provided to Inkatha did not constitute a criminal offence. They also said there was no direct link between the military assistance and the KwaMakutha attack — the basis of the criminal charges.[76]

When it was suggested that the KwaMakutha massacre had been an unauthorised frolic and had nothing to do with higher authority, Captain Opperman told the court: 'In that case it would mean that one person — I — was able to lead the entire South African Security Forces up the garden path . . . It would be impossible for any junior member of the military alone to plan, organise and execute an operation of this type which involved shooting a person.'

At the end of the State's case, all 20 of the accused applied for their discharge on the grounds that the State had failed to provide sufficient evidence to link them to the massacre. The State opposed the applications but Judge Jan Hugo discharged accused number 11 General Tienie Groenewald, accused number 15 Colonel Jacobus Victor and accused number 18 Colonel Dan Griesel, as having no case to answer.[77] He ruled that the remaining 17 had a case to answer. On 11 September 1996 the State withdrew charges against accused number 17, Commandant Jan van der Merwe.

When Judge Hugo asked, at the closing stage of argument, why Chief Buthelezi had not been listed by the State as a co-conspirator, the Attorney General of Natal, Tim McNally, had little to say beyond echoing defence argument that he was known to be a man of non-violence.[78]

On 5 September 1996 Inkatha's leaders submitted a 72-page document to the Truth and Reconciliation Commission in which they denied they had ever planned or authorised acts of violence. Inkatha president, Dr Mangosutho (Gatsha) Buthelezi, added, neverthe-less, that it could not be denied that individual party members had carried out violent acts. 'Although I have not orchestrated one single act of violence against one single victim of the political violence that has cost us many lives, as the leader of the IFP I know that the buck stops right in front of me.'

He claimed that in ongoing violence more than 420 of Inkatha's leaders and thousands of its supporters had been murdered.[79]

On 10 October 1996, at the end of the defence case, Mr Justice Hugo acquitted accused number 4 Peter Msane, accused number 5 Celukwanda Ndhlovu, accused number 6 Martin Thulani Khanyile, accused number 7 Prince Phezukwendoda Mkhize, accused number 19 Hloni Andreas Mbuyazi and accused number 20 Alex Vulindiela Biyela. It was alleged they had all been part of the murder squad at KwaMakutha.

Hugo had rejected the evidence of the key state witness, Captain J P Opperman, who he judged to be a liar. He described his evidence as often contradictory, improbable or absurd, including his 'extremely unlikely' claim that he was appointed by senior military intelligence officers to command the massacre squad — despite having had no combat training or experience. He also accepted the defence contention that as the KwaMakutha attack did not accord with the precision of a military operation, it was unlikely the SADF had anything to do with it. He appeared to have overlooked that the State had not claimed the incident was a true military exercise, but rather the action of an irregular Inkatha unit supported by the military — a big difference.[80]

In his defence General Kat Liebenberg explained that although the word 'offensive' occurred frequently in official SADF documents before the court, in modern military parlance the words 'defensive' and 'offensive' were interchangeable. This did not seem to be the case, however, when Malan deliberately omitted reference to the establishment of an 'offensive unit' in his summary of recommendations to Minister Heunis. Major General Neels van Tonder defined 'offensive steps' as those taken to counteract any potential security threat.[81]

General Marius Oelschig, the SANDF's (South African National Defence Force) Chief Director of Transformation Management, who had been in command of the Ciskei Defence Force when its troops opened fire (defensively or offensively?) and killed 28 marchers and wounded more than 200 at Bisho in 1992, testified for the defence that 'offensive element' could be interpreted to mean a 'protection force'. Offensive did not necessarily suggest 'attack'.[82]

On 11 October 1996 Justice Hugo, acquitted the remaining accused finding that the words 'offensive action' did not necessarily mean aggression and pointed out that the word 'attack' did not appear in any of the documents.[83]

He apparently dismissed its ordinary meaning as defined by the Oxford Illustrated Dictionary: 'Offensive — 1. Aggressive, intended for or used in attack . . . attitude of assailant, aggressive action; attack, offensive campaign or stroke.' If he had looked to

American English for inspiration, Webster's Dictionary says: 'Offensive . . . pertaining to offense . . . used in attack . . . opposed to defensive . . .'

Perhaps he got confused by Charles Dickens, who although surrogate forces would have been beyond his ken, said: 'We are not all arrayed in two opposite ranks: the offensive and the defensive.'

Hans Pienaar summed it up succinctly: 'Indeed, in a passage that could have come from George Orwell's Ministry of Truth in the novel '*1984*', [Mr Justice] Hugo accepts the most grotesque distortion by the army that "offensive" really means "defensive".'[84]

Despite the judge's findings, it seems highly unlikely that 206 men trained in guerrilla warfare and tactics at the request of Chief Buthelezi and with the authority of the State Security Council, were left idle for two and a half years until their final integration into the KwaZulu Police. The unit was recruited to fight Inkatha's battles in the state of virtual open warfare then existing between it and the UDF/COSATU alliance. Specialist training in the SADF's guerrilla training school in the Caprivi was hardly a requirement for static guards on buildings.

SAP/Inkatha collusion: Trust Feed Massacre: 3 December 1988

During the final years in office of the National Party government, allegations of police collusion with Inkatha against the UDF/COSATU alliance were always hotly denied by the police and Inkatha. Yet there were many eye witness reports of police escorting Inkatha impis, of vigilantes wearing red cloths around their heads — *Rooidoekies* — just like the Fathers of Crossroads had used Witdoekies so the police could tell them apart from the comrades. Stories were legion of warlords being briefly arrested and then released and about the most serious of criminal complaints laid against them being neglected or ignored.[85]

During 1988 a security policeman purchased 24 .38 Special revolvers from King's Sports in Durban and licensed them in the name of Inkatha. Some, it was alleged, were subsequently used in political murders.[86]

Funds for other purposes were also secretly channelled to Inkatha by the government over the years. It paid Inkatha R250 000 to conduct two anti-sanction rallies, the first in November 1989 and the second in March 1990. It also paid R1,5 million to the Inkatha aligned trade union, UWUSA. Security Police Captain Louis Botha, of *Operation Marion* fame, was involved in these transactions. The government was also caught out funding an Inkatha Youth Brigade rally near Port Shepstone on 26 January 1991. This resulted in severe cut-backs in the funding of covert operations.[87]

There is no doubt that assistance was extended to Inkatha by the SADF and the SAP during *Operation Marion* and other operations. Then came another well documented case virtually identical to the KwaMakutha massacre. This one occurred in Trust Feed, some 30km from Pietermaritzburg.

Trust Feed, as with the Edendale Valley, is a freehold township owned by about 50 landowning black families. They rented the land to about 5 000 black tenants. In the middle years of apartheid, the area was regarded as a 'black spot' in 'white' Natal and a forced removal of the residents to an established black area was actively considered by the government. The alarmed residents formed the Trust Feed Crisis Committee (TFCC) to resist it. The TFCC was a non-aligned non-political group and in March 1988 they were successful in having Trust Feed declared a black development area.[88]

It is difficult to know whether the suggestion to form a Landowners' Committee originated from Jerome Gabela — a landowner, the Inkatha chairman in Trust Feed and an Inkatha Youth Brigade leader — or from Warrant Officer George Nichas, the station commander of New Hanover Police station. Whoever it was, the TFCC was universally regarded as an obstacle to Inkatha in taking control of the area. Discussions certainly took place between Gabela and Warrant Officer Nichas, because they had a mutual interest in the matter. Gabela, as a landowner, believed the TFCC had no right to make decisions about land it did not own. The police, on the other hand, regarded the TFCC as an UDF affiliate. The question was put down for discussion at the next meeting of the local Joint Management Committee.[89]

Lieutenant Brian Mitchell took command of New Hanover police station in January 1988. He had wanted to join the Security Branch, but his divisional commander persuaded him to accept the New Hanover posting instead.

Like many of his police colleagues he viewed the political unrest in Natal with alarm, believing it had escalated to such an extent that a state of civil war existed. Many policemen had been murdered and many others had had their homes burned down. The official view was that the UDF was a surrogate of the ANC. It was looked on not merely as anti-government or anti-state, but as 'the enemy'. Inkatha on the other hand was regarded as an ally, a friend who was assisting in the fight against the ANC/UDF.

In Mitchell's previous posting as a staff officer at the SAP's Divisional HQ in Pietermaritzburg, he had performed duty as the secretary of the Joint Management Committee. This had allowed him unlimited access to secret government documents that dealt with counter-revolutionary strategies to counter the 'total onslaught' by the UDF against the State.

Part of the local Joint Management Committee's strategy was for paramilitary training to be given to 'special constables'. The men were derogatorily known as *kitskonstabels* — instant constables — by the local populace. They seem to have been a sort of branch or a continuation of *Operation Marion* by the SAP. Lieutenant Mitchell, however, was probably too far down the 'need to know' ladder to be aware of it.[90] A document drawn up in 1987 by Major General M F A Steenkamp of Police General Headquarters in Pretoria compared the special constables to the *Witdoekies* of the Cape and said they should be used to form a 'physical wedge against the tyranny of the UDF/ANC comrades'.[91]

After training, some of the Special Constables were returned to their communities. Others, judging from events in Trust Feed, were placed with the Offensive Group of *Operation Marion* and based with SAP riot units in the area. Riot Unit 8 at Pietermaritzburg, commanded by Captain Terblanche, was probably no different to its counterparts elsewhere. Its function was to combat unrest and maintain law and order within the 'political' sense of the word.[92]

According to Mitchell, the purpose of the (offensive?) special constables was to assist Inkatha in attacks on UDF/ANC strongholds so that the ongoing violence could be portrayed as 'black on black' and the white community would not be affected.[93]

As the new station commander, Lieutenant Mitchell automatically took over as chairman of the local Joint Management Committee. This made him responsible for 'monitoring unrest' and implementing the state's counter-revolutionary strategy. He sincerely believed it was his duty to fight the state's enemies with everything at his disposal.[94]

Throughout 1988 he had regular meetings with Jerome Gabela. As Deneys Coombe said: 'These meetings illustrate the covert collusion between Inkatha and the SAP, a partnership which extended far beyond the boundaries of Trust Feed, and which was to perpetuate the discord that ultimately culminated in the massacre.' [95]

Working in collusion with Gabela through the local Joint Management Committee, Mitchell oversaw the establishment of the Landowners' Committee in April 1988. It comprised nine local members of Inkatha.[96] Its purpose was to oppose the UDF, operating in the guise of the TFCC. While insisting it was neutral, the SAP via Lieutenant Mitchell made it plain they preferred to work through a tribal authority in Trust Feed. Needless to say, the only organisation that could impose a tribal authority was Inkatha. There is reason to believe that the official policy of the Security Forces elsewhere in Natal was identical.

In August 1988 a prominent Inkatha member from Pietermaritzburg addressed a meeting at Trust Feed and lambasted the TFCC whom he called a 'bunch of thugs'. This alarmed the TFCC who sent a written complaint to the SAP, to Inkatha's head office at Ulundi and to the Natal Provincial Administration. Not surprisingly it was ignored.

In October 1988 the TFCC chairman and his assistant were wounded in a shooting. Intimidation was rife and Inkatha vigilantes knocked on doors at night, demanding allegiance and threatening those who demurred. Inkatha gained many members even if the membership did not necessarily spell support.[97]

On the other side of the coin, according to Lieutenant Mitchell, in the same month, UDF supporters forced members of Inkatha to parade through the streets naked and attacked the homes of Inkatha supporters. The police intercepted a truck loaded with weapons that was destined for the UDF.[98] Mitchell believed Inkatha was coming off second best in its encounters with the UDF in Trust Feed.

A major problem, from his point of view, was that Jerome Gabela seemed weak, vulnerable and in need of assistance. At a routine meeting, Mitchell told Gabela he was not doing enough to counter UDF attacks and he should jack himself up. He pointed out that if the police arrested UDF people, they would only have to release them again. One whom he was probably referring to was Emmanuel Mbongwe, a TFCC member who had been arrested on 23 November 1988 and released shortly afterwards. The only solution that Mitchell could suggest, was that UDF people should be killed. Gabela treated Mitchell's remarks as 'mere suggestions' and said he had not expected him to go out and kill people.[99]

The security situation worsened when Inkatha supporters were bussed in from Msinga and Edendale to launch a major recruiting campaign. Cars were stoned, houses were burnt and people were beaten up and stabbed. Four UDF supporting youths were murdered by Inkatha vigilantes on 30 November. Residents fled from the area, many to live as refugees in the veld near New Hanover. By Thursday 1 December Trust Feed had experienced a take-over by Inkatha vigilantes and had been all but denuded of residents.

The SAP, insisting that everything was under control, ordered journalists to leave Trust Feed and confiscated film from photographers who had taken shots of refugees departing the area.[100]

Lieutenant Mitchell discussed the Trust Feed situation with Captain Terblanche in Pietermaritzburg. Captain Terblanche convened a meeting (probably of the Joint Management Committee) at Morawa House, Pietermaritzburg, on the morning of 2 December. Those attending were Terblanche, Mitchell, Gabela and probably some others. They were addressed by an Inkatha warlord of some importance.

It was decided that Captain Terblanche would make six special constables from his unit available to the New Hanover police station. Ostensibly they would be sent to 'protect' Gabela, but the real reason for sending them was to launch an attack against UDF activists in Trust Feed early the next morning. It is not known whether a target was discussed and agreed on at the time, or if this was left to Lieutenant Mitchell to decide.

That evening Captain Terblanche and Sergeant Rose, driving an unmarked Combi, delivered six special constables — all card-carrying members of Inkatha — to Lieutenant Mitchell at New Hanover police station. They were wearing civilian clothes and were all strangers to the area.[101]

Mitchell said he drove them to Jerome Gabela's house and dropped them off. He said he had instructed them to attack and burn the house of Emmanuel Mbongwe. He suspected that activists were using the premises to store petrol bombs and other weapons.[102] Whatever else he was or might have been, Mbongwe owned a store and held title deeds for Trust Feed land. He opposed moves for the incorporation of Trust Feed into KwaZulu. Mitchell told the special constables to target males aged between 16 and 35 who were involved in political violence.[103]

Lieutenant Mitchell professed he had taken no part in the actual attack — which the TRC accepted. In contradiction though, Constables Jason Burton and Stuart Van Wyk of New Hanover police station said they had been drinking with Lieutenant Mitchell late that evening. He mentioned he had to get to a meeting in Trust Feed and drove with them to Gabela's place where he picked up two special constables. Still with Burton and Van Wyk, he drove to Mbongwe's store. Confusion reigns over what followed because it was never established in court if the store was already burning or whether they had set fire to it. Mitchell was later granted amnesty by the TRC for 'arson relating to the destruction by fire of the property of Mbongwe'.[104]

The two special constables faded into the darkness while Constables Burton and Van Wyk remained at the store. Mitchell left but unknown to them, he returned to Gabela's place, picked up two more special constables and apparently rendezvoused with the two dropped off earlier.

Despite Lieutenant Mitchell's denials, the special constables said he accompanied them to the target. This was probably true, even if Mitchell did not take part in the actual attack. The heavily armed special constables were strangers. A guide was essential in an area where houses were jumbled at random across the landscape, as is the pattern of most informal black areas. This ruled out Gabela. He lived in Trust Feed and was unlikely to make a mistake but he was well known. This left o
nly Mitchell, who was probably familiar with the area, but in the dark he might still have lost his way.

Whatever happened, they missed Mbongwe's house and went to house TF83 instead. It belonged to Mr Sithole, a TFCC supporter, who considered himself politically nonaligned. He certainly did not support Inkatha.[105] Inside, a party of 19 people, aged between four and 70, had gathered to pay their respects at the wake of a person who had died of natural causes. The mourners had long gone to sleep, but in accordance with Zulu custom, a candle had been left alight as a mark of respect for the deceased.[106]

At 03:00 on Saturday 3 December 1988 two special constables moved to the rear of the house and the other two to the front. Although Mitchell denied being there, he admitted the attack took place on his directions. The special constables insisted he was there.

A special constable knocked on the front door.

'Open up . . . police!'

A woman got up and sleepily opened the door.

The special constables immediately opened fire through the windows, doors and mud walls at the back and the front of the house.

The two in the front barged inside and moved from room to room, mercilessly shooting men, women and children. One used a torch to illuminate the victims, while the other executed them at point-blank range. For the panic-stricken victims it must have seemed like it was a hell that lasted forever.

A survivor said: 'They just kept on firing brutally. All around me people were crying and screaming. They were running around the house not knowing where to hide. The shooting carried on until all screaming stopped.' There was a sudden pause and a little girl was heard to say: 'Auntie! Wake up, wake up! They have left.' A gunman overheard her as he was leaving. He returned to the room and mercilessly shot the child dead.

By the end of it all 11 were dead, some literally shot to pieces, and two were wounded. The oldest victim was a woman of 66 and the youngest was a little boy of four years.[107]

That Mitchell had either taken part in the attack or at the least had been in the vicinity, was confirmed by Constables Van Wyk and Burton who were waiting for him at the burning store. The sound of distant shots and loud moans startled them.

Soon afterwards Mitchell returned to collect them and they reported the shots and moans to him. He laughed, saying they were 'imagining things'.[108]

It was not long before it was discovered the wrong house had been attacked and that those killed and wounded were not the intended victims. Mitchell immediately reported this to his superiors and 'frantic and feverish attempts' were made 'by some of them' to cover up this 'colossal blunder'.[109]

Police arrived to investigate the next morning, but the little that was done could be dignified as an investigation. The investigating officer, Captain Patrick Wattrus, spoke to the survivors but only noted the names of the deceased. He kept no proper records. Shotgun cartridges found at the scene were not registered as evidence, the assistance of the fingerprint unit was not requested and he did not bother to view a video of the scene taken by another policeman. The actions of Wattrus might be attributable to sheer incompetency, but what followed was a sheer cover-up.

Understandably, there was considerable media interest, but this suited neither Inkatha nor the police. Men armed with stones and knobkerries chased a CBS News team from the area. A reporter from the *Natal Witness* was threatened in the presence of policemen who refused to guarantee his safety. The police gave public assurances that everything was under control, but despite this, more than a thousand people who fled the area remained too frightened to return and collect their belongings.[110]

On 6 December Chief Buthelezi issued a statement denying Inkatha was responsible. He threatened to sue any newspaper that irresponsibly blamed his organisation for the massacre. Later he issued another statement in which he claimed his lawyers had established that the victims were members of Inkatha. This directly contradicted the survivors' statements that they and the 11 dead did not belong to Inkatha. They supported the TFCC, which to them was a politically non-aligned body.[111]

Two weeks later Constables Burton and Van Wyk reported to higher authority that Lieutenant Mitchell and two special constables were involved in the massacre. Doubtless with relief, Wattrus handed the docket over to Brigadier Christo Marx, the CID Divisional Chief in Pietermaritzberg. Marx passed it to his deputy, Colonel W van Zyl who passed it to his namesake, Captain J P van Zyl. On 6 January 1989 warrants were issued for the arrest of Special Constables Khambule, Ndwalane, Ngubane and Sikhosana. Lieutenant Mitchell was briefly questioned by Brigadier Marx. He asked him what had happened 'just to see what his response would be'. Marx said he had been too busy to do more because he had been looking for the wanted special constables.

Despite the brigadier being so busy looking for them, the special constables continued to live at their usual places of residence and drew their salaries every month from the SAP. In April 1989 the SAP's Security Branch cleared them for attestation into the KwaZulu Police. They continued to live openly as members of the KwaZulu Police until August 1991.

Not surprisingly, by the end of 1989 the CID investigation had stalled. In the meantime Lieutenant Mitchell had been promoted to captain, Brigadier Marx had become a major-general and Captain J P van Zyl had risen in rank to major. The Trust Feed massacre docket was on track to become another of those dubiously unsolved murder cases that were filed 'Undetected' at various police stations around Natal.

This undoubtedly would have been its fate had Captain Frank Dutton of the Special Investigation Unit at Wartburg not received information regarding the whereabouts of the wanted special constables. A police general in Pretoria ordered Dutton to take over the case from Major J P van Zyl.

Within two weeks, despite considerable obstruction from his SAP colleagues, Captain Dutton had arrested not only the four former special constables, but Captain Mitchell as well. On their arrest two of the constables confessed that certain policemen, acting on the orders of an unnamed KwaZulu police colonel, had warned them to go into hiding. It emerged that certain senior SAP officers had tipped off the colonel that the arrests were impending.[112]

The Supreme Court trial began on 15 October 1991. The former special constables, Khambule, Ndwalane, Ngubane and Sikhosana, admitted their guilt, but claimed they had been acting under Mitchell's orders. Captain Jacobus van den Heever and Sergeant Neville Rose entered pleas of not guilty. Captain Brian Mitchell initially pleaded not guilty, but on 26 February 1992 he changed his plea to guilty.[113]

Mitchell later called the attack a mistake.

Matthew Kentridge probably came close to the truth when he said: 'This act of violence was neither senseless nor aberrant. It was not a once-off expression of madness, but the culmination of a systematic political process of terror and coercion which had steadily crushed and sapped the resilience of Trust Feed over a period of many weeks.'[114]

If this was true of the Trust Feed massacre, it must also have been true of the KwaMakutha one. The hallmarks were the same.

That a police cover-up had taken place was effectively confirmed when Major-General Marx and Major P J van Zyl refused to give evidence for the State at the trial unless they were legally represented. In addition, Van Zyl also declined to give evidence that might incriminate him. The directive for this had originated from no one less than the Commissioner of Police himself. The judge, rightly, remarked that in all his years on the bench, he had never before experienced policemen asking for legal representation before they would give evidence for the State.[115]

On 23 April 1992 Mitchell, Khambule, Ndwalane, Ngubane and Sikhosana were convicted of 11 counts of murder. They were each sentenced to an effective 15 years imprisonment.

Brian Mitchell was convicted and sentenced to death 11 times for ordering the massacre. On 24 April 1994 the death sentences were commuted by the State President to 30 years' imprisonment.

Van den Heever and Rose were acquitted. The only evidence against them was that they had transported the special constables to and from Trust Feed. There was no evidence showing that they knew what they were there for.

The former special constables were granted amnesty under the Further Indemnity Act, 1992, and released from prison the same year — a truly amazing act of clemency by the National Party government.

Yet this sort of generosity by the government towards matters KwaZulu was commonplace. Detective Constable Khethani Richard Shange of the KwaZulu Police, at his May 1991 trial for the murder of members of the ANC-sympathising Gumede family in KwaMashu in February 1990, was described by Judge Gordon as a 'beast in a policeman's clothes who was one of the main players in the reign of terror in KwaMashu.' He was sentenced to 27 years' imprisonment and refused leave to appeal. Yet on 14 February 1992, a mere eight months later, the prison authorities quietly released 'the beast' on parole. Such generosity was not extended to Mitchell. He obviously had far too high a profile to merit an early release. In December 1996, after serving nearly five years of his sentence, he was granted amnesty by the TRC and released.[116]

10

Operation Katzen
Xhosa Resistance Movement — Iliso Lomzi
MI knows best
1985-1986

1985 was a year of panic and despondency for the Security Forces in the Eastern Cape. The area was burning, political killings were rife, beer halls were burnt down, black councillors were murdered, consumer boycotts were enforced, service dues were unpaid and the black townships became no-go areas. The UDF called for South Africa to be made ungovernable.

At 22:00 one night in August 1985 a large deputation of ministers and officials including Defence Minister Magnus Malan and Minister of Police Louis le Grange and others arrived by air in Port Elizabeth. Civil unrest was at its height. They met with members of the JMC led by Brigadier 'Joffel' van der Westhuizen, the SADF's Eastern Province Officer Commanding, at the military base on at the airport opposite the civilian terminal at the airport.

During heated discussions regarding the unrest, Minister Malan told Brigadier van der Westhuizen in so many words that if he could not get the situation stabilised . . . and he had no intention of telling him how to do it . . . then he would be relieved of his duties and that was that.

He had a field day and also threatened that the senior policeman present would be relieved of his command.

Minister Malan's attitude was so unpleasant and intimidating that the proceedings had to be halted for a time to allow Mrs Vermeulen, the JMC's administrative secretary, to be comforted after she burst into tears. Minister Le Grange stepped in to smooth things over and calmed what had become an ugly scene.[1]

In February 1986 the leader of the opposition, Dr Frederik van Zyl Slabbert, when introducing a motion of no confidence in the South African Parliament, said that the administration of townships in the Eastern Cape was disintegrating and that they were virtually being run by the military. It was impossible to talk to black community leaders because they were either in detention or unable to talk.[2] The situation was much the same in Transkei and Ciskei.

This climate of chaos and the arrival of the Commonwealth's Eminent Persons Group in February 1986 with a broad mandate to seek a settlement to the 'South African question', prompted State President P W Botha to order the Security Forces to stabilise the situation countrywide by December 1986.

It was hardly a Botha decision made in presidential isolation. As journalist and author Brian Pottinger said: 'The securocrats' view was thus very simple: the South African government should ignore foreign pressure and move decisively and as ruthlessly as necessary to restore order domestically and power regionally'.[3]

Army officers worldwide, from fledgling subalterns upwards, are universally nurtured in the comfortable belief that the army knows best; that the military possesses a universal panacea for all ills; that they can rectify by sheer logic, common sense, discipline and training, any chaos or disorder resulting from the bumbling incompetence of lesser beings . . . like civilians. 'Benevolent dictatorships', in this author's experience, are frequently mooted as hypothetical ideals in military circles virtually everywhere. Fortunately, at least in the West, this mostly remains hypothetical because in truth military culture contributes few imaginative ideas on how to deal with situations where soldierly benevolence is reciprocated by hostility and violence.

A T-shirt bearing a slogan popular with soldiers reads: 'Join the Army. Travel the world. Meet interesting people. Then kill them!' This sardonic insight holds more than just a grain of truth.

It is not a new lesson in established democracies where in times of civil unrest the police remain in control, with the military enlisted only as an aid to the civil power. Giving the military *carte blanche*, no matter how democratic the background of its general officers, carries an inherent risk. When they lack a democratic ethos as was the case in South Africa it is a guaranteed recipe for disaster. The Eastern Cape situation in the mid-1980s was a classic example.

In the first half of 1986 Brigadier van der Westhuizen called Colonel Pieter Hall, his Senior Staff Officer Operations, and Colonel Lourens du Plessis, his Staff Officer Intelligence, into his office. Colonel du Plessis was heavily involved in the administration of the National Security Management System (NSMS) and his section supplied the secretariat for the local Joint Management Centre in Port Elizabeth. He had been personally involved in the Eastern Cape for many years and knew all the main role players. He had been the Eastern Cape Command's representative on the committee discussing procedures and so on for Ciskei independence in 1981. Lennox Sebe, whom he had got to know well, had presented him with a book of his speeches personally inscribed: 'Those who trust in the Lord will never be disappointed'.

Brigadier van der Westhuizen issued a command directive for them to prepare an operational instruction based on his ideas of how the unrest situation in the Eastern Cape could be quelled. What it boiled down to was that he envisaged the amalgamation of Transkei and Ciskei as the means by which the Xhosa nation could be united as a pro-government group. To achieve this it would be necessary to remove President Lennox Sebe from office in Ciskei. A Xhosa resistance movement would be formed to combat political unrest. They would deal with dissidents by intimidating them, killing them or whatever, to keep them in line. This would provide the government with the necessary tools to combat the unrest situation. He envisaged Charles Sebe heading the Xhosa resistance movement so his role would be a key one. As a first step it was vital he be sprung from prison. That was the partial plan that Colonels Hall and Du Plessis were given to work on.

The plan was written by Colonels du Plessis and Hall. After it was completed, Brigadier Ferdi van Wyk, Director of Communications Operations at Army HQ in Pretoria, became involved during a routine visit to Eastern Cape Command. It was discussed with him because it had Comops (Communication Operations) connotations. He ran through it with them and made some minor suggestions and changes. Until then it had been unnamed. He suggested that it be called *Operation Katzen* — an anagram from the Kat of General Kat Liebenberg and the 'zen' from Brigadier Joffel van der Westhuizen. So *Katzen* it became.

Brigadier van der Westhuizen rewrote the final plan in his own handwriting.

On 13 June 1986, he submitted his paper on a 'plan' to achieve President Botha's order in the Eastern Cape. It was endorsed 'First Attempt', referenced BEV OP/309/1/, classified 'Top Secret', marked for the personal attention of the Chief of the Army (then Lieutenant-General Kat Liebenberg), and signed. It was hand delivered to Liebenberg by Brigadier Ferdi van Wyk. Brigadier van der Westhuizen modestly stressed that it was not a detailed plan that could stand on its own, but one which should be 'analysed and appreciated by experts' and 'cleared at [the] highest level'.

On 9 July 1986 the Brigadier completed a more polished refinement of the plan. It was designed to address the problem of the 'permanent normalisation of the Eastern Cape situation'. He recommended it should be aligned with existing national and regional plans both 'written and unwritten', to halt the 'onslaught', but tantalisingly made no mention of what those other plans were. His plan, he stressed, should not be viewed in isolation, but as part of the 'total counter-revolutionary attempt'.

He reminded the Army Chief that in November 1985 his command and GB5 had jointly set out to 'win in 1986', which was still their intention. With the adoption of his plan he expected the political climate to show sufficient improvement for the Emergency Regulations in the region to be lifted. Despite this, he cautioned, he did not believe this would complete the counter-revolutionary tasks. Nevertheless, he added confidently, his plan would 'permanently' normalise the situation by December 1987.

His plan was based on a foundation of Xhosa unity and the formation of pro-RSA resistance movements. He contended that the Xhosa people were strongly homogeneous and had a long history of resistance against both Zulu and white domination. Their desire for 'self determination and nationhood was deeply rooted', he continued, indicating that he had not heard of, or maybe not bothered to read, the Quail Commission findings quoted earlier. The latent instability prevailing in Transkei and Ciskei, he said, stimulated the revolution throughout the country. Disregarding the fact that his political masters had already granted Transkei and Ciskei 'independence', he aligned himself with what the opponents of apartheid had always contended — Ciskei and Transkei were inseparable parts of the Eastern Province — which was also 'relatively unstable'. The whole area, he said, should be viewed as one 'front or theatre'.

He stressed the inability of the government 'and its instruments' to curb the continually deteriorating riot and unrest situations. This had led to a mood of defeatism, aggravated economic depression and whites deserting the area.

Attempts to 'activate and keep alive the pro-RSA resistance movements, the Kakanes of Cookhouse, Memese of Somerset East and Maqina's Black Crisis Centre, Port Elizabeth', and efforts to organise black moderates had failed because of intimidation and a lack of moderate leaders.

'The Eastern Cape', Van der Westhuizen continued with resignation, 'is not blessed with dynamic white politicians'.

On the political side, as far as Ciskei was concerned, Chief Lent Maqoma, as a political refugee in Umtata, was a key figure. The Brigadier praised him as a 'blue blooded chief' who had 'held various cabinet posts' and who had been 'booted out' in 1985 by Lennox Sebe who regarded him as a threat. He said Maqoma was 'pro-RSA inclined and [an] esteemed Xhosa leader'.

On what evidence Van der Westhuizen judged him to be 'pro-RSA inclined' is unknown but he was a respected tribal leader. His great-grandfather, a Xhosa national hero, had valiantly fought against the British Army in the 19th Century. This had recently been acknowledged by South Africa which had permitted the disinterment of his remains from Robben Island, where he had died in captivity, and their re-interment in the Amatola Mountains.[4]

On 2 June 1986 Lent Maqoma announced the formation of a new Ciskei opposition party in Port Elizabeth, the Ciskei People's Rights Protection Party (CPRPP). He said it would provide a voice for all who believed in democracy and in Ciskei's constitutional bill of rights. The principles of freedom of thought and expression were 'anathema' to the present leadership, who did not adhere to the bill of rights, he correctly opined.

The new party was in accordance with *Operation Katzen*. In his paper of 13 June 1986 Brigadier van der Westhuizen wrote: 'Maqoma establishes in May 1986 the CPRPP as opposition to Lennox'. In the event, however, the formation of the party preempted Pretoria's approval. The Brigadier's use of the present continuous tense 'establishes' instead of 'established' indicates it was a step in his plan that he had already set in motion.

While Van der Westhuizen was still discussing with Comops in Pretoria the production of anti-Lennox Sebe propaganda leaflets for distribution in Ciskei, Colonel du Plessis involved Commandant Pieter Marais and the Eastern Cape Command Comops and went ahead himself with the leaflets. He was later rapped over the knuckles for doing it without Pretoria's authority, but in truth he had decided they took too long to get things moving anyway.

After examining available artwork, he designed a letterhead for a body called '*Iliso Lomzi*'. The name had been thought up by Namba Sebe and translated roughly as 'the eyes of the nation'. Initially Van der Westhuizen had loosely referred to it in Afrikaans as the *Xhosa weerstandbeweging* (XWB) — xhosa resistance movement. The letter under the *Iliso Lomzi* banner mounted a scurrilous attack on Lennox Sebe's character, exposing his shady dealings and extolling the virtues of Namba Sebe. The Command Comops had its own printing press and qualified printers to operate it and they produced hundreds of thousands of leaflets which were packed into corrugated cardboard cartons.

It was standard practice at the East London Airport for the radar and allied equipment to be shut down after the last flight at about 21:00. This left the airport non-operational and without radar scanning the local skies until it was reopened for the first flight the next morning. Taking advantage of this, Colonel du Plessis called up four or five privately owned aircraft together with their locally based Commando pilots. The aircraft were loaded with the cartons and on 30 September 1986 the aircraft took off to overfly Ciskei. Each pilot was given a sector and these were carefully quartered for the leaflet drop. By the time they had finished it was reckoned that they had left few parts of Ciskei untouched and there were few locals who had not picked up a copy.[5]

Brigadier van der Westhuizen's refined paper recommended that an exercise of 'image building of the CPRPP in the Eastern Cape' be embarked on and arrangements made for the 'involvement of the smaller moderate groups'. Mooted as political allies for Lent Maqoma were Rev Wilson Xaba, Namba Sebe and Ray Mali. Although Mali was serving time in a Ciskei prison for theft and fraud, Van der Westhuizen judged him as 'moderate, very capable and pro-RSA'. Future paramount chief, Sandile, was noted as another possible ally, but there was no further mention of him after this.

Support (by the SADF) would be given to Maqoma and his party, which was tasked with uniting moderates eligible as voters into its ranks, whether they lived within Ciskei's borders or not.

Van der Westhuizen's next objective was to create his pro-South African resistance movement amongst the Eastern Cape Xhosa before December 1986. He explained in his paper that in nature and extent it would be 'similar to Inkatha and must together with our Security Forces form a counter-revolutionary front'. The struggling black resistance movements (fronting for the SAP/SADF) — like the Kakanes of Cookhouse, Memese of Somerset East and the Black Crisis Centre of Port Elizabeth — were mooted for incorporation. This would be the *Iliso Lomzi* movement.

Recommending Charles Sebe as its leader, the Brigadier said he had 'together with [Rev Wilson] Xaba and brother Namba [Sebe] in 1983' unsuccessfully attempted to depose Lennox Sebe and was unjustly sentenced to 12 years imprisonment. He said Charles Sebe was 'a powerful leader' who enjoyed 'a great following' and had status amongst Ciskei and Transkei Security Forces. He classified him as 'strongly pro-RSA inclined' and said he hated Lennox Sebe. He cautioned that although Charles Sebe had the background, ability and stature to activate and lead the *Iliso Lomzi*, he would 'have to be strictly controlled to ensure that the RSA aims/objectives' were realised according to plan.

Ruminating on Charles Sebe's abilities, stature and background later in the paper, Van der Westhuizen said he projected 'traditional authority', so he expected the Security Forces and the older generation to support him. Opposition could be expected from the left, the youth and Lennox Sebe's supporters and he suggested such opposition should 'be wisely and schematically turned around', but offered no ready plan.

In his second paper he noted that Charles Sebe saw 'the interests of Ciskei linked to the RSA', was strongly anti-communist and against trade unions and subversion. He expected him to 'exercise a very strong anti-communist influence in Ciskei' that would also obtain in the periphery, to South Africa's advantage. He failed to mention that others who knew Charles Sebe better than he were less complimentary — like 'a runtish psychopath straight out of a Graham Greene novel and widely loathed', as the *Sunday Times* aptlyput it.[6] Amnesty International regarded him as a torturer.

In the furtherance of *Iliso Lomzi*, Charles Sebe and certain 'identified co-prisoners', apparently his son Khambashe Sebe, Namba Sebe's sons Koli, Toni and Mlotana, were to be sprung from prison either through 'negotiations or [by] covert Security Force action'.

Once he was free, Charles Sebe's 'physical and psychological health condition' would be strengthened and an operation to rebuild his image and those of other anti-Lennox Sebe leaders would be launched by Comops. Transkei was seen as the 'logical place for Charles Sebe's exile' because it enjoyed 'relative stability'. If, for whatever reason, it was discovered that Charles was incapable of establishing and commanding the organisation, then 'suitable officers' like 'Brigadier Holomisa and [CDF's] Major Sandile' would be used. More will be heard of Major Sandile later.

Major-General Holomisa told the author he knew nothing about *Iliso Lomzi* at the time and had no involvement in its planning. He suggested he had probably personally come to Van der Westhuizen's attention through the Combined Management Board (CMB) meetings that he had attended since 1981. Van der Westhuizen usually chaired the meetings and Holomisa regularly brought up training issues. At the time he was concentrating on persuading the SADF to admit Trankei personnel to training courses at its white military institutions because the training at black ones was markedly inferior.[7]

Colonel Lourens du Plessis confirmed to the author that Eastern Province Command had indeed thought highly of Bantu Holomisa. When the policy of allowing senior black officers from the homelands to attend the SADF's staff duties course was finally accepted, Du Plessis was made responsible for administering the initial stages relating to officers of the Transkei and Ciskei defence forces from his offices in Port Elizabeth. He vividly recalls when Brigadier Zondwa Mtirara and Colonel Bantu Holomisa were selected to attend the course. It was an imperative for white SADF officers to pass examinations before they could attend, but it was decided to ease the process for black officers of the homeland forces. In lieu of an immediate entrance examination, SADF officers were identified to coach the black candidates through the syllabus and the material required for the pre-course. This meant that the candidates had at least some prior knowledge of the subjects before attending. Nevertheless, just before the course started, they still had to write the same entrance exams as white officers. To facilitate coaching for Mtirara and Holomisa, Du Plessis travelled twice monthly to Umtata for teaching sessions.

Despite coaching, many officers from the homeland forces barely managed to scrape through the staff duties course. Some failed dismally, a few were given 'diplomatic' passes. Bantu Holomisa, however, passed the entrance examination with flying colours and the course itself with outstanding marks.[8]

Brigadier van der Westhuizen recommended that the movement's headquarters should be within the SADF's Eastern Cape command area, preferably Port Elizabeth, so that a controlled power base could be built up. He later amended this to say its headquarters should be in Transkei. He made the point that a climate had to be created for the acceptance by Transkei's leaders of Namba Sebe, his associate 'traditional leaders' and *Iliso Lomzi*.

If the movement had been based in Port Elizabeth in accordance with Van der Westhuizen's original recommendation, the first step would have been to place it before the Joint Management Centre in Port Elizabeth for approval of the military's recommendation. On internal matters the army and police could not act alone without the involvement of the civil authority, even if it amounted only to a rubber stamp.

Having obtained that approval, the next step would have been to submit it to the State Security Council. When Minister of Defence, General Magnus Malan announced the establishment of Joint Management Committees, sub-Joint Management Committees and Mini-Joint Management Committees on 11 March 1986, he said they coordinated 'joint government action at regional level', but they possessed no executive powers and had no authority to enforce decisions. They reported to General Pieter van der Westhuizen at the SSC[9], an organisation with executive powers and able to enforce decisions. Establishing *Iliso Lomzi* on 'foreign' territory like Transkei circumvented the need to present the concept to the JMC in Port Elizabeth. Being an 'external operation' allowed it to go straight to the State Security Council for approval. Whatever the channels followed, it would surely end up at the State Security Council, no matter how much it is denied.

Formation necessitated the provision of sufficiently operating capital by the SADF, together with reasonable accommodation, facilities and support staff. Xhosa speaking troops would be assigned, especially in the beginning, so the movement would have 'teeth'. Namba Sebe and Lent Maqoma needed to recruit anti-Lennox Sebe dissidents who had fled Ciskei. The initial task of *Iliso Lomzi* was to overthrow Lennox Sebe, but after that it was scheduled to play a leading role in unifying the Security Forces of Ciskei and Transkei. It would work together with the South African Security Forces 'to establish general stability on the Eastern Cape "front"'. The objective would be to use 'influential actions to bring Ciskei and Transkei Security Forces closer together'. This would lead, Van der Westhuizen envisaged, to a (very mini, one thinks) NATO-type organisation - OKMVO — *Oos Kaapse Militêre Verdrag-Organisasie* — the Eastern Cape Military Treaty Organisation. This, he said, would unite them formally on a 'security foundation'. In his second paper he clarified that this would only happen after Lennox Sebe was overthrown.

While open to speculation, it seems reasonable to suppose that if the Security Forces of South Africa, Transkei and Ciskei were offering a united front against the common enemy, i.e., the ANC/SACP/UDF alliance, *Iliso Lomzi*'s role would be purely covert. It would operate under the cover of a front organisation, but the nature of this front was not disclosed. In fact, its *raison d'être* could only have been as a death squad to eliminate UDF/ANC dissidents when the conventional Security Forces had no lawful grounds to arrest or kill them. This would soon have seriously damaged or destroyed the ANC/SACP/UDF alliance's organisation and undermined its operational ability.

This hypothesis was reinforced by Joffel van der Westhuizen's stress that his plan could 'wind up the Eastern Cape case' and 'win in 1986', sufficient for the Emergency Regulations in the Eastern Cape to be lifted; and that it would 'permanently' normalise the situation by December 1987. He possessed no secret weapons other than *Iliso Lomzi* with which to achieve his objectives.

Van der Westhuizen's next objective, after the formation of *Iliso Lomzi*, was the political unification of Transkei and Ciskei before June 1987. Here, *Iliso Lomzi* would play a major role. The success of this move was independent of the success of Maqoma's CPRPP and did not rely on it.

The 'big stumbling block' was Lennox Sebe, who had to 'be removed as a step of this phase or even earlier'. He stressed that Lennox had 'long been an embarrassment to our government — the SP [State President P W Botha] has himself said so'. The brigadier emphasised that Lennox was a 'thorn in the RSA flesh'.

He proposed the following methods of removing him:

(a) Maqoma defeats Lennox in an election.
(b) Charles threatens and "removes" him.
(c) Matanzimas get rid of him.
(d) RSA Security Forces covert action.
(e) Lennox is 'placed on pension' by RSA.

In the meantime, concurrent with the establishment of *Iliso Lomzi*, a 'subtle psychological breakdown of Lennox Sebe and his colleagues' would be commenced. The 'power bases of Lennox, with the exception of the Security Forces' would be 'attacked and made suspicious'.

His second paper mentions electoral defeat and being pensioned off. The more direct phrases — 'remove', 'get rid of' and 'covert action' — are replaced by the blunter and more explicit '*coup d'état*'. He again explained that Lennox Sebe and his colleagues would be replaced by 'moderate pro-RSA members like Lent Maqoma, Namba Sebe, Charles Sebe etc'.

South Africa, meanwhile, would undertake the training and organisation of smaller moderate groups to take over third level authorities in Ciskei.

Having created *Iliso Lomzi*, freed Charles Sebe, got the movement operational, removed Lennox Sebe and installed Lent Maqoma and his colleagues as the new 'democratic' government of Ciskei, attention would be turned to unifying Transkei and Ciskei.

'Climate creation for Xhosa national unity' would be embarked on by all parties involved — Transkei, Ciskei and Eastern Cape. SADF's Comops, who had ample funds for this type of exercise, were heavily involved. The Xhosa 'struggle for unity as a nation (particularly in Transkei) must be exploited or taken advantage of'. The proposed unification, he said, was the best logical means to satisfy the aspirations of the Xhosa in an orderly manner, vaguely adding that the 'general feeling' (and the feeling of the generals!) in the Eastern Cape 'is for Xhosa unity — the question is how and when it must come'. Maximum use had to be made of traditional leaders.

Transkei, with the brothers Matanzima in charge, would become (that is, be made by the SADF) the senior partners. 'Pro-RSA and pro-Transkei/Ciskei leaders' would 'reconcile themselves formally with the Xhosa unity idea primarily under Transkei leadership'. Leaders deposed in the coup would be expected to lend support so they could carve out a 'political niche for the future'. So Xhosaland would be born — at the latest by June 1987 — and recognised by South Africa as an independent state.

This would be followed by the incorporation of the 'white corridor' between Transkei and Ciskei into Xhosaland before December 1987. The corridor would include King William's Town, Berlin and the rest. He appreciated that this would 'upset whites' in the area but suggested it be done in a manner designed to save the government from facing accusations of having sold out the white voter. He agreed it would be a sellout, nevertheless. He also expected the right wing to 'attempt to make political gain', but said the resultant greater economic growth in the area would make everyone happy. This showed that Van der Westhuizen knew even less about economics and his own right wing Afrikaners than he did about the Xhosa people.

Expanding into a mood of runaway optimism, he suggested that 'Xhosaland' would be projected to the world as a 'success story of RSA's (apartheid) policy of independent states. The envisaged Xhosaland could 'become an African power and earn international recognition in the end . . . a formidable Xhosa ally for the RSA is not to be scorned . . . Such a Xhosa government can be asked to keep its people (within or outside their land) in check. Together', he said, 'we can better combat the ANC/UDF onslaught'. These steps would also 'arrest the influx (of blacks) into urban areas, especially into Port Elizabeth and Cape Town'.

Following this, a confederation of Eastern Cape states would be established before June 1987 in the manner of the Kwa-Zulu-Natal concept. Treaties and cooperation agreements would be concluded. Ciskei, Transkei and the Eastern Cape, he stressed, found economic progress difficult. Together, though, possibly with East London as a free port, they would have the means to become economically stronger. Meanwhile, in preparation for this, the Eastern Cape would be granted provincial status to give it second tier government and place it on an equal footing with Transkei and Ciskei.

It was important, the Brigadier said, that the plan 'must entail minimum political risk for the RSA' and 'actions must not be traced back to the RSA'.

What was truly breathtaking was that the plan was a naïve reflection of his personal favour/disfavour of the government's apartheid policy — a policy the world had been pressuring South Africa to scrap for years. Despite this, he as a mere brigadier had set out to radically alter established government policy to coincide with his own narrow military view of things. Amazingly, he nearly succeeded!

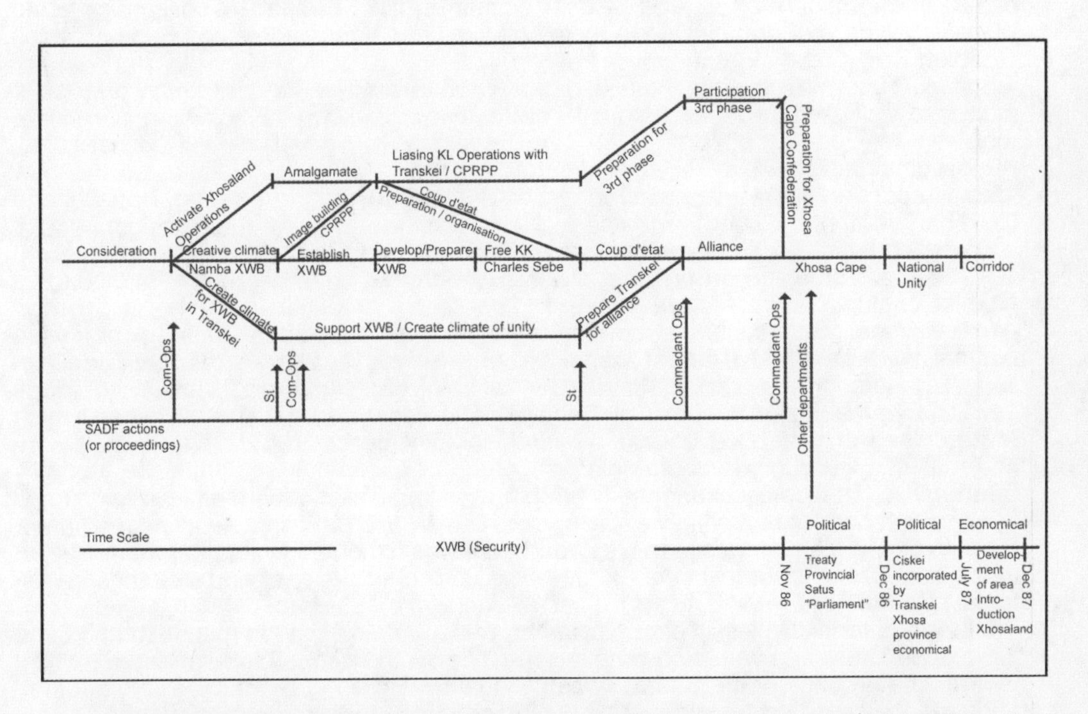

Brigadier Joffel van der Westhuizen's *Operation Katzen* and its anticipated rosy results in diagrammatic form.

The *Operation Katzen* plan was approved by the Chief of the Army, General Kat Liebenberg in July 1986. Later in the month Brigadier van der Westhuizen conducted another presentation for the Chief of the SADF, General Jannie Geldenhuys; the Commissioner of Police, General Johan Coetzee; the East London Security Police Chief, Colonel Jan Griebenauw; the Chief of Staff Intelligence, Vice-Admiral Putter; the Natal National Intelligence representative, Neville Höll; and other senior officers. Verbal authorisation was granted at this meeting for him to proceed with the first phases of the plan. Colonel John More, of the Military Intelligence's Special Tasks Directorate, was appointed Project Officer for the operation. Control over the execution of the first phase commenced with his appointment.[10]

Colonel Griebenauw was ordered to provide intelligence regarding Charles Sebe's imprisonment and so on. He disagreed and wrote to Security Police headquarters and made it clear that as a police officer he objected to being involved in unlawful activities. His letter was ignored by his superiors so he reluctantly went ahead and gave orders to his subordinates to collect the information required. He did not tell anyone, except his immediate subordinate, Major Sakkie van der Merwe, anything about *Operation Katzen*.[11]

Brigadier van der Westhuizen said the Deputy SADF Chief, General Ian Gleeson; the South African Ambassador to Ciskei, General van Deventer and the Dean of the Faculty of Law at the University of Port Elizabeth and later the National Party government Minister for Local Government, Professor Tertius Delport, endorsed the plan although they had only been made partly aware of it.

Appearing on the SATV programme *Newsline* during the run-up to the 1994 election Delport was asked: 'Would you deny you were involved in *Operation Katzen*?'

Instead of answering directly he waffled: '. . . I was involved in trying to bring peace to this country. As also PAC leaders can testify. I spent many hours trying to bring together leaders in the Eastern Cape, both ANC, at the time UDF . . . and PAC people . . . and people from the government side to try to solve the problems we had at that stage. Port Elizabeth was becoming really a city of terror. It was becoming a city in 1985 where people fled from. We lost businesses. If you want to accuse me of trying to do what I could for my city and my region, do so. I was never involved in anything I did not do in the open'.

Question: 'Were you involved in *Operation Katzen*?'

'No, of course not, that's nonsense'.

In a handwritten document, Brigadier van der Westhuizen listed another eight people whom he had briefed on *Operation Katzen*. They included Major-General Joep Joubert, GOC Special Forces, and Brigadier Willem Schoon, the head of the SAP's infamous Vlakplaas unit.[12]

Another meeting on the subject of *Operation Katzen* was held in Cape Town. It was attended by SADF Chief, General Jannie Geldenhuys; the secretary of the State Security Council, Lieutenant-General P W van der Westhuizen; the Commissioner of Police, General Johan Coetzee; the Director-General of the National Intelligence Service, Dr Niel Barnard; the Natal representative of the National Intelligence Service, Neville Höll; and the Project Officer, Colonel John More.

General Johan Coetzee was frankly unenthusiastic, believing the plan was not a new idea and that nothing had come of similar ones in the past. Dr Barnard was not prepared to play a part in the plan because his department was a 'non executing department'. He asked to be kept informed, though, and Neville Höll continued to attend meetings as his representative.[13]

Colonel Lourens du Plessis phoned Namba Sebe and arranged to meet him and Lent Maqoma in Umtata. It would be a covert meeting so the venue chosen was a mobile home in the grounds of the South African Embassy. He and Van der Westhuizen met them and they outlined the plan. They explained that in the interim a Xhosa resistance movement would be formed and headed by Namba until Charles Sebe could be sprung from prison. A new political party to be headed by Lent Maqoma would also be formed. It was envisaged that eventually, once Lennox Sebe had been disposed of, Namba and Lent would take over the administration of Ciskei until its amalgamation with Transkei was achieved. They said the next step was to meet Prime Minister George Matanzima and Namba said he would make the necessary arrangements.

The security relating to this meeting was inadvertently breached by Lourens du Plessis. He smoked Lexington filter-tipped cigarettes. This was generally well known because he had the habit of pinching off the filters. People often asked him why he did not smoke the plain version to save himself the trouble, to which he always replied: 'The taste is different'. After the meeting someone noticed a quantity of filter tips in an ashtray and word got around that Lourens du Plessis had been at the embassy. In the event no harm was done but it could have prejudiced the security of the operation.

That evening Van der Westhuizen and Du Plessis drove from Umtata to Bisho. It was late so they decided to stay the night at the Amatola Sun Casino Hotel. The next morning Van der Westhuizen told Du Plessis to return to Umtata in the car. He was to contact Namba Sebe and arrange an early appointment with Prime Minister George so as to get things moving. He would arrange with Port Elizabeth to send a car to collect the prime minister.

Colonel du Plessis saw Prime Minister George alone later that morning. He explained the plan and the Prime Minister was 'very taken with it'. He particularly liked the bit where he would become either the prime minister or president of the combined Xhosa state. He was in seventh heaven when it was explained that the new territory would also include the 'white corridor' between the two territories and probably the cities of Port Elizabeth and East London.

With George Matanzima's approval a further meeting was arranged. Attending would be Joffel van der Westhuizen, Namba Sebe and Lent Maqoma, plus Colonel du Plessis. For security reasons it was decided this meeting should take place at Prime Minister George's smallholding just outside Umtata, not at his office or official residence as Du Plessis felt it would attract too much attention.

When they arrived, they were astounded to find ten or 12 people already there, waiting in the lounge for interviews with the prime minister. He was nowhere to be seen. They sat around waiting until eventually someone appeared and invited them to wait in the prime minister's office. No mention was made of what had happened to the man himself. There was another long wait until the same person returned. This time they asked what had happened to the prime minister and whether he would be long. They were told he was still in bed. There was another wait and the person returned and invited the four of them to go to the bedroom.

There were insufficient chairs, so when he was invited to sit down, Colonel du Plessis had to sit on the edge of the water bed. He ran through the plan again for the benefit of those present and Brigadier van der Westhuizen gave it his official blessing.

The atmosphere was friendly and everyone was happy. Namba and Lent were even happier when Du Plessis gave them an envelope each via Van der Westhuizen. Namba's contained R10 000 in banknotes and Lent's R5 000.

'You guys must get to work and get things off the ground. Work on the people you know and recruit for the resistance movement. If you need more money just say so. Meanwhile, you can use this money for whatever you like. If you want to buy yourself a nice suit, then be my guest. If you want to spend a few thousand on land then go ahead. It is up to you'.

The money had been provided by Colonel John More, the project officer.

After this local acceptance the Security Police commander in East London, Colonel Griebenauw, was briefed. Major-General Reid Daly was away attending to a contract of Security Specialists International at Sasol II in Secunda. He received a call from Major-General Mtirara who asked that they meet at the Johannesburg Sun Hotel.

General Mtirara explained that he had been involved in discussions between Prime Minister George and Brigadier Joffel van der Westhuizen about a plan to disrupt the Ciskei that would become *Operation Katzen*. He said the P.M. approved of the plan and wanted to discuss its ramifications with him when he returned to Umtata. This happened.[14]

Prime Minister George, who had many homes and who was not particularly enamoured with his official residence sited in Umtata's parliamentary enclosure, allowed Lent Maqoma and Namba Sebe to move in and use its offices. During their ongoing discussions, Colonel Du Plessis was often entertained to a *braaivleis* (barbecue) there.

An undated and unsigned list of code names of the principle personalities involved in *Operation Katzen*, was produced by General Holomisa at a press conference on 11 March 1993. It was written in Afrikaans and presumably used for the purposes of radio messages, correspondence and guarded telephone conversations. It follows the concept of distancing the military from their covert actions by adopting code names drawn from commercial usage. The participants were listed as:

1. Van der Westhuizen — managing director.
2. K D M [Kaiser Matanzima] — co-director.
3. George M [Matanzima] — manager.
4. Colonel (P) Hall — co-owner.
5. Colonel (L J) More — assistant manager.
6. Commandant du Plessis — deputy manager
7. Colonel van Rooyen — book keeper.
8. Charles S [Sebe] — accountant.
9. Lennox S [Sebe] — shareholder.
10. Umtata — head office.
11. Lent M [Maqoma] — attorney.

12 Kwane Sebe — deputy accountant.
13 XWB — Xhosa Resistance Movement — corporation.
14 Namba S (Sebe) — auditor.
15 *Liza [Iliso] Lomzi* — company.
16 SADF's Special Forces — workers.
17 Transkei Special Forces — relief workers.
18 Ciskei Defence Force — pensioners.
19 Port Elizabeth — farm.
20 Bisho — rest camp.
21 East London — holiday resort.
22 King William's Town — new project.
23 Eliminate — bank acceptance.
24 Rig [Brig?] Deyzel — assistant attorney.
25 Pretoria — factory.
26 R R Daily [Daly] — director.

There is always a danger that military code names can be revealing, which is why NATO uses names taken from random lists. *Operation Katzen*'s code names are particularly revealing, including the operational name itself. Brigadier van der Westhuizen as 'managing director' was clearly in charge. Reid Daly as 'director' and Kaiser Matanzima as 'co-director' were obviously key figures but of lesser importance. Umtata as the 'head office' shows the base for its actions. Van der Westhuizen's scarcely concealed contempt for Ciskei is shown by Lennox Sebe being a mere 'shareholder', the CDF being 'pensioners' and Bisho as the 'rest camp'. The list was clearly prepared in the early days of planning, because the Xhosa resistance movement appears twice, once as the XWB and once as *Iliso Lomzi*. In both instances the code names are similar. The only code word, that was significantly vague, was the sinister 'eliminate' for which 'bank acceptance' was used. The titles of company officials were commonly used as code names by the SADF.

The next move came on 23 July 1986, a mere 14 days after the submission of Van der Westhuizen's second paper to Pretoria. Namba Sebe, speaking publicly in Umtata, announced the formation of *Iliso Lomzi*. He said its aim was to counter 'atrocities' by the Ciskei government.[15] It had been decided to form it before Charles Sebe was bust from prison, because of the time it would take to recruit, train, equip personnel and get it off the ground.

Van der Westhuizen's suggestion that *Iliso Lomzi* become the security wing of the CPRPP, if the Party succeeded, had been adopted. Namba Sebe confirmed this by saying it was a 'wing' of Chief Maqoma's CPRPP and was already operational in Ciskei, 'protecting' people against Lennox Sebe's administration. It was, he claimed, 'entirely peaceful'. It was not, of course, 'already' operational. Chief Lent Maqoma announced at the same time that when he and Namba Sebe assumed power they would consider amalgamating Ciskei and Transkei.[16]

Recruiting for *Iliso Lomzi* commenced. It was based with and trained by Transkei's Special Forces at Port St Johns. Various membership figures have been bandied around, with some speculating that it reached as much as 150. It is doubtful, though, that it ever enjoyed a strength of more than 25 to 30 at the most.[17]

The 'subtle psychological breakdown of Lennox Sebe and his colleagues' began almost immediately. On 11 August Chief Maqoma won an action in Ciskei's Supreme Court for the return of land that had been excised from the jurisdiction of his chieftainship. The court found that the proclamation ordering it was *ultra vires* the constitution. He failed in a parallel bid for an order restraining Lennox Sebe or his agents from harassing or unlawfully arresting him.

On 25 August 1986 The Sangoni Partnership of Butterworth, Transkei, wrote a letter to the Speaker of the House, Ciskei National Assembly, Bisho, copying one already sent to Ciskei's Advocate-General (in fact, the Attorney-General), with a schedule attached.

It was a schedule of orders drawn on the Department of Works on the instructions of Lennox Sebe. They concerned construction and maintenance work carried out at his privately owned properties including Two Rivers farm at Izeli, a flat at Tshatshu Village, a beach house at Hamburg and a house at Zone 4. It also included the supply of luxury furniture to those properties. The misuse involved monies in excess of R600 000.

The Sangoni Partnership drew to the attention of the Speaker that he had a duty in terms of Act 118 of 1979 to bring these allegations to the attention of the House.[18]

Lent Maqoma claimed responsibility for the letters saying the actions 'amounted to dishonest use of taxpayers' monies with the resultant effect of enriching the president at the expense of the taxpayers'.[19]

That the costs were financed by the SADF and motivated by Major-General Reid Daly, probably at the suggestion of Comops, is supported by the first section of a four-page paper detailing points for a meeting. It is in the distinctive handwriting of Reid Daly. It is undated but deals generally with planning relating to the attempt on Lennox Sebe's life.

1 A court action has been launched against Lennox Sebe involving the misuse of state funds. The sum of R20 000 (twenty thousand rands) is urgently required to initiate this action.

2 **Questions**:
- a Could this sum of money be made available?
- b If so is it acceptable that this money be paid to Sangoni Bros (Attorneys) Umtata. They have been commissioned to commence the action.
- c How soon can this be made available?'

3 **Ciskei Defence Force. Require urgently**:
- a 1:250,000 map coverage of Ciskei.
- b Locstats and strengths of Ciskei Defence Force at each locstat.
- [c] State of training.
- d Plans of each base.
- e Routine followed in each base, particularly over weekends.
- f Guards and sentries:
- g Numbers by day and by night (each base).
- h Emergency drills — if any (each base).
- i Communications.
  - i Type of radios used;
  - ii Frequencies;
  - iii Radio routine, i.e. radio checks etc;
- j **Clothing and equipment:**
  - i We believe clothing is identical to SADF, is this correct?
  - ii If so can 300 sets be made avail to us?
  - iii Vehicles required:
    - (a) Type.
    - (b) Routine and where parked at night, gds [guards] etc.
    - (c) Locstats.
- k **Command and control:**
  - i Which building houses this?
  - ii Routine:
    - (a) By day
    - (b) By night
    - (c) Home addresses (plus town plan) of all commander[s].
- l **Roads blocks:**
  - i Composition.

ii Tactical layout.
iii Locstats if stationary.
iv Numbers of mobile rd [road] blocks (if any).

4 **Zibi**: Require all aval[able] data on this man as for Lennox Sebe.

5 **Lennox Sebe**

a Plan of official locstat [offices].
b Plan of private locstat [residence]
c Plan of girlfriends' house/s if any?
d Routine:
i By day.
ii By night
e As above of his close friends/confidantes.
f Does he move at night?
g Types of cars/number plates used
h Bodyguards and their routine.
i Alarm systems.[20]

It appears Major-General Reid Daly got the R20 000 he had asked for to pay for the action he was orchestrating against Lennox Sebe.

General A J van Deventer, the South African Ambassador to Transkei who, according to Brigadier van der Westhuizen, had been made 'partly aware' of *Operation Katzen*, was replaced by Chris van Aardt on 1 August 1986.[21] It is reasonable to assume that Van Aardt was given a briefing on the situation by his predecessor.

On 18 September Namba Sebe claimed that 12 men had tried to kidnap him on 13 September. He said he recognised most of them as Ciskei security policemen. Needless to say, Ciskei denied all knowledge.[22]

South African Special Forces were ordered to spring Charles Sebe from Middledrift Prison. This was arranged with the GOC Special Forces, Major-General Joep Joubert. He tasked a group to go ahead with the planning. In all probability the group was supplied by the Civil Cooperation Bureau (CCB) division of Special Forces. An undated intelligence report, probably originating from the SADF's Eastern Province Command Group 8 in East London said that according to Source C3 the task 'was carried out by 3-Recce Commando, three Selous Scouts and one black man'.[23] *Project Barnacle* became 3-Recce for a brief spell before it was changed to the CCB in April 1986. It is possible that someone referred to the unit as 3-Recce without being aware that the name had already been changed.

Another indication that the CCB was involved was that Colonel Griebenauw was told to liaise with Colonel Joe Verster of Special Forces. Colonel Verster took over command of the CCB in 1986. Colonel Griebenauw ordered Warrant Officers Hattingh and Fouche to photograph the prison and sketch Charles Sebe's cell. Someone also bribed prison warders to obtain information on prison routines. The cells of Charles Sebe, Khambashe Sebe and Namba Sebe's sons Koli, Toni and Mlotana were pin-pointed. A duplicate key to Charles Sebe's cell was obtained and probably keys to the other cells as well.

Colonel Griebenauw passed the photographs and all the intelligence gathered to Colonel Joe Verster at Special Forces.[24]

During the evening of 24 September Major-General Kwane Sebe, son of Lennox Sebe and commander of the CDF, and his second in command, Colonel Z 'Bullet' Ngwanya, went to the Amatola Sun in Bisho to meet a white man who had promised to introduce them to an important source. From there they were lured to the Holiday Inn in East London, probably on the pretext that the source had got cold feet at the last moment and had refused to come to Bisho in case he was recognised.

Once in a room in the Holiday Inn the officers were overpowered, handcuffed, leg-ironed, blindfolded, drugged and smuggled out of the hotel. Their assailants, operators from the CCB, drove them out of the Ciskei to Umtata using back roads. Colonel Griebenauw said his role had been to collect information on border posts and safe routes.

With reluctance he arranged for security policemen to take up positions on certain roads. 'We used codes and flickering lights [strobes] to safeguard the route to the border post and get the abducted people to safety'.[25]

In the early hours of the next morning, 25 September 1986, in a slick and well-planned operation, a group of what was called at the time in SADF circles 'white Recce operators' armed with AK47s and PPSH sub-machine guns stormed Middledrift Prison.

4 118

4 LENNOX SEBE

a. PLAN OF OFFICIAL LOCSTAT
b. " " PRIVATE "
c. " " GIRL FRIEND'S HOUSE/S IF ANY?
d. ROUTINE:
i. BY DAY
ii BY NIGHT
e. AS ABOVE OF HIS CLOSE FRIENDS/CONFIDANTES
f. DOES HE MOVE AT NIGHT?
g. TYPES OF CARS/NUMBER PLATES USED
h. BODYGUARDS AND THEIR ROUTINE.
j ALARM SYSTEMS

Handwritten section of General Reid Daly's planning to murder President Lennox Sebe.

Commandant E Hammond, the Staff Officer Intelligence at the SADF's Group 8 HQ in East London, in a 'secret' intelligence report said the raiders used aluminium ladders that were exactly the right height to scale the outside walls. From the top of the wall they dropped rope ladders into the yard and gained entrance. They quickly overcame what little resistance the warders offered, and using a duplicate key in their possession, opened Charles Sebe's cell door and released him. The prison warders threw down their weapons when they saw the attackers were white. This was specifically referred to in Parliament later when the guards were described as cowards for throwing down their weapons and fleeing. Shooting took place but it is unknown by whom. There were, however, no casualties. Middledrift residents made statements to this effect to the Ciskei Police. It was said that Major-General Kwane Sebe and Colonel Ngwanya were driven to the prison and displayed to the warders as bargaining chips. The release of Khambashe Sebe and Namba Sebe's three sons was not facilitated as planned, probably because the intelligence relating to the location of their cells had been incorrect.

Commandant Hammond, in the same intelligence report, said that urban Ciskeians were talking openly about their concerns of an invasion of Ciskei by Transkei. They were also saying 'there will be big trouble in Ciskei' and many doubted that President Lennox Sebe would still be around by the end of November 1986. He said that Lennox drew most of his support from the rural population, particularly the chiefs and headmen. He said the general dislike of Lennox by urban Ciskeians was well known. Commandant Hammond also said it had 'been stated' that General Charles Sebe 'still enjoys the support of 80% of the Security Forces'. 'This factor alone', he suggested, 'contributes to the likelihood of collusion between Ciskei prison officials and Gen Sebe's "rescuers". A possible attempted coup in the future cannot be ruled out.' This indicates that Commandant Hammond was not in-the-know as far as *Operation Katzen* was concerned.[26]

THE SANGONI PARTNERSHIP

Attorneys-at-Law, Notaries Public
Administrators of Estates and Commissioners of Oaths
Also Attorneys of the High Court of Lesotho

lement Temba Sangoni, B. Juris (S.A.)
ctor Zilindile Sangoni, B. Proc. (F.H.)
aptain Paluxolo Noah, B. Proc. (F.H.)
ompleton Mzilwandile Ntsaluba, B. Proc. (F.H.)
ola Mlungisi Petse, B. Proc. (F.H.)
reston Pumzile Majeke, B. Proc. (S.A.)
umisa Buhle Ntsebeza B.A., B. Proc. (S.A.)
ssisted by
obeko Mavis Ntsebeza B. Proc. (F.H.)

Our Ref. CTS/stb/
Your Ref.

P.O. Box 462
BUTTERWORTH

14 Fuller Street
BUTTERWORTH
Tel. (04341) 3291/2

1986/08/25

The Speaker of the House
Ciskei National Assembly,
BISHO

Dear Sir, "BY HAND"

MISUSE OF PUBLIC MONIES : PRESIDENT L.L. SEBE

We forrward herewith a copy of our letter dated the 25th instant to the Advocate - General together with annexures. The said letter speaks for itself.

We are instructed, in view of the allegations against President Sebe, to ask you, as we hereby do, to bring to the notice of the members of the House the allegations against President Sebe. This is a measure that is taken in case there is no Advocate - General appointed in terms of that Act 118 of 1979.

You will appreciate, we trust, that in terms of the said Act you have a duty to table a matter of this nature before Parliament.

We ask you to confirm with us in writing not later than 4pm on the 28th instant as to when you expect to discharge the said duty.

Yours Faithfully
THE SANGONI FARTENRSHIP

Per

Letter from Attorneys The Sangoni Partnership to the Speaker of the House of Ciskei's National Assembly, drawing attention to President Sebe's misuse of public monies. General Reid Daly instigated the action and obtained R20 000 (of taxpayers' money) from Military Intelligence to pay for it. It was a case of a misusing pot calling a misusing kettle black.

On a strict 'need to know' basis only a handful of people were involved in the planning of the jailbreak and Colonel Lourens du Plessis, who had originally drafted the plan and was the principal officer involved in liaison with Namba Sebe and Lent Maqoma, was not one of them.

Early on the morning after the jailbreak, Colonel du Plessis' phone rang and the caller told him to have Namba Sebe at the Holiday Inn in Umtata by 10:00. They were met there and Namba Sebe was directed to drive to somewhere nearby to meet another man. This man handed him a suitcase packed with bank notes and said he should go to another nearby rendezvous where he would again be met. He should hand over the suitcase and its contents and in return he would be given Charles Sebe.

He complied and took over a jubilant Charles Sebe as a free man.The handcuffed and drugged General Kwane Sebe and Colonel Ngwanya were taken over by the Transkei Police. They were detained in Wellington prison on 26 September. Transkei, it must be said, had no grounds to detain them, considering they had been unlawfully and forcibly abducted in South Africa and bundled through to Transkei.[27]

Lieutenant-General Joffel van der Westhuizen told the Truth and Reconciliation Commission that the intention had been to create the impression that Charles Sebe had been sprung by mercenaries. Colonel More had provided the funds and the suitcase so that the play could be acted out. The money was eventually returned to him minus the sum of R250 used to pay an informer.

Colonel Joe Verster phoned Colonel Griebenauw and told him the operation had been successful.[28]

Namba Sebe immediately claimed credit for the jailbreak and the abductions on *Iliso Lomzi*'s behalf'. He said that it formed part of the strategy to unseat Lennox Sebe and dissolve Ciskei's national assembly so that free elections could be held. He added, (one wonders on what legal authority, that General Kwane Sebe and Colonel Ngwanya would be released from prison only if Lennox Sebe resigned, if the national assembly voluntarily dissolved and if Khambashe, Toni and Koli Sebe, and Mlotana were released from Ciskeian detention.[29]

Commandant Hammond, in the same 'secret' intelligence report said it had been suggested that Major-General Reid Daly was the 'master brain behind the execution of the Charles Sebe release and [the] Kwane Sebe kidnap. He added: 'General Reid Daly and members of his staff were on leave when these incidents took place as they are in line for a renewal of contract with the TDF and are very money orientated. It is quite possible that they could have accepted such a task'.[30]

It is unlikely that General Reid Daly was involved except on the periphery of the planning, although he would have been expecting to be because of his involvement with *Operation Katzen*. It is doubtful that any of his ex-Selous Scouts or the employees of Security Services Transkei (Pty) Ltd were involved in the operation. It was in all probability an operation by South African Special Forces.

It is interesting to note that a security report from Eastern Province Command, undated but about this time, reported that a Commandant O J [Oupa] Gqozo of the CDF had been in Transkei seeing Prime Minister George Matanzima. It said Gqozo was in line to be the new Defence Force chief once the government of Lennox Sebe had been replaced.

The reporting officer commented: 'Gqozo was Charles Sebe's plant in the CDF during 1982/83. He worked with Charles in the CCIS [Ciskei Central Intelligence Service]. He is always in the background when CDF matters are discussed. Although the second in command of the CDF neither [General] Mlandu nor [Major] Sandile trust him and openly give him a cold shoulder . . . '[31]

Interviewed on 29 September after his release, Charles Sebe said he had begun 'vigorous military training in preparation for the restoration of democracy and stability in Ciskei'. In a document drafted about the same time, he noted that a Commandant Oupa Gqozo was among those in Ciskei who had 'a positive outlook on a change resulting in a new Ciskei'.[32] It was the ultimate poor misjudgment.

This marked the commencement of a second leafleting exercise. It focussed on anti-Lennox material and extolled the virtues of Charles Sebe. The new leaflets sported a badge with a lion's head and the title *Iliso Lomzi* scrolled below. The artwork came with the compliments of Colonel Lourens du Plessis. The leaflets were distributed throughout

Ciskei in the same way as the first batch, using several commando pilots called up with their privately owned aircraft to do the job.

On 30 September, an upset Lennox Sebe announced that a low flying aircraft had dropped what he called 'derogatory pamphlets' over Mdantsane and other Ciskei townships. He accused Transkei of violating Ciskei's airspace and demanded South African government intervention to facilitate the commencement of mediation between Ciskei and Transkei. He promised retaliatory action if the mediation failed.[33]

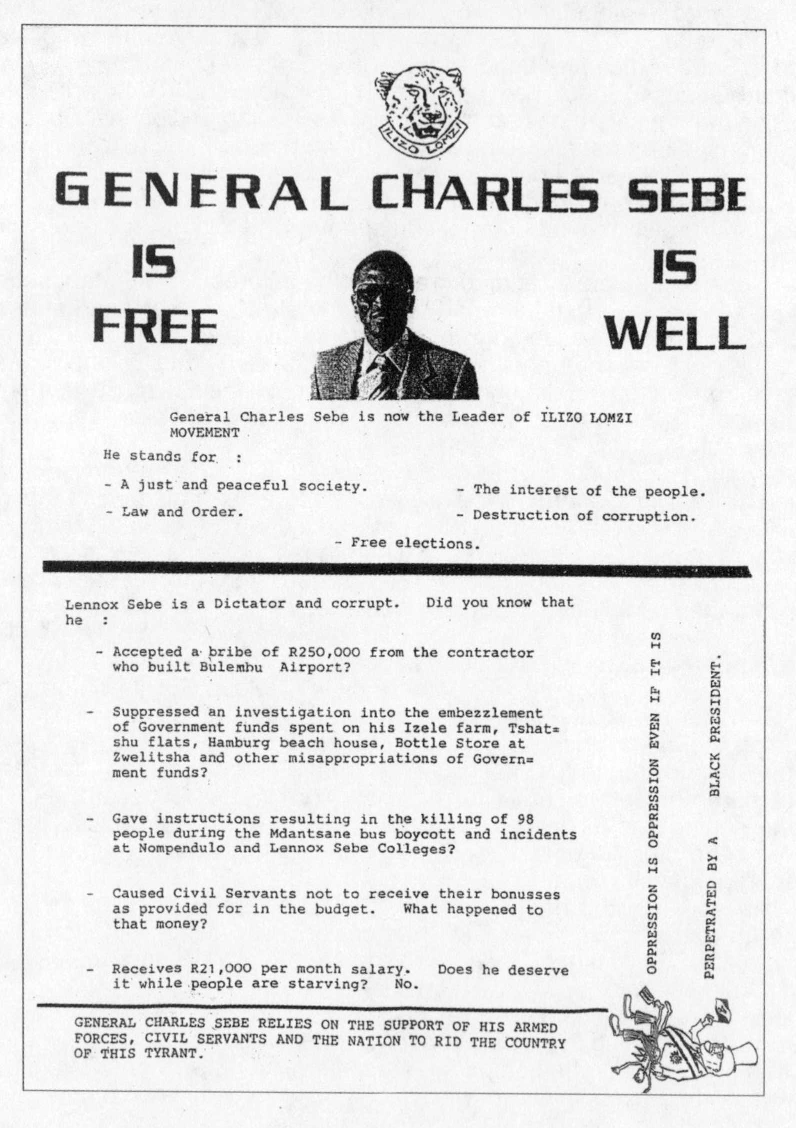

ILIZO LOMZI

GENERAL CHARLES SEBE

IS FREE

IS WELL

General Charles Sebe is now the Leader of ILIZO LOMZI MOVEMENT

He stands for :

- A just and peaceful society.
- Law and Order.
- The interest of the people.
- Destruction of corruption.
- Free elections.

Lennox Sebe is a Dictator and corrupt. Did you know that he :

- Accepted a bribe of R250,000 from the contractor who built Bulembu Airport?
- Suppressed an investigation into the embezzlement of Government funds spent on his Izele farm, Tshat= shu flats, Hamburg beach house, Bottle Store at Zwelitsha and other misappropriations of Govern= ment funds?
- Gave instructions resulting in the killing of 98 people during the Mdantsane bus boycott and incidents at Nompendulo and Lennox Sebe Colleges?
- Caused Civil Servants not to receive their bonusses as provided for in the budget. What happened to that money?
- Receives R21,000 per month salary. Does he deserve it while people are starving? No.

OPPRESSION IS OPPRESSION EVEN IF IT IS PERPETRATED BY A BLACK PRESIDENT.

GENERAL CHARLES SEBE RELIES ON THE SUPPORT OF HIS ARMED FORCES, CIVIL SERVANTS AND THE NATION TO RID THE COUNTRY OF THIS TYRANT.

Leaflet designed and printed by Comops for dropping over Ciskei.

South Africa's Deputy Minister of Foreign Affairs, Ron Miller, met representatives of Ciskei and Transkei separately the next day in a attempt to mediate.[34] His efforts bore no fruit, which was not surprising considering that the leaflet-dropping intruders were South Africans and not Transkeians.

An enraged Lennox Sebe appointed a judicial commission of enquiry to investigate the escapes from Middledrift Prison. He accused the warders and the local police, who had not even fired a shot, of being drunk.

On 2 October Prime Minister George Matanzima of Transkei announced that 'two Ciskei officers' had been detained for complicity in the 18 September attempt to kidnap Namba Sebe. Five days later 'the two Ciskei officers', who turned out to be General Kwane Sebe and Colonel 'Bullet' Ngwanya, appeared before the Umtata magistrate on charges of attempted kidnapping and assault. Their attorney told the court they had been incarcerated in Umtata's Wellington Prison since their abduction on 26 September.

On 5 October, taking up his role in *Operation Katzen*, Ciskei's former vice president, Rev Wilson Xaba, claimed in Umtata that Charles Sebe had been freed to facilitate efforts to bring about an amalgamation of Transkei and Ciskei.[35]

On 7 October Namba Sebe told an Umtata press conference that *Iliso Lomzi* was run by professionals. It had come into being over a 'long-standing family feud', after Lennox Sebe had rejected appeals by the family to negotiate. He announced that General Charles Sebe would 'soon' be taking over as commander of *Iliso Lomzi*. He claimed he had retained the kidnapped Ciskeian officers in his personal custody until they were taken over by the Transkei Police. As a reward for his admissions to the press, Ciskei immediately applied for Namba Sebe's extradition to Bisho.

Chief Lent Maqoma described Charles Sebe's release from prison as the first step towards Xhosa unification and 'ridding our society of an incompetent leader'. He called on Lennox Sebe to resign and for the holding of free and democratic elections in Ciskei.[36]

Relations between Ciskei and Transkei, probably more so than the SADF had planned, plunged further on 13 October. The CNIP's deputy whip warned a meeting of chiefs, headmen, MPs and councillors in Bisho that Transkeian citizens living and working in Ciskei, including civil servants, would be evicted from their subsidised homes and 'deported'. South Africa's Foreign Minister, Pik Botha, said he had held talks with both parties and had urged them to resolve their problems peacefully.[37]

President Lennox Sebe dissolved Ciskei's National Assembly on 17 October in preparation for an election on 19 November — the first since 1978. In terms of the South African-crafted constitution the Ciskeian electorate would be able to vote only for 23 members of the National Assembly. The remaining 48 were chiefs and nominated members, so as an exercise in democracy, it was a farce. To make matters worse the recently promulgated Electoral Amendment Act had increased deposits for candidates from a reasonable R300 to a punitive R10 000. It also laid down that political parties intending to contest the election had to obtain the signatures of 10 000 people who supported their applications.

Lent Maqoma, not currently resident in Ciskei, found it an impossible task to collect the 10 000 signatures necessary to qualify the CPRPP for registration — even with the substantial financial and logistical help of the SADF which sorted out the deposits for him. The day before nominations closed, he lost an urgent application in the Ciskei Supreme for the nomination and polling dates to be postponed or set aside to allow the CPRPP sufficient time to register as a political party so it could contest the election.

The South African taxpayer, through Military Intelligence, paid the substantial costs of this court action, but it saved Ciskei the expense of holding an election, because to no one's surprise, when nominations closed the next day all 23 candidates of the ruling CNIP were returned unopposed.[38]

In adopting this system, unashamedly introduced to minimise the chances of the opposition gaining power, President Lennox Sebe had clearly taken a leaf from Chief Jonathan's book — Lesotho's 1985 elections had just been run in the same manner.

On 21 October General Kwane Sebe and Colonel Bullet Ngwanya were released on bail of R3 000 each into the custody of South African ambassadorial staff. Despite this,

Transkei's Security Police immediately redetained them in terms of the Public Security Act. The following day an urgent application for their release was made to the Transkei Supreme Court. In answer to the application, the Security Police chief produced an affidavit that claimed the subjects had either 'committed an offence or intended to commit an offence', or had information relating thereto. Their applications were turned down.[39]

The Ciskei lodged diplomatic notes with South Africa on 22 and 23 October, protesting at its ambassadorial staff's failure to claim diplomatic immunity for the two men while in their custody. It called the Transkei Security Police's actions 'contempt of court' and an 'abuse of authority'. It also appealed for South Africa's intervention because 'We believe that Transkei by her latest acts of aggression is looking for a pretext to invade Ciskei and enforce her long cherished ambition of amalgamation, which she wants to achieve irrespective of the feelings and sentiments of Ciskeians'.[40]

Ciskei would have felt even more justified in its protestations if it had known about *Operation Katzen* and South Africa's involvement.

On 22 October Charles Sebe told Major-General Reid Daly that on the morning before, Lennox Sebe had ordered the arrest of his own brother-in-law, Chief Simon Hebe. Chief Hebe was picked up from his tribal authority in Whittlesea and dragged before a meeting of cabinet ministers and officers of the Security Forces chaired by the President.

They demanded to know the whereabouts of Charles Sebe. When Chief Hebe failed to answer because he genuinely did not know, Lennox Sebe ordered the Security Police to take him away for interrogation. At their headquarters they kicked, punched and tortured him and poured itching powder on his anus and private parts. At 01:00 the next morning, having failed to break him, they detained him in the cells. Nine hours later he was warned to keep his mouth shut about what had happened, then he was released.

When Chief Hebe got home he found that his wife — Charles Sebe's sister and Lennox Sebe's half sister — had also been spirited away by the Security Police for interrogation and torture.[41]

Lent Maqoma's two daughters were detained at Alice Police station, stripped naked and throttled with a wet towel. Lungi Msuthawana, a girlfriend of Charles Sebe who worked in the post office at Bisho, and who had often accompanied Chief Hebe's wife on visits to see Charles in prison, was also arrested. They stripped her naked and all but suffocated her with an inner tube. When she maintained her denials, an acidic substance was poured on her thighs and vagina, causing severe burns. She was kept in solitary confinement for five days without medical treatment.[42]

The arrests of Chief Hebe's wife and Lungi Msuthawana were confirmed by Major Sandile during discussions with Commandant Hammond on 24 October 1986.[43]

Major Sandile of Ciskei's Military Intelligence had regular meetings with Commandant Hammond at the SADF's Group 8 HQ in East London. Hammond assessed him as 'unquestionably loyal' to President Lennox Sebe. During a meeting on 24 October Sandile maintained that he had operators monitoring the movements of Charles Sebe in Transkei. He spoke of him as the biggest threat known to the Ciskei government and said he was plotting to overthrow the president by force. He did not believe that Namba Sebe posed a particular threat. By Major Sandile's assessment, if a coup attempt was successful, Charles Sebe would resume his old job in the military and Namba would end up as president.

Major Sandile attempted to enlist SADF support against Charles and Namba Sebe but Hammond refused and told him the matter 'could only be satisfactorily resolved by diplomatic means'.

Sandile let it slip that General Edwin Kuta, the Ciskei Police Commissioner, was also about to be detained because he had maintained close ties with Charles Sebe throughout his detention and even after he had fled to Transkei. From the conversation Commandant Hammond gathered that phones of Kuta and others under suspicion had been bugged.

Sure enough, as he had predicted, General Kuta, his deputy, General Fambalele Zozi, and Security Police Chief, General Zebulon Makuzeni, were detained on the grounds that they had failed to return the president's son, General Kwane Sebe, to Ciskei or provide an explanation as to how the prison break had taken place.

Major Sandile had effectively become a source for Commandant Hammond by this time.

Military Intelligence at Eastern Province Command reported that Major Sandile had secretly met 'his agent' from the Transkei in the early hours of 24 October. The agent, who was a paid source of Military Intelligence, reported that Charles Sebe was planning to go to Johannesburg to meet friends. He had been booked in at the Sandton Sun Hotel, room 703, under a false name. He would, however, be easily recognisable because he would be wearing his trademark dark glasses.[44] Whether Charles Sebe paid the proposed visit to Johannesburg is not known, but it can be assumed that Ciskei's Military Intelligence mounted observations in Sandton in an attempt to capture him.

Whatever the case, Major Sandile phoned and arranged to meet Commandant Hammond on 25 October. He said Lennox Sebe was distressed about the continued detention of his son, General Kwane Sebe, in Transkei and wanted him freed before Ciskei's Independence Day celebrations on 4 December 1986. Sandile naïvely explained his plans. Lennox Sebe had ordered the elimination of Namba Sebe, because it was believed Kwane's continued detention was reliant on his evidence.

Meanwhile, Ciskeian agents resident in Transkei had been ordered to kidnap Transkei's Chief Vundu Matanzima and bundle him into Ciskei. A demand would then be made for Charles Sebe to be handed over in exchange for Vundu Matanzima. With Namba Sebe dead there would be no case against Kwane, so there would be no alternative but to release him.

The operation involved despatching to Transkei a three-man hit squad armed with AK47s and Makarov pistols. They knew Namba's house and that he was staying with his wife and children. His eldest son had enrolled for a course at the University of Transkei, but he had been forced to leave after his fellow students discovered that he had failed to matriculate. Namba's home was guarded but the sentries appeared to be untrained and were mostly asleep. It was not thought they would present much of an obstacle. In preparation an operator living in Umtata had struck up an acquaintanceship with Namba. He worked for a removal company and normally parked his vehicle close to Namba's residence. The plan was for him to lure Namba from the house. A team member would shoot him while the other two covered him. Simultaneously, another team would be tasked to capture Chief Vundu. They would explain that he was a hostage and that he would not be placed in detention. Both groups would move in and out of Transkei on foot to avoid roadblocks.

Major Sandile mentioned that because of the real threat posed by Charles Sebe, security arrangements for the president had been stepped up. The military lacked trust in the Ciskei Police, which is why they had not involved them in the discussions.

Sandile said he had contacted Brigadier Holomisa of the TDF to arrange the monthly meeting to be attended by representatives of the CDF, the TDF, the Ciskei Police, the Transkei Police, the Ciskei Security Police, the Transkei Security Police and the South Africans. It had been arranged for 29 October and would be held at the Eastern Province Command's GP8 HQ in East London. He confirmed the approval of President Lennox Sebe.

Major Sandile sought two things from the SADF. Firstly, he requested assistance in planning, training and rehearsing the operation, but stressed that he did not require troops. Secondly, he asked that South Africa tell both the Ciskei and Transkei defence forces that all aid to them would be suspended unless the politicians in both countries solved their problems.

Commandant Hammond told Major Sandile he would refer his requests to higher authority — ultimately Brigadier Joffel van der Westhuizen. The almost immediate result because of the threat posed to Namba Sebe, was for his security arrangements to be upgraded. Sandile's second surprising request clearly brought a realisation that he could probably be manipulated and utilised in regard to *Operation Katzen*. It was noted that Sandile's trust in Hammond could easily be exploited.[45]

The meeting of the military South Africa/Ciskei Joint Management Board, chaired by Brigadier van der Westhuizen, took place on 28 October. Unusually, President Sebe himself arrived to take part. He made it clear that he was aware of the actions planned against him and was adamant that he would never agree to the amalgamation of Ciskei with Transkei.

He told those at the highly charged meeting that he had already taken several steps to prevent the plans against him coming to fruition. He had ordered the arrest and detention of numerous people, including Charles Sebe's sister and had despatched various letters and telexes to the South African government. He also said 'he had established a hit squad to get rid of Charles Sebe'.

Brigadier van der Westhuizen, it seems, took little notice of this tirade.[46]

The meeting between delegations from South Africa, Republic of Ciskei and Republic of Transkei was finally held at Group 8 HQ on 1 November. Chairing the meeting and heading the South African delegation was Brigadier van der Westhuizen. Others in the South African group were Colonels Pieter Hall, Reg Deyzel, A E van Rooyen and Griebenauw (Security Police). From Transkei were Major-Generals Mtirara and Reid Daly. Fom Ciskei were Lieutenant-General D N Mlandu, Colonels F Zibi and M G Pakade and Majors N Sandile and J Zwelibansi. Colonel Lourens du Plessis acted as secretary.

Van der Westhuizen described the situation existing between Ciskei and Transkei as serious, but said that 'no purpose will be served by blaming each other. . . The Security Forces . . . must endeavour to promote stability in the area. Armed conflict must be avoided at all costs'.

The Ciskei delegation might have taken comfort from this, but it should have been cold comfort indeed, considering that everyone else sitting around the table with them was busily plotting their downfall.

The minutes of the meeting under 'summary of decisions' reflect Ciskei's preoccupation with Namba Sebe, Charles Sebe and the release of General Kwane Sebe and Colonel Bullet Ngwanya.

Summary of Decisions

3 It was agreed that the situation regarding Namba, Charles and Maj Genl Kwane Sebe and his second in command be resolved peacefully.

4 That the matter of Namba Sebe and his actions within Transkei as well as his involvement in the kidnapping of Maj Genl Sebe be discussed at the highest diplomatic level.

5 That the Namba Sebe issue not be regarded as a military matter.

6 That it is important that the recommendations regarding Namba Sebe be supported by all three Defence Forces concerned.

7 That Ciskei take steps to have Namba Sebe extradited from Transkei.

8 That the troops deployed by EP Comd in the [white] corridor be seen as being part of the counter-revolutionary actions in that area and not as being there to keep Ciskei and Transkei Forces apart.

9 It was decided that the three Defence Forces concerned will advise each other if any troop movements are going to take place over each other's territories. This matter is to be coordinated at HQ Gp 8 in East London.

10 That the Namba Sebe issue will not be discussed at CMB [Combined Management Board] meetings.

11 That the Defence Forces concerned will use their influence to try and stop further kidnappings and will not become involved with mercenaries.

12 That the meeting supports the establishment of a Southern Africa Treaty Organisation (SATO). The author has no details of the first two minutes[47]

With the Ciskei delegation out of the way the meeting continued with discussions on *Operation Katzen* between the South African delegation and Major-Generals Mtirara and Reid Daly.

Colonel Jan Griebenauw mentioned that Namba Sebe had become a problem since he had publicly admitted his involvement in breaking Charles Sebe from prison and in the kidnapping of Kwane and his second in command. He said that Ciskei was putting pressure on South Africa to force Transkei to extradite Namba because the abduction had taken place in South Africa.

Someone suggested the answer was for Namba to be 'taken out' — murdered, to put it in plain English. It was a suggestion that was apparently well received because there is no record that anyone registered a protest.

With the mood having been set, Colonel F Zibi was the next to be discussed. It seems he must have been outspoken at the meeting, although the minutes do not reflect this. Perhaps he asked too many them questions, because there was a whole raft of awkward ones he could have asked. Whatever it was, it upset the delegates from the SADF and Transkei to the extent that his name was scribbled down to join Lennox Sebe on the *Operation Katzen* death list. Namba Sebe was not added to it, probably because he was conveniently to hand and 'taking him out' posed no problem. After all, he did not even know he had been reclassified as 'the enemy'.

On 5 November a meeting was convened at GP8 HQ in East London at Major Sandile's request. It was attended by Colonel Reg Deyzel, Commandant Hammond and Major Ted Brassell. Ostensibly the meeting was to check Sandile's security plan for the duration of the forthcoming Independence Day celebrations. He was eager to update the SADF officers with intelligence on Charles and Namba Sebe.

He said his source had reported that Namba Sebe had moved to a house across the road from the CID offices in Umtata. His guards had previously lived on the premises in a tent, but they had been exchanged for well-armed TDF soldiers in uniform who worked proper shifts.

Charles Sebe, he said, was living next door to a judge in Umtata's Ministerial Complex. He enjoyed protection from the security guards at the complex and also from the TDF.

His source had visited Charles who had laid out his aims for *Iliso Lomzi*. It would infiltrate agents into Ciskei, assassinate President Lennox Sebe, seize Radio Ciskei and take over military bases and the Parliament building in Bisho. It would then despatch a communiqué to the South African government demanding the inclusion of the white corridor into Ciskei and for the amalgamation of Ciskei with Transkei.[48]

On 10 November another meeting was held at the TDF's disused Msikaba Base in Transkei. It was attended by Generals Mtirara, Reid Daly and Charles Sebe, Chief Namba Sebe, Lent Maqoma, Brigadier van der Westhuizen, Colonels Lourens du Plessis and Van Rooyen, Major Sakkie van der Merwe (representing Colonel Jan Griebenauw), of the Security Police, Bob Milner (real name Moore) of National Intelligence and Major Piet van der Riet.

Needless to say, no invitation had been extended for a Ciskei delegation to attend.

The four phases of *Operation Katzen* were explained by Brigadier van der Westhuizen as:

Phase 1	Charles Sebe's release from prison (completed). The rescue of his three sons (unsuccessful). Kwane Sebe's abduction as a hostage (completed). Resistance movement (Namba Sebe selected the wrong people in Transkei). Campaign to discredit Lennox Sebe (commenced). Shadow cabinet under Lent Maqoma (partially achieved).
Phase 2	Lennox Sebe eliminated and a pre-amalgamation, stable, interim government established. Headman Lent Maqoma must lead it. This must be a short phase.

Phase 3 Transkei and Ciskei work together towards amalgamation. An amalgamation between Xhosaland, RSA and Lesotho concluded.

Phase 4 [White] corridor included in Xhosaland. East London becomes a free port.
To be a success the new states must be: economically, politically [and] militarily strong.

In a future South African context a strong Xhosaland will act as an example for a future Zululand. The other reason for this project is that South Africa will prove to the world that the homelands concept was indeed a success.

Lennox Sebe was an embarrassment for the RSA and they had to get rid of him in a very subtle way. This plan would also encourage a strong unity against the ANC and communism. By this means blacks would also become involved in white politics.

Brigadier van der Westhuizen insisted that the meeting must decide on the immediate priorities relating to phases one and two. To achieve this, a committee of experts had to be formed that would meet regularly. The committee decided on were:

Brigadier Joffel van der Westhuizen,
Colonel Jan Griebenauw,
Major Sakkie van der Merwe,
Colonel Lourens du Plessis,
Colonel van Rooyen,
Major-General Mtirara,
Major-General Reid Daly,
Bob Milner (real name Moore)

It was decided that 'Namba Sebe would 'disappear'. Lent Maqoma would give a press conference where he would announce that Namba Sebe had moved overseas for the purpose of raising funds. That would cut out the 'elimination' of Namba Sebe and at the same time the request to hand him over would be addressed. Meanwhile, Charles Sebe would take control of *Iliso Lomzi*.[49]

Portions of the actual minutes of the meeting classified 'Top Secret' in the author's possession read:

Phase 4: Incorporation of [white] corridor into Xhosaland (can take years). East London becomes free harbour and city. Queenstown not part of incorporation.
Note: Phase 4 very difficult as a result of strong political implications although the economic community is for that. Xhosaland must be accepted in Africa and must become politically, economically and militarily strong. Must be able to counter Zululand to maintain the balance. Natal *indaba* also necessary in the Eastern Cape. As a result the homeland policy will be proved and the total defence burden need not be borne by whites only. Lennox Sebe a great embarrassment. RSA can do nothing to get rid of him — he is 'their' creation. Lesotho is and remains a problem. If the present government [Ciskei] must disappear, a strong Xhosaland must ensure that the entire Eastern Cape is not threatened [by ANC operations] from Lesotho.

Paragraphs a, b and c are missing from the author's copy of the minutes.

d Phase 1 and 2 run concurrently. If stopped at phase 2 and not carried further to 3 and 4, RSA will be satisfied if Ciskei will have nothing to do with Xhosa unity. RSA will help with phases 1 and 2, <u>but not</u> with phrases 3 and 4.

e Aim of meeting:
 i Planning of phase 1 & 2. What will we? (?)
 ii Specialist participation is necessary. Who is involved? Continuous report backs necessary.
 iii Action for phase 1 must be determined.

f **General explanations until (before?) actions**

i Priority 1. Lennox [Sebe] out. This is and remains main aim. Need not take place first.

ii Namba Sebe must disappear from scene. SAP cannot then act against him. Dekatonie (?) Namba is overseas. Stays in exile in Transkei. Charles [Sebe] take over his role. Charles must be strongly promoted with respect to XWB.

iii *Iliso Lomzi* (XWB) must be against Lennox Sebe as an organisation of the people. Actions must be carried out. RSA to provide funds. All Xhosas must identify with the organisation. Namba Sebe to work behind the scenes. The organisation to be a second Inkatha with Charles as a strong 'clean' leader. Success[es] however small must be striven for so that the organisation can capture the attention of the population.

iv Opinion of members — e.g. Col Zibi. With this action the RSA can actually lend support but the 'removal' will be carried out by Transkei. This action can also not be reported to Pretoria.

v Kwane Sebe and his twin brother must never return to Ciskei. If the situation improves, this can be reconsidered. In case they are not locked up forever, they must "disappear".

vi The three sons cannot be exchanged for Kwane and his brother.

vii When Lennox disappears or gives way, there must be a government that can take over to prevent a new leader from emerging from the present cabinet.

viii All actions are interwoven. As soon as one action takes place the follow-up actions must be ready to be proceeded with.

A signal detailing the results of the discussions was despatched to the Chief of the SADF, classified 'Secret' and marked 'personal for Colonel L J (John) More'. It was signed by Colonel van Rooyen, Senior Staff Officer Intelligence, Eastern Cape Command.

1 Actions currently planned, and already in process, as well as funds needed.

2 Actions:

A Gen Campling is blackmailed by Gen Reid Daly to leak certain info to L[ennox] Sebe that will increase pressure on L Sebe'. [The late Major-General Bruce Campling, formerly of the Rhodesian Army, was then resident in King William's Town and involved with the CDF as an adviser.]

B Namba Sebe apparently going overseas to raise funds for the Xhosa Resistance Movement [*Iliso Lomzi*]. SAP (V) shall provide cover.

C Lent Maqoma makes a declaration to provide the necessary support for para 2 B, as well as that Charles Sebe now takes over as leader of the Resistance Movement. Declaration by Lent Maqoma includes that there is a lot of support in Ciskei for the Xhosa Resistance Movement.

D After declarations pamphlets will be dropped to promote Charles [Sebe]. Declaration in two parts:

i Charles will be introduced as a leader and promoted.

ii Attacks on Lennox Sebe to portray him as a swindler and weakling. Also that Namba Sebe enlists funds and support.

E Col Zibi must disappear (permanent). [General Reid Daly had earlier requested 'all available data' on this man. The colonel, a senior policeman, was a close associate of Lennox Sebe.]

F Let [Lent Maqoma] sets up his shadow cabinet and list of supporters.

G Action against Lennox's property.

H Obtains funds.

3 Funds for:

i Clothes and food;

ii Radio, TV and furniture;

iii Car hire;

iv Aircraft hire;

v Financial support to families;

vi Purchase personal weapons for Charles [Sebe];

vii Advertisements;

4 Charles [Sebe], Namba [Sebe] and Lent [Maqoma] in safe house and under guard at Msikaba. Lourens [Colonel du Plessis] on his way to Msikaba'.[50]

Instead of 'taking out' Namba Sebe the arrangement had been changed. It has become clear that by then one reason for wanting him 'taken out' was because of his failure as a recruiter for *Iliso Lomzi*. He was being sent overseas to get him out of the way. It is clear he was unaware of his 'reprieve'. Doubtless when ruminating about the long and pleasant trip he was about to make, he had no idea that he might have been making a longer and rather more unpleasant one!

There were no reprieves for President Lennox Sebe and Colonel Zibi at the meeting.

On 12 November, after the meeting, Colonel John More, Colonel Lourens du Plessis, Lent Maqoma and Major Sakkie van der Merwe visited the *Iliso Lomzi* recruits under training at the TDF's Special Forces base at Port St Johns. The recruits were wearing SADF browns.

The visitors were conducted around by the training officer, an ex-Rhodesian warrant officer and employee of Security Services Transkei (Pty) Ltd. He put the recruits through their paces on the rifle range and explained that the main focus of the training was on minor infantry tactics and the use of explosives. He said the men had already been well-trained in the use of explosives, which would play an important role in any attack on Lennox Sebe.

'Colonel', the warrant officer told Lourens du Plessis, 'those guys can now wire a car with explosives and have it ready to be blown in seven minutes.' If true that was pretty impressive.[51]

On 13 November, following the visit to Port St Johns, a handwritten but unsigned list headed 'Training Requirements' and detailing quantities of firearms, ammunition, grenades, explosives and RPG-7 rockets as 'training requirements' for 'Jim's scene', was prepared by an unidentified member of Security Services Transkei. It was presumably directed to General Reid Daly because it was addressed 'Sir' and is endorsed in Reid Daly's handwriting with 'requirement for squad under training'.[52]

Reid Daly was disappointed with what transpired because he was issued with only a quarter of what he had asked for.[53]

Colonel Jan Griebenauw debriefed Major Sakkie van der Merwe on his return to East London after the meeting. After hearing him out, the colonel said to him: 'They are now talking of killing and physical removal and he agreed with me that we withdraw completely' from the project. Colonel Griebenauw said: 'It worried me and didn't sit right with me as a policeman while trying to combat terror', at the same time as *Katzen* 'was training certain terrorists organisations' like *Iliso Lomzi* over which there was no 'proper control' and which engaged in 'acts of terror'. He informed Brigadier van der Westhuizen accordingly.[54]

On 14 November, following the proposal outlined in the signal to Colonel More on the 10th, a press release purporting to be from Lent Maqoma as the leader of the CPRPP was published in the *Daily Dispatch* in East London. It said that Namba Sebe had gone overseas 'to find strategies for the dismantling of the Current Ciskei government'. Maqoma said the CPRPP had been left with no option but to 'internationalise' the problem. In Namba's absence, he said, Charles Sebe had assumed temporary command of *Iliso Lomzi*.[55]

Colonel Lourens du Plessis, meanwhile, said he was visiting Umtata three or four times a month. At least once a month he took a suitcase with him containing bank notes amounting to at least R150 000 that had been passed to him from Pretoria by the project officer, Colonel John More.

This was pay for *Iliso Lomzi* members and to provide money to be sent to their families for living expenses. The money was passed to General Reid Daly for distribution. Colonel du Plessis began to hear complaints that many of the *Iliso Lomzi* recruits were not receiving their pay.

Brigadier Bantu Holomisa, the acting Chief of Staff of the TDF, and Lieutenant-Colonel Craig Duli, the acting Staff Officer Intelligence, were mystified by what was going on. They had orders to provide troops to guard Charles Sebe and others at various places in Transkei, but they had no idea how they came to be there. The only officers who knew were Major-Generals Mtirara and Reid Daly and they were not taking Holomisa and Duli into their confidence. They planned an investigation to ascertain what was going on, but before they could start it Brigadier Holomisa was faced by a deputation of instructors from the Special Forces base at Port St Johns.

13 . 11 . 86

TRAINING REQUIRMENTS

Sir,

because we do not know as yet how many members we are looking at for Jimi's scene, the list of weapons and explosives below will suffice for the present. Once we have an idea what the recruiting looks like we will re-indent.

REQUIRMENT FOR SQUAD UNDER TRAINING

BEHOEFTE 1-5 REEDS BY J. MORE

SER	TYPE	QUANTITY	ORIGIN	REMAR
1	R4 RIFLES C/W 48 MAGAZINES	12	MIL	
2	9MM UZI SMG C/W 48 MAGAZINES	12	MIL	
3	9MM PISTOLS C/W 48 MAGAZINES	12	MIL	
4	5.56 AMMUNITION	13500 Rds	MIL	
5	9 MM AMMUNITION	9000 Rds	MIL	
6	GRENADES M962	300	MIL	
7	PE 4A PLASTIC EXPLOSIVE	100 KG	MIL	
8	DYNAGEL EXPLOSIVE	50 KG	CIVVY	
9	GELIGNITE	50 KG	CIVVY	
10	TNT	50 KG	CIVVY	
11	SAFETY FUZE	200 M	CIVVY	
12	CORDTEX	800 M	CIVVY	
13	DETONATORS S4	300	MIL	
14	DETONATORS ELECTRIC	300	CIVVY	
15	PENTOLITE BOOSTERS	400	CIVVY	
16	TM 46 LAND MINES C/W DETS	6	TER	
17	RPG 7 ROCKETS	24	TER	

General Reid Daly's shopping list for weapons required for his hopelessly inept *Iliso Lomzi*' operation to assassinate Ciskei's President Lennox Sebe. It was submitted the day after senior SADF officers inspected *Iliso Lomzi* under training at the TDF's Special Forces base at Port St Johns.

They complained that they had not been provided with money to maintain the *Iliso Lomzi* recruits under training at the base.

Shortly afterwards Charles Sebe phoned and asked to see him.

'Man, what is going on here?' Holomisa asked.

Charles explained that he had been sprung from gaol to take over command of the fledgling *Iliso Lomzi* then undergoing training at Port St Johns. The intention was to use the movement to mount an operation to topple Lennox Sebe. He was apparently unaware it was intended to become the nucleus of Xhosa resistance on the lines of the Zulu Inkatha Freedom Party. *Iliso Lomze* had been told they would be paid, but they had seen little money.

Charles had contacted Lourens du Plessis in Port Elizabeth who said he had given money for their support to Reid Daly. Charles pointed out that there was a desperate need for money to maintain the troops and their families. He had insufficient money for food for himself and his own family and to pay his children's school expenses. He displayed a deep distrust of Reid Daly and his ex-Rhodesian military advisers and professed to be frightened of them.

Holomisa and Duli were reluctant to get involved. There was obviously political backing for whatever was going on and they were concerned it might impact adversely on them. Holomisa gave Charles money from his own pocket to cover his personal needs. He and Duli also gave money to the instructors who came to see them so that the recruits could buy soap and so on.

They tried to see Prime Minister George to find out from him what was going on, but he was too busy to see them. So Holomisa phoned Colonel Lawrence du Plessis and asked for a meeting. He went through to Port Elizabeth and was given a detailed briefing on *Operation Katzen*. Du Plessis confirmed he had given Major-General Reid Daly money for Lent Maqoma, Namba Sebe and *Iliso Lomzi*, but he did not say how much. There was little Holomisa could do to pursue the matter, so he left it unresolved.

After this Holomisa made a point of seeing Charles Sebe regularly. Sebe continued to be uneasy about his allies, the former Selous Scouts. On one occasion he called Holomisa and expressed a fear that they might be planning to abduct him. He told Holomisa that 'these people' said he should go to Durban to attend a meeting. It sounded funny to him that he should be asked to step beyond the borders of Transkei. He took Holomisa's advice to stay put.[56] This was particularly wise when it is remembered that the Ciskei's Major Sandile had been tipped off previously about a booking for Charles at the Sandton Sun Hotel.

Brigadier van der Westhuizen, by Lourens du Plessis's account, was getting impatient. He wanted Reid Daly to go ahead with the next stage and assassinate Lennox Sebe, but the former was dragging his feet.[57]

Reid Daly, by his account, was expecting assistance from the National Intelligence Service and the Security Police, but all his requests were met with silence. This concerned him and he asked the SADF what was going on. He was given an assurance that he should not worry because *Operation Katzen* was proceeding. Prime Minister George, meanwhile, was pressuring him to go ahead. This prompted him to phone Admiral du Plessis (Putter?) of Military Intelligence in Pretoria and request a meeting with SADF Chief General Jannie Geldenhuys and Lieutenant-General Pieter van der Westhuizen. Admiral du Plessis (Putter?) confirmed a meeting in Pretoria for 12 December.[58]

After a meeting on 24 November 1986, Colonel Piet Hall, SSO (Ops) at Eastern Province Command, wrote a report on *Operation Katzen* to a Colonel Deyzel (not the Brigadier Deyzel mentioned later in this chapter). He said that Phase One of the plans had already been activated and that 'our people in Pretoria are also worried about SADF involvement. We are going ahead behind the scenes, but low profile'. He added that 'all political front actions (Lent Maqoma) will now be handled by NI (National Intelligence Servic)]. We will continue to cooperate politically/militarily'.[59]

On 3 December, to express solidarity with the points agreed at the meeting at Msikaba Military Base on 10 November, Charles Sebe and Chief Lent Maqoma held a press conference in Umtata. Charles Sebe professed a deep sense of revulsion at the 'atrocities and dictatorship' of Lennox Sebe's rule and said he supported 'democracy'. But he immediately contradicted this contention by advocating that power should be handed over to the 'Ciskei's rightful rulers' — the chiefs. It must have slipped his mind that there were already 43 nominated chiefs in the National Assembly and that Lennox Sebe was himself a chief.[60]

In late November General Makuzeni and Brigadier Bonisile Simandla — the officer in charge of Middledrift Prison — were detained under section 26 of Ciskei's National Security Act for dereliction of duty connected with the escape of Charles Sebe.[61] Brigadier Simandla was severely assaulted and tortured by Ciskei's Security Police to get him to confess to assisting in the breakout.

It seemed to Colonel Lourens du Plessis that there were a myriad of meetings held to discuss details relating to *Operation Katzen*. Most took place at Major-General Reid Daly's official holiday home built within the confines of a military detention barracks complex north of Port St Johns in Transkei. It became a talk shop where nothing happened except that the talk droned on and on, interrupted occasionally by huge plates of eggs and bacon and seafood cooked for the visitors by the inmates.

The get-togethers occurred so frequently it became a joke, so Du Plessis often excused himself. It meant flying there in a light aircraft and he had had too many bad experiences of them during his years of military service.

The operation began to lose momentum.[62]

On 11 December Reid Daly flew to East London for a meeting with Brigadier Joffel van der Westhuizen, Colonel Lourens du Plessis and Colonel Reg Deyzel to discuss his meeting in Pretoria the next day with General Jannie Geldenhuys and Lieutenant-General Pieter van der Westhuizen. He expressed concern at the apparent withdrawal of the National Intelligence Service and the Security Police from *Operation Katzen*.

On 12 December he said he saw General Gleeson and Admiral du Plessis (Vice Admiral Putter?) at Military Intelligence's headquarters in the Liberty Life Building in Pretoria. They offered their apologies for the absence of General Geldenhuys and Lieutenant-General van der Westhuizen who were on leave. It seems that other than pleasantries being exchanged, little was discussed. General Gleeson promised to arrange another meeting in January when General Geldenhuys and Van der Westhuizen would be available. It is clear that nothing was said that suggested the cancellation of *Operation Katzen*.[63]

Meanwhile, Foreign Minister Pik Botha announced on 20 November that the governments of Ciskei and Transkei had agreed to former Chief Justice F L Rumpff, mediating their dispute.[64] As a result of this mediation an agreement on a prisoner exchange was reached. There would be 'a Berlin Wall' type exchange of two batches of detainees in the centre of the Kei River Bridge on 24 and 30 December respectively.

The first, the curtain raiser became little less than comic opera. It took place 'amid handshakes, smiles and pledges of Xhosa peace and brotherhood'. For its part, Transkei released Cecil Vanda — the managing director of Ciskei's People's Development Bank — and a bank employee, E M Bici. Vanda had been arrested in mid-December under the provisions of the Public Security Act while on a visit to Transkei to unveil his father's tombstone. Bici was arrested while trying to negotiate Vanda's release. It appears Transkei lacked prisoners to exchange, so the unfortunate bank officials were hurriedly arrested because no one else was available.

For its contribution Ciskei dutifully handed over John Booi, Lennox Macanda and Diliza Khunjuzwa. John Booi and Lennox Macanda had been in detention for a month over allegations that they had been transporting dissidents to Transkei for military training. Khunjuzwa added a personal touch of comedy to the solemn events by refusing point-blank to be part of the handover. He maintained he was a retired Ciskeian inspector of schools who did not even come from Transkei. He was a Ciskeian through and through. He insisted he be allowed to return to his home and hearth in Ciskei, and was eventually allowed to do so.

This exchange of nonentities was a rehearsal for the command performance which took place on the 30 December. On that earnest occasion — which would have been a delight to spymates of the KGB and the CIA — Ciskei allowed Khambashe, Toni and Koli Sebe to march across the bridge towards the Transkei contingent.

Simultaneously, General Kwane Sebe and Colonel Bullet Ngwanya began to march across in the opposite direction towards the Ciskei party.[65] It was not recorded whether the two sets of released prisoners exchanged pleasantries with each other as they passed the centre point.

The fact that two 'island' homeland states within the greater South Africa had reached a virtual state of war with each other presented an unlikely scenario. It would have been impossible without Pretoria's mischievous scheming. By the same token, it would have been unimaginable for two republics within the old Soviet Union to have reached that impasse without the connivance of Moscow — within its sphere of influence the old Red Army had been all powerful and it would not have allowed such a situation to arise. Similarly, the SADF, within its sphere of influence, was also all-powerful.

It was Brigadier Joffel van der Westhuizen's last working day in the Eastern Cape before being transferred to Witwatersrand Command on promotion to major-general.

His last job in Port Elizabeth before clearing his desk was to send a 'secret' report to Lieutenant-General Ian Gleeson, the deputy SADF Chief, giving details of the prisoner exchanges. He said they had been opposed by both Prime Minister George Matanzima and General Reid Daly, but the SADF who directed the operation, overruled them. General Reid Daly, he pointed out, had asked for an urgent meeting in Pretoria to discuss *Operation Katzen.* Transkei still supported the operation 'in broad principle' but a clarification of methods was required. He proposed a meeting be held in Pretoria on 2 January 1987.

The meeting apparently did take place and was attended by SADF Chief, General Jannie Geldenhuys; the Chief of Staff Intelligence, Vice Admiral Dries Putter; General Pieter van der Westhuizen of the SSC; the Senior Staff Officer Operations at Eastern Province Command, Colonel Piet Hall; the Project Officer, Colonel L J More; TDF adviser, Major-General Ron Reid Daly; the chief of the TDF, Major-General Zondwa Mtirara; and the relevant SAP and Security Police generals.

General Reid Daly, however, said the meeting never took place.[66]

Brigadier Kritzinger took over the Eastern Cape Command from Van der Westhuizen. It is presumed that the ramifications of *Operation Katzen* were explained to Kritzinger by his predecessor, but he wanted nothing to do with it apparently because of its clear unlawfulness. In fact, despite approval for the operation having come from the top, he ordered his officers to have nothing more to do with it. When he discovered later that Colonels Lourens du Plessis and Reg Deyzel were still liaising directly with Major-General Joffel van der Westhuizen in Johannesburg regarding *Operation Katzen*, he was 'most disenchanted'. He told them that if they did not stop, there would be big problems.[67]

Despite Brigadier Kritzinger's objections, planning for the operation continued. It was certainly not dropped by the upper echelons of the SADF. Colonel John More retained his position as Project Officer. Despite what might have been said at the TRC about the SADF's involvement ending in November 1986, it remained involved until the operation's ignominious end in February 1987.

11

Operation Duiker
Conspiracy to murder and attempted murder President Lennox Sebe of Ciskei 1986

Hit men, ransoms and take-outs

Lennox Sebe passed word that he was willing to pay a substantial reward for the assassination of Charles Sebe, or better still, for his abduction and return to Ciskei as a prisoner. Someone from Ciskei met a loud-mouthed white man in an East London pub who spoke about the reward on offer. He claimed he was an ex-Recce and boasted that he could take on anybody or anything. It was suggested that he should speak to Colonel Reg Deyzel, the SADF's Group Commander in East London and volunteer his services. Colonel Deyzel played along. The 'ex-Recce' expounded his ideas about killing Charles Sebe and handing his body over to Ciskei. Deyzel noted his contact number and promised to make a plan. He phoned Brigadier Joffel van der Westhuizen, who in turn phoned Major-General Reid Daly.

Unaware of this, Brigadier Bantu Holomisa was called to Reid Daly's office. By then he knew *Iliso Lomzi* was an instrument designed to overthrow Lennox Sebe. But he still did not know of plans for it to eventually become a more general Xhosa resistance movement that would target the ANC and its associates. Reid Daly told him he was interested in establishing links with people in the Ciskei Defence Force for intelligence purposes.

They discussed the CDF's Major Sandile, a former schoolmate of Holomisa. Reid Daly mentioned that they should try to get money from Ciskei to maintain the *Iliso Lomzi* people and their families. He suggested that Holomisa should contact Major Sandile and make a bogus offer to hand Charles Sebe over for R250 000.

Holomisa agreed and approached Sandile, who after consulting with his superiors, jumped at the chance.

Holomisa briefed Charles Sebe on what was happening and made sure he kept him fully informed as negotiations progressed.

Holomisa and Sandile first met for discussions at Komga. They met twice again after that.

Meanwhile, it appears that Reid Daly had briefed Major van der Riet, an adviser with Transkei's Special Forces, to make contact with the ex-Recce hitman, without telling Holomisa.

A January 1987 situation report, headed *Operation Katzen*, was despatched by Colonel Hall to Colonel More at Army Headquarters. It revealed that General Reid Daly had 'hired' a 'hitman', whom he named as Major Pieter John van der Riet. It seems likely that Colonel Hall had got his story mixed up. If not, it was a strange sort of 'hiring' for Van der Riet, a former lieutenant in the Selous Scouts who had been in the employ of Security Specialists Transkei (Pty) Ltd since 1 June 1981.[1]

Meanwhile, Van der Riet was tasked to contact 'Brigadier Holomisa's friend', Major Sandile of the CDF 'via our man Howse' from King William's Town. The danger, according to Colonel Hall, was that the CDF might arrest Howse and force him to talk, 'compromising both the [Eastern Province] Command and the SADF'. In the event of this happening, Howse's cover story was that he only knew that Major Sandile had asked to be put in touch with Van der Riet.[2]

It appears that Major van der Riet and the ex-Recce hitman made contact with Major Sandile and conducted their own negotiations. They presumably told him that they were fully *au fait* with the negotiations that Brigadier Holomisa had been conducting with him. They set up timings, arranged a rendezvous and confirmed that Charles Sebe would be handed over. Major Sandile should bring R250 000 in cash in payment.[3]

Brigadier Holomisa had the surprise of his life when an unidentified white man (apparently the ex-Recce hitman) phoned and asked to meet him. During their conversation it became apparent the man knew of his contacts with Sandile and spoke of him by name as 'Charlie'. Holomisa became very suspicious because only a few people knew Sandile as Charlie. He felt sure 'something fishy' was going on and declined to meet him.

Sandile phoned shortly afterwards and also asked for a meeting. Holomisa refused, saying he felt nervous because a white man had contacted him and mentioned Sandile by his first name. 'This white man seems to know about these things, Charlie. I am pulling out of that. Sorry! We'll try another time.'

Late that night Sandile phoned Holomisa again, saying he wanted to see him urgently. They could meet anywhere he suggested because he was stranded. He did not explain what he meant by 'stranded'.

'Sorry, Charlie', Holomisa told him, 'I cannot get out of the house now. You can't call me at such awkward hours.'

'I want to see you, now, now', Sandile insisted. 'No, not at this time. I can see you tomorrow morning at 08:00, but not now.'

He terminated the conversation.[4]

Unbeknown to Holomisa a party from the Transkei led by Major van der Riet and probably including the ex-Recce hitman had rendezvoused with a party from the Ciskei led by Major Sandile. They met in the centre of the Bolo Bridge at Tsomo. The Transkei party had a stretcher containing a bulky object covered by a blanket. It was allegedly the body of Charles Sebe. Before bringing the stretcher forward they demanded to see the money. Sandile produced a suitcase with the R250 000. After it was checked, the Ciskeian party relaxed and the stretcher was brought up. To their chagrin the body was a very much alive TDF soldier. Suddenly they found themselves covered by Transkeian guns. They were quickly disarmed and taken prisoner. The whole bunch were driven back to Umtata together with their military vehicles. The vehicles were absorbed into the inventory of the TDF, but the fate of the R250 000 is a matter for conjecture.

A few days later Colonel Lourens du Plessis called in to see General Reid Daly at his offices in Umtata.

'General, that R250 000?', he asked him.

'Now I don't think that he knew that I knew about the planning. Of course I knew about it', Colonel du Plessis told the author. 'And he [General Reid Daly] was quiet for a minute or so. Then he said: "Oh, I am hanging on to it for the time being".'

They never discussed the money again. Colonel du Plessis has no idea what eventually happened to it.[5]

On the morning after the abductions, Brigadier Holomisa heard the arrest of Major Sandile announced on Transkei Radio. The story was that he had led an armed party from Ciskei in an attempt to kidnap General Charles Sebe. It was a public holiday so Holomisa was at home when the Deputy Commissioner of Police, General Kilatili, phoned him.

'How are you, general?' Brigadier Holomisa asked.

'I'm fine. I would like to come and see you at your house.'

'Any time', Holomisa told him.

At 12:00 General Kilatili arrived with a party of armed policemen.

To Holomisa's shocked surprise he was served with a notice of indefinite detention, arrested, taken to prison and locked in a cell. Later on he was moved to the military detention barracks.

Instead of being questioned by the police, which he expected, Colonel Keith Samler, Reid Daly's Intelligence Chief and an employee of Security Services Transkei (Pty) Ltd, accompanied by Colonel Craig Duli, the Staff Officer (Intelligence), came to the prison to record a statement from him. He was told he was facing an allegation that he had planned to murder Charles Sebe and hand his body to the Ciskei for a reward.

Holomisa refused to give a statement.

'You must be crazy', he told them. 'Are you policemen? I am not under military detention. The detention order says I have jeopardised the security of the country. I am not interested in what you want to say. I cannot give you a statement.'

They left and returned on another day with a directive from Prime Minister George which said: 'This is to direct you that you will cooperate and give a statement to Duli and Samler.'

So he gave them a statement. He told them of the arrangements made with General Reid Daly. He suggested they interview Charles Sebe, who would confirm that he had been fully informed about what was going on. He also explained how he had told Major Sandile he was backing away from the operation because of the involvement of a white stranger.

In retrospect, General Holomisa — who was a person of considerable influence amongst the officers and men of the TDF in the 1980s — recalls that over that period he had been continually raising objections amongst his brother officers over the renewal of Security Services Transkei's contract. He knew it was coming up for renewal, but was unaware that the renewal date was as early as 1 March 1987. His anti-renewal views were generally well known. He had often stressed the point that any renewal should have Cabinet and Treasury approval, unlike the original arrangement. He had lobbied President Kaiser Matanzima on that very issue before he retired and the President had also agreed that the contract should not be renewed.

General Holomisa's viewpoint was that the TDF required sophisticated training, which by then was available through the SADF and from other countries. In truth, there was little in the way of professional skills for senior officers that Major-General Reid Daly could offer. He had been one of several senior sergeants-major in the Rhodesian Army who were commissioned to the rank of captain as a reward for long service and because of the exigencies of the time. He eventually retired and was brought from retirement and promoted to major to command the Selous Scouts. He resigned from the Rhodesian Army as a lieutenant-colonel, after being court-martialled for indiscipline. He might have been holding the rank of a general officer in the TDF, but neither he nor any of his white officers had ever attended a staff course.

There were other factors too. Brigadier Holomisa and other TDF officers objected to *Operation Katzen* and the policy of destabilising Ciskei. They also thought little of the TDF commander, Major-General Mtirara, and regarded him as little more than a puppet of Reid Daly and Prime Minister George. Another reason why they objected to the renewal of Security Services Transkei's contract was because it was part of a whole basket of factors relating to the unchecked levels of corruption in the administration. Transkei had become little more than the fiefdom of the Matanzima brothers.

Bantu Holomisa concluded retrospectively that his agitation against the renewal of the contract of Security Services Transkei was the most likely factor in the misfortunes that overtook him.

Even though his story was checked by Colonel Craig Duli and found to be correct, he remained in detention.[6]

Operation Duiker: SADF Plan to assassinate Lennox Sebe

The sub-plan of *Operation Katzen* involving the assassination of Lennox Sebe was designated *Operation Duiker*.

Ciskei had been tipped off that Transkei, with SADF assistance, intended mounting a raid to assassinate President Lennox Sebe. In October 1986 Brigadier Johan Deyzel was assigned by the SADF's Chief of Staff Intelligence, Vice-Admiral Dries Putter, to work for a Johannesburg based construction company, Jalc Holdings. Jalc was used as a Military Intelligence front. It had widespread interests in neighbouring states including Ciskei, Transkei, Mauritius, Botswana and Mozambique. Deyzel was to go undercover to make political and commercial contacts in high places on behalf of the SADF and Jalc. He would also monitor (dissident?) activities in the countries he worked in. Overtly he would be a Jalc employee, but covertly he would report to Vice-Admiral Dries Putter.

Laurie Painting, a director of Jalc Holdings, would say they had employed him because he was useful in promoting 'cooperation between ministers of neighbouring states and the Department of Foreign Affairs'. His duties were to promote dialogue in other countries.

Brigadier Deyzel became friends with President Lennox Sebe towards the end of 1986. At an official reception held at the beginning of February 1987, President Sebe shocked Deyzel by revealing that SADF elements were planning to attack him, Sebe. Deyzel found this difficult to believe, but the president insisted that South African elements were destabilising his country. He said the situation in the border area was fast becoming like Lebanon. He asked if South Africa could launch an investigation and take disciplinary action against those responsible. The brigadier put the president's mind at rest, promising to inform the South African military authorities.[7]

Brigadier Deyzel visited Pretoria on 9 February 1987 and reported the president's allegations to Vice-Admiral Putter. To his astonishment, Putter angrily reprimanded him and said his assessment and views of Lennox Sebe did not coincide with the official ones. He accused him of 'sticking your nose in where it does not belong'.

Deyzel had expected immediate counter-measures to be instituted to protect President Sebe. Instead there was a flaming row. Deyzel said he 'lost all respect' for Putter and other officers because of the SADF's point-blank refusal to act to prevent the impending attack. Putter ordered him out of his office in the heat of the moment.[8]

Putter later handed in a written report to the Harms Commission evaluating Deyzel's allegations. He said he had prepared it contemporaneously, but it is reasonable to assume that he prepared it later especially for the Harms Commission. It said: 'The Ciskei government contend that they are in possession of information that certain RSA elements are involved in the destabilisation of Ciskei. If this is correct then it would be advisable to put a stop to it. The border conflict could deteriorate into a Lebanon-type situation. The RSA will have to take steps to put a stop to the actions of those responsible . . . An investigation of the facts surrounding the conflict must be urgently attended to and punitive measures considered.' [9]

Putter's professed prior ignorance seems odd to say the least, because the Holomisa files reveal he had been scheduled to attend a planning meeting relating to *Operation Katzen* together with General Jannie Geldenhuys, Chief of the SADF, on 2 January 1987, more than a month before Deyzel's visit.

Before he quoted the Vice-Admiral's evaluation, Judge Harms noted: 'The Commission has in its possession categorical [*uitdruklik*] evidence that the accusations are untrue.'[10] He emphasised elsewhere in his report that many secret documents were produced, the contents of which were not revealed to the public, and that his findings were based on them as well.[11] If the evidence was so convincing and of such a categorical nature, one is left to ponder, in view of later revelations, who especially manufactured documents for the occasion. One can safely assume, however, that no mention of *Operation Katzen* appeared anywhere in that 'categorical evidence'. Without seeing it, one can only remain bemused by the findings of Judge Harms.

Significantly on the same day he allegedly wrote his evaluation of Brigadier Deyzel's information, Admiral Putter also prepared a paper setting out guidelines on which that officer's association with Jalc could continue. It contained nothing new and merely reiterated existing guidelines the Brigadier had supposedly ignored. Undoubtedly he was reining Deyzel in, perhaps on his own initiative but more likely on the instructions of someone more senior.

According to Judge Harms: 'He [Deyzel] was requested to sign the letter and he did it on 16 February 1987. He immediately created the impression that these guidelines made it impossible to continue as a Jalc representative and that he decided then, in spite of it being an order, to ignore them.' The judge clearly disproved of Brigadier Deyzel's behaviour, despite basic common sense indicating that Putter's 'work to rule' conditions made it impossible for the Brigadier to continue in an undercover capacity. For instance, Putter said the Brigadier should 'pay his own way'. This meant paying for his own meals when dining with Jalc directors or their associates, paying his own travelling expenses and so on. He was refused permission to fly in Jalc's company aircraft — he had to make his own way.

Brigadier Deyzel maintained that the restrictions were impossible. To function effectively as an undercover agent it was essential that his SADF links were not exposed. Nobody had expected the SADF to be solely liable for his expenses, which in the four months he had been with Jalc amounted to R24 000.[12]

A picture of the Brigadier doling out his share of cash at the end of a business lunch seems more in keeping with teenagers on a 'Dutch treat' at McDonald's than with high-flying executives conducting business worth millions of rands.

Another heated row between the Vice-Admiral and the Brigadier followed, during which the latter was told to take early pension and threatened with an internal investigation if he refused. Deyzel told him to 'have as many investigations as he liked' and for a second time was ordered to leave the Admiral's office. Not surprisingly, he felt 'utterly humiliated and insulted'.

Deyzel's opposition to the assassination of Lennox Sebe, after 33 years of loyal service, cost him his career. After sitting around in an office for five months 'where I did absolutely nothing' he left the service. He first attempted to retire on medical grounds, based on a disc problem in his neck and severe headaches. When this failed he retired on pension and took up an employment offer with Jalc.[13] Jalc was only too glad to have him back, because his quiet endeavours in the few months he had been with the company had generated some R27 million worth of business.

Vice-Admiral Putter conceded to the Harms Commission that the Brigadier's telephone had been tapped continually while he worked undercover and that this had continued even after his retirement from the service.[14] Military Intelligence, the National Intelligence Service and the Security Police had the authority to tap anyone's phone — they merely had to tell the post office that the person concerned was a 'threat to the state'. No messy ministerial orders, no affidavits, no judicial warrants, nothing was required in substantiation. Abuse of power in keeping with a police state was routine.[15]

Putter denied to the Harms Commission that the Lennox Sebe assassination allegation was the reason for Deyzel being shelved, but his evidence was evasive, contradictory and lacked credibility. Judge Harms said the Admiral's affidavit was misleading and contained untruths and that he only gave oral evidence after there had been adverse publicity.[16]

Asked by Judge Harms why he had been so keen to protect President Lennox Sebe, Brigadier Deyzel said it was because he was a head of state and also a personal friend.[17]

Long before the Harms Commission, Deyzel confided in Tony Botha, a George-based business consultant with contacts in high places. He told him about the assassination plot and handed him copies of documents to prove it. Tony Botha presented them to Deputy Foreign Minister Kobus Meiring at a Cape Town meeting attended by Jalc Holdings directors, Chris van Rensburg and Laurie Painting. 'Mr Meiring almost fainted when he saw the documents', Chris van Rensburg recalled later.[18]

Laurie Painting later told Judge Harms that Brigadier Deyzel had volunteered to be President Lennox Sebe's 'bodyguard', adding that he also utilised his experience on security systems.[19]

According to Major-General Jan Griebenauw's 'Top Secret' memorandum submitted to the TRC, Major-General Reid Daly had told him after the raid that Prime Minister George had been put under pressure because Lennox Sebe had threatened to repatriate all Transkei citizens living in Ciskei to Transkei. This resulted in Prime Minister George reprimanding both Generals Mtirara and Reid Daly for having failed to mount the raid into Ciskei.

This was a very strange allegation indeed. Although Ciskei announced on 22 November 1986 that all Transkei citizens travelling to its territory would require valid travel documents, it only issued its ultimatum — that all Transkei citizens living there would have to leave by 31 August — on 17 February, about 48 hours before the raid was launched. By then preparations and planning were well advanced. Reid Daly also alleged that Prime Minister George had told him that a South African cabinet minister had given him an assurance that South Africa 'would look the other way'.

Seeing that Reid Daly had had no recent communications with Pretoria, he continued with planning, expecting a routine approval by the South Africans. He showed his plan to Prime Minister George who assured him that South Africa had given it the green light. It seems very strange that Reid Daly should submit his operational plan for SADF approval via Prime Minister George when he had been dealing with them directly all along.

Whatever the case, and to make doubly sure, he contacted Colonel Nel at Military Intelligence and arranged to meet Admiral du Plessis (probably Putter) at the Royal Hotel, Durban, on 3 February 1987. He showed him the plan and the Admiral said he would discuss it in Pretoria and revert to him later. He phoned Colonel Nel in Pretoria after a week and was told 'the political climate was not right'.

'As a result of pressure from Prime Minister George Matanzima, and still convinced under the impression that his actions were approved by the SADF', Major-General Reid Daly went ahead with the operation.[20]

On Thursday 12 February 1987 Jean-Michel Desble (43) booked into a hotel in Bisho, then approached Headman Somtunzi, Deputy Director-General of Ciskei's Foreign Affairs and Information Department. He produced a business card indicating he was a journalist with the Paris weekly magazine, *L'Express*, and said he intended writing a history of Ciskei. He asked for but was refused an interview with President Lennox Sebe. He was offered but declined a press kit on Ciskei and booked out of his hotel the next day.

On 16 February he telephoned Headman Somtunzi, mentioning that he had spent the weekend hiking in Ciskei and was still wanting a meeting with the president. Somtunzi stalled him, vaguely saying he would try to set it up for 20 February. Desble booked back into the same hotel on 17 February and booked out again the following day. Before leaving he called at Somtunzi's office. There was a representative of the BBC with him who seemed to know Desble. But Somtunzi remained suspicious because he did not act like a journalist. That was the last he saw of him. While there Desble used a cream Mazda hired from Avis in East London.[21]

Desble was a professional soldier. He had served in the French Army, including the French Foreign Legion, for ten years. He was commissioned before his resignation in 1973. He joined the Rhodesian Army in 1974 and served for four years in the Selous Scouts, leaving as a lieutenant on its disbandment in 1980. That year, like many other ex-Rhodesians, he signed a short-term contract with the SADF. He served for a year with 3 and 5-Recces at Phalaborwa.

He joined Reid Daly as a military adviser to the TDF with the rank of captain when Security Services Transkei's contract commenced in 1981. He resigned in December 1984 to work in the Transkei Development Corporation's security division as a training officer. He left in July 1986 and became a security management consultant (Military Intelligence operator) with Craig Williamson's Longreach Ltd in Johannesburg.

In January 1987 Desble applied for permanent residence status in South Africa. It was puzzling why he had not bothered before, but it was probably because he had been working mostly in Transkei since he had left Rhodesia. Nevertheless, in 1980 he had served with the Recces, which should have made him automatically eligible for permanent residence. A character reference supporting his application was signed by Michael Irwin, ostensibly his boss. Another was signed by Craig Williamson who highly recommended him and said he had known Desble for three years.[22]

By his own account, Williamson knew nothing about *Operation Katzen*. Desble, who was not busy at the time, asked for leave from Longreach when Reid Daly or his associates asked him to assist with *Operation Duiker*. He was promised the rank of major in the TDF or CDF if everything went well. He only told Williamson he was going to Umtata on leave.

While there, Desble stayed at the Umtata Club. His accommodation accounts were mailed to Longreach's Bryanston post office box number.[23]

On Tuesday 17 February Brigadier Deyzel again tried to head off the attempt on Lennox Sebe's life. This time he sent a fax to Brigadier 'Tolletjie' Botha, chief of Military Intelligence's Directorate of Covert Collection (DCC), to whom he reported on the Jalc project. Brigadier Botha maintained this only reached him on 19 February, but this is unlikely.

Prime Minister George put out a belligerent statement that the two homelands would soon amalgamate, whether President Lennox Sebe liked it or not.

The Ciskei administration retorted in similar, sable-rattling fashion, vowing that Ciskeians would 'fight to the last man'.

On Wednesday 18 February, in a final attempt to stop the attack, Brigadier Deyzel phoned the secretary of the State Security Council and explained what was about to happen. The secretary, who later denied the telephone call, allegedly said he had no jurisdiction regarding happenings outside South Africa.[24]

And so the matter rested.

Judge Harms in his report slated both Brigadiers Deyzel and Botha for making submissions in writing to him regarding the South African Army's involvement in the assassination attempt, but for not having the 'courage of their convictions' to repeat the statement on oath. The brigadiers obviously had their reasons. Perhaps it was because it was two years down the road from the event. They also knew what Brigadier Deyzel's principles had done for him, so not unreasonably they feared another railroading. They had, after all, bucked the military who were the most powerful people in the land.

In another desperate attempt to stave off the assassination, Lennox Sebe called the South African Ambassador to Ciskei, Christiaan van Aardt, and apprised him of what was about to happen. Van Aardt agreed it was a serious matter and promised to go to Cape Town to inform the government.[25] Whether he did or not is an open question.

So the time for the mounting of the utterly senseless *Operation Duiker* raid came inexorably nearer. By then it was certainly no secret. That it had been 'blown' was surely known to its South Africa Army planners and to the National Intelligence Service which had been handling the political side of the operation but had apparently washed its hands of it.

Ciskei and Transkei continued trading public insults and boasting about what they were going to do to each other when the attack came. Ciskei issued a statement saying it was 'on full alert awaiting the planned invasion of Ciskei by fugitives from justice, backed by the Transkei Battalion'. As a preparatory move, the guards at President Lennox Sebe's palace and offices were reinforced and put on high alert.

One can only speculate whether Military Intelligence alerted Major-General Reid Daly to Lennox Sebe having prior knowledge of the impending raid. Perhaps they just ignored it and kept their fingers crossed, hoping that everything would work out on the night. If Reid Daly knew his raiders were expected, but went ahead against the 'pensioners' anyway, he must have been suffering from a serious dose of overconfidence. If, on the other hand, he had not picked up basic intelligence that they knew he was coining — even by reading the local newspapers, by listening to the local radio stations, or from his own intelligence resources — then his standards of efficiency had slipped a lot since his glory days with the Selous Scouts.

On the evening of 18 February, Chief Lent Maqoma, puppet leader of the CPRPP, was booked into an East London hotel. He would remain there on standby, ready to take over the government once President Lennox Sebe had been killed, his cabinet ministers made prisoner, Bisho's radio station captured and the unfortunate Colonel Zibi located and knocked on the head. It should not prove difficult to kill Colonel Zibi, because Reid Daly had ensured that his men knew details of his office, his residence, his routine by night and day, his girlfriends, other friends and so on. In the confusion, his cold-blooded murder would most likely be put down as just another coup casualty. Lent's first task as the new president would be to broadcast a prepared statement announcing the success of the coup over Radio Ciskei the next morning.

The 22-strong raiding party comprised ex-Rhodesian military advisers working for Security Services Transkei (Pty) Ltd, members of *Iliso Lomzi* and operators from the TDF's Special Forces unit at Port St Johns. They were well armed and equipped.

Major Sandile of the CDF accompanied them. He had been turned Selous Scout-style and was now 'on side' with the Ciskei dissidents. After his 'arrest' and interrogation in Transkei the month before, he had been put on show before the media to reveal that President Lennox Sebe had personally ordered him to abduct or kill Charles Sebe. A mystified Ciskei spokesman, quite correctly, insisted he had been speaking under duress.

The raiders had maps of King William's Town, Queenstown and Bisho, the latter marked with target details. They wore civilian clothes and had two TDF troop carriers, a Toyota Land-Cruiser and a hired Mazda. After a final briefing by Reid Daly at 16:00 at the Transkei Air Wing station, they moved out and passed through Umtata at 19:00.

At the Kei River Bridge border post, the party experienced unexpected difficulties when an officious immigration official refused to let them enter South Africa with military-type weapons. Eventually, after a long delay and considerable persuasion they were allowed to continue.

They rendezvoused with Jean-Michel Desble in East London and he spent a hour briefing them as to the situation on the ground at Bisho. He had familiarised himself with all designated targets, but had failed to gain admittance to Lennox Sebe's palace to conduct a close reconnaissance of the most important target.

Here we have the unedifying spectacle of a private company — Security Services Transkei (Pty) Ltd — with its more than dubious majority shareholder — Major-General Ron Reid Daly — teaming up with the SADF to harvest profitable pickings in the business of manufacturing revolutions and creating instability. One can only speculate whether it was the SADF's intention that Security Services Transkei should later also take over the responsibility for training the Ciskei Defence Force as a reward for its murderous actions.

The raiders left East London at 22:30 in convoy, with Desble and Major Piet van der Riet taking the lead in the hired car. En route they halted briefly and donned uniforms similar to those worn by the CDF.

Reid Daly, meanwhile, took off in a light aircraft that was to be his airborne command post. To his dismay, his radio communications had failed and he lost all contact with the raiding column.

The raiders reached King William's Town shortly before midnight and Desble parked the Mazda at a convenient spot in town. Van der Riet left his briefcase under the seat of the car for safety's sake. It contained R1 400 in cash, operational and political planning for the proposed attack, a map of Bisho marked with the proposed targets, various other maps, a nominal roll of ex-Rhodesian employees of Security Services Transkei serving with the TDF, the identity documents of himself and his wife, plus personal papers. Van der Riet and Desble locked the car and transferred to the TDF trucks.[26]

The first stage of the plan was to attack President Lennox Sebe's palace and kill him. The next task was to capture the radio station, followed by an exercise to round up the cabinet ministers. Only token resistance was expected and they confidently anticipated success on a 'who dares wins' basis. The CDF was woefully inexperienced and its soldiers had never fired an angry shot. The well-trained raiders, in contrast, were led by battle-hardened ex-Rhodesians — men who were veterans of hundreds of contacts.

Their planning was sloppy, however, and their overconfidence self defeating for, in truth, they had underestimated their enemy and taken far too much for granted. Intelligence on the likely reaction of the 'pensioners' was lamentably lacking.

Their vehicles had been over-sprayed in the khaki drab used by the CDF, but they had not bothered with the wheel rims. It is astonishing that they overlooked the basic requirement of checking their vehicles for anything that might connect them with the TDF. A TDF log-book showing that the vehicle had been booked out earlier that day from the TDF's Special Forces base at Port St Johns had been left in a troop carrier's glove compartment. The bogus CDF registration plates on the vehicles were amateurish in the extreme. The numbering sequence bore no resemblance to the genuine ones used by the CDF. In addition, the original TDF plates had been left in place underneath the false ones.

Perhaps the most careless mistake of all was allowing the raiders to keep TDF identity documents on their persons.[27]

At 01:45 on Thursday 19 February 1987 they halted their vehicles about 500m from President Lennox Sebe's palace and debussed with their weapons and equipment.

At 02:00 Major Sandile emerged from the gloom and approached the guards at Lennox Sebe's palace, probably to talk them into surrendering. They recognised him immediately. They were edgy and expecting an attack so they took him prisoner.

Things were not going according to plan. The raiders, probably armed with a preponderance of light machine guns, opened fire and launched an assault to overwhelm the attackers.

To their dismay the CDF fought back with tenacity. There were far more well-armed defenders than expected. They also came under crossfire from two machine-guns. The element of surprise had rebounded on them with a vengeance.

In a fierce one-sided firefight lasting ten minutes, the raiders suffered two casualties. Rifleman Mbuyiselo Templeton Nondela was killed and Rifleman A Ndulu seriously wounded. Others might also have been wounded, but if so, they managed to escape. The assault quickly turned into a rout. Bullets zinged everywhere. One ricocheted around the bedroom of Vicky Clarke just across the border in Queens Road, King William's Town, narrowly missing her.

The raiders fled in disorder. They abandoned their vehicles, a light machine gun, two R-5 rifles, camouflage uniforms and ration packs. Some of the Ciskeian *Iliso Lomzi* cadres escaped into the black townships and lost themselves amongst the locals.

There was a delay while the contingent guarding the palace contacted the barracks of the nearby 1-Ciskei Battalion and asked for reinforcements to mount a follow-up. The troops were reluctant to abandon their defensive positions because it would have left the President and his wife without protection. During what seemed to be an endless waiting period, two helicopters, which soldiers identified by their engine sounds as Alouettes, apparently landed briefly and picked up a few of the much chastened survivors.[28] They were probably TDF choppers.

There was an unconfirmed story doing the rounds in ex-Rhodesian circles that a fully armed light military aircraft of the CDF's Air Wing was airborne and ready to assist in the hunt for the raiders. This and one of the TDF Alouettes, it was said, were both being flown by ex-Rhodesian Air Force pilots. Radio contact was established by one ex-Rhodesian helicopter pilot who identified himself and told his former comrade-in-arms to lay off.

His former comrade, apparently, told him sharply that as their loyalties no longer coincided, he intended to shoot him down. He tried his best and chased the Alouettes in the direction of Komga. Fortunately for them, they had the necessary speed to make good their escape.

Operation Duiker: the aftermath

Headman Somtunzi said South Africa had a lot to answer for. They had not only violated Ciskeian air space, but had allowed Transkei's military vehicles to pass through the Kei River Bridge border post. 'Bearing in mind the time the attackers spent on South African soil as detailed in the plan, and taking into account the precision of the execution of the plan, it is incomprehensible that they were not spotted.'[29]

Lacking confirmation that all, or for that matter any, of the raiders had actually managed their escape by air, Ciskei mounted a massive ground search and follow-up operation.

Chief Lent Maqoma, with the rapid evaporation of his political ambitions and high hopes, was spirited away from his East London hotel and back to the safety of his exile in the Transkei. It was the terminus for his and Namba Sebe's gravy train.

It marked the beginning of numerous phone calls to Colonel Lourens du Plessis from Maqoma and Namba Sebe begging for money.[30] It was a fruitless quest. The SADF's own gravy train with its large cargo of cash aboard had pulled out and would never call at their station again.

A preliminary interrogation of the captured Major Sandile, who had been badly assaulted by his captors and was only too willing to cooperate, quickly revealed the identities of his fellow raiders. He also willingly disclosed that Desble's car had been parked in King William's Town before the start of the raid. A party of soldiers was despatched across the border to investigate and found it exactly where Desble had left it. They smashed a window to open the door and found Major van der Riet's briefcase under the seat with its treasure of raid documentation.

The soldiers, concerned that problems could arise from the car being in South Africa, and to give themselves more time for a thorough search, attempted to start the engine. It failed to start, so they gave up and pushed the vehicle across the border into Bisho. They found little more that was useful. To create confusion about its retrieval from South African territory, they parked it next to the captured vehicles and riddled it with bullets to make it look as if it had been right in the middle of the 'Battle of Bisho'.[31] Headman Somtunzi recognised it as the Mazda used by the visiting journalist who had aroused his suspicions. Avis papers had been discovered during the earlier search and a phone call identified it as one hired by Jean-Michel Desble.

During the course of that day, Brigadier Deyzel spoke to Directorate of Covert Collection Chief, Brigadier Tolletjie Botha, about the attempted coup. He said Ciskei had found documents that proved SADF involvement. Brigadier Botha suggested the authorities show them to the South African Ambassador. A disillusioned Deyzel responded that if they did, he hoped they did not hand over the original evidence.

'This is indeed strange behaviour for a member of the South African Army, especially one with the rank of brigadier', Judge Harms would critically say in his report.[32]

Brigadier Deyzel could afford to ignore this, however, because doubtless similar critical remarks were made by German judges about Colonel Count von Stauffenberg, when *Der Fuehrer* escaped with his life after the failure of the bomb plot of 20 July 1944.

The East London *Daily Dispatch* phoned General Reid Daly at home and asked him if he knew Jean-Michel Desble. Reid Daly lied not very convincingly that he had 'never heard of him'. This set the tone and lying became endemic in Transkei's military circles. A 'spokesman' at Transkei's Special Forces HQ at Port St Johns said: 'We have no members by the name of Mbuyiselo Templeton Nondela (shot dead) and A Ndulu (wounded) in the force . . . even the so-called leader of the raiders, a Major van der Riet, is not known to us'. They declined to explain the TDF identity card found on the body of the late Rifleman Nondela and on the captured Rifleman Ndulu.

Major-General Zondwa Mtirara declined to comment.

Major-General Reid Daly was 'out' when newsmen phoned to quiz him about Major Piet van der Riet.[33] His reticence was understandable when it is appreciated that both Van der Riet and Desble were founder members of his very own Selous Scouts.

Ciskei's spokesman, Headman Somtunzi, had the last word. He said that no funeral arrangements had been made in connection with Rifleman Nondela's body. 'They [Transkei] should see what they intend doing about their dead man', he said.[31]

On 20 February Prime Minister George Matanzima lashed out at Ciskei in a verbose statement. He did not even mention the Bisho attack and refused to answer questions 'in case he was misquoted'. Nevertheless, when asked to comment about his statement that Transkei and Ciskei would amalgamate whether President Sebe liked it or not, he said: 'That is not a question. I'm not replying to any questions but this is being left to your speculation as journalists, but I am not going to incriminate myself or my government'.

He blamed the 'deteriorating political situation' on Ciskei, saying they had been 'uprooting families' from areas where they had lived all their lives. The Ciskei government, he said, lacked legitimacy because it engaged in mass detentions, torture and killings. He accused Ciskei of sending Major Sandile to Transkei to kidnap Charles Sebe, but declined to answer when he was asked if Sandile had subsequently escaped from custody. He ended by saying he appreciated South Africa's neutral stand in the dispute between the two countries.[35]

Ciskei, understandably, did not share his appreciation. It requested the SAP to assist in the hunt for the raiders, to stop them escaping back to South Africa. On 20 February the SAP's liaison officer for the Border region, Lieutenant Dot van der Vyver, confirmed that South Africa's Security Forces were helping to track down the attackers, but said that no arrests had been made. She made the point, sounding somewhat like Prime Minister John Vorster in his heyday, that it was South African practice to assist 'a friendly neighbouring state'.

Colonel Avery Ngaka, a Ciskei Police spokesman, declined to comment.[36] This was probably because he knew, despite the lieutenant's official statement, that the SAP had already arrested and detained Jean-Michel Desble in East London. Amazingly, his arrest was not in connection with the raid, but for his alleged involvement in the abduction of Major-General Kwane Sebe from Ciskei on 26 September 1986. The Ciskeian authorities were baffled as to why he should be detained on the abduction charge when the matter had already been resolved at top level by a prisoner swop in December 1986. If Ciskei was no longer seeking the abductors, why should South Africa be interested? Besides, Ciskei had proof that Desble was one of the Bisho raiders.

Colonel Craig Williamson was markedly unhappy. He visited Desble in custody, but refused to assist him. If he had asked permission to go operational outside the Longreach orbit he would have allowed him to, but he had not. Instead, he had involved himself in a messy assassination attempt which eventually compromised Longreach. At the least it left the impression that Longreach had been involved in the attempt. Williamson said that Desble appreciated his viewpoint.[37]

Ciskei issued a warrant for Desble's arrest on 21 February and had it legally endorsed for service in East London. South Africa rejected it on the grounds that Desble was already in custody on another charge. They also refused an amended request for the warrant to be executed if Desble was granted bail or acquitted. An extradition request was turned down.

About three days after the failed raid, Major-General Reid Daly phoned Colonel Lourens du Plessis and expressed a wish to meet him and brief him on the raid. He said he would fly to East London in a helicopter, but needed a secure place to land and meet. Colonel Reg Deyzel arranged for the target shed at the rifle range to be swept and for the provision of camp chairs. Reid Daly's Alouette landed behind the butts where it was out of sight from traffic on nearby roads. Two white advisers were with him and he asked if they could borrow Colonel du Plessis' car as they wanted to go shopping in East London. This certainly surprised Colonel du Plessis, because a request to go shopping was the last thing he had expected. He shrugged and allowed them to take his car which was fitted with diplomatic plates.

Colonels du Plessis and Deyzel settled down in the target shed with Reid Daly expecting to be told the full and detailed story. Reid Daly, however, gave them a general briefing but was very skimpy on detail. They learned that the radio communications had failed and that several casualties had been suffered, but not much else.

The advisers eventually returned from their shopping trip and drove the car straight to the parked helicopter. To Colonel du Plessis' surprise, a black girl wearing an Afro wig and with a scarf over her face, alighted and climbed straight into the helicopter. Without providing a word of explanation Reid Daly hurriedly said his goodbyes and got into the helicopter which took off immediately.

The armed rifleman who had been provided to guard the helicopter enlightened them by saying that the 'black woman' was a 'white man' in disguise. He had been close enough to be certain of it.

Colonel du Plessis heard later that it was a white warrant officer who had disguised himself as a woman after the failed raid and hidden out amongst the black populace in one of the townships.[38] To get away with that, he must have been assisted by one of the *Ilison Lomzi* cadres from Bisho who had taken part in the raid.

Du Plessis was not charmed by Reid Daly's subterfuge. He felt he had been used. If Reid Daly had told him the truth and asked for assistance, he would have helped, but he resented his underhand behaviour.

On 20 February 1987, asked to comment on the latest developments, the South African Foreign Affairs ministry said they had warned Transkei not to allow its territory to be used as a launch pad for acts of violence against Ciskei. They were then asked how vehicles containing heavily armed men could pass through South African territory without being detected, why armed Ciskei policemen had been seen in the streets of King William's Town on 19 February, what role South Africa had played and was South Africa assisting in the hunt for the gang?

They humph-humphed that they could not take sides in the dispute, even though it directly affected South African interests. The remaining questions were left unanswered.[39]

On 8 April 1987 the abduction charge against Desble was withdrawn on the orders of the Attorney General and he was rearrested as an illegal immigrant — an odd charge indeed when it is considered he had already applied for permanent residence[40] and had served his time in South Africa's armed forces. Both facts would be concealed by the authorities. The former would only come out after a revelation by *The Sunday Star* on 28 February 1988 and the latter on the publication of this book.

The Ciskeian Minister of Justice, this time impeccably adhering to the correct diplomatic channels, asked the South African Justice Minister to issue a provisional arrest order for Desble. The request was ignored and Desble was deported to France on 23 May 1987.

It is difficult to see why Desble was the only man arrested and detained. Why not the others? In the first place it might have been the action of an honest policeman who, like Brigadier Deyzel, was disgusted at the criminal antics of people in high places. But whatever it was, it took months to resolve, with the agenda changing constantly and in the end it probably had nothing to do with the arresting officer.

One is not left wondering for long why Desble was not extradited to Ciskei. If he had been put on trial it would have opened a Pandora's box and it is doubtful whether P W Botha's administration would have been left unscathed.

It must have been for the same reason that the rest of the lawbreakers — those in the South African political hierarchy, those in the SADF and those in Transkei who were all *prima facie* guilty of the common law crime of conspiracy to commit murder, or of attempted murder or of being accomplices — were not handed over. Or why they were not charged in South Africa — where most of the conspiracy took place. If they had been brought to count, it would have left the SADF's hierarchy pretty thin on the ground.

There was nothing in the constitution of South Africa that put them above the law. So one must believe there was a hive of anxious cover-up activity going on behind the official scenes and disinformation was thick on the ground. But fear lingered on in high places

— worries that evidence proving the true story would one day come out, as was ultimately the case.

The late Kit Katzen (no relation to *Operation Katzen*), an ace investigative journalist for *The Sunday Star* and a good friend of the author, was credited with breaking the Information Scandal in the 1970s. He won many well deserved journalistic awards for his work in the media. In February 1988 he revived the story of Jean-Michel Desble. Using information gleaned from 'a highly placed source' he represented Desble as a 'Day of the Jackal' type character who had been the kingpin in the Lennox Sebe palace attack.[41]

This author, when asked his opinion in advance of the publication of the story, told Katzen that the South African government output was definitely disinformation. He opined that the Frenchman was only a minor cog in the machine and certainly no 'Jackal'. He had been set up as the 'fall guy' after the raid had failed, selected because he was a Frenchman, a foreigner without money or influence in South Africa. He had been used as the tool to divert attention from the more important people involved. Katzen, however, preferred the version of his 'deep throat' who, it was rumoured, lurked in the virtually oxygen-less upper stratosphere of the Ministry of Foreign Affairs.

On 19 March 1987 Defence Minister Magnus Malan, Law and Order Minister Adriaan Vlok and Foreign Affairs Minister Pik Botha visited Bisho and were very publicly shown the items captured from the raiders. Pik Botha said he now had 'a very realistic account' of the raid on Lennox Sebe's home.

One can bet that he did.

He gave no intimation, however, of having had a prior briefing on *Operation Katzen*. This seems surprising when one considers that his direct subordinate — General van Deventer, the South African Ambassador to Transkei — had been made 'partly aware' of the plan by Brigadier van der Westhuizen and that another direct subordinate — Christiaan van Aardt, the South African Ambassador to Ciskei — had received a worried advance briefing by Lennox Sebe himself. One would also have expected him to be in the know by virtue of his permanent seat on the State Security Council.

Transkei: exit the mercenaries

Meanwhile, nemesis had crept up on some more of those responsible for the bungled assassination attempt. At 22:30 on Sunday 29 March 1987 the chief of Transkei's Security Police phoned Major-General Reid Daly's home to warn him that 'trouble was brewing in the military base outside the town. People were armed to the teeth and he was concerned about what he had heard.'

Reid Daly phoned the white military adviser responsible for the camp and told him to ascertain what was happening. The adviser drove to the camp but everything was quiet and peaceful.

Reid Daly returned the Security Police chief's call and was told that a deputation of six officers had 'just' seen Prime Minister George. He would let Reid Daly know the next day what had happened.[42]

Instead, the next morning Prime Minister George sent for him and TDF commander, Major-General Mtirara. The latter, wisely, developed a problem at his tribal home so he was unavailable until later that afternoon.

Prime Minister George told Reid Daly that the deputation had demanded Brigadier Holomisa's immediate release from detention, the replacement of Major-General Mtirara and a pay rise for all lieutenants.

Reid Daly cried 'mutiny' and demanded that the six be dealt with 'swiftly and harshly' before the army disintegrated. It was a new role for Reid Daly, who had always cast himself as the conciliatory 'Uncle Ron' — his old Rhodesian Army nickname — rather than in the harsher mould of a Captain Bligh.

The Prime Minister demurred, probably fearing the disintegration had already occurred. He said that in view of various undertakings he had given, he would continue negotiations, bypassing the normal army chain of command. He would attempt to talk them out of their demands.[43]

It became clear that the release from prison of Brigadier Holomisa was the key to settling the situation. Prime Minister George contacted the Commissioner of Police and and asked why Holomisa had not been charged. The commissioner replied that it was nothing to do with him — he had only been told to arrest Holomisa.

'What about evidence?'

'There is no evidence.'

It was eventually decided, apparently jointly by Reid Daly and Prime Minister George, to relieve the tension amongst the troops by arraigning Brigadier Holomisa before the magistrate's court that afternoon and by not opposing bail. This remarkably clumsy piece of crisis management failed, unfortunately for the crisis managers.

The first Brigadier Holomisa knew about it was when the TDF's legal officer came to see him and said he was sorting out bail.

'How come you are doing that when I have not even been allowed to see an attorney?' Holomisa asked.

He told him to leave his cell as he did not want bail.

Next was the Commissioner of Police in person, who also attempted to persuade him to accept release on bail.

Again Holomisa refused.

Later, after being brought to town to appear before the magistrate, the Brigadier forthrightly refused to cooperate. He demanded he be returned to his cell and his military guards obediently complied.

Reid Daly said indignantly: 'This action had a bad effect on the troops, as they had been promised he would be released, and now he was back in the cells. I believe they thought the Prime Minister had gone back on his word.' [44]

A deputation of army officers led by Brigadier T T Matanzima and Colonel Craig Duli visited Brigadier Holomisa in prison. They explained that they had sought an interview with Prime Minister George and asked him to provide them with the grounds on which he had been detained. Colonel Duli confirmed that his own earlier investigations had cleared Holomisa of any wrongdoing. The Prime Minister was unable to oblige.

Colonel Duli said: 'We feel that Reid Daly is messing you about. He's got a project that we don't know about. Why were you arrested? You didn't steal any money. You didn't do anything. So we will tell Prime Minister George that you must be released.' He also told Holomisa that according to his investigations it was probable that Major Sandile was already in the custody of Major van der Riet (and the ex-Recce hitman) when he telephoned that night to ask for a meeting. He believed if that if Holomisa had gone, both he and Sandile would have been arrested. They might also have been shot as both were perceived as obstacles.

That evening the officers returned to the prison and told Holomisa he was free.

Holomisa, always the stickler for regulations, told them to sign the order book to make it official that he was free. He went to his house and Colonel Craig Duli arranged for armed guards to be placed on guard there to see to his safety and well-being.[45]

At 16:30 that day a white adviser phoned General Reid Daly and appealed for help. He said that mutinous soldiers were holding him and four colleagues as hostages. Reid Daly cautioned Major-General Mtirara against doing anything precipitous, but the General ignored his advice and bravely went to the military base and persuaded the mutineers to release the men.[46]

A deputation of senior officers called on Holomisa at his house. They told him they were 'sick and tired of these Selous Scouts. The officers, the other ranks and the troops had decided they should be deported'.

'What does Prime Minister George have to say about that?' Holomisa asked.

'We don't trust him, he's a hypocrite', they said. 'We will sort out Chief George later, but these Selous Scouts need to be sorted out now. They must go. Now! They are dividing us.'

Major-General Reid Daly later said he had 'for some time been aware of a military power play involving Brigadier Holomisa, and I had twice spoken to him regarding his attitude to General Mtirara. He was not showing the loyalty expected of one officer to another. I had even gone as far as taking him before the Minister of Defence, the Prime Minister'.[47] Both general officers, each of whom had been given accelerated promotion from the rank of colonel or below, apparently lacked the necessary abilities to discipline a subordinate. Similarly, they also did not have the perception to see the obvious unlawfulness of their involvement in the execution of *Operation Katzen*.

Reid Daly said: 'We erred in not getting him [Bantu Holomisa] into court quicker when he was arrested in January on a serious charge, about which I am not prepared to elaborate now [and about which he never elaborated]. His detention took too long to execute and a mistake was made in placing him in a military base under close arrest. He then had plenty of time to talk to the men of the battalion he used to command'.[48]

On Tuesday 31 March the secretary to the cabinet sent for Reid Daly and told him that although the Prime Minister 'was saddened' the contract with Security Services Transkei (Pty) Ltd had been terminated with effect from 1 April 1987. This was despite it having been renewed by Prime Minister George for a further three years on 1 March 1987. He suggested that the advisers remain in their houses and keep a low profile. Meanwhile, they could continue drawing normal pay and allowances and use military vehicles until the finalisation of a financial settlement.

The game was up.

Reid Daly called together the 27 white employees of Security Services Transkei, told them to hand in their weapons and any other kit and equipment they might have and to keep a low profile. If anyone wanted to get out of town, or even the country, they could go. Ten of the advisers, wisely sniffing the wind, drove for the border that evening. The remaining 17, less wisely, spent the next two days packing and clearing up.[49]

On Wednesday 1 April Major-General Zondwa Mtirara resigned his command, saying the TDF was receiving instructions from a 'certain politician' and not the Prime Minister. He said later that he had resigned because he 'feared for his life'. In acquiescing with the detention of Brigadier Holomisa by Prime Minister George and Major-General Reid Daly, he had committed the fatal error in African politics of backing the wrong horse.[50]

During the afternoon of Friday 3 April, Fort Gale, the up-market suburb of Umtata where the white advisers lived, was isolated by TDF roadblocks. Reid Daly drove up to one where, despite protestations that he was a civilian over whom they could exercise no jurisdiction, he was arrested and escorted back to his house. Heavily armed soldiers raided the homes of the other employees of Security Services Transkei (Pty) Ltd and arrested them in front of their families. One colonel was given a beating.[51]

The TDF soldiers bundled them into an army paddy wagon and completed their humiliation by trundling them around the town and through Umtata's outlying black townships — like French aristocrats being carted off in the tumbrels to the guillotine.[52] The author was told on good authority that, in fact, many of them had an uncomfortable feeling that a somewhat similar fate awaited them.

Eventually, they were returned to the military base and formed up before an audience of soldiers who were 'in a high state of tension'. Afterwards a 'posse of well-armed soldiers' escorted them to their homes and conducted further detailed searches for 'incriminating evidence'.[53] Reid Daly did not mention the nature of the 'incriminating evidence' they were seeking, but presumably it related to *Operation Katzen*.

From there they were taken to a military detention barracks and locked up five or six to a cell, without charges being preferred. Throughout the night they were subjected to abuses and threats. One soldier threatened to toss a grenade into Reid Daly's cell.[54] The questioning continued well into the next day. Reid Daly says he advised his men to refuse to answer questions unless they were 'nebulous', but he made no mention as to what the questions concerned.

On Saturday 4 April at 18:00 they were served with detention orders, escorted to their homes, given 15 minutes to pack, taken to the border under armed-escort and handed over to the South African authorities.

Before this unceremonious bundling across the border, Reid Daly reminded his captors that 'only a month previously I had been given Transkei citizenship in appreciation of my services, but was now being thrown out of the country like a dog.' [55] He would have been wiser to have kept his righteous indignation to himself and accepted that abrupt terminations of employment are commonplace in the mercenary business. It is not, after all, generally recognised as pensionable employment.

On Sunday 5 April it was announced that Reid Daly had cancelled an expected press conference and left for Johannesburg under police guard. The National Party MP for East London, Peet de Pontes, who was monitoring the situation for the cabinet, declined to reveal the reasons for Reid Daly and his men being escorted to Johannesburg under police guard.[56]

On the following day Reid Daly made a statement from an 'undisclosed location' to the effect that he had deliberately lied about fleeing from East London to 'bamboozle' abductors from Ciskei. 'We apologise for the subterfuge in our statement on Sunday, but it was necessary because of a real threat to our lives.'

Confusingly, he would later deny this, insisting: 'I never apologised — as was reported in the media — about putting out false information regarding our movements. I never said there was any threat to our lives.' [57] Despite his denial, it would be reasonable to assume that Reid Daly and his men spent at least some time in police custody after re-entering South Africa, particularly considering that Desble was still in detention.

Reid Daly's contradictory statements gave Headman Somtunzi, Ciskei's spokesman, a golden opportunity to piously say: 'We respect the norms and procedures of law and will not violate the territory of another country.' He added, with justification, that Reid Daly's 'imagined' fears of abduction indicated his involvement and that of some of his men in the abduction of General Kwane Sebe.[58]

On 8 April Prime Minister George issued a statement saying the white advisers had been expelled for their 'own safety' because of a deterioration in their relationship with the TDF. He also announced the promotion of Brigadier Bantu Holomisa to major-general and said he would succeed Major-General Mtirara as commander of the TDF.[59]

Following negotiations, the South African, Ciskeian and Transkeian governments signed a non-aggression pact in Cape Town on 10 April 1987. They agreed not to allow the planning, inciting or carrying out of acts of violence or terrorism against each other. The pact also provided for the establishment of a three-member 'regional commission for security and co-operation' to resolve security disputes and make recommendations on economic co-operation.

A retired Commissioner of the SAP, General Johan Coetzee — an Eastern Cape man himself — was appointed to play a part as liaison officer to keep the peace between the two territories.

President Lennox Sebe thanked State President P W Botha for having sent three senior ministers of state to mediate and 'check what would have developed into open conflict'. The three senior ministers were Foreign Minister Pik Botha, Defence Minister Magnus Malan and Law and Order Minister Adriaan Vlok. All of them, significantly, were permanent members of the State Security Council and must have known about *Operation Katzen*.[60]

Prime Minister George placed doubt on the efficacy of the proceedings by noting that 47 years ago similar 'peace agreements' (that did not work) had been signed between Britain's Neville Chamberlain and Germany's Adolf Hitler. After the pact was signed, the 'expatriation' of Transkei citizens from Ciskei was halted.[61]

Security Services Transkei (Pty) Ltd instituted an action to sue the Transkei government for breach of contract and damages through Transkei's Supreme Court, but they were prevented from doing so by legislation with retrospective provisions which was hurriedly enacted by the National Assembly. This was obviously done to avoid a messy legal situation, although if the contract had not been subjected to Treasury approval and had been approved by Cabinet, it was of doubtful validity anyway.

Besides that, one is left to speculate how the company would have fared in such an action, considering the clause which allowed the government to cancel the contract if the company was 'guilty of conduct prejudicial to the safety and security of Transkei'. It would certainly have been arguable that the launching of an attack on President Lennox Sebe's palace by Reid Daly's raiders fell within that category.

It was the beginning of the end for Transkei's old guard. On 7 May 1987 Kaiser Matanzima attempted a comeback by forming an opposition party, but was thwarted by his brother, Prime Minister George, who rushed a bill through the national assembly in one day prohibiting 'former state presidents' from sitting as MPs. Four days later Kaiser was served with an order banishing him to a remote corner of Transkei. Kaiser said his brother George was corrupt and accused him of colluding with Reid Daly in the raid on Lennox Sebe's home. He said it had been 'perpetrated in the interests of Ciskeian refugees in our country, from whom the prime minister takes instructions'.

Prime Minister George countered by accusing Kaiser of 'trying to woo the army to overthrow me'.[62]

On 23 September 1987 Prime Minister George slipped out of Transkei and took up residence in Port Elizabeth, only hours ahead of a deputation of TDF officers who came to see him at his residence with a pre-prepared letter of resignation for him to sign. Six ministers and two deputy ministers were not quite so nimble and they had to sign their resignations at gunpoint. Chief Dumisani Gwadiso was appointed as acting Prime Minister and George Matanzima capitulated and resigned as well.[63]

On 25 September the SAP in Port Elizabeth arrested Namba Sebe for extradition to Ciskei on two counts of corruption and two of theft. After publicly apologising to President Lennox Sebe and promising him his full support, the charges were withdrawn and he was released from custody on 23 December 1987. He confessed that he had turned his back on Lennox in 'a misguided moment'.[64] He did not, however, return to Ciskei to fulfil his promise, but scuttled back to Transkei where, for the time being, he continued his life in exile.

On 5 October 1987 the ruling party met and elected Stella Sigcau as Prime Minister and party leader. Major-General Holomisa insisted there had been no coup and pledged his support for the new administration.

With the enactment of the retrospective provisions Security Services Transkei (Pty) Ltd was left out in the cold, their golden contract shattered beyond repair. An unlikely fairy godfather in the person of the Minister of Defence, General Magnus Malan, stepped in to make things good for them. One can be certain this was not due to a streak of inborn generosity, but because of the risk that Reid Daly and his associates might get nasty, go to the press and blurt out the bizarre story of how they had been jointly involved with the SADF in a conspiracy to murder a homeland leader.

On 2 October General Malan authorised that R2 million be paid as a 'closure' — whatever that might have meant — of *Operation Katzen*. General Coetzee handed 'the involved ex-Rhodesians', by then in South Africa, R2,25 million in cash in a suitcase. This was presumably in full and final settlement of Transkei's alleged debt. The money (taxpayers' money) was paid from the Department of Military Intelligence's aptly named 'Scraper Fund'. As is noted in Chapter 10, payments from this fund were also made in respect of the top-secret *Operation Marion*.

By then the only two 'involved ex-Rhodesians' still around were Ron Reid Daly and John Erasmus — the rest had dispersed to centres all over South Africa after the loss of their jobs in Transkei six months earlier. It is open to conjecture whether this money was deposited to the personal accounts of Reid Daly, Erasmus or anyone else, or to the accounts of Security Services Transkei (Pty) Ltd or Security Specialists International (Pty) Ltd. Also whether they as individuals or as responsible directors declared it for the purposes of South African or Transkei taxation. In view of the controversial history of non-payment of taxes surrounding Security Services Transkei (Pty) Ltd, and Reid Daly and his fellow advisers personally, it seems doubtful. One can assume that if the SADF had intended that taxes should be paid they would have paid them by cheque. One also wonders if they contacted their former employees and paid them any salaries still due that they might have forfeited as a result of their undignified exit from Transkei.

Major-General Holomisa, as Chairman of the Military Council, demanded R300 000 which he claimed South Africa still owed Transkei in relation to *Operation Katzen* for vehicles and other equipment that Ciskei captured during the raid. This was conceded and the money from the Scraper Fund was given to him in three equal installments of R100 000. Maybe they had to scrape the bottom of the Scraper Fund barrel to get it, which would explain the three installments. According to a letter sent to the TRC Amnesty Committee by General Holomisa, he handed this money to Transkei's National Intelligence Service for use by the TDF's Military Intelligence. This was undisputed.

As Lieutenant-General Joffel van der Westhuizen testified in his evidence to the Amnesty Committee in April 1999: 'Even though the payments to the ex-Rhodesians and Major-General Holomisa were shown as expenditure relating to *Operation Katzen*, it was not strictly speaking the case. The expenditure was connected only in a broad sense to *Katzen*'s objectives, but because of that reason, and for the lack of a more suitable allocation, it was linked to it.' (Hearings of the TRC's Amnesty Committee at East London in April 1999) What exactly did he mean by that? Was it felt that because Reid Daly was a co-conspirator with the SADF, the South African taxpayer had some sort of moral responsibility to pick up the bill? It seems that Reid Daly did not apply to the TRC for amnesty for his part in the criminal conspiracy. He did, however, submit a post-hearing affidavit which has since gone missing, so its contents are not available for comment.

On 11 November 1987 armed troops forced the departmental secretaries-general of the Transkei Departments of the Interior, Education, Transport, Local Government and Land Tenure and Foreign Affairs to sign pre-prepared letters of resignation.

On 30 November Kaiser Matanzima was detained under the Public Security Act for making statements to the *Daily Dispatch* which Prime Minister Stella Sigcau said could form the basis of a criminal charge. He was released shortly afterwards by order of Transkei's Supreme Court.

At midday on 30 December the TDF took over Transkei in a bloodless coup, ending the 86-day reign of Stella Sigcau. General Holomisa declared martial law, suspended the constitution, banned all political activity and ordered that the country be run by an interim administration comprising a military council and an appointed council of ministers. This had been triggered by the discovery that Stella Sigcau was allegedly counted amongst those who were paid R50 000 kickbacks by the Matanzimas out of the R2 million bribe paid by Sol Kerzner for the exclusive gambling rights of what later became the Wild Coast Sun.

On Christmas day 1987, Peter McNielage, formerly a white adviser with Security Services Transkei (Pty) Ltd, was arrested by the TDF's Special Forces unit at Port St Johns and charged with returning to the country after deportation. He was sentenced to six months imprisonment. Ironically, from being one of the first in at the beginning of the contract, he also ended up as the last.[65]

George Matanzima got his just desserts the next year when he was charged with others in the Transkei's Supreme Court on nine counts of corruption, alternatively bribery. He was imprisoned and his estate sequestrated over debts amounting to R4 million.[66]

Despite the meddling by the South African military that had almost created anarchy in both Transkei and Ciskei, the Eastern Province command was solemnly awarded the SADF's coveted 'Sword of Peace' in both 1986 and 1987.

Was it the peace of death? If it had been a medal instead of a sword, would it have included the '*Iliso Lomzi*' and 'Lennox Sebe' clasps for trying?

It is not the first, nor will it be the last time that honours have been awarded for disastrous failures.

Operation Katzen was not a rogue operation. If it had been, it would have been reasonable to expect that when details of it became public knowledge, those connected with it would have been suspended from duty and criminally charged. This did not happen. Even the prime mover, Joffel van der Westhuizen, by then a lieutenant-general, remained in office sullenly weathering the storm. He was eventually allowed to retire honourably, but very quietly, 'on medical grounds' and with full pension rights on 31 March 1994[67] — less than two months before an inquest finding was due on the murder of Matthew Goniwe and his three UDF colleagues.

When called to give evidence at the Goniwe inquest, he took refuge in his statutory right not to answer questions about *Operation Katzen* on the grounds that it might incriminate him.[68] It most certainly would have done as was confirmed by his later submissions to the TRC.

That President F W de Klerk and his cabinet did not act against General van der Westhuizen by suspending him from duty when his culpability came to light is a serious indictment in itself. But unfortunately, the complete upper structures of the SADF's general staff were involved to a lesser or greater degree and suspending the whole lot in one fell swoop would have proved politically impossible. Nevertheless, the fact that they did not, raises the overwhelming inference that the military acted with the authority of the State through the State Security Council.

But why did it happen at all? Why did South Africa go all out to destabilise Ciskei?

Van der Westhuizen regarded it as part of the 'total response', but what was he 'totally responding' to? The Lennox Sebe regime was not allied to the ANC or the PAC or SWAPO. Certainly it was disastrously corrupt and hopelessly inefficient, but was it so different to the neighbouring Matanzima regime? The National Party government had cast the mould for both and provided an excellent role model in itself.

The trigger was President P W Botha's alleged remark that Lennox Sebe had 'long been an embarrassment to our government'. The governing grip of the National Party cabinet 'yes men' had been meekly handed to the State Security Council which, working as a cabal or group dictatorship with President P W Botha, encouraged the generals to play war games within South Africa. All of them arrogantly overlooked the fact that the law governing the country was civil and not martial.

This loosening of the reins resulted in Joffel van der Westhuizen waging war against an interim objective — not even an enemy — which in his perception was an obstruction on the path to the fulfilment of his flawed and dangerously irresponsible plan. The corrupt Prime Minister George had been brought on side by offering him visions of him becoming prime minister or president of a greater Xhosaland. In return he allowed *Iliso Lomzi* to be based and trained in Transkei. Only Lennox Sebe stood in the way.

The main responsibility, however, lay with President P W Botha who gave his political and military securocrats their heads. President John F Kennedy, when attempting to topple Fidel Castro in the Bay of Pigs debacle, also gave the military the nod to go ahead because Cuba, like Lennox Sebe, had become 'a thorn in the flesh'.

'Cuba might well be a thorn in our flesh', Senator Fullbright, Chairman of the Senate Foreign Relations Committee, warned Kennedy, 'but it is not a dagger at our heart!'

Lennox Sebe was not a dagger at South Africa's heart either.

12

Security Police Death Squads 1985-1989

In the case of Matthew Goniwe the Department of Education and Training (DET) representatives both at the State Security Council and the Eastern Province Joint Management Centre (EPJMC) wanted him reinstated in his old post as headmaster — but Military Intelligence and the Security Branch wanted him dead. Consequently, their representatives on both bodies followed their own agenda.

In October 1983 Matthew Goniwe, the principal of the Llingelihle High School, Cradock, his brother Mbulelo Goniwe and another teacher, Fort Calata, formed the Cradock Residents' Association (CRADORA), affiliated to the UDF, to fight rent and other black township issues.[1]

According to State Security Council documents, Matthew Goniwe, who was born in Cradock in 1946, had been jailed in the Transkei for four years from 1976 for his Marxist leanings. Major-General Bantu Holomisa said Goniwe had 'taught in Transkei for a number of years; he taught at Ngqamakwe and at Holomisa Senior Secondary School, Mqanduli. He was well known in Transkei . . .'[2]

The DET, in an attempt to curtail their political activities, transferred both Goniwe and Calata from Llingelihle High School to posts in Graaff-Reinet. They declined the postings and were dismissed from the service on 27 January 1984.[3] Their supporters, interpreting this as the work of the Security Police, instigated a pupil boycott at Cradock and Graaff-Reinet schools. This sparked widespread unrest, which quickly spread to other Eastern Cape centres.

On 31 March 1984 Matthew Goniwe, Mbulelo Goniwe, Fort Calata and Madoda Jacobs were served with 12-month detention orders. This sparked further unrest which culminated in a pupil being stabbed to death by youths who ran amok in Llingelihle Township. Eighty-one people were charged with intimidation, attempted arson and public violence. After only seven months in detention, Matthew Goniwe and his colleagues were released on 10 December 1984.[4]

When the new school year opened in January 1985, stay-aways continued in Queenstown, Fort Beaufort, Graaff-Reinett, Uitenhage, Grahamstown, Port Alfred and Port Elizabeth. In Cradock pupils vowed to continue school boycotts until Matthew Goniwe and Fort Calata were reinstated. Cradock should not be looked at in isolation, however, as statistics show that 907 schools, involving 674 275 black pupils countrywide, were affected by boycotts during 1985.[5]

Matthew Goniwe's name first appeared on the agenda of the Eastern Province Joint Management Centre, chaired by Brigadier Joffel van der Westhuizen, on 28 March 1985. Colonel Lourens du Plessis was secretary. The meeting, attended by four brigadiers, three colonels, three commandants, a major, a captain, two lieutenants, a doctor and a contingent of public servants, was told the school boycotts in Llingelihle and adjacent areas were total.

At the end of Item 7 (c) of the minutes it was recorded that a number of teachers had agreed to transfers, but had subsequently changed their minds 'evidently as a result of the influence of Matthew Goniwe'.

The meeting spent considerable time dealing with Communications Committee (COMCOM) matters. News reports on unrest in the preceding month were briefly discussed and it was agreed the revolutionary climate had deteriorated dramatically since 1984. Projects relating to Youth Year came up for discussion as did drama festivals, school netball tours, library projects and expenses like the cost of bus tickets etc. Attention was given to a population development programme planned for East London in April and Queenstown in May.

For the two weeks prior to the meeting the SADF had deployed troops in the region in support of the police, but the meeting noted a cabinet announcement dealing with an escalation of their role was expected later that day.[6]

Explaining the 1984/85 situation, Van der Westhuizen told the reopened inquest into the deaths of Matthew Goniwe and his murdered associates, that the Eastern Cape was a flash point for anarchy. He controlled 30 000 troops in his area of responsibility which stretched from Ciskei/Transkei and the Eastern Cape to the north-eastern Cape.

He said Goniwe had been planning 'alternate structures' — street and area committees — for Cradock. This involved holding house meetings and helping residents join UDF-aligned civic associations. Goniwe intended creating black-ruled areas that broached no interference from government — 'liberated areas'. In Cradock and other areas he influenced, he called it his G (for Goniwe) Plan, but no mention of this appears in the March or April minutes of the EPJMC.

It was said that AZAPO was opposed to Goniwe's actions, but it is assumed this was the Maqina faction — an SADF surrogate.[8]

In April 1985 Cradock's class boycott was unexpectedly called off, despite there having been no moves made to reinstate Matthew Goniwe and Fort Calata. Attendances climbed to 72% of the January 1984 enrolment figures. On 22 May 1985, though, classes at Llingelihle High School were suspended for two days after pupils damaged a DET official's vehicle, threatened a teacher with a knife, ejected two more from the school and failed to attend classes.[9]

The EPJMC's meeting on 23 May was again chaired by Brigadier van der Westhuizen. Item 6 on the agenda — class boycotts — evoked grave concern. There was a briefing on the suspension of classes at Llingelihle High School, discussions on the mounting demands for the reinstatement of Matthew Goniwe and Fort Calata,[10] the unrest, the growing influence of the UDF in rural areas, threats to boycott East London's *Daily Dispatch* because of its allegedly poor coverage of UDF affairs, and a boycott of red meat in the Border area, instituted after the sacking of abattoir workers.

Under Item 25 the meeting decided: 'A signal will be sent to the Secretariat of the State Security Council, for relay to the relevant cabinet ministers, recommending that Matthew Goniwe and Fort Calata never be appointed as teachers again.' A signal to this effect was despatched to the head of strategy at the State Security Council's secretariat, Major-General Johannes 'Hans' Janse van Rensburg, two days later.

The Department of Education and Training saw the situation somewhat differently to the police and the army. Jaap Strijdom, Secretary of the DET, met Goniwe at Cradock on 24 May 1985 and concluded he was not 'the brain behind everything' and recommended his reappointment. His report was presented to a meeting of the State Security Council's Joint Security Centre Action Committee on 6 June 1985. It was chaired by Deputy Minister of Law and Order, Adriaan Vlok, and attended by the National Intelligence Service's Mike Louw, various senior SADF and SAP officers and several officials from the DET. They ruled that Goniwe's future should be decided by a task group especially convened by the State Security Council's Secretariat. There was no mention of Fort Calata. It would submit its report to Deputy Minister Vlok by 12 June 1985.

General van Rensburg formed the task group, drawing its members from the SADF, SAP and DET, and placed it under Air Force Brigadier Pieter Johannes Geldenhuys,. The DET representatives were Jaap Strijdom and Johan Vermaak, Deputy Director-General of the DET's Community Communications.[11]

On Friday 7 June 1985, probably in the morning, Brigadier van der Westhuizen in Port Elizabeth and General van Rensburg at the State Security Council in Pretoria discussed Goniwe on the telephone. General van Rensburg said their conversation centred around detaining Goniwe and 'some of his militant lieutenants for an indefinite period in an attempt to defuse the Cradock situation'. This indicates that General van Rensburg and Brigadier van der Westhuizen disagreed with the likely recommendations of the Geldenhuys Task Group and intended going it alone.

Brigadier van der Westhuizen briefed Colonel Lourens du Plessis, telling him that General van Rensburg had offered to assist with the Goniwe 'problem'.[12] It appears Van Rensburg instructed Van der Westhuizen either to convene an emergency session of the EPJMC to discuss Goniwe and get its recommendation, or canvas its members by phone to obtain a consensus for a recommendation.

Whatever happened, Brigadier van der Westhuizen was sure to have consulted his colleagues on the EPJMC, because it seems unlikely he would have spoken on their behalf without having done so. While he could probably circumvent or ignore the high-powered Pretoria-based task group, he probably had close relationships with the members of the EPJMC — people like the Security Police who 'understood' local conditions and were more than willing to go along with him. There would be no incriminating minutes, so members could deny all knowledge later. That afternoon Colonel du Plessis despatched a signal, translated from Afrikaans, as follows:

> FROM: Eastern Province Joint Management Centre (EPJMC)
> TO:
> Secretariat of the State Security Council (State Security Council)
> SECURITY CLASSIFICATION: Top Secret
> ORIGINATOR'S NUMBER: EPJMC/191/7 June 1985
>
> Personal for General van Rensburg
> 1 Telephone discussion General van Rensburg/Brigadier van der Westhuizen on 7 June 1985.
> 2 Names as follows:
> Matthew Goniwe, Mbulelo Goniwe (brother or nephew of the one mentioned above), Fort Calata.
> 3 It is proposed that the above-mentioned persons are permanently removed from society, as a matter of urgency.
> 4 Widespread reaction can be expected, locally as well as nationally, because of the importance of these persons, especially the former, for the enemy, e.g.
> A. Interdicts, such as recently in connection with the disappearance [murdered by the Security Police] of Godolozi, Hashe and Galela (PEBCO — [Port Elizabeth Black Civic Organisation] officials).
> B. Reactions by leftist politicians, such as Molly Blackburn.
> C. Protests such as in the case of Oscar Mpetha in sympathy.
>
> Drafter's name: L du Plessis [Colonel Lourens du Plessis)

It was authenticated by the date stamp of the SADF's Eastern Cape communication centre. Signals officer H J Pretorius recalled transmitting it, but said that signals were normally destroyed after three months.[13]

The phrase 'permanently removed from society', would cause much dissension. At the inquest into the deaths of Goniwe and his colleagues, Colonel du Plessis who had compiled and despatched the signal on Brigadier van der Westhuizen's instructions, described it unequivocally as a death warrant sent to initiate steps to murder the three men. He said that although General van der Westhuizen had not used the word 'kill', he knew it was implied. Fort Calata and Mbulelo Goniwe were not mentioned by name, only as Goniwe's 'helpers', but he knew who they were.[14]

Colonel du Plessis agreed he had originally made an affidavit contending the phrase 'permanent removal from society' was not a death order, but said this was because J Wagenaar of the Attorney General's office in Pretoria and the SADF's legal adviser, General Knipe, had spent 'some hours' convincing him he 'could not have been right'. He later retracted this and made a second truthful affidavit.[15]

Colonel du Plessis paused in his evidence and applied for indemnity from prosecution, necessitating an adjournment for three weeks. The Indemnity Board refused his application, saying there was some dispute as to whether sending the signal amounted to an offence with a political motive. This remarkable stance amounted to a gagging order, because if he continued his testimony incriminating Van der Westhuizen, he would have become liable for prosecution as an accessory. This triggered a furore in the media, which ceased only when President F W de Klerk overruled the Indemnity Board and granted him indemnity.[16]

Brigadier (by then Lieutenant-General) van der Westhuizen, in evidence at the inquest, claimed he could not recall the signal, but he accepted Colonel du Plessis' contention it was sent on his orders to confirm a telephone conversation with General van Rensburg. He insisted, though, that this concerned a proposed written submission to the Geldenhuys Task Group on action to be taken about Goniwe.

He also said General van Rensburg wanted his views on the possible security implications of reappointing Goniwe to the Llingelihle High School. He denied the signal was a recommendation for Goniwe's execution, only for his detention. The presiding judge professed he had 'problems' with this contention. He did not say it but 'lawful detention' to achieve 'permanent removal from society' was impossible, as there were no statutory provisions for it.[17]

Judge Zietsman said that if General van der Westhuizen's contentions were true, the signal was 'altogether incorrect' because it met none of General van Rensburg's demands. 'It does not confirm the telephone discussion you had, the wording was wrong if reappointment was to be discussed, no implications are spelt out and it gives information that was not discussed or asked for.'[18]

Van der Westhuizen denied ordering Colonel du Plessis to send the signal to circumvent the EPJMC or using it as his personal solution to the Goniwe problem. He insisted that killing Goniwe would have been 'unproductive'.[19]

At the reopened inquest in 1993 Major-General van Rensburg suddenly recalled receiving the signal, which he had denied until then, but he could not produce it. 'I may have destroyed it . . . which I would have been within my rights to do as it was addressed to me personally.' Alternatively, he might have handed it to Adamus Stemmet, chief of the State Security Council's Stratcom — Strategic Communications Section — the SSC's propaganda arm.

It was suggested that the destruction of a classified document had to take place in front of the 'holder of the register and an independent witness, and a 'destruction certificate' filed. The general denied this procedure was followed 'to the letter . . . if we had to fill in a form every time we destroyed a document the secretariat would grind to a halt'.[20]

General van Rensburg maintained that he had not seen the signal until Monday 17 June — ten days after it was despatched from Port Elizabeth. He accounted for the delay by saying that at the time he was chairing a task group that was considering the implementation of a National State of Emergency. He did not pass the signal to the Geldenhuys Task Group because they had already completed their task. What was more likely was that as the signal dealt with Goniwe being 'permanently removed from society', he considered it of no concern to the Geldenhuys Task Group. Van Rensburg, however, insisted he had interpreted the signal as a recommendation for detention.[21]

Stemmet denied receiving the signal, but said it might have been in a file passing across his desk. If he had received it he would have signed for it and booked it out afterwards.

He disagreed with Van Rensburg that classified documents were often destroyed without following laid down procedures.

General van Rensburg had, however, drawn his attention to the signal because of its 'dramatic' language. The general had said its language was 'unnecessarily harsh and ambiguous' and he had instructed him to address the matter in training which was his responsibility. Stemmet said terminology like 'eliminate', 'take out', 'neutralise', 'discredit' and 'remove' was undesirable.[22]

Andy cut straight to the heart of what it meant.

Despite his stated disapproval, Stemmet did not consider the signal sinister, nor did he believe it was a recommendation that Goniwe and his colleagues should be murdered. If its author had a sinister motive, he said blandly, he failed to see why it had been sent to the State Security Council which had no executive authority and could not deal with such matters.[23] His highfalutin statement was not in accordance with the evidence, but accorded with his position in the State Security Council.

Significantly, a year later in 1994, General van Rensburg experienced another remarkable recovery of memory and suddenly clearly recalled receiving the relevant signal on Wednesday 12 June 1994 — the day Brigadier Geldenhuys' Task Group submitted its report to him. This, he said, prompted him to compile a supplementary report, incorporating 'parts of the signal', for the attention of Deputy Minister Vlok. The report, he said, was typed by his secretary, Anna Vorster; but she doubted this and said she had never seen the signal. The supplementary report, if it existed, was neither shown to the Geldenhuys Task Group nor produced at the inquest.

General van Rensburg still maintained that he had believed the signal was a recommendation for Goniwe's indefinite detention and not a recommendation for his assassination. He insisted he had had 'nothing, but nothing, to do with the murders'.[24]

Johan Vermaak, the DET's man on the Geldenhuys Task Group, however, testified bluntly that the Security Forces regarded Goniwe as an enemy of the state and opposed his reappointment. The DET, conversely, believed his reappointment was central to defusing the unrest situation in Cradock and the rest of the Eastern Cape. The school boycotts had been going on for more than 15 months and a return to classes was the priority.

Vermaak first saw the EPJMC's signal when it was reproduced in the *New Nation*. If the task group had seen it, he would certainly have queried it. He was 'unfamiliar with military terminology', but believed it meant that Goniwe, Mbulelo and Fort Calata should be killed.

Brigadier Geldenhuys reported dissension within his task group, but said it completed its report and submitted it to General van Rensburg on Wednesday 12 June 1985. Its unanimous recommendation was that Matthew Goniwe be reappointed to his teaching post. He knew nothing about a supplementary report arising from the EPJMC's signal.[25]

General van Rensburg said he supported the Geldenhuys recommendation for reinstatement, which he called a 'breakthrough', but agreed it was at odds with the generally held view of the security establishment. In support he produced a copy of a 'top secret' letter dated 'June' addressed to Deputy Minister Vlok which laid out options for Goniwe. Detaining him, he had suggested, could fan the flames of revolution in Cradock, but reappointing him would subject him to the disciplinary codes of the DET. He recommended reinstatement. This proved nothing, but established that in all probability he was following two contradictory agendas — a dovish one and a hawkish one.

On 13 June Adamus Stemmet wrote to Brigadier Geldenhuys, confirming the recommendation for Goniwe's reappointment, but said it should be in line with usual DET policy. This required the post to be advertised, candidates interviewed and the appointment made on merit. Considering the DET's view on his urgent reinstatement, this bureaucratic move was undoubtedly designed to torpedo it.

On 18 June a DET internal memorandum addressed to five top DET officials, marked 'secret' and signed by the DET's Deputy Director-General, J Nienaber, confirmed that the Geldenhuys Task Force had recommended Matthew Goniwe's reappointment.

Opposition by the securocrats continued unabated. On 25 June Police Commissioner General Johan Coetzee, in a 'Top Secret' report to the then Minister of Police, Louis le Grange, strongly recommended that Goniwe should be removed from Cradock and detained in Johannesburg Prison. Whichever route they followed, whether it was reappointment or detention, they would still be criticised.[26]

Colonel Nic Janse van Rensburg, second in command of the Security Police in the Eastern Cape, discussed the question of eliminating Goniwe and his associates with his subordinates, Captains Herman du Plessis and Johan van Zyl. It was generally believed the Goniwe group were a threat to the security of South Africa.[27]

The Security Police were facing considerable pressure from the State Security Council and the Joint Management Centre to control unrest. Both President P W Botha and Defence Minister Magnus Malan had said publicly that 'we must fight fire with fire'.

The security policeman decided that at an opportune moment Goniwe and his associates would be killed in circumstances suggesting they had been murdered by vigilantes. This was approved by the Eastern Cape Security Police Chief, Colonel Harold Snyman.[28]

Sergeants Fred Koni and Boyce Msoki of Security Branch Cradock were responsible for monitoring the phones and transcribing calls made by Cradock activists. Mr Hattingh, a Security Police officer at Port Elizabeth, visited Cradock regularly to obtain details of phones to be tapped. Matthew Goniwe was one of about 80 of Cradock's 'A Files' — people classified as top security risks.

Sergeant Koni said surveillance of Matthew Goniwe was stepped up after a Security Police meeting with an unidentified cabinet minister in early 1985. Surveillance was achieved not only with bugging devices, but also through informers, field workers and handlers who dogged his every move. Lieutenant Eric Winter, the Cradock Security Branch commander, got daily reports on his movements.[29]

Colonel Lourens du Plessis confirmed this. 'Every day they [the Security Police] would come and tell us [at meetings of the local Joint Intelligence Committee (JIC) of which he was chairman] about Goniwe's movements and activities.'

The Cradock log book noted a call made by Goniwe to UDF activist Derrick Swarts at Port Elizabeth early on 27 June 1985. The transcript read:

Swarts: 'Hello.'
Goniwe: 'Hello . . . how is it?'
Swarts: 'I'm all right and you?'
Goniwe: 'I'm all right. I just want to find out if you are awake.'
Swarts: 'Ja, ja, what is the time now?'
Goniwe: 'Just about half past five. Well, I'll be seeing you, okay?'
Swarts: 'Listen, man, you must phone Barry du Toit. Do you know this guy Barry?'
Goniwe: 'Ja.'
Swarts: '7752 Grahamstown, you know.'
Goniwe: 'When?'
Swarts: 'You can phone him tomorrow morning in connection with the briefing – you know, in connection with that, you know.'
Goniwe: 'Otherwise, I will be seeing you this afternoon, okay?'
Swarts: 'Ja, okay brother, sure.'

Sergeant Koni passed the transcript to Colonel Winter. He phoned Port Elizabeth, then left the office with two colleagues. Unusually for him he did not say where he was going and left no contact number. His destination was the Port Elizabeth Security Branch where he reported to Colonel Harold Snyman. They were joined by Captain Sakkie van Zyl, who had been nominated to lead the operation, Sergeant Gerhardus Lotz and three black security policemen.[30]

Colonel Snyman's briefing was terse and to the point. 'It is between us. Nobody has to know about this except us.' His orders were specific: 'Do not use firearms — stab them and batter them, they must think it is part of the Eastern Cape charterist [UDF/AZAPO] feud. It must not be traced to us.'

Tabs were kept on Goniwe and his friends all day until it was reported they had left UDF activist Michael Coetzee in Port Elizabeth at 21:10 and were on their way home to Cradock.

The team waited for them in two cars on the Olifantshoek Pass. When Goniwe passed by in his Honda Ballade they followed, overtook him and established a roadblock farther on towards Middleton. Goniwe had told a friend earlier he would only stop for uniformed police, but in the event he had no choice.

They were dragged from the car and handcuffed. Sparrow Mkhonto and Sicelo Mhlawuli were bundled into one car, Matthew Goniwe and Fort Calata into the other. They drove in convoy back towards Port Elizabeth, a policeman driving Matthew Goniwe's Honda at the rear.

Near Bluewater Bay they left the road, drove into thick bush and stopped. Eric Taylor remained in one car guarding Goniwe and Calata, while the others shepherded Mkhonto and Mhlawuli into the bush. They were not designated targets, but their companions were, so they could not be allowed to live to tell the tale. Shortly afterwards Goniwe heard what he thought was a gunshot and he asked Taylor what had happened to his comrades. Taylor made no reply. The five policemen returned alone a little while later.

It was Eric Taylor's turn to be blooded. Accompanied by his colleagues he led Fort Calata and Matthew Goniwe separately into the bush and killed them with multiple stabs. Sergeant Lotz told the TRC he beat Goniwe to death with a heavy steel motor car spring, but post mortem results indicated he had been knifed to death. The policemen were highly experienced, but either through downright inefficiency, arrogance or fear, they left a broad trail of clues that pointed to their identities.[31]

According to Sergeant Koni, Lieutenant (later Colonel) Winter returned to his Cradock office only the next day. He appeared 'unusually anxious' and continually asked what was being picked up on the Goniwe telephone tap. During the day Warrant Officer Fanie Els was taped when he phoned from Port Elizabeth and told Mrs Goniwe that her husband's burnt-out car had been found in the bush near Bluewater Bay. Sergeant Koni reported this to Winter, who emerged from his office an hour later and announced briefly: 'AZAPO got them.'

When Goniwe's Honda was found it had a single false registration plate, number CB10627, affixed to it. The correct plates were found some distance away. The false number came from a car that had been scrapped on 19 January 1984. Since then the Port Elizabeth Traffic Department had collectively issued seven parking tickets to a white Ford Cortina and a yellow Datsun, both with the same registration number. In every case the vehicles had been parked in a particular expired meter bay outside the Security Branch's Strand Street offices when ticketed.[32]

The public prosecutor at the magistrates' court had withdrawn all the tickets. Colonel Harold Snyman, the Security Police Chief in Port Elizabeth, who had ordered the killings, confirmed, no doubt with some trepidation, that traffic tickets issued to official cars parked in front of the Security Police headquarters building were routinely withdrawn.He denied his staff utilised false registration plates and insisted that if it had occurred it was irregular.

Colonel Karel Britz of the Port Elizabeth Murder and Robbery Unit, however, contradicted Snyman and said the Security Police did use false number plates under certain circumstances. He had, however, failed to trace details of the ones they had used and when.[33]

The bodies of Sparrow Mkhonto and Sicelo Mhlawuli were discovered in thick coastal bush on the city's outskirts on 29 June 1985. Both had suffered multiple stab wounds from which they had died. The bodies had been doused with petrol and the faces burnt beyond recognition. Mhlawuli's hand had been chopped off at the wrist. Mkhonto had been shot with a ,22 rifle, established forensically to have been a Gevarum — a rare kind of sniper's rifle. Significantly, a Gevarum was said to have been kept in the storeroom of the Hammer Unit, a Citizen Force Special Forces unit, at the Eastern Province Command. However, this line of investigation went no further.[34]

On 30 June 1985 the police invited the press in Port Elizabeth to join a search for the missing Matthew Goniwe and Fort Calata. Within an hour their bodies were found far apart in the bush between St. George's Strand and Bluewater Bay. Both been stabbed to death and their bodies burnt.[35]

In May 1994 at the conclusion of the reopened inquest, Judge Neville Zietsman said it had been 'proved *prima facie* that the signal sent by Colonel Lourens du Plessis on behalf of [then] Brigadier van der Westhuizen to Major General van Rensburg was a recommendation that Matthew Goniwe, Mbulelo Goniwe and Fort Calata should be killed, and that this was the meaning Colonel du Plessis and General van der Westhuizen intended the signal to have'. He found no proof, though, that the, until then, unidentified murderers knew of the signal or its contents. 'Evidence to link the signal with the murders is lacking. What must be borne in mind is that the signal was a proposal, and not an order given to any person or persons.'

The judge found a 'case of suspicion' had been raised against Colonel Harold Snyman, Colonel Eric Winter, Lieutenant-General van der Westhuizen, Colonel Lourens du Plessis and Major-General van Rensburg. 'But suspicion does not constitute *prima facie* proof, which requires at least some evidence directly linking the deaths of the deceased persons to the acts committed by the persons under suspicion. The evidence led at this inquest does not, in my opinion, provide the necessary link', the judge found.[36]

And so the case remained 'unsolved', with the police exhibiting little enthusiasm for solving it, until Eric Taylor stepped forward in 1997. He admitted his involvement in the murders and applied to the TRC for amnesty.

The Security Police had been conducting state-sponsored, or at the very least, tacitly approved murders of activists, for many years. It had certainly not started in 1985 with the formation of TREWITS.

In September 1977 Steve Biko, the Black Consciousness leader, died after being severely beaten by the Port Elizabeth Security Police and transported naked and comatose by Land-Rover to Pretoria. Minister of Police Jimmy Kruger maintained he had starved himself to death after embarking on a hunger strike.[37] It was the same Jimmy Kruger who, when the Rhodesian Police arrested Constable Kriel — a member of the SAP engaged in counter-insurgency duty in Rhodesia — for snatching a black baby from its mother's back and slitting its throat, demanded he be released from custody, failing which the South African contingent would be withdrawn from the country.[38]

In 1982 security policemen Nic van Rensburg, Gerrit Erasmus, Herman du Plessis and Gideon Nieuwoudt (the first two retired as general officers and the latter as colonels) abducted two Eastern Cape activists, Siphiwo Mtimkulu and Topsy Madaka and took them to an abandoned police station at Post Chalmers near Cradock. Mtimkulu had lodged a R150 000 law suit against the Minister of Police for alleged thallium poisoning during his five months detention in 1981, so it would be strange if the minister had no knowledge. The policemen spiked their coffee with sleeping tablets, shot them in the head and dragged their bodies to an already prepared fire. They spent six hours cremating the bodies, after which Nieuwoudt scooped the ashes into a plastic bag and threw it in the Great Fish River.[39]

Undoubtedly there were many other political murders in addition to those brought to public attention by the TRC, but it is unlikely that the rest — the flotsam and jetsam of a dirty undeclared war — will ever be revealed. A particularly distasteful *modus operandi* of certain Security Police operators involved the immediate cremation of murdered victims on funeral pyres built out in the bush. This was clearly to destroy evidence. When the practice was first revealed by former Vlakplaas commander, Captain Dirk Coetzee, it was generally regarded as an aberration, a particularly horrible one it is true, but an aberration nevertheless. Since then it has become known that the practice was commonplace in certain sections of the Security Police. It was far too widespread to be an aberration. It was institutionalised. It was a drill.

In May 1992 Jan van Eck, an Independent MP, asked Parliament for the appointment of an international panel of jurists to investigate claims of political murders by government agencies. He claimed that sources in Military Intelligence and others close to the former President had told him P W Botha had boasted 'on a number of occasions' that he and his government, through the Military Intelligence and National Intelligence Service, were responsible for the summary execution of more than 1 000 black radicals.[40]

When asked in response to this report if he recalled the State Security Council discussing the Goniwe affair, ex-President P W Botha, its chairman in 1985, said: 'I know nothing about it . . . can you know of something you did in 1985? Can you know something you did in 1984?'[41]

The Security Police also turned savagely on their own.

There was a bizarre incident where Colonel Eugene de Kock beat one of his own operators to death in the Vlakplaas pub for losing his issue pistol, then ordered he be given a funeral with full military honours.

There were also the Motherwell Four. On 7 December 1989 Brigadier Fanie Gilbert, Divisional Commander of the Eastern Cape Security Police, since deceased, phoned General Nic van Rensburg in Pretoria and asked for Vlakplaas assistance to 'deal with' several security policemen whose 'suspected' recruitment by the ANC made them a security risk. Gilbert said head office had already given them the okay to 'make a plan'.

Brigadier van Rensburg said it was his perception it had been okayed at police commissioner level (General Johan van der Merwe) or ministerial level (Adriaan Vlok). 'I would also have expected him to get instructions from the [then] head of the Security Police, General Basie Smit.'

It appears that such a request, verbal and unsubstantiated by documentation, was so routine that General van Rensburg did not bother to seek guidance from his superiors.

Captain (later Colonel) Gideon Nieuwoudt flew to Pretoria to brief the General on 12 December 1989. Significantly, the police requisition form for his air ticket was personally authorised by police Commissioner, General Johan van der Merwe. The briefing took place at General van Rensburg's home, not at his office, presumably for security reasons. Colonel Eugene de Kock, who was on 'pseudo suspension' for the public's benefit because of earlier disclosures by Captain Dirk Coetzee about hit squad activities at Vlakplaas, was there. He was forbidden to do paper work, but had been allowed to continue with the planning of an attack in Botswana. Apparently nothing was documented at the meeting.[42]

Captain Nieuwoudt explained that the policemen under suspicion, Warrant Officer Mbalala Mgoduka, Sergeant Amos Faku, Constable Desmond Mapipa and ex-MK Askari, Xolili Sakati alias Charles Jack, had been part of the team who had murdered Matthew Goniwe and his associates. They were threatening to give details to the ANC — including the names of the white security policemen involved. Switching allegiance would seriously jeopardise his intelligence network of agents and informers. Some of his agents had already been killed or captured as a result of leaked information from the alleged turncoats. Now some of his colleagues were at risk because they were planning to plant a limpet mine on a police vehicle as a token of resistance on the Day of the Vow (now Day of Reconcilliation) on 16 December 1989.

Colonel de Kock, on the other hand, said Captain Nieuwoudt had briefed him that it was suspected that *two* security policemen and an informer had intercepted cheques posted to trade unions and other left wing organisations and deposited the money into their own accounts. There was no mention of a third policeman. Nieuwoudt said there was pressure to charge the thieves, but this roused the risk that they would blow the whistle on past violations and offences.

During the briefing there were no explicit orders to kill the men, according to Colonel de Kock. The normal practice was to use euphemisms like 'the people must go' or they 'must say goodbye'. 'In this particular case it was they "should be prevented from talking". I understood they should be killed'.

Colonel de Kock saw General van Rensburg a second time later the same day and queried the need to kill fellow policemen simply because they were involved in fraudulent activities. 'That's when he told me the Goniwe case was involved and many other similar cases. The operation was critically important'. De Kock knew the Security Police were involved in those murders. 'We realised it was an extremely high-profile matter and could be extremely damaging to the Security Police if it leaked out. I personally believed it could lead to the destruction of the Security Police.'

General van Rensburg and Captain Nieuwoudt both denied De Kock's allegations. Nieuwoudt, however, in testimony to the TRC, confirmed that police were considering charges of fraud against Warrant Officer Mgoduka and Askari Sakati for the theft of cheques totalling R76 489. The cheques had been sent from overseas to the Eastern Cape Council of Churches and intercepted by police. He repeatedly denied, however, that this was the reason for their assassination.[43]

'I was satisfied', General van Rensburg said speaking of his own version of Nieuwoudt's briefing, 'that the decision to "eliminate" them was justified. For this reason I was prepared to order De Kock to help Nieuwoudt.'

Colonel de Kock ordered Vlakplaas operatives Warrant Officer (later Major) Martinus Ras, Lionel Snyman and Snor Vermeulen to lend assistance. The plan was to kill them with a car bomb. Brigadier Waal du Toit, commanding officer of the SAP's Technical Unit in Pretoria, arranged for the production of a suitable six-kilogram explosive device.

Brigadier du Toit, Captain Nieuwoudt, Warrant Officer Ras and other security policemen rendezvoused at a farm near Port Elizabeth on 14 December 1989. They examined a white Volkswagen Jetta, registration number SAP65389M, that Captain Nieuwoudt had drawn from the Security Police motor pool. Brigadier du Toit and another officer set the device, to be detonated by an electronic remote, in the boot of the Jetta.

That evening Captain Nieuwoudt ordered that 124 Hintsa Street, Motherwell, be placed under surveillance on the grounds that he had received information indicating that a trained MK guerrilla, Mandla Maqhubela, was using it as a hideout. He contacted Sergeant Faku and Constable Mapipa at the New Brighton Police Station by radio and ordered them to conduct the surveillance. They were to take Xolili Sakati with them to identify the wanted man. He told Faku he would arrange a vehicle for the job, as the Combi the sergeant usually used had become well known as a Security Police vehicle. Sergeant Faku was to drive in the Combi to the Monument Crossroads near Motherwell in the Combi, utilising the lonely Addo Road, and wait for him there.[44]

Captain Nieuwoudt then phoned Warrant Officer Gerhardus Lotz, the son-in-law of General Nic van Rensburg, and arranged to rendezvous with him and the white Jetta at the Monument Crossroads.

At 22:45 Captain Nieuwoudt drove to the crossroads himself, picking up Warrant Officer Mgoduka from his home en route. He ordered him to take command of the surveillance team.

The three vehicles rendezvoused at 23:50. Warrant Officer Lotz saw Sergeant Faku, exchanged the Combi for the Jetta and immediately left for Port Elizabeth. Captain Nieuwoudt briefed Warrant Officer Mgoduka and his team, then watched as the unsuspecting men drove off to perform their allotted duties.

When their car had travelled 100m, Captain Nieuwoudt activated the remote. There was an ear-shattering explosion and all four men were killed. He went to the scene of the blast, ostensibly to collect evidence, but probably to kill any survivors, 'sweep' the scene and collect anything incriminating. He had ample time to suppress evidence or commit any other irregularity. If he missed the chance, though, he was given plenty of time to make good — because he was immediately appointed as the investigating officer.

Not unexpectedly, the scene of crime investigation was sloppy. The crater left by the blast was not even measured and Nieuwoudt did not bother to collect samples for forensic examination.

It was announced later that an ANC spokesman in Lusaka had claimed responsibility for the killings, but in reality the claim had originated from the Security Police, not the ANC.

At the inquest, Captain Nieuwoudt, an acknowledged explosives expert, said that when he was 'about 100m from the cross roads, an explosion occurred. I immediately turned around and rushed to the scene. I found that an explosive device had been placed under vehicle SAP65389M.' He identified it as a limpet mine, suggesting it had been attached to the Jetta's axle. Amongst the wreckage he found a VZD-3M detonator of Eastern Bloc manufacture. The four mutilated bodies were strewn around the veld. The magistrate gave a routine verdict and the incident, for the time being anyway, passed without fanfare into history.

Captain Nieuwoudt, when called to give evidence at the Goniwe inquest, was questioned about the Motherwell explosion. He conceded that the condition of the Jetta's axle and other components after the explosion indicated it was unlikely a limpet mine had been clamped to the axle. The device, whatever it was, had more likely been placed in the boot. He also agreed that its destructive force and the way the blast had distributed the bodies around the scene indicated it was probably 20 times larger than a 300g limpet mine and more than six times the size of a 900g mine. Nevertheless, Nieuwoudt maintained, explosives were unpredictable and it was often impossible to establish exactly what explosives had been used.

Advocate Mostert pointed out that both the inquest magistrate and the district surgeon had concluded the deaths had arisen from multiple injuries caused by the blast of a 'limpet mine'. This was brought up because Nieuwoudt had given misleading and incorrect evidence on no less than six occasions.

Captain Nieuwoudt agreed that neither he nor the other six explosive experts who checked the scene of the explosion had suggested the blast was caused by a device weighing six kilograms or more. Nieuwoudt admitted having misled the inquest magistrate, the district surgeon and the public and asked to be 'forgiven' for his neglect.

When asked by Judge Zietsman why he had neglected to record his opinions in affidavit form he replied: 'I can't give a reason.'

He agreed with Advocate Mostert that it was impossible to accurately target a pre-set car bomb fitted with a VZDM3M detonator — it could be detonated at any point from five minutes to eight days after setting, but it was obviously impossible to anticipate who might be in the car at a particular time. He conceded that a radio activator would have been a more practical initiator, allowing one to control exactly when and where the explosion took place. He conceded that if it had been initiated by radio, he was the only one there who could have done it. But Nieuwoudt contended that the VZD3M detonator he had found there had convinced him a radio transmitter was not used. Advocate Mostert, however, pointed out that the blast must have generated 'a massive ball of fire with temperatures reaching 3 000 degrees centigrade — more than double the heat required to melt cast iron'. Surely, he said, a light alloy detonator, which in any case showed no heat damage, could not have survived such a blast?[45]

In 1996, after extensive investigations by a dedicated police team, charges of murdering the Motherwell Four were brought against Gideon Nieuwoudt — by then a colonel — Brigadier Waal du Toit, Major Martinus Ras and two others. They pleaded not guilty in the Port Elizabeth High Court. Colonel de Kock and his subordinate Lionel Snyman turned State evidence and Nieuwoudt, Du Toit and Ras were convicted and sentenced to 20 years, 15 years and ten years respectively. The rest were acquitted.

They were granted bail pending an appeal, but immediately afterwards they applied to the TRC for amnesty together with General Nic van Rensburg, Colonel Eugene de Kock, Major Gerhard Lotz, Lieutenant-Colonel Kobus Kok, Lionel Snyman and 'Snor' Vermeulen.

Colonel de Kock's amnesty application was unnecessary, because he had been indemnified against prosecution after testifying for the State. But, he said, 'I want to put all the facts on the table . . . and expose the people who gave the actual orders. Many of those who gave the orders never had the experience of pulling the trigger. It is very easy to say to someone to pull the trigger, but to do it yourself is a very different matter.' He decided to testify when he heard the accused were denying involvement and realised this would result in their acquittal. This was reinforced by General Nic van Rensburg's successful High Court application in 1996, when the TRC was interdicted from hearing evidence implicating him in gross human rights abuses. 'It was another case of [the generals] running away. It was time for them to answer for their deeds.' [46]

13

Project Barnacle to Civil Cooperation Bureau
The External Factor
1985-1991

When Major-General Joep Joubert took over command of Special Forces from General Kat Liebenberg in November 1985, *Project Barnacle* was still operating. It was still staffed predominantly by former members of the Rhodesian Security Forces, supplemented by trained Recce operators.

Defence Force Chief, General Jannie Geldenhuys, decided the time had come to decide whether changes were required to the organisation of *Project Barnacle*. Consultations took place between the Chief of the SADF, the Chief of the Army, now General Liebenberg and General Joubert. Colonel Joe Verster, Staff Officer to the GOC Special Forces, was made responsible for the planning. When it was complete the SADF Chief submitted the plan to the Minister of Defence, General Magnus Malan, for the approval of a budget.[1]

Project Barnacle became an approved unit of Special Forces as 3-Recce, but this did not last long because of the name's obvious military connotations. For a short time after this it was known as 'the organisation'.

In his amnesty application to the TRC, Major-General Joep Joubert gave clarity to the reasons behind the changes:

> 'In the mid to late 1980s one of the major goals of national security policy and strategy was to bring the revolutionary organisation and mobilisation by the revolutionary movements, particularly the ANC, to a halt. By this time it was also clear that the ANC was not going to be stopped by normal conventional methods and that revolutionary methods would have to be used.
>
> 'As the institution for external operations, Special Forces would also have to intensify its external operations, since the necessity for unconventional and revolutionary action was already clear. It was also clear that clandestine and covert operations would have to take place internally, for which Special Forces members would be used.
>
> 'It was more or less then that the name CCB was adopted as a replacement for D40 or *Barnacle*. The revolutionary and covert nature of the plan amongst other things, involved:
>
> - That ANC leaders and people who substantially contributed to the struggle, would be eliminated.
> - That ANC facilities and support services would be destroyed.
> - Activists, sympathisers, fighters and people who supported them would also be eliminated.

His application described the CCB as a 'civilian strike force . . . which neither the government nor the SADF would acknowledge publicly'.

Commandant Charl Naudé, the *Project Barnacle* chief, continued in his post after the organisation's reformation. But as with Major Neil, his predecessor at *Barnacle*, he fell from favour and was effectively sidelined to Region 1 as Regional Manager. Colonel Joe

Verster, a more senior officer than he, superseded him as director/commander. To give himself an even deeper cover, Verster actually resigned his commission to distance himself from the SADF. In 1988 Charl Naudé responded in much the same way as Major Neil and resigned his commission. Dawid Fourie took over as Regional Manager in Region 1 with Christo Nel, the CCB's head of intelligence, handling intelligence.

In April 1986 'the organisation' became the Civil Cooperation Bureau (CCB), in Afrikaans the *Burgerlike Samewerkings Buro* (BSB). Within Special Forces it was one of four sub-projects of *Project Triplane*, but the author is uncertain what the other three were. One was probably Electronic Magnetic Logistical Component Technical Consultants and Manufacturers (Pty) Ltd (EMLC), the front company that supplied technical support to Special Forces; another was the chemical and biological warfare (CBW) capacity of *Project Coast*. As had become the practise with the SADF's intelligence arms, the CCB was registered as a proprietary limited company. For the financial years 1988/89 its budget was R22 093 000 and for 1989/90, R28 717 000.[2]

The CCB staff plan, which covered all employee benefits, and the financial plan was prepared by Raymond Pretorius of Armscor. Pierre Theron was appointed as auditor and he acted as consultant in the formulation of the plans.[3]

CCB members derived the same benefits and perks as public servants. There was a car allowance of up to R42 500 and 18c per kilometre for 'work-related' mileage, reimbursement of all out-of-pocket expenses, free medical aid, a full funeral scheme and membership of the attractive Public Service housing scheme.[4]

A policy change resulted in Major-General Joubert and his successor reporting to the Chief of the Army, Lieutenant-General Kat Liebenberg, on ANC matters. When actions were envisaged against any other enemy of the State — the PAC for instance — the orders continued to emanate from Chief of the SADF. Because of the covert nature of CCB operations and the unique position of its members, it was felt the existing Treasury Regulations were inappropriate for the organisation to function effectively. Hence special new financial procedures were drawn up and approved.[5]

The CCB was divided into nine regions, each run by a regional manager, following much the same organisation as *Operation Barnacle*. There was a tenth region, Region 6, but this was a code name referring to South Africa and until 1987 had no regional manager or staff.

The geographic boundaries of the regions were:

Region 1 — Botswana
Region 2 — Mozambique and Swaziland
Region 3 — Lesotho
Region 4 — Angola, Zambia and Tanzania
Region 5 — United Kingdom and Europe
Region 6 — South Africa
Region 7 — Zimbabwe
Region 8 — SWA/Namibia
Region 9 — This was not a geographical area, but the department responsible for supplying support for the intelligence department.
Region 10 — This was not a geographical area either, but the department responsible for providing the CCB with financial and administrative support.

Each region was supposed to have had a manager, a deputy manager and 14 other posts including secretaries, salesmen and two 'black workers', but not all of them had this staff complement. In its heyday the organisation had between 100 and 150 operators.[6]

The CCB's top structure was divided into six sections — production, production planning, security, marketing, support and specialists. Its next line of management consisted of finance, personnel, organisation and methods, training liaison and communication specialists.

'Specialists' included public relations officers, computer experts, pilots, lawyers, shipping experts, translators and printers.

'Organisation and methods' division included at least one doctor, a psychologist, an ethnologist, a social worker, scientists, electronic and mechanical engineers.

'Support' division had panel beaters, mechanics, caterers and communications staff.

Membership of the organisation's social club was compulsory and members were encouraged to join outside sports and recreation clubs — their subscriptions were reimbursed.[7]

The organisation's chain of command comprised the Chairman — the GOC Special Forces, Major-General Joep Joubert, the Managing Director, Colonel Pieter Johan (Joe) Verster, his deputy Colonel Dawid Fourie (organisation name Heiner Muller) and nine Regional Managers. The GOC Special Forces answered to the Chief of the SADF, General Jannie Geldenhuys, who answered to the Minister of Defence, General Magnus Malan.

Major-General Eddie Webb succeeded Major-General Joubert on 1 January 1989 after spending a month understudying him. He said he was given a general briefing by General Joubert, but detailed briefings relating to his command were given by the commanding officers of the various Recce regiments — presumably Dr Wouter Basson regarding *Project Coast* and probably Colonel Sybie van der Spuy regarding the EMLC. Joe Verster briefed him on the CCB. It was Major-General Webb's first experience with unconventional warfare. He came to Special Forces from the post of Commanding Officer of the Infantry School/Army Combat School at Lohatlha — there were few postings more conventional than that.

General Webb professed to having never seen a personnel organogram of the CCB, which was under his command, and he had no idea how many men were serving in the organisation. Nor was he briefed on internal operations by General Joubert, because Region 6 was only activated on the day he took over Special Forces. He maintained — though, although he also contradicted it — that General Joubert had told him that when an operation involved murder, serious injury or serious damage within South Africa he had to seek permission from higher authority. It was an eventuality that never occurred.

When asked at his TRC amnesty hearing many years later why, when talking as one general officer to another, he had not asked General Joubert: ' What are you talking about? Who is going to come and ask me to commit murder, or blow up a building, or play any other dirty trick against any individual that I have to go to higher authority for? What am I letting myself in for? Isn't that the reaction of one general to another?'

General Webb conceded that 'it should be like that'.

When pressed and asked how, when speaking general to general, he 'could leave matters of life and death in the air', he answered: 'I don't know . . . I have no explanation.' He also did not offer any examples of where he had referred such projects to higher authority.

When asked if CCB operators were subject to military discipline and to a court martial for breaches of the military code, he insisted that they were. When pressed and asked if the military code authorised soldiers to commit criminal offences, perjure themselves or employ gangsters to do their work, Webb confessed that it did not.[8]

According to Dawid Fourie, the CCB was a long-term project that required at least a ten-year period of gestation to develop an effective covert capacity. The objective was to create a global subterranean network of companies that would be legitimate businesses as well as fronts for operational intelligence. They would be headed by businessmen well integrated into their communities, who were at the same time skilled operators able to collect intelligence and act on it when this was called for.

Colonel Joe Verster confirmed the long-term aims of the CCB. He described its goal as setting up a 'first line of defence' outside South Africa. He gave as an example ships carrying weapons to South Africa's enemies, arguing that it was counter-productive to wait for the weapons to reach their destinations. It was better to develop a capacity to sink the ships before they left their home ports.

The intention was for the CCB to be fully functional by the mid 1990s. Based on the experience of other intelligence agencies, it was recognised that it would take a long time for a skilled soldier, even with help, to transform himself into a career businessman well integrated into the community. In the event the CCB's operations would be driven by circumstances, which would ultimately contribute to its downfall.[9]

The former Defence Minister, General Magnus Malan, continually denied knowledge of CCB operations, but as Judge Harms said bluntly: 'It is an objective fact that Special Forces' operations have to be approved and authorised. The Chief of the SADF [General Jannie Geldenhuys] may, in given circumstances, grant approval for the execution of operations, but if there are political and strategic implications involved, the matter must be submitted to the Minister of Defence [General Magnus Malan] for approval.' [10]

Colonel Verster said the purpose of the CCB was 'to gather special information in connection with the enemies of the State as well as to execute operations against such enemies "abroad" where no other security forces have access. Operating against such enemies means throwing their plans into confusion to the extent that these plans cannot be carried into effect or that the execution of such plans is ineffective. It also involves support to other branches of the SADF in the execution of their operations. Operation is in all spheres in which the enemy is engaged'.

In essence its tasks and responsibilities were:

a To gather specialist intelligence.
b To operate against the enemy.
c To confine its operations to the enemy abroad [which was a lie].[11]

Chairman, General Eddie Webb, who was suspended from duty in the SADF in March 1990 when the Harms Commission commenced,[12] added the following tasks and responsibilities to Verster's summary. The CCB had to:

a Infiltrate enemy networks (pipelines).
b Disseminate intelligence along the channels laid down.
c Execute specific specialist operations that could not be executed by other branches of Special Forces.

He confirmed Verster's lie that the CCB's activities were restricted to operations abroad.

Regions were structured into inner and outer circles. The inner circles comprised 'overt members' who were full-time employees of the SADF. Outer circles consisted of 'covert members' who, in theory, had no idea they were indirect employees of the SADF.

As Judge Harms put it: 'Persons with serious previous convictions (such as murder) or personality defects were employed in circumstances that point to their being engaged specifically because of, and not in spite of, their previous convictions or defects'.[13] Overt member Christo Nel confirmed this to the TRC, saying the covert members fell into three categories: those who thought they were connected with the government, but were unsure which part, those who were totally ignorant and 'international criminals . . . people who were usable for the type of work that was planned'.[14]

Cover stories, pseudonyms, lies and other stratagems were extensively used by overts when recruiting their coverts to make it difficult, preferably impossible, for recruits to identify their recruiters.

The planning of operations was the sole responsibility of overt members, but the implementation, supposedly, fell within the exclusive province of the covert members.

Security, at least in theory, was foolproof. Not only was there an alphabet soup of code names and aliases, but the overt members were to all intents and purposes civilians with no discernable military connections. Each overt member had what was called a Red Plan and a Blue Plan. The Red Plan concerned the activities and objectives of the CCB, while the Blue Plan was the cover or front behind which he operated. To achieve this, the SADF provided finance to set them up in businesses, all profits of which accrued to them, the operators. To all intents and purposes the overt members were respectable businessmen engaged in a wide range of genuine commercial pursuits. The injection of SADF capital ensured the success of their business enterprises and if they failed, there was always more money where that came from. The regions had no offices, so meeting places were chosen at random.

Overt members were a single safe step away from the military, while covert members who did the dirty work and stood the greatest risk of arrest, were two safe steps away from the military. Thus, the chance of a project being traced back to the SADF was remote. If a covert was arrested, the organisation would draw back into the shadows and make no effort to extricate him. Like the proverbial spy of popular fiction, even though a covert might not have realised he was one, he would find himself alone.

In practice, unfortunately for the system, gross security lapses were commonplace, and many coverts ended up knowing far more about the organisation than they were supposed to. The fact that many were criminals or were recruited from the seedier fringes of society, should not have implied a collective stupidity. It would be truer to say they were characterised by a collective cunning, a sense of self preservation, which prompted most to make it their business to identity their employers.

In essence, the enviously elité South African Special Forces, which until the formation of the CCB had never deviated from a strict selection process, had naïvely abandoned this criterion. They placed their trust in criminals or those treading the thin line between crime and respectability.

Each region had a Regional Manager, who liaised directly with the Managing Director and the Chairman. Below him was the Coordinator, providing the administrative link with the Managing Director. The MD's principal responsibilities concerned finance and the passing on of instructions and details relating to approved projects. Cell members took orders from both the Managing Director and the Regional Manager.

According to General Webb, no files on the CCB were maintained at Speskop, HQ of Special Forces. The organisation kept its own files to which he had access, should the need arise.

The State's enemies were identified as the SACP, the ANC, the PAC and other banned organisations, both to the left and right of the political spectrum.[15]

Region 2: Enter Leslie Lesia November 1986

Leslie Lesia, an art dealer in Bloemfontein, was under constant Security Police surveillance in the mid-1980s. This was stepped up after he attended the funeral of his brother, a MK cadre in Tanzania, in November 1986.

On his return, a man who said he was from the US Consulate, phoned to say he wanted to see him. The man, who turned out to be Ernie 'Tiger' Bekker, and a colleague named Brown, paid for his flight from Durban and met him at Jan Smuts (Johannesburg International) Airport. They opened discussions by expressing interest in investing in his art centre, but after becoming better acquainted they revealed they were working for Military Intelligence and asked who he had met on his Tanzanian trip. He needed the money so he allowed himself to be recruited. But he was unable to say later if he had, in fact, been enlisted by the CCB. His story indicates that he had been recruited as a covert member for the CCB's Region 2 — Mozambique and Swaziland. Ernie Becker and Brown were obviously the false identities of overt CCB operators, but neither has been identified. Lesia had a string of previous convictions for theft, housebreaking and dealing in drugs between 1959 and 1978. Judging by the CCB's recruiting policy, it is unlikely he would have been rejected on those grounds.

He was instructed to work undercover in Mozambique and Swaziland and ordered to eliminate ANC terrorists. To this end Bekker gave him a signet ring with a swivel top in which poison, for tipping into drinks, could be concealed. He was also handed four bottles of a yellow poison, two hypodermic syringes, detonators to booby-trap doors and an unnumbered pistol with a silencer. The poisoning materials were concealed in a hidden compartment behind the dashboard of his car and the pistol in another compartment. He did not say so, but he must also have undergone specialist training, particularly regarding the use of explosives. His general instructions were to ingratiate himself with the ANC, and when the opportunity arose, spill poison into the drinks of high-ranking officials. He might also inject them with poison.

Lesia alleged that in December 1986 he delivered a case of poisoned beer and a present for 'Big Jack' — whom he had been ordered to eliminate — to the Soviet Embassy in Gaborone, Botswana. His cover story was that it was a gift from the ANC. What the result was is unknown.

On another occasion he went with Ernie Bekker to what, he was told, was the SAP's Forensic Laboratory at Silverton. Bekker took over three cases of beer, a case of brandy and a case of vodka from a man called Jakes and gave it to Leslia. Brown briefed him that the bottles had been doctored with a colourless and odourless poison that showed no trace and took up to two weeks to take effect. He was told to donate the liquor to the ANC in Maputo.

Once in Maputo Lesia retained four beers and gave the rest to Sipho, an ANC official. He later saw another official, Gibson Ncube, drinking one of the beers. 'It gave me a shock. There was nothing I could do to him.' Soon afterwards the wife of another ANC official phoned and said Ncube had died — from what seemed like 'a paralysis'.

In June 1987 Bekker provided a television booby-trapped with explosives that was primed to detonate when a signal was transmitted on a certain frequency. He was instructed to present it to the ANC's Chief representative in Maputo. Bekker planned to detonate the charge once Lesia was safely back in South Africa.

He attended Ncube's funeral in Maputo, where ANC top notables like Albie Sachs were pointed out to him. This apparently promoted a change of heart, because instead of presenting the set to the ANC's Chief representative, he neutralised the detonating mechanism and gave it to a Mr Mhlope. From there it found its way into the hands of Frank Chilisi, a minor ANC official, who took it to Harare. There his wife, Tsitsi Chilisi, plugged it into a power point and she was killed by the resultant explosion. So much for Lesia's knowledge of explosives!

After returning to South Africa, Lesia found himself confronted by an angry Ernie Bekker, who demanded to know why he had given the television to Mhlope. He ordered him to return to Maputo and recover it. Unfortunately for Lesia, he could find neither Mhlope nor the television in Maputo. This was not the first time Lesia had been surprised by his handler knowing all about what he had done and even to whom he had spoken while on a mission. Somebody was obviously keeping tabs on him.

Days later four armed men burst into his hotel room. After searching him and his room, he was blindfolded, hustled into a car and driven to the airport. They bundled him aboard an aircraft and flew to Lusaka where the ANC detained and interrogated him extensively. They told him how the television had exploded in Harare and accused him of being responsible. Who had recruited him? When was he recruited? How was he recruited? Who was his handler? Lesia stringently denied everything, maintaining his innocence.

He was then driven to Harare and handed over to the much-feared CIO (Central Intelligence Organisation), who incarcerated him in their detention centre at Goromonzi. The centre, situated in the Goromonzi Police Camp, had been purpose-built for the interrogation of captured guerrillas during the Rhodesian War days. The cells were without windows and soundproofed.

The CIO savagely tortured him, breaking both his legs, until he eventually broke and confessed. Another unpleasant surprise was the discovery that his car had been brought to Goromonzi from Maputo. Under extreme pressure he pointed out the secret compartments and the CIO recovered his poison ring, bottles of poison, detonators, syringes, firearms, ammunition and his bankbook which detailed payments made to him. The CIO took numerous photographs showing him making the indications.

He was formally charged with murdering Tsitsi Chilisi and remanded in custody to Chikurubi Maximum Security Prison. The murder charge was dropped in October 1988, probably because the authorities found it impossible to explain his kidnap from Maputo, but he was re-detained under the Emergency Regulations.

On 26 July 1990, 12 hours before Zimbabwe's 25-year-old state of emergency lapsed, the authorities released Lesia from Chikurubi. Home Affairs Minister Moven Mahachi said they had freed him because 'we no longer have the powers to hold him.' He was the last person to be detained under Zimbabwe's Emergency Regulations.

They deported him and he was flown to South Africa in a light aircraft, probably one belonging to Military Intelligence or the CCB. He spent four months in 1-Military Hospital, Pretoria, recovering from his ordeal.[16]

Like many other CCB operators, Leslie Lesia was soon engaged in suing the SADF for loss of income and suffering while detained in Zimbabwe.[17]

Proposal to eliminate the ANC's Ronnie Kasrils and Pallo Jordan: 1986

Trevor Floyd's area of operation was Region 5 — the United Kingdom and Europe. His code name was Richard Chalmers and his Blue Plan cover was based around a company he established on the Isle of Man. For most of the CCB's lifespan he was the only operator based permanently in Region 5, although other agents moved through in transit. The region was later expanded but it never had more than four agents.

After Major Neil's resignation from *Project Barnacle*, Floyd received all orders relating to eliminations and disposals directly from Major-General Kat Liebenberg. This continued until Liebenberg was transferred and replaced by Major-General Joep Joubert in 1985. The only time he took orders from Major Neil's successor, Charl Naudé, was when he commanded a major raid, coded *Operation Lebanta*, which was launched against ANC facilities in Maseru in December 1982 and another raid into Botswana that followed. (See Chapter 25 The Silent War by Peter Stiff)

In 1986 Colonel Joe Verster ordered him to eliminate top ANC and SACP officials, Ronnie Kasrils and Pallo Jordan, in London. Using a false passport in his code name of Richard Chalmers, he travelled to London on a reconnaissance and returned with a British-made umbrella. He had decided the best way to go about it was to stab at the targets with a poison-tipped umbrella in the same way as Soviet agents had killed the Bulgarian dissident George Markov in London some years earlier.

Floyd explained his idea and gave Joe Verster the umbrella for adaptation.

Mr Q, who ran EMLC's 'James Bond' mechanical and electronics workshop, was called to General Liebenberg's office and told to take a few weeks leave to work on a special project at home. Dr Wouter Basson would visit him and tell him what was required. Basson called at his house two or three times to check on progress and give him guidelines. The final result was a walking stick that could fire a polyurethane pellet about three to four millimetres in diameter. It had a hollow core to accommodate a liquid or powder. Mr Q assumed it would be used to shoot someone.

Meanwhile, Jan Lourens, the only bio-engineer with the Special Forces' medical unit, who for 18 months had been the project manager for the construction of the Delta G Scientific facility in Pretoria, suggested to Dr Phillip Mijburgh that the defensive chemical arm of Delta G be separated and placed in another facility. This was agreed and using funding arranged by Dr Basson, Lourens set up System Research Developments (SRD) in a building in Strydom Park, Randburg.

Dr Basson invited Mr Q to join SRD, explaining that it would be similar to EMLC but separate. Defensive chemical work concentrated on filters and detection apparatus while the SRD Electronics division worked on surveillance equipment and debugging devices. A mechanical workshop was established and Mr Q was placed in charge. He shared the building's basement with QB Laboratory which supplied tear gas canisters to the police. Jan Lourens told Mr Q to draw up a list of machinery and equipment he needed and gave him a cheque to pay for it. Dr Basson and the SAP Forensic Scientist, General Lothar Neethling, also recruited other staff for SRD.

Mr Q's work revolved around the production of silencers, special ammunition and magazines, and the modification of weapons and timing mechanisms. He also modified cars used by Special Forces personnel, mostly fitting them with more powerful engines and enlarged petrol tanks. Another aspect of his work was modifying weapons, by, for example, fitting them with folding butts.

Based on his experience with the walking stick, Mr Q turned his hand to making special applicators. Screwdrivers followed the walking stick. The hollow handle contained a spring loaded plunger that allowed liquid to be sucked up through a small hole at the tip of the blade. The liquid was released by impact when it was jabbed into someone. There were screwdrivers fitted with surgical hypodermic needles, a combination spoon and knife, a folding knife and spoon and a shootable switch blade powered by a blank cartridge that fitted into a cigarette box together with a small amount of toxin. Another deadly device was set into a bicycle pump. Some were activated by an explosive charge.

An evaluation report prepared by Dr James Davies noted that although detonations in a particular device were audible, they would probably be obscured by street noises. It also said that Clostridium and the rabies virus could be used in the applicators. The effectiveness of devices was tested on the rumps of pig carcases.

QB laboratories produced a pen that shot polycarbonate micro balls that were virtually impossible to detect on an autopsy or by security X-Ray machines. Mr Q even designed a trigger for a letter bomb. Leslie Lesia's signet ring, with its secret compartment for poison and unique locking device, was his handiwork too.

Orders for special applicators were passed to Mr Q personally either by Wouter Basson or Jan Lourens, who would also personally collect the finished products. Sometimes Lourens would pass them on to Dr Immelman or Dr Davies at Roodeplaat Research Laboratories for evaluation. Occasionally new designs were returned for modification.

One day Basson handed him an umbrella and requested he fit it with a poison-tip. It would be the only one he would ever make. When complete, Basson told him he wanted to test it at the Roodeplaat Research Laboratories and they drove there together in Basson's car . When they got there, however, Mr Q suddenly realised that he had left the cocking mechanism at his laboratory. Basson became 'quite upset' as the full test could not be done and he had to satisfy himself with testing the substance on a baboon.

Basson instructed Lourens to go to London, meet Floyd and hand over the applicator. He was vague about how the umbrella got itself to England but the implication was that it was dismantled and taken in pieces. Some sections might have been mailed. Maybe they were sent ahead by diplomatic bag. Lourens was handed two glass ampules of colourless watery liquid by Mijburgh. He wrapped them in tissue paper, sealed them in plastic bags and packed those in a toiletry bag which he carried in his hand luggage.

He duly flew to London, met Floyd on a tube station and took him to Warfield Cottage at Ascot. The cottage had been purchased by Dr Wouter Basson and was frequently used by both him and Lourens for holiday purposes and as accommodation during 'business' trips. Lourens handed over the umbrella and the ancillary equipment. A 15cm long false tip had been made for screwing onto the umbrella. Concealed inside was a spring-loaded plastic syringe with a pad of micro needles. The idea was that when the umbrella was jabbed into a target, the needles would penetrate the skin simultaneously and inject the toxin. Floyd believed it had been adapted from the standard SADF issue antidote kit used in case of a chemical attack. He understood the toxin had been supplied by Dr Basson, although Mijburgh was actually the culprit.

Lourens demonstrated how to fit the glass poison vial and the syringe into the false umbrella tip. While doing so he accidentally got some poison on his finger and without thinking licked it.

'He [Lourens] got the fright of his life', Floyd said.

When Lourens got the bitter taste he realised what he had done. He could remember little about what happened next, but his vision became impaired and he began to shiver uncontrollably. For a brief spell he lost consciousness.

Floyd felt completely helpless. He was in a strange environment and did not even know the location of the nearest hospital. Besides, even if he located one, how could he explain the accident to a doctor in a casualty department. He suggested to Lourens that he drink some milk in the hope that it would neutralise the poison. Lourens followed the suggestion and also drank some Dettol antiseptic he found in the bathroom. He then went to lie down.

In the event, he suffered no lasting ill effects and a couple of hours later he had a beer and ate some hot chips. Apparently the poison had to be injected to be effective and so as Lourens had no open cuts or sores in the area of his mouth, he was okay. Nevertheless, it was a lucky escape.

Lourens later discovered that the poison was Silatrane. It had either been synthesised locally or imported. The symptoms of Silatrane poisoning matched precisely what had happened to him.

When he had recovered from the shock of it all, he drove Floyd to the station, then he caught a train back to London.

The umbrella turned out to be a less than ideal weapon. With the false tip fitted, it was too long to hold comfortably while walking and Floyd remained constantly aware that accidental contact between the tip and the pavement might cause a premature release of the toxin. He had nowhere to store the tip, so he bought a curling tong in a case which had a convenient slot where it fitted.

A team of 'covert' Portuguese operators had been recruited to carry out the actual assassinations. Floyd met them, briefed them on the mission and demonstrated how to use the poison-tipped umbrella. He kept them under surveillance 'just in case they shirked their duty'.

In the end they were unable to carry out the mission. Pallo Jordan had changed his address and Ronnie Kasrils 'never seemed to be at home'. Floyd aborted the mission and disposed of the umbrella and toxin by throwing them into the River Thames.[18]

Lourens said that he and Basson had discussed the special applicators manufactured by SRD on several occasions, the last time was on a train in Britain. Lourens was wrestling with his conscience over the morality of his work and expressed this concern to Basson.

'Sort it out with your God . . . I have', Basson told him.

Their relationship soured in 1988 when Lourens returned home from SWA/Namibia unexpectedly early and found Basson's car parked in the driveway of his house. He suspected that Basson and his wife were having an affair. Although he could not prove it, the incident led to his divorcing her. He quit SRD and moved as Managing Director to another *Project Coast* front company, Protechnik. In January 1993, still wrestling with his conscience over non-defensive projects, Lourens sought an interview with Lieutenant-General Dr Niel Knobel, the Surgeon General, South African Medical Service, and the officer in overall charge of *Project Coast*.

Knobel told him he knew nothing about applicators and he did not want to know. Lourens, however, insisted on handing him a computer disc and a document giving full details of the applicators he had made.

He had also discussed his moral qualms with Dr Phillip Mijburgh and other colleagues, but without finding answers. He had increasingly come to realise that the threat of an imminent chemical attack against South Africa that had existed at the commencement of

Project Coast had completely receded. He was no longer deriving satisfaction from his work and his relationship with Basson was tense. He had also become increasingly concerned about the flamboyant lifestyles of the project leaders, which he believed was not in keeping with their positions.

While visiting Taiwan in connection with the proposed sale of defensive technology in March 1993, he decided to resign and did so immediately after his return to South Africa. He offered Protechnik Chairman, Charles van Remoortrere, six months notice, but was told to clear his desk and get out within 24 hours. On leaving, he took a few of the 'screwdrivers' with him and hid them in case he needed them later as evidence. A few days later Van Remoortrere called him and accused him of expropriating company funds. There was indeed a discrepancy, but it had arisen from non-defensive projects that Van Remoortrere knew nothing about.

Two months later Lourens sought an interview with the then Defence Minister, Roelf Meyer, to brief him about the unorthodox projects. Meyer refused to see him and directed him back to General Knobel who also declined to see him. He was referred to General Kat Liebenberg. They arranged a meeting one evening, but General Liebenberg too told him there was nothing to discuss. As far as he was concerned the matter was closed. 'But those are my toys . . . and I want them back', Liebenberg threatened.

He did not get his toys. Lourens eventually handed them to the special investigation team formulating criminal cases against Dr Wouter Basson.

Plan to assassinate Oliver Tambo

After cutting contact with *Barnacle*, Brian remained in contact with Team Juliet and also with Kevin Woods for business reasons. He started a lucrative business of exporting motor car spares to Zimbabwe, legal in South Africa, but not in Zimbabwe. He was paid in Zimbabwe dollars, which he converted into hard currency on the black market, realising a good profit.

One person he was doing business with was Rory Maguire, owner of Mactech Garage, Bulawayo. Kevin Wood had introduced him to Brian at the Sandton Holiday Inn during a Johannesburg visit.

During the course of their business dealings, Brian became uncomfortably aware that Rory knew far more than he should about intelligence operations in Zimbabwe. Someone involved was being less than discreet. In addition, Kevin was engaging in risky business deals. This posed no risk to Brian, who was no longer involved and did not even go to Zimbabwe, but it was dangerous for Kevin.

Other hazardous practices came to his notice. In the Rhodesian Special Branch world, where he had cut his security teeth, sources were inviolate. For safety's sake the only person who knew the identity of a source was the handler.

In Military Intelligence, however, they did things differently. He learned that certain senior officers had demanded details of sources and insisted they meet them in Zimbabwe, Botswana or elsewhere. Brian had always resisted such demands, but those who came after him, had not been so firm. Brian had heard that all types of military 'funnies' had been to Zimbabwe to meet Team Juliet after he resigned, including Colonel Joe Verster's second in command, Dawid Fourie. Team Juliet trusted Brian and they enquired from him if he was 'all right'.

Brian sought out Alan, a Team Juliet member, and warned him: 'This guy Rory Maguire is wheeling and dealing. Kevin is also getting involved and so is Kit. They are taking unnecessary risks. It is business. I can do it because I'm here and not there. I don't trust Rory. I'm doing business with him, but I don't trust him. He is very much involved with these guys and seems to know exactly what they are doing. Is he working for you?'

Rory, Allan said, was supplying fuel and motor spares to the teams on an as required basis and was being reimbursed in South African rands at a very favourable rate, but he was not a source.[19]

Guy Bawden, who had been quietly enrolled into Juliet by Kit Bawden without permission shortly before Brian left *Barnacle*, lived in Virginia Close, Borrowdale, Harare. He had established a truck rebuilding business in Harare and also held an interest in the family ranch at Fort Rixon.

Kit and Guy, on Pretoria's instructions, made plans to assassinate the ANC leader, Oliver Tambo, when he visited Hero's Acre, a portion of the Warren Hills Cemetery in Harare. Hero's Acre had been set aside, officially to commemorate the dead on all sides in the Rhodesian War, but in reality it commemorated only the 'heroes of the revolution' — Robert Mugabe's ZANU-PF 'martyrs'.

The plan, authorised in terms of *Operation Mixer* or a succeeding operation, called for a huge explosive charge to be detonated on the side of the Harare-Bulawayo road as Tambo passed by on his way to the cemetery. The operation was called off for unspecified reasons.[20]

Region 2: Sergeant-Major Dave Tippett, KIA: June 1987

On 17 June 1987 Sergeant Dave Tippett, operating under his organisation *nom de guerre* of David Horne and posing as a businessman, went to the Namaacha Border Gate between Swaziland and Mozambique to meet certain agents or informers.

It was possible at the time to enter the no-mans-land between the two countries and conduct meetings with people from across the border without going through passport control.

It is uncertain what happened, but whoever met him shot him in the head with a Tokarev pistol fired at close range and downed him. His assailants tried to drag him across the border into Moçambque but the Swaziland Police intervened and fired shots and they ran back across the border.

He was flown to Pretoria and was still alive when admitted to the Eugene Marais Hospital in Pretoria. Regrettably the bullet had fragmented considerably and had caused massive brain damage. He died three days after the shooting on 20 June.

He was the only CCB operator ever killed in action.[21]

Attempted assassination of Jeremy Brickhill: Zimbabwe 13 Oct 1987

Team Juliet was ordered to assassinate Jeremy Brickhill. Bulawayo-born Brickhill had fought with ZIPRA during the Rhodesian Bush War. He worked as Dumiso Dabengwa's assistant in ZAPU's Lusaka-based Department of Analysis and Research. This very effective organisation was responsible for the analysis of operations conducted by both ZIPRA and the Rhodesian security forces and the ongoing provision of intelligence reports relating to Rhodesia's Security Forces, lines of communication and so on, for ZIPRA's Military High Command.

They analysed newspaper reports, magazines and books published in Rhodesia, South Africa and elsewhere. They were also responsible for organising assistance from foreign sympathisers. They established and maintained regular liaison with the ANC and MK — their brothers-in arms, the Soviet missions in Zambia, Defence and Aid, the World Council of Churches, the Palestine Liberation Organisation and a rag-bag of Soviet-backed terror organisations.[22]

With the expert help of the Soviets and other communist surrogates, they invariably beat the Rhodesians on the propaganda front, although their victories on the battlefield were sparse.

When the war ended it is believed Brickhill assisted with the establishment of the Harare offices of Aeroflot, the Soviet Union's state airline.[23]

In *The Hidden Hand*, a television documentary he wrote and presented for Britain's Channel 4 in 1991, he modestly played down his role in the Bush War, saying merely that he had 'allied himself to the cause of majority rule'. Of the war's closing years when he was with ZIPRA in Zambia he said: 'I was a schoolboy when all this [certain events in 1977] was happening'. By his own account he was ten at UDI time in 1965. By 1977 he was 22, so he must have been a mature schoolboy.

His subsequent activities are unknown, but according to him he had been 'involved in Zimbabwean nationalist movements for a long time and as a writer and journalist I have written extensively on politics in the region — including South Africa. I have also supported the South African liberation movements, which is why the South Africans came after me.' He has also been described as a 'veteran anti-apartheid activist'.[24]

South African Intelligence believed his support for the ANC went far beyond mere lip service. Their information was that he had been involved in the bomb blast outside the SAAF's HQ in Pretoria in May 1983. Whether they believed he had been an active participant or whether they thought he was involved only in the planning is unclear. Brickhill, in any case, maintained he had been in Harare when the bomb exploded. South African Intelligence was not always accurate. For instance they noted his wife down as a Russian, whereas she was a Durban girl!

Whatever the truth regarding his involvement in the Pretoria bomb blast — and most intelligence officers interviewed by the author believed he had nothing to do with it — the CCB decided Brickhill had to go.

Two members of Juliet were involved. Kit Bawden travelled from South Africa by car, smuggling in three bombs through the Beit Bridge customs post. In Harare he stayed with Guy.

Guy was provided with money to buy a car and he helped Kit turn it into a car bomb and wire it for command detonation. The device was boosted with commercial gelignite. Much of it had probably been obtained locally and was old stock. Afterwards Kit told Guy to get rid of the stuff that was left because 'it was probably weeping'.[25] Gelignite, when kept for a long time, starts sweating small and highly volatile beads of nitro-glycerine.

They conducted various reconnaissances of the target's home, where Kit intended detonating the bomb. Guy, however, was against this, because it was close to a crèche and the blast could have injured many children. Abandoning this plan they began checking Brickhill's daily movements. Were they erratic or was he a creature of habit? In one aspect, they found, he was certainly a creature of habit. Every day he visited a restaurant for early morning coffee in the Avondale Shopping Centre.

Their plan was simple. On the morning of the hit they would wait for Brickhill to arrive at the shopping centre. When he had parked his car and entered the restaurant, they would pull the mobile bomb in next to his and await his return from a safe distance. When he was back in the driver's seat, they would command-detonate the charge. The SADF had offered a reward of R70 000 for Brickhill's head.[26]

On 13 October 1987, as planned, Jeremy Brickhill got into his car and the bomb was detonated. Brickhill survived the explosion but sustained ghastly injuries. His stomach and groin were ripped open and his spleen and diaphragm ruptured. His left leg and hip were smashed, his eardrums perforated and his body peppered with shrapnel. He was left permanently disabled and disfigured. Three years later he was still receiving treatment for his injuries in London.

Eighteen others were injured in the blast.

No one got the R70 000.[27]

Assassination of Dulcie September: 29 March 1988

The tempo to assassinate the ANC's top 50 leaders gained momentum in 1988. Cassius Make, an official of the ANC's National Executive and a senior member of MK, was assassinated early in the year after he disembarked from an aircraft at Swaziland's Matsapa Airport. He was the most senior ANC member to go since Joe Nquabi. Both Alfred Nzo, the ANC's Secretary-General and Thomas Nkobi, the Treasurer General, escaped assassination attempts.

There was another attempt when Albie Sachs, a leading academic and senior ANC member, was blown up by a car bomb in Maputo on 7 April 1988. He had been detained in South Africa under the 90-day law and had left the country in 1966 to lecture in law at Southampton University. He was employed in Mozambique's Ministry of Justice and had played a leading role in the ANC's legal section. Sachs survived the blast, but lost his right arm.[28] He is now a judge with South Africa's Constitutional Court. The TRC suggested that Indres Naidoo, the ANC's diplomatic representative in Maputo, had been the target of this attempt. Sachs had borrowed Naidoo's car in which the bomb had been planted. Nevertheless, Sachs was a high profile ANC member, so the operation was regarded as successful. The operative who placed the bomb was paid R4 000.[29]

On 2 February 1988 two shots were fired through the office window of Godfrey Motsepe in Brussels. Motsepe was the ANC's diplomatic representative for the BENELUX countries. The shots missed. On 27 March 1988 a 17kg explosive device was disarmed in his office before it could explode.[30]

Dulcie September (45), based in Paris, was the ANC's representative for France and Switzerland. On the morning of 29 March 1988, only two days after Godfrey Matsepe's bomb, her body was discovered at the entrance to her dilapidated fourth floor apartment, which also served as the ANC's office, in the Rue des Petites Ecuries near the Gare du Nord.

Press reports indicated that the gunman, apparently working alone, surprised Miss September as she opened her door. He shot her five times in the head using a silenced pistol. When they found her body the key was still in the lock and her mail was clutched in her hand. No one in the vicinity heard shots.[31]

Various groups, including a delegation representing French President Mitterrand and his Socialist Party, cancelled attendance at the funeral at the last minute because they objected to the way France's *Parti Communiste* had taken control of the event and the vigil arrangements, even to the extent of providing their own security officers.

10 000 anti-apartheid campaigners joined the ANC's entire executive committee, including Oliver Tambo and Joe Slovo, at her grave side in the historic Pere Lachaise cemetery.[32]

Dulcie September was a former teacher from Cape Town. She became a member of the National Liberation Front, an ANC front organisation, and with others was convicted of treason and sabotage by the Cape Supreme Court in 1964 and sentenced to five years imprisonment. She was released in 1969 and placed under house arrest, but left South Africa on an exit visa in 1972.[33]

Foreign Minister Pik Botha said the South African government could not be held responsible for her death. 'While details about the assassination are not yet known, the South African government must bring attention to the fact that serious quarrels arise within the ranks of organisations who employ violence in order to achieve political aims.'

French Security Minister Robert Pandraud unsympathetically described the murder as a 'settling of account between terrorists'. The respected investigative magazine, *Actuel*, said the assassination had been carried out by South Africa's Military Intelligence Directorate, under the overall command of General van der Westhuizen in Pretoria. It had been set up, it said, by a French mercenary, Captain J Dessales, then serving in the Comoros with Colonel Bob Denard.

South African born musician Martin van Geems, who left South Africa in 1984 to evade the draft, was arrested by the French 'political police' and briefly held until he was cleared of involvement and released.[34]

A 'top Western intelligence source' suggested the murder was the work of a group of highly trained hit-men — known as a Z-Squad — working for South Africa's National Intelligence Service.

The Netherlands Institute for Southern Africa, an amalgamation of three former anti-apartheid bodies, submitted a 16-page report to the TRC. It detailed an alleged assassination plot, convoluted like the plot of a novel and linked to back-door arms deals between France and South Africa which, South Africa feared, September was in a position to thwart. It named Dirk Stoffberg, an arms dealer and alleged South African agent who headed 'Z-Squad Incorporated', an organisation created by BOSS and perfected by the NIS. It was apparently staffed by 'highly-trained hit-men with a virtually unlimited range of action and operational funds'. It said that Stoffberg, who arrived in France two days before the assassination, gave the nod for September to be killed. 'He said he paid two former members of the French Foreign Legion to kill her' . . . 'Stoffberg said he had no idea why she was to be assassinated . . . he activated these two hit-men through the Adler Group.' It also suggested Stoffberg had been asked to facilitate the assassination by the South African Security Police.

The Institute said that just before her death, September 'phoned Aziz Pahad [ANC], asking him to come to Paris for a very sensitive matter'. Pahad thought Dulcie had stumbled on some sort of nuclear secret. September also said she feared for her life.

'Although there have been suggestions that members of the French secret service were directly involved in the murder of September, Glaser [a French investigator] doesn't think that the French themselves planned or executed this murder.' They believed the French only created space 'for South African agents to eliminate DS [September]'.

The report also pointed a finger at the CCB, suggesting the hit had been 'directed' by Eeben Barlow, head of the CCB in Europe. It appears the Netherlands Institute had many ideas but little evidence and were intent on covering every possible option. In reality, it is highly unlikely that the operation was conducted by a combination of four organisa-tions, the NIS, military intelligence, the Security Police and the CCB.

The author's information, on the other hand, suggests the assassination was carried out by a captain in Special Forces seconded in the normal way to the CCB. Posing as an ANC sympathiser he spent several months 'getting close' to Dulcie September, gaining her trust and friendship. What this meant in real terms is unknown. He waited for the word from Pretoria, then struck.

On the morning of 29 March 1988 he accompanied her to the fourth floor of the building, then shot her five times in the head as she inserted the key in the lock. She was taken by surprise and did not stand a chance.

Where had she come from? Her office also served as her residence, so she was probably returning home after spending the night elsewhere, probably with the assassin. If he had got close enough to become her lover, it should astonish nobody that she was taken by surprise.

The suggestion by the Netherlands Institute that she was targeted because she had stumbled on important information relating to French/South African military links does not stand up to examination. Such links had existed openly for many years and had long been the focus of the anti-apartheid lobby. The most likely motivation for the hit, other than the original intentions of *Operation Mixer,* was that it was meant as a signal to the ANC that wherever their officials might be, there was no safe place to hide.

The socialist mayor of Vitrolles, near Marseilles, named a street, *Rue Dulcie September*, in her honour, but this and another street named after former Chilean president Salvador Allende were abruptly changed when a National Front candidate took office as mayor in 1997. This probably prompted the renaming of a Paris square as *Place Dulcie September* and a major memorial service in the town of Arcueil on the tenth anniversary of her death.[35]

Operation Crawler: 'fishing' vessel Margit Rye

It was common and frustrating knowledge in South African security circles that the Soviet KGB possessed a large number of small ships, often fishing vessels or coasters, that operated continually on intelligence gathering missions. They were capable of going anywhere in the world, entering harbours without arousing suspicions, dropping and picking up agents, carrying arms and supplies for surrogates, conducting communication surveillance, and the like.

Soviet techniques in this regard were well known and were often the subject of discussions and lectures.

In late 1987 or early 1988 it occurred to the SADF that they could operate in exactly the same way as the Soviets if they found themselves a suitable vessel. It would be particularly useful on the African east coast in support of RENAMO.

A suitable fishing vessel, the *Margit Rye*, was located in Denmark. It was the property of Roger Gunnar Nielson of Esjberg. The *Margit Rye* Shipping Company was formed in Malta as a front with CCB overt agent, Andre Wilhelmus Groenewald, organisation name Kobus Pienaar, as the owner and Managing Director. His address on the company documents was shown as P O Box 1658, Maputo. Although everything was registered in his name, it was made clear to Groenewald that the assets remained the property of the SADF. To cover the eventuality of Groenewald leaving the CCB, he signed undated change of ownership/directorship papers and handed them to the CCB.

The sensitive negotiations to acquire the ship were channelled through legitimate business and South African government organisations abroad. One of several agents used was a man of considerable influence, Knud Enggaard, the then Danish Minister of the Interior and later Minister of Defence.

Eventually, R2,5 million was forwarded to Groenewald for the purchase and the deal went through in February 1988. A further R250 000 to cover general expenses was made available to him and he was instructed to open various bank accounts in Europe and deposit the money.

Raid that went wrong: Botswana 20 June 1988

Johannes Basson, formerly a Recce operator, had worked undercover for four years, first for *Project Barnacle* and then for the CCB. In 1988 his area of responsibility was Region 1—Botswana. His cover was import/export and he 'worked' for a Military Intelligence front company, Essem Import and Export. Most of his friends thought he was unemployed and he lived as a civilian in Lebombo Street, Claremont.

On Wednesday 16 June 1988 his superior, a Mr Rowe, briefed him on a mission. He would drive to Botswana on Sunday 19 June, in a vehicle supplied by Military Intelligence and rendezvous with another operator, Theo Hermensen, who would be in charge of the operation.

On the night of Monday 20 June they would rendezvous with and pick up an assault group of five fully armed and equipped Recce operators who had covertly crossed the border from South Africa on foot. Using two cars they would transport them to a drop-off point near Kgale Mission, six kilometres south of Gaborone and west of the Gaborone Dam.

The assault group would make their own way into Gaborone and 'capture or kill' an ANC official called 'Oupa' who lived in the Borakanelo area of central Gaborone. Later, it is presumed, they would rendezvous with Basson and Hermensen who would get them back to the border.

Basson was using a false South African passport in the *nom de guerre* of H J Smit, the name he always travelled under.

Theo Hermensen shared a house in Cyrildene, Johannesburg, with Paul Kemp whom he had met in a Hillbrow pub. To Kemp he was an 'ordinary guy' who had asked to share his house because he 'went to Botswana on business and was only home one or two weeks a month . . . As far as I know he did national service in Durban and had a slack time — never went to the front — and he certainly has not done camps since I've known him.'

On the surface he was a sales representative for a Germiston company, Interstate Traders and Representatives. This was linked to a Botswana company, Intercontinental Traders, which dealt in brick-making machinery.[36] Like Essem Import and Export, Interstate Traders and Representatives was also a Military Intelligence front. The telephone numbers for both fronts were handled by answering services.

Hermensen travelled on a false South African passport under his organisation name of Dirk van Niekerk.

On 19 June Johannes Basson crossed the border into Botswana.

Theo Hermensen, meanwhile, contacted a friend, Barry Viviers, who managed a Spar supermarket in Broadhurst, Gaborone, and told him he was coming. Botswana-born Viviers had lived most of his life in South Africa, but had recently moved back to his country of birth. It remains a matter for conjecture as to how much he knew about Hermensen's covert activities.

Hermensen and Basson rendezvoused in Lobatsi as planned, then picked up the five-man Recce team at the arranged point. There were two white and three black operators whom they knew as Phil, Willie, Teffo, Kas and John.

After stowing their kit and equipment in the vehicles they drove to the Kgale Mission, a Roman Catholic girls' school, where they dropped the team off close to a railway line. As they pulled away a police Toyota Land-Cruiser, crewed by a sergeant and six constables, approached from the opposite direction.

Constable Morutwa's attention was drawn to the vehicles because both ignored the stop sign at the rail crossing. He saw they had South African registrations and noted the number of one as MMF195T.

The police vehicle stopped where the Recce team had taken cover in the bushes. Coincidentally the sergeant intended dropping off three of his men there, so they could perform a routine foot patrol on the road back to Gaborone.

The Recces, however, mistakenly believed they had stopped to look for them — that the operation had been blown. They took the initiative and opened fire. Constable Mlhabano took ten rounds in his body and was seriously, almost fatally, wounded. Constable Morutwa who was shot in the thigh was manhandled from the truck and thrown in the road. A third policeman was also wounded.

The operators took over the police vehicle, drove straight to the border and escaped on foot into South Africa. When the police recovered the vehicle it was riddled with 24 bullet holes.

When word of the shooting got back to the police control room, they reported it to the BDF which alerted all their patrols and roadblocks. Hermensen and Basson were stopped at one and arrested. There is little doubt that the policemen, incensed at the shooting of their colleagues, beat them up badly.

At 06:00 on the morning of Tuesday 21 June an explosive device destroyed a vehicle and damaged a house belonging to Allison Seeketso, a Gaborone building contractor. The windows of nearby houses were also shattered. This raised understandable suspicions that this was the raiders' target, but the police failed to prove a connection.

The SADF issued a statement saying: 'A patrol, which was gathering information in Botswana near the South African border, was involved in a shooting incident with the Botswana Police early this morning.

'The Botswana Police fired on the patrol, which was forced to return their fire. In this process members of the Botswana Police were wounded.'

The statement added that Hermensen and Basson were not involved in the shooting.

Botswana Police Commissioner Simon Hirschfeld denounced this as a lie, saying his policemen were unarmed as was the normal practice when conducting routine patrols. He also pointed out that all seven South Africans involved, including Hermensen and Basson, had been wearing civilian clothes. A priest, Father Arthur of St Joseph's College at Kgale, who aided the wounded men after the shooting, confirmed that they were unarmed.

On 27 June the Botswana Police arrested Barry Viviers under the Arms and Ammunition Act for the unlawful possession of a grenade and for having been in contact with Hermensen before the Recce incursion. He protested that the grenade was harmless and purely ornamental, but was still remanded in custody pending a report by BDF experts.

Barry Viviers (29), Olaf Iva Bergh (33) and his wife Elizabeth Gertruida Bergh appeared in the High Court on 7 September and pleaded not guilty to high treason in connection with the SADF incursion. Olaf Bergh faced a second charge of illegally possessing ammunition to which he pleaded guilty.

Barry Viviers' case concerned the concealment of information relating to the abortive raid and communicating with Theo Hermensen.

The Berghs were accused of hiding a SADF uniform, cameras, a kitbag and a set of SADF 'dog tags'. Mrs Bergh was alleged to have burned the uniform after Basson and Hermensen were arrested.

During the trial Major Toteng Lesedie of the Botswana Defence Force testified that the military equipment produced before the court belonged to a foreign army but he did not know which one. With a certain quaintness, he described the dog-tags as a 'necklace . . . commonly used by soldiers for identification purposes in the event of the soldier dying or being killed in action'.

On the 11 October Viviers was convicted and sentenced to 18 months imprisonment, Elizabeth Bergh to a suspended sentence of two years imprisonment and Olaf Bergh to a 200 pula fine for possessing ammunition of war.

Yvonne Viviers, Barry Viviers' mother, insisted a bizarre set of coincidences had landed them in trouble. Barry, she said, had let Hermensen stay in his flat for a few weeks after meeting him at a disco. He then disappeared and the next Barry heard was that he had been arrested.

Barry was questioned, then arrested after police searched his flat and found an old grenade that had been rendered harmless and used as an ornament.

Elizabeth Bergh, a friend of Barry, concerned he might get into more trouble, burned part of the SADF uniform that he kept for compulsory Citizen Force service, then hid the rest of it at her husband's firm. Her domestic servant, however, reported the matter to the police and she was arrested with her husband. They were both charged with treason.

On 20 September the Botswana Police arrested Duncan Morotsi, a Botswana national who was the attorney representing Johannes Basson and Theo Hermensen. They alleged he had been found in possession of undisclosed 'undesirable items' that linked him to a plan to spring the South Africans from prison before their trial began on 26 September 1988. On 22 September Duncan Morotsi and a South African, Johannes Muza Zitha, were remanded without bail on a charge of treason arising from the plot.

The charge sheet alleged the accused had, on different days between 15 and 19 September 1988, with intent to commit treason, failed to give information to the President or to a police officer. A third plotter, 'Dudley' of Johannesburg, who was not before the court, was also named.

The State did not allege it, probably because they could not prove it at the time, but Johannes Zitha was a Recce operator. They merely contended he was an SADF agent. Zitha was convicted and imprisoned. The fate of Morotsi is unknown.

Theo Hermensen, Johannes Basson and Barry Viviers appeared in the High Court in Francistown on 12 October. Troops with machine guns and rifles ringed the tiny courthouse, while scores of policemen and prison guards took up positions within the packed courtroom. Two trucks each with ten heavily armed soldiers, established a block on the road leading to the courthouse. Only pedestrians were allowed to pass.

Hermensen and Basson were charged firstly with acting in concert with others not arrested and attempting to murder or cause the death of, or cause grievous bodily harm to, three Botswana Police constables. They were also charged under the National Security Act with committing acts 'prejudicial to the safety or interests of Botswana' and with one count of the unauthorised use of a government motor vehicle. Hermensen was also charged with making, or conniving to make, a false statement after entering Botswana using a false name. The more serious charges carried the possibility of life sentences.

Viviers was charged with one count of contravening the National Security Act for permitting Hermensen to 'meet' at his residence. The judge dismissed the charge on the grounds that the indictment made no sense and failed to disclose an offence.

On 8 December both Hermensen and Basson were found guilty of causing grievous bodily harm to the three policemen and sentenced to ten years imprisonment and eight strokes of a cane. The prison sentences were confirmed on appeal in July 1989, but the sentences of caning were set aside.

On 8 December 1991, three years after Hermensen and Basson had been sentenced, an SADF spokesman announced that the Botswana authorities had freed Hermensen, Basson and Zitha. He confirmed they had been captured during an 'authorised' cross-border operation, 'but in the interests of their own safety and that of their families', he declined to release any further details. He said all three were still members of the SADF and would be treated as such. The statement confirmed that Johannes Zitha had been involved in an abortive rescue operation.

Their release apparently resulted from a deal struck between the South African and Botswana governments.[37] No mention was made of Duncan Morotsi, and it is not known whether he was also freed.[38]

Formation of Executive Outcomes: 1989

During 1989 Eeben Barlow, formerly of 32-Battalion and by then a member of the CCB, together with a nucleus of CCB and other Special Forces operators, formed Executive Outcomes which was destined to become the world's largest and most sophisticated private army.

There are several scenarios regarding its formation.

The first is that it comprised a number of disgruntled former operators who felt betrayed by an ungrateful government which had dumped them, and decided to go into the mercenary business on a privateering basis in pursuit of the only career they really knew — soldiering.

The second is that it was a CCB operation which would facilitate the entrance of their military training teams into virtually every African or other country where military forces required a brushing up of skills. There could be no better way of gaining intelligence on such military forces and on their standard of efficiency, their leadership, their readiness, their weapons and their equipment. The lessons they taught them would in no way compensate that invaluable intelligence.

It was not a new concept. The British SAS had been doing it for years in the guise of organisations known as 'firms'. They consisted of ex-members or current members on a secondment who trained praetorian guards for presidents, sultans or whoever else was in need of them. When it suited British government policy, they also acted as 'mercenaries', as when they fought alongside Royalist guerrillas deep inside Yemen during the 1960s, when the Yemeni administration was assailing the borders of what was then Britain's Aden Protectorate.

Little is known of Executive Outcomes' early history but at the Idex 97 Defence Exhibition held in Abu Dhabi in the United Arab Emirates, Eeben Barlow told *The Star* newspaper 'Our track record since 1989 is well known by world governments and much of the interest we have received here stems directly from governments for whom we have worked since that time'.[39]

It is known that after Eeben Barlow's connections with the CCB were severed when that organisation was disbanded, he officially moved to a position with Armscor. Many *Operation Barnacle* operators had drawn their salary cheques from Armscor. Whatever his job there, because of his foreign connections, it positioned him to sign point-of-exit sales to obtain any armaments he might need.[40]

Nevertheless, it appears little of EO's equipment was sourced from South Africa because, again according to Eeben Barlow: 'We have no formal links with the SANDF and it is sad our own people did not want to do business with us. South Africa could have made a fortune out of the equipment, including two helicopters [that] we were forced to buy from outside sources.'[41]

14

Veterans for Victory versus End Conscription Campaign 1986-1992

Conscription in South Africa: a history

Because of often deep-seated points of contention between Afrikaans and English speakers — which had even resulted in war on two occasions — conscription in South Africa was never a factor. The old Boer Commando system was, perhaps, a form of conscription, but call-ups were rarely strictly enforced, mainly because of a cantankerous objection amongst the *volk* to 'English' authority and to being subjected to any kind of sanctions except for family ones. The Defence Act of 1912 made provision for compulsory military training for male white citizens, but again it was never enforced.

Bitterness as a hangover from the Anglo-Boer War of 1899-1902 created impossible political obstacles to the introduction of conscription in World War I. After the British conferred 'Responsible Government', leading to the Union of South Africa in 1910, the divisions in South African white society became even more apparent. Prime Minister General Louis Botha, his Defence Minister General Jan Smuts and the South African Party believed a united South Africa could be achieved by Boers and English-speakers burying their past quarrels. General Hertzog and his National Party, however, vehemently opposed this, believing it would lead to the swamping of the Afrikaner. It was a belief that would remain undisturbed over the years.

In 1914, Boers led by many of the old Boer War generals went into an armed rebellion over South Africa's decision to declare war against Germany in support of Great Britain. The rebels were quickly defeated, but this made the introduction of conscription impossible. Nevertheless, it did not stop thousands of Afrikaans and English speakers from volunteering and fighting shoulder-to-shoulder as comrades-in-arms. Many South African soldiers of both language groups distinguished themselves in that war and at the same time found reconciliation. Deneys Reitz, a Bitter-ender who had gone into exile after refusing to accept the British peace terms at the end of the Boer War in 1902, joined the British Army as a private soldier in 1917. Less than two years later in November 1918, when the Armistice was signed with Germany, he was colonel in command of the 1st Battalion Royal Scots Fusiliers — a regiment commanded by Winston Churchill earlier in the war.[1]

In 1939 there were sharp differences in the cabinet over the question of South Africa declaring war against Nazi Germany. On 6 September 1939, after a bitter debate, the pro-war faction led by General Smuts won a narrow majority of 80 votes against 67. Prime Minister General Hertzog promptly resigned, General Smuts was appointed Prime Minister and South Africa declared war on Germany.

This divided the country into two opposing camps. The vast majority of Afrikaners, particularly those belonging to the *Ossewa Brandwag* (Ox Wagon Sentinels) commonly known as OBs, were violently opposed to South Africa's participation. The *Ossewa Brandwag* was originally formed as an innocuous cultural organisation during the 1938 centenary celebrations of the Great Trek to perpetuate the Afrikaner's *Ossewagees* (ox wagon spirit). By 1940, though, it had become a pro-Nazi movement. It initiated an active campaign of sabotage and became a thorn in South Africa's side for the rest of the war.

The Defence Act of 1912 made no provision for the Union Defence Force to serve beyond the country's borders. From 1939 new volunteers and serving members were required to sign an 'Africa Oath' that declared they were prepared to fight anywhere in Africa. Those who signed were distinguished from the rest by red (actually dark orange) shoulder tabs on their uniforms. The Africa Oath, as a result, was soon derisively referred to as the 'Red Oath'. The Oath was later extended to permit the UDF to fight in Italy where, as in North Africa, it fought with distinction.

Needless to say, as was the case in World War I, conscription never became a factor.[2]

A ballot system of national service conscription for white males was introduced in the early 1950s. This was apparently done because the government had a commitment as a member of the Commonwealth to supply an armoured division for service in North Africa if another war broke out. It was said that there were insufficient volunteer soldiers to staff the Citizen Force units. A more pertinent reason, however, had come about as a result the *Ossewa Brandwag* hangover because it had actively discouraged Afrikaners from joining the services. With the National Party government assumption of power in 1948, though, times had changed. Despite the National Party and its allies having brought this situation about themselves, it concluded that all the Citizen Force units were essentially 'too English' for comfort. The only way this imbalance could be rectified, they concluded, was to introduce compulsory military service. This would effectively draw young Afrikaners into the net.

The Defence Act of 1957 made it an offence to refuse to serve in the Defence Force if called on to do so, unless one's bona fide religious denomination was opposed to participation in war. In that instance, it provided for such persons to be assigned to non-combatant duties.

In 1967 the Groenewald Committee rejected the ballot system, which it considered was something of a lottery and basically unfair. Resulting from its recommendations, with effect from 1 January 1968, it became compulsory for every white male to undergo 12 months military service on attaining the age of 18 years.

South Africa's secret involvement in Angola during 1975-1976 under the code name *Operation Savannah* resulted in the periods of service of the current national service intakes being increased by one month until the exercise was terminated.

In January 1978, with the SADF's increased commitment in Namibia and Angola national service was increased to two years.

Churches' stand on conscientious objection: 1974-1982

In July 1974 at the national conference of the SACC (South African Council of Churches), a motion regarding conscientious objection to military service was proposed by the Rev D Bax (Presbyterian Umtata) and seconded by the Rev D Beyers Naudé, director of the Christian Institute. The motion was adopted by 48 votes to nil.

In summary, the motion maintained that Christians should strive for justice and peace. It did not accept that it was the automatic duty of Christians to engage in violence and war. Both Catholic and Reformation theology, it said, regarded the taking up of arms as only justifiable when fighting a 'just war'. This excluded war in defence of an unjust and discriminatory society — which it considered South Africa to be. The motion noted the primary institutionalised violence which had provoked the counter violence of 'terrorists or freedom fighters'. It was hypocritical, it continued, to deplore their violence while South Africa prepared to defend its society with institutionalised violence.

Amongst those identifying themselves with the resolution were NUSAS (National Union of South African Students), the United Congregational Church of South Africa, the

Evangelical Lutheran Church (Transvaal Region), the Anglican Diocese of Johannesburg and the Bantu Presbyterian Church.

Some churches made no definite pronouncement, or decided to reflect on the situation. Those taking this stance included the Presbyterian Church of Southern Africa, the Methodist Church of South Africa and the Anglican Diocese of Cape Town. The Baptist Union of South Africa dissociated itself from the resolution.

The Northern Transvaal Moderator of the Nederduitse Gereformeerde Kerk, Dr O'Brian Geldenhuys, attacked the resolution saying it had slammed the door between the SACC and the Dutch Reformed Churches in South Africa.

Prime Minister Vorster said in response to the resolution that it was clear that it was intended to bring about a confrontation with the State. 'I want to warn very seriously that those who play with fire in this way must consider very thoroughly before they burn their fingers irrevocably', he said.

The Defence Minister announced that he was seeking a legal opinion on the resolution.

Commenting in the Assembly, Sir De Villiers Graaff, said the United Party believed it was the duty of every South African to assist in the defence of the country against aggression, including terrorism, and that the encouragement of conscientious objection would only serve the cause of violence.

Speaking for the Progressive Party, Dr Frederick van Zyl Slabbert, MP, said that although his party had repeatedly said the government's present policy was unjust, it had always urged that the socio-political system that had resulted from it could and should be changed by non-violent means. Therefore, the very institutions — political, economic and social — which could serve as instruments of peaceful change had to be defended against attack and violence from the outside. He said that a clear distinction had to be drawn between loyalty to South Africa and what she could become, and a commitment to the policy of apartheid.[3]

The question was raised again at the Southern African Catholic Bishops' Conference in February 1977 when it urged the State to make provision for alternate forms of national service for those who regarded it as participation in unjust oppression.[4]

The annual General Assembly of the Presbyterian Church of Southern Africa held in Johannesburg in October 1981 was attended by 140 delegates from the Church's 12 regions which included Zambia and Zimbabwe. The Assembly's view was strangely ambivalent regarding the taking up of arms and conscientious objection. It recognised the bona fides of Christians 'who in good conscience before God' take up arms to fight either for 'liberation' or for 'law and order' in South Africa. It paid tribute to those who suffered or died in doing so. It also paid tribute to those who had taken a stand 'for peace and reconciliation' by refusing to do military service on the grounds of conscientious objection.[5]

In 1982, by 165 votes to six, the Provincial Synod of the Roman Catholic Church, expressed 'serious doubts about the legitimacy of a military system whose role is increasingly seen as the protector of a profoundly immoral and unjust social order in which the majority of the people suffer gross oppression and exploitation . . . A vital function of the SADF has become the protection of those unjust structures . . . Synod therefore wishes to make it clear that allegiance to Christ demands of every Christian that before he takes up arms for any purpose, or enters the military, he should face our Lord and ask him whether this is truly what he should do.'[6]

Organisations opposing military conscription

In May 1978 it was reported that a publication called *Omkeer* (About Turn) was being distributed in South Africa by SALSCOM — the South African Liberation Support Committee. The publication provided advice to deserters and draft dodgers and offered them assistance to leave the country. This was part of its general aim of weakening the

SADF. SALSCOM was part of an underground organisation called *Okhela* or Atlas — formed as an overseas-based white wing of the banned ANC. Its aim was to bring about revolutionary change under the leadership of the black revolutionary movements by the use of armed struggle and underground activities.[7] *Okhela* never quite got off the ground.

In September 1981 it was reported that an agent of Military Intelligence, Colin Westgaard, had succeeded in infiltrating SAMRAF — the South African Military Refugees Aid Fund, a New York-based anti-military draft organisation. Documents stolen by him and handed over to the SADF revealed that SAMRAF had links with SALSCOM, SWAPO and the ANC. Westgaard confirmed that SALSCOM was organising a campaign to undermine the morale of white soldiers and to encourage them to resist military service.[8]

In April 1982 SAMRAF announced that the US cities of San Francisco, Oakland, Berkeley and Santa Cruz had resolved to offer refuge to South Africans who were resisting military service because of 'their refusal to participate in the military forces of apartheid.'

The initiative had not been sanctioned by the US State Department.[10]

SADF and conscientious objection

There were ructions in January 1981 when it was announced that military service, on a selective system, would be compulsory for male citizens of SWA/Namibia between the ages of 18 and 24.

About 100 members of SWANU (South West Africa National Union), fled to Botswana on the grounds that the struggle against SWAPO was not their war. It was then announced that compulsory call-up would be waived for black men living in the border areas of Owamboland, Kavango and the Caprivi. The excuse was that there were sufficient volunteers there who were already serving in the regional battalions of the SWA Territorial Force. Another important reason was that black political parties and churches had expressed strong misgivings about a call-up in the areas concerned, saying that some men might be forced to fight their own brothers who belonged to SWAPO's military wing. This culminated in the GOC SWA Territorial Force announcing that SWAPO supporters in the Force — bearing in mind that the internal party was not banned — would be treated as conscientious objectors and employed in non-fighting capacities.[10]

In May 1982, the Minister of Defence, in answer to a question in Parliament, said 312 men were in detention barracks for refusing to undergo military training. Two conscientious objectors had been sentenced to imprisonment and discharged with ignominy from the SADF. One, a Mr Viveiros, had maintained that he found it impossible to take up arms because of his faith in Christ. The other, a Mr C Yates, was sentenced to prison terms for refusing to do military service and later for refusing to wear the standard military uniform while in detention. Two others, a Mr N Mitchell, a Catholic conscientious objector and a Mr B Paddock, were also imprisoned for refusing to serve on religious grounds.

This triggered the PFP (Progressive Federal Party) into calling for a change in SADF policy. It suggested the creation of a statutory tribunal to assess the sincerity of objectors. If it found that the objectors were genuine, they should be given the opportunity of serving South Africa in a non-combatant or non-military capacity for periods longer than the laid down statutory periods of continuous service.

Die Kerkbode, the official organ of the NGK (Nederduitse Gereformeerde Kerk), supported this view. Similar support also came from the Southern African Catholic Bishops' Conference, the Baptist Union of South Africa and the Presbyterian Church.

Shortly afterwards, in October 1982, the SADF established the SADF Committee on Persons with Conscientious Objections to National Service under the chairmanship of Brigadier C Naudé, to investigate the manner in which objectors could be accommodated. Its findings were incorporated in the draft Defence Amendment Act, 1983.

The Act provided for four categories of objectors together with relevant sanctions:

1 Religious objectors whose religious convictions prevented them from serving in a combatant capacity.

Required to wear military uniforms and perform tasks beneficial to the SADF for a period of two years continuous service (to match national service), followed by 720 days service (to match Citizen Force service).

2 Religious objectors whose convictions prevented them from serving in a combatant capacity, performing any maintenance task of a combatant nature or wearing uniform.

Required to serve one and a half times the normal call-up period performing maintenance tasks for the SADF unrelated to combat activities. Refusal entailed a gaol sentence of an equivalent period.

3 Religious objectors whose religious convictions prevented their performing any military service or training or any tasks connected with the military.

Required to perform in continuous service one and a half times the length of the normal call-up period in community, public or municipal service. This was conditional on the objector not engaging in political activities or publishing any written political material. Refusal entailed an equivalent gaol sentence.

4 Non-religious objectors refusing to perform any type of military service.

The sanction was a six-year prison sentence.[11]

There was no provision for the so-called 'just war' theory. To have included it on the terms demanded by pacifists with political agendas, would have effectively meant that an objector could pick and choose whether to serve his country or not. It would have allowed him latitude to decide if the war had been declared by a legitimate authority; if its cause was just; if it had been undertaken as a last resort; if it had just goals; if the means employed were just; and if it promised a reasonable chance of success.

It would have been a recipe for social chaos.

The Board for Religious Objections as provided for in the Act comprised three theologians of different denominations and two members of the Defence Force, one a chaplain. It was chaired by a judge or a retired judge. It fell under the Minister of Manpower, not the Minister of Defence.

In January 1983, a spokesman for COSAWR (Committee on South African War Resisters), based in England, said it expected the number of 'war resisters' leaving the country to increase when the new Defence Act was passed. He claimed that several thousand South African 'war resisters' were scattered all over the world, with at least 300 in Great Britain, 100 in the Netherlands, 30 in Australia and 20 in the USA.[12]

SADF Chief, General Constand Viljoen, accused South Africa's opponents of attempting to discourage its youth from doing national service by persuading them to become 'draft dodgers'. It was a calculated attempt to undermine the whole concept of national service and the necessity to defend the borders.[13]

End Conscription Campaign

In March 1983, at the Black Sash's national conference, a motion calling for an end to conscription was carried. Following this, in July 1983 a conscientious objectors' support group of the Black Sash (a women's anti-apartheid movement) decided to launch an organisation that would be known as the ECC — End Conscription Campaign.

By January 1984 committees had been formed in Cape Town, Durban and Johannesburg to take up the campaign and in July 1984 the ECC formulated its declaration. It said that South Africans lived in a society that denied basic human rights to most people and was in a state of civil war. Young men were conscripted to maintain South Africa's illegal occupation of Namibia and to wage war in foreign countries. Conscripts had to assist in the implementation and defence of apartheid policies, it claimed. It said that it was the 'moral right' of people to 'exercise freedom of conscience and to choose not to serve in the SADF'. Meetings aimed at ending compulsory military service through the weight of public opinion were held in Cape Town, Durban and Johannesburg.

Some 40 church, student and civil rights groups lent support to the campaign. They included the SACC (South African Council of Churches), Diakonia in Durban, the Western Province Council of Churches, Women for Peace in Cape Town, NUSAS (National Union of South African Students), JODAC (Johannesburg Democratic Action Committee), NEUSA (National Education Union of South Africa) and the Cape Town area committees of the UDF (United Democratic Front).

Mr Vause Raw, defence spokesman for the New Republic Party and deputy chairman of the parliamentary standing committee on defence, described the campaign as 'subversive and extremely dangerous'.

Philip Myburgh, Progressive Federal Party defence spokesman acknowledged the right of people to campaign for an end to conscription, but said he did not approve of the ECC. 'There is a distinct impression being given by the people supporting the campaign that it is aimed at diminishing the strength of the SADF.' He emphasised that PFP policy was to phase out conscription in favour of an all-regular army, but not at the expense of the strength of the SADF.

Despite these remarks, the ranks of the PFP were divided. After decisions taken by its provincial congresses, the party's federal council committed the party to work for an end to compulsory military service. This resulted in its finance spokesman, Harry Schwarz, refusing to accept the resolution because he believed the country needed strong defences as an 'umbrella of peace' to allow political reform to take place. Four PFP MPs, Harry Schwarz, Philip Myburgh, Alf Widman and Reuben Sive resigned from the party's defence group in a revolt against the decision.

PFP leader, Dr Frederick van Zyl Slabbert, commented that while it was morally wrong to apply conscription only to whites, if it became applicable to other race groups which did not enjoy the same privileges as whites, it would prove to be provocative and dangerous. Conscription for whites introduced a racial dimension into sensitive domestic activities, particularly as the SADF had been deployed to quell disturbances in black townships. While the phasing out of conscription would take time, a start should be made.

Professor Deon Fourie, head of strategic studies at the University of South Africa, described the PFP's decision as unrealistic because South Africa could not afford a solely permanent force. The SADF had about 200 000 people available from the ranks of national servicemen, the Citizen Force and the Permanent Force. The Permanent Force comprised only 30 000 people. Abolishing conscription would permanently remove about 100 000 people from the economy.[14]

The Defence Amendment Act, 1983, came into effect at the beginning of 1984. In July the secretary of the Board for Religious Objection, Major David Fourie, said there had been an increase in people applying for religious objector status. He believed this had nothing to do with the activities of the End Conscription Campaign, but was happening because the board had become better known through countrywide visits to churches by the board's chairman, Judge M T Steyn. It was significant that during 1984, the board received 341 applications of which only four were refused.[15]

During 1985 the ECC steadily increased its activities and additional branches were established in Grahamstown, Pietermaritzburg and Port Elizabeth.

In June 1985 the ECC held a 'peace festival' at the University of the Witwatersrand, Johannesburg, that was attended by a 1 000 people. Messages of support were received from about 100 organisations both within and outside South Africa. Speakers at the festival included Dr Beyers Naudé; Molly Blackburn, a member of the PFP's provincial council and the Black Sash; and the Right Rev Desmond Tutu, the Anglican Bishop of Johannesburg. Dr Naudé argued that the campaign to end conscription was really a battle against the entire unjust apartheid system that was dependent on enforced military service to bolster it.

During a debate with the ECC in June l985 on the topic 'The SADF — Shielding the Nation or Defending Apartheid', Dr Frederick van Zyl Slabbert said his party believed that conscription should be phased out in favour of a non-racial volunteer army.

He accused the ECC of being 'dangerously romantic, extraordinarily naïve and counter-productive in its campaign'. He emphasised that it was the duty of the SADF to combat terrorism and violence, but it was not its duty to maintain law and order or to combat crime. He said it should get out of the townships.

The report of the ANC's National Consultative Conference held at Kabwe, Zambia, in June 1985 under the heading 'Mobilisation of the White Community', said:

> To ensure that democratic whites become active participants in the struggle we recommend that:
>
> - They work increasingly to popularise the End Conscription Campaign. The issue of conscription can be explained and the community be convinced politically why they should not join the SADF.
> - The formation of support groups for conscientious objectors, war resisters and supporters.
> - The Movement to draw these people into our ranks and persuade those who are prepared to fight a just war rather than act as cannon fodder for apartheid to become active combatants of MK.[16]

In September 1985 the Security Police detained four members of the ECC in terms of section 29 of the Internal Security Act, 1982. They were released 11 days later without being charged. Shortly afterwards the ECC claimed that more than 50 organisations had expressed their support for its call to end conscription

On 20 September 1985 the Deputy Minister of Defence, Adriaan Vlok, said that people who approved of and promoted the ECC were being used by the ANC to promote its 'evil goals'. He said the organisation aimed to break down law and order by weakening the State's machinery. He accused the Black Sash, the UDF, the ANC and the 'radical leftist ECC' of aiming to influence servicemen to become draft dodgers and to rebel against their military duties.

The ECC rejected this, saying the ANC was a banned organisation and 'the ECC has never had, nor will it have, links with it.[17]

Addressing a gathering in the Cape Town city hall on 7 October, Molly Blackburn claimed there was a growing militarisation of 'our society'. She questioned whether the damage to race relations by white troops would ever be repaired. 'If you are black and living in the Eastern Cape, you can honestly say you are living in a state of civil war'.[18]

Enter Rob Brown

Rob Brown although British-born had lived much of his life in Australia where his family was domiciled. He was a soldier's soldier. At 18, while the Vietnam War was still raging, he volunteered for the Australian Army's elite 2-Commando Company — a unit similar in many ways to Britain's Royal Marines. He became a commando and was trained in minor tactics, demolitions, parachuting, jungle warfare and small boat operations. Frustratingly though, he was not allowed to go to Vietnam where many of his comrades were serving as advisers to local troops. The Australian Army's policy was to send only sergeant-instructors aged 26 or more to Vietnam. He was neither a sergeant nor even close to 26 years of age.

Kicking his heels in a peacetime army did not suit him and he resigned. He travelled as a civilian firstly to Singapore, then to Malaya and up the peninsula into Thailand. In Thailand he applied for a visa to enter South Vietnam. Whilst waiting for this to come through he stayed in the small town of Chiang Mai some 400km north of Bangkok. He was not a drinker and he frequented a small cafe there that sold cold milk because it was one of the few places that had a fridge. There he struck up an acquaintanceship with a friendly Thai national — an educated man who spoke Thai, Malay, five Chinese dialects and a little Urdu in addition to English. During conversations he asked Rob what he did and why he was in South-East Asia. When he discovered his military background, he offered him a job. On enquiring what the job entailed, he was told it was for the provision of military training.

Although it was never confirmed because the Thai was his 'cut-off' and he never dealt with anyone above him, he became certain the man worked for the CIA. The CIA employed only US citizens as full-time operators, but they did employ what they called 'indigenous employees' in overseas countries. Such employees, in turn, were allowed to recruit their own operators, which is how Rob came to work for the CIA.

He formed part of a three-man team that consisted of himself and two locals and they operated up country in Thailand and into Laos. His Thai superior pre-designated the villages they should go to provide military training. They were also to set up protected villages. Once, because of his small boat experience, he conducted an operation into Cambodia via the islands.

After leaving Thailand, Brown went to the United Kingdom and joined the British Parachute Regiment. Amongst other duties he served as an operator with an SAS-led covert unit known as the Military Reaction Force (MRF)conducting intelligence operations in Northern Ireland. From Britain he moved to Rhodesia where he passed selection for the Rhodesian SAS.

While serving with them, he took part in the most successful Security Forces' ambush of the war. A group commanded by Lieutenant Martin Pearse lay in ambush for several days until a large ZANLA group walked into the killing ground on 14 March 1975. The bodies of 22 ZANLA guerrillas were counted afterwards, but there were many more than that because their screams could be heard for many hours afterwards as they died in the surrounding bush.

Rob Brown and his team mate, Trooper W R 'Rocky' Walton, were badly wounded by machine-gun fire. Casevac help was not immediately to hand and Rocky died some hours later.

Brown spent several weeks in hospital recovering from his wounds. Rhodesia was a small country and it was not geared to provide much aftercare for those wounded in action. Consequently, when their condition allowed it, the wounded were sent home to convalesce with their families until they were again ready for active operations. But Brown could not go home because his was thousands of kilometres away in Australia. He'd had a rented flat, but had been forced to relinquish it because of his lengthy spell of hospitalisation. Eventually, after being discharged from the hospital, he moved into an old house in Salisbury (Harare) with a lady friend and spent the next six weeks lying flat on his back on a couch.

This gave him time for reflection. One morning he began to wonder why he was still alive. Others with similar wounds had died, but he had survived. Why had he been saved? He had always been a Christian, but had never taken religion seriously. It was a Sunday and his lady friend was out of the house training her dogs. He walked around the corner to a small church where he got involved in the service and eventually made a commitment to Christ. Thereafter he became what he called 'a Bible-believing Christian'. In essence this meant he subscribed to the fundamental belief that everything in the Bible, from Genesis to Revelation, was absolutely true and beyond question.

Brown became involved in other military operations, until he was wounded a second time when his vehicle struck a landmine. This time he was discharged from the army on medical grounds.

By 1980 he had fully recovered. He joined South Africa's Special Forces and became a member of 6-Reconnaissance Commando which was formed from the remnants of the Rhodesian SAS after Rhodesia became Zimbabwe. Another close friend, Sergeant Ian Suttill, was killed in action during the Recce raid on ANC facilities in Matola on 30 January 1981(*Operation Beanbag).*[19] The loss of two close friends in action resulted in Brown developing a protective attitude towards young soldiers. This shaped what would soon become an important part of his life.

After serving for a year, Brown left the Recces. His first job was as a manager at a game ranch. After this he sought work in a Christian 'safe-house' in Hillbrow, Johannesburg called The Lord's Place, where he was unpaid except for small donations that came his way. He had been married and divorced by this time. The Lord's Place ministered to alcoholics, drug abusers, prostitutes and other down-and-outs. He got involved in church work and street evangelism. For a time he worked at the YMCA. He involved himself in basic preaching, but because he was not an ordained minister, he preferred to call it lecturing.

From there he joined Frontline Fellowship in Cape Town, recently established by a young 22-year-old missionary and evangelist, Rev Peter Hammond. Frontline Fellowship was anti-communist and organisations allied to communism, like SWAPO in SWA/Namibia, FRELIMO in Mozambique, the ANC/SACP alliance in South and the MPLA in Angola.

Frontline Fellowship was not anti-military and certainly not a pacifist organisation. It was more a 'praise the Lord and pass the ammunition' type of mission. Rob Brown later became its deputy director.

Enter Veterans for Victory: 1986

Rob Brown, although still with Frontline Fellowship, had begun to cast around to see if he could get back into soldiering. He put out the word on the grapevine and made various contacts. Eventually he was contacted by an anonymous English-speaking officer who spoke with a London accent. He was interviewed at a small unmarked office in Johannesburg's Carlton Centre. The recruiter regretted that he was unable to offer Rob a post in Military Intelligence because they were only interested in people with university degrees and he did not have one.

One day Rob and John, another ex-soldier, went to a well-attended meeting of the End Conscription Campaign at Sea Point in Cape Town. They listened out of sheer curiosity. A man related how he had already performed his national service in the army, but although he was obliged to respond to Citizen Force call-ups, he no longer intended going. He would rather be arrested and imprisoned. He lambasted the army and was full of horror stories, most of which by the reckoning of the two former soldiers, were patently false.

Eventually, unable to take it any longer, Rob stood on his chair and interrupted. He told the audience that if they carried on the way they were about destroying their army, they would surely all lose their freedom. There would be anarchy in South Africa and there would be no one left to protect society.

Eventually both men stormed out in protest, followed by a group of heavies from the ECC. It was obvious that they intended to assault them, but when the two obviously dangerous ex-soldiers turned at bay, they changed their minds and returned to the meeting.

Brown discussed the objectives of the ECC with many people who agreed with him that the organisation could be very damaging to the country. Rob, having been a soldier all his life, concluded that the ordinary servicemen of the SADF needed help and that it might as well be he who organised it. He resigned from Frontline Fellowship, believing a pro-military campaign might prove damaging to it, and moved to Hillbrow where he established himself in a small flat.

His organisation, he decided, would be called Veterans for Victory. He would print and put out leaflets, write letters to newspaper and do anything else that would assist the SADF. The only problem was that he had virtually no money. He approached and discussed this with Aida Parker, a journalist who produced a right wing newsletter. He told her what his intentions were and she made a major feature of it in the next edition of her newsletter. This brought in a few public donations which were sufficient to get him started in his Hillbrow flat. He wrote out copy in longhand, then a young girl volunteer typed it for him on an old electric typewriter and another volunteer proofread it.

A man called Tobie Vermaak had been leaving messages and trying to get hold of him. When he succeeded, Rob learnt that he was an officer from Military Intelligence. Much later he discovered he was an officer from the sub-division of Comops (Communication Operations) of the Chief of Staff Intelligence of the SADF. Vermaak, he found, was directly concerned with psychological operations or psyops, as it was more commonly known. Through him he was introduced to Brigadier Ferdi van Wyk, the Director of Psychological Operations based at Military Intelligence's headquarters in the Liberty Life building in Pretoria.

They confided that the SADF had a major problem — which was the campaign being waged by the ECC. They were literally terrified that a similar situation could arise in South Africa to the one that had occurred in the USA and Australia during the Vietnam War era. There, pacifist campaigns became so effective that soldiers returning home — even though they were often conscripts and not volunteers — were intimidated, scorned and sometimes beaten up and generally treated like common war criminals. It was so serious that a serving president of the United States had to put up with the continual badgering of war protesters chanting: 'Hey, hey, LBJ [Johnson], how many kids have you killed today?' It was many years before a United States administration deemed that sufficient time had elapsed for it to be politically acceptable to erect of a war memorial commemorating the honoured dead from that war.

The psyops people had nightmares of huge rolling street demonstrations against conscription and the military. The problem was they did not know the identities of the people likely to be behind such actions. They had concluded that although the SADF had an abundance of equipment to fight and win any land war on the African continent, they were babes-in-the-wood when it came to psychological warfare. But it was clear to them, from watching events overseas, that there was considerable profit to be accrued from propaganda and psychological operations. Senior Comops' officers had already been despatched for training to Taiwan's Military Academy for Psychological Warfare. This was probably one of the world's best institutions of its kind, because of the undiminished communist threat that Taiwan faced from mainland China.

They pointed out that most of the conventional English churches — although not the Afrikaans ones — to a lesser or greater degree had come out in open support of the ECC's concept that exemption should be allowed for conscientious objectors who believed the SADF was engaged in fighting an unjust war. There was also a greater acceptance of the so-called 'liberation theology' — which was alarming.

They had noted that at the ANC's Second National Consultative Conference held in Kabwe, Zambia, from 16-23 June 1985, the setting up of a Department of Religious Affairs had been mandated 'to lead and initiate an active and meaningful participation of the religious community in the struggle for a new democratic South Africa'.[20]

Other more conservative churches which were openly anti-communist and were not in sympathy with the aims of the ECC, had been unaffected so far. There were many such churches, both black and white, but the churches that fell under the United Christian Action umbrella were considered particularly important. They were Africa Christian Action of Cape Town, Betel Group of Ministries of Innesdale, Cape Christian Action of Cape Town, Centre for Reformed and Contemporary Studies in Pretoria, Free State Christian Act of Bloemfontein, Frontline Fellowship of Cape Town, Gospel Defence League of Cape Town, Ligstryders of Pretoria, Namibia Christian Action of Otjiwarongo, Operation Corinthians of Somerset West, Pro-Life of Cape Town, Signpost Publications and Research Centre of Pretoria, Theocentric Christian Education of Cape Town, World Federation of Doctors who Respect Human Life of Cape Town and Zambia Christian Action of Lusaka.

Military Intelligence had been conducting brainstorming sessions to find solutions to the problems they were facing. They were wary of ECC infiltration into schools. They were worried that the mothers of national servicemen could be got at and organised into an anti-war lobby. To combat this, SADF female personnel working overtly in civvies organised the mothers, formed committees and organisations outside the SADF and provided a support system. Military Intelligence decided that it was safe to say that any group of people, whether it was a ladies' sewing circle, a book club or a cycling club could be utilised to serve the enemy's ends . . . or one's own. It all depended on who got to them first.

That, they concluded, was what had happened to the mainstream English churches. The enemy had got there first. They were determined to ensure that this did not become more widespread. They assured Rob Brown that they were in the process of infiltrating their agents into the more conservative churches to report what was going on, but more importantly, so they could influence opinion. In some cases the actual church leaders, where they identified themselves with the SADF's cause, had been brought on side.

It is probable that most churches in South Africa — conventional or unconventional, Afrikaans or English, black or white based — were infiltrated to some degree by Military Intelligence agents by the early 1990s. The degree of success they achieved is questionable.

There was considerable discussion regarding the Rev Peter Hammond's Frontline Fellowship. They were wary of making a direct approach to him for assistance, despite his openly anti-communist stance, because they regarded him as a loose cannon. He always did as he pleased and he went off at unexpected tangents whenever he felt like it.

In July 1986 Peter Hammond did an excellent job for Frontline Fellowship, and unwittingly for Military Intelligence as well. He entered Mozambique with the reluctant permission of FRELIMO on what he anticipated would be a routine bible teaching, bible distribution and evangelistic mission to the north of the country. While it did in fact result in many church services and the distribution of a large number of bibles, it also became a research trip when Peter heard about atrocities committed against the people by the ruling FRELIMO.

This resulted in his hiving off on a side trip and travelling many hundreds of kilometres by motorbike, Land-Rover, dugout canoe and on foot. He interviewed about 300 tribesmen, including 100 pastors and church leaders and visited villages in nine different districts of Tete, Zambezia and Niassa Provinces.

Accepting only sworn eye-witness testimonies confirmed by first-hand accounts of separately interviewed witnesses, he documented evidence confirming that FRELIMO had razed at least 42 villages to the ground, torched 74 churches and burnt over 60 cases of bibles. He uncovered 28 instances where Zimbabwean or FRELIMO troops had massacred the occupants of whole villages down to the last infant. Every village surveyed reported people being taken away without reason and placed in FRELIMO's 're-education' camps. Many children, some as young as 12, had been rounded up and inducted into the FPLM, FRELIMO's military wing. He encountered countless instances of crop destruction and the wholesale theft of clothing and other property by FRELIMO.[21]

Whilst the Military Intelligence people were jubilant at the adverse publicity and discomfort this created for the Marxist FRELIMO regime, they were concerned that he might try to do a second missionary trip to Mozambique. This would undoubtedly result in his arrest and imprisonment.

In view of his previous position as a director of Frontline Fellowship and the positive influence he had over Rev Hammond, Rob Brown was asked if he could act as Hammond's handler without his being aware of it. The important thing was not to let him return to Mozambique and to influence him positively in schemes approved by Military Intelligence. Brown agreed.

Many projects were discussed where it was believed Frontline Fellowship could be steered towards them in the future. Most of the projects involved SWA/Namibia and the SADF-controlled areas of southern Angola. Brown pointed out that they would require extensive funding as Frontline Fellowship was generally run on a shoestring. Military Intelligence saw no difficulties in this. It arranged for the payment of 'donations' from 'anonymous well-wishers' into Frontline's bank account. This included money not only from local sources but also from the United States and Europe. It was always in cash, sometimes a few hundred dollars, pounds or rands, but more often than not sums as high as US$7 000. In this way some R500 000 rand was paid into Frontline Fellowship's bank account over the next five years. They believed, correctly as it turned out, that Rev Peter Hammond and his fellow missionaries would attribute their increase in funds to their anti-communist cause attracting increased support.

Hammond and his colleagues were also belatedly right. By the time Military Intelligence's covert funding was cut off it was no longer required because the organisation had advanced considerably since the days when it ran on a shoestring. Hammond had conducted several fund-raising trips to the United States and his cause had indeed proved popular. So popular, in fact, that he might not even have noticed the dip caused by the sudden cut-off of MI's contributions.

MI approved Rob's idea of establishing Veterans for Victory and confirmed that the ends he wished to serve were identical to their own. They wanted to get aboard and fund it. They were confident that if the organisation was properly handled, it would act as an effective counterbalance to the ECC.

Rob Brown was a ground soldier, not a trained intelligence officer with a degree — which is what MI would have preferred. Yet he had recognised the threat facing the SADF. Somehow he had scraped together his pennies, inspired some donations, and started an organisation, albeit small, to combat the machinations of the ECC — something MI had so far not managed to do themselves. They recognised talent. And he had other advantages. He was an ex-soldier with a culture similar to their own. He was also used to working in the conservative church environment, an area they wanted to infiltrate and control.

The Veterans for Victory Association, he was told, would be positioned as an organisation of ex-servicemen. According to the association's 'organisers' manual' that was later prepared by Military Intelligence for Brown, it was 'dedicated to preserving the Christian, democratic, capitalist system.' It was a 'multiracial interdenominational group of mostly former ex-servicemen and women' who held 'fundamental beliefs of freedom'.

This freedom was a 'God-given gift' that had to be preserved at all costs. The punch line was that 'the preservation of this free society' came from 'having a strong SADF/SAP'.

Brown's line function, he was told, was to 'destroy' the ECC and any other 'peace organisation' that might come into being. The word was 'destroy', not just 'disrupt'. The headings for chapter 2 of the organisers' manual illustrate the intensity of its focus on the ECC. The other chapters gave detailed instructions on 'successful organising', 'fund raising', 'legal advice' and 'The Media' (which gave advice on disinformation campaigns, manipulation of the press and so on).[22]

Brown's handler or Project Officer, as Military Intelligence preferred to call him, was an English-speaking major called Jamie. Brown never discovered his real name,

They went to appraise Brown's set-up at his Hillbrow bachelor flat. The officers sniffed when they saw his single battered electric typewriter on a side table. Nor were they impressed when he explained his use of a volunteer typist, his occasional proof-reader and the friendly guy who allowed him use of his photocopier.

Naturally, they as Military Intelligence knew how to run things, how to organise in true military fashion, how to squeeze maximum juice from the lemon. What was more than obvious was that poor old Rob Brown, as well intentioned as he might be, did not have a clue. He was certainly going to need some sorting out and some help.

'You need a proper office. You need this, you need that. You will definitely require a full-time secretary to relieve you of administrative work and other employees as well. We will arrange the advertisements. Decent typewriters need to be sorted out. We have no idea how you have been managing without a fax machine. What sort of car do you have?'

Brown shook his head. He had only recently gone through a divorce and he had been left with very little of anything, not to mention the luxury of a car, any car.

'Okay, we will get you a new car. You will have a lot of travelling to do working for us. At least you can travel in comfort.'

'Now wait a minute', said Brown.'Where will the money for all this come from?'

'From us, of course', exclaimed a puzzled officer. 'Where do you think?'

'No, hang on', said Brown. 'At the moment I am living in a flat in Hillbrow. I have an electric typewriter, a telephone and a couple of volunteer helpers. Now next week I am going to be working from a smart office, with a fax machine, two or three telephones, a dolly bird as a full-time secretary sitting at the reception desk and a brand-new car parked under the carport outside. Isn't that going to attract attention? Isn't someone going to say that someone has given me something?'

Brown insisted on doing things his own way, not the Military Intelligence way. Veterans for Victory would grow slowly, organically. A single telephone was okay to start with and the flat would suffice for the moment. He would manage without a car.

They insisted he had to have one, but he just as insistently said that he could not afford it. Eventually, as a compromise, they got him an old banger that ostensibly came as a donation.

Money was required to expand, but he took and used it parsimoniously. It was brought to him in cash in brown paper bags. To get the cash into his system, he used small cheques of one or two thousand rand paid to him as donations by certain banks and companies. He padded the amounts with SADF cash before banking it. He also advertised literature and intelligence gathering equipment for sale in magazines. The proceeds of the transactions, whether real or not, were also padded with SADF money before banking.

Eventually, when he believed the time was right, Brown moved Veterans for Victory to offices in Yeoville, Johannesburg. They remained there, until on the instructions of Military Intelligence, he took a three-year lease — later changed to a five-year lease — on more upmarket offices in Yazaki House, 31 De Winnaar Street, Halfway House, on 1 February 1990.

Military Intelligence pumped much money and expertise into the organisation. A monthly magazine was introduced. It was called *Stand-To* and its title was effectively underlined by a soldier with a rifle lying in a prone position. Its often scurrilous articles were virulently anti-pacifist, anti-communist, anti-ANC, anti-SWAPO, pro-SADF, pro-Christianity, pro-Western civilisation and so on. Mailing lists with thousands of addresses were purchased to facilitate widespread distribution.

The monthly print bill for *Stand-To* and other propaganda literature emanating from Veterans for Victory eventually amounted to a substantial R60 000 per month. For security reasons a commercial printer selected by Brown was used instead of the Government Printer. Comops began to use the same printer for one of their own projects. This was for a series of picture comic books developed around the subjects of Marx, Lenin, Mao and Christ. They were produced by the millions as giveaways in both English and Afrikaans. They were crude propaganda aimed at the black anti-liberation movements. They bore no dates and showed neither the name of the printer nor the publisher. It was so obviously a Military Intelligence project that Rob immediately switched printers to ensure the projects were not linked. A cursory investigation would have quickly revealed the likely background.

By the time Veterans for Victory and *Stand-To* got off the ground, Brown had three employees — a secretary, a lay-out artist and a writer. Only the writer was aware of what was going on, but he never had contact with anyone above Brown. They would sit around a desk as a team and have brainstorming sessions. Brown was neither an artist nor a writer but he suggested ideas and these would usually form the basis for whatever they came up with for the monthly publication.

Counter-revolutionary propaganda and psychological warfare have certain basic tenets, many interlinked with the others. One tenet is that if you wish to destroy an enemy organisation, it is better to tackle it during its embryo stages before it gains strength. Another tenet is that if an enemy organisation is established to oppose you, the best way to control it is to form an opposing organisation. This is effectively what Veterans for Victory did with the ECC. There was, in fact, relatively little time between the formation of the two organisations.

The difference between the two was that the ECC regarded Veterans for Victory as a right wing irritation. It never realised that it had been specifically formed by Military Intelligence to infiltrate and destroy it and that it had virtually unlimited financial resources at its disposal. No one tried to infiltrate the organisation and no one bothered to find out exactly who and what Rob Brown was. He was occasionally referred to as a 'shadowy figure' in newspaper articles, but that is as far as it went and no one attempted to discredit him. Although he was in deep cover, if anyone had bothered to make a concerted effort they could have found out his background and so on, but no one did. He was just dismissed as the cranky leader of a right-wing ex-serviceman's organisation.

This was not the case as far as the other side of the coin was concerned. The ECC operated from the English-speaking university campuses drawing its primary support from white students. Later, it also spread its influence to some of the Afrikaans universities. But it would be fallacious to say it had widespread support amongst students. In Rob's experience, most white students considered they had a duty to perform their national service and looked forward to doing it. Many had already done their initial periods of service. Students, both male and female, generally regarded the ECC and its pacifist lobby as weirdos. As a result, there was never a shortage of volunteers eager to infiltrate the ranks of the ECC and report back to Veterans for Victory on what was going on. Some reached very high positions within the organisation and Brown got documents and often brilliant information across his desk that had often only just come out of secret meetings. He often saw it long before it got down to the ECC's branches. Veterans for Victory knew what was happening the whole time. They also got to know full details of the considerable funding EEC was getting from overseas organisations like South African Military Refugees Aid Fund (SAMRAF), the Committee on South African War Resisters (COSAWR), and the Anti-War League.

Much of this was published in *Stand-To* to embarrass the ECC, but some was too sensitive to publish and such documentation was immediately collected by Military Intelligence. If published, it would have blown the covers of those Veterans for Victory operatives working within the ECC.

The accuracy of information about the organisation was confirmed by Dr Crispian Oliver, chairman of Cape Town ECC, who complained in a press statement that 'a particular level of intelligence work with respect to the ECC is also evident. There is often prior knowledge of organisation activities and knowledge of ECC members' particulars'.[23]

This became particularly evident at the Grahamstown Arts Festival in 1988. A series of pamphlets targeting students who belonged to the ECC were distributed. They were numbered, 1/10, 2/10 and so on. Each showed a student's photograph with details of his criminal convictions, like possession of cannabis, etc. 'Who is next?' was printed beneath each photograph. According to reliable sources within the ECC, the pamphlets caused havoc amongst its membership. It also prompted an abortive advertisement in a local newspaper offering a reward to get information that would identify the culprits.[24]

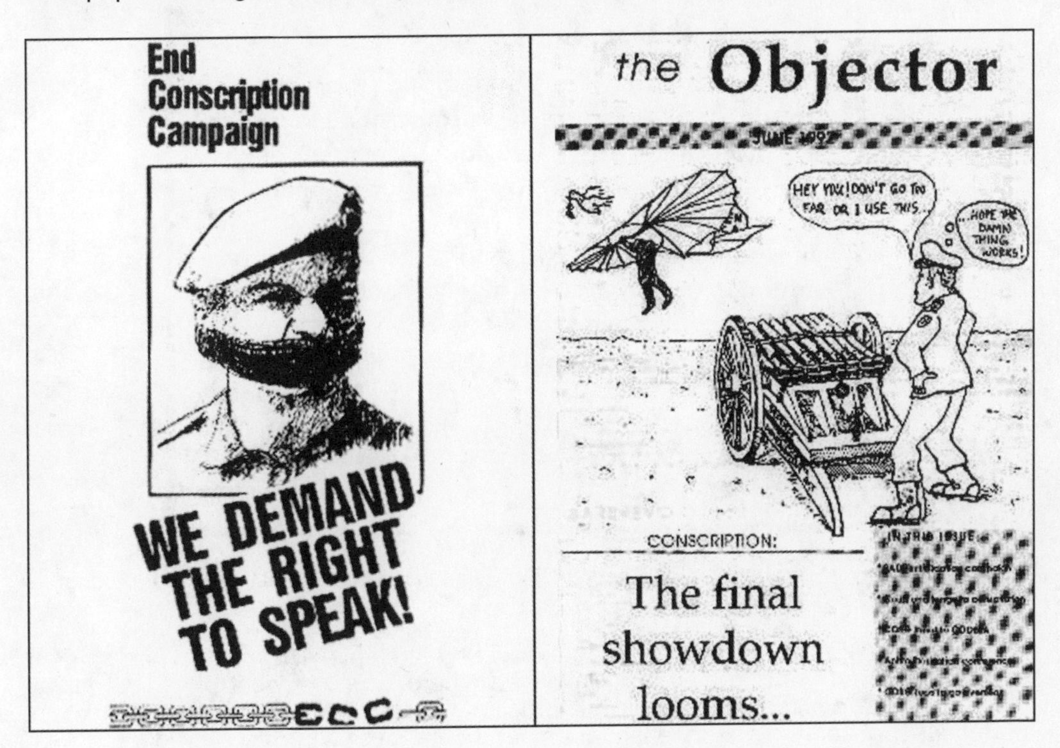

The End Conscription Campaign's agenda. (Left) ECC pamphlet which is self explanatory. (Right) Front cover of the ECC's 'The Objector' magazine. In addition to their pacifist and 'just war' agendas, they also attempted to undermine morale by attacking the SADF's credibility as a fighting force.

ECC meetings and stands on university open days were regularly monitored. People attending were photographed using telephoto lenses so they could be identified later. The number plates of cars parked in the vicinity were also photographed to link them with ownership. Dossiers were built up. Meetings were rarely well attended, except when they had a hard-hitting speaker like Bishop Desmond Tutu or someone of similar calibre.

There were some occasions, after intelligence had been assessed, when certain people connected with the ECC were identified as posing a proximate danger to the State. Veterans for Victory recommended to Military Intelligence that they be eliminated by assassination. Detailed plans were submitted as to how this could be achieved.

Each time such plans were vetoed from the top.

To protect his own cover and that of Veterans for Victory, Brown used a system of cut-offs. Students directly recruited by him — call them the inner circle — would know about him and his connections. Those students, however, would be the cut-offs when they recruited others to perform tasks and their own recruits would have no idea who was above them. Similarly, if those students in turn recruited other activists, the latter would also be unaware of anyone above their own recruiter. By this means Veterans for Victory had dozens of students working clandestinely against the ECC.

REWARD

The Grahamstown End Conscription Campaign is offering a reward for any information leading to the prosecution of the individual(s) responsible for distributing Veterans for Victory pamphlets on Saturday.

The pamphlets - which contain factually incorrect information and may be highly defamatory, were distributed in town and illegally on campus.

Please contact Pauline (28131) or Sylvia (22023 x 337).

ECC

End Conscription Campaign

There were times when the ECC became highly incensed over the activities of Veterans for Victory.

In Cape Town Brown once directly ran four young students. They in turn had students working for them, who in their turn employed others. Much of what they did could be categorised as common vandalism, but the activists regarded them as acts of sabotage. They cut speaker wires at meetings, damaged cars, put super glue into door locks or padlocks, phoned up people and anonymously intimidated and threatened them, put dog's excreta through letter boxes, let down tyres and performed many other often serious acts of harassment. ECC posters advertising public meetings were ripped down within hours of their being put up.

There were numerous occasions when Military Intelligence told Rob that his people were going too far, that he should rein them in. He found it very difficult to control them, however, because of his system of cut-offs. He had to pass his appeals down the line and they did not always reach the people they were meant for, because he genuinely had no idea who was responsible for what.

To this day Brown is surprised that no one was seriously hurt considering that he was running 18-year-old students who were taking part in meetings where other participants were not averse to using violence. If covers were blown, there is little doubt that the students concerned would have been seriously assaulted. Worse still, although blacks were not eligible for conscription, many black ANC and UDF activists attended the ECC meetings. This was a time when 'necklacing' by the UDF was a strategy and a commonplace occurrence, so the results could have been tragic.

The SADF embarrassingly diverted responsibility for ECC harassment away from its surrogate, Veterans for Victory, to itself. This occurred during the trial of three national servicemen charged with contravening the Official Secrets Act. While under cross examination Colonel J J Claasen, the Officer Commanding Comops (Communications Operations) at Western Province Command, conceded that the SADF had mounted a campaign that was aimed at discrediting the ECC. This was intended to undermine its goodwill and damage its ability to attract members and funds.[25] As a result, in September 1988 the ECC applied for an interdict in the Cape High Court to restrain the SADF from harassing and interfering with the organisation or its members.

In a reply affidavit lodged with the court, Brigadier A K de Jager, the Officer Commanding Western Province Command, admitted that members of the SADF had taken part in a campaign to discredit the ECC by printing derogatory slogans and dropping pamphlets by helicopter at an ECC meeting. The Chief of the SAAF, General van Loggerenberg, maintained that the actions were 'necessary military measures because South Africa was in a state of war'. He submitted that because of this the courts had no jurisdiction to rule on the actions of the SADF.[26]

This prompted reactions demanding whether the Minister of Defence believed the SADF was above the law in a country where an undeclared state of war existed. Mr Justice S Selikowitz found that the deliberate propagating of false information about the ECC went far beyond legal opposition and he granted a restraining order against the Minister of Defence, the Officer Commanding Western Province Command and all those under him prohibiting them from harassing the organisation. The docket was forwarded to the Attorney General to decide whether prosecution would follow.[27] It did not, of course.

The military often urged Rob Brown to mount pro-SADF public demonstrations, but he was never able to. From the outset he sensibly realised that Veterans for Victory's following was insufficiently large to support major demonstrations.

The ECC in contrast, while it also had a small core membership, possessed the capability of calling for the public support of church groups, organisations like the UDF and its affiliates, the Black Sash and a host of other anti-government bodies.

This was always the basis of a dilemma for Brown. If he wanted to break, destroy or burn anything, he invariably had a queue of young men and girls who were willing to do it for him. If, on the other hand, he was planning a passive demonstration of any sort, he had to scratch to find even a scantling of volunteers. They had joined Veterans for Victory because they diametrically opposed the ECC's creed of pacifism. Standing on street corners with placards did not interest them. They wanted to fight!

To retain the interest of his inner circle and others who had come forward and openly joined the association as members, it became necessary to find ways to keep them interested. This was achieved by arranging weekend bush camps in cooperation with the SADF at which Brown gave them basic military training. He put them through their paces with pistols, R4 and R5 rifles, sub-machine guns like the Uzi, the general purpose machine gun or MAG, and even support weapons like 60mm and 81mm mortars and the 50 calibre Browning heavy machine-guns. Some members became sufficiently well-trained to provide Veterans for Victory with the capability for both covert and overt military operations.

The organisation's main thrust lay in the direction of propaganda and in discrediting the ECC, not in vandalism and the disruption of meetings. The letters-to-the-editor columns of newspapers were bombarded with letters of support for Veterans for Victory. Not all were published, but those that were showed a groundswell of ex-service opinion. Remarks in newspaper columns supporting the ECC or trashing the SADF were quickly repudiated. Posters were printed and put up. Leaflets were prepared for putting under the windscreen wipers of cars or for use as inserts in newspapers. Millions were distributed in this manner.

A series of posters was printed based on the ECC's 'Out of Step' logo — stickers saying 'ECC peace off', 'ECC: Every Cowards Choice' and 'KGB approved' stamped over the ECC's symbol.

Such campaigns created controversy, but their effectiveness cannot be doubted. People who supported the ECC were enraged and many wrote letters to newspapers deploring the content of the leaflets. It did not make any difference. As someone once said, there is no such thing as good publicity or bad publicity, there is only publicity. A campaign of 'Tell them (the troopies) we care' bumper stickers supported by brightly coloured posters was launched. It was a particularly effective campaign. Large quantities were printed and distributed to national servicemen and their families.

With Trust Bank as the sponsor, Brown arranged for the then current Miss South Africa, Michelle Bruce, to give a glamorous farewell to an intake of national servicemen when they reported for service at Johannesburg's Sturrock Park. She braved the cold for three hours, chatting and smiling happily as the lads stood patiently in long lines waiting to be photographed with her.

Resulting from the thousands of flyers and copies of *Stand-To* sent out to addressees on mailing lists that had been bought, Veterans for Victory's propaganda campaigns soon bore fruit. Donations poured in, particularly from America. The organisation was frequently contacted by US church groups and conservative organisations who identified with the anti-communist cause. They wanted to see the southern African situation for themselves. They came out in groups and Brown arranged tours of the Namibian border areas. They were flown in SAAF transport aircraft or in C-160s hired by the SADF from *Safair* to visit and talk to Jonas Savimbi at his Jamba headquarters in southern Angola. If he needed a C-160 for such a purpose, all Brown had to do was ask Military Intelligence for one and he got it.

In the same way, on instructions from MI, he facilitated trips by Rev Peter Hammond and his missionaries of the Frontline Fellowship to SWA/Namibia, which were indirectly in line with MI's aims. They reported on the estimated 30 000 Angolans in the south who had lost limbs to Soviet-supplied landmines. Peter Hammond wrote about FAPLA's Soviet supplied MiG strike aircraft machine gunning and bombing villages with napalm. He reported that the Cubans were forcibly removing children as young as seven years of age from their Angolan parents and shipping them to Cuba for communist indoctrination, and so on.[28] In all, teams of missionaries from Frontline Fellowship, until independence in 1990, spent up to three months a year paying MI-orchestrated visits to SWA/Namibia for evangelistic purposes.

The publicity regarding the evils of communism generated by those visits was welcomed by Military Intelligence.

Australian Operation: May-June 1987

In May 1987, Rob Brown was nominated to undertake an operation in Australia. This was apparently because he was an Australian resident and had a British passport endorsed for entry into that country. Military Intelligence briefed him that it wanted him to reconnoitre the ANC's offices in Sydney, which were shared with a trade union. It was planned, he was told, to plant a bomb there designed to blow up on 20 May 1987 — the fourth anniversary of the ANC's Church Street, Pretoria, bomb. Like the earlier bombing of the ANC's offices in London by the Security Police and assassinations overseas by the CCB, it was intended to demonstrate that no matter how far away ANC cadres were from South Africa, the SADF could always reach out and attack them. It was also intended as a high profile operation designed to bring awareness to Australians of terrorist atrocities being committed by the ANC and its affiliates in South Africa. It was hoped this would serve to lessen support for the ANC amongst the Australian populace. The third motivation was to make Australians aware that by offering hospitality and sustenance to a terrorist group, it could bring repercussions like the transplantation of a covert war onto their own soil.

He was briefed by the project officer, a woman, who did not introduce herself. He was given air tickets and travellers' cheques and told that he was to fly to Sydney on 15 May. He was given the address of the ANC's offices and the names and telephone numbers of contacts who would assist him. It was an old building near Number 1 Quay, Sydney harbour, close to where the monorail runs. There were two little sandwich bars/takeaways on the opposite side of the road. She explained the layout of the offices which were on the fifth floor and difficult to get into. On the day designated for the recce, his contacts would arrange a demonstration with placards outside the building. While everyone was busy watching, he would slip inside and do the recce. He was given the impression that arrangements for the actual blasting had already been finalised. He just needed to do the final recce to check that everything was in order.

Strangely enough, instead of leaving the country as soon as he had completed his recce and before the blast took place — for security reasons his project officer ordered him to remain in Australia. He was to take a return flight to South Africa on 9 June, three weeks later.

On his arrival in Sydney he phoned his contacts who were indeed real people, but he was mystified when they indignantly denied all knowledge of him. He apologised for bothering them and put the phone down.

Without anyone to turn to in South Africa, because his project officer had told him he would report only to his contacts in Australia, he was at a loss as to what to do. Eventually he decided that although something had apparently gone wrong, he should go ahead and do the recce because time was slipping away. He fully expected someone to contact him anyway. After all, his project officer knew how to get hold of him and he fully expected her to do so.

The day after his arrival he went to the building to conduct the recce. Everything appeared in order from the outside. But there was no one to organise a diversionary demonstration, so he decided to enter and climb the stairs to the fifth floor. The initial part until he reached the fifth floor should have posed no problems, because according to his project officer's briefing, there was no security guard or a doorman on duty in the hall. He passed through the front door and was shocked to find himself faced by a reception desk manned by a stern-faced old lady. Recovering himself, he blithely attempted to walk past her to the stairs as if he belonged there.

'You can't go there', she said.

She called him back and firmly told him to leave the building.

He could not make a fuss because that would have attracted attention. So he left.

The date of the proposed bombing came and went, but nothing happened. He remained in Australia visiting his family until his scheduled date of departure. Puzzlingly no one from South Africa or Australia contacted him. He just assumed the operation had been called off.

On his return to South Africa his project officer debriefed him, but she made no comment as to why he was not contacted, nor why the operation had not gone ahead. Unusually she demanded his air ticket and all original vouchers in respect of his expenses while abroad. He explained that the system was for him to give copies to project officers and retain the originals for the Military Intelligence accountant who audited his books. When she insisted, he handed her the originals thinking that she was probably new to that sort of thing. The accountant merely shrugged when he explained this to him later.

Prisoners in Zambia: October 1987

In October 1987 Rob Brown was briefed for another external mission that fell outside the Veterans for Victory brief by Military Intelligence. He was ordered to make contact with a small group of missionaries in Malawi. One of its personalities was a man called Ian Grey. Grey, he was told, had established good communications with the rebel RENAMO organisation in northern Mozambique. Brown's brief was to contact RENAMO through Grey and open a land line to their bases by which South Africa could supply and train them.

He was told to involve the Rev Peter Hammond of Frontline Fellowship in the trip, for he was well connected with missionary groups in Malawi. They said he would probably also be keen to get involved in Mozambique again. They were right — he jumped at the opportunity.

Brown, working in conjunction with Hammond, arranged it as a normal missionary trip. Brown's plan was to travel to Malawi by the most direct route through Zimbabwe. Military Intelligence, however, forbade it and insisted that he take the group there by the long route through Botswana and Zambia. He objected but they insisted he should obey orders. They gave no reason for the routing.

The group comprised Rob Brown, the Rev Peter Hammond, a missionary called Chris and a young student from Cape Town. They travelled through Botswana without experiencing a problem and entered Zambia via the border post at the Kazungula Ferry.

They were stopped and arrested at the first military roadblock. It was apparent to Brown that they had been expected. The Zambians were placed in detention and brutally tortured and interrogated in a quest to make them reveal military information. They were convinced the group was on a military mission and treated them accordingly. It did not help that Brown's body was badly scarred from old wounds, so they always addressed him as 'major'.

Brown, Hammond and Chris, although South African residents, were all British passport holders. They managed to sneak word of their detention out to the British High Commission and the torture abruptly ceased. They were told the South African authorities had refused to assist because they were British nationals.

Meanwhile, unbeknown to them in their straitened circumstances, on the international political front matters regarding the future of the South African government were balanced on a razor's edge.

South Africa had been a country in turmoil since 1984, with civil unrest and violence in African areas reaching new and unprecedented heights. This had again focussed the eyes of the world on the apartheid system, resulting in calls for the imposition of further sanctions on South Africa and creating more potential problems and headaches for the National Party government.

Because the Commonwealth Heads of Government Conference was scheduled for October 1985 in Nassau in the Bahamas, the increasing chorus of demands for the tightening of sanctions on South Africa was first channelled to that body for discussions and recommendations, rather than to the UN. Depending on what was agreed there, UN involvement would come into the picture later.

In terms of an accord formulated at the conference, the Commonwealth called on South Africa to dismantle the apartheid system, end the state of emergency, unconditionally release ANC leader Nelson Mandela and everyone else detained for opposing apartheid, establish political freedom, lift the ban on the ANC and other political parties and initiate a process of dialogue across colour lines to end violence and establish a non-racial representative government in South Africa.

If South Africa refused to comply, it was intended to recommend the implementation of a whole raft of new sanctions. If South Africa made no progress towards complying with the demands, many of the Afro-Asian nations were recommending the adoption of even harsher measures.

The British government recommended the formation of a committee of eminent persons to go to South Africa and investigate the situation with a view to seeing what could be done to implement the Commonwealth's recommendations. This became known as the EPG — Eminent Persons Group.

Representatives of black-ruled African states viewed the proposal with alarm, believing it was a product of the British government's wish to resist sanctions against South Africa and a device to postpone effective international sanctions. A majority were finally persuaded to support the British proposal, mainly because most believed the EPG would not be allowed to set foot in South Africa anyway.[29] They were mistaken, however, and in a letter dated 24 December 1985 President P W Botha said the EPG was welcome to visit South Africa and consult with the government and the various population groups. It was clear from this letter that he disagreed with the Commonwealth's objectives, but those concerned read what they wanted to in it.[30] It was all in the eye of the beholder.

It is reasonable to assume that Botha was persuaded to extend the invitation by British premier, Margaret Thatcher. It was undoubtedly a delaying tactic, even though the diplomatically experienced British government denied it. The South Africans had nothing to lose and the time spent by the EPG in South Africa would provide a breathing space and give it room to manouevre on the international front. More importantly, it would give time for the troublesome internal situation to cool down.

These exchanges led President Botha to give South Africa's Security Forces' commanders orders to stabilise South Africa's internal situation by December 1986. It did not work.

The EPG comprised Malcolm Fraser (co-chairman) — a former Prime Minister of Australia, General Olusegun Obasanjo (co-chairman) — the man who headed Nigeria's military government from 1976-1979, Lord Barber of Went Bridge — a leading British Conservative, Dame Nita Barrow — President of the World Council of Churches, John Malecela — a former Tanzanian cabinet minister, Sardar Swaran Singh - a former Indian cabinet minister and the Rev Walter Scott — formerly Bishop of Kootenay.

It is beyond the scope of this book to detail the political implications of the EPG. When they arrived in South Africa, they embarked on their task with boundless enthusiasm. As promised by President Botha, they were given absolute freedom of access to see anyone they wished, including political prisoners in gaol. Their enthusiasm, however, was a one-way street.

The EPG's zeal was quickly curbed when, without notice, Recce strikes were launched against ANC targets in Zimbabwe and Botswana simultaneous with the SAAF mounting an air strike against targets in Zambia. (For greater detail see Chapter 30 *The Silent War* by Peter Stiff)

Speaking in confidence after the event, a senior Recce officer told the author: 'One must see it against the background of the EPG at the time, padding around here firmly believing we were about to hand over to the ANC. They would like to have been seen as the instruments of peace — the instruments which crystallised in putting the ANC in the chair. There was an overall political desire [of the South African government] to have an ANC scalp to brandish around, but on my level it appeared to be a deliberate attempt to cock a snook at the EPG. The approval came down right from the top [President P W Botha].'

As Robin Renwick, British Ambassador to South Africa, succinctly put it, the moves the EPG wanted the South Africans to make were 'several bridges too far' for P W Botha.[31]

The bubble burst, as P W Botha had no doubt expected, and the EPG withdrew in righteous indignation on 20 May 1986.[32]

This was followed shortly afterwards by a confrontation between the US Congress and President Ronald Reagan when the Congress overrode a presidential veto by passing the Comprehensive Anti-Apartheid Act. The act banned the import of South African coal, iron, steel, uranium, arms and ammunition, textiles and agricultural products. New investments and the export of oil were also banned and the US landing rights of South African Airways were revoked. The Act also directed the President to impose further sanctions if Pretoria made no progress towards ending apartheid in the next year.

As he was compelled to do by the Act, Reagan reported a year later that there had been no significant progress towards the ending of apartheid. He claimed that the legislation's impact had proven negative by 'causing increased unemployment for blacks and worsening the country's economic situation without having a positive effect on the government itself'. Instead of additional sanctions, Reagan proposed — using the language of diplomatic gobbledygook — that the US embark on 'a period of active and creative diplomacy' to bring about negotiations. He was severely criticised by those who advocated tougher sanctions, but attempts to have Congress adopt stronger measures were abandoned.

The next move in the international debate occurred at the Commonwealth Heads of Government Conference held in Vancouver, Canada, in October 1987. A new element was the presence of Mozambique with observer status. Britain's Conservative government led by Margaret Thatcher had developed a close relationship with Mozambique since Zimbabwe's independence. Britain's aim, along with that of the European Community, the United States and the Scandinavian countries, was to reduce the Front Line States' dependence on South Africa by restoring the transport routes through Mozambique which had been disrupted since Rhodesian War days.

At Vancouver Margaret Thatcher laid great emphasis on Britain's aid to the SADCC States and said her aim, more or less echoing President Reagan, was to 'work for peaceful dialogue in South Africa' to end apartheid.[33]

This far from satisfied the vociferous proponents of the imposition of more sanctions, led by of President Kenneth Kaunda of Zambia. Kaunda was somewhat knocked off balance, though, when Margaret Thatcher launched a counter-attack by accusing him of the detention and torture of three harmless British Christian missionaries — none other than Brown, Hammond and Chris. She demanded their immediate release.

This, combined with the growing British and Western regional commitment which was imposing significant constraints on Pretoria, served to take the heat out of the sanctions issue.

After the conclusion of the conference, Rob Brown and the missionaries were freed and allowed to return to South Africa.

A sacrificial lamb?

Many years later Rob Brown discovered that the SADF had not been in need of a line of communication with RENAMO, because it had well-established ones already. He concluded that this factor, together with Military Intelligence's insistence on his taking the long route to Malawi through Zambia, indicated it was likely he had been set up as a ploy to ease Premier Margaret Thatcher's progress through the Vancouver talks. This was clearly in the South Africa government's interest, but whether it was set up in connivance with Britain's MI6 remains an unanswered question.

It also led Brown to re-examine the Australian operation. What had happened to his contacts? Why was the reception area of the office block not the same as he had been led to expect? Why was he deployed to Sydney to conduct a recce only five days before the proposed bombing? Surely he should have been allowed more time? Why was he told to remain in Australia for so long?

He concluded that the explosion had been planned by someone within the ANC based in Sydney, not by his non-existent contacts as his project officer had led him to believe. If this was true, it is likely he would have been remembered by the receptionist. It is also probable that after the explosion, information of his presence would have been fed to the Australian Police who would have fingered him as a suspect. His Special Forces background would have pointed to his culpability. He became convinced he had been deployed as a decoy duck, not to conduct a recce. After all, the bomber would surely have known everything there was to know about the premises.

But what was the purpose? While he undoubtedly would have been arrested, it is unlikely he would have been convicted because there was nothing to connect him to any blast. His arrest, however, would have diverted attention away from the real culprit. There was also the real probability of turning his visit around into a psychological or a media operation. His family in Australia would have created a row by wanting to know what was going on. The Australian Serviceman's League would have created a storm demanding to know why one of their members had been detained on such flimsy evidence. The British would have enquired about their national.

It was highly likely, too, that he would have been interviewed by the media and his own protestations of innocence would have created a media furore.

It would have been the second high profile event after the bombing itself. What more could Military Intelligence want?

Whatever the case, Rob Brown was not the first to discover that the SADF was not averse to using English speakers as sacrificial lambs when it suited their purpose.

Visit to Namibia: 1989

On 22 December 1988 the Protocol of Brazzaville was signed in New York by representatives of the governments of Angola, Cuba and South Africa. This cleared the way for the implementation of Security Council Resolution 435 on 1 April 1989 which would bring independence to Namibia. The SADF would make a scheduled withdrawal from the territory, clearing the way for free and fair elections to be held under UN supervision in November 1989. Independence would follow in 1990.[34]

During January 1989 Rob Brown was ordered to orchestrate a visit to SWA/Namibia by Frontline Fellowship. Colonel Jan Breytenbach (retired), the founding commander of the Recces, 44-Parachute Brigade and 32-Battalion joined the group at Peter Hammond's invitation.

Brown was instructed by Military Intelligence that while they were engaged in evangelism around the territory, the missionaries should be persuaded to give a positive slant to the forthcoming independence campaign. Unfortunately for MI things did not work out that way. Jan Breytenbach was vociferously against the idea of South Africa giving SWA/Namibia away to SWAPO. So much so, in fact, that the mission was a complete failure as far as MI were concerned. They even considered banning Breytenbach from entering military bases there.

The end of Veterans for Victory

On 2 February 1990 President F W de Klerk made his bombshell address to parliament, that he was lifting the bans of various black nationalist organisations including the ANC. He also announced that Nelson Mandela would be released from prison.

It did not affect Military Intelligence, as far as the running of Veterans for Victory was concerned, for another two years. Tobie Vermaak visited its offices when Rob Brown and his staff were busily engaged in 'putting to bed' the December 1991 issue of *Stand-To*. Hard-hitting articles slamming the ANC and Bishop Tutu had been planned, but Vermaak said it was no longer politic to publish it. He also objected to the front cover which showed a cartoon of a soldier slamming a Russian bear labelled 'ANC' on its backside with his rifle butt with the heading: 'Hit them where it hurts!'

After several acrimonious arguments Brown agreed to drop the articles, but he refused point-blank to change the cover. Military Intelligence eventually agreed it could remain as long as 'ANC' was deleted from the bear's behind. But when the issue appeared in print, despite a half-hearted attempt to remove 'ANC', it was still clearly visible. Brown also retained the anti-ANC article, but he had spiked the one on Bishop Tutu. The fact that he had ignored instructions created bad feelings between himself and MI.

Shortly afterwards in January 1992, he was again visited by MI. They told him that the December 1991 issue of *Stand-To* was the last. Furthermore they demanded that Veterans for Victory be closed down forthwith. It had served its purpose, but now that negotiations for a new constitution were taking place, it had lost that purpose.

Brown told them it was impossible to close it down just like that. He made it clear that he personally did not recognise the political changes. The ANC/communist enemy of yesterday remained his enemy of today. The government might have policy changes, but he did not. He was still a Bible-believing Christian and the communists were the enemy.

'I am not part of your government', he told them.

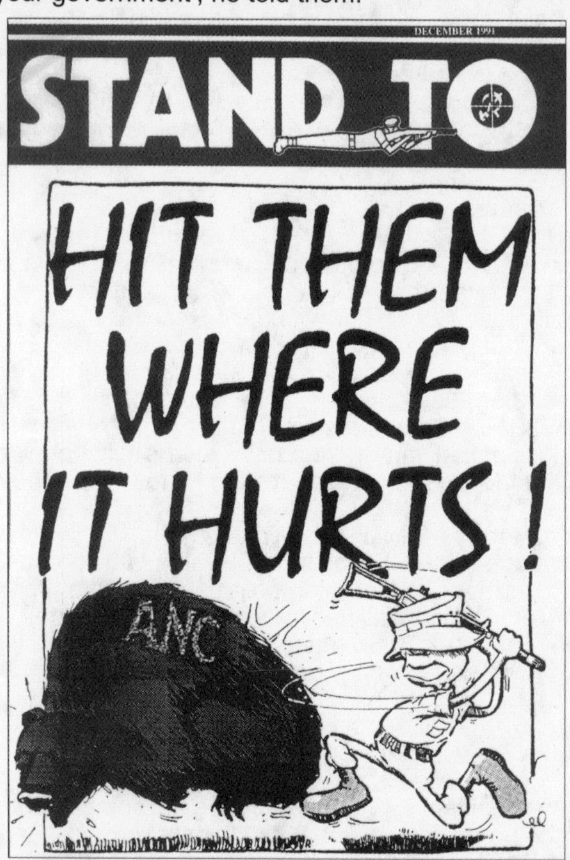

Military Intelligence vetoed the front cover of the final December 1991 issue of 'Stand To' because it was no longer politically acceptable. They finally allowed it to go ahead conditional on 'ANC' being removed from the Russian bear's backside. In a gesture of defiance Rob Brown published it how it was.

'You do not understand', they told him. 'Nelson Mandela was released from prison because we could not let him die there. Despite that, he will be dead in ten years.'

There were other reasons why he could not close the operation, he pointed out. His agents were deployed on the ground and they had to be paid. They had worked hard in the SADF's cause and he had no intention of letting them down.

'Why are you being so difficult?' they asked him.

Then they fired him but he refused to accept it. However, he realised that if he was cut off from finance, further publication of any kind would be impossible. He was personally owed considerable sums of money by Military Intelligence and he had no intention of losing out. By arrangement, MI held signed cheques relating to the Veterans for Victory's bank account in case something happened to him. For the same reason, they also had duplicate keys to his offices, filing cabinets and the safe. He worked out that he was personally owed at least R105 000. So on 25 February 1992 he drew a cheque for this sum and cashed it to ensure Military Intelligence did not get to the account first and empty it. There was a lot more than that in the account.

One morning shortly afterwards, Vernon, his landlord, who had offices next door, complained that someone had broken into them. Nothing had been stolen, but he was highly indignant. A few days later he told Brown that two thuggish looking men had called to see him while he was out.

Brown, who was under pressure at the time, paid no particular attention. He should have because the next day he arrived at his offices to find they had also been broken into and ransacked. Anything and everything that related to Military Intelligence, no matter how remote the connection, had been cleared from his safe, his filing cabinets and his desk drawers. The bank account had also been emptied of any funds that remained.

Yet the days of Veterans for Victory were not yet over. While there could be no further issues of *Stand-To* because of a lack of finance, Brown concentrated on writing letters to newspapers and getting articles into them where he could.

By April 1992 the stance of Veterans for Victory had changed. Now it cared only for the troops themselves and had turned on the Comops division of the SADF which had nurtured it. In a story in *The Citizen*, Brown accused the South African Army of brainwashing national servicemen attached to the Commando system. He said an organisation called Montage was allowed unlimited access to military camps in the Cape. Commando members were apparently called up and urged to accept National Party policy as the only viable option for a future South Africa. They were told to forget the dangers of communism because as a philosophy it was dead. The lectures, it appears, were arranged by a certain Colonel Claasen, the Commanding Officer of Comops at Western Cape Command. One group said they had received a telex from him telling them to stop complaining or they would face disciplinary action.

A South African Army spokesman confirmed that seminars had been held to inform SADF members of the current situation. They included information on the negotiating process, on change and the management of change in the country. Various constitutional models were explained. Its aim, the army said, was to equip members to better perform their tasks as soldiers. It denied any political involvement.[35]

In a follow-up letter to this article, Brown, still signing himself as chairman of Veterans for Victory, asked why, after President de Klerk had explicitly said that all secret projects had been terminated, the SADF continued to spend upwards of R7 million on an operation designed to brainwash and manipulate the troops. In particular, he said, Veterans had pointed out that the lectures were being delivered by the same people who had orchestrated the handover of Namibia to SWAPO.

He demanded equal time to inform the troops on the situation as viewed by Veterans for Victory and 'concerned and patriotic South Africans' as opposed to those whose sympathies lay with 'some sort of informal NP/ANC/SACP alliance.[36]

After this the activities of Veterans for Victory tailed off. By the time of the Goldstone Commission raid on the DCC's (Directorate of Covert Collection) headquarters in Momentum Mews, Pretoria, in November 1992, Rob Brown had effectively closed down the organisation.

15

Civil Cooperation Bureau
The Internal Factor
Pre-Region 6 days
1986

Assassination of Piet Ntuli: 29 July 1986

On 24 April 1985 KwaNdebele's Chief Minister, Simon Skosana, announced after negotiations with Pretoria that the homeland would take 'independence' towards the end of 1986. In true Orwellian fashion he announced that a new department, the Department of Citizen Liaison, would be established to liaise with KwaNdebele citizens resident in urban areas designated for white occupation. He declared smugly that Pretoria had agreed to the incorporation into the new state of the tin-pot dorp of Ekangala next to Bronkhorstspruit, population 4 708. The development of their future capital, Zusterhoek, had begun.

In Pretoria Cooperation and Development Minister Dr Gerrit Viljoen confirmed 'anew that the government actively pursues independence for National States. The enthusiastic and positive attitude of the government of KwaNdebele in regard to independence is, therefore, sincerely welcomed.' He said an inter-governmental working committee headed by the director-general of his department, was already engaged in consultations and preparations with a view to independence.

The announcements of coming independence and rumours of incorporation prompted an angry mob to burn down Ekangala's local government offices. A reign of terror against those opposing incorporation began. 'Vigilantes who are KwaNdebele supporters have been given *carte blanche* by the local SAP to assault and terrorise . . . travelling in cars with KN registration numbers, wearing balaclavas, and armed with pangas, sjamboks and clubs, these men roam the township and mete out "justice" to all seen to oppose KwaNdebele rule.'

Parliamentarian Colin Eglin (PFP) called the creation of a state only 30 to 40km from Pretoria 'a farce'.

State President P W Botha visited the homeland on 7 August 1985 and in an orchestrated display of mutual back scratching, praised its leaders. They, in turn, praised his constitutional proposals and his strong stand on law and order.

The homeland had four chiefs, one of whom, Chief Lazarus Mahlangu, wanted no truck with independence and had already 'resigned' from the homeland and applied officially for the amalgamation of his tribal lands into Bophuthatswana. In terms of its constitution there had to be four chiefs in KwaNdebele's legislative assembly. Having only three stymied Simon Skosana's ambitions for independence. He solved this by firing Chief Mahlangu on 9 July 1985. Chief Mahlangu, however, was reinstated after winning an action, opposed by respondents Skosana and Dr Gerrit Viljoen, in the Pretoria Supreme Court.[1] Moutse 1,2 and 3 were incorporated into KwaNdebele, evidently against the wishes of the majority of people there and strong opposition by the Lebowa homeland. At least 40 people were killed during protests.

In January 1986 Simon Skosana blessed extra-legal activities by launching the Mbokotho Vigilante Group. He became Mbokotho's president and his Minister of Internal Affairs, Piet Ntuli, vice president. Its 25-strong executive council was given sweeping powers to 'protect the interests of the community . . . deal with people who enforced boycotts' and 'handle troublemakers' — euphemisms for the opposition. Collectively they were classified as 'comrades', whether UDF/ANC supporters or not. In this 'with us or against us' atmosphere, such imagined divisions soon led to their becoming a reality.

The actions of Mbokotho degenerated into mob rule with criminal incidents too numerous to describe. In late December 1985 they beat up members of a Mamelodi youth organisation who had been in conflict with taxi drivers causing several serious injuries. In February 1986 the principal of Siyabuswa School decided to discipline pupils who had held a meeting and the police and Mbokotho arrived in Casspirs to assist. Five teachers and five pupils were arrested and handed over to Mbokotho who tortured and stabbed them with assegais. The teachers were released two days later, but the pupils disappeared.

In March Chief Mahlangu survived an assassination attempt by Mbokotho gunmen. In April seven vigilantes tried to force their way into the ward at GaRankuwa Hospital to assault or kidnap his wife, Princess Nonhlanhla — sister of Zulu King Goodwill Zwelithini — who was a patient there.

They attacked Benginhlanhla High School, Siyabuswa, seized ten students and forced them to perform balancing acts on soap-covered floors. When they inevitably slipped, they were tortured, beaten and electric shocks were administered as punishment. In Vlaklaagte 1, Mbokotho conducted house-to-house searches for 'troublemakers' after students had presented grievances to their chief. The police freed 30 of their captives, but Jacob Skosana, father of one of the pupils, was taken to Kwaggafontein where he was tortured and killed and his wife was sexually assaulted.

Colleen McCaul, author of a political and economic survey of KwaNdebele, reported that the events 'outraged the communities that witnessed them, leading to the involvement of many hitherto politically unorganised or uninvolved people in the resistance waged against the Mbokotho, and those who they protected, in the months that followed'.

On 7 May 1986 the government announced the homeland would become independent on 11 December 1986. This prompted the KwaNdebele royal family to convene an indaba on 12 May 1986 for the people to discuss the issue. Some 20 000 to 30 000 tribes people and many chiefs attended. Youths hijacked the entire fleet of the Putco Bus Service operating in the homeland's northern area to get to the meeting. Demands were made for the entire legislative assembly to resign and for Mbokotho to be disbanded. Fighting broke out and homes and businesses belonging to those with suspected Mbokotho affiliations were put to the torch.

On 13 May Jacob Skosana's funeral sparked widespread violent anti-independence demonstrations. Troops were deployed in virtually every village. On 14 May 25 000 tribes-people gathered for a meeting which, unknown to them, had been banned the previous day. Security Forces fired tear smoke and rubber bullets from Casspirs and a helicopter to disperse the crowd. Widespread violence flared between villagers on the one hand and Mbokotho supported by the SADF on the other. Fighting lasted for two days, leaving at least 12 people dead. 43 youths were captured by Mbokotho and a further 11 were abducted by a cabinet minister's brother. The 54 were held and tortured in a 'concentration camp' outside Siyabuswa, the homeland's capital, until the police attacked it on 20 May and released them.

Hundreds of youths left their villages to join organised resistance against Mbokotho, gathering under the banners of KWAYCO — KwaNdebele Youth Congress, and the Moutse Youth Congress. 200 village committees were set up to oppose independence. Tim Skosana, son of the Chief Minister a leader of KWAYCO, accused his father of losing direction and 'misleading the Ndebele people into accepting the apartheid laws of

Pretoria'. There is little doubt, too, that the UDF grasped the opportunity and climbed on the bandwagon.

The next two months saw a rapid escalation of violence with work stayaways and widespread acts of violence. In one incident, Minister Piet Ntuli led Mbokotho in an armed attack against villagers in Tweefontein. During a shooting in which he took part, at least six villagers were killed.

On 12 June 1986, Pretoria's nationwide state of emergency came into force. Additional restrictions on reporting actions by the Security Forces in KwaNdebele were imposed by the police commissioner there, Brigadier C M van Niekerk. 300 people were detained under the Emergency Regulations, many of whom were charged with public violence, arson or looting. There were rumours of midnight raids on homes by Mbokotho and people disappeared without trace. The police discovered the partially burnt bodies of nine young African pupils from Mamelodi, all had been shot with an AK47 .

On 2 July a group of senior church officials met Constitutional Development Minister Chris Heunis to express 'deep concern' about the KwaNdebele situation. Heunis said he was also concerned and intended doing something about it, but he had difficulties. Later in the month South Africa's Commissioner General for the homeland, Gerrie van der Merwe, said independence was on schedule for December 1986 and that the troubles resulted from 'purely domestic power struggles'.

On 15 July an indefinite work stay-away commenced to protest the presence of the Security Forces in the villages, the activities of Mbokotho and to support demands that detainees be released, the cabinet resign and 'independence' be cancelled. Civil servants, including nurses, teachers and even magistrates responded and by 18 July a strike by KwaNdebele's entire workforce was in progress.

Mbokotho went on the defensive. Its vigilantes travelled in SADF Casspirs, pointing out 'comrades' to the soldiers instead of taking action themselves. Many of them were killed or went into hiding, others defected to the anti-independence lobby. By the end of the month 70% of KwaNdebele's business premises had been burnt down.

The Black Sash reported that although the police often showed reluctance in taking action against Mbokotho, they were not actively working with it, but the SADF were.

A priest's diary recorded that about 120 people had died between 12 May and 25 July 1986. He estimated a third had been killed by the Security Forces, a third had died at the hands of Mbokotho and the rest had been killed by the 'comrades' — most of them 'necklaced'. The authorities, however, claimed 42 people had been killed between 8 May and 8 June and 32 between 13 June and 18 July. This, the authorities said, had resulted from 'black on black violence' — the Security Forces had not killed anyone.

In late July the police arrested Minister Piet Ntuli after his home was searched and 50 stolen cars and an arms cache were found. He was already facing charges of murder and three assault charges connected with Mbokotho activities. One of the victims was his own night watchman. He was released on bail.

The Weekly Mail claimed he had become an embarrassment to the administration. Senior officials acknowledged that 'many of KwaNdebele's problems would be eased if his power was effectively eliminated.'

Northern Transvaal's Security Branch commander, Colonel Jack Cronje, had come to the same conclusion by a different route. He suspected Ntuli was an ANC double agent, who was deliberately destabilising KwaNdebele to stave off independence. He was certain his violent behaviour was turning the populace against independence, which played into the hands of the UDF/ANC.

On Colonel Cronje's recommendation, several representations were submitted to Minister Heunis for Ntuli's detention, but he turned them down because it would have embarrassed the government. Ntuli was a supporter of independence, so how could they detain him?

Following this Colonel Cronje 'in all probability' recommended to a meeting of TREWITS — (Counter-Revolutionary Intelligence Target Centre) that Ntuli should be killed. He had also raised the question at the Joint Information Centre, on which representatives of the police, military and NIS (National Intelligence Service) sat. In the end, the order to kill Ntuli came down either from TREWITS or the Joint Information centre, Colonel Cronje could not recall which. General Johan van der Merwe, then the Security Police Chief and later Police Commissioner, confirmed to the TRC during his testimony on 5 June 1998 that the assassination had been sanctioned by the State Security Council.

Meanwhile, in the wake of the National State of Emergency, SADF Chief, General Jannie Geldenhuys, had instructed all units to 'make a plan' to provide support for the Security Police to combat internal dissidence. Special Forces Commander, Major-General Joep Joubert, said he was told this would involve 'unconventional and revolutionary methods'.

General Joubert identified three 'trouble spots' — Northern Transvaal, the Witwatersrand and the Eastern Cape — and decided to liaise with the relevant security branch and army commanders to identify 'targets of importance in getting the areas under control'. He allocated two CCB five-man groups commanded by senior officers to support the police in the Northern Transvaal and the Witwatersrand. This was before the formation of Region 6, so he co-opted personnel from other regions.

Joubert's plan, designed to cause the 'maximum disruption of the ANC', involved the 'elimination of ANC leaders, destruction of their facilities and support structures and elimination of their supporters and collaborators'. It was 'a very busy time' and he was unable to secure a formal meeting with General Geldenhuys to discuss his plans, but he spent 15 minutes explaining them at a farewell function for the Armscor chairman's retirement. 'All he [Geldenhuys] said to me', General Joubert explained, 'was that it sounded good and that he had never had any problem with my integrity and my judgement. If the SAP agreed, the plan could go ahead.' [2] General Joubert took that as an authorisation to implement his plans.

General Geldenhuys, however, denied General Joubert had explained the full details of his plan to him, or that he had authorised the elimination of activists, but he conceded his instructions could have been misinterpreted.[3]

Joubert said he was approached by either Colonel Joe Verster or Sergeant Major Trevor Floyd with an SAP request that Special Forces supply an explosive device with which to blow up Piet Ntuli.[4]

Trevor Floyd, however, said he was summoned to the General's office and told to go and see Colonel Cronje and Captain Hechter and assist them with an operation they were busy with. He had no idea what it was all about and where they were. Colonel Joe Verster, the Senior Staff Officer Special Forces, told him how to find their offices in Pretoria. He went there and they briefed him about the planned elimination of Piet Ntuli. They told him that although he was the Minister of the Interior in KwaNdebele, he was also a member of the ANC and responsible for various acts of terrorism.

Captain Hechter took Floyd on a reconnaissance. They went to the KwaNdebele government offices where Piet Ntuli's Toyota Cressida was pointed out as well as the bay in which it was normally parked. He was shown the entrances to the complex and noted that the main gate was unguarded. The nearby police station was also indicated to him. He decided the best way to tackle the job was to place an explosive device under the car's front seat that could be command detonated by radio from a distance. It would be important to ensure that nobody else was in the vicinity when the explosion took place.

On his return to Pretoria, Floyd reported to Major-General Joubert and told him his basic plan, but said another reconnaissance would probably be wanted. He explained the kind of device he needed and said he required two arming devices as a failsafe.

General Joubert said he should leave it to him. He passed on the instruction to Colonel Joe Verster, who presumably passed it on to the EMLC.

Shortly afterwards he was told the device was ready for collection. General Joubert told him to give it to Colonel Cronje and Captain Hechter, explain how it worked and how to operate it, but not to get involved further. 'He said the reason was, or as I remember at that stage, was that he was not sure if he had got the authority to do the operation. He wanted no further involvement from our side', Floyd recalled.[5]

General Joubert said: 'I was under the impression that I had to support the police. I felt satisfied that . . . it would be a South African Police operation and I knew that Ntuli was a key figure in the ANC struggle. I was satisfied that this would disrupt the ANC and I gave permission that an explosive device would be given to the SAP. I did not want any person of Special Forces involved in this operation, because I was of the opinion that this would be a simple operation that did not need any special abilities . . . I did indeed give permission that a member of the SAP be trained in the use of the device . . .'

General Joubert apparently personally discussed Piet Ntuli with Colonel Jack Cronje, who assured him the police had authorised the operation. Despite this, the general remained unsure from how high up the police ladder the authorisation had emanated.

Captain Abraham Kendall, the commander of the Security Police at Bronkhorstspruit, was well aware of the grassroots opposition by traditional leaders to the idea of KwaNdebele being declared an independent homeland. They felt that the area was not traditional land where the graves of their forefathers were situated, but land allocated to them by the government, so it was not appropriate. Part of the proposed homeland also contained segments of land occupied by Sotho and Tswana speaking people.

In efforts to promote peace, Captain Kendall explored many avenues. He discussed the situation with the cabinet and traditional leaders, particularly Prince James Mhalangu, with whom he had a good relationship. He even arranged the release from Security Police detention of a Catholic priest, Father Shaun O'Leary, because he could play a positive role in arbitrating between the opposing groups. At one public meeting Piet Ntuli swore at Kendall because he refused to throw his weight behind the independence move.

While he was convinced that Ntuli should be removed from office in the interests of peace in the area, it had never occurred to him that he should be killed, and he would have opposed the plan, if he had known about it.

On 29 July 1986 Captain Kendall, accompanied by a Lieutenant de Beer, returned to Siyabuswa Police Station from a morning patrol of KwaNdebele. He noticed a white Toyota Hi-Ace Combi parked opposite the police station and recognised Colonel Cronje, Captains James Hechter and Jaap van Jaarsveld who were braaiing meat beside the vehicle. He stopped and they introduced him to two detectives, Andries Oosthuizen and Deon Gouws from the Murder and Robbery unit. They were with the SAP's Unit 19 and were assisting locally based detectives in the investigation of some 300 politically inspired murders in the area. While trying to get to the bottom of these murders, several of the witnesses they had interviewed were murdered.

They expressed an interest in Piet Ntuli and asked where he was. Kendall assumed, as Murder and Robbery detectives were there, that he was being sought on criminal charges. Shortly afterwards Kendall and De Beer left to see if Ntuli was at the government offices. He was not, nor was his car parked in his official bay. Kendall dropped De Beer off at the police station and returned to Colonel Cronje. Cronje told him that Ntuli was at the house of Chief Minister Simon Skosana. They discussed Ntuli's criminal antics for quite some time and had a few drinks in the process.

Captain Kendall had previously arranged to see Chief Minister Skosana to discuss local unrest, school boycotts and traditional leaders and eventually decided to go to his house. Cronje asked Kendall if he could go with him to meet the Chief Minister and he agreed. The two got into Kendall's car followed by Captain Hechter who lay down on the floor in the back. This mystified Kendall who suspected they were 'busy with dirty tricks' but he did not have the slightest idea that a bomb was involved. Several vehicles were parked in front of the Chief Minister's house, including a brown Toyota Cressida that Cronje identified as Ntuli's car. He told Kendall to park as close to it as possible.

Kendall entered the house, but Cronje said he would wait at the garden gate. After tea with the Chief Minister and a short discussion the latter walked him to the gate. Cronje moved forward to introduce himself.

As Kendall drove from the security fenced area, Cronje asked Hechter in the back of the vehicle 'if he had managed'.

Hechter replied in the affirmative.

They joined Oosthuizen, Van Jaarsveld and Gouws who were awaiting them at the Toyota Hi-Ace. It was only then that they told Captain Kendall about the bomb. Oosthuizen and Gouws both had detonating devices and they were discussing who would actually activate the bomb. Kendall left for Bronkhorstspruit, not wanting to have anything to do with what was about to happen. He received a radio message shortly afterwards saying that a bomb had exploded at Siyabuswa Police Station.

When he had finished his business at the Chief Minister's residence, Piet Ntuli had got in the driver's seat of his car, closed the door, started the engine and drove out of the government compound. The arrangement was that the explosive device would be detonated 30 seconds after Ntuli left the place. There was also a delay to ensure that the car was well clear of all houses in the area. It exploded and killed him just as the car reached the S-bend beyond the Siyabuswa police station.

Chief Minister Simon Skosana and his cabinet sent for SAP Commissioner, General Johan Coetzee, from Pretoria. They accused Colonel Cronje of the murder in his presence. The accusation was indignantly denied. Captain Kendall was also accused of setting off the bomb and the police authorities told him never to set foot in KwaNdebele again. Presumably as a sop to the Chief Minister, General Coetzee appointed a high-powered Detective Branch team under the command of General Schutte to investigate the murder.[6]

For the next six week they ran around in the proverbial small circles, finally completing their investigations and reporting the negative result and lack of arrests to General Coetzee on 11 September 1986. It is unknown whether General Schutte mentioned in his report that he had failed to question Colonel Cronje. Whether the fact that he didn't was by his own omission or on the instructions of General Coetzee, is a matter for conjecture. Whatever the reason, no orders were given to correct the omission. An inquest absolved Colonel Cronje of any blame.

According to Captain (later Colonel) Kendall the 'general and popular opinion' in the Bronkhorstspruit and KwaNdebele area was that he, Kendall, was the prime suspect in the murder. This played on his mind so much that it became necessary for him to undergo psychiatric treatment and then electro convulsive therapy. The incident destroyed his life and he was eventually discharged from the SAP 'on medical grounds' because of it.[7]

News of Ntuli's death prompted an air of celebration in KwaNdebele. He had been variously regarded as the 'power behind the throne', the 'notorious strongman' and the prime mover behind Mbokotho and moves for independence.

In August 1986 the ANC's Chris Hani claimed an MK unit had carried out the assassination as part of their strategy of identifying with local struggles. He described it as the elimination 'of one of the worst collaborators with the regime'.[8] Locals, however, continued to believe that people within the KwaNdebele administration or 'agents of Pretoria' had planted the bomb and they were correct.

Piet Ntuli's death marked a turning point. It boosted the morale of the anti-independence forces and terrified Mbokotho and the pro-independence lobby who feared the same fate awaited them. On 12 August 1986 the KwaNdebele Legislative Assembly abandoned moves for 'independence' and banned Mbokotho. Residents of Siyabuswa, lining the streets in anticipation, greeted the news with jubilation. In the days that followed, rejoicing and celebrations took place throughout KwaNdebele.

It is impossible to say if there was any connection with recent events, but Chief Minister Simon Skosana died of diabetes complications on 17 November 1986.

Judging by the late Chris Hani's comments, and by Piet Ntuli's general behaviour around Mbokotho, it seems unlikely that he was a double agent. What is more probable is that the security establishment decided to kill him because of the trouble he was causing in the homeland. Ironically, his assassination utterly destroyed all chances of KwaNdebele becoming an 'independent state' in pursuance of the National Party government's agenda.[9]

Murder of Nietverdiend Ten: 27 June 1986

Although Special Forces commander Major-General Joep Joubert maintained his cooperation with the Security Police on internal operations began in mid-July, the first such operation occurred a few weeks earlier in late June 1986.

It was prompted by the activities of undercover security policeman Joe Mamasela who, in the guise of an MK operative, infiltrated the ranks of UDF/ANC 'comrades' in Mamelodi Township, Pretoria. Ten of them, Thomas Phiri (22), Elliott Sathege (20), Morris Nkabinde (19), Steven Makena (18), Abraham Makulane (17), Jeremia Ntuli (17), Samuel Masilela (16), Jeremiah Magagule (16), Sipho Sibanyoni (15) and Matthews Lerutla (15) asked him to smuggle them to Botswana for military training by MK. They were all politically active, but only two had ever been arrested by the Security Police.

Mamasela reported this to his security branch commander, Colonel Jack Cronje. It appears, judging by subsequent events, that he brought the matter to the attention of TREWITS. TREWITS, it further appears, authorised the assassination of the activists. The police's point of view in summation was that they had to stop the activists from being trained. While scholars might leave the country as untrained innocents, when they returned as trained MK guerrillas they posed great dangers to the State. It seemed wiser to kill them at the earlier rather than at the later stage. Prosecuting them in terms of the security legislation was possible, but it was rejected as it would have blown Mamasela's cover.

Colonel Cronje approached General Joep Joubert who referred him to CCB commander, Commandant Charl Naudé. A meeting was held, perhaps at Speskop perhaps at Renosterspruit Farm, where a plan was formulated to kill the activists. The planning was conducted jointly by Commandant Naudé, Colonel Cronje and Captain Jacques Hechter. It was approved by General Joubert.

The idea was for Joe Mamasela to transport the recruits in a minibus to Zeerust, near to the Botswana border. He would take a large quantity of liquor and encourage the recruits to celebrate their pending training. Hopefully, by the time they neared Zeerust they would be very drunk. Joubert authorised Charl Naudé to obtain 'drugs' to put in their drinks. Joubert was vague about its origin saying: 'I cannot say with certainty, but it comes from one of the laboratories or it could have come from the Police Laboratory . . . '[10] In reality it must have come from *Project Coast*. Sergeant-Major Dave Tippets arranged for the procurement of the drugs.

Naudé, Cronje and Rudi Crause, another security policeman, reconnoitred a farm road near Zeerust and found a suitable spot for the operation to take place.

During the evening of 26 June 1986 Mamasela left Mamelodi in the minibus and set off for Zeerust with the ten recruits. Following him in a car, within radio contact, were Cronje and Hechter. One can only assume that Mamasela explained his possession of the radio by saying he was in contact with MK in Botswana.

On reaching Zeerust Cronje directed Mamasela to head for the border post at Nietverdiend (meaning 'not deserved' in Afrikaans) and turn on to a deserted road in the Madikwe area. Mamasela's passengers, by this time, were hopelessly drugged.

Charl Naudé, Dave Tippets and the experienced Danie Phaal awaited them at the prearranged rendezvous. Tippets filled the syringes. The trainees, who were too drugged to offer resistance, were covered with guns and told to get out of the minibus one by one. Over the next 15 minutes each was forcibly injected with an unidentified substance by Naudé and Phaal, while Cronje and two other security policemen, Crause and another looked on. Cronje assumed, rightly, that the substance was meant to kill them. This, he said, was to eliminate any possibility of their surviving their forthcoming ordeal.

After being injected they were ordered back into the vehicle where all fell unconscious. In all probability, judging by what happened in previous incidents of prisoners being injected, they died almost as soon as they were back in the vehicle.

With Major Derek Vorster driving the minibus with the comatose or dead activists aboard, they headed in convoy for another spot where it was intended to stage an 'accident'.[11]

The Security Police and CCB operators pushed the minibus down an embankment and it crashed into a ditch. Major Vorster splashed the interior with petrol. To add authenticity and to create an explosion, a limpet mine was placed in the vehicle along with an AK47. The vehicle was then set alight. It blew up when the limpet mine detonated from the heat. The impression they wanted to create was that the recruits had brought explosives with them from Botswana for sabotage purposes, but instead their vehicle crashed and they were blown up.

Except for a short report in the *Sowetan* seven days later saying that ten people had died in a car explosion in the Madikwe area, the incident received no media coverage.[12]

Colonel Cronje said that Brigadier (later Major-General) Johan Viktor, variously described as second-in-command of the Security Branch's Intelligence Desk/Security Branch's counter-insurgency unit, phoned and congratulated him on the success of the operation.

Colonel Cronje said a Bophuthatswana Police investigation proved inconclusive and they were unable to identify the victims. At a TRC hearing on 31 October 1996, however, the names were submitted by Attorney Brian Currin.[13]

Colonel Charl Naudé, a veteran of 141 contacts while serving with the Recces, went to Major-General Joubert afterwards and told him that neither he nor his men wanted to be involved in such an operation again. They were soldiers who shot at the enemy and the enemy shot back. When the shooting finished, they treated each other's wounds and 'the war would be over'. The Nietverdiend sort of operation was against their nature.[14] It is likely that this attitude led to his replacement as head of the CCB by the more ruthless Colonel Joe Verster.

Charl Naudé was a brave and honourable soldier. The author remembers, when he was researching *The Silent War: South African Recce Operation 1969-1994*, how Naudé expressed his personal regret and said how awful he felt over the killing of about 190 guerrillas at SWAPO's Shatotwa Base in Zambia in August 1976.

'What could we do', he asked the author, 'it was war.'[15]

Projects Checkers/Le Roux: Assassination of Dr Fabian and Mrs Florence Ribeiro: 1 December 1986

Although it is now denied, there is little doubt that Dr Fabian Ribeiro had a history of political activism. He had been tried but acquitted on charges of terrorism in 1977 and had also spent time in detention under the Emergency Regulations. But how much of an activist he was and how much of a danger he posed to the security of the apartheid state remains controversial.

Security Police records described him as 'a high profile' activist who had been detained 'several times'. He had financially assisted 'comrades' escaping the country to join the ANC in exile as well as 'terrorists' returning to conduct operations. He had allegedly given medical treatment to (wounded) 'activists and terrorists' and had shown banned films in his garage, including Richard Attenborough's *Cry Freedom* — the story of Steve Biko, founder of the Black Consciousness Movement who was murdered by Security Police. It is bizarre that viewing a movie should have become a contributing factor in a State motivated assassination.

Florence Ribeiro had no particular political reputation, but her brother was the late PAC leader, Dr Robert Sobukwe.[16] Colonel Cronje and Captain Hechter of the Security Police said that as a matter of convenience entries relating to her activities appeared in her husband's file. They said she supported her husband in his underground activities and occasionally, when he was absent, she had personally assisted 'comrades'. Neither could recall specific instances of her alleged illegal activities, but in fairness, they no longer had access to the file.

Chris, their son, was adamant that neither of his parents were activists. He agreed that prior to his detention 'they had aided comrades [from all liberation movements] who were going to exile, logistically and financially'. After his release from detention in 1981, his father had stayed away from politics. Yes, he did treat 'comrades' wounded in clashes with police, but he was a doctor — that was his job. He did not say if he treated the wounded of those opposing the 'comrades'. He said that describing them as 'high profile' activists who rendered assistance to MK guerrillas was a 'blatant lie'. 'If he had shown *Cry Freedom* in our garage', Chris said, 'then I would not have seen the film for the first time after it was unbanned in the 1990s'.

Moss Chikane, a political activist in Mamelodi during the 1980s and later an ANC MP, described Dr Ribeiro as 'a respected person in the Mamelodi community, widely known as the "People's Doctor". He was not the sort of person who organised meetings or marches. A concerned person, yes, a sympathiser, but not an activist.' He said Dr Ribeiro was often invited to speak at commemoration meetings — because of his standing in the community, not because he had a leadership position in political structures.Chikane confirmed, though, that the doctor treated injured comrades on a no questions asked basis and with an assurance he would not betray them to the police. This might have included his treating wounded murderers on the same basis, so whether this would classify him as a political activist or not is a moot point.

Florence Ribeiro, Chikane said, had nothing to do with politics. 'She was a good wife and a good mother, but she was not an activist.'[17]

Colonel Jack Cronje, Northern Transvaal's Security Branch commander, said that towards the end of 1986 he was approached by Commandant Charl Naudé of the CCB and asked for a 'memorandum' on Dr Ribeiro. Commandant Naudé told him Special Forces had identified Ribeiro as a target. 'I later learnt', Colonel Cronje said 'that the order to eliminate Ribeiro came from TREWITS, Law and Order Minister Adriaan Vlok and/or the SSC.' He gave Charl Naudé and an operator called Paddy access to Security Police files on Ribeiro and designated a subordinate, Captain Jacques Hechter, who was responsible for Mamelodi, to assist with planning. Captain Hechter, he said, told him the operation involved the murder of Ribeiro.[18]

Special Forces commander, Major-General Joep Joubert, however, contradicted Cronje's version of the events, saying the motivation for the operation came from the Security Police, not Special Forces. He insisted that Special Forces never acted alone within South Africa, but only in support of the police and only 'when requested by the police'. He did not seek approval for the operation from SADF Chief, General Jannie Geldenhuys, 'because I was under the impression he had [already] given me authorisation to do that'.

Planning for the assassination was conducted jointly by Commandant Charl Naudé, Noel Robey and Jaques Hechter.

Noel Robey, a former sergeant in the Selous Scouts and by then an operator in Region 4 (Zambia), had earned a formidable reputation as a pseudo group leader. He was reputed to have accounted for more guerrillas during the Rhodesian War than any other Selous Scout. After the independence elections brought Robert Mugabe to power, he moved to South Africa and joined 7-Recce, which briefly became 3-Recce, then 5-Recce. Within two hours of his first deployment from Ondangwa in SWA/Namibia with 3-Recce, his pseudo group engaged in a successful contact with SWAPO guerrillas. From 5-Recce he transferred to *Project Barnacle* which became the CCB when its designation changed.

Captain Hechter wanted to 'take out' Ribeiro himself,[19] but it was finally decided to shoot him at his Mamelodi home. There was no question of Florence Ribeiro being targeted. Hechter told Cronje that Special Forces were flying in two black 'Angolese', who could only speak Portuguese, from SWA/Namibia especially for the job. Charl Naude said 'they needed operators who had never been to Mamelodi and who will never return to Mamelodi. I then requested from headquarters that I want Portuguese [speaking] Special Forces operatives from the operational area. This request was conceded . . .' They were operators from 5-Recce Regiment who had formally served in 32-Battalion.[20]

Comprehensive reconnaissances were conducted to ascertain when the target would be at home. Much of this was probably done by the Security Police, but Special Forces had learned from experience that it was wise to supplement this with their own reconnaissance.

The two operators flew in from SWA/Namibia. Robey collected them from Speskop and pointed out the Victoria Hotel and the Manhattan Hotel. He gave them R2 000, dropped them off at the station nearby and told them they could book into whichever they wished. They should call him on his pager and let him know which one so he could find them. They ended up staying at the Manhattan Hotel. He made arrangements to pick them up at 08:00 the next morning.

Robey collected them in a blue VW Golf. He showed them the route to Mamelodi from Pretoria, along Church Street to the turnoff at Silverton. He made sure they knew the rendezvous where they would meet after the hit. He drove them backwards and forwards, six or more times, from the Manhattan Hotel to the rendezvous.

By the morning of the second day a red Opel Kadet had already been positioned at the Palm Hotel — the last building outside Silverton. It had been fitted with false number plates so it could not be traced. Engine and chassis numbers had been ground off. Most of the day was spent with the two operators driving the Opel backwards and forwards to the Manhattan Hotel. Robey followed behind to ensure there were no hiccups en route.

On the third day he picked them up from the station at 08:00. The operators were fully briefed by Robey and shown air photographs of the immediate area of Ribeiro's house. There were also pictures taken from the ground supplied by the Security Police. After poring over the photographs, Robey sent them into Mamelodi to familiarise themselves with the target area on the ground. They checked out the house and also Ribeiro's surgery which was a distance away.

'They then came back and they were quite happy with the area and the target areas. Again I followed them back to the station area where they went back to the hotel. I then got hold of Mr Naudé and said that the chaps know the area. They have familiarised themselves with it. There are no hiccups to and fro. They know the route etc., so everything is all right from our side. On the fourth day [1 December 1986] Mr Naudé phoned to say that: "It's carry on with the operation." It was around 11:30, but we must wait until the afternoon, from 16:00 onwards, because that is when Dr Ribeiro and his wife would return home after hours.'

Robey made preparations. He collected two Colt .45s, wrapped them in towels and placed them in a duffel bag. 'I picked up Mr Vlietstra in my vehicle [Land-Rover] and then went to the Schoeman Street parking garage where I parked the Blue Golf. I used to park it there after work, pick up my own vehicle and drive home in that . . . I first phoned the chaps to meet me at the station at 15:30.' He parked the Land-Rover away from the station because Vlietstra was with him and walked to the station on foot. He handed over the duffel bag with the weapons and told them the operation was on. They were to take the Opel and go on the route they had practised.

Robey then returned to the parking garage, parked his Land-Rover and transferred to the Blue Golf. It would not start and after about 15 minutes of trying he gave up and transferred back to the Land-Rover. He was running out of time to rendezvous with Charl Naudé and the Security Police at the Palm Hotel.

He told them his problems with the Golf and the operation was almost aborted. But it was then decided to go ahead and he was told to take his Land-Rover to the rendevous point. Captain Hechter was not taking an active part in the operations. He was waiting in a field outside Mamelodi in case the assassins were stopped by police while escaping. It would be his job to effect their release.

Robey waited at the rendezvous until he believed sufficient time had passed for the operators to complete the operation, then stood out in the road ready to wave them down. They were expecting him to be in the blue Golf, not the Land-Rover. Fortunately for them they saw him and pulled in. They jumped out, leaving their weapons and duffel bag in the Opel, and got into the Land-Rover. Vlietstra jumped into the Opel and drove off. It was later broken up and destroyed.

Chris Ribeiro was chatting to a friend about 15m away from the house. He saw his parents park their van in the driveway. He vaguely noticed an Opel halt at the stop sign close to the creche on the opposite side of the road. He heard a series of bangs, but took no notice. The bonnet of his parents' 20-year-old van was difficult to close so he thought they were trying to slam it shut.

He glanced at the house and suddenly saw three people wearing balaclavas running from his home to the Opel which was by then stopped in front. Chris ran to the driver's door, wrenched it open and grappled with the driver, attempting to pull him from the car. He heard bangs but the sound did not register until he noticed that the person in the front passenger seat had a pistol and was shooting at him. When the third shot was fired, the shooter was almost spreadeagled across the seat. Chris registered that he was a white man despite the balaclava over his face.

Chris broke away and fled for his life in a westerly direction. The Opel sped past him moments later. He turned around and ran back towards the house to tell his parents he had been shot at by thieves. He was convinced they had been robbed. He was shocked to find his father's body sprawled over the drain in the yard. There were about 20 to 25 bullet wounds in his head. His mother's body lay close by. She had been shot only once.

His father was already showing a blue tinge. Nevertheless, Chris tried to resuscitate him by talking him back to life. His mother appeared uninjured and he cradled her in his arms until she sighed her last breath. An ambulance arrived and the crew confirmed that Ribero was well past saving. They felt there was still a faint chance for Mrs Ribeiro and they put an oxygen mask on her face. They were loaded into the ambulance and Chris got in with them. The vehicle had to be push-started. It took a long route to the hospital instead of going by the shortest way. To this day the Ribeiro family is convinced that this was part of a deliberate plan by the Security Police to ensure the ambulance would take too long for the successful administering of medical attention. Fabian and Florence Ribeiro were certified dead on arrival at the hospital and were taken to the mortuary.

Charl Naudé had cruised past the house while the ambulance was there. He saw a large crowd of people who appeared very tense and excited. He drove directly to Mamelodi Police Station and saw the commander.

'Do you know that Dr Ribeiro has been shot? There are problems. You had better get there', he told him.

Naudé made radio contact, via the Special Forces radio room and alerted the police Reaction Unit, the Murder and Robbery Squad, the fingerprint people and so on. He then accompanied the station commander to the murder scene. He left shortly afterwards.

It was all going wrong for the assassins.

They escaped in the Opel, but two witnesses raced through the township after them in hot pursuit. The Opel stopped next to a Land-Rover. They watched as the assassins scrambled from the car and into the Land-Rover. A bearded white man alighted and climbed into the driver's seat of the Opel. Both vehicles drove off. Another vehicle was thought to be involved, but no one recorded its registration number or noted its description. The witnesses, however, wrote down the registration numbers of both the Opel and the Land-Rover.

Robey drove back to Pretoria by his normal route, then went circuitously around town to ensure no one was tailing him. He dropped the killers off at the station. He instructed them to pay their hotel bills and be ready for collection at 05:00 the next morning. He duly picked them up and left them with their kit and equipment in the foyer of Speskop, Special Forces HQ. The men returned to Ondangwa in Owamboland on the next scheduled C-130 flight. Robey, who had more to do with them than anyone else, recalled that their names were Johnny Pinta and Louis da Silva. He had introduced himself to them by his organisation name, Lionel Kirby, so it likely they also went by false names for security reasons.[21]

When Chris Ribeiro arrived back home it seemed like hundreds of soldiers were there. He was refused entry, but insisted he had a right to go into his own home to see what was happening.

'Kaffir, we will shoot you as well', one told him.

After waiting around for what seemed like a couple of hours he was eventually allowed in. Security Branch policemen were inside. They had collected cartridge cases and removed certain documents. Drawers were open and they were still searching the place.

'What happened?' one of them asked.

'We cannot tell you what happened', Chris said. 'We cannot give you a statement because it's you who killed my parents.'

He was convinced they knew the killers and that there would be 'one big cover up' which, in the end, is what happened. He had few reasons for optimism.

It was the third attack on Dr Ribeiro that year. In the early hours of a March morning, petrol bombs were thrown into his home causing extensive damage. A witness said he had seen police alight from a Casspir and throw the bombs over the yard wall before speeding off.

In September Ribeiro's sons apprehended a man watching the house. He had a bomb in a carry bag. He confessed he had been ordered to plant it in the doctor's surgery.[22]

Brigadier (later General) Basie Smit, a renowned criminal investigator, was assigned to investigate. It was not long before his team produced results. The Opel's Pietermaritzburg registration plates were false. The Land-Rover's number, KYK899T, belonged to the SADF but the vehicle was registered in the name of Noel J Robey. This was not released to the press, but reporters from *The Star* had obtained the vehicle numbers independently from witnesses. Their own enquiries at the licensing office confirmed the Land-Rover was registered to Noel Robey who lived near Hartbeespoort Dam. When they made further enquiries, both Robey and his wife ducked into hiding, probably on the instructions of Major-General Joubert or the new CCB commander, Colonel Joe Verster. This did not prevent the police from locating and arresting him.

Panic stations was the order of the day at Speskop. General Joubert contacted Colonel Jack Cronje and Captain Jacques Hechter and called them to Speskop for a meeting with himself, Joe Verster and Commandant Charl Naudé. The five discussed the situation. The General said there were 'problems'. He was aware Basie Smit had established that the Land-Rover belonged to the SADF and he asked Cronje if there was any way he could obstruct the investigation. Cronje promised hesitantly to 'do what I can', but stressed it was an area in which he lacked influence.

This did little to cheer up Joubert who, after Cronje left, made a report to Lieutenant-General Ian Gleeson, second in command of the SADF.

Gleeson took the bull by the horns and went with Joubert to see the Commissioner of Police, General Johan Coetzee. Joubert explained the circumstances surrounding the murders to Coetzee and was 'surprised' (probably more like horrified) to hear the commissioner deny he had authorised the operation. Joubert had assumed that Colonel Cronje, as the senior security policeman involved, had the backing of his chief. Cronje, on the other hand, later said there had been no need to get authorisation for what was essentially a Special Forces' operation. His only responsibility was to check from time to time with his subordinate, Captain Hechter, to see how the planning was progressing.

Ultimately, who exactly motivated the assassinations will probably never be known, but whoever it was both the CCB and the Security Police bore equal responsibility.

Captain Hechter heard about the Gleeson/Joubert/Coetzee discussions on the Security Police grapevine and tipped off Colonel Cronje. Forewarned, he was called to a meeting later that day with General Johan Coetzee and Brigadier Willem Schoon — head of the Security Police's C units, including the infamous C1 at Vlakplaas.

Coetzee spoke of his meeting with Generals Gleeson and Joubert and asked him what he knew about the murders. Cronje told Hechter later that Coetzee was 'furious' that they had assisted Special Forces. Despite this, in an obvious damage control exercise, Coetzee ordered that Brigadier Smit be replaced on the investigation by Brigadier Daantjie van Wyk. In evidence to the TRC in 1997, General Coetzee denied all knowledge of the assassinations and maintained that Colonel Cronje had never briefed him about them.[23]

Some days after taking over, Brigadier van Wyk went to the scene of the crime to see for himself, but a crowd of 200 to 300 people prevented him from entering the Ribeiro house. Police had briefly been allowed entry an hour after the crime was committed, but after that access was refused. Brigadier van Wyk was also denied access to witnesses, because the family believed the police were involved. He first interviewed them 18 days after the event. His investigation, he told the TRC, was also hampered by the Security Police withholding important information, i.e. that the assassinations were a Special Forces' operation. He did not say when he first became aware of this.[24]

In a move designed to ensure that justice did not prevail and that the press, by accident or design, did not solve the murders by default, Minister of Law and Order, Adriaan Vlok, banned the publication of any further details of the case five days after the attack.[25] In testimony to the TRC in October 1997, ex-Minister Vlok said that during his term of office, he neither authorised nor *condoned* unlawful actions. If his clampdown on the press over the Ribeiro murders was not a condonation, it is difficult to see what was.[26]

On 14 January 1987, more than a month after the assassinations, the two witnesses who had pursued the Opel pointed out Robey's Land-Rover as being similar to the one in the car-switch. An identification parade was held, but they did not pick out the clean-shaven Robey. It is common knowledge in ex-Rhodesian and Recce circles that Robey had sported a beard for many years. Beards were a culture of the Selous Scouts. A Rhodesian Air Force pilot had once jokingly nicknamed them 'armpits with eyeballs' — a name that stuck.

Instead of being brought to trial, Robey was arraigned on a preparatory examination — a pre-trial examination of evidence that had not been used in South Africa for many years. It was ordered by the then Attorney-General of the Transvaal, Don Brunette. According to Captain Hechter, both he and Noel Robey reported to a state advocate, who was acting as prosecutor, and a state attorney, the day before the preparatory examination commenced. He could not remember their names.

'The prosecutor handed us a list of questions and answers he had compiled and said: "Learn these. If you stick to them in court tomorrow, the magistrate knows what to do." It was abundantly clear to me . . . that everyone involved knew the matter would never go any further', Captain Hechter testified.[27]

Noel Robey, whose defence was an alibi, gave no evidence in his defence and was discharged as having no case to answer at the conclusion of the preparatory examination. Major General Joep Joubert, Commanding General Special Forces, arranged for the payment of his defence costs, amounting to R33 700.[28]

SADF Chief, General Jannie Geldenhuys, admitted General Gleeson had told him about Special Forces involvement in the Ribeiro murders. He also agreed he had instructed Major-General Joubert to support the Security Police, but denied he had authorised murder. He conceded, however, that Joubert might have interpreted his instructions as an authorisation to eliminate government opponents.

General Gleeson had also told him the police had been informed about the role played by Special Forces in the murder. 'I didn't want to meddle because there was already a police investigation. If I had ordered a board of enquiry or a court martial, that would have amounted to interfering with the judicial process', General Geldenhuys said. When the 'inquest' (preparatory examination) failed to find anyone responsible he had accepted the finding.[29] He obviously did so with relief, clearly hoping the case would go away. But it didn't.

The Harms Commission found the Ribeiros could have been monitored by the CCB. They also proved Robey's legal expenses had been authorised by the then Chairman of the CCB, Major-General Joep Joubert, and the Managing Director, Colonel Joe Verster. The administrator of the funds (Parsons — the CCB's security manager) and Verster had certified that the expenditure was incurred 'for *bona fide* activities in pursuit of the organisation's aim'.

The expenditure was intelligently concealed from the prying eyes of the Auditor General and the prescribed procedures for the payment of the legal expenses of an officer of the State were circumvented. The expenses debited were at first to *Project Checkers* (a foreign project) as 'unforeseen expenditure for services rendered', then changed to 'project expenses'. From there the amount was transferred to *Project Le Roux* as furniture purchases. In the short time between the money being authorised by the CCB and the attorney handling the matter getting it, someone creamed off R1 000.[30]

A CCB member called Van Deventer offered to sell his story about the CCB's involvement in the murders, but when called by the Harms Commission he refused to answer questions on the grounds he might incriminate himself.[31] This prompted Judge Harms to describe him as a witness who wanted to make money out of his evidence, or merely an extortionist.[32] This was despite General Joubert having confirmed that Van Deventer and Robey had worked together in the CCB.

Van Deventer's fiancé also said she knew about the killings. When she was served a subpoena to appear before the Harms Commission, the CCB's attorney offered to represent her free of charge. She accepted with alacrity, but before her examination commenced it was drawn to the attorney's attention that at the very least, there was a potential conflict of interest between his client and the CCB. He withdrew. She not unexpectedly denied knowing anything about CCB activities or the murders.

The attorney's seemingly improper intrusion makes Judge Harms' assessment of Van Deventer 'as a witness who was in it for the money' seem harsh. The residual impression is that both witnesses, like others, had been seriously intimidated.

The investigating officer, Colonel Brits, tried to track down the black CCB members involved. He ultimately reported to the TRC that one had died and the other was in Botswana and out of reach. To complicate matters, Brits' car, complete with the Ribeiro docket in its boot, was conveniently stolen on 5 May 1990.

The Commission's officers finally gained access to the CCB's strongrooms on 29 March 1990. On 30 March a large sum of cash was put through Robey's bank account and his bank manager noted that Robey would be abroad for six months. It was established that he had gone to England and could not be traced. The *Saturday Star*, however, suggested he was involved with Kaliso Safaris, a company offering fishing safaris to tourists in the Caprivi.[33]

Judge Harms suggested that 'when the Ribeiro murders were committed, the CCB was not yet fully developed' and that Robey might have been acting as a member of *Barnacle*. In fact the CCB was operational when the Ribeiros were murdered and had been so from April 1986.[34]

Judge Harms found there were grounds for believing that Noel Robey might have been involved in an official capacity in the Ribeiro murders, but he could not determine whether his actions were authorised or not. He nevertheless believed there were sufficient grounds for the Attorney-General to order a further investigation. However, no further investigation of any effectiveness occurred. The *status quo* remained until Colonel Cronje and Captain Hechter applied to the TRC for amnesty for both murders in early 1996.[35] After that everything came out.

The Ribeiro killings had proved a nasty experience for SADF Chief General Jannie Geldenhuys, particularly as on his own admission he took part in the subsequent cover-up.

He very likely also authorised Major-General Joubert to eliminate enemies of the state in cooperation with the Security Police. General Joubert believed 'everyone of importance' in 'the government of the day' was aware of the clandestine and covert operations.

After the Ribeiro killings 'corrective' steps were taken to 'establish proper authorisation channels' (with the Chief of the SADF). The approval mechanism, General Joubert said, was in place in early 1987. This was confirmed by General Geldenhuys.[36]

Operation Dual: The killing machine kills on: 1986-1987

Victor de Fonseca was an ex-Moçambican who had served in the Portuguese Army. He was a trained and experienced operator with *Project Barnacle*. He worked at Speskop in a building known as *Die Gat* (the hole) which was occupied by the remaining *Project Barnacle* operators who were then in the throes of setting up the CCB.

De Fonseca developed brain cancer. He was given both surgery and treatment, but he became a security risk because he suddenly started to talk about covert operations, not only to fellow SADF members but to civilians as well. He had many contacts in the Portuguese community and several investigations were conducted into his security breaches. This resulted in his being detained in the detention barracks at Phalaborwa.

Captain Danie Phaal was told by Johan Theron that it was vital that De Fonseca be brought under control. He was sent to collect him from Phalaborwa and bring him back to Speskop. At Speskop Phaal gave him a cup of tea into which he had stirred powder supplied by either Theron or Dr Kobus Bothma.

Killing De Fonseca was not easy to do because Phaal considered him a friend and comrade. After stirring the doctored tea, Phaal unconsciously bent the spoon almost double in his anguish.

But the anguish was premature because De Fonseca did not succumb.

Theron gave Phaal some bottled fluid and told him to try again. He took De Fonseca to the centre of Pretoria and sent him to the licensing office to renew a licence while he waited in the car. The moment he was out of sight, Phaal went and bought two cartons of fresh orange juice. He injected one with the poison and handed it to De Fonseca on his return. He must have had a strong constitution because he still did not die.

Dr Wouter Basson and Theron discussed De Fonseca's fate and decided against admitting him 'to the system'. He was married to a South African woman and if he went missing it could create problems. It was felt preferable, because of his serious illness, to 'accommodate' him at 1-Military Hospital. Accommodate, by Theron's definition, meant that 'Basson would treat him in such a way that he died'.

On 13 August 1986 either Basson or Theron told Phaal that De Fonseca had died. Basson apparently spoke to Theron about 'dramatic' scenes at the hospital where De Fonseca's widow had been sobbing hysterically. Phaal never discovered whether De Fonseca died from the disease or was poisoned, but he believed it was the latter.

Also on 13 August, Theron and Van der Linde flew to Barberton in *Project Barnacle*'s new Cessna Caravan aircraft — that had replaced the Piper Seneca — to pick up a black 5-Recce operator who, it was euphemistically said, had become 'an outcast'. When they reached Barberton, it was to find the operator sleeping from the effects of drinking a can of doctored 'Game' energy drink. He was docile and posed no problem as Theron injected him with Scoline and Tubarine.

He was dumped into the Indian Ocean off St. Lucia.

On another occasion Theron sent Phaal to Phalaborwa in a VW minibus to take care of a security risk. He did not know the victim whom he took over as a prisoner from Sergeant-Major Chris Pretorius. Phaal won the prisoner's trust by telling him he was being released from custody because he had been selected to accompany him on a special operation. The man had eaten supper shortly before which meant a sedative would have been ineffective on a full stomach. To hasten digestion Phaal — who had once been a physical training instructor — put him through a vigorous session of exercise. This was done on the pretext that it was a test to ensure he was fit enough for the bogus operation.

Afterwards he gave the unsuspecting victim a cool drink laced with a sedative. When he passed out, Phaal tied him to the rear seat of his minibus and drove to Barberton. En route the victim regained consciousness and made a halfhearted and unsuccessful attempt to overcome Phaal. It is assumed that Phaal injected him with another sedative to keep him quiet when he arrived at Barberton because he had to wait there overnight.

Van der Linde and Theron landed in the Cessna Caravan at 07:00 the next morning. The victim was loaded aboard and Phaal injected him in the neck to kill him. They flew to Dukuduku, removed the aircraft's door, flew out over the Indian Ocean and dumped the body. It was the first time that Phaal took part in a body dumping exercise.

Some time after this, Van der Linde was transferred from Speskop to SAAF HQ. By then Special Forces had its own helicopter in addition to the Cessna Caravan. Before leaving, he spoke to his successor, HAP Potgieter, and briefed him that he would have to carry out certain operations with Johan Theron. He did not say what the flights entailed, but warned him to always make sure they were authorised. He said 'don't do it unless you get a direct order'. He said he did this because it had been 'unpleasant' to work on such missions with Theron and he wanted to warn him what to expect.

December 1987 marked Theron's final operation. 5-Recce faxed and asked him to conduct a security investigation into the activities of a black operator who had been detained by the Security Police after he tossed a hand grenade into a shebeen, killing five people. The operator was Corporal Mack Anderson, a mulatto who had served as an intelligence officer in the Portuguese Army in Mozambique. Theron arranged for the Security Police to transfer him to the custody of 5-Recce and promised that he would be 'handled' and never seen in public again.

Theron flew to Phalaborwa in the Special Forces helicopter piloted by HAP Potgieter and took over Anderson from 5-Recce. Theron injected him with Ketelaar, Scoline and Tubarine and killed him. After stripping the body it was loaded in the helicopter. They flew east over the Kruger National Park and dumped the body just across the border in Mozambique.

Theron was posted from Special Forces shortly afterwards. After spending a year on a staff duties course, he moved to Military Intelligence as the Senior Staff Officer Project Security, probably as a colonel. This put him in security-charge of all secret SADF projects including *Project Coast*.

Whether somebody else was appointed in his place as the 'chief executioner' for Special Forces is not known.

Operation Dual: Who carried the can?

The numbers eliminated were unimportant to Johan Theron and he made a conscious effort to wipe the killings from his mind. When asked during an investigation into Dr Wouter Basson's activities how many victims he had been responsible for eliminating, he could only say: 'It must have been hundreds.' With the exception of a lone black woman, all the victims were black males. It appears that Theron was haunted by the killings because many years later he became a born-again Christian and confessed his role in the murder of prisoners. One wonders whether he is still haunted by it.

It can be said that proper command and control were exercised in relation to the *Operation Dual* murders. It is difficult to know where the information that led to the victims 'being put in the system' came from, but it must be assumed it was from the intelligence organisations. In some cases it clearly originated from Special Forces' Intelligence, particularly 5-Recce when the 'packages' concerned were turned SWAPO guerrillas who had re-turned or when it was feared there was a danger they would. Other information probably originated from Military Intelligence itself and perhaps from the Security Police. Some came from the Koevoet Police Counter-insurgency Unit in SWA/Namibia.

Without exception, the intelligence was channelled to the Commanding General Special Forces in Pretoria. In the beginning that was Major-General Fritz Loots who initiated *Operation Dual*. On 1 October 1982 he was followed by Major-General Kat Liebenberg who remained in office until 1 November 1985 when he was promoted to lieutenant-general and appointed Chief of the Army. Major-General Joep Joubert took over from him and commanded Special Forces until 31 December 1988 when he was posted to become second-in-command to the Chief of Staff Intelligence.

Again without exception, the responsible general officer decided whether or not the victims should be killed. For a short time Major-General Loots passed the order jointly to Major Neil and to Johan Theron, but after that only Theron was given the order and he passed it on to the pilots and others down the line who became involved.

Several general officers who the author spoke to emphasised that strict command and control was always maintained by the SADF and that no one was allowed to just go around killing people, which according to most of them, was what occurred with the Security Police. What they overlooked, of course, was that whether command and control existed or not, the intentional killing of a human being is still murder. That the killing of helpless prisoners was unlawful is beyond question. Everyone who was part of the murderous chain — from the people who supplied the intelligence to the general who approved the suggestion to the operators who did the deed including the pilots — was an accessory before or after the fact to murder or was guilty of murder *per se*.

The defence of 'I was only obeying orders' was well explored at the trials of the major Nazi war criminals in Nuremberg after World War II. It was held that not only was it not a soldier's duty to obey an unlawful order, he actually had an obligation to disobey it. If he did not he might find himself facing the full consequences of his actions in a court of law.

Most of the prisoners were murdered in SWA/Namibia. The South African Administrator-General administering Namibia before the territory came to independence in 1990 granted a general amnesty to all members of the South African Security Forces for matters committed 'in the heat of an armed struggle'. He believed these acts were comparable to the various deeds of terrorism and other crimes committed by SWAPO guerrillas freed in terms of UN Security Council Resolution 435 in July 1989.[37]

Consequently, those involved in the murder of prisoners in terms of *Operation Dual* did not apply for amnesty under the provisions of the Truth and Reconciliation Commission. Those giving evidence for the State in the Dr Wouter Basson's case were, in any event, granted indemnity from prosecution by the High Court. This was purely academic though, because the judge also found that no one could be prosecuted for the Namibian matters because of the amnesty granted by the Administrator-General.

All Special Forces' operations, particularly those relating to *Project Barnacle*, were handled on a strict need-to-know basis. This applied particularly to *Operation Dual*. In fact, the only officer with immediate access to *Operation Dual* files was the man who did most of the actual killing — Johan Theron. The author has spoken to many former Special Forces and *Project Barnacle* operators and none of them knew anything about *Operation Dual*. Colonel Eugene de Kock, who as a captain was a group leader with Koevoet from 1979 to 1983, told the author of his astonishment when he learned about it. De Kock, whatever else might have been said about him, has held nothing back and has revealed more than anyone else about the often murderous workings of the Security Police machinery. The author had no reason to doubt his astonishment. He assumed it was a strict need-to-know situation involving only a few nominated Koevoet members.[38]

Dr Basson said he had never taken the Hippocratic Oath — only the latter day Physicians Oath — but despite this he saw no moral or ethical questions arising from operations such as kidnapping where it formed part of a military operation directed at 'enemies of the State'. He did, however, have a problem where operations took place within South Africa and could lead to his prosecution. This dichotomy obviously arose from a fear of arrest and had nothing to do with morality or ethics.

He admitted that he had occasionally supplied police operators with incapacitating drugs for use in cross-border 'snatch' operations. He said that this had been on the direct orders of the late General Kat Liebenberg.

'These people were a direct threat to South African society. I saved many lives. The target was not my patient — I took care of the South African population . . . I was not part of the political game. I was a soldier with orders.'

He said he supplied tranquillisers and sleeping medication on only four occasions.

When asked if it was all the same to him if a person was killed in a foreign country with a weapon or with poison, Dr Basson replied that the Defence Force was entitled to use 'any weapon available' when launching operations on foreign soil. He refused to speculate on the use of poison, saying that no one had ever asked him for it.[39]

Top level planning meeting of CCB: 28 April 1987

On 28 April 1987 there was a meeting at a CCB farm in the Eastern Transvaal to discuss 'the coordination of planning and actions relevant to the administration of the CCB and for the Chief SADF to prescribe guidelines'. Present were SADF Chief, General Jannie Geldenhuys; the Commanding General Special Forces and Chairman CCB, Major-General Joep Joubert; Chief SADF (PSO), Brigadier Sonnekus; the Managing Director CCB, Colonel Joe Verster; and the Regional Manager for Region 2 and acting secretary for the meeting, Commandant Corrie Meerholz.

General Geldenhuys said he did not believe it necessary for the CCB to have a formal structure, but he expected this aspect to become clearer when the second stage of development planning had been completed. He did not detail what the second stage was.

That a duplication of facilities between the CCB and Military Intelligence might result caused him no concern. If this created friction at a lower level, his ruling would prevail.

Paragraph 9 of the minutes reveals that there was already an ongoing dispute between General Joubert and the incumbent CSI, Vice-Admiral Putter. It was suggested, probably to keep the peace, that an officer from Military Intelligence be posted to the CCB but remain on CSI's strength.

General Geldenhuys stressed that the CCB was a long-term project, so short and medium term operations must not be allowed to undermine its principal objectives. He rejected suggestions (he did not say by whom) that the CCB had a control problem and said the decentralisation of projects was essential. Control, he believed, depended entirely on the level of know-how of the relevant Regional Manager. He approved the type of operators so far employed but regarded recruiting as a long term process.

Paragraph 7 of the minutes headed 'Methods employed' notes that 'Chief SADF does not see the actions as murder and defines it as follows: "An attack on an individual enemy target with non standard issue weapons in an unconventional manner — so as not to affect the innocent." '

He was clearly referring to operations within South Africa, as the killing of an enemy during an external raid was considered an act of war. Besides, unless they were taken prisoner, raiders were beyond the reach of the target country's legal system.

This exercise in military semantics by General Geldenhuys would return to haunt him and he would find that, like Shakespeare's rose in Romeo and Juliet, there was little in a name and murder would remain murder no matter what the euphemisms.

In paragraph 9 Geldenhuys confirmed that he had ordered the Commanding General Special Forces to double the CCB's domestic capabilities. A channel for the elimination of special targets was being arranged and this would be further discussed at the next meeting on 12 May 1987. It seems he was referring to 'special targets' within South Africa.

Paragraph 10 considered the 'protection of CCB operators' — apparently protection against prosecution for criminal acts committed in South Africa — and a presentation was arranged for discussion on 12 May. General Geldenhuys made the following points:

10.1 The broad mandate for projects not envisaged by him. (sic)
10.2 The CCB may suggest targets, but this must be channelled directly to Chief SADF via Commanding General Special Forces.
10.3 They must not attempt to take protective actions too far, but they must, however, ensure the job is done;
10.4 Members of Auditor General's Department: Chief SADF determines that their inspection of documents is totally wrong. This aspect must be discussed with Admiral Bekker through Commanding General Special Forces and the problem solved as speedily as possible; and
10.5 Purchasing procedures: Chief SADF instructs that it must be handled as in para 10.4 [without subject to audit by the Auditor General].'

General Geldenhuys' other comments were summarised in paragraphs 11 to 15:

11 Requires professional action based on a healthy doctrine.
12 Research must be conducted and a doctrine must be developed.
13 Recruitment of operatives must be done according to a specific concept or doctrine.
14 Principles for undercover action must be researched and members must be trained. Maybe it will not be a formal type of training.
15 Know-how is a factor that must not be overlooked. Where we have deficiencies it must be bought or made available in some other manner. The following aspects count:
15.1 Finances;
15.2 Legal aspects;
15.3 Company and organisational aspects;
15.4 Handling of funds undercover; and
15.5 The possibilities of learning from Comops must be investigated and Commanding General Special Forces must liaise with CCB to capitalise on Comops contacts.'

Commandant Corrie Meerholz signed the minutes.

Major-General Joep Joubert later swore an affidavit for purposes of the inquest into the death of the activist Matthew Goniwe in the Eastern Cape saying: 'The contents of this document are self explanatory and mean exactly what they say. This document attests that there was always command and control over the CCB.' [40]

General Joubert said that after approval mechanisms for Special Forces to work with the Security Police for the elimination of enemies of the State were in place, the police no longer requested their support in covert operations.[41] From then until he handed over command of Special Forces to Major-General Eddie Webb in November 1988, neither the Special Forces nor the CCB were involved in internal covert operations, either jointly with the Security Police or on their own. They only conducted conventional operations.[42]

In July 1995 Chief of the SANDF, General Georg Meiring, told a media briefing that before February 1990 — when former State President F W de Klerk announced the unbanning of the ANC, the PAC and the SACP — '. . . the SADF was one of the instruments of the State and was involved in certain officially authorised projects. These projects were in line with the circumstances prevailing at the time . . . the former SADF followed these instructions to the letter'. Such projects, he said, had since been evaluated and those not in accordance with the SANDF's function were closed down.[43] The inference is that he was referring to internal operations of doubtful legality carried out by the CCB and other SADF intelligence arms.

General Eddie Webb, in testimony to the Harms Commission, said no CCB internal operations were submitted for authorisation to any authority higher than himself while he was in command of Special Forces. Principally, the CCB's targets were those that posed a danger to the safety and security of the State, against whom the SAP could not act within the scope of the law. General Webb's testimony led to his facing a charge of perjury, for which he was eventually granted amnesty by the Truth and Reconciliation Commission.[44]

16

The Boys from Brixton
Formation of CCB's Region 6
1988

Establishment of Region 6: 1988

In 1988 it was decided to create a new internal region for the CCB — Region 6. It was tasked to internally disrupt the enemy and gather intelligence with a view to the maximum disruption of the enemies of South Africa within South Africa. 'Maximum disruption could conceivably consist of anything from breaking a window to killing a person, depending on the priority class.' It appears the new region was to act independently, not from intelligence supplied by TREWITS.

The suave Lieutenant-Colonel 'Staal' (Steel) Burger, nicknamed after an Afrikaans James Bond-type super hero Staal Burger, a series broadcast on the defunct Springbok Radio, was the high profile commander of the SAP's elite Brixton Murder and Robbery Squad. Until 31 March 1988 he was the blue-eyed boy of the Force.

The change began on 28 September 1987. That evening, two men claiming to be policemen knocked on the front door of Bernie Ogle, a drug dealer and receiver of stolen property. They lured him out on the pretext that they needed to check his car documents, then shot him dead with a ,22 calibre firearm.

Three hours later Ernest Molokoane of Soweto was also called outside by 'policemen' demanding documents for his Porsche. He was shot four times with the gun used in the Ogle slaying, but he survived.

On 4 October Peter Pillay, the late Bernie Ogle's brother-in-law and partner in crime, borrowed R5 000 before keeping a 20:00 appointment with Captain Jack Le Grange, commander of the East Rand Murder and Robbery Squad. Pillay's bullet-riddled body was found the next morning.

Captain le Grange and Sergeant Robert van der Merwe of the Brixton Murder and Robbery Squad were arrested on two charges of murder and one of attempted murder. Le Grange denied all knowledge, but Van der Merwe confessed he had shot the suspected 'ANC members' on the lawful orders of his superior officer (Le Grange). He alleged that such actions were commonplace, a contention rejected by the court, but proved in later years to have been true — certainly in the case of certain sections of the Security Police during the 'total onslaught' years. They were contract killings, carried out at the behest of the deceased's drug-dealing rivals. The police elite, supposed to be at the sharp end of fighting organised crime, had been caught doing the crooks' dirty work.

Both were convicted and sentenced to death twice for the murders and to ten years imprisonment for attempted murder. The sentences were later commuted to life imprisonment — apparently as a *quid pro quo* to the Afrikaner right wing after the so-called Sharpville Six were reprieved as a sop to world opinion.[1]

Staal Burger suggested there was a difference of opinion between himself and the commander of the detective branch, General Schutte, relating to the Le Grange and Van der Merwe cases. General Schutte, he said, believed their convictions tainted the integrity of the Brixton Murder and Robbery squad. Obviously, on a 'where there's smoke there's fire' basis, he decided the time was ripe to get rid of several members of staff on transfer, including Burger himself.

Burger was extremely unhappy with this. His view was that Le Grange and Van der Merwe had acted entirely on their own initiative. What they had done was nothing to do with anyone else. If others were transferred, it would give the unfair impression that they were also suspected of being involved in the murders. Burger apparently also thought that the posting the police authorities had in mind for him — perhaps a transfer back to uniform branch — was an insult.

However, he had done little to advance his police career or his public image. In an impassioned speech at a public meeting in support of the two former policemen, he compared them to Rambo (in the Sylvester Stallone movies) and Chuck Norris (another movie tough guy). 'Jack le Grange and Robert van der Merwe were prototypes of those two movie stars.' President F W de Klerk and those in authority within the National Party government apparently shared his view, for three years later both were released on parole.[2]

Burger looked for other career opportunities. He knew that Colonel Joe Verster was in Special Forces. They had known each other since childhood and were at primary and high school together. They were good friends, but they had lost contact with each other when their career paths diverged, with Verster joining the army and his joining the police.
He contacted Verster who arranged to meet him at his office in Johannesburg's Ponti Building. Burger asked him if there was any chance of a transfer to Special Forces.

Verster, of course, was intent on staffing the CCB's new Region 6. It was of no concern to him that the Brixton Murder and Robbery Squad detectives were tainted by association with two convicted contract killers, or that they might occasionally have stepped over the legal white line. If they had, an advantage — after all, a soldier's culture demands that he kill the enemy, not arrest him. Verster needed men capable of recruiting agents from the criminal underworld — and who had better contacts than the Brixton Murder and Robbery Squad? If they were not as straight as they should have been, it was all to the good. As a policeman, Burger also had expertise in the urban environment, which most soldiers lacked. Verster probably recalled General Geldenhuy's specific instruction at the meeting of 28 April 1987: 'Know-how is a factor that must not be overlooked. Where we have deficiencies, it must be bought or made available in some other manner.' So they were in the marketplace for skills and buying.

He told Burger there was indeed an opportunity for a transfer. He explained that he was running a new civil section of Special Forces, which was why he was operating in civilian clothes from the Ponti Building instead of from Special Forces headquarters. They discussed Burger's rank and how it would be adapted to Special Forces. Verster explained that although it would be a civilian appointment, salary and so on would more or less equate with salaries in the SADF's officer corps. He was told the organisation was secret and that he should not talk about it to anybody. The work he would be doing would also be secret. He was told, however, that he would be utilised in the war against enemies of the State, but he would fight as a civilian.

Staal Burger completed an application form and was later contacted and told he had been accepted. He still had no detailed knowledge regarding his future duties. He went to see Verster again. He was informed that there were more vacancies in the organisation and could he make proposals in that regard?

That way Verster would not only get Burger as the new Regional Manager, but he came as part of a package. This indeed suited Burger, who promised to bring 'the best' over with him. Effectively, the CCB would staff the new region in one fell swoop. What was overlooked — and what the SADF should surely should have seen — was that the concept of Region 6 was rotten, its operations were wholly illegal and it contained the seeds of its own destruction. It would turn out, as Major-General Joep Joubert told the author later, to be 'a bad mistake'.[3]

Detective Warrant Officer Chappie Maree and Detective Sergeant Carl Casteling 'Calla' Botha agreed to resign and go across with their former commander.

Lieutenant Abram 'Slang' (snake) van Zyl, highly regarded as an up-and-coming young officer, had enjoyed a high profile, although at times controversial career. He was currently on transfer to the Pietermaritzburg Murder and Robbery Unit. Van Zyl was a member of the team that had searched for ex-police captain Andre Stander — bank robber extraordinary — who was finally shot dead in Fort Lauderdale, USA, in February 1984.[4] Van Zyl and Jack le Grange were among the last to question former professional boxer and gangland leader James Meiring before his charred remains were found in what appeared to be a 'necklace' murder. The case was unsolved, but his family remain convinced he died during police questioning.[5]

Staal Burger explained that he, Maree and Botha were resigning to join the Matthysen Bus Service, a Special Forces' front. They would retain their police ranks, but get more money. Van Zyl agreed to accompany them for an interview with Joe Verster at the Ponti Building.

Verster spoke to each separately and introduced them in turn to Wouter J Basson (organisation name Christo Britz — not to be confused with his cousin Dr Wouter Basson of *Project Coast*), Region 6's newly appointed Coordinator. He had previously been Coordinator for Region 9 (supplying support for the Intelligence Department) and Region 2 (Mozambique and Swaziland). Basson, who had transferred from 1-Recce to the CCB in 1987, brought with him a number of incomplete or ongoing projects, including *Project Crawler* (concerning the fishing vessel *Margit Rye* used for intelligence missions off the east coast of Africa) to Region 6.[6] In addition, his 1989 diary shows he also remained involved with various unnamed projects in Swaziland, Botswana, Zambia, Zimbabwe and Malawi.

Verster introduced himself as a SADF colonel and the organisation's managing director. The CCB, he explained, comprised civilians operating with the SADF. Speaking generally and without detailing the unit's objectives, he said their task would be to disrupt South Africa's enemies. Until then, he explained, the organisation had consisted only of regions with external responsibilities. But now Region 6 would handle domestic operations.

Verster said that as the 1980s had progressed, the emphasis had swung from crime to security. He said Van Zyl knew from personal experience that the ANC and UDF had engaged in a violent campaign to overthrow the government. It had resulted in widespread loss of life and the destruction of property. Conventional warfare practised externally to keep the enemy at bay had become ineffective, so Special Forces had turned to secret warfare. He played on Van Zyl's loyalty as a South African, as an Afrikaner. Van Zyl in turn felt honoured that he had been selected for such an elite unit.

He was told that salary would be better than his police one, but full details would only be provided on acceptance. He completed an application form and was subjected to routine security clearance. In addition to his salary the organisation paid a year's pension contributions in advance, a telephone allowance, generous home loan facilities and medical aid for both himself and his family. He would also get out-of-pocket expenses. If he qualified, 'production bonuses' would be paid half yearly in May and November.

Burger, Van Zyl, Chappie Maree and Calla Botha were inducted simultaneously into the CCB on 1 June 1988, after swearing an oath in terms of the Protection of Information Act. All CCB activities were secret, they were told, and on a need-to-know basis they would not be told anything about projects of their colleagues.

There was an understanding between the SADF and the SAP. On inter-service transfers a period of six months non-involvement was observed to avoid friction. Mr Matthysen, the owner of Matthysen Bus Company based close to the Escom offices in Megawatt Park in the Johannesburg area, was an old friend of Burger's from the time they had done their national service together. He approached Matthysen, took him into his confidence, and explained that he and some colleagues were joining Special Forces. They needed employment as a cover for their activities for the foreseeable future. He explained to

Matthysen that it would not cost his company anything. They would effectively be working for nothing. The operators would be paid their salaries in cash and they would hand this to the bus company. After deducting tax the company would return the money by way of salary cheques drawn on their account.[7]

Matthysen agreed as a personal favour to Burger and they took up a variety of cover posts with his company. Burger became a director, Maree joined technical services, Botha was appointed as an inspector and Van Zyl became the marketing manager.

R30 000 was laundered through the Matthysen Bus Service for Van Zyl to purchase a BMW 318i. It was registered in his name, but he signed a blank 'change of ownership' form so the authorities could recover it if he resigned. He could use it for both his Red and Blue Plans, but an allowance of 18 cents per kilometre was paid for the former.

Another R30 000 was laundered to enable Botha to buy a used VW Golf. He was a rugby player of some repute, had represented SA schools in 1979, Rand Afrikaans University, Transvaal under 20s, the SAP and Transvaal 'B'.[8] He joined the CCB 'for the adventure . . . I understood and believed there was a war raging inside South Africa and it was about the survival of moderate South Africans. I saw it as a struggle involving South Africans, and that formed part of my motivation'.[9]

Their monthly salaries, net after deductions as at the end of January 1989, were as follows: Burger R4 978.96, Van Zyl R3 852.15, Maree R3 805.15 and Botha R2 871.40. By May 1989 they had risen meteorically. Burger was getting R11 220.63 + R701.40, Van Zyl R9 118.42 + R701.40, Maree R9 547.36 + R701.40 and Botha R9 685.37 + R701.40.[10]

The Region 6 operators met Joe Verster and Wouter J Basson at the Ponti building on various occasions during the next six months. They also saw Major-General Joep Joubert, the Commanding CCB chairman, there twice.

In early 1989 they were sent on a five-day course at Renosterspruit, Botha called it the 'shed' (*skuur*). Their instructors included Verster; Theunis Kruger; Dawid Fourie; the CCB's deputy managing director; Wouter J Basson; and Barries (organisation name), the CCB's logistics manager, Lafras Luitingh, the Production Manager; and Danie Phaal. Verster and Basson were serving officers, but in a tactical move in late 1989 to distance themselves from the SADF, they took mock discharges and embarked on their own Blue Plans. Wouter J Basson's Blue Plan involved the selling of vacuum cleaners and he established an estate agency in his Pretoria home. He found it hard to break ties with his past life in the military. 'I lived the life of a hermit and I broke all ties with friends. I tried to prevent people asking me: 'What are you doing?' [11]

During the course they were briefed on what was expected of them. Primarily the CCB was an intelligence gathering unit, but it had a secondary responsibility of launching disruptive actions (approved projects) on the strength of such intelligence. This was their most vital task.[12] Within their region they had complete freedom of movement and were expected to infiltrate 'pipelines' leading to external enemies. They also monitored people within the country to get information on pipelines leading outside.[13] Phaal presented a course on cover stories and on techniques of how to conceal their links with the SADF.[14]

Staal Burger and his men were former policemen and they knew about criminality. They asked what would happen if they committed criminal acts like murder and so on. It was explained that they had no need to worry as they 'would be protected by State structures'. The words 'indemnity' or 'indemnify' were not used. Burger did not understand that the 'protection' offered involved legal process. It was more a question of being protected by government influence.[15]

A confused soup of code names was used for everything. The establishment of Region 6, and its code name thereafter, was *Project Choice*. Operators were given pseudonyms for operational, administrative, pay and other purposes. Burger became Bert Brummer, Wouter J Basson was Christo Britz, Van Zyl became Andries Rossouw, Maree used the name Stefan le Roux, Botha was Deon Calitz and Joe Verster variously used Jack (or Rick) van Staden and Dave Martin. Dawid Fourie's organisation name was Heine Müller, Financial Manager Theunis Kruger was Jaco Black and the Regional Manager for Region

8, Roelf van Heerden, was Roelf van der Westhuizen. When dealing with their covert members they adopted other *nom de plumes*.[16] Claims for petrol expenses etc. were coded as *Project Tourist*.

Verster told the TRC that the organisation consisted of about 100 overt and about 150 covert members. Altogether the CCB was involved in perhaps 170 to 200 projects, including the setting up of Blue Plans for overt members.[17]

Overt operators compiled intelligence reports suggesting targets, human or otherwise, together with related motivation, and submitted them to the Regional Manager. He passed them to the Managing Director via the Coordinator. If the MD decided the intelligence justified a project, he returned the file to the region for the compilation of a preliminary study.

This would include recommendations on the roles nominated covert members would play. Their tasks would be detailed and an estimated financial budget would be prepared. When complete the responsible overt member would sign and pass it to the Regional Manager via the Coordinator. If the Regional Manager approved, he added his recommendations and passed it to the MD.

If the preliminary study was approved by the MD he would instruct a so-called 'in-house' to be convened. This would be attended by the Regional Manager, the Coordinator and the responsible overt member. The Coordinator would open the in-house with a verbal presentation which would be followed by general discussion. If the MD believed the preliminary study merited more work, it would be returned to the overt member for attention. When he had done whatever was required, a second in-house would be convened. This would be attended by himself, the MD and the Coordinator to allow further discussions. If this failed to gain the MD's approval, it would spell the end of the exercise. If he approved it, a paper would be submitted to the Chairman, who had the final say on whether the project went ahead or not.

According to Major-General Webb, he normally set aside about an hour a week to discuss projects with Joe Verster requiring his approval. Such meetings were normally in the nature of open discussions between the two of them. If he had queries or any point required enlargement, he would ask Verster. No minutes or any other records were kept of the meetings for security reasons. Generally speaking, he had no contact with any member of the CCB except for Joe Verster.

Monitoring operations did not require his approval, but any that involved the elimination of targets or the use of any kind of force did.[18]

During lectures Joe Verster emphasised they would be given automatic indemnity if they became involved in acts of violence while executing approved projects. The reasoning was that the SADF, therefore the State, had approved the execution of projects so prosecutions would be untenable because a state of internal warfare existed. Despite this, they should make every effort to ensure such things could not be traced back to the SADF.

Slang van Zyl explained later: 'I was 26 years old. In my opinion just about every member of the army and the then structures of the police force and other structures were brainwashed by the government and [about] what the government advocated and so forth. I think I was naïve and if you would table the same proposition to me today, I would not accept it . . . At that stage I was aware how the prosecution structures worked and how the investigative structures worked, but that is what I believed. I think it is no secret, certainly, that in most countries of the world organisations like the CCB existed and probably still exist. Over the course of time they look after those people . . . so they are not exposed to prosecution. It is in that light that I believed we would be indemnified from prosecution.'[19]

Their first Blue Plan, effectively a joint one with the Matthysen Bus Company, lasted for only 11 months because Staal Burger and Chris Matthysen fell out. The four operators cleared their office desks and left.

For the implementation of their next Blue Plan, Burger turned to shady Greek millionaire Alexandros 'Big Alex' Kavouras — a Hillbrow hotelier and night club owner who was reputed to be the untouchable 'Don of Johannesburg'. The formation of 'Staal Burger and

Partners Security' resulted. Burger commented: 'He [Kavouras] is known as somebody who is involved in drugs and such substances, but I don't know if he had been found guilty, but he had many contacts with the underworld. We made use of this opportunity to make contacts in this underworld of Mr Kavouras.' In effect, Burger later admitted that few, if any, contacts were made and utilised by Region 6 through this medium.[20]

Chris Nel (organisation name Derek Louw), the CCB's Intelligence Officer, and Wouter J Basson — both trained Special Forces operators — agreed that the use of criminals as covert members — in the hope that whatever job was done would not be traced back to the State, was a forlorn one. Chris Nel called it the 'biggest waste of money ever'. He estimated that approximately 80% of the operations had to be stopped because of a lack of effective cut-offs that would block the State from being implicated.[21]

Burger used the Park Lane Hotel as Region 6's HQ. Kavouras set aside two rooms, which Burger furnished with money provided by the CCB, and set up his detective agency. Between March and June 1989 Botha, Van Zyl and Maree breakfasted or lunched there on most days. They were often seen deeply engrossed in conversation in the restaurant or in the basement parking garage.[22]

As a joint Blue Plan it was not long before Staal Burger and Partners Security foundered because of serious personality clashes between Burger and the other three. Following this double debacle, Joe Verster instructed them to form their own Blue Plan front companies. He approved financial assistance to the amount of R75 000 under the code name *Project Patriotic* for this purpose.

Kavouras also appointed Burger as the general manager of his Park Lane Hotel and paid him a salary of R3 000 per month. A former accountant said: 'There is no way a man like Alex would hire someone like Staal without some kind of connection.' [23] The connection, according to the *Sunday Times*, arose from Kavouras' close relationship with Brigadier Krappies Engelbrecht whom Burger succeeded at Brixton. Perhaps he took over the relationship along with the job.

They were not Kavouras' only police friends. He boasted that through connections with the 'fourth floor' (senior police officers at John Vorster Square police station — now Johannesburg Central) and the Liquor Board', he had 'organised the police to turn a blind eye', so underworld boss Joe Kgasi could get a liquor licence for his New York City night club in 1975. He regarded himself as above the law and when he opened his 'In the Mix' night club in 1986, the invitations were illustrated with line drawings of mandrax tablets.[24]

In 1978 his 20th Century night club mysteriously burnt down. Accounts vary as to whether he received an insurance pay-out. But whether he did or not he resurfaced in Zambia in 1980 as a partner of President Kaunda's son, Panji, a colonel in the Zambian National Defence Force. Both were fingered when the Zambian government clamped down on illicit drug trafficking and Big Alex was deported.[25]

He re-established himself in Hillbrow, acquiring hotels and opening night clubs. In 1991 the *Sunday Star* ran a story saying his Quirinale Hotel was the focus of prostitution and drug dealings and detailed why he had been deported from Zambia. Kavouras complained to the Media Council, saying the report was defamatory and a breach of their code of conduct. After a protracted two-year enquiry, punctuated by serious intimidation of the *Sunday Star*'s witnesses, his complaint was dismissed when documents refuting his deportation, purporting to emanate from the offices of the Zambian President and Immigration Department, were proved to have been typed on one of his own typewriters.[26]

Burger said: 'I was known to Mr Kavouras from [my] Brixton Murder and Robbery Squad days. I arrested and detained him at one stage. He went to Zambia and when he returned he came to Brixton offices and we checked if they were looking for him in the country. I think Commercial Branch was looking for him and I delivered him to them. Later on, we had an amicable relationship. So my involvement at Park Lane was not strange in the eyes of the police. They knew that I knew Mr Kavouras.'

Doubtless the SAP's hierarchy took cold comfort from that. If they were concerned during the murder trial of Le Grange and Van der Merwe that the chief of their crack Brixton

Murder and Robbery Squad had been associating with undesirables, Burger's 'Big Alex' connection must have confirmed their worst nightmares.[27]

In November 1988 Slang van Zyl hired a pager on a 12-months contract at CCB expense, to use when contacting his Red Plan covert members. Calla Botha hired one from Executive Communications, pager number 011-331-3561, channel 1200, code 18, using Johan Malherbe as a *nom de guerre*.

Under his Blue Plan, *Project Bliss*, Van Zyl started a private detective agency, Incom Investigations, [28] which became sufficiently successful to take in a partner. His partner's salary etc. was paid by the business, and according to Van Zyl he had no idea Incom was a CCB front.

Van Zyl and Maree, according to Calla Botha, rented a second floor flat in some 'mansions' in Louis Botha Avenue, which in the early stages of Region 6 was used as a meeting place. They terminated their tenancy abruptly when they heard the NIS had been nosing around there. After this they held meetings in hotel rooms at random venues. When there was no specific purpose like an in-house, general matters like the state of the nation, security reports from Military Intelligence and settlements and adjustments were discussed.

Project Toddler allocated Chappie Maree R40 200 with which he started Lema International, a business that exported electronic appliances, calculators, computers, watches and so on to other African countries. The money was to buy furniture and initially pay staff wages, but he handed most of it back when he rented furnished offices. From there he expanded and opened a second business in Durban as a ship's chandler under the name Capall and took in a partner. He followed this with another company, Lema Namibia, in Windhoek. The CCB was delighted with his activities. It regarded them as long term, because it gave him an excuse to move freely into neighbouring countries. In August 1989 Burger called him into his office and asked him how he would feel about opening a business in Germany and settling there. Maree visited Germany, advertised in newspapers, contacted business people, looked into schooling for his children, checked out a house and sought out office space.

'My Blue Plan entrapped me in the sense where I found myself in a situation for a number of months where I didn't know anything about business, but I had to deal with business and staff members. I was caught up in the whole idea of running a business, rather than delivering production.'

For this reason Maree was hardly involved in CCB activities.[29]

Calla Botha's Blue Plan, *Project Hilton*, involved the establishment of a marketing company, Cabot International cc. Its purpose was to distribute promotional items bearing company logos. It was more humble than the rest and an opening budget of only R1 055 per month was approved. He later switched to the insurance business.

The Region 6 operators addressed each other by their Christian names, although Staal Burger insisted he be called 'colonel' or 'sir'. Botha said that while there was no rank structure, 'there was definitely seniority and the seniors clearly made the subordinates feel subordinate'.[30]

Region 6 was officially activated in January 1989.

Enter Ferdi Barnard: December 1987

Ferdi Barnard, son of a retired police colonel, was a former West Rand Narcotic Bureau sergeant. On 10 December 1984 he was sentenced to 20 years imprisonment, of which 14 years ran concurrently — giving him an effective (and totally inappropriate) sentence of six years imprisonment for the murder of two drug dealers, for the attempted murder of another and for three counts of car theft. The case involved inciting Peter Ward (19) and Edward Joffe (19), both addicts and alleged drug runners, into breaking into a pharmacy, where he shot the former dead and wounded the latter. In the second murder case he stole a car with an accomplice and gave it to an addict to frame him. When he got into the vehicle, they shot him dead.[31]

On 10 December 1987, after serving only three years, he was released on parole and offered employment as a claims assessor by Willie Smit, a former Springbok athlete and owner of President Insurance of 11 Rose Street, Florida. The story was that Ferdi's fiancé of long standing, Brenda Milne, who worked there, was instrumental in him getting the job.

Willie Smit, however, said he was approached by his 'brother', Botha, who asked him to use his influence to get Barnard out of prison.

Whatever the truth of the matter, Smit offered him a job. Barnard needed more excitement and once he was free he asked Theunis Erasmus Kruger, who was working for the CCB in a financial capacity, to enquire about an 'intelligence gathering job'.

In the early 1980s Kruger was convicted of murder, committed while serving in Owamboland with an informal SADF counter-insurgency unit, the Tekkie Squad. He was sentenced to 15 years imprisonment. The police officer who arrested him was Floris Mostert. It would not be the last time he intruded in Kruger's life.

Well thought of as a soldier, Sergeant Kruger had been especially transferred to SWA/Namibia from 44-Parachute Brigade's Murrayhill base, where he was an infantry instructor, at the request of Brigadier 'Witkop' Badenhorst, then Commanding Officer of Sector 10.

After discharge from prison after serving only five years, he qualified as an accountant and was enrolled in this capacity into the CCB on the recommendation of General Badenhorst. That he was a convicted felon who had served time, posed no problem to the SADF.[32] Joe Verster described him as someone 'detained by the State, but he was a soldier who was detained wrongfully and then through the official channels of the Defence Force he got work with us'. The SADF certainly looked after its own — no matter the rights and wrongs.

Ferdi Barnard and he were prisoners together. They were in daily contact for three years and became good friends. Barnard had noticed that 'highly placed Defence Force persons' were amongst Kruger'sregular visitors.

What Kruger told Barnard about the CCB is not on record, but it appears he was frank.

Whatever the case, the friendship led to his meeting Louis Yssel (actually Lafras Luitingh), a former 5-Recce operator, at a Pretoria Hotel.[33] 'Yssel', he alleged, at first said he was working for a business syndicate which required information to safeguard its investments. The work involved clandestinely monitoring various political organisations. Later, he was told he was working for the 'organisation'. Barnard was considered suitable material as a covert member because of his wide-ranging underworld contacts.

He was offered a generous salary of about R4 000 which included benefits but not operational allowances. He was allowed R30 000 to buy a car. He could spend more but the rest would have to come from his own pocket. His salary continued without interruption until his Section 29 detention in late 1989. He was also told to establish a Blue Plan front as a cover for his Red Plan activities. He formed a company called Profsure, and used his police experience to establish himself in the business of investigating insurance scams. He worked on an ad hoc basis for Willy Smit.

It was impressed on him that both MK and APLA liaised closely with criminal networks. He was told to infiltrate those networks and he was given *carte blanche* to recruit whoever he wanted. It was important, though, that they had the right type of access to foreign countries and preferably held other than South African passports. While the Department of Home Affairs willingly issued false travel documents to Military Intelligence and Security Police operators, they had drawn a line at issuing them to agents who might be criminals.

For contact purposes Barnard hired a pager from Executive Communications, using the name H J van Staden, although his organisation name was Rud Erwee. The pager's number was 011-331-3561, channel 784, code 18. To all intents and purposes it seems he was treated in the same way as other overt CCB operators, except that he was not posted to a region. That he was an overt operator has been consistently denied by the SADF authorities, but the large number of projects he was involved in indicates otherwise.

Barnard said he was handled differently because although he was hired for his intelligence gathering expertise, he was also well known as a ruthlessly efficient killer. This seems consistent because killing was, after all, the CCB's *raison d'etre*. His killing duties were broached to him gradually as he became better known and more trusted.

Yssel arranged the issue of false identity documents, a false passport and a false police appointment certificate in the name of H J van Staden. On instructions, Barnard rented an apartment in the Ponti Building in Hillbrow using his alias.

He was anxious, because breaking his parole conditions could result in his immediate re-incarceration. But he was given the fullest assurances that support systems had been created by the SADF. If he encountered a situation where he had committed an illegal act during the course of his duties, he would not be prosecuted.

Barnard, who was nobody's fool, quickly checked with his friend Theunis Kruger and ascertained that Louis Yssel was in reality Lafras Luitingh. He also learned that his boss, Jack van Staden, was actually Joe Joubert and that Major-General Joep Joubert, as the Commanding General Special Forces was in overall command. He also heard about it when Major-General Eddie Webb took over from Joubert. Needless to say, even in the beginning, Barnard did not swallow Luitingh's story about the business syndicate and so on.[34]

Although Barnard knew of the organisation's military/Special Forces' connections, he was unaware it was called the CCB. His handler — although overt members did not normally have a handler — Luitingh, was another overt member whom Joe Verster had taken on as a 'production manager'. Verster had tasked him to write a 'pseudo plan' and to plan operations for which the ANC, PAC and SACP would be blamed. His region remains unknown.[35]

Barnard, whose big mouth eventually brought about his downfall, in any case blew all the cover stuff by telling Willy Smit he had been offered a job by 'NI' (presumably MI — Military Intelligence). Smit, like most civilians at that time, was probably unaware of the extent of the intrusion of Military Intelligence into civil life and understood N1 to be the Security Police. Barnard, who completely ignored the 'need to know' principle, said his new job entailed monitoring and eliminating activists — employment more to his taste. He continued his relationship with Willy after he joined the CCB.[36]

To maintain contact, Luitingh arranged the use of a post office box as a drop point. Barnard rented a box at the Florida Hills post office in the name of H J van Staden and gave Luitingh a key. Andrew Voster, Willy Smit's brother-in-law and a printer by trade, forged a police ID in the name of a Captain van Staden, mounted with Barnard's photograph.[37]

Eventually, he said, he was called in for a personal interview with Joe Verster and Danie Phaal. His belief at the time was that anything was justified, as long as the government was involved. He went there as if for an ordinary job interview, carrying a briefcase containing his references and qualifications. There was his matriculation certificate, legal certificates and others pertaining to various courses, many of them advanced, that he had undertaken while in the police. There was also his BA degree from the University of South Africa. He sat down at Joe Verster's desk and spread them out, but neither Phaal nor Verster were interested in looking at them.

'Congratulations', Verster said, 'you've got the job. What cars can you steal? What cars can you open? What weapons can you work with?'

He could indeed steal cars and that was mostly what they wanted to know.

He was given a one-on-one instructional course on CCB operations, operational procedures and so on by both Luitingh and Phaal. It was later confirmed that he was taught the same subjects as the new operators recruited for Region 6.

Barnard recruited an important agent, a Zimbabwean with a military background called McQuillan. He met him through a gold deal with the local 'mafia' involving 10kg of unprocessed gold. He gave him the CCB's cover story (that it was a consortium of businessmen), but McQuillan did not buy this and accused Barnard of working either for Military Intelligence or the Security Police. He offered to provide intelligence in Europe and in London, but not in Zimbabwe because his family was there.

Barnard said that Luitingh was very interested. He was told to 'chase' McQuillan and find out if he had 'hard line' people who could operate in Europe, planting bombs and poisoning people.

McQuillan was despatched to London in October 1988 with US$15 000 that Barnard had drawn for him. He returned and contacted Barnard, but Luitingh told him to break contact and demanded McQuillan's number in London. Despite this, while still in South Africa McQuillan continued to contact Barnard on his pager. He handed over an envelope that contained a written breakdown showing how he had spent the US$15 000. He also reported that a safe house had been established, contacts put into place and a car purchased. He mentioned an Australian had been flown in to do a project. Barnard was highly upset. What was happening had arisen from his initiatives but despite this, someone else had taken over as McQuillan's handler.

He resealed the envelope and handed it to Luitingh who was unhappy that Ferdi had made contact with McQuillan. Barnard said, however, that he wanted to continue handing McQuillan who also did not want to deal with Luitingh. Things continued for a while until Luitingh told him the project had to be suspended because the 'whole world' knew about the US$15 000 that had been paid to McQuillan.

In February 1998 McQuillan phoned Barnard's pager from Athens and said he had important information from the London network. Barnard called Luitingh who instructed him to call McQuillan and find out what he had. McQuillan reported that a member of his family who belonged to the IRA had an Angolan Intelligence officer, Alvaro Figerido, with him. Figerido had documents that detailed the Soviet, Angolan and Cuban five-year plan against South Africa. He also had a map that showed the locations of previously unknown MK training camps in Angola.

This resulted in the South Africans getting much valuable intelligence.

Within a month Luitingh told Barnard he required information about one Anton Lubowski, a Windhoek resident. Barnard, who had never heard of him, thought he was a Russian. Luitingh enquired if he had Security Police contacts in SWA/Namibia who could provide Lubowski's address and information on his SWAPO connections. SWA/Namibia, he said, was a priority area.

'Yes', Barnard replied, 'I have a few contacts of people who worked with me in a certain branch. I had contact with them from time to time, but they were not the type of people I could approach for this project.'

The enquiry 'came out of the blue', as it did not relate to the work Barnard had been doing until then. Oddly enough, Barnard said, Luitingh never mentioned Lubowski again.

Peaches gets the cream

Slang Van Zyl was responsible for the Cape. In October 1988, before the unit's activation, he phoned his brother and said he was seeking someone in the criminal fraternity to recruit as a source to report on thefts at the Matthysen Bus Company. He made no mention of the CCB. His brother suggested a gangster, James Edward 'Peaches' Gordon, a member of the 'Dixie Boys' gang, who, after an initial phone contact, met Van Zyl and Calla Botha in Cape Town. Van Zyl introduced himself as Tinus de Wet and took him to meet Staal Burger at a hotel. This was contrary to CCB policy as the identities of covert members — like police informers — were supposed to be sacrosanct. Burger, however, insisted on meeting him, despite the breach of security.

Burger conducted the interview, saying they were protecting the interests of certain overseas businessmen, and asked if Gordon had any contacts with the ANC and UDF.

This was of interest to their clients because radicals posed a risk to their investments. Gordon acknowledged he had such contacts and agreed to work for them. He was given R20 as a sweetener. Van Zyl prepared a report, countersigned by Burger, which was passed to Wouter J Basson. He passed it to Joe Verster who approved Peaches Gordon as a covert member. He was given the code name Diago.

When Van Zyl phoned Gordon two weeks later he was accused of being a security policeman. Van Zyl hotly denied it.

He visited Gordon in January 1989 to check on his reliability. At lunch Van Zyl handed him a sealed parcel and told him to deliver it to a certain café at 10:00 the next morning. It contained, he said, a firearm (in reality two flat stones) and under no circumstances was he to open it. Calla Botha observed the parcel's reception at the café and collected it afterwards as had been arranged. Van Zyl, after satisfying himself it had not been tampered with, paid Gordon R200. Everyone felt so good about Gordon afterwards a salary of R1 480 per month was approved for him.

In early February 1989 Van Zyl flew to Cape Town and gave Gordon a list of six SWAPO members and told him to confirm their addresses in the Cape. Gordon reported a few weeks later that he had traced one to an Athlone address. He said the subject was transporting ANC and UDF sympathisers daily in a micro-bus to an ongoing terrorist trial in Cape Town. He described the bus and where it was parked at night.

He handed over the names of two coloured males, Ismael and Isgak alias Gakkie Hardien, who wanted to work for Van Zyl. Gordon arranged a meeting where Van Zyl introduced himself as Thinus de Wet and gave the usual 'overseas businessmen' cover story. He agreed to employ them, gave them his pager number, an advance of R200 each and told them to infiltrate the ANC and UDF.

Wouter J Basson instructed Van Zyl to embark on a preliminary study for a project to burn the SWAPO man's micro-bus. Van Zyl submitted it with a recommendation that Ismael do the job in Athlone where the vehicle parked at night. The project was approved at an 'in-house' and Van Zyl was given R1 500 to pay Ismael when the job was done.

Van Zyl flew to Cape Town and briefed Ismael, who reported the next morning that he had completed the task. Van Zyl asked Gordon to verify this and afterwards paid Ismael his fee. Much later, the reliability of both Gordon and Ismael came into serious question when it was discovered that not only had the micro-bus not been burnt, it had not even existed. While this still lay in the future, for various other reasons Van Zyl had come to doubt Gordon's trustworthiness and he decided that paying him a monthly salary was a mistake. After discussing it with Staal Burger, he returned to the system of paying him only for results.

Gordon was told to produce information on political radicals. He came up with Advocate Dullah Omar (later Minister of Justice in the first ANC government), saying he was the UDF's regional secretary in the Western Cape and was serving on the executive councils of various banned organisations. Van Zyl submitted a report and discussed him with Wouter J Basson. After confirming Omar's political status with Military Intelligence, Basson told Van Zyl to embark on a preliminary study to eliminate him.

Staal Burger told a TRC Amnesty hearing that Omar was only one amongst many in the hierarchy of the ANC and its allied organisations who were on a hit list.

Van Zyl instructed Gordon to produce a plan to kill Omar. Gordon suggested recruiting two covert members to shoot him at his house. Van Zyl detailed a project and submitted it for approval. At an 'in-house' held at the Rosebank Hotel, Johannesburg, attended by himself, Verster, Burger and Basson, the project was approved. Gordon was authorised to recruit two covert members. Their identities would remain unknown to the cell. They would be provided with a Makarov pistol fitted with a silencer and seven rounds of ammunition. Gordon would be paid R15 000 from which he would pay the killers. The CCB chairman, Major-General Joep Joubert, approved the plan. Burger produced a Makarov with a loaded magazine, wrapped in a blue plastic bag, and gave it to Van Zyl after demonstrating how it worked.

In Cape Town a few days later, Van Zyl handed Gordon a briefcase containing the Makarov. It was still in its blue plastic bag. Gordon professed familiarity with the weapon, so a demonstration was unnecessary. He confirmed he would recruit the assassins for the fee of R15 000. Three days later he paged Van Zyl and said he had recruited two suitable assassins, but each had demanded an advance of R2 500.

Van Zyl completed an application for the amount of R15 000 on Burger's instructions and handed it to the Coordinator, Wouter J Basson. Shortly afterwards he was given the money in cash. He paid R5 000 into Gordon' bank account and locked the rest in his safe at home. It was arranged that when Omar had been effectively disposed of. Gordon would contact Van Zyl via his pager and leave the message: 'The sun is shining'.[38]

Four months dragged slowly by, but the sun never shone.

Staal Burger: Something in the pipeline

Staal Burger, while still with the Matthysen Bus Company, also engaged in the recruitment of covert members. Calla Botha said Burger and 'Big Alex' Kavouras flew to London to recruit someone from Zambia. The plan, the other cell members heard, was for the covert member to establish a business in Zambia importing and exporting pipes. Kavouras' involvement aroused hilarious speculation within the cell as to what might end up being stuffed in the pipes.

R70 000 was budgeted for the project, but it all came to naught. This was probably *Project Maxie* which, according to Wouter J Basson, concerned the gathering of information in an African state about the movements of 'enemies' of South Africa.

Burger later denied he had flown to London with Kavouras.[39]

CCB and SWAPO

In late 1988, while still with the Matthysen Bus Company, Calla Botha was sent to SWA/Namibia to assess SWAPO's chances of winning the independence elections in 1989. He returned with the impression that SWAPO would probably attain a majority.

His report outraged Joe Verster, Wouter J Basson and Staal Burger. They told him that perhaps he had visited the wrong country because as far as they were concerned, SWAPO was definitely not going to win the election.[40]

Planned assassination of Michael Gavin Evans: March/April 1989

During March 1989 Staal Burger, Chappie Maree and Slang Van Zyl met in the 'Mansions' flat in Louis Botha Avenue to discuss a project that had been passed from the CCB's intelligence structures via Wouter J Basson to Staal Burger.

Slang Van Zyl was told an in-house had already been held to discuss the elimination of *Weekly Mail* journalist Michael Gavin Evans. Evans, son of Bishop Bruce Evans of Port Elizabeth, was purportedly a friend of Heinz Grösskopff — wanted for a MK bombing atrocity that occurred in Johannesburg.[41] Evans was also thought to be a SACP member and an arms smuggler as well as a prominent member of the End Conscription Campaign (ECC). Members of the ECC, as previously explored, were considered enemies of the State because their aims were to create division, lower morale and influence the youth not to join the SADF.

Evans' elimination had been approved on those grounds. It was Chappie Maree's project but he was busy with external projects. Evans' address had been obtained by the simple expedient of phoning the *Weekly Mail*, posing as a friend asking for his address. Van Zyl was told to send for Peaches Gordon and another person to do the job. Gordon had to stab him or gun him down and make it appear to be a robbery.[42] Van Zyl gave Gordon R2 000 to cover expenses and promised him another R5 000 when the task was complete.

Then there were suggestions that Evans' address was incorrect, causing Joe Verster to cancel the project. This was not the end it, however, because the following appeared in Wouter J Basson's diary for 9 May 1989: 'Stephen [Chappie Maree] — Evans' and on 1 August 1989: 'Bert [Staal Burger] must chase Grosskof [Grösskopff] and attack his followers — G Evans.'

Ultimately, it turned out that the CCB's intelligence was incorrect and that Evans was not even associated with Grösskopff. Nor was he a prominent member of the ECC.

Nevertheless, his assassination remained on programme as a priority, but nothing happened because his address was not traced and Region 6 had insufficient personnel to handle it.

The Chairman at the time, Major-General Eddie Webb, denied that he had approved this project.

Checking SWAPO's leadership: March 1989

In March 1989 Ferdi Barnard found typed instructions and R3 000 in cash from Louis Yssel (Lafres Luitingh) in his post office box. He was to fly to SWA/Namibia and investigate where Danny Tjongarero — a member of SWAPO's central committee — was living, the vehicles he drove and his daily routine. There was no explanation, but Luitingh had told him previously that the organisation intended driving a wedge between SWAPO's internal and external parties. Various journalists had been helping. SWAPO, Luitingh said, posed a threat because of its ties with the ANC. Barnard was sure they intended to kill Tjongarero.

Barnard located his home in the up-market section of Katutura Township and discovered he drove a white Toyota Cressida. According to Barnard, Luitingh was pleased with the result and paid him a production bonus of R2 000.[43]

In direct contradiction, Luitingh said Barnard was 'fired' by the CCB in February 1989 for committing a 'security breach' [44], presumably for talking too much. If this was so, what was he doing in Namibia?

Assassination of Dr David Webster: 1 May 1989

Zambian born Dr David Joseph Webster (44), a social anthropologist at Witwatersrand University, had been conducting ongoing research in the Kosi Bay area. It had started with a few brief visits, but in 1986 his field work began in earnest. His interest was the tribal structures and village systems of the Themba-Tonga people, who straddle the border of northern Natal/Mozambique.

Friends said he was 'in love with Mozambique'. He had links with Maputo's Eduardo Mondlane University through Sergio Veira — a former Minister of Security in the FRELIMO government and by then a professor of politics — regarding his academic research and his interest in RENAMO. Webster had recently phoned Veira to report the illicit movement of ivory from Mozambique into Natal.

Webster was obsessed with exposing the SADF's ongoing support of RENAMO. He had established that the SADF were training them in South Africa and clandestinely infiltrating them back into Mozambique. He had discussed this with a fellow academic who had close ties to the FRELIMO government and was supposed to have compiled notes concerning his discoveries. The notes never turned up. Two years before a KwaZulu agricultural officer had reported seeing three mobile RENAMO bases in the Kosi Bay area. Another was believed to be in the Ndumu Game Reserve on the Mozambique border. An SADF intelligence report leaked to the *Weekly Mail* in 1992 confirmed the existence of a covert RENAMO training base in the Tembe Elephant Park near Kosi Bay.[45]

Webster's girlfriend, Maggie Friedman, believed he had many political enemies because of his left-wing affiliations.

He had planned to take journalist Eddie Koch with him to Kosi Bay in May 1989 to illustrate his discoveries, but he never made it.[46]

Glenda Webster, his ex-wife to whom he had been married for 20 years, said he had sworn her to secrecy in 1978 and told her he had joined the ANC. But the ire of the SADF was probably aroused by the leading role he had played in the End Conscription Campaign. This organisation, 'the enemy' to the SADF, had been prohibited under the 1988 State of Emergency from 'carrying on or performing any activities or acts whatsoever'. As late as October 1992 when conscription was winding down, the SADF persisted with its threats to prosecute the ECC for urging national servicemen to ignore call-ups.[47]

Webster was an executive member of the Five Freedoms Forum and a passionate campaigner against detention without trial. He was a member of the UDF's cultural committee, the Restricted Detainees Parents' Support Group, JO-DAC (Johannesburg Democratic Action Committee) and DEW (Detainees Education and Welfare). His interventions on their behalf brought him popularity amongst former detainees and their relatives. He arranged gatherings — known as Webster's tea parties — at which people were comforted while they sang and prayed.[48]

Dr Webster did not realise it, but he was being closely monitored by personnel of the Security Department of the Johannesburg municipality, which had close links with Military Intelligence and the Security Police via the Joint Management System. Military Intelligence personnel including Major Roy Laubscher, Piet Cronje, Dick Greyling, Sergeant Paul de Swardt, John Eagen, Nic Vlok, Piet Assenmacher and others were attached to the department. One of their briefs was to 'establish and maintain a detailed list of all subversive leaders'.

As the 1980s progressed the department, although funded by ratepayers, became an extension of Military Intelligence. Virtually everyone was taken at face value as a potential enemy, even members of the ruling party. They infiltrated the radical *Afrikaner Weerstandsbeweging* (AWB), the liberal Progressive Federal Party (PFP) and even the governing National Party. They maintained a watch on the Pope during his September 1988 visit, reported on unrest in black areas, monitored industrial unrest, tapped telephones and much more. *The Star* newspaper claimed they spied on at least 48 organisations. Dr Webster fitted easily into their definition of 'a subversive' and intelligence detailing his activities was classified Top Secret.

Tony Naude, a Security Department employee, was ordered to get friendly with Dr Webster. He managed to become his jogging partner. In one report, Naudé disclosed his home address — 13 Eleanor Street, Troyville — and detailed his general activities, including the title of a video shown at his house on a particular evening. This titbit, like the rest, was passed to Military Intelligence and the Security Police.[49]

It appears that until then, it was believed that he lived in Kibler Park south of Johannesburg, because since November 1988 a D J Webster living there had been getting threatening phone calls. 'We are going to kill you', was one of the threats by a male caller. On other occasions there was heavy breathing or silence. While he was at work two white men called and asked the maid who lived there. Significantly, someone phoned his sister-in-law on 1 May 1989 and asked if Dr David Webster lived there. They were told he did not. Someone, it appears, was making certain of his facts, before turning his attention to another address. Significantly, it signalled the end of the threatening calls.

David Webster and Maggie Friedman were never the recipients of such phone calls, but they were awakened by night-time calls with heavy breathing. It is unknown if the Security Department of the Johannesburg Municipality liaised with the CCB, but Petrus Botes, an overt member, said at least one full time member of the CCB worked in the Pretoria City Council — so why not Johannesburg?[50]

Ferdi Barnard made a point of reading newspapers like *Die Vrye Weekblad*, the *Weekly Mail* and the *New Nation* to keep up to date with leftist and black nationalist politics. When he was called to Joe Verster's office in Ponti by 'Louis Yssel' and the subject of Dr David Webster was broached, he knew all about him.

They handed him a file with an A4-size recent black and white photograph of Webster. There was also a list of three to four car numbers, two addresses — one in Dunbar Street and the other in Eleanor Street — and a few newspaper clippings. Barnard was told to check on Webster's movements but warned against making obvious enquires or drawing unnecessary attention to himself.

They told him emphatically that Webster was an absolute priority and that he was going 'to fall' (be killed).

He was also assigned prominent trade unionist, Jay Naidoo (later a cabinet minister), and told to check up on him. He received information that Naidoo lived at 93 Hopkins Street, Yeoville, Johannesburg and he reconnoitred the place. He got into a nearby block of flats and from an upper floor balcony was able to get a bird's eye view of the house's layout. A yellow Ford Escort fitted with an old Port Elizabeth registration plate was parked in the driveway. Barnard passed on all the information he had gathered to Luitingh, but he was given no further tasks in that connection.

Dr Webster was the priority so he concentrated on him. He explained to Luitingh how difficult it was to maintain observations on Webster's residence in Eleanor Street because of its situation in a one-way street. Staying around for too long drew unwelcome attention. Luitingh told him it would be necessary for him to make a full presentation for the benefit of Joe Verster and himself at the Ponti offices.

There was nothing on paper, only writing on a white board with a felt pen. Barnard explained to them that Dr Webster could only be killed as an 'occasional target' because he did not follow a set routine. His working environment of Witwatersrand University was not a viable option for an assassination because of high traffic density in the area. There was also the problem that the area was well covered and effectively patrolled by uniformed security guards — with probably some in civilian clothes as well. He recommended an opportunist drive-by shooting that could take place by day or night. He said a shotgun should be used, because one shot of SG or SSG would kill the target and he would be difficult to miss at close range. In traffic it would also be taken as an engine backfiring. Another advantage was that ballistics experts could not identify the weapon from which a shotgun cartridge was fired. Barnard said 'Luitingh was "like Mickey Mouse who had seen a snake". He didn't say anything, Joe Verster did all the talking . . . there was no specific time frame or schedule, but I was told it was absolutely urgent. I must add that I made enquiries regarding why Dr Webster had to be killed. I wanted to be certain I was killing a terrorist . . . The most serious stipulation was the fact that apparently he had been busy with the compilation of a report that would be sent by him or presented by him to the United Nations. It had something to do with something that Dr Webster had discovered that emanated from his field of study, which was anthropology. This was in the Kosi Bay vicinity. It had to do with arms supplies and I don't know what else. It was a transaction between RENAMO and the South African government. They wanted to stop that. It was so serious by nature that if I could not kill Dr Webster under convenient circumstances, I was told to penetrate his home and kill him.' [51]

Barnard approached Calla Botha in April 1989 and showed him the photograph of Dr Webster. He had a file and an investigation diary relating to Webster and said he had been given a project to eliminate him. He explained he had been collecting information over a period of time since an in-house had been held at Ponti. He asked Botha to assist him. Botha, who was familiar with 'in-houses' and suchlike took him at his word and agreed to assist. He did not speak to anyone about it, because it was not his project and it would have been a breach of security.

He accompanied Barnard in monitoring Dr Webster at his house on three or four occasions, both by day and by night. Each time, they were operationally ready with false number plates fitted to the vehicle and balaclavas available in the car but the opportunity for a hit never presented itself.

Calla Botha and Ferdi Barnard were using the same gym, playing rugby for the same club and jogging together. They had known one another since 1977 when Botha was a schoolboy and Barnard a policeman. Botha gained the impression that Barnard was trying to recruit him. This led to their playing open cards and mutually revealing to each other that they were working for the same organisation. Botha assumed Barnard was an overt member from another region.

Brenda Milne, who lived with Barnard after his release from gaol in December 1987 until they broke up in early 1996, had also accompanied him on several of these monitoring missions. She knew — because he had told her — that he worked for a secret government organisation, but only discovered much later it was the CCB. He had told her that he passed intelligence gathered about subjects to his superiors who decided whether they should be eliminated or not.

Despite this '. . . he specifically told me . . . if he ever got the opportunity he would kill Dr Webster. He talked about substances they had in the CCB and such things', Milne said. 'I knew there wasn't a shortage of ways to kill him, but he didn't specifically tell me how Dr Webster would be killed. He did tell me, though, that he didn't have orders to kill the man.' He said he had a 'bag of tricks' with items like balaclavas and gloves readily available in case the opportunity arose to kill him. He also had a computer printout of information on Webster given to him by a policeman at the Brixton Murder and Robbery Squad.[52]

Barnard had borrowed a sawn-off shotgun from George Mitchell, ex-Rhodesian Special Branch attached to Selous Scouts and by then a captain with the KwaZulu Police Murder and Robbery Unit. Barnard was on his way to a friend's farm in Natal and said he wanted to shoot guinea fowl. In fact, he wanted to practise shooting at moving targets from the back of a car with a shortened shotgun. A normal shotgun would have proved difficult to manoeuvre in a car.

Mitchell said his gun was returned to him before Webster was killed. Barnard said the configuration of Mitchell's shotgun proved satisfactory, so he modified a shotgun from his own private stock of weapons by removing the butt and replacing it with a Pachmeyer pistol grip. He also shortened the barrel by about 12cm so it matched the length of Mitchell's weapon.[53]

Barnard told his wife, Maryna (she reverted to the surname of Language after their divorce) he would be paid to 'take out' Webster, because Webster had a high profile in the ANC. He said he took along his girlfriend Brenda Milne when he monitored Webster. 'I didn't believe it at first, because I thought he was living in a dream world . . .'[54]

Monday 1 May 1989 — International Labour Day — was one of those overcast autumn days when, as Maggie Friedman put it, houses look half asleep and nothing seemed to move very fast.

In the morning Barnard took Brenda Milne's white Ford Laser sedan and left her house. It suited him because every second or third vehicle was white, so it was nondescript. He told her he was picking up Calla Botha and they were going to monitor Webster. They drove around the block two or three times because it meant driving down three street blocks to get back to 13 Eleonor Street. Eventually Botha, who was driving, stopped the car by a corner café at the start of the one-way. They waited, balaclavas on laps, hands gloved and the shotgun held down out of sight, for 45 or 50 minutes.

Then Dr Webster's Ford Cortina van approached from the rear and continued past them down the street.[55]

David Webster and Maggie Friedman had been shopping. They bought plants at a nursery, stopped at a bakery to get bread and returned home at 10:20. The air was chilled from Sunday's rain and there were the mixed smells of freshly baked bread, plants and dogs in the back of the enclosed Cortina van. Only days before, Webster had sent his newly completed manuscript on right-wing death squads to a publisher. In a bitter irony, he had concluded his study with: 'It is very rare that such assassinations are solved'. Oddly enough, the manuscript never resurfaced in public.

They intended to spend a long and lazy day gardening, talking, making lunch and talking some more. They let the dogs out and were about to unload plants from the rear of the van. 'I wasn't expecting anything to happen', Maggie said.[56]

Ferdi Barnard focussed on his target, cocked the weapon and took off the safety catch. Both he and Calla Botha slipped on their balaclavas. Botha put the Ford Laser into gear and drove down the street, slowing as they neared the target.

Webster alighted from the van, walked to the rear and opened the back flap.

'We moved towards him very slowly. We were approximately two metres away from him. He was standing with his back towards me.'

'Webster!' Barnard called.

'He then turned around, as he did so, I stuck the shotgun out of the window and shot him at point-blank range. I fired one shot. Dr Webster collapsed on the ground. We drove away somewhat faster, but we didn't want it to look as if it was a car chasing away [escaping]. We removed our balaclavas. I looked back and saw there was a vehicle coming after us. I reloaded the weapon, but I had another weapon in the car as a back-up. I thought it might be somebody wanting to make a citizen's arrest. I would have shot the occupant if he had continued to pursue us, but the car stopped.'

They made good their escape.[57] Barnard said he admonished Botha because he drove off at speed, which drew unwelcome attention to them.

Barnard got rid of the balaclavas, gloves, shotgun and the car's false number plates. He variously said he had thrown the shotgun into a dam, given it to his father or that it was his favourite, nicknamed Buks Benade, and that he still had it. He said he had originally stolen it during a housebreaking and theft, carried out by himself and his associate, Eugene Riley. Botha said Barnard had told him he had broken the gun into pieces and disposed of it. Whatever he did with it, it was never found.[58]

'I heard the car — later I thought perhaps it was two cars', Maggie Friedman said. 'Something seemed to have back-fired. Suddenly David was stumbling. I thought he'd twisted his ankle. He had a bad ankle, you know.' She went to help him and he said he had been shot and told her to call an ambulance. 'Even when he said he'd been shot I couldn't believe it. There was just a small hole in his back. I thought they'd just take the bullet out.' Bystanders helped turn him on to his back to stem the bleeding. 'It was only when we turned him over that I saw blood coming out of his chest.' [59]

Cornelius du Plessis happened to be following what he thought was a white Opel Ascona or Monza sedan as he drove along Eleanor Street. It slowed by number 13, a shot rang out and a man collapsed. The Opal's white driver and a rear seat passenger glanced back at Du Plessis as they sped off. He knew he could recognise them if he saw them again. Identikits were prepared from his descriptions, but for some unknown reason they were not published until revealed at the Webster inquest three years later.[60]

Du Plessis stopped his car and helped Maggie Friedman administer mouth to mouth resuscitation. 'All those neighbours — most of whom didn't even speak to us, came out and started gawping and tut-tutting and trying to pat me on the shoulder', Maggie said. 'They kept saying, he's gonna be fine, he's gonna be fine, he's gonna be fine. It took me a while to understand that he wasn't . . .' Sadly, their efforts were fruitless and when the ambulance arrived a half hour later he was dead.[61]

The police investigation was complicated from the outset by a national serviceman falsely alleging he had witnessed the shooting as an excuse to delay his return to the army from leave. The imaginary identikits he compiled were widely circulated. Three months later, when his statement and identikits were proved to be false, the police inexplicably failed to advise the general public. On 19 May 1989, though, Brigadier Mostert had announced they had traced an eye witness (Cornelius du Plessis) and had 'improved identikits', but he refused to release them to the press. It was odd that, as the most obvious witness to the shooting, more credence was not given to Cornelius Du Plessis' evidence earlier. It was also strange that one of the identikits showed a striking resemblance to a Donald Acheson, who comes up later in this story.

The police showed the Du Plessis identikits to eye witness Loretta Mnamatha, who said: 'I am sure that two of the sketches look like the men in the car. I would make some changes to them', and she suggested a small cut on the driver's crew-cut head and more stubble on their faces. The second drawing, she said, was of the man in the back seat. 'His window was still open when they drove past me . . . I was ten to 12 yards away from where it happened. This man at the back then started to close his window.' Asked how she could be so certain, she said: 'Because I saw them.'

A third witness, Shirley Rousseau, also of Eleanor Street, was shown the Du Plessis identikits only three months after the shooting. She said one of the sketches resembled the driver.[62]

Ferdi Barnard arrived at Brenda Milne's home at lunchtime on the same day and announced he had killed Webster with a shotgun. The chance had come, he said, while Webster was unloading plants from the back of a van. He called out his name and shot him as he looked up.

'He [Ferdi] was very excited, agitated and nervous', Brenda Milne said. 'I think he was scared as well. I wasn't surprised when he told me, but I didn't expect it to happen in broad daylight. I thought it was part of his work, that it was inevitable. He still worked for the CCB . . . He did not receive authorisation to kill Dr Webster, because his instructions were to monitor the man. He would only afterwards have gone through all the channels and then been approved. He 'jumped the gun . . . He wanted to show the organisation he had what it took to be an assassin. He wanted to rise up in the organisation and wanted to be a handler [overt member].' [63]

Barnard told a later girlfriend, Amore Badenhorst, whom he set up as the madam of a brothel to gather information for Military Intelligence's Directorate of Covert Collection (DCC) many years later, that Calla Botha was so shocked by the murder he had to threaten to shoot him if he did not drive.[63] He also gave the unlikely story that Webster was 'an ANC activist who had on the day he was shot planned to blow up a bus full of people. He said Joe Verster had phoned and given him the order. I did not know Verster, but I knew he had contact with Ferdi', Amore said. 'Ferdi once received a call from him at the start of the [Webster] inquest.'

Barnard also spoke to his wife Maryna on the night of the murder and told her there had been three of them in the car. Calla Botha was driving, Eugene Riley was in the front passenger seat and he was in the back. 'Webster was unloading plants and was standing in the street and Barnard saw it as an ideal opportunity to do the hit. He shot Webster with a shotgun and told me [that] Webster's wife screamed like a stuck pig. He told me he had disguised himself with a blond wig. Ferdi used to have a badly made blond wig that he used to keep in a cupboard at my house. I sometimes jokingly put the wig on', Maryna testified. She said an identikit compiled by Cornelius du Plessis looked very similar to Ferdi wearing that wig. Barnard, however, denied he had worn a wig. Another looked just like Eugene Riley.

Eugene Riley, formerly of the SAP's Internal Stability Unit, had been on 'sick leave' on full pay from the force since 10 April 1989. When questioned later by the media, the police coyly refused to divulge the nature of his sickness, calling it 'an internal matter'. The truth was somewhat different. Riley had been suspended from the force after being charged with two counts of murder at Taung Regional Court in the then Bophuthatswana homeland. The charges were eventually withdrawn. Riley's girlfriend, Elmarie Wilkin, said she recalled overhearing Barnard and Riley planning Webster's murder in her flat. Riley suggested the use of a high-powered rifle, but Barnard disagreed.[65]

The killing was supposed to be unauthorised, but Barnard, according to Maryna, was paid a production bonus of R90 000 which he used as a deposit to buy them a house in Roodepoort.[66]

Barnard said he listened to and watched numerous reports about the killing on radio and television and read every newspaper going and was shocked by the public reaction. He had expected some because he had shot people before, but nothing like what happened. It bothered him and he tried to contact his handler.

Cornelius du Plessis, an eye witness to the Webster murder, prepared identikits of three of the culprits. (Right above) Is unmistakably Ferdi Barnard wearing a long blond wig — a witness said he had access to one. (Left above) Shows a remarkable similarity to Eugene Riley — a close associate of Barnard. (Below) Sketch shows remarkable similarity to the photograph of Donald Acheson — probable murderer of Anton Lubowski — whom Barnard supposedly only met and introduced to the CCB *after* the Webster murder. Strangely enough, the police did not release these excellent identikits until several months after the murder. Even more strange, neither Riley nor Acheson were seriously investigated. By the time Barnard was charged a remarkable number of those around him, including Riley and Acheson, had been murdered or were missing. The unfortunate Cornelius du Plessis probably paid for his public spiritedness with his life. He died, supposedly of 'natural causes' in Johannesburg General Hospital.

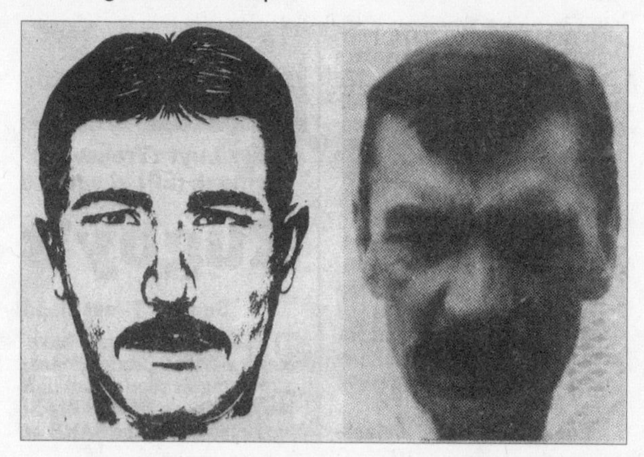

Lafras Luitingh, who was in Cape Town on 1 May, said Barnard left him five pager messages. He assumed he was after outstanding payments for CCB work done. He said they met the following day, 2 May 1989. Barnard, however, said he struggled to get hold of Luitingh and only managed it after three or four days of leaving messages. Eventually, Barnard said, contact was made and it was arranged they meet in the car park of the Hyperama at Roodepoort, where previous meetings had taken place.

The delay bothered Barnard because 'Lafras Luitingh and I didn't really get on very well. I cannot say I didn't trust him, but there was something about him that bothered me'. This mistrust prompted him to ask Calla Botha to accompany him. He had been told previously 'that one could do a job and then simply be taken out just like that. I had just killed Dr Webster from a moving vehicle and the same thing could happen to me'.

Botha confirmed that he went along and that he lay down on the car seat to avoid being seen. The implication was that he went armed to cover the meeting in case of problems, but neither of them spelt this out.

Barnard said he made his report to Luitingh and said: 'Listen, you've got some damage control here. You've said that you've been able to squash things.'

Luitingh, he said, 'congratulated me and asked me to tell him briefly what had happened. He wanted to know what I did with the vehicle and the firearm. I told him I had destroyed the items. I didn't tell him what vehicle I had used. I didn't tell him exactly what I had done with the firearm. He wasn't really interested in any further details. He then went to the boot of the car where he removed a brown A4 envelope and handed it over to me. He said it was a production bonus and also that Joe [Verster] was very happy.'[67]

Barnard, Luitingh said, blurted out that he had 'floored' Webster. Luitingh professed that he had never heard of Webster and asked if it was a CCB-related killing. Barnard replied in the negative, so Luitingh told him he did not want to hear any more about it. He found the killing incomprehensible, but believed Barnard might have done it to prove he could still play a role in the CCB.[68] He said nothing about handing him an envelope.

Botha confirmed that Barnard had an envelope on his return to the car. Ferdi drove off and when they were well away from the car park he stopped and opened the envelope. They examined the contents and Botha saw R15 000 in cash. Barnard said it was his payment for the successful execution of the Webster project. He gave Botha R5 000 as his share and said that Luitingh 'was impressed'.[69] Whether this was indeed a payment for killing Dr Webster, or whether it was an 'outstanding payment for CCB work done' is an open question.

Luitingh shared Barnard's revelations with some of his CCB comrades and finally with the Chief of Staff Intelligence, General Rudolph 'Witkop' Badenhorst, who threatened both him and Joe Verster and warned them to 'keep quiet'.[70]

'It was the strangest thing', Barnard said. 'Nobody ever approached me. Joe Verster did not approach me [although] Lafras [Luitingh] knew what I did.' The investigative team as he got to know it, '[Police General] Krappies Engelbrecht and Witkop Badenhorst still today haven't spoken to me about it. Nobody asked me about it.'[71]

Living with his wife Maryna in one house and with his girlfriend Brenda Milne in another — with both apparently knowing of the existence of the other — showed the extremely convoluted lifestyle that Ferdi Barnard led.

David Webster's funeral was attended by hundreds of blacks from trade unions and civic bodies, who paraded in the streets, sang freedom songs and prayed at the service. Firoz Cachalia, a Johannesburg attorney and the publicity secretary of the Transvaal Indian Congress — a close friend and former student of Dr Webster — announced that he had 'died a soldier of the ANC'. When asked to explain he said: 'I'm not in a position to say who has formally joined the ANC, but David was a member of the ANC in spirit.' That he had died for 'the cause', is supported by the inscription on his tombstone: *Greater love hath no man than this, that a man lay down his life for his friends*. This, from the Gospel of St. John, is customarily used on the headstones of soldiers killed in action.[72]

Two unidentified white academics with confirmed Military Intelligence links — one from Potchefstroom University — visited the Kosi Bay area shortly after the murder. Purporting to be members of a research team, they questioned field workers about Webster's activities in the area. This aroused the suspicions of Dr Webster's former assistant and he reported it. Warrant Officer Rousseau spent 'several weeks' conducting investigations there. Police believed the academics had been seeking Dr Webster's simple grass and tin hut, to search it for documents he might have left behind. Although highly suspicious, no evidence connecting them to the murder was found.[73]

Significantly, though, the day after the *Sunday Times* report on this incident appeared, Joe Verster and a CCB henchman walked into the home of the journalist responsible, De Wet Potgieter, and told him 'in no uncertain terms' in front of his wife and a terrified three-year-old son, to retract claims of CCB involvement in Webster's murder in the next edition, or face the consequences. 'I retracted nothing, and happily, survived to tell the tale'.[74]

As his ex-wife, Maryna Language so aptly said, Barnard told 'the world and his wife' he had killed David Webster.

A few days after the murder, a Region 6 meeting, attended by Staal Burger, Chappie Maree, Calla Botha and Slang Van Zyl, was held in a hotel room. It started late because Joe Verster had sent for Wouter J Basson to discuss the Webster case. Verster, Burger said, suspected it had been the work of Region 6. Van Zyl maintained he knew nothing about the killing, which had never been discussed within their cell. Nevertheless, he could not say if other members of the cell were involved or not.[75]

It was suspected that Ferdi Barnard was the culprit. It was said he had been used once to conduct an authorised reconnaissance of Webster and it was thought he had murdered him to get back into the good books of the CCB after he was sacked.

Calla Botha kept quiet about the part he had played. He personally thought the killing had been an approved project on which Joe Verster had back-tracked. 'I saw how they reacted . . . he [Verster] asked people if we were involved and that made me realise that this project would not be admitted, either by himself or any other party. So it was a closed book . . . it was my fear that Joe Verster would exonerate himself and Luitingh and apply a so-called cover-up operation and sell Barnard and I out. I wasn't prepared to take that chance'. It would be many years before Botha admitted the part he had played in the killing to Pretoria's Attorney-General, Dr Torie Pretorius.[76]

This Region 6 meeting was probably prompted by Lieutenant-General Jaap Joubert, the head of the SAP's Detective Branch, who had summoned Major-General Eddie Webb to his office.

'Are your [Special Forces] people involved or not [in the Webster murder]?' he asked him bluntly.

Webb emphasised it was not a discussion between officers of equal rank. Joubert was senior to him. Nor was it a chummy discussion between two members of the Security Forces.

'I don't think any detail was discussed. For me the important thing was that he directed his enquiry at me. Perhaps he wanted to look me in the eye when he asked me this? Perhaps he didn't want to mention it on the phone? He summoned me to his office and I went.' He surmised that in his senior position, General Jaap Joubert had most likely known about the involvement of Special Forces in previous incidents — like the murder of Dr and Mrs Ribeiro — which had probably prompted his enquiry.

Major-General Webb was personally convinced that the CCB was not involved, but he nevertheless checked with Joe Verster, who presumably asked Staal Burger of Region 6, who asked his men. Webb eventually reverted to General Jaap Joubert with the answer that Special Forces was not involved.[77]

For the next eight years Ferdi Barnard lived a charmed life, claiming innocence at both the Harms Commission and at the Webster Inquest. Many were willing to testify he had admitted murdering Webster, but all withdrew their willingness to testify after death threats.

Barnard had many allies, albeit reluctant ones like his CCB colleagues because he knew too much about their own criminal activities, but it saved him from arrest. Once a crack drug buster with the police, he ended up as a loose-tongued crack addict.[78]

Anthony Rosskam's car burnt

Calla Botha recruited Jeffrey, a coloured dagga dealer from Randfontein, as a covert agent. Jeffrey suggested that Anton Rosskam, a leftist activist, be marked for attention. Botha sought further intelligence from the CCB's information officer which revealed that Rosskam was Chairman of the Wits University Student Council, a member of the End Conscription Campaign, the Johannesburg Democratic Action Committee and other left-leaning organisations.

A project to burn his vehicle was approved after an in-house. Botha tasked Jeffrey to do the job, but decided at a certain stage that he had overestimated his capabilities. He asked Ferdi Barnard for his assistance and one night they went to Rosskam's home, poured petrol on the car and burnt it out. This was confirmed by newspaper photographs.

Afterwards Rosskam received several threatening letters, warning him that if he continued his left-wing activities he would end up dead like David Webster.[79] They obviously originated from the CCB.

The project was financed and filed under Region 6's code name, *Project Choice*. Staal Burger approved payment of R5 500 for Jeffrey. Botha believed this was stingy and an acrimonious argument resulted. Perhaps this was because — as came out in the Webster murder trial — that his friend Ferdi Barnard, and not Jeffrey, was his accomplice in the burning incident. It seems certain a relatively paltry sum like that would certainly not have satisfied Barnard!

Rev Frank Chikane and Roland Bruce White: June 1989

In June 1989 Calla Botha was told to place two people under surveillance and gather intelligence about them. The first, Bruce White, had been instrumental in the formation of the UDF in the Eastern Cape[80], and the second, Rev Frank Chikane, was the General Secretary of the South African Council of Churches. Botha obtained a printout of Chikane's activities from Military Intelligence. It showed that he had been the prime mover in the foundation of the Independent Board of Enquiry into Informal Repression, established with the assistance of the Lawyers for Human Rights and the Human Rights Commission. In the end his instruction to monitor Chikane was overtaken by events and he never did anything beyond his initial enquiries.

Shortly afterwards the Rev Chikane fell inexplicably ill while in Namibia en route to the United States. After his arrival in America, he was struck down three times with the same malady — which was symptomatic of a malarial attack, and hospitalised. 'In all cases I felt nauseous, I started sweating, salivating and vomited. My body started shaking and twitching. My eyes became watery and my vision was blurred. I could hardly walk, or turn my body when in a sleeping position', Chikane said.

Tests established the cause. Traces of organophosphate anticholineesterase — an insecticide which prevents the function of one of the body's vital enzyme systems — was impregnated into his clothing. The poison had been absorbed into his body through the hair follicles.[81] A urine sample taken at the Wisconsin University hospital showed the presence of diethylphosphate which indicated the presence of parathion. The presence of paranitrophenol indicated that paraoxon, as the metabolised form of parathion, was also present.

Towards the end of 1988, Dr Wouter Basson introduced Dr Immelman of Roodeplaat Research Laboratories (RRL) to three men whom he described as 'collaborators and colleagues', and called Chris, Manie and Gert. Immelman gained the impression that Chris was a colonel. To protect RRL's cover, Immelman was introduced as 'Willem', a farmer who was in the business of supplying toxins for cash on a part-time basis. Basson said he should give the men anything they wanted. 'Willem' had about nine meetings with them, usually in restaurants. When they observed that he had an extensive knowledge of toxins for a farmer, he laughed and ascribed it to him having 'good contacts'. Immelman assumed the men belonged to 7-Medical Battalion, but they were obviously with the CCB. Orders were normally fulfilled within two or three days of their being placed.

When Willem delivered paraoxon to them on 4 April 1989, they asked him to describe at length how best it chould be applied to clothing. He told them to spread the substance over the widest possible area of a garment where it directly touched the skin. The most sensitive areas of the human body for the absorption of toxins were the scrotum and eyelids, hence underwear fitted the bill. In particular, he suggested the contamination of the waistband of underpants and the collars of shirts.

DrImmelman said his co-directors knew he was supplying toxins on Dr Wouter Basson's orders. He discussed the incident with Dr Schalk van Rensburg after the story of the poisoning of Rev Chikane broke in the newspapers and he suggested that paraoxon was the probable culprit.

Dr van Rensburg put it differently, saying that after he read a newspaper report of the poisoning he confronted Immelman and demanded: 'What on earth are you people doing?'

Immelman explained that the operation had been a gigantic failure because of mistakes. The operator had dabbed the poison on the fabric of five pairs of underpants, instead of spreading it thickly over the widest possible surface area of one pair. Intelligence had also been inadequate. The information was that Chikane had been travelling to Namibia, where forensic facilities were virtually non existent, but in reality he was flying to America via Windhoek.

Dr Immelman told him the CCB was furious.

Immelman denied that such a conversation had taken place, but agreed that Van Rensburg had asked a great many questions about the Chikane incident. He could not fully recall everything that had passed between them. Nevertheless, because of Van Rensburg'a persistent questioning, he began to harbour doubts about his loyalty. This was reinforced when Van Rensburg begged his fellow directors never to reveal to his wife that RRL was a SADF front company.

Dr Immelman maintained that he could not say with certainty that any toxic substances supplied to Basson or anyone else had been used to poison people, but his suspicions were strong as far as Rev Chikane was concerned. He quoted from an article on organophosphate pesticides which confirmed the American FBI report had indicated that Chikane had been the victim of paraoxon poisoning.

Dr Mike Odendaal of RRL, although never informed about the attempt on Rev Chikane's life, also harboured suspicions. He remembered a discussion he had with Dr Immelman about a plan to poison someone 'important'. He later concluded through media reports that Chikane must have been the person he was referring to.[82]

Although suspended by the CCB, there was no shortage of offers for Ferdi Barnard's services from amongst his ex-police colleagues in Region 6. It seems likely, though, that they believed he was still serving the CCB in some capacity. Calla Botha and he worked out together twice daily in the gym and were also playing rugby in the same team.

Botha mentioned to Barnard that he had been asked 'to work on Bruce White'. Barnard said Botha 'had a problem or problems'. He was working alone and he did not have much detail except for a photograph, a little general information and knowledge that White worked at the Urban Foundation based in the United Towers Building in Fox Street, Johannesburg. Barnard offered to assist with a surveillance of the building and they went there two or three times together.

In Barnard's opinion Bruce White was being monitored for eventual elimination, although no one told him so. 'The whole purpose of the CCB was the maximum disruption of the enemy. You cannot disrupt someone to the maximum if you do not kill [him] and I think that's what they wanted.'

Barnard said he 'made a mistake' on 9 June 1989 by asking a security guard at the building where White parked his car. 'We were a little frustrated' and he had not realised how sensitive Mr White was and that it was likely his enquiry would be reported. White's suspicions were indeed aroused when he was told about it and he complained to the police. Detectives from the Brixton Murder and Robbery Squad sped to the scene and confronted Botha and Barnard on the street corner.

They gave an impromptu lame excuse that they had been waiting for a lady. This was passed by radio to Captain Gert Zeelie at Brixton, but he brusquely rejected it. He instructed his men to bring them in for questioning and the detectives told them to follow their car to Brixton.

While en route Barnard thought up a more acceptable excuse. They told Captain Zeelie they were not looking for a 'Mr White' but for a 'white BMW' that his ex-employer, Willy Smit, had asked them to trace and seize. The police let them go saying that they would check it out. Barnard got to Smit first and asked him to confirm their story. In the end the police accepted the excuse and charges were dropped.[83]

Staal Burger was livid when Calla Botha reported what had happened. He accused him of discussing top secret information with Barnard which he obviously had, but he denied it. Botha's regional colleagues told him in confidence that Burger had demanded his instant dismissal. Instead, Joe Verster called him in, severely reprimanded him and 'put him on ice' — an effective suspension with full pay. Burger took his 'Red' pager — rented in the name of Johan Malherbe — and gave it to Chappie Maree. Botha's relationship with Burger, which was not a happy one anyway, continued to deteriorate.

Non-arson at a non-existent Cape printing works: June 1989

In early June 1989 Slang Van Zyl heard that a Cape Town printer was producing material for the ANC, the UDF and COSATU. A project was approved and orders were given for the place to be burnt down. Van Zyl nominated Peaches Gordon for the job and told him how to tackle it.

Gordon reported in due course that he had successfully torched the factory and was paid R2 000. Van Zyl heard much later from Isgak Hardien that there had been no fire at the factory. What was more, the factory did not even exist![84]

More Peaches, no cream and Advocate Omar

Ferdi Barnard met Slang Van Zyl at the Witwatersrand Police Rugby Club at the beginning of 1989. He got to speak to him because he knew his wife who had been a prosecutor when he was a detective. 'At a certain stage', he said, 'I contacted him upon numerous occasions. We had telephonic conversations, ultimately we met in a restaurant, if I recall correctly. It wasn't clear to him, but from the discussion we realised that both of us were working for the CCB. I also told him that I was working for them and I told him that sometimes I would receive information that was favourable. What basically happened [was that] we decided to assist each other when we could.'

One can be certain that Barnard's reputation as a ruthless killer was well known to Van Zyl.

The lack of progress on the Dullah Omar project was discussed at Region 6 level and it was decided to get a sample of his heart tablets. The CCB's medical man suggested he duplicate them with a poisonous alternative, which could be substituted for the real thing. After ingestion Omar would die, apparently from a heart attack. The Chairman gave his approval and Van Zyl tasked Peaches Gordon to get a sample. Van Zyl also paged Barnard and tasked him to recommence his monitoring. Gordon got some pills and Van Zyl gave them to the medical man.

Van Zyl contacted Gordon on several occasions while on leave in Cape Town and the latter reported that Omar's movements were returning to normal. A few days later Van Zyl was called to a meeting at the Holiday Inn at Jan Smuts (Johannesburg International) Airport. 'Tilly' Smit (organisation name Nick Nienaber), by Van Zyl's account, handed him a small bottle of white powder. Tilly said Staal Burger had given it to him because duplicating the heart tablets had proved impossible. He did not give a reason, but in fact it was because Roodeplaat Research Laboratories did not have the necessary machinery to press out tablets. If sprinkled on food the powder would cause a heart attack.

Calla Botha, however, said Van Zyl was given pills, not powder. Van Zyl, he said, mentioned a R50 000 budget for the project, but by chance he caught sight of the project's settlement/adjustment form in the hotel room on which R70 000 was noted. It made him wonder what the other R20 000 was for.

Van Zyl said he passed the powder to Peaches Gordon who shortly afterwards phoned and said the task was impossible. There was no way he could get that close to Omar.

Ferdi Barnard claimed that Van Zyl approached him in July 1989 regarding the Omar incident. 'We discussed it and he told me that such a project had been registered, and it had been approved as a CCB project on the highest level . . . Advocate Omar had to be assassinated . . . he also informed me that the persons who had been tasked had been provided with a Makarov pistol fitted with a silencer . . . The project had been pending for quite some time and there had been problems in executing it. He wanted to know if I would be prepared to assist with the project.' Barnard agreed. He insisted that he had never been asked to monitor Omar, only to kill him.[85]

Major-General Eddie Webb, the CCB Chairman, maintained that he had never approved a project to murder Omar. He knew he was being monitored, but his approval was not required for that.[86]

Ferdi Barnard flew to Cape Town and booked in at the Inn on the Square. Van Zyl joined him shortly afterwards. Barnard, as loose mouthed as ever, mentioned his Cape Town activities to Calla Botha. Botha knew Slang had been working on a project relating to Omar, but he did not know until he learned from Ferdi that Peaches Gordon had been tasked to shoot him. Botha was still 'on ice' and not allowed to attend meetings of Region 6. In the meantime he busied himself with activities connected with his Blue Plan company.

Van Zyl briefed Barnard further and explained that Gordon's reliability was suspect. They met Gordon at the Cape Sun Hotel that evening. Staal Burger confirmed that Van Zyl had reported his suspicions that Gordon was a double agent and maybe a UDF supporter.[87]

On Van Zyl's instructions Gordon returned the silenced Makarov pistol. It was passed to Ferdi Barnard who hid it in the ceiling of his hotel room. The next day they met Gordon who took them to Athlone and pointed out Omar's residence. From that point on it was understood that it had become Ferdi Barnard's task to dispose of the target.

Barnard established his own liaison with Gordon and tasked him to steal a vehicle for him. He paid him R500 and Gordon undertook to have the vehicle available the next day. At 10:00 the following morning they rendezvoused in a nearby parking lot and Gordon indicated a cream-coloured Nissan. Barnard inspected the vehicle and noticed it had its original key. It had only 2 600km on the clock and it still smelt new, although the radio was missing. Gordon said an associate had taken the vehicle from a dealer for a test drive and had kicked the driver out. Barnard knew how the police surveillance system functioned. This car was not only 'hot', it was brand new and too easy to identify. Nevertheless, he gave him another R500 and took over the car.

Later that afternoon he drove to Cape Town Airport, got an exit ticket from the machine, parked the Nissan and stole a more suitable Ford station wagon with a roof rack. He had previously reconnoitred the car park of a large block of flats close to his hotel where there was a lot of traffic moving in and out day and night. He parked the Ford there. He watched the traffic until he saw another Ford similar to the one he had stolen and noted its registration number. He then called Gordon and paid him R300 to obtain a set of registration plates which he fitted to the stolen vehicle.

He was now ready to operate. Keeping in daily touch with Slang Van Zyl by phone, he began to reconnoitre the area of Athlone where Omar lived. He noted traffic densities at various times of the day and night. His first thought was that the best time for a hit was in the morning, because the target would have to leave home at about 07:15 to get to his office. The high density of bumper-to-bumper traffic at that time was not conducive to escape. He drove past the target's residence on several occasions and at various times without spotting him.

He had problems from the first day he commenced observations. Athlone was predominantly a Cape Malay, coloured and Indian neighbourhood. In that environment people soon picked up when a vehicle or a person did not belong. It had its own pulse and rhythm and anyone who was not part of the place stuck out like a sore thumb — particularly a white man. For this reason he could never leave the car and walk around. He had the additional difficulties of having a stolen car with false number plates and ten litres of petrol on the back seat with which to burn it after leaving the murder scene, to say nothing of the Makarov with silencer. He had not even had a visual observation of Omar and the longer he stayed in the area the more his security situation deteriorated. He phoned Van Zyl, pointed out the risks and he told him the CCB should obtain specifically orientated pin-point information about Omar's movements and so on. He then returned to Johannesburg with the task unfinised.

Van Zyl discussed the lack of progress on the Omar project with Staal Burger, but he was directed to continue. Pressure began to mount for him to finish the job. He contacted Barnard and told him he was being pressured from high up on the matter. Barnard asked what the hurry was. Van Zyl said some documents had been stolen from Omar which indicated he was involved in underground structures and a bombing campaign being waged in Cape Town.

Once again Barnard flew to Cape Town and booked in at the Inn on the Square. He recovered the Makarov from its hiding place and found the stolen car still at the block of flats where he had parked it. He repeated his process of observation and experienced even more problems than before. For instance, he would be waiting outside Omar's house in the car when someone would come out ostensibly to check the post box — at 21:00! It was obvious people were suspicious. All he needed was for the police to come and arrest him on suspicion! He returned to Johannesburg.

In September, on Van Zyl's insistence, he once again flew back to Cape Town. He retrieved the pistol and the stolen car. Amazingly, it was still at the block of flats.

One night he parked the car and waited in the shadows. He had his pistol cocked and ready to fire and was wearing a balaclava. After he had been there for more than an hour, Omar's car appeared and stopped in front of the house. He got out with a female passenger. Barnard's instructions were to make the killing look like a robbery. He was to shoot the target, clean out his pockets and take his wallet and wristwatch. He knew that if he shot Omar he would have to shoot the woman as well.

Killing David Webster in front of Maggie Friedman had badly affected him and he had been drinking heavily ever since. Memories of the incident haunted him and probably still do. He also knew that if he shot only Omar, the woman would raise a hue and cry and he would not even get as far as the highway. He made his decision — he could not shoot the woman. He clicked the safety catch of his pistol to safe and ducked down in the car.

Slang Van Zyl was in Cape Town on leave and Barnard saw him the following morning. He explained that Omar had arrived home with a female companion. This was unforseen and he had decided not to shoot the target as he did not want to kill the woman.

Van Zyl, Ferdi said, 'nearly went mad. He wanted to know why I hadn't shot him. He said I had lost my chance. I told him he had wanted it to look like a robbery, on which he retorted that I should have killed the woman as well. I told him that I wasn't prepared to do this and I was upset.' [88]

Shortly afterwards Omar suffered a heart attack which thwarted the project. Barnard returned to Johannesburg a few days later and suggested a postponement until Omar recovered. He said he handed the Makarov back to Van Zyl.

Staal Burger, Calla maintained, never found out about Ferdi's involvement.

The furore resulting from the Lubowski assassination caused the complete cancellation of the Omar project.

Archbishop Desmond Tutu: Project Apies: July 1989

In July 1989 an in-house was held in a Sandton hotel to discuss *Project Apies* (Monkey). This project had been passed to Major-General Eddie Webb by 'higher authority'. He passed it to Joe Verster who passed it to Region 6. The in-house was attended by Staal Burger, Wouter J Basson and Chappie Maree. It involved hanging a jam jar containing a monkey foetus from a tree at Bishop's Court, the official Cape Town residence of the Anglican Archbishop and Nobel Peace Prize laureate, Desmond Tutu. It was intended to give him a psychological jolt — to get him to reach back to his African roots and to make him believe he was being bewitched. It was later suggested that it was not the Archbishop himself who was targeted, but his black employees. It was hoped they would believe he had been bewitched and leave his employ. This would start to erode his support base. An ethnologist, whom someone in the CCB had consulted had come up with the idea.[89]

Meanwhile, according to Dr Immelman of Roodeplaat Research Laboratories, Dr Wouter Basson requested he obtain a baboon foetus that was required for research. He passed the request to Dr Stian Wandrag who understood it was required for tissue culture research in the Far East. Wandrag performed a Caesarian section on a pregnant baboon and removed two foetuses which he placed in a plastic bag and packed it with ice in a polystyrene container. He gave it to Immelman who passed it to Basson.[90]

Staal Burger, on the Chairman's instructions, ordered Chappie Maree and Slang Van Zyl to accompany him to Cape Town for actioning the project. At the last moment, though, something came up and neither Burger nor Maree could go. Van Zyl flew there alone, a bottled foetus and four nails treated by a witchdoctor in his suitcase. He linked up with Ferdi Barnard, who was there on the Omar project, and early the next morning they rendezvoused with Peaches Gordon and an unidentified coloured male. This man drove them to Bishop's Court in his car, where Van Zyl, Barnard and Gordon got into the yard by climbing the fence. While Van Zyl furtively tied the jar to a tree, Barnard, following Burger's instructions, completed the 'spell' by pushing two nails into the ground on each side of the driveway. Van Zyl gave Gordon R200 to pay the driver, then phoned Staal Burger and reported the project's completion.

What must have been a particularly unsuperstitious black gardener found the jar and tossed it in the dustbin. He did not deem the matter of sufficient importance to report it to the Archbishop.[91]

Ferdi Barnard later testified during his trial for murdering David Webster, that the depositing of the foetus at Bishop's Court was supposed to be only the first part of an operation directed against Archbishop Tutu. It had been intended to also leave the carcass of a dead hyena in the grounds as a follow-on and then to ultimately poison his son, Trevor — presumably with toxins obtained from *Project Coast*. Someone who had access to the house through a servant had been tasked to carrying out the poisoning. It never happened.

The purpose, Barnard said, was to create a record of events which would indicate that Bishop Tutu's own people, his own tribe, were angry with him because he had supported the call for sanctions against South Africa and they were losing their jobs as a consequence.[92]

Limpet mine at Early Learning Centre: 31 Aug 1989

Elections were pending on 6 September 1989. Isgak Hardien told Slang Van Zyl that prominent ANC and UDF activists in the Cape were planning violent disruptions. Secret meetings, where acts of sabotage and terrorism were the topic, were being held at the

Early Learning Centre hall in Athlone by the Kew-Town Youth Movement, a newly formed subversive organisation.

The organisation, Hardien said, had already been responsible for planning school boycotts, acts of terrorism and bombings, including the planting of limpet mines at Athlone's Magistrate's Court and Post Office. The mines at the Magistrate's court had exploded prematurely, killing two of those responsible. Hardien provided documentary proof that a Kew-Town member had been involved and also that further bomb blasts were planned to intimidate people into boycotting the forthcoming election. The Movement had also written to a candidate, Alex Anthony, warning him to take part in 'racist elections' at his peril. Isgak's information was that the organisation would be meeting on 31 August to plan further acts of terror.

Van Zyl prepared a preliminary study and passed it to Wouter J Basson on 10 August 1989. Despite the obvious urgency, Staal Burger only arranged an in-house for 25 August 1989. After discussions, a project was approved to destroy the Early Learning Centre on 31 August 1989 — the day of the intended Youth Movement meeting. A budget of R30 000 for expenses was recommended. Van Zyl suggested using a limpet mine detonated with a remote device. He opposed random detonation as this might cause the loss of innocent lives. Its purpose was to deter, disrupt and frighten the Movement into discontinuing its campaign of intimidation and violence. Hardien had already agreed to both plant the limpet in the hall and to detonate it. Van Zyl intended to lend his assistance if problems arose.

On the morning 30 August Major-General Webb met Joe Verster at the latter's office to discuss the project. A high degree of urgency was involved because the attack was planned for the following day, so Verster's submissions were oral and not written. The idea was not to kill anyone but to give the plotters a severe fright, so it was planned to detonate the device as soon as possible after they left the hall. He hoped that those concerned would say: 'Look, I'm done with this. I'm not going to take part in this kind of thing.' Despite this, the project provided for the possibility of lives being lost.

General Webb had access to other intelligence sources, presumably Special Forces' Intelligence and Military Intelligence, but there was no time to seek confirmatory information. So after listening to Verster, he approved the project. He phoned the Special Forces engineering and technical officer, Colonel Hekkies van Heerden, and instructed him to procure a Soviet manufactured limpet mine and arrange for a remote detonating device for the job. This, Webb said, was the first 'physical' operation that he approved in Region 6.[93]

That afternoon Slang Van Zyl attended a meeting held in a room at the Protea Gardens Hotel, Johannesburg. Staal Burger, an unnamed medical man and the CCB's newly appointed financial manager, 'Tilly' Smit (Nick Nienaber), were already there. Burger opened the meeting by saying that Joe Verster had warned that if the Kew-Town Youth Movement activated one more bomb, Van Zyl would be held personally responsible. Wouter J Basson arrived during the course of the meeting with a cardboard carton containing a large grey SPM limpet mine. The detonating mechanism, fitted with an aerial, had been made from a pocket calculator. The charge was activated when the minus sign was depressed.

Van Zyl was a novice with explosives, so he requested the assistance of Calla Botha who had qualified as a demolitions expert while with the Security Police. Burger phoned him personally. Although still under suspension, he gladly agreed to assist. He was anxious to return to the CCB structure, although he harboured the feeling that he would probably be tossed out again at a later stage.[94]

They drove to Cape Town, the limpet mine snuggled in its carton in the boot and the remote in Van Zyl's briefcase. They arrived in the early hours of 31 August. They slept in Van Zyl's brother-in-law's flat for four hours, after which Van Zyl phoned Isgak Hardien and arranged to meet him in the D F Malan (Cape Town International) Airport's car park.

Hardien was given two identical bags, one empty and the other containing the bomb. A coloured woman, with the empty bag within the bomb bag, would enter the Early Learning

Centre and plant the bomb bag in a cupboard. She would leave carrying the empty bag as a precaution in case someone asked her where her bag was.

Van Zyl retained the detonating device, intending to hand it to Hardien when they met later in the nearby Bellville Holiday Inn. Van Zyl developed second thoughts. He was worried that Hardien might just detonate the bomb in the veld, so after discussions with Botha they decided to personally supervise the operation.

Van Zyl said they met Hardien as planned and he drove to them to the Early Learning Centre. They arrived around 19:45 and parked the car about 400m away. Hardien indicated the hall, pointed out cars in the car park and explained that the Kew-Town Youth Movement's meeting was already in progress.

Van Zyl despatched Hardien on a recce, telling him to check that children from an earlier karate class had left. He returned shortly afterwards and reported the place clear — only executives of the Youth Movement were still around. They found a spot where they had a good view of the hall and waited. At 21:00 the Kew-Town executive members, after idling around talking for while, made their way to their cars and left. When satisfied the place was absolutely clear, they drove a block away and Van Zyl depressed the button. There was a loud explosion and they drove off.

Calla Botha, on the other hand, said they were driven to the hall by Isgak Hardien in his car, because only he knew where it was. En route Hardien confirmed the bomb was already in the cupboard, so Van Zyl passed him the calculator. Botha explained that the remote device had to be activated no farther than 500m from the target.

Hardien dropped them off some distance away, then left for the hall. He returned shortly afterwards, complaining the remote did not work. Botha checked it, but found it faultless. He suggested Hardien had been too far away and said he should get closer and try again. He once again returned a short while later, insisting the device was faulty. Botha told him to get even closer and try again . . . this time an explosion resulted. Hardien returned and drove them straight to the airport and they flew out. Van Zyl, he said, left his car with his brother-in-law in Cape Town.

Staal Burger and Chappie Maree met them at Jan Smuts (Johannesburg International) Airport in the early hours of 1 September and Slang reported success. Later he presented a full written report to Staal Burger, Wouter J Basson, Maree and 'Tilly' Smit at the Rosebank Hotel. He returned the detonating device to Wouter J Basson, sorted out Isgak Hardien's payment which amounted to R18 000,[94] and returned to Cape Town to resume his leave. Calla Botha heard later that R100 000 had been approved for the project, not the R30 000 he had been led to believe. What had happened to the balance is left to the imagination.

Peter Williams, who with Osmond Alexander, was the joint leader of the Kew-Town Youth Movement, denied the organisation was subversive and described it as merely a youth club. He told the TRC that both he and the Movement were anti-gangster and anti-gangsterism. Nor was he a political activist; he pointed out that his half-sister, Colleen Williams, had died in the Athlone bombing. He denied the bomb had only exploded after the Early Learning Centre had cleared and the cars had left. He said the meeting was still in progress and the cars were in the car park when the detonation took place. It was only by quirk of circumstance that those in attendance were not in the hall at the time. Fortunately, the meeting had earlier been moved to the boardroom by the principal, because she had promised the hall for a football meeting which, in the event, did not take place. Three people were injured in the explosion.

Williams described Hardien as a gangster — an *agent provocateur* — who had offered to supply the Kew-Town Youth Movement with weapons and hand grenades which he said he had access to. Williams told him categorically he was not interested as they were not involved in acts of sabotage.[96]

When asked during his amnesty hearing if he would still have approved an operation to blow up the premises where a subversive meeting was believed to be taking place if those premises had been the Sanlam Insurance Building in Cape Town, Major-General Webb said: 'It's possible, yes.' As with the Early Learning Centre he would not have approached the owners and warned them: 'Hey, your building is being abused'. That was not the way the CCB did things.[97] One can only assume this was because it would have breached its deep cover.

After this attack, Calla Botha was taken 'off ice' and resumed duties within Region 6. Wouter J Basson said he was reactivated because 'we had a dire need for his services'.[98]

17

Civil Cooperation Bureau/National Intelligence Service Disaster in Zimbabwe 1988

Project Barnacle's cells and agents: Zimbabwe: the 1980s

There were several *Project Barnacle* cells and individual sources working independently in Zimbabwe. The members of one such cell, code named Juliet, lived in various parts of Zimbabwe. They were in deep cover and normally only came together for operations.

The group leader was Kit Bawden, who like many others, had been hardened by the Bush War. He lived in Kumalo, one of Bulawayo's upper class suburbs, in what was described as 'a flash house with flash furniture' and always drove good cars. Kit, a tall, athletically built and hard living man, was a dedicated polocrosse player. After watching his first game he bought a pony and soon afterwards was representing Bulawayo with a handicap of two.

He emigrated to South Africa in 1985 and settled in Johannesburg with his wife and two children. Despite this he continued going in and out of Zimbabwe, spending at least six months of the year in Bulawayo. He was a free spender but the source of his finance was unclear, especially since W B Holdings, the timber business in which he had an interest, went bankrupt. Nobody was particularly concerned. The Bawdens were of 1890 pioneer stock and everyone assumed he was still financially involved in Glenorchie Ranch, the family business at Fort Rixon.

Next came Bulawayo-born Michael Smith, who had joined the Rhodesia Light Infantry in 1973 and later passed SAS selection. Like so many others he had left Rhodesia on Robert Mugabe's assumption of power and joined 6-Recce, in which he served for a year. At his later trial he refused to disclose the type of work he did in the SADF, saying: 'I can't discuss it. I am not allowed to discuss it.'

After returning to Zimbabwe he took employment as a farm manager at Balwearie Estates, Chakari, where he lived with his wife Eileen. They had no children. He was recruited into *Project Barnacle* in 1983 by Brian after he returned to Zimbabwe.

Kit recruited his cousin Barry Bawden into the cell as the third member of the team. Barry managed the White Kopje Ranch in Shangani and had served in the Rhodesian Light Infantry during the war years.

Kevin Woods, who had served in the Special Branch of the British South Africa Police before independence, was recruited as an agent by South Africa's National Intelligence Service. He was tasked, by Woods' account, to supply information on ANC activities and the 'bandit situation' in Matabeleland.

Major Brian knew Kevin from his BSAP days, so he assisted him by arranging his appointment to the Central Intelligence Organisation (CIO) in Bulawayo through existing sources within the organisation. After leaving he took up a position as manager of a security company and lived in Burnside, Bulawayo. He was divorced with two children, but still lived with his ex-wife, Jane. Although not a member of the cell, he worked in close liaison with them because they had sophisticated radio equipment that he did not have.

It was not the sort of thing he could have kept in town because there was a danger of it being located by direction finding equipment.

At least once or twice a year, by arrangement, Brian came up from South Africa and rendezvoused with the members of Team Juliet at camps on the Zambezi River, usually the Chobe or the upper Zambezi. The idea was to conduct a major debriefing in an area impossible to subject to electronic surveillance. At the same time it gave them an opportunity to unwind and have a break. The strain of constant engagement in intelligence operations is intense and a two-week fishing trip with cold beers readily to hand was guaranteed to relax anyone.

Another source, freelance and unattached to a team, was Phillip Conjwayo, a South African born Xhosa, who had served in the Special Branch of the British South Africa Police from 1954 to 1979. He was a fine policeman who became disenchanted at the country being taken over by a bunch of terrorists. He was based in Harare.

Kit wanted Brian to authorise the recruitment of his younger brother Guy Bawden into Juliet. He was working at Renosterspruit Farm as a mechanic and wanted to return to Zimbabwe. He had served in the Selous Scouts during the bush war days, but as a mechanic and not as an operator. He had, though, gone on some of the big external operations conducted by the Scouts. Brian would have none of it, he had known Guy since he was a youngster and believed he did not have the right temperament for intelligence work.

Brian kept a tight rein on his men, believing this and good security were essential for their own safety and well-being.

Attack on ANC transit facility: Bulawayo: Jan 1988

In December 1987 intelligence gained by the Security Police from an MK capture in South Africa established that a bungalow at16A Jungle Road, in the run-down Bulawayo suburb of Trenance, was being used by MK as a transit facility. This was passed to the National Intelligence Service which ordered Kevin Woods to reconnoitre and photograph the target. He confirmed it was occupied by young men of military age, presumably MK fighters, and passed the information back to Pretoria. It was decided it that would be dealt with by the CCB's Team Juliet. He knew of the existence of Team Juliet, so he was instructed to liaise with them.

Team Juliet was ordered to attack and destroy the Jungle Road facility and cause the maximum number of MK casualties. An extra CCB operative was to be parachuted in to assist.

Operator Barry Bawden got the message from Kit and passed it on to Guy. He was to go to the family farm at Fort Rixon and arrange a DZ into which Henry Thompson, together with weapons, equipment, stores and suchlike would be parachuted. On the designated night, Guy marked it out, using infra red strobes invisible to other aircraft and waited for the C-130 to appear overhead.

The strobes were activated when he heard the distant growl of aircraft engines. Once the aircraft had danced into position overhead, the green light flashed on and Thompson jumped through the rear, parachuting in with enough clothing, grenades and firearms for six men and a supply of explosives and chemicals for the manufacture of bombs. He was met by Guy on the ground and together they disposed of the parachutes and carried the stores into hiding.

An interim operation concerned the kidnapping and smuggling into South Africa of Jabulani, an ANC cadre. This apparently involved Mike Smith, Guy Bawden and Henry Thompson, but what transpired is unknown.[1]

Kit Bawden and Henry Thompson drew up the plan of attack.

At first it was intended that Kevin Woods would obtain a car from an ex-girlfriend and this would be converted into a car bomb. Instead Philip Conjwayo, an intelligence agent probably with the National Intelligence Service who had become involved in the team's activities, was given cash byThompson to buy one elsewhere. It was obviously believed that a buying expedition by a black man would be less likely to attract attention than one by a white man. Conjwayo, using the pseudonym James Sibanda, bought a yellow Renault R5 sedan from Francis Kapfidze, a Bulawayo office worker, for Z$5 000. Unfortunately for him, Kapfidze had a retentive memory.

Kit Bawden, Mike Smith and Henry Thompson packed the Renault with explosives and fitted a remote control detonating device. Their instructions were to file all identifying numbers off the vehicle, but for some inexplicable reason they failed to do so.

Kevin Woods, in the meantime, having completed his reconnaissance mission, left for South Africa to take his child back to boarding school in Irene near Pretoria.

On 8 January Kit Bawden drove Henry Thompson to a rendezvous near Beit Bridge. He was picked up by a SAAF helicopter and flown to South Africa.

On D-day, Monday 11 January 1988, Philip Conjwayo went to the Vungu Labour Exchange, Bulawayo and enquired amongst the unemployed people gathered there for a casual driver.

Amon Obert Mwanza, an unemployed Malawian, stepped forward. Conjwayo took him on, paid him a retainer and told him he would be getting Z$50 per week.

Conjwayo gave Mwanza the address of the ANC facility in Trenance, handed him Z$10 and the keys of the Renault and told to drive there and pick someone up. He should pull into the drive, hoot twice and the person requiring the lift would give him directions to his destination. It is assumed that Mwanza was unaware the house was an ANC facility. He was also unaware that Kit Bawden and Mike Smith, armed with a remote detonating device, were in another car a safe distance away.

The unsuspecting Mwanza pulled into the driveway and hooted twice, unaware that he had signed his own death warrant. An ANC cadre heard the hooting and went outside to investigate. His next recollection was waking up in hospital. There was a gaping hole where his right eye should have been and he had serious multiple injuries. When testifying in court later he denied he had received military training. He said he was a refugee who had left South Africa in 1985 for the Dukwa Refugee Camp in Botswana. After leaving Dukwa he moved to the ANC's headquarters in Lusaka and stayed there for two years. He was in Bulawayo, he said, 'to visit, to see Zimbabwe'. He described the other five people in the house as ANC 'comrades'. He explained that they 'were afraid that if our names were known South African agents amongst us might make reports on what we were doing.' [2] That such elaborate arrangements were made to conceal identities indicated they were more than just tourists. Another ANC cadre was badly injured and hospitalised and two others received lesser injuries. The blast damaged houses 200m away.

Kevin Woods saw the news on television in Pietersburg while en route back to Zimbabwe.

The police investigation commenced immediately and they were soon on the blundering trail the CCB operatives had left for them to follow. Their mistake, as in the Brickhill operation, was to buy the car openly. If Conjwayo had not bought it from Kapfidze, then Woods would have got his ex-girlfriend's car, which would have left an even clearer trail. The main difference between the Jungle Road bombing and the attempt to kill Brickhill was that the police traced the car used in the former case.

It would have been wiser to use stolen vehicles, which is routine in such matters. The IRA, for one, certainly did. Some senior professionals put it down to arrogance. There was a belief that since independence, investigational standards in the Zimbabwe police force had dropped so low they were hardly worth bothering about. It was a serious mistake that would cost the operators their freedom, almost their lives. There were still some detectives around who had learned their trade in the old British South Africa Police. Two of the investigating officers had served with Philip Conjwayo. Detective Inspector Liberman Ndhlovu, when as constable, had trained under Sergeant Conjwayo. 'I respected him as a father. His approach and dedication to duty was an inspiration to me.' Chief Superintendent Blessing Mvandiambira knew him as a 'brother' and a hard interrogator.[3]

Francis Kapfidze identified the front bumper and number plate found amidst the wreckage as originating from his yellow Renault. He remembered Philip Conjwayo.[4]

The driver of the car bomb was so badly mutilated that the pathologist was unable to tell if it was a male or female. Only a foot and a hand remained intact.

Fingerprint impressions were taken from the severed hand and compared with records at the Foreigners Identification Bureau in Bulawayo. The hand belonged to Amon Mwanza.

With that information, they located Mwanza's landlord, Victor Ndhlovu and showed him what remained of his former tennant. Ndhlovu positively identified Mwanza by the foot: '. . . he used to walk barefoot so I knew his feet.' He also identified clothing found as being that worn by Mwanza when he had left for the employment office that morning. He confirmed, too, the deceased's identity card.[5]

They located a work seeker, Christopher Muchatsi, who had witnessed Mwanza being recruited by Conjwayo. He remembered the incident and both men involved.

On Friday 15 January 1988 the police swooped and arrested Conjwayo at the high density township of Mabvuku in Harare. CIO — Central Intelligence Organisation — detectives might have learned their investigational procedures under the old Rhodesian system, but in the new Zimbabwe the old checks and balances that had been in place to stop the torture and abuse of prisoners had been swept away with independence.

Such abuses often had ministerial approval. Note the efforts of Minister of Justice and Legal and Parliamentary Affairs, Dr Herbert Ushewokunze, to amend Zimbabwe's criminal code after the acquittal of the Thornhill 'Air Force Six' — senior white air force officers who were falsely accused of blowing up the Air Force of Zimbabwe's strike jets. (They had been destroyed by *Project Barnacle* operators — see Chapter 10 *Cry Zimbabwe: Independence Twenty Years On* by Peter Stiff) The idea was to render confessions extracted under torture admissible in court.

Then there was the case of the South African Security Police spy, Odile Harrington, puzzlingly convicted for contravening Zimbabwe's Official Secrets Act and sentenced to 25 years imprisonment for attempting to infiltrate the ANC. How such an act amounted to a breach of an official Zimbabwe secret is beyond comprehension. At the appeal hearing Chief Justice Enoch Dumbutshena noted that the prosecution had made no attempt to rebut evidence that Harrington was:

- Repeatedly flogged with wire flex until she lost consciousness or soiled herself.
- Stripped naked and indecently assaulted before five male interrogators.
- Starved.
- Kept in solitary confinement for the ten months before her trial.
- Subjected to water torture with her head crammed into a water-filled bag until she almost drowned.

No attempt was made to bring to book the CIO members who had so savagely tortured her. The trial judge, Mr Justice Wilson Sandura, did not care a jot about the torture either. He merely ignored it, expressing regret he could not sentence her to be put before a firing squad and shot, instead of just 25 years imprisonment.[6]

So Philip Conjwayo, and later his comrades in the CCB cell, were earmarked for a torrid experience. After arrest he was driven to the Harare Central Police Station and taken to the CID offices where a CIO officer and a detective began interrogating him at 20:00. They questioned him the whole night without respite. They wanted to know about bomb attacks in Harare and Bulawayo, but he denied all knowledge.

They handcuffed him so tightly it stopped the blood flow. When he persisted in his denials they used the water torture, continually submerging his head in a bath of water and pulling it out only just before he drowned. When this failed to break him they attached electrical leads to his penis and administered powerful electric shocks with a hand-operated dynamo. They also worked him over with rubber straps.[7]

On Saturday 16 January Conjwayo, unable to take any more, broke down and confessed. The police, as could be expected, denied he was tortured. They said he willingly volunteered to phone his controller in Johannesburg, Ms Mary Baker, because he wanted his white accomplices arrested. Conjwayo, on the other hand, said he was in fear of his life. It seems he had no way of making direct contact with either Smith or Woods.

'Help me, you must get me out', he told Mary Baker on the phone. 'I want money and assistance . . . You said if there was going to be any trouble you were going to be so fast and pick me up.'

He then called an unidentified man in Johannesburg. 'It's very, very bad. My sons, my daughter and my wife have been picked up. They want me.'

On Sunday 17 January he phoned Mary Baker again. 'We are very worried about you', she said. 'Everything will be fine.' 'Is it a trap?' she asked with concern.

Presumably satisfied, she told him to go to Mactech Garage in Bulawayo, spelling it out phonetically to ensure he got it right.

'You will find stuff in a plastic bag in the toilet. You know, the little tank in the toilet', she told him. He was then to make his way to Francistown, Botswana.

Mary Baker was later identified as a former Rhodesian policewoman, Katriona Marilyn Burger.

The CIO laid on a team to keep Mactech Garage under observation.

Kevin Woods's NIS (National Intelligence Service) handler, meanwhile, had phoned and asked him to arrange a dead letter drop of Z$1 000 in the toilet cistern at Mactech Garage. Why the Mactech Service Station owned by Rory Maguire was chosen for the dead letter drop, instead of a spot out on the main highway or some other isolated out of town place, is beyond comprehension.

The observers saw Woods arrive at the service station and enter the toilet. After he had left, a check revealed Z$1 000 in the cistern. The police arrested him at his Burnside home on the morning of Monday 18 January. During a search they found a high tech Textel machine on the premises, supplied by the NIS to transmit typed coded messages to South Africa at high speed. When connected to a telephone, it could store and transmit 7 400 characters virtually instantaneously. Its memory was erased at the touch of a button.[8]

By his own account Woods cooperated after his arrest because he feared what would happen to him if he did not.[9]

A senior police officer had shouted: 'You are dead!'

Another said: 'I am very glad that you are an ex-member [of the CIO] because you know what happens to people who do not cooperate.'

They threatened to interrogate his ex-wife if he did not cooperate and he was terrified they would torture both her and his children to make him talk. They told him he could forget about a lawyer because 'you will never see one.'[10]

Recalling his days with Zimbabwe's CIO, he told of the interrogation of an innocent man suspected of involvement in the abduction of six tourists in Matabeleland in 1982. 'Because he was innocent, he could not say what they wanted to know. The last time I saw him he was a completely rotten piece of living flesh.'

Woods led the police to the house used by Kit Bawden when still living in Zimbabwe — 1 Blane Road, Waterford — where they recovered a large quantity of arms of war.[11]

Rory Maguire was also arrested and he soon broke under pressure and offered to give State evidence. He was already pending trial for contravention of the Customs and Excise Act, concerning R300 000 worth of motor spares smuggled in from South Africa by Brian — the ex-Rhodesian police officer and South African Special Forces operator. Brian had to write this off as a total loss.

Despite Brian having been uninvolved for a long time, an old source close to the police in Bulawayo phoned him during the afternoon of Monday 18 January 1988.

'They've nailed Maguire and Woods. They arrested them this morning. Something to do with money going into a toilet at a garage.'

Brian's first reaction was that it was bucks. Big bucks. They had been smuggling, got greedy and had been caught. He telephoned Alan at the farm.

'Do you know that Rory and Kevin were arrested this morning?'

It was the first Alan had heard about it.

After that his phone rang incessantly. Suddenly he was the intelligence and liaison man between Special Forces and what was happening in Bulawayo.

He phoned his source two hours later. He had promised to do some digging to find out what was going on.

'Brian', he told him, 'those guys are in the shit. They are involved in all sorts of things.'

'What?' Brian asked.

'I don't know exactly, but some black has been arrested and he has blown it. There has been a killing in Trenance'.

'You've got to get Mike Smith and Barry Bawden out', he told Alan on the phone. 'Some black has blown things, so you can't leave them there.'

In fact, Special Forces had realised it was Philip Conjwayo who had been arrested and compromised the moment they heard Rory and Kevin had been arrested. Brian did not discover this until later, nor that Philip Conjwayo had been operating with Team Juliet.

Special Forces and the CCB dithered.

They contacted Mike Smith by phone and guardedly warned him of the arrests, but said he should sit tight because it was probably nothing to worry about. They contacted neither Barry nor Guy Bawden.

Sand in the hourglass began to run out.

It ran out for Mike Smith on Tuesday 19 January, when dozens of policemen and a platoon from the police support unit descended on Balwearie Estates, Chakari. They also arrested his wife, Eileen, and the farm's owner.

He was handcuffed, leg-ironed and driven to Bulawayo where he was intensively interrogated. He had no idea what had happened to his wife and was confused when his interrogators threatened to make her disappear never to be seen again, unless he confessed . They added that the same would happen to him. He had no doubt they intended carrying out their threats.

Barry and Guy Bawden were also arrested. Barry's wife was pregnant and gave birth after he was in custody. Kit Bawden escaped the net and skipped the country.

Attorneys were denied access until 28 January, but even then it was conditional on their not discussing the allegations with their clients. They could only talk about business affairs and welfare matters. During this and subsequent interviews, policemen or prison officials were always present and listening. Michael Smith's attorney was not permitted a private consultation with his client until 22 February 1988.

Operation Direksie (Direction) 1 and 2: attempt to spring prisoners: 1988

In late January 1988 Brian approached General Joep Joubert at Speskop.

'I know I'm out, but I have worked with these guys. I'd like to get them out.'

He was promptly whisked downstairs, out of the building and into a collection of buildings to the left of the gate boom at the entrance to the complex. This was where Colonel Joe Verster had established his offices. Verster, from what he could gather, had taken over as the commander of *Project Barnacle*.

He and Brian had never seen eye to eye.

'So you have come to join us, eh?' he asked.

He opened his desk drawer, took out what was apparently a contract some 30 pages long, and shunted it across his desk. Brian only realised later it was a contract for the CCB, the organisation that had succeeded *Project Barnacle*. He was unaware his old organisation had ceased to exist — nobody had bothered to enlighten him. He was aware another organisation of some sort had come into being, however, because after his resignation he had heard that many of his former black staff had transferred to it, but he had no idea of its name. He assumed the new and the old were running in parallel. He only discovered the truth when media publicity about the CCB broke in 1990.

He glanced at the papers and saw they constituted an employment contract, although no employer's name appeared. He later discovered that it was obligatory for everyone recruited into the CCB, and those who transferred from *Project Barnacle*, to sign this contract on resigning from the army. It was supposed to guarantee pensions and that sort of thing, but judging by the large number of its members who threatened court action in later years it didn't achieve its objective.

Brian pushed the contract back across the desk and told Verster he was not interested in signing anything. His only desire was to get his friends out.

Verster warned that if he did not sign he would not get a salary.

'A salary doesn't interest me', Brian replied. 'I will help as much as I can. Just refund any expenses I incur.'

This was agreed.

Brian reactivated his connections with former sources in Zimbabwe and tasked them to watch, monitor and report on what was going on as far as the prisoners were concerned.

It was decided that two teams, an internal one and an external one, were required for the operation. Brian would recruit the internal team and Joe Verster would be responsible for the external one. There were numerous conferences and think-tanks at Speskop, to discuss ways of springing the operators from Chikurubi Maximum Security Prison. Probably as many as 100 ideas were explored, then discarded. Initially it was intended to use Recce operators proper, with a mixture of *Project Barnacle* (CCB) operatives for the external team.

One of the many ideas developed involved a ground team storming the prison gates. With the element of surprise in their favour, it could have worked. Brian cautioned against this because the Depot of the Police Support Unit, the famed 'Black Boots', was just down the road from Chikurubi. They were a highly professional unit with heavy support weapons and not to be tangled with lightly, although their present quality of leadership was unknown. Although most white policemen had resigned after the Mugabe takeover, a senior and highly disciplined black leader element which had fought throughout the Rhodesian Bush War remained. Some of the more senior members had also fought in Malaya. If things went wrong, a nasty punch-up was inevitable.

The idea of using Special Force operators proper was discarded because the powers-that-be demanded that the rescue mission be deniable. This was of particular importance since they had already denied knowledge of the unfortunate prisoners.

With every plan discussed, they kept returning to one factor. An aircraft was essential, either a chopper or a fixed wing. It would be required to land close by, so the prisoners could immediately be flown out of the country.

One idea, calling for a helicopter, envisaged landing on the heavy gauge mesh covering part of the prison, cutting through it with heavy power tools and getting the men out that way. Something similar had apparently been planned to rescue the 'Air Force Six', following the sabotage of aircraft at the Thornhill Air Base in August 1982. The major hazard in the use of a fixed wing was that the Hunters could be scrambled to shoot it down. A helicopter was more suitable. SAAF Pumas had the necessary range to get in and out, but if one was spotted or shot down it would be completely undeniable. The alternative was to hire a helicopter, but this was not as easy as it seemed. They were not hired out to all and sundry and even if this was done through a front company of Military Intelligence, fingers would still be pointed at South Africa if things went wrong.

In early February 1988 Mike Smith's wife, Eileen, flew from Harare to Cape Town. The two-week visit was ostensibly to visit relatives, but in reality it was to make contact with Brian on Mike's behalf. Brian did not know her, as she had only met and married Mike after his resignation from *Project Barnacle*. Eileen proved to be a brave woman, whose only desire was to get her husband out of prison.

Brian took the next flight to Cape Town, where they spent long hours exploring possibilities. Brian had in mind a rescue similar to Patrick Gericke's, and he asked her if she knew anyone who was serving in the Zimbabwe Security Forces. Maybe a policeman? Someone with a valid reason to be in contact with the prisoners? Perhaps it was somebody who was already in contact. It could be anyone who might be useful.

Eileen promised to think about it. She was staying in Cape Town for two weeks, so Brian suggested she phone him from Jan Smuts Airport when she passed through on her way home to Harare.

Brian up-dated Colonel Verster and they both flew to Cape Town so Brian could introduce him to Eileen.

Later she duly rang Brian and they met at Jan Smuts (Johannesburg International) Airport. Eileen had thought of a possible solution. If they needed a helicopter, what about one belonging to the Air Force of Zimbabwe?

She knew a ZAF helicopter pilot, Air Lieutenant Gary Kane. They were friends long before she had met Mike. They were never romantically involved, but they moved in the same circles. Eileen thought he might be open to suggestions, but one could never tell. Stealing a helicopter, she knew, was a lot to ask. She was certain, however, that he would not report her to the authorities if she did ask. It was a matter of waiting for the right moment, then sounding him out. It was not something that could be approached like a bull at a gate.

She returned to Harare. It took about a month, as she had expected, before she got the opportunity to ask Gary Kane. He turned out to be sympathetic and to her relief agreed to help. Besides, he was planning to resign from the Air Force and leave Zimbabwe anyway.

Kane was flown to Swaziland to see Brian. They had an in depth discussion at Matsapa Airport. Gary explained that for a pilot, booking out an Augusta Bell helicopter for a practise flight did not pose a problem. The Air Force had become very sloppy in its administration and security. It was done all the time.

Brian reported back to Joe Verster. He decided to see Eileen again, this time with Kane. To ensure maximum security, he asked Brian to arrange for both of them to fly to Europe. He would see them there.

Deon, a former policeman from Bulawayo who worked for Brian in his business of exporting motor spares, frequently travelled back and forth to Zimbabwe. He had been uninvolved since the end of the Bush War and had played no part in *Project Barnacle*.

Quite coincidentally, just after the arrest of the agents, he had casually mentioned to Brian that he knew Mike and Eileen Smith well – he had even been a guest at their wedding. For youngsters of his age in Zimbabwe, the arrests had been a major talking point. Brian trusted him implicitly and he seemed the ideal liaison link between himself and the internal team.

Brian asked Eileen, during one of her frequent visits to South Africa, what she thought of Deon. Did she know him well? Could she get on with him?

Surprised to learn that Deon was working for Brian, Eileen assured him that they were great friends. He was also very reliable and she would be glad to work with him. Having got the okay from Eileen, who had become a crucial element in the planning, Brian recruited Deon into the scheme.

In April Eileen suggested he recruit 'Des' for the internal team. During the Bush War he had fought with the Rhodesian African Rifles, but he was no longer involved. He was tough and had the right qualities. She knew him well because he had been her sky diving instructor. Brian remembered Des from the war days and he asked Eileen to see if he was amenable. If he was, she should ask him to fly to Johannesburg to see him. He flew down and was recruited.

Subsequent to his discussions with Gary Kane in Swaziland, Brian had nothing further to do with him directly, because Joe Verster took over as his handler. Gradually, too,

Verster eased Eileen away from Brian and took over as her handler as well. This was unsatisfactory and Brian found he had to conduct an important element of the planning third hand, by communicating with both Eileen and Gary through Deon, instead of directly as Verster was doing.

Deon did much of the leg work, sorting out funds for the operation from personal monies held by Brian in Zimbabwe. It had been the practice of the prisoners' families to take food to Chikurubi Maximum Security Prison for them daily. They were not allowed to see the prisoners because only one short monthly visit was allowed. They merely handed in the food at the reception for onward transmission to the prisoners.

Deon took over this daily chore. It gave him an excuse to be in the prison area and the guards and prison authorities soon got used to him. It also gave him time to check on procedures and routines there. He reported to Brian that the prison itself was impregnable. A break-in seemed impossible.

He noticed a weak point in the system, however. The prisoners were transported from the prison to the magistrate's court in the centre of Harare for further remand every two weeks. They travelled in a locked prison van. The driver was unarmed and only one guard sat in the back with them. He was lightly armed with a single shot Martini-Henry Greener shotgun. It would be easy to stage a hold-up en route, spring the prisoners, load them into a helicopter and fly them out.

Deon began to coincide his prison visits with the times when remand prisoners were being transported to town. He followed the vans noting timings how long it took to travel from point A to point B to point C and so on.

Brian's plan, adopted by the CCB, called for Gary Kane to sign out an Augusta Bell helicopter for a practise flight early on the morning of D-day. He would fly alone which was not unusual. Once airborne he would cruise around the general area of Domboshawa and Chikurubi, awaiting a hand signal from Deon on the ground pointing out the truck they had to intercept. They had practised the manoeuvre on several occasions and it presented no difficulties.

On getting the signal Gary would radio the ambush party consisting of Des plus three white and two black operators from South Africa. They would immediately establish their roadblock at the intersection of Harare Drive and Arcturus Road, Greendale, and await the prison truck. Two black operators in police uniforms would wave down the truck. When it came to a halt, the other operators would spring from cover, overpower the guards and release the prisoners.

Gary, closely monitoring the situation from above, would land the chopper nearby and pick up everyone, including Deon who would be following the truck in his car. He would fly them to the ZISCO landing strip at Redcliff, just outside of Kwekwe in the midlands, where they would be picked up by a fixed wing aircraft and flown to South Africa.

An Augusta Bell can accommodate eight fully armed and equipped soldiers, so there was room for everyone plus a few hangers-on should the necessity arise. Des and Deon had also plotted escape routes to five or six emergency pick-up points. They were a contingency option in case something happened to the helicopter. If that occurred, or for some reason there were so many people that weight became a problem, those not choppered out could be driven to an alternative pick-up point for later uplift by a fixed wing aircraft.

For the prisoners, one 14-day remand was followed by another. No date had been set for their High Court trial, so there was no particular urgency in putting the plan into operation. But things changed abruptly when Gary Kane was told he was scheduled for rotation to the Beira Corridor for operational duty in mid-July. This would have been his second tour in Mozambique, where the ZNA (Zimbabwe National Army) was acting in support of FRELIMO.

The helicopter was an essential element, so the final date for D-day was set for Thursday 30 June 1988, when the prisoners were due for remand. The remand date after that, 14 July, would be too late. Preparations were accelerated.

In early June Joe Verster phoned Brian. Behaving very mysteriously he told him to contact Des and tell him to fly to Matsapa Airport in Swaziland, via Jan Smuts (Johannesburg International) Airport. Brian was also to fly there in an aircraft chartered at Lanseria Airport north of Johannesburg and meet him. Verster declined to provide more details.

On the appointed day Brian flew to Matsapa Airport. The chartered aircraft dropped him off and returned to Lanseria. He met Des and to their mutual surprise they discovered that a second chartered aircraft, a Learjet, was waiting to fly them to Otjiwarongo in SWA/Namibia. The mystery was deepened by the pilot assuming they fully appreciated what he was doing. He dog-legged back to Lanseria and collected Kit Bawden. Kit said Joe Verster had personally driven him to the airport.

Brian, an experienced intelligence professional, was perplexed by the unnecessary mystery. Verster had already spoken to all three of them in connection with the pending operation, so the flights to Matsapa Airport and back to Lanseria, presumably as a security measure, appeared unnecessary to say the least.

While the aircraft was taking off Kit whispered to Brian: 'We are going to look at farms, okay?'

Brian shrugged.

He discovered that Kit would not to take part in the rescue attempt. He was there because it was his brother and cousin . . . his team . . . who were in gaol.

After an hour in flight the pilot struck up a conversation with Brian.

'Why are guys going to Otjiwarongo?'

'We're looking at game farms . . . we want to buy game farms.'

There was a pause while the pilot digested the information.

'Where you from?'

'Zimbabwe', Brian replied.

'Oh', the obviously puzzled pilot said, 'if you're from Zim, why did we have to pick you up in Swaziland?'

Brian mumbled a non committal reply, inwardly cursing Verster for not briefing him. He could understand why the pilot was puzzled — their cover story did not gel.

'I've been told to stand by to pick you up', the pilot said after a pause. 'When is that likely to be?'

'Well . . . maybe . . . it depends . . . we'll let you know', Brian mumbled and fell victim to another bout of silently cursing Verster.

'I've got some good friends involved in the Otjiwarongo farming scene. Perhaps I can introduce them to you', the pilot suggested helpfully.

'Thanks . . . but well . . . no . . . we'll be okay.'

Brian was understandably relieved when the aircraft landed at Otjiwarongo. He did not have the slightest idea what to expect and neither did his companions. A vehicle was parked just off the airstrip. Waiting in the driver's seat was Danie Phaal of Special Forces' security. They asked where they were going, but he merely gestured that they should get in. They drove south on the Okahanja road, turned east towards the Botswana border and negotiated the Klein Waterberg mountain range. Eventually he stopped and indicated a dirt track leading off the main road.

'Walk up there for about a kilometre and you'll find someone you know', Phaal told them.

They unloaded their luggage and briefcases and trudged up the track until a farmhouse came into view. Awaiting them was 'Aussie', Dennis 'Sammy' Beahan, 'Big Jim' Maguire and two black operators. Brian had met neither the Australian nor the two blacks, but he knew Sammy and 'Big Jim'. They all knew him, though.

Sammy Beahan had served in the British Army and then the Rhodesian SAS during the Bush War. After that he joined Chief Superintendent Mac McGuinness of Special Branch, who was responsible for Selous Scouts' intelligence and who also ran various 'funnies' from his Bindura base.[12] After leaving Rhodesia he served for a brief spell in 6-Recce, then returned to Zimbabwe where he served for a short time in the ZNA.

Big Jim Maguire shared a similar background.

Brian had not seen either of them for ten years.

'Aussie', a big man like Maguire, was also a former military man, perhaps in the Australian Army, perhaps in the British Army, and had seen some involvement in African conflicts.

Brian did not have a high opinion of any of them. He regarded Sammy and 'Big Jim' as low quality operators and recalled instances from the Bush War days when jobs they had been involved in had ended up with unnecessarily inconclusive outcomes. Aussie proved to be bombastic and argumentative.

The two blacks were 5-Recce operators who had taken part in the first Maseru Raid, *Operation Lebanta*. They remembered Brian from pre-raid briefings conducted by Pete and himself. They were seasoned operators, but former guerrillas. Fortunately their English was satisfactory, but neither of them was particularly well educated. They had to pose as policemen, which was not easy considering that they had not served in the police. He had specifically asked for two ex-policemen who had worked with him in *Barnacle*.

Brian gained the uncomfortable impression that Colonel Verster had recruited a team of 'expendables' — people who could be sacrifice if things went wrong — instead of tried and tested operators to guarantee success. Brian was right but, of course, he had no knowledge of the 'overt' and 'covert' member system adopted by the CCB.

Joe Verster had appointed Sammy as the leader of the external team. The most worrying thing for Brian about Sammy, 'Big Jim' and Aussie — all recruited from civvy street — was that none of them had been 'involved' for many years.

The recruitment of Sammy Beahan, who was working as a security manager at the Sandton Sun Hotel in Johannesburg, was a geographic saga. Alan flew to Frankfurt, phoned him at Sandton, asked if he was interested in a one-off job for R8 000 and paid his air fare to Germany to talk to him.[13] Sammy accepted the job in Germany and returned to Johannesburg to stand by until required for training.

Back at the farmhouse, Brian received a call on the radio. The caller did not identify himself, but Brian recognised the voice. It did not fool any of the other operators either.

'Hell', said one, 'what's Joe Verster up to now?'

The voice instructed Brian to walk back to where Danie Phaal had dropped him off earlier and said he would be met there. He was picked up shortly afterwards by Joe Verster himself, who drove a confusing route of lefts and rights for an hour. They ended up at a bush camp set up by Verster and some of his CCB colleagues. He asked Brian what he thought of the team.

Brian replied bluntly that he was unimpressed and did not believe they were capable of doing the job. They were yesterday's heroes.

'Surely we can put together a more professional team?' he asked.

Verster was visibly annoyed.

'Your job', he snapped, 'is to recruit and train the internal team. The external team is my responsibility.'

Brian requested the two black operators of his choice, instead of the two he had been saddled with. Verster refused and told him to train the ones he had got.

Give them tips on police procedures. Show them how to conduct themselves at a roadblock. Tell them what to do after stopping a vehicle. Teach them what to say. And so on.

Brian, Kit and Des remained at the farm for about a week, training the black operators and assisting the others. The black operators were fitted out with Zimbabwe National Police uniforms.

Des threw himself into the training with enthusiasm, firing thousands of rounds from a heavy automatic weapon, similar to that mounted on the Augusta Bell they expected to be riding in. Maybe he might have to use it during the escape bid.

Much equipment had been brought to the farm. There were bolt cutters, angle grinders and cutting machines with petrol powered generators for breaking the lock on the prison truck. They also practised with small explosive charges, blowing off locks and so on. They thought up and experimented with many new ideas, discarding them if they did not work as well as anticipated. Much of the equipment needed was not immediately available, because it had only been decided on after they gathered at the farm. Specialised items had to be made or adapted, silenced weaponry needed to be sorted out and radio equipment from the range available had to be selected and tested.

They issued the black operators with FN rifles, the basic weapon of the Zimbabwe National Police. The rest chose whatever weapons they fancied. It mattered little because they would only appear and act in support once the prison van had been stopped by the pseudo policemen.

There was a mountain of equipment stashed in Zimbabwe, but much of it had been buried for years. Its condition was uncertain and it might well have deteriorated. They wanted to be sure that what they used was functional, so they decided to smuggle in new stuff. Besides, they did not know whether any of the caches had been lifted by the Zimbabweans — or if any were under observation.

Brian was tasked to infiltrate the two black operators and get them to Bulawayo. Joe Verster's people were to arrange the infiltration of Sammy, 'Big Jim' and Aussie and get the equipment into Zimbabwe. This was to be packed inside windsurfers that would be moved by heavy trucks transiting Zimbabwe on routine runs to Malawi. The designated transport company was part of the Military Intelligence set-up. The consignment would be unloaded at Masvingo (formerly Fort Victoria) and taken over by an internal team, which would get it to Des in Bulawayo.

Brian remained distrustful of Verster's three white operators, a feeling he shared with Des and Kit. During what turned out to be daily visits to Verster's bush base, Brian again suggested they drop all three. He would gladly do the job with Kit and Des. They were sure they could handle it without the others.

Verster, of course, would not hear of it. The last thing the South Africans needed was for Brian and Kit to be arrested in Zimbabwe.

Meanwhile, Brian and Kit had discovered the precise location of Verster's bush camp after conducting a recce in the general vicinity of the farmhouse. Despite the lengthy detours taken by Verster to get there, it was only a few hundred metres away from the farmhouse.

This deception, considering Verster was known to all the operators involved including Des, plus the poor quality of the external team and the elaborate system of flights used to get everybody there, worried Brian. There was an unnecessary sense of the dramatic — like someone had been reading too many books on Mossad and MI6. It probably looked good on the operations board, but it dented Brian's confidence. Instead of making complicated things straightforward and simple, they made straightforward and simple things complicated.

It was Mickey Mouse.

This atmosphere prompted Brian to suggest a complete duplication of all equipment being transported to Zimbabwe, so a back-up set would be available if things went wrong. He accepted responsibility for its delivery, but Verster rejected his offer out of hand.

The Otjiwarongo farm, being isolated and far from Johannesburg, spawned complex communication difficulties. Brian found it impossible to maintain links with his sources in Zimbabwe, nor could he liaise with Deon to keep in touch with happenings on the operational front.

Deon by then had been taking food to the prisoners daily for more than a month. He had become a familiar sight at the prison, as had been intended.

Time was slipping by and D-day was near, so Brian decided to get Des back to Zimbabwe. Borrowing a vehicle from Joe Verster, he drove to Windhoek and put Des on a scheduled flight to Johannesburg and on to Zimbabwe.

Brian arranged for Z$80 000 to be drawn from his business account in Zimbabwe. This was to buy a Mazda pick-up for the ambush team and to hire a sedan for Deon's last few visits to the prison. It was appreciated that Gary Kane would have to flee the country afterwards too. Obviously it would not be healthy to hang around, particularly after the unusual use of an Air Force of Zimbabwe helicopter. Gary would do the hiring and buying. If they traced the vehicles back to him later, it would not matter. Besides, it was intended to abandon both vehicles in the general area, but they would be swept first to ensure nothing incriminating was left in them. So it is doubtful they would play a major part in the police investigation.

Providing everything went well, there was no reason why the covers of Deon and Des should be blown. Nor was it believed Eileen Smith's involvement would be revealed. She would not even be there when it happened. Her task was to move the prisoners' families to Europe and then get out herself so that reprisals by the authorities would be avoided.

What Brian had overlooked, working by fairly remote control, was that Gary, Des, Deon and Eileen were young and foolishly indiscreet. The plotting, the planning and the danger had drawn them close together, probably because they needed each other's reassurance.

Over the months, whenever Deon and Des were in Harare for discussions with Eileen and Gary, their conferences invariably took place at the New Sarum air base officers' mess, where they drank and socialised together. This might well have resulted in tragic consequences for all of them.

To dig the CCB's cover as deep as possible, Colonel Verster arranged, at no little cost to the South African taxpayer, for Sammy Beahan, Big Jim Maguire and Aussie to fly to Europe after finishing their training at the farm. When the time came they would individually journey to Zimbabwe from Europe, carrying pristine but false passports identifying them as businessmen or hunters on safari. Sammy Beahan was transformed into Henry Coleman.

The final leg of Aussie's journey would be a flight to Bulawayo. Des would pick him up from the airport and take him to Gray's Inn where he would stay until needed. Sammy and 'Big Jim' would fly to Maun in Botswana via London, Johannesburg and Manzini. At Maun they would pick up a prearranged car and drive via the Kazungula border post to Bulawayo, where they would rendezvous with Des at a caravan park.

Des reported by phone that Aussie had duly arrived in Bulawayo and booked in at the Gray's Inn. He was deeply concerned about him, though, because he had been on the bottle ever since. He had also been gratifying his sexual needs in Bulawayo's red light district, where a whore had stolen his wallet and all his money. Fortunately, he still had his passport and Des was able to replenish his funds. Nevertheless, he could hardly go to the police and make a fuss about the theft.

Brian took the black operators to Halfway House, between Johannesburg and Pretoria, from where they were driven to Botswana, which they entered using false passports. From there they were driven to Botswana's far north and dropped off at the Zimbabwe border. After bypassing the formalities of Customs and Immigration they were met by an internal team who dropped them off in Bulawayo. In the afternoon they rendezvoused with Des at a bus stop in Hillside. It was his responsibility to accommodate them in a safe house and look after them.

Joe Verster asked Brian to make arrangements for a 4x4 type vehicle to be delivered to Maun Airport for Sammy and Big Jim. An ex-operator friend of Brian who was going to Maun on safari, volunteered to do it. Unbeknown to Brian or his friend, but known to Sammy and Big Jim who had been briefed, the CCB had snugly styro-foamed the team's radio equipment into the vehicle's doors.

Brian gave Sammy and Big Jim's ETA at Maun to his friend and asked him to leave the vehicle's keys at the Duck Inn, outside the airport. He was to tell the barman a 'Mr Smith' was collecting them and maintain observation until Sammy and Big Jim picked them up. Under no circumstances was he to make himself known. The two were easy to recognise — one was a really big man and the other a little short guy.

When they appeared from the airport building it was evident they had taken full advantage of the CCB's deep cover — both were visibly drunk, loud and boisterous. It must have seemed like a publicans' outing, with free booze all the way from Johannesburg to Europe, more from Europe to Johannesburg, top-ups between Johannesburg and Matsapa Airport and some refills en route to Maun.

They picked up the keys from the Duck Inn, had a few more drinks and bought some takeaway bottles to guard against dehydration. More than just merrily they set off for Kazungula, continuing their mobile party past the Moremi Wildlife Reserve and through Chobe National Park. Somewhere along the route they picked up two Irish nurses hitchhiking north and ended up with them at the Kazungula border post.

The border post officials judged the operators' sobriety, or lack of it, at a glance. They routinely questioned them about their destinations, but a customs officer decided to search their car for contraband and directed it be taken to the police station. It was later suggested they had attracted the suspicion of the Zimbabwe officials because 'they seemed of dubious character and were placed under arrest'. They might indeed have been dubious, and they were certainly drunk, but they were not arrested.

The conducting of vehicle searches at the Kazungula police station was routine. Unlike the customs post it possessed an inspection pit which simplified searches. Sammy and Big Jim probably had no reason to worry because it was unlikely a routine search would have turned up anything. They should have remained cool, calm and collected but this was inconsistent with their inebriated state.

Instead of brazening it out, their guilty consciences got the better of them. They made a run for it, jumped into the Zambezi River and swam to the Zambian Bank. When they thought it was safe, they swam back across the river to the Caprivi Strip. This was South African controlled territory and safe ground.

They should have walked westwards, looking for help until they reached the military base at Katima Mulilo. Instead, they moved from north to south across the eastern tip of the Caprivi, swam the Chobe River and re-entered Botswana.

They made their way back to Kasane ten kilometres away, phoned their CCB handler in Pretoria and reported they were on the run. Their handler, instead of telling them to hot-foot it back to the Caprivi, inexplicably suggested they use some of the ample funds they had been provided with to pay someone to fly them south to Gaborone.

At 02:00 on Tuesday 28 June 1988 Joe Verster phoned Brian. Beahan and Maguire, he said, had been compromised on the Zimbabwe side at Kazungula, but had escaped. They were in the Kasane area and intended making their way to Gaborone. Did he know anyone there who could help them?

If they got to Gaborone, Brian told him shortly, help was unnecessary as it was only 19km west of the South African border. He asked why, seeing they were in Kasane, they had not crossed the Zambezi River into SWA/Namibia. It was only a 200m swim.

'No, no, no . . .' Verster said firmly, 'it is not possible. Their handler has already told them what to do.'

He refused to enlighten him further. Brian gathered it was another of the elaborate, geographic and secret plans he had become used to of late.

'All right', Brian told him, 'contact me when they get to Gaborone and I'll see what I can do.'

At 09:00 Verster phoned again.

They had chartered a light aircraft at Kasane and had been dropped off in Gabs. What should they do now?

'Sit tight', Brian told him, 'no matter where they were. They must wait until dark, find the power lines and follow them for 19km until they reach the South African border near the Kopfontein Gate.' This route was safe because it cut through the bush. Whatever they did, Brian stressed, they should stay away from the main road where the BDF had a permanent roadblock.

The situation was verging on farce but it was compromising the whole operation. Despite this, Aussie, minus his wallet, was in place at Gray's Inn, the black operators were in a safe hide, Gary and his chopper were standing by and Des and Deon were raring to go. It was up to them — they were taking the risks.

Brian phoned Des and told him there was the possibility of a major compromise. Sammy and Big Jim were still on the run, but they might be captured at any moment. Anything or everything could go wrong at short notice. Meanwhile, as a precaution, they should stay clear of the Bulawayo rendezvous where they were scheduled to link up with Beahan and Maguire. Anyway, there was no way they could get to Bulawayo in time, even if they got out of Botswana.

Did they want to cancel or continue?

Des and Deon drove to Harare to see Gary Kane. They talked it over and decided to go ahead.

'We can do it', Des told Brian from Harare.

In fact they were happier now that doubtful heavies like Sammy and Big Jim were out of the way.

Could they leave Aussie out of it, too? They had had enough of his drinking. Des was sure he could handle the ambush with the two black Recce operators. There was only one lightly-armed guard to deal with.

Brian gave him the bad news. Aussie was the only white survivor of Joe Verster's external team and he had ordered that he take command of the ambush in place of Sammy Beahan. Verster would broach no argument — that is the way it was.

Eileen Smith and the families of the prisoners had flown to Europe a week earlier.

Another major problem reared its head. The windsurfers had been collected from Masvingo, but a check of their contents revealed everything was there except the radios. Communications were an essential element. Where were the radio sets?

Brian phoned Joe Verster's office.

'There are no radios. What the hell is going on?'

'The radios were hidden in Beahan and Maguire's car. We didn't think . . .'

'What about back-up equipment. You will recall I wanted to send in a second set of stuff?'

There were a host of excuses, but nothing could change the fact that there was no back-up equipment. They were lucky it was only radios they were short of.

Brian phoned Des and asked if Gary could 'borrow' a radio from the Zimbabwe Air Force.

He managed to get a TR-28 set, which worked when tested. They should have had fancier and more reliable radios complete with ear pieces, but the TR-28 met their minimum needs. It was essential that the ambush team had radio communications with the helicopter and it was desirable for Deon, but at a push he could get by using hand signals.

It was 36 hours to H-hour.

Early on Wednesday 29 June 1988 a member of Colonel Verster's staff phoned Brian. Instead of following orders and sticking to the power lines, Beahan and Maguire had marched straight along the main road leading to the Kopfontein Gate border post. Not surprisingly they had blundered into the BDF's permanent roadblock.

'Big Jim' Maguire managed to evade his pursuers, escape into the darkness and get back to South Africa. But Sammy Beahan was another story. He was in the custody of the Botswana Police and he knew too much — like the whole plan.

Once again the operation faced cancellation.

Fortunately the South African Security Police had paid informers in the ranks of the Botswana Police. They began monitoring the situation through their sources. By that evening Beahan had not broken under interrogation, although there was always the possibility that he might at any moment. Or maybe he would hold out until after the rescue deadline.

A bright spot was that the ZNP had not yet managed to put two plus two together. It was a mystery to them why Beahan and Maguire had run away. They had searched their vehicle thoroughly, but had not located the radios foamed into the doors. Neither had they commenced a liaison with the Botswana Police.

Still, it was very chancy.

The rest of the ground team had arrived in Harare.

Brian phoned them.

'Sammy has been lifted in Botswana. There is a possible compromise, although we have been assured there is not. Are you still prepared to go ahead?'

The operators remained determined to give it a go.

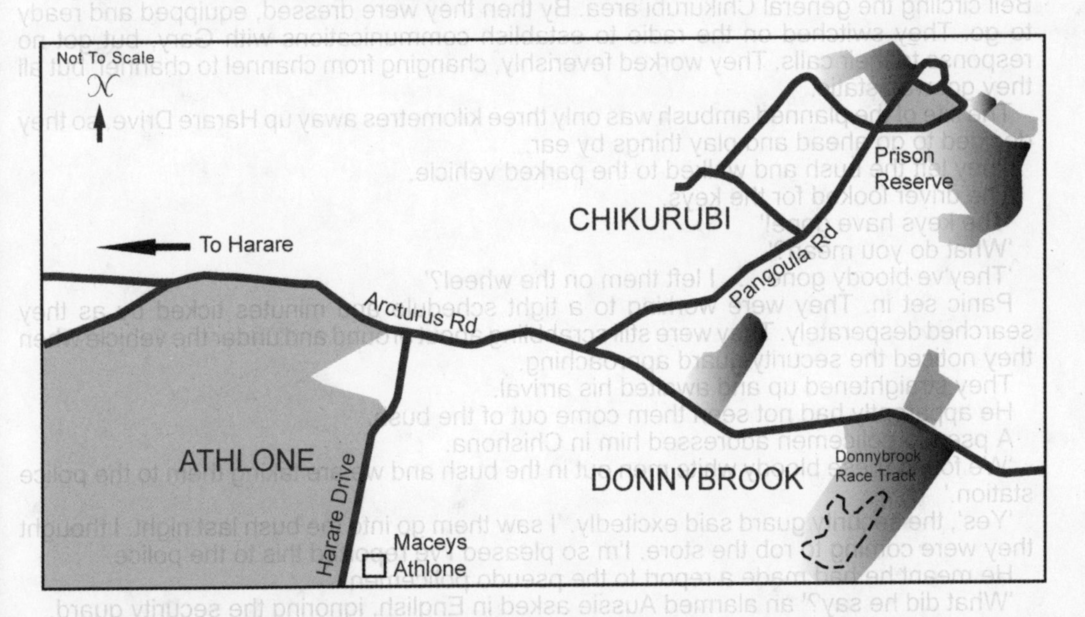

Map of the general area of the CCB's failed attempt to rescue the Chikurubi Five plus Odile Harrington from Chikurubi Maximum Security Prison

The ambush team consisting of Aussie, Des and the two black operators took over the radio set from Gary and stashed their weapons and other equipment in the back of the Mazda pick-up bought by Gary. Much of the weaponry was still concealed in the wind surfers and they placed them in the back with the cutting equipment, camping stuff and so on. The plan called for them to drive to the general area of Cleveland Dam, where they would sleep out in the bush for the night.

They parked the Mazda in the parking area of a disused supermarket, Maceys in Harare Drive, in the early evening. This was in the Athlone/Greengrove area just to the west of Cleveland Dam. It seemed deserted — dry leaves were scuffing about in the wind and no one was around.

Taking the weapons, the uniforms for the two black 'policemen', the radio and other kit, they penetrated about 200m into the thick bush and settled down for the night. Inexplicably, the driver left the ignition keys on top of the vehicle's rear wheel. It can only be assumed he was being extra careful, worried he might drop them in the bush.

Unbeknown to them a security guard was on duty at the supermarket and he observed the vehicle drive into the parking area and stop. He saw four persons alight and go into the bush, but could not identify them because it was too dark. He did not make his presence known, because he was alone and afraid they had come to rob the supermarket which his employer, Sam Levy, used for bulk storage.

Later that night, when no one returned, the security guard plucked up enough courage to go and inspect the Mazda. Quite by chance he glimpsed the ignition keys perched on the rear wheel. This was distinctly odd, so he took the keys to hand to his employer the next morning. While he could do little on his own to prevent a robbery, he could at least ensure they lacked transport with which to cart stolen goods away.

He could not report the suspicious goings on to the police, because the nearest police station was nine kilometres away at Rhodesville and he was not allowed to leave his post.

On Thursday 30 June 1988, shortly before 07:00, the ground team heard Gary's Augusta Bell circling the general Chikurubi area. By then they were dressed, equipped and ready to go. They switched on the radio to establish communications with Gary, but got no response to their calls. They worked feverishly, changing from channel to channel, but all they got was static.

The site of the planned ambush was only three kilometres away up Harare Drive, so they decided to go ahead and play things by ear.

They left the bush and walked to the parked vehicle.

The driver looked for the keys.

'The keys have gone!'

'What do you mean?'

'They've bloody gone . . . I left them on the wheel?'

Panic set in. They were working to a tight schedule and minutes ticked by as they searched desperately. They were still scrabbling about around and under the vehicle when they noticed the security guard approaching.

They straightened up and awaited his arrival.

He apparently had not seen them come out of the bush.

A pseudo policemen addressed him in Chishona.

'We found these bloody white men out in the bush and we are taking them to the police station.'

'Yes', the security guard said excitedly. 'I saw them go into the bush last night. I thought they were coming to rob the store. I'm so pleased I've reported this to the police.'

He meant he had made a report to the pseudo policemen.

'What did he say?' an alarmed Aussie asked in English, ignoring the security guard.

'He says he's happy he's reported this to the police', the pseudo policeman said.

Both Aussie and Des thought he meant the real police had been told they were there and were on their way to investigate.

They did not ask the guard if he had seen the ignition keys.

The radio had failed, so they could not contact the helicopter.

Now this!

They panicked.

Des, being a mechanic, could easily have hot-wired the Mazda and started it, but he, like Aussie, thought they had run out of time.

'We'll bombshell', said Aussie, deciding to abort the operation.

He ordered they split up and make their way individually to the crash rendezvous at Lake Chivero. They would be lifted out of the country from there. The black operators demurred, insisting on making their own way back to South Africa. They were Mashonas and it was clear they believed they stood a better chance of escaping without whites in their company. Without ceremony everyone tossed their weapons and equipment into the back of the Mazda. The black operators disappeared into the bush to change out of uniform, while Aussie and Des trudged off to make their way to Lake Chivero.

They left behind a very puzzled security guard.

For Deon, on the other hand, everything had gone according to plan.

He took the prisoners' food to Chikurubi Maximum Security Prison at 06:30, but after handing it in at the reception he hung around the car park, watching and waiting.

It was easy to identify the correct prison vehicle because it was scheduled to depart from the main prison for the women's prison to pick up Odile Harrington. This had been timed previously at half an hour.

Gary Kane's chopper appeared overhead and began circling the prison area in a very wide orbit. Deon indicated by hand-signals that the truck had departed for the women's prison.

Gary would have no difficulty in identifying the correct vehicle because Deon would fall in behind and follow it out.

Again everything worked according to plan and as the truck was driven towards the Arcturus road it was followed discreetly by an unseen procession. There was Deon immediately behind in the car hired by Gary and Gary cruising overhead in the Augusta Bell.

Deon had managed to get a message through to the prisoners that they could expect a rescue attempt. Everyone they wanted was in that prison van: Barry Bawden, Mike Smith, Philip Conjwayo, Kevin Woods, Guy Bawden, a South African who had been arrested for an unrelated offence and the additional bonus of Odile Harrington.

A prisoner poked a single finger through a rifle port in the side of the truck. It was unmistakable. It confirmed there was only one guard in the rear. They knew he would only be armed with a Greener shotgun and the driver, as usual, would be unarmed.

On reaching the roadblock the prisoners would leap on their guard and disarm him.

Gary had made several unsuccessful attempts to contact the ambush party by radio. He could only assume the set had become unserviceable, which considering its age was not surprising.

The prison van, with its ground and air tail, drove south from the prison on Pangoula Road, then turned right on to the Arcturus Road.

Gary, enjoying a bird's eye view from the helicopter, looked both east and west along the Arcturus Road. He could scarcely believe his eyes. It was empty of traffic, no roadblock had been erected and not a vehicle was in sight.

What had happened to the ambush party?

With a sinking helpless feeling he watched the prison van trundle past the roadblock site at the intersection of Arcturus Road and Harare Drive.

Deon and Gary continued tracking it, hoping that by some mischance the roadblock had been set up closer to Harare.

Gary saw the whiteness of fingers being prodded through the rifle ports as the prisoners appealed desperately for rescue.

They were so near, yet so far.

The heavy van entered the densely populated area of Greendale and headed on towards Highlands.

Deon stopped his car by an open area and Gary swooped down briefly and picked him up.

Gary again picked up the trail of the prison van and despondently tracked it the whole way to the magistrate's court in the centre of town. After that there was nothing more he could do. He pealed off over central Harare and returned to the Athlone/Greengrove area.

What had gone wrong?

He circled the bush around Cleveland Dam, seeking some sort of indication as to what had happened. Deon spotted the Mazda in the old Maceys' car park. There was no one around and it seemed abandoned. Gary landed down and they clearly identified the jumble of weapons and other kit in the back.

Why had they abandoned the stuff?

What had happened to them?

The shit must have hit the fan.

The plot was too far advanced to abort and await another opportunity. If the ambushers had been arrested — probably as a result of Beahan's arrest in Botswana — then the operation was blown. The CIO might be hours away from arresting them, or it might be only minutes. What if the Air Force Hunters appeared and tried to force them down?

Their only chance of escape was to fly low and fast for the ZISCO airfield at Redcliff. Hopefully, the aircraft from South Africa would be waiting for them. Gary set course for Redcliff. The chopper had been fully refuelled before take-off that morning, so he had plenty of range.

And there it was. A Dakota in the colours of one of the Wonderboom 'funny' air charter front companies of Military Intelligence and crewed by Special Forces personnel was sitting on the strip. It had an armed protection team aboard in case of trouble.

Gary and Deon climbed aboard and it took off. An irresponsible member of the protection team fired through the door and raked the Augusta Bell with AK bullets. A young black girl, Doubt Chinhamo (11), who was innocently rubber-necking at the strange goings on, was wounded by a stray bullet. They blamed Gary afterwards, but it had nothing to do with him. They flew to Katima Mulilo and transferred to a waiting Learjet which flew them to Lanseria near Johannesburg.

In Harare things proceeded at the leisurely pace of an ox and none of the urgency experienced by the failed rescuers manifested itself among their opposition. The Zimbabwean authorities first became aware there was a problem when the Maceys' supermarket security guard walked into Rhodesville police station at 11:00.

'I don't know what's going on', he reported, 'but there's a vehicle parked out there with big guns in it.'

The police exhibited moderate interest, but they were short of transport so they took no action. At 15:00, after a four-hour delay, a car was despatched to the scene.

Meanwhile, the prisoners had been formally remanded at the magistrate's court and returned to the Chikurubi Maximum Security Prison. They returned in the same prison truck accompanied by the same lightly-armed guard and driven by the same unarmed driver.

Later that afternoon the Air Force of Zimbabwe realised a helicopter was missing. The police had received a report earlier about a shot-up helicopter and a wounded child at Redcliff, but they had not got around to telling the air force.

The next day the Zimbabwean authorities claimed they had prior knowledge of the rescue attempt and hinted that with much derring-do their forces had thwarted it. The truth can be judged on its merits.

Brian heard that things had gone horribly wrong. The black operators of 5-Recce were the first to return. They jumped the border at Beitbridge and walked into an army base at Messina late on 30 June 1988. Gary and Deon were also out — but the rest were missing. That night Des phoned Brian from Harare. He had gone to the crash rendezvous at Lake Chivero, been picked up and was being looked after. Brian up-dated him on who had got out and asked him how he felt.

'Do you want to lie low, or do you want out?'

Brian had gathered from his Harare sources that the authorities had no idea what had happened. There was no way the Mazda or the hired car could be tied to Des because Gary had handled the transactions. There was no hue and cry for him and his cover seemed safe.

What Brian did not know was that Eileen, Des and Deon had regularly socialised with Gary at the New Sarum officers' mess. Within a week the CIO would discover this and be searching for them all. Fortunately, they were all clear of Zimbabwe by then.

Des was nervous and worried about Aussie, who was panic-stricken and had gone to pieces. Despite being the leader he had become irrational and was continually making rash suggestions. Brian believed it would be safe for them to fly out to South Africa using a scheduled flight. Sending in a light aircraft for an emergency pick-up seemed unnecessary.

Des agreed, but insisted he travel alone. The way Aussie was behaving he would get them both caught. He took the first flight out of Harare the next day.

Aussie had no wish to stay in the company of Des either and also wanted to travel alone. He planned to fly north to Malawi, as he believed a flight to South Africa posed too much danger. He refused to accept help and insisted on making his own way to the airport to catch his flight. The CCB debriefed him in Blantyre, where he was full of stories about how the internal team had let him down. He kept quiet about the loss of his wallet in the Bulawayo whorehouse, his perpetual drunkenness and that it was he who had called off the ambush.

Brian has seen neither Big Jim Maguire nor Aussie since.

Quite by chance Brian saw the two black operators a few months later and they confirmed the truthfulness of what Gary, Deon and Des had told him.

After a robust interrogation, the Botswana Police pushed Sammy Beahan across the border into the hands of the Zimbabweans on 2 July 1988, presumably at their request. After questioning by the CIO, he admitted being the leader of the failed rescue team and revealed that radios had been sealed with plastic foam into the doors of the vehicle abandoned at Kazungula. On 30 June 1989, he was sentenced to life imprisonment for contravening the Law and Order (Maintenance) Act. This was reduced to 20 years on appeal.

The unfortunate hitchhiking nurses Beahan and Maguire had picked up suffered a hard time in the hands of the Zimbabwean authorities, but they were eventually cleared of involvement and released.

The CCB, through the SADF, embarked on a disinformation campaign, designed to show the operation had been a freelance one conducted by 'renegade' Rhodesians without South African authority. They chose the mass-circulation *Sunday Times* as the vehicle for this campaign. The failed rescuers were dubbed, the 'Crazy Gang' and it was said that 'furious South African security sources' had claimed that 'Pretoria's intelligence network in Zimbabwe could be damaged because of the exploit' and 'it's about time these heroes realised the Rhodesian Bush War is long over and gone.'

In fact the 'heroes' — both the bombers and those attempting to rescue them — were South African agents on missions authorised at the highest level by the President of South Africa and the State Security Council. Their exploits had nothing to do with the Rhodesian Bush War, which was indeed long over and done with.[14]

According to a press report the failed rescue bid cost the CCB an astonishing R6 million.[15] This expensive price tag included the costs of accommodation, equipment, transport, bribes, food and payments to the '15 operatives' of the rescue team. If true — considering that nowhere near 15 operatives were involved, and that a key operator was working for expenses only — it seems likely that the free spending CCB diverted lavish sums to other purposes.[16]

Trial of Woods, Smith and Conjwayo: 'Dropped like a dead rat'

The trial of Kevin Woods, Michael Smith and Philip Conjwayo opened in the Harare High Court on 12 October 1988 before Judge-President Mr Justice Sandura. They entered pleas of not guilty to charges of murder and to the statutory alternatives of causing explosions or committing acts of terrorism.

The proceedings were marked by unprecedented security measures involving hundreds of troops and police and even an anti-aircraft gun. A motorised column of six armoured personnel carriers packed with heavily armed commandos escorted the three men from Chikurubi Maximum Security Prison and back daily. Sharpshooters were posted on the roof of the High Court and surrounding buildings, others armed with AK47s patrolled the corridors or sat within the courtroom itself. The authorities were taking no chances in case of another rescue attempt.[17]

Much of the evidence against the three depended on the 'free and voluntariness' of their confessions, but once the judge found they had not been subjected to undue influence, it was all over. On 19 November 1988 he convicted them of murder with constructive intent.

Kevin Woods, speaking on his own and Michael Smith's behalf before sentencing, he admitted their guilt saying: 'We have no quarrel with Zimbabwe', and adding that they were sorry that Amon Mwanza was not a member of the ANC's military wing. 'The six people in that house', he said, 'were no more refugees than anyone in this court today. Our only motivation was on behalf of the people of South Africa who suffer mayhem and death on a daily basis at the hands of these ANC murderers.'

Philip Conjwayo staunchly maintained his innocence to the end and accused the police of framing him.

Judge Sandura sentenced them all to death.[18]

Rory McGuire was tried in the magistrate's court for failing to report the presence of enemy agents. He admitted knowledge of *Operation Kodak*, the May 1986 Recce raid on the ANC's Angwa Street offices and their safe house in Eves Crescent, Ashdown Park, but said he had played an unknowing part.[19] He was found guilty and sentenced to seven years imprisonment.

His admissions led to the interrogation of Kevin Woods and Michael Smith regarding their involvement in that operation. Barry Bawden admitted playing a part, but Guy Bawden adamantly maintained his innocence.

The trial of Kevin Woods, Michael Smith and Barry Bawden began in the Harare High Court on 20 February 1989. They pleaded not guilty to three charges and three alternate charges under the Law and Order (Maintenance) Act. The State alleged they had acted in concert with South African commandos in an attack on the ANC's offices and their Ashdown Park facility on the night of 19 May 1986 by providing crucial back-up and logistics. It was also alleged they had helped South African saboteurs possess 'offensive weapons or material' between 1 May 1987 and 19 January 1988.

Finding them guilty of three charges under the Law and Order (Maintenance) Act on 7 June 1989, Mr Justice Ahmed Ebrahim said the evidence indicated the three accused had made common cause with South African commandos over a considerable period.

He lashed out at the country's CIO chiefs for 'inefficiency' because, although forewarned, they had made no effort to capture the South African raiders when they came to attack the Harare targets. He was referring to an ANC member who had given evidence anonymously that he had evacuated the Ashdown Park facility two hours before it was attacked because the CIO had phoned and warned him three times that the raid was imminent.

On 9 June 1989 Justice Ebrahim sentenced them to 25 years imprisonment for the attack on the ANC office, 30 years for attacking the ANC house with explosives and 15 years for unlawful possession of arms of war and explosives. With portions of their sentences running concurrently, each would serve 40 year terms. This was reduced on appeal in April 1993 to 25 years after the Chief Justice Anthony Gubbay ruled that the term imposed was 'a punishment unprecedented in the context of post-independence' and was 'manifestly excessive, justifiable only occasionally and in the rarest of cases.'[20]

On 18 October 1988 it was announced that Guy Bawden would stand trial for the car bomb attack in which Jeremy Brickhill and others were injured.[21]

After his arrest, CIO operatives kicked him in the kidneys and lower stomach for over an hour at the Highlands Police station in an attempt to force him to confirm a 'confession' before a magistrate. They also held a loaded Uzi sub-machine gun to his head and threatened to shoot him, but he still maintained his innocence.

They made several more attempts at Chikurubi Maximum Security Prison. 'I'd refuse and tell them to take me to court', he said. 'I wasn't going to cave in . . . What could they do to me? Kill me? So what. I really couldn't give a damn. After a while in there, nothing matters any more.'[22]

In August 1990 the prosecutor conceded he had insufficient evidence to charge him with concealing arms caches or with assisting in the Avondale bombing, and withdrew the cases against him.[23] However, he remained in Chikurubi Prison under a preventative detention order without being brought before the Detainees' Review Tribunal.

The kicking triggered the onset of a severe bladder condition. Prison doctors consistently refused to treat him, although he was bleeding and in pain. 'They said I should have hanged, that they would be happy when I died.' They also denied him medicines provided by his family.

Proper tests were only carried out after he threatened to take legal action, but even then he was only given antibiotics and pain killers. He was taken to hospital under armed escort after his condition drastically deteriorated.

'It was ridiculous', he said. 'I think people must have thought there was a military coup because of the armoured cars, the antiaircraft guns, the sirens and all the fuss. The government had to issue a statement explaining that it was taking "highly dangerous prisoners" to hospital for humanitarian treatment.' [24]

His bladder condition deteriorated into cancer. Zimbabwe's Home Affairs Minister ignored appeals for his urgent release, so his lawyers considered an appeal to the High Court. Then Zimbabwe's only practising urologist stepped in and personally pleaded with President Mugabe for his release. The specialist insisted his condition would prove terminal if he did not undergo surgery within a month. He was released unconditionally in February 1990, after 25 months in Chikurubi Maximum Security Prison.

After surgery in South Africa he told the *Sunday Times*: 'I have been through a living hell for the last three years. I cannot return to Zimbabwe because my life would not be worth a damn. I have lost my farm, my business, my home, my livelihood, my family — everything. I suffered torture at the hands of the Zimbabweans in prison, which has left me permanently weakened. And all of this was because of the actions of the SADF — a force of which I have never even been a member. I have been trying for several months now to talk to senior officers in the Defence Force to try and organise some kind of compensation which I was promised.

'So now I'm suing the Minister. Considering what I've been through, I don't think I'm being unreasonable.' [25] I have tried to speak to everyone from Foreign Minister Pik Botha to the State President, but I've been blocked all the way'.

He accused the SADF of failing to warn him that other members of the ring had been arrested, which deprived him of the opportunity to flee Zimbabwe.[26] He also revealed that operators had been guaranteed that if they were caught during an operation they would never have to serve more than two years in prison — the SADF would get them out. Furthermore they would be properly compensated for anything they lost in Zimbabwe as a result of such an arrest.[27]

He claimed more than R1 million from Defence Minister General Magnus Malan in compensation for time spent incarcerated in Chikurubi Maximum Security Prison as a result of covert operations, the loss of a farm, his home, his business and for pain and suffering. Affidavits prepared for the Supreme Court revealed his involvement in the attempted assassination of Brickhill and in a plot to kill ANC deputy leader, Oliver Tambo.[28]

Guy Bawden was interviewed by the State Attorney who threatened him with five years imprisonment if he went ahead with his suit and revealed details of covert cross-border operations.[29]

At the same time Special Forces warned operator Alan that if he did not keep Bawden quiet, they 'would laugh off' the others in Chikurubi and their families in South Africa. He was ordered to tell him 'not to rock the boat'. He apparently tried, but Bawden would have none of it. The South African government eventually settled out of court, without admitting liability, and paid him R250 000.[30]

On 6 September 1990 Kevin Woods, Michael Smith and Philip Conjwayo petitioned the High Court in Harare for relief from 'inhuman and degrading treatment' in contravention of Zimbabwe's constitution. They said that for 24 hours a day they were kept in separate windowless cells under lights and only allowed 30 minutes exercise on weekdays. From 16:00 to 07:00 they were kept naked, which was especially gruelling during winter. It took six months for anything to happen, but on 21 February 1991, after five judges had inspected their imprisonment conditions, Chief Justice Anthony Gubbay ordered they be allowed outdoors for an hour each morning and afternoon. They were also to be allowed an hour a day out of their cells on weekends and public holidays.[31]

On 9 May 1991 the five convicted agents, in a written statement, appealed to the ANC to help secure their release from prison in Zimbabwe in terms of the release of political prisoners under way in South Africa. They asked it to give the matter immediate attention 'as an act of good faith during the process of reconciliation'. They said the offences of which they had been convicted concerned operations against the ANC and were of a purely political nature.[32]

In October 1991, in an obscene display befitting a banana republic, Zimbabwe's Director of Prisons allowed cameras into 'Chikurubi Maximum Security Prison for the first time'. A BBC Channel 4 team was there to film Jeremy Brickhill interview the three death row prisoners and Barry Bawden about their connection with South Africa's destabilisation activities for a TV documentary titled *The Hidden Hand*. The spectacle was reminiscent of the Romans putting prisoners on public display in the Colosseum before doing them to death. A television documentary, certainly, is very public exposure. The condemned men were escorted in chains in and out the interview room.

The Director of Prisons was present.

When viewing this heavily edited film it became patently obvious that the prisoners were shocked and reluctant participants. What was particularly obnoxious was that the interviewer was in the process of suing the interviewees for damages.

The first prisoner in was Barry Bawden.

Brickhill: 'Was the attack against me organised by the South African government?'

Bawden: 'It's hard to say . . . I can't put my head on a block . . . Wouldn't . . . I can't answer that, it's unfair. I still can't believe it's you. I am not being stupid. I'm pleased to see that you have recovered . . . I must admit I have become a Christian. I've actually been praying for you. I am not saying that just to be nice. I've generally been praying for everybody.'

The next was Michael Smith.

Brickhill: You helped identify my residence. Then one of your colleagues tried to kill me. As far as I am concerned you're involved. As far as I'm concerned you're accountable.'

Smith: Well, then we see it differently.'

Brickhill: 'You're a Zimbabwean. How did you get involved in attacks being ordered by the South African military?'

Smith: Let's just say I was asked to help. I felt it was the thing to do.'

Brickhill: 'How do you expect to get out of here?'

Smith: 'I don't know. My hopes are that . . . through some political bargaining.'

Philip Conjwayo was next.

Brickhill: 'Mr Conjwayo, did you work for the South Africans?'

Conjwayo: 'I don't . . . I don't even know . . . I don't . . . I once even . . . even a little but I don't even know where their intelligence offices are. If I had seen you, or known you . . . straight, no ways, there is no point of denying that. If at all I had done that myself you were going to die. Straight I am not denying that. I am a trained person. I was in the police, as a whole . . . including Special Branch . . . for 26 years and 52 days.'

Kevin Woods provided the final interview.

Brickhill's first question was not shown.

Woods: 'I was sentenced to death because according to the court I was involved with the bomb attack on the ANC house.'

Brickhill: 'Were you working for the South Africans?'

Woods: 'I can't answer that now, Mr Brickhill. I can't answer that. If I've been dropped like a dead rat well then that's . . . that's my tough luck. I certainly believe that . . . I certainly hope that I will not be forgotten somewhere along the lines in the negotiations that are taking place.'

Brickhill: ' Where would you suggest I have to look if I want to find the answers to why I was attacked?'

Woods: 'In a crystal ball . . . and I say that without any facetiousness . . . because you are not going to get the answers from me. I don't know what the other guys told you. I can't give you the answers that you want. I am sentenced to death. My life is worth nothing any more. I don't even have to sit and listen to you any more. So Mr Director of Prisons, I thank you very much, sir. I have nothing else to say.'

Brickhill suggested afterwards they had all been abandoned by their South African handlers. It was difficult to disagree.

The four men afterwards sought a High Court interdict against the Zimbabwe government and Jeremy Brickhill to prevent the interviews being broadcast. An affidavit from Attorney-General Patrick Chinamasa denied that any prison regulations had been flouted by the conduct of the interviews. Jeremy Brickhill contended that the four prisoners had cooperated willingly[33] — which was obviously untrue.

It is unknown to the author whether *The Hidden Hand* was viewed in Zimbabwe, but it was certainly broadcast in Britain.

In July 1993 relatives of the five prisoners protested against the failure of the South African Department of Foreign Affairs to obtain pledges that the men would be released in return for the freeing of ANC saboteurs including the 'Magoo Bar bomber', Robert McBride.[34]

They had a point. When compared to the massive governmental effort undertaken to gained the freedom of Recce Captain Wynand du Toit, captured in Cabinda during *Operation Argon*, relatively little was done to negotiate the freedom of the five *Barnacle*/CCB operators. The Du Toit case, it might be recalled, involved a French-brokered swop of him alone for 133 FAPLA prisoners held by UNITA, plus Klaas de Jong — the Dutch-born ANC activist who had been holed up in the Dutch Embassy in Pretoria since 9 July 1985 and Pierre-Andre Albertini — a French communist and ANC activist who was serving a prison sentence in the Ciskei for refusing to testify against persons accused of terrorism offences. Du Toit's return was treated as a triumphal occasion, with Foreign Minister Pik Botha meeting him at Maputo and personally escorting him to Cape Town for a reception with President P W Botha.[35]

Was the difference, perhaps, that the *Barnacle* operators were not Afrikaners, not even South Africans, but ex-Rhodesians? Would the situation have been different if the Recce operators taking part in *Operation Kodak* had been captured and incarcerated in Chikurubi Prison with them? Whatever the rationale the National Party government gave away all its cards without demanding their freedom in return.

It took five years for the appeals of Woods, Smith and Conjwayo against the death sentence for the Bulawayo bombing to be heard. This was mainly because it took the Ministry of Justice three years to produce a typescript of the trial record. It was finally heard in October 1993, when the Judges of Appeal dismissed their applications because they had been 'enthusiastic participants' in the operation.[36]

They immediately lodged another appeal against the death sentence on the grounds that their five years wait on death row constituted 'cruel and inhuman suffering' in contravention of the constitution. This followed a ruling by Chief Justice Anthony Gubbay in an unrelated but successful appeal lodged on behalf of death-row prisoners by the Catholic Commission for Justice in Zimbabwe. It resulted in the death sentences of 20 condemned prisoners being commuted to life imprisonment because of their long wait in the shadow of the gallows.[37] The ruling infuriated President Mugabe's ZANU-PF regime which accused the judiciary of attempting to 'hijack' the government's executive powers. Justice Minister Munangagwa said the government was keeping the death penalty and intended amending the Declaration of Rights so that delays in carrying out death sentences were specifically excluded from the constitutional definition of 'inhuman treatment'.[38]

The third reading of the amendment, aimed at stripping those condemned of an automatic claim for clemency was hurriedly, almost indecently, enacted. It was passed on a voice vote only, although a constitutional amendment required at least 100 'aye' votes to line up during a formal division. When the error was realised, parliament failed to formally annul the first vote but put the amendment up again on 6 October 1993. This time it was passed by 101 votes and signed into law on 5 November 1993.

Despite this indecent rush by the government to snuff out the lives of Woods, Smith and Conjwayo on the gallows, Chief Justice Gubbay held that their appeal, as well as the appeals of another two condemned murderers, had been lodged before the constitutional amendment became law. The appeal would therefore be heard in terms of the previous law, which regarded delays in carrying out hangings as unwarranted punishment.

On 10 December 1993 he ordered 'the sentence of death be set aside and substituted by life imprisonment'.[39] It can be said they owed their lives not only to a judge who refused to be browbeaten by the government, but also to the appalling inefficiency of the Justice Ministry's typing pool.

The first ever meeting between President F W de Klerk and President Robert Mugabe occurred in Gaborone on 26 January 1994. It signalled the end of the hostile climate that had separated Harare and Pretoria since Zimbabwe's independence in 1980.[40] Following this, South Africa's Justice Minister, Kobie Coetzee, held wide-ranging talks in Harare with Zimbabwe's Justice Minister, Emerson Munangagwa, and Home Affairs Minister, Dumiso Dabengwa, to formalise the normalisation of relations.

Mr Munangagwa said afterwards he had discussed the fate of the five with Kobie Coetzee 'in general terms . . . They will be released at an appropriate time, not because of South African interference but because we want to release them.' He refused to be drawn on the timing of their release and inferred that a speedy resolution was unlikely.

Mr Coetzee refused to say if the men were South African agents, saying in reply to a reporter's question: 'Sorry, I can't answer that one.' [41] A source close to the ministry was adamant that Coetzee had stuck to his guns during negotiations and insisted the men had not been involved in authorised operations. If this were so, it probably contributed to the Zimbabweans keeping them in custody.

In May 1994 the new South African Foreign Minister, Alfred Nzo, delivered a letter to President Robert Mugabe from President Nelson Mandela requesting that Kevin Woods, Michael Smith, Philip Conjwayo, Barry Bawden and Sammy Beahan be freed.[42]

Relatives announced on 17 August 1994 that Woods, Smith and Bawden had renounced their Zimbabwean citizenship and 'adopted' South African citizenship in the hope it would facilitate their freedom. Philip Conjwayo is a South African by birth, while Sammy Beahan is British. The simple 'adoption' of South African citizenship without going through the necessary bureaucratic process is of interest, because this would hardly have been allowed if the men had not been South African agents.[43]

President Mugabe, addressing an international press conference at the end of a four-day state visit to South Africa on 19 August 1994, said crimes committed for political reasons during the Zimbabwean and South African conflicts would be more favourably reviewed. 'Both Zimbabwe and South Africa are now free. We feel that those who were party to the quarrels of the past should have their cases reviewed. I don't see why those specific cases should not also be reviewed.' [44]

On 19 March 1995 it was reported that President Mandela had again asked Zimbabwe to release the five. The matter had been the subject of ongoing diplomacy since his inauguration.

A senior SANDF spokesman, General Gert Opperman, described their plight as 'extremely sensitive'. While the SANDF had refused to confirm the agents were their men, some sources suggested it had been privately admitted to President Mugabe. There is however, nothing to confirm this.

Foreign Affairs Director-General Rusty Evans said publicity about the case could jeopardise their release. In real diplomatic double speak he said: 'There is a sense in South Africa that the Zimbabwe government is sensitive and prepared to be sympathetic and disposed to these people being released in the context of the indemnity programme here.' There was, however, an underlying suggestion that Zimbabwe would only let them go when South Africa drafted legislation allowing its nationals to be returned to serve sentences in South African prisons for offences committed in Zimbabwe.[45] South Africa drafted such legislation shortly afterwards. It would have been ironic if the five had ended up serving sentences in South Africa for operations authorised by the State Security Council and conducted under orders of the SADF. In the end it was purely hypothetical, because Mugabe made no move to allow their transfer anyway.

It is also ironic that in 1982, as a CIO officer Kevin Woods, it was said he was involved in Dumiso Dabengwa's arrest and lengthy incarceration in Chikurubi Maximum Security Prison. In fact, though, other than being involved in the discovery of a substantial ZIPRA arms cache at the wonderfully scenic Silalabuhwa Dam near Filabusi, he had nothing to do with Mugabe's round up of ZIPRA officials. It is possible a direct connection with Dabengwa was discovered at Silalabuhwa, because his home area of Gwatemba is to the east of Filabusi. If that is so, it was outside of Woods' knowledge and he had nothing to do with it. Whatever he might have become involved in later, at the time he was just a police officer doing his job.

With a reversal of roles, a rehabilitated Dumiso Dabengwa became Zimbabwe's Minister of Home Affairs and Kevin Woods was condemned to become a prisoner in the same Chikurubi Maximum Security Prison. The author was told that Dabengwa has never forgiven Woods for his own travails and those ZIPRA was subjected to. He has said privately that so far as he is concerned, Woods will *never* be released from prison and he can rot there.[46]

When touring prisons during 1996, Minister Emerson Munangagwa told the prisoners that they should stop writing to President Nelson Mandela and others to secure their release. 'Salvation will come from Zimbabwe, not from outside', he told them.[47]

A beacon of hope appeared, however, when Sammy Beahan was suddenly released without fanfare in October 1997, five years earlier than his due release date in 2002. Zimbabwe's state controlled *Sunday Mail* suggested that Barry Bawden would be released in two years time instead of well into the next century, because he qualified for increased remission in terms of an amnesty granted by President Mugabe in 1996.

In an open letter to Zimbabwean and South African newspapers on 8 December 1997 signed by the four remaining prisoners, they expressed their gratitude to 'His Excellency President Mugabe and his government for allowing Beahan's release. We have been jailed since 1988. We are the only former South African agents, from a political era now long past, who remain incarcerated, and we sincerely hope and pray that the same benevolence, understanding and statesmanship that saw Beahan's release, will soon be afforded to us remaining four. We would like to take this opportunity to reiterate, as per our numerous petitions for clemency to President Mugabe, our sincere apology to him, his government and the people of Zimbabwe for the destabilisation, insecurity and the death that we caused.'

President Mugabe dismissed this appeal too.

When President Mugabe met President Thabo Mbeki during 1999, sources said the former was amenable to granting clemency to the prisoners, but apparently Minister Munangagwa advised against it.[48]

In early 2000, President Mugabe decided to extend his 1996 Clemency Order to cover Barry Bawden, which reduced his 25-year sentence by a quarter. This, together with time off for good behaviour, qualified him for immediate release and this was done.

Justice, Legal and Parliamentary Affairs Minister Emmerson Munangagwa, (now speaker of the house and probably heir apparent to Robert Miugabe) said of the remaining three prisoners that they would have to serve their life sentences. He made no secret of his hatred for the three, whom he has accused in the past of conspiring with foreigners to tarnish the image of the Zimbabwean government. Woods is very ill and in desperate need of surgery for a heart bypass, but even this has been ignored.

And so the last three POWs of the South African conflict — for that is what they are — remain, at the time of writing, incarcerated without a hint of mercy in the hell that is Chikurubi Maximum Security Prison.[49]

18

'Free and fair' elections in Namibia Military Intelligence/CCB Involvement 1989

Recruitment for CCB's Region 8

Johan Niemöller served with 5-Recce from 1976 to April 1981. After discharge he had obligations for Citizen Force call-ups, but they were always deferred. Although he denied it, press reports suggested he was a 'founding member' of *Project Barnacle*.

After leaving Special Forces, he said he had helped his father on the farm. In 1984 he opened a factory in Upington, Northern Cape, producing a camouflaged back-pack — designed and patented by himself — and various items of camouflage uniform and webbing. He was unable to market his products in South Africa because the sale of military equipment was prohibited by law, but he found a ready market in 'ex-army' surplus stores in the UK. His attempts to exploit the vast US market were thwarted by anti-South African trade sanctions.

His representative in England, an ex-Rhodesian called Evan Evans, two Norwegians — Frank Larson and his son John Larson — and a Jonathan Weekly, made plans to kidnap and eliminate ANC leaders Oliver Tambo, Joe Slovo and others. In 1987 the British police arrested Evans and his co-conspirators for this and for plotting yet another coup in the Seychelles. Much unwelcome attention was focussed on Niemöller, who was widely fingered as a South African Intelligence operative. The bottom dropped out of his UK market because no one wanted to trade with him. He was forced to close his factory and was sequestrated.

Whether he was involved in the London conspiracy or not is open to speculation. He certainly protested his innocence, which one would have expected whether he was guilty or not — particularly as he was safe from arrest in South Africa. He later maintained that he had passed information about both plots to his uncle, Colonel Joe Verster, at Special Forces.

During 1988 Niemöller was employed as a transport manager in Upington, which was work not to his taste. Charles Neelse, a coloured driver working with him, had written several unacknowledged letters to State President P W Botha begging to be allowed to join the army. He was totally preoccupied with military life. Niemöller mentioned that if he really wanted to join the army, he could organise it through Colonel Verster. Niemöller also felt like a change and phoned Verster who travelled to Upington to meet him.

Whether Neelse met Verster is unknown. Niemöller certainly did and signed an employment contract with an unnamed organisation which he assumed was a section of Special Forces. Presumably he became an overt member. Significantly, he told Verster he had no wish to get involved in criminal activities and stated a preference for working in SWA/Namibia, which suited the CCB. His commencing salary was R3 200 per month and he was allowed R27 000 cash to buy a Ford Sierra station wagon. He was given the organisation name of Gerhard.

They no doubt discussed his Blue Plan at length. The London kidnap debacle and the resultant collapse of his business made his re-establishment difficult and expensive. In the northern Cape he had been widely known and respected as an entrepreneur and a man of substance. Bankruptcy, however, is frowned on, particularly in conservative Afrikaner circles. Setting him up in a corner café in Upington or Windhoek would hardly have achieved either his or the CCB's aims. Besides, Niemöller believed the SADF owed him a debt 'because they never paid me for what I've done for them concerning the Seychelles situation . . . I would certainly have expected it from them to put me back on my feet'. A budget of R800 000 was approved for his Blue Plan. The generous funding available to the CCB, and his relationship with Joe Verster, ensured haggling was kept to a minimum.

In December 1988 both Niemöller and Neelse left their jobs. While Niemöller had become a member of the highly secretive CCB, the closest Charles Neelse had got to soldiering was a job as a driver and general factotum at a salary of R1 500 per month. Niemöller said he was to do as he was told and ask no questions.

In March 1989 Neelse drove Niemöller firstly to Krugersdorp and then to Pretoria. Niemöller had arranged to meet his handler, Hannes Coetzee (organisation name), in Krugersdorp to collect his Blue Plan money. He had a telephone and a pager number to establish contact. They rendezvoused at a shopping centre and Coetzee passed him a bag containing R600 000 in cash. The remaining R200 000, he was told, had been diverted to another project. Niemöller signed an agreement to return the money or hand over the assets of his Blue Plan company if he resigned.

In Pretoria Niemöller bought R7 000 worth of photographic equipment, including video and still cameras. He told Neelse that he was replacing equipment lost through his insolvency, but did not mention he required it for his Red Plan. Afterwards Coetzee visited Upington monthly to pay him his salary in cash.

Mrs Niemöller had already established a company in Windhoek, Niemcor (Pty) Ltd, so he banked the cash in Krugersdorp for credit to that account. His wife was in nominal control of the company, because as an unrehabilitated insolvent he was prohibited from holding directorships or opening bank accounts.

Niemöller bought a house in Upington for R140 000, spent R160 000 on cattle and began a ranching operation on rented properties straddling the Northern Cape/Namibian border. He also commenced explorations seeking marble and granite deposits in the Opuwo area of Namibia's Kaokoland. Niemöller intended selling the cattle to finance his mining operations if the need arose. A major problem was that the deposits he had found were on state-owned land. SWA/Namibia was in a state of political flux and he had no idea whether he would be allowed to exploit the claims if a SWAPO government came to power. SWAPO was Marxist, so they might opt for mass expropriations.

His Red Plan was a long-term proposition. He was to establish himself in Namibian society, but his real work would only begin after independence. Effectively, he would be a 'sleeper' until he was established. If and when intelligence was required, he would be well placed to provide it. In the short pre-independence term he would restrict himself to gathering low-key intelligence, reporting on what people were talking about, on predictions of Namibia's future, the state of the nation, the likely results of the coming elections and so on. He was also to systematically photograph and video all public buildings and installations, radio stations, bridges and anything else of importance in case it proved useful later — perhaps in ten years time. This was a lesson learned after Zambia, Mozambique and Zimbabwe became independent, when it was discovered there was a shortage of basic material for operational planning.[1]

Namibian settlement and UNTAG

Since the fall of Angola to the communists in the mid 1970s, South Africa could envisage no end to its war against SWAPO. UN proposals for a negotiated settlement were unthinkable. It would have brought the Soviets and their surrogates nose to nose with the SADF on South Africa's western border. Then, instead of fighting in the interior of far off Angola, they would have been fighting on their own doorstep. So if there had to be a struggle with the Soviets in a war for South Africa, it was better that it took place in Angola with SWA/Namibia as a buffer. The US thought the same.

The situation began changing in the late 1980s when the seemingly invincible Soviet Empire started to crumble. Effectively it was going insolvent and could no longer keep up in the East-West arms race. It wanted out in Afghanistan, where its nose had been well and truly bloodied, and it wanted an honourable exit from Angola.

In Geneva in March 1988, a peace settlement that had eluded negotiators and baffled world statesmen for four decades suddenly came within grasp. Foreign Minister Pik Botha and US Assistant Secretary of State Dr Chester Crocker reached agreement on a new initiative to open the way for Namibian independence. After much hard bargaining a trilateral agreement between South Africa, Angola and Cuba was signed on 22 December 1988. It provided for the implementation of UN Security Council Resolution 435/1978 and settlement proposals regarding UN supervised free and fair elections leading to independence for Namibia and the staged withdrawal of all Cuban troops from Angola. The Namibian elections were scheduled for November 1989, with independence to follow in 1990. 1 April 1989 was to be the first day of peace — the day UNTAG took charge of the transition process.[2]

South Africa had stuck strictly to the letter of the agreements, and more. It had demobilised the powerful SWA Territorial Force, drastically reduced the strength of the SADF and confined what remained to its Namibian bases.

When the sun rose on that fateful 1 April, it would catch the shadows of only five SAAF Alouette helicopter gun-ships, emasculated of their deadly cannons, and dispersed along 400km of Namibia's border with Angola.

SWAPO's leader, Sam Nujoma, knew all about the cut-backs, for the knowledge was international property via the UN. Nujoma had transmitted his written agreement to a cease-fire to the UN Secretary General in late March. But while professing he was for peace, he was secretly planning to bolster his political position by force of arms. It appears he had fallen victim to South Africa's propaganda war and, like the SADF, had come to believe he stood little chance of winning power in a 'free and fair election'.

More than 1 600 of his PLAN fighters, who should have long before been removed under UN supervision to camps north of the 16th parallel, were massing along the Angolan/Namibian border. They were heavily armed with everything from anti-tank to sophisticated anti-aircraft weapons.

Indications suggest the plan, inspired by ZANU- PF's intimidatory successes in the run-up to Zimbabwe's independence election in 1980, was Robert Mugabe's idea. Zimbabwe provided PLAN with sufficient camouflage uniforms, much of it over-printed ex-Rhodesian camouflage, to give the 1 600 PLAN fighters three sets each. Included, too, were suits of Kenyan camouflage — which casts serious doubts about Kenya's impartiality when it is remembered they had supplied a battalion of infantry to UNTAG.[3]

On the night of 31 March-1 April 1989, PLAN surged south across the border in what they thought was an unstoppable wave. Once the wave broke into pools, they believed, they would be allowed by a weak and vacillating UNTAG to establish base camps within Namibia. Civilian supporters would flock to the camps and be uniformed and equipped with the extra kit brought in by the fighters and from arms dumps clandestinely established earlier within the country. The black electorate would then be subverted by a brutal intimidation campaign.

But they overlooked a wild card. It was a thin blue line of some 1 200 lightly armed but battle-hardened SWA Policemen of the northern border command. They were mostly former members of the counter-insurgency unit, Koevoet, whose hands had been tied by their heavy weapons being removed from their Casspir fighting vehicles in terms of the peace plan. But what those policemen — 95% of whom were Namibian blacks with a sprinkling of white group commanders — lacked in weaponry, they more than made up with sheer guts, awesome fighting skills and undying courage. For nine bitter days until the signing of the Mount Etjo Agreement, they fought the PLAN insurgents to a grim standstill, beating them hands down. Air support and military assistance by the UN was only provided in the latter stages of the conflict.[4]

The battered and bloodied survivors of the PLAN incursion withdrew in disorder or were repatriated back to Angola by UNTAG. SWAPO's dream of establishing PLAN base camps within Namibia dissipated in the smoke of battle when they were defeated in the Nine Day War. It would be the last lethal kick of a dying white South African horse.

Details of the armed incursion were soon obscured by the propaganda of SWAPO and their sympathisers, but British Prime Minister Margaret Thatcher was explicit when she answered questions in the House of Commons on 4 April 1989: 'The Secretary-General's report to the Security Council', she said, 'specifically confirmed there had been large-scale incursions from Angola to Namibia by armed SWAPO personnel. It is a most serious challenge to the authority of the UN and the internationally agreed arrangement for Namibia's independence and I certainly condemn it. There has been no provision in the UN plan for SWAPO to have bases in Namibia, indeed SWAPO committed themselves to the Geneva Accord under which they are required to stay north of the 16th parallel in Angola. It is this breach by SWAPO which has led to the most regrettable fighting and loss of life. I would emphasise that the South African units involved are acting with the authority of the United Nations . . .'[5]

The SADF had regarded SWAPO with barely concealed distrust before the 1 April incursion — afterwards they trusted it even less. A senior Foreign Affairs official told the author his department's assessment was that SWAPO would sweep the forthcoming polls and South Africa would be lucky to retain even trade representation status in Windhoek. The SADF and the SWA Police, on the other hand, optimistically expected SWAPO's main political opponents, the DTA, to win at least a simple majority. What was more, the relevant military and security departments were ordered to make every effort to ensure it did.

Following an effective propaganda campaign by SWAPO and its allies, all former members of Koevoet, by then engaged in routine police duties in the northern border area, were suspended from duty on August 1989 and confined to their bases on Pretoria's orders. Their weaponry, large reserves of ammunition and their fighting Casspirs were secured under UNTAG's seal. In early October 1989, bowing to UN pressure, South Africa went further and ordered the demobilisation of former members of Koevoet as 'unsuitable' for police duties. Considering their heroic actions only five months before, this was at the least astonishing, at the most disgraceful. The blacks in Koevoet had been recruited on short term contracts from the special constabulary, so they were easily discharged, but why besmirch them as unsuitable? The whites, all SAP or SWA Police regulars, could have demanded boards of enquiry to assess their suitability in terms of the Police Act.

Nobody, however, raised a murmur of protest. This was because all of them, black and white, had been told the demobilisation was a mere political move designed to keep the UN happy and ensure the peace process remained on course. They had been assured, on the authority of no less than State President P W Botha himself, that in the unlikely event of things going sour, the black members and their families would be trans-located to South Africa and the white members would be transferred to the SAP, keeping their same ranks. So although 'discharged' they remained under discipline within or near their bases.

South African Intelligence believed that *when* SWAPO lost the election, they would counter-punch with a cross-border attack from Angola with powerful armoured forces. SWAPO believed that, with the support of 2 000 PLAN fighters already repatriated to the country as 'returned refugees' who had been secretly reformed into units, and perhaps with the help of troops from sympathetic African states flown in to 'restore order', they would snatch control by *force majeure*. This possibility of help was not far-fetched either, because the author personally saw some (but certainly not all) captured SWAPO soldiers wearing uniforms identical to those worn by UNTAG's Kenyan component. Few UN members wanted to believe that PLAN had any effective armoured forces left in Angola, but after the hoo-ha of independence had subsided, SWAPO quietly repatriated an estimated R2,6 billions worth of Soviet supplied tanks, armoured personnel carriers and anti-aircraft pieces from Angola.[6]

SWAPO knew a major military intervention would be required to halt their attack, but they also knew UNTAG lacked the mandate, the strength and the will to intervene and prevent a takeover becoming a *fait accompli*. The once invincible SADF was no longer a threat. Only 1 500 troops remained and they would be withdrawn shortly after the polls.

Disruption of SWAPO: Operations Heyday and Victor

What SWAPO failed to realise was that the SADF had no intention of caving in. They knew that *when* the DTA and its allies formed the new government and SWAPO launched its invasion there was no one else to call on. In expectation of this scenario the battle-hardened Koevoet was poised to politely brush aside their UNTAG monitors and re-equip themselves within hours from their armouries and transport parks. With the remaining 1 500 SADF troops they would hold the line until massive reinforcements could be brought in from South Africa. If the 1 500 troops had been withdrawn by then, Koevoet would do it alone with the help of SWATF's remobilised 101 and 102 Battalions. Appeals for their recall would be broadcast over *Radio Owambo*. This system had proved its worth after the 1 April incursion, when the first units of 101 Battalion were re-mustered and operationally deployed within 48 hours.[7] Together with Koevoet they would constitute the army for the new DTA government.

During the election run-up the 'demobilised' men of 101 Battalion and Koevoet had a specific task. It was to assist the DTA in their campaign to beat SWAPO at the polls. They bolstered attendances at party rallies — the SADF laid on food and drink to woo voters away from SWAPO rallies — and spread DTA's word. Effectively they were civilians and Namibians, so they were only exercising their political rights, but their efforts were officially coordinated and they reported back daily to their officers and NCOs at their bases.

It would be naïve to believe that the black 'ex-members' did not seriously intimidate SWAPO supporters. It was the name of the game and SWAPO seriously intimidated DTA supporters in return. Brawling often flared between rival supporters, despite the parties having pledged themselves to a disciplined and clean campaign free of intimidation. On 6 November 1989, PLAN cadres, taking umbrage at political messages broadcast over Owamboland by a DTA 'sky shout' light aircraft, shot it down. Intimidation is an important factor in African political campaigning.[8]

On 20 April 1989 the Administrator-General appointed a Commission of Enquiry under the chairmanship of Acting Justice Bryan O'Linn to investigate allegations of intimidation by the police, the defence forces, political activists and even UNTAG. It was SWAPO's complaint that the SADF and the demobilised SWATF had conspired with the DTA and its allies to effect SWAPO's defeat at the forthcoming elections. On 26 July 1989, after due deliberation, the Commission announced that they had cleared the SADF and SWATF of such a conspiracy, as the evidence presented had amounted almost exclusively to 'hearsay and speculation.' The hearsay and speculation, however, had been correct.[9]

Like its earlier abortive financial support of the moderate Bishop Abel Muzorewa and his allies during Rhodesia's twilight days, South Africa did the same and more for the DTA. The party had been formed as South Africa's moderate hope, its foil to the communist SWAPO. What this support cost the South African taxpayer will never be known with certainty, but three estimates are available. Foreign Minister Pik Botha said afterwards South African support for about seven moderate political groupings (including the DTA) had cost about a R100 million.[10] The TRC put the SADF's budget for *Operation Heyday* and the police's budget for *Operation Victor* — both dealing purely with the destabilisation of SWAPO during the election run-up — at R125 million and R36,5 million respectively.[11] A senior South African official at Oshakati, however, ruefully remarked to the author immediately after the announcement that the DTA had only polled 9 000 votes in Owamboland against SWAPO's 196 169, that the real cost over the years was about a million rand per vote.[12]

The nerve centre for Comops'(Communication Operations) anti-SWAPO campaign was the Bastion building in central Windhoek. Theirs was a propaganda war, a war of words, much of it waged with leaflets widely distributed to disrupt SWAPO's election campaign. SWAPO embarked on a widespread campaign to recruit members, raising funds at the same time by selling membership cards. There was a considerable degree of intimidation involved in such transactions and most blacks bought the cards as insurance. To disrupt both activities Comops printed many thousands of forged cards, complete with a forged signature and date stamp, and distributed them free of charge.Amongst those they targeted with leaflets were Anton Lubowski and Gwen Lister.

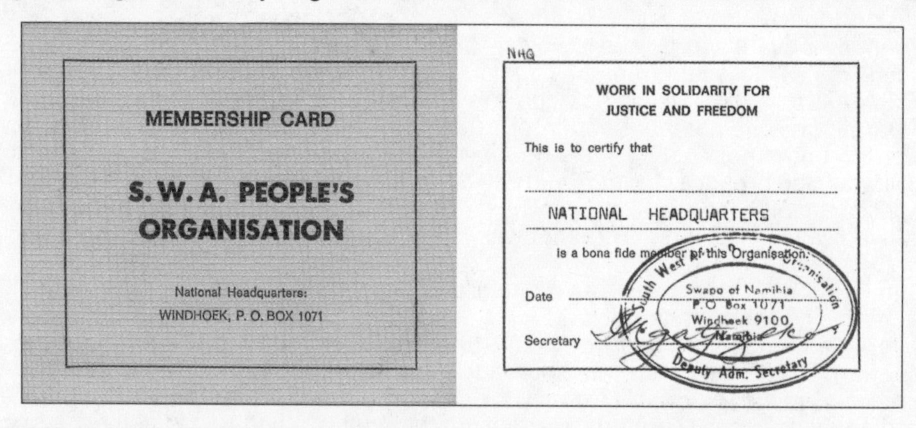

MEMBERSHIP CARD

S. W. A. PEOPLE'S ORGANISATION

National Headquarters:
WINDHOEK, P. O. BOX 1071

NHQ

WORK IN SOLIDARITY FOR JUSTICE AND FREEDOM

This is to certify that

NATIONAL HEADQUARTERS

is a bona fide member of this Organisation.

Date

Secretary

South West Africa People's Organisation
Swapo of Namibia
P.O. Box 1071
Windhoek 9100
Namibia
Deputy Adm. Secretary

Free SWAPO membership cards provided by courtesy of the SADF's Comops.

Advocate Anton Lubowski, whose father was Polish born, in 1984 became the first white to openly declare himself for SWAPO. 'He was ignored socially as though he was a contagious disease and he was publicly harangued as a "white kaffir" ', his mother recalled. There had been an unsuccessful attempt on his life and he had been detained six times. The last time he was kept in solitary confinement for 22 days in a corrugated iron hut deep in the desert, wearing only his underpants. He had represented SWAPO at various meetings with Western leaders, was awarded the Bruno Kreisky Prize for human rights achievements in 1988 and had assisted in the establishment of SWAPO's Windhoek HQ. Appointed deputy director of finance and administration in SWAPO's election directorate, he was expected to become a cabinet minister if SWAPO took power.[13]

Gwen Lister, through her *The Namibian* newspaper, was also a long-time SWAPO supporter. She had also been shunned as an alleged communist by her fellow whites while trying to raise money to launch her newspaper. Eventually funding was provided by the European Community.[14] While correctly critical of many government actions — which is the duty of any journalist, and for which Lister rightly received much acclaim — a study by the author showed that much of the copy published by *The Namibian* during the 1989 election run-up was sheer SWAPO propaganda.[15]

Comops (and undoubtedly they were not alone in the ranks of the SADF) regarded both as *kafferboeties* — white traitors who consorted with the black Marxist 'enemy'. Because of their political alignment with blacks, it followed to the Afrikaner mind-set that they must also be miscegenating with them. To a loyal *Boer* what could be more outrageous than that?

The result for Anton Lubowski, Gwen Lister and others was an ongoing campaign of crude leaflets of a scurrilous and intimidatory nature. The Anton Lubowski leaflet, illustrated with his photograph, called on whites to shoot it full of holes and mail it to him to show their disapproval. He received many such riddled leaflets in his mailbox. This was an incitement to murder, if anything was.

TAKE A SHOT AT COMMUNISM IN SOUTH WEST AFRICA

LET SWAPO'S ANTON "V.D." LUBOWSKI AND HIS COMMUNIST LACKIES KNOW HOW YOU FEEL. JUST FOLLOW THESE STEPS:

1. Write down this address on an envelope:

   Anton "V.D." Lubowski
   P.O. Box 3714
   WINDHOEK 9000
   South West Africa

2. Take this target to your nearest shooting range and ventilate it. Invite your friends along too.
3. Fold up the remains of the target, slip them into the envelope and post it to "V.D." Lubowski. We are sure he will enjoy receiving the target as much as you enjoyed shooting at it.
4. Incidentally – you can also ask him why he now has the additional initials "V.D." to his name.

This scurrilous leaflet, targeting white SWAPO official, Advocate Anton Lubowski, was widely distributed by the SADF's Comops. Lubowski was murdered by the CCB shortly afterwards.

One ploy that badly backfired was a Comops reprint of a SWAPO campaign leaflet, illustrated with a photograph of Sam Nujoma and calling on the electorate in English to vote for SWAPO. The Comops version retained the photograph, but replaced the caption with insulting epithets. Comops had unlimited funds so their print run far outstripped SWAPO's and they distributed it more widely. It appeared on billboards, was pasted to shop windows and nailed to trees throughout Windhoek and other towns. What Comops overlooked was that most Namibian blacks were either illiterate or only literate in Afrikaans. So what registered most strongly with them was Nujoma's face with an inference that they should vote for SWAPO.

Comops experienced widespread success when they publicised SWAPO's brutal treatment of its own cadres, suspected of spying against it in the war years. Confined in hell holes dug in the ground in Angolan and Zambian detention camps, they had been starved, beaten, tortured and murdered. 200 SWAPO 'orphans', aged between two and six — many probably the children of women prisoners raped by guards in SWAPO concentration camps — were discovered in an institution in the Gastrow area of East Germany. They had been placed there at the request of SWAPO's Solidarity Committee 'for educational purposes'. Hundreds of ex-prisoners remain unaccounted for to this day and are presumed dead. The publicity caused SWAPO much embarrassment and it still does. It cost them many votes in the election.[16]

To keep pace with what the opposition was up to, and without the knowledge of UNTAG which had prohibited it, the South African authorities tapped 300 telephones in Windhoek.[17]

There were some red faces in June 1989 when *The Namibian* published extracts from top secret minutes of a SWA/Namibian National Security Council meeting held at Bastion in late 1988. Chaired by the DTA's Dirk Mudge, it was attended by army top brass, the police and senior civil servants. It gave details of a proposed strategy to torpedo SWAPO in the coming elections. The Security Police confiscated the minutes from the newspaper's offices after rushing through a search warrant.[18]

There were more red faces when Sue Dobson, a press officer seconded to the office of the South African Administrator-General, defected to London. She had been secretly answerable to a seven-member interdepartmental government team in SWA/Namibia and had a budget of R3,5 million to manipulate publicity about South Africa. Dobson, a 'loyal' public servant who had been recommended for a position in the President's office, had been a covert member of the ANC (a 'sleeper' in intelligence terms) since the 1976 Soweto uprising.

Whoever it was who conducted her security check overlooked that her husband Peter was the brother-in-law of former ZAPU intelligence officer and ANC activist, Jeremy Brickhill.

Speaking of her duties in Windhoek she said: 'Our [the committee's] broad aims were to promote the image of South Africa, promote anti-SWAPO political parties and play on allegations of splits and power struggles within SWAPO itself.' They were to publicise allegations of torture by SWAPO, develop good relations with UNTAG and its chief, Martti Ahtisaari, smear UNTAG personnel and cast doubts on their impartiality. Needless to say, the Administrator-General denied it.[19]

Comops officer, Major Nico Basson, in a top secret project personally approved by SADF Chief General Jannie Geldenhuys, took full-time employment with the DTA as a cover. Opening a company called African Communications Projects (Pty) Ltd, he established an office in Windhoek's Kalahari Sands Hotel and set up an international press centre. Basson's task was to seek support from foreign missions and international journalists for the SADF's role in the run-up to independence. To assist,he sub-contracted foreign lobbyists to sell the SADF's 'positive image' to politicians and governments abroad. He was to promote the 'democratic process' in SWA/Namibia, inform and educate the local populace on the basic principles of democracy, and campaign against growing intimidation by SWAPO.

The project was launched with initial funding of R304 000, boosted by monthly payments of R64 000 until March 1990 — R1 072 000 in all. To help get their message across, twin engined aircraft were chartered to ferry DTA leader Dirk Mudge and his colleagues countrywide to address meetings. Dakotas were also chartered to cart journalists and photographers around after them.

Through African Communications Projects Nico Basson published *Call Them Spies*, a book co-authored by himself and Ben Motinga on the question of SWAPO's ex-detainees. For the SADF, Basson did all he was asked to do and more.

He claimed that after the CCB's cover was blown by the media, there were three attempts on his life. In Namibia he was badly beaten up twice and in Pretoria someone tried to run him down with a car. His story only came to light when he filed a claim against the SADF for R700 000 in back pay. Defence Minister Malan, in an unexpected turn, agreed to pay him an undisclosed sum actually (R133 000) as an out of court settlement. The SADF also threatened to prosecute him under the Protection of Information Act, but this never materialised.[20]

The CCB's part in disrupting SWAPO: April to Sept 1989

After SWAPO's defeat in the Nine Day War, the CCB, like Comops and others, was ordered to prioritise the disruption of its election campaign.

In May 1989 Colonel Joe Verster called in the respective CCB Regional Managers and ordered the deployment of personnel from Regions 6 and 2 and a third region into Region 8 — SWA/Namibia. The projects of the various regions were compartmentalised for security reasons.

The Coordinator (or Regional Manager) of Region 2 — Mozambique and Swaziland — was Petrus Jacobus Botes (organisation name Marius). He was formerly a paratrooper, a member of 32-Battalion and an operator with 5-Recce. Botes had originally been assigned to the Zimbabwe Region, with the administrative name of Bobby Greef, but after a difference of opinion with Verster, he was moved to Region 2 under Corrie Meerholz. Here he developed both Region 2 and Region 4 and eventually took over the former completely. He ran his front company offices from Verwoerdburg (now Centurion) near Pretoria.

Botes knew nothing about *Project Coast*. He knew poisons were available from 'Doc Wouter's [Basson] team' and that they could be obtained from a medical coordinator through liaison officers, Danie Phaal or Joof Booysen. He never knew precisely the origination of such substances, but he had been frequently told that 'Doc Wouter's team' had the ability to provide anything that might be needed. He met Dr Basson only once when he took a lion cub to his home and Basson's cousin, Klein (Little) Wouter, introduced him, saying: 'This is Doc Wouter and he works in XXX section of the organisation.'

Substances were available that would take effect within minutes or long-term toxins that would strike within hours, days or even up to three months, depending on the time required for an operator to exit the area of operation. Requests were made at final briefings and approved by the commanding general before being passed to the medical coordinator with instructions to supply. With an increase in seniority, Botes started to bypass Phaal and Booysen and began to collect orders for toxins personally from the medical coordinators. He knew three of them. There was De Wet who was not an MD and Gerrie Odendaal and Frans Brink who were.

Botes collected such stuff on three occasions. Once it was a clear liquid in a small brown eye-drop-type bottle that he was told was tasteless, odourless and that a single drop could kill a man. On two occasions it comprised ampules of clear liquid. Once De Wet drove him to Centurion and dropped him off about a five minute walk away from the headquarters of the South African Medical Service (SAMS). He returned 15 minutes later with an ampule.

Before the independence elections in 1989, Botes, like all other CCB coordinators, was told to suspend operations in his own region and concentrate on Namibia.

One of his tasks was to organise the assassination of Hidipo Hamutenya, the Secretary for Information and Publicity in SWAPO's Politburo and later Minister of Information in the SWAPO government. Botes deployed a team of operatives to Windhoek. They planned to murder Hamutenya at the Namibian Nights Nightclub. Three SWAPO members were recruited as covert operators to do the job, but nothing ever came of it.

He was told to arrange for bombs to be planted and grenades to be thrown at SWAPO meetings. Snakes were also to be released amongst audiences to create chaos. Fifty cars belonging to SWAPO were targeted for destruction. Another proposal was to firebomb the car of the UN Special Representative, Marthi Ahtisaari, although he was to come to no personal harm.

Botes flew to Windhoek to identify opportunities for anti-SWAPO operations. While there he received an order from Joe Verster to contaminate the water supply at the Dobra refugee camps in northern Namibia with cholera bacteria and yellow fever virus.

There was an entry in the official diary of Wouter J Basson, Region 6's coordinator, on 10 July 1989 which said: 'Spread sickness in camps — Frans/Heiner', and one on 14 July which read: 'Look at drinking places to use medicine — atmosphere — possible methods.'

Botes ordered one of his operators, Charlie, to collect a parcel from Joe Verster in Pretoria and convey it to him in Windhoek. Charlie collected what he described as a 'box wrapped in paper' from Verster, drove to Windhoek in a light delivery vehicle and handed it to Botes. According to Botes, inside were four brown glass jars. Two contained cholera bacteria and the other, yellow fever germs.

It appears that contaminating water supplies with yellow fever is a futile exercise, because it can only be spread by mosquito bite.

Botes was not convinced the cholera would work either because he had established that the water reservoirs at the camps were connected to municipal water supplies, so it followed that they were chlorinated. He said he gave the jars to another operator, José Daniels, and had him go with Charlie to infect the reservoirs. He said they returned in due course, reported to Botes that the task had been completed and returned the bottles to him. He destroyed the bottles. According to Charlie, though, he did not accompany Daniels on the mission. As Botes had expected the bacteria did not survive, presumably because of the chlorination.[21]

The CCB, Botes said, bought its own weapons from RENAMO contacts in Mozambique. At the Harms Commission he produced a shopping list in Verster's handwriting which instructed him to buy illegal arms to the value of R2 million. The organisation used fishing boats and bribed officials to smuggle weapons into South Africa.[22]

Johan Niemöller said he was tasked to photograph houses of SWAPO officials to establish an information bank, but this must have been target reconnaissance, because otherwise an address book would have sufficed. In most cases he selected structures on his own initiative for photographing, but occasionally he was ordered to photograph or video particular places. During various forays he videoed or photographed at least 200 structures. He was ordered to retain all the material until he was asked for it.

Charles Neelse said Anton Lubowski's house was one of those videoed and the results were handed in at the SADF's main base at Grootfontein the next day. Niemöller said this was possible, but he could not remember.

On 4 April 1989, three days after SWAPO's April Fools Day incursion, Neelse, driving the Ford Sierra with a caravan in tow, chauffeured Niemöller from Upington to Windhoek and registered at the Daan Viljoen resort outside town. On subsequent visits he stayed either there or at the Safari Motel caravan park. Niemöller told Neelse he was there to sell gravestones and to inspect mines producing marble and granite in Karabib. Before leaving for Karabib he hired two pagers from Telecall to maintain contact. His number was 33180, Neelse's 33165.

Niemöller paid R10 000 for a secondhand Ford Cortina for Neelse so he could attend political meetings and make reports. Niemöller instructed him to keep pace with current events, because if everything worked out, he would move to Namibia after the elections. Neelse also looked after the caravan when Niemöller was away. Shortly afterwards Niemöller gave the old caravan as a present and bought a new one for himself. Niemöller spent two weeks a month, six to seven months in all, in SWA/Namibia during 1989.

Niemöller said the CCB's Regional Manager for SWA/Namibia, organisation name Frik, met him once or twice a month in Windhoek.

Neelse first noticed Frik when he entered the Safari Motel bar when he was drinking with Niemöller. When Niemöller saw him, he abruptly finished his drink and left, closely followed by Frik.

Frik, Niemöller said, instructed him to video the road from Tsumeb to Windhoek including the towns, villages, factories, road signs, bridges, buildings, caravan parks, rivers, towers and any other feature. Niemöller insisted he had no idea of its purpose, but it was clearly a photographic reconnaissance. He thought it was 'ridiculous', but agreed it could be of strategic value to the CCB. Neelse drove the car while Niemöller filmed. He said he was after a marble concession in the area, so he had to check the road to see it could take the weight involved in transporting stone blocks.

Niemöller maintained he handed the videos to Frik — the only ones he ever passed to him. Frik, however, returned them saying they were not needed, so he copied over them.

Niemöller first met Advocate Anton Lubowski, then the deputy director of finance and administration in SWAPO's election directorate, in Johannesburg in early 1989. Lubowski addressed a seminar for the shareholders of a listed company. Niemöller had shares so he received an invitation to attend. He insisted he had bought the shares of his own volition, but it seems more likely the purchase was contrived by the CCB.

Niemöller introduced himself during the interval and they discussed whether it would be safe to invest in Namibia and continue doing business there if SWAPO assumed power. He made an appointment to see Lubowski at his home in Windhoek to continue their discussions. He kept the appointment, but Lubowski was not there. A second appointment also fell through. On both occasions, he said, Neelse chauffeured him there.

Neelse said that during discussions about Lubowski Niemöller said: 'This *bliksem* (bastard) wants to steal the assets from our mines and I am not going to allow that.'

Niemöller eventually saw Lubowski at SWAPO's Windhoek HQ. They spoke of mining rights near Opuwo that interested Niemöller. He queried rumours suggesting SWAPO was going embark on a programme of nationalisation if itcame to power, but Lubowski assured him SWAPO had no intention of nationalising land. Niemöller, for his part, said he told Lubowski frankly he was an ex-Recce with SADF connections, but it seems unlikely that he imparted this information. To provide a particular answer, Lubowski introduced him to Toivo ya Toivo — Secretary General of SWAPO's Politburo.

Niemöller submitted a report saying he had been impressed by Lubowski and had concluded SWAPO would probably win the forthcoming poll. This, he maintained, was the only report he submitted on Lubowski — which also seems unlikely. Lubowski was a CCB target and it was Niemöller's duty to report on him.

Frik expressed interest in meeting Neelse, so Niemöller took the latter to the Safari Motel bar. When Frik arrived, Niemöller finished his drink and left.

According to Neelse, Niemöller told him they were meeting Nick Verbeeck — Staal Burger — whom Neelse recognised from the last occasion. Suddenly Frik became Nick, although Niemöller insisted press photographs of Staal Burger bore no resemblance to Frik.

When asked at the Lubowski inquest if Frik and Nick were one and the same person, Niemöller variously said: 'I don't know . . . It can be, but I don't know . . . I assumed that [Nick/Staal] was Frik . . . I doubt it whether Frik would have approached, or whoever, would have approached Neelse while I was sitting there, it would have compromised him I suppose'.

When questioned about his lack of curiosity regarding the Neelse/Nick (Staal) meeting he said '. . . the working method of the organisation was such that you do not ask many questions'.

When Niemöller left the bar Staal (Nick) introduced himself and offered Neelse a job. Neelse accepted and was given a post office box number in Krugersdorp and contact phone numbers in Pretoria and Krugersdorp.

Niemöller, however, claimed he had discharged Neelse because he negligently allowed the Ford Cortina to be stolen. It is more likely Neelse sold it. While Niemöller was understandably disgruntled about the loss of his car, their parting probably resulted from orders to pass him on to another handler.

Neelse, no doubt on Staal Burger's instructions, took employment as a temporary driver in Johannesburg. In June 1989 Burger phoned and left a message that he was wanted for a job and arranged to meet at the Johannesburg railway station. He booked him into the

Karos Hotel, Hillbrow, for the night, gave him R1 200 for expenses and told him to return to Windhoek the next morning. Burger made a telephonic reservation for him to stay at the Hansa Hotel there.

In Windhoek they met for a drink at the Safari Motel bar. Burger opened his briefcase and Neelse noticed that it contained the *Who's Who In Namibia* and bundles of R50 notes.

Burger gave out that he was employed by International Holdings, a company which believed it vital, because of substantial financial investments in the country, that SWAPO did not win at the polls. He raised the subject of Anton Lubowski and Danny Tjongarero and said he wanted their testicles on the table.

He offered Neelse a salary of R1 500, the same as that paid by Niemöller. He was always paid in cash and on at least three occasions, collected it from a tree near the Truckport. Burger said he would provide cash for him to buy a combi for use as a taxi, which would be his cover. He would also be paid funds to translocate his wife and family from Upington to Windhoek.

They met again at the Kalahari Sands Hotel the next evening and drove to Brakwater for a braai. Neelse thought Burger had been there earlier, because the fire was already burning. He was given R11 500 to buy the taxi, R1 500 as salary, R500 for a deposit on a house, R2 800 to transport his furniture to Windhoek and R500 for petrol. Probably it was a convivial evening with drink flowing freely, because Burger loosened up. He abandoned his 'International Holdings' story and admitted he was working for the army, like his father before him who had been a colonel. It was the last time they would meet because Johan (Ferdi Barnard) was taking over as his handler. Barnard, he said, was also a soldier — a sergeant or lance sergeant.

Neelse bought a Toyota Hi-Ace for R11 500 for use as a taxi. He rented a house in Rehoboth — about 85km south of Windhoek — and moved his family from Upington on 8 July 1989. He began operating a taxi service between Windhoek and Upington.

Contradictorily, Barnard said he became involved in Namibia at the instigation of a Kobus le Roux who approached him in June 1989 and introduced himself as a CCB operator. Le Roux, he said, was his real name. At various times he used the aliases 'Dewald' and 'Willie'. Le Roux said he was responsible for SWA/Namibia and was based there. He asked if Barnard was prepared to serve or function in that territory.

Ferdi Barnard was still trying to re-establish himself following his release from prison and he was in the process of buying a house. He told Le Roux he could not see his way clear to moving there permanently, but he was prepared to assist on a part time basis. After a few more meetings it was arranged that Barnard would fly to Windhoek. He was given about R8 000 and told to book in at the Continental Hotel. He reported his arrival by phone to Le Roux in Pretoria and gave him his room number.

The next day Le Roux came to his room and told Barnard that the SWAPO-supporting advocate Anton Lubowski was a priority target. Namibia was his region and he had been authorised to deal with him. Barnard gained the impression that Le Roux had already done extensive work on the Lubowski project.

Le Roux said the plan was to kill Lubowski in Namibia and asked if Barnard was willing to do the job. He revealed that Charles Neelse (Barnard called him Nielsen), a coloured long distance taxi driver had already been recruited as a covert member of the CCB.

He told Barnard to contact Neelse and check to ensure the address he had provided was indeed his true residential address. Le Roux arranged the meeting. Barnard said they met Neelse outside a hotel somewhere in Windhoek where Le Roux handed him an unspecified amount of money.[23]

Neelse said that after meeting they drove to the Truckport outside town, where Barnard gave him R1 375 to hire a pager from Edumeds in Windhoek. Neelse was a friend of the manager, Morkel Vermeulen, which prompted Barnard to suggest they use Edumeds as a 'letter box' when he wanted Neelse to call him. Pager records indicate that Neelse frequently phoned the paging service from Edumeds and left messages for 'Johan'.[24]

After Le Roux had left Barnard went off with Neelse so he could point out a few places to him. Barnard deliberately set out to manipulate him, taking him to a few clubs and several bars. They ended up at 02:00 the next morning at Rehoboth. After a few whiskies, Barnard was satisfied that it really was Neelse's house. Everyone there knew him and he had a key to the front door. They made arrangements to meet the next day.

Barnard reported to Le Roux that he had confirmed Neelse's address. Le Roux, he said, handed him a video camera and showed him how it worked. It was sophisticated and even had night vision capability. He told Barnard to see Neelse, hand over the camera and task him to video Lubowski's house in the Windhoek suburb of Sanderburg from every possible angle. He said he saw Neelse, handed him the camera and instructed him accordingly.

Neelse was already familiar with Lubowski. He handed Barnard a note on which he had written 'Mr L [Lubowski] is a late mover and he moves alone', and asked him to pass it to Le Roux — although he did not know him by that name. Several days later Neelse returned the video camera. Barnard and Le Roux viewed the tape together. There were images of Lubowski's residence taken from various angles, all of them shot by day. Some were obviously taken from a moving vehicle. Le Roux, Barnard said, was well satisfied with the results and told him to withdraw and return to South Africa. He (Le Roux) would continue with the project, himself. Barnard was paid R1 200 for his work, above his expenses. He said he had nothing more to do with the Lubowski project.[25]

Neelse's account varied considerably from Ferdi Barnard's. He said the next time they met was in Kaiser Street (now Independence Avenue). Barnard was driving a blue Ford Cortina and accompanied by a man disguised by a stocking drawn over his head. Barnard, taking directions from Stocking Head, drove to the Katutura African Township. Stocking Head pointed out a house as Danny Tjongarero's. Their next stop was Sanderburg Street, Klein Windhoek, where he pointed out number 7 as Anton Lubowski's residence.

Neelse told Barnard he had to know everything about Tjongarero and Lubowski. Where were their offices? What time did they leave for work? When did they return home? Who visited them? Whom did they visit? Everything they could find out.

Neelse hired a video camera from Edumeds on Barnard's instructions. They cruised up and down Sanderburg Street in Neelse's taxi, videoing Lubowski's house and the general surrounds. Barnard said afterwards: 'Now I have everything on Lubowski, now we will show him.' A few days later they kept observation for an hour and a half, noting the registration numbers of vehicles calling at the house.

Neelse drove past Tjongarero's place a few days later, but it was too public to establish an observation position. Instead he paid a personal visit to check out the geography of the house, boldly introducing himself to Tjongarero as a 'comrade' from Upington. He was invited into the sitting room and they had a friendly conversation.

He received an urgent message from Barnard, instructing him to fly to South Africa. He met Barnard in Pretoria and was told to forget about Tjongarero and Lubowski. He was given a list of 13 SWAPO vehicles and the names and addresses of those using them and told to sabotage them. It was suggested that he remove the sump plugs so the oil would drain out and the engines seize, adulterate the fuel systems with sugar, or insert lighter-type (explosive?) devices in their exhausts.[26]

When Neelse returned to Windhoek he presumably decided it was too hazardous a task and destroyed the list. He avoided further contact with Ferdi Barnard. He said he heard Barnard had been looking for him in Rehoboth and at the Windhoek Hospital and said he sent a message to him which was unanswered. This, however, seems improbable.

Significantly, after a tip off, police searched a caravan at the Safari Hotel on 14 September 1989, finding 16 cans of oil and a note written in English which said:

> 'I am sorry I can't be here myself, I have unfortunately other commitments in Owambo. Please take the oil to the taxi rank and give each SWAPO vehicle a can of oil which are going to the airport. Make certain that it is SWAPO vehicle. Obtain the full particulars of the drivers of the vehicles so that I can later follow it up and if you fulfil this task to the

satisfaction I will strongly consider to make use of you again. Your compensation is under the mattress.'

R500 in R50 notes was under the mattress.

The oil was contaminated with acid and copper chloride, which would have seriously damaged a car engine. The originator was not traced.[27]

There is an element of mystery surrounding the fate of the Ford Cortina Niemöller bought for Neelse, but there is none concerning the caravan (obviously not the one mentioned above) he was given and the Toyota Hi-Ace bought as a taxi with CCB funds. Neelse sold them both. He probably did the same with the Ford Cortina.[28]

Donald Acheson: Covert CCB member: recruited June/July 1989

Donald Acheson (51), an Irishman from Belfast's Catholic Castlereagh Road area, held an Irish Republic passport issued in Dublin in 1983. For a Northern Irish Protestant, this was an unusual background, to say the least. After Zimbabwean independence he moved to South Africa, where it was said, he served with 5-Recce.[29] He contended that he had trained as a cartoonist in Canada and had worked for *Playboy*, *Mad Magazine*, *The Sun* and the *Daily Mirror*. Divorced, he had a daughter and two grandchildren in England and other family in the Irish Republic.

In Johannesburg he had held several part-time jobs selling advertising. He had once owned and operated the short-lived Johannesburg-based monthly magazine *What's On*, which went to print in December 1987 and closed its doors two months later. He had also worked part-time for an international trading company, in Johannesburg's Carlton Centre. He told friends he was involved in sensitive business deals 'north of the Limpopo'. He lived with his girlfriend, Cynthia Leo, in her modest one-bedroom flat in Bedfordview. Leo professed she was well off, having got a 'very good settlement' when her Italian husband divorced her seven years before. This, she said, enabled her to support Acheson and financially back some of his abortive business ventures. Despite her alleged wealth Acheson usually drove an old Volksie Beetle belonging to Leo's mother.[30] Generally, he cut a pathetic figure, elderly in appearance and seemingly down and out.

In May 1989 he was arrested for shoplifting and taken to Cleveland Police Station. Detective Sergeant Willie Knox alleged the security personnel at the store were reluctant to press charges against Acheson as he appeared to be mental. Knox remembered him as 'Irish', but he probably identified himself as Donald Dolan. Acheson said they discussed his service life in Rhodesia for about three hours. He said he had served for two and a half years with the police, two years with Grey Scouts and for an unspecified time with an unnamed army anti-terrorist unit. Knox questioned him about his political views and finally told him to forget the shoplifting charge.

The next day he returned and resumed his discussion with Knox, who told him there were people in high places, intelligence people, who were not happy with the political situation which they regarded as a sell-out. He asked if Acheson would be willing to help South Africa. He expressed interest, but said that any work he did had to be for the military, not some cowboy organisation. He was not prepared to work for the *Afrikaner Weerstandsbeweging* (AWB) or anything like that. Knox assured him there was no question of that, the work would be for people in the top hierarchy. Could he travel to Zimbabwe, Mozambique, Zambia and other African countries without a problem? He could, with the exception of Zimbabwe, but he preferred Europe as a destination.

Knox said someone was needed to monitor SWAPO and the run-up to the forthcoming Namibian elections. He would be untouchable, even by the police. Someone, he added, was coming to see him.

Knox had already contacted Ferdi Barnard who he knew was involved in some sort of intelligence unit. They were friends and had worked together on private investigations.[31] Barnard did not introduce himself, saying his name was unimportant, but flashed what seemed to be a Military Intelligence ID. He later used his organisation name of Harry van

Staden. Barnard, Acheson said, again asked if he wanted to work for Military Intelligence. Barnard, conversely, said he told Acheson he represented a consortium of businessmen who might offer him a job involving extensive travel. Whatever the case Barnard noted Acheson's phone number, gave him his pager number for contact purposes and a R500 sweetener.

Barnard reported his meeting to Lafras Luitingh (louis Yssel) and was told to submit a written background report. He asked Acheson for his CV, but because he was a prohibited immigrant, he was reluctant to reveal his real name. Barnard told him to use any name he liked. Two days later Acheson produced a CV in which he called himself 'The Cleaner'. It elaborated on his Rhodesian military service, claimed he had served as a mercenary, been involved in 'bounty hunting' in SWA/Namibia and had 'loan sharked' in the USA. He would, he wrote, do anything, even act as a 'hit man' if the money was right.

Acheson began making a nuisance of himself, phoning Barnard's pager number sometimes five times a day to find out what was happening. Barnard urged him to be patient, explaining that his appointment did not vest in him, but someone else. Eventually Barnard ignored his calls and suddenly they ceased, which prompted Ferdi to ask Lefras what had happened. He said that Acheson was unsuitable and Barnard should not contact him again. Barnard knew Lefras had Acheson's phone number, so he assumed he had phoned him and turned him down.

Despite this negative reaction Barnard passed Acheson's CV to Calla Botha, who was still 'on ice' following his clash with Staal Burger. It was a friendly gesture, as the recruitment of a useful covert member by Botha might help him to re-establish himself. Burger, however, told him that Joe Verster had already involved Acheson elsewhere.

In early July 1989 Chappie Maree phoned Acheson, introduced himself as Derek and said he was his Security Police controller. He asked if he was really serious about working for 'them'. If he did want to, he should insert a particular advertisement in the personal column of the next *Saturday Star*. Acheson could not accurately recall the copy required, but he thought it included something like the 're-adoption of the POL' — whatever that might have meant.

Chappie Maree phoned the Monday following and told Acheson to look in a pot plant at the entrance to his block of flats. He went downstairs and discovered a sealed envelope that contained R5 000 in R50 notes. While he was in the process of opening it, he noticed two men driving away in a BMW. Maree phoned almost immediately afterwards to confirm that he had got the money. This marked the beginning of Acheson's career as a covert member.

Enter the Outjo 3: the AWB/CCB connection: August 1989

Leonard Veenendal (23), a swimming pool attendant and a staunch member of the AWB — whom its leader Eugene Terreblanche had once referred to as 'my little fanatic' [32] — said he became involved in intelligence activities during 1989. A 'Mr Brown' had recruited him for various assignments. Some involved the collection of information, some related to the supply of weapons to RENAMO and one concerned intelligence required for the planned assassination of an undisclosed person. The file was supposedly destroyed. Sometimes Mr Brown contacted him direct, sometimes through a go-between. Payments for services were always made in cash. Veenendal made no mention of the subjects of his intelligence gathering activities, but said he had never spied on right-wingers. If Veenendal was telling the truth, it had all the hallmarks of his being a covert member of the CCB.

A plan to attack the UNTAG offices and barracks in Outjo was finalised in Johannesburg and the required weapons were smuggled across the border into Namibia. The originator of the plan, according to documentary evidence held by the TRC, was the CCB's Coordinator or Regional Manager for Region 2 (Mozambique and Swaziland), Petrus Botes. It was a continuation of CCB's plan to destabilise the Namibian situation before the elections, in the hope that UNTAG might withdraw its troops if it encountered armed opposition. Those involved were an 'action group'.

Horst Klenz had been involved in German right-wing politics from an early age, when his family had been interned in concentration camps, presumably by the communists. A promising career in West German Intelligence was terminated because of his political activities, so he emigrated to SWA/Namibia in 1985 and became involved in opposition to the UN settlement. A Johan Coetzee introduced him to Leonard Veenendal and Darol Stopforth (22) during a visit to Johannesburg.[33]

In August 1989 Veenendal, Klenz, Stopforth and two others travelled to SWA/Namibia for the UNTAG operation. Klenz acted as liaison officer between the action group and Namibian right-wing activists. It is possible the attack resulted from an AWB plan or that of another right-wing organisation. The fact that its objectives were closely aligned to the CCB's plans to destabilise Namibia might have been purely coincidental. What appears beyond coincidence, though, was that the long road used to reach their target area — except for the short haul between Otjiwarongo and Outjo — had only recently been the subject of a very thorough video reconnaissance by Johan Niemöller and Charles Neelse on CCB orders. Besides that, white Afrikaner extremists made ideal coverts when dirty work was afoot.

At 21:20 on 12 August 1989 they attacked UNTAG's regional HQ in Outjo, using rifles and hand grenades. They killed a COIN Security guard, Michael Hoseb (22). Witnesses suggested the attack was mounted by two whites and a black. Simultaneously, a second attack was launched against Outjo's drill hall where weapons handed in by disbanded units of the SWATF were stored. Kenyan troops in barracks next door were taken by surprise and failed to retaliate. Only minor damage was achieved.

Horst Klenz, who took part in the second attack, said: 'We could have destroyed the whole [Kenyan] unit, if that had been the aim.' It was probably no idle boast as the Kenyans were ill-disciplined and presented an easy target. The attackers used a stolen white Opel Ascona car with false UN registration plates. They crashed through a police roadblock and disappeared.[34]

The attack failed dismally in its prime purpose of intimidating UNTAG into leaving Namibia. It was condemned by both the Administrator-General of Namibia, Louis Pienaar, and UN Special Representative, Martti Ahtisaari. He called it a 'callous and cold blooded murder' and vowed UNTAG would not be diverted from its task. Identikits of the assailants appeared on SWATV and in the press.

Neelse, meanwhile, probably on a high from selling the Toyota Hi-Ace and the caravan, had entered the used car business. He had imported four items of stock from South Africa, which necessitated engine and chassis numbers being cleared by the Police Vehicle Theft Unit before they could be registered in Namibia. Immediately following the Outjo attack, he took an import to Chief Inspector Willem Terblanche, whom he had met on an earlier visit, for clearance. Coincidentally, Terblanche was involved in the Outjo investigation.

Neelse, for an unexplained reason, blurted out to Terblanche that one of the identikits appeared identical to Johan Verwey (Ferdi Barnard). He explained how he had been approached by a white man and offered work entailing the denigration of SWAPO in the eyes of the voters. They (presumably Neelse and others) were to sabotage SWAPO vehicles and eliminate their more prominent leaders, including Anton Lubowski. When using the word 'eliminate', he drew a finger graphically across his throat.

His contacts, he explained, were Johan Verwey (Ferdi Barnard) and Nick Verbeeck (Staal Burger). They could be contacted at *Die Nes* (The Nest), in Krugersdorp, phone number 011-795-3539, which was connected to an answering machine. Mrs Bouwer and Morkel Vermeulen at Edumeds could confirm his story because his contacts had bought or hired a 'TV camera' there.

Terblanche questioned him briefly, asked for more information and enquired if he had carried out any tasks for his contacts. Neelse was reluctant to say. Terblanche said he gained the impression that Neelse was bragging, trying to show himself in a good light, so he did not follow it up or report it. Soon afterwards there was a breakthrough in the Outjo case, so he forgot about it entirely. He only mentioned it three months later when Deputy Commissioner 'Jumbo' Smit confronted him after Lubowski had been assassinated. When questioned about this at the Lubowski inquest, Terblanche insisted it was because the Outjo Three had already been arrested. Neither the judge nor the myriad of advocates and instructing attorneys representing everybody imaginable, picked up the point that the Outjo Three were not arrested until late September 1989 — more than a month after Neelse approached Terblanche.

Monitoring vehicles of SA Council of Churches: Namibia: Aug 1989

On Staal Burger's orders, Slang van Zyl despatched Isgak Hardien to Windhoek in early August 1989. Hardien was ordered to monitor the movement of four micro-buses belonging to the South African Council of Churches that had been reported there.

On 25 August Hardien returned to Windhoek with the particulars of one micro-bus and was told to wait there for orders to damage or destroy it. The day after his arrival, though, he was instructed to return immediately to Johannesburg because all Namibian projects had been cancelled.

Another of his tasks had been to monitor the movements of Anton Lubowski, but his efforts uncovered nothing of particular significance.

Donald Acheson: Mission to Windhoek: July/August 1989

Chappie Maree, who had recently opened his Blue Plan company, Lema Namibia, in Windhoek, was instructed to arrange for Donald Acheson to be settled there.

On a Friday in July 1989 Maree phoned and arranged to meet Acheson at 19:00 in a third floor room at the Ascot Hotel, Norwood, Johannesburg. Acheson arrived early and settled down in the foyer to await his appointment. Coincidentally, he knew the receptionist, so he asked and was told three men were in the room. Just before 19:00 the lift arrived at the ground floor and two men alighted. One, an African American who paid regular visits to South Africa on the pretext he worked for the American Student Exchange Plan, had tried to recruit Acheson to work for the ANC a few months before. Acheson thought he was CIA. He did not know his companion.

They left the hotel without noticing him and he took the lift to the third floor. When the door opened he found himself face to face with Derek (Chappie Maree). Maree invited him into the room, then picked up three dirty glasses and went to the bathroom. Acheson noticed a half open briefcase under the bed and while Maree was rinsing the glasses in the bathroom he lifted the lid with his foot. There was a file on top, covering bundles of US$100 bills.[35]

Maree told Acheson to prepare to move to Windhoek. Later, he said, he would arrange for his 'wife', two children and household effects to follow him. He should rent a house in its own grounds close to the city centre, using estate agents Joseph and Snyman in the Kalahari Sands Hotel complex.

Maree phoned the following Monday and told Acheson to fly to Windhoek the next morning. Maree still had Calla Botha's Executive Communications pager and he instructed Acheson to contact him through that. He also provided the pager number of 'Taxi', who would arrange transport if it was required. Taxi was probably Charles Neelse, although he denied it.

Acheson stayed at the Kalahari Sands, the highest profile hotel in Windhoek, for two nights. On the third he moved to Youth With a Mission hostel (YWAM). It was a Christian welfare organisation dedicated to religious teaching. Occasional visitors were charged tariffs more applicable to charity cases than former residents of the Kalahari Sands. He introduced himself to the secretary, Hilda Basson, as Donald Acheson — Canadian citizen, journalist and *Time* magazine trouble shooter.

Maree rang him twice on YWAM's public telephone. He told him to evaluate the current political situation, assess the feelings of the general public and report on SWAPO rallies. In response to a query on his house-hunting activities, Acheson said vacant houses were scarce and rents highly inflated because of the flood of UNTAG personnel in town. Maree said he should keep looking.

Acheson said he stayed at YWAM for a week, but Hilda Basson said he only stayed two nights on his first visit. Later, she said, he stayed for another night, but he visited there frequently to use the public telephone — often twice a day. Acheson said he went there daily between 07:00 and 19:00 daily to await phone calls from Maree. Hilda Basson's natural but wrong conclusion was that wherever he went after leaving the mission, he did not have the use of a phone.

Acheson was of great interest to Hilda because of his alleged employment with *Time* magazine. She was a journalism student herself, so she regarded him as a fountain of knowledge. But she soon found he knew little or nothing about the subject and she began suspecting his *bona fides*.

Mrs Waltraud Ratzke rented a furnished garden cottage to Acheson at 3 Ahrens Street, Klein Windhoek. As with Hilda, he told her he was a *Time* magazine journalist. She thought this odd because he walked everywhere and had no car. He stayed there from 27 to 31 July then left. Where he stayed the next night is unknown, but Maree phoned him at the mission and told him to fly to Mbabane, Swaziland, where a room had been reserved for him at the Swazi Sun Hotel.

He flew there on 2 August via Jan Smuts (Johannesburg International) Airport. Maree visited him at the hotel and said he was to return to Johannesburg by road. To circumvent his illegal immigrant status, he had arranged for him to re-enter South Africa at the Oshoek border post. The situation in Windhoek, Maree said, was moving fast and there was no longer the need to find a house. Acheson stayed at the hotel until 5 August, then hired a car and drove to Johannesburg.

On 16 August Maree phoned him at Cynthia Leo's flat and told him to return to Windhoek. He would contact him by phone at YWAM. Acheson reported his arrival via Maree's pager. He insisted he stayed at the mission, but Mrs Ratzke said he rented her cottage on 17 and 18, was absent on 19, but returned on 20 to 27 August. The cottage had its own telephone and Acheson's phone bills were high, but he paid in cash as the amounts fell due. The Namibian telephone system lacked the sophistication necessary to trace the destinations of calls.

One very hot day in mid August, Friederich Brandt and his wife were out driving when they saw an 'old man' walking along Gobabis Road. Mr Brandt disliked picking up strangers, but his wife was more compassionate. They stopped and Brandt asked the walker where he was going. He replied that he was 'a journalist from *Time* magazine . . . looking for accommodation at a place called YWAM.' Brandt gave him a lift.

While conversing en route the old man complained about the difficulties of finding accommodation and how he was unsure if he would find anything at YWAM. *Time* magazine, he said, sent him to all the world's trouble spots. 'I have been in Beirut, in South America and such places and I have been incarcerated for many weeks and brutally assaulted and mistreated. Look at my face and body!' Brandt protested that Namibia was not a trouble spot, but the man replied: 'But it will become one. Namibia has been dished out to the Russians long ago.'

When they arrived at YWAM Mrs Brandt scribbled down their address — 42 Gever Street, Ludwigsdorf, Klein Windhoek — and phone number and said he should call them if he needed help. He phoned the next day, thanked them, and said he had come right. Brandt saw him again briefly at the central post office in late August. He later identified him as Acheson.

Chappie Maree phoned Acheson on 20 August and told him to meet him in the restaurant at Kalahari Sands Hotel the next morning. Acheson sat down and was approached by a man who said he was there on Derek's (Maree's) behalf and introduced himself as 'Campbell'. He handed over an envelope containing R4 000 in R50 notes and another with photographs of roads and an intersection. Campbell said Derek would tell him later how to get to the intersection, where he was to meet a Combi.

Anton Lubowski had a premonition of death. As a white senior member of SWAPO he knew he was a target. His elder sister, Jolene du Plessis, presenter of the SABC's Afrikaans programme *Uit en Tuis*, saw him when he visited Pretoria in late August 1989. 'Anton had had an increasing number of death threats recently . . . people kept telephoning him. At some stage we had talked about dying and he had mentioned to my mother that, should anything happen to him, the family should not bury him too soon', as he wanted friends from far away to attend his funeral. His younger sister, Anneliese Beukman, said: 'It was almost as if he had a feeling something was going to happen.'[36] His parents confirmed his gloomy expectations. When dining in restaurants, he sat with his back to the wall as 'if they shot him he wanted to see them — he didn't want to be shot in the back like a dog'.[37]

Lubowski's feeling that he was being watched was correct. On 25 August 1989 Joe Verster addressed a Region 6 cell meeting about Lubowski visiting South Africa between 25 and 30 August. Slang van Zyl was ordered to monitor his movements and note the people he visited in Johannesburg and Cape Town.[38]

Ferdi Barnard said he was contacted by Van Zyl and they met at a business complex in Florida on the West Rand. Van Zyl said he had been tasked to monitor Lubowski's movements, find out the vehicle he was using and obtain any other useful intelligence. Van Zyl gave Barnard some cash and a photograph, although he already knew what Lubowski looked like from his Namibian trip. His face was seen in Namibian newspapers and on television with regular monotony. Lubowski's first engagement, Barnard was told, was at the world-renowned Mount Nelson Hotel in Cape Town where he would address a gathering at a formal dinner party.

Barnard booked into another hotel and took a taxi to Mount Nelson on the day of the dinner. He presumably had tea and took the opportunity to check the place out to get a feel of its physical layout and to try to ascertain the venue of the dinner party. He returned at about 18:00. Later, people began to arrive, dressed in formal evening wear. Ferdi did not say so but it appears his own attire did not match that of the guests. He failed to gain access to the dinner venue, although at one stage he found himself only three or four metres away from the target. When the dinner was over, Lubowski came out with a group and they climbed into a Combi. Barnard took the registration number and tried to follow it. But by the time he got into his own vehicle and edged out to follow, he had lost it in the traffic. Barnard then withdrew because he was afraid he was becoming conspicuous.

He contacted Slang van Zyl by phone. He said Lubowski was flying to Johannesburg where he was scheduled to address a meeting the next afternoon at the Johannesburg Country Club. They knew the flight he would be on. It was also thought he would be staying at the club. It seemed clear to Barnard that the CCB either had pin-point information on Lubowski's agenda or they had a source very close to him.

Barnard took an earlier flight and Brenda Milne met him at the airport with his car. He watched Lubowski's arrival at the domestic terminal and saw him rent a car at either Avis or Imperial Car Hire. He followed him to the parking area and saw him pick up a red BMW. He tailed him to the Rosebank Hotel and watched him check in.

'I found out his room number by phoning from a call box in the hotel lobby . . . I asked if my friend, Lubowski, [had] checked in. They gave me his room number and I said: "I will go to his room." I hung around for a while. Later that afternoon I drove to the Johannesburg Country Club. I observed the layout . . . to see if I could get access . . . and find out where they were having the function. I was in position at about 17:00 . . . The outside area is quite big . . . there were a lot of trees. Lubowski arrived alone, but there were other people moving around . . . He parked quite far from the front entrance . . . that was just after 18:00.'

He tailed him as he had done at Mount Nelson but could not get close. The guests, once again, were formally dressed. Barnard, big fellow that he is, stood out and because there were many security people around, he decided to wait outside and follow the target if he went anywhere afterwards. At 23:00 'something strange happened. Someone came out and climbed into Mr Lubowski's vehicle, a blond woman . . . switched on and drove off. I was confused and I wondered how I could have missed him because he was quite a large man.'

He decided to wait instead of following the woman. Approximately ten to 15 minutes later Lubowski and three men came out. They dawdled around chatting for a short time, then moved to a V8 Rover in the parking lot and got in. They stayed for another ten minutes and then drove off. Barnard followed the car to the Rosebank Hotel. The four went into the cocktail lounge and ordered drinks. They settled down for what seemed to be a long stay.

Barnard phoned Van Zyl: 'Listen', he said, 'I have monitored him all day. I have all the information you wanted. What do I do now?'

Van Zyl decided to meet Barnard in the parking lot. While waiting, Barnard went upstairs to locate Lubowski's room. He tried the door, but it was locked. Van Zyl arrived about 40 minutes later.

'I am ready. I have *things* here with me', Barnard said. He had a modified bayonet on him and an AK47 in the car. 'This man is meek and he has been walking around the parking area by himself in the dark', he continued. He pointed out that he made an easy target of opportunity and he could easily have killed him earlier at the country club. Barnard said that Van Zyl 'nearly had a heart attack and said: 'No, never, there was no such order.' He stressed that he should only monitor Lubowski. This order had come from the highest level and added that 'Staal Burger would have me for breakfast if something went wrong with this'.

Barnard was astonished. 'There was no doubt in my mind that they wanted to kill him in South West during that excursion. I thought: here is the ideal opportunity. This is the sort of work I do. Why don't I just take him out?'

Barnard was debriefed later by Van Zyl. He provided a detailed report on Lubowski's movements, the registration numbers and description of the cars he used and descriptions of the people who had been with him. He also mentioned that Lubowski was a large man, much taller than one thought, light on his feet and in shape. He conveyed the impression of having been through some sort of military training.

Van Zyl submitted his report to Staal Burger. Major-General Eddie Webb's impression was that the observations had proved fruitless.[39]

On 23 August 1989 Chappie Maree phoned Donald Acheson. Acheson said he had rented a cottage, but would continue to use the mission phone. Maree asked for his address, but Acheson refused to give it. Maree, ignoring his refusal, said he was also in town and gave his phone number.

Two evenings later, to Acheson's surprise, Maree arrived at his cottage but did not say how he had tracked him down. He told him plans had changed and they had to move fast to disrupt the elections. He handed him a camera, a briefcase packed with US $100 bills with a folder on top, three small incendiary devices in hardboard boxes and three 'panic bombs'.

SWAPO had opened offices at the airport to deal with returnees. Acheson was to maintain observation and photograph any whites who entered. He was to monitor Gwen Lister, photograph her house, the car she drove, her servants and any visitors. He was to check on Lubowski's visits to SWAPO's offices, to Gwen Lister or anyone else. Maree assisted by providing particulars of Lubowski's BMW and photographs of Lubowski, Lister and three unnamed SWAPO blacks. When a film spool was completed, he was told he should phone, then leave it behind the motoring magazine section in the Kaiser Street Central News Agency for collection.

He was to take the briefcase to the Kalahari Sands Hotel restaurant the next morning, place it in a prominent position on the floor next to him and order breakfast. Afterwards he should pick up the briefcase and take it to the basement garage and conceal it behind a refuse skip.

He was to give the incendiary devices to 'Taxi' and show him how to use them. Acheson was also to supply him with SWAPO and DTA IDs for leaving at scenes to create the impression that both organisations had been involved. The incendiary devices, fitted with time delays, were for placing beneath vehicle fuel tanks. They were armed by pulling a tag. After a timed delay, a ball bearing shot up and punctured the tank. Fuel leaked through the rupture and saturated the device, ensuring the vehicle would burn when the detonation occurred. The 'panic bombs', dummies of the real incendiaries, were to be planted beneath SWAPO vehicles parked at UNTAG's Windhoek Airport base. Their purpose was to create panic and confusion.

After the briefing Maree told Acheson to phone for a taxi. While awaiting its arrival outside, Werner Ratzke appeared and offered them a lift in his car. Ratzke remembered dropping them at the Municipality, but Acheson said it was the Kalahari Sands Hotel. Wherever it was they parted immediately, because Maree had no wish to be seen with Acheson. Neither Mr nor Mrs Ratzke could describe Maree, but Mrs Ratzke remembered Acheson describing Maree as his boss.

While breakfasting at the Kalahari Sands the next morning, Acheson's noticed five black men, one sporting a brassy-looking SWAPO lapel badge, at a nearby table. After breakfast Acheson left the briefcase in the garage as instructed, but dawdled around to see what happened. To his surprise SWAPO Lapel Badge appeared, walked slowly to the skip, picked up the briefcase, threw it the back of an ageing BMW sedan and drove off.

A few days later Acheson gave Taxi the incendiary devices and panic bombs and commenced his own tasks of photographing SWAPO's airport offices and the rest. He disposed of the completed spools in accordance with Maree's instructions, but never saw the results.

Exit Regional Manager Petrus Botes (Marius)

Petrus Botes returned from Namibia on 23 August 1989 to give a progress report on his region 's Namibian projects. Colonel Verster accused him of mismanaging funds — Calla Botha suggested it was R500 but Botes said it was R200 000. According to Botes, Verster threatened to kill him. Botes stormed from the office and resigned. His Namibian disruption plans, including the assassination of Hidipo Hamutenya, were scrapped. He tried to make an appointment to see the General Officer Commanding Special Forces, Major-General Eddie Webb, but he was continually 'unavailable'.

Shortly afterwards a bomb exploded in Botes' Blue Plan business premises — clearly an unsubtle warning to keep his mouth shut.

Frightened, he sought an interview with Minister of Law and Order, Adrian Vlok, and it was granted. He reported the existence of the CCB, identified himself as a member and said they had murdered David Webster. Vlok who, it seems, knew nothing about the CCB, promised to have it investigated by the Commissioner of Police, General Johan van der Merwe. The information filtered down the chain of command until it reached Brigadier Mostert. This was the first Mostert had heard of the CCB's existence too. Vlok apparently made no effort to halt the investigation or influence it. Judging by the way the investigation progressed, it appears that he did not query the organisation's existence with his cabinet colleague, Defence Minister Malan either. One can be certain, though, that Vlok and Malan had much to say about it later.[40]

Threats were made against the school attended by Botes' child so Botes made contingency plans to murder Joe Verster should any harm come to him. He intended to use 'indirect members' (coverts) of the CCB who were loyal to him and 'who ate out of his hands' to get at Verster and his family.[41]

He also took an additional precaution by exposing the CCB to Jacques Pauw, a journalist with the *Vrye Weekblad* newspaper. He scoffed at suggestions of the CCB's professionalism and that assassinations were planned down to the last detail. He said the unit had operated efficiently when Major-General Joep Joubert was the Commanding General Special Forces, but after Major-General Eddie Webb took over the situation became chaotic. While Webb was a good conventional soldier he knew little about covert warfare and Verster took advantage of it. A tail wagging the dog situation developed and Verster regularly misinformed Webb regarding projects and operations and told him only what he believed he should know.

'Verster became a prima donna, blinded by his new-found power. I was supposed to have a meeting with him every 14 days. I had to wait for hours to see him. I once did not see him for two months. Because of this, Verster lost touch with his operatives in the field. He gave unauthorised instructions that Webb did not know about. Not all operations were referred to Webb for approval.'[42]

Judge Harms, in his Commission's report, variously damned Botes as someone wanting to 'make money from his evidence', as an 'extortionist' and a 'perjurer'. He refused to call Minister Vlok to testify before his Commission, but found that 'Botes did not inform the Minister of any unlawful activities of the CCB in the RSA' — a difficult conclusion to arrive at since he did not order Vlok to be subpoenaed for cross-examination. The judge also concurred with the unlikely conclusion of a police investigation 'that Botes very probably blew up his own premises'.[43]

One wonders if ex-Minister Vlok's 1997 application to the Truth and Reconciliation Commission for amnesty for crimes committed by him while in office, has prompted Judge Harms to re-examine his decision not to call Vlok as a witness 'because there was no reason to believe the Minister could give any relevant evidence'.[44]

Countdown to murder: Anton Lubowski: 12 September 1989

On 1 September 1989 Slang Van Zyl attended a Region 6 meeting at the Rosebank Hotel, Johannesburg, with Staal Burger, Wouter J Basson, 'Tilly' Smit (organisation name Nick Nienaber), Calla Botha, Chappie Maree and an unnamed logistical officer. Van Zyl was aware that Burger and Maree had been paying regular visits to Namibia.

After Van Zyl's projects had been discussed, there was a break to await Verster's arrival. Maree and Wouter J Basson, meanwhile, were jotting down notes. Maree mentioned as an aside that they concerned Lubowski. Van Zyl said he had also worked on a project concerning him, but Basson interjected and said it was of no concern to him. There was about to be an in-house submission, so both he and Calla Botha should get out. They left, and Van Zyl assumed that the in-house concerned Lubowski.[45]

Late in September at another Region 6 meeting attended by Verster, Burger, Van Zyl, Maree, Botha and 'Tilly' Smit. Verster told Van Zyl that he was to attend a second training course in October. Van Zyl said there was little point as he was resigning. He had been influenced by the operators having been ordered to finalise their projects by 1 September 1989 as F W de Klerk was replacing P W Botha as president and he had not yet been told about the CCB's existence. His resignation was a bombshell. They thought he was joking at first, but when they saw he was serious, Staal Burger lost his temper and accused him of misusing the organisation to establish his Blue Plan business.

Van Zyl denied it angrily and pointed out that his resignation meant the loss of his November production bonus, his 13th cheque due at Christmas and that he would become liable for all medical expenses relating to his wife's pending confinement.

He offered no explanation, but said later he had reconsidered his connections with the organisation while he was on leave in Cape Town. South Africa was entering a new era of negotiation under a new president. Talking to the ANC meant not only the end of armed conflict, but the redundancy of the CCB, in particular Region 6. Van Zyl supported negotiations, believing it better for South Africa and for his family's future. It is probable, too, considering his police experience, that he had suddenly realised Region 6's activities were blatantly criminal.

Burger tersely told him to get out . . . he was no longer part of the organisation.

It was Slang Van Zyl's last formal contact with the CCB, but he returned his BMW, his telephone scrambler, his shredder and other office equipment to the organisation.[46]

On Wednesday 6 September 1989 Chappie Maree phoned Donald Acheson and told him to return immediately to South Africa. When filling in immigration forms on departing Windhoek Airport, he wrote that he had been in Namibia on business and had stayed at 3 Ahrens Street, Klein Windhoek. He stopped-over in Johannesburg for one night, then flew to Swaziland and booked in at the Swazi Sun Hotel where Maree had reserved a room. Maree met him and paid him R5 000 in R50 notes, mentioning again that 'things' needed speeding up and he was to return to Windhoek as soon as possible.

Acheson had settled into the 'geographic' pattern beloved by the CCB that Brian had found so 'Mickey Mouse' while involved with *Operations Direksie 1 and 2* — the abortive attempt to break Kevin Woods and company from Chikurubi Prison. Despite Maree having only recently seen Acheson in Windhoek, the latter suddenly had to be routed to Swaziland via Johannesburg for a briefing. To return to Windhoek, he flew from Swaziland to Johannesburg on Saturday 9 September and to Windhoek the following day.

Acheson obviously knew something criminal was in the offing. On arriving at Windhoek International Airport he noted on the immigration forms that he would be staying at 42 Gever Street, Ludwigsdorf — the home of the Brandts who had been kind to him in mid August. This was the only time he wrote a false address on Namibian immigration papers. That it was false is evidenced by his having phoned Mrs Ratzke's son before departing from Johannesburg to book her cottage for 10 September.

Acheson's first stop was the Kalahari Sands Hotel, where he was saved from going 'geographic' again by bumping into Maree in the foyer. In the basement garage Maree slipped him R1 000 to rent a car from Imperial Car Hire. He gave him his number and told him to phone and report the type of car hired.

He also gave him a box containing a slow-acting white and odourless poison and a syringe. He suggested he inject some into Gwen Lister's toothpaste, put drops on her *Tampax* or lace her food with it. Lister, he said, would 'keel over' within 48 hours. Maree denied this at the TRC Amnesty hearing.[47]

Acheson rented a Windhoek registered white VW Fox sedan from Imperial, drove to 3 Ahrens Street and hid the poison kit in the cottage. He telephoned Maree and described the car he had rented. After this he drove to *The Namibian*'s offices to look for Gwen Lister. She was not there and neither was she at her house. The Fox's brakes developed an irritating squeak, so he returned to Imperial to exchange it. A replacement was not immediately available, but they said he should come back the next morning.

Mrs Ratzke who was away on Sunday 10 September, noticed the white Fox parked in front when she returned home at 22:30.

The next day 'Taxi' turned up unexpectedly and went with Acheson to Imperial Car Hire. The Fox was exchanged for a red Toyota Conquest, registration CA 183000. Before its release Imperial's Dennis Nautoro conducted a routine check, noting a scratch and a dent on the right hand rear door. Acheson phoned Maree and reported the exchange.

Maree was furious and wanted to know why Acheson had done this so close 'to the time'. Why hadn't he kept the first car. Acheson slammed down the phone and waited for Maree to call back. He had calmed down by the time he did and he said Acheson should get on with his mission. Acheson argued saying that breaking into Lister's house was impossible. Maree replied that he should 'just jab the bitch'. Acheson, with little confidence, promised to see what he could do.

He found a parcel at the back door of his cottage, concluding by its shape that it held 'a rifle of sorts'. Wary of leaving fingerprints, he drove to town and bought a pair of rubber gloves. Slipping them on he opened the parcel and found an AK47 and two charged magazines. Maree had not warned him to expect this, but it could only be for assassination purposes. The magazines, oddly enough, were charged with a mixture of ball and tracer ammunition. Prising open a few tracer rounds, he found they contained cotton wool and an unidentifiable powder.

Maree phoned and Acheson confirmed he had opened the parcel. Maree, he said, told him to take it to the basement garage of the Kalahari Sands Hotel the following evening between 20:00 and 21:00 when he would be met.

During the evening of Tuesday 12 September, Acheson said, he set off for the Kalahari Sands Hotel with the AK in his car. En route he saw a profusion of blue lights and the urgent movement of police vehicles ahead, so he U-turned and went back to the cottage. Twenty minutes later he tried again, but police were still around in force. Concerned by this unusual activity, he turned around again and drove out towards the airport. At a quiet spot he buried the AK in the sand and returned to the cottage. Switching on the TV he saw a news flash announcing that a top SWAPO official had been gunned down. He phoned Maree and asked what was going on. He was told to sit tight in the cottage for a few days and not worry. He was going to Lusaka and would see Acheson there later, but neglected to name a rendezvous. Acheson complained bitterly as he did not feel inclined to hang around, but Maree said he must. He obeyed, but as a precautionary measure disposed of the poison and the hypodermic syringe.[48]

Possibly the CCB intended Acheson to stay in Windhoek and take his chances, believing it unlikely that he would be connected to the organisation if he were arrested. Wouter J Basson's diary entry for 12 September 1989, which probably concerned Chappie Maree, may confirm this. The page had been ripped out, but forensic tests showed indentations which read: 'Disguise, don't phone, change clothes — new clothes, act only according to plans, don't use pager, alibi to go to Zambia — stay for two days, no personal contact after the incident'. Well, Chappie Maree certainly had no personal contact with Acheson after the shooting, nor did he seek his company on the flight to Zambia.[49] If they had been arrested together, it would undoubtedly have proved disastrous for the CCB.

Mrs Ratzke's version of the day's events was different. In the early afternoon she was watering the garden when Acheson arrived in the Toyota Conquest. They exchanged pleasantries, but as he walked to the cottage she noticed he was carrying a narrow brown paper parcel about 20cm long which he seemed to be trying to conceal. Almost immediately afterwards he returned to the car holding a dark-brown hessian sack, about half a metre long, by its neck. Her impression was that it contained a heavy object, somewhat larger than the parcel. Judging by the bag's contours, she thought it was a car jack and vaguely wondered why he had taken it to the cottage and then returned it to the car.[50]

On Tuesday 12 September Staal Burger, travelling under the name of Gagiano, flew into Windhoek. He had borrowed the name of a journalist whom, he would insist later, he hardly knew. What he did while in Windhoek remains a mystery.[51] Slang van Zyl had dined with him the previous evening in Johannesburg, but Burger had not mentioned he was flying to Windhoek on the morrow. He was aware, though, that both Burger and Maree had frequently visited Windhoek. Staal Burger later maintained that he had only spent a single day in Windhoek during the whole of 1989. He had flown in during the morning and out again in the afternoon.[51]

Michaela Clayton, an attorney by profession, lived with Anton Lubowski at 7 Sanderburg Street, Klein Windhoek. At 19:00 on 12 September the phone rang as she walked into the house. It was Lubowski calling from his office to tell her he had arranged they have dinner with a colleague, Hans Geingob. He asked her to reserve a table at the Gourmet Inn for 20:30 and said he would soon be home.

At 19:30 a Rob Calesky arrived for an appointment which Lubowski had forgotten. Michaela phoned Lubowski and Calesky spoke to him, leaving immediately afterwards.

Then Leon Raath appeared for an appointment, which had also slipped Lubowski's mind. Michaela phoned him again and after a fleeting conversation, Raath also left.

At 20:20 Lubowski phoned back. 'I'm running late, please phone Hans Geingob and tell him we'll pick him up at 20:45, not 20:20 as arranged. I'll be home shortly.'

At about 20:35 Lubowski arrived at the front of his house. He got out of the car, walked to the front pedestrian gate and pressed the intercom button. Michaela walked to the bedroom and picked up the handset to check that it was Lubowski and to open the gate electronically. As she picked up the handset there were loud crackling noises.

Lubowski was being shot to death at the gate, but she did not realise it. She thought someone outside was causing trouble by setting off fire crackers. She was alone and all the outside doors were open, so she locked herself in the bedroom and phoned a colleague, Andrew Corbett.

'Please phone the police and come and help me.' While speaking she heard a car pull away. As she replaced the handset, the phone rang.

'Is everything all right?' a neighbour asked.

Olaf Krause (16) was watching television with his mother in the sitting room of 6 Sanderburg Street, opposite. It was above a garage and had its own balcony. Krause heard what he thought were fireworks, then realised seven or eight shots had been fired from a semi automatic weapon. He and his mother ran to the balcony and saw what they thought was a new red VW Golf with tinted windows outside Lubowski's house. The rear lights were bright so they could see there was no rear registration plate. The car moved south along Sanderburg Street, slowly at first and then faster. They tracked its progress by its rear red lights, despite bushes and trees intermittently masking them. It turned south-east into Feste Road and for a few moments they lost sight of it. The lights came back in view as it turned south into Gobabis Road. It was the only moving vehicle in the vicinity.

Folkert Meeuw (42) heard automatic rifle fire while he was watching television at 15 Frieden Street. He instinctively glanced at his watch . . . 20:36. He thought of Anton Lubowski, because he was politically controversial. Stepping onto the balcony he looked towards Lubowski's house, some 250m away as the crow flies across open veld. He glimpsed what he thought was a new red VW Golf as it passed a street light some 30m to 40m south of Lubowski's house, but had no idea where it went. He also thought it had tinted windows because he could not see the occupants.

Wynand Vermaak (15) of 133 Gobabis Road was another watching television at about 20:30. His house was on the western side of Gobabis Road, close to the intersection of Feste Street and Eadie Road. He heard rifle shots, but could not place their origin, so he rushed outside and saw a car with only sidelights showing stop at the intersection of Eadle and Gobabis. It turned south into Gobabis Road and as it passed him and gathered speed, he identified it as a red Toyota Conquest. He was a 'vehicle enthusiast' and he made no mistake about it. He did not see the registration number, but the driver was a white male with hair 'a little bit light'. He watched the car until it disappeared from sight, but was unable to say if there were passengers.

Mrs Ratzke was in the bathroom when she heard four to six shots. She did not note the time, but immediately afterwards she began watching the programme *Hart to Hart* on television with her husband. It started that night at 20:30 and ended 45 minutes later. They briefly discussed the shooting, but did not go out to investigate.

Mrs Ratzke could see the front garden gate through a glass door from her chair. Acheson's Toyota pulled up in front. The door was slammed hard several times, which irritated Mrs Ratzke.

When is he going to stop slamming and come inside? she asked her husband.

Recalling events later they concluded that Acheson had done it deliberately to draw attention to his arrival. The gate opened and Acheson, who was not carrying anything, walked towards the cottage. Mr Ratzke put it at 20:50, but his wife believed it was only a 'couple of minutes' after the start of *Hart to Hart*.

Police plan of Lubowski murder scene supported by photographs.

Key to plan and photographs

A = Anton Lubowski's home at 7 Sanderburg Street.
B = Witness Olaf Krause's home, corner Frieden and Sanderburg Streets.
C = Witness Dr Folkert Meeuw's home, 15 Frieden Street.
D = Cross roads at Gobabis Ave, Feste Street and Eadie Street
E = Witness Wynand Vermaak's home,133 Gobabis Avenue.

After the programme they retired to bed. The cottage was on the same side as their bedroom. At about 22:40 Mrs Ratzke heard someone going past their bedroom window and heading for the front gate. Her husband got up and looking through the front living room window, he saw Acheson climb the 'fence' — a low wall surmounted by two wooden poles about 1,5m high — to get into the garden. Ratzke assumed he was coming from his car and wondered why he had not used the gate. This time Acheson detoured to the rear of the house to get to the cottage, instead of walking down the side of the house as usual.

Folkert Meeuw, certain there had been a shooting at Lubowski's house, drove there, arriving about six minutes after the shots. He stopped in front of Lubowski's BMW and saw a man sprawled on his right side by the gate. He returned to his house, phoned the police and came back with his wife, a medical doctor. Dr Meeuw immediately saw Lubowski was dead. She noted several gunshot wounds on his body and an exit wound on the right cheek — which looked like a *coup de grace* shot.[52] Keys lay on the ground beside him, but his briefcase was still tightly gripped in his left hand.

The neighbour who, had phoned earlier arrived at the same time as the police. He spoke to Michaela through the intercom and gave her the bad news.

Deputy Commissioner 'Jumbo' Smit took over the investigation. Twelve 7,62-mm short cartridge cases, fired from an AK47, were found at the crime scene and there were bullet scars on the wall and gates. The window of a car parked in a neighbouring yard had been smashed by a bullet. Ballistic tests showed all cartridge cases had been ejected from the same weapon.

On Wednesday 13 September, the day after the murder, Staal Burger alias Gagiano, returned to South Africa on a scheduled flight.

Mrs Ratzke spoke briefly to an unusually cheerful Acheson in the garden just before 08:00 the same morning. She excused herself to listen to the television news and heard that Anton Lubowski had been shot. In a state of unease, the Ratzkes checked where Acheson had climbed the fence the previous night, and noted his footprints in the flower bed. Lubowski was dead, they had heard the shots, there was the strange business of the sack and Acheson's unusual behaviour. Something 'was wrong with him'.

At 10:30 she went to the police and suggested his implication in the murder. Deputy Commissioner Smit returned to the house with her at 13:00 and questioned Acheson, who stuck to his story that he was a reporter with *Time* Magazine. Deputy Commissioner Smit searched the cottage, but found no evidence of his involvement. In his suitcase, though, he discovered R3 500 and another R500 in R50 notes in his wallet. He found a scrap of paper with a Johannesburg pager number — 331-3561, channel 784, code 18 — scrawled on it in his pocket.

There were traces of *Wonder Glue* on the rear number plate of Acheson's Toyota Conquest. This implied something had been stuck there, but there were no corresponding glue traces on the front plate. There were fresh paint scratches on the left- hand side rear, on top of the right front door and on the right-hand front corner of the roof. They were consistent with the marks an AK47's magazine would have made during recoil if the shooter had used the car as a dead rest.

Deputy Commissioner Smit arrested Acheson on suspicion of murder, learning later that a warrant had been issued in South Africa for his deportation as a prohibited immigrant. It was not long before Acheson retracted his story about being a reporter with *Time* and said he was a freelance cartoonist. Then he said he was there to explore his chances of immigrating to Namibia. After that he decided to go as a professional shoplifter, there to form a syndicate of shoplifters. Retracting this, he said he worked for Derek (Chappie Maree) of National Party Broadcasting and was there to find a 'safe house'.[53]

Asked about his movements on the evening of 12 September 1989, he said he had gone to the *Spur* for a meal, but it was full so he dined at the Central Café. Afterwards he window-shopped at the Gustav Voigt Centre and returned home. The police were unable to confirm his story.

Deputy Commissioner Smit kept Acheson in solitary confinement and gave him writing materials. He could only hold him for 48 hours and he needed time to arrange for an immigration warrant to detain him in Windhoek Prison. After the cell was vacated he searched it and found two undated and unsigned sheets of writing paper under the mattress.

It was an account of Acheson's meeting with Van Staden (Ferdi Barnard), the story of his travels to Johannesburg, Swaziland and Windhoek, his dealings with Derek (Chappie Maree), how he met 'Campbell', the large amounts of cash he was given and finally, that he was watching *Hart to Hart* in his cottage when Lubowski was murdered.

Deputy Commissioner Smit questioned Acheson until 29 September 1989, when he agreed to make a warned and cautioned statement, but refused to have it reduced to writing. He repeated much of what he had written in the police cell, but denied he was carrying a bag when he met Mrs Ratzke, or that he had climbed the fence and gained access to his flat via the rear. He reiterated that he was watching *Hart to Hart* at the time of the murder.

Acheson's arrest prompted Comops to embark on a major damage control exercise and conflicting stories were cleverly fed to the press. *The Namibian* suggested he was a mercenary with experience as a paramilitary operator with Protestant extremist organisations.[54] Other reports said he was a hired gun employed by dissident SWAPO factions opposed to Sam Nujoma.

A police spokesman insisted they had the right man, but another contradicted this and said they had nothing on him. A rumour went the rounds that Lubowski's resignation from SWAPO to join the opposition United Democratic Front had been imminent. Another story was that he was seen leaving a girlfriend's home, tears streaming down his face, muttering angrily about SWAPO.[55]

Senior SADF intelligence, SWA Police officers and other Intelligence staff, who should have been fountains of correct knowledge, were convincing in circulating these stories.

Sue Dobson, after her defection to the ANC from the Bureau for Information, confirmed: 'We were briefed to perpetuate the allegation that Anton Lubowski was killed by SWAPO elements who supported Hidipo Hamutenya, rather than Sam Nujoma, whom Lubowski was supposed to have been close to. My briefing was to find as much dirt on Lubowski as possible to play on the theme he had been murdered by SWAPO.' [56]

One of the many who accepted this information at face value was the author who was in Windhoek at the time writing the book *Nine Days of War — And South Africa's Final Days in Namibia*. He wrote at the time:

> 'There are sinister divisions coming to light within SWAPO itself and it would not be surprising if a few heads amongst the leadership, perhaps even Nujoma's himself, rolled before the election in last minute power struggles.
>
> 'It seems probable that white SWAPO leader, Anton Lubowski, who was assassinated outside his Windhoek home on 12 September, was murdered by SWAPO as a sacrificial lamb. 'There is much to suggest he had been killed by an IRA hit man brought in especially for the job, on orders of SWAPO's top leadership, as an example to those agitating against Nujoma's presidency of SWAPO. It is doubtful Lubowski was involved in such plotting, but he was generally resented within SWAPO and undoubtedly regarded as expendable.
>
> 'The warning was probably directed at the highly placed Hidipo Hamutenya, who it is said, is being backed for the SWAPO presidency by PLAN's top military commanders. Windhoek, a sleepy hollow until now, seems to have a violent future lying ahead.' [57]

The time was good for disruptive disinformation — Sam Nujoma was due to make a triumphant return to Namibia within 48 hours.

The Comops campaign continued unabated. A mystery man calling himself Eric du Plessis inveigled Jolene du Plessis into a meeting and claimed her brother had been assassinated by PLAN elements. This, he said, was due to unhappiness in SWAPO circles about the alleged misappropriation of SWAPO funds, jealousy about his friendship with Sam Nujoma and because he was white.[58]

Panic in the ranks

It was the headline in all the major South African newspapers. An 'Irishman'— undoubtedly Donald Acheson — had been arrested for Lubowski's murder. An emergency meeting was convened at the Rosebank Hotel. Everyone except 'Theo' was there. There was virtual pandemonium. Acheson's arrest was a concern to everyone, but especially to Staal Burger and Chappie Maree. Maree and Calla Botha were told to lie low.

A second meeting followed, this time at the Train Restaurant, Midrand. Burger, Wouter J Basson, Maree and Botha attended. Botha mentioned that Acheson had originally been recruited by Ferdi Barnard, which no one else seemed to know. Everyone, he said, was 'very dissatisfied with him'. Burger demanded to know whether Barnard knew anything of Botha's involvement. Botha said he didn't, but they believed he was lying.

There was concern about Botha's Red pager, which Chappie Maree had returned to him. Botha was told to destroy it, but being just as concerned, he had already done so. Another worry was that Acheson's last stay at the Royal Swazi Sun had been booked in Maree's name.

Staal Burger phoned Joe Verster and Tilly Smit (organisation name Nick Nienaber) and this made him happier. He announced confidently that Acheson's prosecution was a lemon and would be stopped 'at the top'.

Lafras Luitingh (Louis Yssel) warned Ferdi Barnard that 'his Irishman' had been arrested for murder in Windhoek. Lefras, Barnard later said, showed no concern for Acheson's fate. He had been well paid and another R70 000 awaited him in Canada. It was more important to ensure the organisation was not implicated. Barnard, upset that Acheson had been abandoned, asked what had happened to the State's protection they had always boasted about. Lefras shrugged and said Acheson had been briefed in Swaziland, so the organization was in the clear. He told Barnard to destroy his pager, which he did.[59]

Staal Burger ordered Botha to steal the register from the Ascot Hotel, Norwood. He did not say why but Botha guessed Acheson had been interviewed there. Botha got Barnard to accompany him and while he distracted the black receptionist, Barnard slickly removed the register from the desk and slipped outside.

As Botha was leaving, he passed 'Big Alex' Kavouras and a woman on their way in. He concluded gleefully that he had also been sent by Burger to get the register. In the car, however, they discovered they had the wrong book — they had stolen the table reservation book for the restaurant.

During this escapade, Barnard said, Botha told him that Maree was Acheson's handler and that the Lubowski hit was an approved Special Forces' operation. Using the *nom de guerre* of Derek, Maree had briefed Acheson in Swaziland. He had been promised the sum of R70 000 paid to him in Canada once he had done the job.

Botha also said that General Eddie Webb, the Commanding General Special Forces and Chairman of the CCB, was seeing Staal Burger and Wouter J Basson that evening to discuss putting a stop to the police investigation. Everyone, he said, was confident Webb would succeed.[60] This turned out to be a case of misplaced optimism.

Exit the Outjo Three: 4 December 1989

On 27 September 1989 Leonard Veenendal, Darol Stopforth, Arthur Archer, Craig Barker and Horst Klenz were arrested in southern Namibia after information regarding their whereabouts was provided by the Brixton Murder and Robbery Squad. They appeared in the Otjiwarongo magistrate's court in connection with the attack on UNTAG's regional HQ at Outjo on 24 August. Charges against Barker were withdrawn and he was released. The remaining four were remanded in custody until 11 October.[61]

AWB leader, Eugene Terreblanche, speaking of Veenendal's arrest said: 'If it is true, I am shocked.' He insisted the AWB had neither taken part in the attack, nor sanctioned it.[62]

On 3 October 1989 police arrested Johan Coetzee — who had introduced Klenz to Veenendal and Stopforth — for questioning. Charges against both Coetzee and Archer were eventually withdrawn, but they were kept in protective custody as State witnesses. Sources suggested that Coetzee, suspected of being a Military Intelligence spy, had been kicked out of the AWB.[63]

On Monday 4 December 1989 Veenendal, Stopforth and Klenz — the Outjo Three as the press called them — were moved 270km from Windhoek to Otjiwarongo for further remand. They were charged with murder, malicious injury to property, unlawful possession of firearms and ammunition, unlawful possession of hand grenades and theft of a car. Acting magistrate Quentin van Rooyen further remanded the prisoners. He suggested to Constable Ricardo van Wyk (21), who would be escorting them to Okahandja, that they be allowed to 'stretch their legs from time to time'.

At the courthouse 'people from South Africa' told the prisoners that a pistol had been hidden in a toilet cistern.[64] Before getting in the police van, Veenendal asked permission to go to the toilet. Constables van Wyk and Boois waited innocently outside, while Veenendal entered and armed himself. After locking the prisoners in the rear of the van, Constable Van Wyk took the wheel. Neither Van Wyk nor Boois noticed the green Nissan following them.

Ten kilometres south of Otjiwarongo, the prisoners banged on the dividing window demanding to be let out to urinate. The unsuspecting constables obliged. But as the van stopped, the Nissan drew alongside. Two men, Bredenhann and Cliffie Barnard, both members of the AWB's *Ystergarde* (Iron Guard), overpowered the policemen with the help of the prisoners. Constable Ricardo van Wyk was shot in the back and suffered chest and spinal injuries. Leaving him for dead by the side of the road, they bundled Constable Boois into the back of the police van and escaped in both vehicles. They abandoned the police van about 30km away. Constable Boois broke out of the back, hitchhiked to Otjiwarongo and raised the alarm. Constable van Wyk died in hospital.

A hue and cry was raised and an intensive land and air search was launched. Roadblocks were set up on all major routes, but the fugitives had disappeared without trace.

Veenendal and Stopforth only surfaced in South Africa after Namibian independence in 1990. The Namibian government applied for their extradition, but it was only in 1992 that a Johannesburg magistrate ruled they were extraditable. They appealed the decision. They argued that SWA/Namibia was part of South Africa in 1989, so they could not be extradited for offences committed before independence. The Minister of Justice finally ordered their extradition in November 1996. An appeal to the High Court for a stay pending the outcome of an amnesty application to the TRC was refused, because the commission had no jurisdiction to entertain amnesty applications for offences committed in a foreign country.[65]

The extradition question remains unresolved at the time of writing.

CCB: Beginning of the end

Deputy Commissioner Smit in Windhoek looked towards Johannesburg after receiving a fax from Mrs Rankman of the Black Sash. She reported that a man speaking English with an Afrikaans accent had phoned her anonymously.

Lubowski's killers, he said, had also murdered Dr Webster. Their instructions had come from high government authority, as high as ministerial level.

Deputy Commissioner Smit, isolated from Johannesburg and the happenings there by thousands of kilometres, had only vaguely heard of David Webster. He had long suspected, however, that the Lubowski killing was politically motivated.

Phoning the Brixton Murder and Robbery Squad, he told them about Rankman's letter and arranged to escort Acheson to Johannesburg so they could jointly question him about both murders. Smit was confident he would get genuine assistance, because of Brixton's help with the Outjo Three.

At Brixton, Acheson's initial questioning took the investigations no further. Smit personally carried out enquiries with Executive Communications regarding two pager numbers taken from Acheson. The first, 011-331-3561, channel 1200, code 18, hired by a J Malherbe (Calla Botha) of a hotel at 75 De Villiers Street, Joubert Park, Johannesburg, came to a dead end. Indeed, a J Malherbe had once stayed there, but the Krugersdorp residential address provided proved fictitious. The second pager, 011-331-3561, channel 784, code 18, rented by H J van Staden of 11 Rose Street, Florida proved more promising. The address was an empty house once rented by a Willy Smit for his insurance brokerage. A check with the Executive Communications' accounts department established that rentals had been paid through the cash account of one Ferdi Barnard. Barnard, he established, had once worked at 11 Rose Street.

With the assistance of Warrant Officer Rousseau — the investigating officer of the Webster murder — and other Brixton detectives Deputy Commissioner Smit located and interrogated Barnard. Barnard said he had been recruited by 'Hans' for clandestine work after his discharge from prison. He had used the false name of Van Staden on his instructions for the hire. He admitted obtaining a CV from 'Donald Dolan' — who he agreed was identical to Acheson — and passed it to Hans. Acheson had paged him a few times before contact had ceased.

Barnard denied knowing 'Derek' or 'J Malherbe' and maintained he had no idea what Acheson had been doing in Windhoek. He cooperated in the preparation of an imaginary identikit of Hans. Smit decided against confronting him with Acheson and returned to Windhoek with his prisoner.

Acheson had frequently asked Deputy Commissioner Smit to find him an attorney. Smit did his best, phoning various lawyers in Windhoek, but they were either unavailable or would not touch the case because of its political sensitivity. The Irish Consulate in Johannesburg declined a request for legal aid. Smit's efforts had reached a dead end when, suddenly, Jennes Scholtz and Pierre Botha, from a Roodepoort firm of attorneys which Acheson said he had neither instructed nor paid for, appeared and represented him with vigour. This convinced Smit that some kind of shadowy organisation was behind the murder.

In October 1989 Deputy Commissioner Smit returned to Brixton for further enquiries. He interviewed Willy Smit who related how Ferdi Barnard and Calla Botha had visited him. They had been arrested while monitoring a man called (Roland Bruce) White and needed an alibi. In a turn of words he suggested they had been trying to trace and seize a 'white' BMW from him. Willy Smit said Barnard had expressed his intention of 'taking out' out White because killing people was his job.[66] Both spoke of Webster's murder with familiarity.

Deputy Commissioner Smit told Brigadier Floris Mostert and Warrant Officer Rousseau the results of his enquiries. They both recalled the arrest of Ferdi Barnard and Calla Botha after Roland Bruce White had complained he was being followed. The link between

Webster and White was also of interest, because they belonged to the same left-wing organisations. It was vital for the success of Deputy Commissioner Smit's South African investigation that he convince Mostert and Rousseau that the Lubowski and Webster murders were connected. They could act against Barnard and Botha, but as a Namibian police officer he could not.

They discussed detaining Barnard and Botha under Section 29 of the Internal Security Act. Its provisions were truly draconian in that it effectively infringed on an accused person's right to remain silent. Certainly a prisoner could remain silent if he wished to and (in theory) could not be forced to talk, but he could be detained indefinitely in solitary confinement in a soundproofed cell, without the benefit of legal counsel, until he did! The investigation was tailor-made for section 29, because if a sinister 'murder incorporated' kind of organisation existed, it must pose a threat to the safety and security of the State, which was a defining reason behind Section 29.

Deputy Commissioner Smit returned to Windhoek in a hurry. Attorney Jennes Scholtz had lodged an urgent application with the Supreme Court in terms of the Immigration Act, demanding Acheson's release. The application was granted on 6 November 1989. Deputy Commissioner Smit knew both Ferdi Barnard and Calla Botha were about to be arrested by Brixton, so he could not allow Acheson to slip through his fingers. He rearrested him on the court steps and had him remanded in custody for the murder of Lubowski.

On 31 October 1989, meanwhile, a team of detectives led by Warrant Officer Rousseau arrested Ferdi Barnard on a section 29 Internal Security Act warrant and spirited him away to the police station at Hartbeesfontein, where there were special facilities for the detention of such prisoners. Barnard's father, former SAP Colonel Piet Barnard, asked the Brixton Murder and Robbery Squad about the whereabouts of his son but, as was par for the course, they denied all knowledge.[67]

Calla Botha told Staal Burger about Barnard's detention. Burger, however, was unperturbed, confidently predicting that General Eddie Webb or Colonel Joe Verster would halt the investigation at high level. He reassured him further by saying Verster had reported that Webb had passed a list of Region 6 members to Deputy Commissioner Smit or CID General Jaap Joubert, instructing they were to be left alone. Barnard, however, was not released so Botha badgered Staal Burger continually. Burger said he should not worry.[68]

On 14 November 1989 Deputy Commissioner Smit again escorted Acheson to South Africa where he was also detained at Hartbeesfontein. With Warrant Officer Rousseau, he questioned Barnard for two weeks, sometimes alone and sometimes with Acheson present.

On 24 November Colonel Barnard, Ferdi's father, submitted an urgent application to the Supreme Court for his son's release from Section 29 detention. The CCB had deposited funds with Attorneys Scholtz and Botha in Roodepoort. They contacted Colonel Botha and told him the costs of the action had been covered.[69] They also gave him R4 000 a month for Brenda Milne and he wrote out cheques for her.

The application was opposed by the Minister of Law and Order, the Commissioner of Police and the Divisional Commander SAP Witwatersrand. Brigadier Floris Mostert filed an opposing affidavit giving the first public hint of the existence of a 'secret group'. He alleged Ferdi Barnard was withholding vital information concerning the Webster and Lubowski murders. He said the murders and other incidents where the property of leftist political activists had been damaged were designed to frustrate government's policies. If Barnard was prematurely released it could jeopardise his investigation.[70]

Finally, on 27 November 1989 Ferdi Barnard made an affidavit to Deputy Commissioner Smit, in which he admitted he had been employed by a nameless military organisation. His controller was not 'Hans' but Louis (Lafras Luitingh) and the organisation had been seeking information about Lubowski. He provided details of anti-SWAPO operations in Windhoek, including the involvement of Charles (Neelse) in the sabotage of vehicles. He agreed he had recruited Acheson (Donald Dolan), but said Louis had told him they had rejected him and he never saw him again. Nick Verbeek (Staal Burger), he said, controlled Namibian operations. He had hired a pager in Windhoek, No. 37110, for communications purposes. Deputy Commissioner Smit returned Acheson to Windhoek on 28 November.[71]

Colonel Piet Barnard withdrew his urgent application on the same date. A statement by Attorney Piet du Plessis said Ferdi Barnard had told his father to drop it because he was afraid of being killed by 'interested parties'. He also told his father that innocent people, like Calla Botha, had been falsely implicated. Suggestions that a far-right murder squad existed were false and had been made to protect 'certain people' in authority.[72]

Calla Botha's wife said that Warrant Officer Rousseau came to her home on 30 November. Botha sought advice from Staal Burger who referred him to Piet du Plessis of Attorneys David H Botha, Du Plessis and Kruger. Calla Botha said that Piet du Plessis had threatened him and warned him to remain silent. He was 'very scared' knowing full well what had happened to Marius (Petrus Botes) when he tried to blow the whistle on the organisation. The last thing he wanted was a bomb in his own back yard.

Calla Botha accompanied Attorney Piet du Plessis to the Brixton Murder and Robbery Squad and gave himself up. He insisted he had done nothing wrong. Brigadier Mostert arrested him in terms of Section 29 of the Internal Security Act for questioning about the Lubowski and Webster murders. The police refused to release his name to the press, but Attorney du Plessis did so without qualms, saying: 'Mr Botha absolutely denies that he is a member of any right-wing organisation. He is a supporter of the National Party and its reform policies and denies taking part in the alleged crimes.'[73]

Botha said the CCB allocated R15 000 to pay for the costs of an interdict to effect his release, but he accused Staal Burger of repeatedly stalling the process.

Botha was interviewed in detention by Brigadier Krappies Engelbrecht and a 'Brigadier van Rensburg'. Disingenuously, General Badenhorst, it appears, was Brigadier van Rensburg because Botha only mentioned two visitors. Brigadier Engelbrecht said he had a message for him.

'Remain silent!' he told him.

'How long?' Botha queried.

'Six or seven months', Engelbrecht replied.

'Arrange my release', Botha demanded.

'The investigation is out of my hands', Engelbecht said. He told him again to keep silent, or . . . and drew his finger across his throat in an unmistakable gesture.

Warrant Officer Rousseau who witnessed Engelbrecht's astonishing behaviour, reported it to General Jaap Joubert and Brigadier Mostert, who had been nominated to question senior officers of the Security Forces. Badendorst and Engelbrecht had pulled rank to gain access to the Section 29 prisoners, despite a standing instruction that only members of the investigation team could be admitted. To stop a reoccurrence, General Jaap Joubert ordered the fitting of extra locks to the cells.[74]

General Badenhorst crumbled under cross examination at the Webster inquest and conceded he had been present at the Calla Botha interview.

Why was Brigadier Engelbrecht not withdrawn from the investigation after his extraordinary behaviour? he was asked.

'I personally questioned Botha about this aspect', Badenhorst stumbled. 'He denied he had said this [that Engelbrecht had told Botha to shut up about the CCB].'

'Didn't you think Engelbrecht's presence would inhibit Botha?'

'No', Badenhorst replied unconvincingly.

General Badenhorst insisted that 'as a result of my own enquiries, I heard of the CCB for the first time during the last week of November 1989'.[75] However Vice-Admiral Dries Putter, his predecessor as Chief of Staff Intelligence, certainly knew about it because the minutes of the CCB meeting attended by Chief of the SADF Jannie Geldenhuys on 28 April 1987 showed he had complained about the CCB encroaching on his territory. If Putter knew, it is difficult to believe he did not properly brief his successor when handing over command.

Calla Botha eventually became so claustrophobic from solitary confinement that he felt he would do anything to speak to anyone, just to get a visit. 'I said on a certain day that I would like to clear my conscience, that I was prepared to tell them everything that I knew, but I wouldn't speak to any of them but the general. They brought the general in by helicopter. He arrived there and he said: "Son, can we talk to you, what's your position?" And I said, yes General, I would like to discuss a few things with you. They took me out of the cells and treated me like a decent well-educated person. They allowed me to have a cup of tea and then they said: "Well, are you ready to speak?" I said yes, I would like to talk about the food, I would like to talk about my detention, my freedom and a few other aspects. "No," they said, "we'll change everything for you, but let's talk about the involvement of others." I said: No General, I have got nothing to say about that. Naturally, he expressed his disapproval and departed, but that hour of escape bought me another day.' [76]

The Section 29 detentions threw the CCB into turmoil. Chappie Maree was contacted in Germany and told to stay where he was. He was to put the company on hold and send his partner back to South Africa. He had no option but to break the news to his partner that he had become involved in a SADF front company.[77]

Deputy Commissioner Smit, in the meantime, returned to Windhoek and tracked down Charles Neelse. Neelse admitted working for Military Intelligence after being introduced to Nick Verbeek (Staal Burger) by Johan Niemöller. Burger had demanded Lubowski's 'testicles on the table'. Through Burger he was introduced to Johan Verwey (Ferdi Barnard) and they reconnoitred the homes of both Tjongarero and Lubowski together. Barnard had used a video camera hired from Edumeds, Windhoek, to film Lubowski's home. Deputy Commissioner Smit's enquiries confirmed much of Neelse's story.

On 2 December 1989 Major-General Herman Stadler, SAP Public Relations chief, hinted that more arrests could be imminent. He said a 'secret' right-wing organisation was closely linked to hit squad activities, and the police knew the identity of the forces behind it.[78]

On 3 December 1989 the story broke that Ferdi Barnard was claiming to be a member of Military Intelligence. This was denied by an SADF spokesman, who said there was no record of his ever having been employed in any capacity.

On 4 December 1989 Namibian Attorney General Pretorius told Deputy Commissioner Smit he was withdrawing the case against Donald Acheson. Smit persuaded him to fly with him to Johannesburg where they met CID Deputy Chief, General Jaap Joubert and Brigadier Floris Mostert. What he heard from them was sufficient to persuade him that Acheson should be further remanded.

On the 19 December 1989, according Defence Minister General Magnus Malan, 'the moment' he learned of the CCB's existence, he ordered SADF Chief, General Geldenhuys, to conduct an internal probe of the CCB with special emphasis on the Webster murder. Geldenhuys nominated Chief of Staff Intelligence, General Rudolph 'Witkop' Badenhorst for the job with Brigadier Krappies Engelbrecht, deputy chief of the Security Police, assisting.[79]

The inference was clear: neither Generals Malan nor Geldenhuys knew anything about the CCB's involvement in murders or other 'dirty tricks'. General Geldenhuys certainly knew about it and Police General Jaap Joubert said both Malan and Law and Order Minister, Adriaan Vlok, had known about it at least as early as 3 December 1989. This was confirmed by a letter dated 5 December 1988, regarding an officer who was 'retiring' from the SADF to join the CCB, signed by General Malan and produced in the Pretoria Supreme Court on 7 March 1991 in support of a civil claim. Malan denied that its purport sunk in when he signed it.[80]

General Badenhorst said that during their section 29 Internal Security Act detention, Calla Botha and Slang van Zyl had both admitted that Region 6 had monitored Roland Bruce White, deposited a monkey foetus at the home of Archbishop Desmond Tutu and blown up the Early Learning Centre. But they had denied knowledge of the Webster murder and Badenhorst said he was satisfied they had told the truth, but he omitted to ask them who had given the orders. When asked why he had not confronted General Webb and Colonel Verster, he replied lamely that both had already denied knowledge of the CCB's internal activities. 'I was keen to get finished [with the investigation] as soon as possible. I wanted to establish the CCB's involvement . . . but the head of the CCB denied it . . . in spite of the utmost efforts . . . we could not make any progress on the Webster murder . . . everyone we questioned denied that the CCB was involved.'

By the end of it all his internal probe into CCB's activities had been laid bare for what it was — a sham. It was just a cover-up. Badenhorst soldiered on, but having been completely discredited, he took early retirement in 1991.[81]

On 21 December 1989 Deputy Commissioner Smit recorded a second affidavit from Ferdi Barnard at Hartbeesfontein. This time he revealed that Staal Burger, Calla Botha, Slang van Zyl and Chappie Maree were members of the organisation's Region 6. The coordinator was Wouter J Basson. He named other cell members, Baker, Theo and Tilly Smit, but he had not met them. It was long after he had recruited Acheson that he heard Chappie Maree had become his handler. Whatever he knew about the Lubowski murder he had learned after the event. This included Calla Botha telling him Lubowski's murder had been a CCB operation controlled by Chappie Maree.[82]

Tensions soon developed between Witkop Badenhorst and Joe Verster. One night in January 1990 when Lieutenant-General Badenhorst, Major-General Webb, Brigadier Engelbrecht and Wouter J Basson were in his office, Verster told Badenhorst: 'General, you must know this. I don't trust you.' Verster said he tried to maintain a normal relationship with him, but Badenhorst lost his temper 'because I did not want to play along [with the SADF's Webster enquiry]. Badenhorst tried to chase me out of the office. I said it was my office and I stayed seated. He then got up and in front of Krappies Engelbrecht and Wouter J Basson, he assaulted me. I did nothing back — I just left him.' General Badenhorst denied the assault.[83]

Eddie Webb claimed that at this meeting, Joe Verster admitted ordering the assassinations of Dullah Omar and Gavin Evans. When testifying before the Harms Commission, though, Webb perjured himself by denying it to protect Verster. Verster, supported by Badenhorst, denied he had ever said it.

During the evening of 6 February 1990 Brixton detectives accompanied by Deputy Commissioner Smit arrested Slang van Zyl on a Section 29 Internal Security Act warrant. Smit interviewed him briefly at Brixton when he said he could 'help a great deal' as he was present when the planning for Lubowski's assassination was finalised. Smit, however, did not record a statement, intending to do so the next morning. By then, however, things had changed and he was blandly denied access to Van Zyl because he was detained under the security laws.

Deputy Commissioner Smit appealed directly to General Jaap Joubert, emphasising the importance of Van Zyl's testimony, but access remained blocked. General Joubert told him, however, that *if possible*, information would be made available to him. Smit enlisted the aid of Namibian Attorney General Pretorius to secure him access, but this also failed. In the end Deputy Commissioner Smit was convinced Van Zyl had been placed in Section 29 detention in a deliberate move to block access to him.[84]

On 16 February 1990 Slang van Zyl's wife, Brenda, brought an urgent action before the Supreme Court for the release of her husband, but it was dismissed. A tearful Mrs van Zyl insisted her husband had only obeyed orders and maintained that as 'Brigadiers and generals in the army gave him orders — they must explain.' The SADF, she said, had offered to assist her with legal costs and personal finance, but nothing had been forthcoming.[85]

Acheson: Going geographic

When Staal Burger and Chappie Maree reappeared from hiding after Namibian independence on 21 March 1990, Deputy Commissioner Smit asked the SAP to arrest them for murder in terms of a Namibian warrant issued on 2 February 1990. The SAP refused and both subjects declined to surrender voluntarily to the Namibian authorities.

Subpoenas were served on Ferdi Barnard, Calla Botha, Detective Sergeant Knox and Slang van Zyl for them to attend the High Court in Windhoek as witnesses in the case of the State versus Acheson, Burger and Maree. They all refused to attend.

On 18 April 1990 Acheson appeared before Judge Mahomed. Prosecutor-General Heyman applied for a further adjournment to allow him time to get the absentees to Namibia by 'diplomatic initiatives'. The judge ordered the proceedings adjourned until 7 May 1990, but the State had still not complied by then so the charge against Acheson was withdrawn and he was released from custody.[87] He had not entered a plea to the indictment, so he could be rearrested and charged again in the future.

Understandably, Acheson and his legal team saw no sense in hanging around for a Namibian holiday after his release, so they hightailed it to Johannesburg on the next available flight. Atchson went to Cynthia Leo's flat. An 'official from Jan Smuts' arrived at the flat and returned him to the airport where he stayed overnight in the transit area. The official version was that he was refused entry because he was a prohibited immigrant. The next morning he was joined by Cynthia Leo and his legal team, Pierre Botha, Ben van der Merwe and Herman Oosthuizen (from Windhoek) and they flew to Swaziland together.

In Windhoek, Johannesburg and at the Royal Swazi Sun hotel, Acheson volubly protested his innocence to the press and anyone else who cared to listen. His attorney reminded the press that the matter had not reached the stage where his client could have presented his defence — an alleged alibi proving his innocence.

The *Sunday Times* reported that for the rest of the week Acheson's legal team were engaged in 'frantic telephone negotiations' about his future, but they did not say with whom.

The day after his arrival an unidentified white male phoned Acheson and instructed him to go to a particular room and collected something. A cleaner opened the door for him, but there was nothing. The next morning he got a call asking if he had got the money. Acheson replied in the negative and was told he had gone to the wrong room — he should check the same room number in the hotel next door. This time he found R20 000 in R50 notes.

An attorney released a statement that Acheson had decided to go to America 'for a couple of months', then to Europe for a year, before attempting to re-enter South Africa. 'Don also considered a number of island groups to go to. I advised him to be practical — he is a cartoonist and the only place where there is an abundance of that work is America and Europe.'

The *Sunday Times* came up with the unlikely story that an Irish human rights organisation had paid for most of Acheson's legal bills, contributed towards his stay in Swaziland and presumably the expenses of the legal team accompanying him like 'minders'. Cynthia Leo, harping as usual on her 'very good divorce settlement', also took credit for paying his legal bills.[87] Acheson, however, admitted later that he was never billed for legal fees and he had no idea who paid them, but he suspected it was the CCB.

Acheson flew out of Swaziland on 10 May 1990, leaving Cynthia Leo behind. On the advice of Attorney Pierre Botha, he headed not for America, but for Athens. Botha, he said, told him to register at the Congo Palace Hotel and keep in touch with his office. The *Sunday Times* said he left Swaziland with Attorneys Ben van der Merwe and Herman Oosthuizen, but he travelled alone on the onward flight from Johannesburg.

In Athens, a woman with a British accent slipped him a toiletry bag containing US$4 000 in US$100 bills. He liaised, he said, with Jennes Scholtz by phone. From there he moved to Crete and then on to London and Scotland. He wanted to return to South Africa, he said, but was told to stay away for 18 months to two years — at least until the Harms Commission was over. He was reminded that he was still on the payroll. Eventually he insisted on returning to South Africa and Jennes Scholtz reluctantly agreed.

Attorney Pierre Botha, he said, was on the return flight with him on 9 August 1990, but they did not communicate. Whilst waiting at customs, he said, Botha muttered instructions for him to go to Leo's flat and await orders.

Acheson laid lay low for two months, expecting to be contacted and paid R250 000, the balance allegedly promised to him for going to prison. Like tomorrow, the money never came.[88]

In response to media reports that Acheson was illegally in the country visiting Cynthia Leo, 'informed intelligence sources' told *The Citizen* that although Acheson had been convicted of shoplifting, he had not been declared a prohibited immigrant. He was an Irish passport holder so was welcome to visit the country at any time without fear of arrest.[89]

On 9 January 1991 a journalist from *Die Beeld* recognised him in a hotel and interviewed him. The resultant story, in which he claimed he was innocent of Lubowski's murder and said he had been set up by a senior Namibian police officer with CCB connections, was published the next day. He suggested they wanted to hang him so the real culprits could go free. His only task in Namibia, he said, was to eliminate Gwen Lister who was regarded as a trouble maker. The organisation, he said, still existed.[90]

Acheson said he panicked when the article appeared. He phoned Attorney Jennes Scholtz and claimed the story was nonsense. Scholtz, he said, professed to believe him, but said 'they' were having a meeting about it in Pretoria and he should phone back in half an hour. 'I telephoned him again at 10:30 and he said they were mad at me. I repeated that I did not say what was reported in the paper. He repeated that while he believed me, they had found me guilty and I had to leave South Africa immediately. He did not elaborate on why I had to leave.'[91]

A day later, on 11 January 1991, the bloodied corpse of James Edward 'Peaches' Gordon, who had so boldly boasted to the Harms Commission that he had creamed off R25 000 from the CCB for operations never carried out, was found in a stolen car in Cape Town. In an execution-style killing he had been stabbed twice in the throat and shot in the head, back and chest. A couple who witnessed his killing were murdered a few months later and so was his suspected killer. The murders remain unsolved.[92] Whoever was responsible, his exemplary death was clearly designed to frighten others.

It certainly frightened Acheson.

A dawn telephone call warned him to 'run for it'. Former CCB operatives, under investigation for various crimes, intended to kill him for speaking to the press. Terrified, he skipped Leo's flat with only the clothes he stood up in, 50 cents in cash and an air ticket to Athens that he dared not use for fear of being tracked down.

He shaved off his distinctive moustache and begged sanctuary from the *Sunday Times*. They put him in a safe house. They tried to persuade him to make a full statement to the police, but he skipped and disappeared. A former CCB member described him as 'a walking time bomb' — because he could bring Anton Lubowski's killer to book and pull down the pillars on the CCB.[93]

The authorities, however, had no intention of letting him do a 'Samson' on them by pulling down their pillars of secrecy. His status as an Irish passport holder who 'could visit the country at any time without fear of arrest' suddenly reverted to his being a criminal not wanted in South Africa. On 6 February 1991 he was arrested and detained pending deportation as 'an illegal alien'. A spokesman said: 'At the moment he has been granted an opportunity to complete his personal affairs — this is being done under supervision.'

On 1 April 1991, instead of an underling, no less a personage than the Director-General of Home Affairs himself, Piet Colyn, announced that Acheson had been deported — put on a SAA flight for London. 'There was no more reason for him to remain here', Colyn said. 'His work permit expired in December. That's the end of it.'[94]

And so it was.

It appears highly likely that once he was overseas, Acheson was hunted down and murdered. He posed too much of a danger to the organisation to be allowed to live. Whatever the case he has not been heard of since.

As a footnote to Anton Lubowski, an attempt was made by the Minister of Defence General Magnus Malan to portray him as an SADF informer. The general opinion of operators in the security services was that it was a frame up. Ferdi Barnard said the Directorate of Covert Collection (DCC) had tried to recruit him but he was unrecruitable. He insisted that 'if he was an informer, he was an informer posthumously'.[95]

19

Civil Cooperation Bureau Countdown to Disbandment 1989/1990

Appointment of CCB accountant: October 1989

In October 1989 retired Brigadier Heinrich Pfeil was appointed accountant to Special Forces and the CCB. On tackling the CCB's accounts he used the SADF's *Financial System* — the procedure for internal audits approved by the Treasury and Auditor General — as a guideline. He was refused access to offices and was forced to rely on a single contact, Theunis Kruger, who could only be reached by telephone. Kruger provided him with computer printouts and evidence of expenditure, but because of the CCB's covert nature his access to files was strictly limited. Effectively, he could only compare advances against accounting documents to see if they balanced and check totals of cash drawn against the totals expended.

Those receiving cash signed a receipt which was countersigned by the Regional Manager who certified its correctness. It was impossible, however, to verify signatures or check that the recipients were actually entitled to the money received. The system was wide open to abuse and the money could have been given to anyone.

Brigadier Pfeil did what he could, demanding authorities for expenditure, querying the insufficiency of information on accounting documents and requesting explanations for advances unaccounted for. But he fought a losing battle and was given satisfactory explanations for only about 50% of his queries. Conducting an effective audit of monies expended on projects was impossible.[1]

An entry in Wouter J Basson's diary on 15 May 1989 said: 'Stay clear of any indications of a fight [in the financial] area. Financial problems in organisation . . .'.

Financial mismanagement, it seems, was the rule, not the exception.

On 24 November 1989 Colonel Alwyn 'Corrie' Meerholz, HC, was killed in a road accident a few kilometres west of Phalaborwa. Meerholz was a strong character and a fine soldier. He had previously been a CCB regional manager and had been posted back to 5-Recce as commanding officer in January 1989. According to several accounts received by the author, there had been a major clash of personalities between him and CCB's managing director, Joe Verster.

Nevertheless, it was said, he was hardly transferred in disgrace. He was a highly intelligent man who had edged himself into a powerful position — but to many in the SADF he knew too much. There was a story that when items for an operation had not been forthcoming — which he believed had endangered the lives of his subordinates — he stormed into Speskop and punched the commandant responsible for operational logistics. The author is uncertain if this occurred before or after he left the CCB.

The lower ranks and most of his Recce contemporaries loved him — in the way that hardened fighting men have always loved a brave and proven warrior leader. Others, it was said, including Major-General Eddie Webb, the then commander of Special Forces, respected and sometimes even feared him. When Corrie wanted something for his men

— whether at 5-Recce or in the CCB — he was never averse to pounding the table.

In his time — and no one would say quite when that time was — it appears he built up things in his unit and did things no one else had done before. Several sources in Special Forces described his position as 'unique' and advanced the theory that he had been 'taken out' because he knew too much.

According to Petrus Botes, Corrie Meerholz received a phone call at 02:00 on the morning he died. He got up and left in his car. Ten kilometres outside Phalaborwa, his car left the road, crashed into a tree and burst into flames.[2]

According to his brother, Johan: 'Corrie was on his way to Tzaneen [from Phalaborwa], where he had been called to pick up someone outside the police station. Apparently the person to be picked up was still waiting there long after the accident. No other vehicles were involved and the crash occurred on a long, straight road. He apparently left the road and hit a tree. It was a horrible accident. Corrie's BMW was totally burnt out. Even the tree was totally charred. He could only be identified by the *Rolex* watch on his wrist.'

His father said: 'I have been twice to the site of my son's accident, and I've seen the tracks where the car left the road. I've seen what is left of the car. It was folded completely around the tree on the side where Corrie was sitting.' [3]

Strangely enough, the investigation into the accident was done by the CID — odd procedure indeed unless foul play was suspected. It is unknown if the services of a forensic scientist was used.The investigation was still ongoing three months later but the results were inconclusive.

The SADF conducted its own internal probe. General Webb flew to Phalaborwa the next day, briefly visited the accident scene and then addressed the officers and men of 5-Recce. He said he had checked everything out and it had obviously been an accident and everyone should forget about it.[4] An SADF spokesman refused to comment on the internal findings when asked by the *Sunday Times* three months after the accident.

The author, a former senior police officer with 20 years experience in the investigation of traffic accidents, attended the scene some months later. The lack of trees on the verges of that stretch of road was particularly noticeable. It was on the road to Gravelotte, only 29km from Phalaborwa, so it appeared unlikely he had fallen asleep at the wheel. The most unusual features were that, firstly, the car caught fire and, secondly the blaze was so ferocious. Unlike in the movies, vehicles burn in only a small percentage of accidents and when it does happen, it is usually associated with insurance fraud.The cause of Meerholz's death was probably indeterminable, because his body was burnt to a cinder. Even the fillings in his teeth had melted. The generation of such intensive heat indicated that the fire had received some help from the addition of highly flammable material. This could, for instance, have been phosphorous oil which had been used by the CCB because it was particularly effective in setting cars on fire.

A Recce operator phoned the author in 1990 and gave him a genuinely friendly warning. He said there were rumours that the author had been enquiring about the death of Corrie Meerholz. 'I would be very careful if I were you as if you dig too deep it could prove dangerous to your health because certain international organisations with nasty habits might take you out'.

In retrospect, now that *Operation Dual* has finally been brought out into the cold clear light of day, it becomes a matter for conjecture whether or not Corrie had become a 'package that needed to be put in the system'. And which was the 'international organisation' the author's caller was talking about? Could it have been the CCB?

Whatever the case, Corrie would not be the last man with close CCB connections to die in suspicious circumstances. Petrus Botes, the Regional Manager for CCB's Region 2, survived a bomb explosion outside his business premises after he resigned from the CCB following a fall-out with Joe Verster. There were several more.

The likelihood of assassination in those times of change was not far-fetched. In the trial of Dr Wouter Basson that commenced in 1999 and is still ongoing at the time of writing, the prosecutor Dr Torie Pretorius applied to the judge for a ruling to protect the identity of certain witnesses. Dr Pretorius told the judge that the elimination of those threatening to expose covert operations or units featuring in the trial was done as a matter of course. The clear inference was that such risks still existed and had not passed into history.

At a passing out parade of national servicemen in Oudtshoorn, General Magnus Malan announced that the SADF would no longer mount cross-border raids. This 'particular role' was no longer necessary. 'Over the last few decades the situation demanded that the SADF engage in cross-border operations, not only in Angola but in other countries. These were preventative measure aimed at flushing out revolutionaries and terrorists.' Significantly — and probably referring to internal operations of the CCB, Military Intelligence and SADF surrogates — he said: 'During the height of the revolutionary climate in the mid 1980s . . . the Security Forces and especially the army, went out of their way to stabilise and normalise the situation. This led to a situation where, strictly speaking, we were performing tasks that did not fall within the ambit of our duties.' [5] He did not elaborate.

Joe Verster said that in January 1990, SADF Chief Jannie Geldenhuys had told him that State President F W de Klerk had given his assurances that there would be no witch hunt over CCB operations.[6]

By mid-January, however, the heat was on the CCB and Joe Verster activated an 'emergency plan' for all project and financial files to disappear. There was a general anxiety amongst the operators about the changing political situation and misgivings that they might be prosecuted. Verster's story about the activation of this emergency plan was extremely unlikely. He said he called an unidentified person at CCB's HQ on his 'care' phone and told him to move the files, contained in locked suitcases in a strongroom, to a safe place. The person, he said, could have been any one of 20 or 30 people who worked there and it would be impossible to determine where the files were taken to. CCB Chairman, General Eddie Webb, also denied knowing where the files went.[6]

Two and a half years later, in a letter to President F W de Klerk, Joe Verster said four generals, including General Kat Liebenberg who took command of the SADF after General Geldenhuys retired, had influenced their CCB subordinates to make the files disappear.[7]

Following a successful application to the Supreme Court in early February 1990, Calla Botha was released from Section 29 Internal Security Act custody.[8] Ferdi Barnard's release followed.

On 12 February 1990 the SADF admitted that the CCB was a covert operation of Special Forces aimed mainly at conducting surveillance of elements aggressive towards South Africa. It was not customary, the statement said, to comment on covert operations. This was followed by a statement in Parliament by Defence Minister Malan that the Chief of the SADF had suspended all the activities of the CCB pending the outcome of a judicial enquiry.[9]

On 15 February a police spokesman confirmed that two coloureds — obviously Isgak Hardien and probably 'Peaches' Gordon, had been arrested under Section 29 in connection with the blast at the Early Learning Centre.[10]

'Harms Commission of Inquiry into certain murders' appointed: February 1990

The judicial Commission of Inquiry 'into Certain Alleged Murders' with Judge Louis Harms as the sole commissioner, was appointed by the State President on 2 February 1990.

On 2 March Joe Verster was arrested and detained for questioning. He was released on 8 March by ministerial order along with Slang van Zyl, Theunis Kruger, Isgak Hardien, Ferdi Barnard, Calla Botha and whoever else remained under Section 29 Internal Security Act detention. The reason given was that they were required to give evidence before the Harms Commission.[11]

Ferdi Barnard found a bonus of R6 000 awaiting him at his attorney's office, with a message that he should go on two weeks leave. When he returned he was told to phone the Chief of Staff Intelligence, Lieutenant-General 'Witkop' Bardenhorst, on a vehicle phone. He did and it was arranged for them to meet at an advocate's office in Pretoria. Badenhorst told him the CCB was being disbanded. People would contact him and appoint him to the Military Intelligence's Directorate of Covert Collection (DCC). The transfer was arranged within two weeks.[12] Other CCB operators, including Staal Burger and Calla Botha, were also transferred.

During the long years of the National Party government's rule, commissions of inquiry, by reason of their ponderous procedures, had become instruments of a cover-up, rather than instruments of exposure. This was particularly true with the criminal activities of the CCB, because the appointment of a commission effectively removed it from the hands of policemen, who were doggedly determined to pursue their investigations to a satisfactory conclusion. It also gave the government time to fend off embarrassing questions on the shaky grounds that a matter was *sub judice*.

On 9 May 1990 Brigadier Floris Mostert told the Harms Commission he believed that at least three members of the CCB — Ferdi Barnard, Calla Botha and Joe Verster — were involved in the murders of David Webster and Anton Lubowski. Information to this effect had originated from several sources, but he had not been able to gather sufficient hard evidence to stand up in court.

'Do you want to arrest the whole organisation?' Judge Harms asked sarcastically.

'No, only those named in the case', Mostert replied.

'I must say, you astound me. If this is the way you use your discretion, you astound me', said Harms.

It was put to Brigadier Mostert that he wanted to use detention on Joe Verster as a means to 'wring a confession out of him'.

'No, not a confession', Mostert replied. He still wanted a lot of information from Verster including the true names behind the large number of aliases used in the CCB. 'I will not arrest him or the others again. I now have ministerial orders not to do it.'[13]

Judge Harms in his report, dismissed Brigadier Mostert's evidence saying that 'as a whole it was unsatisfactory and contradictory.'[14] This appears ill considered, remembering that if it were not for Brigadier Mostert and his team and the press (which Harms also strongly condemned), it is unlikely anything about the CCB would ever have seen the light of day.

The establishment of the commission led both Brigadier Mostert and Warrant Officer Rousseau to conclude that it would seriously prejudice their investigations into the Webster murder. Their fears became reality when a joint SAP/Harms Commission investigation team, headed by the SAP's General Ronnie van der Westhuizen and Colonel John Wright, raided Theunis Kruger's smallholding and seized CCB files. They grabbed more from the CCB's HQ at Renosterspruit Farm.

Van der Westhuizen and Wright, however, refused to allow Mostert and Rousseau access to them on the frankly ridiculous grounds that they were not members of the investigation team. Van der Westhuizen mollified them, however, by saying that if any documents relevant to the Webster murder were found, Warrant Officer Rousseau would get them once the commission's work had been completed.

It was a thin promise.

Instead, the files were subsequently returned directly to the CCB, without giving the investigating officers an opportunity to examine anything. Brigadier Mostert and Warrant Officer Rousseau heard later that the CCB had destroyed them in an 'emergency exercise'. Thanks to this action, many questions remained unanswered. Trying to continue the investigation into the CCB link once the Commission was disbanded proved hopeless. The evidence had either been destroyed or put out of reach. Brigadier Mostert remarked: 'I can't say what we would have uncovered if our investigation had continued.'

The influential Witwatersrand Attorney General, Klaus von Lieres und Wilkau, in overall charge of the Webster investigation, also expressed his concern to Brigadier Mostert that the Harms Commission would hamper rather than help the investigation. When he realised it was also taking over the Webster investigation, he remarked that it spelt 'the end'.[15]

The Hiemstra Commission established to investigate hit squad allegations by *The Star* newspaper effectively blocked other avenues of investigation. Brigadier Mostert explained: 'We can't proceed in this case in the normal way. Before a witness at either commission can be questioned by the investigating officers trying to solve murder cases, the police have to get permission from one of the presiding judges and then subpoena the witness'.[16]

Warrant Officer Rousseau's access to prime suspects in the Security Forces was limited at first, then completely blocked when General Jaap Joubert ordered him to cease all enquiries involving CCB operators. He warned the tenacious Rousseau that if he arrested any CCB operators they would quickly be released.[17]

Not surprisingly, Brigadier Mostert surrendered his quest in despair, announcing on 10 May 1990 that Ferdi Barnard, Calla Botha and Slang van Zyl were no longer suspects in the Webster murder.[18]

After the Harms Commission, Ferdi Barnard told Warrant Officer Rousseau that the CCB had used its agents' deeds in the line of duty 'as a sword over their heads' to force them to tone down their evidence. 'Obviously', Barnard said, 'if you have been in the game you have done certain things. They say straight to your face that you must cooperate or you're in the shit.' He revealed that Slang van Zyl and his family had been subjected to serious intimidation after his frank testimony to the Harms Commission. A notice advertising a large white sow and a small white piglet, and carrying his telephone number, appeared in a newspaper. The threat to his wife and child by chilling innuendo was obvious. Van Zyl got some 70 calls in response to the ad.[19] The Comops officers involved must have felt very proud and powerful. One wonders how powerful they are now!

Slang van Zyl and Calla Botha, the only Region 6 operatives who testified honestly before the Harms Commission without claiming privilege, were denied legal counsel by the SADF and had to pay their own fees. The SADF, however, paid the legal fees of those who refused to testify on the grounds of self incrimination.[20]

The Harms and the Hiemstra Commissions dragged on. Numerous witnesses were heard, many investigations were conducted not very efficiently and there was considerable legal pontificating. A report was finally issued in November 1990.

To the surprise of few of those who had been following the proceedings, Judge Louis Harms found there was no evidence that the CCB was responsible for the murder of David Webster.

There was another finding that should surely regularly return to haunt Judge Harms. He found that there was no evidence of a state-sanctioned police hit squad at Vlakplaas.[21] Judge Harms had earlier been guilty of a shockingly inappropriate outburst in London, when hearing the evidence of former Vlakplaas commander, Captain Dirk Coetzee. When Coetzee confessed to the Commission that he had murdered numerous political activists and cremated their bodies at the behest of the State, Judge Harms slammed back that he was talking 'a lot of crap'.[22] More seriously, without calling for expert medical testimony, he branded Coetzee as showing 'strong psychopathic tendencies', not to mention paranoia and delusions of grandeur.

The judge recommended in his report that the responsible attorneys-general give attention to the murders of Fabian and Florence Ribeiro, the bombing of the Early Learning Centre in Athlone, the plot to kill *The Weekly Mail* journalist Gavin Evans, the conspiracy to murder Dullah Omar, the disappearance of CCB documentation and other matters.

The media in Britain was highly vocal in its criticism of Judge Harms for using such unseemly language. The South African press, particularly the English language newspapers, adopted the same stance. Astonishingly, some of them, maybe because Afrikaans was the judge's home language, questioned whether he had realised the true meaning of 'crap' at the time of his outburst. The author finds it difficult to believe that a judge of the High Court would have experienced difficulties in this regard. If he did then maybe he should not have been appointed to the bench.

Shortly afterwards, of course, thanks to the media, the secrecy bubble burst. Coetzee was revealed as the murderer he had freely admitted he was to Judge Harms and the infamy of the Vlakplaas death squads reverberated around the world.

It is unfortunately not known how Mr Justice Harms viewed the stories in the media that reflected adversely on his behaviour. He never commented at the time, but he had made clear his views on the English language press when speaking to an *Afrikaanse Sakekamer* (Chamber of Commerce) meeting in Pretoria during 1989. He characterised the English language media's treatment of recent corruption scandals involving Afrikaans people as '*Boere* bashing'. He pointed out that for every corrupt official there was, in theory, at least two corrupt businessmen or members of the public. If there were no bidders the officials would have nothing to sell. Referring to the major scandal surrounding the founding of *The Citizen* newspaper, he said it was generally accepted that the row would have been over — possibly wrongly — if the facts about its birth had been revealed together with an appeal to national interest.

It appeared that Judge Harms had lined himself up with those who believed that the closing down of newspapers that did not toe the National Party line — and the spending of millions of taxpayers' rands to covertly open up new ones that did — was in the 'national interest'. He seemed to have overlooked the fact that press freedom is the most important nutrient feeding the roots of democracy. It is disquieting to speculate on what else the judge might have believed could be sacrificed to the expediency of 'national interest'.

Chris de Jager, MP, (Conservative Party Bethel) thought the same. Speaking to Parliament during the debate on the Justice Vote, he described Judge Louis Harms' remarks that the public should not be too concerned about corruption in South Africa as inappropriate and not at all reassuring. He called it disturbing that the judge had entered the field of politics with such remarks.[23]

CCB: Sanctions Busting

According to testimony by Chappies Maree during court proceedings in Johannesburg during 1990, part of his CCB brief was to operate as an agent covertly importing high-tech military equipment into South Africa. In early 1990 he undertook a four month trip to six European countries brokering business deals for the acquisition of such material for the SADF.[24]

CCB disbanded: 31 July 1990

On 31 July 1990 SADF Chief, General Jannie Geldenhuys, announced that the CCB had ceased operations and was being disbanded. Its affairs were being administratively wound up, which meant that the transfer, dismissal and other aspects, like benefits due to members, were being finalised. Businesses and other assets were disposed of. CCB members were being transferred from Special Forces to the Army.

The saga, however, was far from over. Some of its 200 members accepted the retirement packages offered or transfer to other branches of the SADF. Others, however, demanded retirement packages which the SADF considered excessive.

A few announced intentions of launching civil claims against the government for sums amounting to some R30 million. In response the government announced it intended introducing legislation to indemnify the State against such claims. This indicated that the claims were probably valid, because otherwise they would have told the men to go to court and do their worst. No such legislation was introduced, but it would be a long saga before settlements were finally reached.

Ferdi Barnard also falls: June 1998

Ferdi Barnard would probably never have been brought to justice but for the determination of State Advocate Anton Ackermann SC, and Senior Superintendent Casper Jonker's crack team of incorruptible police investigators. Because of their professionalism, Barnard's luck ran out on 1 September 1997 when he was arrested for murder (2 counts), attempted murder (3 counts) fraud (6 counts) and other charges of housebreaking, robbery, arson and the illegal possession of weapons — 24 counts in all including the murder of Dr David Webster.

The charge sheet alleged Barnard had monitored Webster on CCB orders for some time before his death and that on 1 May 1989 Calla Botha drove the car while Barnard pulled the trigger. Named as co-accused were Slang van Zyl, Joe Verster, Staal Burger, (the late) Peaches Gordon, Calla Botha and Wouter J Basson.[25]

By then many of those who would have been called to testify had died, many in strange circumstances. Cornelius du Plessis, the most important eye witness, had died in Johannesburg General Hospital, apparently of natural causes. One can only wonder whether he was poisoned with one of the great variety of undetectable toxins that were available through *Project Coast*. Ferdi Barnard's criminal associates, the brothers Corrie and Johannes Goosen, died in separate motorcycle accidents in 1996 and 1997. The girlfriend of Mark Francis — another criminal associate of Barnard and Eugene Riley whom they had beaten to death with a baseball bat — Carol Anne Harris, was kidnapped and murdered by two unknown men in 1994. Riley, in turn, was himself found dead with a bullet in his head in 1994. Peaches Gordon had been murdered in Cape Town. 'Crunchy' Johnson, another witness, was attacked and murdered by intruders at his Pretoria home the day before he was due to testify against Barnard. There were far too many deaths for all of them to have been coincidental or accidental.

On 4 June 1998, despite the loss of these witnesses, Ferdi Barnard was sentenced in the Pretoria High Court to two life terms for the murders of David Webster and Mark Francis and to a further 63 years on 23 other charges. Amongst those charges was the attempt to murder Dullah Omar.

After sentencing he told reporters he would 'follow in the footsteps of President Mandela . . . When President Mandela was sentenced in the Rivonia trial he did not go the next day and turn on all his comrades. I'm going to take a page from his book. I'm not going to turn on my friends. I will just serve my time . . . I bear no grudges, not even against those who testified against me . . .'[26]

20

De Klerk's political bombshell 2 February 1990

President F W de Klerk's bombshell: 2 February 1990

On 2 February 1990 President F W de Klerk, when opening Parliament, in a watershed speech said only negotiations among the representative leaders of all sectors of the *entire* population would ensure lasting peace in South Africa. To achieve it the government was taking certain steps, the most important of which were:

1. The banning orders on the ANC, PAC, the SACP and their subsidiary organisations were lifted forthwith.
2. People serving prison sentences arising from their membership of those organisations would be released.
3. Restrictions on 33 banned organisations were rescinded.
4. Emergency Regulations relating to the media and the reporting on education matters were lifted.
5. The death penalty, in future, would be limited to extreme cases and all executions were suspended until Parliament had made a final decision on capital punishment.

The announcement, a radical reversal of National Party government policy, astonished the world. It released the brakes of an unstoppable roller-coaster. On 11 February 1990 Nelson Mandela was freed from prison after 27 years.

De Klerk commented: 'I want to emphasise that there can no longer be any doubt about the government's sincerity to create a just dispensation based on negotiations. I call upon Mr Mandela and all other interested parties to make their contribution towards a positive climate for negotiations.'

Mandela expressed confidence that negotiations between the ANC and the government would soon take place. In a gesture of what would become his personal crusade for reconciliation between the races, he committed the ANC to a policy of allaying white fears of domination by the black majority. At the same time, obviously until the talks bore fruit, he recommitted himself to supporting the 'armed struggle' and the continuation of economic sanctions against South Africa.[1]

South African Army's contingency plans to take control of South Africa

President de Klerk's speech left the SADF stunned. Commandant Gerrie Hugo, by then Intelligence Officer at Group 8 Headquarters in East London, was one of them. The higher command levels exhibited a deafening silence. It seems that not only the lower ranks had been left in the dark, but the higher echelons as well. Everyone talked about it. Some shrugged and said that it was up to the politicians. Others not at all favourably inclined towards the reform issue adopted a 'to hell with it' attitude.

After waiting for a few days without receiving any clarifying signals, Commandant Hugo decided to seek guidance from higher authority. He despatched signals to Eastern Province Command in Port Elizabeth and to Army Intelligence in Pretoria to enquire who the enemy was in view of the self-evident changes brought about by the unbanning of the black nationalist parties.

What was the new policy the military should adopt towards these entities?

The deafening silence continued unabated. The idea of changing policies from killing to kissing was apparently just too much for the SADF's general staff to handle. In the end comprehensive instructions on how the recently unbanned African nationalist parties should be handled did not come through for about four months.

Nevertheless, within a month of De Klerk's announcement a coded signal addressed to all Group Officers Commanding and all Group Intelligence Officers was received at Group 8 Headquarters. It had been despatched through intelligence and not operational channels. Although given the highest security classification of 'Top Secret', it was emphasised in the body of the signal that its classification was considered to be far higher than that. It was marked strictly for the eyes of addressees only. Despite this Colonel Thys Buitendag thought it essential to involve the Officer Commanding East London Command in the planning, because much of the contents of the signal dealt with his physical area of responsibility — places like Duncan Village and so on.

Another indication of its secrecy was an instruction that an office should be set aside for the planning of its directives. Before it was used, however, the office had to be debugged. The only people with the facilities and the correct equipment to do this were the Security Police. This was highly embarrassing because the Security Police were colleagues on the local Joint Management Committee, where all top secret operations were planned. Now they had to tell them they needed an office debugged because the planning they were undertaking was too secret for them to be told anything about it.

Commandant Gerrie Hugo recalls that the signal had peculiar wording. It said that Groups were to prepare detailed contingency plans to facilitate a declaration of martial law in the event of 'the blacks revolting'. The planning involved the mobilisation of Citizen Force troops, clamping down on township areas, the organisation of logistics, the control of food supplies and so on. It also involved moving into and taking control of the independent homelands, but contingency plans for that already existed. They had been routinely prepared long before when Brigadier Joffel van der Westhuizen was still in control of Eastern Province Command.

While the military, wherever they are in the world, have a preoccupation with contingency planning for even the remotest of possible scenarios, both Gerrie and his officer commanding, Colonel Thys Buitendag, recognised that the signal was something far removed from the mundane and routine.

Gerrie Hugo was no fool. The message told him that a group of generals were instructing their subordinates to plan for a military takeover of the country, including the homelands.

Anyway, orders were orders, so they called in the Security Police to debug the room chosen for the planning. There were many questions and many sideways glances from the Security Police, but eventually the debugging was achieved and the planning was completed.[2]

This was most likely the root from which rumours of a military coup began to circulate.

Consternation at Mandela's release was felt in both military and police circles. As Colonel Eugene de Kock said: 'There was confusion and a sense of total sell-out by the government. Some of the police generals were fast off the mark ingratiating themselves, obviously already thinking of themselves, but those of us on the ground knew that we were sold out totally. We had just to look at what had happened in SWA/Namibia to see a mirror image of what was about to happen to us. There were generals who were in favour of Mandela's release, some who were against it, but the majority sat around lamely muttering to themselves the whole day, hitting at their calculators to check their pensions, and dumping the past as fast as possible. As for those who had carried them up until then, especially those at Vlakplaas, well they constantly told us everything was okay. But we knew it was not. Previously we had been the dependables: now we were the expendables.'[3]

A political coup d'etat

Arguments that the State Security Council was a sinister cabal unhampered by the rule of law have often been heard, but have always been denied. Every minister who served on it, excepting former Law and Order Minister Adriaan Vlok — who was caught with his fingers in the blowing up of the Khotso House cookie jar and given amnesty by the TRC — has denied being responsible for illegal actions.

Yet if the SSC was so harmless, so impotent, what was it doing there? This author believes it was indeed a government within a government which ran the country the way it saw fit and rode roughshod over the meek and mild well-disciplined elected representatives who were supposed to speak in Parliament for the people.

It was a cabal, long run by the four permanent political representatives — State President P W Botha, Foreign Minister Pik Botha, Defence Minister Magnus Malan and Law and Order Minister Adriaan Vlok — and the service chiefs. When President F W de Klerk took the chair as president, he replaced P W Botha, but other than that the membership remained unchanged.

After President de Klerk held out the hand of reconciliation to the ANC in February 1990, there were persistent rumours of an imminent coup either by the military and the police supported by the right wing or by the right wing supported by the military and the police. All were just as persistently denied.

If such a coup was a possibility, its most likely chance of success would have been if it had been orchestrated by the political heads of the Security Forces, namely the Defence Minister and the Minister for Law and Order — both permanent members of the State Security Council. If it had come to the crunch, because they were in hands-on control of the generals, their authority would surely have counted more than that of the State Security Council's chairman, President F W de Klerk and the self-described moderate, Foreign Minister Pik Botha.

De Klerk has never admitted concerns that a right wing coup could have been in the offing, although subsequent events have shown the dangers of one were omnipresent. Nor has he ever conceded that his position as president had become well nigh impossible due to cabinet and party divisions. But he said in his autobiography that he was never properly briefed by the responsible ministers about covert organisations run by the military — and the police Unit C10 at Vlakplaas.[4]

Sacking Malan and Vlok outright would probably have precipitated a chiasmic split in both his cabinet and the National Party. Worse still, it might have sparked a military or police *coup d'état* and a right wing revolution. De Klerk, however, took a cleverly devious route. Instead off sacking them he retained them as ministers, but shunted them sideways. Effective from 1 September 1991 Malan was moved from Defence to the innocuous Housing and Works and Water Affairs and Forestry Departments and Vlok from Law and Order to Correctional Services (Prisons).

General Malan took it on the chin as befitted an old soldier. 'Now I have been called to serve in a different capacity, I will do so with devotion', he said. But after being barred from the wafting smell of gun-smoke for a mere 17 months, his devotion had dissipated along with his enthusiasm and he retired from politics in February 1993.

Vlok taking it more emotionally, burst into tears.

Maybe it was because he suspected that the grim-faced Mussolini-type portraits of himself in a heroic pose which he had caused to be hung in the foyers of all police stations would end up being consigned to the tip. He was correct.

Eminent political analysts like Professor David Welsh, of the Department of Political Studies at the University of Cape Town and Professor Willem Kleynhans, a political analyst and former head of Political Science at the University of South Africa, agreed that the sideways shifts were effective demotions. They believed it was a sop to the ANC — a way to defuse the crisis in relations besetting the government.

Senior officers of both services were upset at losing their ministers. Senior military officers regarded Malan as Mr SADF. He had led them as commander, then minister, and had moulded the SADF into the formidable fighting force it was. Senior police officers spoke of Vlok as an exceptional minister, who had shown leadership and loyalty and had always done his best for the force.

Professor Lawrence Schlemmer, Director of Political Studies at the Wits Business School, was unsure of the effect it would 'have on the morale of the army'. Prof Herman Giliomee, head of Political Studies at the University of Cape Town, called the changes an 'astonishing performance by the State President', but suggested their replacements would 'have a hard time winning the trust of the people around them'.[5]

In the end no one twigged what President de Klerk had really achieved.

In one fell swoop he had kicked the permanent chairs on the State Security Council out from under the posteriors of both Malan and Vlok. Their successors in office, Roelf Meyer (Defence) and Hernus Kriel (Law and Order) — both moderates — effectively neutralised any danger there might have been of a *coup d'état*.

But can anyone seriously suggest that Vlok or Malan would have led a coup?

Malan told Hilton Hamman he had had approaches to help organise a coup.'A lot of people say to me: "You had a lot of power." But that's not the way you approach it. You're there as part of a team, you're serving the leader — and now they expect you to get rid of the leader and get rid of the team and take over. My whole way of thinking is that you serve the government of the day and that this is a democratic country', Malan told him. 'If you want to change it, you use the ballot box. You don't change it through military might. I had *a lot* [author's emphasis] of approaches from South Africans living in South Africa, saying: 'We'll supply the money, you do the coup." My reply was always: "are you trying to escape from the present situation by arranging a coup and are you then sure you'll accept the new situation or are you just trying to find an escape route? Forget it. Do it through the ballot box." '

Malan said the approaches were usually from South African business people. Some were well-known but no top or really influential people were included. 'The first approach was always jokingly. They did it light-heartedly to test the water — once you test the water you can get serious. So they always tested the water first. I still maintain the military I belonged to would accept my way of thinking and would never be part of a coup. You might find the odd person talking about it but in his heart of hearts he wouldn't say: 'Let's do it!' [6]

Malan was a minister of state, initially Minister of Defence and later the Minister of Housing and Works and Water Affairs and Forestry. On his own admission several approaches were made to him to mount a coup. The plotters tested the water to see his attitude. His attitude was surely ambivalent, otherwise they would not have continued. Did he immediately report the approaches and the apparent grumbles of discontent in the Defence Force to President de Klerk — his political head and the Commander-in-Chief of the Defence Force — so that action could be taken, as was his duty? He certainly did not tell Hamman that.

The truth was it was out of line that a minister of state should have involved himself in discussions about a coup even if it was done idly.

Sir John Harrington said it better than this author:

Treason doth never prosper: what's the reason?
For if it prosper, none dare call it treason.

When questioned by the author about his sideways shift of ministers at a public meeting to promote his autobiography in early 1999, De Klerk avoided being pinned down by directing his questioner to his autobiography. But in it, making no mention of the SSC, he said revelations arising from the Harms Commission of enquiry into political murders made the removal of Malan and Vlok from their security portfolios unavoidable. His reasons for not sacking them outright from his cabinet were because, firstly, he 'wished to avoid any impression' he was surrendering to ANC demands; secondly, because a political storm was looming over long-term government aid to Inkatha; and thirdly, because both ministers had 'solemnly and repeatedly' assured him they had no personal knowledge or involvement in 'totally unacceptable criminal activities — such as murder, assassination, torture and the instigation of violence . . . '[7]

The reasons advanced by the author, in combination with De Klerk's reasons, most likely reflects the truth. It would be difficult to believe De Klerk did not hold the view that the SSC — even in the amended form he had shaped it into when taking power as President — had run out of control and, more to the political point, that it had outlived its usefulness.

Interestingly, he also wrote in his autobiography: 'If I had known then what I know now, I would certainly have exercised greater vigilance within the State Security Council during the P W Botha period — although in those days the ability of outside ministers to influence the decisions of the security departments was strictly limited.' Like the born and bred politician and lawyer that he is, he carefully avoided any suggestion that any SSC baggage from the P W Botha days had been carried forward to his presidential era[8] — although that clearly was the case.

Whatever the situation, he quietly finished the job by disbanding the SSC altogether before the election that brought the ANC to political power in 1994. He effectively broke the SSC's stranglehold on government and returned the bewildered SADF, SAP and National Intelligence Service securocrats reluctantly to desks at their own headquarters. The machinery for planning a total response had been blown away by the winds of change.[9]

Referendum, CODESA, CODESA 2 and all that

On 17 March 1992 the last 'exclusively white referendum' was held to provide De Klerk with a mandate to continue reforms. If he received a majority of support from white voters, he would take it as a mandate to enter into binding agreements at CODESA — Convention for a Democratic South Africa. If the vote conveyed a thumbs down to the government, he would resign.

An overwhelming 69% of the white electorate voted 'yes'.

The first hiccup occurred in June 1992 when the ANC and its allies withdrew from CODESA. Meanwhile, the government was holding bilateral talks with the Azanian People's Organisation (AZAPO), the Conservative Party (CP) and the Pan Africanist Congress (PAC) to discuss conditions under which they would enter into constitutional talks with the government.

When the government and the ANC agreed to resume talks in March 1993 at what became known as CODESA 2, further problems arose when the Inkatha Freedom Party (IFP) declined to attend because the Zulu king had not been included in the process.[10]

The PAC and its armed wing, the Azanian People's Liberation Army (APLA), took a limited role in the CODESA 2 talks because of their refusal to suspend the armed struggle. Unlike the ANC which immediately engaged in 'talks about talks' with the National Party government, the PAC took the stance that negotiations could only be undertaken from a position of strength. Instead of negotiating a constitution before an election was held, it wanted a coalition of the unbanned liberation movements to form themselves into a Patriotic Front. This would provide a 'level playing field' for them to fight the Nationalists in an election for a constituent assembly. The elected assembly, which would obviously consist overwhelmingly of Patriotic Front members, would then devise the new constitution.

This was totally unacceptable to the National Party government for it would, in effect, be an unconditional surrender by itself. The more pragmatic ANC, for the same reasons, regarded the PAC's aspirations as a pipe dream.

Not getting its own way, the PAC stood aloof from the CODESA negotiations.

In the end, PAC president Clarence Makwetu only announced his organisation's suspension of the armed struggle in January 1994. This and the decision to take part in the elections had been resolved, he said, by the organisation's national working committee 'in the light of the promulgation of the Electoral Act' of 1993 and after resolutions had been passed at its December 1993 annual congress. Makwetu, however, refused to rule out further APLA attacks as 'it would take some time' before all cadres could be notified of the decision. Besides, although he avoided mention of it, the PAC had resolved to abandon the armed struggle *only* when all the land occupied by whites had been returned to the African people.[11]

But before all this could happen, and before there was an election based on universal adult suffrage, South Africa still had a long way to go.

21

MK's Operation Vula And its aftermath 1987-1993

Although the ANC's *Operation Vula* was only revealed in July 1990, its roots were firmly embedded in the past.

At the ANC's National Consultative Conference held at Kabwe in Zambia in June 1985, the ANC's president Oliver Tambo called for the struggle to be brought into white areas. Civilians would no longer be safe from the crossfire.[1]

This was followed in 1986 by a report prepared by the ANC's Commission on Strategy and Tactics headed by Joe Slovo. Under the heading 'Action against the Enemy's support base' it said:

> 'We have always gone out of our way to avoid a confrontation along racial lines and we will continue to do so. But those among the white community who constitute the core of its social base for race domination are increasingly being mobilised in support of brutal suppression. In particular, the enemy has begun to transform almost every farm into a military outpost. Certainly in the countryside there are more and more blurring [of the] distinction between what is civilian and what is military.
>
> 'In many other ways, both in the urban complexes and in industry, it is also militarising its civilian support base.
>
> 'Up to now our dedication to the avoidance of racial confrontation, has often prevented us from dealing telling blows against the enemy and his installations for fear that white civilians would be caught in the cross-fire or be killed or injured in the vicinity of an enemy installation. We have even inhibited ourselves inflicting blows against whites who are ostensibly civilians but who are, in fact, part of the military, para-military or [another section of] the security machine.
>
> 'The escalating brutality perpetuated daily against our people is now creating a new situation. We can no longer allow our armed activities to be determined solely by the risk of such civilian casualties. We believe that the time has come when those who stand in solid support of the race tyranny and who are its direct or indirect instrument, must themselves begin to feel the agony of our counter-blows.' [2]

The first public hint to South Africans that an escalation of violence was pending, occurred for those who listened, on 16 February 1987 when the ANC's *Radio Freedom* broadcast the following:

To the accompaniment of martial music:

'The time has come to take the battle to the white areas. The African National Congress calls on our workers in the factories, mines farms and suburbs to form underground units and combat groups and take such actions as sabotage in our places of work.'

To the accompaniment of martial music with a background of explosions:

'Disrupt the enemy's oil, energy, transport, communication and other vital organs.'

Return to martial music:

'We call on our people to spread the consumer boycott to all areas of our country. Organise well-planned demonstrations in white suburbs and central business districts.'

To the accompaniment of machine gun fire:

'The time has come to carry out systematic attacks against the army and police and the so-called 'defence units' in the white areas. We must start organising well-planned raids on armouries and arms dumps of the army, police, farmers and gun shops to secure arms for our units.

'In this battle we call on the white democrats to participate in mass action in white democratic movements. Spread the voice of democracy through your anti-apartheid organisations and win as many whites as possible to the side of freedom and non-raciality. We must intensify campaigns against conscription, repression, the tri-cameral system, racist education and the mass challenge by the army and police in the townships.'[3]

About this time an element of the ANC's National Executive Committee, its members drawn almost exclusively from the SACP's Central Committee, created the President's Committee (PC). The PC was tasked to form components to conduct covert activities both within South Africa and externally under the code name *Operation Vula*. Its purpose was to create internal structures and underground bases for the establishment of a 'People's Army'. It would be trained and provided with logistical support so that it could play the major role in a 'People's Revolt'. The PC also became known as the *Vula* Head Committee.

The ANC's Commission on Strategy and Tactics, chaired by Joe Slovo, reported in 1986 and discussed the relationship between 'People's War' and insurrection.

'By People's War we mean a war in which a liberation army becomes rooted amongst the people who progressively participate actively in the armed struggle both politically and militarily, including the possibility of engaging in partial or general insurrection . . . the actions of the enemy's forces and our own determines the protracted nature of the struggle in which we need to reduce the enemy's resources, reserves and endurance, whilst gathering our own strength to the point where we are capable of seizing power.'[4]

Siphiwe Nyanda had been in charge of MK's Transvaal machinery since 1983 or before. His house had been targeted in the SAAF's *Operation Skerwe* (splinter) air strike on Maputo's Matola suburb on 23 May 1983. It was not hit.[5]

Nyanda was definitely based within South Africa on 20 May 1987, because he ordered a team of three MK operators to plant a car bomb with 100kg of explosives outside Johannesburg Magistrate's Court in tandem with a decoy limpet mine. The objective was to draw policemen from the court by detonating the limpet mine and hopefully kill many more in the bigger detonation. The second explosion was timed to take place minutes after the first. The trap worked and four policemen, Constables Weyers Botha, Andre Duvenhage, Kobus Wilkins and Chris Botha, were killed. Another three policemen and 11 civilians were injured.[6]

Some time during 1988 Nyanda was in Moscow with Mac Maharaj. Arrangements had been made, with Soviet assistance, to smuggle them back to South Africa for the purposes of *Operation Vula*. It was decided as a cover to put out that both were to remain in the Soviet Union. Maharaj, who suffered from knee problems, had already spent several weeks in a Soviet hospital in 1985. Disinformation was spread that he had developed tuberculosis and was under treatment at a sanatorium in a remote place in the eastern Crimea. Maharaj gave the Soviets a batch of letters for posting to his family at regular intervals. Nyanda's cover was simpler. There were numerous military training institutions in the Soviet Union, many of them far from Moscow. *Africa Confidential* of 8 September 1989 picked up the story and reported that 'leading Umkhonto commander Siphiwe Nyande [Nyanda] has left the beleaguered military to study in the Soviet Union, disenchanted with the ANC leadership'.[7]

'Only Tambo, Slovo and a handful of others knew the truth', Kasrils said.

Joe Slovo flew to Moscow to brief them. With forged passports and identity documents provided by the Soviets they made their separate ways to South Africa where they would rendezvous and begin operations.

According to Kasrils, Maharaj and Nyanda (known as Comrade Joe) 'had successfully built underground ANC structures and were at last providing the kind of leadership that had been absent for many years. They had a variety of disguises, safe house and identity documents to assist them in their work. A computerised telephone communications network, using encoded messages, kept them in close touch with the external leadership. They were also in contact with Mandela and with leaders of the internal democratic movement [the United Democratic Front (UDF)].'[8]

Doubtless this was true, for Nelson Mandela had been in regular contact with Oliver Tambo in Lusaka by smuggled letters, even during the harshest days of his imprisonment. By December 1988 he was living in a cottage in the grounds of the Victor Verster Prison at Paarl. He was allowed regular visitors and subjected to a bare minimum of authoritarian hassles.[9]

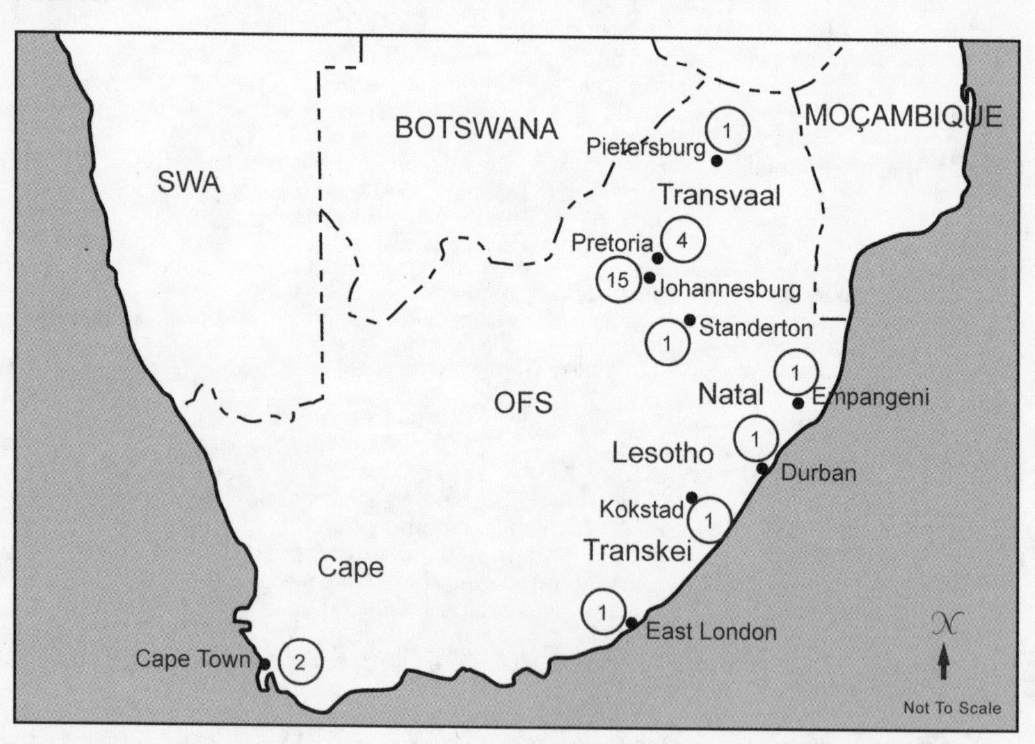

Twenty-three bomb blasts were attributed to MK between 23 January and 2 July 1988.

There was a marked increase in MK activity in 1988. Between 23 January and 2 July there were 23 bomb blasts around the country. They were flagrantly targeted at civilians: 20 were killed and 160 injured in the blasts. Amongst the fatalities were two babies — one newly born and the other aged 12 months. In two instances, the bombers were themselves killed when devices exploded prematurely. Amongst the targets were railway stations and snack bars. On 2 July a car bomb planted in a German luxury car exploded at the Ellis Park Stadium in Johannesburg after a rugby match just as the crowd streamed into the streets. Two were killed and 35 injured.[10]

MK chief Joe Modise and Ronnie Kasrils visited Moscow in March 1988. They told the Soviets that MK had carried out more than 250 operations in 1987.[11] This figure and the effects on the South African government of MK's actions were optimistically exaggerated. The optimism, however, was tainted ' by numerous problems: lack of discipline, the leaking of information by captured fighters — and especially the appearance of Askaris , turncoats who created great difficulties for MK members returning to South Africa.'[12]

US Assistant Secretary of State, Chester Crocker, writing about it in 1992, said: 'The armed struggle never amounted to much more than a costly inconvenience to the Security Forces — an inconvenience that was gradually eliminated during the course of the 1980s.' [13] The official South African figures for the 18 months ended June 1988 revealed that the Security Forces had killed 86 and captured 333 MK and APLA guerrillas inside the country.

Kasrils, by his account, only joined Maharaj and Nyanda in the latter stages. '. . . no sooner had I joined', he wrote, 'than events began to speed up'. On 2 February 1990 President F W De Klerk lifted the ban on the ANC, the SACP and 54 other organisations. The following week Nelson Mandela was released from prison.[14]

The ANC's director of information, Pallo Jordan, announced that the ANC would not halt its military campaign because of the unbanning. 'We have always said that the notion of unilaterally abandoning the armed struggle is out of the question. Any cessation of hostilities will have to be negotiated and will arise out of a mutually binding cease fire.'[15]

After three months of haggling and posturing by both sides in efforts to gain advantages before talks took place, it was agreed during one-on-one discussions between President de Klerk and Nelson Mandela that talks between the government and the ANC would begin in May. To facilitate this the government granted temporary immunity to members of the ANC's National Executive Council (NEC). This allowed them to return from exile to take part in negotiations.

Both Maharaj and Kasrils were members of the NEC. Kasrils had been appointed in July 1988. He became only the second white member after Joe Slovo, who despite being MK's chief of staff, had only been appointed to the NEC in 1985.

The granting of immunity posed a security problem for *Operation Vula* because both Maharaj and Kassrils had already returned! They could not reveal themselves. They were instructed to leave South Africa covertly and report to London or Lusaka. After that they would make a public return. Kasrils, using a false passport and posing as a businessman, flew to London. Both returned to South Africa as planned. Siphiwe Nyanda had remained in place because he was not an NEC member.

In early May 1990 an ANC delegation including Nelson Mandela and Walter Sisulu held talks with the government at Groote Schuur, Cape Town, to discuss obstacles to negotiations. While the ANC did not say outright that the armed struggle would be suspended, both parties agreed on a common commitment towards a resolution of the existing climate of violence. A document, the Groote Schuur Minute, intended to facilitate the negotiation process, was signed by the government and the ANC on 3 May 1990.[16]

Hot on its heels, the SACP held a secret Consultative Conference at Tongaat in Natal on 7 May 1990 to plot the way forward. The minutes make it clear there was a general consensus amongst those attending that the space created by the onset of negotiations should be utilised creatively. An extract reads:

> 'Taking the thesis seriously, we should be wary that we do not think that now with negotiations, we have arrived in Babylon. The legal space now creates the possibility of this kind of uprising much more than before.

'Those who do not sign the cease-fire are not bound by the terms of it. We are fighting the regime and its subsidiary forces and from our side, it is our forces. In a cease-fire it will be these two parties who will agree on something.

'We need to bear in mind that there is tremendous uncertainty about a smooth and simple negotiated solution. We dare not allow ourselves to believe that the path to the transfer of power to a democratically elected government of the people will proceed unhindered. Because of this, we must build our revolutionary forces side-by-side with the negotiation process.These revolutionary forces cannot simply be legal ones. Neither can they simply be forces that apply pressure on the government so as to force it to make the necessary concessions demanded [by] our negotiating team. But a great deal of work is going to have to be planned and organised in a clandestine way. This brings us to our strategic perspective. Where is the limit to the pressure of the masses to be exerted against the existing power block? The only logical answer is a nationwide uprising . . . '

'We must steadfastly avoid the situation where we feel that everything and all things depend on negotiations. A strategy which must encompass the uprising perspective means that we must have a strong U/G [underground] machinery which is an active rather than a passive 'reserve' function. Last but by no means least, it is the underground that insures the ANC's political leadership and control over the 'Revolutionary Army' and 'Popular Militia'. It is not possible for the legal ANC and its branches to handle this essential task or (sic) [on] the ground.'[17]

In *The African Communist*, Journal of the SACP, number 12, First Quarter, 1990, an article headed 'A single spark can start a veld fire: The perspectives of the armed seizure of power' appeared. It was contributed by Siphiwe Nyanda, using the pseudonym Tebogo Kgope. The following illuminating extracts are quoted:

- 'Seizure is a forcible act. It is clear immediately [when] we talk about seizure that we envisage struggle entailing varying degrees of force. There can be no peaceable or friendly seizure . . .
- 'What, therefore, are the main forms that our movement identifies? The first is mass mobilisation. It aims at militant and united mass action, for central government power. Passivity does not contribute towards seizure of power. Negotiations for power are not part of an agenda to increase the militancy of the masses. Negotiations can only be conducted from a position of strength derived from militant action and other revolutionary activity by the oppressed . . .
- 'If the masses of the people in certain quarters have been negotiating with the regime's representatives and councillors over certain issues, it is not, as certain people would have us believe, an indication of the strategy of negotiations. It is because our people, through militant action, have won a certain measure of real power, that forces the regime and its puppets to negotiate with them . . .'
- 'A spark can start a veld fire. Insurrection, in order to take place, relies on a stimulus. The objective conditions can be present, but this is no guarantee that an uprising will take place. The suffering, frustrations and grievances are pent-up until a stimulus arises. The stimulus or "spark" can come in many forms. It can arise from some high-handed action by some official, sparking protests which spread; the killing of a child; a massacre; unpopular legislation; rent evictions etc. It can even arise out of the most unexpected circumstances like a training accident. The uprising in 1988 [possibly 1948] started with a tearoom brawl. Hence the famous saying by Mao Tse-tung: "It is only the tiny spark that sets the prairie afire." This stimulus can also come from the revolutionary movement making a call, the response to which triggers a chain of events leading to insurrection or a direct call to the masses to rise . . .' [18]

In early July 1990 the Security Police, acting on information received, moved to conduct search and seizure operations in Durban relative to *Operation Vula*. This resulted in the arrest of Siphiwe Nyanda and other local and foreign-trained MK operatives. Several secret compartments were located in Nyanda's Toyota Cressida sedan. A M3A1 ,45 calibre sub-machine gun with an optical night sight and a silencer was found in one of them. More than 1 000 documents, including the minutes of the SACP's secret conference on 7 May 1990, and approximately 4 000 pages of computer printouts were seized. On analysis it became apparent that the ANC was proceeding to utilise the space and freedom of movement created by the negotiating process to go ahead with plans to bring about a revolutionary and violent overthrow of the government. There was also an indication that the group had kept a 'hit list', subject to continual updates, although the list itself was not found.

Plans to bring about an insurrection using a People's Army were at an advanced stage. Natal (as it was then) had been divided into zones, each with its own 'zonal' or area commanders. Military training courses, identical to those given to cadres in Angola, Tanzania and East Germany, had already been presented and were ongoing for recruits in the various zones. Training manuals were found on the computer discs seized.

Six operational safe houses and two covert offices were located in Durban, three safe houses in Johannesburg and another three in Cape Town.

The following armaments were seized: 7,2kg of TNT, ten Soviet 158 mini limpet mines, 21 F1 hand grenades, two SPM limpet mines, four Stechkin 9mm machine pistols, three Makarov 9mm pistols, one AKM 7,62mm assault rifle, a large quantity of electrical and mechanical timing mechanisms and detonators, two-way radio sets and components for car bombs.

Documentation retrieved indicated that the following had been ordered or had already been distributed to operatives: Strela ground-to-air missiles, RPG7 rockets launchers, radio controlled detonating devices, SPM limpet mines, mini limpet mines, hand grenades, plastic explosive, Stechkin 9mm machine pistols, AK47 7,62mm assault rifles and Scorpion 7,65mm machine pistols. It became apparent that a large quantity of war material had been removed from a secret underground cellar in a Johannesburg 'safe house' before the police could get to it.

The difference between *Operation Vula* and previous MK operations within South Africa was the high level of secrecy maintained within the ANC's external high command, the expertise used in its planning and execution, and the sophistication of the equipment, including computers, utilised. The high level of 'need-to-know' was obviously instituted because the ANC's external structures had been so deeply penetrated by the Security Police. The measures succeeded and the organisation operated for more than two years before the police broke it up.[19]

Arrest warrants for Maharaj and Kasrils were issued because of their involvement. Maharaj was arrested and detained for a while, but the warrant for Kasrils was never executed. Siphiwe Nyanda was detained until November 1990. After being released, he served as MK's chief of staff from 1992 until 1994 when he was appointed to the new South African National Defence Force as a general officer. After a brief stint as Commanding Officer Gauteng Command, he was appointed Deputy Chief of the SANDF. He became its first black commander in May 1998.[20]

The cracking of *Operation Vula* by the Security Police did not signal the end of efforts by the ANC and SACP to engineer an insurrection. The following document was prepared probably in the middle of 1993. The organisation was still heavily infiltrated, which explains how the document came into the hands of the Security Police.

SACP discussion document on the prevailing situation: mid 1993

Comrades:

Let me be very frank and let us have a closer look at what is going on in our country at the moment. First of all, I want to give you some background which is important to keep in mind in order to understand what is taking place now.

In 1988, when the Regime and their National Intelligence came to us, in London, with the approach that they wanted to negotiate and that we should stop the armed struggle, it sparked a lot of debate in our own ranks about the possibility of negotiating. Some people argued that we were getting nowhere with the armed struggle and the chances for an insurrection were very small. It was suggested that we should look at ways to get the leadership back into the country. We were sitting there so far away and not in a position to keep ourselves up to date with what was going on inside the country. The leaders of ANC structures within the country, like the UDF and the MDM, were increasingly following their own heads and were less inclined to adhere to the guidance of the leadership in exile. Our logistic lines were stretched very long and we were experiencing considerable difficulties in getting men and material into the country and many of our people were getting arrested and locked up in apartheid jails.

The Regime was leaving no stone unturned to suppress us. The Security Forces, armed with the Draconian legal measures formulated by the Securocrats in 1984 -1987, could do anything to wipe us out. But, in spite of all this, our internal struggle was making good progress and we knew that the power of the people was there and that it was waiting to be re-activated by us. We also understood that the chances of utilising the power of the people to affect an insurrection were slim.

So, the discussion in our own ranks went on and we started strategising around this point and it was decided that we should embark on a dual strategy: To negotiate but to use this opportunity to intensify our armed struggle to prepare for an insurrection. The Regime was very weak at this point and this was when we held our 7th annual congress. The path to power, which was and still remains one of our most important documents on strategy and tactics, was adopted at this congress of 1989. Still today, we are using the same strategy document, with minor changes to it. But, we realised also that if we entered into negotiations, the Regime would relax its security measures and that the result would be a lot of confusion amongst the Security Forces themselves. We know that through the creation of this confusion we would be able to come into the country and prepare for an insurrection.

Operation Vula was launched as the final phase of the struggle and we were so confident that this strategy would be successful. So, we entered into the negotiations, but we never changed our objectives. We said: All right, we will enter into negotiations and we will make a few compromises, but negotiations will be a form of struggle to weaken the Regime — because they have the security power and we have the political power, lying there waiting. We needed to find ways of destroying their security power, while at the same time, building our political power. It was also important that we should build our armed capability at the same time. This is the reason for our double agenda — to talk and to fight.

Talking means fighting and the armed struggle also means fighting. It is similar to what the PAC is trying now recently. But they are too small and too weak to have any real success. We realised that the Regime was with its back against the wall — facing economic collapse, sanctions were really getting tough. This was an opportunity for us. We realised that we could build our strength on their weakness. To be honest, our strength was multiplied by the Regime's weakness. We knew that De Klerk was looking for national and international recognition in order to achieve economic revival and that he would compromise a lot to be successful.

Building the underground.

Our first priority was to build the underground and to arm the masses, to prepare them for an armed insurrection. *Operation Vula* formed the backbone of our strategy. *Vula* was partly successful because large quantities of arms were smuggled into the country at the time and most of these caches are still in place and available to us.

MK, the SDUs and the youth in general were prepared to form the underground military structures. It was at this time that we introduced the manual "For the sake of our lives" for the purpose of training SDUs. It is still in use today.

The defeat, which the SADF suffered in Angola, had a seriously demoralising effect on the rank and file of the SADF. De Klerk's talks coming so soon after the defeat, only served to increase the disillusionment amongst the Security Forces. In addition to that, the police were steadily losing credibility and could no longer control the violence in the Townships. This was a serious setback and the plan had to be shelved.

Emphasis on negotiations:

Negotiations now became the main terrain of the struggle. There were different opinions within our own camp: There were those who said "No, we should not let this interfere with our objectives and the armed struggle should be intensified" and there were others who believed that we can obtain power through negotiations. But our underground actions continued, although on a smaller scale than before. Then the Harare conference was called, to pave the way for negotiations. At the conference it became clear that the Regime would accept anything as long as they got us committed to negotiations. We though at first that they had a hidden agenda — we did not trust them. But the SACP played its normal strategising role and a plan was mapped out for the conduct of the negotiation process and the period of transition which would have to develop from the process.

A major victory:

The unbanning of the democratic forces in South Africa and the release of Nelson Mandela and other political prisoners were a major victory for the freedom struggle. The return of the exiled leadership to the country gave our strategic planners the opportunity to assess the prevailing situation within the country at first hand. This afforded the SACP the initiative to mobilise and unleash the masses in their thousands. By means of mass protest action, we were able to prove the extent of our support to the whole world.

Then we played one of our trump cards: We suspended the armed struggle — but Comrades, I say again suspended. The suspension of the armed struggle served to "blur" the mandate of the Regime's Intelligence Organisations, and they had to change their priorities. The confusion, which has been created in this manner, is actually giving us manoeuvrability, which we might otherwise not have had, to establish and to strengthen the underground. We have plenty of evidence that these organisations are no longer as effective as they used to be.

Then we embarked on a full programme to weaken their security power and to expose their underground activities and their hidden agendas and to distract attention away from our own activities of which *Vula* is an example. The exposé of the CCB and the Askaris provided us with a golden opportunity to challenge the Regime on this terrain of hit squads and hidden agendas. We were able to sensationalise the issue to such an extent both locally and internationally by means of our contacts in the media, that De Klerk had no alternative but to disband these dangerous elité forces.

Attention was deflected from *Vula* to the Regime's hit squads in this manner. Naturally in the process the Security Forces were discredited to such an extent that our accusation that they were illegitimate was accepted universally. You must remember that although we had the political power, the fact that the Regime controlled the Security Forces still put us at a disadvantage and it was essential that this power had to be weakened by any means at our disposal in order to strengthen our position so that we could achieve our main objective which was, and still is, to seize power.

Building and strengthening the SACP:

During 1991 and 1992, we concentrated on building our constituency be means of mass action. The SACP used this period to confirm and develop our control over the National Democratic Revolutionary Forces. We secured a leadership position in the ANC; COSATU; SANCO and in Women's, Youth and other organisations. By means of COSATU we established a mass action machine which could be set into motion at will — whenever we felt that such mass action would serve as the necessary pressure to force the Regime into compromise at the negotiation table. (You will remember how we held the CODESA talks hostage with our constant threat of mass action).

As the talks progressed at CODESA, we realised that the balance of forces was not in our favour. De Klerk had a lot of Allies at CODESA, i.e. the IFP; Bophuthatswana; Ciskei and others and they were able to out-vote us in some of the working groups that were established. We had to act quickly to break this developing uniting amongst the enemy. It was clear to us that there was no joint strategy between them and that it would be possible to drive a wedge between them, provided we could find a way of buying the time that was necessary. Boipatong provided us with the right opportunity. (You have to break eggs if you want to make an omelette).

Insurrection in our grasp:

During the deadlock at CODESA, we unleashed a campaign against De Klerk's allies — IFP; Bop and Ciskei. Our mass action campaigns went from strength to strength. In July/September of 1992, there was much talk of the insurrectionary perspective amongst our leaders.

Ciskei was to be a test ground for the insurrectionists within our party. The aim was to develop a domino effect of partial insurrections in Ciskei, Bop and KwaZulu. Venda and Transkei were ours already and if we could manipulate events so that the other three collapsed, it would be possible to instigate a national insurrection. We went for this option because we were beginning to lose our mandate for negotiation from the people. There were many indications that the people were becoming very impatient with the slow pace of change in our country. The people had many sacrifices and yet they were still not seeing any benefits from the unbanning of the liberatory (sic) organisations.

Resumption of talks:

The Bisho event and some significant compromises made by the Regime in the record of understanding moved us back to the table. When we went back to the table, the Regime had been divided from at least some of its allies, especially the IFP.

Our immediate objective was to pull the Regime closer to our side so that COSAG could be destroyed.

We offered the Regime the 'Sunset Clause' which was conceived by Comrade Slovo. The whole idea of power-sharing was offered to the Regime and although they wanted ever-lasting power-sharing, a compromise was achieved when they agreed to power-sharing during the transition, because we needed some experience and expertise to be transferred from them to our people to enable us to govern the country. We were not surprised when the Regime took the bait which we held out to them. Some opportunists in the Regime's camp would do anything to retain the position of power.

What the Regime did not know was that while we offered the 'Sunset Clause', we at the same time launched *Operation Sunrise* which is in fact low intensity armed activity within the country, to ensure that our struggle through the masses and specifically through the worker forces, will emerge. This strategy is based more or less on the *Vula* formula, but not so strongly on the armed activity as *Vula*.

The Regime agreed that the negotiations must be pushed into top gear. In order to get rid of the spoilers, we have to take the Regime with us and bind them to us as much as possible. Our immediate objective, at this stage was to:

- Get the TEC in place in order to dominate the transitional process.
- Secure an election date in order to demonstrate progress to our constituency.

As part of our strategy, we kept the Regime happy by handing out "Lucky Packet" compromises and by promising the lifting of sanctions. At the same time we stood firm on the issue of federalism and self-determination. On these two issues there can be no compromise as we are working for a unitary socialist South Africa!

In spite of the death of Chris Hani, which created another opportunity for the realisation of the insurrectionary perspective, we decided to continue with our negotiation strategy (COSAG was too strong at this point and the Security Forces had not been weakened sufficiently). In any case, if we had followed this option, we would have driven the Regime back into the arms of COSAG. We were happy with the major compromises which had been made by the Regime so far and we knew that we would be able to push for more, faster. The Regime would do anything to keep the process going and this meant that we were negotiating from a position of strength.

In our bilaterals with the Regime, we reached agreement on the TEC [Transitional Executive Council] ; the election date; media commission and electoral commission. This meant that our pre-election strategy had worked and the foundation for victory had been laid. Once the election date had been set, all other negotiations became of less importance. Our move to allow the lifting of economic sanctions was simply the carrot with which we wanted to entice the Regime into the TEC. The Regime was blind to the long term implications of their decisions. Their only "success" in the negotiations, the lifting of sanctions, was actually an ANC handout and therefore constituted no victory in the real sense of the word. Now the time had come to divide the spoilers so that even they would become weaker.

The AVF and the formation of the Freedom Alliance:

It was at this point that a red light started flashing . . . A new debate was opened in our ranks on the issue of the manifestation of reactionary forces, under the banner of the AVF. This is a threat which we have to analyse very carefully, especially now that the Freedom Alliance has been formed. We surely do not want to repeat the mistakes of Angola and Mozambique.

Our immediate strategy to deal with the Freedom Alliance:

- Expose the Freedom Alliance as a force with an insignificant constituency.
- Continue efforts, with the help of the Regime, to discredit and divide their members.
- Taint them in the eyes of the people as a force that cannot provide a constructive alternative (the only solution which they offer is war).
- Discredit the IFP and other black groups with their constituencies on the issues of aligning themselves with white racists.
- Utilise the TEC mechanisms in order to render them irrelevant to the transitional process.
- Direct all intelligence gathering capabilities of the Regime against the Freedom Alliance, thus giving us more manoeuvrability in our underground work.
- Build the image of the National Party nationally and internationally, to enable them to re-capture their constituency and thus weaken the right wing.
- Discredit the Freedom Alliance as warmongers, so that big business will not support them and their resources will be limited.
- Mobilise the AAM, so that international support for the Freedom Alliance will be limited.
- Ridicule their call for self-determination as a continuation of apartheid. Discourage people who want to join them by creating the spectre of 'enemies of the state' — a concept which is psychologically difficult to accept for the ignorant whites.
- Ensure that the Freedom Alliance does not succeed in creating a split between the 'Doves' and the 'Hawks' in the NP.

The way forward:

All the mechanisms are in place to achieve victory:

The TEC will give us effective control over the National Party government — specifically over the Security Forces. Although the multi-party negotiating forum has achieved international recognition, it would be better to have the IFP back in the process. At the same time it would divide the Freedom Alliance.

We will deal with the reactionaries after the elections but we will do what we can during the TEC to frustrate all their efforts.

We must get MK more organised in the National Peace Keeping Force. At the same time we must spare no effort to get our arms back into the country. The struggle must be intensified. This means that they have to be defeated politically by all the means and resources available to us. The SDUs and civics must play their role in achieving the total liberation of these areas.

In the meantime our election list has to be prepared. We must see to it that the majority of the candidates are SACP members. It is also important that the Tripartite Alliance be kept intact in this period. COSATU must not be allowed to break away. We must intensify the workers' struggle through COSATU.

The right people have to be prepared for the right jobs after the elections. A decision has to be taken on who must go to Parliament and who should remain outside in order to drive the National Democratic Revolutionary machinery after the elections.

The ability of the Security Forces of the Regime to counter our efforts has to be minimised. We must also guard against the possibility of attempts by the Security Forces to expose our agenda. It should be relatively easy to control the Security Forces via the sub-councils of the TEC.

We must be seen to make compromises on certain relatively unimportant issues while we must stand firm on others like the clauses in the Bill of Rights which pertain to land and property rights. Such issues can only be finalised after the reconstruction phase. (We cannot allow farmers to own land that belongs to the people).

We must persist in obtaining consensuses on the need for major reconstruction after the elections. Affirmative action has to be implemented in all walks of life especially with regard to the training of senior civil servants and our own parliamentarians.

Our demand for the reincorporation of the homelands has to be repeated and everything should be done to achieve this, even before the elections. We should concentrate on those homelands which refuse to implement the TEC laws and which refuse to participate in the elections. If we have the interim constitution and the boundaries of the future regions have been demarcated, there will be no reason for them to remain outside the process. (At the moment Ciskei provides a good opportunity for weakening the Freedom Alliance, with the imminent court hearing of Oupa Gqozo's orders to kill [Charles] Sebe. The outcome of the court case could provide us with an opportunity to demand the immediate reincorporation of the Ciskei.

Of course the major players of the Freedom Alliance like KwaZulu, Bop and Ciskei will all lose their power-base as well as their access to resources after the election. This will be turned to our advantage. In the meantime we have to prevent any efforts by members of the Freedom Alliance to secede from the rest of our country. The Regime and the NPKF [National Peacekeeping Force] must be used to deal with such an eventuality. The threat of blocking their funding must constantly be held before these homelands.

December 16 must see the start of unprecedented mass action. This must be utilised to precipitate election fever. We will deal with the IFP and other black reactionaries in the townships. Of course the violence will increase. Our people will have to be ready to defend themselves. De Klerk hopes for a capitalist up-swing after the lifting of sanctions, but this will not materialise before the elections. Any new investments must be accepted on our terms. Investors have to accept the reconstruction idea.

We must accept that we will not be able to control the SDUs and other grassroots structures. Only the fittest and the strongest will survive. Our underground structures will have to deliver during this period. We must secure a ⅔ majority. A big event just before the elections will help greatly — perhaps something similar to the death of Hani will do it for us. The anger that such an event will precipitate amongst the people will serve as a powerful stimulus. There are those amongst us who argue that if the situation around the elections turns out to be unsatisfactory, such an 'event' could serve to create an insurrectionary 'moment' during which we, who will be ready, will be able to seize power immediately.

Ramaphosa's Kabal (sic) Group disagrees with this perspective, because they believe it is important that the method and the result should be acceptable to the international community.

The SACP/ANC after the elections:

The process which I have described to you before i.e., the National Democratic Revolution, which is aimed at getting into Parliament and rendering the present government ineffective by changing its status to that of a minority group in the transitional government, is regarded by us as the First Phase of the transformation of South Africa from a capitalist state to a socialist state. A similar strategy was used with great success in both Cuba and Vietnam.

The Second Phase will start right after the elections. If all goes according to plan, we will have majority control in both the Constituent Assembly as well as in the Interim Government. We do not need the majority of the votes for the SACP because the ANC NEC will in actual fact be our shadow parliament. (This is why we have no problem with fighting the elections under the ANC banner — it serves our purpose perfectly that all concerned think that they are dealing with a nationalist movement!) No individualistic approach in parliament by ANC members will be accepted. Anyone who does not toe the line will simply be replaced. Comrade Suttner's document of 14 October 93 explains how we will be able to control parliament from the outside.

We see that the transformation from capitalism to socialism will take place during the Second Phase. The main pillar of the transformation is the reconstruction pact. The capitalists have agreed to this in principle because they want to reconstruct in order to improve profits. That is of course not our aim. We want to use reconstruction as a vehicle with which to transform South

Africa into a workerist (sic) state — not to make unjust profits (by exploiting the people!) The bosses will have to realise that there is no compromise position somewhere between Capitalism and Socialism. There can only be Capitalism or Socialism — and we are well on the way to establish Socialism. Comrade Jeremy Cronin explained this concept in his paper : "The Boat, The Tap and the Leipzig Way." No compromise can be made.

Even if we do not achieve the majority in parliament that we hope for, it will not be a serious setback, because we will still be writing the constitution in the same manner in which our people are taking the lead in the negotiations at the World Trade Centre.

During this period we will concentrate on removing their reactionaries from the civil service and from the Security Forces. This in itself will pave the way for the insurrectionary/Leipzig option if we are not happy with the constitution. It is however, very important that the alliance should remain intact during this time. Our members are very capable and as Comrade Suttner points out: The SACP will manipulate the constitution writing process as well as the reconstruction process to our own advantage in order to realise our ultimate aim of a Socialist South Africa.

All the emphasis during this phase will be placed on the workers' struggle under the guidance and direction of COSATU. It is vital that the power-base of the workers be broadened so that people can be empowered and thus break the shackles of apartheid. Our promises to the people must be fulfilled in the shortest possible time. Those who doubted the vanguard role played by the SACP in the National Democratic Revolution, will have to come to grips with our leading influence at this time, because this is where our strategy will be implemented to the last letter.

Some political observers and even some intelligence organisations say that we are insignificant because our membership is around 40,000. Through the years we have recruited quality members who possess the skills and the discipline required for dedicated party work. Besides, in all the workerist revolutions which have taken place, it was always just a handful of communists who saved the people from oppression.

The possibility of a counter-revolution:

There can be no doubt that some of our actions which will be taken during the rapid transformation phase will anger elements within the NP as well as other conservatives. They will then join the reactionary forces. The Freedom Alliance (if it sill exists by then) will grow with the support of other people who benefited from apartheid and who will now be asked to pay the price for reconstruction. We plan to accommodate De Klerk's constituency during the Government of National Unity phase.

One of the aspects of the rapid reconstruction phase is to empower our people to assist us in dealing with the reactionaries. The majority of weapons for so-called self defence will not be in the hands of a few whites anymore. Our citizens force and commando systems will be well established in the townships and in the rural areas. In the work place our workers will deal with the reactionary elements in business. Some of the reactionaries like Bop, Ciskei and KwaZulu, will be marginalised when they lose their 'independence' in the new regional system. The Afrikaner homeland will never be allowed. The reason is that we know that the reactionaries will use it as a base from which to launch attacks against us. We must not let all their expansionist ideas bear fruit. We will divide and rule.

The final phase:

Once the socialist struggle has been completed, the third and final phase will start. This is a long-term strategic phase and a lot of strategic thinking must still go into this phase, in order to transform our socialist South Africa into a classless, Communist State. Great care will have to be taken to avoid a repetition of the mistakes made in the Soviet Union and Eastern Europe.

We will develop a unique system for South Africa by learning a lot from the Cuban experience. We have already sent a delegation to Cuba to study the structure of Castro's office so that it can be implemented in a similar manner in our own country.

But, we cannot see South Africa in isolation. We have to consider the struggle in a regional context — the SADC countries have to be included in our vision for a socialist South Africa. This could develop into an Africa concept.

The ultimate plan for world politics exists. After the East European debacle many people regarded it as the death of socialism. But we see these developments as a temporary setback and we are already strategising to develop the struggle between the southern impoverished countries and the rich northern countries. It is a well-known fact that capitalism is in a deep crisis. As more people realise that capitalism isn't the answer, a rebirth of international socialism and communism will become possible.

The armed struggle:

We need to deal with this very carefully. The armed struggle has always been a 'Golden Threat' (sic?) throughout the National Democratic Revolution phase and it will also be like that during the transition after the election. This strategy of low intensity warfare in the townships and of arming the masses, suits our strategy. Some elements in the ANC are totally opposed to it, so that we have to accuse the enemy of low intensity warfare to justify this direction. You must know that the insurrectionary possibility always exists. Insurrections are normally not planned and are usually coupled to a big event — but we must be ready for it. Say for instance the death of Mandela. If there is anything sinister about his death, it could suit us at that stage.

Currently, we are involved in several underground operations to reach our political objectives. There is specifically an operation against the reactionary elements. *Operation Hunter*, and we hope to get rid of the bad elements in the Police. With the help of POPCRU we will be able to make a success of this. We also have *Operation Prickly Pear* which is aimed at enemy agents in our own ranks — intelligence agents who are trying to gain information from us. One of the big operations, which includes all the SDUs and in future will incorporate the Peace Corps and the Marshals as well as elements from MK, is *Operation Breakthrough*. This National Democratic Revolution, through the first phase, to protect our leadership, to defend our people and to deal with reactionaries. There are some smaller operations i.e. *Operation Trench* which is aimed specifically at the IFP in Natal. So, most of these operations are based in the Transkei and co-ordinated in Johannesburg. The most important operation for us goes with *Operation Sunrise* — it will carry us through the second phase of the revolution. The sun is setting for the Regime and the sun is rising for us. We will make sure that our military power supports our political strategies through this period.

These actions will increase after the elections, but they will then be legal. We will use our Special Forces' abilities in the Security Forces to deal with the reactionaries and to achieve our political objectives.

Dangers for us:

There are certain dangers which lie ahead and for which we must prepare:

- The formation of a coalition between the NP and the Freedom Alliance.
- If the NP loses the bulk of its constituency to the Freedom Alliance.
- If the Freedom Alliance obtains international recognition.
- If the Freedom Alliance receives significant support from big business or if formations like the ZCC join the Freedom Alliance.
- If civil war breaks out before the elections can take place.
- The unwillingness of international forces to intervene in Africa.
- If we get less than 50% of the vote in the elections.
- If the agenda of the SACP is exposed to the international community.
- A right-wing *coup d'etat*.
- If De Klerk is forced to call a referendum and then loses his mandate to negotiate.
- If the Freedom Alliance develops rapidly and bonds so strongly that we cannot divide it.
- If elements from the Security Forces join the Freedom Alliance in large numbers.
- If the MPNF loses international recognition.
- If the NDR loses momentum after the elections so that the transition to socialism does not take place as intended.
- If the Alliance breaks up after the elections and individual factions decide to 'Go it alone'.
- If the PAC gets much more support than expected.
- If a major anti-communist black party is formed within the ANC.

- If the international community declares the elections as not free and fair.
- If we fail to attract substantial investment after the elections.
- If the people decide that socialism will not serve their expectations.
- If our own MP's become self-centred and put their own interests before the interests of the people.[21]

22

Goodbye Lennox, Hello Oupa
Ciskei
1989/1990

In the late 1980s the Ciskei homeland, along with Transkei, became an easy target for crooks, confidence tricksters and those after an easy buck. Corruption, aided and abetted by Ciskei officials — with President Lennox Sebe in the vanguard — was endemic. It was not as if Sebe, like his neighbours the Matanzimas in Transkei, was hindered by such mundane constraints as the balancing of budgets. Thanks to the South African government, this was totally unnecessary because it was only too happy to assist as long as the apartheid credo was kept alive. In the fiscal year 1988/89, for instance, Ciskei's total revenue amounted to R191 million. To balance its budget the central government happily provided subsidies of South African taxpayer's money amounting to R910 million — almost a billion rand — to tidy things up.[1]

The central government's Minister of Home Affairs, Stoffel Botha, refused a visa to multi-millionaire Italian national, Vito Roberto Palazzolo, who had been convicted of drug smuggling and sentenced to a prison term in Switzerland. Following this in March 1987, Peet de Pontes, the National Party MP for East London and Palazzolo's attorney, in a flagrant abuse of political power used his contacts with Lennox Sebe to secure his client permanent residence in the Ciskei. This effectively circumvented Palazzolo's South African status as an illegal immigrant and allowed him to enter the country legally.

The ground had apparently been softened by Douw Steyn, Ciskei's ambassador plenipotentiary, who had visited Palazzolo at his Swiss prison in September 1986. A company, Papillon International, was formed in which Palazollo and De Pontes were partners. Papillon was created as a vehicle to move funds into various business ventures proposed by De Pontes and his associates. This included a bank in the Ciskei for which Lennox Sebe verbally granted them rights.

Steyn told the Harms Commission, that was investigating 'certain alleged cross-border irregularities', that Palazzolo had offered to invest US$2 million in the Ciskei in exchange for citizenship. Because of the deteriorating (financial) conditions in the territory ' we had to clutch at straws'. De Pontes sat down and assisted Lennox Sebe with the drafting of legislation that enabled Palazzolo to apply for citizenship — after fulfilling a residence qualification of a mere two weeks! Palazzollo got his citizenship but the US$2 million payment failed to materialise. De Pontes, however, was handsomely rewarded by Palazzollo for his work.[2]

Peet de Pontes was later charged with multiple counts of theft, bribery, fraud and forgery.

The Harms Commission also investigated the affairs of South African businessman Albert Vermaas who had extensive financial interests in the Ciskei. In March 1989 his estate and his companies were sequestrated, except for the Ciskei-registered Eurobank, after he was charged with 22 counts of fraud involving R300 million. In May 1989 at the first creditors' meeting of his liquidated Ciskei-registered Eurotrust, claims amounting to R28 million were accepted.[3]

The much sought-after casino rights in the Ciskei, after considerable haggling and protracted negotiations, were finally split three ways after Brigadier M Deyzel who was working undercover for Jalc Holdings — the Military Intelligence front company — personally intervened with Lennox Sebe. As a result Sebe split the rights among Lentin (a subsidiary of Jalc), Sun International and the Ciskei administration.

In 1988 the Ciskei administration declared 19 February a public holiday — Heroes' Day. This was to commemorate the CDF's 'heroic' repulse of Transkei's *Operation Katzen* attack in 1987.[4]

Political violence: Ciskei

UDF-inspired political unrest in the mid 1980s had soon washed over South Africa's invisible frontier with the Ciskei. There had been a marked escalation in detentions of members of political opposition groups and civic organisations under section 26 of the Ciskei National Security Act. Most detainees were associated with such organisations as the United Democratic Front (UDF), the Azanian National Youth Unity, the Border Council of Churches, the Council of Union of South Africa (CUSA), the Ciskei Teachers Union, the East London Youth Congress, the South African Allied Workers' Union (SAAWU) and the SADA residents' association.

In late 1989 Lennox Sebe displayed some ambivalence by releasing from prison the Secretary-General of the UDF's Border region, Rev Arnold Stofile, on 'humanitarian grounds'. He called it 'a contribution towards a new dispensation in the broader southern Africa'. Stofile had been serving an 11-year sentence.

There were numerous signs indicating that the Ciskei's Security Police were running out of control. Six of its members were awarded prison sentences ranging from two to 12 years for culpable homicide and for attempting to defeat the ends of justice in connection with serious assaults on prisoners. In some cases security policemen had been acquitted by the courts, but it became patently obvious that abuse was widespread.

This was so obvious that Ciskei's former ambassador plenipotentiary, Douw Steyn, announced that he intended to approach the International Red Cross and appeal to them to inspect all places of detention in the territory because he feared for the lives of detainees, including that of his successor V Mafani.

The Ciskei administration retorted that an inspection had been conducted in September 1986 and that the Red Cross had had 'nothing but praise for the conditions, facilities and amenities in Ciskeian prisons'.

In April and May 1989, though, the Ciskei Police were ordered to pay thousands of rands against damages claims for assault, torture and police brutality. Amongst the claimants was a man whose arm was left paralysed when he was assaulted while taking part in industrial action.

Plans for Ciskei coup: August 1989

General Charles Sebe's Umtata home was attacked with hand grenades on 11 July 1989. Following this incident and after discussions involving Pretoria, Bisho and Umtata, it was agreed that Charles Sebe, Namba Sebe and Lent Maqoma would be allowed to move to South Africa and continue their political exile there. Their presence in Umtata had become too much of a bone of contention between the two homelands.[5]

Rainer Maria Moringer, an Austrian businessman and long-term permanent resident of South Africa had between 1984 and 1988 tried to establish a small aircraft factory in southern Africa. His first approach was to the Transkei government and he had several meetings with President Kaiser Matanzima, but nothing materialised. The conditions for establishing a factory both in Transkei and in Botswana did not suit Moringer's requirements.

Eventually, with the assistance of Chris van Rensburg of Jalc Holdings, he established contact with the Ciskei government. This led to his getting financial assistance from the Ciskei People's Development Bank. He established his factory at Bisho Airport, but continued to live in Johannesburg. Most of the finance for the project came through the 'financial rand'. This system operating in South Africa at the time permitted approved foreign investments to be brought into the country at an exchange rate 30% higher than normal. Unfortunately for Moringer, he had recently married an Austrian journalist, a relationship that soon soured and proved disastrous. He claimed that during the break-up, on a 'hell hath no fury like a woman scorned' basis, she despatched anonymous letters to his business associates and every institution he dealt with. This resulted in his arrest, remand and incarceration for 299 days on allegations of fraud involving R50 million.

Eventually, when the case came to trial before the Supreme Court in Johannesburg and after the State closed its case, the judge dismissed the charge on the grounds that Moringer had no case to answer.

However, the episode resulted in the collapse of his business for, as he said: 'You cannot run a business from Johannesburg Central Prison.' It also caused a souring of relations with President Lennox Sebe who had supported the setting up of his factory at Bisho with enthusiasm. He was no longer welcome in Ciskei. This led to his making contact with Charles Sebe because 'we might have mutual interests that we should discuss and maybe find out what we could do.' Charles Sebe introduced him to Transkei's Director of Military Intelligence, Major Mzwaiba.

During June 1989 there were initial discussions in Butterworth between Moringer, Charles Sebe and Major Mzwaiba on the question of mounting a coup attempt to overthrow Lennox Sebe. It was agreed that as a reward for assisting, Moringer's aircraft business would be returned to him after Lennox Sebe had been toppled from power.

Charles Sebe and Moringer met again for further discussions at the Royal Hotel in Durban during July 1989. Sebe said he had further discussed his plans with the Transkeian authorities and personally with Major-General Bantu Holomisa. Another meeting had been arranged in Umtata for the beginning of August and he wanted Moringer to attend.

When the time came, Moringer picked up Charles Sebe and drove with him to Umtata. They stayed for two days and discussed the proposed coup with Major Mzwaiba, TDF Chief Brigadier TT Matanzima and other members of the TDF, including the commander of Transkei's Special Forces. The plan entailed Lennox Sebe being taken prisoner by Moringer. Charles Sebe's *Iliso Lomzi* men who were still based at Port St Johns, with the support of Transkei's Special Forces, would invade Ciskei and occupy strategic places like the Radio Ciskei building and so on.

The discussions did not involve Major-General Holomisa, but Brigadier Matanzima and Charles Sebe both said they would be reporting the results of their discussions to him.

During the evening of 30 August 1989, on the instructions of Attorney-General Klaus von Lieres and resulting from information emanating from the Harms Commission of Enquiry into cross-border financial irregularities, the SAP raided Moringer's home in Bryanston, Johannesburg. Amongst others found there were Charles Sebe, by then living in Durban, and Johan Vosloo, an employee of Moringer. After searching the house and confiscating numerous documents and an audio casette, they arrested Moringer. At his specific request the police did not speak to anyone else present.

When the audio cassette was checked it was found to contain a recording by Charles Sebe relating to a proposed takeover of the government of Ciskei.

As Moringer told an amnesty hearing of the TRC: 'We were planning a joint operation where I was involved, where Charles Sebe and his people were involved and where Transkei Military Intelligence was involved, which objective was to overthrow Lennox Sebe . . . I don't know how long this whole operational planning took place. I was frequently in the Transkei, we spent time there, we were training people there and during this period the person I was dealing with was Major Mzwaiba. So we established, call it personal trust, but definitely a working relationship based on trust.'

Following Moringer's arrest Charles Sebe fled back to Transkei.

Needless to say, the plans for the coup attempt collapsed.[6]

More unrest in Ciskei

In 1989 there was an increase in UDF/ANC-inspired political incidents. There was a bombing in Bisho, three bombings in Bulembu, a bombing in Frankfort, a bombing in Keiskammahoek, a bombing in Zwelitsha, three bombings and three armed attacks in Mdantsane and an attack on the Potsdam Police station.

A State of Emergency was declared in the Balasi area of Bisho and in East Peelton on 16 October 1989. This had come about because of the excision of East Peelton from the Eastern Cape in 1988 and its incorporation into Ciskei against the wishes of residents. The spectre of removal to make way for an expansion of Bisho also hung over the Balasi residents. East Peelton residents were repeatedly harassed by the Ciskei administration during the first year of incorporation. Many, including elderly people, were detained and assaulted. Over 200 were charged with offences like erecting illegal structures, but this resulted in the conviction of only two. In late September the homes of four Ciskei administration supporters in Balasi were petrol bombed. Seven youths were detained. Residents complained that those who opposed the removals were being attacked by vigilantes calling themselves 'Inkatha'.

The day after the declaration of the State of Emergency, the Ciskei Police supported by the army, forcibly moved most of the inhabitants of the largest village, Nkqonkqweni, across the border into South Africa. The South Africans objected and the SAP made them take everyone back into the Ciskei. Half the homes in Nkqonkqweni were bulldozed and more than 100 people arrested. Many were badly assaulted by the Security Forces and at least 55 hospitalised. In December 1989 the vigilantes were seen assisting the Ciskei Police. Meetings were broken up and in January 1990 a member of the Balasi Youth Congress was murdered, apparently by vigilantes.

Many residents fled to King William's Town and refused point-blank to return to Ciskei until it was re-incorporated into South Africa.[7]

In November 1989 25 000 Thornhill residents marched through the streets of Queenstown (outside Ciskei but close to Thornhill) demanding the return of their South African citizenship and protesting against the ongoing incorporation of communities into the homelands. In December a march by pensioners to the Home Affairs office in Queenstown was stopped by police, but a delegation was allowed to meet the Commissioner of Home Affairs. They wanted to be South Africans again and demanded that the central government resume responsibility for their pensions. They said the pensions in Ciskei were considerably lower; in addition taxes, levies and compulsory membership fees for Lennox Sebe's Ciskei National Independence Party (CNIP) were automatically deducted from their pensions. In February 1990 Thornhill's 12 000-strong Group Four community threatened to move from Ciskei to South Africa if the central government did not honour a 15-year-old promise to return land that they claimed.

The desire for re-incorporation into the Republic arose because of a general perception that South Africa was 'a paradise' in terms of state-provided services — as compared to inadequate pensions, understaffed clinics, a shortage of schools and the inadequacy of wholesome water supplies in the rural villages.

In the immediate aftermath of independence, a large portion of Ciskei's budget was earmarked for the improvement of services in the rural villages. Funds dried up when it was decided that as a matter of prestige, the priority lay in the construction of Bisho as the capital. This resulted in the local tribal authorities extorting 'voluntary taxes' from local residents. Included were levies for the tribal administration (including one for the entertainment of visiting cabinet ministers), contributions to a variety of funds and for a 'security fund tax'. This was in addition to the compulsory payment of CNIP membership fees. Non-payment of any levy resulted in the denial of access to resources, including old age pensions.

January 1990 marked the start of a defiance campaign that involved the burning or the return of CNIP membership cards to the administration. It began in the south-east and spread to the villages around Alice and Keiskammahoek in central Ciskei and to peri-urban areas around Bisho itself. The membership card was the key to several essential services and its rejection was equated by those involved as a rejection of Ciskei's independence. The campaign infuriated Lennox Sebe who said he would not tolerate it and warned that those taking part would be charged and sentenced to ten years imprisonment.

On 2 February 1990 — the day President F W de Klerk lifted bans on the various liberation movements — a state of emergency was declared in the districts of Mdantsane (which incorporates Khambashe) and Zwelitsha (which includes Kwarini, Nkqonkqweni, and Tambo — the villages making up East Peelton — and Balasi where a state of emergency already existed).

Brigadier Avery Ngaki, the Ciskei Police's head of community relations, said the purpose of the state of emergency was to counter lawlessness. In particular it was to combat violence in Khambashe where a gang of youths had burned the homes of a chief and a headman a few days before.

'It has been noted that they don't like the chief . . . the police will make them love the chief', the brigadier threatened ominously.

Questioned about vigilante activities in the unrest areas, Brigadier Ngaki described them as members of the community who assisted the police. While the police briefed them before they went to the villages on operations, they did not monitor their activities.

On 12 February 1990 celebrations over Nelson Mandela's release from prison the previous day turned violent in Mdantsane. During the disturbances the Ciskei Police shot ten people dead and wounded 20, some critically. In Alice the chief of Ciskei's Security Police panicked and drove into a crowd, killing a child and injuring another 21 people. Municipal rent offices were torched and the looting of businesses continued for four days.

A rally to protest the deaths of those shot was banned. Police caused panic amongst shoppers when they used a helicopter and a light aircraft to fire teargas shells at a shopping centre and a taxi rank near the Independence Stadium. The home of a Ciskei police officer in Mdantsane was attacked with hand grenades and the home of another in Peddie was burned. Hospital workers in Mdantsane went on strike in protest.

Heroes' Day on 19 February was marked by widespread rioting and unrest.

On 29 February priests led 15 000 residents on a march through Keiskammahoek to protest against Ciskei's independence. The Security Forces broke up the demonstration with teargas and sjamboks. Priests later reported that two children had died from inhaling teargas and that 18 people had been injured.

Residents in Peddie refused to be bussed to the national shrine of *Ntaba ka Ndoda* where Heroes' Day celebrations were being held. The attending crowds were scheduled to be addressed by President Sebe. Instead they handed in their CNIP cards en masse. Police retaliated with sjamboks, killing one person and injuring several others. Later, the Police baton-charged a congregation attending a church service and seriously injured a school child. That night they fired random shots while patrolling the area. A child was wounded by one such shot. The authorities cut off water supplies to punish the recalcitrant villagers.

Enter Brigadier Joshua 'Oupa' Gqozo: 4 March 1990

On 4 March 1990, while President Lennox Sebe was away in Hong Kong, his administration was overthrown in a bloodless coup by disgruntled officers led by the Ciskei Defence Force's intelligence chief, Brigadier 'Oupa' Gqozo.

At about 09:00 the SADF's Military Attaché in the Ciskei, Commandant B H 'Mias' Muller, phoned Colonel Thys Buitendag, Officer Commanding the SADF's Group 8 HQ, East London, and reported the coup. He said Buitendag and his Intelligence Officer, Commandant Gerrie Hugo, were required to report to the residence of the South African Ambassador to the Ciskei, Christiaan van Aardt, in King William's Town. Unusually, the embassy and the residency were sited in South Africa and not in the Ciskei. The officers were required for urgent discussions to decide on South Africa's reaction to the coup. Obviously the existing contingency plans for a South African takeover of the Ciskei were relevant. — if that option was decided on.

The force level immediately available to the Group 8 HQ in East London was a single company of paratroopers. The only other forces it controlled were local Citizen Force units like the Kaffrarian Rifles, Commando units and so on, but they had to be called up and mobilised before they could become operational. As it happened, both officers were in such a hurry to get to King William's Town that they forgot to collect the contingency plans from the safe. Forty-five minutes later they drove into King William's Town.

Ambassador van Aardt, Commandant Mias Muller and two National Intelligence Service operators were at the residency. They got straight down to business. The question was what to do about the coup. Should the SADF intervene? There were two precedents. South Africa had intervened and helped President Lucas Mangope retain power after the coup attempt in Bophuthatswana in February 1988. That intervention had eventuated because Mangope was regarded as a solid ally of the apartheid state. The same factors had been considered regarding the toppling of the Matanzimas by General Bantu Holomisa, but for some inexplicable reason it was decided not to intervene — to the lasting regret of Military Intelligence.

The fact that a coup had occurred in Ciskei hardly surprised anyone. The general population had long been dissatisfied with Lennox Sebe's rule, and so was the Ciskei Defence Force. It also went without saying — considering its involvement in *Operation Katzen* and so on — that the SADF felt the same way. So it was a political question rather than a military one.

Foreign Minister Pik Botha came on the telephone from Pretoria. Ultimately it would be his decision. Botha needed a briefing so that the next move could be planned. Everyone took part in the discussions and made contributions. On the King William's Town side, Commandant Muller did most of the talking and passed on the Minister's comments to the rest as the phone lacked conference facilities. Ambassador van Aardt gave the task to Muller because he was suffering from throat cancer and found it difficult to speak. It was a condition that eventually killed him.

The discussions had been going on for about half an hour when an anxious Brigadier Gqozo appeared. For Commandant Hugo it was their first meeting, but he got to know him well later on. Brigadier Gqozo took great pride in his appearance and he was always immaculately turned out. On that day, however, Hugo recalls he was dishevelled, almost bordering on scruffy. There was even a glimpse of a pyjama jacket peeking from the neck of his tunic. He had obviously dressed in a great hurry.

Gerrie Hugo and the other South Africans gained the impression that Gqozo had not been the prime mover in the coup. It seemed more likely that it had been mounted by a committee of officers. Maybe Gqozo had not even initially known about it. Having put the wheels in motion, though, the committee suddenly realised the serious consequences of their actions and decided they needed a figurehead acceptable to the South Africans — someone who could talk the SADF out of a military intervention.

That could only be Oupa Gqozo. It was well known that he was a favourite amongst the SADF's general staff. He had assisted with the formation of the SADF's first black battalion, 21-Battalion, based at Lenz outside Johannesburg. When his tour of duty as Ciskei's Military Attaché in Pretoria ended on 8 January 1990, the South Africans had awarded him the Order of Good Hope. That was only two months previously.[8] He was also reputed to have links with SADF Military Intelligence. All this made him the only officer who fitted the bill.

In the circumstances, it seems likely the coup committee themselves had decided to roust him out of bed to request he take over the coup.

What was also obvious was that the coup committee had despatched him to speak to the ambassador, to tell him that everything was all right and persuade him that there was absolutely no reason for the SADF to interfere.

The South African officials listened to what he had to say, but he needn't have worried because the decision had already been made before he arrived. It just needed a tidying up of the detail. The SADF would not get involved. They would support him because he was known to have strong pro-South African sentiments. Besides that, he was certainly preferable to Lennox Sebe whom they had wanted to 'take out'.

So Brigadier Gqozo was told to stand easy. The South Africans would not interfere.

It was suggested by various sources that South Africa had probably played a part in the coup. Commandant Hugo who was there and had had the benefit of the group phone discussion with Foreign Minister Pik Botha, is convinced otherwise.[9]

Lennox Sebe had been warned by the central government of an imminent coup minutes before he left for Hong Kong. He continued his journey, however, leaving the South African government puzzled as to why he disregarded the warning. *The Weekly Mail* suggested it was because he thought the coup they were referring to was one he had planned with his son, Lieutenant-Colonel Kwane Sebe, of the Ciskei Elite Unit. Lennox wanted to retire and had planned for Kwane to seize power while he was absent abroad. That would have circumvented the need for a democratic election. It seems, though, that the President and his son had boxed a little too cleverly.

This scenario was effectively confirmed by Foreign Minister Pik Botha who said: 'Brigadier Gqozo said his action was essential to pre-empt a coup which was already being implemented by another branch of the Security Forces who intended to entrench the rule of President Sebe. His interest, he said, was to save Ciskei from a corrupt and repressive regime . . . He had only acted at a critical moment in history when the wrong elements were intent on seizing power, which would have plunged Ciskei into chaos.'[10]

Brigadier Gqozo's first move was to disband the Ciskei Elite Unit and arrest Lieutenant-Colonel Kwane Sebe and two other prominent members of the Security Forces.[11] Kwane Sebe soon got his just deserts. He was tried and convicted for ordering the bombing of the Keiskammahoek Bottle Store and a private home in Peddie. He was given a prison sentence of 21 years. He applied to the TRC for amnesty on the grounds that he had been convicted of 'political crimes' connected with his duty of combatting *Iliso Lomzi*. Witnesses dispelled this illusion and testified that the bombings arose from personal vendettas.

They testified how he had thought nothing about ordering the arrest and detention of people who disagreed with him. He even detained a man under Section 26 of Ciskei's Security Act for a long time because he regarded him as a rival for a woman's affections. In another instance he was instrumental in the detention of a senior civil servant because he was a suspected sympathiser of a banned organisation. Yet during his 108-day detention the unfortunate detainee was not even questioned. When he was released, he discovered he had been demoted from departmental secretary-general to principal clerk.

Kwane Sebe's second in command, Major-General Bullet Ngwanya later confirmed that 'he was feared by everybody in Ciskei. Nobody could touch him'. Sebe openly pillaged state coffers. Amnesty was correctly refused, so he will be sitting in prison for a long time yet.[12]

Within days, two statues of ex-President Lennox Sebe that had cost R90 000 each, were removed from their plinths by the Public Works Department.[13] Lennox Sebe appealed unsuccessfully for the South African government to intervene. Instead, Foreign Affairs provided him with a luxurious mansion in Waterkloof, Pretoria, where he could remain in comfortable exile.

Major-General Bantu Holomisa welcomed the coup and hoped it would result in the gradual improvement of the relationship between Transkei and Ciskei.[14]

Brigadier Gqozo said he had mounted the coup because of corruption, nepotism and widespread violence by Lennox Sebe's regime. He said that all units of the Security Forces, including the police and the prison service, had pledged their support.

Thousands of Ciskeians took to the streets to celebrate.

Standing beneath the draped flags of the ANC and the SACP — to the horror of South African Military Intelligence — Gqozo addressed a boisterous crowd of 100 000 at Mdantsane's Sisa Dukashe Stadium where in the days of Lennox Sebe hundreds of people had suffered unspeakable tortures at the hands of his vigilantes.

Gqozo told the cheering crowd that Lennox Sebe's appeal for South African intervention had been rejected. He announced that his administration's ultimate goal was to see to Ciskei reincorporated into South Africa. Detainees held for security offences would be released and political organisations would be permitted to operate freely.

'We are looking for a new future', he said.

The next day, to emphasise Ciskei's new political maturity, Gqozo asked the UDF to share a platform with him the because, he said, he knew it was what the people wished.

But while Oupa Gqozo was grandstanding with his newly-found comrades, his bloodless coup had deteriorated into bloody shambles. The cheering news that he had rid them of Lennox Sebe became an excuse for mobs to embark on a rampage. For the two days after the coup there was massive destruction, plundering and arson. Factories and shops at Mdantsane, Dimbaza, Phakamisa and Zwelitsha were looted and torched. The looters dragged away television sets, furniture and food.They called it a refund for what they had paid in development tax over the years.[15]

An employee of the Amatola Sun Hotel told *The Star*: 'All the shops and factories were burning. Everybody was looting and there was complete chaos. There was no evidence of the police and little of the military. The people seemed completely happy.'[16]

One can be sure they were.

The 27 who died and the hundreds more who were injured were probably not so ecstatic. Whether the casualties were rioters shot by the Security Forces, by people defending their property, or whether they were supporters of Lennox Sebe attacked to work of old scores is unknown.

On 5 March Brigadier Gqozo declared a State of Emergency and invited the SADF to move in and stop the looting and destruction. The SADF's Group 8 HQ in East London established a Tactical HQ at King William's Town and Commandant Gerrie Hugo was positioned there. Those paratroopers available were deployed into Bisho to back-up the CDF.

The paratroopers had orders to restore calm, in particular to protect South African property, but virtually all property and businesses in Bisho fell into that category. The soldiers faced mobs of thousands of excited rioters and the CDF did nothing to assist. CDF soldiers, in fact, were seen drawing petrol from service station pumps and handing it out in bottles and cans for the use of arsonists![17]

Faced with such a chaotic situation, a token company of paratroopers could do little. Playing the heavy hand would have worsened an already tense political situation. The problem was that bringing in additional forces would not only have taken time because they were not immediately available, but it might also have ended up with their taking over Bisho as the only option for restoring law and order. South Africa, instead of remaining on the sidelines, would then have had to live with the embarrassment of later handing back control to a leader who had seized power by means of a coup.

Lennox Sebe's private home in Zwelitsha was razed to the ground. Ninety percent of commercial enterprises in Mdantsane were destroyed, including Sun International's Entertainment and Hotel Centre. The damage in Mdantsane was conservatively estimated at R60 million. Twenty-seven factories were comprehensively looted in the Fort Jackson industrial area — nine were gutted by fire. The cost of the damage and the looting was estimated at R130 million rand. This did not take into account the human cost — the deaths, the injuries and the at least 3 000 people who were thrown out of work because their places of employment had been razed to the ground or cleaned out by looters.

Gqozo's military administration opened discussions with the locally based UDF. A delegation from the UDF's national executive, including its general secretary, Popo Molefe, met his Military Council in Bisho. Talks were dominated by the need to restore order. The UDF delegation promised to change the people's negative attitudes towards the police and the new military rulers.

'The police were yesterday's enemies, but they can be today's and tomorrow's friends', Molefe said.

A UDF rally held in Bisho two days later called for a major clean-up. Mdantsane Residents' Association helped the police to conduct door-to-door searches for stolen goods and apprehended looters.

Speaking to Durban's *Sunday Tribune*, Brigadier Gqozo said that 'all progressive movements existing in the interests of the people, including trade union movements, will be allowed to operate. Their leaders must come forward, discuss their plans with us, and together we will be able to solve the problems'. Asked about Ciskei's place in the South Africa of tomorrow, he said: 'This depends on negotiations between Pretoria and Mr Mandela . . . whether they can carry on while homelands continue to exist, we will have our structures patterned to keep in accordance with what is decided at the negotiating table'.[18]

General Charles Sebe, speaking from exile in South Africa, said he was overjoyed at the news of the coup and announced that he was returning to Ciskei as soon as possible. The fact that Ciskeians had moved to return their CNIP cards to the administration, he said, meant that Lennox Sebe was no longer governing the country by the will of the people. He expressed absolute confidence in Brigadier Gqozo whom 'he had known for many years'.[19]

He changed his mind shortly afterwards when Chief Lent Maqoma pre-empted him by becoming the first to make a triumphal return to Bisho from exile. Maqoma was somewhat put out when the Ciskei's Security Police arrested and deported him.[20] Charles Sebe was left with no doubt that a similar fate awaited him if he tried to emulate his colleague.

Almost a year later in February 1991, according to *The Weekly Mail*, South African Foreign Minister Pik Botha took Oupa Gqozo aside during a Cape Town meeting and urged him to step down in favour of Lent Maqoma. Gqozo tentatively agreed, but changed his mind on his return to Bisho. Pik Botha, who had a warm relationship with Maqoma, was furious at being thwarted.

Shortly afterwards, after more pressure from Pretoria, Gqozo relented and allowed Maqoma to return and take up residence in Ciskei. Foreign Affairs had brokered an agreement with Maqoma that he would stay out of politics.

Brigadier Gqozo's behaviour was often erratic, but he could also be foolishly gracious. It was this, presumably, that led him to appoint Maqoma as his Minister of Manpower shortly afterwards. It was a move he would soon regret.[21]

On 8 March 1990, 11 members of the ruling Military Council were sworn in by Ciskei's Chief Justice, Benjamin Pickard. It comprised Brigadier Gqozo, Colonel Onward Guzana, Commandant S S Pita and Major Peter Hauser — an Austrian who had been seconded to the CDF in 1982 as director of music. No members of the Sebe cabinet were appointed.

Gqozo suspended the constitution, abolished Ciskei's National Assembly and ordered that all prisoners held under section 26 of the Ciskei's National Security Act, 1982 be released.[22]

Colonel Guzana was dropped from the Council and detained less than two months later. Major Hauser, no doubt sniffing what had become very variable winds indeed, announced that he was returning to Austria.[23]

On 30 April 1990, the day before Nelson Mandela was due to address an ANC rally in Bisho, the Military Council unbanned the ANC, SACP, PAC, the South African Allied Workers' Union (SAAWU) and *Iliso Lomzi*. Gqozo obviously still did appreciate that the last was a South African Military Intelligence front organisation.

In early June 1990 Ciskei's Commissioner of Police, General L B Madolo, was dismissed and detained for his involvement in an alleged plot to overthrow the Military Council and install Charles Sebe as head of state.

Brigadier Gqozo said Charles Sebe had 'arrogantly assumed that he would be welcomed back in Ciskei by a grateful nation' and 'was supported in this fallacy by people who should know a lot better'.[24]

Proposed reorganisation of the CDF

There were bi-monthly meetings between officers of the SADF and the Combined Management Boards (CMBs) of the homeland states. They took place under the guise of being concerned with the development and training of the homeland's defence forces, but in actuality they were joint operational and intelligence briefings. The venues for the meetings in the Eastern Cape alternated between Bisho and Umtata.

It was at one such meeting that Brigadier Gqozo mentioned that he intended to recruit an SADF officer for secondment into the CDF. He needed one to assist in knocking the organisation into shape. This immediately sparked interest in Lieutenant-Colonel Gerrie Hugo who had recently been suffering from an increasing lack of job satisfaction in the SADF. He mentioned to some of his colleagues that he intended to apply. A senior officer heard about it and told him dismissively not to bother as an officer from the Directorate of Covert Collection (DCC) — Lieutenant-Colonel John Mawdsley — had already been nominated for the posting. Military Intelligence were absolutely intent on having one of their own men in place in Bisho.

Gerrie Hugo was unhappy with this and sought an interview with the CDF Chief, Brigadier Andrew Jamangile, in Bisho. He told him he had intended to apply for secondment to the CDF, but the SADF had decided on their own nominee. Gerrie had an excellent rapport with the CDF's officers and with Brigadier Andrew Jamangile in particular.

'In that case why don't you resign from the SADF and join us?'

He pointed out that if he did so, the CDF would no longer need a seconded officer.

Jamangile took him around Army Headquarters for the next half an hour and introduced him to everyone as his new Chief of Staff. He was told he would commence duties there as a full colonel. Hugo returned to East London and resigned, giving the mandatory one month notice. Many in the SADF were upset with him, particularly the DCC which were chagrined that he had foiled its plans to implant its man into the CDF. The post earmarked for Gerrie Hugo was Chief of Staff Intelligence. After a month spent wrangling over the amount of pension contributions that should be refunded to him, Gerrie moved to his new job in the Ciskei in August 1990.

Ciskei: The scramble for intelligence

About a month later, Brigadier Gqozo, who after the unbanning had become progressively more pro-ANC and pro-reform — even sharing a platform with Nelson Mandela — suddenly experienced a change of heart. He started worrying about subversive activities and wondering whether his position was being undermined. Much of his focus was on

Charles Sebe and those perceived to be allied to him. He began to talk about forming his own intelligence organisation, instead of relying on the SADF as he had been doing.

It seems clear that the South Africa's intelligence community, the NIS, Military Intelligence and the Security Police were jockeying for position in the Ciskei. The territory was important. While their political masters had decreed that the war against the ANC and the other black nationalist political movements was over, they regarded it as still ongoing. It had been their ambition in the Transkei, when the surrogate *Iliso Lomzi* was established, to use it as an island in the Eastern Cape from which they could foray out and attack the ANC and the PAC . Now they could substitute Ciskei instead — with the added bonus of being able to target Transkei from there too. Under Major-General Holomisa's Military Council, Transkei had become too ANC and PAC friendly for the intelligence community's liking.

Ciskei: Enter the National Intelligence Service

The National Intelligence Service (NIS) was first on the scene, initially in the person of Kobus Botha. He was a man of many talents, having pursued such occupations as hairdresser and insurance salesman during his working career. Brigadier Gqozo had met him when he became involved in some sort of decorating work at State House. They struck up a friendship and from this Gqozo appointed him as director in the Office of the Chairman of the Military Council. Botha's elevation was regarded askance, particularly when he moved into State House and took up residence with Gqozo and his family. It is doubtful that Botha was a former NIS officer. It is more likely that the NIS took advantage of his friendship with Gqozo and recruited him. Botha influenced Gqozo on various issues, including Christianity.

Around September/October 1990 Brigadier Gqozo clashed with the Mdantsane-based and UDF-inclined Border Civic Congress (BOCCO). They organised a march to the magistrate's court in Mdantsane to present Gqozo with a list of their grievances. He called them 'rabble rousers' — people who regarded themselves as a parallel government and who had no respect for authority. He declared the march illegal and threatened to deploy his Security Forces to break it up if it went ahead. The ANC's regional convenor, Rev M A Stofile, intervened at the last moment and persuaded Gqozo to allow the march to take place and to accept the memorandum.

This angered Gqozo and probably made him aware that he could have achieved better results if he had more finely honed negotiating skills. Kobus Botha took advantage of this and was instrumental in organising, through the National Intelligence Service, Gqozo's attendance at a one-week course in Pretoria. It involved instruction on thinking skills, speech writing, note taking and on the handling of the media. It appears apparent that he was also brought into contact with the NIS.

Shortly afterwards, Brigadier Gqozo submitted a proposal for a system of local government that was answerable to Bisho and called a meeting of the House of Assembly to discuss it. It became clear during the meeting that Gqozo was not there to discuss things. He merely wanted his proposals ratified. By this time he had become dictatorial in his handling of government affairs, and often did not even consult with his cabinet ministers on important government policies. This brought him into conflict with the ANC and with BOCCO, which also rejected his ideas. Ministers and senior CDF officers expressed surprise when Gqozo began to make scathing attacks in the media on the ANC and its allies. This set the stage for more confrontation between him and the ANC alliance.[18]

About this time, Brian Campbell, a senior NIS officer, accompanied by an operator, 'Bossie' Bosman, and the NIS' Regional Director in East London, visited Gqozo in Bisho. They suggested arranging an NIS operation course for some of his officers as a forerunner to establishing an intelligence capability for Ciskei.

Campell suggested that Brigadier Gqozo personally arrange the recruitment of civilians to work as intelligence operatives, for the NIS was intent on forming an organisation that was a mirror image of itself. Gqozo agreed a course would be desirable, but said he would have soldiers trained to become the nucleus of his new intelligence service. The venue for the course was the 12th floor of Dukumbana House in Bisho which also housed the CDF's Military Intelligence branch. Ten Military Intelligence operators attended the three-week course which was personally conducted by Brian Campbell, assisted by two instructors from Pretoria.

Campbell moved to King William's Town and took an office in the South African Embassy where he established his own secure communications set-up — something he was very particular about. Campbell's seniority can be judged by the fact that his previous posting was in Washington — which indicates the importance the NIS attached to Ciskei.

Brigadier Gqozo was treated like royalty and he became very pro-NIS, because he desperately wanted an effective intelligence service. He was even invited to attend an NIS course in Pretoria and by all accounts he thoroughly enjoyed himself while on it.

It certainly appeared that initially, at least, the NIS had edged out its rivals in its efforts to gain predominant influence in the homeland.

Military Intelligence, however, had not retired from the race and was still waiting in the wings. It had taken a bruising when Gerrie Hugo pre-empted their man Mawdsley in its efforts to take control of the office of Ciskei's Chief of Staff Intelligence, but it had by no means run out of ideas.

23

Transkei and Politics
Military Council Years
1987-1994

Corruption in Transkei

By January 1989, 70 civil servants had been brought before Transkei's courts on theft or fraud related charges. Two South African residents, formerly businessmen in Transkei, were extradited from South Africa to face 59 counts of theft, fraud and reckless trading.

Major-General Holomisa said fraud and embezzlement amounting to more than R8 million had been uncovered by his administration since it assumed power. He also said that considerable progress had been made in the recovery of unpaid taxes by former political office bearers and businessmen. Some traditional leaders had been convicted of corrupt practices in the selling of land in rural areas.

South African judges and advocates had been co-opted to speed up prosecutions and he hoped that the courts would deal with all outstanding cases by the end of 1990.[1]

Re-interment of the late Chief Sabata Dalindyebo: October 1989

Chief Sabata Dalindyebo, a cousin of Nelson Mandela and the deposed paramount chief of the Tembus, died in exile in Zambia on 7 April 1986. Shortly afterwards his remains were returned to Transkei for burial in the Umtata district. The Release Mandela Committee, the UDF and the Soweto Civic Committee arranged buses to transport mourners to Umtata.

The Transkei Commissioner of Police, General R S Matanga, decreed that the Bumbane Great Place where the funeral was to take place and the surrounding areas would be 'prohibited areas' from 19-21 April, in an attempt to halt the anticipated influx of mourners. People from outside Transkei, including journalists, were refused permits to enter the area.

On 20 April the Transkei Supreme Court granted an interim order to Chief Sabata's son, Buyekhaya Dalindyebo, and Sabata's widow halting the funeral and granting them custody of the body. They intended to return the body to Lusaka because agreements entered into before the body was returned to Transkei had been violated. They objected to restrictions placed on non-Transkeians attending the funeral, to the grave not having been dug in the intended place and to the fact that other relatives had ousted them from the funeral arrangements.

In defiance of the court order, Chief Kaiser Matanzima had the body snatched from the funeral parlour and buried under tight security at Bumbane while hundreds of armed soldiers, policemen and government officials looked on.

The chief's relatives, including Winnie Mandela, refused to attend.

The Dalindyebo family lodged papers with the Supreme Court seeking an order for the body to be exhumed and returned to the them. They called on K D (Kaiser) Matanzima and Chief Bambilanga Mtirara (the deceased's brother) to show cause why they should not be held in contempt and punished.

Matanzima replied by immediately lodging an application with the Court to order Buyekhaya Dalindyebo and the late chief's widow to show cause why their application halting the funeral should not be withdrawn because of 'fraud and misrepresentation'. Buyekhaya Dalindyebo and Mrs Sabata fled the Transkei in fear of their lives.

General Zondwa Mtirara, the sacked commander of the TDF, was installed as Paramount Chief at the instigation of Kaiser Matanzima. He was eventually forced to resign when the Dalindyebo Tribal Authority refused point-blank to confirm him. Following this, Chief Bambilanga Mtirara, took over as regent until the rightful heir, Buyekhaya Dalindyebo, could take over the paramountcy.

This left the way clear for the exhumation of the chief's remains and for its re-interment in a manner befitting the leader of the tribe. 40 000 people attended the funeral on 1 October 1989. Many of them were waving ANC and SACP flags.

Major-General Bantu Holomisa shared a platform with Peter Mokaba, chairman of the restricted South African Youth Congress; Murphy Morobe, publicity secretary of the UDF; Elijah Barayi, COSATU's president; and Mrs Winnie Mandela. Holomisa said:'Regimes have come and gone. If the people want to be part of South Africa, we shall hold a referendum.' [2]

Transkei's relations with KwaZulu deteriorate: 1989

In September 1989 KwaZulu's Chief Minister, Chief Gatsha (Mangosuthu) Buthelezi, turned down an invitation extended by Transkei to attend a meeting of heads of homelands. In his reply he criticised Transkei for having taken its 'independence' in 1975. He demanded the reincorporation of Transkei into South Africa before he would join such talks. He also expressed irritation about a meeting in Lusaka, Zambia, between General Holomisa and the ANC earlier in the month.

A month later Chief Buthelezi, when addressing the Inkatha Women's Brigade, remarked that Murphy Murobe had commented at Chief Sabata's funeral that Transkei's military had carried out a mission in the struggle for liberation by deposing the Matanzima administration.

'Let me challenge General Holomisa thus: you speak boldly, sir, and it is said in your presence on your soil that your Transkei *coup d'état* was orchestrated by the ANC working in collaboration with Mr Marobe. Be man enough, sir, to complete your work and undertake to take over the Ciskei through a coup . . . Use this as practise and then dare a *coup d'état* in KwaZulu. If your coup was orchestrated and sanctioned, your hands are already very filthy and they cannot be soiled more by orchestrating a coup in innocent KwaZulu.'

He suggested that General Holomisa should stop 'peddling his political arse'.

General Holomisa wrote to him expressing his 'disbelief and amazement'. The chief, he said, had an 'unfortunate knack of annoying friend and foe alike'. He had 'alienated everybody seriously engaged in the body politic of the region'. Was he truly concerned with South Africa's future or was he just safeguarding his position and 'the purse attached to it . . . People will respect you if you resign as a homeland leader and pursue the national liberation struggle from another platform'.[3]

Labour problems in Transkei: October 1989

October 1989 was marked by a series of wildcat strikes that affected at least 11 factories in Butterworth and Umtata. They were categorised as 'spontaneous' protests over poor pay and working conditions, but they were behind-the-scenes evidence of attempts to establish trade unions which had been banned in the territory since 'independence'. Major-

General Holomisa and administration officials met employers' and workers' representatives to discuss the strikes. General Holomisa said afterwards that it had been agreed there had been a breakdown in communication between workers and employers. He said there was a need for bodies to represent workers and that ill treatment of them should cease. The administration said a new labour policy would be announced, but in the meanwhile a delegation was appointed to monitor progress and ensure that the striking workers were not dismissed.

On 23 October there was a general flexing of labour's muscles when 10 000 workers marched to Major-General Holomisa's Umtata offices and presented a list of grievances. They complained about the lack of trade unions and demanded an end to the state of emergency imposed on 30 June 1989. The demonstrations were marred by serious intimidation and police took action after several shops and a bank were forced to close. At Ngangelizwe Township a policeman was hauled from his car and badly beaten by a chanting crowd. He was one of several admitted to hospital.[4]

Transkei moves closer to ANC: October 1989

Two days later 25 000 people marched to the offices of the State President Tutor Ndamase and presented him with a petition for the abolition of the death penalty and for the reprieve of two prisoners, P Mayaphi and N Ndzamela — convicted of murder in respect of a bomb blast at the Wild Coast Sun Casino Hotel which killed two. The march formed part of the 'Save the Patriots Campaign' of the South African Youth Congress (SAYCO). The Transkei Executive Council met ten days later and imposed a stay on all executions, pending an investigation by a special committee to examine whether the death penalty should be abolished.

On 26 October 1989 at the annual 'independence' celebrations, President Ndamase announced that Transkei would review its security legislation to enable its Security Forces and legal personnel to function normally. He said: 'Transkeians have never been found wanting when it comes to the vanguard of spearheading the liberation of the black people'.[5]

He also announced that the ban on the formation of trade unions would be lifted and that new ones would be encouraged to register with the Department of Manpower Planning and Utilisation. In the interim, until enabling legislation was passed, a wage board and an industrial council would be established.

On 8 November Transkei lifted its state of emergency and its ban on 15 organisations including the Azanian People's Organisation, the Black People's Convention, the African People's Democratic Union of South Africa, the Azanian Students' Organisation, the Prisoners' Welfare Programmes, the South African Allied Workers' Union, SWAPO, the UDF and COSAS.

On 25 November seven ANC leaders recently released from prison, including Walter Sisulu, Govan Mbeki and Andrew Mlangeni, addressed a gathering of about 400 supporters at a church hall in Umtata. The Transkei Police tear-gassed the crowd and two elderly supporters subsequently died. A policeman was attacked in retaliation and murdered.

A special welcome-home rally attended by between 45 000 and 80 000 people was held in Umtata's Independence Stadium the following day. Major-General Holomisa shared a platform with the leaders, together with the general secretary of the National Union of Mineworkers, Cyril Ramaphosa.

General Holomisa submitted a written apology for police behaviour the previous evening and announced he had ordered the formation of a special commission of enquiry to investigate it. He blamed the incident on 'renegade' police.

Walter Sisulu praised the actions of the Military Council, the unbannings, the release of political prisoners, the lifting of the state of emergency and the re-interment of Chief

Dalindyebo. He hailed the idea of a referendum on Transkei's 'independence' and urged chiefs to become members of the Congress of Traditional Leaders of South Africa. Sisulu praised Holomisa for advancing the 'struggle against tribalism and for his efforts in seeking to reunify the homelands with South Africa'. He called on other homeland leaders to emulate Holomisa's example.

Govan Mbeki said: 'The government of Transkei has begun to set the people free.'

Andrew Mlangeni pointed out that 'many of the leaders of the ANC come from Transkei which has an early tradition in the fight for freedom. *Umkhonto we Sizwe* (MK), the ANC's army, is alive and well in the Transkei, alongside the army of General Holomisa and it is my personal belief that Holomisa is a spiritual member of *Umkhonto we Sizwe*'.[6]

In a report on the 25 November incident issued later, the investigating commission's chairman, P Magid, said the police had overreacted and run riot. The two people who had died were suffering respectively from an advanced lung disease and an advanced heart disease and it had been impossible to establish if they had died directly or indirectly from the inhalation of tear gas. The report recommended that senior police officers 'root out' those who had brought the Force into disrepute. The report was sent to the Attorney-General with a view to possible prosecution.[7]

President de Klerk visits General Holomisa: 10 January 1990

On 10 January 1990 State President F W de Klerk accompanied by the Minister of Foreign Affairs, Pik Botha, visited Umtata for talks with Major-General Bantu Holomisa. It was obvious that Pretoria was concerned about Transkei's recent intercourse with the ANC.

'We want you to renounce that you are contemplating unbanning the ANC', they told him.' We are unhappy that ANC and PAC people are already being allowed to wear their colours in the territory. You seem to be working alone.' [8]

President de Klerk described the proposed referendum on incorporation as 'untimely and unsuitable'. Transkei, he advised, should keep its options open with an eye to forthcoming developments in South Africa. He pointed out that with positive constitutional changes in South Africa, Transkei could receive the benefit of greater international recognition. He stressed that it was vital the territory return to civilian rule as soon as possible.[9]

'Go back to the barracks', they told Holomisa.

Holomisa reminded them that they had been involved in plans to assassinate him. Despite this he was still around.

'We [Transkeians] are the children of the fathers whom you deceived in 1975 when you sold them independence. You are talking to the wrong people. There will be no return to civilian rule [manipulated by you] on your conscience. You are not going to tell us how constitutional matters will be handled in Transkei. You talk of reforms but this is not in line with what you are saying in Pretoria.'

'You must return power to the civilians', Pik Botha repeated adamantly.

'No, you are out of order', General Holomisa told him. 'We never asked the National Party for permission to topple Matanzima. So there will be no return to civilian rule. We will go to the people of Transkei [by referendum]. They will decide where they want to go in the future. We will do this at the right time and not on your terms.'

As General Holomisa put it, 'the relationship soured' after that meeting.[10]

Pretoria immediately accused Transkei of breaking the Customs Union agreement by banning imports of sorghum beer from Natal. It also accused General Holomisa's administration of attempting a coup against Lennox Sebe in Ciskei in August 1989. It disputed the necessity for the continued detention of seven South Africans, who Holomisa claimed, belonged to two hit squads sent to assassinate him.

Holomisa pointed out in his reply that Pretoria was refusing to extradite to Umtata the alleged masterminds behind the plots.

Pretoria replied that Transkei had not followed the correct procedures in their efforts to extradite former Transkei businessman, Vulindlela Mbotoli, the chairman of Temba Construction and a director of Jalc Holdings, wanted in connection with the coup attempts by Colonel Craig Duli.

Holomisa said that in that case the interrogations of the other seven suspects would continue until Mbotoli had been handed over to Transkei for trial.

Another accusation laid at General Holomisa's feet was that he had interfered in several labour disputes, in every case on behalf of the workers, and that this was driving companies from the homeland.

After talks between General Holomisa and South Africa's Ambassador to Transkei, both agreed that the atmosphere of distrust was not benefiting either country.[11]

Unbanning of political parties in Transkei: 7 February 1990

On 7 February 1990 Major-General Holomisa followed President F W de Klerk's example and announced that he had unbanned the ANC, the PAC, the SACP, the South African Student's Union (SASU), the Marxist Front, COSATU and the Azanian Liberation Movement. He also announced the release of political prisoners — including those convicted of murder in connection with the bombing at the Wild Coast Sun Casino Hotel — for the purpose of promoting dialogue. Prosecutions relating to 'politically motivated crimes' were shelved. In was later announced that laws restricting political activity were under review.[12]

Also on 7 February, a committee investigating the feasibility of a referendum held its first open meeting. Holomisa told the committee: 'It is an open secret that Transkeians have always identified themselves with the struggle for liberation in South Africa. All our symbols of independence have no significant meaning; the Transkei passport is a document of no significance and Transkei citizenship has become a symbol of denial, deprivation and further disadvantage.' He said that President de Klerk's speech and the unbanning of various organisations, irrevocably committed South Africa to fundamental change with implications of a unitary state. 'If apartheid is to be abandoned, it follows that all its cornerstones and structures will be systematically relinquished.'

The committee decided that all Transkeians over the age of 16 would be allowed to vote in the referendum. A special cabinet committee was set up to work out details of how to conduct the referendum.

The PAC met representatives of the Military Council in Tanzania. They applauded the referendum as 'progressive and most democratic'.[13]

Until 1987, the SAP had free movement in and out of Transkei, looking for and arresting suspects whether they were involved in criminal or political activity. When Major-General Holomisa took over as Chairman of the Military Council he stopped all that. He demanded that Transkei be treated as an independent country. If the SAP wanted something or someone they would have to put a request through proper channels — as the Transkei Police had to do if they wanted the same thing in the greater South Africa. There would be no more raids and arrests in Transkei as had occurred in the past.

This was the reason why over the period 1988 to 1994 but particularly after 1990, ANC and PAC people were able to seek safe refugee in the territory. As far as Holomisa was concerned, apartheid was a South African doctrine and had nothing to do with Transkei. If South Africa was fighting a war against people determined to overthrow apartheid, it was of no concern to Transkei. He never allowed his forces to go and fight side-by-side with the SADF in the Namibian/Angolan operational area.[14]

The SAP made various attempts at cooperation with the Transkei Police. Mostly they were rebuffed, but occasionally they were successful. Major-General Griebenauw of the Security Police in East London noted the following operations where cooperation was successful.

On 6 February 1988 during a joint operation between the SAP and Transkei's Security Forces, an armed MK guerrilla was spotted in Umtata. During the follow-up he was shot and killed. The SAP in the Eastern Cape noticed a distinct cooling of attitude towards them by General Bantu Holomisa.

Information from an MK guerrilla arrested in the Western Transvaal (North West Province) during October 1988 led to a senior MK officer, Aga Tiyo, in a house in Umtata. The house was attacked, Tiyo was arrested and an AK47 was recovered. The arrest also led to the discovery of a large weapons cache. General Holomisa later ordered that Tiyo be released.

On 21 January 1991 during a follow-up by Transkei Police, an MK guerrilla was cornered at Lutwayizo Trading Station in the Willowvale district. The guerrilla opened fire and wounded a policeman. The Transkei Police requested SAP assistance but three guerrillas evaded capture. In a further follow-up by a unit of the SAP Task Force supported by a SAAF helicopter gunship, an arms cache was discovered.

Resulting from information supplied by the SAP, Captain Ngidi and Constable Simon checked a suspected MK safe house at Mcubazi in Butterworth. A guerrilla opened fire with his pistol and killed them both. The Transkei Police requested assistance and the SAP mounted roadblocks across Transkei's borders. When a car was flagged down at a roadblock at Elliott, occupants opened fire. Two guerrillas were shot dead, two escaped and two were captured. Two policemen were wounded.

In continuing operations at Mount Shadows, during a joint follow-up by the SAP and Transkei Police, two guerrillas were shot dead and another two arrested. Two SAP constables were wounded. Investigations confirmed that the guerrilla gang concerned had been responsible for the killings of Captain Ngidi and Constable Simon.[15]

After this there was little co-operation — to the chagrin of the Transkei Police and the SAP.

On 25 March 1991 a Directorate of Covert Collect (DCC) report said the ANC had opened 28 branches in Transkei. It was actively involved in organisation, recruiting and influencing protest marches. Alternative structures like civic and residents' associations were also being set up. It said that returned MK members were playing an important role in recruiting supporters, mostly juveniles, to undergo training in the Transkei or in foreign countries. Many were also being given 'military quick training' in the handling of AK47s and limpet mines. It also reported that 30 MK recruits were currently undergoing a 'combat fitness course' at the TDF's Ncise Base.[16]

In June 1991 the South African government (presumably Military Intelligence) received information that MK had established two training bases in Transkei 100 members of the Transkei Defence Force had been trained by MK.

The ANC denied the report.

A top secret report by the DCC's IR-CIS in Ciskei suggested that MK was using the TDF's training facilities. For security reasons such facilities had been coded as follows:

Port St Johns/Libode	=	Mandela Camp.
Idutywa	=	Slovo's Command.
University of Trankei	=	Kaunda's Installation.
Lady Frere	=	MK Gardens.
Ezibeleni	=	Nyerere Shield.[17]

Major-General Holomisa subsequently accused the South African government of trying to topple his administration and of attempting to kill him and the MK chief of staff, Chris Hani, who was resident in Transkei at the time.[18] According to IR-CIS reports, Hani was staying at Minister Titus' house in Durrow Street and at 6 Ebony Street, Umtata.

Operation Abbott: Plan to topple Major-General Holomisa

General Holomisa was correct. By the beginning 1991 the SADF was indeed looking for a reason to justify military intervention in Transkei. Holomisa's military government openly supported the ANC and PAC and interfered with the SADF's divide-and-rule strategy that had proved so effective in other homeland states.

To justify intervention, it was necessary for South Africa to invent dissatisfaction with the military government. It had to create a rebellious attitude amongst Transkeians towards their government.

During 1991 repeated allegations that the TDF was training MK cadres were just as repeatedly denied. In return, Transkei accused South Africa of destabilising it by withholding budgetary aid for months at a time — which it certainly was doing. In January Holomisa said he was using his power base in Transkei to fight apartheid and that he would be prepared to relinquish his position in favour of a centralised South Africa.[19]

Comops had a disinformation heyday. To create uncertainty in the territory, articles were placed in newspapers saying that civil servants would not be paid.

Operational order 1/91 was directed to the SADF's Task Force A. Translated from Afrikaans and reduced to its salient points, it read:

OPSO [Operations Order] 1/91. Operation Abbot 1 (Task Force Alpha)

Situation: The Transkei government is experiencing a financial crisis and civil servants will not receive their salaries by 15 June 1991. Indications are that unrest/violence could result, spilling over into South Africa. It can be expected that one or more of the following will have to be dealt with:

- Local population becoming violent.
- TDF interference with South African Security Forces.
- MK attacking South African Security Forces.
- Military Council members orchestrating action against South African Security Forces.

Mission: Task Force A is to do contingency planning to prevent violence/unrest spilling over from Transkei and Transkei island into southern Natal by 12 June and thereafter continue normal tasks in company areas of responsibility.

General idea. The operation will be conducted in four phases:

Phase 1: Preparation and initial deployment in Task Force A area of responsibility.
Phase 2: Closing of southern border and Transkei island on receipt of code word 'close up'.
Phase 3: Entry into Transkei on code word 'sort out'.
- Scenario 1. With permission and cooperation of Transkei government.
- Without approval of Transkei government.

Phase 4: Mopping up and withdrawal of forces to own areas of responsibility.

Operational instruction 20/91 was directed to the SADF's Group 9. Again translated and abbreviated it read:

OPS Instruction 20/91: GP9 — Operation Abbot 1

Situation: Same as Task Force Operational Order.

Mission: Planning to be done according to the following scenarios:

- **Scenario 1:** Aid is requested and South African forces enter with permission — in other words in cooperation with the TDF and Transkei Police.
- **Scenario 2:** The SADF enters Transkei without approval. It must be accepted that the TDF and the Transkei Police will resist.

Tasks (Task Force Alpha):

- **Scenario 1:**
    - **Priority 1:** Protection of lives of South African citizens in Transkei and adjoining areas.
    - **Priority 2:** Protection of South African property etc.

- **Scenario 2:**
    - **Priority 1:** Protection of lives of South African citizens in Transkei and adjoining area. When resistence from Transkei Security Forces is experienced, such resistance must be eliminated.
    - **Priority 2:** Protection of South African property.
    - **Priority 3:** Transkei key points of importance to South Africa.
    - **Priority 4:** Other Transkei key points.
    - **Priority 5:** Stabilising the situation.

The following is evident from the above operational orders:

- The mock financial crisis was created by the South African government withholding funds from Transkei.
- Its hopes of an unrest situation in Transkei were fuelled by Comops using the media to spread alarm and despondency.
- The operation involved an attack on an independent homeland, so approval must have come from the highest level.
- Orders must have come from the highest level of the SADF because the Army, Air Force and Medical Services were involved.
- The JMC Port Elizabeth (Communications Committee (COMCOM), the Security Committee (SECCOM) and the SAP) were involved as was Natal SECCOM — which also indicates the State Security Council had approved the operation.
- Armed reaction was approved if resistance was met.
- Despite the ban on the ANC and other organisations having been lifted in February 1990, a military operation that was effectively anti-ANC was being planned as late as June 1991.[20]

Other moves in the same direction were also afoot. Brigadier Wouter Basson who was effectively working undercover on the SADF's chemical and biological warfare programme, *Project Coast*, claimed in August 2001 at his trial that in the early 1990s he was despatched by Comops to Natal's south coast with a King Air aircraft that was especially equipped for air photography. He took his bank manager and his family along with him to disguise the real reason for his flights to and over Transkei — which was to photograph military bases and record military activities.[21]

PAC/APLA's command structure

Members of the PAC's National Executive Committee and APLA served on the PAC's Military Commission under the chairmanship of Johnson Mlambo, the PAC's first deputy president. The commission was responsible for the formulation of the PAC's military policy as carried out by APLA.

APLA's High Command (External) in Tanzania, was responsible for all APLA operations both inside South Africa and abroad. It comprised about 30 members under the chairmanship of Jonathan Mlambo as commander-in-chief. The army commander, Sebelo Phama, was also the Defence Secretary until the Second National Congress in 1990 when the PAC's constitution was amended. Barney Hlatswayo was APLA's chief of Staff, Daniel Mohato Mofokeng, *nom de guerre* Romero Daniels, was its chief commander and chief of security and Raymond Fihla was its director of intelligence.

The High Command (Internal) was commanded by Enoch Zulu who also commanded APLA in South Africa. Lawrence Vumenkosi Nticinka was chief of operations in Transkei until November 1992 when he was replaced by 'Happy' Moses Mmphalala Lethlapa. Lethlapa was also Enoch Zulu's deputy on the High Command. Zulu and Lethlapa were both based in Transkei.

APLA divided South Africa into three military regions each of which had a regional command structure. Below the regional structures were local structures that comprised units of three to eight persons, each commanded by a unit commander.

The chain of command operated as follows.

The PAC's military policy as decided by the Military Commission was passed to the High Command (External) which issued the orders to the High Command (Internal). These were passed to regional commands who passed them down to local commands. The local command identified the target, planned the operation and ordered a unit to carry it out. Regional commands were responsible for supplying arms, ammunition or any other equipment required to local commands. Reports back followed the same chain — from local commands, to regions, to the High Command (Internal) to the High Command (External) and back to the Military Commission.

Despite this, as APLA attacks escalated, the PAC's hierarchy attempted to distance itself from its military wing. When interviewed on the SABC's 'Agenda' programme, the PAC's secretary-general, Benny Alexander who later styled himself as Khoisan X, said:

'The constitution of the PAC gives us very clear guidelines as to the responsibility and role of the National Executive Council and within the functions, the constitutional functions, the question of military operations and liability or responsibility in that regard is clearly outside of the mandate of the political leadership constitutionally.' [22]

PAC/APLA's Operation Great Storm

APLA's military commission, which included the leadership of both PAC and APLA, laid plans for *Operation Great Storm* after the unbanning and the PAC's refusal to enter negotiations. Its most important phase involved stepping up attacks on white farmers, because PAC/APLA believed that not only had the farmers participated in dispossessing the African people of their land, they had also become the beneficiaries of it.[23] The primary objective was to drive the farmers from their land and rob them to raise money for financing future operations. They were considered part of the security system, because many belonged to the police reserve or local commando units.[24]

In February 1992 the Katlehong branch of the Pan Africanist Student's Organisation (PASO) passed a resolution condoning attacks on white teachers, saying it was an element of the liberation war. The PAC refused to condemn the resolution.[25]

APLA bases in the Transkei were simple to locate. A *Sunday Times* investigation in early December 1992 by a team headed by Wiseman Khuzwayo, confirmed that APLA was training recruits at informal camps there. They discovered a house and two bush camps at Sterkspruit near the Transkei/Lesotho border where cadres had been seen undergoing military training a few days before. Sources confirmed that a spate of attacks on white motorists in the Lady Grey area near Sterkspruit, had been carried out by APLA cadres operating from those camps. Their intention was to drive whites from the area so that blacks could take over their businesses and shops. The campaign, the *Sunday Times*' team was told, was being masterminded by a Sterkspruit supermarket owner who stored APLA's weapons at his shop.

Locals directed the journalists to the house of headman Tshekedi Pitso Ndhlovu — an admitted PAC member — about ten kilometres away. The locals said it was used as a barracks for APLA fighters, who trained there frequently and openly during daylight hours. Training courses lasted for three weeks. When the *Sunday Times* team drove into Ndhlovu's yard, a man ducked into the house and locked the door. They knocked and he allowed them in, his hand resting on a pocketed pistol at all times.

Two training camps in the dense forests of Mboniseweni and Qhoboshane, near Herschel were also utilised and locals reported many more along Transkei's north-eastern border in the vicinities of Engcobo, Cala, Komga, Umtata and Bolotwa. APLA, they said, had been operating in the Transkei for two to three years. It was common knowledge that APLA had weapons, but they were reputed to be short of cash. Their high command in Harare, it was said, had ordered them to raise money to finance missions by stealing weapons, vehicles and money.[26]

The SADF and the SAP had also long been aware of the bases. A Special Forces covert reconnaissance operation conducted in Transkei to look for MK camps in May 1991 revealed the Nyerere Shield camp at Ezibileni, the Umkhonto we Sizwe camp at Cacadu, the Slovo Command camp at Idutywa, the Mandela camp at Port St Johns/Libode, the Hani Front camp at Tabankulu, the Fisher Battlefields camp at Matatiele, the Mao Front camp at Sterkspruit, MK gardens camp at Lady Frere and the Kaunda Installation camp at Umtata. It also alleged that Soviet, Cuban, Libyan and Algeria officers were in the territory helping to train MK cadres.[27]

Intelligence uncovered their planned terror campaign against whites, after arresting and interrogating 20 PASO members following a petrol bomb attack in Ficksburg on 29 September 1992. They revealed they had been acting under the orders of a senior APLA commander in Bloemfontein, but the campaign was masterminded by a Commander Sizwe in the Transkei. Soft targets like sporting events, cinema shows, schools, churches and buses in the Eastern Cape, Free State and Natal had been designated for attacks over the Christmas period.[28]

The SADF and the Security Police formulated plans to raid APLA bases in the Transkei, but these were cancelled by their political masters[29] because they were anxious to recruit the PAC into the CODESA negotiations.

Minister of Law and Order, Hernus Kriel, however, met the PAC on 11 November and warned them he was aware of APLA's training bases in the Transkei and of their planned attacks. But instead of threatening counteraction he appealed to them, as a gesture of goodwill, to send their APLA cadres 'on a holiday for some months'.[30] Their reaction is not on record, but Kriel was apparently satisfied with their response. It is doubtful that the security chiefs were.

Prior to the meeting, however, Kriel had instructed police headquarters to issue a precautionary warning to vulnerable white communities in the Border region regarding the threat posed by APLA. The SAP confirmed that the Commissioner, General Johan van der Merwe, had issued a directive to his provincial commissioners in October 1992, instructing them to warn the public. He also ordered police stations to liaise with community leaders and businessmen, alerting them to be on the lookout for suspicious-looking people and dangerous objects. Extra police were drafted to the region.

The warning, however, failed to reach the civilians on the ground. Border SAP spokesman, Lieutenant-Colonel Christo Louw, contrary to Pretoria's story, insisted he had received no specific instructions or warnings regarding the onset of an APLA terror campaign.

'After the spate of attacks on police on the Reef and in other parts of the country a couple of months ago, we were told to warn our men to be on guard against attacks on policeman — but there was no mention of APLA or soft targets. We were not guarding schools or shops or anything like that. In fact, the first time we realised soft targets were being attacked was this week.' [31]

Colonel Louw was referring to a particularly callous incident on 28 November when three APLA cadres launched an attack with grenades and automatic weapons on the King William's Town Golf Club while a Christmas party for senior citizens was in progress. They admitted they had intended causing as many deaths and as much damage to property as possible. They succeeded, killing four and wounding 17.[32]

There was an attack on a restaurant in Queenstown, a spate of attacks on white farmers in the Eastern Cape and on policemen in various areas, for which APLA claimed responsibility. During 1991/1992 APLA murdered 16 people in all.

In early 1993 State President F W de Klerk ordered Judge Richard Goldstone to investigate APLA's activities. The Transkei, the PAC and APLA refused to cooperate, saying they would ignore subpoenas issued by the commission of enquiry.

In their submissions, the SADF revealed that the PAC had received US$14 million from Libya in 1991, when Colonel Moammar Gaddafi had contemplated becoming their primary source of finance. PAC/APLA's aim was the total liberation of South Africa by armed revolution and the replacement of the government with an 'African Socialist Democracy'.

To promote its armed struggle, the SADF said, PAC/APLA used both political and military structures, which were intertwined and complementary. Their military structures, both internal and external, were also intertwined to further their aims in South Africa. APLA had adopted a Maoist approach, placing more emphasis on the country areas than the towns, in an attempt to create footholds so the struggle could be exploited by local 'underground' fighting units and local 'task force' self defence units.

Their strategy was for the military and political wings (PAC) to work together. The PAC's task was to create a climate in which APLA fighters returning to South Africa could survive. It provided logistical support and established new branches where necessary to further this strategy.

The following quotes emanated from APLA:

'The SAP and SADF remain enemy number one of the African people and must be destroyed.[33]

'The SAP remains the primary target of the APLA forces'.[34]

'APLA would continue to target security members until its immediate objective, the establishment of a constituent assembly, has been realised'.[35]

'The SAP together with the SADF are fully armed enemy organs. For any revolution to succeed they should be wiped out.' [36]

APLA's strategy was to wage 'full-scale war' by attacking white farmers, members of the Security Forces and white residential areas. Their 'swift attacks', mostly using grenades, were directed at targets where the 'enemy' congregated in large numbers, like in barracks or at parties. Their 'mobile warfare' involved operations launched from 'liberated zones'. Evidence of their strategy, the SADF said, was manifested by details of their operations.[37]

The Goldstone Commission heard SAP allegations that APLA had conducted at least 41 attacks in South Africa during 1991/1992, using the Transkei where their High Command was situated as a rear base. The SAP said that Transkei should hand over to the Commission all 9mm firearms loaned by them to APLA since April 1992 to determine if any of them had been used in attacks on whites.

The Commission invited the Transkei administration to respond to the allegations, but the chairman of its Military Council, Major-General Bantu Holomisa, rejected the invitation, saying it would not give evidence of APLA activities in the territory before the Commission. 'If Mr Justice Goldstone's investigation indicates that Transkei is being used as a training ground and launching pad for attacks against South Africa, the Goldstone Commission and the South African government officials are welcome to present evidence to the proposed Transkei commission of enquiry.' [38]

The Goldstone report positively linked APLA to 34 attacks involving 16 murders and numerous injuries. Their primary targets were indeed members of the Security Forces. The

Commission found that APLA was involved in 15 attacks on police, 13 on farmhouses, three attacks in Ficksburg, the murders at the King William's Town Golf Club and attacks on restaurants in Cape Town and Queenstown. The 16 murders did not include an undisclosed number of people who had died in recent attacks on cars in the PWV (Pretoria/Witwatersrand/Vereeniging) area. It found:

1 Both the PAC and APLA still propagate the armed struggle.
2 APLA is the military wing of the PAC.
3 APLA uses Transkei as a springboard for attacks into the Republic of South Africa. Arms and ammunition are stored in Transkei for use by APLA units. The presence of armed APLA members in Transkei was known to members of the Transkeian Police.
4 The Transkeian government has supplied APLA with arms allegedly for VIP protection purposes.
5 APLA's operational activities are aimed at members of the SAP, the SADF and white civilians in general.
6 The PAC controls APLA's budget.
7 APLA members have received training in Transkei.
8 Arms and explosives are being smuggled into the Republic of South Africa and Transkei for use by APLA members.
9. APLA's internal High Command for the Republic is based in Transkei.

Despite the blame for such incidents having been laid squarely at the feet of PAC/APLA, their attacks escalated. They became the target of considerable criticism.

Chris Hani, former MK Chief of Staff, urged the PAC leadership to 'bite the bullet', accept negotiations and scale down or suspend APLA operations. They should drop their slogan 'one settler, one bullet' because it was not only racist but encouraged the perception that it was alright to kill whites.

'We are involved in negotiations for democratic elections and cannot condone any form of violence' said Hani. The killing of innocents served only to fuel the emotional outbursts of right wing and left wing extremists. 'I can't understand why it should be in the interests of our struggle to look around for a school bus carrying white children or to open fire on a highway used by everybody. Such attacks are very cowardly and not revolutionary at all. Revolutionaries value life.' [39]

In February 1993 Major-General Holomisa claimed that South Africa was training Africans to pose as members of APLA. He claimed that such men were used in attacks on civilians in South Africa to provide 'proof' that APLA was at war with MK.

A spokesman for South Africa's Ministry of Law and Order dismissed the claim as 'malicious propaganda' and suggested that if the general had evidence to support this he should produce it.

In the same month 80 PAC supporters picketed the South African Embassy in Umtata to protest at the alleged presence of members of 32-Battalion and Koevoet along the frontier with Transkei. They dispersed when the Transkei riot unit fired tear gas at them.[40]

During March 1993 three APLA cadres based in Transkei attacked the Yellowwoods Hotel near Fort Beaufort. One guarded the back door to prevent escapes, while the other two went in through the front door with guns firing, killing an 18-year-old white student and wounding others.[41]

At the end of the month the SAP and SADF sealed off the Transkei/South African frontier and set up roadblocks on all roads leading into the Transkei to 'protect South African citizens from cross-border attacks'. Border patrols were intensified.

The South African government issued a statement saying the moves were designed to 'improve [the] security of its borders with Transkei'.[42]

Tensions between the South African government and Transkei eased after talks late in April. An immediate consequence was that South African border controls were 'adapted' to ensure there was less disruption of traffic crossing between Transkei and South Africa.[43]

When addressing police officers in Transkei shortly afterwards, APLA army commander, Sebelo Phama said the organisation targeted children because it wanted to 'strike at whites where it hurt the most.' The South African government sharply criticised Transkei for providing him with such a stage. Simultaneously Transkei released the draft terms of reference for its own commission of enquiry into APLA's activities in the homeland.[44]

In April four people including two German tourists were wounded in armed attacks in Transkei. The Germans were driving from Cape Town to Durban when they were attacked near Mount Ayliff. A Lusikisiki businessman, Richard Pretorius, and his companion, who were travelling to Kokstad, were attacked in a separate incident.

In May APLA cadres operating from Transkei, burst into the Highgate Hotel in East London. They opened fire with AK47s and tossed in grenades, killing five white civilians and wounding seven. According to the TRC the attackers returned to Umtata afterwards to report to their commander, Moses Lethlapa, known as 'Happy'.[45]

After a South African, Abraham Cilliers, became the victim of the third attack on whites in May 1993, the South African Department of Foreign Affairs warned local motorists to 'as far as possible' avoid travelling through Transkei.

At the multi-party constitutional negotiations during May, Minister of Law and Order, Hernus Kriel, produced documents naming Happy Lethlapa as head of APLA operations in Transkei. The documents disclosed that he had been named by several APLA cadres who had been arrested as the one who had instructed them to kill whites and policeman. Some of those arrested said they had been trained in Transkei and others in foreign countries.

Towards the end of the month Major-General Holomisa dismissed as disinformation a South African Military Intelligence report that linked him to the infiltration of a nine-man killer squad of mixed APLA cadres and TDF soldiers. The objective of the action, codenamed *Operation Trench*, was to kill whites. He accused Military Intelligence and the newspaper that published the report of conspiring to defame him, adding that if hard evidence existed linking him to the killer squad, then 'surely they should prove it in court'.[46]

By June the killing of whites had become frequent in Transkei itself. This prompted Holomisa to express 'grave concern' after the murders of two South African businessmen during armed robberies at Coffee Bay and Idutywa.

'The perpetrators of these cowardly acts do not have the interests of Transkei residents at heart', the general said. 'If white investors already operating in Transkei gained the impression that lawlessness and civil mayhem are reigning supreme in the streets, they are likely to pull out of the Transkei with the resultant loss of scarce job opportunities.' He added that his administration 'accordingly enjoins political organisations, interest groups, the dispute resolution committee and civic organisations to help us fight this cancerous development in society'.[47]

Transkei's Security Forces did nothing to curb APLA's activities.

On Sunday 25 July, while Bishop Frank Retief was leading a 1 000 strong multiracial congregation in prayer, an APLA gang burst into St. James Church, Kenilworth, Cape Town. They tossed two grenades and sprayed the congregation with automatic fire, killing 11 — four of them visiting Russian seamen — and wounding 56. The PAC later admitted the assault had been ordered by APLA's operations director, Happy Lethlapa. The grenades were forensically sourced to a batch supplied to the Transkei Defence Force.[48]

On 20 August four Cambodian-trained APLA cadres based in Transkei attacked the Engen oil depot in East London with RPG-7 rockets. Explosions rocked the surrounding suburbs, but damage was limited because the fuel tanks hit were empty. Police fired on a car fleeing from the scene.[49]

In the same month US Fulbright scholar, Amy Biehl (27), an exchange student studying at the University of the Western Cape, was set on by a mob of young PASO members while driving black friends to their homes in Guguletu Township, Cape Town. They mercilessly knifed, stoned and beat her to death with rocks and bricks. PASO's regional executive later admitted they had approved the murder.[50]

On 27 August four APLA cadres from Transkei fired on a Translux bus with R-4 rifles as it drove into Beaufort West in the Karoo, wounding eight passengers.[51]

On 6 September five APLA cadres armed with automatic weapons walked into the Riverside Lodge Hotel, Ladybrand, in the Free State. They forced the staff and black clientele to lie on the floor and told them they were only looking for *Boere* or 'whites'. After failing to find any, they hurled petrol bombs and shot-up the buildings, causing an estimated R1 million worth of damage.[52]

APLA's internal commander, Carl Zimbiri, said they would continue attacking civilians. Their policy, he said, had been to attack members of the Security Forces, but attacks on civilians had achieved far better results and had been necessitated by 'developments and trends'.[53]

On 30 December three APLA cadres armed with automatic weapons and rifle grenades, burst into the Heidelberg Tavern, Observatory, Cape Town, and emptied their weapons at the patrons who were mostly students, many of them coloured. A rifle grenade failed to explode. This was traced to a batch supplied to the Transkei Defence Force. Four people were killed and four wounded.[54]

There were many other APLA attacks during 1993.

In Daveyton on the East Rand, a white man was dragged from his van and burnt to death; two policemen were abducted from the Kokstad, Transkei, charge office and shot to death; a gang of eight APLA cadres murdered a farmer's wife at Tzaneen, Northern Transvaal (Northern Province); four APLA cadres were arrested after a 'fund raising' robbery at City Deep, Johannesburg; a detective was killed at his Krugersdorp home; two policemen were fired on at Eldorado Park, Johannesburg; the Randfontein home of a police lieutenant was attacked with AK47s and R-4 rifles; two policemen died and another was seriously wounded when a police patrol was ambushed in Mabopane, Pretoria; two flats and the district surgeon's consulting rooms at Beaufort West were petrol bombed; a white-owned supermarket at Cala in Transkei was torched; an Elliot, Eastern Cape, farmer and his daughter were shot dead while delivering milk.[55]

Umtata raid: 8 October 1993

With the escalation of APLA attacks, the SADF and the SAP re-examined the possibility of striking APLA facilities in Transkei. The problem was that their training bases were will-o'-the-wisp — here today and gone tomorrow. There were no permanent barracks, little in the way of permanent housing and no large groups to be targeted. Most cadres were locally trained — youngsters drawn to or persuaded to the movement and regarded as expendable by the leadership. Very few were from the hard core — the type the Security Police had been monitoring for years.

Clearly APLA's leadership were keeping a wary eye over their shoulders, aware that if any degree of permanency was attained at particular training camps, it was almost certain they would be targeted by the Security Forces. This was evidenced by the constant stream of information gathered on APLA by the Security Police. They experienced few difficulties and garnered it in from an abundance of sources, including many Transkei police officers and soldiers who did not share the overt enthusiasm for APLA, as was the case with Major-General Bantu Holomisa and his Military Council.

A breakthrough came in July 1993 when police arrested two locally recruited APLA cadres at the Kei River bridge border post. During questioning one revealed he had been given a crash course in weapons handling at Port Elizabeth and had made several trips to the Transkei to collect weapons and money. During one visit he had stayed several days at a transit facility at 47 Jordan Street, Umtata. While there, he had witnessed the issue of weapons to APLA cadres on at least three occasions. Cadres slept there regularly — one night 18 shared the place with him. The State Security Council discussed the situation in August 1993, apparently without coming to a conclusion.

Police arrested an externally trained APLA cadre in Elliot on 15 September. He confessed he had taken part in an attack on the Wesselsbron Supermarket in the Free State on 3 July when five people were killed. When staying in Umtata, he also lodged at 47 Jordan Street. He said that up to 18 APLA operatives stayed there.

SADF Chief, General Georg Meiring, later told the TRC he relied on the then Director of Operations, Brigadier Castleman — a senior staff officer for the intelligence aspects — and Colonel Gibson for the planning of any raid that might take place.

With the approval of Defence Minister Kobie Coetsee, 5-Recce (then temporarily known as 451-Parachute Battalion) launched a reconnaissance mission to keep observation on the premises, a mission that lasted from 2 to 7 October 1993. All comings and goings were recorded and the Security Police's intelligence confirmed that it was indeed an APLA facility. They were unable to confirm, however, that weapons were stored there.[56] In anticipation, 5-Recce had in the meanwhile been ordered by the Commander Special Forces to place a 12-man team on standby to raid the facility.

On 7 October a meeting of the State Security Council attended by the State President F W de Klerk, Foreign Minister Pik Botha, Defence Minister Kriel and senior members of the Security Forces was held and authority given 'to conduct a limited strike on the house . . . to neutralise the target'.

The reconnaissance team was ordered to withdraw at 20:00, the same time that the attack force left their South African base by road. They crossed the border into Transkei at 24:00 reaching the target at about 02:45 on 8 October. They were armed with Uzi sub-machine-guns and pistols fitted with silencers.

Little detail is known of the raid except that nine operators were on target and the other three provided backup away from the scene. Former unit C10 commander at Vlakplaas, police Colonel Eugene de Kock, claimed that his men also played a part in the raid.[57]

A neighbour, in bed but awake at the time, heard a vehicle pull up nearby. He did not look out, but thought it was a Toyota van.

'I heard shots being fired from an automatic rifle, which seemed to have been fitted with a silencer because the noise was not so loud. I thought it was just people shooting somewhere, as sometimes happens here in Umtata. The vehicle drove away but came back again and pulled up next to my own house. There was a noise again as if the people were loading things on the vehicle and I could hear shouts sounding like "go, go, go".'

According to General Georg Meiring in testimony to the TRC, the house was in darkness: 'The door was kicked open and because of security reasons, they did not switch on the lights . . . but used flashlights, they were prepared to find as many as 12 people. There were actually only five persons in the house and all were killed because they acted hostilely.'

Immediately afterwards the SADF also claimed the occupants had resisted, prompting the operators to open fire and kill them. Whether this was true or not is difficult to say, but the *modus operandi* of Special Forces when on target makes it likely they would have opened fire anyway. General Meiring confirmed this to the TRC when asked if the operators had a licence to shoot to kill, saying: '. . . a soldier is never trained [to do] anything but shoot to kill. There is no way of asking how to shoot, you shoot for effect if you do shoot.'

Whatever the case, when they opened fire, they fired effectively. One of the dead had 23 bullet wounds, another 12 and another 11. Four had been shot in the head execution style. The Transkei Police docket revealed that 78 cartridge cases and 26 expended 'projectiles' of a type not mentioned were found at the house. The expected large arms cache did not materialise, but the raiders found an AK47, an R-1 carbine and pistols, some of them handmade. There were indications that 'provision had been made' for the storage of a large quantity of weapons.[58]

The SADF press statement afterwards said the raid had been on 'a confirmed APLA facility', adding that intelligence indicated it was being used 'as a springboard for criminal acts of terror on unarmed South African civilians. This intelligence was obviously obtained, *inter alia*, from sources in the custody of the SAP.' [59]

In support of this contention, the SADF said a quantity of documents had been seized from the house. They produced handwritten poems — including one titled *Azania is Not for Sale* and another called *Africa for the Africans*. There was an 'APLA Code of Discipline' which included the following clauses: 'Do not surrender to the enemy or hand over arms or information; speak politely to all people; pay fairly for all you buy from the people; and do not hit or insult people.' There were documents dealing with the 'principles of pan-Africanism', and a PASO application form. A document titled: *We Fight* gave APLA's definition of the enemy, 'types of ambush' and 'the seven deadly sins of a political fighter'. Some documentation related to a meeting of the Patriotic Front in 1991. There were also school study notes, telephone messages, receipts, a letter to an aunt and examination questions on Louis Leipoldt's play *Die Heks*. They also discovered a loose ID photograph of Jabu, a trained APLA cadre who had been positively linked to three attacks in the Free State in which a 15-year-old white girl was murdered and two women were wounded. The raiders, who suffered no casualties, were on target for 27 minutes.[60]

The house was owned by Sgqibo Mpendulo (57). Mpendulo was a former prisoner who had been convicted of political offences and had spent five years on Robben Island. After his release he was arrested in Transkei and with seven other people charged with offences relating to PAC activities. They were all acquitted after a marathon trial lasting two years.

Strangely enough, neither Mpendulo nor his wife were at 47 Jordan Street that night, which raise the possibility that they lived elsewhere — particularly as he refused to tell the *Sunday Times* afterwards where he and his wife had spent the night. This indicates that the premises were indeed an APLA facility. Mpendulo told *The Citizen* that his neighbour, who had heard the raiders during the night, came to 'his house' at 06:00 to tell him he had discovered his children dead.

'Inside the first room', the neighbour told *The Citizen*, 'I found three of the children. Two of them were lying on the ground and one was still in bed. Their bodies had been raked by bullets. In the second room I found the other two. One was lying on the floor and the other was lying halfway on the bed with his upper body on the floor. All the children had bullet wounds at the back of their heads and three had wounds at the back of their legs. It was a typical commando raid. The house was riddled with bullets. It was littered with 9mm spent cartridges.' [61]

Mpendulo insisted that although he was a PAC member, his relatives and visitors were not. He said the youths comprised a study group who had been studying there for school examinations. When finished they would have laid mattresses on the floor of the lounge and TV room, watched TV and gone to sleep.[62]

PAC's Deputy President, Johnson Mlambo, identified the dead as Mpendulo's twin sons, Sadat and Samora, another Mpendulo child Mziwandile (12) (actually Mziwandile Mfeya — not a son of Mpendulo) and their two cousins, Tando (actually Thando Mthembu) (19) and Sxeshe (actually Sandiso Yose) (12). Whether the last two were really cousins of the Mpendulo twins is unknown.

Not unexpectedly, APLA's information officer, Johnny Majozi, speaking from its HQ in Tanzania, said the house was not an APLA hideout. 'APLA has never used the house in question, and the people involved were not APLA members.' Transkei PAC chairman Gilbert Sereke said it was possible one or two of the dead were members of PASO, but not the 12-year-olds.[63]

The row over whether those killed were innocents or whether they were APLA cadres deepened. At a news conference in Pretoria on 8 October Defence Minister Kobie Coetsee and his generals came under fire regarding the ages of the targets. General Georg Meiring said those shot appeared to be adults, but the strike force did not wait to find out. They brandished weapons at the operators and were shot.

Kobie Coetsee said President F W de Klerk and his senior ministers had authorised a 'limited strike' against the 'verified' APLA facility. The decision was made against the background of the Goldstone Commission's finding that APLA was using Transkei as a springboard for attacks into South Africa, that their cadres were being trained in Transkei and their High Command was based there. The strike had been justified because APLA had announced the continuation of its armed struggle. It was unacceptable that APLA continued its killing spree while the PAC took part in negotiations which effectively protected APLA.[64]

Deputy Law and Order Minister, Gert Myburgh, said it was a tragedy that youths were killed during the SADF raid, but 'the raid has provided additional proof that APLA is, in fact, recruiting, training, and deploying juveniles for terrorist operations against innocent soft targets'.

SADF sources told the *Sunday Times* that the raid had been pre-emptive after they had received extensive intelligence of plans to attack soft targets in South Africa. 'We got the people we were going for. We had to be 105% sure of what we were doing, otherwise we could never have gone in — not at a [politically difficult] time like this.' [65]

ANC president Nelson Mandela called the raid barbaric.[66] He later accused President F W de Klerk of terrorism.

The presiding bishop of the Methodist Church of Southern Africa, the Rev Dr Stanley Magoba, said the strike 'could well prove a serious setback for the process of negotiations in South Africa'. Bishop Magoba called on the government to institute bilateral negotiations with the PAC and offered to mediate if required. He also urged the PAC to abandon its armed struggle. It is significant that not long afterwards, the Bishop replaced Clarence Makwetu as PAC president and was responsible for converting the PAC from a liberation movement into a political party.[67]

Foreign Minister Pik Botha shook his ministerial colleagues by conceding in reply to hostile questions at a public meeting that the attack had been a 'bad mistake'. He admitted he was involved with the decision to mount the raid. General Kat Liebenberg, he said, had assured him the premises from which many attacks in South Africa had been carried out, had been under surveillance for weeks. Rifles were stored there. 'I personally queried the facts before the attack and I was assured there was nothing to worry about. The killing of people was not authorised — only the seizure of weapons. When the most senior member of the Defence Force assured me, I believed him.' [68]

This was another of those numerous opportunities presented to Pik Botha when he could have resigned as a minister as a matter of principle. Needless to say, he did not.

There was tit-for-tat diplomacy following the raid when General Bantu Holomisa expelled South African Ambassador, Horace van Rensburg, and the 12 SADF personnel guarding the Umtata Embassy. In retaliation South Africa expelled Umtata's Ambassador to Pretoria, G S Magazi.[69]

A more serious tit-for-tat was an attack on the Bhongolethu Police Station near Kokstad by four MK cadres after they had attended the funerals of those killed in the raid. They disarmed Sergeants Mbhele and Ngubo, dragged them from the police station and callously executed them.[70]

During the ongoing row afterwards, lawyers for the Mpendulo family arranged for an international US forensic expert to examine the seized weapons. The SADF failed to produce them and said they had been destroyed. This was disbelieved by the TRC which led to its finding that the raid and the killings were a 'gross violation of human rights'.[71]

During the furore that followed the raid, few of those protesting about the SADF's actions in killing 'children', castigated the PAC and APLA for subjecting children as young as 12 to military training and using them to mount terrorist attacks against civilians, including women and children. That they had regularly done so is a matter of record.

It must be added that APLA was not alone in Africa and elsewhere in their methods. It is well documented that ZANLA used children in combatant roles during the Rhodesian War; so did RENAMO in Mozambique. Four thousand child combatants were given government amnesties in Sierra Leone in 1998 and there have been many more cases since.[72] Children were and still are being used in combatant roles in Rwanda, Burundi, Angola, by the Lord's Resistance Army in Uganda, in Burma, Sri Lanka, the Democratic Republic of Congo, Southern Sudan and many other countries. There are numerous other examples.

In 1999 Amnesty International launched a campaign aimed at plucking children out of war zones, where they have become deliberate targets of war, whether as victims or as child soldiers. Their report, *Children in the Firing Line*, was timed to coincide with an UN working group meeting in Geneva to discuss raising the minimum age for recruitment into the armed forces from 15 to 18.[73]

In 1995 the Government of National Unity, formed after the 1994 general election in South Africa, issued the following statement: 'The raid on the house in Umtata was authorised on the strength of intelligence provided by the Security Forces that it was being used as an arms cache for attacks against civilians in other parts of South Africa. That information was inaccurate at the time of the operation and the killing of the youthful occupants was unjustified and inexcusable.' According to Justice Minister Dullah Omar, the statement was drawn up in consultation with President Mandela and Deputy President F W de Klerk.

President Nelson Mandela apologised to the families of the five youths killed during the raid.[74]

APLA's attacks continue

After the PAC and APLA had 'officially' suspended their armed struggle, attacks on policemen, white farmers and other whites continued unabated.

An APLA commander, wishing to remain anonymous, told the *Sowetan* on 18 January 1994 that he and his subordinates would continue military operations despite the PAC suspending the armed struggle. They were convinced the leadership had abandoned the cause because of 'cold feet'. The feeling that there were dissidents in APLA was reinforced when three senior PAC members, including the National Director of Publicity and Information, Waters Toboti, were suspended for challenging the suspension of military operations.[75]

During February 1994 three APLA cadres were summoned to Umtata, issued with automatic weapons and grenades and instructed to travel to Newcastle to select a soft target frequented by whites. On the night of 14 February — Valentine's Day — they attacked the Crazy Beat Disco, killing a white woman and wounding two others.[76]

In a joint statement on 18 March 1994 the Transkei Defence Force and APLA leaders said the TDF was making its training facilities available to APLA in preparation for its integration into the South African National Defence Force (SANDF).[77]

By the end of March 1994, as a direct result of TDF assistance to MK and APLA, the homeland was dissolving into anarchy. On 28 March the once idyllic resort town of Port St Johns became a war zone. According to Transkei Police spokesman, Colonel Solly Mkiwane, the violence began in the town when APLA members led by a PAC branch official and local prosecutor, Gwebelentlanzi Mposelwa, attacked ANC members holding a voter education workshop at a local school. An ANC member was killed. The shooting spread to the town and the bodies of a TDF member, a security guard and two APLA cadres were discovered near the post office.

APLA cadres led by Mposelwa fired several shots at an ANC supporter hitchhiking from Port St Johns to Umtata. He escaped unharmed and reported the shooting to the police.

Transkei Police supported by Special Forces operators from the unit in town went to Mposelwa's house to arrest him. He resisted and there was an exchange of gunfire lasting until late into the night.

Early the next morning Mposelwa and four of his comrades emerged from the house and attempted to drive to Second Beach, but they drove into a roadblock set up by the Security

Forces. They opened fire on the roadblock and the Security Forces returned it. Mposelwa was shot dead and the other four were arrested.

The story appears to be a little too pat. The more likely truth is that APLA and MK cadres undergoing joint training at the Special Forces depot turned on each other and a shootout resulted.

Whatever the case, General Holomisa could not be reached for comment. A statement was released from his office that said soldiers would be deployed in Umzimkulu, Bizana and Western Transkei to check for and arrest anyone found in possession of firearms without permits.[78]

With the forthcoming general election on 27 April 1994, the grip of General Holomisa and his Military Council on the Transkei loosened. The amalgamation of the territory into a greater South Africa became a *fait accompli* in waiting.

One would like to think that the Transkei Police, who until then had been forced to stand helplessly by and watch APLA's bloody excesses without being able to do anything about it, enthusiastically launched a crackdown. But it is a probability that until the re-amalgamation became a fact — as with their ruling political authority — they had been indifferent to APLA's murderous activities.

Whatever the case, Transkei's Murder and Robbery Squad Chief, Lieutenant-Colonel Ronald Dlanjwa and his deputy, Captain Dumisa Magadlela, announced the arrest of 18 cadres of two Transkei-based APLA groups and said they were looking for a third group that had fled to Ciskei. Captain Magadlela said the 18 had been implicated 'in almost all the murders, especially around Butterworth/Idutywa, and all the highjackings on the N2 highway. They were all singing the same song'. They had been linked to the murders of four white businessmen in the Transkei and positively identified as involved in an attack on the Willowvale Police Station, where they stole weapons. The local community, who viewed APLA's criminal activities with disfavour, had carried out the arrests.

Captain Magadlela said: 'They are claiming to be APLA and are APLA members . . . They started by attacking white motorists, but as time went on they attacked any motorist entering the territory, black or brown.'[79]

All APLA operatives convicted or facing trial for murders committed during their pre-1994 election murder sprees were eventually granted amnesty by the TRC. It was accepted that their activities had been politically motivated and that they had made full disclosures. Far from expressing remorse for their actions, the hearings were frequently punctuated by laughter and shouts of encouragement by their comrades of 'One Settler, one Bullet!'

The stock used in many of APLA's terror-motivated grenade attacks was traced back to Transkei's military armouries, but even more tangible evidence of the support given to it by Transkei's Military Council emerged later.

The Kroon Inquiry, headed by Judge Frank Kroon, was established by the Eastern Cape government after the 1994 general election and the reintegration of Transkei into South Africa. Its brief was to investigate the root causes of violence in the strife-torn Tsolo area of Transkei where more than 285 people had been killed in violence since January 1993. Kroon singled out Major-General Holomisa — by then deputy minister in the South African government — and former TDF Chief, Lieutenant-General T T Matanzima — later Chief of Staff Personnel in the SANDF — for criticism.

He said Generals Holomisa and Matanzima had acted unlawfully in sanctioning the 'common practise' of issuing TDF weaponry, including automatic rifles, to civilians. Not all of them had been recovered.

He quoted an example that occurred in January 1993 when the PAC's Dr Malizo Mpehle reportedly asked the TDF for protection after he had allegedly 'heard' that a group of white men had been enquiring about his whereabouts. This scenario was highly unlikely in itself. A 'group of white men' wandering around the Transkei of that time asking questions about the PAC or the ANC would soon have found itself behind bars. Be that as it may, the TDF issued him with an Uzi sub-machine gun and two R4 rifles for use by five young men he had chosen as bodyguards. The men were given a two-week crash course on weapons-training.

Dr Mpehle later asked for more men to be trained. The TDF rejected this but agreed to replace the R4s with G3 carbines on the strict understanding that he return the R4s. They were never returned. Mpehle also ignored an instruction by General Matanzima in May 1994, after the election, that all weapons given to civilians be returned to the SANDF into which, by then, the TDF was in the process of being absorbed.

At least one of the R4s was used in the murder of two people in Tsolo. Police seized the Uzi in August 1994 after the violent death of someone else. When the police eventually recovered the missing weapons, it was found that a 'substantial amount of ammunition' issued with them was missing.

By 1995 Dr Mpehle was occupying the unlikely position of MEC for Safety and Security in the Eastern Cape government. The Kroon Enquiry recommended his dismissal from the post and it was done.[80]

In another earlier instance, on 1 September 1992, the TDF issued Lawrence Vumenkosi Nticinka, APLA's chief of operations in Transkei, with 12 9mm Z.88 pistols and three 9mm Beretta pistols together with 225 rounds of ammunition for 'protection purposes'. Significantly, attacks in which 9mm ammunition figured prominently showed a marked increase during 1992.[81]

24

Enter IR-CIS
Murder of Gen Charles Sebe & Col Onward Guzana
Ciskei
1990/1991

Enter International Researchers — Ciskei Intelligence Service (IR-CIS)

Ted Brassel, a one-time deputy Town Clerk in East London and a former senior member of the Directorate of Covert Collection (DCC) had retired as a major. His last posting had been the DCC's field office in East London where he worked for Lieutenant-Colonel John Mawdsley. He was contacted and asked to approach Brigadier Oupa Gqozo, whom he knew well, and suggest he set up his own intelligence agency. It appears likely he suggested the NIS could not be trusted and that Gqozo would be better off with an organisation that he could personally control.

Ted Brassel became a frequent visitor to Brigadier Gqozo's office. Gqozo's staff became aware from conversations and by Gqozo's general utterances that he had very sensitive information at his disposal, but he kept the source to himself. The information suggested that the Transkei under Major-General Bantu Holomisa, the MK controlled by SACP leader Chris Hani, *Iliso Lomzi* under Charles Sebe and Major-General Teitlefer Minnaar were conspiring to oust him from office.

An intelligence organisation for Gqozo would not come free, because although it would use the expertise of experienced ex-military officers, it would be a civilian-run commercial company. It would be a business and those working for it would have to be paid. In the way of Military Intelligence, Brassel quoted a cash figure to set it up and it must have seemed very attractive. Gqozo, of course, would have been unaware that in reality it would be run by Military Intelligence, which would be only too happy pick up the tab. Of course Military Intelligence would have run it for nothing, but Brassel was not going to say that.The beauty of it for Gqozo was that its employees would owe total loyalty to him and would not be looking over their shoulders at Pretoria, like the NIS. Gqozo, a highly gullible man, should nevertheless have known better.

Gqozo was even more amenable to the suggestion when Brassel said he could get an ex-commandant, Jan Anton Nieuwoudt, to run the organisation for him. Gqozo knew Nieuwoudt well, which was the main reason he had been nominated for the job. In 1978 he had been Gqozo's instructing officer in his 21-Battalion days and they had served together for a long period.[1] They were also good friends. Gqozo accepted at face value Brassel's inference that Nieuwoudt was a retired officer. This was untrue. He was a serving officer with the rank of Commandant and at the time was the second-in-command to Colonel At Nel on the DCC's terrorist desk.

The DCC arranged Nieuwoudt's 'retirement' from the SADF, but in reality it was a sham. He would merely be going undercover. To reinforce the ploy he was even given a retirement package of R46 922,28 to give him personal capital. This was obviously 'on account' although the SADF — as often became par for the course with its covert operators — would later treacherously deny it and turn its back on him.

Officially Jan Anton Nieuwoudt was offered an appointment as a 'civilian intelligence adviser' by the Council of State's director-general, Kobus Botha. His contract was signed by Brigadier Gqozo in his capacity as the Head of State with the agreement of the Central Personnel Administration.

Ted Brassel was also instructed to come out of retirement and join Nieuwoudt in the Ciskei. Several other captains and lieutenants also went undercover with the organisation.

There have been suggestions that the unit first became operational in September 1990, working from a safe house in Gonubie, East London. If so, in its early stages it was probably run by Brassel.

Whatever the case, Jan Anton Nieuwoudt's CV shows his last working day with the DCC was 31 October 1990. The next day, he joined International Researchers-Ciskei Intelligence Services (IR-CIS).[2]

In late October 1990, the daily meeting of Ciskei's Council of State was scheduled to be held in Brigadier Gqozo's office. To the surprise of the senior military and police officers attending, they saw Gqozo usher two bearded white men into an adjacent conference room. Gqozo told them the men were members of his own personal covert intelligence unit, formed to advise him on covert issues. He emphasised that he was the boss and that no one had the right to question his decisions. Everyone, he said, should cooperate with the unit.

After making his point, he called in the white men and formally introduced them, but no one remembered their names.

Interestingly enough, Colonel Mias Muller, the South African Military Attaché to the Ciskei — later to be Gqozo's military adviser — spoke immediately afterwards to Lieutenant-Colonel Zantsi — Ciskei's joint Chief of Staff Intelligence — alerting him to the imminent arrival of Jan Nieuwoudt as Gqozo's intelligence adviser. This surprised both Zantsi and CDF Chief, Brigadier Jamangile, for it was the first they had heard about it. Colonel Muller was concerned about Nieuwoudt's appointment because he regarded him as the wrong material for a position in Ciskei as he had no understanding of the circumstances there.

It seems it was just another example of a Military Attaché's right hand not having the slightest idea what Military Intelligence's left hand was doing.[3]

IR-CIS at first set up their offices on Blacklands Farm outside Bisho, which belonged to Brigadier Gqozo. From there they moved to House 14 in the Ministerial Complex, although they continued to get some use out of Blacklands Farm.

Jan Anton Nieuwoudt and another Military Intelligence operator, Clive Brink, were not seen much in the IR-CIS offices in Bisho during the days before the 22 November coup attempt in Transkei by Colonel Craig Duli. Major Ted Brassel was invariably alone in the office. When asked about the other two, he claimed they were attending meetings in East London. On 21 November Nieuwoudt attended the daily meeting of intelligence organisations, but stayed only long enough to listen to the input of the Security Police and the SADF Military Intelligence. He left immediately afterwards to attend what he described as an important meeting in East London. In passing, he said he would not be in the office on 22 November.

On the early morning of 22 November Jan Anton was certainly not in his office. He was elsewhere with Brigadier Gqozo monitoring events relating to the coup bid as they unfolded. The following document dated less than a week later signed by DCC Director, Brigadier J J 'Tolletjie' Botha and counter-signed as 'approved' by the then Chief of Staff Intelligence, SADF, Lieutenant-General 'Witkop' Badenhorst, confirms it.

Memorandum

27 November 1990

From: DCC [Directorate Covert Collection]
To: HIS

Purchase of communications: National KXF120 fax machine

The objective of this memorandum is to obtain authority to purchase communications equipment.

During the failed coup in the T/skei [Transkei] Brig Gqozo as well as Mr Nieuwoudt were kept informed of activities. Mr Nieuwoudt kept this Directorate continually informed telephonically. This method of communications is unsafe. Therefore, a safer means of communicating is required. Due to the above a fax machine is considered to be the best means of communication.

The fax machine is commercially available and [purchasing it] will not draw any attention. The cost of two fax machines and two decoders is R16 950,00.

Authorisation [required] for two fax machines at: R11 300,00.

Installation of two decoders: R5 650.00.

Signed
J J Botha [Brigadier]

Approved and signed R [Witkop] Badenhorst [Lieutenant-General][4]

On 22 November, after news of the coup's failure had come through, Colonel Gerrie Hugo attended a meeting with IR-CIS personnel. Clive Brink was almost in tears because, he claimed, the SADF had not intervened as promised. Clearly referring to Colonel Craig Duli, he said he had lost 'a dear friend.'

Transkei's Major-General Bantu Holomisa asked for South African assistance in getting statements from people connected with the coup attempt. Included were Jan Anton Nieuwoudt, Ted Brassel and Clive Brink.[5]

The request was ignored.

The unit continued to feed sham intelligence to Brigadier Gqozo that suggested the ANC, Charles Sebe and the Transkei were jointly or severally plotting a *coup d'etat* to overthrow him. He began to submit regular intelligence reports of unknown origin to routine meetings of the Council of State that dealt with alleged plots to oust him. This was in itself unusual. The Head of State was supposed to be briefed about intelligence matters at the meetings and not the other way around.

Apparently it was also suggested that the NIS was involved in the plotting and scheming. It was effective brainwashing. The disinformation transparently lacked foundation, but Gqozo became paranoid and refused to listen to reason or accept evidence to the contrary. Within a month he underwent a 180 degree change — from being supportive of the ANC and the reform initiatives to being completely anti-ANC. He discussed omnipresent threats of coups and plots openly and continually with his officers.The information was invariably unconfirmed and no one took it seriously except for Gqozo himself.

Colonel Gerrie Hugo recalls that in CDF intelligence circles, it became a standing joke with officers rushing around, particularly on Friday afternoons, shouting: 'They [the ANC or Transkei] are coming! They are coming!' [6]

Gqozo eventually accused the NIS of cooperating with his enemies. He told Campbell bluntly that he could forget about establishing his proposed National Intelligence Service for Ciskei. Furthermore, they were to cease all operations in and around the territory. Eventually, because of a total lack of cooperation from Gqozo, Brian Campbell had no option but to give up and pull out of King William's Town in January 1990.

According to Colonel Hugo, a NIS source who worked for the Southern Sun hotel group in the Ciskei accused him of smearing the NIS with Brigadier Gqozo, and vowed to get even. It is something he still strenuously denies. It later transpired that he had fallen victim to a Military Intelligence disinformation campaign designed to destroy his position.

An IR-CIS signal from '[Sergeant] Clive [Brink]' to someone code-named *Ouboet* (Older brother) at the DCC on 23 June 1991, confirmed who was responsible. It said amongst other things: 'NI is very cross with us because we influenced Brig Gqozo to chase Campbell away.' [7]

Colonel Hugo had no idea that he was also being watched by IR-CIS. A signal sent to DCC read: 'Colonel G Hugo — on three months trail. He has really started working. I trust him now, but I first want to fire the CDF members that I do not trust. I will then trust him fully.' [8]

Brigadier Gqozo announced at a Council of State meeting that he had changed his policy to one of being anti-ANC. He said the ANC was behaving as if it was running the country, but he intended to show them that he was in charge in Ciskei.

In November 1990 Gqozo wrote a strongly worded open letter to the ANC's Border Region convenor, Mr Stofile, accusing him and his colleagues of acting against the interests of Ciskei. He accused them of frustrating government plans to regain control in villages and rural areas which he claimed was to the benefit of the community. He said they were inciting people to reject and attack traditional leaders and accused them of playing a leading part in fuelling a strike of civil servants that was then ongoing. Stofile described the letter as 'an unfounded and vitriolic attack on the ANC'.

This led to a further strain in relations between Gqozo and the ANC.[9]

Military Intelligence embarked on a second tack to gain influence in the Ciskei, presumably in case the IR-CIS operation failed. Basie Oosthuizen, a fluent Xhosa speaker who was running the Comops front company, Dynamic Teaching cc, a subsidiary of Adult Education cc, approached Gqozo and proposed he conduct an 'enrichment course' for CDF officers. Its purpose would be to turn them into Christians, teach them to respect authority and respect their African cultures.

The opposite end of the scale to all this, obviously was communism.

Gqozo liked the idea and referred Oosthuizen to CDF Chief, Brigadier Andrew Jamangile, to arrange timings and sort out nominations for the courses. It was only then it was learned that the courses were intended for blacks only — white officers were not required. Two courses of about a week's duration were conducted by Oosthuizen and two assistants. One of the assistants was Kussa Kruger, who later joined the staff of IR-CIS. The courses, each attended by about 24 CDF members, were conducted at a facility at Kologha near Stutterheim on the other side of the border in South Africa. It was set in a secluded forest with a gravel road leading to it. It comprised prefabricated military-style barracks with kitchen and mess facilities (there were two chefs, one a white and the other a coloured), lecture rooms, an administration block and ablution blocks. Rations and logistics were supplied via the SADF's Eastern Province Command and laundered through Oosthuizen.

It was not much of a military course.

In the mornings and evenings students were dispersed throughout the complex and told to listen to nature — the singing of birds, the sounds of trickling water in streams and other such nonsense. After they had done with the listening, the dictates of the course demanded that they settle down and pray individually.

During lectures students were placed in syndicates, each with an instructor, and given a topic for which they had to provide a solution. This would be followed by a presentation period. If their solutions were considered unacceptable, the instructors would propound their own views, suggesting 'wise and correct' solutions that students on previous courses had apparently provided.

Most thought the courses were marvellous. Those not so naïve saw through it. Several of the more canny students suggested (rightly) that its underlying purpose was to inculcate them with an anti-communist attitude and to portray the ANC and its associates as the anti-Christ intent on eroding and destroying the Christian religion and African cultures.

Ciskei paid Dynamic Teaching cc large sums of money for conducting these courses. If NATO had used courses like that during the Cold War days, it is doubtful the world would have ended up celebrating the fall of the Berlin Wall. More likely it would have been commemorating the fall of Western democracy instead.

Basie Oosthuizen next separately approached the joint heads of the CDF's Military Intelligence — by then Colonel Hugo and Lieutenant-Colonel Zamunsi Zantsi — without telling the other. He proposed a programme that would allow his staff to go into the rural areas of Ciskei and teach the unsophisticated populace about culture and local government. Neither Hugo nor Zantsi were enthusiastic — Hugo, because he was well aware that Dynamic Teaching cc was an SADF front company, and Zantsi because he rightly suspected there was a larger and deeper strategy behind the proposed moves. It puzzled both of them, however, that Oosthuizen had not gone directly to Brigadier Gqozo and used his influence to bulldoze his wishes through — as he had done before with Brigadier Jamangile.

Questioned by Lieutenant-Colonel Zantsi as to who was funding his organisation, Oosthuizen vaguely replied that it was 'big business'. Shortly after this he disappeared from circulation and he was not seen in Ciskei until the second half of 1991.[10]

The NIS was not the only organisation crossed by the SADF's Military Intelligence. Alan Lindner, a former intelligence officer with the Selous Scouts in Rhodesia, had a company specialising in covert intelligence training. Lindner negotiated a deal for a three-module training course worth R120 400. He maintained that the CDF had accepted the complete course, plus a computer record-keeping service, for R100 000. The CDF reneged on the contract, undoubtedly at the instigation of IR-CIS, which forced Lindner to resort to civil action through the Supreme Court in Bisho.[11]

Assassination of Charles Sebe and Onward Guzana

On 16 January 1991 Commandant Jan Anton Nieuwoudt telephoned Lieutenant-Colonel Zantsi, Ciskei's joint Chief of Staff Intelligence, and asked him to attend a meeting at the IR-CIS offices at House 14, Ministerial Complex, Bisho at 18:00. He said that Brigadier Gqozo would be there, which implied the meeting had been called by him. Colonel Gerrie Hugo, the other Chief of Staff Intelligence was not involved and he knew nothing about it.

CDF Chief, Brigadier Jamangile, also lived in the Ministerial Complex and Zantsi paid him a courtesy visit while en route to the meeting. He was astonished to discover that the brigadier had neither been told about the meeting nor had he been invited to attend. Despite this, Brigadier Jamangile instructed him to attend. There was already deep distrust between the CDF and IR-CIS and he was told to report back on what happened.

Sergeant Clive Brink met Lieutenant-Colonel Zantsi outside House 14. He told him he would take him to the house of the South African Military Attaché, Commandant Mias Muller, to see Jan Nieuwoudt and get his permission to enter House 14. Zantsi noticed the official cars of both Brigadier Gqozo and Colonel S S Pita — the second-in-command of the CDF — parked outside the house when he returned with Nieuwoudt. Nieuwoudt asked him to wait in the lounge while he briefed Gqozo and Pita.

Zantsi was surprised to see Lieutenant-Colonel Poyo, the CDF's welfare officer, and former CDF Lieutenant-Colonel Mlandeli Kula, there. Nieuwoudt explained that the two had been working for IR-CIS for a long time. A meeting in Jan Anton's office, attended by Brigadier Gqozo, Colonel Pita, Lieutenant-Colonels Jantisi and Poyo, Mlandeli Kula and Major Ted Brassel, followed.

Nieuwoudt briefed them on a meeting that had taken place in Transkei attended by General Charles Sebe, Colonel Onward Guzana, Poyo and Kula. Charles Sebe, he said, planned to mount a coup to topple Gqozo from power on the night of 27 January. The CDF soldiers who would support it, Charles Sebe was told, had been recruited by Poyo and Kula. Another meeting between the role players had been scheduled for 18 January at Ezibeleni near Queenstown.

Nieuwoudt asked Gqozo when Brigadier Jamangile would be briefed about the pending 'intelligence operation', as it would be his responsibility to deploy roadblock personnel on the night of the coup attempt.

Gqozo replied that only those present would be told about it, until he deemed the time was right.

On 17 January at about 16:30 Gqozo sent for Lieutenant-Colonel Zantsi who went to his residence where he met Lieutenant-Colonel Pita there. Pita said that Nieuwoudt needed two drivers for covert work. It was essential that neither Charles Sebe nor Onward Guzana were likely to know them. They also had to be able to keep their mouths shut and should preferably be drawn from the Military Intelligence Division. Pita said it would be difficult to ensure they were unknown to Guzana because he (Guzona) had been serving in the CDF until recently and knew a lot of people. Guzana's brother, a rifleman in the CDF, was another problem. He was currently suspended from duty, so it was possible he was in Transkei and might be accompanying Guzana. He would certainly know more soldiers than his brother would.

Rifleman Khahla, a recruit under training at the Ntaba ka Ndoda Military Base, was selected. Khahla was related to Pita and was a good driver. He was also relatively unknown. Pita told Zantsi to arrange with his company commander for Khahla's detachment. He should also look for another suitable driver.

When Zantsi reported to Nieuwoudt at the IR-CIS offices, he was told a second driver had already been nominated. The two were needed to drive Poyo and Kula to a lunchtime meeting with Charles Sebe and Onward Guzana the following day. The vehicles would be fitted with electronic recording equipment for the monitoring of conversations.

On 18 January Zantsi collected Rifleman Khahla from the training company and handed him over to Sergeant Clive Brink.

On 21 January Zantsi phoned Brink to get the results of the Ezibeleni meeting. Brink told him that unfortunately the recording equipment had developed a fault, so they would only be able to find out when they saw Poyo and Kula later in the week.

On 25 January Lieutenant-Colonel Zantsi was again called to Nieuwoudt's offices for a briefing. Nieuwoudt told him that the meeting with Charles Sebe and Guzana had gone ahead as planned. It had been confirmed that the coup would proceed according to schedule on 27 January. Poyo and Kula had assured them they could rely on the complete support of the CDF. Most officers, they told them, were eager for Guzana to replace Gqozo as Head of State.

Charles Sebe and Onward Guzana would be waiting at a bridge outside Stutterheim at about 02:00. They would be driving a red VW Golf sedan, hired for them in Durban by Mr Nohashe, the mayor of Fort Beaufort.

Sergeant Simiselo Ralo and Lieutenant Sipho Mguzulwa, driving a Military Police van fitted with a blue lamp, would meet them at the bridge. Guzana and Sebe had been told the two would escort them to Bisho's police station. Once they were there, arrangements would be made for all CDF officers and all senior police officers to report to 1-Ciskei Battalion. Guzana would address them and announce that he was the new Head of State. Sebe and Guzana had asked that Brigadiers Gqozo and Jamangile, Colonel Pita and Lieutenant-Colonel Zantsi be arrested as a precautionary measure before their scheduled time of arrival in Bisho.

Nieuwoudt tasked Zantsi to arrange for Lieutenants Ngculu and Kleinbooi plus six Military Intelligence personnel to report to the IR-CIS offices at 08:00 on 26 January. Zantsi phoned from Nieuwoudt's office to make arrangements, only to learn that Ngculu was away on a course. Lieutenant Mguzulwa, he discovered, had already left the base to go home. He phoned Military Intelligence's offices and tasked Lieutenant Kleinbooi to detail six members to await him at the offices.

Using a map, Nieuwoudt explained to Zantsi that Sebe and Guzana could drive from Stutterheim to Bisho by any one of three routes. The first was the Stutterheim-King William's Town Road, the second the Stutterheim-Ndakana-Frankfort gravel road and the third the Komga-Bisho Road. He asked him to arrange for three sections of troops to be available to man roadblocks on all three roads.

Zantsi refused, having had enough of being ordered around, and told him that troop deployments were the responsibility of the Chief of Staff (Operations).

Nieuwoudt retorted angrily and tersely ordered him to personally instruct the Chief of Staff (Operations), Lieutenant-Colonel Nelson Naka, to report to House 14 the next morning. Zantsi should return with him.

Zantsi located Lieutenant Kleinbooi, Lieutenant Mguzulwa and Lieutenant-Colonel Naka and told them to report to House 14 the next morning.

That night he was awakened by a driver who told him that Brigadier Jamangile wanted to see him urgently at his house in the Ministerial Complex. Jamangile had just returned from Brian Campbell's farewell *braai* (barbecue). Campbell had asked him if he was aware that a coup was due to take place on the coming Sunday. Embarrassingly for Jamangile, he was forced to admit that it was the first he had heard of it. Not surprisingly, he excused himself from the party and sent for his Chief of Staff Intelligence to find out what was going on.

Without hesitation Lieutenant-Colonel Zantsi briefed him on the situation. He explained that he had been unable to tell him before, because Brigadier Gqozo had specifically ordered that the information should be restricted to only those present at the meeting.

Brigadier Jamangile thanked him and excused him.

At 08:00 on 26 January there was a large gathering at the IR-CIS offices. Representing that organisation were Commandant Nieuwoudt, Lieutenant-Colonel Poyo, Major Ted Brassel, Mr Kula, Captain Funani, Warrant Officers Soci, Barnes and Melani, Sergeant Clive Brink, Charles Bongani Wana and Mbejeni. From the CDF side there were Lieutenant-Colonels Naka and Zantsi, Lieutenants Kleinbooi and Mguzulwa, Sergeant Ralo, Riflemen Notshe and Mboniswa and five details from Military Intelligence.

Commandant Nieuwoudt called Lieutenant-Colonels Zantsi, Naka and Poyo, Kula, Lieutenant Kleinbooi and Sergeant Clive Brink into a separate meeting. An AK47 and a Scorpion sub-machine gun lay on the floor next to his chair. He briefed them on the pending operation. The roadblock details, each comprising a section of CDF personnel and two members of IR-CIS to look after the morale of the troops, would be established as planned. The roadblock commanders were Clive Brink — the Stutterheim to King William's Town Road, Jan Anton Nieuwoudt — the Komga to Bisho Road and Lieutenant Kleinbooi — the Stutterheim to Ndakana to Frankfort gravel road.

Major Ted Brassel would take over command of the Protection Unit at State House as a precautionary measure. Mr Kula would join Brigadier Gqozo, Lieutenant-Colonel Pita and members of the Council of State at State House. As another precautionary measure, Lieutenant-Colonel Poyo would take up position with 1-Ciskei Battalion.

Lieutenant-Colonel Naka was tasked to organise the three roadblock sections and report with them to Blacklands Farm at 23:00 for a briefing. Lieutenant-Colonel Zantsi was placed in charge of deception operations. In the early hours of the morning he would arrange for two Military Police vehicles, with blue lights flashing, to move from 1-Ciskei Battalion to State House and the Ministerial Complex and after a pause, back to 1-Ciskei Battalion. They had no idea how many sources and supporters Charles Sebe and Onward Guzana had keeping watch in Bisho. The deception operation was designed to give the impression that Brigadiers Gqozo and Jamangile and Lieutenant-Colonels Pita and Zantsi had been arrested and detained as requested by Charles Sebe. The movements would probably be relayed to Sebe and Guzana and allay any misgivings they might have.

After an initial briefing, Nieuwoudt instructed the officers to report to State House to be present when he briefed Gqozo and the Council of State. Brigadier Gqozo, Brigadier Jamangile, Lieutenant-Colonels Pita and Commandant Mias Muller — by then Gqozo's adviser — were in attendance. So were General Z Makuzeni, Brigadier L Nhonhonho and Brigadier Marele of the Ciskei Police.

Commandant Nieuwoudt outlined his plans to foil the coup attempt. Lieutenant-Colonels Zantsi and Naka would join Lieutenant-Colonel Poyo in the operations room at 1-Ciskei Battalion after the roadblock details had been dropped off at Blacklands Farm. They would be jointly responsible for controlling or regaining control of the troops at 1-Ciskei Battalion if the plan went awry. Details involved were issued with civilian-type walkie-talkie radios. This was a back-up in case of failure of the military radio communications between the roadblock details and State House.

At question time both Jamangile and Nieuwoudt asked Gqozo for clarity on the course of action to be taken by the roadblock sections when Sebe and Guzana appeared.

Brigadier Gqozo was categoric. They must be shot and killed. He could not take the risk of imprisoning them in Ciskei and facing a constant threat that someone might try to spring them.

Nieuwoudt had not been told, but the commander if 1-Ciskei Battalion, Lieutenant-Colonel Mteti, had arranged with Lieutenant-Colonels Zantsi and Naka for an additional section of troops to be deployed to reinforce the State House guards. This was a precautionary measure to guard against 'unforseen developments'. The officers were not well disposed towards Nieuwoudt and his IR-CIS. In particular they distrusted the prominent role it was playing in the planning and execution of the operation — which was based solely on information that it had gathered and tested without any other inputs. Nieuwoudt had ridden roughshod over the usual CDF chains of command and no checks or balances had been built into the operation. They suspected a hidden agenda. Maybe Brigadier Gqozo was, after all, the true target and the real purpose of the operation was to remove him from office?

Lieutenant-Colonels Naka and Mteti assembled the roadblock sections and gave them an initial briefing. From there they were taken in three Buffels by a roundabout route to Blacklands Farm by Lieutenant-Colonel Naka. This was a precaution to avoid detection by Sebe and Guzana sympathisers who might be out and about.

Lieutenant-Colonel Zantsi addressed the roadblock details once they got there. He introduced the IR-CIS personnel as troops from Brigadier Gqozo's personal intelligence service. It was the IR-CIS's first official contact with the lower echelons of the CDF. He explained that, with the approval of Brigadier Gqozo, IR-CIS personnel would command the roadblock parties. After this he handed over to Commandant Nieuwoudt for a detailed operational briefing.

Lieutenant-Colonels Zantsi and Naka drove to King William's Town and noted a significant SADF presence at the Amatola Commando HQ. Police and military units were patrolling the streets in strength and two SAP Casspirs were deployed in stationary positions south of Bisho's Independence Stadium. This, of course, was very unusual at that time of night in a quiet country town like King William's Town. Neither doubted that the South Africans were in a state of readiness because they were aware of the forthcoming operation. They had obviously been told by Nieuwoudt.

On 27 January at 01:00, Mguzulwa and Sergeant Ralo drew their military police vehicle and left to keep their rendezvous with Sebe and Guzana. Sergeant Ralo was armed with an AK47, but no one mentioned it because Nieuwoudt had been similarly armed earlier.

Clive Brink routinely reported that Lieutenant Mguzulwa's vehicle had passed through his roadblock en route to Stutterheim. This was Lieutenant-Colonel Zantsi's signal to order the deception plan to swing into operation. At 01:30 two military police vehicles, blue lights flashing, moved from 1-Ciskei Battalion to State House, from there to the Ministerial Complex and back to 1-Ciskei Battalion. The drivers were provided by the elite Parachute Unit based at Bulembu Airport.

Clive Brink reported by radio that Lieutenant Mguzulwa and Sergeant Ralo had returned to his roadblock and that Sebe and Guzana had not appeared at the rendezvous. He told them to go back and wait.

At 02:05 he came back on the air.
'Contact! Contact!' he yelled.
Gunfire could be heard in the background. He reported that Sebe and Guzana were returning fire and asked for reinforcements.
The two other roadblocks groups responded. Lieutenant Kleinbooi said he was on his way.
Nieuwoudt came on the air and said he was returning from a briefing at State House and would be at the scene shortly.
Brigadier Gqozo broke in and asked for a sitrep.
Where exactly had the contact taken place?
On the Stutterheim-King William's Town road opposite Mxhalanga Village.
Nieuwoudt came back on the air and reported that he had found the body of Onward Guzana in the driver's seat of the red VW Golf in a field close to the roadblock. Charles Sebe was on the run and he requested that the CDF's only Alouette helicopter be deployed to mount a follow-up. However, Brigadier Jamangile and Colonel Penhall had flown to Port Elizabeth earlier so it was not immediately available. Lieutenant-Colonel Naka was ordered to locate the pilot and get them to return immediately.
At about 06:30 Lieutenant-Colonel Zantsi arrived at the shooting scene. It was crawling with troops, police and Brigadier Gqozo's bodyguards. Clive Brink showed him the vehicle and indicated where it had left the road and ended up in the field. Onward Guzana was slumped dead over the steering wheel, a lumber jacket covering his head. The car was riddled with bullets and the seats were covered in blood. Charles Sebe's spectacles were on the passenger seat and two pistols and an Uzi sub-machine gun were on the floor.
Brink reported that he had removed two briefcases from the Golf before the police had arrived. He suspected they contained sensitive information. He suggested that Zantsi join him at the IR-CIS offices once the follow-up had been completed and then inspect the briefcases.
Zantsi conducted an on-the-spot investigation to ascertain exactly what had happened. To his surprise he experienced considerable difficulties with his own Military Intelligence staff deployed at the roadblock. They evasively maintained that they had been away with the stopper groups when the shooting occurred and had seen nothing. He sensed this was probably untrue, but they would not budge from their stories.
Warrant Officer Melane of IR-CIS (an informer of CDF's Military Intelligence) explained the actual circumstances later. He said that Lieutenant Mgulzulwa and Sergeant Ralo had rendezvoused with Sebe and Guzana as planned. They had driven from the rendezvous towards Bisho with Sebe and Guzana following in the red Golf. The military van halted when it reached the roadblock and the red Golf slowed behind it but did not stop. Sergeant Ralo leapt out with his AK and fired on the Golf. The driver tried desperately to escape, but the vehicle left the road, careened through a fence and came to a halt in the field. The other troops there also opened fire on the Golf. Sergeant Ralo got into a Buffel with Rifleman Xhotyeni and ordered him to pursue the Golf. When they reached it, Sergeant Ralo opened fire again. Charles Sebe had made good his escape, but Guzana was still in the driver's seat. He was still alive but wounded. Sergeant Ralo boasted later that he had finished him off.
Brigadier Jamangile and other senior military and police officers arrived by helicopter shortly afterwards. The CDF took over the follow-up of Charles Sebe.
At the IR-CIS offices, Clive Brink showed Lieutenant-Colonel Zantsi a speech prepared by Onward Guzana in which he announced that he had taken over as the new ruler of Ciskei. Zantsi also examined Sebe's and Guzana's diaries which contained various lists of people with telephone numbers from across the political and social spectrum.
The two men had been carrying a lot of money.
Charles Sebe managed to evade his pursuers until the early morning of 28 January. Then a village headman, Tese Dwashu, phoned 1-Ciskei Battalion and reported that Sebe was hiding in a shop behind his house in Gubevu Village.

Right – President F W de Klerk's press conference after his bombshell announcement on 2 February 1990.

President F W de Klerk and ANC leader Nelson Mandela during the constitutional talks in 1992.

ıe referendum of the white ectorate held on 17 March 92 returned a resounding 69% affirmative votes for the ntinuation of the reform ocess.

Left – the Krugersdorp Post Office after Dries Kriel's bomb.

Right – the Verwoerdburg (now Centurion) Post Office after Dries Kriel's bomb.

Left – Dries Kriel is decorated by the then Commandant General of the AWB, Servaas de We (an ex-police colonel), fo blowing up the Hillview High School and COSAT House in Pretoria and th Verwoerdburg and Krugersdorp post offices Ironically, the medals parade was held in the grounds of the Union Buildings in Pretoria.

Right – in the late 1980s Rob Brown was giving military training to supporters of Veterans for Victory.

Left – and women, too.

Below – by the early 1990s, at the behest of Military Intelligence, Brown was training right-wing anti-communist members of black churches in KwaZulu.

INFANTERIESKOOL BESOEK

INFANTRY SCHOOL VISIT

eft page top – AWB leader Eugene erre'Blanche, 12 of his generals and other ght-wingers were guests of the SADF for the urposes of a four-day 'Christian visit' in October 993. 'General' Mossie Mostert said he only eard about the Christian aspects afterwards.

eft page bottom – Eugene Terre'Blanche (with crambled eggs' on his camo cap) and CP eader Ferdi Hartzenberg.

Above – *Afrikaner Volksfront* leaders wearing AWB swastika rosettes look cheerfully forward to a right-wing future.

Left – AWB leader Eugene Terre'Blanche and AWB secretary-general, General Nico Prinsloo, show the rest how to stop cars at AWB roadblocks.

Below – General Constand Viljoen (right) found he was not always in agreement with his colleagues in the *Afrikaner Volksfront*.

Sunlight mildness

ɪft page top left – SADF Chief General Georg Meiring. ɦhen asked by right-wingers if he would allow Afrikaners fight Afrikaners he said: 'Yes, the soldiers are already place.'

ɪft page top right – One wonders how General Constand ljoen would have replied if he had still been the ɒmmander of the SADF.

ɪft page bottom – Bophuthatswana police Constable enyatsoea shoots dead AWB General Nic Fourie and ɤo others.

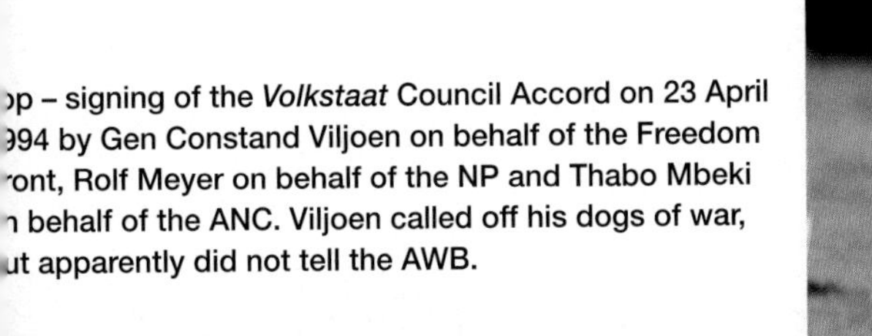

ɔp – signing of the *Volkstaat* Council Accord on 23 April ɔ94 by Gen Constand Viljoen on behalf of the Freedom ront, Rolf Meyer on behalf of the NP and Thabo Mbeki ı behalf of the ANC. Viljoen called off his dogs of war, ut apparently did not tell the AWB.

ight – Gen Constand Viljoen was surprised that President e Klerk did not attend to sign such an important document ɪr Afrikaners. He later learned he was playing golf.

Above – the AWB's Bree Street bomb on 24 April 1994.

Below – the AWB's Germiston bomb on 25 April 1994. There was another after that at Jan Smuts (Johannesburg Internationa
Airport.

Soldiers led by CDF Chief, Brigadier Jamangile, surrounded the shop and called on Charles Sebe to surrender and come out with his hands up. He came out naked, unarmed and seriously wounded. Jamangile ordered Warrant Officer Thozamile Veliti, a member of Brigadier Gqozo's bodyguard, to radio for instructions.

Gqozo radioed back and ordered that Sebe should be shot.

Sergeant-Major Veliti raised his rifle and shot him. This sparked a chain reaction and prompted the rest of the patrol to open fire. Charles Sebe's body was riddled with bullets.[12]

Times had changed since the junior Oupa Gqozo had been General Charles Sebe's plant in the CDF.[13]

Tese Dwashu was given a reward of R5 000.

The Commissioner of Police, Zebulon Makuzeni, claimed that Brigadier Gqozo initially refused the investigating officers permission to interview Veliti.

During press interviews Brigadier Gqozo said indiscreetly: 'People loyal to me fooled Charles into believing he had their support. They wanted to trap him because he had caused the country a lot of misery . . . I said search and destroy when you find him. So they did exactly that. It was an operation to take him [Sebe] out. I don't see why we should back down and even regret it . . . He was poison . . . we blew him.'[14]

Gqozo did an abrupt about-turn when an inquest into the deaths of Sebe and Guzana was ordered. He did everything he could to avoid giving evidence. He submitted three affidavits to the court, variously saying he was too busy to give evidence, denying he had ordered the deaths and arguing that his order to 'search and destroy' did not necessarily mean Sebe should be killed.

When this failed to have the desired result, he issued two decrees that exempted him from giving evidence in any court or to any quasi-judicial proceedings. Ciskei's Appeal Court rejected his decrees because the homeland's Bill of Rights did not exempt a head of state from the due processes of law.[15]

During the inquest, Jan Anton Nieuwoudt declared under oath that neither he nor his IR-CIS were linked to the military. He later contradicted this in affidavits laid before the High Court in South Africa in connection with a civil claim against the SADF. He unequivocally said: 'At all relevant times to date, since January 1974, [I] was a member of the Permanent Force and an officer involved with various units of the SADF.'

In his finding the presiding judge, Mr Justice Michael Claassens, said that Charles Sebe and Onward Guzana were lured into a trap 'like lambs to the slaughter'. Hours later when Charles Sebe was unarmed, wounded, in pain, unarmed and in the process of surrendering, he was murdered — shot down in cold blood on Gqozo's orders.[16] The judge added: 'Nieuwoudt and company knew there was no inside component [in the Ciskei to the coup attempt] and knew there was no danger to any interested party in Ciskei. The trap was set for one purpose only: to rid the regime in Ciskei under Brigadier Gqozo of any further threat from Sebe and Guzana. I have thought very seriously of the possibility of Nieuwoudt, in particular, being party to a conspiracy to murder.'[17]

Judge Claassens made no finding in regard to the killing of Onward Guzana.[18]

In November 1990 many Ciskei civil servants who had flocked to join the ANC-backed National Education, Health and Allied Workers Union (NEHAWU) embarked on a strike demanding recognition for NEHAWU and salary parity with their counterparts in South Africa. Brigadier Gqozo vilified NEHAWU, accusing it of causing instability and promoting poor work ethics in the public service.The strike was evidence of the deteriorating relations between Gqozo and the ANC.

25

Colonel Craig Duli
Attempted Coups
Transkei
1989/1990

Conspiracies to commit coups: 1989/1990

In April 1989, Colonel Craig Duli, General Holomisa's second in command on the Military Council, was arrested and detained. It was alleged he had plotted to oust the general by discrediting him with false accusations of adultery.[1] According to General Holomisa, Duli had come under suspicion and agents were infiltrated into the group that he was working with. When General Holomisa finally confronted him, he was able to quote chapter and verse the subversive activities he had been engaged in.[2]

Major-General Holomisa maintained that Colonel Duli had been subverted by ex-President K D Matanzima to whom he was related. 'He fell into a trap through blind loyalty to Matanzima, not because he had anything against him [Holomisa].' [3]

Major-General Zondwa Mtirara, the Chief of the TDF in Reid Daly's day, who was in exile in South Africa was also alleged to be involved in the conspiracy. He was abducted from Daveyton in the Transvaal [now Gauteng] in July 1989 and bundled back to the Transkei and detained. Both were released after successful court applications in December 1989. Colonel Duli left the Transkei and took up residence in Stutterheim, outside Transkei in the Eastern Cape.

Meanwhile, in July 1989 six black South African agents were arrested after a shootout in Umtata for their involvement in a suspected plot to assassinate General Holomisa. They confessed under interrogation that they had been sent to kill General Holomisa by the Chairman of Temba Construction, who also had close links with the Military Intelligence front company, Jalc Holdings, Vulindlela Mbotoli.

This led to Colonel Booi of Transkei's Security Police being mandated to form a team of operators to seek intelligence and investigate people intent on the overthrow of Transkei's Military Council.[4]

On 27 December 1989 two South Africans, one a serving South African Police officer, were arrested in the Transkei for their alleged involvement in a plot to kill General Holomisa. The car in which they were travelling belonged to Jalc Holdings.[5]

Shortly after they were released from prison in Port Elizabeth, Colonel Craig Duli and Mbotoli again began planning for a coup to topple General Holomisa.

In January 1990 Colonel Duli sought out Mazizi Thomas Ntisana, formerly a member of parliament under ex-Prime Minister Stella Sigeau before the latter was deposed by General Holomisa's Military Council. He was one of a deputation of 30 who went to see General Holomisa after the Military Council had been in operation for six months to demand that the country be returned to civilian rule.

General Holomisa had told them he was not ready for it.

Those in the deputation decided to wait and see what happened, but gradually most of them were arrested, one by one, and removed from the centre of political activity. This caused Ntisana to flee to East London to escape arrest. He was still on Transkei's wanted list. Ntisana was determined to fight politically for a 'people's government that would be mandated by the people and who would be mandated by the people.' He firmly believed it was in the interests of Transkei that military rule be terminated.

They both agreed that they could not return to the Transkei while the military remained in control, but Mazizi did not want to be involved in anything which involved the spilling of blood.

Colonel Duli asked Mazizi to contact certain soldiers in the TDF based in Umtata and request they visit him at Stutterheim. Those concerned were Mazizi's brother, Sergeant Sidwell Mzwamadoda Ntisana, Rifleman Bongo Ndamase, Rifleman Hlumelo Mxutu, Rifleman Sandisile Bongweni and two others. Contact was made through Mazizi's brother, Sidwell. They had no transport, so Mazizi collected them and took them in his car to Stutterheim.

Colonel Duli explained that since his release from prison he had concluded that soldiers should overthrow the Military Council and return Transkei to civilian rule. He pointed out that that General Holomisa had promised to do this within six months of his takeover, but that time frame had long elapsed.

Sergeant Sidwell Ntisana and some others had been with Colonel Duli in Military Intelligence when Stella Sigcau was deposed as Prime Minister. Colonel Duli told them to go to Port St Johns and pass the word to their contemporaries of similar rank to themselves. They were also to instructed to recruit two Special Forces operators, Warrants Officers Xweta Ndeleni and Zamikaia Armens. Duli said that most of the senior officers knew what was happening and would lend their support. He promised there would be no bloodshed. It would be just like Stella Sigcau when she was deposed in a bloodless coup. The soldiers believed him.

Details of the plan are unknown, but on the 14 January 1990 Sergeant Sidwell Ntisana and his colleagues in Umtata were tipped off that information regarding the pending coup had leaked to the authorities from Port St Johns. The story was out, so they knew the coup would not be supported.

They pretend that everything was normal and went to work on 15 January as if nothing had happened. They thought they had got away with it, but when they did the same on the 16 January, they were arrested at their desks. They were detained for two years, before being brought for trial before the Supreme [now High] Court and charged with conspiracy to commit treason. They were convicted and sentenced to terms of imprisonment.[6]

Prominent Transkeians like ex-President Kaiser Matanzima and others began to beat paths to the doors of Foreign Affairs and Military Intelligence in Pretoria, asking for assistance to overthrow Major-General Bantu Holomisa's Military Council. The South Africans listened with interest because they were convinced Holomisa was supporting the ANC. Once, after Transkei's Security Police arrested some dissidents who were returning from Pretoria after they had trekked there to discuss the forcible overthrow of General Holomisa, Foreign Minister Pik Botha phoned him personally.

'General', General Holomisa can imitate the gravelly little voice of Pik Botha with perfection, 'I have heard that you have arrested people who came to us for military assistance. I want to assure you that whatever was discussed, bottom line was that we advised these people to go and speak to you and to live harmoniously in Transkei once there is stability there.' He was particularly concerned about former prime minister, Stella Sigcau, and he begged General Holomisa not to order her arrest.

General Holomisa assured him he had no intention of doing so.[7]

The author believes the plots to assassinate Major-General Holomisa detailed in this book were genuine. Some have suggested that if there had been so many genuine plots against the general, it is doubtful that the Transkei's Security Police and Military Intelligence would have been capable of dealing with them.

General Holomisa explained that breaking the plots had proved fairly simple, but only because he had a high level informant in the National Intelligence Service, called Riaan. Riaan would contact Major-General-Holomisa's military intelligence Chief and say: 'This is the plan. The authorities are sending . . . I'm in charge of the operation. Intercept them at so and so . . . I have been in a conference with . . . This is what is happening . . .'

Holomisa was unaware of his identity at first, but he is convinced that without his assistance he would have been killed long ago. Riaan was responsible for revealing at least three assassination plots targeting Holomisa. Eventually, the general made a particular point of flying to Johannesburg to meet and thank him. Riaan was a man who, unlike many of his contemporaries in the intelligence community, did not believe that intelligence operators had a licence to break the law.

Riaan played no part in uncovering the Colonel Craig Duli coup attempts. Colonel Duli was aware of Riaan's existence, so he made sure he avoided any intelligence regarding his own activities coming to his notice.[8]

Colonel Craig Duli's coup attempt: April 1990

Colonel Eugene de Kock was the commander of the Security Police's C1 (counter-insurgency and counter terrorism) Unit based at Vlakplaas Farm near Pretoria. C1 (at one time called C10). It had several facets. It was responsible for covert and sometimes overt internal operations and for cross-border operations into neighbouring states. It was also the home of former ANC and PAC askaris who after capture had been 'turned' to the government's side. In achieving this its *modus operandi* was much the same as the Selous Scouts of Rhodesia.

Two shipping containers served as repositories for the mostly Soviet-style weapons captured during police operations. Much of it originated from the Koevoet counter-insurgency unit in Namibia which accounted for many tons. In particular there were many thousands of weapons, pistols, carbines, machine guns of a variety of calibres, grenades, plastic explosive, TNT, a whole spectrum of anti-tank launchers, light artillery weapons and even SAM-7s. All had been captured during SWAPO's last fling incursion on the 1 April 1989 and were transferred after that debacle to Vlakplaas' stores. Some of the weapons were later transferred to the COIN (counter-insurgency) armoury at the Police College in Pretoria.

A written agreement of cooperation existed between C1 and Military Intelligence's DCC — Directorate of Covert Collection. It was this that led to Jan Anton Nieuwoudt approaching him at Vlakplaas during March 1990. De Kock knew him as Commandant Nieuwoudt, whom he understood was a senior staff officer serving under the command of Brigadier Tolletjie Botha and Colonel At Nel at Military Intelligence's Directorate of Covert Collection (DCC).

He asked for rifles, hand grenades, mortars and ammunition to be used in a proposed coup to be mounted from a farm near Queenstown to overthrow General Holomisa. The quantity requested was arranged by a Sergeant Steve Bosch of the Security Police's C1 and it was collected by someone from Military Intelligence's DCC.

Training commenced. Meanwhile, though, the TDF's Military Intelligence had picked up information as to what was happening and General Holomisa instructed that undercover agents from Transkei's Security Police be sent to infiltrate the trainees.Information as to what was going on was reported to General Holomisa by them.[9] General Holomisa claimed he reported Colonel Duli's plans to Pretoria after which the South African Security Police took action.[10]

On 6 April they arrested a group of 25 armed plotters, including Colonel Craig Duli and Vulindlele Mbotoli, on the Queenstown farm where they were undergoing military training. Many weapons and a large quantity of ammunition was seized. Major-General Griebenauw, by then commanding the Security Police in the Eastern Cape, conveyed the impression that it was his motivation that resulted in the arrests. He said that those arrested were photographed and copies were sent to the Security Police in Umtata. It elicited no response.

This prompted Security Police chief, Lieutenant-General Basie Smit, Major-General Griebenouw and Lieutenant-Colonel F J M Venter to visit Umtata on 8 May 1990 for discussions with Major-General Holomisa, 'his military advisers', and other senior officers of the Transkei Police and Defence Force.

General Smit told the Transkeians that initial investigations had revealed that those held in custody had been involved in planning a coup in Transkei although it had not been confirmed. He invited the Transkei Police to nominate officers to join the SAP's investigation team so they could jointly get to the bottom of what was going on. The invitation was made in good faith to put an end to almost continuous allegations that South Africa was intent on destabilising Transkei.

General Holomisa immediately appointed Police Major-General Damois to form and lead the Transkei team but no further reaction was received. Finding this strange the invitation was repeated in writing through diplomatic channels, but it brought no response.[11]

These events had coincided with Colonel de Kock and Commandant Nieuwoudt flying overseas to recruit a senior ANC member as an informer.

These events had coincided with Eugene de Kock and Jan Anton Nieuwoudt flying overseas to recruit a senior member of the ANC as an informer. When they returned, they heard about the arrests.

This prompted DCC Chief Brigadier Tolletjie Botha and Jan Anton Nieuwoudt to go and see General Basie Smit to sort things out. Smit listened in silence while they explained the circumstances that lay behind the proposed coup. The general was particularly unhappy when he heard about Colonel de Kock's involvement, especially because the Harms Commission of Enquiry into hit squad activities, under Judge Louis Harms, had just got underway. It did not help either that he had effectively already made a fool of himself over it in Umtata.

Jan Anton Nieuwoudt later told Eugene de Kock later that General Smit was so angry that he 'walked around like a sheep and bit the carpet'.[12]

In August 1990 Colonel Craig Duli, Vulindlele Mbotoli and Duli's bodyguard Boetie Davis were convicted by a Port Elizabeth magistrate of being in unlawfully in possession of weapons of war. Each was convicted and gaoled for six years, but they were released on bail of R1 000 each, pending an appeal. The police did not oppose bail, despite protests by Umtata. Umtata demanded they be extradited to Transkei for trial. South Africa did not refuse, it merely ignored the request. Obviously the embarrassment of the left hand not knowing what the right was doing precluded any action in that direction. This and other parallel issues caused a serious deterioration in relations between Transkei and South Africa.[13]

Colonel Craig Duli's second coup attempt: 22 November 1990

Soon after Colonel Craig Duli's first coup attempt, General 'Krappies' Engelbrecht of the Security Police, approached Colonel de Kock. He told him of a discussion he had had with Chris van Rensburg who headed Jalc Holdings — a Military Intelligence Front Company. The name Jalc was put together from the names of the four directors, 'J' was from John Strong, 'A' was from Athos Poulos, a Greek, 'L' was from Laurie Painting and 'C' was from Chris van Rensburg.[14] Chris van Rensburg, General Engelbrecht said, had provided proof that there was an economic slump in the Eastern Cape. This was especially so in East London and adjoining areas. It had arisen from General Holomisa allowing the ANC and PAC to use Transkei as a safe haven.

The next week General Engelbrecht took him to a house in Sandton to meet Vulindlela (Vuli) Mbotoli. He introduced him as a Butterworth businessman. He was the managing director of Temba Investments and Temba Construction, both subsidiaries of Jalc Holdings. He told Colonel de Kock to act as Mbotoli's handler to collect information about General Holomisa's involvement with the ANC and PAC in Transkei.

Colonel de Kock allocated Mbotoli a false name and registered him as a C1 source. This cleared the way for putting him on the pay roll as an informer. He arranged for the issue to him of two South African passports and matching identity documents. One set was issued in his real name and the other in his *nom de guerre*.

Colonel de Kock arranged for Sergeant Chait of C1 to be his handler. Sergeant Chait reported to Colonel de Kock who reported to General Engelbrecht. Mbotoli made regular flights from the Eastern Cape to Johannesburg, with C1 paying for his flight and accommodation cost. A regular flow of intelligence on the Transkei resulted.

One day Mbotoli told Colonel de Kock that Colonel Craig Duli wanted to see him. They had never met but De Kock had heard of him. He contacted Commandant Jan Anton Nieuwoudt, whom he was aware was involved in the Ciskei. Nieuwoudt confirmed that Duli 'was on our side' and that it was safe to speak to him.

He met Colonel Duli and his coloured bodyguard, Boetie Davies, in a room at the Jan Smuts (Johannesburg International Airport) Holiday Inn. Vuli Mbotoli introduced them. Afterwards Craig Duli asked Mbotoli and Sergeant Chait to leave the room, but insisted that Davies remain because he felt safer with him there. They worked out code names and Duli provided a telephone number where he could be contacted. The drill was for him to give his code name to the woman that answered. She would provide a time for him to call back when he could speak to Duli.

'I have a shopping list', Colonel Duli told him.

He certainly had. He wanted AK assault rifles, hand grenades, rifle grenades, machine guns, RPG-7 rocket launchers, a SAM-7 launcher with missiles, ammunition and demolition equipment. The SAM-7 was needed because the TDF had limited air power in the form of a helicopter and several fixed wing aircraft.

'What about radio equipment?' Eugene de Kock asked.

It was something that Craig Duli had overlooked and it was added to the shopping list.

He explained that he needed the stuff to mount a *coup d'etat* to overthrow General Holomisa and reestablish Kaiser Matanzima as President. If successful it would provide the South African government with a friendly head of state in power with Craig Duli commanding the TDF. It would give South Africa's Security Forces, particularly the Security Police, unrestricted access to the territory to deal with MK and APLA who were becoming entrenched.

'Who is supporting you? Is it SAP Intelligence or Military Intelligence?' Eugene de Kock asked him.

'Both', he replied.

Eugene offered some general advice, but Craig Duli seemed disinterested.

Eugene asked General Engelbrecht for directions. He detailed Craig Duli's shopping list and explained that it was required to mount a coup against General Holomisa.

General Engelbrecht said bluntly that he thought it was high time Holomisa was toppled from power and gave the operation his unequivocal support. He cautioned Eugene to be careful not to get caught.

It was about this time, before the formation of International Researchers-Ciskei Intelligence Service (IR-CIS) in Ciskei (dealt with elsewhere in this book), that Brigadier Gqozo told police officers attending the daily meeting of Ciskei's Council of State to leave the room. He told the CDF officers remaining that Colonel Craig Duli had visited him the evening before and asked for his assistance in making a training area available. He needed one for seven days to train an armed group for a coup he intended mounting against Major-General Bantu Holomisa.

Brigadier Gqozo told the meeting that Colonel Duli had explained that he had no problems as far as weapons and logistics were concerned. He only needed the training area. They all knew that Transkei was harbouring General Charles Sebe and helping his *Iliso Lomzi* with training facilities at Transkei's Special Force's base at Port St Johns. Gqozo wholeheartedly approved the request and suggested that Colonel Duli be allowed the use of facilities at the Sandile Military Base at Peddie.

A heated argument ensued and surprisingly most of the CDF officers objected to the idea of helping him. Eventually, Brigadier Gqozo withdrew his proposal and he never mentioned it again in the Council of State.[15]

Eugene de Kock gathered together the war material required, finding it necessary to get a lot of stuff not only from the Vlakplaas stores but also by rounding up various weapons that members of C1 had been utilising for their personal use. He also had to recover stuff stored at the Counter-insurgency (COIN) Armoury at the Police College, Pretoria. Serial numbers were ground off the weapons to hinder any attempts to identify and trace them later.

The items were sealed in plastic bags and loaded into two closed vans. He arranged to rendezvous with Colonel Craig Duli in a room at the Ostner Hotel in East London. He was using as his base from which to launch his coup attempt. He left Pretoria, accompanied by C1 operatives Warrant Officers Willie Nortje, Lionel Snyman and Snor Vermeulen, he left Pretoria for East London with the two vans loaded to the brim with material.

In East London they booked into a holiday home. They were staying there for an indeterminate time because no time had been set for the hand over of the weapons. Colonel de Kock contacted Craig Duli and arranged to see him at the Ostner Hotel. Eugene introduced his men.

Colonel Craig Duli said there had been a change of plan. He needed four AK47s, ammunition, spare magazines and 16 hand grenades immediately. The rest could come later. Eugene demurred because all the material had been sealed in watertight plastic packages. To separate certain items entailed unloading the vans and opening the packages. This posed a major security problem as they might be seen by the local police or by members of the public. The C1 operators were in East London incognito and without the knowledge of the local Security Police.

Craig Duli shrugged but insisted that he needed them. He did not volunteer the reason.

Eugene also shrugged. After all, it was not his coup. He was there to facilitate, not to obstruct.

He ordered Warrant Officers Lionel Snyman and Snor Vermeulen to go to the holiday home and retrieve the advance requirements. They got it and handed it over to Colonel Duli.

It did, as anticipated, cause a problem because it meant breaking the waterproof seals. After this, Eugene decided the holiday home was inappropriate as it had no lock-up facilities for the two vans containing the arms consignment. No date had been set for the coup attempt and a theft would have proved disastrous. He knew they would be spending at least another three to four days in East London.The next day they moved to beach-front cabanas which had secure lock-up garages where the vehicles and the arms consignment could be kept out of sight.

Willie Nortje recalled that at about this time he accompanied Eugene de Kock to the Ostner Hotel where they met Jan Anton Nieuwoudt and Clive Brink and discussed strategies. Colonel de Kock denied that such a meeting took place.[16]

During another meeting with Colonel Duli at the Ostner Hotel, the question of means to transport the weapons to Umtata arose. It was impossible to use the vans, because they were registered SAP vehicles. Eventually it was decided that Colonel de Kock would hire a Combi under a false name and the weapons would be transferred into that.

Colonel Duli told them the coup would be going ahead on 22 November. Eugene arranged to rendezvous with Colonel Duli's group at a particular dirt road between Ugie and Maclear and hand over the Combi and its cargo of weapons at 21:00 the evening before. Afterwards Colonel Duli and his men would continue to Umtata and mount their attack.

In the meantime, they needed to find a quiet place where the weapons could be discreetly transferred from the vans into the Combi. Eugene de Kock eventually decided to use the East London race course which was virtually deserted at the time. The transfer went ahead without a hitch.

Eugene and his men arrived at the rendezvous early. Colonel Craig Duli's party was very late. His group of about 15 men dressed in SADF browns arrived in a small convoy of four vans five hours later at 02:00 and Eugene handed over the Combi. He was very anxious about the lateness of the hour, believing that the cover of night was a vital element contributing to the success of the assault. He advised Craig Duli to postpone the attack — cancel and lay it on for another night. He stressed how important it was that they gain control of the telephone exchange and the radio station in the early stages.

Craig Duli was obstinately optimistic. He would go ahead anyway. There was nothing more to discuss. It was Eugene's impression that he was working on an absolute need-to-know basis. He gathered from his general attitude and demeanour, that his plans were already firmly in place and that he was not prepared to consider further suggestions from anyone.

During earlier conversations with others, though, he had said he had been 'called' by the TDF and believed he had something like 75% support amongst them. He wanted the government to be removed from the control of the Military Council and handed back to the people. He said nothing about it to Eugene de Kock, but he had divided the operation into two phases. The first phase, involving the toppling of Holomisa's regime by military force, was *Operation Sacrifice*. The second, involving the installation of a civilian administration, was coded *Operation Dawn*.[17]

It seemed he had a premonition before they parted company, because he hesitated at the last moment. He removed a chromium-plated mini Rugar 14.223 calibre from his pocket. It was a beautiful weapon, one that any fighting man or gun collector would have wanted to own.

'Do me a favour. If anything happens to me, please give this to my son.'

Eugene took it and nodded.

There were brief waves and shouts of 'good luck' as Colonel Craig Duli's convoy moved out and headed towards Umtata.

'It really is too late', Eugene said to his men. 'He should have cancelled.'[18]

Unbeknown to Colonel Duli his group had been heavily infiltrated, not only by members of the Transkei's Security Police, but also by operators of South Africa's Military Intelligence and the National Intelligence Service.

Warrant Officer Pumelele Gumengu, acting in deep cover, was tasked to travel ahead of the group to scout for TDF roadblocks and so on. He did not find any roadblocks but he took the opportunity to phone his handler, Captain Mfazwe, of the Transkei's Security Police to tip him off that the coup attempt had started.[19] According to Major-General Holomisa, though, they were taken completely by surprise. Somehow, it seems, Gumengu's message did not get through. Obviously the Military Intelligence and NIS operators were not interested in blowing the operation to Transkei, so security was maintained.[20]

Mazizi Thomas Ntisana, and three other civilians, were also involved in the operation. They were on the periphery in Ntisana's vehicle and it was their job was to enter Umtata when the fighting was done to mount *Operation Dawn*. They would form the foundation of the planned new civilian administration. In the event, Mazizi and his companions never even entered Umtata.[21]

Sabelo Wana, who was later convicted in the Umtata Supreme (now High) Court for his role in the attempted coup, told the TRC that TDF commander, Major-General Matanzima and other senior officers had assured Colonel Duli that his assault force would not be resisted by their forces. Colonel Duli had intended replacing Major-General Holomisa and his Military Council with an interim structure headed by Transkei's Chief Justice, Ted Beck, and nine traditional leaders. This would have included ex-President Kaiser Matanzima.

'He [Craig Duli] said we are not going to fight, we are just going to take Holomisa out. He told us we would not meet any resistance. However, we were betrayed at the eleventh hour by members of the TDF', Sabelo Wina said.[22]

General Holomisa, rejected his submission with contempt, saying that if his senior army officers had been determined to oust him, they would have done so without waiting for people 'to come in the middle of the night from South Africa'.[23]

Colonel Duli planned to neutralise the home forces by attacking the Ncini Military Base in Central Umtata (garrisoned by the TDF's 1-Battalion) and the KD Matanzima Airport outside town to isolate the airstrip. In the event he did not succeed with either endeavour.

Private Themba Pokwana was with the 'D' Company recruit intake at the Ncise Base in Umtata. Some were sleeping in barrack blocks and others were in tents.Pokwana was in a barrack block with about 80 other recruits. They were unarmed. Between 03:00 and 04:00 there was gunfire and the recruits hurriedly got up, turned the lights on and dressed.

Private Kwele of 'E' Company staggered through the door into 'D' Company's barrack block, his face covered in blood.

'What's happening?' they asked.

'There is shooting outside', he said

Privates Pokwana and Peter got to their feet, but as they did a mortar bomb crashed through the roof of the bungalow. It detonated and killed Private Peter and wounded Private Pokwana. There was a bedlam of noise with men crying and moaning.

When Pokwana recovered consciousness he saw that Private Gungu was also dead. Privates Nombida, Mogoduga and others were wounded.

There was a lot of gunfire and much shouting outside.

Soldiers wearing SADF browns, which were different to the Transkei uniform, came to help the wounded. They wrapped them in blankets and took them outside, saying that those capable of doing it, should try to crawl away from the barrack blocks as it was likely more mortar bombs would fall. The wounded came to appreciate that their helpers were, in fact, the attackers. Two mortar bombs landed nearby almost simultaneously and two privates were killed in the explosions. Those assisting the wounded told them they would now have to help themselves as best they could because they had to go. They left. Thirty-three soldiers were wounded in all.

Soldiers within the barracks began returning the fire of the rebels.

Colonel Duli, speaking through a loudhailer at the gates of the barracks, shouted that he had come to overthrow the Military Council.

'Everyone come and join me. I am in power now, ' he shouted. 'The Military Council has been toppled. Holomisa is no more.' [24]

General Holomisa told the author that in the general excitement Colonel Craig Duli got too close to a RPG-7 when it was fired and the backblast scorched his face. It is unknown how badly burnt he was.[25] In the meantime, his troops had hijacked at gunpoint an ambulance used to transport early morning workers from the town centre to Ncise Base.

According to Major General Holomisa, 'the first I knew of the coup attempt was when I saw it on [SABC] television' early in the morning.[26]

At about 06:00 the ambulance was used to transport Colonel Duli, Boetie Davies and Sabelo Wana to the Botha Sigcau Building in central Umtata. This housed most of Transkei's government offices. It also included General Holomisa's offices, the cabinet room and the offices of the Military Council. They bumped into General Holomisa's personal secretary, Colonel Mbulelo Xaba, in a passageway as he arrived to open the 11th floor offices. They opened fire on him. He returned fire with his pistol, but they captured and made him to open the doors of General Holomisa's office suite which they entered and took over.

The reason for such a takeover was never revealed, but it was apparently a symbolic gesture of control like the attempt to capture the airport. Strangely enough, no effort was made to capture the radio station and the telephone exchange.

Colonel Duli ordered Colonel Xaba to telephone Major-General Holomisa to tell him they had captured his offices.

'Thank you', General Holomisa told Colonel Xaba coolly. 'We have been looking for Colonel Duli and now we know where he is. Just stay there and relax.'

The rebels moved from the offices to the cabinet room.

At 07:00 General Holomisa ordered the streets around the Botha Sigcau Building to be cordoned off. The area was quickly surrounded by troops. He told the author he ordered that the rebels should be captured alive.[27]

Shortly afterwards a journalist, in an attempt to find out what was going on, phoned General Holomisa's office. It was answered by an unidentified man: 'Colonel Duli has taken over the government. General Holomisa will not be at work today', he told the reporter.

By 08:00 it appears that Warrant Officer Pumelele Gumengu had been properly debriefed by his handler. He must have mentioned the transfer of arms from Colonel de Kock to Colonel Duli's group, but it became enlarged in the telling. This prompted the mounting of a manhunt for 'six whites' reportedly with the rebels. When asked about this afterwards, General Holomisa said he had no proof of white participation but said that 'maybe they ran away after they found their palace coup was a cock-up'.[28]

During a lull in the fighting around Ncise Barracks, TDF soldiers came to collect the, wounded and take them to hospital using a variety of commandeered vehicles.[29]

At 12:00 Major-General Holomisa ordered the cutting of all telephone links between South Africa and Umtata. This was done after it was discovered that Colonel Duli, during his last desperate hours while holed up in the Stella Sigcau Building, had dialled seven South African telephone numbers. This included calls to several unnamed officers in South Africa's Security Forces, including a brigadier and a colonel. He also telephone Chris van Rensburg of JALC Holdings.[30]

Significantly, it was revealed by a Ministry of Law and Order spokesman during the course of the day, that a 'crack force' of the SADF and SAP had been sent to East London to protect national interests and citizens in Transkei. It had been necessary to dispatch the force 'as we wanted them nearby', the spokesman said.

This was SADF-speak for saying that they had already been deployed and were poised to follow up on Colonel Duli's successes.

At 12:30 General Holomisa warned South Africa not to send police or troops, which brought any idea of a South African intervention to a halt. Obviously it might have proved messy because it was highly likely that TDF would have capitalised on their successes against Colonel Duli by fighting back. If this had resulted in the deaths of young national servicemen, it would have been difficult to explain, particularly when the white electorate were only too well aware that a handover of government was in the offing.

About this time Major-General Holomisa heard that ex-President Kaiser Mantanzima was strutting around Umtata dressed in white announcing to all and sundry who mgith have wanted to listen that he would soon be back in power.

Major-General Holomisa told the author he was reluctant to fire on the Botha Sigcau Building, because he wanted the rebels to surrender. He sent several messages to Colonel Duli asking him to surrender, but each time he was met with a refusasl. Eventually at 15:00, TDF commander, Major-General Matanzima, asked for his permission to storm the building.

'Go ahead', General Holomisa told him.[31]

He told the *Sunday Times* he had no option but to order his troops to shoot to kill.[32]

The press said the building was mortared, but it was more likely that RPG-7 rockets were used.

General Holomisa told the author:'So the building was raided and Duli was apprehended. I believe he died on his way to the Military Hospital because he had been shot in the body . . . shrapnel.'

The *Sunday Times* dramatically said that 'blinded by shrapnel and dying from multiple bullet wounds, Colonel Duli was pulled out feet first from the office he coveted . . . thick smears of blood traced the 11th floor passage, strewn with debris and wreckage'.[33]

Witnesses to the storming said Colonel Duli was alive when he finally emerged from the building. In an interview with *The Star* General Holomisa repeated that Colonel Duli had been wounded. Asked how he had died he replied: 'He was wounded in the face and body'.

Some witnesses told *The Star* that they had seen no blood on the colonel's chest and face. *SAPA* reported claims that Duli was taken away in the boot of a car after a hostile crowd closed in to attack him.[34]

The SABC news said that Colonel Duli 'had been murdered by [Transkei] government soldiers while on his way to a place of detention'.[35]

Sabelo Wana in evidence to the TRC, said that during the battle within the building Boetie Davies was killed and Colonel Duli was wounded by a bullet in his right thigh and by shrapnel in his left eye. Both he and Colonel Duli surrendered to government troops and were escorted from the building. The colonel appeared unwounded except for slight scratches.[36]

Colonel Duli's widow, Mrs Nontobeko 'Topsy' Duli, told the TRC, and the author, that after the revolt had been crushed her husband had been summarily shot in the back of his head at the Ncise Military Base. This was witnessed, she said, by Colonel Wildon Mbulawa, then head of the Umtata Murder and Robbery Unit — later Deputy Commissioner of Police in the Transkei — who reported it to her.

Lieutenant-General Mbulawa was assassinated outside his home in Umtata in 1994.[37]

Eugene de Kock told the TRC that several weeks afterwards Jan Anton Nieuwoudt of IR-CIS (see later) had told him that Craig Duli had been wounded during the coup attempt. After he was allegedly tortured, there was a discussion between General Holomisa, Brigadier T T Matanzima and Holomisa's driver, Whiteboy, after which someone shot him to death.

During a subsequent interview, Colonel Eugene de Kock told the author that from information gained from sources who were present, in addition to those he had previously mentioned, SACP leaders Joe Slovo and Chris Hani were also at the scene. Armed MK operatives wearing blue overalls had apparently assisted in putting down the coup. This, he said, led to Joe Slovo allegedly saying that it would be impossible to keep Craig Duli alive. He not only knew too much, he had seen too much.

Whiteboy then shot him.

In an interview with the *Saturday Star*, General Holomisa dismissed ongoing allegations that Colonel Duli had been murdered. 'Colonel Duli was seriously injured and lost both his arms in the violent exchanges between his men and the Security Forces, ' he said. 'The bodies of the rebels were displayed to the media because we did not have anything to hide.' [38] He threatened to take court action against the TRC for listening to those who continued to make unsubstantiated allegations that he was somehow involved in a plot to murder Colonel Duli.

Later on the afternoon of the coup attempt, General Holomisa addressed an impromptu gathering at Umtata's Independence Stadium. He announced that the coup attempt had been put down and that the rebel leader, Colonel Craig Duli had been killed. He expressed his suspicions that South Africa was behind the attempt and he called for an urgent meeting with the South African government to discuss it. He railed against South Africa's Ambassador to Umtata, Gert Terblanche, 'who had the audacity not even to phone me' before going public about the coup attempt. He also questioned the presence of SABC-TV newsman, Danie Malan, who was poised in Umtata early on 22 November although no newsworthy events had been planned for that day.[39] An Umtata lawyer said it was clear from the thousands of people who flocked to the stadium that General Holomisa was widely supported by the average man in the street. Whether this was due to his public association with the ANC or not is a matter for speculation.[40]

The next day the torn bodies of Colonel Duli and ten of his comrades were unceremoniously dumped on the hot tarmacadam of the car park in the Ncise Military Base. Those of Duli and his bodyguard Boetie Davis were set slightly apart from the rest, next to an arsenal of captured rifles, machine guns, mortars and ammunition. Four captives, two severely wounded and the others manacled, sat disconsolately on a nearby embankment overlooking the grisly exhibition. On a podium 50m away, General Holomisa, his back firmly turned on his one-time friend, thanked the assembled troops for their help in putting down the attempted coup.[41]

General Holomisa told them he had forgiven Colonel Duli and called on them to attend his funeral. This statement did not go down well with the troops who responded by booing. He told the *Sunday Star* that it had been 'a very sad incident' and he had no personal grudges against Duli whom he believes was 'misled and manipulated . . . I understand Colonel Duli because he was a man trapped by his loyalties to the Mantanzimas and he was easily influenced. I have a lot of sympathy for the man because I don't think his heart was in it.'

Speaking professionally, he said Colonel Duli had made a bad mistake in ordering his rebels to mortar the Ncise Military Base because that would have served to anger the troops whose support he needed for his coup to succeed.[42]

Ambassador Terblanche stated flatly that his government was not involved in the coup bid. In Pretoria, Foreign Affairs Minister, Pik Botha, said: 'The South African government is shocked at Major-General Holomisa's allegation that the South African Embassy in Umtata had knowledge of the attempted coup. It is not only unfounded, but extremely irresponsible.' [43]

He would have said that, of course.

On 25 November 1990 President F W de Klerk bluntly warned Transkei's President Tudor Ndamase that the territory stood to lose R1,8 billion in aid unless General Holomisa ceased making false allegations that South Africa was involved in the coup bid.

General Holomisa replied: 'I stand by my statements and nothing will be retracted. I am not changing one slight word.'[44]

The factors indicating that South Africa knew of the plan were:

- The SABC's Danie Malan was in Umtata as early as 06:00 on the day of the coup.
- He (General Holomisa) was unaware of events until the early morning SABC broadcast — despite his phone lines being free.
- The coup was launched from South African territory.
- The conspirators were mostly South Africans.
- The weapons used originated from South Africa.
- Colonel Duli had recently been released on bail after being sentenced to imprisonment for possession of arms and ammunition intended for another Transkei coup.[45]

There are many more reasons revealed by the author. During discussions with President F W de Klerk and other cabinet ministers at the Union Building in Pretoria, Major-General Holomisa presented a document which revealed the involvement of South Africa and name those members of the South African Security Forces involved. SAP Major-General Fischer was appointed to lead a team investigate Major-General Holomisa's allegations.[46] With this achieved South Africa and Transkei papered over their differences by reaffirming the bonds of friendship binding them to the sovereignty and inviolability of each other's territories; their rejection of the use of force to resolve differences; and their commitment to the 1976 non-aggression pact between them. In a joint statement made afterwards the two countries recorded that alleged prior knowledge of the attempted coup by the South African Ambassador in Umtata had been jointly resolved 'to the satisfaction of both delegations'.[47]

In spite of several invitations Transkei refused to participate in Major-General Fischer's investigation. The investigation team failed to find anything that corroborated General Holomisa's allegations.[48]

Later in the month General Holomisa appealed to the South African government to have over three Transkeian citizens implicated in the Duli coup attempt. He named them as Vuklindlela Mbotoli, Mazizi Ntisana, as well as the homeland's former Ambassador to Austria, Amos Somdaka.[49]

As was par for the course, the request was ignored.

On 13 December 1990 former President Kaiser Matanzima was detained by the Transkei police in connection with his involvement in the Duli coup attempt. For the reasons of disloyalty to Transkei he was suspended as the Paramount Chief of Western Thembuland.[50]

Vlakplaas, the DCC and IR-CIS: after Colonel Craig Duli's coup attempt

According to Eugene de Kock, on the morning of 22 November 1990 he and his team monitored radio reports for news of the coup, eventually hearing that it had failed and that Colonel Craig Duli and others had been killed.They anxiously monitored radio broadcasts the rest of the day but details remained sketchy. Asked how a successful coup would have benefited the government of the time, Eugene de Kock speaking generally told the TRC: 'It would have established a friendly government in the Transkei' with 'Kaiser Matanzima as the head of state and Colonel Craig Duli as the military head . . . It would have given us unconditional access to the Transkei where Vlakplaas in particular would have been used very effectively with regard to the identification of PAC and ANC members . . . We would be able to arrest these persons and recruit them. We would also be able to neutralise [arms] stockpiling locations . . . '[51]

Captain Ras of C1 who was in East London on another operation said, however, that Eugene de Kock and his men went to a safe house used by the Security Police in East London. He was also there and so were an undisclosed number of ex-ANC and ex-PAC askaris. If the coup had been successful, Captain Ras said, 'we would have entered the Transkei with the ANC and PAC members to assist with the identification of ANC and PAC persons who resided in the Transkei and worked from there, with the exclusive purpose of arresting them and handing them over to the Transkei Security Police . . .'[52]

It appears from this, particularly as the askaris were in the safe house apparently awaiting deployment, that a follow-up operation by C1 into the Transkei was more imminent than Eugene de Kock had made it out to be.

During the afternoon Eugene de Kock took his men to have a few beers at the Ostner Hotel. Commandant Jan Anton Nieuwoudt and Sergeant Clive Brink appeared shortly afterwards. Nieuwoudt, he said was depressed and disappointed at the coup's failure. He said, though, that things were all bad as the covers of four of his agents had not been blown. It seems these four men had been given the four AK47s and the hand grenades that Craig Duli had demanded without explanation earlier. He failed to explain whether the four were supposed to have taken part in the actual coup attempt, or whether they were in Umtata as some sort of contingency plan.

Eugene de Kock said this was a coincidental meeting, but it seems unlikely. Colonel de Kock had liaised regularly with Commandant Jan Anton Nieuwoudt. This was both before and after the latter set up IR-CIS (International Researchers — Ciskei Intelligence Service), in Bisho, Ciskei, as a front company for Military Intelligence's DCC in October 1990. When staffing the unit he attempted to recruit Warrant Officer Willie Nortje of C1 and get him to resign from the Police Force. He even made an offer to Eugene de Kock. Both offers were refused.

Colonel de Kock told the TRC that Jan Anton Nieuwoudt 'was very committed in this attempt to overthrow General Holomisa or to neutralise him in the Transkei'.

It was put to him that although Craig Duli had come to the fore as the one who would execute the coup, there had been continual planning in which Jan Anton Nieuwoudt and the DCC had played a role.

De Kock replied: 'It was a continuous situation . . . Just before [the Duli coup attempt] Nieuwoudt, [Clive] Brink and I met at a holiday house at the coast . . . I would not be able to find it again, but it was where [Jan] Anton Nieuwoudt told me that there were 22 men who acted as sources for him and received salaries on that basis, that they were former members of the Transkei Security Forces . . . and were well trained.'

He added that during the Duli coup attempt 'some of them were killed and some were caught, but that he still had to support the families financially. It [the Duli coup attempt] was not an impulsive attempt to usurp General Holomisa's government.' [53]

Mbotoli: abducted to the Transkei

After moving to Johannesburg Rayner Maria Moringer had remained in contact with Transkei's Military Intelligence Chief, Major Mzwaiba, and had regularly passed him low-key political intelligence. He was engaged in establishing a new business that sold equipment. In early 1991 Major Mzwaiba contacted Moringer and said they were anxious to track down and kill Vuli Mbotoli because of his involvement in the Craig Duli coup attempt. Moringer knew Mbotoli from his association with Jalc Holdings in the days when he trying to set up business in Transkei. Mbotoli had facilitated his first meeting with Prime Minister George Matanzima. Major Mzwaiba said they had tracked Mbotoli down by monitoring the telephones of his friends and associates in Transkei.

Moringer told the major he thought it was a bad idea to kill Mbotoli. Besides, he wanted nothing to do with an assassination. Surely, he reasoned, it would be more sensible to kidnap him and get him back to Transkei. Once he was in custody in Transkei, he could be comprehensively debriefed to find out who in the South African government was behind the various coup attempts. His suggestion was accepted, so Moringer agreed to assist.

Major Mzwaiba gave him a Johannesburg telephone number, obtained by monitoring, where it was believed Mbotoli was staying. He found it was the office of John Strong, a director of Jalc Holdings whom he had met when he had first contacted Chris van Rensburg. He phoned Strong to renew his acquaintance and arranged to call at his place. When he got there, he found Vuli Mbotoli. He arranged to keep in touch with him and expressed sympathy with his anti-Holomisa stance.

During the next two to three months he established close a close relationship with Mbotoli. He discussed progress with Major Mzwaiba over the phone and met him once at the Wild Coast Sun Casino Hotel and once Transkei's Embassy in Pretoria. Eventually, from conversations with Mbotoli, he established that another anti-Holomisa coup was due to go ahead in the next two to three weeks. This made it essential his abduction be accelerated. Mbotoli, for his part, had been trying to establish if General Holomisa held a numbered bank account in Switzerland, which there had been rumours about. Moringer assured Mbotoli that he would do his best to find out. After discussions with Major Mzwaiba it was decided to use the Swiss bank account issue as bait for a trap.

A five-man snatch team of five men from Transkei's Military Intelligence had been standing by at Transkei's Pretoria Embassy, ready for action should the opportunity arise.

On 12 April 1991 Moringer phoned a friend and asked to borrow his house for the evening for an important business meeting. The friend agreed. This was not a particularly unusual request because Moringer had only a small and insignificant home at the time.

He phoned Mbotoli and told him he had made contact with an official from a certain Swiss bank. This official, he told him guardedly, had some information that would be of interest to him. He suggested that he pick up Mbotoli that evening and bring him to his house when he could meet the man. Mbotoli jumped at the bait.

Mbotoli had no idea where Morenger lived, so it did not arouse his suspicion when after being picked up in Rosebank, he was driven to the friend's house. Waiting in hiding within the house was the five-man snatch team. They were equipped with chloroform and five injections, each of which, they had been told, would keep the prisoner helplessly sedated for about two hours. They each had a leisurely Coke to drink in Moringer's friend's bar.

Moringer eventually stood up and said he was going to get something from the kitchen. This was the signal for the snatch team to rush into the room and grab Mbotoli. He was overpowered and went out like a light after a chlorine-soaked pad of cotton wool was held over his mouth. He was then injected with the special injection . Unfortunately it did not work as efficiently as expected which created problems later. From there he was carried from the house to three waiting cars and driven via Durban to the TDF's Special Force's base at Port St Johns. Moringer was not involved in the car trip.

Mbotoli was held incommunicado for six months. Eventually, General Holomisa held a press conference at which he produced Mbotoli. He said the military had abducted him from South Africa, but he was handing him over to the police to be tried before the High Court on charges of treason with 18 co-accused involved in the coup attempt.

Following this Mbotoli was allowed access to his attorney, a doctor and consular officials from the South African Embassy. Predictably he fingered Meringer as being involved in his abduction. Shortly afterwards, while he was out, Meringer got an urgent but surreptitious phone call from his wife. She whispered that the Security Police had arrived and were waiting at their home to arrest him for the abduction.

He phoned Major Mzwaiba who advised him to flee to Transkei. Acting on his instructions, he contacted the military attaché at Transkei's embassy in Pretoria. Fortunately, the attaché was travelling to Transkei the next morning to take up an appointment as the Minister of Police. He said that if Moringer could hang around and stay out of the way of the security police until then, he would gladly drive him to Umtata.

Moringer had no option but to remain in the Transkei for the next two years living in a house provided by the government . When the Truth and Reconciliation Commission was established, he immediately applied for amnesty.[54]

After a trial that lasted two years, Transkei's Chief Justice Ted Beck, convicted Vulindlela Mbotoli on12 counts that included treason, conspiracy to overthrow the government and murder. He was sentenced to an effective 20 years imprisonment. Seventeen of his co-accused were sentenced to a total of 800 years between them. One of them, Msimelo Mpakati, was found not guilty and discharged.[55]

On 3 July 1995 they were pardoned by President Nelson Mandela and released from prison.[56]

26

IR-CIS Ciskei
Framing of the Few
February/March 1991

Arms cache at IR-CIS base

After the murder of Charles Sebe and Onward Guzana, IR-CIS operators Jan Anton Nieuwoudt and Clive Brink submitted intelligence to the DCC to say the only remaining threat to Brigadier Gqozo was posed by the ANC and its alliance partners.

They began compiling details and addresses in the Ciskei of returned MK guerrillas and ANC activists. By early February the list comprised 156 names and addresses.

On Friday 1 February 1991 a unit of South Africa paratroopers conducted a parachute exercise. It was carried out on South African territory but adjacent to Bisho's Ministerial Complex. After gathering up their kit the paratroopers left immediately after the drop. This was unusual because there had been no liaison with the CDF beforehand as was normal. The military attaché in King William's Town and apologised after a protest was lodged. He said Eastern Province Command had not notified the CDF due to an oversight.

On 3 February 1991, two days later, a statement by Brigadier Gqozo was published in the *Sunday Times*. In it he accused Major-General Bantu Holomisa of the Transkei, the ANC — in particular SACP leader Chris Hani, and the late Charles Sebe and Onward Guzana of plotting a *coup d'etat* to topple him from office. He threatened to shoot Chris Hani if he ever entered the homeland again. This statement concerned most of the CDF's command element because, as far as they were concerned Sebe and Guzana had been lured to their deaths by IR-CIS, which they were convinced was a surrogate of the SADF's Military Intelligence. No one believed it had been an ANC plot.

CDF Chief, Brigadier Jamangile and Lieutenant-Colonel Zantsi attempted to contact Brigadier Gqozo to seek an explanation. He was not available and they were told he was at the IR-CIS' base at Blacklands Farm. After failing to get him, they sought out Brigadier Gqozo's second in command, Colonel Pita. He expressed surprise on being shown the *Sunday Times* report. He told them that on 1 February Brigadier Gqozo had been in his office with Jan Anton Nieuwoudt and a *Sunday Times* reporter. He had heard Nieuwoudt attempting to persuade Gqozo to make a statement to the journalist much along the lines reported in the newspaper. Brigadier Gqozo, however, had steadfastly refused to do so. They were still discussing things in his office Colonel Pita left later that afternoon.

On Monday 4 February Brigadier Gqozo told those attending a Council of State meeting that no one had the right to question him about what had appeared in a Sunday newspaper. It was his prerogative to say what he liked to anyone. After that senior officers who were members of the council stopped attending meetings in protest and sent along juniors as proxies. This was because Gqozo had allowed himself to be manipulated by the SADF.

On 7 February the SADF's 32-Battalion carried out a parachute drop at the old Bisho Airfield. Strangely enough none of the black officers, including the commander, Brigadier Jamangile, were told about it or invited to watch until the day before it happened. Brigadier

Jamangile was briefed by the Senior Staff Officer (Operations) in the Eastern Cape, Colonel Dirk van der Bank — who coincidentally happened to be Nieuwoudt's cousin. The Officer Commanding of Group 8 in East London, Colonel Phillip Hammond, was there and South Africa's newly appointed Military Attaché to the Ciskei, Colonel Bill van der Linde, took part in the actual jump.

This made it apparent that the exercise had been planned well in advance. Everyone who mattered in the SADF in the region knew about it. The only ones kept in ignorance were the officers of the CDF. It became patently obvious, however, that Brigadier Gqozo knew about it. While the purpose of the exercise remains unclear to this day, it was most likely a 'show of force' to demonstrate to the CDF's hierarchy that the SADF through IR-CIS was still in control.

Lieutenant-Colonel Zantsi attended the parachuting exercise along with the other senior officers. He sent Lieutenant Kleinbooi to take his place at the daily Council of State meeting. Kleinbooi reported back that Brigadier Gqozo was furious about the absence of the senior officers. He said that it was apparent that most officers had a negative attitude towards him and were either ANC supporters or sympathisers. So, he said, he was going to Pretoria to see the Minister of Defence, Magnus Malan, the Minister of Law and Order, Adriaan Vlok, and other powerful men so he could get new soldiers with new weapons. He threatened to dismiss any Ciskei soldier who failed to cooperate with him.

He left for Pretoria that afternoon.

After watching the parachute drop most of the CDF's senior officers, less Brigadier Jamangile and his Chief of Staff, Colonel Pita, retired to the Officers' Mess at 1-Ciskei Battalion for lunch. The SADF officers who took part in the demonstration were not invited.

After lunch those there assembled for a meeting in the office of 1-Ciskei Battalion Commander, Lieutenant- Colonel Mteti. Lieutenant-Colonel Zantsi proposed that they draw up a petition calling on Brigadier Gqozo to resign as Head of State. This was agreed to unanimously. They listed their grievances. Their main complaint related to his day-to-day politicking and particularly how he was allowing himself to be manipulated by IR-CIS.

The letter was given to Lance Corporal (Mrs) Mkhosana in the Military Intelligence offices to type. When ready it would be signed by all the senior officers who had participated in the drafting, including the CDF Chief and his Chief of Staff. A deputation would present the letter to Gqozo when he returned from Pretoria on 9 February.

On 9 February the dissident officers were astonished by an article in East London's *Daily Dispatch*. Brigadier Gqozo had sent the newspaper a hand-written press release saying that if he should be incapacitated, the Chief Justice would act as Head of State. They concluded a leak had occurred and that Gqozo knew about the pending petition. Nevertheless, they felt so strongly about it that they decided to go ahead with signing the petition and handing it over as planned.

Brigadier Jamangile went to King William's Town to have a chat with the South African Military Attaché, Colonel Bill van der Linde. He asked if he had any idea what lay behind the letter to the *Daily Dispatch*. Van der Linde said he knew nothing about it, but suggested that it was normal for a Head of State to nominate someone to act in his absence.

On 9 February at about 05:30, Lieutenant-Colonel Zantsi, paid a social visit to the house of Lieutenant-Colonel Naka in north Bisho. Naka was a musician and that he and his group had intended to have an all-night session, so he knew he would be awake. To his surprise he was met by Warrant Officer Melane of IR-CIS and Staff Sergeant Mputa-Mputa. They told him that Lieutenant-Colonel Mteti, Captain Qamata and Naka had been looking for him at his home village.

They told him a large cache of weapons had been discovered at the IR-CIS' House 14, Ministerial Complex. Melane said it included about 50 AK47 rifles, seven RPG7V rocket launchers, and seven SAM7B ground-to-air missile launchers.

Two bearded white men dressed in khaki drill and driving two white vans had been seen to arriving at the house on 7 February while the SADF parachuting exercise was on. Jan

Anton Nieuwoudt, Clive Brink and Warrant Officer Melane were there at the time. The vans were unloaded, the contents taken into a room inside and the curtains drawn. Afterwards the white men left.

Shortly afterwards Lieutenant Qamata and Staff Sergeant Ralo of Brigadier Gqozo's bodyguard had arrived there. Nieuwoudt ordered them into the room where the weapons were stored together with Warrant Officer Melane and Clive Brink. Nieuwoudt and Brink lectured and gave them practical demonstrations on how to operate the weapons.

'Your next job will be across the [Kei] river against that comrade general [Holomisa], 'Nieuwoudt told them.

He warned them not to repeat this to anyone, particularly the senior officers of the CDF. He threatened them saying that if this information leaked out the person responsible would suffer the consequences.

According to Colonel Eugene de Kock, he had supplied the weapons from stocks at Vlakplaas at Nieuwoudt's request. Nieuwoudt said his request had been approved by Brigadier Tolletjie Botha of DCC, by Brigadier Oupa Gqozo and by his own commander. He mentioned that Transkei had helicopters and it was planning to use them in an attack designed to overthrow Ciskei. The missiles were for use against the helicopters.[1]

Lieutenant-Colonel Zantsi drove to the Ministerial Complex to report the latest developments to Brigadier Jamangile, but en route he met Lieutenant-Colonels Naka and Mteti and Lieutenant Qamata. They told him that the brigadier was not at home and that no one knew where he was. Qamata confirmed what Warrant Officer Melane had said about the weapons and also that it was rumoured in the bodyguard unit that the CDF's senior officers were planning a coup.

They discussed what to do and agreed they should break into House 14, remove the weapons and place them in storage in the armoury at 1-Ciskei Battalion. This could be used as evidence to prove the nefarious activities of the IR-CIS. All senior officers involved in the petition calling for Brigadier Gqozo's resignation would be shown the weapons for their information and to strengthen their resolve. Afterwards, they would call in journalists from the *Daily Dispatch* and other newspapers and show them the cache. It was felt this was essential otherwise Nieuwoudt would just deny everything. It was also the only way they could get the South African government to answer publicly about the origin and purpose of the cache.

Breaking into the premises provided no difficulty because it was Saturday and IR-CIS did not man the place over weekends. Three vehicles to transport the weapons and details to load them were organised with the duty officer at 1-Ciskei Battalion. Warrant Officer Melane and Staff Sergeant Mputa-mputa were ordered to stand by at House 14 and guard the weapons until the transport came. They were unloaded at the Standby Armour Store and inspected. The weapons were freshly oiled and wrapped in black plastic.

Lieutenant-Colonel Zantsi and the other officers busied themselves phoning their colleagues who were signatories to the petition and getting them to come to inspect the weapons. Eventually they got hold of the CDF commander, Brigadier Jamangile who said he would be coming immediately to look at the weapons.

Lieutenant-Colonel Naka, meanwhile, had phoned the Paratroop Unit at Bulembu and arranged for two sections of troops to report to 1-Ciskei Battalion. They were required to deal with any eventuality that might arise.

While en route they were flagged down by Warrant Officer Veliti of Brigadier Gqozo's bodyguards. He asked where they were going. On being told their destination, he said the officers there were preparing for a coup. He added that there was going to be a big fight because neither the bodyguards nor IR-CIS would allow Gqozo to be overthrown.

Brigadier Jamangile was shown the weapons by Lieutenant-Colonel Mteti and he left to see his military adviser, Brigadier Mias Muller, to find out what was going on.

Lieutenant-Colonel Zantsi, meanwhile, after breakfasting with other officers at the officers' mess, sent Staff Sergeant Mputa-mputa to his house to fetch his uniform, personal firearm and money as he was running low on petrol. Lieutenant Kleinbooi arrived and Zantsi sent him to see the weapons.

A signaller then called Zantsi to the operations room. To his surprise he discovered that Colonel Mgwebi of the Transkei Defence Force was on the line for him. He wanted to know if it was true that Brigadier Gqozo was ill and that no one knew where he was.

Zantsi said he did not know what he was talking about, but told him the senior officers of the CDF were puzzled and surprised by the article in the *Dail Dispatch* the previous Friday.

'Are Brigadier Jamangele and Colonel Pita well?' Colonel Mgwebi asked.

Zantsi told him that to the best of his knowledge they were.

Shortly afterwards Staff Sergeant Mpeta-mpeta arrived with his uniform. Lieutenant Manekwane, the acting commander of the Parachute Unit, and Staff Sergeant Jelman of Military Intelligence also arrived. He briefed them while he was dressing, but suddenly there was a volley of gunfire in the vicinity of the administration block.

Lieutenant Manekwane went to investigate, but ran back shouting that the troops were firing at the officers. He had seen Warrant Officer Melane shot and fall.

The shooting continued and there was much shouting in the corridors.

'Zantsi is inside the operations room', someone shouted. 'Come out or we will throw a grenade through the air-conditioning vent.'

The operations room was windowless, so it was impossible to see what was happening outside.

The troops outside kept chanting that Zantsi was the mastermind behind the coup and that they were going to kill him.

Lieutenant-Colonel Zantsi shouted that he was coming out and that they should not shoot.

He opened the door and walked out with his hands up, but the firing continued.

Rifleman Jerry Qhawe confronted him with an R4 rifle. He indicated with it which way he should go. He told him he was to join the rest of the officers who were all laying face down on the parade group.

While being escorted there with his hands up he passed a group of soldiers who were recklessly firing R4 rifles and sub-machine guns from a sandbagged bunker. A stray shot hit him in the right leg and he went down.

'Get up!' Rifleman Qhawe snarled and kicked him to his feet.

Zantsi limped to the parade ground and joined the other officers. In front of him was the transport officer, Lieutenant Lawana, who had only come to the base to give Lieutenant-Colonel Mteti the keys of the Transport Section. The wild firing continued and a bullet wounded Lawana in the thing.

Warrant Officer Melane, badly wounded as he was, was forced to crawl from the administration block to join the rest of the prisoners on the parade ground to the accompaniment of taunts by the mutineers.

More troops arrived at the base and lined the parade ground gawking at their officers. The ambulance from the sickbay arrived to pick up the wounded and take them to hospital. An argument ensued between the medical orderlies and the mutineers. They refused to allow the wounded, Lieutenant-Colonel Zantsi, Lieutenant Lawana and Warrant Officerb Melane, to be moved to hospital. They wanted them sent straight to the Military Detention Barracks in a Military Police Vehicle. Alternately, they would finish them off then and there.

Someone tried to restore order, but this only attracted shouts of defiance.

'Nonsense! *Voertsek*!

At last the firing subsided and finally ceased.

Only Colonel Mias Muller, Major Mzayiya and Lieutenant Kleinbooi escaped being rounded up with the rest. Brigadier Jamangile initially escaped detention arrested, but he was later arrested and dealt with like the rest.[2]

Finally, the unwounded officers were taken to the detention barracks at Jongumsobomvu Military Base and the mutineers were persuaded to allow the three wounded men to go to Cecilia Makiwane hospital for treatment. This was conditional on the ambulance going under military escort.

En route to hospital a drunken escort admitted to the officers that the troops really had no idea what had happened. Most of the troops had been to an all-night party at Skobeni Village, held for the benefit of the returned inmates of a circumcision school. When they drifted into the base the next morning, they were addressed by Sergeant Vinta Gqirana who told them the officers at the unit were intending to overthrow Brigadier Gqozo. He pointed out the weapons that had been brought to the base and said they belonged to the officers, who intended to use them to shoot all the soldiers. He ordered the troops to shoot the officers before they could shoot them.

When the troops opened fire, they were saying amongst themselves that it served the officers right. They wanted to be cabinet ministers. They were just greedy and were not satisfied with the privileged lives they already led.

The drunken rifleman was correct. What he was not clever enough to realise was that IR-CIS had capitalised on the removal of its weapons cache by spinning the story so that it appeared the weapons had been taken by the officers to be used to mount a coup against Brigadier Gqozo. This, of course, was in conformance with Brigadier Gqozo's earlier statements to the *Sunday Times*. Now he could celebrate that his very own IR-CIS had rescued him from yet another ANC/Transkei-inspired coup.

At about this time Colonel Gerrie Hugo, the Joint Chief of Staff Intelligence, who fortunately for him had been out of town arrived back in Bisho. He found an urgent message for him to contact another white CDF officer, Colonel Jaco Rossouw, who was in charge of signals. He phoned and Rossouw told him what had happened and advised him to stay well away from 1-Ciskei Battalion. If he had been around earlier, it was likely he would also have ended up in the bag.

While the doctor was attending to Lieutenant-Colonel Zantsi's wounds, Warrant Officer Barnes and Sergeant Gqirana appeared and demanded his car keys as they wanted his briefcase. He told them the keys were with Staff Sergeant Mputa-mputa and they left. More soldiers came after them, amongst them Rifleman July Mqungqutho, who said he had orders from the Council of State to take Zantsi to State House. The doctors and nurses protested that he was a patient under treatment, but they still removed him from the hospital. Instead of taking him to State House, however, they took him by ambulance to 1-Ciskei Battalion and then removed him by truck to the detention barracks.

At about 19:30 Ted Brassel and Clive Brink arrived at the detention centre. They spent some time inspecting the separate cells that the officers were locked in. They reserved most of their attention for Lieutenant-Colonel Zantsi, accusing him of thinking he was 'too clever' when they (the IR-CIS) had done its homework a long time ago. One can be sure they had.

On 11 February the nine officers were removed from the detention centre and sent to different prisons for detention under Section 26 of Ciskei's Internal Security Act. Most went to Middledrift Prison, but others were sent to police stations at Tamaarha, Punzana and Ntoleni. Lieutenant-Colonel Zantsi alone was taken to Mdantsane Prison.

Meanwhile, Lieutenant Qamata had been found dead, his body floating in the Yellowwoods River. He had been killed execution-style by a bullet in the head. It was said that after the weapons were removed from the Ministerial Complex, the officers involved breakfasted together at 1-Ciskei Battalion's officers' mess. It seems the unfortunate Lieutenant Qamata was not amongst them because the post mortem revealed no signs of food in his stomach. It appears he probably lagged behind and was caught by IR-CIS personnel. Like any good intelligence organisation they had their own informers and had obviously been tipped off as to who was involved in the removal of their weapons. They were angry and they probably interrogated and afterwards executed him. Ciskei at the time was a Banana Republic, so no proper investigation was conducted. Later, though, during unrelated court proceeding, somebody connected to IR-CIS actually admitted having killed

Qamata. Unfortunately, for some kind of legal procedural reasons, this could not be used in a trial so no prosecution resulted.[3]

Whilst detained in Mdantsane Prison, Lieutenant-Colonel Zantsi was moved to the offices of the Ciskei Security Police's offices at Mdantsane for interrogation by Jacques Seaward of the SADF's Military Intelligence Division in the Eastern Cape. He alleged that Seaward, who had never served in the Ciskei's Security Forces, brutally tortured him. His questioning revolved around how the CDF officers had learned about the weapons caches at IR-CIS' offices and why they had removed them. He also demanded to know the identities of those in the ANC and in Transkei who were working with CDF officers to overthrow Gqozo. He later interrogated and tortured other detainees.

The detained officers were later charged with treason and terrorism. These charges were dropped on 8 March 1991. On the 22 April they were called to CDF headquarters to face a disciplinary enquiry, but instead they were served with letters of dismissal by Colonel S S Pita.[4] By September 1991Jan Anton Nieuwoudt was submitting reports to DCC suggesting that he had proof the badly wronged Brigadier Jamangile was liaising with the ANC's Chris Hani. Another matter for 'suspicion' was that the brigadier had also met with the Eastern Cape Security Police, Chief, Major-General Griebenhau in East London on 20 August 1991.[5]

A few years later the detained officers sued for wrongful dismissal and won. They had never been prosecuted, simply because there was not a shred of evidence of wrongdoing against them.

This, of course, caused no loss of sleep to Jan Anton Nieuwoudt and his IR-CIS or to Military Intelligence in Pretoria. From Nieuwoudt's point of view it was a job well done. He had turned the loss of the weapons to his own advantage (and no doubt got them back). In a masterstroke he had rid himself of the unsympathetic majority amongst the officers in the CDF — officers intent on foiling the IR-CIS' nefarious aims in the region — and furthered the aims of Military Intelligence in establishing Ciskei as Tac HQ for the fight against the ANC.

After the weapons cache incident blew IR-CIS's cover at House 14 Ministerial Complex, the organisation moved its base to another farm outside Bisho.[6]

With the CDF's senior officers out of the way, Jan Anton Nieuwoudt did not find it difficult to persuade Brigadier Gqozo to fill all the vacant (and strategic) post with seconded or retired South African officers. In terms of an agreement signed between Gqozo and South Africa's Foreign Minister Pik Botha on 27 February 1991, Brigadier Marius Oelschig, ex-Special Forces and Military Intelligence, was seconded in June 1991 to take over the CDF in place of the unfortunate Brigadier Jamangile. Colonel Dirk van der Bank was moved from East London to take over as his second in command.[7] Nieuwoudt had actually identified Deon Ferreira — a former 32-Battalion commander — for the post but he was unavailable.

In the event, Marius Oelschig did not last long because of Brigadier Gqozo's paranoia.

Nieuwoudt also arranged for the ubiquitous General Jan Viktor — the renowned former police commander in Soweto — to take over as Commissioner of Police.

Military Intelligence's policy, through IR-CIS, was undoubtedly based on fears arising from the report on the ANC's National Consultative Conference in June 1985 where it said:

> 'One of the questions most extensively debated was whether we should seek to advocate the overthrow of the Bantustan administrations or whether we should focus exclusively on the struggle against Pretoria. If the former applies, it would involve the establishment of (if only for a short time) a radical administration with sympathies for the liberation movement. Would such an approach weaken our correct policy of unconditionally rejecting the legitimacy of the Bantustans? It was generally felt we should be flexible in our approach.
>
> 'There is no doubt that Pretoria would intervene immediately to save its puppets. Such intervention would reduce the whole Bantustan policy to shambles. By removing the puppets we would bring the people into direct confrontation with the racists, opening up these areas into bases for the advancement of [the] People's War.' [8]

They obviously felt that MK and APLA had both ensconced themselves in Transkei through the offices of a sympathetic Military Council and they were determined to head off the same thing happening in Ciskei.

The founding commander of the Recces, Colonel Jan Breytenbach, also arrived in Ciskei from retirement to retrain Ciskei's Parachute Unit and get it battle-ready. There was not, of course, any battles in the offing to get it ready for, but that did not concern anyone. His letter of appointment said he was 'attached' to the CDF 'to provide specialist advice in the upgrading' of a parachute unit.[9] There were suggestions that Breytenbach was another Nieuwoudt nominee, but this did not seem to be the case because he followed his own track by really knocking the paratroopers into shape, instead of bothering himself with the agendas of Military Intelligence. Many of them are now notable soldiers in the Parachute Brigade of the new SANDF.

According to him his appointment in Ciskei resulted from a letter he wrote to Gqozo congratulating him for taking a stand against ANC Self Defence Units (SDUs). This eventually resulted in Gqozo personally inviting him to come to Ciskei to take over the paratroopers. They got on famously until the Amatola Sun Hotel in Bisho was held up by armed robbers. This led to a suggestion that the paratroopers, when they were not doing anything more useful, could be rented out as highly trained security guards. This did not go down well with the highly principled Colonel Breytenbach who dismissed the suggestion out of hand.

After this the Gqozo/Breytenbach relationship deteriorated rapidly.

Jan Breytenbach was convinced the South African Department of Foreign Affairs had a lot to do with his final departure from the territory, but it seems likely that Brigadier Oelschig might also have had a hand in it.

Colonel Gerrie Hugo defects to Transkei

After about 60% of the personnel of CDF's Military Intelligence had either been detained or discharged, some for placing sources in IR-CIS, Colonel Gerrie Hugo felt extremely apprehensive regarding his future. He was also extremely angry that his black colleagues had been out-maneuvered by IR-CIS and Military Intelligence, resulting in their illegal arrest and detention. In the case of Lieutenant Qamata it had ended in his death.

Colonel Hugo also had no staff and no authority to recruit more. A week after these terrifying events, Hendrik 'Christo' Christophel Nel and Ockert Swanepoel, both former CCB operators — Nel had been its Chief of Intelligence — reported to him for duty at the Military Intelligence's offices. They said he had to assist them.

'I don't know you', Gerrie told them.

'Oh, well, Jan Anton Nieuwoudt recruited us and we are here to get intelligence', they replied.

He discovered that Brigadier Gqozo had sanctioned their employment as civilian staff. Later, on 1 October 1991, both were appointed as officers in the CDF, Nel as a lieutenant-colonel and Swanepoel as a colonel and Director of Intelligence. Swanepoel's three-year contract was only signed on 26 August 1992. In December 1992 his political dealings upset Brigadier Gqozo and he fired him without notice. August 1995 saw him filing papers in the Bisho High Court claiming R313 188,86 in back salaries from the South African government because of wrongful dismissal.[10]

Nel, however, stayed for much longer. He continued IR-CIS's operations and took over and ran their networks until the Ciskei homeland was finally apartheid history.

In the meantime, Colonel Gerrie Hugo found it intolerable working with two people whom he knew were only pretending to work for Ciskei — despite what Brigadier Gqozo believed. Their loyalties lay with the SADF's Military Intelligence. Colonel Hugo, however, owed his loyalty to his employer — the Ciskei homeland. It was impossible to share intelligence with them because they were there only as a conduit for it to be passed to DCC in Pretoria. It would have been a rare for any of this to have been Ciskei's interest.

Colonel Hugo began notice that his classified documentation was disappearing. At the least they were moved or files had been tampered with. People working in intelligence are naturally suspicious people. If colleagues are not trusted, little traps are set. Things are placed in certain ways and checked later. The computer is set up to invite someone to go into a programme and so on.

Eventually, Gerrie could take it no more. His problem was that to bust open the situation as had happened and was happening in Ciskei he had to have someone to blow it to. Brigadier Gqozo was an impossible choice because he was in cahoots with South African Military Intelligence — even if he was unaware of it. Besides, he would not believe him. The South African authorities were out of the question because whatever he said would get straight back to the DCC. If he blew the cover story to the press he knew the DCC would provide so many covers stories that no one would believe him.

Gerrie was driving to his office one morning, when on sudden impulse, instead of turning off into Bisho, he drove into the Transkei and headed for Umtata and the Military Intelligence's undercover office. He had never intended to become a whistle blower, but suddenly it seemed the right and only thing to do. Major-General Bantu Holomisa was likely to believe him because it was in his interest to do so. Gerrie was nobody's fool and he knew the consequences would probably be very grave for him, but he would take his chances. He walked into the offices, asked for a senior intelligence officer and told him he wanted to talk about what was happening in Ciskei.

The Transkei's Security Police were alerted and they came almost immediately. They gave him a hurried debriefing, then locked him in a solitary confinement cell. It was obvious he was not trusted to the slightest degree.

Inevitably Gerrie Hugo became the star at a well-attended press conference in Umtata. He exposed the activities of IR-CIS, the involvement of Jan Anton Nieuwoudt, its connections with Pretoria, its involvement in the Craig Duli coup attempt, its involvement in the deaths of Onward Guzana and Charles Sebe, the unlawful arrest and detention of his army colleagues, the death of Lieutenant Quamata and so on.

The SADF flatly denied all knowledge involvement.

It was well reported in the press, but because there was no concrete proof little notice was taken off it. The story became a seven-day wonder. This was particularly so after the SADF responded that Colonel Hugo was a common thief who had fled Ciskei to escape an audit that had revealed the misappropriation of substantial amounts of CDF funds. There was no attempt to submit proof, because as the SADF said, the matter was *sub judice*. Gerrie Hugo denied an audit had been pending and asked where the normal Part 1 orders were. This was overlooked by the media because of its limited knowledge of military procedures.

The SADF were determined to get him. They even had a helicopter standing by at Umtata ready to airlift him to Pretoria. The Transkei authorities regarded him as an embarrassment, someone to be got rid of, so they would not stand in the way. Suddenly the SADF took a step back, realising that flying him to Pretoria would indeed create many problems later — like illuminating their involvement in IR-CIS. They had forgotten that Colonel Hugo no longer belonged to the SADF. He was Ciskei's man.

The Ciskei's Commissioner of Police, General Jan Viktor, one of South Africa's men there as a result of IR-CIS' activities, had the standing that enabled him to skip petty legalities like deportation proceedings and so on. It an obviously synchronised effort, The Transkei Police put Colonel Hugo across the border into South Africa one weekend. The South African Police immediately arrested him on theft charges and bundled him across the border into Ciskei. This effectively kept him out of the way of the media because he was immediately detained.

Colonel Hugo, as the CDF's Chief of Staff Intelligence, handled large sums of informer money and as so many proceedings of the Truth and Reconciliation Commission of South

Africa have revealed, accounting procedures were not always what one might expect on the London Stock Exchange.

The Ciskei, by then effectively controlled by SADF Military Intelligence's puppeteers, was determined to discredit Colonel Hugo so that his revelations about IR-CIS would be ignored. The first tack was a court martial. Colonel Hugo won that round but was immediately placed on suspension from the CDF without pay. He was then remanded on bail on charges of stealing R180 000, which was progressively reduced to R80 000, then to R18 000. His bail condition was that he was not permitted to leave the magisterial district of King William's Town.

With such a restriction where could he find work?

Where could he live?

How could he support himself?

Almost two years had passed before he was arraigned before the Supreme Court (now High Court) in Bisho, on a charge of theft. By then he was flat broke and virtually down-and-out. Acting on poor legal advice he pleaded guilty to theft of R18 000. He did so because he no longer had access to the CDF's Military Intelligence records and he could not prove that monies had been properly receipted. He was also concerned a plea of 'not guilty' might cause further delays. This resulted in his being convicted and awarded a suspended sentence.

Later, he laid a civil claim against the SADF for unfair dismissal from the CDF and won. By then the CDF no longer existed. Despite the lapse of time the SADF remained intent on discrediting him for the same reasons as before. In recording his findings the judge pointed out that although Colonel Hugo had pleaded guilty to the theft charge, he had not stolen anything, so he was definitely not guilty. He should not have been convicted.

The court ordered the SADF to pay him R300 000, but the SADF were unhappy with the decision intended to appeal. This was crisis time for Colonel Hugo as he was flat broke and owed a lot of money. This resulted in his attorney negotiating with the SADF and striking a deal by which they would pay him just over R200 000. Of this he had to pay his lawyers R18 000 and use most of the rest to repay family and other people who had helped him through the hard times he had been experiencing.

His criminal record reduced his chance of getting future employment. Currently lawyers are working to correct the miscarriage of justice and get him a Presidential pardon.[11]

27

Diary of a white terrorist
Dries Kriel
1991-92

Origins of Afrikaner resistance

Dries Kriel had been inculcated with a hatred of the 'English' since he was dandled as a child on his grandfather's knee. His grandfather, wounded by a British lance at Colenso and locked up in the Johannesburg Fort after the failure of the 1914 rebellion, had extracted a promise from him.

'The struggle for our nation's freedom will never end. One of these days you will be grown up and I will be dead. You must promise me that you will continue the struggle, my boy.'

Dries promised on his honour and he never forgot it.

In 1969 he joined the right-wing *Herstigte Nasionale Party* (HNP — Reformed National Party) and became an organiser at a salary of R300 per month. The problem was that an organiser had to collect at least R300 in donations before he could draw his salary. He was sent to Middelburg in the Transvaal (now Mpumalanga) along with another organiser, one Eugene Terre'Blanche, to assist with certain organisational tasks and collect donations. It was the first time they had met. Two others, Piet Rudolph — an ex-policeman, and Jan Groenewald, a former lieutenant in the Security Police and the brother of General Tienie Groenewald of Military Intelligence, also joined as organisers later.

'How are you doing this month?' Terre'Blanche asked after mutual introductions.

'I spent the last two nights sleeping in the car and had a late meal the day before', Kriel replied.

Terre'Blanche looked at the balding tyres on Kriel's car.

'How much have you collected this month?'he asked.

'Nothing', Kriel answered. 'And you?'

'Also nothing', he answered and showed him his receipt book to prove it.

Kriel left his car in Middelburg and continued in Terre'Blanche's Colt bakkie. Terre'Blanche had only R12 left in his pocket and he insisted they take a room at the Morgan Hotel in Lydenburg so they could have a bath and freshen up. The bed and breakfast tariff was R5 per person. The next day they visited the wealthy owner of a sawmill and he wrote out a cheque for R400 in favour of the HNP. Terre'Blanche insisted that Kriel write out the receipt so that his monthly salary was safe, even though he had no donations to his own credit.

Terre'Blanche had only just left the police force, but he was already planning to go into politics. He spoke of his experiences as a bodyguard with Prime Minister John Vorster. After this he was selected for the SAP's 'Cultural Division' (believed to be part of the Security Police) where he was instructed in politics. He was also taught drama and public speaking. When on their way home he took Kriel into his confidence and told him he believed the time was ripe to establish an Afrikaner resistance movement. In those days Kriel trusted Terre'Blanche implicitly and despite the hint it never crossed his mind that maybe Terre'Blanche's special training in the police had been for a specific purpose — that he might actually be under orders to establish a political organisation.

Prime Minister John Vorster was very politically aware and was not averse to using the police for his own political ends. His great friend, General Hendrik van den Bergh, the commander of the SAP's Security Branch and later the head of the Bureau of State Security (BOSS) was clearly an ally in such moves.

Vorster and Van den Bergh, like most other members of the National Party of that time, had had no sympathy for the Allied cause during World War II. Mostly, their hearts and minds had been with Hitlerite Germany and the Nazis. Both had actively sabotaged the Allied war effort and had both ended up in detention for the duration. Vorster had been a 'general' in the pro-Nazi *Ossewa Brandwag* (OB) movement.[1] It is not difficult to find similarities and point at it as the predecessor of the AWB.

It was said that Vorster was highly upset when an element of the National Party broke away to form the HNP. Besides being no democrat, he also knew that violence was often the result when splits occurred in Afrikaner politics. An attitude of 'live and let live' was alien to the Afrikaner's political culture. Vorster (and Van den Bergh) had a need to know what was going on in the breakaway camp. An obvious way to find out was to infiltrate it, and doubtless that was done. But an even cleverer way was for the Security Police to establish another organisation closely allied to the HNP. They would even put in one of their own security men to lead it. It would obviously draw all the anti-Nationalist opposition under its umbrella and keep the Security Police informed on what was going on.

That was the rumour about how the AWB came to be founded, according to Kriel and other members of the AWB the author interviewed. Kriel had also heard it said that Military Intelligence took over the handling of the AWB from the Security Police in about 1983.

Nevertheless, not even suspecting such things when the AWB was finally established in 1973, Kriel extended his unstinting support to Terre'Blanche.

By 1980 Kriel, by then working on the Free State goldmines and an elected representative in the Mine Worker's Union, with the assistance of Terre'Blanche led the first successful disruption of a National Party meeting. It was addressed by the then Minister of Public Affairs, Dr Andries Treurnicht. Kriel, who became well known as a radical, instigated the tarring and feathering of Welkom's mayor, Gus Gouws. Gouws had upset the Afrikaner right wing by using his casting vote to allow the establishment of a black taxi rank in the city centre. Continually badgering what Kriel called the 'English money magnates' who owned the mines, through his position with the union, it is not surprising that they breathed a collective sigh of relief when in 1988 he was found to be medically unfit to work on the mines anymore. It did not put a stop to his trade union activities, though, and he began to forge a loose alliance between his trade union and the AWB. They were concentrating on the same thing — the deprivations of the Afrikaner *volk*.

Blast at Hillview High School, Pretoria

During 1991, as Kriel put it, 'the government, encouraged by the ambivalence of right-wingers, went ahead in leisurely fashion with its policy of forced integration'. In July he noted with alarm that the 'white' Hillview High School in Pretoria, which was being run on a caretaker basis, was about to be opened to blacks because of the acute shortage of places in schools. It was close to the city centre and he felt, 'without doubt, the ANC would utilise this institution as a terrorist base from which the public would be intimidated'.

He regarded it as a direct threat to the residents 'of this Voortrekker city'.

At the same time he was bemused by the activities of right-wing Afrikaner politicians. 'One minute they would announce the start of the third freedom struggle [the first two being the First and Second Anglo-Boer Wars] and then a few months later condemn violence. This curious cycle of declarations and contradictions was repeated to distraction and resulted in great confusion amongst right-wing membership.'

Kriel had met Koos Botha through his trade union activities. They discussed the Hillview question and decided the school should be blown up to prevent it falling into black hands. Botha's agreement was in itself surprising, for in Conservative Party circles he was regarded as a leftist. He was the son of a well-known church minister and a Conservative Party Member of Parliament. From Kriel's point of view this was all to the good, for unlike him, Botha had no history of militancy, so it was unlikely he would become a suspect in an act of terrorism. The two of them reconnoitred the Hillview High School on several occasions, the last time on the day of the blast.

Initially it had been planned that the job would be carried out by Botha and Kriel alone, but others were eventually brought in. The bombers met for the last time before the operation in the car park of the *Adelaarsklub* (Eagles Club) on the Friday before. Kriel briefed them in full, spelt out the dangers and the likely consequences, and said that if anyone was scared or was experiencing second thoughts there was still time for them to withdraw. 'Johannes van der Berg, the son of Mossie van der Berg, was clearly terrified and withdrew.' Such cowardice, he said, 'was inexcusable and in any other terrorist organisation would have been punishable by death. Perhaps this weakness in the removal of traitors and cowards contributed to the short-term failure of our struggle.'

On the Saturday Kriel left for Carltonville to collect explosives from a friend. His friend had been delayed at work, however, and he did not return home until 16:00. He handed over the requested quantity of 'Tovex' explosive together with the necessary fuses and everything else needed. He did not ask questions.

Kriel put the stuff in his car. When one is in such a position there are two hazards to be avoided — roadblocks and road accidents — but fortunately for him he got home without encountering either. Kriel knew what he was doing. As a former miner, who had worked with explosives on a daily basis, he knew exactly how to place the charge to cause maximum structural damage.

He took the stuff into an outbuilding at his house and began to prepare the bomb. He had already bought a yellow plastic 25 litre cooking oil drum from a fish and chip shop. 'Tovex' is packed in sticks and covered with plastic. He cut off the plastic and packed the sticks in the drum. If left in packets, even though it might appear otherwise, the sticks exploded in succession instead of simultaneously. When stripped of the plastic packaging and packed tightly in a drum, though, its explosive power was dramatically increased. Another advantage was that no fragments of plastic would be left behind for forensic examination. He placed the fuse and detonator in the drum with the latter to the front. After scrubbing the exterior of the drum clean and drying it, the bomb was ready.

He showered, dressed in dark clothes and strapped on his .38 Special. After a short prayer he loaded the bomb in his car and drove to the rendezvous point at the *Adelaarsklub*. The others were not yet there and when they did arrive, they were noticeably tense. Another man had withdrawn and had sent a message accordingly. The rest were talking about postponement. Suddenly they were full of ideas. Kriel, however, was having none of it and told them it was too late — there was no turning back.

There was a perceptible tenseness in the car. Koos Botha, who was unfamiliar with explosives, was afraid the device would explode prematurely in the car. The more Kriel tried to reassure him, the less he was prepared to believe him. When Kriel said he would light the fuse while they were still in the car because there was an abundance of time, Botha nearly had hysterics. This, Kriel mused, was probably why Botha refused to accompany him on any further bombing missions.

They got to the school at 02:00 and stopped the car at a place where there was a hole in the fence. The driver got out and lifted the bonnet to make it appear the car had broken down. Kriel had a last long look around the area to ensure it was clear, but everything was unbelievably quiet. The petrol station immediately across the road was deserted.

The blond youngster who carried the 25kg bomb was short and stocky. He impressed Kriel because of his calmness and because he never spoke unnecessarily. They moved through the opening in the fence into an area of relative darkness. Near the main entrance they entered a floodlit area. It was then that the youngster inadvertently kicked some loose tiles and the sound seemed to echo like thunder.

Koos Botha gestured nervously that he should be quiet, but with a heavy bomb in his arms and his vision partially obscured by it there was little the youngster could do.

They reached the second floor. Kriel had predetermined a place that he had deemed to be ideal for the bomb to cause maximum damage. He gestured to the blond youngster where to put the bomb and then jiggled it into the exact position he wanted. He removed the cap to expose the safety fuse. He lit it. It hissed as it ignited. There was a four and a half minute delay.

The hissing proved too much for Koos Botha and his fears got the better of him. Kriel had warned him about it, but it made no difference. He sprinted for the stairs. Fear was contagious and Blondie bolted after him. To Kriel's dismay they made an enormous racket as they rushed from the building and made for the car. It was a miracle they were not seen or heard.

The driver gestured that everything was okay and closed the bonnet.

They moved off and stopped at the traffic light which was showing red. It was as if this was a signal because suddenly the lights went on at the service station behind them and early morning traffic started being noticeable in the streets.

They got back to their rendezvous and dispersed to go home in their own cars.

The school building was destroyed.

Kriel had planned the operation without the prior knowledge of AWB leader, Eugene Terre'Blanche, but he reported to him afterwards. Terre'Blanche approved the operation in retrospect because it was the kind of operation he wanted the AWB to engage in.

It was a turning point in Dries Kriel's life — he had become a white terrorist.

Blast at COSATU House, Brown Street, Pretoria

It was clear that none of those who had helped at Hillview High School were prepared to continue, so Kriel looked around for others. Piet Judeel was a Mine Workers Union representative at a mine in Brits and was a staunch AWB member. Kriel also found it difficult to source explosives. So he broached the subject bluntly with Piet, who jumped at the chance of helping the Afrikaner cause. In turn he recruited Andre Odendaal.

The Congress of Trade Unions (COSATU) House was in Brown Street, Pretoria. It was closely allied to the ANC and Kriel chose this as his next target. He spoke to Koos Botha who promised to cooperate and even get explosives for the job — as long as he was not personally involved in the operation.

One day in December 1991 Koos Botha arrived at Kriel's home with 12kg of 'Tovex' explosive in the boot of his car. That night Kriel built another bomb, similar to the Hillview High School one, but with a smaller charge. When he was finished he phoned Judeel who came to the house with Odendaal and another. They took the plastic covering into the veld and burnt it.

They went in two vehicles with Judeel and Odendaal leading in a bakkie with the bomb in the back. and Kriel and the other man following in his unreliable Japanese union-owned car. In Waverley, Pretoria, a police Flying Squad car unexpectedly appeared from a side street, did a 'U' turn and followed them. It's over, Kriel thought, they are going to pull us off the road and catch us red-handed with a bomb.'

They remained calm, however, and continued to drive at a steady speed well within the limit. Eventually, to their great relief, the police car turned off.

Kriel parked his car by the Wonderboom Post Office and got in the front passenger seat of the bakkie next to Judeel. The other two got in the back and lay down next to the bomb.

Judeel was composed and whistling happily as he drove. It was 02:00 but there was considerable traffic in the city centre. They turned into Brown Street and Kriel tapped on the back window to signal Odendaal that he should light the fuse. The smell of burning safety fuse wafted past Kriel's nostrils.

They stopped in front of COSATU House. They had firearms at the ready, but everything was quiet and the place was deserted. The bomb was lugged from the bakkie and placed in its pre-determined position. They drove off.

The place was completely destroyed.

Kriel had a continuing requirement for explosives. He had known Gawie Volschenk from when he had been the AWB's chief commandant in the Eastern Transvaal (Mpumalanga). After that, Volschenk established his own Boer commando and moved to Pretoria. In the old days they had accumulated quite a lot of explosives among themselves. In an effort to get some, Kriel arranged to meet him secretly in Heidelberg where he explained his urgent needs and said it was required so he could continue the struggle. To gain his trust, he told Volschenk that he had blown up Hillview High School. Volschenk came through and supplied him with 20kg of Pentolite and various detonators

Blasts at Verwoerdburg (now Centurion) and Krugersdorp Post Offices

Kriel's brother-in-law, Dirk Hattingh, was boarding with Piet Judeel. He explained that Hattingh had been asking awkward questions and he thought he suspected what they were up to. In the end Kriel took him into the team because it was difficult to exclude him.

Kriel decided to hit really high profile targets. When one sabotaged an Eskom power line or something like that, it attracted little or no publicity. In fact, the authorities deliberately kept it quiet. This did not serve the right-wing cause because it was essential that people learned what was going to encourage further resistance.

He and Koos Botha decided to go big and attack ten post offices in one night. Such a bold move, he thought, would certainly create chaos and attract the publicity he was seeking. He selected the ten targets which included the Central Post Office in Pretoria, the post offices at Witbank, Middelburg, Sinoville, Brits, Krugersdorp and Verwoerdburg (now Centurion). He brought in extra AWB members and gave them a basic course in the handling of explosives. In all he had 15 eager volunteers which he deemed was sufficient to handle all the operations.

Kriel made up ten bombs similar to the device laid at Hillview High School, but somewhat smaller — each weighing only about 18kg. Most of the explosives had been obtained by Piet Judeel . On Christmas Eve 1991 he took volunteers underground at the mine where he worked. While others were enjoying Christmas Eve dinners, he and his men each lugged 50kg of explosives and a large quantity of detonators to the surface from four levels underground. When they delivered it to Kriel he scarcely recognised them because they were battered and bruised from the effort and filthy from the mud and dust. It was deemed highly dangerous to store such a large quantity of explosives in Kriel's garage, so Koos Botha found storage space on a farm near the Rooiwal Power Station.

D-Day was set for 2 January 1992. The bombs were ready. Kriel and his usual team — Judeel, Odendaal and Hattingh — were ready, but none of the other volunteers appeared.

Kriel decided to go ahead with just two targets, the post offices at Verwoerdburg and Krugersdorp. The MP for Verwoerdburg was the high profile National Party Cabinet Minister, Adriaan Vlok and for Krugersdorp it was a Mr Wessels, a man regarded as despicably leftist by the AWB.

They went to Verwoerdburg first, lit the fuse while still in the car, and set the bomb on the post office's verandah. They drove for the highway to head for Krugersdorp, believing correctly that there was less chance of being stopped by the police on the highway than on back roads. They heard later there had been a huge explosion at Verwoerdburg. It was heard as far away as the Union Buildings in central Pretoria.

The Krugersdorp bomb, fitted with a three minute fuse, was placed in the area of the post office boxes and a cash machine. Kriel reckoned it must have rained money. There was a huge explosion as they reached the outskirts of town.

It was planned that Kriel would phone Koos Botha when the operation was over. Botha would arrange for an anonymous press release by the Boer Republican Army claiming responsibility for the blasts. It would be coupled with a demand for the 'self determination of the Boer nation'. Kriel phoned at 04:00 but Botha's phone was off the hook.

A few days later Kriel read in a newspaper that Gawie Volschenk had been arrested. He had been linked with an explosion at a Melkrivier school. Kriel had read about the attack and had condemned it as a 'dumb action' with seemingly little purpose. Kriel realised there was a danger that he might talk. He was also tipped off that the Security Police had a tap on his phone. He contacted his group and told them to go into hiding. It was arranged for them to be accommodated on a sympathiser's farm in the Karoo.

During the evening of 14 January, before they could action their plan to flee, a stranger arrived at Judeel's house and told him that Piet Rudolf (a senior AWB member) wanted to see him and Hattingh urgently. The security policeman, for that is who he was, took them by car into the veld where they were quickly surrounded by a group of policemen. Judeel drew a pistol intending to resist, but he was quickly disarmed.

They were assaulted tortured, given the water torture — where bags of water were placed over the subject's head, sealed and kept on until they almost drowned or lost consciousness. The whole time they were questioned about bombings and the whereabouts of their associates.

Andre Odendaal had spent that night at Kriel' home. Early in the morning on what was Dries Kriel's 47th birthday, the Security Police knocked on his front door. They had surrounded the house. His wife, mother and two daughters looked on silently as the men were arrested.They were taken out of town to the Nylstroom Police Station. A Security Police colonel told Kriel he had Volschenk in custody. He had revealed details of their secret meeting at Heidelburg, that he had given him explosives and that he had confessed to bombing Hillview High School. He also told the police that Kriel and Koos Botha had asked him to assist in blowing up post offices.

Kriel refused to admit his involvement. After being cleared of the Melkrivier bombing, he was escorted back to Pretoria and questioned there. They told him they knew the farm where he had been storing his explosives and also that Koos Botha was involved. As a trade off to prevent harassment of the elderly couple living on the farm and the arrest of Botha, Kriel offered to take responsibility for the bombing of Hillview High School, the bombing of COSATU House, the bombing of Verwoerdburg Post Office and the bombing of Krugersdorp Post Office. He refused to incriminate anyone else.

Later, he discovered that Koos Botha had never been arrested, had never spent even a minute in detention. He thought: I should have told them to go ahead and arrest them! He conjectured that the Security Police (and the National Party government for that matter) were actually pleased he had blown up COSATU House and probably Hillview High School as well. It gave them something to flourish in front of the ANC and say: 'Look how dangerous the right-wing is.'

On 23 January 1992 Kriel and his group were released on bail. Kriel decided he would never go back to gaol. For seven months, accompanied by his wife Lettie, he went on the run, evading capture, camping in the primaeval depths of the great Knysna Forest and hiding with friends around the country. Then he turned himself in. A week later he was again released on bail. Kriel started working for the Iron and Steel Union and moved to Welkom in the Free State. He was promoted to colonel in the AWB, made commander of the Northern Free State, and given instructions to expand its structures.[2]

28

Ciskei under Brigadier 'Oupa' Gqozo And another surrogate: African Democratic Movement 1991-1994

Civil Service strike and Gqozo's ministers sacked: February-April 1991

In February 1991 Ciskei's civil servants went on strike again, with demands similar to the unfulfilled ones they had made in November 1990. They also demanded the resignation of Brigadier Gqozo. After the arrest of the CDF's senior officers on 9 February, strike action intensified and continued throughout February to April 1991. Public institutions came to a standstill as nurses, court officials and even announcers on Radio Ciskei joined the strike.

The Minister of Justice, also a practising advocate in the Amatola Bar Council for Bisho, Keith Matthee, and the Minister of Public Works, Linda Sallie, recalled that two or three unidentified white men frequently interrupted cabinet meetings with demands to see Brigadier Gqozo privately. Afterwards, Gqozo invariably returned to the meetings with a hardened attitude towards the matters under discussion. Without mentioning names he would imply obliquely that several of his cabinet ministers were ANC agents. It was assumed the interrupters were IR-CIS agents using electronic listening devices to eavesdrop on cabinet meetings. They would then interrupt as necessary to give Gqozo running advice on how to handle particular situations.

Finally, the Ciskei government gave its civil servants an ultimatum to report to work by 5 April 1991, failing which they would be summarily dismissed. Some heeded the call and reported for work, but the estimated 3 000 who failed to were fired. Some posts were filled by individuals perceived as supporters of Gqozo and with relatives of others in power, but many posts were left vacant.

Two months after this Gqozo sacked Ministers Keith Matthee and Linda Sallie for unspecified reasons. Matthee was a former magistrate's court prosecutor in Natal. While a university student he had been a Bureau for State Security (BOSS) informer and had reported on anti-government activities. He was probably motivated by his father, a senior policeman in the SAP's detective branch. In 1981, resulting from his experiences as a prosecutor, he had a change of heart and resigned his job because he could not continue to prosecute 'apartheid crimes' and live with his conscience. He qualified as an advocate, got involved in the activities of Lawyers for Human Rights and the Legal Resources Centre and became a lay preacher in his church.

As a minister, Keith Matthee was instrumental in drafting and promulgating Ciskei's Constitutional Decree and its judicial Bill of Fundamental Human Rights and Responsibilities. In retrospect, it appears that Brigadier Gqozo had little understanding of what it was all about. It fundamentally allowed the courts to intervene and limit Gqozo's ambitions of total despotism and absolutism, but he did not realise this at the time. Matthee's work would be responsible for Gqozo being forced to testify at the inquest of Charles Sebe and Onward Guzana. It also frustrated IR-CIS' wish to do as it pleased. Matthee could also claim credit for abolishing the death penalty. More pertinently he was instrumental in Ciskei's Attorney-General dropping charges of terrorism and treason against the eight senior officers of the CDF who had been unjustly suspended by Gqozo. Both he and Linda Sallie had displayed much sympathy for the plight of the discharged civil servants and they had both urged Brigadier Gqozo to reconsider his decision.

Gqozo found criticism intolerable. IR-CIS quickly reminded him of Matthee's connections with the NIS. It said he could not be trusted and suggested Gqozo get rid of him. So he did. The IR-CIS' report to DCC prior to this happening dismissed him as 'totally liberal' and said he would 'be dismissed in the next two to three days.'[1]

African Democratic Movement (ADM)

In mid-1991 Brigadier Oupa Gqozo announced the formation of a political party, the African Democratic Movement (ADM). He said it would represent 'the silent majority of southern Africa on a realistic and moderate basis.' As its leader he rejected nationalisation and a unitary state. He dismissed claims linking it to Inkatha, and said it gave him a mandate as to what the people needed 'even to the negotiating table.'

It was undoubtedly formed at the suggestion of Military Intelligence (via IR-CIS) because of the sudden reappearance of Basie Oosthuizen of Dynamic Teaching CC. Brigadier Gqozo appointed him as the ADM's first general secretary. Blacks loyal to the National Party government who had been working for agencies in the Eastern Cape, like Linda Tamsanqa, were also appointed to the organisation.[2]

Shortly after taking power in 1990 Brigadier Gqozo had scrapped the tribal headman system and in their stead recognised Residents' Associations as the proper representatives of rural residents. He also stopped salaries paid to chiefs.

With the formation of the ADM Gqozo immediately reappointed the deposed headmen without bothering to consult the people. Payments of stipends and salaries for headmen and chiefs were reintroduced. Membership of the ADM became compulsory for headmen, chiefs, senior government officials and cabinet ministers. The problems and complaints of rural people, including the payment of social grants and old age pensions, could not be processed without claimants being members of the ADM. Headmen reported to chiefs and chiefs to Gqozo on all matters that occurred in their tribal areas.

It appears the IR-CIS had made Brigadier Gqozo aware that residents' associations, civic associations and so on were invariably affiliates of the UDF and ANC. So his earlier recognition of them as the true representatives of rural people meant that he was losing control of the population at grass roots level.

Gqozo made his views clear at a meeting in Johannesburg in July 1991 when he was asked to comment on a Lawyers for Human Rights's claim that he was violating human rights. In his reply he described the organsiation as 'a very curious lot close to the ANC' who were guilty of 'grossly misleading and inaccurate propaganda'. He suggested it should change its name to 'Lawyers for ANC Human Rights'. He described Ciskei's human rights situation as 'good'. 'We only want to stop people bullying people. We want school children to go to school and workers to work.' He claimed that industrialists had fled Ciskei because of the ANC's intimidation. He was merely applying the rule of law and protecting those wanting to work.

Gqozo said the ADM catered for the needs of 'those who did not want to toyi-toyi [a sort of political protest dance] and jump around raising flags and AK47s'. People were sick and tired of being hauled out of their houses and made to attend political rallies. He claimed there was an orchestrated move to destabilise the country. People were feeling neglected and lost.[3]

The stage was set for rural confrontations between supporters of the ADM-cum-tribal system and supporters of the UDF/ANC. The houses of chiefs and headmen and their supporters were torched and the properties of the opposing groups were burnt in retaliation. Hit squads were formed and many people on both sides were murdered.

IR-CIS covertly weighed in by launching a rifle attack on the house of the ANC's regional president, Smuts Ngonyama (later spokesman for the Thabo Mbeki presidency). Ngonyama was at home at the time but he was unharmed.[4]

Brigadier Gqozo's response to all this was to declare a State of Emergency and detain scores of those who opposed his ADM. Refugees from the violence fled to King William's Town, East London, Stutterheim, Queenstown and Fort Beaufort. The State of Emergency was only lifted just before Christmas 1991 after ANC leader Nelson Mandela personally intervened.

Colonel Silence Pita, Brigadier Gqozo's deputy, said the establishment of the ADM led to violent clashes with the ANC and sparked a wave of killings. 'People were killing each other. They were dying. The ADM and the ANC were fighting each other. It was a very difficult time. The ANC wanted things done a particular way and the ADM wanted things to be done another way altogether.'[5]

Mutation of IR-CIS: October 1991

By mid 1991 considerable unwelcome media attention had been drawn to IR-CIS, much of it, as we have seen, due to the courage of Colonel Gerrie Hugo. He had taken his career in his hands to make its agenda public, partly to right the wrongs perpetrated by its parent, SADF's Military Intelligence against the black senior officers of the CDF, and partly because what was happening was just plain wrong. His efforts effectively ruined him.

Nevertheless, although much of the media initially ignored Colonel Hugo's allegations because of a lack of proof and because they seemed far-fetched, it prompted some top investigative reporters to begin seriously digging to find out what was really going on in Ciskei. In the vanguard was the redoubtable Louise Flanagan writing for *Weekly Mail*, *The Saturday Star* and the *Daily Dispatch*.

A flow of stories followed, accusing the IR-CIS of involvement in a host of violent incidents. This included Colonel Craig Duli's attempted coup in Transkei, the murder of General Charles Sebe and Colonel Onward Guzana and much more.

Ciskei's administration displayed remarkable ambivalence.

In April 1991 Minister of Police, Zebulon Makuzeni, confirmed the existence of a group of 'security personnel operating under the title of International Researchers'. This was in answer to affidavits submitted to the Supreme Court in Bisho by three disaffected CDF officers who asked for protection from IR-CIS. They claimed that IR-CIS had lured Charles Sebe and Onward Guzana to the homeland and murdered them. The IR-CIS Warrant Officer, Vuyo Melane, described how the organisation operated. The relevant sections of his affidavit were struck out by order of the judge on the grounds of the organisation's secret classification. The judge had overlooked journalist Louise Flanagan, however, who published the deleted sections in full in an article in East London's *Daily Dispatch* — because South Africa was outside the jurisdiction of Ciskei's Supreme Court.

Shortly afterwards, Ciskei announced it was disbanding an 'intelligence service' but omitted its name. It said a decree was pending which would outlaw covert units. The decree never materialised.

During May and June 1991, in an effort to get a tame reporter aboard to combat the disastrous publicity the organisation was attracting, Clive Brink and Paul Oeschger attempted to recruit *Daily Dispatch* journalist Andrew Trench to the IR-CIS cause. This rebounded badly when Trench splashed the story in the press.

The Ciskei administration was taking a public relations battering and it did not know how to deal with it. In July, in answer to another query, the Council of State said: 'A company search has revealed no evidence of an organisation called International Researchers' within Ciskei's borders. This bland denial was based on the difference between 'Research' and 'Researchers'.

A clampdown on Radio Ciskei ordered by Brigadier Gqozo was vehemently denied by the station. It said in a statement: 'The fact that we are in agreement with Brigadier Gqozo in pursuit of a clean administration and a propaganda-free station, is incidental [to the clampdown]'.

Ciskei's response to media criticism vacillated from periods of sullen silences, interspersed with contradictory statements to furious counter-attacks. It became virtually impossible for the press to get comment from Ciskei on almost any issue. In August, probably on advice from Pretoria, it began to repair its image and again began responding to queries by journalists.

The media revelations sparked Army Chief General Kat Liebenberg and the Deputy Director-General Foreign Affairs, Rusty Evans, into paying a flying visit to Bisho on 6 August 1991. They met the Council of State and held what Evans called 'wide and constructive discussions' covering a 'whole range of activities'. He insisted that nothing 'sinister' should be read into the meeting, nor was it sinister that General Liebenberg had been part of it. The general had merely gone because of his keenness to meet Brigadier Gqozo.[6] The press conversely suggested they had gone there to press for IR-CIS to be restructured or disbanded to ensure greater accountability. The press, however, was still relatively naïve regarding the way in which Military Intelligence ran its surrogates and front companies. They found it difficult to get away from the standpoint that IR-CIS was completely under the control of Brigadier Gqozo and that Kat Liebenberg and Rusty Evans had just gone there to lean on him. This was far from the truth. They were there on a damage control exercise.

The press was right in one way, though, General Liebenberg did have a restructuring in mind. His motive was to get the organisation or its replacement back into deep cover as soon as possible, to enable the SADF to continue and enhance its programme of controlling Ciskei. This had nothing to do with accountability to the public, only with accountability to the SADF.

It was decided that Comandant Jan Anton Nieuwoudt and his IR-CIS had to go, because their cover had been badly blown. Subsequent to this decision, Nieuwoudt (under the codename Rawhide) telexed Colonel At Nel at DCC (under the codename At) in a signal dated 4 September 1991 saying that arrangements had been completed for them to get out of the territory. 'Myself, Clive [Brink], Piet Pienaar, Kussa Kruger and Paul Oeshger are going. Chris Nel, Ockert Swanepoel and Zane Brassel [Ted Brassel's son working with the] ADM [African Democratic Movement] would be staying.'

Nieuwoudt would remain with Ted Brassel until the auditor, Colonel White, had completed the account books. To continue IR-CIS's work, he suggested that Chris Nel should take over Clive Brink's 'channel'. Alternatively, Brink could retain his channel and his (Nieuwoudt's) typist could stay on with him. He added: 'I am satisfied that RSA is now managing Ciskei effectively and my role is done. The flow of information can go ahead with or without Gqozo . . .'[7]

He was right. His job was indeed done as by then most key positions in Ciskei, both political and military, had been taken over by SADF nominees. IR-CIS had effectively absorbed Ciskei's military intelligence and continued DCC operations in the more respectable guise of the latter. That meant the ANC would continue to be treated as the enemy by the SADF, political settlement or no political settlement.

The last job conducted by IR-CIS was to persuade Brigadier Gqozo that they had uncovered 'yet another plot by the ANC and Transkei' to topple his regime. This resulted in the homeland's withdrawal from a conflict resolution committee set up during the Codesa negotiations.[8]

Jan Anton Nieuwoudt claimed as his successes:

- The successful penetration of the ANC in the region.
- The successful penetration of the PAC in the region.

- The scrapping of an agreement between Brigadier Gqozo and Austria for the storage of atomic waste in Ciskei, by publicising it.
- The appointment of an SADF officer as Chief of CDF.
- The appointment of a retired SADF general as Commissioner of Ciskei Police.
- The appointment of selected South Africans as cabinet ministers in Ciskei.
- The prevention of four ANC-inspired coups in Ciskei.

It is beyond question that when IR-CIS lured General Charles Sebe and Colonel Onward Guzana to their death it was not an ANC-inspired coup attempt. It was a set-up designed to kill them. Nor was the discovery of the IR-CIS' weapons cache by senior CDF officers at the Ministerial Complex an ANC coup plot. The unfortunate repercussions that IR-CIS manipulated so that it rebounded on the officers was nothing to do with the ANC either. These incidents cast doubt on the remaining two 'ANC-inspired coup' attempts.[9]

In April 1991, due to the 'sensitivity' of his appointment in Ciskei, Commandant Nieuwoudt was moved to another Military Intelligence front company, Pan Afrik Industrial Investment CC (PAIICC). While he had undoubtedly served Military Intelligence with loyalty when running IR-CIS, it was not reciprocated. When the time came for his retrenchment in 1993, the SADF denied that he had remained a serving member after his 'resignation' to run IR-CIS. He claimed he was due a R900 000 retrenchment package. The SADF used what was known as the 'Robert Koch formula' to calculate a package of R646 000 for him, but this was turned down by the finance authorities. Nieuwoudt offered to settle for R400 000, but the SADF could only offer R213 000 — a shortfall of R187 000 and R713 000 less than he originally claimed.

Lieutenant-General C P van der Westhuizen in a 'Top Secret' letter to Army Chief Kat Liebenberg, said Nieuwoudt might embarrass the SADF and the government if the case went to court where he could reveal details of operations carried out by IR-CIS. He was also in possession of compromising information relating to certain senior SADF officers and cabinet ministers. Still, General van der Westhuizen insisted bravely, the SADF would not submit to blackmail.

Nieuwoudt in desperation appealed directly to Minister of Defence Coetzee for assistance. 'I am a *Boereseun* (Boer son) and a specialist covert collector (DDC man) (who has been blown) and I ask to make a new beginning. I know Africa is Lion Valley, but enough is enough.' Beneath his signature he wrote 'Isiah 54, verse 17' ('No weapon that is formed against thee shall prosper; and every tongue that shall rise against thee in judgement thou shalt condemn. This is the heritage of the servants of the Lord, and their righteousness is of me, saith the Lord.').

Nieuwoudt's eloquent appeal for ministerial (or divine) intervention was effectively ignored and he had no other option but to take his claim to the Supreme Court. The SADF remained not unduly concerned because classified SADF documents were to be produced, so the case would have to be held in camera.

Amongst his embarrassing discoveries was a revelation that after he had left Ciskei, DCC Director Brigadier Tolletjie Botha had visited him in Cape Town. He had revealed that Alan Lindner had commenced an action against the Chief of the Ciskei Defence Force in the Supreme (High) Court at Bisho. He was claiming for losses and damages relating to the breach of his training contract with the CDF at the instigation of Nieuwoudt. Botha said it necessitated the CDF Chief giving evidence to say that Nieuwoudt was not in the DCC's employ.

'I suggested that we prepare a letter saying that I did not accept the offer of the PAIICC and back date it to October 1991 so as not to put the Chief CDF and the RSA government into a predicament. We did so', Nieuwoudt wrote.[10]

The SADF experienced an immediate panicky change of heart when the judge unexpectedly ordered that the case should be heard in open court. The SADF settled, paying the additional R187 000 that Nieuwoudt had asked for to prevent the embarrassment that General CP van der Westhuizen had been so concerned about.

General Liebenberg suggested the shortfall of R187 000 be (quietly and illicitly) made up from 'project funds'. He probably had in mind utilising that good old fall-back position, the 'Scraper Fund'. After all, why should it be necessary to bother the taxpayer about the odd couple of hundred thousand rand used to cover up the SADF's criminal activities.[11]

Ciskei during 1992

During 1992 Brigadier Oupa Gqozo began to display an ambivalence towards the question of reincorporating Ciskei into a greater South Africa. In February he told the media that most homeland administrations, including Ciskei, wanted 'some form of self rule within a federal system', not a unitary state as proposed at Codesa.[12] In March Ciskei signed the National Peace Accord.

In April Gqozo exhibited another change of heart and a policy document submitted to Codesa said Ciskei no longer considered a referendum was necessary 'to test the will of the people' on the question of reincorporation. It said Ciskei was committed to reincorporation into a 'democratic united South Africa', provided this only occurred after the new South Africa had taken shape so that people would know what they were rejoining.

A month later Gqozo said: 'I now believe that reincorporation or an interim government now is like entering a dark tunnel. You get in and think there is peace and safety. But people mug you and you are not seen again.' He added that if the Ciskei administration was disbanded in favour of federal elections and he was not elected, he would be very angry.[13]

In March 1992 Ciskei denied ANC allegations that its officials were using the headman system (through the African Democratic Movement) to undermine the authority of tribal chiefs. The ANC's publicity secretary for the Border Region, Marion Sparg, said this undermining of chiefs was the major reason behind the ANC's political campaign against the homeland administration.[14]

By mid-1992 there were signs that the CDF was mounting covert deployments in support of the ADM. Many attacks on ANC supporters bore the hallmarks of military professionalism. In June and August the home of senior ANC leader Skenyana Roji was attacked twice, once with rifle fire — when the windows were smashed and the interior riddled with bullets — and once with rifle grenades that failed to explode. No one was injured. Cartridge cases and the grenades found at the scene appeared to originate from the CDF.

Another armed attack launched with military precision was against the village of an ANC supporter called Ngece. It was common knowledge that he was at loggerheads with the headman and other ADM supporters. Houses were burned and several people, including children, were killed or injured. Two CDF sergeants and a corporal were arrested and tried for the attack. The homes of the ANC-supporting Skiti family in Dimbaza and Quzini were attacked with rifles and grenades, resulting in injuries. Other armed attacks also bore the hallmarks of the CDF.[15]

The ANC, for its part, remained determined to topple Brigadier Gqozo's regime.

One night in October 1992, 'Kolela' and three other MK cadres were instructed by the local MK commander, Xoliswe Sotyifa, to join him in an attack. They would be armed with a Russian machine pistol and two hand grenades and would go by car to the Frankfort Hotel about 15km from King William's Town. Information suggested that soldiers drank in the bar there every night. The operatives would wait until it was almost closing time, when most of the soldiers would probably be drunk, then lob in grenades. Covering fire would be provided by the machine pistol. The objective was to capture weapons, which were desperately needed to arm the ANC's local self-defence units (SDUs). Properly armed, they would be able to fight back against the homeland's Security Forces. The prime objective was to capture weapons, not kill the soldiers. If it became necessary, though, they would kill them.

The bar was empty of soldiers when they arrived, so the mission was aborted.

Killing a policeman named Mxolise Ngqolazana was a secondary mission. Ngqolazana had been interrupting ANC activities, disrupting meetings and generally making a nuisance of himself. He had also openly allied himself to the Ciskei administration. He was therefore designated as an enemy of the people. Because he was against 'democracy', he had to die. The four cadres had been ordered to check the village where he lived, then locate and recce his house. It was important that he alone was killed and that his family and other innocents were not harmed.

The target was not at home, so they waited outside the village for his return. Eventually, at about 24:00 he was spotted sitting in a car with a woman nearby what they believed was his house. Having positively identified him, they debated whether they should open fire and risk killing his female companion. They also had niggling concerns that they might have been led into a trap, as locating him had seemed almost too easy. The target appeared set to remain in the car for a while, so they set off to check the area for possible ambushes. On their return they discovered, to their chagrin, that the target had gone. They were unsure if he had entered a room and if he had, which one? They could hardly throw grenades at random, so they aborted the mission.

They were stopped at an army roadblock while driving back to King William's Town. After discovering weapons in their car, the soldiers stripped them naked and beat them so severely that they broke Kolela's arm. Beating up ANC suspects was standard procedure for CDF soldiers at the time. They were ordered back into the car and told to go. They heard the soldiers whispering amongst themselves, saying that they would shoot them for 'attempting to escape' as they drove off. Fortunately for them, a police patrol appeared and arrested the cadres. The men were charged and convicted of the unlawful possession of arms of war. They were later given an amnesty by the TRC.[16]

The Bisho Massacre: 7 September 1992

The ANC/SACP alliance began to mobilise the black masses in the Eastern Cape to take part in a protest march on 7 September 1992. The route would be from King William's Town across the Ciskei border into Bisho. They claimed that Ciskei was an 'illegal Bantustan' and that it had no legal right to exist. They demanded free political activity and the replacement of Brigadier Gqozo and his ruling Council of State. An advertisement in the *Daily Dispatch* called on people to join the march. It listed ten well-known ANC personalities who would be taking part, including eight prominent communists like Chris Hani, Ronnie Kasrils, Harry Gwala and Jeremy Cronin. All of them played important roles in planning the march.

Speeches by Hani and Kasrils in villages around Bisho left little doubt that the intention was to oust Gqozo, even if it became necessary to use a measure of force.

'We are not going to talk much today. We are preparing for battle tomorrow. The battle is to remove parasites', Chris Hani told a crowd at Ndevana Village the day before the march.[17]

The march was intended as a precursor to mass action that would cause the overthrow of other homeland governments and self-governing states, in particular Bophuthatswana and KwaZulu. No mass action was planned for neighbouring Transkei, because the ANC regarded it as already being 'on side'.

There was a legal requirement for the ANC to apply to the local magistrate for a permit to hold the march. At first, permission for the marchers to cross the border into Ciskei was flatly refused.

In the days preceding the planned march the government received representations from the clergy and South African government ministers who sought to persuade the reluctant administration to allow the march. Ciskei's Minister of Foreign Affairs, Mickey Webb, said they all 'promised proper controls and behaviour. Tragically, history has proved that the Ciskei authorities' understanding of the purpose of the march was indeed correct and that promises of a peaceful, controlled march could not be sustained.'[18]

According to Webb, South Africa's and Ciskei's Military Intelligence had fed the Ciskei administration with misinformation that 'could only have ended up in confrontation between the authorities and the ANC'. The Ciskei had been manoeuvred into the situation, he said. 'The cross-fertilisation of mystery and intrigue would have done justice to a best-selling suspense novel. But at the time it was serious business conveyed with urgency in clandestine calls and covert messages.'

Eventually, on the morning of the march, reluctant permission was given for it to take place subject to certain conditions. One was that the ultimate destination had to be the Independence Stadium. The marchers were allowed to enter the stadium for a rally, but not go beyond into Bisho itself. Andrew Hendricks, the ANC's vice-chairman for the Border Region, said dismissively before the march started that the ANC intended to defy the magistrate's order and march into Bisho.[19]

Significantly, the ANC's secretary-general, Cyril Ramaphosa, told the TRC later that the ANC had planned to occupy Bisho's central business district to hold a 'people's assembly' in a public show of unhappiness with the Gqozo regime. This confirms that from the outset, the ANC had intended to ignore the conditions imposed by the magistrate. We can only speculate about exactly what Ramaphosa meant by 'a people's assembly'. It sounded much like it was intended to announce the toppling of the government and the takeover of the territory. Controlling a large crowd of demonstrators in such a built-up area — effectively the heart of Ciskei — and with such limited forces available would likely have proved impossible without mayhem resulting.

Brigadier Oupa Gqozo said he received a security report on the day of the march saying that MK planned to use to the march to overthrow his government. Colonel Silence Pita, Gqozo's deputy, confirmed this saying they had been informed that MK was planning a coup that 'would take us where we didn't want to be'. The sources of the information were unclear but it is understood they were in the ranks of the ANC's top hierarchy. Whatever the case it confirmed the large volume of information from other sources.

The CDF was ordered to deploy in support of the police, who retained their prime function of maintaining law and order. Lieutenant-Colonel Archibald Mkosana was appointed field commander for the operation.

On the morning of 7 September a crowd of demonstrators, variously estimated at anything from 50 000 to 100 000 and comprising men, women and children of all ages, congregated in King William's Town in preparation for the march. It would be naïve to suggest all of them were there voluntarily, because as is the way of African politics, a large proportion were undoubtedly seriously intimidated into attending.

It was significant that senior notables of the ANC/SACP/COSATU alliance, including Chris Hani, indeed took part. That so many were there emphasises its importance to the alliance. Hani was later assassinated but if that had not happened, he would very likely have become deputy president to Nelson Mandela in place of Thabo Mbeki.

Lieutenant-Colonel Mkosana said the security situation in Ciskei was tense and the potential for violence between the ANC and the government of Ciskei was rife. 'It is public knowledge that during 1992 soldiers serving in the Security Forces of the Republic of Ciskei were regarded as traitors and puppets by their fellow black people including one's own family and friends. In whatever neighbourhood one resided, attacks upon soldiers and their families and friends and social and political pressures directed against soldiers were nearly unendurable.'

His commander had briefed him that 'a march was planned by the ANC/SACP/COSATU alliance which was, so we were told, to take over the Ciskei State under grave and very tense circumstances . . . the marchers will take over Ciskei and we will be attacked by MK'. He was ordered to protect Bisho at all costs.

The lieutenant-colonel, his officers and his troops were tense and afraid, which was understandable considering the large crowd of demonstrators they were expecting to face. None had been trained in crowd control.

Before permission to cross the border was granted to the marchers, the troops were kept out of sight within the Independence Stadium. When permission came through for the marchers to proceed into the stadium, the troops withdrew and were deployed to protect Bisho.

A platoon of 36 men under Major Ndaniso in two Buffel infantry fighting vehicles took up station in Jangilanga Crescent — a route that led from the stadium into town. Lieutenant-Colonel Mkosana and his second in command, Major Mbene, positioned themselves with this group.

A 108-strong infantry company was deployed to block Parliament Street and protect the Ministerial Complex and Fort Hare University. Another company was kept in reserve at Yellowwoods Farm outside town.

Because of the anticipated attack by MK, they were equipped with lethal weapons — R4 rifles, 40mm grenade launchers and light machine guns. This had been ordered by the CDF Commander, Brigadier Marius Oelschig, and his deputy Colonel Dirk van der Bank. Both had adopted a vantage point on top of the Parliament building as their HQ. Lieutenant-Colonel Mkosana seemed to remember that Van der Bank had been in a CDF helicopter that was circling the area, but with the passage of time he could be wrong.

Lieutenant-Colonel Mkosana looked on as the marchers filed by their thousands into the Independence Stadium. He was puzzled when he suddenly noticed that the numbers occupying a particular grandstand appeared to be diminishing instead of increasing. He could not understand why.

The SACP's Ronnie Kasrils was at the head of the marchers. When they reached the stadium at 13:30, instead of heading through the nearest entrance, he led them around the outside perimeter to the far side. Access to Bisho by that route had been barred by rolls of barbed laid across the road and the adjacent veld. Kasrils urged the marchers to force a path through the barbed wire.[20]

Kasrils still agonises over that decision. 'I accept in a profound moral sense that I was an element in the events that culminated in the massacre, and it still haunts me that perhaps *we* could have done more to avoid the terrible outcome.'[21] The *we*, according to Tokyo Sexwale, was the ANC leadership present at King Williams's Town which jointly made the decision to lead the marchers through the gap.[22]

The Goldstone Commission of Enquiry criticised the organisers of the march for acting in bad faith by not informing members of the National Peace Secretariat at the scene that they intended to break the magistrate's conditions by leaving the stadium. The commission called on the ANC's leadership to 'publicly censure' Ronnie Kasrils and other ANC officials for leading marchers out of the stadium and 'knowingly or negligently exposing them to the danger of death or injury'.

Needless to say, there was no public censure by the ANC.

Ciskei's Chief Justice Pickard's Commission of Enquiry was even blunter. It said the march leaders had led the marchers towards the CDF's guns 'like lambs to the slaughter'.[23]

Ronnie Kasrils' section of the crowd rushed down Jangilanga Crescent towards Lieutenant-Colonel Mkosana's group. He first saw them when they were about 200-300m away. Meanwhile, other sections had hived off towards the south and the east and were seeking alternative routes to the centre of Bisho.

Lieutenant-Colonel Mkosana, despite the noise of two helicopters circling the area — one belonged to the SAP and he had no communications with it — distinctly heard two or three shots which he believed had been fired from the crowd at his group. No one was hit. He was not alone in hearing shots. He had been expecting MK to attack, so shooting had been expected. There had been earlier reports over the radio that some of the marchers had been seen carrying AKs carved from wood. If some had carved replicas, others probably had the real thing.

It all happened in split seconds.

Lieutenant-Colonel Mkosana called Colonel van der Bank on the radio and asked for instructions.

'Colonel van der Bank', he said, 'the marchers are now out of the stadium and they are storming in our direction. What must we do?' He added that some shots were 'being fired in our direction.'

He heard Van der Bank consult briefly with Brigadier Oelschig. He kept the transmitter button down so the radio line remained open.

'Archie', he replied to Mkosana in Afrikaans, 'If you are being shot at, shoot back [*skiet terug*].'

Meanwhile, Major Ndaniso had debussed his platoon, which left Lieutenant-Colonel Mkosana, Major Mbene, Major Zulu and a few others in the command Buffel.

'Major Mbeni', Lieutenant-Colonel Mkosana ordered, 'minimum force fire!'

He explained later what this meant. 'There are a lot of stages of minimum force. It's firstly when you make a show of force. Secondly you throw teargas to the crowd. Thirdly, you again make a show of force. You debus from the vehicle so that the people can see there are people there . . . there are soldiers there.' He explained that only enough fire was required to make the person or group withdraw.' He said the crowd was far too close for him to go through all the stages. Also, he had no teargas.

There is confusion over what followed.

Lieutenant-Colonel Mkosana said Major Mbene called Major Ndaniso by name on the radio and ordered: 'Single shots, fire!'

Major Mbene told the board of enquiry: 'I pressed the [radio] switch and shouted loud to open fire. All company commanders on the net could hear this and the members in the vicinity heard my verbal command. The company commanders, all of them confirmed the same way when I ordered "cease fire".'

Lieutenant-Colonel Mkosana denied it.

Whatever happened, all units opened fire.

Rifleman Gonya, who was standing next to Mkosana in the rear of the Buffel, fired two grenades from his launcher at the ground by the feet of the approaching demonstrators.

'This fucking tube has fired!' Major Zulu exclaimed in astonishment.

'Why have you fired? Why? Who gave you the order?' Lieutenant-Colonel Mkosana asked Gonya.

Mkosana said that all units, except Major Ndaniso's platoon, fired against orders. There was firing over by Parliament and everywhere else. An investigation revealed that 185 rounds had been fired in Jangilanga Crescent and another 240 at Fort Hare.

After 'a second' he ordered 'cease fire' and everyone obeyed.[24]

Colonel van der Bank, however, said the shooting continued until he intervened. He thrice ordered a 'cease fire' before he was eventually obeyed.

Rifleman Gonya narrated a different story. He said that when Lieutenant-Colonel Mkosana called Colonel van der Bank on the radio the latter asked if he could see a certain tree. Mkosana replied in the affirmative and Van der Bank told him to report when the advancing marchers drew level with it.

'Fire!' Mkosana yelled when they did.

The soldiers glanced at each other, unwilling to fire.

He repeated his order, but still nothing happened.

'I am saying, fire!' Mkosana ordered for a third time.

Everyone, including Rifleman Gonya, opened fire. He was convinced the order had also been directed at him. He fired one grenade to the left front of the advancing crowd and another to the right. The riflemen continued firing until the order to 'cease fire' was given.[25]

29 people, including a soldier hit by friendly fire, lay dead and another 200 were wounded.

The ANC blamed the South African government for the killings.

President F W de Klerk replied that it was the ANC and not the South African government who started the 'mass action'.

The Goldstone Commission's report, after criticising Kasrils and the ANC for their part in the tragedy, stressed that this in no way excused the conduct of the Ciskei soldiers. It added that 'continued and prolonged' firing even after the crowd turned and fled was 'quite unjustified and unlawful'.[26]

Judge Pickard's report said that the troops who had fired at the demonstrators led by Ronnie Kasrils may 'well have been justified in firing some shots', but the conclusion was 'inescapable that the shooting on the southern and eastern sides of the stadium should never have occurred, that matters got entirely out of hand and that the soldiers overreacted considerably.'

The ANC rejected his report 'without consideration or qualification.' [27]

The Goldstone Commission found there was only one firearm amongst the marchers. Ballistic tests showed that it had not been fired. There were, however, 50 000 marchers there at the lowest estimate . The shooting created panic. People ran for their lives and in the chaos of the moment the Security Forces could hardly have been expected to conduct body searches. They were too involved with the aftermath of the shootings to bother with that. If several dozen armed MK cadres were amongst the crowd, they would hardly have waited there to be checked out for weapons.

In any case the en masse shootings by Gqozo's troops made a far more effective tool to discredit him than anything MK could have done. The ANC's expectation afterwards was that Gqozo would fall within a matter of days.

This turned out to be wishful thinking though, because Gqozo continued to cling tenaciously to office.

In the days following the massacre an even greater public anger was exhibited against the CDF. Some off duty soldiers were caught and beaten and a few were murdered. Married personnel living in civilian areas of Bisho and its surrounds hurriedly moved into the military bases for safety.

Personnel of all ranks stopped wearing uniform when outside barracks. The sight of a uniform became an invitation to violence. The local populace frequently vented their anger on soldiers, pelting them with rotten fruit or even worse.

It was a recipe for anarchy.

For safety's sake, Rifleman Marambana adopted the habit of returning to his home in Bisho only late in the evenings. On the night of 11 September he and his girlfriend routinely arrived late and went to bed. He awoke from habit at about 03:30, aware that he had to report for early duty at 1-Ciskei Battalion. He was about to light the lamp when a bedroom window caved in and a petrol bomb was lobbed inside. Luckily for him the flaming wick went out as it was thrown. Marambana rushed to the window, noticing a strong smell of petrol as he did, and found himself face-to-face with someone striking a match. It was apparent he planned to toss it through the window to ignite the petrol.

He shouted realising at the same time that the arsonist was his neighbour. They had played and gone to school together as children and hunted in tandem as teenagers. They had been good friends, but the pervasive aurora of violence had changed all that.

Rifleman Marambana was furious. His shouts startled the attacker who fled panic-stricken into the night. Marambana felt sure the man had not been alone. Attacks like that were always carried out by groups.

For safety's sake he left his girlfriend at his sister's house. He tried to phone the police but the lines were down. He drove to 1-Ciskei Battalion's barracks and took his service pistol from his locker. Feeling more capable of looking after himself, he returned to his house and went to seek his neighbour.

He found him and demanded to know why he had tried to kill him. At first the neighbour blandly denied it, but after questioning, he eventually admitted it and begged forgiveness.

Rifleman Marambana was very angry. Two of his comrades had been horribly murdered in the past few days — one had been necklaced with a burning motor car tyre thrown around his neck.

He was afraid to let his neighbour go free, because he might embark on a second attempt to kill him and maybe succeed. He was no longer a friend. Marambana was in fear of his life. It was war and the enemy stood before him. He drew his pistol, told his former schoolmate it was his turn to die and pumped ten shots into him.

Marambana was convicted of murder and sentenced to imprisonment, but was granted amnesty by the TRC.[28]

In the aftermath of the massacre, South Africa's Department of Foreign Affairs invited Brigadier Gqozo to lead a delegation for discussions in Cape Town. As he entered the conference room he was appalled to see his own Minister of Manpower, Lent Maqoma, sitting at the table. He had gone there at the invitation of Foreign Affairs without Brigadier Gqozo's knowledge.

South African diplomats immediately urged Gqozo to 'take a holiday' and let Maqoma take over in his stead.

Gqozo was understandably incensed and he got up and stormed from the meeting. He took an official car and headed straight for D F Malan (Cape Town International) Airport. South African officials followed him in an attempt to pour oil on troubled waters. A meeting was held at the airport, needless to say without the presence of Maqoma, and unsuccessful attempts were made to placate him.

A year later *The Weekly Mail* tried to confirm these events with Dr Allan Sharp, head of the 'independent' TBVC [Transkei, Bophuthatswana, Venda, Ciskei] States Desk in the Department of Foreign Affairs. He strenuously denied that Gqozo and Maqoma had attended such a meeting in Cape Town, saying sanctimoniously: 'I cannot imagine that the Department of Foreign Affairs would make such a suggestion to the leader of another country.'

The author could certainly imagine it.

A few days after the alleged Cape Town incident, a mini-limpet mine exploded in Lent Maqoma's Department of Manpower building in Bisho. Brigadier Gqozo fired him from his position of Minister of Manpower shortly afterwards.[29]

Former Foreign Affairs Minister Pik Botha, testifying to the TRC about the Bisho massacre, admitted he had considered ways of having Gqozo removed as Head of State. This was particularly after the murder of General Charles Sebe and Colonel Onward Guzana. After his advisers told him there was no constitutional provision for this, 'I personally suggested to him on more than one occasion that he should resign.'[30]

He chose the wrong man to pressure. Botha should have focussed on the SADF's Military Intelligence. They were pulling out all stops to keep Gqozo in office and ensure Ciskei was preserved as a final bastion against the advance of the ANC's influence in the Eastern Cape.

Not long after the Bisho Massacre, Brigadier Marius Oelschig's secondment as the CDF commander was terminated on his promotion to major-general. His second-in-command, Dirk van der Bank, took over command with the rank of brigadier.

And so the SADF continued to control the CDF.

The TRC granted amnesty to all those involved in the Bisho massacre, with the exception of Lieutenant-Colonel Mkosana and Rifleman Gonya. At the time of publication of this book both were on remand on murder charges.[31]

Politically inspired trouble was ongoing. The authorities and the African Democratic Movement's paramilitary units regarded the ANC and its associates as the enemy. ANC supporters were routinely attacked and many were rounded up and arrested. Others left their homes and lived in the bush or fled across the border into South Africa. As Mthethele Crosby Kolela — an MK section leader and later an ANC councillor — said: 'Most of the people were living like animals.'

Another plot against Gqozo: January 1993

In January 1993 Brigadier Gqozo accused the military wings of the ANC and PAC of plotting with the TDF to attack both the KwaZulu and Ciskei administrations. By his account, the SACP had instructed APLA and MK recruits under training in Transkei to mount the attacks.

The ANC described his claims as a 'mixture of outright lies and pure invention'. The PAC called it 'ludicrous' and 'full of professional lies'. General Holomisa said Gqozo was 'conducting a propaganda campaign against Transkei in collaboration with the South African Security Forces'.

General Holomisa probably had it right.

In February 1993 Ciskei's Council of State followed this by saying that a 'comprehensive and detailed report of a plan' to overthrow Brigadier Gqozo had been forwarded to the Goldstone Commission of Enquiry. The plan, it alleged, had been jointly drawn up by MK and APLA.

In January 1993 section 43 of the Ciskei National Security Act of 1982, which prohibited the holding of meetings and protest marches without the permission of a magistrate and the local headman, was found to conflict with Ciskei's Bill of Rights by the Bisho Supreme Court and declared invalid.[32]

In May 1993 Ciskei's Attorney-General, Willem Jurgens, announced that charges would be laid against 70 people, including Ciskei soldiers and the ANC's Ronnie Kasrils, for their roles in the Bisho Massacre. A few days later the Ciskei administration followed this with an announcement that it had granted 'unconditional indemnity' to all those members of the CDF who were involved in the massacre.

'It is the considered opinion of the Ciskei Council of State that criminal prosecution of persons in this regard would simply impact negatively on the multiparty negotiations in process', the announcement said.

The Supreme (High) Court later found the indemnity unconstitutional.

A new political organisation aligned to the Ciskei administration, to be known as the Christian People's Movement, was launched at a rally later in the month. A spokesman said the rally had been held to consult African Democratic Movement members 'regarding a possible change in the aims of the movement' which had been 'prompted by a 'spate of attacks on ADM members and their families'.

The ANC and its alliance partners called it just 'another trick' by Brigadier Gqozo to deceive the people after his 'failure' to present the ADM as a 'genuine political movement'.[33]

Whatever the case, the ADM remained in being.

In June 1993 CDF Chief, Brigadier van der Bank, announced that two officers and two NCOs had been arrested for 'conduct prejudicial to good military discipline'. He declined to provide details, but denied they were involved in a plot to overthrow Brigadier Gqozo. In view of the ongoing unrest at that time, it is an open question as to whether this was true or not.

African Democratic Movement hit squads: 1993/1994

A report in the *City Press* on 1 August 1993 said the CDF had trained and armed 100 youths as the nucleus of a 'secret militia' to support Brigadier Gqozo's administration. Ciskei denied the report. Later the same month, in contradiction, Gqozo warned that his administration would establish its own 'private army' unless MK ceased its activities in the territory and was disbanded. He maintained the ANC was 'to blame for 99% of the violence in the Ciskei' and that he had statistics to prove it.[34] It is unknown if this played a part in what followed.

In September 1993 Titus Mcoyiya, a director in Ciskei's Department of Foreign Affairs and the chairman of the ADM, concluded that the time had come to forcibly retaliate against the ANC. He sought the advice of Somtsora, a friendly MK member from Port Elizabeth, and asked how to form a self defence unit. Somtsora suggested he use the armed guards provided to protect the headmen as a nucleus. Mcoyiya did not agree as he believed they were insufficiently trained.

Somtsora (who had obviously changed sides) and Madikane were the first recruited into the unit. Mcoyiya armed them with an AK47 and a 7,65mm pistol. They were utilised at Dimbaza on 16 December, when they shot and wounded the ANC's Sam Kwelita. Mcoyiya's official BMW was used to get them to Dimbaza. On 23 December Mongezi Ndudula, also of Dimbaza, was less fortunate. He was shot and killed.

In early January 1994 Jeffrey Moshumi and Xolani Dywili were brought from Cape Town as reinforcements and as instructors to train recruits. Shooting practice was conducted at the CDF's Mapasa Base rifle range. Mongezi Reuben Solani, stationed with Brigadier Gqozo's bodyguard unit, was the next recruit. Mcoyiya, meanwhile, had managed to get hold of another three AK47s and a Smith and Wesson .38 revolver.

On 8 January four of the recruits hijacked an Opel Record and shot and wounded the driver. They had become concerned that Mcoyiya's BMW might have become compromised. While en route for shooting practice, they spotted seven people in ANC T-shirts, apparently on their way to a political rally. In an opportunistic crime, they stopped and opened fire, killing one and wounding another. Following this they dumped the Opel into the veld and set it on fire.

On 19 January the gang planned to attack a Mr Gantolo at Dimbaza because he had made disparaging remarks in the press about the ADM. En route they hijacked an Opel Ascona for use in the attack, holding up the driver, Bonisile Tose, and his girlfriend, Nomsa Tyuku, at gunpoint. As they made their getaway in his car, Tose drew his own pistol and shot at them. The gang fired back, but nobody was hit. After hiding the BMW they went to a house they wrongly believed was Gantolo's house. They fired through the windows with AKs on automatic and lobbed in a grenade. Solani used his own CDF R5 carbine. One occupant was wounded but the remaining three escaped unharmed. The Opel Ascona was abandoned in the veld after the attack.

During the evening of 21 January they attacked the house of ANC member, John Gamzana, at Phakamisa. Using the same modus operandi, they fired their AKs on automatic through the windows and lobbed in several grenades. Gamzana, his wife and his daughter were injured, but others in the house escaped unharmed.

On 25 January police flagged down Mcoyiya's official BMW in Zwelitsha. Somtsora was driving and Madikane and Moshumi were passengers. A search of the car revealed a 7,65mm pistol and a .38 Smith and Wesson revolver and ammunition. They rounded up the rest of the gang, including Mcoyiya, and the weapons used at the various shooting scenes were recovered.[35]

Exit Brigadier Joshua 'Oupa' Gqozo: March 1994

In November 1993 — in spite of his making every effort to thwart the due process of law — the trial of Brigadier Gqozo on a charge of being an accomplice in the murder of Charles Sebe opened in Bisho's Supreme Court.[36] His legal representative said that as Head of State he could not be 'held responsible in a personal capacity' for the murder'. In reply the Attorney-General for Ciskei, Willem Jurgens, said if the chairman of the Ciskei Council of State — which was Gqozo — committed a crime he could not be immune from prosecution.[37] Gqozo was acquitted after a lengthy trial, but with the tribulations and pressures he had been subjected to, it had become increasingly obvious that he would be unable to cling to power and stop the re-amalgamation of Ciskei into South Africa.

By mid March 1994 Brigadier Gqozo had made no arrangements for the general election due to take place in Ciskei in terms of the Codesa agreements. What's more he refused to discuss it with anyone. Despite this, he enjoyed widespread support in the territory — but this was probably out of fear.

In the lower ranks of the Ciskei Police and in the civil service, however, there was widespread dissatisfaction with Gqozo. It was felt that he was only interested in the army. When the troops had complaints, he made a point of speaking to them and addressing their problems. When the police complained, he ignored them. Much of the dissatisfaction in the police and civil service stemmed from dissatisfaction relating to pension issues. They wanted their pensions paid out to them before re-incorporation in case the money disappeared.

It was a widely held belief that no matter the posturing that was going on, it was inevitable that Ciskei would eventually be re-incorporated into a greater South Africa. Civil servants had already launched an action in the Bisho Supreme Court to compel the administration to pay them out. Many middle ranking policemen wanted the police to join the action but the commissioner was against it. The inspectorate, in particular, had continually asked the commissioner to meet and discuss pension issues with them. Meetings were arranged, but were invariably cancelled at the last moment.

Another burning question was what kind of future they could expect in the Ciskei Police. They believed their officers were too chummy with Brigadier Gqozo and were disinterested in their welfare. They had frequently been warned that failure to cooperate with Gqozo's administration could result in their discharge.

Another bone of contention concerned a senior officer suspended from duty for theft. Despite being charged and convicted, the commissioner had allowed his return to duty.

Demands became more strident. In mid February Commissioner Nqoya made an arrangement to meet the inspectors at Bisho Police College at 08:00 on 22 March. The inspectorate assembled on the day, but instead of Commissioner Nqoya being there, they were addressed by Inspector Suys and Captain Falteng of the Police College about the forthcoming general elections and the mechanics on how it would likely work.

Detective Inspector Mfene, acting as spokesman, objected and insisted they were not there to talk about elections. They had come to be addressed by Commissioner Nqoya. Where was he?

The two hurriedly exited when they saw the mood of the assembled officers. They returned shortly afterwards with the commanding officer of the Police College, Brigadier Kuwuza. The assembled officers repeated their grievances and told him to fetch the commissioner. He left, promising to do so.

They inspectors sang 'freedom songs' while awaiting him.

Commissioner Nqoya eventually appeared at 11:00. He seemed to be very angry.

Detective Inspector Mfene asked him about the future of the Ciskei Police and demanded information about their pensions.

Nqoya said he had no time to answer questions because he was already late for an 11:00 appointment with Brigadier Gqozo. He promised to discuss their grievances with him and return later with answers.

Detective Inspector Mfene asked if policemen of all ranks could be called to the college so they could also hear the news on his return. Commissioner Nqoya agreed.

While they waited, radio control notified all police stations as to what was going on and numerous policemen, including senior officers, joined them at the college. Some officers came voluntarily but others refused and were rounded up and brought there at gun-point. Officers were made to sit on chairs on the stage apart from their men. Effectively they were held hostage. In the interests of solidarity, no one of whatever rank was allowed to leave the college. By that time a universal but apparently unspoken demand had developed that Brigadier Gqozo should be removed from office.

When Commissioner Nqoya failed to return by 14:00, men were sent to look for him. They returned and reported that they had seen him and he told them he would be coming soon.

By 16:00 when he had still not arrived, Sergeant Nkwenkwe and a few others took a Casspir and drove into town to find him. His offices were closed and deserted. Assuming he had gone home, because his offices normally closed at 16:00, they returned to the college to check if he was there. He wasn't.

At about 18:00 Sergeant Nkwenkwe and his companions drove to State House in their Casspir. They planned to persuade the guards to let them in to speak to Brigadier Gqozo, but to their surprise the guard huts were deserted. Going inside they looked around until they eventually found Gqozo himself. He greeted them and said he had been sold out by the police. Instead of maintaining law and order they were in revolt. He described it as a sure sign that his government was no longer needed. He also said he had been deserted by his military bodyguards who had returned to their base. He had already phoned Foreign Minister Pik Botha in Pretoria and told him he had resigned.

Sergeant Nkwenkwe and the rest were shocked. They sheepishly explained that they had come to fetch Commissioner Nqoya whom they thought might be hiding there.

Brigadier Gqozo assured them he had last seen the Commissioner at 11:00 that morning.

They asked him to accompany them to the Police College and address the assembled policemen. He refused, saying he could not do it as he no longer held office since he resigned.

They asked for proof. He replied that there was a large SADF contingent of troops standing by just across the border in King William's Town. They should go and ask them not to move into Ciskei because there was no longer a need for them. The CDF and the police had taken control. Before returning to the college they detoured through King William's Town and confirmed there was a large concentration of SADF troops there. They reported the resignation on their return to the Police College, but no one was prepared to believe them. The very idea of Brigadier Gqozo voluntarily resigning seemed too far-fetched to be believed.

At 20:00 a government official, a Mr Goosen, appeared and confirmed that Brigadier Gqozo had resigned and suggested they go to their homes They thought he was lying too as a ruse to get them to disperse. Various other officials, including the Minister of Police and Attorney-General, Willem Jurgens, appeared and listened to their complaints. Jurgens warned that if they persisted with their demonstration, they could end up being charged with mutiny. By then about 75% of the Ciskei police's junior ranks had assembled at the college.

In the end they stayed at the Police College all night, singing freedom songs, hesitant to leave in case the Commissioner used it as an excuse not to see them.

At 04:00 on 23 March four soldiers arrived and asked for permission to join them because they also had complaints. They confessed they had actually been despatched to disrupt the meeting, but they had no intention of doing that. They confirmed the resignation of Brigadier Gqozo and said it was because of what had happened at the Police College. The policemen, distrustful of the army, chased them away because they thought they were spies. In fact, the very appearance of soldiers frightened the assembled policemen, so men went to the college armoury to arm themselves with R4 and R5 assault rifles. They would fight back if there was army interference.

Soon after, more soldiers appeared and asked permission to join them. They still thought they were spies, but allowed them to stay. Later they came to realise that the soldiers also had genuine grievances.

A posse of policemen was sent to collect Commissioner Nqoya. They found him hiding at the Ministerial Complex and escorted him to the college. He calmly apologised for the delay, but confessed that he had been too frightened to come. When questioned about the future of the Ciskei Police, he was evasive and also avoided mention of his discussions with Brigadier Gqozo.

Thoroughly disillusioned, most policemen left the college during the course of the morning and made their way to the Independence Stadium. They joined 20 000 stomping and singing civil servants who were waiting for Brigadier Gqozo to address them regarding their grievances.[38] The stadium was bristling with the weapons of dissident soldiers and policemen. Loyal army officers feared for Brigadier Gqozo's safety and on their advice he did not appear.

At about 14:00 Transitional Executive Council (TEC) official Zam Titus, union negotiator Phillip Dexter and the ANC's Border president, Smuts Ngonyama, appeared and attempted to placate the angry crowd. Unfortunately the public address system broke down. This proved to be the last straw and the crowds streamed from the stadium in disgust.[39]

Brigadier Gqozo announced during the course of the morning that he had fired all his ministers. He said he had personally stepped down because he had no desire to see Bisho burn. He had watched the demise of Bophuthatswana and Mangope's presidency from the wings just more than a week before (see later) and he had bowed to the inevitable and resigned as Ciskei's head of state.

There was a near crisis that evening when a committee of soldiers and policemen demanded that Brigadier Gqozo retract his resignation. They wanted him restored to office. Their demands came to naught when a search disclosed that he had already left the territory for the proverbial 'undisclosed destination'.

Whatever other measures the committee might have had in mind to retain the Ciskei as an independent homeland, they were foiled when on 24 March at 09:30 — to the accompaniment of jeers of derision from the CDF — an SADF armoured column rolled into Bisho. But while they jeered, the SADF moved swiftly and secured the military headquarters, the Parliament building, Radio Ciskei and the two industrial areas at Dimbaza and Fort Jackson. It was determined that this time there would be no repeat of the near anarchy that resulted when Brigadier Gqozo first grabbed power.

Many off-duty soldiers and policemen, who were determined to face down the SADF, smashed open armouries at military bases and distributed weapons. They were too late because the South Africans already controlled all key areas. By mid-afternoon Ciskei's Security Forces had capitulated and they handed in their weapons without firing an angry shot.[40]

The South African government and the Transitional Executive Council appointed two administrators, South African Ambassador, Piet van Rensburg, and the ANC's Rev Bongani Finca to oversee the territory until the April elections.[41]

The Republic of Ciskei passed into history like a damp squib.

29

Consolidation of Afrikaner resistance Formation of Afrikaner Volksfront 1993-1994

The *Afrikaner Volksfront* (AVF) was a political organisation initiated by a committee of generals. The committee comprised General Constand Viljoen, a former Chief of the SADF; General Mike Geldenhuys, a former Commissioner of Police; General Kobus Visser, ex-SAP; and Generals Tienie Groenewald and Dries Bischoff, both former army generals. They first met on 5 May 1993 to enquire into the possibility of forming an umbrella association to bring the Afrikaner *volk* under a single banner. They had been asked to look into this after an initial meeting of various right-wing organisations in April 1993.

General Tienie Groenewald, outlined the AVF's proposed objectives:

1 To unify the fragmented right wing.
2 To maximise pressure for a *Volkstaat* during negotiations.
3 To bolster COSAG — Concerned South Africans Group at the multiparty talks.

Groenewald sketched a three-phase plan of action for supporters of a *Volkstaat*:

A Political pressure for the establishment of a system of national states.
B Passive resistance, including mass action, boycotts and strikes.
C As a last resort, secession from South Africa by an Afrikaner state.

The official launch of the AVF by 21 right-wing parties and organisations, including the *Afrikaner Volksunie* (AVU), the *Afrikaner Vryheidstigting*, the *Afrikaner Weerstandsbeweging* (AWB) and the Conservative Party (CP), took place on 19 May 1993. CP leader, Dr Ferdi Hartzenberg, was elected chairman of the executive committee. While not formed as a political party, its council was dominated by the CP because it had been decided that serving MPs would each have a seat on it. The CP was the only movement within the AVF that had representation in Parliament. At their founding meeting they rejected the concept of a unitary state and demanded an Afrikaner *Volkstaat* to form part of a confederation of South African states. Welcoming General Constand Viljoen's entry into Afrikaner politics, Eugene Terre'Blanche said he would willingly serve as his corporal.

As a soldier, General Viljoen had been fighting various communist-backed black nationalist forces since 1960. He regarded it, correctly, as an extension of the Cold War. He and his four general officer colleagues — but particularly himself — were students of revolutionary warfare and salted by experience. They believed that such a war could not be fought on military lines because it was a fight for the hearts and minds of the people.

They devised a number of strategies. They addressed violence aspects, military aspects, economic aspects, propaganda aspects and psychological aspects. From that they devised a negotiation strategy, a political strategy and so on.

The primary objective was the mobilisation of Afrikaners to the AVF's banner to prove that the Afrikaner people were unhappy with the manner in which political events were unfolding.
They rejected the idea of South Africa becoming a unitary state, with the re-incorporation of the black homelands.They believed that re-incorporation would result in a major diminishment of Afrikaner influence. Afrikaners wanted a *Volkstaat* where they could live and organise themselves in the manner they wanted to without interference. It would become part of a confederation of states. Afrikaner self determination was not negotiable.

They set out to gather substantial proven support, so that notice would be taken of them. To achieve this they began to stomp the country. At meetings, the generals — particularly Constand Viljoen, Tienie Groenewald and Kobus Visser — were always prominent amongst the speakers. Supporting speakers were from the AVF's member organisations, particularly the CP and the AWB. They set out to create unity and a feeling of togetherness amongst Afrikaners — to win their hearts and minds and 'scare the hell out of De Klerk and the ANC'. Field organisers fanned out in the country areas to mobilise support. Cells were formed and secret meetings took place. Their efforts, which were designed to attract military, political and economic support, proved successful. Within six weeks the AVF, according to General Viljoen, had enrolled 150 000 members in areas all around the country. Large numbers had expressed their willingness to take up arms in support of the AVF.

On 6 June an AVF deputation met the government to discuss its call for a temporary suspension of multiparty constitutional negotiations until political violence had abated. It demanded that:

- plans for a general election on 27 April 1994 be dropped;
- the government restore law and order;
- the government take steps to accommodate the right to self-determination;
- a white election or referendum be called before any constitutional changes were made.

It promised to consider a government proposal that it take a seat at the negotiating forum, or alternately, submit proposals on how regions should be defined.[1]

The restoration of law and order was an important plank in the AVF's platform. Yet was it was more than the continued existence of Afrikaners that was threatened by a breakdown in law and order?

On 6 May 1993, when discussions with farmers were taking place relating to the formation of the AVF, the *Sowetan*, understandably, was giving more prominence to news items of interest to their 99,9% black readership than to the plight of white farmers.

It revealed that the crime situation was pretty frightening for blacks as well. The story headlined on the front page concerned an APLA ambush of a truck containing black policemen going off duty in Soweto the previous morning. Four, including a policewoman, died and five were wounded.

In a Pretoria suburb two black men were forced from their car by unknown assailants, made to lie face down on the ground and shot execution-style with single shots to the back of the head. An 18-month-old toddler was left unharmed in the back of the car.

In Soweto a black schoolteacher narrowly escaped death when six young armed black men hijacked his car. He managed to run away, which saved him from being shot.

Three black men attacked and shot a black police sergeant travelling home on a bus in Natal. The other passengers in the bus arrested the attackers.

The editorial said 'mindless criminality' in the Vaal townships had got out of hand, with the police being unable to control the situation. It said people were reverting to vigilante action, which the newspaper certainly did not condone. It highlighted the tragic case of a black man in Soweto who shot dead three black youths and wounded another three after they wantonly damaged his house and shot and killed his 16-year-old daughter.

It seemed that the radical right-wing Afrikaners who demanded greater protection from violent crime and called for the formation of armed self defence units, were little different to their black fellow countrymen who were demanding the same.

On 24 June the AVF held a protest march outside the World Trade Centre where constitutional negotiations were in progress. They demanded a halt to negotiations and that Afrikaners be granted a *Volkstaat*. The crowd, estimated at 2 000 and comprising a large number of AWB supporters, stormed through a police cordon chanting 'AWB! AWB!'

General Viljoen tried in vain to stop them.

They smashed a civilian landmine-protected vehicle through the front glass doors, poured inside and briefly occupied the centre. Members of the negotiating teams fled. Outside the crowd rocked cars as they arrived at the centre and ripped off their windscreen wipers.[2]

At a news conference afterwards General Viljoen said the AVF had pleaded with the government to slow down negotiations so that the right-wing could negotiate its aims, but its efforts had been ignored.[3]

On 8 July the AVF, as an outgrowth of its discussions with government on 6 June, produced a provisional map for a future constitutional dispensation in which South Africa would be divided into eight regions. It said that the opinion of Afrikaners in each region would be tested separately to find out where they wanted a *Volkstaat*. Until Afrikaner opinion had been ascertained, it said, the organisation would refuse to draw up proposals for a new regional dispensation.

Hennie Bester, the chairman of the Democratic Party's policy advice committee, said the AVF had not defined an 'Afrikaner' which indicated 'the political poverty and dishonesty of the organisation'. Its proposals were based on the same economic incoherence as the 'Verwoerdian dream' and that it could never support autonomous and credible regions.

The National Party said the AVF's proposal for an Afrikaner poll confirmed what the bulk of voters already knew — 'that they don't have a plan'. It added that the majority of Afrikaners had already decided to share the country with other South Africans.[4]

Shortly afterwards the *Sunday Star* claimed that an AVF document leaked to it called for the outlawing of political parties in the proposed *Volkstaat*. Representatives in its parliament, it said, would be elected as independents and be accountable to their constituents only. An executive state president would be elected by a simple majority of MPs. It distinguished between *Volksburgers* and *Staatsburgers*. *Volksburgers* were defined as Afrikaners or members of related ethnic groups who would have the vote. *Staatsburgers* were defined as members of other ethnic groups like 'Zulus, Tswanas and coloureds'. They would have all civic rights except for the vote.[5]

On 2 August General Groenewald said that South Africa had never been so close to a civil war. He added, however, that the AVF was confident that a constitutional compromise would be reached before it broke out. The AVF, he said, was involved in intensive bilateral talks and the ANC and the government realised that 'Afrikaners and the Zulus' would not permit a communist government to take power.[6]

On 19 August General Groenewald said the AVF was demanding that political power be vested in separate states. The states would decide what powers should be allocated to a central authority.[7] General Viljoen announced that the AVF and the government had established a committee to determine ways to promote Afrikaner self-determination within the constitutional framework. He said that when the AVF deemed it 'sensible and in the interests of Afrikaners' it would take part in the constitutional negotiations, but said there was little hope for that at that moment. Viljoen urged Afrikaners to reject the negotiating process and the scheduled general election and prepare to defend themselves. He added that the negotiators had rejected all of the AVF's proposals, including its demand for a *Volkstaat*.

The Transitional Executive Council Bill, passed in September 1993, applied to South Africa and all 'independent' homelands and was designed to ease the transitional process. General Tienie Groenewald said that if the government and the ANC attempted to implement the bill, the AVF and other COSAG (Concerned South Africans Group) members would refuse to accept the TEC's authority. The adoption of the bill, he continued, would be considered a declaration of war. On the other hand, General Constand Viljoen, chairman of the AVF's directorate, said however, that war was not necessarily the best way of achieving Afrikaner self determination, as negotiations would have to follow even after a war.

During the September parliamentary session, only the CP and IFP opposed the bill. The CP walked out, labelling the legislation 'a constitutional revolution that will transfer power to the ANC/SACP alliance'.

On 8 September General Viljoen said the AVF had failed to achieve its goals at multiparty talks, so it had now turned to trying to sell its *Volkstaat* ideals through meetings with the leaders of other parties. He said talks were going well and he was hopeful they would be able to bargain something for the Afrikaner and achieve peace.[8]

Shortly afterwards the *Christian Science Monitor* reported that the AVF had agreed to take part in the elections in return for a semi-autonomous Afrikaner state. It said the agreement had resulted from secret negotiations between General Viljoen and ANC leader, Nelson Mandela.

The AVF, however, denied a deal had been struck. It said that if anything emerged from the current negotiations with the ANC or the NP it would be communicated publicly. Despite this, a joint statement issued by the AVF and the ANC confirmed that proposals for an Afrikaner homeland had been tabled during a series of bilateral discussions. Both parties described the talks as 'encouraging' and said they would be continued as a matter of urgency.

The CP subsequently issued a denial that there was a split in the ranks of the right-wing.[9]

AWB and AVF prepare for war: May 1993

Following the formation of the *Afrikaner Volksfront* in May 1993, Dries Kriel was nominated to become its second-in-charge in the Free State.

Shortly afterwards Eugene Terre'Blanche called him to his Ventersdorp farm. He told him they must prepare for war to stop the ANC and the communists from taking power. He was told to form secret cells comprised of reliable people who could be trained in sabotage techniques.

This was followed two days later by an approach by Jaco de Villiers, the commander of the AVF in the northern Free State and Kriel's immediate superior. He belonged to the *Boere Krisis Aksie* (Crisis Action) component of the AVF and was a prominent member of the Conservative Party. He did not belong to the AWB.

He told Kriel that he had orders from General Viljoen. Feeling that he could not take orders from everyone Kriel went to the AVF's offices in Hatfield Pretoria and spoke to Commandant Pretorius there. He confirmed there had been discussions with the AWB and it had been decided the AWB would be responsible for urban terrorism. The AVF, it is assumed, was responsible for rural terrorism.

Having seen people suddenly fade from the scene when action was in the offing, Kriel did some straight talking to Jaco de Villiers. He told him he did not want to end up with only his own people involved. Everybody should be involved.

'No, everybody is ready', De Villiers said. 'The bombs are going to go off and everybody is going to start now — the *Boere Krisis Aksie* as well.'

Kriel saw Terre'Blanche and spoke of his discussions with the AVF. That was fine, Terre'Blanche, assured him. He should just go ahead and establish cells.

He embarked on a recruiting drive to select suitable people from within the ranks of the AWB. Everything was classified 'secret' and dealt with on a need-to-know basis. Training camps were established and brought into operation on farms in Bothaville and in the western Free State. Cells were formed in the Northern Cape, the Eastern Free State, the Eastern Transvaal (Mpumalanga) and the Northern Free State. The Northern Cape cell comprised the cell leader, Wynand de Villiers and Eugene Groenewald. The cell leader of the Northern Free State cell, which also operated in the Western Transvaal (North West Province), was Neils Labuschagne — Kriel's second in command in the local AWB. His members were Jaco Botes and Dan van der Watt. The Eastern Transvaal cell never got off the ground. All the cells were based in rural areas, despite the arrangement that the AWB would be responsible for urban terrorism.

Kriel was given assurances that cells were being formed in other areas by member organisations of the AVF. In the end, though, except for an AWB *Ystergarde* (Iron Guard) cell, trained and run by Cliffie Barnard and Koper Myburg at Ventersburg and another that became known as the Ridora Group at Randfontein under Phil Kloppers, no other cells were formed. The Ridora Group was activated only in December 1993 and the Iron Guard cell only came into operation just before the April 1994 election. This, of course, was unknown to Kriel. He accepted that there were many other cells within the AVF and assumed they were operating on a need-to-know basis, which was why he knew nothing about them.

Two of Kriel's recruits, Mossie Mostert (not the AWB general) and Wally Joubert, were tasked to procure explosives. They were miners in Welkom and they stole high explosive from underground, smuggled it from the mine and passed it to Kriel. While this was a useful start, they did not have enough and it was necessary to supplement it with 'low' explosive made from ammonium nitrate fertiliser mixed with dieseline. This was freely available in farming areas. It had to be used in combination with cortex, because its detonating process was far slower than that of high explosive.

Right wing visit to the SADF: October 1993

Kriel discussed various matters with Terre'Blanche during October 1993. Generals Nico Prinsloo, Japie Oelofse and a couple of other senior officers were present. Terre'Blanche mentioned that the SADF had invited a party of right wingers including himself, the AWB's general staff, members of the Conservative Party and officials of the AVF to pay a four-day visit to various military facilities in the Cape.

Terre'Blanche mentioned that he got on very well with certain SADF officers and that the relationship was important to the AWB. He nominated those who would be attending and passed on the necessary orders. They were told to assemble at the Waterkloof Air Base near Pretoria on 6 October 1993. He told them what they should take with them, which included their AWB uniforms. They should wear civilian clothes when they reported to Waterkloof.

Terre'Blanche, his officers and their fellow right-wingers duly assembled at Waterkloof. There were 33 of them in all. They were met by an SADF liaison officer who would conduct the party around. He issued them with files on the SADF and gave them note pads. Afterwards they filed out onto the apron and took their seats aboard a SAAF C-130 transport aircraft.

Their first stop was the Army Women's Training College at George. After drinks they were given lunch. By this time those of the AWB who were not already in uniform put them on. After lunch they were conducted around the college and the training programme was explained to them.

From George they flew to the Infantry School at Oudtshoorn.

That night in the bar the AWB people, who kept much to themselves, got talking to the SADF liaison officer. Until then he had spent most of his time with Terre'Blanche. He said he was a former commanding officer at Potchefstroom, but was currently based at Defence Headquarters in Pretoria.

Terre'Blanche was garrulous. He had long suffered problems with alcohol and had drunk far too much whisky. While the officer was away for a few moments, he spoke excitedly to some of his cronies grouped around him.

'This is Dr Van Vuuren. His code name is Dr Van Vuuren, but his real name is the one he has been introduced as. He is the Defence Force officer that I always refer to.'

The clear implication to Kriel was that Terre'Blanche had liaised with the officer before and that he was the SADF's liaison officer with the AWB. That explained his use of the *nom de guerre*, Dr Van Vuuren.

His close cronies appeared to understand what Terre'Blanche was saying, but Kriel who was not included in the conversation, was mystified. He had once enjoyed a close camaraderie with Terre'Blanche, but had lost that in the late 1980s. Terre'Blanche, at that time, was having a rather public affair with an English-speaking lady jounalist. His Calvinistic colleagues were outraged. This did little to influence Terre'Blanche who expelled his critics from his inner circle and surrounded himself with sycophants.

Kriel, because of his relationship with Terre'Blanche, was consulted by a medical doctor, also a member of the AWB. The doctor told him confidentially that Terre'Blanche had spoken about divorcing his wife and marrying the other lady. The doctor had responded firmly, saying divorce was impossible, because he 'belonged to the people — to the Afrikaner *volk*'. Terre'Blanche refused to terminate the affair, but he was amenable to the idea of subjecting himself to treatment for alcoholism. He also thought it a good idea that his lady friend should undergo the same treatment, because he believed she might be addicted to slimming tablets.

The doctor told Kriel that he feared a major scandal, a scandal that would inevitably damage the organisation and asked him to intervene. Kriel promised to broach the subject. He took the opportunity the next time he was alone with Terre'Blanche, which was at a braaivleis. He spoke bluntly, telling him 'that he belonged to the people and he could not carry on' with this woman. For the sake of the movement he had to break off the affair.

Terre'Blanche swore at him and told him to mind his own business. The relationship between the two was never quite the same again. The affair eventually ran its course and came to a messy end after AWB zealots attempted to assassinate the lady. Terre'Blanche, it seems, did not act on the suggestion that he seek treatment for alcoholism either.

That night at Oudtshoorn, Dries Kriel had much to think about. He wondered with misgivings about 'Dr van Vuuren'. What was going on?

He told the author: 'I realise today that he was up to dirty things, working with others. He was scared to get me involved because I was very loyal to the cause. The way I felt at that time, I know that if I had thought he was betraying the cause, I would have 'buried' him. I know there are others who would have done the same. So I think that is why I was not included in the conversation about Dr van Vuuren.'

The next morning he approached Terre'Blanche and asked him to be frank about Van Vuuren. Terre'Blanche evasively replied that he knew nothing about him. When pressed he stonewalled Kriel's every question and lost his temper.

'I realised something was wrong, but I thought it might be something good. Maybe people were planning an uprising or something like that. That's the way I thought at the time', Kriel told the author.

They spent the day at Oudtshoorn, watching infantry, range firing and weapon demonstrations. The officers treated them with the utmost courtesy. They addressed the AWB generals and brigadiers by their ranks as if they were commissioned officers of the SADF. The same courtesies were extended wherever they went. The rankers did not salute them, however, probably because most would have refused anyway if they had been ordered to.

The next morning they flew to the Ysterplaat Air Base in Cape Town. From there they were taken to the Simon's Town Naval Base as guests of the South African Navy.

They were met on arrival by the Chief of the Navy, Vice-Admiral R C Simpson-Anderson, who explained the functions of the South African fleet to them. According to AWB General

Mossie Mostert, he also thanked them 'for everything you have done'. He told Terre'Blanche and his officers: 'When you take over this land, you must see to the Navy because we have no money for equipment.' Mostert's impression was that the Admiral's sympathies lay in the direction of the AWB. They were entertained for dinner one evening at the Cape Town Castle. On another day they were taken out to sea in a minesweeper.

From Cape Town they flew to the Air Force Base at Langebaan Road. Training was demonstrated and they were shown various weapons systems. They were treated to a flight and aerobatics demonstration by a Harvard aircraft. The Air Force was in the process of being down-sized and it was experiencing budgetary problems. After being well entertained in the mess they slept in the barracks and returned to Pretoria the next morning.

AWB General Nico Prinsloo commented that their hosts were 'extremely positive about everything [the right wing cause]'. Subsequent to the visit the military took both Terre'Blanche and Prinsloo around the Western Transvaal 'to investigate stockpiling locations [arms dumps etc] that had been established'.

Mostert told the author that the right-wingers' tour had followed a similar one in September by politicians to the left of the political spectrum, like the ANC, the SACP, the PAC and the Democratic Party. A senior officer said in confidence that the tours had been arranged to enable the SADF authorities to get an idea of where the sympathies of their officers lay. Mostert's distinct impression was that they favoured the Afrikaner right-wing, not the ANC.[10]

It seems somewhat bizarre that the SADF had gone out of its way to entertain a radical organisation like the AWB. Military Intelligence well knew that it was dedicated to bombing campaigns and to the overthrow of South Africa's established system of government.

Astonishingly too, the visit was given major prominence on the leader page of the November 1993 issue of the SADF's magazine *Paratus*. It called it a 'Christian' visit and a 'peace mission to the people of the Western Cape'. The visitors, it said, had concluded there was still a chance for peace for South Africa'. It was illustrated with a photograph of some of the 'peacemakers'. Dominating the centre of the picture is a smiling Eugene Terre'Blanche. To his right is General Japie Oelofse, who would gain infamy as the commander of the Ridora Crossing killers, who demanded they bring him a victim's ear.To his left is a partially obscured picture of a man in AWB uniform emblazoned with its Nazi-style insignia. Mossie Mostert told the author that they had only heard afterwards that it was supposed to have been a 'Christian visit'.

The author believes that the visit, and the visitors for that matter, must have been personally approved by the Chief of the SADF for an article such as that to have been given prominence. The Chief of the SADF at the time was General Kat Liebenberg, an officer with known right-wing persuasions, who was due to retire on 31 October 1993. He would be replaced by the incumbent Chief of the Army, General Georg Meiring.

Freedom Alliance formed: October 1993

The Freedom Alliance comprising the *Afrikaner Volksfront*, the Inkatha Freedom Party, determination for the people of southern Africa. It replaced the Concerned South Africans Group (COSAG) formed in October 1992 with a somewhat similar agenda. General Constand Viljoen took on a pivotal role in the Freedom Alliance. The AVF, through this organisation, intended to perpetuate the 'homelands' system as a means by which Afrikaners would get their own *Volkstaat*. If the need arose, they would fight for it. They would be the 'USA' in the Freedom Alliance's particular brand of NATO, although this was not seriously evident at the time.

On 2 December 1993 the Negotiating Council approved a draft bill providing for the return of South African citizenship to residents of the 'independent' homelands, effective from 1 January 1994, and for the re-incorporation of the territories into South Africa on election day, 27 April 1994. Venda and Transkei approved the bill, but Bophuthatswana and Ciskei rejected it.

Dries Kriel's bombing campaign: November 1993 to February 1994

By September 1993 Dries Kriel's training was in full gear.

From November 1993 his cells were responsible for numerous bombings.

They attacked targets like the Regina Farm School at Orkney — because it had integrated blacks with its white pupils. They detonated bombs close to informal settlements occupied by black squatters at Viljoenskroon, Hoopstad, Potchefstroom, Wesselsbron and Bothaville.

'They were getting kind of vicious in Wesselsbron . . . having all kinds of toyi-toyi, marches and things', Kriel said. 'We decided to sort of teach them a small lesson. It was more something to scare them, because if we [had] wanted to, we could have killed quite a lot of them. It was only intended as a warning. At that stage I didn't feel like going in and killing innocent people. I couldn't make peace with that. A black woman and a child were slightly injured. Nobody [was] killed, but it shocked them. It was quiet for quite a while after that.'

Railway lines were the most frequently struck targets. They blasted the line of rail between Orkney and Leeudoringstad on 22 December 1993, on 14 January, 26 January, 28 January, 31 January and 4 February 1994 and sabotaged the line between Potchefstroom and Klerksdorp on 18 January. They struck at the line between Hennenman and Kroonstad on 21 January, the line between Kroonstad and Jordaan on 1 February and the line between Leeudoringstad and Makwassie on 7 February.

'Okay, and did you damage the railway line?' the author asked.

'*Ja*, some of those trucks are still lying there [at Orkney]. We stopped the whole route through Western Transvaal to Kimberley. Eventually, the trains started going by day . . . with a bloke going in front. We were just at the stage where the drivers started refusing to go to work when we were arrested. We hammered the railways. They were all derailments — the whole lot. There was millions [of rands worth of] damage. It was derailed trucks all the way. They called it the bombing route. They said you've got the wine route in the Cape and this is the bombing route . . .'

The only charge to misfire was at the Anglo American Corporation's offices in Reinett Building in Welkom. Neils Labuschagne's cell had made what seemed to be a highly effective bomb. Once it was in position in the building's entrance, though, they disagreed over whether or not the fuse length would allow them sufficient time to clear town before detonation. Deciding it was too short, they cut and joined another section before igniting it. If they had possessed more expertise or experience, they would have replaced the whole length of fuse. As it was, Anglo American was spared the experience of a badly damaged or perhaps utterly destroyed building.

Kriel never attributed responsibility for any of the blasts to any organisation. However, the Boere Republican Army run by right-winger Andrew Ford claimed the responsibility and credit for them all. The BRA, though, existed in name only. It had never conducted a single operation. So claim what may, Ford remained safe from harassment by the Security Police because he had done nothing. In later years Kriel jokingly remonstrated with him. Ford replied that Kriel had actually been with the Boere Republican Army — he just didn't know of it! [10]

Afrikaner war talk: 1993

In 1993 Nico Prinsloo was an AWB general and the secretary-general of the general staff at its Ventersdorp head office. Apart from liaison between Eugene Terre'Blanche and his generals, he was also in charge of administrative services and acted in a liaison capacity with the media, the general public, the SADF and other right-wing political organisations worldwide. He liaised with the police to make arrangements when AWB or other right-wing organisations held public marches, demonstrations or meetings.

He attended all the meetings of the general staff.

In the second half of 1993 a closed meeting was held by Terre'Blanche and his generals on a farm near Ottosdal. The question of the *Volkstaat* was raised and the areas where it could be declared were discussed. Certain towns controlled by right-wing councils had declared them to be part of the *Volkstaat* and awarded the AWB and other right-wing organisations the 'Freedom of the Town'. 21 of them were in Western Transvaal and others were in the Free State, the Eastern Transvaal and even two in Natal. Naturally, with major towns controlled by AWB sympathisers, the Western Transvaal offered the best prospects of becoming the first *Volkstaat*. What they overlooked, needless to say, was that the majority of townsfolk were black. White businessmen soon became painfully aware of it when, at the instigation of the ANC, black residents imposed consumer boycotts on white-owned businesses.

On 9 October 1993 a *Volkskongres* (People's Congress) was held at Klerksdorp. It was attended by thousands of right-wingers. All of the AWB's general staff attended, including General Nico Prinsloo. There was a parade of uniformed members through the streets, followed by the congress itself.

Conservative Party leader Ferdie Hartzenberg, was the first speaker, followed by Eugene Terre'Blanche and General Constand Viljoen. In a three-hour address, Terre'Blanche told the meeting how he and his senior officers had visited army, air force and naval institutions at the invitation of the Chief of the SADF. The unmistakable implication was that the SADF was backing the AWB. He told the crowd he would refuse to negotiate the future of a *Volkstaat*, except over 'the barrel of a gun'.

'If the government of the ANC does not grant us a free republic we will fight throughout South Africa and win the country entirely. We will pursue them to their homelands until all of South Africa is ours. Furthermore', he added, 'if we have to fight it will be foolish to pay such a high price for such a small piece of land. We will fight for the entire South Africa. We will pay with lives, it's war. This thing has broadened into a war in which we will fight. It is a war we will win . . . We want a free state. The *volk* will determine the boundaries. The war will also determine the boundaries.'

He rejected the constitutional negotiations at the World Trade Centre in Kempton Park. He spoke of the Western Transvaal as an area for the *Volkstaat*. It did not have to be seized by violence, because the majority of towns had already been given to the right-wing by the ceremonial granting of the 'freedom of the town' to the AWB, the Conservative Party and the *Afrikaner Volksfront*. Committees, he said, comprising city councillors, city secretaries, financial experts, employees of traffic departments, those running civil protection services and so forth plus members of the local army Commando have solemnly handed these areas to the *Volkstaat*. The AWB would fight to prevent anyone attempting to take back that land from the *Volkstaat*.

During December 1993 a National Party MP, Johan Steenkamp, produced a 16-page AWB war plan in Parliament. Details included the provision of mass graves for blacks and plans for the mass mobilisation of right-wing forces loyal to the AWB.

On 19 December Captain Craig Kotze, a spokesman for the Department of Law and Order, said that right-wing organisations were being monitored. Action would be taken if evidence emerged that they were committing crimes.[11]

General Constand Viljoen: Planning for war

General Viljoen described his war plans to the author as follows:

> **General Viljoen:** We were building a massive military capability. We had field organisers going throughout the country. Don't ask me how many, but they were throughout the

country. There were secret meetings, cell meetings. Let me put it quite clear about the military strategy. I was quite prepared to enter into a war if that, in my opinion, would be the only solution. I said that unless I could say to myself, my God and my people: "This is the only answer", I would not go to war. The CP and the AWB especially were mad about going to war, reacting and talking about reopening the Anglo-Boer War.

I kept saying: 'Look, you don't know what you are talking about. You don't know what war is.' I said I thought I could gather about 50 000 people. We had organised them into groups. We had all their names. We had the 'not so sure' groups, we had their names. We had realised that if you start a war like this, it can only survive if you have good support. They saw themselves as the military wing of the Afrikaner *Volksfront*. The real force was the farmers. They could have fielded about 15 000 people.

Question by the author: You know yourself, when you are talking about calling up 50 000 people, you are talking about transport, logistics, you are talking ammunition. Did you use the Commando call-up system?.

General Viljoen: I could not use the Commando system, but naturally there were people who had developed with the Commandos. I could not go to them and say I intended to use their call-up system. But naturally, many people were with the Commandos. I never had any contact with the Defence Force for the purpose of organising things. I had a lot of contacts at the time. I was absolutely convinced that I still commanded a lot of support in the Defence Force. But I did not split the Defence Force. I did not, at that stage, start undermining the Defence Force. I would never have done this, but I realised that if I started a war I would have got a lot of support from there.

Question by the author: In other words, the leadership cadres?

General Viljoen: Yes, not only the leadership, maybe complete units. We had the AWB, they were a force on their own. Then we had the farmers that we had organised country wide and they were the root of it. They were very well disciplined, most had gone through their two years national service system. Many were still part of the SADF, either with the Citizen Force or the Commandos. That's when we realised we needed heavy weapons. We did not have a single Casspir. We had light arms. Most of the farmers had rifles and things so we could produce a lightly-armed force, but we had no armour or support weapons. Some complete units could have walked over to us, but that was not organised. Our planning had two kinds of war in mind.

Military Plan A: Was more a conventional type war. The kind of war that we would use to do everything possible to get a unanimous agreement on a *Volkstaat*. Let us say the Eastern Transvaal, the northern Cape or wherever. The forces would go there and we would tell the government that unless they talk to us about making it a *Volkstaat* within the new South Africa, we will fight you.

Question by author: But you would have been flattened by the SADF?

General Viljoen: No, I don't agree. My personal feeling was that loyalty to me still existed in the SADF.

Question by author: But you must have tested the water?

General Viljoen: Of course, when I met my people, I would tell them what I had in mind. But I never went to a unit commander and said: 'Listen you have some nice Casspirs. How about letting me have some?'

Question by author: But surely you could not have been engaged in wishful thinking only? You must have had something more concrete in mind?

General Viljoen: I think my presence would have split the Defence Force. They would either have come [over] to me, or they would have abstained. 50 000 men would have posed a major threat if there had been an area for them to take. It was difficult, but we were continually looking for an area where we could use that strategy — so we could declare it as a *Volkstaat*. Now, let us say we were unanimous about declaring the Eastern Cape or the Northern Transvaal as *Volkstaats*, then we would have occupied that area. We would have declared that we wanted the area and were declaring a UDI there. We would say: 'We are prepared to fight if necessary. If you attack us, we will retaliate. But we are prepared to negotiate. So Military Plan A could have worked wonders, if we had been able to find such an area. We were also very worried whether we would be able to maintain a *Volkstaat* after it had been declared. Not militarily, but economically. If they had sealed off the area and refused to allow farmers to take their cattle or crops to the markets and cut off food and diesel supplies, it would have lasted less than two months. Meanwhile, of course, there was MK who might have exercised its own IRA option. Exercising Military Plan A would nevertheless have put us close to a solution.

Military Plan B was the IRA tactic. That's the one I really had in mind. Do you know that when the IRA was at its peak there were never more than about 300 trained terrorists in the organisation? But they could maintain a lot of pressure. I realised this and this was where I differed with the CP. This was the most viable option because if the large forces envisaged in Military Plan A had been committed, the Americans might have come to Mandela's assistance. They had made preparations in Botswana and a large contingent of marines, with all their equipment, had been secretly deployed to an air base there. With this 'Mandela factor' in mind, it would have been foolish to challenge the world. I realised it but my political masters [the CP] could not grasp it. I said I would make the going to war decision, because I would carry the responsibility and not them.

The second option could have been exercised not only during but after the election. The idea was to apply pressure to get what we wanted. That is the purpose of a war.

I was visited once by [Police Commissioner] Van der Merwe and [Security Branch commander] General Basie Smit. They told me they had a lot of information regarding AVF activities and they hoped I would not force them to move against me. That is why I dealt with only a limited number of people when making plans. It was because of leaks. Cells were completely independent. The organisers would come and report back to me.

I dared not open my military planning to the AWB. My greatest problem was to get planning done for the farmers without letting the AWB know what was going on. I was in a very difficult situation. There was no unity in our military plans.[12]

The killing fields: Ridora Crossing: 12 December 1993

Orders, allegedly emanating from Eugene Terre'Blanche, were passed to Chief Commandant Phil Kloppers of Randfontein. The AWB should prepare for war. They were to arm themselves, even if it meant stealing the weapons. They would allow the election to take place on 27 April. Kloppers said: 'I received an order that the revolution will start that night [12 December]. Our duty was to sow chaos in the urban areas. All the men understood what I meant by the "real McCoy" because General Oelofse wanted to see corpses. Our target group was the ANC-SACP alliance.'[13] The revolution was scheduled to commence countrywide that night.

Kloppers ordered his group to assemble at Uncle Harry's Café — a Randfontein road house. On Commandant Martin's instructions Badenhorst collected Assistant Commandant Visser from his girlfriend's house and passed on Martin's orders. They went first went to Badenhorst's house where Visser kept his uniform.

The group, mostly dressed in the AWB's camouflaged uniforms, assembled at the roadhouse. Those present were Commandant Deon Martin, Assistant Commandants Martinus van der Schyff (25) and Andre Visser (39), Jaco Badenhorst (20), Petrus Matthews (26), Etienne Visser (23), Kallie Meiring and Gert Diedricks (34). Kloppers arrived last. Martin brought the men to attention and saluted.

Oelofse had warned them two weeks before to make preparations for the revolution. This had prompted them to hold a preliminary meeting to decide on what actions they should take when it started. Several possibilities had been discussed. One suggestion was that they 'penetrate' houses in a black squatter camp, force the occupants of shacks to lie on the floor and search them for weapons. The problem was that no one had the slightest idea how to go about it. Another idea was that they should 'clean up' a certain hotel that was being frequented by blacks. Eventually, they decided to establish a roadblock. They would stop all black-driven cars and search them for unlicensed firearms. Originally, there was a vague suggestion that they should hand confiscated unlicensed firearms to the police.

Everyone had guns except for Diedricks, Visser and Van der Schyff. Kloppers produced two homemade shotguns that Oelofse had given him. Initially he handed them to Visser and Diedricks. Van der Schyff, however, intervened and took the gun from Diedricks. He said he would show him 'how to shoot a kaffir'.

They first went to Badenhorst's house because his parents were on vacation. They had five cars altogether, but Kloppers decided they would use only two, Martin's Mercedes and Visser's Nissan Sentra. The rest would be left there. The registration numbers of the two chosen were covered with masking tape. From there they went to Andre Visser's flat where they polished off a bottle of 'First Watch' whisky to boost their courage. At Martin's smallholding, their next stop, they drank a few brandies. Martin issued them with a reflective chevron board, a blue light, yellow reflective jackets and torches.

Martin knew that what they were about to embark on was illegal. He also knew it would be necessary to use force to get people to stop their cars and hand over their weapons. The purpose of the action, he said in a moment of truth, was to stop, assault and intimidate 'kaffirs'. It was also designed as a protest against the recent killings of whites by black political groups. His role, he said, was purely a supervisory one.[14]

En route to the Ridora Crossing close to Randfontein on the Johannesburg to Mafikeng Road, where they had planned to establish the roadblock, they paused briefly while two of them got out and beat up a couple of black pedestrians. Matthews heard a shot and Visser shouted: 'I shot a kaffir.'

When they reached Ridora Crossing Meiring, who knew about roadblocks from his days as a traffic policeman, instructed them on their duties. He told them where to stand, where to position the reflectors and so on. The blue light, which became Visser's responsibility, was fixed to the roof of the Nissan Sentra.

Kloppers and Martin intended to drive up the road to look for targets. When they found a good prospect, they would turn around and follow it back to the roadblock and flash their car lights as a signal that it should be stopped. About four or five cars were stopped and allowed to proceed because the black occupants appeared to have no connections with the ANC or SACP. Some professed to belong to Inkatha, which the AWB regarded as an ally.

Suddenly, Kloppers flashed a signal for them to stop two approaching vehicles. Visser switched on the blue light and the cars slowed down and halted about 250m before the roadblock.

Kloppers, who had passed them and returned to the roadblock, warned them 'to be careful because people might climb out of the vehicles and get rid of things'. The cars drove slowly towards the roadblock.

The first, a Honda Ballade sedan, was occupied by three students. Theo More (25), Gabriel Shabangu (22) and Teboho Lordly Makhuza ((21) had come from Mafikeng and were en route to Springs. Seeing the blue light flashing, they assumed it was a police roadblock.

Matthews, in a camouflaged uniform, waved them down with his torch. The car stopped and pulled over. A second camouflage-clad man, probably Kloppers, pulled Theo More from the car, dragged him to the side of the road and punched and kicked him. Other whites in camouflaged uniforms and armed with pump action shotguns, ran up and joined in the beatings.

Martin forced the students to sit by the side of the road. Diedricks asked them why they had reduced speed when approaching the roadblock. He also asked them whether they belonged to the ANC.

'We were confused. We did not know what to answer. The man said we had no respect for the "bosses", because we did not answer', Gabriel Shabangu said.

They accused them of being ANC supporters and used this as an excuse to assault them with batons and gun butts.

One searched Shabangu and found a gold-plated watch and a R100 in cash which they confiscated. Some rooted around in the boot of the Ballade and stole items like a tool box, an audio cassette and various miscellaneous items. Matthews, Van der Schyff, Visser and Matthews all carried stolen property home with them.

The second car, a Toyota Cressida was driven by William Segotsane. His passengers were brothers Petrus and Abram Mothupi, Patrick Gasemane, Simon Nkompone and his two young children. They dragged them from the car and forced them to join the students. They were also assaulted and kicked while being questioned about their membership of the ANC. Kloppers rapped those on the head who did not answer fast enough.

According to Visser Martin called a group to the chevron board and spoke to them.

'This is the target, SACP and ANC people', he said. 'This is our target to shoot at.'

When he opened fire, it would be a signal for the rest to follow suit. Visser walked to Van der Schyff where he was searching a car.

'Get your gun ready, we are going to shoot these people.'

Some said they formed themselves into a firing line, which confirms they planned to murder their victims. Martin fired first and the others joined in.

Matthews said Martin was his brother-in-law. He was frightened he would assault him if he refused to shoot. He claimed he fired six shots over the prisoners' heads.

Van der Schyff said he fired two shots into the ground, because he did not want his commandant to think he was a 'yellow belly'.

Some said they fired because they were shocked and afraid and thought the prisoners were going to attack them. The shooting was over in a few seconds. Immediately afterwards, some of the men jumped into the Nissan Sentra and drove off in the direction of Krugersdorp.

Kloppers told the rest that it was nothing to worry about.They would meet the others at the Town Hall later.

Someone shone his torch and Martin, who denied he had been a major role player, said he saw three or four dead blacks and realised they had been shot by his people.

'Take his ear!' Martin heard Kloppers say.

He drew a hunting knife from its sheath and cut off a victim's ear. He could not remember wiping the blade clean of blood on a dead man's jersey, but said he might have done.

'I'm talking about something that gives me nightmares . . . It seemed to me he was dead . . . I cannot believe I did such a thing', he said at his trial.

'What the fuck is that?' Kloppers said he asked as he got into the car. He denied he had told him to take the ear. He asked: 'Are you mad?'

Shabangu saw a white man cock the action of his shotgun and open fire. 'I saw a child fall. I fell to the ground and I covered my head with my hands. I heard more shots. The shots went on for about two minutes.' The child who fell was 13-year-old Patrick Gasemane. When he looked up, it was to see flames coming from the boot of the Honda Ballade. At the same time he saw the whites responsible leaving the scene in a Nissan Sentra and a Mercedes Benz.

He only realised that Theo More was hurt when he heard his laboured breathing. He then noticed he had been shot in the head. Teboho Makhuza was lying 'dead still'. Poor Teboho, who was due to graduate in 1994 and take up a scholarship for further engineering studies in Germany, would never do that now. 'I saw a man who looked horrible in his face. I think he had been shot in the face.' It was Thembane Nkompone. Contributing to this horrible look was the bloody gap left by the ear that Martin had slashed off.

A passenger in the Cressida had been shot in the arm and another in the leg.

Patrick half dragged and half-carried Theo into the veld. He returned to the roadside and tried to flag down passing cars to get help. No one stopped. 'I returned to Theo and put him on my lap because I thought he would be more comfortable like that, but when the police came I ran away in my blood-soaked clothes because I did not trust them. All the policemen were white — and whites had shot us.'

For Sergeant Hendrik van Heerden, a member of Randfontein Emergency Reaction Unit, it was like a war. The Honda Ballade was ablaze. Close to it were the bodies of a man and a young boy. He tried to reach them, but was beaten back by the heat. 'A tall black man appeared from the darkness. He was wounded in the face, his nose and upper lip were missing and he was bleeding badly. I thought he had been shot in the face with a heavy calibre shotgun. He told me there were more injured people. Later I saw a paramedic bandaging the head of a man with a missing right ear. He had a long cut on the side of his face and a huge hole in his shoulder.'

He checked inside the Toyota Cressida and found another wounded man and two small children. Understandably, both children were suffering from severe shock. Another three wounded men were discovered in the bush a distance from the road.[15]

Theo More and Thembane Nkompone died from their wounds in the Paardekraal Hospital in Krugersdorp. Loss of blood caused by his ear being cut off was a contributing factor in the death of Nkompone. William Segotsane, Petrus Mothupi and Abram Mothupi all had serious gunshot wounds.

Matthews said that on their return to base, Kloppers claimed that he had cut off the ear. He said it was in a plastic bag in the Mercedes and he sent Badenhorst to collect it. Matthews said he 'laughed like a pig'.

Kloppers, however, said he handed the severed ear to Oelofse at the AWB's area headquarters the next day. He reported that they had got into 'big trouble'.[16] General Oelofse's and Eugene Terre'Blanche's reactions can be judged by their subsequent behaviour. The Day of the Covenant, 16 December, held sacred by Afrikaners as the day the Voortrekkers defeated the Zulus in the Battle of Blood River. As was customary, it was celebrated by a huge gathering of Afrikaner right-wingers at the Voortrekker Monument in Pretoria.

The AWB's Ridora Group, as it became known, had achieved a famous victory. Their shooting of the 'communists' was the talk of the gathering. Dries Kriel personally congratulated Oelofse on his men's achievements. Oelofse accepted his congratulations graciously.

They were formed into an honour guard for their leader, Eugene Terre'Blanche to inspect. They were immaculately turned out and apparently rapturously acclaimed by the assembled crowd.

That moment of dubious glory, however, was short-lived. Christmas 1993 would be the last they would spend in the comfort of their homes for many years. Twenty days after the atrocity, they were arrested and charged with multiple counts of murder, attempted murder and theft. They were convicted and everyone except for Diedricks was sentenced to death. Afterwards they spent many anxious months in cells on death row in Pretoria Central Prison. Fortunately for them, moves were already in progress to abolish the death sentence. Their sentences were eventually commuted to life imprisonment.

They applied to the TRC for amnesty, but their applications failed.

Their leaders, Eugene Terre'Blanche and 'General' Japie Oelofse, stayed away from the hearings, obviously because they feared cross examination.

Disagreement at the Assembly Hotel: 16 December 1993

After prayers, celebrations and a braai at which great quantities of meat were consumed at the Voortrekker Monument on 16 December, about 30 of the AWB's senior officers left and assembled for a meeting at the Assembly Hotel in Pretoria. It was an often-used meeting place and various matters were discussed.

Dries Kriel shocked the gathering by making a proposal that the AWB's general staff should be immediately disbanded and replaced. He said they needed people with military or police experience, officers who could reorganise the para-military *Wenkommando* into an effective fighting force.

Eugene Terre'Blanche responded angrily by accusing Kriel of 'buggering up' the meeting. Everyone agreed with his sentiments.

Kriel scornfully told them that they had safety in numbers, but unless they heeded his warning and recruited professionals for its leadership, the AWB stood no chance of halting a communist takeover of South Africa.

Terre'Blanche ordered him to leave the meeting.

Kriel ceremoniously ripped off the brigadier's insignia from his khaki uniform, threw them contemptuously on the floor and stomped out. He was furious that no one was prepared to listen.

Despite this fallout with Terre'Blanche and the general staff, Kriel continued his bombing campaign. He believed it was his sacred duty to the Afrikaner *Boerevolk*. At the end of January 1994 Terre'Blanche phoned and asked Kriel to come and see him. He emphasised that while Kriel should not have acted as he did at the Assembly Hotel, he was still doing an excellent job with the bombing campaign. They resolved their differences and agreed that, as a cover for his activities, he would continue to operate outside the organisation's structures and not openly resume his rank of brigadier.

The Security Police arrested him shortly afterwards.

Kriel was later given amnesty for his bombing campaign by the TRC.

An ANC rebuff, talks and meetings: January 1994

In January the AVF suspended negotiations with the ANC after a statement by Nelson Mandela that Afrikaners should not expect self-determination in a *Volkstaat* before the general election.[17] Justifying the suspension, Dr Ferdi Hartzenberg, chairman of the AVF and CP leader, said the establishment of an Afrikaner homeland was inevitable. The Afrikaner nation would now use other methods to gain its freedom.

The AVF responded by setting up a transitional authority for Afrikaners. The authority, Dr Hartzenberg said, would seek a mandate from Afrikaners to establish a *Volkstaat*. Each region that was considered to be part of the *Volkstaat* would be represented by ten members. They would decide whether they wanted a *Volkstaat* and where its borders would be.[18]

Despite the breakdown, however, talks between General Viljoen and Thabo Mbeki continued in an effort to find a way to prove the strength of Afrikaner support for a *Volkstaat*.[19]

On 29 January General Constand Viljoen told a large AVF meeting in Pretoria that there were no simple solutions to the complex problem of demands for a *Volkstaat*. If the people wanted it before the election, they would have to 'seize it violently'.

Despite broaching the war option, Viljoen professed he was still hoping for a political settlement. Eugene Terre'Blanche, however, adopted his customary rabble-rousing mode at the meeting and insisted that the Afrikaner could not live without freedom. If necessary, it would be acquired violently.[20]

'The meeting was badly organised and emotions took over', General Viljoen told the author. 'I carried on believing that apart from the military option there was also a political solution that could be negotiated.'[21]

SADF Chief General Georg Meiring: Another rebuff

Towards the end of January 1994, the AVF requested a meeting with the recently appointed SADF Chief, General Georg Meiring. They wanted to clarify whether his attitude was sympathetic towards the right-wing. It was arranged that a meeting would take place at the SADF's Intelligence College at Observatory in Waterkloof, Pretoria. The arrangements were covert and the meeting was kept secret because of the sensitivity of the times.

AVF members including CP leader Ferdi Hartzenberg, his deputy Dr Willie Snyman, Agricultural Union leader Dries Bruwer, Advocate Jurg Prinsloo, general secretary of the AVF Joseph Chiole and Colonel Piet Uys assembled at the college. AWB leader, Eugene Terre'Blanche, was not told about the meeting and was not there.

They were met by General Meiring, an Air Force general and a general in Military Intelligence. The atmosphere was friendly. They were served with coffee and biscuits and treated hospitably. Ferdi Hartzenberg had to leave unexpectedly because something urgent came up, but the rest of them remained.

Eventually they got down to questions and answers.

Willie Snyman opened by bluntly asking the general if he was prepared to serve under a communist president like Nelson Mandela. It was clear he was expecting a positive answer.

General Meiring was furious.

'How dare you ask me a question like that?' he responded. 'I am the commander of the SADF and take orders from the president of the day.'

'What are you going to do as the Chief of the SADF? What are you going to do if we engage in armed resistance to the political process?' someone interjected.

'I will shoot you', Meiring replied.

'Do you want to tell me, general, that you will use Afrikaner soldiers against brother Afrikaners — your own people?'

'Yes', replied the general. 'The soldiers are already in place.'

Joseph Chiole said Meiring did not say specifically which soldiers were in place.

By this time there was uproar in the room.

Piet Uys recalls that someone demanded to know what units he would use.

'I will first use my English [Citizen Force] regiments.'

'And then?' another asked.

'I will use my black soldiers.'

It was clear to everyone by their attitudes that his brother general officers also supported him.[22]

General Meiring, while not mentioning this meeting in particular, told Hilton Hamman: 'In fact, since the previous year, in the process of time we had a lot of footwork going on where we tried to have discussions with the other political role players, or thought themselves to be — the General Viljoens of this world, the Ferdi Hartzenberg, the Buthelezis. Everyone had an axe to grind and was a major player in this thing and from time to time threatened to pull out and go to war. The Zulus were trying to arm themselves, the far right were trying to arm themselves, and I had to talk to a lot of them from the PAC right through to the CP at the time. I never spoke to Eugene Terre'Blanche, because he was a nonentity. But we were really very seriously trying to let the people see the wisdom of working together and not pulling out of this whole thing. We had these contingency plans at the time and I told many of them: "If you are really going to do what you say you are going to do, we'll have to stop you." I even had to say that to Constand Viljoen. He said he understood and for a long time we never discussed it. We never antagonised one another, but we were very clear in understanding what we actually meant',

Meiring said the SADF kept the lid on controlling everyone, left or right, who wanted to derail the electoral process. He made sure that everyone knew they were playing with fire. 'I warned everyone before the election: "*As julle 'n ding gaan doen gaan ons julle opvok: julle moet pasop.*" [If you're going to do something, we'll fuck you up. Watch out!] So everybody knew the success and stability was as a result of this.'

It was later said that General Meiring had also plotted a military coup, an accusation that still rankles. 'I mean, I saved the bloody country — I didn't coup it! Then they come and say I was going to instigate a coup', he told Hilton Hamman.[23]

General Viljoen, when interviewed, made no mention of this to the author. While he had not attended personally, Chiole had reported the results to him. He also had personal discussions with General Meiring. This surely should have made it clear that his Military

Plan A was no longer an option. It must also have become clear that his hopes of members of the Permanent Force flocking to the banner of a right-wing rebellion, was a pipe-dream. Maybe he could have gained some support from Commando units in rural areas and from some soldiers in the Citizen Force reserve. But what hope of success did his Military Plan A have without armour and support weapons? The rural Commandos were equipped only with R1 automatic rifles. Even 50 000 riflemen, assuming he had that many, could hardly have stood against a trained and disciplined military force equipped with armour and heavy support weapons. As the author told General Viljoen: they would have been flattened.

There is no doubt that General Viljoen had been depending on the SADF coming to his aid if the call went out. While the late General Kat Liebenberg — a former subordinate of Viljoen's and an officer with sympathies towards the right — was still the chief, he might well have got that aid. Liebenberg had retired prematurely only three months before, on the face of it because of failing health. He later developed cancer from which he died. But this was not the only factor that prompted his retirement.

On 16 November 1992 the Goldstone Commission issued a press statement about a raid it had made on Momentum Mews, an office building in Pretoria. It turned out to be the headquarters of the Directorate of Covert Collection (DCC), operating behind the facade of a front company. Files were found that indicated, as F W de Klerk put it, 'that elements in the SADF might be contravening the direct undertaking that I had given after the Inkatha-gate imbroglio that the Security Forces would no longer involve themselves in actions in favour of, or against, political parties'.

Despite this, De Klerk was not charmed by Judge Goldstone revealing what he called 'preliminary untested findings' by 'precipitate and sensational statements to the media'. Instead, he said, the judge should have submitted it to him as the State President 'after all the evidence had been properly tested and weighed'.

The Cabinet considered Goldstone's statement on 18 November. De Klerk commented: 'It was clear to me that we would have to intervene — more directly than before — to get to the bottom of allegations regarding the clandestine activities of the SADF. Even though Judge Goldstone would continue with his investigation, more was needed.'[24]

What he meant, of course, was that the last thing he needed, at that particular delicate political time, was precipitate action that would destroy the effectiveness of the Security Forces. He said as much to Judge Goldstone when the latter visited him on 20 November, to ask for further resources to investigate his discoveries. The implication is that the judge came perchance, but the most likely explanation is that he was sent for.

De Klerk explained that he had appointed Lieutenant-General Pierre Steyn, the Chief of Defence Force Staff and a 'widely respected air force officer with an impeccable record' to 'carry out an in-depth investigation into all the intelligence activities of the SADF'. 'I told him', De Klerk said 'we would have to find some way of ensuring that his investigation did not harm the bona fide activities of the Security Forces'.

They discussed the means by which the Goldstone Commission 'would, in future, liaise with General Steyn to ensure that it received any information that might be relevant to its mandate and offered to make additional resources available as and when required'.

The judge hardly needed to be a mind reader to realise he was being nudged off the case. As De Klerk said: 'Judge Goldstone agreed that his commission already had sufficient powers to carry out its mandate.' This was particularly so, as his mandate now included a sideways shift away from the investigation into Military Intelligence.

De Klerk mandated General Steyn to provide him 'with a complete and comprehensive analysis of all the SADF's intelligence activities' and to report to him as soon as possible 'on the advisability of restructuring these functions. To facilitate his task, I placed him in direct immediate command of all the intelligence functions of the SADF. I also ordered him, in conjunction with a senior police general [Lieutenant-General Alwyn Conradie], to ascertain whether any activities had taken place which might be in contravention of the law or of government policy'.[25]

On 26 November 1992, only four days later, President de Klerk called a meeting at the Union Buildings in Pretoria. It was attended by the newly appointed Minister of Defence Gene Louw, the Minister of Justice Kobie Coetsee, the Chief of the Defence Force General Kat Liebenberg, and General Steyn.

General Liebenberg was transparently discomforted over the wide-ranging powers the commission had given to his subordinate. De Klerk commented that it 'no doubt wrought havoc with the traditional SADF lines of command and authority'.

President de Klerk insisted that General Steyn's appointment was not a sham. It would involve a thorough review of Military Intelligence. 'At the same time we did not want to throw out the baby with the bath water. I said I wanted a proper division of responsibility between the intelligence activities of the SADF, NIS and SAP. I wanted Military Intelligence to get rid of any function that did not belong to it, so that I would be able to state categorically that it was no longer involved in any unacceptable activities. We had to take firm action against any of those who had been guilty of any form of misconduct. I needed an absolute assurance that the SADF's activities had been fully cleaned up. I stressed that these things had to happen — and they had to happen quickly. I had given General Steyn a hands-on instruction with direct authority over all the relevant commanders.'[26]

It was clear to President de Klerk that General Liebenberg, 'by his body language' was still unhappy and he asked if he had a problem.

Liebenberg raised procedural difficulties and called the whole thing a plot to discredit the SADF.

De Klerk replied grimly that he was 'wrestling with the image of a defence force that could evade scrutiny of the auditor-general; that had been accused of sinking the Harms Commission and of frustrating the government's attempt to gain information'.

Nothing had happened, he said. 'Hardly anyone had been disciplined.' He said that care would be taken to see the SADF's image was not damaged. But he insisted that the 'SADF should for once get its house in order'.

It would surely not be the best Christmas that President de Klerk had known. General Steyn brought him a preliminary report on 10 December. He had begun to uncover 'a veritable rat's nest of unauthorised and illegal activity within Military Intelligence'. He was also nervous and concerned that his personal safety was being placed at risk by the investigation.

President de Klerk urged him to press ahead and complete his investigations. He offered him any support he might need. He also instructed the SADF's long-time rivals, the National Intelligence Service, to provide him with any assistance necessary.

On 18 December General Steyn addressed a hurriedly called cabinet meeting in Cape Town. He briefed them from a staff report prepared by the subdivision of Counter-Intelligence. After the briefing, according to the author's information, the report was given to President de Klerk to peruse and he passed it for safekeeping to Brigadier Muller of Counter-Intelligence. President de Klerk, however, insisted that 'no written report was submitted to me, as was alleged outside Parliament'.[27]

Whatever the case, the 'Top Secret' Steyn Commission report was blunt in its findings. It divided the culprits into three categories.

A Personalities in command positions who carry albatrosses from the past around their necks that they cannot escape from. Personalities in that category are:

i General Kat Liebenberg — the SADF Chief.

His personal albatrosses, amongst other things, were the conspiracy to murder Chief Minister Lennox Sebe of Ciskei in terms of *Operation Katzen* and *Operation Dual* arising from *Operation Coast*.

ii Lieutenant-General Joffel van der Westhuizen — the Chief of Staff Intelligence.

He was responsible for the DCC and without acting against him it would be impossible to act against his subordinates.

B Commanders who could be discredited because of the manner in which they had managed their subordinates' activities:

Lieutenant-General Georg Meiring was included together with another general officer and two brigadiers — one was Brigadier 'Tolletjie' Botha, the DCC's Director.

C Officers who were following their own agendas against the interests of the State:

This concerned officers of lesser ranking whose names are irrelevant to this issue. Included were three brigadiers, five colonels and three commandants.

These individuals in all categories, the report recommended, 'should be asked to take early retirement or be forcibly retired if necessary'.[28]

President de Klerk, as he put it, was 'dumfounded'. He likened the SADF and the SAP to having inherited a savage Rottweiler and a bull terrier from a previous owner (P W Botha) who had doted on them. Despite having curbed their former free ranging habits, there were still times when they slipped their leashes and went after cats.

While the SADF's command structure generally supported the negotiation process and accepted that it ultimately fell under political control, it believed that civilian politicians 'were naïve about the true nature and intentions of the ANC/SACP alliance and that, under these circumstances, it would be irresponsible to dismantle all their covert anti-ANC capabilities . . . the initiators of the Security Forces covert projects against the ANC probably decided that the less the civilian political leadership knew of such activities, the easier it would be for them to pursue the negotiating path without being contaminated by the realities of the continuing underground struggle'.[29]

De Klerk omitted to mention that the Steyn Commission report had bluntly recommended he fire his three top military commanders — the Chief of the SADF, the Chief of the Army and the Chief of Staff Intelligence. He mentioned, though, that he had 'seriously considered the option of dismissing General Liebenberg and a few other generals in the top structures of command'.

He faced a serious dilemma. The SADF was the government's ultimate power base. Only it could provide a final guarantee for the constitutional process then under way. Anything could happen. The ANC might try to unleash mass action again, *Operation Vula* and the armed struggle could be revived, KwaZulu might try to secede and right-wingers might go into rebellion. Under such circumstances, dismantling the SADF's top command structures and replacing them with a possible vacuum — combined with a certainty of disarray — would cripple morale and reduce its effectiveness. It would be a folly to take such a risk.

He summoned Minister of Defence Gene Louw and the three top generals named in the report — General Kat Liebenberg, Lieutenant-General Georg Meiring and Lieutenant-General Joffel van der Westhuizen — to his office.

Asked to comment on the report Liebenberg said he was 'surprised and shocked and had no knowledge of such illegal activities', but agreed that immediate action was necessary to cut SADF malpractices to the root.

The services of a limited number of members, contract members (members of the SADF who had 'resigned' to work in front companies) and collaborators (sources) involved in alleged illegal and/or unauthorised activities and malpractices were disposed of. A further 16 members, including two generals and four brigadiers, were placed on compulsory retirement and another seven officers were sent on compulsory leave pending the conclusion of the investigation.[30]

General Liebenberg and General Meiring survived the purge.

'Only later when I was Chief of the SADF and got to see aspects of the Steyn Report, did I see that Kat Liebenberg and I were also named', General Meiring said.

ANTICIPATED PASSAGE SHOULD MILITANT BEHAVIOUR INCREASE

	1994	1995	1996	1997	1998	1999		
Militant Left	Conditional Acceptance	Passive Rejection	Active Rejection	Active Resistance	Active Opposition	Active Opposition	Violent Opposition	Militant Left
	SPIRIT OF NATIONAL RECONCILIATION			ELECTION				
Main Stream	EXPECTATIONS CREATED BY RDP		Economic Growth Social Contract Industrial Peace	Economic Growth Social Contract Industrial Peace	Economic Standstill Social Disillusionment Industrial Unrest	Economic Stagnation Social Unrest Industrial Unrest	Economic Shrinkage Social Collapse Industrial Unrest	Main Stream
	POLITICAL AND RACE TOLERANCE			ELECTION				
Militant Right	Passive Acceptance	Passive Rejection	Passive Rejection	Passive Rejection	Active Rejection	Active Opposition	Active Resistance	Militant Right
	1994	1995	1996	1997	1998	1999		

Military Intelligence's gloomy 'Top Secret' predictions of South Africa's future before the 1994 elections.

Doubtless the cabal of retired senior officers in the AVF — led by General Viljoen — had strongly sympathised with Generals Liebenberg and Meiring over their travails at the hands of the politicians. De Klerk said: 'General Steyn was ostracised by his former colleagues and was ejected from the inner circle of the SADF culture.' As retired senior officers whose sympathies undoubtedly lay with the SADF's old regime, they would certainly have been at one with the rest in deploring General Steyn's so-called 'disloyalty and treachery'. General Meiring said: 'Steyn did this because he wanted to become Chief of the Defence Force. He wanted to get Liebenberg and myself out of the way and figured he'd be in like Flint.'[31]

General Leibenberg, however, in spite of surviving the purge had been put on a very short leash, as can seen by his 'voluntary' retirement less than a year later. Lieutenant-General Meiring, it seems, had been cleared, or whatever he was supposed to have done had been forgiven. He was promoted to full general and designated to take over from General Liebenberg as the next SADF Chief.

It is not unreasonable to speculate that the AVF's right-wing military cabal were confident that General Meiring's sympathies lay in their direction. When they found out that he was in fact true to himself and to his oath of allegiance to South Africa, it must have come as a body blow.

This did not mean, though, that Military Intelligence as a whole had accepted that the route to real multi-party democracy as instigated by President de Klerk and as agreed during the CODESA 2 negotiations, was likely to lead to a rosy political future in South Africa. This can be seen by the 'top secret' progression chart prepared by them in January 1994 just before the election. This was after the initial publication by the ANC of its strategy regarding its 'Reconstruction and Development Programme' following a conference in January 1994.

Right-wing talk shops: February 1994

Addressing the annual congress of the National Union of Mineworkers on 9 February 1994, Nelson Mandela said the ANC had rejected Afrikaner demands for a *Volkstaat*. Such a homeland would never be granted. He added, however, that the ANC was prepared to discuss with the AVF ways to accommodate the fears of the Afrikaner.[32]

On 28 February Eugene Terre'Blanche said he had '60 000 soldiers of God' trained and ready to fight for a *Volkstaat*.[33] In retrospect it is uncertain if he was referring to the AWB alone, or whether he was also including the farmer militias of the AVF. On the same day the Pretoria *Boerekomando*, an ultra right-wing Afrikaner group led by Willem Rätte, a former officer in 32-Battalion, occupied and fortified the municipal offices at Rayton, about 30km east of Pretoria. Rätte said he had been asked by the local community to do this as 'a first step towards [the establishment of] a *Volkstaat*'. The barricades were removed by the police.[34]

In February President F W de Klerk refused to consent to a referendum to gauge Afrikaner support for a *Volkstaat*. It was after a meeting held at General Viljoen's request to discuss this issue that De Klerk said to him: 'I hope it will never be necessary for you and I to face each other over the barrel of a gun.'[35]

At about this time it was leaked to General Viljoen that the government had been making plans to round up about 5 000 right-wingers and lock them up in preventative detention centres.[36]

30

Intervention in Bophuthatswana AWB and Boere People's Army March 1994

President Lucas Mangope remained adamantly opposed to Bophuthatswana's reincorporation into South Africa. Civil servants, teachers, nurses, the police and defence force, however, were concerned that if the territory chose to go it alone, they would lose their pensions and a large part of their salaries — because 71% of its budget was subsidised by the South African taxpayer.

In January 1994 President Mangope announced he intended retrenching public servants and those found to be ANC members would be dismissed first. A meeting convened to discuss strike action was forcibly broken up by the police. There seems little doubt that by this time the ANC had infiltrated rabble rousers to stir up trouble and implement 'rolling mass action'.

In February the employees of some 52 government departments, but not the police and army, went on strike, causing a total collapse of the public service. President Mangope remained intransigent. Bophuthatswana would not be incorporated and neither would he allow its people to vote in the forthcoming election. ANC spokesman, Matthews Phosa, said militantly that if any of the independent Homelands failed to reincorporate, 'the tanks would roll in' as a last resort.

The AVF took exception to this threat by the ANC and Dr Ferdie Hartzenberg warned that if there was any attempt to reincorporate Bophuthatswana by force, it would be interpreted as a declaration of war against the CP as well.[1]

By 8 March dissatisfaction was mounting in Bophuthatswana's Security Forces. When they expressed fears for the future during meetings with President Mangope, he accused them of disloyalty and threatened to fire and replace them. It was against this background of unrest that a meeting of Bophuthatswana's National Security Council was called on Tuesday 8 March 1994. It was presided over by President Mangope and attended by its executive officer, J J L Esterhuizen — who liaised closely with South African intelligence services; Police Commissioner, General Seleke; his deputy, Brigadier 'Fats' Waller; BDF chief General Jack Turner; and several cabinet ministers including Defence Minister Rowan Cronje — a former minister in Ian Smith's Rhodesian Front government.

Present by the express invitation of President Mangope was General Constand Viljoen, representing the AVF. He was there to fulfill the solemn Three Musketeer's 'one for all and all for one' promise of the Freedom Alliance. They discussed the rapidly deteriorating situation and examined a report from Bophuthatswana's Intelligence Service. It said the ANC intended bussing some 6 000 armed MK cadres to Mmabatho/Mafikeng during the weekend of 12-13 March to forcibly overthrow the government.

General Viljoen offered what he called the Boere People's Army (BPA) for deployment in a defensive capacity. They would guard key buildings and installations and keep the situation stable to free the Security Forces for more important tasks. It was obviously a wonderful opportunity to test the call up system he had been planning. It was agreed the BPA would fall under General Turner's command. Viljoen said he would discuss the matter with CP leader, Dr Ferdi Hartzenberg, and make 'a few thousand [white Afrikaner] farmers' available.

His offer, subject to the situation deteriorating, was accepted. The purpose of their involvement would be to stabilise the situation until Tuesday 15 March, when the Bophuthatswana Parliament would reconvene to make a final decision on reincorporation and whether the homeland should participate in the 27 April general election. It was made clear to General Viljoen, however, that should he be called, the invitation would not include his fellow right-wingers, the AWB. Mangope regarded them, not unreasonably, as undisciplined and militantly racist. He feared that their sudden appearance in their distinctive uniforms might well trigger a mutiny in his own armed forces. The agreement to the possible deployment of the Boere People's Army was not conveyed to black members of Bophuthatswana's Security Forces.

General Viljoen reported the results of his discussions to his colleagues in the Freedom Alliance, after which he and Dr Ferdi Hartzenberg told AWB leader Eugene Terre'Blanche that if the BPA was called in, he was under no circumstances to deploy the AWB. Terre'Blanche assured them the AWB would not interfere — an assurance he later denied, although he agreed he was asked. General Viljoen called on the Recce's retired founding commander, Colonel Jan Breytenbach and former Recce officer, Commandant Douw Steyn, to take command of the BPA.

By 10 March civil unrest had escalated and spread throughout Bophuthatswana. The administration was in a state of virtual collapse. The situation became so bad that it was decided to evacuate President Mangope by helicopter from Mmabatho to his tribal home at Motswedi.

During the afternoon a police officer, Lieutenant Lethlogile, led a peaceful march of disenchanted policemen to the South African Embassy. They called for the resignation of Police Commissioner Seleke, the reincorporation of Bophuthatswana into South Africa and the right to vote in the forthcoming election. Simultaneously, a second group of policemen mutinied and joined protesting university students who torched their Nyala mine-protected vehicle. This effectively brought police operations in the contiguous towns of Mmabatho and Mafikeng to a halt, although some police officers tried, mostly in vain, to continue with their duties.

With the removal of police restraint a rapid descent into chaos followed. Rioting mobs rampaged through the shopping complexes of Mega City in Mmabatho, Central City in Mabopane and those in Ga-Rankuwa, Temba, Makapaanstat, Itsoseng and elsewhere, looting, trashing, devastating and burning. That afternoon President Mangope instructed Rowan Cronje to ask General Viljoen to deploy his BPA. Cronje told Viljoen he had received confirmation that ANC cadres were moving into the area.

The call to arms in the white farming areas was achieved by use of the Marnet radio communications system, installed on many farms as a security measure and also used by the smaller local authorities, by telephone and by word of mouth. The call was certainly not restricted to the rural areas, because many people answered the call from the towns. Others pitched up from as far afield as the Free State and the northern Transvaal.

It was impossible for General Viljoen, or anyone else, to know who really belonged to his BPA. The word was passed around in Afrikaner circles to anybody and everybody, including members of the AWB who hijacked the call-up for their own ends. Eventually, 350 Afrikaner right-wingers responded to the BPA's call-up, while 600 to 1 000 answered the AWB's call to arms. It was arranged that the BPA would be deployed unarmed, except for sidearms and shotguns carried for personal protection while en route to Mmabatho. They would be armed and equipped there by the Botswana Defence Force (BDF) and fall under the command of and receive orders from its officers.

Eugene Terre'Blanche phoned President Mangope and offered his services the same afternoon. Mangope later said he told him he was not wanted, but despite this he suggested he phone Bophuthatswana Defence Minister, Rowan Cronje. This indicates he was still somewhat ambivalent about the AWB. Rowan Cronje denied that Terre'Blanche phoned him.

It appears that the AWB commenced its call-up on Tuesday 8 March, probably immediately following Terre'Blanche's assurances of non intervention to Viljoen and Hartzenberg. Whatever the case, two contingents of AWB — one from Zeerust and the other from Lichtenburg — converged on Mmabatho/Mafikeng and pre-empted the arrival of the BPA.

The Zeerust contingent arrived in the late afternoon of Thursday 10 March. Most wore khaki uniforms with the blood-red swastika-type insignia of the AWB. Others wore camouflage uniforms. Some brought their women along.

Mmabatho's City Secretary, Peter Waugh, said the Zeerust crowd pitched up at the Riviera Park suburb of Mafikeng where he lived. They were in sedan cars, pickup trucks, one-ton trucks and other vehicles — about 300 in all. They had come well prepared with food-packed cool boxes, rifles, shotguns, pistols, hunting rifles — some with telescopic sights — and military issue R4 and R5 carbines. A 'Commandant' with a loudhailer marshalled the vehicles into sections, directing Free Staters to their assembly point, Transvaalers to theirs and those from various towns to other points.

Peter Waugh asked what they were up to and was told President Mangope had called for them to help put down 'the uprising'. They ignored Waugh when he said they were not wanted and suggested they leave town.

They immediately embarked on a shooting spree. A convoy of cars filled with armed white men wearing khaki shot and killed at least two black women that afternoon.

At 18:00 the AWB presence was reported to an operations room in Pretoria via the South African Embassy in Mmabatho. At 21:00 an operations room was set up in the Embassy.

Throughout the evening and that night Waugh heard vehicles departing and arriving at the encampment and he assumed they were going into Mmabatho and Mafikeng. He heard sporadic shooting during the night and many people observed armed khaki-clad whites patrolling Mmabatho and Mafikeng in civilian vehicles.

Seven people, either looting at the Mega City shopping complex or fleeing from the authorities in the Mmabatho/Mafikeng area for whatever reasons, had been shot dead by the Bophuthatswana Police the previous afternoon and night. Another two burnt to death or died of smoke inhalation while looting blazing shops at Mega City.

The spirit of lawlessness that prevailed and, no doubt, the excitement of the moment, heralded a marked increase in sudden deaths in Mmabatho/Mafikeng. One man was shot and killed during an armed robbery, another was crushed beneath the wheels of a low-loader while joy-riding with friends.Three were bludgeoned or stabbed to death by unidentified assailants. The cumulative result was a proliferation of bodies in the mortuaries and an escalation in the number of casualties in hospitals and clinics suffering from gunshot wounds.

Meanwhile, the AWB's Lichtenburg contingent under the personal command of Terre'Blanche, was mustering throughout the night at Rooigrond on the Bophuthatswana-South African border, between Lichtenburg and Mafikeng.

General Jack Turner heard of this and despatched Colonel Botes and a deputation of senior officers to instruct Terre'Blanche to withdraw his men and not to enter the territory. They made it plain that the AWB was not welcome in Bophuthatswana. Terre'Blanche dismissed Botes arrogantly, refusing to take orders from a mere colonel.

Colonel Botes suggested to Terre'Blanche that he discuss the matter with General Turner personally. He escorted him and two of his 'generals' to the BDF HQ at Malopo Base. General Turner told him again that neither he nor his members were wanted or welcome. There were several BDF officers present, including a black captain and a black lieutenant.

Terre'Blanche angrily insisted that he was there by President Mangope's invitation and refused to withdraw. When contacted, presumably by phone, Lucas Mangope strenuously denied he had invited an AWB intervention. He insisted later that he would not have thought 'of touching the AWB with a barge pole'.

Sundry phone discussions, lasting several hours in all, occurred between Terre'Blanche and Defence Minister Rowan Cronje and between Cronje and General Turner. It was finally agreed that the AWB could remain, conditional on their insignias being removed from their uniforms and that they place themselves under the command of Colonel Jan Breytenbach and Commandant Douw Steyn. It was insisted that Eugene Terre'Blanche personally withdraw. It was a difficult decision for Terre'Blanche and his hot-headed general staff, who said angrily that they had left their farms and the bosom of their families to help out. Now they were 'being chased away like dogs'. Colonel Botes described their mood as ugly. He believed that if they had attempted to force the AWB from the territory a bloodbath might have resulted.

In the early hours of Friday 11 March the BPA contingent under Commandant Douw Steyn moved from Lichtenburg to Mafikeng/Mmabatho, pausing briefly at Rooigrond to allow the AWB contingent to tag on at the end of the convoy. Before moving, however, the AWB's dominee, called his people to prayer, asking that '*die Here ons moet bewaar, want dit sal van ons verwag word vandag om kaffers dood to skiet* — the Lord must protect us because today it will be expected of us to shoot kaffirs dead'.

The SAP's Internal Stability Unit had set up a checkpoint at Rooigrond and another at nearby Buhrmannsdrif, to monitor the movement of right-wingers into Bophuthatswana. Legal opinion was that Bophuthatswana was still an independent state, so they could not impede the freedom of cross-border movement, only monitor it. The BPA/AWB column of civilian cars, pickups and trucks was met at the border by BDF military vehicles which escorted them to Mmabatho.

There was another brief pause in Riviera Park to allow the AWB's Zeerust contingent to join the column. Before doing so the AWB's dominee again asked them to join him in prayer. He read a verse from the scriptures, prayed for the safety of all those present and asked for God's help in carrying out the task given to them as 'Afrikaners'. He repeated his earlier prayer that '*die Here ons moet bewaar, want dit sal van ons verwag word vandag om kaffers dood to skiet*'. Finally, he asked for forgiveness for their sins and asked God to lead them forward along the path into the future in which the existence of the Afrikaner was being threatened. This particular 'man of God' remains unidentified.

Having done with their prayers, they continued to the Mmabatho Air Force Base. Following about five minutes behind them was an SADF convoy, en route to take up a precautionary station at the South African Embassy.

At the air base 140 members of the BPA were issued with R1 rifles and ammunition and deployed to guard key points like Mega City, the post office and so on. Their deployment at Mega City, although there was no shooting by them, effectively curbed the looting.

Colonel Breytenbach arrived at the Air Force Base at 10:00 and took command. General Viljoen had instructed him to get the AWB out of Bophuthatswana as soon as possible. Despite their earlier agreement they had refused to remove their insignia, or place themselves under the command of Jan Breytenbach and Douw Steyn. Breytenbach forcibly told AWB 'Generals' Cruywagen and Nick Fourie that whether they liked it or not they fell under his command, and they were all under the command of the BDF which did not want them. He criticised their lack of discipline. They would be withdrawn and guided out by routes that avoided built-up areas to avert a confrontation with the local population. They could certainly not leave by the direct route via Mafikeng.

'Generals' Cruywagen and Fourie refused to comply, mustered their men and abandoned the discussions in a huff. It would cost Fourie his life. As the morning progressed, the AWB drifted away from the Air Force Base, some in dribs and drabs and some in convoys, all intent on making their way home. They refused escorts to guide them out the 'back way' and deliberately and provocatively chose to leave via the main streets of Mmabatho and Mafikeng.

General Turner, meanwhile, saw President Mangope at 10:00. Mangope had heard of the shootings of blacks by the AWB and said the Security Forces must eject them from the territory. The Boere People's Army, however, could remain. General Turner remonstrated with him, saying that the general public and the army resented the presence of *all* right-wingers and wanted them out.

He suggested they call in the SADF who were ready, willing and waiting at the South African Embassy for the order to deploy. President Mangope appeared to agree, but while they were talking, Dr Ferdi Hartzenberg arrived. He told Mangope that under no circumstances should he allow the SADF to intervene. If he did, they would probably topple his regime which would spell the end of Bophuthatswana. He persuaded Mangope to keep them out. Hartzenberg clearly realised that if the territory was re-incorporated into South Africa, it would spell the end of his dream of an Afrikaner *Volkstaat*. If none of the black tribes remained with homelands, there would be no justification for the 'white tribe' to get one. It was a decision that would substantially increase the butcher's bill in Bophuthatswana during the coming hours.

At 11:00 Lawrence Seupe (26), a medical technologist at Bophelong Hospital, and a colleague, Johannes Mokoma, were standing on the corner of Voortrekker Road and Shippard Street, Mafikeng. They paused at the Total service station on the north-east corner of the intersection to greet a friend, Ernest Lekhobe.

A convoy of open pickup trucks and lorries approached along Voortrekker Road. They were packed with whites, some standing and some sitting. Most were dressed in khaki, with AWB badges on their sleeves. Some were armed with rifles and others had pistols. A few vehicles turned towards Zeerust, but the majority continued towards Lichtenburg.

Without provocation, an AWB member in a Mazda Drifter stood up and opened fire on the five or so people at the service station. Others joined in. Ernest Lekhobe was shot in the ankle. Lawrence Seupe took cover behind a petrol pump, but was shot in the leg. Johannes Mokoma checked his condition, then ducked into cover at the back of the garage. Lawrence Seupe died later from his wounds.

Some time after 12:00, Joel Mokaleng (25) and his cousin Thulo hitched a lift on a pickup in Mmabatho to go to Mafikeng and buy milk. BDF soldiers at a bridge were stopping people from entering Mafikeng, including a group of between 80 and 200 marchers. Thulo alighted from the pickup to urinate against a tree, leaving Joel standing in the back. He saw a convoy of 12 or more pickups loaded with khaki-clad AWBs armed with rifles, appear from the direction of Mmabatho.

When they were 200 to 300m from the roadblock, they opened a general fire on blacks in the vicinity. Joel was shot in the chest from a range of about 100m and died on the spot. Thulo fled for his life, while the shooting continued behind him. He could not say if the soldiers returned the fire of the AWBs.

Anna Nakedi (50) was standing opposite her house in Kgotleng Street. Her niece Sophia Mogale was nearby. At about 12:45 a green truck, either a police or an army vehicle, drove along the road, its uniformed occupants warning people to go indoors. They were fighting 'the Boers' who were 'killing people with guns'. No one took much notice — if anything it aroused their curiosity.

At 13:00 a young boy ran up to Sophia.

'The AWB are coming!' he called in alarm.

She retreated into her aunt's yard from where she saw two pickups, one a beige/yellow Isuzu and the other a red Toyota Land-Cruiser, coming down the street. They were crewed by white AWBs armed with rifles and pistols, wearing balaclavas and dressed in khaki. They began to fire indiscriminately at black pedestrians. People scattered in panic, leaving a young boy on the ground with a gunshot wound to his leg.

The Land-Cruiser swung towards Anna Nakedi and an AWB blasted her with his shotgun. She died of multiple pellet wounds in her breasts, thighs and legs. Sophia ran across the road to aid her but it was a fruitless effort. The whites swore and tracked her with their guns, but did not open fire. A crowd of marchers were farther up the road and the boy who had alerted Sophia ran to warn them. They scattered into the National Development Corporation industrial area.

Thapelo Motsumi, a coloured who was almost white in appearance, had just finished loading cabinets on to a truck at the *Furncraft* factory. His employer, Abraham Davids, was already in the driver's seat. Motsumi opened the front gate for him to leave.

'Here come the AWBs!' someone shouted.

Two pickups drove past and Motsumi ran for his life pursued by a hail of bullets. He was shot in his left arm and a second round lodged in his back near his spine. He crawled agonisingly into a nearby room where women were sewing. The AWBs fired into the room, but fortunately did not hit anyone.

Abraham Davids, meanwhile, panicked, lost control of his vehicle and knocked down a black worker. A bearded white man with a hunting rifle, one of five or six aboard a pickup, jumped down and ran over to Davids' vehicle. He pointed his rifle at the accident victim. 'Let me finish him off', he demanded in Afrikaans.

'Why are you shooting my workers?' Davids demanded.

The bearded AWB swung the barrel of his rifle towards him. Davids saw by his expression he was about to kill him. He was certain his last moment had come. His proximity to death focussed his thoughts and Abraham Davids knew that if he survived he would never forget that bearded face. Something caused the thug to change his mind. He hesitated briefly, then lowered his rifle and returned to his companions.

'*Kom*', he said, '*laat ons die ander Kaffertjies gaan skiet* — Come, let's go and shoot the other little kaffirs.'

They drove off, firing on people at a nearby filling station. They were behaving, Davids said, as if they were on a hunting trip.

Constance Kutoane and Sylvia Leinana (32) were walking from Mmabatho to Mafikeng when a police vehicle sped past broadcasting a warning on its public address system.

'People, run into your houses . . . the *Boere* of Terre'Blanche are coming from Mmabatho and are shooting.'

Constance, Sylvia and others scattered into a nearby village to seek cover. As they did they saw vehicles crewed by white AWBs pursuing them. They tried to seek refuge in a large brick house, but the occupants had locked the door, so they ran into an adjacent mud and thatch house. Shots were fired outside, but the shooting soon ceased.

'I want to see the boys of Terre'Blanche', Sylvia said peeping through the door. 'There they are!' she said and ran outside.

Constance followed and they looked towards the Vryburg-Mafikeng Road. Police and soldiers in armoured vehicles, probably Casspirs and Mambas, were fighting a pitched battle with AWBs. It was a firefight in which both sides gave as good as they got. Sylvia cried out and dropped dead, a bullet in her back. It could only have been fired by the AWB, because they were behind her and the police were in front.

Leinie Moeng (32), another who was unfortunate to be in the area, was also shot dead at about 13:00 as she ran for cover in a hostel.

Lieutenant Dikobe and Lance Corporal de Koker were part of a BDF section supported by police travelling in Mamba infantry fighting vehicles. They had been told by radio that a large crowd was congregating at the TPA building and had been ordered to prevent them entering Mafikeng in case they ran amok. Lieutenant Dikobe addressed them over the loud hailer, but they failed to disperse.

There was distant sporadic gunfire and a convoy of eight or ten civilian vehicles — pickups, Combis and motor cars with headlights blazing — appeared from the direction of Mmabatho and headed towards them. They were packed with armed khaki-clad whites wearing AWB insignia.

The crowd began to stone the vehicles, but the distance was too great to be effective. The AWB fired in reply, shooting not only at the crowd but at the soldiers as well. Lieutenant Dikobe, Lance Corporal de Koker and others returned fire. De Koker and two privates left their Mambas to assist two wounded civilians. One had been seriously wounded in the back and the other in the thigh.

An old blue Mercedes sedan in the convoy came to a halt at a four-way stop after it was hit by several shots. The rest of the convoy continued without it. The driver, a big bearded man — later identified as Alwyn Wolfaardt — alighted with his hands up.

'Don't shoot!' he yelled.

A soldier ordered him to lie on the ground on the passenger side of the car.

When Lance Corporal de Koker, who was still helping the wounded, next paid attention he saw a second white man — later identified as Jacob Stephanus Uys — propped against the left rear wheel. A third man, AWB General Nic Fourie, was in the front passenger seat with his head on the dash and clutching a chest wound. He soon joined the rest on the ground.

Police Sergeant Mokgoko ordered his subordinates to search them and the Mercedes for firearms. They seized two pistols, a shotgun and ammunition. Sergeant Mokgoko asked them what they wanted in Mmabatho and where they came from. Uys said evasively that they came from different places. Wolfaardt volunteered that he came from Naboomspruit. They said their officers had sent them to Mmabatho, but they had not been told what their duties were.

Sergeant Mokgoko handed control of the scene to a BDF officer and returned to his office in the TPA building where he secured the exhibits, then returned to the scene.

Colonel Marx of the BDF appeared briefly, but left to call an ambulance. There were reporters around, some photographing and videoing the scene.

Alwyn Wolfaardt appealed continually for someone to render first aid to Uys, because he was badly injured.

When Sergeant Mokgoko returned, he was in time to intercept Constable Gaobepe, who was unarmed, from approaching the three AWB men. He threatened to 'kill those Boers' and told them that if he felt like it 'he could do away with them in a second'. Sergeant Mokgoko felt certain that if the constable had been armed he would have shot them. He restrained Gaobepe and led him away from the cluster of reporters to calm him down.

'We are leaving people who have been killing our people. Now who are the people who are going to protect our people?' he asked.

Twenty minutes later an unarmed police sergeant and Constable Ontlametse Menyatsoea, who was armed with a rifle, appeared. Constable Menyatsoea was upset and aggressive. He shouted that the white men did not deserve to live because they had killed people, even children.

'What are you doing here? What does the AWB want in Mmabatho?' he demanded.

The crowd chanted: 'Kill them, man! Kill them, man!'

Constable Menyatsoea raised his rifle and shot Fourie in the head and neck. The sergeant tried to stop him, but Constable Menyatsoea swung his rifle and he backed off. He then calmly shot Uys in the chest and face and Wolfaardt in the back of his head. All three died on the spot.

Meanwhile, the black soldiers of the BDF who, unwisely, had been given no advance warning of the BPA's planned deployment by their political and military leaders, were incensed. Mmabatho was in flames, looting was rampant and many black people were dead. There was a dearth of precise information, so it was understandable that they laid the blame for most of the deaths and the mayhem in general on Terre'Blanche and his AWB. Lumping the Boere People's Army in with the AWB was not difficult. For the most part they wore khaki, drove civilian cars, pickups and trucks and spoke Afrikaans. As far as they were concerned, they were one and the same.

A deputation of about 400 angry BDF troops, which included platoon and unit commanders as well as private soldiers, asked their white officers what the AWB was doing at the Air Force Base. The AWB had fired on their homes and families and were still roaming around. If the answers given were unsatisfactory, they would attack the base and wipe them out.

General Turner's second in command, Brigadier Jordaan, passed word to Colonel Breytenbach to withdraw his BPA from guard duties forthwith. He complied, mustered his men and told them their assistance to the BDF had ceased. Furthermore, a confrontation was looming and they did not have the weapons to deal with it. They only had 140 R4 rifles, a sprinkling of shotguns and a single 20mm machine-gun they had removed from an aircraft to defend themselves against attack. If an attack did come it would likely be spearheaded by Casspirs and Mambas fitted with heavy weapons. So Brentenbach confined his men to the Air Force Base, saying that if the threat became imminent, Colonel Swart of the BDF had promised to escort them from the area with one of his units. In the meantime they should prepare to defend the base against possible attack.

Shootings of blacks by the AWB continued as elements continued their leisurely withdrawal from Mmabatho and Mafikeng. It is difficult to preclude the thought that some of them perhaps delayed their departure just to get the opportunity to shoot a few more blacks.

Lebogang Brown Manyeneng was being driven by his foreman from their place of employment in Ottosdal to Mafikeng. He was due to be dropped off at the taxi rank by the railway station. They could hear shooting in town, although not from near the railway station, so the foreman offered to drive him to his home. Lebogang, however, declined because he had shopping to do. His body, with multiple gunshot wounds, was found in the mortuary the next day.

Between 15:00 and 16:00 Joseph Mokgosana (24) was walking in Station Road, Mafikeng, with his friends, Eliot Tlalang and Bridgley Motshabi. A red Toyota Hilux with two whites in front roared up as they walked into an alleyway. The front seat passenger opened random fire with a pistol at any black people around. Eliot ran in one direction and Joseph and Bridgley in another. Joseph was shot three times and died instantly. His body, together with the bodies of four unidentified men, was found later near the Wanda Furniture Shop.

Oarabele Joseph Mokgosana was another who died in Station Road after he was shot by an unidentified white man in a red Toyota pickup.

At about 16:00 Petrus Saul (33) was in the front passenger seat of a Nissan Combi taxi as it entered Mafikeng via Shippard Street. The driver, Petrus Mathola, noticed three vehicles travelling from the opposite direction with white people pointing rifles and pistols through the windows. His windscreen shattered and Petrus Saul slumped against him, a fatal wound in his chest.

At 16:30 Gaobolel Isaac Mokgalapa and other workers were being transported by a company Combi to their homes in Mafikeng. At a four-way stop in Shippard Street, an unidentified assailant fired three shots. One penetrated the windscreen, wounding Benjamin Gopane and killing Mokgalapa.

Wilhelmina Nnunu Kgwadinyane was another who died from a shot in the head in central Mafikeng.

The AWB did not escape unscathed. AWB Generals Alex Cruywagen and Roelf Jordaan maintained that in addition to Fourie, Uys and Wolfaardt being killed, other members were wounded by elements of the BDF who ambushed them as they left town. The bakkie carrying three AWB generals, Ferris Munro, Nico Prinsloo and Mossie Mostert, was near-missed by a 40mm projectile.They and one other man ended up with shrapnel wounds. Eugene Terre'Blanche was nowhere around. He had tucked himself away in the safety of a rear base well away from Mmabatho/Mafekeng. He had probably concluded that as he 'belonged to the *volk*', it would be prudent to look after their interests and keep his substantial rear end well away from the firing line.[2]

Mac Maharaj (ANC) and Fanie van der Merwe (NP), Joint Executive Secretaries of the Transitional Executive Council (TEC), were mandated to fly to Mmabatho to assess the situation. At 15:00 they met SADF Chief General Georg Meiring, SAP Commissioner General Johan van der Merwe, Foreign Affairs Director Rusty Evans, General Turner and Brigadier Jordaan at the South African Embassy. General Turner described the situation as desperate. The Bophuthatswana Police had lost control, the BDF was verging on mutiny, the government administration had collapsed and law and order had ceased to exist. He wanted the SADF to step in to restore order, but he had to clear it with President Mangope first.

General Meiring was willing to deploy troops immediately, clearance or no clearance, but Mac Maharaj felt that he and Fanie van der Merwe should report back to President de Klerk and Nelson Mandela first to get a mandate before pursuing any radical course of action. While they scrupulously followed the proper channels, General Turner tried unsuccessfully to contact President Mangope. How hard he tried is a matter for conjecture.

Then, in his capacity as BDF Chief, and acting in accordance with an Inter-State Agreement between South Africa and Bophuthatswana, Turner made a formal request to General Meiring to deploy troops to restore law and order. General Meiring immediately acceded to his request.

Colonel Breytenbach, meanwhile, had instructed Commandant Steyn to take the main body of the BPA out of the territory, leaving the remaining 90 men to guard the Air Force Base. Douw Steyn was given a map and instructed to use back routes and avoid built-up areas. They left at 16:00. At the same time Colonel Breytenbach was called to a meeting of generals at the South African Embassy. He told General Meiring he was moving his men out. The general agreed to provide troops to take over guard duties at the Air Force Base and to escort the rump of the BPA out of Bophuthatswana. With this assurance, Colonel Breytenbach returned to the Air Force Base.

Major Chris Serfontein was ordered to occupy the Air Force Base and provide the escort. He was met by Colonel Burger of the BDF, General Constand Viljoen, Colonel Jan Breytenbach, Leonard Veenendal, other AVF leaders and a group of men dressed in khaki and armed with R1 and R4 rifles. They had about 80 pickups among them.

Major Serfontein arranged for four Casspirs to take the lead, followed by the 80 pickups, with three more Casspirs as the rearguard. He refused to accept responsibility for any of their activities. The long convoy travelled from the Air Force Base as far as the Mmabatho Sun Hotel and turned right into Voortrekker Road.

Shortly afterwards the BPA element came under fire from a disused airfield. Major Serfontein thought it originated from several automatic weapons, which as tracer was used, were obviously military weapons. The BPA hurriedly debussed, took cover and returned fire. The shooting stopped after about two minutes and the men returned to their vehicles. There were three casualties. One had been wounded in the hip, another through the shoulder blades and the last, Francois van Rensburg (36), through the jaw. He died later while undergoing treatment in an SADF field hospital.

The main body of the BPA under Commandant Douw Steyn had also run into trouble. While wending their way from Bophuthatswana by back route dirt roads, an unidentified Mamba of the BDF fired on a vehicle of the Hartswater contingent and killed Francois Venter (54).

At 17:00 SADF troops under the command of Brigadier Johan Coetzee deployed from the South African Embassy to the BDF's Malopo Base. The BDF troops were paraded by their officers and told the unrest situation would be stabilised jointly by SADF and BDF troops operating together.

The disorder in the territory also stirred up a xenophobic reaction towards black foreigners, who at the best of times are not high in the popularity stakes of the Tswana people. In Mmabatho, where many government employees came from Central and West African states, the SADF intervention was in time to stop the looting of many of the expatriate's homes.

General Turner reported his actions to President Mangope, who told him in no uncertain terms what he thought of him and his decision. But it no longer mattered by then.

By Saturday 12 March, with the South African Security Forces in firm control, Bophuthatswana began to awaken from its two-day nightmare of civil unrest. In addition to the dead about 200 to 250 people in the Mmabatho/Mafikeng area had suffered gunshot wounds of which no detailed records were kept. The AWB were responsible for many of them.

In the other ink spots of land that made up Bophuthatswana on the map of South Africa another 49 black people had died in the uprising and many more wounded. No intrusion of white right-wingers had taken place in those areas. Most of the casualties were looters who had been shot by the police or by security guards.

Eugene Terre'Blanche's vainglorious view of the AWB's murderous incursion into Bophuthatswana became crystal clear when he was interviewed on the SABC's *Agenda* programme. There he called it a '*skitterende oorwinning*' — a brilliant victory . . . '*en die uitslag van die aanval is presies dit — 11 ongevalle aan die kant van die AWB waarvan vyf dood is en aan die anderkant 50 dood en 295 gewond*' — and the result of the attack is precisely this — 11 casualties on the side of the AWB of which five are dead and on the other side 50 dead and 295 wounded. He even claimed the casualties of General Viljoen's equally chastened Boere People's Army as his own.

Willem Rätte, the ex-32-Battalion major, made another futile demonstration of Afrikaner right-wing unity on 13 March when he and members of his Pretoria *Boerekommando* made a token occupation of the old Wonderboom Fort at Pretoria. Rätte called it a protest against the neglect of the cultural and military heritage of the Afrikaner, the slow progress of establishing a *Volkstaat* and against the 'barbaric slaughter' of the AWB in Mmabatho. No one took much notice.[3]

As President F W de Klerk said about the Bophuhatswana episode: 'If General Viljoen's operation had not been sabotaged by the precipitate action of the AWB and if he had been able to reestablish order in Bophuthatswana at the invitation of a government to which we still gave legal recognition, we would have been confronted with a very serious situation.Under such circumstances would we have been prepared to send the SADF in to seize control of the country? And would they have been prepared to fire on their former comrades and their former commander?'[4]

The answer to that was probably 'yes'.

Whatever else the Bophuthatswana episode might have been, it was a historic moment. For right or for wrong it was the last ride of South Africa's Boer Commandos. It was not yet, however, the AWB's final fling.

End of the Afrikaner Volksfront: Birth of the Freedom Front

It should surprise no one that the Tebbutt Commission of Inquiry into the Bophuthatswana troubles found that Eugene Terre'Blanche and AWB 'Generals' Cruywagen, Jordaan, Etsebeth, Nico Prinsloo and Andries Terre'Blanche, based on the legal principles of common purpose, conspiracy or incitement, had *prima facie* cases to answer arising from the murder of innocent civilians. Despite this finding, no prosecutions have resulted.

The finger of connection with atrocities was not pointed at the Boere People's Army. Judge Tebbutt said they had remained under discipline the whole time. Nevertheless, the Commission found that 'a large measure of responsibility' for what happened on 10-11 March 1994 rested with the '*Afrikaner Volksfront* and on its leaders Dr Ferdi Hartzenberg and General Viljoen.'

On the evening of Saturday 12 March 1994 South African Ambassador Tjaart van der Walt phoned President Lucas Mangope at his lavish country retreat at Motswedi near Zeerust.

'Will you receive Foreign Minister Pik Botha?'

President Mangope answered that he would. This was so far, so good, but how would he react when he discovered Botha's mission was to depose him? Intelligence suggested that a 100-strong force of supposedly loyal BDF troops was guarding him. Precautions were put in place to ensure the tables were not turned and Botha and those with him taken hostage. It was impossible to predict the mood or intentions of the BDF troops.

At 20:30 three Puma helicopters took off from the South African Embassy at Mmabatho. One carried a delegation led by Foreign Minister Pik Botha and including TEC executive members Mac Maharaj and Fanie van der Merwe, General Georg Meiring and others. They were escorted by a unit of 'fighting soldiers', probably Special Forces operators. They were ready to deal with (the unlikely situation where) a loyal praetorian guard of the BDF was getting ready to fight to the death in defence of their leader. The helicopters were blacked out, just in case, for a helicopter makes a prime target for an RPG-7 rocket.

The troop-carrying Puma swooped down and landed. The troops deplaned, deployed and secured the area. It was an anticlimax, because there was no one to oppose them. The chopper with the VIPs aboard landed shortly afterwards. It was followed by the third Puma, probably a gunship with more troops.

They must have felt more than a little sheepish when they were graciously met by a reception committee of President Mangope (in safari suit and slippers), his wife Rosemary (attractive in a dress), his son Kwena (wearing shorts and sandals) and his son Eddie, head of the Bophuthatswana Broadcasting Corporation.

Pik Botha expressed appreciation for Mangope's willingness to receive them. Then, as Roland Darroll described it, Botha began to intone the last rights. The president was unwilling to comply with the requirements for a free and fair election, Botha remarked Many people had died or were wounded and property damage was widespread. Although still president, Mangope was no longer in control, so the time had come to restore law and order. Accordingly, Botha said, it was his painful duty to inform him that South Africa no longer recognised his government, so he could no longer continue as its head. The territory's administration was being placed under the control of Ambassador van der Walt forthwith.

President Mangope responded, his eyes moist, his hands trembling and a tremor in his voice. 'I have done nothing unlawful', he said. 'I have followed the constitution to the letter.' He asked for time until his Parliament met on Tuesday 15 March. He promised that on his recommendation, it would then satisfy all the election requirements. Time, however, had run out for both himself and for Bophuthatswana.[5]

Dr Ferdi Hartzenberg had been proved correct in his earlier assessment that calling in the SADF would spell the end of the territory.[6] His CP executive, by a vote of 73 to 20, reinforced its dogged determination not to take part in the election.

General Constand Viljoen experienced a last minute change of heart after the inglorious eviction of the AVF's Boere People's Army from Mmabatho. He resigned as head of the AVF's directorate of generals to become the leader of a new party — the Freedom Front — which *would* take part in the election. Exactly 20 minutes before the deadline for the registration of political parties for the poll, his party, drawing into its ranks Afrikaner right-wingers of all persuasions, handed in a provisional list of candidates to the electoral authorities, with a promise to flesh it out later. Its platform remained the creation of a *Volkstaat* and self determination for the Afrikaner people. It would be achieved, he said, by negotiation and constitutional means.[7]

The move spelt the end of the *Afrikaner Volksfront*. It also savaged the CP's membership, as many notables switched allegiance to Viljoen, including eight of its 11-person provincial executive in Natal.[8]

General Viljoen said conflict between himself and the leadership of the AVF had reached a stage where there was no easy solution to their differences. He was no longer 'politically acceptable' in the AVF and 'maybe it is time that we rather accept the facts'. He strongly criticised the undisciplined and uninvited intervention in Bophuthatswana of the AWB, whom he accused of leaving him in the lurch. Turning his attention to the ANC and the National Party, he declared in rather Churchillian fashion: 'I will fight them on the beaches. I will fight them on the plains.' He made no mention of the particular beaches and plains he had in mind.

An AWB spokesman called General Viljoen 'a political Judas goat sent by the Broederbond/ANC/NP/Communist Party alliance to lead us to the slaughter'.[9] He also criticised General Viljoen's handling of the Bophuthatswana situation and said the AWB had lost confidence in him.[10]

Judge Tebbutt in his report called the events in Bophuthatswana a watershed in the political history of South Africa. 'The resistance of the black armed forces to the *Afrikaner Volksfront* [BPA] and the AWB, resulting in the deaths of some of the members of those organisations, brought with it a realisation on the part of the right-wing organisations that an ill-equipped, in terms of military equipment, largely untrained minority of civilians without proper arms and armoured vehicles, cannot hope to succeed in an armed confrontation with a well-equipped, well-trained and disciplined army of professional soldiers. It also brought with it the realisation that assaults upon and the killing of blacks will result in retaliation with, in many instances, fatal results. Those realisations led to the cessation of the militant activities and the demise of the militant right-wing elements in the South African political milieu.'[11]

In finality, Judge Tebbutt was correct in his assessment although he only submitted his report in late 1994. The right-wing forces withdrew from Bophuthatswana in March 1994, but the right-wing game would not be finally played out until the end of April, more than a month later.

31

On the brink of Civil War
April 1994

AWB meeting: at Trim Park Ventersdorp: 2 April 1994

An AWB meeting was held at the Trim Park (the local caravan park) in Venterdorp on 2 April 1994. The first part was open to the general public and covered by the media in general and by television in particular.

The AWB's chaplain-general opened with a prayer with an undertone of war. 'You and I must remember we got this country by means of the vow . . . This is the country our predecessors, our descendants, left to us . . . I want to say . . . that God has given us this country already. You and I must occupy and conserve that which God has given us, even though the world says whatever it says. We must remain thankful that I should never have to report to Mandela or De Klerk. You and I will answer to God and answer His question: "What did you do to the property that I gave you?"'

Manie Maritz followed and explained how God had helped the Afrikaners at Blood River. 'I am a white man and proud to be white. I have nothing against the black man, but he is not my neighbour, he is not a member of my *volk*. That is why I say to my people that we should take each other by the hand as well as those who will fight with us.' He ended with: 'I want to say to you that the revolution is to hand. Let us begin it.'

Eugene Terre'Blanche came next with a rambling tirade in which he claimed victory for the AWB during the Bophuthatswana invasion fiasco. He spoke critically of General Constand Viljoen for his role in getting the AWB to withdraw. He called his murderous rabble who had taken part 'proud soldiers, men of courage and determination. There was never any retreat, cowardice or lack of order. There was always discipline . . . they deserve the admiration of the world.'

He said most members of the Permanent Force of the SADF supported the right wing. Of those and the '250 000 members of the Commandos and the Citizen Force' at least 180 000 were right wingers. The South African Police, he said, was 80% right wing. If these were added to the 65 000 AWB members, 'then we are prepared.'

He said the whites were in the minority, but they had the most soldiers. MK, on the other hand, represented 28 million people, but they only had a mere 7 000 soldiers. 'Next month this time we will have become part of a new state . . . or we will have our *Volkstaat*, no matter how big or how small . . . I have told you that I will never accept an ANC government. Since then I have never changed my mind . . . when we ultimately obtain a much bigger *Volkstaat* than Mandela had ever planned for us. I promise you that when we have won the war, Mandela will ask us for land. Then we will decide whether or not we could do away with a centimetre or two.' The AWB would negotiate only over the barrel of a gun. He would not vote in the forthcoming election and would ensure it was completely disrupted.

The meeting became a closed one and the journalists were told to leave.

The AWB members were divided into groups responsible for communications, medical and so on, allowing the generals and commanders to sort out and check their equipment to see that it was in order.

Chris van der Heever, an AWB fighting general (a former army staff sergeant), was in charge of the AWB's Special Forces and responsible for medical equipment and supplies. He was also the commander of the AWB's Witwatersrand command and professed to have good channels of communication with the SADF. He maintained he could get whatever equipment was needed through those channels.

He had supposedly arranged to obtain Ratel armoured cars from the infantry base near Zeerust. The AWB foot soldiers had no reason to disbelieve this, because Eugene Terre'Blanche had often spoken about his close relationship with the SADF.[1]

A map of the old Boer republics — Northern Natal, the Free State and the Transvaal — had been drawn up and displayed as the future *Volkstaats*. The Western Transvaal (North-West Province) was proposed as the first *Volkstaat*. The maps had been drawn up by General Nico Prinsloo and were discussed at the meeting. Prinsloo said he had drawn the borders using information supplied by the military and the 'SAP's special information'.

It was generally accepted at the meeting that the revolution would quickly spread throughout the country — and that the *Volkstaat* would soon be the whole of South Africa and not just a small piece of land.

Terre'Blanche made it clear that the AWB was preparing for war. It was just around the corner and members would soon be getting their call-up instructions.

'General' van den Heever spoke to a group of officers after the closed meeting and told them that the move to the Western Transvaal would probably take place on 15 April. He reiterated that no one should worry as they would be well supported by the SADF and the police. At least 40 000 members of the AWB would be moving to the new *Volkstaat*. They should bring their caravans, tents, power generators and anything else they might need to establish themselves in the state.

If they were short of money en route, they could engage in 'affirmative shopping'. They could buy whatever goods they needed, or fill their cars with petrol, then refuse to pay. If that caused problems, they could 'shoot their way through or out of the situation'. Once in the *Volkstaat*, no one would be able to touch them. It is unknown if anyone took advantage of this suggestion, but several people amongst them expressed a rooted objection to the idea of stealing.

Meanwhile, a war hysteria was sweeping a large section of the white population. People were digging cellars under their houses to use as shelters and stocking up on *oorlogkos* (war food). By mid April most of the larger chain stores had sold out of things like corned beef, baked beans, candles and so on.

This hysteria was fanned by a flood of leaflets, originating from right-wing Christian organisations, that were mailed, faxed or slipped under doors. Extracts from one such leaflet read as follows:

> Make sure you have all your medical supplies. People on permanent medication to ensure they have sufficient supplies on hand for at least three weeks — one week prior to the election, two post the election.
>
> Stock up on non perishable goods, i.e, tinned foods. There will definitely be no milk and bread deliveries. Candles, oil for lamps, gas etc. Milk powder recommended. Run deepfreeze stocks down as power failures are a certainty.
>
> Because of the above, Hyperamas, Spars etc. are doing the same — also because of looting like happened in Bophuthatswana. Check with your local store.
>
> Petrol — fill up on Friday before the election. Confirmed by Engen etc. that their trucks will not deliver because of the risks. Garage stocks will be low and some will close.
>
> Confirm with your doctor whether he will be available during this time. Doctors will probably laugh at this question, but they will probably be the first to close their rooms at the first hint of trouble. Record telephone numbers of local paramedics.
>
> Banks — ensure sufficient funds on hand both before and after because they will close if there is any trouble.

There will definitely be roadblocks and they will be heavily manned. Beware of roadblocks with only one or two policemen or vehicles. Turn around, even if you have to travel against the traffic. The authorities have given assurances that all roadblocks will be heavily manned.

Post election — uncontrollable celebrations and retaliations will occur.

Meeting of AWB's general staff: Fyndoringtjies Nature Reserve: 16 April 1994

On 16 April 1994 a further meeting was held in the Fyndooringtjies Nature Reserve near Ventersdorp. Present were Eugene Terre'Blanche and the AWB's general staff, including Generals Kiewiet Roodt, Cruywagen, Japie Oelofse, Dirk Ackerman and his brother, Eugene's brother Andries and Nico Prinsloo, All the generals had been briefed on their tasks. They each had an area of operation and had been given maps. Everyone was behaving in a war mode. Prinsloo was allocated the area north-east of Ventersdorp, including Rustenburg. It stretched as far as the PWV (Gauteng) area. The elite *Ystergarde* (Iron Guard) was placed under his immediate command.

After consultations and discussions, Commandant-General Dirk Ackerman instructed Prinsloo to find someone in the AWB's special forces and get him to assemble a car bomb. On Sunday 24 April the bomb should be deployed and detonated in Johannesburg. He specifically wanted Johannesburg targeted. It contained the largest congregation of people (mostly blacks) likely to vote for the ANC. It was also the most international city in the country and 'the most liberal'. Ackerman said it would be the first of many bombs. Black taxi ranks, restaurants and such other similar targets would also be attacked.

He was told to go for soft targets. The NP offices in the Western Transvaal, including the offices in Ventersdorp, had already been bombed. It would have been nice to target the ANC's national offices in Shell House, but the complex was too well guarded.The purpose was to create chaos, terror and generate a psychosis of fear. They wanted the bomb to create the same effects as had occurred with the ANC's Church Street, Pretoria, bomb.

Quintessentially, the AWB wanted to send a message that it would not submit to rule by a black government, and certainly not by an ANC/SACP government. If that should happen, there would be a general uprising of the Afrikaner *Boerevolk*. They demanded self determination and the creation of a *Volkstaat*. The bombings would demonstrate that they were willing to fight and die for such a cause.

The message was aimed at the National Party government in office and the ANC/SACP, which they regarded as the government-in-waiting. They wanted to make people too frightened to vote in the forthcoming election. Tagged on to it was the hope, which the AWB still clung to, that such actions would influence the SADF into swinging its weight behind it. This was despite news just in that the Ratel armoured cars at the infantry base near Zeerust, which they had hoped to appropriate, had been moved to an unknown location. It appears likely that the SADF had heard news of the AWB's intentions through intelligence channels.

The bombing campaign, it was decided, would be followed by national and international announcements by Terre'Blanche where he would claim responsibility on behalf of the AWB. It would be coupled with a demand for the secession from South Africa of the Western Transvaal as a *Volkstaat*. It was expected that Dr Ferdie Hartzenberg and General Constand Viljoen would make announcements in support.[2]

Terre'Blanche commented that if Afrikaners did not get a *Volkstaat* by 27 April, or if the constitution was not amended to allow for one, 'then all hell will break loose and neither me nor Ferdi Hartzenberg will be able to stop that'.

The AWB issued a press statement saying it had drawn up a strategy to secure the Transvaal and the Free State as bases against a future communist government. Thousands of its members were already moving into such areas to 'ensure sufficient manpower was mustered to ward off any persecution or action' against right-wing supporters.[3]

Mustering for war: 10-23 April 1994

Some AWB members got call-up instructions as early as 10 April and moved to Ventersdorp on the 12th or 14th. This was to avoid the 'huge buildup' of traffic later, when it was anticipated everyone would set out on the mass move to the *Volkstaat*. In the event nothing remotely resembling a traffic jam was encountered by anyone, either then or later.

Another reason for the hurry was because they had been told a fax had been intercepted that revealed threats to the bodily well-being of members of the *Ystergarde*, their wives and children. They had already been told to desist from wearing badges of rank on their uniforms, because of the risk that it might make them easy targets for sharpshooters.

Major Johannes Smit of the Iron Guard lived in Vanderbijlpark. He got his call-up instructions on 19 April and was told to contact the members of his unit and move with them to the Western Transvaal. They were instructed to leave their employment, abandon their houses whether rented or otherwise, collect up all their food and weapons and bring everything with them to Ventersdorp. They were required to protect the *Volkstaat*. If the government did not accede to the demands of the Afrikaner *Boerevolk*, they were told, it would be prevented from holding the election. Smit passed on the message to the rest and personally collected some of his people and their families from Pretoria. They ultimately assembled at Commandant Abie Fourie's smallholding at Vereeniging. Fourie was the AWB commander in the Vaal Triangle. They stayed there overnight, then set off in convoy for Ventersdorp.

Etienne le Roux and his wife, for their part, decided before they set out for Ventersdorp that the *Boerevolk* had only one option left — that was to fight for its future and its survival.

People from various centres arrived at the Trim Park. Many had quit their jobs and sold everything they owned in the excitement of becoming part of the new *Volkstaat*. It was surely the promised land. Some 30 members of the Iron Guard had arrived by then. Their commander, Brigadier Leon van der Merwe, said they would be responsible for looking after the integrity of the borders of the future *Volkstaat* and seeing to the safety of farmers during the period of the forthcoming elections.

They were prepared to make war to obtain a *Volkstaat*. They would first demand that the government of the day give it to them, but if need be they would take it by force. Further instructions would be issued later. In the meanwhile it was emphasised they were now in the *Volkstaat* for good.

The Iron Guard's somewhat dramatic oath taken while a loaded gun was held to their heads was: 'If I walk ahead, follow me. If I turn around, shoot me. So help me God.' The oath was taken very seriously, despite no one so far having been taken outside and summarily shot. Nevertheless, the circumstances made it clear that by coming to Ventersdorp they had reached a point of no return. Whatever happened, there was no turning back. Besides that, with inflammatory slogans like 'Kill the Boer — Kill the farmer' being bandied around by several ANC notables at the time, many genuinely believed they were already at war with the ANC.

Leon van der Merwe assured them there would be employment aplenty in the *Volkstaat* for Iron Guard members. Commandant Abie Fourie, who had resigned from his employment of 14 years to answer the call-up, was promised a job as head of security with the Klerksdorp municipality; 20 others were also promised jobs there. It was generally accepted that Iron Guard members who participated in the struggle would become the founding members of the *Boere Afrikaner Volkstaat* Police

Other AWB groups, they were told, had mustered in the other provinces. Some no doubt did, but the suggested number of 50 000 men appears highly unlikely. If that was so, why had men from centres as far afield as the Free State and Natal mustered at Ventersdorp instead of reporting to local assembly points?

The Iron Guard personnel were moved to Kloof Barnard's farm and a camp was established. Most had brought tents or caravans. They settled in and prepared themselves, their provisions and their weapons for the 'war that was to hand'. The wives, however, were less than happy with living conditions out in the bush, especially as only a single toilet was available. A deputation of wives interrupted the war and complained, so they and the children were moved to less austere surroundings at Jan de Wet's farm at Ottosdal. From Kloof Barnard's farm the men were 'called up' for active duty and moved to a 'base' at Brigadier Leon van der Merwe's game farm.

Commandant Abie Fourie was appointed camp commandant. He ordered that rubbish and latrine pits be dug. A radio mast was erected but communications were unsatisfactory and continued to remain so. Major Smit was put in charge of guards and guarding systems. If anyone wanted to leave the farm, even temporarily, special permission had to be sought. There was a fear that planning information might be leaked by informers to the police or other intelligence agencies.

Commandant Johan du Plessis had been 'called up' up by the Iron Guard from Ficksburg in the Free State. His command in Ficksburg was about 30 men, but without exception they had refused to leave the Free State and move to Ventersdorp.

At the game farm, because of his former SADF experience, Du Plessis was placed in command of patrols and of certain operations that might take place. He had no idea what such operations were likely to entail, but thought he would probably be used to liaise with the SADF. He did have an inkling that it might include 'war deeds'. He was given the title of 'commandant operations'.

There were about 35 men of the Iron Guard there when he arrived. Most hailed from Vereeniging, Johannesburg and Pretoria, but there was a sprinkling of men from elsewhere. Their numbers would be considerably enhanced when about 40 'Natalers' joined them on 25 April.

The ordinary rank and file AWB members found places to stay around the province. The Germiston and Boksburg groups moved to a small holiday resort at Koster. It had ceased trading years before and was dilapidated. The owner allowed the group to move in. Some suggested there were about a 1 000 or more congregated there, but it was nowhere near that many. Jan de Wet suggested that altogether there were between 200 and 400 families spread out amongst a total of seven assembly points. One was Manie Maritz's farm near Brits, another was a farm near Mooinooi and a third was the farm of Koos Hough close to Ottosdal.

Brigadier Anton van Zyl commanded the Germiston, Alberton and Johannesburg detachments of the *Wenkommando*. Unlike other commanders, he attempted to dissuade his members from going to Ventersdorp and did not answer the call-up himself. Despite this, he frequently ran supplies out to those who had gone there. Some listened to him and did not go, but others just packed up and went anyway.

Van Zyl's military experience told him that massing people in camps in the Western Transvaal prior to a proposed rebellion was suicidal. Supposing it had been suggested, encouraged and arranged by government agents within the organisation? If the government decided that such concentrations posed a threat to the security of the State, it could easily move in and decimate them. They would be completely vulnerable to air strikes by ground attack jets or by helicopter gunships — to say nothing of an assault by ground forces. Equipped as they were with handguns and pump action shotguns, they would hardly be able to offer an effective resistance either way. He thought it would have been wiser to leave those living in the urban environment in position in the towns. From there they could have engaged in a far more effective guerrilla war.

He and a few others had long before come to realise that mounting an insurrection with handguns and pump-action shotguns would be seriously futile. Some of those on the fringe of naïve Christian fundamentalism, however, saw no problem in one AWB warrior armed with a pistol effectively tackling 200 'heathen and communist' MKs armed with AKs.

They would, no doubt, have been in for a nasty surprise.

Nevertheless, the question of AWB elements arming themselves with more effective weapons had come under intense scrutiny by some members. Local police stations, where ample supplies of automatic rifles, grenades and even Casspir fighting vehicles were readily

available, had been surveyed. At Alberton, for instance, it had been discovered that one could walk into the charge office late at night and invariably find the personnel asleep.
Why the AWB had never even managed to re-arm itself with large quantities of AK47 rifles, considering the country was awash with them at the time, and they were supplying some to the IFP, remains a moot point.
Perhaps those pulling the AWB's strings were ensuring it did not happen?

General Constand Viljoen: War or peace?

General Viljoen kept his warfare and political options open right to the end. He told a press conference in November 1996 that a force of 'many thousands' had been on standby before the elections. His intention had been to seize an area by using military force, but refused to identify the area except to deny it was Bophuthatswana — the territory most journalists opted for.
The general impression is that General Viljoen had not cooperated with Terre'Blanche and the AWB since the Bophuthatswana debacle, but there appears little doubt that his chosen *Volkstaat* and Terre'Blanche's were identical — it was the Western Transvaal (North-West Province).
The author believes it likely they cooperated right up until 23 April 1994.
General Viljoen's claim that he had thousands of troops standing by, presumably for his implementation of Military Plan A, is doubted. If he had a force available, it was probably an elite and small group of experienced ex-soldiers. This is confirmed by media reports at the time which suggested there was a force of ex-Recces, former Koevoet fighters and members of 32-Battalion available to him. That would certainly have been numbered in the hundreds rather than the thousands. He might well have had many volunteers available to crowd temporarily into the *Volkstaat* to establish some sort of residential occupation status. But he would still have kept a wary eye over his shoulder at the US Marines that he believed had been flown into that Botswana base. The Americans denied that such a force existed and the author tends to go along with that.
On the political side, although President de Klerk had turned down the concept of an Afrikaner referendum in February — basically because defining an Afrikaner was fraught with impossible difficulties — Viljoen still soldiered on trying to find a way around this.
Eventually, after the formation of the Freedom Front, he and Thabo Mbeki agreed on a way to confirm 'substantial proven support' by Afrikaners. The provincial votes cast for the Freedom Front in the election would count as if it was a referendum. The votes for the party in the different polling stations would also be kept separate, so it would be possible to determine support in particular areas. This would assist with the assessment of which areas of South Africa could be developed as a national home for the Afrikaners.
When asked, Mbeki at first defined 'substantial support' as 50% plus one of the votes. He later amended this so that 35% could be regarded as substantial proven support.
It was agreed that the National Party government, the ANC as the government in waiting, and the Freedom Front would sign a tripartite agreement on Afrikaner sovereignty that would allow for the formation of a *Volkstaat* Council that would investigate the advisability of establishing a *Volkstaat*.
The accord was originally to be signed on Saturday 16 April. It was to be witnessed by two diplomatic representatives, one of them the UK High Commissioner. The German Ambassador declined to get involved. The US Ambassador, Princton Lyman, was particularly helpful during the negotiations. Suddenly the ANC came up with an excuse, so the signing was put off until Monday 18 April. Then something else happened and there was another delay until Tuesday 19th. Then it was Wednesday 20th.
On the 20th when the signing was delayed yet again, Viljoen was furious. He got the distinct impression that the ANC was being evasive so they could pull out of the agreement.
'Okay', he told US Ambassador Lyman', I am going to let the dogs go.'

As in Shakespeare: 'Cry havoc and let slip the dogs of war.'

A nod was clearly as good as a wink to Ambassador Lyman. General Viljoen has no idea whom he spoke to but within half an hour someone contacted him from the ANC and told him the accord would be signed without fail, on Saturday 23 April. Saturday came and the agreement was duly signed by Mbeki on behalf of the ANC, Viljoen on behalf of the Freedom Front and Roelf Meyer of the National Party. Viljoen was surprised that President de Klerk had not attended to personally sign such an important document for Afrikaners. His surprise turned to anger when he heard later that the President had been playing golf, a game he described in his memoirs as 'one of my favourite pastimes'. In truth De Klerk, as he made clear in his memoirs, believed the quest for a *Volkstaat* was an exercise in futility. He believed that Mandela was stringing Viljoen along and that in the end, nothing would result from the exercise. He was proven correct for nothing did come of a *Volkstaat*, even with a *Volkstaat* Council in place. The problem was basic. Where there were many Afrikaners, there were even more people of colour.

So General Viljoen called off his dogs of war, but it appears he neglected to tell Eugene Terre'Blanche — who was still crying 'Havoc!' and about to let slip his own dogs of war.

General Viljoen should sometimes ponder, perhaps, on what might have happened if his rebellion had gone ahead and if it had failed. World history is littered with instances of respected former chiefs of staff leading rebellions against established governments. Some have prevailed, but how many more have ended up being put against a wall and shot the day after it started?

War of Terre'Blanche's Volkstaat: Saturday 23 April 1994

General Prinsloo sought out Cliffie Barnard and briefed him on the general staff's requirements. He told him to select the men he needed for the operation. To Prinsloo's surprise he found that Barnard already knew there was to be a bombing mission targeting Johannesburg. Whether he had heard it from someone on the general staff, or whether Terre'Blanche had told him personally, he never found out. Barnard, he said, was one of the best trained men they had. Many believed he had been an operator with the Recces and that he had also seen service with the SAP. Most of the rank and file believed he was a colonel in the Iron Guard but were unsure. He never wore uniform, apparently because he had long hair and was reluctant to cut it. It was common knowledge that he worked closely with Eugene Terre'Blanche who held him in high regard.

Barnard went to the game farm and sought two volunteers. He needed a man familiar with Johannesburg and another who was experienced with explosives. Etienne Le Roux volunteered and said he knew Johannesburg. As far as explosives were concerned, he recommended Pieter Koekemoer who had once attended an Iron Guard training camp with him at Clocolan. Koekemoer worked as a master blaster on the mines.

Barnard, soon joined by Koper Myburgh, showed Le Roux and Koekemoer a quantity of commercial explosives and some pipe bombs in a VW Golf. On Barnard's instructions this was transferred into Le Roux's car and the four of them drove to Koesterfontein Farm. The farm belonged to Myburgh's parents. It had a house, a workshop and various storerooms. They unloaded the explosives into the workshop.

There was an old Audi there. A man called Breytenbach had given it to Barnard and told him he could use it for anything he wanted to. Barnard told the men he wanted it turned into a car bomb. Shortly afterwards a Corrie Botha and his son 'Klein' Corrie drove up with a trailer in tow. They had more explosive with them and it was unloaded and taken into the workshop. The Bothas left to join the Iron Guard at the game farm.

They looked around the farm for something to use as the bomb's foundation. Koekemoer discovered a lawn roller which showed possibilities. They cut a square hole in the top and packed it with commercial high explosives. There was insufficient to fill it, so it was supplemented with low explosive contrived from a mixture of ammonium nitrate fertiliser and dieseline. A length of cortex was placed in the centre and a length of safety fuse with a detonator was added. The result was a highly powerful bomb.

Removing the spare wheel to make space, they loaded the roller into the boot of the Audi. P4 plastic explosive was packed around it to boost the charge. Koekemoer led the safety fuse from the boot to the front of the car so it could be ignited from there.

The actual site of the blast in Johannesburg had not been finally decided, but Barnard said he needed an inner city area dense with buildings. That would serve to heighten the effects of the blast. The suitability of the Carlton Centre and its environs was discussed, but the idea was discarded because there were too many open spaces around it. It was eventually decided the Bree Street area provided the best option because there were many tightly positioned office blocks there. Another positive factor taken into account, according to Le Roux, was that it was a 'bad area' with an abundance of escort agencies, massage parlours and brothels.

First day of war: Sunday 24 April 1994

They left first thing in the morning to mount the operation. Koekemoer remained at the farm to work on improving fuses for the pipe bombs. Myburgh's parents were away so Koekemoer was alone. This should have proved critical — because he was a Security Police source and a police reservist. He was considered so valuable a source that not only was he paid, but the police also spoiled him by providing extra luxuries like expensive clothing for himself and his fiancé. He had been sent to Ventersdorp to infiltrate the call-up and report back.

Although there was a telephone to hand and the farmers' emergency radio system was at his elbow, he made no attempt to contact his handlers. The road routes from Ventersdorp to Johannesburg were limited and traffic on them was quiet, particularly on a Sunday morning. If he had contacted them, roadblocks could have been mounted immediately, which would have ensured the bombers were arrested.

Not only did he know the identities of the bombers and where they were going, but the old Audi was easily identifiable, too. It would have stuck out like a sore thumb. If he had taken action, it would have saved many lives and prevented a great deal of human suffering. But in the event, he did nothing. As Le Roux would say: 'He really did his bit [for the *Volkstaat*].'

Le Roux took the lead in the pilot car and kept well ahead on the drive to Johannesburg. His task was to clear the way. He had radio communications with Myburgh and Barnard, who followed in the Audi at a safe distance. If he ran into a roadblock or came up against any other problems, there would be time to warn them.

Positioning the bomb had been left to Le Roux, who knew the geography of Johannesburg. He would make an *ad hoc* arrangement when they reached the city. He eventually drove into Bree Street, found a suitable parking space and turned into it. For some reason best known to themselves Myburgh and Barnard failed to follow his example and did not park. Le Roux pulled out and drove on, looking for another spot. The traffic was fairly busy for a Sunday morning and for a while the cars became separated. Le Roux turned a corner to enable them to regroup. Eventually he found somewhere else and parked for the second time. It was in front of the Monte Carlo Hotel on the corner of Bree and Von Wielligh Streets, midway between the ANC's national and regional headquarters and not far from the PAC's regional offices. The situation of such plum targets apparently played no part in his selection, probably because he was unaware they were there.

Either Myburgh or Barnard ignited a fuse-lighter and applied it to the safety fuse. They got out of the Audi, ran to Le Roux's pilot car and got in. Le Roux slipped the car into gear and drove off. Several witnesses reported seeing smoke emanating from the parked Audi and two white men running away.

Two black street children called after them.

'Mister, your car is burning!'

'That car is not burning . . . there is a bomb inside', one replied.

At 09:53 the device, estimated by the police to contain between 70 and 90kg of explosive, detonated. The blast, the largest in the country until then, left a two metre deep crater in the street. Nine people were killed and at least another 92 were injured. Damage to buildings in the area was extensive.

The street children had not understood the warning and had made no attempt to escape. A witness who overheard the conversation ran away and this saved her life. Tragically, the children died later in hospital from their injuries.

Susan Keane (41), an ANC candidate in the forthcoming election, and regional executive member Joan Fubbs were hurrying to the ANC offices in Lancet Hall to deliver material for a workshop on local government.

'We got to the robot at Bree and Von Wielligh Streets. The lights changed and in a split second it was like all hell breaking loose', Fubbs said. 'There were flames in front of us and Susan said: "Oh, God, a bomb blast." Bleeding from the nose, she added: "I can't drive." She struggled from the car, collapsed and died.

Two women groaned in pain as medics attended to them. A handful of other injured sat beneath the shade of roadside trees awaiting attention. Fifty-three people were treated at Hillbrow Hospital and 39 — including a critically injured four-months-old baby — at the Johannesburg Hospital. Most were suffering from minor shrapnel wounds and shock.

The Times of London reporter, Simon Walker, who was driving past the scene was another who was injured in the blast. He was thrown several metres and suffered a fractured shoulder blade and other injuries. His car was virtually destroyed.

Mike Martins, whose shop was only metres from the site of the explosion, was more fortunate. 'I was standing at the till, just inside the entrance, when I heard a big bang and the glass doors and windows of my shop shattered . . . Everybody was screaming, but none of us [in the shop] were injured.' [4]

Mrs Sifiso Ngwenya was at the corner of Bree and King George Street when the bomb exploded. She suffered permanent injuries to her jaw and to her leg. Despite numerous surgical operations it has proved impossible to rectify her disabilities.

An anonymous caller claimed responsibility for the bomb in the name of *Boere Krisis Aksie*. This meant little as most members of that organisation were also members of the AWB and vice versa. The promised claim of responsibility by Eugene Terre'Blanche on behalf of the AWB never materialised.

During the return trip to Koesterfontein Farm, Myburgh mentioned that he planned to plant a second bomb in a Johannesburg residential area, but he did not say where he had in mind. The three showered and cleaned up at the farm.

Before their return, Prinsloo visited Ventersdorp to discuss problems relating to the breakdown of radio communications between the game farm and the head office. He sought out Eugene Terre'Blanche, reported the successful deployment of the Bree Street bombers and discussed radio reports that had come in about the attack. He had not, of course, seen the bombers to debrief them so he had no first-hand knowledge.

The AWB had made plans to steal cars for use as car bombs and 4 x 4s for use as vehicles for 'military' purposes. Commandant du Plessis and Jannie Kruger briefed the men about garages and dealers in Klerksdorp that could be targeted. Kruger lived there so he explained the area and the local environment.

A vehicle-stealing party was despatched but the car they were travelling in broke down en route. Jan de Wet sought out Prinsloo at the game farm. He had heard on the grapevine that a car was needed for an operation, so he offered his own, conditional on his driving it — he was certainly not about to trust somebody else in the driver's seat of his precious car. Prinsloo accepted his offer and told him to be available with the car the next morning. De Wet did not know until later in the day that he had been earmarked for a bombing mission. Barnard decided to utilise the AWB's trailer (some said it belonged to Terre'Blanche personally) as a bomb, so it was collected from Prinsloo's farm on the Klerksdorp road outside Ventersdorp. Prinsloo said he would tell the *Oubaas* (old boss — Terre'Blanche).

Myburgh, Barnard and Le Roux arrived at the AWB's Ventersdorp headquarters with the trailer. They drew petrol money for the operation, but it is not known who gave it to them. Captain Johan Vlok of the Iron Guard was the guard commander. Myburgh told him he needed him at Koesterfontein Farm to assist in the making of a second car bomb. At some later stage he was told it was intended for detonation at a black taxi rank in Germiston. Myburgh said it was an order of the general staff.

Vlok returned with them to Koesterfontein Farm. Koekemoer was working on the bomb. He was sitting at a table and binding cortex around a full gas bottle that would be an integral part of the bomb. Barnard explained to Vlok that the bomb would be packed in the trailer. Loose pieces of iron and steel would be placed on top to create a shrapnel effect. Vlok and the rest helped with the mixing of dieseline and ammonium nitrate fertiliser to make low explosive. Koekemoer said that it would be detonated electronically. He showed Vlok how to connect the wires and explained that they had to be disconnected when the trailer was uncoupled, otherwise the bomb would fail to detonate.

Koekemoer demonstrated to Vlok, who professed to know nothing about bombs, how to activate the detonating mechanism; there were two — one fitted to the tow bar and the other inside the towing vehicle. He passed him a battery and explained how contact was made. When the poles were connected, the bomb would detonate. There was a time delay and he was assured there would be ample time to escape before the bomb exploded.

De Wet called while work was in progress, but he did not stay long.

Targets in Germiston were discussed and Le Roux suggested the railway station. Cliffie Barnard, who had the final say, favoured this as it was near a black taxi rank and close to a fairly high-rise Volksas Bank building. That would help to enclose and heighten the blast effects. It was also next to the largest shopping complex in the city. The main target, though, was the taxi rank — in Le Roux's own words: 'Those taxis stood there packed. If you drove through Germiston the taxis were always there. There were a lot of vehicles there.' Germiston also offered easy access to a highway which facilitated the getaway afterwards.

Barnard explained to Vlok that Jan de Wet would be driving his own car with the trailer in tow. Vlok would travel with him in the front passenger seat with the detonating device held at the ready. His instructions were that if they ran into a roadblock, he was to activate the detonating advice to blow up the car, then evade capture. The explosion would be huge and unexpected, so it would most likely deter the roadblock details from giving chase.

Because of the breakdown in radio communications between the game farm and Ventersdorp, four members of the general staff, including Generals Kiewiet Roodt and Cruywagen, visited Prinsloo at the game farm. They were pleased with what had happened and instructed him to continue his bombing campaign, saying 'it was too late to turn back'. The next target, they said, should be a high profile one that would serve to focus the attention of the international community on South Africa. They wanted to create an international incident. Jan Smuts (Johannesburg International) Airport, they said, would meet the bill. They said it had been approved as a target by Eugene Terre'Blanche and the general staff.

A closed meeting of officers was held at the game farm that evening. It was chaired by General Prinsloo and Brigadier Leon van der Merwe, Commandant Abie Fourie, Commandant Johan du Plessis and Major Smit were in attendance. Prinsloo, Fourie said, dropped a bombshell. He said that everyone there had to take part in the next operation. They could 'forget about a *Volkstaat*' because there was no longer going to be one. The time for that had passed. Now they had to create chaos to stop the election. 'People must be forced to panic so the election cannot be held.'

The message, he said, had come from 'a person he trusted'.

The only feasible explanation is that General Viljoen had passed a message to Ventersdorp, advising that he had called a halt to the Freedom Front's participation in the armed insurrection because of the accord signed with the ANC. Although Viljoen and the other generals had resigned from the AVF, they had clearly taken the armed farmers of the

AVF with them to the Freedom Front. Otherwise, General Viljoen would not have been cooking up war plans until the last moment.

The men would deploy the pipe bombs that Koekemoer had been fitting with fuses. They would concentrate on black taxi ranks. There would be no attempt to destabilise the forthcoming elections in white areas. Blacks were the enemy. The ANC drew 99% of its support from them, so disrupting that sector would disrupt that organisation.

An open meeting of those at the game farm followed. They were ordered to form themselves into task groups. Koper Myburgh briefed them on what they had to do. He explained how to light fuses and demonstrated how the bombs should be thrown.

Commandant Johan du Plessis, who was in charge of deployments, watched them collect their pipe bombs. He told them to choose the towns they intended going to and also left the selection of targets up to them.

'I came from the Free State', Du Plessis explained, 'and I did not know where the taxi ranks were. I did not even know where most of the towns in the PWV [Gauteng] area were. When I told the people to go and throw the pipe bombs at the taxi ranks, I asked them what towns they knew well. They could specify or choose to which town they want[ed] to go. Some of them, or most of them, could choose the groups in which they wanted to go.' The groups left for Randfontein, Carltonville, Krugersdorp and Pretoria.

Du Plessis classified three of the pipe bomb throwing operations as successful. One was thrown at a black taxi rank at Westonaria, Carltonville; another at a black taxi rank in Randfontein. Another target was Sannie's Café in Marabastad, Pretoria, a place that enjoyed a black clientele. In a fourth incident the bomb misfired.

Second day of war: Monday 25 April 1994

On 25 April the Koesterfontein Farm party awoke early. Once more Koekemoer would not be playing an active part in the forthcoming operation. The trailer bomb was hitched to Le Roux's car. Barnard, Vlok and Le Roux got in and the latter drove to nearby ploughed land where the soil was loose and sandy. They unhooked the trailer and shovelled soil on top of the explosives and scrap metal to compact it and increase the force of the explosion.

While they were at it, Jan de Wet, who had been told to meet them, arrived by car. He was accompanied by Commandant Johan du Plessis, whom General Prinsloo had ordered to go with De Wet to Koesterfontein Farm. Barnard told him he would be going on a bombing mission along with De Wet, but provided no details. Du Plessis assumed it was intended to give him experience. He was also an outsider, a Free Stater, so they probably wanted to commit him to the bombing campaign so he would be unable to back out later. De Wet reversed to the trailer and someone hooked it to his tow bar.

Le Roux, with Du Plessis in the passenger seat, led the way with his vehicle as the pilot car. He would once more guide them to where he believed the bomb should be placed. Initially the vehicles were in radio contact, using SADF radio sets of unexplained provenance, but communications failed soon after they started out. During the drive Le Roux briefed Du Plessis on the intended target. They spoke very little apart from this. Du Plessis was scared they were going to be stopped by a police roadblock. He was also busily trying to strip and fix the errant radio. Another little worry was that the trailer bomb might explode en route.

They drove into Germiston followed by De Wet and Vlok with the trailer bomb. Le Roux, by a parody of hand signals and indications over his shoulder, indicated a suitable place to unhitch and leave the trailer. The others failed to understand his gesticulations. He tried again and indicated an alternative place and this time De Wet appeared to understand. He stopped, then started again and drove into a one-way street. Le Roux lost sight of them temporarily, but shortly afterwards they were shocked by the sight of the car and its trailer bomb approaching from the opposite direction. This was unsettling as they had no idea what was happening because of the breakdown of inter-vehicle communications. But they did know the bomb was due to be detonated and they were scared they might be caught in the blast. Conscious of this, they rushed to get out of town and headed for the highway.

Meanwhile, De Wet and Vlok had found a suitable parking bay. They unhitched the trailer bomb and manhandled it into the bay. De Wet got back in his red car and watched as Vlok set the bomb to detonate. They drove off but the traffic lights seemed to conspire against them. After stopping at the second set, the device exploded to their rear with an ear-shattering roar.

The bomb caused great destruction. Some bodies were thrown ten storeys up on to the nearby Volkskas Bank building. Ten people were killed and many more were injured.

They headed for Ventersdorp and then Koesterfontein. They picked up Koekemoer and went to the game farm.To their relief, De Wet and Vlok had arrived shortly before. Once again, despite having had numerous opportunities, Koekemoer had made no attempt whatsoever to contact his Security Police handlers.

Again there was no claim of responsibility by Eugene Terre'Blanche on behalf of the AWB. Nor, needless to say, were any statements in support of the bombing made by Ferdie Hartzenberg or General Viljoen.

Third day of war: Tuesday 26 April

General Prinsloo sought out Cliffie Barnard and Koper Myburgh and briefed them that the general staff had determined that Jan Smuts Airport should be the target for the next bomb.

Concern had developed because the group who had gone to pipe-bomb Sannie's Café in Marabastad had not returned to the game farm. It was feared they had been arrested. If that was so, there was a danger they had broken under interrogation by the Security Police and revealed their operational base. This meant the police would probably raid the place and round up everyone. General Nico Prinsloo and Brigadier Leon van der Merwe decided they should move and establish a new base at the Waterval Rifle Range close to Rustenburg.

Barnard got his hands on a stolen Peugeot sedan that was available for use as a car bomb. Barnard, Myburgh and Koekemoer drove it to the rifle range.

At the range some men called a meeting and demanded permission to visit their wives and children at Jan de Wet's farm. Many opposed the idea, especially those who had been involved in the bombing. What would happen if they were arrested and interrogated by the Security Police? If people started doing as they pleased, it would defeat the object of moving bases.

Those who wanted to see their wives were not concerned about that. This was democracy *Volkstaat* style. So despite the 'iron discipline' of the Iron Guard — who would shoot you for cowardice or disobedience — men packed into two vehicles and accompanied by camp commandant Abie Fourie, went off to visit their womenfolk. In the event two of the wives decided they had had quite enough of the 'struggle' for that week and demanded their husbands take them home to Johannesburg.

Abie Fourie appointed Commandant Mike Miles-Sharp, a Nataler, to act as camp commandant in his absence.

Jan de Wet arrived at the rifle range in his distinctive red car. General Nico Prinsloo and Brigadier van der Merwe called him over and told him it had been reported on television that a similar one had been spotted at the scene of the Germiston bombing. They suggested he remove the tow bar to make it less conspicuous. De Wet demurred, saying that whatever he did with it, his car was still red. He took the tow bar off anyway.

Meanwhile, Barnard passed on the general staff's instructions that they should turn the Peugeot into a car bomb and detonate it at Jan Smuts Airport. Koekemoer was once more put in charge of building the bomb. As had become the drill, everyone buckled down to help him.

The Peugeot had been 'hot wired' when stolen, which had caused the coil to burn out. Prinsloo expressed his concern that the car might break down during the operation. Barnard passed this on to Le Roux and told him to 'make sure the car is fine'. Le Roux replaced the burnt-out coil with one from his own car. They were interchangeable. One tyre had a slow puncture, so Le Roux and 'Weeskind' Hattingh, the car thief, drove to a garage in Swartruggens and bought a replacement.

The bomb would only be completed late that night, so when Le Roux returned from Swartruggens, Barnard told him to get some sleep as he would once again be driving the lead car. Le Roux reminded him that the coil had been removed from his car, so it was arranged that he would use Jaco Nel's blue Toyota.

Barnard discussed the placement of the bomb at the airport. It needed to be close to either the International Arrivals or the International Departure hall to have the maximum effect. Foreign officials, visitors and media representatives, who were perceived as generally sympathetic to the ANC, were currently pouring into South Africa to pay their respects to the politicians. Also, because the election was on the morrow, Barnard stressed that it was important the world learnt there was widespread resistance to its being held. He emphasised, though, that no foreigners were to be targeted.

That evening Prinsloo drove to Ventersdorp. Someone — he did not say who — told him that all operations were to be stopped forthwith. Information had been received that the police were on to them and arrests were imminent. But for some inexplicable reason, he did not pass this on to the team that was heading for Jan Smuts the next morning. He could offer no explanation, but maybe he just stayed in Ventersdorp and had too many drinks with his leader.

The last strike: Election Day: Wednesday 27 April 1994

Cliffie Barnard awakened Etienne le Roux early. He found Johan du Plessis and Jannie Kruger, who had been nominated to go with the car bomb, already at the farm. They discussed radio procedures and the route they would take to the airport. Le Roux explained to Du Plessis that he would take the slip road immediately before the terminal building and wait for them there. Du Plessis and Kruger would continue to a suitable drop-off point at the international terminal, park the car bomb, light the fuse and walk briskly down to where he was parked to make good their escape.

Initially, at least, everything happened as planned. Le Roux pulled off and Du Plessis and Kruger drove straight to the upper level International Departures Hall. Of course, there had been no reconnaissance. Le Roux, in accordance with what he remembered of the airport layout and not being an international traveller, anticipated being able to keep the car bomb in view from his position. But he found it had disappeared from view. He got out of the car and walked towards the terminal building to intercept the others. He met Du Plessis on the way and asked where Kruger was.

Du Plessis said he had somehow got lost. Le Roux took out his watch and estimated that they could allow another two minutes for Kruger to find the car.

Within that two minutes —15 minutes after polling stations opened throughout South Africa — there was a deafening explosion as the car bomb detonated.

Le Roux and Du Plesses raced for the car and got in. They knew that if they did not get away quickly, they would be caught. They drove towards the exit, but the place seemed to have come alive as police and security personnel rushed towards the site of the explosion. Some quick thinking ones, it seems, ran towards the exit to stop cars from leaving the airport. They were too late. Le Roux paid his parking ticket at the exit barrier and they were back out on the highway.

Airport workers, two traffic officers, bystanders and people in transit were among the 21 injured. The casualties were rushed to Kempton Park's Arwyp Medical Centre. Seven were admitted to hospital and two critically injured casualties underwent immediate surgery. The others were treated for minor injuries and shock. If it had not been for shatterproof windows in the terminal, far more casualties would have been caused by flying glass.

Braam Loots, managing director of the Airports Company, which had recently taken over the operation of the airports from the State, said planes had circled the airport for an hour and a half before being allowed to land. Only a Lufthansa flight, was diverted.

The general area was devastated by the explosion. Ceilings had fallen or were sagging. Glass and great chunks of concrete littered the ground. Six cars were badly damaged. The Peugeot used in the explosion was unrecognisable.[5]

The police, meanwhile, had indeed arrested the Pretoria bombers. They had also received information that a contingent of the Iron Guard was camped at the Waterval rifle range and that the bombing campaign was being orchestrated from there.

A large contingent of policemen raided the rifle range at 06:30, narrowly missing the Jan Smuts bombers who had only just left for Johannesburg. They made 27 arrests and confiscated a pipe bomb, commercial explosives, homemade time switches, a large quantity of firearms, 30 450 rounds of ammunition, 17 vehicles — one fitted with a false bottom and another with false registration plates — radios, clothing, and of all things, nine parachute packs.

Another six men were arrested at their homes in Ventersdorp, Rustenburg, Benoni and Pretoria. Police announced that they were seeking at least another ten men.[6]

The bombers had arranged to rendezvous with Cliffie Barnard at Venterdorp, but en route a car flashed its lights and the driver flagged them down. He said they should avoid the rifle range. It had been raided by the police and about 50 people, including General Nico Prinsloo and Brigadier van der Merwe, had been arrested. They had also been identified as the Jan Smuts Airport culprits and were being hunted by the police.

Throughout the campaign Eugene Terre'Blanche remained silent and made no attempt to claim responsibility for the bombing as had been arranged with the AWB's general staff. The closest he came to it was the submission of an affidavit to the TRC much later on.The affidavit was not subject to cross examination. In it he said: 'I accept that in the difficult time which preceded the election I made several public speeches that could have been interpreted by AWB members as instructions.'

General Prinsloo when asked for an explanation said: 'Well it is my view they [the AWB leadership] were afraid of prosecution . . . Well, I can't say why Mr Terre'Blanche didn't do it. He was supposed to have done [it].' When asked why the general staff didn't approach and tell him: 'Look, go and talk to the people', he replied: 'It could be possible that members of the staff approached Mr Terre'Blanche and [they] directed such a request to him. I think it is highly possible [but] I don't know about it . . . They [Terre'Blanche and the general staff] should have taken responsibility for the actions.'[7]

End of the Volkstaat dream: Aftermath

The dream ended with the widespread arrests of right-wingers.

Le Roux was on the run for two months before he was arrested. He was convicted and sentenced to death for multiple counts of murder and attempted murder. This was ultimately commuted to 29 years imprisonment. Cliffie Barnard and Koper Myburgh were less fortunate. They escaped from prison and were responsible for another fatal bombing in the Cape. There would be no amnesty by the TRC for them because the offences had been committed after the cut-off date. Both were convicted and sentenced to long terms of imprisonment.

Many Afrikaners left their homes, their jobs and abandoned everything they owned to follow the *Volkstaat* dream in the Western Transvaal. That dream turned into a nightmare after the first free election with universal suffrage in South Africa on 27 April 1994. Those not arrested were abandoned and left to their fate by AWB leader Eugene Terre'Blanche and his generals. Many were reduced to begging from their relations for succour. Some unfortunates were reduced to working for certain Afrikaner farmers (who had almost become their fellow *Volkstaaters*) for their keep only. Effectively they were treated as slave labour, but many had nowhere to return to.[8]

Many of them, poor already, never recovered the little they possessed before disaster struck. The promised jobs in the right-wing controlled '*Volkstaat*' councils and municipalities came to naught. That the AWB and the AVF had once marched proudly through the streets after being granted the 'Freedom of the Towns' was of no relevance once white right-wing councillors had been voted from power by a majority black electorate.

The former commandant at the Iron Guard's game farm base, Abie Fourie, was one of those who never recovered. 'I made provision during my years of working . . . that in ten years time I would retire and spend the rest of my life in peace with my wife, children and grandchildren', he told a TRC amnesty hearing. 'I sacrificed all that and also the money when we went to the *Volkstaat*, where they had promised we would live in peace. Since my arrest I lost everything. I got bail but I had problems finding work because people think you are horrible when you come out of prison. After being sentenced, I sold everything I owned in order to live. I had a responsibility towards my family . . . I was stopped from going to my own father's funeral to pay my respects because everyone thought I was so bad. My mother died from a broken heart because of it.'

But what about the true victims?

The unknown street children who attempted to warn the Bree Street bombers that their car was on fire — their bodies lie in unmarked paupers' graves.

Mrs Seako lost her cousin Thokozile to the same bomb. Her mother died of a broken heart.

It changed the way of life of Mr Makhuza, a schoolteacher whose son Teboho Makhuza was brutally murdered by the Ridora Crossing killers. He said afterwards: 'Whenever I see an Afrikaner I think AWB and I hate them — for the brutality with which our children were murdered.' He had taught Afrikaans as a subject for 25 years but he no longer felt comfortable doing so. 'I wouldn't do it justice. My attitude has changed completely.'[9]

Countless other tragedies have been forgotten amidst the mayhem of bomb blasts, the sounds of falling masonry and the rattle of gunfire. Every person killed or maimed was a personal tragedy either for the victim or their loved ones, or both. The maimed still live with the effects of the atrocities and will do so for the rest of their lives.

Yet some appear to have got away with it completely.

What has happened to master bomb maker, Pieter Koekemoer? Despite being a source who the Security Police had sent to Ventersdorp to find out what was going on, he willingly manufactured all the bombs deployed by the AWB during that tragic weekend. He culpably failed to report back to his handler to ensure the bombers were headed off and arrested. He has never been arrested, nor did he appear before the TRC to claim amnesty for his deadly deeds. Instead, the story goes, he has been protected by the Security Police and given a new identity.

While many of the AWB bombers and killers are serving long prison sentences, the same questions can be asked about the hierarchy of the AWB as have already been asked about the hierarchy of the SADF and the SAP. What has happened to those who gave the orders? What about Eugene Terre'Blanche and his braaivleis generals? Only one, Nico Prinsloo, gave evidence before the TRC and accepted responsibility as part of the command structure that ordered the bombings.

The rest, including Eugene Terre'Blanche — who had long been publicly ranting about the forthcoming war over the *Volkstaat* issue — had been reduced to making cowardly miserable mumbles that it was not them — that they had never given the orders. When formally warned that they might be incriminated by the evidence of former subordinates applying for amnesty at TRC hearings — at which they had the right to give evidence on oath in reply — each preferred to submit brief affidavits of denial. This saved them from the indignities and the perils of cross-examination. Sure, at the time of writing, Terre'Blanche is serving a prison sentence, but that is for two convictions for racist assaults completely unconnected with his leadership of the AWB.

It has been said with good reason that the top leadership of the AWB was riddled with paid informers of the Security Police, the NIS and Military Intelligence. Such agents were paid rewards for arrests and convictions. There can be no quarrel with that. It is standard procedure. What is disturbing is a suggestion that at least five of them were *agent provocateurs*. They planned criminal missions and ordered their subordinates to go on them, passing information about it to their handlers. Then they collected rewards at the going rate of R250 000 when they fingered them for arrest. The author has no quarrel with the concept of the protection of police informers. *Agents provocateurs*, however, are true accessories to the crimes and should be prosecuted to the fullest extent of the law.

On 23 April 1998 criminal charges were laid with the then Commissioner of Police, George Fivaz, against certain individuals by former AWB brigadier, Dries Kriel. The charges concerned allegations that they were *agents provocateurs*. The docket was passed to two senior retired CID officers, Brigadier Frik Nel and Colonel Hennie Britz, who had been brought from retirement to form an investigation team. They were and still are investigating many hundreds of serious criminal cases committed by political activists, both to the left and right of the political spectrum. Some cases, consolidated at their offices for convenience, date back to the 1960s. They concern culprits who either had not applied to the TRC for amnesty, or had their applications refused. There are more still to come, because at the time of writing the amnesty committees are still deliberating.

At least 500 police dockets, of which the AWB complaints form a small part, are on the desk of the Deputy Director of Public Prosecutions in Pretoria, awaiting a decision regarding prosecution. The whole matter is complicated by an issue of common justice. Many who merit being charged criminally are currently holding high office in the ANC's political dispensation. The question is: why should such people be let off the hook (as they most certainly will be) while others are prosecuted? Maybe the previous National Party administration of President F W de Klerk should have shown greater wisdom and demanded a general amnesty for everyone, as happened in the former Rhodesia.

So when and if the cases against the alleged *agents provocateurs* ever see the light of day in a court of justice, is anybody's guess.

The IFP: The last stumbling block

The last major stumbling block to the electoral process was the IFP's adamant refusal to take part in the general election despite lengthy negotiations. With a quarter of the national voting population refusing to take part, it would be difficult to classify the elections afterwards as free and fair.

On 28 March 1994 the IFP moved its election boycott to centre stage when 50 000 Zulus, many armed with traditional weapons and some with automatic weapons, marched on the ANC's HQ in Shell House and its Lancet Hall Regional HQ in Jeppe Street, Johannesburg. Fire was exchanged between both groups and at least 31marchers were killed and 276 wounded.[10]

Efforts to achieve international mediation involving former US Secretary of State, Dr Henry Kissinger and former British Foreign Secretary, Lord Carrington, fell through before they had even started.[11]

During March and April 1994 stories surfaced of a 5 000 strong KwaZulu Self Protection Unit, formed with the authority of King Goodwill Zwelithini and Chief Mangosuthu Buthelezi, being equipped and trained with automatic weapons at KwaMlaba camp near the Mozambique border. Its commander, former intelligence officer Phillip Powell, openly admitted the brigade was being prepared for the day when the IFP-controlled KwaZulu authority would be stripped of its powers. It was then that resistance to an ANC-led government would continue underground.[12]

Powell was not the only one who was training troops. The AWB had been providing instructors to train units with weapons supplied by the Security Police through its C1 unit at Vlakplaas. Rob Brown, once of Veterans for Victory, was also constantly in the province on training missions. The Zulus he was training, however, were not connected with Inkatha. They were the members of anti-communist black conservative churches. The money for the training, so he was told, came from right-wing church groups in the United States. He felt certain, however, that it was in reality Military Intelligence money.

He was undoubtedly right. Former President FW de Klerk, in his memoirs, said when referring to the Steyn Commission that followed the Goldstone Commission's raid on the DCC's offices in Pretoria, that some units 'had been providing arms and assistance to elements within the IFP; that they were involved in the instigation and perpetration of violence; that they were involved in activities to discredit the ANC and to sabotage the negotiation process'.[13]

Military Intelligence had worked well with Brown before throughout the anti-End Conscription Campaign of Veterans for Victory. It obviously decided that training and arming right-wing black anti-communist church groups in KwaZulu, as an adjunct to assisting Inkatha — a matter which had become embarrassingly highly publicised — was a good trick indeed. De Klerk's phrase 'to discredit the ANC and sabotage the negotiation process' does not, the author believes, illuminate the story fully. There had to be an end game to Military Intelligence's agenda. Perhaps looked at it against General Constand Viljoen's firm belief — particularly in late 1993 and early 1994 — that the SADF would stand with him in the case of a right-wing revolution, one comes closer to the truth.

The training manual Brown was given to use commenced with the paragraph: 'War is waged by small revolutionary groups by means of ancient tested techniques and principles.' At first glance one would say it was a normal counter-insurgency manual, but it went deeper than that. It was concerned more with waging revolutionary war, rather than instructing one on how to combat it. And that was what Brown taught his students. Military Intelligence's end game agenda plans apparently reached far beyond the election.

Brown also instructed some groups from white right-wing churches with an anti-communist agenda in the handling of firearms.

Finally, after lengthy wrangling, the IFP agreed to enter the process. This was literally at the last minute, and only after the new constitution was amended to recognise the institution of the Zulu monarchy in KwaZulu-Natal — its role, authority and status — and after provision was made for the King to have such rights and powers as determined by Zulu customs and traditions.[14]

Eighty million national and regional ballot papers had already been printed in full colour with portraits of the leaders and the symbols of the parties taking part, but the deficiency was overcome by affixing a sticker with the IFP emblem and a photograph of Chief Buthelezi at the base of the ballot papers.[15]

It is history that the ANC won the election with a large majority.

Many whites had sufficient *oorlogkos* (war food) to last them for years.

Bibliography

Books:

Barber, James, Barratt, John. *South Africa's Foreign Policy: The search for status and security 1945-1988*; **Basson, Nico and Motinga, Ben.** Call them Spies, (African Communications Projects, Windhoek — A Military Intelligence front company); **Crocker**, **Chester A**. *High Noon in Southern Africa : Making Peace in a Rough Neighbourhood*, (Jonathan Ball, Jhb, 1992); **De Klerk, F W**. *The Last Trek: A New Beginning*, (Macmillan, Basingstoke, 1998); **De Kock, Col Eugene**, as told to **Jeremy Gordin**. *A long night's Damage: Working for the Apartheid State* (Contra, Saxonwold, 1998); **Dippenaar, Marius de Witt**. *The History of the South African Police, 1913-1988*, (Promedia Publications, Pretoria, 1988); **Ellis, Stephen and Sechaba,Tsepo**. *Comrades Against Apartheid*: *The ANC and the South African Communist Party in Exile*, (James Currey, London, 1992); **Flower**, **Ken**. *Serving Secretly: Rhodesia's CIO Chief on Record*, (Galago, Alberton, 1987); **Gastrow**, **Shelagh**. *Who's Who in South African Politics*, Number 4 (Ravan Press, Jhb, 1992); **Hanlon, Dr Joseph**, *Beggar your Neighbours*, (Catholic Inst for International Relations, James Currey, London, Indiana University Press, Bloomington, USA, 1986); **Kasrils**, **Ronnie**. Armed and Dangerous: *My Undercover Struggle Against Apartheid*, (Heinemann, Oxford, 1993); **Kentridge, Matthew.** *An Unofficial War: Inside the Conflict in Pietermaritzburg*, (David Phillip, Cape Town, 1990); **Kriel, Dries**. *Diary of a White Terrorist* (unpublished manuscript); **Hamman, Hilton**. *Days of the Generals*, (Zebra Books, Cape Town, 2001); **Hoare, Col Mike.** *The Seychelles Affair*,(Bantam Press, London, 1986); Hugo, Gerrie, Snel, S. *Military Intelligence and the Counter-Revolutionary War in the Eastern Cape*, (UMAC, Cape Town, 1998); Jaster, Robert S, *The Defence of White Power: South African Foreign Policy under pressure*, (Macmillan, Basingstoke, 1988); **McAleese, Peter**. *No Mean Soldier: The autobiography of a professional fighting man*, (Orion, London, 1993); **Mahoney, Richard D**, JFK: Ordeal in Africa, (Oxford University Press, New York, 1983); **Mandela, Nelson.** *Long Walk to Freedom*, (Abacus, London, 1995); **Martin, David, Johnson, Phylis**, Destructive Engagement: Southern Africa at War, (Zimbabwe Publishing House, Harare, 1986); **Military Balance, The**, (International Institute for Strategic Studies, 1987); Minnaar, Anthony, et al **(**editors). *Conflict and Violence in Natal/KwaZulu: Historical perspectives*, (HSRC, Pretoria, 1991), *The Hidden Hand: Covert Operations in South Africa*, 1st ed (HSRC, Pretoria, 1994); 2nd ed 1998; **Mockler, Anthony**. *The New Mercenaries:The History of the Mercenaries from the Congo to the Seychelles* (Sidgwick & Jackson, London, 1985); **Mission to South Africa**: The Commonwealth Report (Penguin, London, 1986); **Moorcraft, Paul & Cohen, Mike**. *Stander: Bank Robber*, (Galago, Alberton, 1984); **Morris, Donald R**. *The Washing of the Spears; The Rise and Fall of the Zulu Nation*, (Simon and Schuster, New York, 1965); **Moyo, Isaac.** Moyo's Highway To Hell, (Unpublished manuscript); **Pauw, Jaques**. *In the Heart of the Whore*, (Southern Book Publishers, Jhb, 1991); **Potgieter, De Wet**. *Contraband -South Africa and the International trade in ivory and Rhino horn*, (Queillerie, Cape Town, 1995); **Pottinger, Brian**, *The Imperial Presidency*, (Southern Books, Jhb, 1988); **Pryce-Jones**, **David**. *The War that Never Was: The Fall of the Soviet Empire 1985-1991*, (Weidenfeld & Nicholson, London, 1995); **Puren**, **Col Jerry**, **as told to Pottinger**, **Brian**. *Mercenary Commander* (Galago, Alberton, 1986); ***Race Relations Annuals.***. (SA Institute of

Race Relations, Jhb),1974,75, 76, 78, 80, 81, 82, 83, 84, 85, 86, 1987/88, 1988/89,1993/94, 1994/ 95; **Reitz, Deneys**. *Trekking On*, (Faber and Faber, London, 1934); **Renwick, Sir Robin**. *Unconventional Diplomacy in Southern Africa* , (Macmillan, Basingstoke, 1997); **Rhoodie**, **Eschel**. *The Paper Curtain*, (Voortrekkerpers, Jhb, 1969), *The Real Information Scandal* (Orbis, Pretoria, 1983); **Shubin, Vladimir**. *ANC: A view from Moscow*, (Mayibuye Books, Cape Town,1999); **Stadler, Maj-Gen Herman D.** *The Other side of the Story: a True Perspective*, (Contact Publishers, Pretoria, 1997); **Stiff**, **Peter**. *Tommy Goes Home*, (Jacaranda Press, Salisbury, 1977), as told to by **Lt Col Ron Reid Daly**. *Selous Scouts: Top Secret War*, (Galago, Alberton, 1982), *See You in November: Rhodesia's no-holds-barred Intelligence war*, (Galago, Alberton, 1985), *Taming the Landmine* (Galago, Alberton, 1986), *Nine Days of War and South Africa's Final Days in Namibia*, (Lemur, Alberton, 2nd ed 1991); *The Silent War: South African Recce Operations 1969-1994*, (Galago, Alberton, 1999); *Cry Zimbabwe: Independence: Twenty Years on*, (Galago, Alberton, 2000); **Streek, Barry and Wickstead, Richard.** *Render unto Kaiser: A Transkei Dossier*, (Ravan Press, Jhb, 1981); **Taylor, Stephen**. *Shaka's Children: A History of the Zulu People*, (Harper Collins, London,1994); **Truth & Reconciliation Commission of SA Report**, (TRC, Cape Town, 1998), Vols. 2 & 3; **Uys, Ian**. *Survivors of Africa's Oceans*, (Fortress Publishers, Germiston, 1993); **Veterans Association of South Africa**. *Organiser's Manual,* (Military Intelligence); **Visser, George Cloete**. *OB: Traitors or Patriots*, (Macmillan, Jhb, 1976);

WEB SITES:

www.ccrweb.ccr.uct.ac.za./cbw/, www.truth.org.za.

NEWSPAPERS AND MAGAZINES:

Azania Combat, Beeld, Business Day, Cape Times, The Citizen, Daily Dispatch, Eastern Province Herald, Focus, Frontline Fellowship News, Natal Mercury, The New American (USA), *New Nation, The Phoenix,* (Ireland), *Pretoria News, Rand Daily Mail, SAPA, Saturday Star, Scope Magazine, Stand-To, The Star, Sunday Express, Sunday Independent, Sunday Nation, Sunday Star, Sunday Times, The Weekly Mail.*

OTHER DOCUMENTARY SOURCES:

ANC's Kabwe Conference and related ANC documents from its Dept of Religious Affairs, report of; **Court Record.** *State versus Wouter Basson*; *The Forgotten Ones*, (Agenda, SABC, April 1995); **Goldstone, Hon Justice RJ**. *Commission of Enquiry regarding the Prevention of Public Violence and Intimidation*, (Pretoria 1/6/93, 6/1/293, 18/3/94); *Commission of Enquiry re Kwazulu*, (9/9/93); **Gould, Chandré and Burger**, Marlene. Reports on the CBW research project of the Centre for Conflict Resolution; **Harms, Hon Justice L TC.** Commission of Enquiry into certain possible irregularities or illegalities, Commission of Enquiry into certain alleged murders; **Hidden Hand, The.** (BBC Channel 4 TV documentary, 1991); **Hugo, Col Gerrie**. *Colonel Gerrie Hugo papers*; **Holomisa, Maj-Gen Bantu**. *The Holomisa papers*; **Lubowski, Adv Anton**. *Inquest into the death of*, (Windhoek, 1992); **South African Law Reports**, 1982-83, Vol 3, State v Hoare and others; **Steyn, Lt-Gen Pierre**. *Steyn Commission Report*; **Tebbutt.** Commission of Inquiry. *Report into the incidents that led to the violence in the former Bophuthatswana on 11 March 1994, and the deaths that occurred as a result*, Vols 1 & 2 dated 23/3/98.

NOTES

Chapter 1

1 Mockler, Anthony. *The New Mercenaries*, p262-264.
2 *Ibid* p264.
3 *Ibid* p266; *Sunday Times*, 30/5/82.
4 Puren, Col Jerry and Pottinger. Brian. *Mercenary Commander*, p 322.
5 *Ibid*, p324.
6 *Ibid*, p323; *The Star*, 25/6/82.
7 *Ibid*, p326.
8 *Ibid*, p328.
9 Hoare, Col Mike. The Seychelles Affair, p16-18.
10 Puren, Col Jerry and Pottinger, Brian. *Mercenary Commander*, p328.
11 Hoare, Col Mike. *The Seychelles Affair*, p18, 19.
12 Puren, Col Jerry and Pottinger, Brian. *Mercenary Commander*, p328-329.
13 *The Star*, 5/5/82.
14 *Rand Daily Mail*, 13/4/82.
15 Hoare, Col Mike. *The Seychelles Affair*, p23.
16 Mockler, Anthony. *The New Mercenaries*, p268-269
17 Puren, Col Jerry and Pottinger, Brian. *Mercenary Commander*, p329.
18 Mockler, Anthony. *The New Mercenaries*, p277.
19 *Rand Daily Mail*, 24/6/82.
20 Hoare, Col Mike. *The Seychelles Affair*, p28.
21 Puren, Col Jerry and Pottinger, Brian. *Mercenary Commander*, p329-330.
22 Hoare, Col Mike. *The Seychelles Affair*, p21.
23 *Ibid*, p32.
24 Mockler, Anthony. *The New Mercenaries*, p275.
25 *The Star*, 2/3/82
26 Hoare, Col Mike. *The Seychelles Affair*, p33.
27 Mockler, Anthony. *The New Mercenaries*.
28 *Ibid*, p275-276
29 Hoare, Col Mike. *The Seychelles Affair*, p32.
30 *Ibid*, p32.
31 Mockler, Anthony. *The New Mercenaries*, p268;*The Citizen*, 29/5/82.
32 *The Citizen*, 29/5/82.
33 Hoare, Col Mike. *The Seychelles Affair*, p333-334.
34 Interview Maj Gen Daan Hamman, 31/3/88.
35 *The Citizen*, 29/5/92.
36 Hoare, Col Mike. *The Seychelles Affair*, p34.
37 *Ibid*, p38.
38 *Mockler, Anthony, The New Mercenaries, p275.*
39 Hoare, Col Mike. *The Seychelles Affair*, p39,40.
40 *The Citizen*, 29/5/82.
41 Hoare, Col Mike. *The Seychelles Affair*, p45,46.
42 *The Citizen*, 29/5/82.
43 Hoare, Col Mike. *The Seychelles Affair*, p42, 46.
44 *The Citizen*, 28, 29/5/82; *The Star*, 2/5/82.
45 Hoare, Col Mike. *The Seychelles Affair*, p44.
46 *Mockler, Anthony. The New Mercenaries,* p244.
47 *Sunday Times*, 30/5/82.
48 Hoare, Col Mike. *The Seychelles Affair*, p43.
49 Conversation with former Rhodesian Intelligence officer, 1982.
50 Hoare, Col Mike. *The Seychelles Affair*, p46.
51 Mockler, Anthony. *The New Mercenaries*, p283.
52 *Rand Daily Mail*, 3/6/82.
53 Hoare, Col Mike. *The Seychelles Affair*, p44.
54 *The Star*, 29/5/82.
55 Hoare, Col Mike. *The Seychelles Affair*, p45; *The Citizen*, 11/6/82.
56 *Ibid*, p47.
57 *Ibid*, p47-49; *The Citizen*, 4/5/82.
58 *Ibid*, p49.
59 *The Citizen*, 4/5/82.
60 *Rand Daily Mail*, 4/5/82.
61 Hoare, Col Mike. *The Seychelles Affair*, p50.
62 *Ibid*, p47-51; *Rand Daily Mail* 4/5/82.
63 Interview Maj-Gen Daan Hamman, 31/3/88.
64 *Pretoria News*, 4/5/82.
65 *The Citizen*, 3/6/82.
66 Hoare, Col Mike. *The Seychelles Affair*, p51, 52; *Rand Daily Mail* 4/5/82; *Pretoria News*, 4/5/82; *The Star*, 4/5/82.
67 *The Citizen*, 4/5/82.
68 Hoare, Col Mike. *The Seychelles Affair*, p55
69 *The Citizen*, 6/5/82; *Rand Daily Mail* 6/2/82; *The Star*, 24/6/82; *Sunday Times*, 18/4/82.
70 *The Citizen*, 24/6/82.
71 *The Star*, 24/6/82.
72 *The Citizen*, 11/6/82.
73 Hoare, Col Mike. *The Seychelles Affair*, p66; *The Citizen*, 22/5/82; *The Star*, 22/5/82.
74 *The Citizen*, 24/6/82.
75 *The Star*, 10/2/82; *Rand Daily Mail* 6/2/82.
76 Hoare, Col Mike. *The Seychelles Affair*, p65-66.
77 *The Citizen*, 9/6/82.
78 *Ibid*, 9/6/82.
79 *Ibid*, 27/5/82.
80 *Ibid*, 3/6/82.
81 *The Star*, 5/5/82.
82 Hoare, Col Mike. *The Seychelles Affair*, p54.
83 *Ibid*, p55.
84 *Ibid*, p55.
85 *The Star*, 25/6/82.
86 Hoare, Col Mike. *The Seychelles Affair*, p56; *The Citizen*, 16/6/82.
87 *The Citizen*, 16/6/82.
88 Mockler, Anthony. *The New Mercenaries*, p284-286.
89 Hoare, Col Mike. *The Seychelles Affair*, p59-61, 67.
90 *Ibid*, p67
91 *Ibid*, p103; *Rand Daily Mail* 4/5/82, 18/6/62.
92 Interview with Col Jan Breytenbach, Jan 1992.
93 Hoare, Col Mike. *The Seychelles Affair*, p61; interview with Maj-Gen Daan Hamman, 31/3/88.
94 Rhoodie, Eschel, *The Real Information Scandal*, p863.
95 *The Citizen*, 25/5/82.
96 Hoare, Col Mike. *The Seychelles Affair*, p66,67.
97 *Ibid*, p67; Mockler, Anthony. *The New Mercenaries*, p297.
98 Hoare, Col Mike. *The Seychelles Affair*, p67; *Rand Daily Mail* 8/6/82.
99 *The Citizen*, 6/5/82, 4, 9, 15, 22/6/82; *Rand Daily Mail*, 4/6/82, 9/6/82; *The Star*, 27/5/82, 3, 9, 15, 22, 24/6/82.
100 Mockler, Anthony. *The New Mercenaries*, p290, 294, 295.
101 *Ibid*, p290; *The Citizen*, 12/6/82.
102 *The Citizen*, 5/6/82, 12/6/82.
103 Interview Col Sybie van der Spuy, 1987; *The Star*, 24/6/82.
104 Hoare, Col Mike. *The Seychelles Affair*, p68; *The Citizen*, 4/5/82,
105 Mockler, Anthony. *The New Mercenaries*, p294; *The Citizen*, 18/6/82; *The Star*, 24/6/82.
106 *Ibid*, p295; Hoare, Col Mike. *The Seychelles Affair*, p70,
107 Hoare, Col Mike. *The Seychelles Affair*, p68; Mockler, Anthony. *The New Mercenaries*, p296; *Rand Daily Mail* 26/6/82.
108 Mockler, Anthony. *The New Mercenaries*, p294-296; Hoare, Col Mike. *The Seychelles Affair*, p68; *The Citizen*, 25/5/82.
109 Hoare, Col Mike. *The Seychelles Affair*, p68; *The Star*, 29/6/82.
110 Puren, Col Jerry and Pottinger, Brian. *Mercenary Commander*, p287, 332, 335, Hoare, Col Mike. *The Seychelles Affair*, p69.
111 *Ibid*, (Puren p334); (Hoare), 71, 72.
112 *Ibid*, (Puren) p335; (Hoare) p73-74; *The Citizen*, 25/6/82.
113 *The Citizen*, 22/5/82, 27/5/82, 28/5/82, 4/6/82, 24/6/82;*The Star*, 24/6/82, 26/5/82.
114 Puren, Col Jerry and Pottinger, Brian. *Mercenary Commander*, p336; Hoare, Col Mike. *The Seychelles Affair*, p73; *The Citizen*, 4/5/82.

Chapter 2

1 Puren, Col Jerry and Pottinger, Brian. *Mercenary Commander*, p337; Hoare, Col Mike. *The Seychelles Affair*, p74,75; *The Citizen*, 4,25/5/82.
2 *The Star*, 28/5/82; *The Citizen*, 28/5/82, 11/6/82; *Sunday Express* 27/6/82.
3 Hoare, Col Mike. *The Seychelles Affair*, p75; Puren, Col Jerry and Pottinger, Brian. *Mercenary Commander*, p338; *The Citizen*, 28/5, 9/6/82; *Rand Daily Mail* 9/6/82; *Sunday Express* 7/4, 27/6/82; *The Star*, 28/5/82.
4 Puren, Col Jerry and Pottinger, Brian. *Mercenary Commander* p359; *The Star*, 18/5/82; *The Citizen*, 12, 16/6/82.
5 Hoare, Col Mike. *The Seychelles Affair*, p18, p76; *Rand Daily Mail*, 16/6/82; *The Citizen*, 5/6/82.
6 Puren, Col Jerry and Pottinger, Brian. *Mercenary Commander*, p358; *The Citizen*, 27/5/82; *The Star*, 15/4/82; *Sunday Times*, 20/6/82; *Rand Daily Mail* 16/6/82.
7 Hoare, Col Mike. *The Seychelles Affair*, p17;*The Star*, 26, 27/5/82; *The Citizen*, 26/5, 5/6/82.
8 *The Citizen*, 28/5/82.
9 Hoare, Col Mike. *The Seychelles Affair*, p76.
10 *The Citizen*, 25, 27,30/5/82, 5/6/82.
11 Puren, Col Jerry and Pottinger, Brian. *Mercenary Commander*, p340.
12 *The Citizen*, 29/6/82; *Rand Daily Mail*, 10, 15/6/82; *The Star*, 19/5/82.
13 Puren, Col Jerry and Pottinger, Brian. *Mercenary Commander*, p339, 340; *The Citizen*, 20, 25/5/82, 18/6/82; *The Star*, 4/5/82; *Sunday Express* 9/5/82; *Rand Daily Mail*, 9/6/82.
14 *The Citizen*, 28/5/82.
15 Puren. Col Jerry and Pottinger, Brian. *Mercenary Commander*, p342; *Rand Daily Mail* 16/6/82.
16 Hoare, Col Mike. *The Seychelles Affair*, p79; *The Citizen*, 22/5, 9/6/82.
17 *The Star*, 25/6/82.
18 *The Citizen*, 5, 12/6/82.
19 Hoare, Col Mike. *The Seychelles Affair*, p80, *The Citizen*, 15/4,4/6/82.
20 Puren, Col Jerry and Pottinger, Brian. *Mercenary Commander*, p342.
21 *Ibid*, p342-344; Hoare, Col Mike. *The Seychelles Affair*, p81; *The Citizen*, 20,28/5, 9/6/82.
22 Hoare, Col Mike. *The Seychelles Affair*, p82; *The Citizen*, 28/5/82.
23 *Ibid*, p82; *The Citizen*, 28/5/82.
24 *Ibid*, p83,84
25 *Ibid*, p82, 83, 85; *The Citizen*, 27/5, 4/6/82; *The Star*, 19/5/82; *Rand Daily Mail* 10/6/82.
26 *Ibid*, p84, *Rand Daily Mail*, 15/6/82; *The Citizen*, 15/4, 4, 29/6/82; *Pretoria News* 23/3/82.
27 *Ibid*, p86; *Rand Daily Mail*, 16/4/82; *The Citizen*, 16/4, 4,11,15/6/82.
28 *The Citizen*, 11/6/82; *The Star*, 26/5/82; *Rand Daily Mail* 26/5/82.
29 *The Citizen*, 17/3; 5, 25, 27, 28/5/82; *Rand Daily Mail*, 16/4, 27/5, 11/6/82.
30 Hoare, Col Mike. *The Seychelles Affair*, p87; *The Argus* 11/3/82; *The Citizen*, 5, 20/5/82.
31 Hoare, Col Mike. *The Seychelles Affair*, p89; *Rand Daily Mail* 18/6/82; *The Citizen*, 28/5/82.
32 *The Citizen*, 5/5/82.
33 *Rand Daily Mail*, 29/6/82.
34 *The Citizen*, 25/5/82; *The Star*, 25, 26/5/82; *Rand Daily Mail* 26/5/82.
35 *The Citizen*, 26/6/82; *Rand Daily Mail*, 27/5, 2, 10/6/82.
36 Hoare, Col Mike. *The Seychelles Affair*, p97; *The Citizen*, 6, 28/5/82; *Rand Daily Mail*, 2/6/82.
37 Hoare, Col Mike. *The Seychelles Affair*, p93; *Sunday Times*, 2/5/82 *The Star*, 5/5, 3/6/82, *Rand Daily Mail*, 10, 11/6/82.
38 *The Star*, 25/5/82; *Natal Mercury* 28/7/82; *Rand Daily Mail*, 9/6/82; *The Citizen*, 23/6/82.
39 *Pretoria News*, 5/5/82.
40 Puren, Col Jerry and Pottinger, Brian. *Mercenary Commander*, p359
41 *Ibid*, p359; Hoare, Col Mike. *The Seychelles Affair*, p93, 97; *Sunday Times*, 20/6/82.
42 Hoare, Col Mike. *The Seychelles Affair*, p94, 95, *The Citizen*, 17/3/, 5/5, 18/6/82.

Chapter 3

1 Hoare, Col Mike. *The Seychelles Affair*, p95; *The Star*, 5, 25/5, 4/6/82; *Rand Daily Mail*, 18/3/82; *The Citizen*, 11/6/82.
2 Hoare, Col Mike. *The Seychelles Affair*, p98; *The Argus* 11/3/82; *Evening Post* 11/3/82; *The Citizen*, 12/3, 5/5, 11/6/82; *Sowetan* 12/3/82; *Rand Daily Mail*, 13/3, 5/5/82; *Natal Mercury* 27/7/82; *Cape Times*, 12/3/82.
3 *The Star*, 15/6/82.
4 *The Citizen*, 28/5/82.
5 Rand Daily Mail, 2/6/82.
6 *Pretoria News* 10/3/82;*The Citizen*, 9/3/82; *Sunday Express* 11/9/82; *Rand Daily Mail*, 12/2/82; *Sowetan*, 8/3/82.
7 *Rand Daily Mail*, 17/6/82; *The Citizen*, 9, 11/3/82; *Sowetan*, 11/3/82; *Sunday Express* 7/3/82.
8 *The Citizen*, 6/5/82; *The Star*, 8/5/82.
9 *The Citizen*, 6/5/94; *Rand Daily Mail*, 10/6/82.
10 *The Star*, 17/6/82; *The Citizen*, 17/6/82; *Rand Daily Mail*, 17/6/82.
11 *Sunday Express*, 9/5/82.
12 *SA Law Reports, 1982-83*, Vol 3, State v Hoare and others.
13 *Natal Witness* 28/7, 6/8/82; *The Citizen*, 5, 6/8/82; *Rand Daily Mail*, 5/8/82.
14 Puren, Col Jerry and Pottinger, Brian. *Mercenary Commander*, p364.
15 *The Star*, 29/7/82; *Daily Dispatch* 2/8/82.
16 Puren, Col Jerry and Pottinger, Brian. *Mercenary Commander*, p344
17 *Rand Daily Mail*, 18/6/82.
18 *Ibid*, 16/6/82.
19 *The Citizen*, 26/3/82.
20 Hoare, Col Mike. *The Seychelles Affair*, p104; Puren, Col Jerry and Pottinger, Brian. *Mercenary Commander*, p345, 346; *Rand Daily Mail*, 24/3/82.
21 *Rand Daily Mail*, 16/6/82.
22 *Rand Daily Mail*, 18, 20/6/98; *The Star*, 29/6/82.
23 Puren, Col Jerry and Pottinger, Brian. *Mercenary Commander*, p346, 347, 359; Phone conversations with Col Puren, 1986; Hoare, Col Mike. *The Seychelles Affair*, p106; *Rand Daily Mail*, 16/6/82.
24 *Pretoria News* 30/3/82; *Sunday Times*, 18/4/82; *Rand Daily Mail*, 19/4/82.
25 *Rand Daily Mail*, 13/4/82.
26 *Pretoria News*, 15/4/82.
27 *Sunday Times*, 20/6/82.
28 *The Citizen*, 30/3/82; *The Star*, 30/3/82; *Pretoria News* 30/3/82; *Rand Daily Mail*, 19/4/82.
29 *The Citizen*, 24, 27/4/82; *Pretoria News* 27/4/82; *The Star*, 23/4/82.
30 Hoare, Col Mike. *The Seychelles Affair*, p155.
31 *The Citizen*, 18/6/82; *The Star*, 17/6/82.
32 *Sunday Express*, 27/6/82; *Sunday Times*, 20/6/82; *Rand Daily Mail*, 18, 23/6/82; *The Star*, 21/6/82; *The Citizen*, 22/6/82.
33 Puren, Col Jerry and Pottinger, Brian. *Mercenary Commander* p361, 362; *Rand Daily Mail*, 5/6/82.
34 *Sunday Star*, 2/8/92; *The Citizen*, 15/12/97.
35 *The Citizen*, 5/12/97.
36 Conversations with various people.
37 Interview Col Sybie v d Spuy, 1987.
38 Uys, Ian. *Survivors of Africa's Oceans*, (Fortress, Germiston, 1993), p158;
39 Hoare, Col Mike. *The Seychelles Affair*, p196.
40 *The Star*, 9/6/82; *The Citizen*, 9/6/82.

Chapter 4

1 *Rand Daily Mail*, 5/5/82.
2 Rhoodie, Eschel. *The Real Information Scandal*, p865.
3 *Rand Daily Mail*; *The Citizen*, 6/5/82.
4 Interview Col Sybie van der Spuy, 1987. *The Argus* 1/2/83; *Cape Times*, 1, 3/2/83; *The Star*, 2, 3, 4, 5,10, 17, 24/2/83; *Rand Daily Mail*, 2, 3, 4, 5, 8, 25/2, 3/3/83; *The Citizen*, 3, 5, 10, 17/2, 26/3/83; *Pretoria News* 8, 17/2/83.
5 *Race Relations Annual*, 1984, p747.
6 Puren, Col Jerry and Pottinger. *Mercenary*

Commander, p379.
7 *The Phoenix*, Ireland, 24/7/92.
8 Interview Col Craig Williamson, 1998.
9 The *Sunday Independent*, 16/7/95.
10 Interview Col Craig Williamson, 1998; *Sunday Times*, 7/2/88; *Sunday Star*, 14/2, 6/3/88.
11 *Sunday Star*, 28/2/88.
12 Interview Col Craig Williamson, 1998
13 Puren, Col Jerry and Pottinger, Brian. *Mercenary Commander* 379, 380 ;*The Phoenix*, Ireland, 24/7/92.
14 Interview Col Craig Williamson, 1998

Chapter 5

1 Mahoney, Richard D. *JFK: Ordeal in Africa*, p10.
2 *Ibid.*
3 Rhoodie, Eschel. *The Paper Curtain*, p113.
4 Mahoney, Richard D. *JFK: Ordeal in Africa*, p19.
5 Bryce Jones, David. *The War That Never Was*, p74.
6 *Ibid.*
7 Minnaar, Anthony, et al. *The Hidden Hand*, (James Selfe, paper in), p103-105.
8 *Ibid*
9 Pottinger, Brian, *The Imperial Presidency*, p41
10 *Ibid*, p42
11 *Ibid*, p43
12 Pottinger, Brian, *The Imperial Presidency*, p41; Jaster, Robert S. *The Defence of White Power* p29 &36; Hugo, G, Snel, Stef. *Military Intelligence and the Counter-revolutionary War*, p8-9.
13 *Race Relations Annual* 1984, p771.
14 *Ibid*, 1985, p484.
15 *Ibid*, 1985, p771
16 Martin, David, Johnson, Phylis. *Destructive Engagement*: p332-338.
17 *Race Relations Annual* 1984, P771
18 Jaster, Robert S. *The Defence of White Power*, p35-38.
19 Jaster, Robert S. *The Defence of White Power*, p38; Hanlon, Dr Joseph. *Beggar your Neighbours*, p9; *Race Relations Annual* 1985, p53.
20 Jaster, Robert S. *The Defence of White Power*, p38.
21 De Kock, Col Eugene and Jeremy Gordin. *A long night's Damage*, p90.
22 *Race Relations Annuals* 1985, p464; 1986, p85.
23 Hugo, G, Snel, Stef. *Military Intelligence and the Counter-revolutionary War*, p15.
24 Interview Col Lourens du Plessis, 8/3/2000.
25 *Race Relations Annual*,1986, p846.
26 Jaster, Robert S. *The Defence of White Power*, p35-39.
27 Renwick, Sir Robin. *Unconventional Diplomacy in Southern Africa*, p121.
28 *The Star*, 8/4/88.
29 Rhoodie, Eschel. *The Real Information Scandal*, p72.
30 *Rand Daily Mail*, 23/2/1984.
31 The Military Balance 1987-88, (International Institute for Strategic Studies,1987), p138.
32 Hanlon, Dr Joseph. *Beggar your Neighbours*, p14-16.
33 *Ibid*, p17, 19.
34 *Race Relations Annual*, 1987/88, p544.
35 *Ibid*, 1986, p810.
36 *The Citizen*, 5/12/97.
37 *Sunday Times*, 30/3/97.
38 *The Citizen*, 15/10/97; *The Star*, 17/10/97.
39 *The Citizen*, 15, 16/10/97.
40 *The Star*, 16/10/97.
41 *The Citizen*, 16/10/97.
42 *The Star*, 9/10/96.
43 *Ibid*, 22/10/86.
44 *The Citizen*, 18/9/96.
45 *The Star*, 10/10/97; *The Citizen*, 10/10/97.
46 *The Star*, 23/10/96; *The Citizen*, 29/10/96; *Sunday Times*, 27/10/96.
47 Hugo, G, Snel, S, *Military Intelligence & the Counter-Revolutionary War*, p8-11.

Chapter 6

1 Evidence: State versus Dr Wouter Basson.
2 *Ibid.*
3 Interview Colonel Dr Wouter Basson, 1987.
4 Interview Col Andre Bestbier, 1987.
5 *Race Relations Annual*, 1982, p194.
6 *Ibid*, 1983, p595.
7 Stiff, Peter, *The Silent War*, p379-383.
8Evidence Trevor Floyd and Dr Daan Goosen, State vs Basson.
9 Stiff, Peter, *Cry Zimbabwe*, Chapter 4.
10 *Ibid*, Chapter 5.
11 *Ibid*, Chapter 10.
12Evidence Major Neil, State vs Dr Wouter Basson
13 Interview with Johnny (*nom de guerre*), 12/4/91.
14 TRC Reports, Vol 2, p86.
15 Stiff, Peter and Reid Daly, Lt-Col R. *Selous Scouts: Top Secret War*, p369
16 Moyo, Isaiah. *Moyo's Highway To Hell* (unpublished manuscript).
17 Interview Col Bert Sachse, 1994.
18 Interview Major Brian (*nom de guerre*), 1995.

Chapter 7

1 Streek, Barry and Wickstead, Richard. *Render unto Kaiser*, p239.
2 *Ibid*, p15.
3 *Ibid*, p26.
4 *Ibid*, p27.
5 *Ibid*, p26.
6 *Race Relations Annual*, 1981, p291.
7 Streek, Barry and Wickstead, Richard. *Render unto Kaiser*, p12.
8 *Ibid*, p30-31.
9 *Sowetan* 2/4/93.
10 Streek, Barry and Wickstead, Richard. *Render unto Kaiser*, p9
11 *Ibid*, p239.
12 *Ibid*, p113.
13 *Ibid*, p86.
14 *Ibid*, Cap 8.
15 *Ibid*, 1988/89, p137.
16 *Ibid*, 1987/88, p937-938.
17 *Ibid*, 1986 (Part 2), p698.
18 *Ibid*, 1978, p287-289.
19 *Ibid*, 1980, p403-405.
20 *Ibid*, 1980, p402-407.
21 *Ibid*, 1981, p297.
22 *Ibid*, p300.
23 *Ibid* 1981 P301
25 *Ibid* 1981 P300
26 Hugo, G, Snel, S, *Military Intelligence and the Counter-revolutionary War*, p34
27 *Race Relations Annual*, 1981, p301.
28 *Sowetan*, 2/4/1993.
29 Streek, Barry and Wickstead, Richard. *Render unto Kaiser*, p91-92.
30 *Ibid*, p91-92 .
31 Interview Maj-Gen Bantu Holomisa, 24/11/99.
32 Flower, Ken. *Serving Secretly*, p220.
33 *Ibid*, p220.
34 *Scope* Magazine, 20/5/88.
35 Stiff, Peter and Reid Daly, Lt-Col R. *Selous Scouts: Top Secret War*, p422.
36 Flower, Ken. *Serving Secretly*, p220
37 Stiff, Peter and Reid Daly, Lt-Col R. *Selous Scouts: Top Secret War*, p423
38 Film *Rebellion*; *Sunday Independent*, review of *Pamwe Chete*.
39 Note by General Bantu Holomisa, 12/8/88.
40 Company Office records, Pretoria.
41 Interview Col Lourens du Plessis, 8/3/2000.
42 Interview Gen Daan Hamman, 31/3/1988.
43 TRC Reports, Vol. 5, p129.
44 Interview Gen Banrtu Holomisa, 24/11/99.
45 *Race Relations Annual*, 1985, p93.
46 *Ibid*, 1985, p277.
47 Attorney's letter to the *SundayTimes*, dated 15/9/88.
48 TDF paysheet for white advisers, April 1986.
49 Transkei Public Accounts Committee: Minutes of Evidence, 1983, p36.
50 Contract between Transkei Government and Security Services Transkei.
51 *Scope* Magazine, 20/5, 3/6/1988
52 *Race Relations Annual*, 1982, p391, 392.
53 Transkei National Assembly Reports of Sessional Committee on Public Accounts 1983, 1985, 1986; Republic of Transkei Reports of the Auditor-General on the Appropriation and Miscellaneous Accounts and on the Accounts of the Lower Authorities for the financial year 1981/82 and 1984/85.
54 Letter to Receiver of Revenue, Pretoria.
55 *Scope* Magazine, 20/5, 3/6/88; Transkei government's file on ABC negotiations.
56 Transkei's Public Accounts Committee: Minutes of Evidence 3 May 1983, p38.
57 Interview Maj-Gen Bantu Holomisa, 24/11/99.
58 Hanlon, Joseph. *Beggar Your Neighbour*, p110.
59 *Ibid*, p113.
60 *Race Relations Annual*, 1983, p58.
61 'Top Secret' memorandum submitted to the TRC by Maj-Gen J L Griebeneuw.
62 *Race Relations Annual*, 1982, p195.
63 *Ibid*, 1982, p195.
64 TRC Reports, Vol. 3, p343-344
65 Ellis, Stephen & Sechaba, Tsepo. *Comrades Against Apartheid*, p126
66 *Race Relations Annual*, 1983, p195.
67 Ellis, Stephen, Sechaba, Tsepo. *Comrades Against Apartheid*, p177.
68 Gastrow, Sheila. *Who's Who in SA Politics*, No 4, p93.
69 Ellis, Stephen, Sechaba, Tsepo. *Comrades Against Apartheid*, p126; Stiff, Peter, *The Silent War*, Chapter 25.
70 'Top Secret' memorandum submitted to the TRC by Maj-Gen J L Griebeneuw.
71 *Race Relations Annual*, 1981, p302.
72 *Ibid*, 1982, p385.
73 *Ibid*, 1982, p385.
74 *Ibid*, p332.
75 *Sunday Times*, 18/3/90.
76 *Race Relations Annual*s, 1983, p334; 1984, p519.
77 *Ibid*, 1985, p515
78 *Ibid*, 1983, p334-335; 1984, p519.
79 *Ibid*, 1983, p334; p514, 519.
80 *Ibid*, 1983, p334;1984, p519.
81 *Ibid*, 1985, p290.
82 *Ibid*, 1985, p291-292.
83 *Ibid*, 1985, p289-290.
84 *Ibid*, 1985, p289-290.
85 *Ibid*, 1985, p290.
86 *Ibid*, 1984, p548.
87 Interview Colonel Lourens du Plessis, 8/3/2000; Hugo, G, Snel, Stef. *Military Intelligence and the Counter-revolutionary War*, p32; 'Top Secret' memorandum submitted to the TRC by Maj-Gen Griebenauw.

Chapter 8

1 *Race Relations Annual*, 1983, p281.
2 *Ibid*, 1983, p277.
3 *Ibid*, 1984, p395.
4 Ellis, Stephen, Sechaba, Tsepo. *Comrades Against Apartheid*, p156.
5 *Race Relations Annual*, 1983, p281, 395, 396, 449-451.
6 *The Argus*, 16/2/83.
7 Ellis, Stephen, Sechaba, Tsepo. *Comrades Against Apartheid*, p155-156.
8 Related to author by a senior olice officer, Pretoria, 1987.
9 *Race Relations Annual*,1985, p540.
10 *The Citizen*, 12/6/97.
11 *Ibid*, 11/6/97.
12 *The Star*, 28/5/86.
13 *The Citizen*, 12/6/97.
14 *Race Relations Annuals*,1986, p524-525; 1988/89, p526.
15 *Ibid*, 1986, p495.
16 *Ibid*, 1988/99, p525.
17 *Ibid*, 1989/90, p196.
18 *Ibid*, 1989/90, p196.
19 *Ibid*, 1984, p7-9, 77.
20 *Ibid*, 1984, p20.
21 Ellis, Stephen, Sechaba, Tsepo. *Comrades Against Apartheid*, p155.
22 *The Star*, 22/5/96.
23 *Ibid*, 22/5/96.
24 *Race Relations Annual*, 1985, p549
25 *The Star*, 22/5/96, *The Citizen*, 24/5/96.
26 *Race Relations Annual*, 1986, p539; *The Citizen*, 26/8/93.
27 *Ibid*, 1985, p289, 549.
28 *Ibid*, 1986, 539; Ellis, Stephen, Sechaba, Tsepo. *Comrades Against Apartheid*, p155.
29 Minnaar, Anthony, et al. *The Hidden Hand*, p275.
30 *Ibid*, p263-276
31 *Ibid*, p239; *Sowetan*, 26/8/93
32 *The Weekly Mail*, 3-9/1/92.
33 *Sowetan*, 26/8/93.
34 *The Weekly Mail*, 3-9/1/92.
35 Minnaar, Anthony, et al. *The Hidden Hand*, p276

Chapter 9

1 Taylor, Stephen. *Shaka's Children*, p345.
2 *Ibid*, p341.
3 *Ibid*, p342.
4 *Ibid*, p308-9.
5 *Ibid*, p346, 347.
6 *Ibid*, p347, 349.
7 Minnaar, Anthony, et al (editors). *Conflict and Violence in Natal/KwaZulu*, p71.
8 Taylor, Stephen. *Shaka's Children*, p340-352.
9 *The Citizen*, 6/9/96.
10 Minnaar, Anthony, et al (editors). *Conflict and Violence in Natal/KwaZulu*, p75.
11 *Sunday Independent*, 3/12/95; *Sunday Times*, 10/3/96.
12 Minnaar, Anthony, et al (editors). *Conflict and Violence in Natal/KwaZulu*, p40-41.
13 *Ibid*, p43-44.
14 *The Star*, 30/11/95.
15 Morris, Donald R. *The Washing of the Spears*, p308, 376-384.
16 Minnaar, Anthony, et al (editors). *Conflict and Violence in Natal/KwaZulu*, p87.
17 *The Star*, 5/11/95; *Saturday Star*, 22/6/96; *Sunday Times*, 10/3/96.
18 *The Star*, 21/6/96; *The Citizen*, 21/6/96; *Sunday Times*, 8/9/96.
19 *The Citizen*, 7/8/96; *The Star*, 7/8/96.
20 *Sunday Times*, 3/12/95.
21 *The Citizen*, 25/3/96.
22 *The Citizen*, 18, 26/3/96; *The Star*, 14/3, 13/6/96; *Saturday Star*, 15/6/96; *Sunday Independent*, 17/3/96.
23 *The Citizen*, 19/6/96.
24 *Citizen*, 13/3, 24/4/96; *The Star*, 24/4/96.
25 *The Citizen*, 14/3/96.
26 *Ibid*, 14/8/96.
27 *The Star*, 13/6/96; *Saturday Star*, 15/6/96; *Sunday Times*, 17/3/96; *The Citizen*, 3/8/96.
28 *The Citizen*, 24, 25/4/96;*The Weekly Mail*, 13-18/12/91.
29 *The Weekly Mail*, 13-18/12/91 *The Citizen*, 26/3/96.
30 *Sunday Times*, 5/5/96.
31 *The Weekly Mail* 13-18/91; *The Citizen*, 13/3/96.
32 *Saturday Star*, 4/5/96.
33 *The Citizen*, 9/8/96; *Sunday Independent* 3/12/95.
34 *The Weekly Mail*, 13-18/12/91; *The Star*, 20/3, 14/4/96.
35 *The Citizen*, 3/8/96.
36 *The Star*, 21/3/96; *The Citizen*, 14/3/96.
37 *The Citizen*, 3/8/96.

38 *Sunday Times*, 5/11, 3/12/95; *Sunday Independent*, 3/12/95; *The Star*, 24/4, 13, 21, 26/6, 7/8/96; *Saturday Star*, 30/11, 3/12/95, 4/5, 15/6, 17, 21/3, 7/8, 8/9/96; *The Citizen*, 25, 26/3, 12, 13, 15, 19, 20, 21, 28/6, 3, 6/8/96.
39 *Ibid*, 19/3/96.
40 *Ibid*, 2/12/96.
41 *Ibid*, 19/3/96.
42 *Sunday Times*, 17/3/96.
43 *The Citizen*, 14/3/96; *The Star*, 15/3/96.
44 *Ibid*, 2/8/96.
45` *Ibid*, 14/3/96.
46 *The Citizen*, 14/3/96 *The Star*, 27/3/96.
47 *The Star*, 18/4/96; *The Citizen*, 18/4/96.
48 *The Citizen*, 22/8/96.
49 *Ibid*, 24/4/96.
50 *The Citizen*, 12/3/96, *The Star*, 12/3/96
51 *The Citizen*, 12, 13, 20/3/96; *Sunday Independent* 5/11/95; *The Star*, 12/3/96; *Sunday Times*, 13/10/96.
52 *Sunday Independent*, 31/3/96.
53 *The Citizen*, 29/3/96.
54 *Sunday Independent*, 31/3/96.
55 *The Star*, 28, 29/3/96; *The Citizen*, 28, 29/3/96.
56 *The Star*, 27/3/96.
57 *The Citizen*, 14,16/3/96.
58 *Ibid*, 14, 20/3, 23/5/96; *The Star*, 11/9/96.
59 *Ibid*, 14/3, 2, 9, 20/8/96, 20/8/96.
60 *Ibid*, 16/4/96; *The Star*, 16/4/96.
61 *Ibid*, 26/3/96.
62 *Ibid*, 26/3/96.
63 *The Star*, 25/4/96.
64 *Sunday Independent*, 21/4/96.
65 *The Citizen*, 14/6/96.
66 *The Star*, 11/6/96; *The Citizen*, 14/6/96.
67 *The Star*, 14/3/96.
68 *The Citizen*, 26/3/96.
69 *The Star*, 29/11/96.
70 *Ibid*, 14/3/96.
71 *Sunday Times*, 3/12/95; *Saturday Star*, 4/5/96.
72 *Sunday Times*, 5/5/96.
73 *The Star*, 29/11/96.
74 *The Star*, 12/3/96.
75 *Saturday Star*, 20/4, 15/8/96; *The Citizen*, 30/4, 15/8, 21/9/96.
76 *The Star*, 17/5/96.
77 *Ibid*, 23/5/96.
78 *Ibid*, 29/11/96.
79 *The Citizen*, 6/9/96.
80 *The Star*, 29/11, 11/10/96; *The Citizen*, 11/10/96.
81 *The Citizen*, 13/8/96.
82 *The Citizen*, 27/8/96; *Sunday Independent* 1/9/96.
83 *The Citizen*, 12/10/96.
84 *Sunday Independent*, 27/10/96.
85 Kentridge, Matthew. *An Unofficial War*, p6-11.
86 *The Star*, 25/7/91.
87 *The Citizen*, 22, 24/7, 25/9/91; *The Star*, 13/12/91.
88 Kentridge, Matthew. *An Unofficial War*, p84.
89 Kentridge, Matthew. *An Unofficial War*, p85; *The Star*, 17/10/96.
90 *The Star*, 11/12/96.
91 *Ibid*, 17/10/96.
92 *Ibid*, 11/12/96.
93 *Ibid*, 17/10/96.
94 *Ibid*, 17/10/96.
95 Minnaar, Anthony, et al. *The Hidden Hand*, p194
96 *The Star*, 17/10/96; Minnaar, Anthony, et al. *The Hidden Hand*, p193.
97 Kentridge, Matthew. *An Unofficial War*, p85.
98 Minnaar, Anthony, et al. *The Hidden Hand*, p195.
99 Minnaar, Anthony, et al. *The Hidden Hand*, p195 *The Star*, 11/12/96; *The Citizen*, 26/7/96.
100 Kentridge, Matthew. *An Unofficial War*, p84, 87.
101 *The Star*, 17/10/96, 11/12/96.
102 *The Star*, undated clip.
103 *The Citizen*, 26/7/96 *The Star*, 11/12/96.
104 Minnaar, Anthony, et al. *The Hidden Hand*, p19; *The Star*, 11/12/96.
105 Kentridge, Matthew. *An Unofficial War*, p88.
106 Minnaar, Anthony, et al. *The Hidden Hand*, p197.
107 Kentridge, Matthew. *An Unofficial War*, p86; Minnaar, Anthony, et al. *The Hidden Hand*, p198.
108 Minnaar, Anthony, et al. *The Hidden Hand*, p200.
109 *The Star*, 11/12/96
110 Kentridge, Matthew. *An Unofficial War*, p87.
111 *Ibid*, p88.
112 Minnaar, Anthony, et al. *The Hidden Hand*, p201-203.
113 *Ibid*, p203, 204.
114 Kentridge, Matthew. *An Unofficial War*, 84.
115 Minnaar, Anthony, et al. *The Hidden Hand*, p204.
116 Minnaar, Anthony, et al. *The Hidden Hand*, 204-206; *The Star*, 11/12/96; *Sunday Independent*, 15/12/96.

Chapter 10

1 Hugo, G, Snel, S, *Military Intelligence and the Counter-revolutionary War*, p40; Interview Col Lourens du Plessis, 8/3/2000.
2 *Race Relations Annual*, 1986(Part 2).
3 Pottinger, Brian. *The Imperial Presidency*, p330
4 *Race Relations Annual*, 1978, p288.
5 Interview Col Gerrie Hugo, 8/3/2000; Interview Col Lourens du Plessis, 8/3/2000.
6 *Sunday Times*, 14/3/93.
7 Interview Gen Maj-Gen Bantu Holomisa, 24/11/99.
8 Interview Col Lourens du Plessis, 8/3/2000.
9 *Race Relations Annual*, 1985, p464.
10 TRC testimony Lt Gen Joffel van der Westhuizen.
11 'Top Secret' memorandum submitted to the TRC by Maj-Gen J L Griebenauw.
12 *The Citizen*, 25/3/93.
13 TRC testimony Lt Gen Joffel van der Westhuizen.
14 'Top Secret' memorandum submitted to the TRC. by Maj-Gen J L Griebenauw.
15 *Race Relations Annual*, 1986 (Part 2), p671-672.
16 *Ibid*, p671-672
17 Interview Col Lourens du Plessis, 8/3/2000.
18 Col Gerrie Hugo papers.
19 *Race Relations Annual*, 1986 (Part 2), p672.
20 Maj-Gen Bantu Holomisa papers.
21 *Race Relations Annual*,1986 (Part 2), p675.
22 *Ibid*, p672.
23 *Sunday Times*, 21/3/93; Col Gerrie Hugo papers.
24 'Top Secret' memorandum submitted to the TRC by Maj Gen J L Griebenauw.
25 *Eastern Province Herald* 8/10/1986; *Daily Dispatch* 8/4/99.
26 Col Gerrie Hugo papers.
27 Interview Col Lourens du Plessis, 8/3/2000; *Eastern Province Herald*, 8/10/86.
28 TRC testimony Lt Gen Joffel van der Westhuizen; *Daily Dispatch*, 8/4/99.
29 *Race Relations Annuals*, 1986 (Part 2), p673.
30 Col Gerrie Hugo papers.
31 *Ibid*.
32 *The Citizen*, 25/3/93.
33 Interview Col Lourens du Plessis, 8/3/2000.
34 *Race Relations Annual*, 1986 (Part 2), p673.
35 *Ibid*.
36 *Ibid*.
37 *Ibid*, p674.
38 *Ibid*, p672.
39 *Ibid*, p674.
40 Col Gerrie Hugo papers.
41 Maj-Gen Bantu Holomisa papers.
42 *The Citizen*, 18/3/97.
43 Col Gerrie Hugo papers.
44 *Ibid*.
45 *Ibid*.
46 *The Star*, 9/4/99.
47 Col Gerrie Hugo papers.
48 *Ibid*.
49 'Top Secret' Memorandum submitted to the TRC by Major-General J L Griebenauw.
50 Col Gerrie Hugo papers.
51 Interview Col Lourens du Plessis, 8/3/2000.
52 Col Gerrie Hugo papers.
53 Interview Col Lourens du Plessis, 8/3/2000.
54 'Top Secret' memorandum submitted to the TRC by Maj-Gen J L Griebenauw; *Daily Dispatch* 8/4/99.
55 *Daily Dispatch*, 14/11/86.
56 Interview General Holomisa, 24/11/99.
57 Interview Col Lourens du Plessis, 8/3/2000.
58 'Top Secret' memorandum submitted to the TRC by Major-General Jan Griebenauw;
59 Maj-Gen Bantu Holomisa papers.
60 *Race Relations Annual*, 1986 (Part2), p675.
61 *Ibid*, p673-674.
62 Interview Col Lourens du Plessis, 8/3/2000.
63 'Top Secret' memorandum submitted to the TRC by Major-General Jan Griebenauw
64 *Race Relations Annual*, 1986, (Part 2), p674.
65 *Ibid*, p675
66 Maj-Gen Bantu Holomisa papers; 'Top Secret' memorandum submitted to the TRC by Maj-Gen Jan Griebenauw; *Sunday Times*, 21/3/93.
67 Interview Col Lourens du Plessis, 8/3/2000.

Chapter 11

1 TDF Pay sheet.
2 Maj-Gen Bantu Holomisa papers.
3 Interview Col Lourens du Plessis, 8/3/2000.
4 Interview Maj-Gen Bantu Holomisa, 24/11/99.
5 Interview Col Lourens du Plessis, 8/3/2000.
6 Interview Maj-Gen Bantu Holomisa, 24/11/99.
7 *The Star*, 12/5/89.
8 *The Citizen*, 10/5/89;*The Star*, 14/5/89.
9 Harms Commission (Into certain irregularities/illegalities), p99.
10 Harms Commission (Into certain irregularities/illegalities), p99.
11 Harms Commission (Into certain irregularities/illegalities), p87.
12 *The Star*, 14/5/89.
13 *The Citizen*, 10-11/5/89.
14 *Sunday Star*; 14/5/89.
15 Rhoodie, Eschel, *The Real Information Scandal*, p678.
16 Harms Commission (Into certain irregularities/illegalities), p85,86.
17 *The Star*, 11,12/5/89; *Sunday Star*, 14/5/89; *The Citizen*, 12,13/5/89
18 *Sunday Times*, 14/3/93.
19 *The Citizen*, 15/3/89.
20 'Top Secret' memorandum handed to the TRC by Major-General Griebenauw.
21 *Daily Dispatch*, 21/2/87.
22 *Sunday Star*, 28/2/88.
23 *Ibid*.
24 Harms Commission (Into certain irregularities/illegalities), p101.
25 *Sowetan*,12/3/93.
26 Conversation with ex -Selous Scout/ex-TDF adviser.
27 *Daily Dispatch*,20, 21/2, 20/3/87.
28 *Ibid*, 20,21/2/87.
29 *Daily Dispatch*, 20/2/87.
30 Interview Col Lourens du Plessis, 8/3/2000.
31 Story related by ex-Selous Scout.
32 Harms Commission (Into certain irregularities/illegalities), p102.
33 *Daily Dispatch*, 20,21/2/87.
34 *Ibid*, 21/2/87.
35 *Ibid*.
36 *Ibid*.
37 Interview Col Craig Williamson, 1996.
38 Interview Col Lourens du Plessis, 8/3/2000.
39 *Daily Dispatch*, 21/2/87.
40 *The Citizen*, 10/4/87.
41 *Sunday Star*, 28/2/88.
42 *The Star*, 12/4/87.
43 *Ibid*.
44 *Ibid*.
45 Interview Maj-Gen Bantu Holomisa, 24/11/99.
46 *The Star*, 12/4/87.
47 *Ibid*.
48 *Ibid*.
49 *Ibid*.
50 *The Citizen*, 6/4/87.
51 *The Citizen*, 6, 7/4, 7/11/87.
52 *The Citizen*, 6/4/87; *The Star*, 12/4/87.
53 *The Star*, 12/4/87.
54 *Ibid*.
55 *The Citizen*, 6/4/87.
56 *The Star*, 7/4/87.
57 *The Star*, 12/4/87.
58 *The Star*, 8/4/87
59 *Race Relations Annual*, 1987/88, p930-931.
60 *Ibid*, 1987/88, p914.
61 *Ibid*, 1987/88, p914; *Saturday Star*, 11/4/87
62 *Ibid*, 1987/88, p935.
63 *Ibid*, 1987/88, p936.
64 *Ibid*, 1987/88, p915.
65 *Ibid*, 1987/88 P932,110.
66 *Ibid*, 1988/89, p80,137.
67 *The Star*, 8/4/94.
68 *The Citizen*, 7/9/93; *Sowetan*, 7/9/93.

Chapter 12

1 *Race Relations Annual*, 1984, p68.
2 *New Nation*, 8-14/5/92.
3 *Race Relations Annual*, 1984, p68.
4 *Ibid*, 1984, p70, 761.
5 *Ibid*, 1985, p389.
6 State Security Council document produced at Goniwe Inquest.
8 *The Star*, 10/3/93.
9 *Race Relations Annual*, 1985, p390.
10 *Sunday Star*, 7/3/93.
11 SSC document produced at Goniwe inquest; *Sunday Times*, 7/3/93; *The Citizen*, 31/3/83.
12 *The Star*, 27/8/93.
13 *The Citizen*, 2/3/83;*New Nation* 8-14/5/92.
14 *The Star*, 27/8/93.
15 *Ibid*, 24/8/93.
16 *Sunday Times*, 6/6/93; *The Citizen*, 7/6/93.
17 *The Citizen*, 9/2/94
18 *Ibid*. 4/9/93
19 *The Citizen*, 8/9/93; *The Star*, 8-9/9/93.
20 *The Citizen*, 10/3/93.
21 *Sowetan*, 10/3/93; *The Star*, 10/3/93, *The Citizen*, 30/3/93.
22 *Sowetan*, 30/3/93; *The Citizen*, 30/3/93.
23 *Ibid*, 31/3/93.
24 *The Citizen*, 10/3, 3/9/94; *The Star*, 3, 10/3/94.
25 *The Star*, 10/3/94.
26 SSC document produced at Goniwe inquest; *The Star*, 2/3/93; *Sunday Times*, 7/3/93.
27 *The Citizen*, 4/3/96.
28 *The Star*, 26/2/98.
29 *The Citizen*, 16/6, 21/9/93; *Sowetan*, 16/6, 21-22/9/93; *The Star*, 21/9/93.
30 *The Star*, 3/3/98.
31 *Sunday Independent*, 4/5/97; *The Star*, 6/3/98.
32 *Sunday Times*, 22/8/93.
33 *The Star*, 4/3/93.
34 *Sunday Star*, 16/8/92; *The Star*, 2/3/93.
35 *Sunday Times*, 10/5/92; *Saturday Star*, 9/5/92.
36 *Sunday Times*, 29/5/94.
37 *The Star*, 12/9/97.
38 Flower, Ken. *Serving Secretly*, p161.
39 *The Star*, 25/9, 27/9/97; *The Citizen*, 25/9/97.
40 *The Star*, 27/5/92; *The Citizen*, 29/5/92.
41 *The Citizen*, 15/5/92.
42 *The Star*, 16/5/96.
43 *Ibid*, 16/11/95.
44 *The Star*, 16/11/95; *The Citizen*, 2, 30/1**0/97.**
45 *Sowetan*, 15/6, 13, 18/8/93; *The Citizen*, 15/6, 12, 13, 17, 18, 20/8/93; *Sunday Times*, 20/6, 22/8/93; *The Star*, 15/6, 20/8/93; *Saturday Star*, 14/8/93; *The Weekly Mail* 13/8, 3/9/93.
46 *The Citizen*, 2/10/97.

Chapter 13

1 TRC testimony Col Joe Verster, 15/3/2000.
2 *The Citizen*, 20/2/91.
3 *Sunday Times*, 10/3/91.
4 *Sunday Star*, 25/2/90.

5 *The Citizen*, 7/3/90.
6 TRC testimony Col Joe Verster, 15/3/2000.
7 *Sunday Times*, 10/3/91
8 TRC testimony Maj-Gen Eddie Webb, 20/6/2000.
9 TRC Reports, Vol 2, p137.
10 Harms Commission (into alleged murders), p42
11 *Ibid*, p39
12 *The Star*, 30/5/90.
13 Harms Commission (into alleged murders), p55-56
14 TRC Reports, Vol 2, p140.
15 TRC testimony Maj-Gen Eddie Webb, 20/6/2000.
16 *The Citizen*, 26/7, 23, 25/11/90; *The Star*, 26/7, 23, 27/11/90; *New Nation*, 23-29/11/90.
17 *New Nation*, 1/3-7/3/91.
18 Evidence Trevor Floyd: State versus Dr Wouter Basson.
19 Interview Major Brian (nom de guerre), 1995.
20 *Sunday Times*, 4/11/90.
21 Discussion with Mike Tippett, Oct 2001.
22 Stiff, Peter, as told to by Lt Col Ron Reid Daly. *Selous Scouts; Top Secret War*, p406; Interview ex-Det Insp John Birch, BSAP/SB., 1982.
23 Interview ex-Det Insp John Birch, BSAP/SB, 1982.
24 *The Citizen*, 28/10/90, 9/10/91.
25 *Sunday Times*, 4/11/90.
26 SABC programme: Agenda:The Forgotten Ones: April 1995.
27 *The Star*, 10/11/91.
28 *Business Day*, 8/4/88.
29 TRC Reports, Vol 2, p121.
30 TRC Reports, Vol 2, p119
31 *Business Day*, 30/3/88; *The Citizen*, 31/3/88.
32 *Sunday Times*, 10/4/88.
33 *The Star*, 31/3/88.
34 *Ibid*, 14/4/88.
35 *The Star*, 14/10/97; *The Citizen*, 1, 6/4/98.
36 *The Star*, 23/6/88.
37 *The Citizen*, 9/1/91.
38 *The Citizen*, 22, 23, 24, 28, 30/6, 5, 6/7, 3/8, 8, 21, 23, 29/9, 12, 13, 14, 15, 22/10, 5, 8/11, 9/12/88; *The Star*, 22, 23, 28/6, 6/7, 12, 13, 16/10/88, 9/12/91; *Sunday Star*, 9/7, 16/10/88; *Business Day* 28/6, 6/7, 13/10/88.
39 *The Star*, 18/3/97.
40 *The New American*, Vol 11, No 18, 4/9/95.
41 *The Star*, 18/3/97.

Chapter 14

1 Reitz, Deneys, Trekking on, Faber and Faber, London, 1934.
2 Dippenaar, Marius de Witt. *The History of the South African Police*, 1913-1988, Chapter 4; Visser, George Cloete. *OB: Traitors or Patriots*, Chaps 1-4.
3 *Race Relations Annual*, 1974, p46-48.
4 *Ibid*, 1977, p42.
5 *Ibid*, 1981, p41.
6 *Race Relations Annual*, 1982, p576
7 *Ibid*, 1975, p64; 1978, p54.
8 *Ibid*, 1981, p60.
10 *Ibid*, 1982, p198.
11 *Ibid*, 1983, p576.
12 *Ibid*, 1983, p577-578.
13 *Ibid*, 1983, p578.
14 *Ibid*, 1984, p748-750.
15 *Ibid*, 1984, p750.
16 ANC's Kabwe Conference Report, 1985.
17 *Race Relations Annual*, 1985, p420-421
18 *Ibid*, 1985, p420
19 Stiff, Peter. *The Silent War*, p317-338.
20 ANC's Kabwe Conference Report and related ANC documents.
21 *Frontline Fellowship News*, Sept 1986.
22 The Veterans Association of South Africa, organisers' manual.
23 *Sowetan*, clip, date unknown.
24 Hugo, G, Snel, Stef. *Military Intelligence and the Counter-Revolutionary War*, p65.
25 *Sowetan*, 1988, clip, date u/k.
26 *The Citizen*, 3/9/1988.
27 *Business Day*, 18/10/1988.
28 *Frontline Fellowship News*, Vol 3, 1987.
29 *Mission to South Africa*, p20.
30 *Ibid*, p148
31 Renwick, Robin. *Unconventional Diplomacy in Southern Africa*, p111.
32 Business Day 21/5/86, Stiff, Peter. *The Silent War*, Chapter 30.
33 Barber, James, Barratt, John. *South Africa's Foreign Policy: The search for status and security 1945-1988*, p333-334.
34 Stiff, Peter. *Nine Days of War*, Cap 13.
35 *The Citizen*, 24/4/1992.
36 *Ibid*, 19/5/92.

Chapter 15

1 *Race Relations Annual*, 1995, p306-309.
2 TRC testimony Maj-Gen Joep Joubert, 6/4/1999.
3 TRC testimony General Geldenhuys, 9/10/97.
4 TRC testimony Maj-Gen Joep Joubert, 21/1/99.
5 TRC testimony Trevor Floyd, 21/1/99
6 TRC testimony Col Cronje; *The Star*, 1/11/96.
7 TRC testimony Col Abraham Christoffel Kendall, 21/01/1999
8 *The Star*, 1/11/96.
9 *Race Relations Annual*, 1986 Part 2, p546- 549, 635-639, 655-658, 681-692.
10 TRC testimony Maj-Gen Joep Joubert, 6/4/99.
11 Evidence in State vs Dr.Wouter Basson; TRC testimony Col Charl Naude, 7/4/99.
12 *Sowetan*, 2/7/86.
13 *The Star*, 1/11/96; *The Star*, 10/10/97; *Sunday Independent*, 3/11/96.
14 TRC testimony Col Charl Naude 7/4/99.
15 Stiff, Peter, *The Silent War*, p222.
16 *Race Relations Annual*, 1986 (Part 2), p535.
17 *The Star*, 7/3/97.
18 *Sowetan*, 31/10/96; *The Star*, 7/3/97.
19 *Sunday Times*, 2/3/97.
20 TRC testimony Col Charl Naude, 7/4/89.
21 *The Star*, news clip, date unknown.
22 TRC testimony Chris Ribeiro, 28/2/1999.
23 *The Star*, 31/10/96, 4/3, 10/10/97; *Sunday Times*, 2/3/97; *Sowetan*, 31/10/96.
24 *Saturday Star*, 1/3/97.
25 *Sunday Star*, 7/12/86.
26 *The Star*, 15/10/97.
27 *Sunday Times*, 2/3/97.
28 *Sunday Star*, 26/10/90.
29 *The Star*, 9/10/97.
30 Harms Commission (into alleged murders), p184.
31 *Saturday Star*, 4/8/90.
32 Harms Commission (into alleged murders), p181-186.
33 *Saturday Star*, 4/8/90.
34 Harms Commission (into alleged murders), p181-186
35 *The Citizen*, 31/10/96.
36 *The Citizen*, 9/10/97;*The Star*, 9, 10/10/97.
37 Stiff, Peter. *Nine Days of War*.
38 Interview Col Eugene de Kock in C-Max Prison, 3/4/2001.
39 *The Citizen*, 4/10/01; *The Star*, 5/9/2001.
40 *The Citizen*, 4/10/01.
41 *Ibid*, 9/10/97.
42 *Ibid*, 9/10/97.
43 *The Star*, 17/7/95.
44 *The Citizen*, 4/11/92; *The Star*, 9/11/92.

Chapter 16

1 *The Star*, 9/7/91
2 *The Star*, 5/12/89, 18/2/90, 8/7/91; *The Citizen*, 6/7/91.
3 Discussion with Maj-Gen Joep Joubert.
4 *Stander : Bank Robber*.
5 *The Star*, 9/2/90.
6 *The Citizen*, 10/5/90, 5/11/92.
7 TRC testimony of Slang van Zyl, 16/3/2000; TRC testimony of Joe Verster, 15/3/2000; and TRC testimony of Staal Burger, 21/6/2000.
8 *Sunday Star*, 3/12/89.
9 *The Star*, 7/4/90.
10 Diary of Wouter J Basson.
11 TRC testimony of Wouter J Basson, 3/6/2000.
12 Lubowski inquest: Slang van Zyl's Section 29 statement.
13 *The Citizen*, 10/5/90.
14 Evidence of Phaal: State vs Dr Wouter Basson.
15 TRC testimony of Staal Burger, 21/6/2000.
16 Diary of Wouter J Basson.
17 TRC Report, Vol 2, p140.
18 TRC testimony of Maj-Gen Eddie Webb, 19/6/2000.
19 TRC testimony of Slang van Zyl, 12/6/2000.
20 TRC testimony of Staal Burger, 21/6/2000.
21 TRC testimony of Wouter J Basson, 23/6/2000.
22 *Sunday Star*, 25/2/90; Star, 8/2/91.
23 *The Star*, 8/2/91; *Sunday Star*, 25/2/90.
24 *The Star*, 8/2/91; *Sunday Times*, 16/3/97.
25 *Sunday Star*, 25/2/90; *Sunday Times*, 16/3/97.
26 *The Star*, 28/2/90, 8/2, 8/10/91; *The Citizen*, 28/8/90; *Saturday Star*, 9/2/91; *Sunday Star*, 8/3/92.
27 TRC testimony, Staal Burger, 21/6/2000.
28 *The Star*, 20/1/93.
29 TRC testimony of Chappie Maree, 27/9/2000.
30 TRC testimony of Calla Botha, 2/10/2000.
31 *The Citizen*, 1/12/89; *Sunday Times*, 3/12/89.
32 *Sunday Times*, 11/3/90.
33 Lubowski Inquest; *The Citizen*, 20/10/92.
34 TRC testimony of Ferdi Barnard, 27/9/2000.
35 *The Citizen*, 19/3/98.
36 *The Star*, 29/10/92.
37 *The Star*, 31/10/92; *The Citizen*, 18/11/92.
38 TRC testimony of Slang van Zyl, 16/3/2000.
39 TRC testimony of Staal Burger, 22/6/2000.
40 TRC testimony Calla Botha, 2/10/2000.
41 *Saturday Star*, 24/3/90.
42 *The Citizen*, 31/10/92.
43 Lubowski Inquest: Section 29 statement of Ferdi Barnard.
44 *The Citizen*, 19/3/98.
45 *The Weekly Mail*, 4/12/92.
46 *The Citizen*, 15/10/92; *The Star*, 15/10/92; *The Weekly Mail*,16-22/3/1990.
47 *The Citizen*, 9/10/92.
48 *The Mail and Guardian*, 21-27 Nov 1997
49 *Saturday Star*, 28/4, 27/9/90; *Sunday Star*, 25/3, 8/4/90; *The Star*, 30/4, 17/5/90, 27/9/90; *The Weekly Mail*, 27/4- 3/5/90,18-24/5/90; *The Citizen*, 5, 24/5/90.50.
51 TRC Amnesty Hearing, CT, Ferdi Barnard, 27/9/2000.
52 *The Star*, 31/3/98, *The Citizen*, 31/3/98, 2/4/98.
53 TRC testimony of Ferdi Barnard, 27/9/2000.
54 *The Citizen*, 18/3/98.
55 TRC testimony of Ferdi Barnard, 27/9/2000.
56 *Saturday Star*, 24/2/90.
57 TRC testimony of Ferdi Barnard, 27/9/2000.
58 TRC testimony of Calla Botha, 2/10/2000; *The Citizen*, 5/2, 7/3, 1/4/98; *The Star*, 31/3/98.
59 *Saturday Star*, 24/2/90; *Sunday Times*, 6/5/90; *The Star*, 15/10/92; *The Citizen*, 24/4/92.
60 *Sunday Times*, 11, 18/10/92.
61 *Sunday Times*, 6/5/90, 11/10/92; *The Star*, 15/10/92.
62 *Sunday Times*, 18/10.92; *Saturday Star*, 17/11/90; *The Star*, 13/10/92.
63 *The Citizen*, 31/3/89.
65 *The Citizen*, 25/2/98.
66 *The Citizen*, 18/3/98.
67 TRC testimony Ferdi Barnard, 27/9/2000.
68 *The Star*, 20/11/92; *The Citizen*, 20/11/92.
69 TRC testimony of Calla Botha, 2/10/2000.
70 *Saturday Star*, 23/1/93; *The Citizen*, 2/12/92.
71 TRC testimony of Ferdi Barnard, 27/9/2000.
72 *The Citizen*, 24/4/92; *Sunday Star*, 3/12/89; *Saturday Star*, 17/10/92.
73 *Sunday Times*, 3/5/92; *The Citizen*, 4/5/92.
74 Potgieter, De Wet. *Contraband*, p186.
75 Lubowski inquest: Slang's van Zyl's Section 29 statement, 18/3/90.
76 TRC testimony of Calla Botha, 2/10/2000.
77 TRC testimony Gen Eddie Webb, 19/6/2000.
78 *The Weekly Mail and Guardian*, 5-11/9/97.
79 *The Star*, 31/3/98.
80 *The Star*, 3/9/97.
81 *The Weekly Mail*, 1-7/12/89.
82 Testimony Dr. Immelman, Dr. Schalk van Rensburg and Dr. Odendaal of RRL: State vs Dr Wouter Basson.
83 Lubowski inquest: Testimony D/C Smit; TRC testimony of Ferdi Barnard, 27/9/2000; *Sunday Times*, 3/12/89; *The Citizen*,14/10/92, 4/3/98.
84 TRC testimony of Slang van Zyl, 12/6/2000.
85 TRC testimony of Ferdi Barnard, 28/9/2000.
86 TRC testimony of Maj-Gen Webb, 19/6/2000.
87 TRC testimony of Staal Burger, 21/6/2000.
88 TRC testimony of Ferdi Barnard, 28/9/2000.
89 TRC testimony of Maj-Gen Eddie Webb, CT, 20/6/2000.
90 Testimony of Dr Immelman and Dr Stian Wandrag: State vs Dr. Wouter Basson.
91 TRC testimony of Maj-Gen Eddie Webb, 20/6/2000.
92 TRC testimony of Ferdi Barnard, 28/9/2000.
93 TRC testimony of Maj-Gen Eddie Webb, 20/6/2000.
94 TRC testimony of Calla Botha, 2/10/2000.
96 TRC amnesty hearing, 15/3/2000.
97 TRC testimony of Maj Gen Eddie Webb, 20/6/2000.
98 TRC testimony of Calla Botha, 2/10/2000; Wouter J Basson, 23/6/2000.

Chapter 17

1 *Sunday Times*, 4/11/90.
2 *The Star*, 15/10/88; *Sunday Star*, 16/10/88; *The Citizen*, 15/10/88.
3 *The Star*, 25/10/88.
4 *The Citizen*, 14/10/88.
5 *Ibid*.
6 *Sunday Times*, 16/10/87.
7 *The Citizen*, 2/11/88.
8 *Ibid*, 22/10/88.
9 *The Star*, 1/11/88.
10 *The Citizen*, 25/10/88
11 *Ibid*, 7/4/89
12 McAleese, Peter. *No Mean Soldier*, p120-154.
13 *The Citizen*, 22/6/89.
14 Interviews Major Brian, April 95; *Sunday Times*, 10/7/88; *The Citizen*, 1/7, 22/8/89; *The Star*, 3, 4, 5, 6, 25/7/88, 5/9/91, 12/10/88; *Sunday Star*, 16/10/88; *Business Day* 6/7,18/10/88.
15 *Sunday Star*, 2/9/90.
16 *Sunday Star*, 2/9/90.
17 *The Star*, 13/10/88.
18 *Sunday Times*, 16 , 23/10/88; *The Citizen*, 30/8, 12-15, 18, 20-22, 25-27/ /10/88, 1, 2, 4, 5, 8, 9, 12, 15 & 19/11/88, *The Star*, 19/2/88, 12, 13, 14, 15, 18, 20, 25, 1, 20/11/88; *Sunday Star*, 16/10/88; *Business Day*, 21/10/88.
19 *The Citizen*, 22/6/88.
20 *The Citizen*, 28/4/93 Second trial *The Citizen*, 21/1/88, 27/2/88, 28/5/88, 22/6/88, 11 & 24/8/88, 21/9, 11,16/11, 10, 21, 22, 30/3, 1, 4, 5, 7, 8, 11, 13, 14, 21, 22/5, 5, 6, 8, 10/6/89, 28/4, 28/8/93; *The Star*, 6/6/88, *Business Day*; 4, 7/4/89.
21 *Business Day*, 19/10/88; *The Star*, 19/10/88.
22 *Sunday Times*, 4/3/90.
23 *Business Day*, 23/2/90.
24 *Sunday Times*, 4/3/90.
25 *Sunday Times*, 23/9/90.
26 *Sunday Star*, 10/1/91.
27 *The Hidden Hand* - interviews - BBC Channel 4 TV documentary, 1991.
28 Supreme Court case No 20322/90 — file empty.
29 *Sunday Times*, 4/11/90.
30 *Sunday Star*, 10, 17/2/91; *The Star*, 23/2, 8/11/90,

10/11/91; *The Citizen*, 9/10/91; *Sunday Times*, 18/2, 4/3, 23/9, 28/10, 4/11/90; *Business Day*, 23/2/90.
31 *The Star*, 21/2/91;*The Star*, 7/9/90.
32 Star, 10/5/91.
33 *The Citizen*, 9/10/91.
34 *Sunday Times*, 18/7/93.
35 Stiff, Peter.*The Silent War*, Chap 27.
36 *The Citizen*, 5/11, 11/12/93.
37 *Ibid*, 16/7/93.
38 *Ibid*, 3/8/93.
39 *Ibid*, 9, 20/11, 11/12/93; *Sunday Times*, 18/7, 21/11/93.
40 *Ibid*, 8/2/94.
41 *The Citizen*, 8/2/94; *The Star*, 8/2/94.
42 *The Citizen*, 20/8/94.
43 *The Star*, 17/8/94; *Sunday Times*, 19/3/95.
44 *The Citizen*, 20/8/94.
45 *Sunday Times*, 19/3/95.
46 Intelligence grapevine.
47 The Star, 20/1/2000.
48 *The Star*, 20/1/2000.
49 *The Star*, 8/12/97, 20/1/2000; *The Citizen*, 15/12/97.

Chapter 18

1 Lubowski inquest: Testimonies of evidence Johan Niemöller and Charles Neelse;
2 Stiff, Peter. Nine days of War, p175-187.
3 *Ibid*, p270
4 *Ibid*, p11-134.
5 Ibid, p90.
6 *The Citizen*, 24/5/90, Nine Days P272
7 Stiff, Peter. Nine Days of War, p64.
8 *The Star*, 13/9, 2/10, 7/11/89.
9 Stiff, Peter. Nine days of War, p201, 207; *The Star*, 27/7/89.
10 *The Citizen*, 26/7/91.
11 TRC Reports, Vol 2, p79.
12 Stiff, Peter. *Nine Days of War*, p283.
13 *Sunday Independent*, 28/4/96; *New Nation*, 15-219/89.
14 *Saturday Star*, 23/3/91.
15 See Stiff, Peter. *Nine Days of War*.
16 Stiff, Peter. Nine Days of War, p 232-247; *Sunday Times*, 8/10/89.
17 *The Citizen*, 27/6/92.
18 *The Star*, 9/6/89.
19 *New Nation*, Oct 27-2 Nov 1989; The Namibian (Windhoek), 23/10/89; *Sunday Times*, 8, 22/10/89; *Sunday Star*, 22/10/89; *The Citizen*, 7, 19, 20, 21/10/89;*The Star*, 7-9, 19-20/10/89.
20 Basson, Nico and Motinga, Nico. *Call them Spies*; *Sunday Star*, 24/3/91; *The Citizen*, 22/4/91; *The Star*, 1/7/89.
21 *The Star*, 5/11/92, 20/1/93; *Sunday Star*, 8/11/92; evidence in State vs Dr Wouter Basson.
22 *The Star*, 14/8/92.
23 TRC testimony of Ferdi Barnard, 28/9/2000.
24 Lubowski inquest: evidence of Charles Neelse.
25 TRC testimony of Ferdi Barnard, 28/9/2000.
26 Lubowski inquest.
27 Lubowski inquest: testimony of D/C Smit.
28 Lubowski Inquest
29 *Sunday Star*, 26/11/89; *The Citizen*, 2/12/89.
30 *Sunday Star*, 13/5/90; *Sunday Times*, 12/11/89.
31 *Sunday Star*, 13/5/90.
32 *Sunday Times*, 1/10/89.
33 *The Citizen*, 14, 16/4, 3/9/92.
34 *The Citizen*, 12/8/89;*The Star*, 12/8/89, 16/4/92.
35 Lubowski inquest record, p78.
36 *Sunday Times*, 17/9/89.
37 *Sunday Independent*, 28/4/96.
38 TRC testimony of Slang van Zyl, 19/6/2000.
39 TRC testimony of Maj-Gen Eddie Webb, 19/6/2000.
40 *The Star*, 9, 16/5/90; *Sunday Star*, 8/11/92.
41 *The Citizen*, 24/5/90.
42 Pauw, Jaques, *In the Heart of the Whore*, p178.
43 Harms Commission (into alleged murders), p65-66.
44 Harms Commission (into alleged murders), p65.
45 Lubowski inquest: section 29 statement of Slang van Zyl, 22/3/90.
46 *Ibid*.
47 TRC testimony of Chappie Maree, 27/9/2000.
48 Lubowski inquest: statement by Donald Acheson, p 66-71.
49 *The Star*, 5/11/92; *The Citizen*, 5/11/92.
50 Lubowski inquest: testimony of Mrs Ratzke.
51 *Saturday Star*, 31/3/90; *Sunday Star*, 13/5/90; TRC testimony of Staal Burger, 21/6/2000.
52 *The Star*, 15/9/89.
53 Lubowski Inquest: testimony of D/C Smit.
54 *The Star*, 16/9/89.
55 *The Star*, 16, 24/9/89.
56 *New Nation*, 27/10 - 2/11/89.
57 Stiff, Peter. *Nine Days of War*, 1st Ed, p299-300.
58 *The Star*, 9/3/90.
59 Lubowski inquest: section 29 statement of Ferdi Barnard, 27/11/89.
60 *Ibid*, 21/12/89.
61 *The Star*, 29/9/89.
62 *Ibid*.
63 *Sunday Times*, 10/12/89; *The Citizen*, 3/10/89.
64 *The Citizen*, 14/4/92.
65 *Ibid*, 14/3/97.
66 *Ibid*, 14/10/92.
67 *The Star*, 24/1/90.
68 Lubowski inquest: Section 29 statement of Calla Botha.
69 TRC testimony of Ferdi Barnard, 2/10/2000.
70 *Ibid*.
71 *Saturday Star*, 2/12/89.
72 *The Star*, 1/12/97; *Sunday Star*, 3/12/89; *Sunday Times*, 3/12/89.
73 Lubowski inquest: section 29 statement of Calla Botha; *Sunday Times*, 3/12/89.
74 *The Citizen*, 14/10/92; *The Star*, 14/10/92; *Sunday Times*, 8/11/92.
75 *The Star*, 6/3/90.
76 TRC testimony of Calla Botha, 2/10/2000.
77 TRC testimony Chappie Marais, 27/9/2000.
78 *Sunday Times*, 3/12/89.
79 *The Star*, 6/11/92; *The Citizen*, 24/11/92.
80 *The Citizen*, 9/3/91.
81 *Sunday Times*, 29/9/91.
82 Lubowski inquest: testimony of D/C Smit.
83 *The Citizen*, 6, 22/1, 2/12/92; *Sunday Times*, 22/11/92.
84 Lubowski inquest: testimony of D/C Smit.
85 *The Star*, 15/3/90; *The Citizen*, 17/2/90.
87 Lubowski inquest: findings, p78-86.
88 Lubowski inquest findings, p71-76.
89 *The Citizen*, 29/10/90.
90 *The Star*, 10/1/91.
91 Lubowski inquest record: statement of Donald Acheson, p79.
92 *Sunday Times*, 13/1/91.
93 *Ibid*, 13/1/91.
94 *The Citizen*, 2/4/91.
95 TRC testimony of Ferdi Barnard, 28/9/2000.

Chapter 19

1 *The Citizen*, 7/3/90.
2 Pauw, Jacques. *In the Heart of the Whore*, p181.
3 *Sunday Times*, 11/3/90.
4 Interview with anon 5-Recce officer.
5 *Sunday Star*, 3/12/89
6 *Sunday Times*, 22/11/92.
7 *The Star*, 27/11/92; *The Citizen*, 17/5, 4/11/92.
8 *Saturday Star*, 10/2/90.
9 *The Citizen*, 1/8/90.
10 *The Star*, 16/2/90.
11 *Sunday Times*, 11, 18/3/90.
12 TRC testimony of Ferdi Barnard, 2/10/2000.
13 *The Star*, 9/5/90; *The Citizen*, 9/5/90.
14 Harms Commission (into alleged murders), p50.
15 *The Citizen*, 14, 15/10/92.
16 *Sunday Times*, 29/4/90.
17 *The Weekly Mail*, 16-22/10/92.
18 *The Citizen*, 10/5/90.
19 *The Star*, 2/12/92.
20 *The Citizen*, 3/12/92.
21 Harms Commission (into alleged murders).
22 *The Star*, 4/5/90.
23 *The Star*, undated clipping.
24 TRC Report, Vol 2, p143.
25 *The Citizen*, 4, 18/9/97.
26 *Ibid*, 5/6/89.

Chapter 20

1 Stiff, Peter. *The Silent War*; Race Relations Annual, 1989/90, p215-216.
2 Interview Col Gerrie Hugo, 8/3/2000.
3 De Kock, Col Eugene, Gordin, Jeremy. A *Long Night's Damage*, p286.
4 De Klerk, FW.*The Last Trek*, p194-203.
5 Stiff, Peter. *The Silent War*, p557-558.
6 Hamman, Hilton, *Days of the Generals*, p212-213.
7 De Klerk, F W. *The Last Trek*, p208-210.
8 *Ibid*.
9 Stiff, Peter. *The Silent War*, p557-559.
10 *The Citizen*,; *The Star*: undated news clips.
11 *Race Relations Annual*, 1994/95, p428.

Chapter 21

1 ANC's Kabwe Conference Report, June 1985.
2 ANC's Commission on Strategy and Tactics.
3 Radio Freedom transcript 16/2/87.
4 ANC's Commission on Strategy and Tactics.
5 Stiff, Peter, *The Silent War*, p393.
6 *Ibid*, 505.
7 Shubin, Vladimir. *ANC: A View from Moscow*, p332-339.
8 Kasrils, R. *Armed and Dengerous,* p30.
9 Mandela, Nelson. *Long Walk to Freedom*, p638-648.
10 *The Star*, undated clip.
11 Shubin, Vladimir Shubin, *ANC: A view from Moscow*, p329.
12 *Ibid*.
13 Crocker, Chester. *High Noon in Southern Africa*.
14 Kasrils, R. *Armed and Dangerous,* p301.
15 *The Citizen*, undated clip.
16 *Race Relations Annuals*, 1989/90, p679.
17 Security Police document.
18 Stadler, Maj-Gen Herman D. *The other Side of the Story*, p95.
19 *Ibid*, p90-98.
20 Stiff, Peter. *The Silent War*, p505.
21 SACP discussion document, undated.

Chapter 22

1 *Race Relations Annual*, 1989/90, p61.
2 *Ibid*, 1988/89, p83.
3 *Ibid*, 1989/90, p485.
4 *Ibid*, 1988/89, p99.
5 *Ibid*, 1989/90, p531.
6 Top Secret' memorandum submitted to the TRC by Maj-Gen J L Griebenauw.
7 *Race Relations Annual*, 1989/90, p469-470, 487-488.
8 *The Star*, 6/3/90.
9 Interview Col Gerrie Hugo, 8/3/2000.
10 *Ibid*.
11 *Race Relations Annual*, 1989/90, p493.
12 *The Citizen*, 26, 30/7/96.
13 *Race Relations Annual*, 1989/90, p493.
14 *Ibid*, 1989/90, p531.
15 *Ibid*, 1989/90, p487-490
16 *The Star*, 5/3/90.
17 *Sunday Tribune*, 11/3/1990.
18 *The Citizen*, 5/3/90.
19 *Daily Dispatch*, 17, 20/3/90.
20 *The Weekly Mail*, 19/5/1993.
21 *Daily Dispatch*, 9/3/90.
22 *Race Relations Annual*, 1989/90, p493.
23 *The Citizen*, 5/6/90.
24 Hugo, Gerrie, Snel, Stef. *Military Intelligence and the Counter-revolutionary War*, p81.

Chapter 23

1 *Race Relations Annual*, 1989/90, p518.
2 *Ibid*, 1989/90, p527.
3 *Ibid*, 1989/90, p531.
4 *Ibid*, 1989/90, p525.
5 *Ibid*, 1989/90, p523.
6 *Ibid*, 1989/90, p527-528.
7 *Race Relations Annual*, 1989/90, 527-528.
8 Interview Maj-Gen Bantu Holomisa, 24/11/99.
9 *Race Relations Annual*, 1989/90, p529.
10 Interview Maj-Gen Bantu Holomisa, 24/11/99.
11 *Race Relations Annual*, 1989/90, p530.
12 *Ibid*, 1989/90, p522-523.
13 *Ibid*, 1989/90, p529.
14 Interview Maj-Gen Bantu Holomisa, 24/11/99.
15 'Top Secret' memorandum submitted to the TRC by Major-Gen Griebenauw
16 Colonel Gerrie Hugo papers.
17 *Ibid*.
18 *Race Relations Annual*, 1991/92, p481.
19 Hugo, G, Snel, S. *Military Intelligence and the Counter-Revolutionary War*, p34,48.
20 *Ibid*.
21 *The Citizen*, 21/8/2001.
22 *Ibid*.
23 *Ibid*, 23/6/98.
24 *The Star*, 28/8/97.
25 *Focus*, Feb 1992.
26 *Sunday Times*, 13/12/92.
27 Col Gerrie Hugo papers.
28 *Sunday Times*, 6/12/92.
29 *The Star*, 5/2/93.
30 *Sunday Times*, 6/12/92.
31 *Ibid*, 6/12/92.
32 *The Citizen*, 7/4/98.
33 APLA press release, 11/9/92.
34 Daniels, Romero, editor of *Azania Combat*, 14/8/92.
35 Johnny Majozi, APLA's Chief of Publicity, Feb 1992.
36 Statement by PAC Youth Dept, AZANYU, 3/1/92.
37 *Eastern Province Herald*, 5/1/93.
38 *Race Relations Annual*, 1993/94, p341, p641, Report of Goldstone Commission.
39 *Sowetan*, 26/3/93.
40 *Race Relations Annual*, 1993/94, p 641.
41 *The Citizen*,15/4/98, *The Star*,15/4/98.
42 *Race Relations Annual*, 1993/94, p314.
43 *Ibid*, 1993/94, p641.
44 *The Citizen*, 6/4/93.
45 *Daily Dispatch*, 5/5, 9/5/93.
46 TRC Report, Vol 2, p690.
47 *Race Relations Annual*, 1993/94, p 314-315.
48 *The Citizen*, 29/7/93, 31/3/95, 27/1/96, 12/6/98; *Business Day* 16/5/93; *The Star*, 31/3/95, 12/6/98; TRC Report, Vol 2, p690.
49 *The Argus*, 20/8/93.
50 *The Citizen*, 31/8/93, 7/5/97; *The Star*, 27, 31/8/93.
51 *The Citizen*, 28/8/93.
52 *The Citizen*, 7/8/93, 6, 8/9/93, *Business Day* 7/9/93; *Sowetan* 7/9/93.
53 *The Citizen*, 30/8/93.
54 *The Citizen*, 29/10/97, 15/1/98; TRC Report, Vol 3, p510.
55 *The Citizen*, 21/5, 23/7, 4, 31/8, 7/9/93, 23/6/95; *The Star*,13/10/93; *Sowetan* 18/10/93; TRC, Vol2, p600.
56 *The Citizen*, 20/10/93; TRC Report, Vol 2, p600.
57 *The Citizen*, 19/9/96.
58 *Ibid*, 9/10/93.
59 *The Star*, 8/10/93.
60 *Ibid*, 8/10/93.
61 *The Citizen*, 9/10/93.
62 *The Star*,10/10/93.
63 SAPA report, 9/10/93; *Sunday Times*, 10/10/93.
64 *The Citizen*, 9/10/93.
65 *The Star*, 9/10/93; *Sunday Times*, 10/10/93.

66 *Sunday Times*, 8/10/93.
67 *The Citizen*, 9/10/93.
68 *Sunday Star*, 31/10/93.
69 *The Citizen*, 18/10/93.
70 *Ibid*, 14/8/98.
71 TRC Report, Vol 2, p601.
72 *The Star*, 10/7/98.
73 *The Citizen*, 11/1/99.
74 *Ibid*, 11/1/99.
75 *The Weekly Mail*, 28/1/94.
76 *The Citizen*, 4/6/98.
77 *Race Relations Annual*, 1994/95, p429.
78 *The Star*, 30/3/94.
79 *Ibid*, 31/3/94.
80 *Ibid*, 31/10/95.
81 Stadler, Maj-Gen Herman, *The other side of the Story*, p115.

Chapter 24

1 *Daily Dispatch*, undated clip.
2 Col Gerrie Hugo papers; Hugo, Gerrie, Snel, Stef. *Military Intelligence and the Counter-Revolutionary War*, p77.
3 Hugo, Gerrie, Snel, S. *Military Intelligence and the Counter-Revolutionary War*, p77-78.
4 Col Gerrie Hugo papers.
5 *The Weekly Mail*, 15/8/91.
6 Interview Col Gerrie Hugo, 8/3/2000.
7 Colonel Gerrie Hugo papers.
8 *Ibid*.
9 Hugo, Gerrie, Snel, Stef. *Military Intelligence and the Counter-Revolutionary War*, p81-82.
10 *Ibid*, p67-68.
11 *Daily Dispatch*, 29/12/91.
12 Hugo, Gerrie, Snel, Stef. *Military Intelligence and the Counter-Revolutionary War*, p84-89.
13 Col Gerrie Hugo papers.
14 *Sowetan*, 3/8/93.
15 *Ibid*, 3/8/93.
16 Minnaar, Anthony, et al. *The Hidden Hand*, p219-220; *The Star*, 31/8/93; *The Weekly Mail*, 3-9/9/93; *The Citizen*, 31/8/93.
17 Minnaar, Anthony, et al. *The Hidden Hand*, 1st ed, (paper by Flanagan, Louise) p223-226.
18 *Race Relations Annual*, 1993/94, p26, 636-637.

Chapter 25

1 *Sunday Star*, 25/11/90.
2 Interview Maj-Gen Bantu Holomisa, 24/11/99.
3 *Ibid*.
4 TRC testimony of W/O Fundikile Blackie Nombanga, , 31/1/2000.
5 *Race Relations Annual*, 1989/90, p520-521.
6 TRC testimony of Sgt Sidwell Ntisana, Mazizi Ntisana, W/O Hlumelo Mzwane Mkhulu Mxutu, W/O Sandisile Edwin Bongweni, 31/1/2000.
7 Interview Maj-Gen Bantu Holomisa, 24/11/99.
8 *Ibid*.
9 TRC testimony of W/O Fundikile Blackie Nombanga, 31/1/2000.
10 Interview Maj-Gen Bantu Holomisa, 24/11/99.
11 'Top Secret' memorandum submitted to TRC by Maj-Gen J L Griebenouw
12 TRC testimony of Col Eugene de Kock, 19/4/1999.
13 De Kock, Col Eugene, Gordin, Jeremy. *Long Night's Damage*, p179, *Military Intelligence & the Counter-Revolutionary War*, p34 *Sunday Times*, 25/11/90.
14 TRC testimony of Rayner Maria Moringer, 15/4/99.
15 Hugo, Gerrie, Snel, Stef. *Military Intelligence and the Counter-Revolutionary War*, p79.
16 TRC testimonies various, 19/4/99.
17 TRC testimony of Mazizi Thomas Ntisana, 31/1/2000.
18 Interview Col Eugene de Kock at C-Max Prison, 3/4/2001; TRC testimony of Col Eugene de Kock, 19/4/1999.
19 TRC testimony of Pumelele Gumengu, 31/1/2000.
20 Interview Maj-Gen Bantu Holomisa, 24/11/99.
21 TRC testimony of Mazizi Thomas Ntisana, 31/1/2000.
22 *The Star*, 20/9/96; *The Citizen*, 20/6/96.
23 *The Citizen*, 20/6/96.
24 Interview Maj-Gen Bantu Holomisa, 24/11/99.
25 *Ibid*.
26 *Ibid*.
27 *Ibid*.
28 *The Citizen*, 23/11/1990.
29 TRC testimony of Privates Pokwana and Nombida, 1/2/2000.
30 *The Star*, 6/12/1990.
31 Interview Maj-Gen Bantu Holomisa, 24/11/99.
32 *Sunday Times*, 25/11/90.
33 *Ibid*.
34 *The Star*, 23/11/90.
35 *The Citizen*, 23/11/90.
36 *Ibid*, 20/6/96.
37 Interview 'Topsy' Duli,1995; *The Star*, 20/6/96.
38 *Saturday Star*, 24/11/1990.
39 *Ibid*.
40 *Ibid*.
41 *Sunday Times*, 25/11/90.
42 *Sunday Star*, 25/11/90.
43 *The Citizen*, 23/11/1990; *The Star*, 23/11/90.
44 *Business Day*, 26/11/90.
45 *Saturday Star*, 24/11/90.
46 'Top Secret' memorandum submitted to TRC by Major-Gen Griebenauw.
47 *The Citizen*, 4/12/90.
48 'Top Secret' memorandum submitted to TRC by Major-Gen Griebenauw.
49 *The Citizen*, 20/12/1990.
50 *The Star*, 27/6/91.
51 TRC testimony of Col Eugene de Kock,19/4/99.
52 TRC testimony of Maj Ras, 20/4/99.
53 TRC testimony of Col Eugene De Kock, 19/4/99.
54 TRC testimony of R M Moringer, 15/4/99.
55 *The Citizen*, 17/11/93.
56 *Ibid*, 4/7/95.

Chapter 26

1 De Kock, Col Eugene, Gordin, Jeremy. *A Long Nights Damage*, p182
2 Interview Col Gerrie Hugo, 8/3/2000.
3 Interview Colonel Gerrie Hugo, 8/3/2000.
4 Hugo, Gerrie, Snel, Stef. *Military Intelligence and the Counter-Revolutionary War*, p90-95
5 Col Gerrie Hugo papers.
6 Interview Col Gerrie Hugo, 8/3/2000.
7 *Daily Dispatch* 8/91;*The Weekly Mail*, 11-17/9/92.
8 ANC's Kabwe Conference Report, June 1985.
9 *Daily Dispatch*, 15/8/91.
10 *The Citizen*, 16/8/95.
11 Interview Col Gerrie Hugo, 8/3/2000.

Chapter 27

1. Stiff, P, *The Silent War*, p19; Interview Dries Kriel 1999; Kriel, Dries. *Diary of a White Terrorist*. (Unpublished m/s).

Chapter 28

1 Hugo, Gerrie, Snel, Stef. *Military Intelligence and the Counter-revolutionary War*, p97-99; *Race Relations Annual*, 1991/92, 479; Col Gerrie Hugo papers.
2 Hugo, G, Snel, Stef. *Military Intelligence and the Counter-revolutionary War*, p68; *The Weekly Mail*, 15/8/91.
3 *Race Relations Annual* 1991/92, p479-480.
4 Hugo, G, Snel, S. *Military Intelligence and the Counter-revolutionary War*, p103.
5 SAPA, 10/9/96.
6 *The Weekly Mail*, 15/8/91.
7 Col Gerrie Hugo papers.
8 *Race Relations Annual*, 1991/92, P480, *Race Relations Annual*, 1992-93, p440
9 Col Gerrie Hugo papers.
10 *Ibid*.
11 *Ibid*.
12 *The Citizen*, 6/2/92.
13 *Race Relations Annual*, 1992/93, p438.
14 *Daily Dispatch*, 28/3/92.
15 Hugo, G, Snel, Stef. *Military Intelligence and the Counter-revolutionary War*, p102-103;
16 TRC testimony of Crosby Kolela, 25/5/99.
17 *Daily Dispatch*, date unknown.
18 SAPA, 10/9/96.
19 *The Star*, 7/9/92.
20 Stadler, Major-General H D. *The Other Side of the Story*, p98-100.
21 SAPA, 9/9/96.
22 *Ibid*, 7/9/96.
23 *Race Relations Annual*, 1992/93, 440-441.
24 TRC testimony of Col Vakele Archibald Mkosana, 3/2/2000.
25 TRC testimony of Zamile Thomas Gonya, 4/2/2000.
26 *Race Relations Annual*, 1992/93, p440.
27 *Ibid*, 1992/93, p441.
28 TRC testimony Themba David Marambana, 9/10/98.
29 *The Weekly Mail*, 19/3/93.
30 SAPA, 9/9/1996.
31 *The Citizen*, 1/6/2001.
32 *Race Relations Annual*, 1993/94, p312.
33 *Ibid*, 1993/94, p636.
34 *Ibid*.
35 Hugo, Gerrie, Snel, Stef. *Military Intelligence and the Counter-revolutionary War*, p102-106.
36 *Daily Dispatch*, undated news clips.
37 *Inid*.
38 TRC amnesty hearings at Bisho, 14-17/6/1999.
39 *The Star*, 24/3/1994.
40 *Ibid*, 25/3/94.

Chapter 29

1 *The Citizen*, 12/6/93.
2 *Ibid*, 25/6/93.
3 *Sunday Star*, 27/6/93.
4 *The Citizen*, 9/7/93.
5 *Sunday Star*, 18/7/93.
6 *Beeld*, 3/8/93.
7 *Business Day*, 20/8/93.
8 *Ibid*, 9/9/93.
9 *The Citizen*, 25/9/93.
10 Interview Dries Kriel, 1999, 2001; Interview Mossie Mostert,1/11/2001.
11 *Race Relations Annual*, 1994/95, p119.
12 Interview Gen Constand Viljoen, 17/4/01.
13 *The Star*, 11/6/98.
14 *The Citizen*, 18/5/94.
15 *Ibid*, 17/3/94.
16 *The Citizen*, 18, 23, 26, 30/3, 13/4, 18/5/94; *The Star*, 18/3, 19/4/94; *The Weekly Mail and Guardian*, 25-30/3/94; *Sowetan*, 22/3,14,20/4/94.
17 *The Citizen*, 11/1/94.
18 *Ibid*, 20/1/94.
19 Interview Gen Constand Viljoen, 17/4/01.
20 *The Star*, 31/1/94.
21 Interview Gen Constand,Viljoen 17/4/01.
22 Discussions with Joseph Chiole and Col Piet Uys, 17/4/01.
23 Hamman, Hilton. *Days of the Generals*, p210, 213.
24 De Klerk, F W. *The Last Trek* p260.
25 *Ibid*, p260.
26 *Ibid*, p261-262.
27 *Ibid*,p263.
28 Steyn Commission Report.
29 De Klerk, F W. *The Last Trek*, p264.
30 *Ibid*, p266.
31 Hamman, Hilton. *Days of the Generals*, p206, 209.
32 *Race Relations Annual*, 1994/95, p423.
33 *Ibid*,1994/95, p427
34 *Ibid*, p431.
35 Interview Gen Constand Viljoen, 17/4/2001.
36 *Ibid*.

Chapter 30

1 *Race Relations Annual*, 1993/94, p35.
2 Interview Mossie Mostert, 1/11/2001.
3 *The Star*, 26/4//94; *The Citizen*,26/4/94.
4 De Klerk, F W. *The Last Trek*, p316.
5 *Sunday Times*, 20/3/94.
6 Tebbutt Commission of Enquiry Report;
7 *Sowetan*, 25/3/94.
8 *The Star*, 15/3/94.
9 *Sunday Times*, 13/3/94.
10 *The Citizen*, 12/3/94.
11 Tebbutt Commission of Enquiry Report.

Chapter 31

1 TRC testimony of Nico Marthinus Prinsloo,15/9/98.
2 *Ibid*.
3 *Race Relations Annual* 1994/95, p427.
4 *The Star*, 25/4/94; *The Citizen*, 25/4/94.
5 TRC testimony of Etienne J Le Roux on 17/6/98, Johan Wilhelm du Plessis on 23/6/98
6 *The Star*, 28/4/94.
7 TRC testimony Nico Marthinus Prinsloo on 14/9/98, Jan B de Wet on 22/6/98, J H Vlok on 23/6/98, Johannes Coenraad Smit on 14/9/98 and Johannes Coenraad Smit on 14/9/98.
8 Interview Anton van Zyl, 18/12/99.
9 TRC testimony Abraham 'Abie' Christophel Fourie on 18-19/6/1998, Yaliswa Rita Seako (victim) on 15/9/98, Archie Khumalo (victim) on 15/9/98, Joan Keene Cambanis (victim) on 15/9/98, Sifiso Freda Ngwenya (victim) on 15/9/98, Mrs Gumbi (victim) on 15/9/98 and John Keene (victim) on 15/9/98.
10 *The Citizen*, 29/3/84; *The Star*, 29/3/94.
11 *The Citizen*, 18/3/94.
12 *The Weekly Mail and Guardian*, 25-30/3/1994.
13 De Klerk, F W. *The Last Trek*, p263.
14 *The Citizen*, 20/4/94.
15 *The Star*, 28/4/1994.

Index

N

W

X

Y

Z